## COUNTER THE COUNTERFEIT & BUILD A STRONG FOUNDATION FOR SUCCESS

***Books are our best friends***, is the adage we have grown up with. However, the pirates of piracy are continuously forging 'our best friends'. Our books and their supplementary online resources are copyrighted, and we don't lend any right-to-copy. Piracy is synonymous to stealing books.

Knowledge comes real, let's not encourage its counterfeit. Therefore, we appeal all our readers to discourage pirated books and **choose authentic ones**.

## HOW TO IDENTIFY THE PIRATED BOOKS?

### 1 COVER AND SPINE

- Look and feel (new or used book)
- Blurred images on the cover
- Hologram pasted on front
- Defective spine (wrinkles) or air pocket at its bottom
- Unclear ISBN/bar codes
- Missing/non-operational access codes for supplemental online or e-learning materials

### 2 TEXT/PRINTING/BINDING

- Uneven inking of pages
- Poor quality or blurred photographs/images/charts
- Substandard paper quality and opacity
- Misaligned pages
- Missing pages
- Inferior binding quality

You can further watch this video on How to identify a pirated book

For more information about identifying piracy, visit **https://www.mheducation.co.in/piracy**

To report a pirated book, send 'Hi' on WhatsApp code given on the back cover or write to us at **support.india@mheducation.com**.

Reported pirated books are examined to combat their piracy.

Let's fight the Pirates of Piracy and resolve to go for original!

# About the Author

**Madhukar Kumar Bhagat** is an officer of the 1995 batch of the Indian Revenue Service (I.R.S.) in the rank of Commissioner of Income-tax. Currently he is also nominated by CBDT as an information security expert in the panel of OECD, for assessment of countries/tax jurisdictions under the ambit of Automatic Exchange of Information (AEOI).

He is the author of several popular books, many of which pertain to preparation for aptitude tests. Some of these which are published by McGraw Hill Education are:

(a) ***Civil Services Interview: How to Excel***
(b) ***CSAT: How to Excel***
(c) ***Prelims, Mains & Interview What...? When...? How...?***
*(d)* ***General Studies: Paper II***
(e) ***Concise CSAT***

Besides, he has also contributed several articles on the personality test, the civil services aptitude test (CSAT) and other areas of civil services preparation, published by; The Times of India, The Hindu, The Hindustan Times, The Indian Express and other leading dailies.

He started his career as a mechanical engineer in the Indian Railways after qualifying the S.C.R.A. examination conducted by the U.P.S.C. Later he joined the Indian Revenue Service after successfully clearing the Civil Services examination. In the personality test conducted by the U.P.S.C, he scored 246 out of 300 (82%) marks. He was awarded the Finance Minister's Gold Medal for the best probationary officer in the 50th batch of the I.R.S. He also has a degree in law and master's degree in economics and has authored books pertaining to taxation which have been published by the Income-tax Department.

For suggestions and queries, he may be contacted at **madhukarbhagat@gmail.com**

HOW TO EXCEL

**Madhukar Kumar Bhagat**

**McGraw Hill Education (India) Private Limited**

Published by McGraw Hill Education (India) Private Limited
Registered Office: Anjana Complex No: 5/90 A, Butt Road, St. Thomas Mount, Chennai – 600016

**CUET: How to Excel**



First reprint 2022



**Print Edition**
ISBN-13: 978-93-5532-146-6
ISBN-10: 93-5532-146-5

**e-Book Edition**
ISBN-13: 978-93-5532-154-1
ISBN-10: 93-5532-154-6

**02 03 04 05 06 RAJ 26 25 24 23 22**



Typeset at Insight Publishing Solutions, C-3, West Vinod Nagar, Delhi 110092 and printed and bound in India at Rajkamal Electric Press, Kundli, Sonepat, Haryana.

Cover Image Source: McGraw Hill's Digital Asset Library
Cover Designer: Neeraj Dayal

Visit us at: www.mheducation.co.in
Write to us at: info.india@mheducation.com
CIN: U80302TN2010PTC111532
Toll free Number: 1800 103 5875

*Dedicated*

*to*

*My Gurus*

*My Parents*

*&*

*the Educational Institutions,*

*as these enabled me*

*to be what I am*

# A Word to the Reader

Embarking on college life has always held a special significance for the young; for it marks the transition from school education to higher education and in a way from teenage to adulthood. Aspirations soar high as to which university/college to seek admission to and which course to join; for the foundations of the future career and life would be laid here. Understandably, the young value and cherish this milestone of education and endeavour to secure the best platform for themselves. However, the onward journey has to pass through the cramped gateways of admission in the prestigious universities and colleges. In the past, their score of the $12^{th}$ board examination, would be the ticket to this entrance. But the process of securing entry to their dream courses was hardly rosy or smooth. The anxiety of securing decent grades in the board examinations was crushing, to say the least. Of late, even a resoundingly high score of 98%-99% was not a guarantee to secure the stream of choice in the very best of colleges. Could the perfect score of 100% guarantee the premium course and the top college and was this the new benchmark of success for university admissions?

The year 2022 is indeed a landmark in the annuls of higher education and admission to the central universities. The Common University Entrance Test (CUET) was announced, the scores of which would determine, the admissions to 44 prestigious central universities for the undergraduate courses for the academic year 2022–23. Many private and deemed to be universities also decided to accept these scores for admission to their respective undergraduate courses. With these, nearly 75 universities and lakhs of college seats would fall under the ambit of CUET in its very first year of launch. The entrance test is to be conducted by the National Testing Agency; a specialised organisation under the Ministry of Education, Government of India, which is engaged in conducting of tests for admissions to premier institutions of higher learning. However, this is not the first examination conducted by NTA for college admissions. Earlier too, CUCET (Central Universities Common Entrance Test) was conducted by the NTA. But there were only a handful of participating universities and the seats of many prestigious universities, like the Delhi University(DU) and Jawahar Lal Nehru University (JNU) were not in the fray.

A key feature of the CUET and admissions to the participating universities is, that the marks of the respective class $12^{th}$ board examinations would not be reckoned and only the performance in the CUET would count. Board marks would only be essential to the extent, that the candidate should have passed the $12^{th}$ board examination. Thus, what CUET offers, is a single examination for admissions to the central universities, for all candidates coming from central and different state boards. The added benefits are: a level playing field, wide reach to the seats of the prestigious universities and relief from the vagaries of differential marks award of different boards. Besides, now the pressures of climbing cut-offs to the prestigious universities wouldn't loom large. But what would be the fate of class $11^{th}$ and $12^{th}$ education? Would the students pay sufficient heed to them? After all the marks scored over there may have little bearing on the admissions in the colleges of the participating universities and mere passing of the board examinations may not be much of an ask from the students. Further, would this radical change of course offer an opportunity to the coaching industry to cast its web? Debate would go on and only time would tell the pros and cons of the new test. But for the aspirants, who have to go on with their business of studies, CUET is now the test to crack. Their goals are now set and it is success in this new examination, which would be the determinant of their prospective careers.

The structure of CUET divides the entire evaluation into three broad areas comprising four sections. The 1st section (Section IA and Section IB) are the tests of language and comprehension skills; the 2nd section (Section II) is the test of core or domain subjects; while the 3rd section (Section III) is the general test of aptitude. The sections and core subjects the candidates need to opt for in this examination, will depend on the course and the university the candidate proposes to apply for and its requirement. The applications for the CUET are to be made online. The examination will be in computer-based test (CBT) mode and the questions in the examination would be multiple choice (MCQ) objective type.

This book offers comprehensive guidance for the test of **English for Section IA** and the **General Test of Section III.** It brings out as to what are the **specific requirements of each of these test domains, the nature of questions to expect, the material required to study and how to go about the preparation. Over 2700 questions, 20 practice papers (10 of each of the two sections), hints and solutions to the challenging problems and many illustrative examples** are included in it. The study material incorporated is optimal for the preparation, without burdening the candidate with too much of superfluous theory to wade through and yet offering quality questions for practice, identical to what may be expected in the test. Thus, the hall mark of the book can be said to be **quality, preciseness and optimality.**

It is often said that a true guide is difficult to find. We have endeavoured to make this publication, as true a guide for the CUET as it is possible to be. To the readers, we wish the very best in their endeavour and hope that this sincere effort would be a definite aid to their toil in their quest for success. But the guide also charts the direction and walks along, only for a part of the journey. It is the seeker who has to tread the path and in this, his own intellect and hard work are the abiding companions. As it is said, *'sapientia et labore'*, meaning, 'through wisdom and labour', may you find success.

Best wishes

Madhukar Kumar Bhagat

# CUET: An Introduction

*"Man often becomes what he believes himself to be. If I keep on saying to myself that I cannot do a certain thing, it is possible that I may end by really becoming incapable of doing it. On the contrary, if I have the belief that I can do it, I shall surely acquire the capacity to do it even if I may not have it at the beginning."*

**—Mahatma Gandhi**

*"You have to dream before your dreams can come true."*

**—A.P.J.Abdul Kalam**

*"Many people have the ambition to succeed; they may even have a special aptitude for their job. And yet they do not move ahead. Why? Perhaps they think that since they can master the job, there is no need to master themselves."*

**—John Stevenson**

*"Success is 80% attitude and 20% aptitude."*

**—Funmi Wale-Adegbite**

The year 2022 can truly be said to be a watershed year for the aspirants' seeking admission in the various central universities in the undergraduate courses. A **Common University Entrance Test (CUET)** to be conducted in 13 different languages, was introduced for admission to all undergraduate programmes of central universities, for the academic session 2022–23. Besides the Central universities, several other deemed to be universities and private universities also decided to accept the scores of CUET for admission to their respective undergraduate programmes. The objective of this sweeping change was to provide a common platform and equal opportunities to the candidates across the country. The single test was also to be beneficial as it would provide a wider outreach for admission in the central universities, in an education system where hitherto the testing and evaluation was compartmentalised in the education framework of different State Boards.

The responsibility of conducting the CUET has been entrusted upon the **National Testing Agency** (NTA). This is an independent autonomous organisation established by the Ministry of Education, Government of India, for efficient and transparent conduct of standardised tests, for admission to premier institutions of higher education. Vide notification dated 26.03.2022 (see notification given later), the NTA has further brought out the broad contours of the entrance test. The CUET is to be conducted in a **Computer Based Test (CBT) Mode**, with questions which would be **objective type multiple choice** (MCQ), comprising different sections and diverse areas of evaluation. (website: https://cuet.samarth.ac.in/ ). Further, vide notification dated 06.04.2022 NTA has invited application for the test, thus opening a new chapter in eligibility evaluation at the undergraduate level.

**The Structure of the CUET**: The test has been designed to evaluate three broad areas which are divided into four distinct sections. (See notification 26.03.2022.) The Sections IA and IB incorporate the evaluation of language skills; Section II is the test of different core subjects; while Section III is referred to as the General Test. Out of these sections, the tests which the aspirants would be required to undertake, would depend on the university and the course being opted for by the candidate.

Section 1A enlists 13 languages, out of which any of the languages may be chosen by the candidate. Section IB includes 20 languages and any additional language apart from the Section IA language needs to be chosen from here. Any of the languages of Section IA can be opted for, as the medium of the candidate. The test of domain papers of Section II, will be bilingual, i.e., their question would appear in this medium as well as English. Besides, any of these 13 languages of Section IA can also be opted for the purposes of the test of language skills. However, those languages which are there in Section IB, will not be eligible to serve as the medium of instruction for the candidate and can be opted only for the purposes of test of the language.

The broad syllabus of the languages and the areas of evaluation has been brought out by NTA (see the notification of syllabus later). Section II comprises the evaluation of the core subjects, which are the domain specific subjects. There are 27 enlisted domain subjects including different sciences, mathematics, different social sciences, arts, legal studies, environmental science, physical education/NCC/Yoga etc. These are specified as per the list in notification dated 26.03.2022. The syllabus of these subjects is to be broadly based on the syllabus of Class $12^{th}$, the details of which are given for each subject on the website of CUET. The candidates can pick a maximum of six domain subjects from the list as required by the applicable university. The third section is referred to as the General Test and comprises questions from different areas of aptitude, general knowledge and awareness. This book is designed to fully cover the preparation of candidates for **English in Section IA** and the **General Test of Section III of the CUET**.

**Language Comprehension, Literary Aptitude & Vocabulary:** Sections IA and IB are essentially the tests of language, literary comprehension and vocabulary. The syllabus of language papers in these two sections (as announced by NTA), specify as to how these attributes would be evaluated viz. the nature of questions to expect. It mentions as below:

*Questions from the Language Section will be from the following topics but are not limited to:*

1. *Reading Comprehension: There will be three types of passages (maximum 300-350 words): (i) Factual (ii) Narrative (iii) Literary*
2. *Verbal Ability*
3 *Rearranging the parts*
4. *Choosing the correct word*
5. *Synonyms and Antonyms*
6. *Vocabulary.*

Thus, the detailing of the syllabus succinctly brings out, that **comprehension skill, and grasp over the language** (grammar and syntax) besides **vocabulary**, would be the core areas of evaluation. Knowledge of lessons/text portions as covered in the readers/supplementary readers of the class $12^{th}$ etc. would not be covered. The notification further specifies, that the test would comprise 50 questions out of which **40** would have to be attempted. The time available to complete this section would be **45 minutes** only.

**General Test or Aptitude:** The third section referred to as the General Test is essentially a test of aptitude where by different abilities of the candidate are evaluated. The syllabus for this portion specifies as below:

*The test consists of FIVE Sections. Each Section has 15 Questions. Candidates have to attempt 12 questions from each Section.*

*Section A: General Knowledge and Current Affairs*

*Section B: General Ability*

*Section C: Numerical Ability*

*Section D: Quantitative Reasoning (Simple application of basic mathematical concepts arithmetic/algebra/geometry/mensuration/stat taught till Grade 8)*

*Section E: Logical and Analytical Reasoning*

Thus, as can be seen the test **evaluates general knowledge and awareness, besides certain specific abilities of the candidates**. Overall, there would be 75 questions (15 from each sub-sections) while **60 questions** are required to be attempted (12 from each subsection) in a time frame of **60 minutes** only. For each of the questions in all the sections, **5 marks** would be awarded for a right answer, no marks would be given for an unattempted question, while a wrong response would entail **deduction of one mark (negative marking).**

Thus, the Sections IA/IB and Section III are essentially designed to be **test of aptitude**, be it aptitude for comprehension and language or that of reasoning and other basic abilities. The tests are also designed to be performed in a specific time limit which is barely **a minute per question**. This further distinguishes the candidates with sharper aptitude and skills from those whose effort is laboured and time taking. But first let's understand what is this aptitude.

## What is Aptitude and What are Aptitude Tests?

The term aptitude refers to the intrinsic abilities and intelligence of a person that determine his/her overall competence. It also reflects his/her capacity to perform a specific kind of work at a certain level. It is distinct from knowledge and understanding which are more in nature of information and knowledge gained.

Aptitude tests aim at evaluating the innate ability of the candidates with a view to assess his/her suitability for certain kinds of tasks. Usually, these tests appraise a candidate's linguistic ability, comprehension skills, numerical aptitude, logic and reasoning, abstract thinking, spatio-visual abilities, intra-personal and inter-personal skills, sense of rhythm and kinesthetics etc. The CUET also aims to evaluate most of these attributes, though not all, owing to the limitation of it being a computer-based classroom test.

Does aptitude imply a set of intrinsic but static abilities? Aptitude should not be presumed to be mere inflexible inborn abilities or inclinations of a person towards certain skills which remain inherently static. Aptitude as a set of human traits, is always dynamic and evolving. It offers scope for growth and improvement and like other human abilities is subject to the human endeavours of practice and preparation. Given the constraints of time, especially the multiple examination the candidates are likely to face and the demand of time posed by the preparation for core subjects, the candidates are invariably hard pressed for time as far as preparing for the sections of aptitude are concerned. They are also faced with the dilemma as to how to go about their preparation while optimising the time and maximising the returns. **This book aims at striking this balance by offering the optimal preparation material for the above two sections.** More in all circumstances does not mean merrier, and optimality is essential in certain situations. This is a key feature of this publication that optimality and balance have been emphasised upon. Truly this book can be said to be a **precise as well as concise repository of quality guidance and preparation material for CUET.** The details of the different sections and the nature of the questions likely to arise in the CUET are briefly discussed below.

## Reading Comprehension

The test of Comprehension is undoubtedly the single **most important topic** as far as Section IA is concerned. One can expect nearly 50-60% of the questions of this section to arise squarely from the comprehension passages. Thus, in the 50 questions of this section, one can expect 25 to 30 question to emanate directly from the comprehension passages. The notification clearly specifies that the passages appearing in the examination would be usually of **maximum 300-350 words.** Thus, the passages are likely to be from short to medium length. Further, depending on the length, content density and complexity of issues, a single to five questions may be asked from each such passage. The passages are likely to of varied types; factual, literary, narrative. The questions may also be of varied types, ranging from those requiring comprehension of words and expressions, to those evaluating the understanding of the substance/import of the passages, from those assessing comprehension of the logical structure of sentences to those, which arise from the various issues entailed in the passage.

In many elementary aptitude tests, the evaluation of comprehension is usually about the ability to locate an answer from somewhat long passages. Further, questions are generally factual in nature and the answers are easily discernible. This may especially be true for the school level comprehension exercises. However, in CUET some of the questions may be such that the answers may not be obvious or explicitly locatable amidst the stated facts. This would call for **understanding of issues**, besides the meaning of every line and word stated in the passage. As such to be proficient in this section, apart from the **comprehension of language**, the traits most essential, are the **ability to concentrate and ability to understand issues.**

Different types of questions, types of passages and how to tackle them, are explained with illustrative examples, in the Chapter-1 of this book on reading comprehension. Besides, nearly 200 comprehension passages with hundreds of questions are included in the exercise sets. These are designed keeping in mind the nature of the passages as mentioned in the notification of CUET, the passages appearing in the previous year's papers of the CUCET (conducted by the NTA) and comprehension passages of other aptitude tests.

**Language, Literary Aptitude & Vocabulary:** This is the other area of evaluation of Section IA. As brought out in the syllabus of languages, this section would incorporate questions pertaining to verbal ability, rearranging of parts, choosing the correct words, antonyms and synonyms and vocabulary. Thus, the questions emerging from this portion would broadly entail evaluation of grammar and vocabulary which are direct and salient tests of the language skills. One can expect 20 to 25 (out of 50) questions to arise from this area. The questions would be of diverse nature. These may require the aspirants to directly pick synonyms and antonyms or to find words which best suit a given definition. Spotting of grammatical mistakes in a sentence, selecting appropriate words to fill in the blanks, identifying meaning of idioms and other such questions are also likely to arise.

**Chapter- 2** of this book titled, **Language, Literary Aptitude & Vocabulary** brings out the different categories of questions likely to arise and explains the approach to solving them with lucid illustrative examples. An annexure of nearly 400 words their meaning, antonyms and synonyms, and another annexure of 125 idioms with illustrative sentences indicating their usage, has also been provided. Further, exercise set containing 225 questions of varied nature (based on past CUCET papers and other aptitude examinations) is also provided. Added to it, a set of **10 practice papers** which incorporate 50 questions each of both comprehension passages as well as language and vocabulary are included in the Part 1 of the book. Practising these will help the candidates simulate an examination like environment and evaluate their own strengths and weaknesses vis-s-vis different areas of the aptitude.

**General Test**: Section III of the paper is the General test, which is inherently a test of different aptitudes, besides that of general knowledge and current affairs. This section is divided into five distinct parts which are (a) **General Knowledge and Current Affairs (b) General Ability (c) Numerical Ability (d) Quantitative Reasoning (e) Logical Reasoning and Analytical Reasoning.** The inter-sectional weightage is likely to be the same, that is equal number of questions are likely to figure from all the five sections. The second part of the book covers the preparation required for section III of the CUET.

**General Knowledge and Current Affairs**

As highlighted earlier, the topic of 'General Knowledge and Current Affairs' is among the five broad areas which are included in the Section 3 (General Test) of the CUET. From the perspective of the examination, it is a significant area of the examination and indeed a challenging one. The ambit of both the topics, general knowledge as well as current affairs, is very vast. But the time of the aspirants for the preparation of CUET is limited and the effort and time which may be needed to master this area would be considerably demanding. The chapter has been accordingly designed to help the candidates understand as to what are the most crucial areas of preparation for this topic and what are the nature of questions to be expected.

The **nature of questions** can be broadly divided into those related to current affairs and others which fall within the ambit of general knowledge. The latter can again be further broken up into those which relate to the study of social sciences and general sciences and those which are outside the domain of formal studies. The last ones come in the purview of general awareness. While the chapter offers a reasonable concise material for preparation in form of some handy tabular information, specific chapters of some of the NCERT books, which would aid the preparation for this area, have also been identified. The chapter also contains 200 practice questions, which emanate from current affairs as well as the general knowledge portions. These are specifically as per the pattern and standard of questions as appearing in the previous CUCET papers.

## General Ability

General Ability, also referred to as General Mental Ability (GMA), is an important area of the section III. Its significance lies in the fact, that to the candidates this section often appears relatively easier. This is so perhaps due to familiarity with some of the questions which may arise over here. However, this should not let the aspirants become complacent about this topic and due preparation time and adequate practice for it must be budgeted in one's schedule. With good grasp over the types of questions and how to tackle them, General Mental Ability can otherwise be a scoring topic where a candidate may even save some time.

GMA broadly comprises three abilities: visuo-spatial ability, verbal ability and numerical ability. The first category involves problems requiring one to visually perceive spatial relationship between different objects. Verbal ability problems in the context of GMA, require understanding of words and their context of use/relationship between a set of words. Problems on numbers usually require understanding of relationship between numbers in a given set or matrix of numbers, such as in a sequence or series.

The chapter brings out the different types of questions one can expect in the examination ranging from the types, requiring determination of the next in sequence to code breaking ones, from those requiring analysis of figures and their movements to those requiring three-dimensional visualisation. Solved examples are provided to highlight as to how to approach each type. 100 questions of different types are also provided in the exercise sets.

## Numerical Ability and Quantitative Reasoning

The two topics are among the most significant area of Section III evaluation. Although considered as separate sub-sections, these are clubbed under a single omnibus chapter in this book for the sake of ease of preparation. Clearly, from the perspective of scoring decent marks in CUET, preparing well for these two topics is extremely important. As the problems of this sections are of numerical types, one is very sure to have got the right answer once the solution matches one of the options given. Hence the dilemma of whether the response was right or not, does not arise. But to be accurate and score well in this section, one surely needs practice. The need for preparation becomes essential if one has not been in touch with this area for a long time. This may be particularly true for the students from the arts background. Even if one is from science background, brushing up the fundamentals, especially the formulae and techniques of solving the problems, would be helpful, considering that the candidates would get merely a minute to solve the problem. As such candidates should get as much practice as possible, for this section.

The chapter on numerical ability and quantitative reasoning brings out the various types of problems which can be expected in the examination. Over 45 solved examples have been provided in the chapter with requisite formulae and theory to handle such problems. Besides, the exercise sets incorporate over 400 problems of varied nature with hints and solutions to many of these.

## Logical Reasoning and Analytical Reasoning

From the perspective of CUET, the twin topics of logical and analytical reasoning are indeed a challenging one. 20 % of questions from this area, half of which would be arising from each of the sub-topics. The significance of this topic specifically lies in the fact that unlike other topics of the CUET, which the candidates usually encounter in other examinations, questions on 'logical reasoning and analytical reasoning' may be new to many of the candidates. Besides, the questions may not appear to be straightforward which can be solved with a given formula or can be approached in a straight jacketed manner. Besides, the time required to solve each question may be more than a minute which is otherwise the time budgeted for in the examination, for each of the questions of this section. As such, these two topics would warrant concerted effort in preparation to attain proficiency in solving them, specially within a reasonable time.

The questions of 'logical reasoning' and 'analytical reasoning' are distinct from each other. Logical reasoning questions are those which entail application of logic and argument to a given statement, usually called a logic stimulus, to arrive at a conclusion. On the other hand, questions on analytical ability consists of a matrix of conditions or constraints, to which by means of deductions and analysis a desired solution is to be arrived at. Many candidates may find it difficult to get a hang of questions of logical reasoning. While for some, analytical deductions required in the latter topic may appear to be their waterloo. A word of advice to such candidates, do not loose heart at the outset or try to evade these topics. Just persist with your preparation. With time you will surely notice a definite improvement in your grasp of both the topics. The chapter on logical and analytical reasoning brings out the different types of questions with illustrative examples, which one may expect in the examination. How to approach them, tips for solving, theory of topics as such as syllogisms etc. are duly explained. Besides nearly 260 questions as per the standard of the previous CUCET and other aptitude tests, are also included in the chapter.

**Practice Papers**: The book also includes **10 practice papers** on Section III. Each paper has 60 questions covering the five broad areas of preparation. The questions are specifically designed considering the standard and nature of the questions which have appeared in the previous CUCET examinations conducted by NTA. It will be advisable to attempt these papers once one has gone through the chapters and solved the exercise sets. It is also advisable to solve this paper in a simulated examination like environment in a time bound fashion. One must also make note of, as to which are the subsections where one faced greater difficulty or got the answers wrong. Noting the time, section-wise / question wise (at least in some papers) would also be helpful in analysis of the time requirement and time constraint, the candidate is likely to face in the examination.

## How to Prepare

In each chapter, tips and the techniques about preparing that topic have been given in detail. However, in the following paragraphs some salient points about overall preparation of the CUET have been discussed.

***When to begin Preparation:***

The year 2022 being the first year for CUET, the candidates did not get the expected time to prepare for the examination. Considering the expanse of coverage required, a period of at least 6 to 8 weeks may be needed for an average aspirant to reasonably cover, the topics of Section 1 and Section III. This book has accordingly been designed. Here is what should be done in this period.

Prepare a plan/schedule for preparation, ear-marking days/weeks for specific topics and sections. Check out your progress regularly. Keep the last two weeks prior to the examination free for solving practice question papers, working on weaker areas and revision. A well thought out preparation plan helps to keep your preparation on a tight leash and prevents you from becoming complacent and going astray.

***Need for Concentration***

Concentration is a key virtue for being successful in any examination and it is more so in an aptitude test. In a test of a specific subject, what is important is whether or not you know the right answer or the technique to solve the question. But in an aptitude test, even if you know how to solve a particular question, your focus and attention will be pertinent in enabling you to pick the right choice and sticking to the time schedule. Techniques like *pranayam*, relaxation exercises, etc., are tested methods to improve concentration.

***Coping with Anxiety***

During the entire course of preparation, some degree of anxiety and nervousness is likely to take place. A bit of anxiety is normal and even helpful, as it peps up our system and prevents us from becoming casual and complacent. But it is important not to let anxiety besiege us. Techniques such as taking walks, listening to light music, mild exercising or simply taking a break from studies for a short while, can be helpful to some. One has to find what suits and helps him or her. But, it is important to build in some activity in your daily routine which helps you to cope up with your anxiety and helps you relax.

***Taking Care of Health***

Never take your health for granted, specially, during your preparation schedule. A bout of illness can make your plans go awry and pin you down psychologically. Take proper and timely meals. Incorporate some physical exercises and activity in your schedule. Drink sufficient quantity of water. This is especially true as the day of the examination nears. If you are pursuing some course, have joined some coaching or go out frequently for pursuing your job, then make it a habit to carry a bottle of drinking water. Avoid taking untreated drinking water or eating tempting unhygienic food from the market place.

## Dos and Don’ts Before and During the Examination

- The application to the examination is to be made online. The website (https://cuet.samarth.ac.in/) has detailed instructions for making the application besides the earlier issued notifications. Go through the notifications and the instructions to the candidates. Note the details of the documents required to be uploaded and the format and maximum size in which these should be. Also carefully go through the information bulletin brought out by NTA and the syllabus of the core subjects.
- Read very carefully the instructions with the admit card. These often contain information regarding the examination, particulars of the examination centre, things permitted to be carried in the examination hall and the time for reporting.

- Prepare a small pouch/box before going to the hall and keep in it all relevant documents, pen/pencils,, admit card, identity card etc.
- Examination is to a be computer-based test (CBT). For those candidates who haven't appeared in any such examination, taking a mock test would be advisable (if possible and available at the CUET website or at the test practice centres of NTA ).
- Have a good sleep, especially the night before the examination and preferably since a week prior to it. Researches have shown that 'a night's sleep', has profound impact on mental alertness and efficiency. Please remember that the questions in the aptitude test will not be like solving a worked-out example or picking the answer of an identical question which you have already encountered. Perhaps you can manage such questions even with somewhat compromised mental alertness levels. But each question in the aptitude test is going to be akin to a freshly encountered problem requiring you to think and concentrate. As such your focus and mental alacrity in the last few days and especially on the day of examination, is really going to matter.
- On the day of examination do not skip your breakfast or have too heavy a breakfast. Eat normal breakfast preferably of fruits and cereals. In case you are in a hurry to reach the examination centre, then at least carry some fruits with you, which you can munch on your way or during the "paper break".
- Do not carry mobile phones or other such items which are expressly prohibited.
- Ascertain beforehand the location of your examination centre and reach suitably before the reporting time. Keeping sufficient time margin is essential lest your vehicle breaks down, you are caught in a traffic jam or you take more than the anticipated time in locating the examination centre.
- At the examination centre, locate the examination hall, check the seating plan and take your seat as and when the time permits. Do not keep waiting till the last moment, lest you find that your chair is broken which needs to be changed, you have entered the wrong room, or there are some glitches with the computer system assigned to you etc. All of these small niggles can be a bit upsetting at the last moment.
- If you have a problem with your seat/table/computers or any other such issue, speak to the invigilator and try to resolve it before the examination begins. If it cannot be resolved and is not a major issue, then bear it. Do not fret over it, upset yourself mentally or waste your valuable time on it during the examination.
- If you feel the urge to answer natures call, do not feel awkward or try to hold it. It is important to relieve yourself mentally and physically before you enter the examination room.
- During the examination read the question paper and the directions given therein very carefully and follow it. For instance, if a particular question requires to select one of the options which is not correct in terms of what is stated in the passage, then do not select an option which is correct.
- Read each question and all the options very carefully before deciding which is the right option.
- Keep a tab on the time you are taking and the progress you are making. Remember that each question should be solved ideally in 60 seconds. If you are getting stuck on a question, then it is prudent to leave it and come back to it if the time permits. What matters is that how many questions (worth how many marks) you have solved right and not which ones you have solved.
- In case you are not able to pick the right option straightaway then apply the technique of 'selection by elimination'. Cross out those options which you are confident, are incorrect. Even if you cross-out two out of the four given choices, decision making becomes simpler and quicker. If you are unable to further narrow down your selection, then you can consider marking that option as correct which you consider to be probably the right one. However, for each wrong answer one negative marks would be incurred. As such guess work should not be employed casually or frequently.
- If the test appears tough to you; then do not be unduly perturbed by it. The paper will be tough perhaps for many others . In such moments, maintain your composure and try to do your best.

# Important Notifications of National Testing Agency

**PUBLIC NOTICE: CUET (UG) - 2022**

**Dated: 26.03.2022**

**Subject: Conduct of the Common Universities Entrance Test CUET (UG)-2022 for Under Graduate Programmes in Central Universities for the Academic Session 2022-23**

The National Testing Agency (NTA) is established by Ministry of Education, MoE (Earlier known as Ministry of Human Resource Development-MHRD) as an independent/ autonomous, self-reliant and self-sustained premier testing organization.

National Testing Agency has been entrusted with the responsibility of **conducting the Undergraduate entrance tests for all the Central Universities (CUs)** for the academic session 2022-2023. CUET will provide a **single window opportunity to students to seek admission in any of the Central Universities (CUs) across the country**.

The CUET (UG) - 2022 will be conducted in **Computer Based Test (CBT) Mode**. The aspirants who desire to appear for the test, may refer to the Information Bulletin for admission to **Undergraduate programmes** of the desired **Central Universities (CUs)** for admission into the **Undergraduate Programmes**.

**The details of the programmes offered by Central Universities (CUs) is being made available on their respective websites.**

Online Application Forms for Undergraduate Programmes will open from **02.04.2022**, the link for the same will be made available on the official website https://cuet.samarth.ac.in/. Candidates who wish to appear for CUET (UG) – 2022 are advised to go through the required eligibility of the desired University/ Universities for selecting the options from UG Programmes being offered. The Application will be open from **02.04.2022 to 30.04.2022**.

**Examination Structure for CUET (UG) - 2022:**

CUET (UG) – 2022 will consist of the following 4 Sections:

- **Section IA** – 13 Languages
- **Section IB** – 19 Languages
- **Section II** – 27 Domain specific Subjects
- **Section III** – General Test

Choosing options from each Section is not mandatory. Choices should match the requirements of the desired University.

**Broad features of CUET (UG) - 2022 are as follows:**

| Section | Subjects/ Tests | Questions to be Attempted | Question Type | Duration |
|---|---|---|---|---|
| Section IA - Languages<br><br>Section IB - Languages | There are 13* different languages. Any of these languages may be chosen.<br>There are 19** Languages. Any other language apart from those offered in Section I A may be chosen. | 40 questions to be attempted out of 50 in each language | Language to be tested through Reading Comprehension (based on different types of passages–Factual, Literary and Narrative, [Literary Aptitude and Vocabulary] | 45 Minutes for each language |
| Section II - Domain | There are 27*** Domains specific subjects being offered under this Section. A candidate may choose a maximum of Six (06) Domains as desired by the applicable University/ Universities. | 40 Questions to be attempted out of 50 | ■ Input text can be used for MCQ Based Questions<br>■ MCQs based on NCERT Class XII syllabus only | 45 Minutes for each Domain Specific Subjects. |
| Section III General Test | For any such undergraduate programme/programmes being offered by Universities where a General Test is being used for admission. | 60 Questions to be attempted out of 75 | ■ Input text can be used for MCQ Based Questions<br>■ General Knowledge, Current Affairs, General Mental Ability, Numerical Ability, Quantitative Reasoning (Simple application of basic mathematical concepts arithmetic/algebra geometry/ mensuration/s tat taught till Grade 8), Logical and Analytical Reasoning | 60 Minutes |

***Languages (13):** Tamil, Telugu, Kannada, Malayalam, Marathi, Gujarati, Odiya, Bengali, Assamese, Punjabi, English, Hindi and Urdu

****Languages (19):** *French, Spanish, German, Nepali, Persian, Italian, Arabic, Sindhi, Kashmiri, Konkani, Bodo, Dogri, Maithili, Manipuri, Santhali, Tibetan, Japanese, Russian, Chinese.*

*****Domain Specific Subjects (27):** 1. Accountancy/Book Keeping 2. Biology/Biological Studies/ Biotechnology/Biochemistry 3. Business Studies 4. Chemistry 5. Computer Science/Informatics Practices 6. Economics/Business Economics 7. Engineering Graphics 8. Entrepreneurship 9. Geography/ Geology 10. History 11. Home Science 12. Knowledge Tradition and Practices of India 13. Legal Studies 14. Environmental Science 15. Mathematics 16. Physical Education/ NCC /Yoga 17. Physics 18. Political Science 19. Psychology 20. Sociology 21. Teaching Aptitude 22. Agriculture 23. Mass Media/ Mass Communication 24. Anthropology 25. Fine Arts/Visual Arts (Sculpture/ Painting)/Commercial Arts, 26. Performing Arts – (i) Dance (Kathak/ Bharatnatyam/Oddisi/ Kathakali/Kuchipudi/ Manipuri (ii) Drama- Theatre (iii) Music General (Hindustani/ Carnatic/ Rabindra Sangeet/ Percussion/ Non-Percussion),

27. Sanskrit [*For all Shastri (Shastri 3 years/ 4 years Honours) Equivalent to B.A./B.A. Honours courses i.e. Shastri in Veda, Paurohitya (Karmakand), Dharamshastra, Prachin Vyakarana, Navya Vyakarana, Phalit Jyotish, Siddhant Jyotish, Vastushastra, Sahitya,Puranetihas, Prakrit Bhasha,Prachin Nyaya Vaisheshik, Sankhya Yoga, Jain Darshan, Mimansa,AdvaitaVedanta, Vishihstadvaita Vedanta, Sarva Darshan, a candidate may choose Sanskrit as the Domain*].

- A Candidate can choose a maximum of **any 3 languages** from Section IA and Section IB taken together. (One of the languages chosen needs to be in lieu of Domain specific subjects)
- Section II offers 27 Subjects, out of which a candidate may choose a **maximum of 6 Subjects**.
- Section III comprises **General Test**.
- For choosing Languages (upto 3) from Section IA and IB and a maximum of 6 Subjects from Section II and General Test under Section III, the Candidate must refer to the requirements of his/her intended University.

| **Mode of the Test** | Computer Based Test-CBT |
|---|---|
| **Test Pattern** | Objective type with Multiple Choice Questions |
| **Medium** | 13 languages ( Tamil, Telugu, Kannada, Malayalam, Marathi, Gujarati, Odiya, Bengali, Assamese, Punjabi, English, Hindi and Urdu) |
| **Syllabus** | **Section IA & IB:** Language to be tested through Reading Comprehension (based on different types of passages–Factual, Literary and Narrative [Literary Aptitude & Vocabulary] |
| | **Section II:** As per NCERT model syllabus as applicable to Class XII only |
| | **Section III:** General Knowledge, Current Affairs, General Mental Ability, Numerical Ability, Quantitative Reasoning (Simple application of basic mathematical concepts arithmetic/algebra geometry/mensuration/stat taught till Grade 8), Logical and Analytical Reasoning |
| **Registration** | Registration will be online at https://cuet.samarth.ac.in/. (*available from 01.04.2022*) |

### Level of questions for CUET (UG) – 2022:

All questions in various testing areas will be benchmarked at the level of Class XII only. Students having studied Class XII Board syllabus would be able to do well in CUET (UG) – 2022.

### Number of attempts:

If any University permits students of previous years of class XII to take admission in the current year also, such students would also be eligible to appear in CUET (UG) – 2022.

### Choice of Languages and Subjects:

Generally the languages/subjects chosen should be the ones that a student has opted in his latest Class XII Board examination. However, if any University permits any flexibility in this regards, the same can be exercised under CUET (UG) -2022 also. Candidates must carefully refer to the eligibility requirements of various Central Universities in this regard. Moreover, if the subject to be studied in the Undergraduate course is not available in the list of **27 Domain Specific Subject** being offered, the Candidate may choose the Subject closest to his choice for e.g. For Biochemistry the candidate may choose Biology.

Candidates are advised to visit the NTA CUET (UG)-2022 official website https://cuet.samarth.ac.in/ (after 02.04.2022), for latest updates regarding the Examination.

For any queries/ clarifications, candidates can also call at the NTA Helpline number 011-40759000 or 011-6922 7700 or write to NTA at cuet-ug@nta.ac.in

**(Dr. Sadhana Parashar)**

**Senior Director (Exams)**

# Important Notifications of National Testing Agency

**Public Notice**
**06 April 2022**

**Sub: Inviting Online Applications for Common University Entrance Test [CUET (UG) – 2022] – Reg.**

In pursuance of the **UGC Public Notice dated 21 March 2022**, the National Testing Agency (NTA) is conducting the Common University Entrance Test **CUET (UG) – 2022** for admission to the undergraduate courses in Central Universities, for the academic year 2022-23.

CUET (UG) – 2022 will provide a single-window opportunity to students seeking admission to the Central Universities (CUs) across the country for various Undergraduate Programmes.

CUET (UG) – 2022 is a bouquet of tests in various Languages, Domain-specific Subjects, and General Test. Candidates can select any one or more of the tests offered under CUET (UG) - 2022, as per the requirements of the University/ies where admission is sought.

The CUET (UG) – 2022 will be conducted in **13 languages**, i.e. English, Hindi, Assamese, Bengali, Gujarati, Kannada, Malayalam, Marathi, Odia, Punjabi, Tamil, Telugu, and Urdu.

The CUET (UG) – 2022 will be held in **547 cities** within India and in **13 cities** outside India (**Annexure-I**), as per the details given below:

| **Online submission of Application Form** | | **06 April 2022 to 06 May 2022 ( up to 05.00 PM)** | | | |
|---|---|---|---|---|---|
| Last date of successful transaction of fee through Credit/Debit Card/Net Banking/UPI/Paytm | | 06 May 2022 (up to 11.50 PM). | | | |
| **Correction in particulars** | | **To be announced later on the website** | | | |
| | | Slot I (Morning) | | Slot II (Afternoon) | |
| **Fee payable** | **Category of candidates** | Centres in India (Fee in ₹) | Centres outside India (Fee in ₹) | Centers In India (Fee in ₹) | Centres outside India (Fee in ₹) |
| | **General/Un-Reserved** | 650/- | 3000/- | 650/- | 3000/- |
| | **General-EWS/OBC-NCL*** | 600/- | | 600/- | |
| | **SC/ST/PwBD/Third Gender** | 550/- | | 550/- | |
| | Processing charges and Goods and Services Tax (GST) are to be paid by the candidates as applicable | | | | |
| **Announcement of the City of Examination** | | To be announced later on the website | | | |
| **Downloading of Admit Cards from the NTA website** | | To be announced later on the website | | | |
| **Date of Examination** | | First/Second week of July 2022 | | | |
| **Duration of Examination** | | Slot I- 3 hours and 15 minutes (195 minutes)<br>Slot II-3 hours and 45 minutes (225 minutes) | | | |
| **Timing of Examination** | | To be announced later on the website | | | |

| Mode of conducting the Examination | Computer Based Test (CBT) |
|---|---|
| Pattern of the test | Multiple Choice Questions |
| Centre, Date, and shift of the test | As indicated on the Admit Card |
| Display of recorded responses and answer keys | To be announced later on the website |
| Websites | www.nta.ac.in, https://cuet.samarth.ac.in |
| Declaration of result on the NTA website | To be announced later on the website |

**OBC-NCL (Other backward classes)- NCL(Non creamy layer) as per the central list of other backward classes available on the website of the National Commission for Backward Classes. The candidates falling in this list (available on https://www.ncbc.nic.in) may mention OBC-NCL in the category column. State list OBC-NCL candidates who are not in OBC-NCL (Central List) must choose General.*

**Important Instructions**

i. Candidates can apply for CUET (UG) – 2022 in the online mode only though the website https://cuet.samarth.ac.in

ii. The Application Form in any other mode will not be accepted.

iii. Only one application is to be submitted by a candidate.

iv. Candidates must strictly follow the instructions given in the Information Bulletin and on the NTA website. Candidates not complying with the instruction shall be summarily disqualified.

v. Candidates must ensure that the e-mail address and mobile number provided in the online Application Form are their own or of their parents/guardians only as all information/communication will be sent by NTA on their registered e-mail address or by way of SMS on the registered mobile number only.

Candidates who desire to appear in CUET (UG) – 2022 may see the detailed Information Bulletin available on the website https://cuet.samarth.ac.in.

The list of Participating Institutions is available on the NTA website https://cuet.samarth.ac.in

Candidates are advised to visit the website of the University/ies where they intend seeking admission, for the courses offered by them, eligibility criteria, reservation, tests in CUET (UG) – 2022 to be selected for admission to the desired courses, admission policy, etc. and ensure that they fulfill the eligibility criteria before they apply for CUET (UG) – 2022.

For further clarification related to CUET (UG) – 2022, candidates can contact **011-4075 9000 or 011-69227700** or send e-mail at cuet-ug@nta.ac.in

**(Dr. Sadhana Parashar)**

**Senior Director (Exams**

# Contents

# Part-I

## English Language

(Section IA of CUET)

# Reading Comprehension

# 1

*"Vacillating people seldom succeed. Successful men and women are very careful in reaching their decisions, and very persistent and determined in action thereafter."*

**—L. G. Elliott**

## 1. Introduction

The test of language skills is an integral and crucial part of the CUET and is incorporated as separate portion in the section-1A of the examination. As to how the language skills are to be evaluated, the CUET notification, species as below.

*'Language to be tested through Reading Comprehension (based on different types of passages–Factual, Literary and Narrative, [Literary Aptitude and Vocabulary]'.*

Further the syllabus for the languages, as notified for sections IA and IB of the CUET, specifies as below.

*Questions from the Language Section will be from the following topics but are not limited to:*

1. *Reading Comprehension: There will be three types of passages (maximum 300–350 words): which will be; **(i) Factual,(ii) Narrative, (iii) Literary***
2. *Verbal Ability*
3. *Rearranging the parts*
4. *Choosing the correct word*
5. *Synonyms and Antonyms*
6. *Vocabulary*

Further, it also specifies that there would be 40 questions to be attempted out of 50 and the time to be allowed would be 45 minutes each. Thus, what emerges from the notification is, that **reading comprehension test** would be the basis for evaluation of the language skills. Further this would be done through passages of different categories viz. factual, literary and narrative. Besides, the notification also specifies that the test of literary aptitude and vocabulary would also be incorporated. Thus, two broad areas of evaluation emerge, which are reading comprehension test as well as test of literary aptitude and vocabulary. Accordingly, the preparation for the language section is divided into two separate chapters, which are (a) **Reading Comprehension** (b) **Literary aptitude, language and vocabulary**. Both the sets of skills are integral to the test and interrelated to each other. While this chapter deals with the preparation for the reading comprehension skills the next chapter is devoted for the latter.

## 2. Reading Comprehension

The word 'comprehension' is derived from the Latin words *comprehendre/prehendre*, which mean to seize. The contextual meaning of the word is to understand or to perceive. This ability is indeed a *sine-qua-non* in virtually every academic field. Understanding of the facts and seizing of the issues at hand is of practical application in all realms of life. Little wonder then, that the skill of comprehension is the foremost attribute, which the aptitude test evaluates. From the perspective of the CUET, this test is undoubtedly one of the most important areas of assessment of a candidate's aptitude, as highlighted earlier.

The next logical question is, what skills would be required to be evaluated and how it would be done? The test of comprehension assesses a person's ability not only to understand an issue, but also to analyse it and to distinguish what is relevant from what is not. It comprises a comprehension passage followed by a set of questions. The candidate is required to read and comprehend the passage and answer the ensuing questions, which are multiple choice objective type. The nature of the questions is such that they test not just the candidate's literal understanding of what is written, but more importantly, the ability to absorb and analyse the issue at hand, to apply his own thought to the subject and to take a decision as to what should be the most appropriate choice in the given context.

## 3. Features of Comprehension Passage

The comprehension passages incorporate subjects of varied nature. As stated they me be factual, literary, narrative or of other types. Further, these may incorporate a diverse range of issues which may vary from a literary piece to a scientific report from an historical account to a concurrent international issue, from present day social challenges to a vision of the future.

But, notwithstanding the diversity of issues, the nature of the selected passages is such that they would not presuppose any prior in-depth knowledge of the subject on part of the candidate. Thus, even a candidate having little previous exposure to the issue, but having the basic comprehension ability, will be able to well understand the passage and attempt the questions. The length of the passage is likely to be from 100 to 350 words. Depending on the length and nature of the passage, the candidate may be required to answer a single to even five questions from each passage.

## 4. Essential Abilities

### 4.1 Ability to Comprehend

Primarily, candidates are required to have the ability to comprehend the passage, understand the import of the question and select the appropriate choice. But reducing the skills necessary to these three broad categories will perhaps be too simplistic. Each of these abilities in turn require several skills and abilities, the important ones of which are being discussed here.

### 4.2 Careful Reading

The reading of the comprehension passage has to be careful and meticulous. Unlike the perusal of storybooks, magazines and newspapers where one tends to go through the matter rather cursorily, or at best casually, comprehension passages require very focused and thorough reading.

Every sentence and every word has to be meticulously gone through to grasp what the author is trying to say. There are times when, while reading in ordinary course, we are not able to fully comprehend what is implied in a sentence or in a paragraph. Although we have visually perused such a portion, we choose to move ahead without waiting to completely understand what has been said or without making a diligent effort to do so. Such an approach is likely to backfire in the test of comprehension ability. As a result of improper comprehension, either we may not be able to pick the correct choice or lose valuable time in re-reading the relevant portion and then deciding the choice of answer. So **careful and focused reading** has to be made your second nature.

### 4.3 Comprehension of Language

Comprehension of language means, having the ability of literal understanding of the passage. This requires a basic command over the language and a reasonable vocabulary.

**A good vocabulary and command over language is a definite aid in quicker and better understanding of the passage**. This is especially true about your vocabulary. If you do not happen to know the meaning of a word used in the passage, then it is possible that your understanding of what the word implies is only a contextual conjecture, which may or may not be right. So if you are not hard-pressed for time, working on your language skills is likely to be doubly helpful. The subsequent chapter, 'literary Aptitude, Language and Vocabulary' will be of immense help in this regard.

## 4.4 Ability to Concentrate

Concentration is one ability, which is of utmost importance in the entire examination and more so in this section. Even a momentary lapse of concentration can mean that you will lose grasp on the subject or waste valuable time again in having to go through the portion where your concentration wavered. This occasionally does happen even with the best and the most alert readers. While the eyes keep on perusing the text, the mind loses connection with the subject and by the time we become aware of the concentration lapse, we have already marched ahead to another line or a paragraph. And then comes the quandary. Whether to keep on reading ahead and risk not understanding the passage fully, or whether to return to the portion where we mentally strayed off and spend more time in grasping it. While the first choice is fraught with the possibility of loss of marks due to improper comprehension, the second one entails loss of precious time. In either case what is adversely affected, is the candidate's performance.

Thus, **it is essential to fully concentrate on the passage**, to be aware of the occurrence of concentration lapse (if that happens) and to come back to the course as quickly as possible.

## 4.5 Visualising What is Being Said

The previous section dealt with the significance and need for rapt concentration while going through a comprehension passage. While the necessity for concentration can hardly be over emphasised, the significant question is how to achieve it or improve upon it. An important skill, which prevents the concentration from wavering is the ability to visualise what is being said. In simple words, this means trying to picturise the letter and import of the text. This is converse of 'imagery', where vivid descriptions in words are used to produce a mental image. In fact visualising what is being said or written, is a usual feature of our brain's ability to interpret text and language. However, generally we are not conscious of this to be happening, or at times the process is so quick and subtle that we fail to, or hardly take note of it. As such, a **conscious effort has to be made to be aware of that visualisation process** or to induce the conscious portion of our brain to picturise the text. To understand what is implied by visualisation, consider the following news item.

*"The Supreme Court has noted with grave concern that lakhs of tonnes of food grain are rotting in government godowns. It has directed the government that food grain should not be allowed to rot and if need be it should be distributed free amongst the poor."*

Did you notice any mental images getting evolved? If not then read again and try to take note of the images coming before you, or make a conscious effort to picturise what is being said. The word 'Supreme Court' may evolve the image of the court room or the Supreme Court building, which we see on television or in pictures, or that of judges sitting in a court room. The words, 'grave concern' may induce images of some grim judges. The word, 'government', evokes different images in different persons. While rotting food grain may produce a picture of piles of sacks of grain lying in the open.

Though all words and ideas may not and cannot be converted into images, still the ability to visualise a reasonable portion of what is contained in the passage helps in the following ways:

(a) It helps in easier and better understanding of the letter and import of the text.

(b) It enables a clearer and quicker recollection of the significant points when you read and answer the questions.

(c) It helps in remaining focussed on to the task of reading and understanding the passage. This is so, as our mind remains engaged in multiple activities, reading, understanding and visualising. Further, whenever concentration wavers and the visual images stop being generated, the brain takes note of the concentration lapse and sets out for course correction.

## 4.6 Understanding the Import

Understanding the import, implies **grasping what is the essence or the central theme of the passage and the underlying meaning that is being conveyed by its detailed contents**. This is essential as the questions following the passage may not to be straightforward, where the correct choice can easily be picked by identifying the relevant portion of the passage from where the question has originated. More often than not, the reader will have to analyse and apply his understanding of the substance of the passage to arrive at the right answer. As such, while reading the passage, if need be, halt between lines or paragraphs and ask yourself whether you have **understood the logic and the line of reasoning** being adopted by the writer. Do not be in a haste to proceed reading further without fully comprehending the previous portion.

As mentioned earlier, the passages in the aptitude test are to assess the comprehension of the issue and not merely the letter. Therefore, the candidate will be required to apply his understanding to pick the correct choice of answer. This can only be done by understanding fully the text as well as the theme and essence of the passage. It is noteworthy that **not only the passage as a whole, but its paragraphs and sub-parts also have themes and sub-themes, which the author is trying to convey**. It is essential to understand each part of the passage, its theme, essence of the entire passage and the line of argument adopted by the author.

Consider the small news item quoted in Para 3.5. Though it consists of only two sentences it conveys many facts and ideas, which are:

(a) *Lakhs of tonnes of food grains are rotting in government godowns.*

(b) *The Supreme Court has taken note of it and expressed serious concern.*

(c) *It has given two directions to the government:*

  (i) *To prevent the rot*

  (ii) *If required distribute it to the poor*

The passages in the aptitude test will similarly contain many ideas, facts, etc., which are knitted in a core theme of the passage. As a reader, one has to understand what these ideas are and themes of the paragraphs and the core theme of the passage.

But why is this essential? Not merely to keep your mind occupied and prevent a concentration lapse. As mentioned earlier, though the question may spring from the passage itself, the answers are not going to be straightforward. They have to be discerned by applying the touchstone of your understanding.

Consider the following question pertaining to the news item about Supreme Court's direction.

(i) *What do you consider is the most important reason for which the Supreme Court has given the aforesaid direction to the government?*

  (a) *There is loss of valuable resource of the country, which is food grain.*

  (b) *People are dying of hunger.*

  (c) *Government has failed to discharge its duties properly.*

Here the choice is not simple. The actual reason is apparently a combination of above all. As such, if Choice (d) 'all of the above', were to be there then the answer would have been obvious. But in the absence of an obvious choice, to come to a conclusion, one has to understand the theme of the passage.

The Supreme Court has expressed grave concern. This concern is not merely limited to the loss of resources and government's purported inefficiency, but more so at the loss of lives, which could be saved if the rotting food reaches the poor and hungry. Perhaps that is why it is directed to be distributed free amongst the poor, if need be. So the most important reason should be Choice (b).

## 4.7 Reading Speed

Reading speed is one aspect, which is often thought to be an area of concern by some aspirants. They believe that a better reading speed would translate into their ability to solve the comprehension passage questions, quicker. Therefore, the faster they read the better it is. However, this assumption is only partly true.

Reading faster would translate into being better, provided speed does not compromise the comprehension ability. If it does, then speed instead of being an advantage becomes a liability. After all marks are awarded for the right answers and if comprehension of the passage and choice of correct answers is sacrificed, then quick reading may save you a few minutes but cause the loss of valuable marks.

As such, be wary of courses or techniques, which offer you 'high speed reading' skills. Such skills may work on text in newspapers, magazines or story books, where you would like to quickly go through what has been written, but not on comprehension passages where the essence has to be understood and then applied to answer the questions. Besides, unlike the categories mentioned above, the comprehension passages have high information and content density. Skipping or improper understanding of a portion or a keyword can impair your comprehension and the choice of the correct option.

But the converse of 'speed reading' is also not the correct option. First, slow reading may not always mean the best comprehension of the subject. Second, the aptitude test paper will not give you the luxury of a lot of time. Extra time taken on comprehension passages would mean lesser time left for other sections. Therefore, **you need to read at an optimal speed, which is your fastest, without compromising your comprehension ability**.

But then what is this optimal speed. Well, this may vary from person to person. But on an average, a speed of 150–160 words a minute can be considered to be reasonable. So find out what is your own optimal speed and try to gradually improve upon it. This can be done with **more practice and better concentration.** But do always remember, **it is the quality of the comprehension, which matters most**.

## 5. How to Prepare: Developing Comprehension Skills

Having known what skills and abilities are expected of you, the next logical step is to develop and hone them. Here are some suggestions and tips, which you may find handy.

### 5.1 Improving Language Skills and Vocabulary

Proficiency in language and vocabulary forms a fundamental aspect of comprehension. Improving on these skills pays you doubly. This is especially true, if English language and repertoire of words has not been your forte or, if these skills got neglected in the past few years in your pursuit of professional studies. Candidates, at times do not get sufficient opportunities to work on these skills during the course of regular studies. As such, it is advisable for them as well as for others, to brush up these skills prior to the CUET. Here is what can be done.

- Go through the subsequent chapter on language and vocabulary diligently. Besides the exercise on language syntax and grammar, it also contains exercises on vocabulary as well as antonyms and synonyms.
- **Read Good Books and Articles ( if time permits),** which have rich and fluent language specially those on topical issues, which whet your thought process. Reading editorials of leading national dailies and articles of substance on concurrent and relevant issues can also be very helpful. These are also an aid in attempting the current affairs and general knowledge questions.
- While reading newspapers or articles in magazines **do not skip those portions which appear to be heavy in terms of the contents or complex because of the language** (such as business, editorial etc). Be patient with yourself and make a sincere effort to grasp what is said. Do not try to skip these and move to sections which are easy to comprehend (such as sports, fashion, page 3 news etc.). Rather, it makes good sense to make a transition to such sections or such newspapers which are dense in content and rich in language.
- **Note the Words whose Meanings You are not Aware of or Sure About.** Check them up in a dictionary, specially the usage of the words in different contexts. Jot them down in a diary or notebook and revise them occasionally. This steadily but surely enriches your vocabulary.

### 5.2 Improve Comprehension Ability

Comprehension ability refers to a number of attributes, which have been discussed earlier, such as understanding the literal text, theme and essence, ability to think on an issue, etc. Here is what you can do to hone it.

- **Grasp the Essence.** Whenever you read an article in a magazine, an editorial in a newspaper or a thought-provoking essay, ask yourself what is the author trying to say? What is the main theme? What are the sub themes of different paragraphs (if any). This instills an ability to grasp the salient aspects of any write up.

- **Visualise while You Read.** As discussed in the previous section, try to picturise what the author is trying to convey. This also gives a boost to your skill of mental imagery and ability to co-relate words, with thoughts and ideas.
- **Reflect and Ponder over what You have Read.** Merely passive reading is not sufficient. Ask yourself whether or not you are in agreement with what the author has to say. Is the expressed view balanced? Such an exercise sharpens your analytical abilities and understanding of the issues.
- **Practice and Practice More.** Please remember there is no substitute for actual practice. No matter how much of theory you have mastered, it is meaningless unless you have tested your abilities on the touchstone of actual practice. Practice reveals your shortcomings and helps you to overcome them. It indicates where do you stand and with time and learning, whether you have shown improvement or not. It helps you understand what your areas of strength and weakness are and how to plan your strategy.

In this chapter, several exercise with nearly 200 have been given to give you good practice. These are organised on the basis of types of passages and nature of questions emanating from them. While attempting the first few exercise sets, your objective should be to get in the grove and to identify the areas of comprehension ability (if any), you need to work upon (viz. vocabulary, understanding the import, concentration, identifying the correct choice, etc.). Do not be in a hurry to complete all exercises within a few days. Try to work upon your skills and then proceed to the next set. Progress to the latter exercise sets when you feel you have got a hang of the test of comprehension. At this stage **it will be prudent to time your practice sessions** so that you are aware of how much time you are likely to take in attempting a comprehension passage and could plan you strategy of attempting the paper accordingly.

## 6. How To Answer

Here are some suggestions and tips, which will be helpful while answering, in ascertaining the right option, saving time and avoiding mistakes.

- While going through the passage try to **underline the relevant words, portions and key concepts, which you consider the passage is trying to convey**. This not only helps in better understanding of the passage but helps you in quickly locating the relevant portions, if you need to refer to, while answering. Besides, it is possible that some questions may emanate from them.
- **Read the questions and options properly**. Once you have read the question, pause for a second and repeat the question to yourself, or ask yourself what you have understood. This helps in clearing any misconceptions bred by your own haste. Do not hesitate to read the question again or to go back to the relevant portion in the passage to recollect, if need be.
- **Look out for expressions**, such as '*which is **not** the correct reasoning*' (a question in negative) or, '*which is not the suggestion made by the author*'. In haste one is likely to miss the word '**not**' and select the wrong choice.
- In certain cases the question states, *"what as per the author/passage are the reasons....?"*. Here the question has to be answered strictly as per views expressed/facts stated in the passage. Question in such cases should not be answered on the basis of a commonly known fact, which may otherwise even be true.
- **Read all options carefully** before deciding your answer. Do not jump to a conclusion just after reading the first or the second choice. The answer choices offered may be quite similar to each other with only a fine difference between them. As such, an incorrect choice may also appear to be the right answer, until you read the subsequent choices and realise that one of them appears to be a better option.
- Many a time the choices of answers are such, that all or **more than one of them, may be partly correct.** The fully correct one or the right option in such cases can only be picked up by very careful reading and understanding the theme and the essence of the passage.

- In some questions, one or more than one of the options may be totally illogical or patently incorrect. Here the technique of **selection by elimination may** be applied. After the first reading of the options, strike out those ones which are totally incorrect. Choosing amongst the remaining options becomes easier. Besides, this saves some time in arriving at a conclusion, as one does not have to go through again over the struck-out options.
- **Pre-judging or pre-phrasing** your reply is also a technique, which works well in some cases. If the question is such that you can articulate/frame your reply without having to look at the given options, then it is called pre-judging or pre-phrasing the reply. Once you have pre-judged the reply and you do find an option closely matching to your reply, then the probability of it being the correct choice is quite high. This helps in saving time as you are able to conclude about the right option rather quickly.
- **Budgeting your time for various sections** and chalking out beforehand a time strategy is always very helpful. This means how much time do you propose to allot to each section and to each question in that section should be planned beforehand. In this case since you have to attempt 40 questions to attempt in around 45 minutes so you would have marginally more than a minute for a question. Hence for a passage with say 3 questions you may like to devote 3 minute or at most 5 minutes. If you are stuck at a question or have already over shot the time but cannot figure out the correct answer, then it is always prudent to leave the question and not to waste further time on it. You may revisit the question later (if time permits) or make an intelligent guess between the possible choices. However, guess work is ill advised where your confidence is low about the correctness of the choice, as negative marks will be awarded for wrong answers.
- Some questions may not be factual or may not be arising from a specific portion of the passage. They may involve understanding the theme or summary of the passage or what is the intent of the author. Some questions may even seek to assess your understanding of the underlying conditions described in the passage. Viz. where is the protagonist located (outdoors, indoors), what time of day it was, etc. There may not be explicit answers to such questions in the passage, but the answers may be required to be **deciphered by understanding the passage and reading between the lines**.
- **In case of short passages of 100 to 150 words read the questions first** before reading the passage. The questions in the short comprehension passage are usually limited in number, may be **one or two** at the most as the passages are short. As such, it would not be too difficult to read the questions first and remember it, while subsequently reading the passage. However, such a technique is difficult to employ in the long comprehension passages where the number of questions are more. The passages may take a good three to four minutes to read. This makes it difficult to remember the questions and yet concentrate on the passage.
- **In short passages reading the question first helps you to know what exactly you are required to do.** Whether the question is emanating from a specific part of the passage, or is it asking you to identify the subject/ summary of the passage, or it wants, the contextual meaning of a word or a phrase to be explained. This technique helps in saving time. This way, one is clear at the very outset as to what is required to be done. One need not have to go to the passage for a second time, to locate the portion from which the question has arisen. However, if questions are more in number or it is difficult to remember them, then it would be advisable to read the passage first and then attempt the questions.
- After having read the questions and knowing what you are looking for, go to the passage and read it from the perspective of finding the

answer/locating the portion from which question has arisen and understanding the passage where the import/view of the author is asked for. Read **the passage carefully and concentrate fully.**

- **Read the question once more and then read all options carefully** before deciding your answer. Do not jump to a conclusion just after reading the first or the second choice.

## 7. Comprehension Passages: their nature and preparation

The comprehension passages appearing in this section are likely to be short to medium ones and usually of 100 – 350 words. These may be excerpts from articles, reports, biographies and even from works of fiction. The short passages may have a single question while the long ones may even have four to five questions depending on the nature and the length of the passages. Each of the questions will have four answer choices from which the correct option is to be picked.

The questions will be aiming at assessing the candidate's **comprehension of language and grasp of what has been stated in the passage**. This may be done in a variety of ways which are;

(a) Questions may emanate from a specific part of the passage or may involve **understanding of fact(s)** stated therein.

(b) Questions may be aimed at gauging the candidate's **understanding of the summary** of the passage.

(c) Questions may require **understanding of the main theme** or the subject of the passage.

(d) Questions may test the **understanding of the words, expressions** and phrases used in the passage.

(e) Questions may require the **understanding of the logical structure of the narration** in the passages.

The exercises on the comprehension passages contains a variety of different categories of passages and questions, which well elucidate what to expect in the examination.

### 7.1 Categories of Comprehension passages and questions

Based on the pattern of the different aptitude tests and the nature of the questions of the previous CUCET papers, the comprehension passages and questions which are likely to arise, can be categorised as below.

(a) **Passages with questions requiring the comprehension of words and expressions**:

This category incorporates passages which are usually literary or even narrative and are medium to long length. The questions require the reader a comprehension of the passage as well as its literal understanding. What is implied by a word or an expression is the specific thrust area of such passages. Such questions may require a contextual understanding as well, besides grasping the literal meaning of a word, expression or a part of the passage.

**7.1 Illustration**

*Climate science has rightly taken up an important position in the public debate. Even as the science of climate change grapples with uncertainties, the world is witnessing more extreme events. The urgency for action is felt more than ever before. In contrast, though the Doha Gateway on climate change agreed upon in December 2012 ensured that there is continuation of a multilateral and rule-based regime to reduce emissions, the emission pledges on the table by the developed country, Parties lacked ambition. With rising extreme events, and rising citizen demand, the world has little option but to listen to the voice of evolving science and respond adequately with strategies and policy rooted in the principles of multilateralism with equitable and fair burden sharing.*

**The climate science is ________ with the uncertainties.**

**(a) managing** **(b) fighting**

**(c) anticipating** **(d) bogged down**

**Question: Which of the above four options best fits in the blank space in the context of the passage?**

**Solution:** As can be seen, the above blank space in the question corresponds to the word grapple in the passage. Thus, the question seeks to assess the comprehension of contextual meaning of grapple as it is used in the passage. The option which best suits the contextual meaning of grapple, is 'fighting'. As seen from the passage science is not able to 'mange' the uncertainties of climate change, neither the two other options fit here. Hence option (b) is the right choice.

Passages of this kind are given in the '**Exercise Set A**'.

**(b) Passages requiring understanding the chronology of sentences and unjumbling of their order.**

In certain questions, a passage is broken down into several sentences. These sentences are presented to the reader in a jumbled manner. Such passages are often of narrative type. The question requires the determination of the correct order of the sentences in the passage. In such passage, usually the correct positions of the first and last sentences are specified and the position of the remaining four sentences of the middle are required to be unjumbled. Such questions require the comprehension of the meaning as well as the logical composition structure.

## 7.2 Illustration

(1) *Another challenge is how to maximise agricultural income while adopting a more sustainable agricultural strategy.*

(a) *There are concerns arising also from over-exploitation of water resources, especially in the Green Revolution belt.*

(b) *The concerns here are land and water degradation due to soil erosion, soil salinity, water logging and excessive application of nutrients.*

(c) *Measures must be taken to promote use of quality seeds, cultivation of drought resistant varieties of crops, judicious use of available water, balanced use of fertilizers, farm mechanisation to improve efficiency levels, and wider use of irrigation facilities.*

(d) *Better management practices for rehabilitation of degraded land and water resources hold the key.*

(6) *Expenditure on agricultural research also needs to be stepped up substantially.*

**Question: Arrange the sentences in the options (a), (b), (c), (d) in the correct sequence to form a logical and coherent passage.**

**Solution:** In the example above the correct position of the 1st and 6th sentences of the passage are given. The four sentences in the middle are jumbled. Their correct order is to be determined. In order to solve such problems, one must read all the sentences thoroughly and comprehend fully their import. Clues as to the order of the sentences are there in the sentence structure as well as their meaning.

The 1st sentence is talking about the challenges for maximising the agricultural income. Sentence (b) which talks about the concerns pertaining to agriculture would logically follow. Sentence (a) would follow suit as it talks about the additional concerns in the field of agriculture. Sentences (d) and (c) would come next as seen from their context. Thus, the correct sequence would be (b) (a) (d) (c).

While reading the sentences in the order (1) (b) (a) (d) (c) (6), we get a logical chronology of a passage.

While solving such questions **cues** may also be taken **from the chronology of events or reference to times** which are often contained in the narrative type passages. Sentence connectors and keywords like, moreover, also, besides, nevertheless, because; also help to identify as to which sentence will precede and which will follow.

Some of such passages are given in the '**Exercise Set B**'.

**(c) Passages requiring understanding of the key message, summary, import, logical inference etc.**

There are certain passages in which the questions require the reader to comprehend and identify the key message, summary or the import of the passage. At times the logical inference which can be drawn from the passage is also required to be identified. Usually, such passages are short to medium length (100-200 words) and encapsulate a key idea or a thought. Further unlike the conventional passages, the answers are not to be identified from any specific part or paragraph of the passage, rather the answer is to be derived through proper comprehension of the meaning and message of the passage.

**7.3 Illustration**

*I believe that man has little need to drug himself. 999 cases out of a thousand can be brought round by means of a well-regulated diet, water and earth treatment and similar household remedies. Instead of using the body as a temple of God we use it as a vehicle for indulgences and are not ashamed to run to medical men for help in our effort to increase them and abuse the earthly tabernacle. The great deal of truth in the saying that man becomes what he eats. The grosser the food the grosser the body.*

**Question: In terms of what is said in the passage, which of the following conclusions can be drawn about the views of the author?**

(1) The author believes that modern drugs are useless in most of our ailments.

(2) The author believes that worshipping our own body as a temple of God is the key to good health.

(3) The author is a staunch believer in traditional system of medicine in treatment of our ailments.

(a) 1, 2, 3
(b) 1, 3
(c) 3 only
(d) None of the above.

**Solution:** The question requires identification of the appropriate conclusion from the passage. This essentially requires comprehension of the key message or the import of the passage. The key message is to have a well-regulated life and diet and to avoid indulgences. The author is neither critical of the modern system of medicines nor a supporter of the traditional system. The conclusion, of the author believing that the body is to be worshipped as a temple of God, can also not explicitly be drawn. The author is only emphasising the significance of a natural and balanced lifestyles bereft of indulgences. Hence amongst the given conclusions none are reflective of the views of the author or can be logically concluded. Hence the correct option is (d).

A number of such passages are given in **'Exercise Set C'**.

**(d) Passages requiring the comprehension of the facts and issues entailed:**

There are certain passages in which not only the key message and its overall logical comprehension is pertinent but the narrative, description of facts and issues are also relevant. These include the conventional passages where the questions often arise from the subject matters which are a part of the passage. Such passages are of variable length but usually of 100 to 400 words. These may be narrative, literary, descriptive, expository or of other types. Invariably these passages are self-contained or at least do not expect the reader to have any additional knowledge of the subject to answer the ensuing questions. Depending on the length of the passage, one or multiple questions emanate from it. Proper and thorough reading of the passage specially the subparts is essential for its comprehension and answering of the questions.

**7.4 Illustration**

*Climate science has rightly taken up an important position in the public debate. Even as the science of climate change grapples with uncertainties, the world is witnessing more extreme events. The urgency for action is felt more than ever before. In contrast, though the Doha Gateway on climate change agreed upon in December 2012 ensured that there is continuation of a multilateral and rule-based regime to reduce emissions, the emission pledges on the table by the developed country Parties, lacked ambition. With rising extreme events, and rising citizen demand, the world has little option but to listen to the voice of evolving science and respond adequately with strategies and policy rooted in the principles of multilateralism with equitable and fair burden sharing.*

**Question1: Why is the urgency of action with respect to climate change felt more today than ever before?**

(i) The developed countries have not taken serious steps to fulfil the emission reduction pledges undertaken by them.

(ii) Extreme events on account of climate change have become more frequent.

(a) For reason (i) only.
(b) For reason (ii) only.
(c) Both reasons (i) and (ii) only.
(d) For neither reason (i) nor (ii).

**Solution:** The current urgency vis-a vis the climate change, is on account of the rise in the extreme events. Hence the right answer is option (b).

**Question2: Which amongst the following are the principles espoused in the passage, on which the policies to fight climate change should be based upon?**

(i) Equal burden on all

(ii) Principle of multilateralism.

(iii) Equity and fairness.

(a) (i), (ii), (iii)

(b) (i), (ii)

(c) (i), (iii)

(d) (ii), (iii)

**Solution:** In the last line of the passage the answer to this question can be found. It mentions the principles of multilateralism and equitable burden Hence points (ii) and (iii) are incorporated and the right answer is option (d)

## 7.5 Illustration

*I am a firm believer in the principle of free and compulsory primary education for India. I also hold that we shall realise this only by teaching the children a useful vocation and utilising it as a means for cultivating their mental, physical and spiritual faculties. Let no one consider these economic calculations in connection with education as sordid or out of place. There is nothing essentially sordid about economic calculations. True economics never militates against the highest ethical standard, just as true ethics to be worth its name must, at the same time, be also good economics.*

**Question 1: Which of the following inferences can be drawn about the author's view?**

(1) He does not see any inherent contradiction between good economics and good ethics.

(2) He wants education to be totally free.

(a) Only inference 1 can be drawn.

(b) Only inference 2 can be drawn.

(c) Both inference 1 & 2 can be drawn.

(d) Neither inference 1 nor 2 can be drawn.

**Question 2:** Why does the author believe that objective of free and compulsory education can only be achieved by incorporating a useful vocation?

(1) Vocational training would help to acquire a skill and earn a livelihood later in life. This would attract the students.

(2) Vccational training would help in growth of mental and physical skills.

(3) Vocational training is a successful model followed elsewhere in the world.

(4) Vocational training is the only means for spiritual development of children.

(a) 1, 2, 3, 4 (b) 1, 2, 3

(c) 1, 2 (d) 1 only

**Solution:** Question (1) wants you to evaluate which of the two, or both, or neither of the inferences can be drawn from what is stated in the passage. The evaluation of the correctness of the inference (1) is based on the understanding of the passage. In the last portion of the passage, the author states that true economics does not militate against highest ethical standard; implying thereby that there is no inherent contradiction between true and good economics and ethics. As such inference (1) can be drawn.

Inference (2) requires evaluation of a factual statement. In the opening lines of the passage the authors views are indicated that he believes in provision of free primary education. The question uses the word education and not primary education. Education would include the entire gamut viz. primary, secondary, higher education etc. in its fold. Therefore such an inference would be factually incorrect.

As such only inference (1) can be drawn and the correct answer would be option (a).

This question (2) is not a plain factual one and the answer is not explicitly located in any portion of the passage. The answer has to be inferred based on what is stated in the passage.

The question gives four options. It is seen that the reason (1) is present in all four options therefore its correctness need not be evaluated.

Reason (4) can be done away with be applying elimination technique. It states that vocational training is the only way of spiritual development of children. Such assertion has nowhere been made in the passage.

What remains to be evaluated is correctness of reason (2) and reason (3). There is no supporting assertion regarding reason (3), as the passage does mention anything about educational model incorporating vocational training anywhere in the world. But the contents of the passage clearly support reason (2). Therefore reason (1) and reason (2) are correct and the appropriate choice would be option (c).

Nearly a 100 of such passages are contained in the **'Exercise Set D'.** The passages are of different nature viz. literary, scientific, narrative, expository etc. besides ranging from short to long passages with single to multiple questions. The set is so designed, that completing this exercise set in itself would give an aspirant, sufficient practice for the examination.

## Exercise Set A

***Read the following passages carefully and answer the questions that follow. Each passage is followed by a sentence with a blank space and four options. Pick the option which best fits in the blanks space.***

### Passage 1

The ultimate goal of economic policy is to create a sustained renaissance of high growth in which hundreds of millions of good quality jobs are created. Good quality jobs are created by high productivity firms, so this agenda is critically about how firms are created, how firms grow, and how firms achieve high productivity.

Labour laws create strong incentives for firms to avoid hiring a large number of low skill workers. An array of problems holds back the entry and maturation of new firms. This protects existing businesses, even if inefficient, and limits entry and competition. It is imperative to use India's unique demographic moment wisely and unleash the second generation of reforms.

The pursuit of long-term initiatives will feed back into the economy in the short term, with a rise in consumption and investment. In India today, there is a coincidence between the priorities for the long term and the priorities for the short term. At the same time, the deeper impact of these policy initiatives will kick in with a lag. When there is an open array of opportunities for individuals and firms, it will take some time for economic agents to understand the new landscape and how they should optimally act in it. Firms will require time and commitment in order to build up organisational capital. Hence, we may envision a five-year period within which the reforms are put in place, followed by a period within which the economy has fully absorbed the new environment and achieved a higher trend growth rate.

1. The ultimate growth of economic policy is considered to be _______ of high growth.
   (a) a sudden revolution
   (b) a continuable resuscitation
   (c) a manageable beginning
   (d) None of the above
2. Creation of good quality job______ the creation new firms.
   (a) crucially depends on
   (b) related to
   (c) has a relationship with
   (d) is not related to
3. The deeper impact of the policies initiatives will_______.
   (a) come into play with a phase lag
   (b) show effect immediately
   (c) kick the economic agents into activity
   (d) reinvigorate policy dormancy

### Passage 2

I would say that if the village perishes India will perish too. India will be no more. Her own mission in the world will get lost. The revival of the village is possible only when it is no more exploited.

Industrialisation on a mass scale will necessarily lead to passive or active exploitation of the villagers as the problems of competition and marketing come. Therefore, we have to concentrate on the village being self-contained, manufacturing mainly for use. Provided this character of the village industry is maintained, there would be no objection to villagers using even the modern machines and tools that they can make and can afford to use. Only they should not be used as a means of exploitation of other.

4. The revival of the villages is possible only if its ________
   (a) people are not abused.
   (b) its farms and fields are not wasted.
   (c) its economic resources and markets are not exploited.
   (d) None of the above.
5. The term 'self-contained', implies ______
   (a) a separate geographical unit.
   (b) an economic entity, separate from the manufacturing centres.
   (c) a centre fulfilling its needs on own.
   (d) None of the above.
6. If villages perish India's _____ to the world will be lost.
   (a) economic objective
   (b) social purpose
   (c) military dominance
   (d) cultural message

**Passage 3**

Private Sector Investment in data-related endeavours is higher than even before. The trend holds across industries as disparate as healthcare and financial services and across geographies and company. In fact, in the last two decades, the world has witnessed the emergence of companies, such as Facebook, Amazon, Instagram, etc., who earn revenue exclusively from people's data. But there are several areas where data is not as ubiquitously harnessed and used. Consider, for example, the agriculture market. If the marginal benefit to a farmer of acquiring price information is higher than the marginal cost of that information, he would pay for that information. Consequently, the private sector would cater to his need by gathering and selling him the information he wants. This would eventually lead to a nationally integrated agriculture market, which should have happened if the marginal benefit of data today is indeed higher than the cost. Why has the corporate sector's data wave not found a parallel in the agriculture sector?

7. Private Sector Investment in data-related __________is higher than even before.
   (a) Enterprises
   (b) Retail businesses
   (c) Start ups
   (d) Markets
8. There are several areas where data is not _________ and used.
   (a) relevant and deployed
   (b) economically viable
   (c) largely feasible for collection
   (d) omnipresent and channelised
9. Agriculturist would pay for the information if the _____ to the farmer of acquiring price information is higher than the marginal cost.
   (a) benefit of every extra unit
   (b) lumpsum gain
   (c) medium term benefits
   (d) none of the above

**Passage 4**

When people come into possession of political power, the interference with the freedom of the people is reduced to a minimum. In other words, a nation that runs its affairs smoothly and effectively without much State interference is truly democratic. Where such a condition is absent, the form of Government is democratic in name.

Democracy and violence can hardly go together. The States that are today nominally democratic have either to become frankly totalitarian or, if they are to become truly democratic, they must become courageously non-violent. It is a blasphemy to say that non-violence can only be practiced by individuals and never by nations which are composed of individuals.

The very essence of democracy is that every person represents all the varied interests which compose the nation. It is true that it does not exclude and should not exclude special representation of special interest, but such representation is not its test. It is a sign of its imperfection.

10. When people come into possession of political power, the __________ freedom of the people is reduced to a minimum.
    (a) multiplicity of
    (b) ambit of
    (c) restrictions to
    (d) legal encumbrance to

11. The reference, 'democratic in name', implies:
    (a) a failed democracy
    (b) democracy in form but not in substance
    (c) a written democracy
    (d) a weak democracy

12. It is a__________ to say that non-violence can only be practiced by individuals and never by nations which are composed of individuals.
    (a) Insult (b) Incorrect
    (c) Impolite (d) Imprudent

**Passage 5**

A robust and resilient infrastructure is fundamental and essential for budding industries. While India has invested in its infrastructure over the years, the challenge is to mobilise adequate investment in infrastructure sector which runs into several trillions of dollars. The investment gaps in the infrastructure would have to be addressed through various innovative approaches with the collaboration of both public and private sector.

13. A robust and resilient infrastructure is essential for ______ industries.
    (a) building (b) upcoming
    (c) sunset (d) sick

14. The investment_______ in the infrastructure would have to be addressed through various innovative approaches.
    (a) shortfall (b) need
    (c) opportunity (d) loss

**Passage 6**

With the world's population estimated to be nine billion by 2050 and one third of world's soils already degraded. There is an imperative need to protect the soils so that adequate safe food can be provided to human kind. Most of the pollutants are due to anthropogenic factors. The importance of preventing both soil pollution and soil degradation is also emphasised by the fact that four sustainable development goals are directly impacted with soil degradation and food security. Soils also hold three times as much carbon as the atmosphere and acting as carbon sinks are important also for mitigating the impacts of climate change. The focus on soils on a particular day encourages the farmers to adapt to more sustainable systems of agriculture.

15. One third of world's soils are already________.
    (a) lost (b) eroded
    (c) deteriorated (d) polluted

16. Most of the pollutants are due to _________ factors.
    (a) Industrial
    (b) human and animal combined
    (c) fossil related
    (d) human induced

17. Soils acting as carbon sinks are important for _________the impacts of climate change.
    (a) eliminating (b) abating
    (c) undoing (d) recovering

**Passage 7**

To me political power is not an end but one of the means of enabling people to better their condition in every department of life. Political power means capacity to regulate national life through national representatives. If national life becomes so perfect as to become self-regulated, no representation becomes necessary. There is then a state of enlightened anarchy. In such a State everyone is his own ruler. He rules himself in such a manner that he is never a hindrance to his neighbour. In the ideal State, therefore, there is no political power because there is no State. But the ideal is never fully realised in life. Hence the classical statement of Thoreau that government is best which governs the least.

18. By the term, 'a state of enlightened anarchy', what is implied is_______
   (a) confusion amongst intelligentsia
   (b) control yet chaos
   (c) awareness in population and deregulation.
   (d) None of the above

19. But the ideal is never fully _________ in life.
   (a) understood (b) implemented
   (c) realistic (d) attained

**Passage 8**

Most importantly, data carries some of the characteristics of public goods. It is non-rivalrous, i.e., consumption by one individual does not reduce the quantum available for others. In principle, data can be made excludable, i.e., it is possible to exclude people from accessing data, as many database firms do by erecting pay walls. However, there are some kinds of data—particularly data gathered by government on issues of social interest—that should be democratised in the interest of social welfare. Such data should be made public goods. As the private sector would fail to provide an optimal amount of any non-rivalrous, non-excludable good, government intervention is required.

20. Passage suggests that some kinds of data-particularly data gathered by government on issues of social interest should be _________ in the interest of social welfare.
   (a) subject to vote
   (b) freely available to everyone
   (c) accessible to political parties
   (d) available to those who are needy

21. Data gathered by government on issues of social interest should be made _________.
   (a) non available to private people
   (b) government property subject to taxation and accessible by all
   (c) freely accessible government property
   (d) None of the above

**Passage 9**

I recognise no God except the God that is to be found in the hearts, of the dumb millions. They do not recognize His presence; I do. And I worship the God that is Truth or Truth which is God, through service of these millions. We are either ignorant or negligent of the divine law by virtue of which man has been given only his daily bread and no more, with the result that there arise inequalities with all the misery attendant upon them.

22. We are either ignorant or ________ of the divine law.
   (a) remiss
   (b) unaware
   (c) deliberately violative
   (d) none of the above

23. There arise inequalities with all the misery __________ them.
   (a) incurable by (b) following
   (c) caused by (d) accompanying

**Passage 10**

Innovations in science and technology are integral to the long-term growth and dynamism of any nation. The pursuit of science also creates a spirit of enquiry and discourse which are critical to modern, open, democratic societies. Historically, India can point to many contributions to global scientific knowledge and technological achievement. However, India under-spends on research and development (R&D), even relative to its level of development. A doubling of R&D spending is necessary and much of the increase should come from the private sector and universities. To recapture the spirit of innovation that can propel it to a global science and technology leader, from net consumer to net producer of knowledge, India should invest in educating its youth in science and mathematics, reform the way R&D is conducted, engage the private sector and the Indian diaspora and take a more mission-driven approach in areas such as dark matter, genomics, energy storage, agriculture and mathematics and cyber physical systems. Vigorous efforts to improve the 'ease of doing business' need to be matched by similar ones to boost the 'ease of doing science.'

**24.** The author feels that, India ____________ on research and development (R&D),

(a) makes no expenditure
(b) makes unscientific expenditure
(c) makes inefficient expenditure
(d) makes less expenditure

**25.** For India to be a producer of knowledge, it should invest in educating its youth in science and mathematics, reform the way R&D is conducted, engage the private sector and the Indian ________.

(a) immigrants (b) emigrants
(c) citizens (d) residents

## Answers To Exercise Set A

| | | | | | | | | | |
|---|---|---|---|---|---|---|---|---|---|
| **1.** (b) | **2.** (a) | **3.** (a) | **4.** (c) | **5.** (c) | **6.** (d) | **7.** (a) | **8.** (d) | **9.** (a) | **10.** (c) |
| **11.** (b) | **12.** (a) | **13.** (b) | **14.** (a) | **15.** (c) | **16.** (d) | **17.** (b) | **18.** (c) | **19.** (d) | **20.** (b) |
| **21.** (c) | **22.** (a) | **23.** (d) | **24.** (d) | **25.** (b) | | | | | |

## Exercise Set B

***The passage below consists of six sentences. The first and the sixth sentences are given in the beginning and the end respectively in correct chronological position. The middle four sentences are given in a jumbled manner in the options PQRS. Find the proper order of the four sentences.***

**1.** It was an extremely hot day.

(P) He had already covered 12 kilometres of the journey.
(Q) The cyclist was sweltering while pedalling the bike in this heat.
(R) Now the last three kilometre's only had to be travelled.
(S) But it was the last part of journey which was the most difficult.

He could not carry on any further and stopped.

(a) PQRS (b) RSQP
(c) QPSR (d) QPRS

**2.** In India authorities always look to store maximum amount of water in reservoir during the monsoon season.

(P) This is so that when monsoon rains come there is space to store the excess rainwater and also so that water can be released in a regulated manner.
(Q) It is an internationally accepted practice that the water level of a reservoir should be kept below a certain level before the onset of monsoon season.
(R) But the authorities store the maximum amount of water in reservoir before the close of the monsoon.
(S) This stored water is then used for irrigation and generation of electricity during the summer months.

This practice is only to ensure greater electricity generation and irrigation.

(a) SPQR (b) SQPR
(c) SRQP (d) PQRS

3. Consumerism is today the driving force of economy.
   (P) The more we consume the greater is the demand for goods and services.
   (Q) But in the cycle of economic growth the concern for environment is often not integrated.
   (R) The greater demand leads to economic growth and creates jobs which feeds the billions.
   (S) Hence the economic growth is not that can be considered sustainable.

   As a result, we are leaving behind environmental poverty and hardships for our children.

   (a) SRQP (b) PRSQ
   (c) PQSR (d) PRQS

4. Culture is a term which is understood as a set of tangible and intangible values of a society
   (P) It is also varyingly understood as different manifestations of human intellectual and other expressions, particularly of ideas beliefs customs and social behaviour
   (Q) At times urbane life styles and discerning tastes of material subjects are also considered archetypal of what culture embodies.
   (R) At a more granular level this conception incorporates different art forms, languages and literature, traditions and values and even religious norms and practices.
   (S) Above all are definitely elements of culture.

   But the most important element of any culture is the human goodness, bereft of which the other elements are mere bodily manifestations without a soul.

   (a) SRQP (b) PRQS
   (c) PSQR (d) RQSP

5. It was an evening of March in New Delhi.
   (P) The shadows had lengthened and people were ready to leave the offices for their homes.
   (Q) In her haste she forgot that she has to go to Bengali market today rather than to her home directly.
   (R) Seema was making a dash to the nearest bus stop from her office at North Block.
   (S) She was worried that she may miss the bus at 6 PM if she does not hurry.

   It was better to take an auto rickshaw for the Bengali market rather than a bus.

   (a) SPQR (b) PRSQ
   (c) PRQS (d) PQRS

6. It was a dark and cold night.
   (P) The beggar was stoking the fire and occasionally petting the mongrel.
   (Q) The beggar was lying on the footpath with a small bonfire lit next to him.
   (R) The dog would emit a soft sound whenever the beggar would pet it.
   (S) A mongrel was also lying near the fire.

   The warmth of the fire was the lifeline of the beggar and the dog in the bitter cold.

   (a) PQRS (b) QRPS
   (c) QPRS (d) QSPR

7. The practice of dieting has become an epidemic; everybody is looking out for a way to attain the perfect body.
   (P) Thereby we also differ in what foods we tolerate or are sensitive to.
   (Q) This explains the failure of diets across the world in curbing obesity.
   (R) We all are different with respect to our ethnicity, genetics, family history, gender, age, health, life styles and preferences.
   (S) So we cannot reduce so many complexities into one diet or diet look.

   Unless the reasons for weight gain are well understood and addressed and unless habits are changed permanently, no diet is likely to succeed.

(a) PQRS (b) QRPS
(c) RPQS (d) RPSQ

**8.** Access to schooling for those coming of age is close to universal.

(P) However, access to quality education exhibits a sharp gradient with socio-economic status.

(Q) The quotas have imposed a debate on the issues of social integration and equity in education that private actors had escaped by and large.

(R) Quotas for weaker sections in private schools is a provision introduced by the Right of Children to Free and Compulsory Education Act 2009.

(S) The idea of egalitarian education system with equality of opportunity as its prime goal appears to be outside the space that the private schools principals exhibit.

Therefore, the imposition of quotas have led to resistance sometimes justified.

(a) PQRS (b) PRQS
(c) PSQR (d) PRSQ

**9.** In India the current focus on the right to privacy is based on some new realities of the digital age.

(P) But the role of state is also to actively ensure that private parties are not able to block it

(Q) A right to free expression of an individual about her exploitation, for instance is meaningless without actual availability of security that guarantees that private force cannot be used to thwart this right.

(R) A right is a substantive right only if it works in all situations and for everyone.

(S) The role of state therefore is not just to abstain from preventing the rightful free expression.

Without this the right of free expression is meaningless.

(a) PQRS (b) RQSP
(c) RQPS (d) SPQR

**10.** The train was chugging out of the platform.

(P) Suddenly with sharp whistle the train started to slow down.

(Q) Apparently someone had pulled the alarm chain.

(R) As the train again came to a stop, a group of passengers deboarded the train.

(S) The scene of the vendors on the platform and the various signages were receding.

It was obvious that the group was not here to travel but to see off the others and had overstayed in the compartment.

(a) PQRS (b) SQRP
(c) SPQR (d) SPRQ

## Answers To Exercise Set B

| **1.** (d) | **2.** (b) | **3.** (d) | **4.** (b) | **5.** (b) | **6.** (d) | **7.** (c) | **8.** (b) | **9.** (b) | **10.** (c) |
|---|---|---|---|---|---|---|---|---|---|

## Exercise Set C

*Read the passages and answer the questions that follow*

**Passage 1**

My patriotism is both exclusive and inclusive. It is exclusive in the sense that in all humility I confine my attention to the land of my birth, but is inclusive in the sense that my service is not of a competitive or antagonistic nature.

**1.** Which amongst the following are in consonance with the message of the passage?

(1) The call to make one's nation economically strong and vibrant.

(2) The call to annex hostile countries.

(3) The call to assert oneself as the greatest nation on the earth.

(a) 1, 2, 3 (b) 1, 2

(c) 1, 3 (d) 1 only

**Passage 2**

A robust and resilient infrastructure is fundamental and essential for budding industries. While India has invested in its infrastructure over the years, the challenge is to mobilise adequate investment in infrastructure sector which runs into several trillions of dollars. The investment gaps in the infrastructure would have to be addressed through various innovative approaches with the collaboration of both public and private sector.

**2.** Which of the following corollaries can be drawn in terms of the message of the passage?

(1) Public Sector funding would not be enough for infrastructure finance.

(2) High cost foreign investment would not be appropriate for infrastructure finance.

(2) Domestic resources would not be sufficient for the infrastructure finance.

(a) 1, 2 and 3 (b) 1 and 2

(c) 1 and 3 (d) 1 only

**Passage 3**

With the world's population estimated to be nine billion by 2050 and one third of world's soils already degraded, there is an imperative need to protect the soils so that adequate, safe food can be provided to human kind. Most of the pollutants are due to anthropogenic factors. The importance of preventing both soil pollution and soil degradation is also emphasised by the fact that four sustainable development goals are directly impacted with soil degradation and food security. Soils also hold three times as much carbon as the atmosphere and acting as carbon sinks are important also for mitigating the impacts of climate change. The focus on soils on a particular day encourages the farmers to adapt to more sustainable systems of agriculture.

**3.** Which of the following conclusions can be drawn in terms of what is stated in the passage?

(a) Human activity has been exclusively responsible for soil pollution.

(b) The current level of good soil will be insufficient to meet the food demand of nine billion people by 2050.

(c) Both (a) and (b).

(d) Neither (a) nor (b).

**Passage 4**

To me political power is not an end but one of the means of enabling people to better their condition in every department of life. Political power means capacity to regulate national life through national representatives. If national life becomes so perfect as to become self-regulated, no representation becomes necessary. There is then a state of enlightened anarchy. In such a State everyone is his own ruler. He rules himself in such a manner that he is never a hindrance to his neighbour. In the ideal State, therefore, there is no political power because there is no State. But the ideal is never fully realised in life. Hence the classical statement of Thoreau that government is best which governs the least.

4. As per the author's views in the passage, which of the following statements are correct?
   (1) A state in anarchy is the final stage of an evolving ideal state.
   (2) Self-regulation by the citizens is the key to an evolving state.
   (3) An ideal state is never realised.
   (a) 1, 2, 3 (b) 2, 3
   (c) 2 only (d) 1, 2

**Passage 5**

Most importantly, data carries some of the characteristics of public goods. It is non-rivalrous, i.e consumption by one individual does not reduce the quantum available for others. In principle, data can be made excludable, i.e. it is possible to exclude people from accessing data, as many database firms do by erecting pay walls. However, there are some kinds of data-particularly data gathered by government on issues of social interest-that should be democratised in the interest of social welfare. Such data should be made public goods. As the private sector would fail to provide an optimal amount of any non-rivalrous, non-excludable good, government intervention is required.

5. Consider the following statements and identify which is/are the **most crucial** message(s) the passage is conveying.
   (1) Private sector is interested only in rivalrous and excludable data.
   (2) Government as yet has failed to make data available as a public good.
   (a) 1 only (b) 2 only
   (c) Both 1 & 2 (d) Neither 1 nor 2

**Passage 6**

I recognize no God except the God that is to be found in the hearts, of the dumb millions. They do not recognize His presence; I do. And I worship the God that is Truth or Truth which is God, through service of these millions. We are either ignorant or negligent of the divine law by virtue of which man has been given only his daily bread and no more, with the result that there arise inequalities with all the misery attendant upon them.

6. What is the key message which the author wants to convey in the passage?
   (a) Human desire to accumulate more than his daily need leads to misery.
   (b) God is truth.
   (c) Both (a) and (b).
   (d) Neither (a) nor (b).

**Passage 7**

The adverse impacts of indoor air pollution also fall disproportionately on women and children who are directly involved in cooking or spend a major portion of their time indoors. According to a study around 4.3 million people die annually worldwide due to household air pollution resulting from the burning of solid fuels. Not only does using inefficient fuel like firewood and dung cakes cause health hazards, they require a considerable amount of time to be devoted for their collection. One of the estimates of the amount of time spent on collecting firewood in India suggests that on an average, women spend around 374 hours every year for collection of firewood. Thus, access to modern energy sources can reduce the amount of time spent on collection of firewood thereby leading to a positive impact on girls' education and employment.

7. The most crucial message conveyed by the passage is:
   (a) Availability of modern energy sources impact indoor pollution as well as gender equity.
   (b) Indoor air pollution is the most serious challenge in rural India affecting health of women and children.
   (c) India lags other counters in provision of clear fuel source for domestic cooking.
   (d) None of the above.

**Passage 8**

Let me begin by saying that we often make or create confusion between federalism and decentralisation and I have seen quite a number of studies where the two terms have been used interchangeably. To me it appears that federalism has to be defined separately from decentralisation. Federalism is the coming together of equal partners who come with a common goal and share power and jurisdictions. In the case of decentralisation, it is one superior entity which is partly decentralising its powers to the units below and there is a spirit of condescension.

**8.** Which is the most important message the speaker wants to convey?

(a) There is lot of confusion as to what is federalism.

(b) Federalism and decentralisation are distinct from each other and cannot be equated.

(c) Decentralisation involves delegation of powers.

(d) Federalism and decentralisation differ in the status and power of entities coming together but are being mistaken as one and the same.

**Passage 9**

Two paths are open before India today, either to introduce the Western principle of 'Might is Right' or to uphold the Eastern principle that truth alone conquers, that truth knows no mishaps, that the strong and the weak have alike a right to secure justice. The choice is to begin with labouring class. Should the labourers obtain an increment in their wages by violence, even if that be possible? They cannot resort to anything like violence howsoever legitimate may be their claims. To use violence for securing rights may seem any easy path, but it proves to be thorny in the long run. Those who live by the sword die also by sword.

**9.** Why does the author not believe in labourers seeking increment in wages by violence?

(a) He believes that labourers are not strong enough to succeed by use of violence.

(b) He believes violence would beget violence and not their rights.

(c) Both (a) and (b).

(d) Neither (a) nor (b).

**Passage 10**

Innovations in science and technology are integral to the long-term growth and dynamism of any nation. The pursuit of science also creates a spirit of enquiry and discourse which are critical to modern, open, democratic societies. Historically, India can point to many contributions to global scientific knowledge and technological achievement. However, India under-spends on research and development (R&D), even relative to its level of development. A doubling of R&D spending is necessary and much of the increase should come from the private sector and universities. To recapture the spirit of innovation that can propel it to a global science and technology leader – from net consumer to net producer of knowledge, India should invest in educating its youth in science and mathematics, reform the way R&D is conducted, engage the private sector and the Indian diaspora and take a more mission-driven approach in areas such as dark matter, genomics, energy storage, agriculture and mathematics and cyber physical systems. Vigorous efforts to improve the 'ease of doing business' need to be matched by similar ones to boost the 'ease of doing science.'

**10.** Which amongst the following conclusions can be drawn in terms of what is stated in the passages?

(1) India conducts little research in areas such as cyber physical storage, genomics, energy storage etc.

(2) India's under spending on R&D can be partly attributed to there being little contribution of the private sector in development of research infrastructure.

(3) India has the potential to become a net producer of knowledge.

(a) 1, 2 and 3 (b) 2 and 3

(c) 3 only (d) None of the above

**Passage 11**

Access to affordable, reliable, sustainable and modern energy is the sine-qua-non of achieving all the sustainable development goals due to its deep inter-linkages with all the other goals. Its importance in achieving economic prosperity is straight forward. However, it is also directly and indirectly linked to other sustainable development objectives such as good health and well-being, gender equality, industry, innovation and infrastructure, sustainable cities and communities. To understand this, consider an example of the linkage between access to energy and gender equality. This happens through various channels. In India, the burden of collecting fuel wood and water and cooking falls disproportionately on the female members of households.

11. Based on what is stated in the passage which of the following conclusions can be drawn?
    (a) Development of modern sustainable energy has a deep impact on human development parameters.
    (b) India lacks in many human development parameters such as gender equality on account of lack of access to reliable and sustainable sources of energy by certain sections of population.
    (c) Both (a) and (b).
    (d) Neither (a) nor (b).

**Passage 12**

To engineer an inclusive and sustainable growth for India, the social infrastructure like education, health and social protection are being given utmost priority by the Government. The Government has been enhancing the expenditure on human capital along with adopting measures to improve the efficiency of expenditure by convergence of schemes. Several labour reform measures including legislative ones, are being implemented for creation of employment opportunities and for providing sustainable livelihoods for the population who are largely engaged in the informal economy. Bridging the gender gaps in education, skill development, employment, earnings and reducing social inequalities prevalent in the society have been the underlying goals of the development strategy to enhance human capabilities.

12. Consider the following statements and examine which of them can be considered as correct in light of what is stated in the passage?
    (1) Multiplicity of social schemes impacts equity or redistribution of wealth in society.
    (2) Labour reforms are critical for bringing sustainable employment growth across all sections of economy.
    (3) India's economic growth has not been sustainable.
    (a) 1, 2 and 3 (b) 1 and 2
    (c) 1 (d) None of the above

**Passage 13**

Some scholars, however, prefer to use the term 'regionalism', referring to any kind of regional cooperation; whilst other focus more on 'integration', often meaning economic integration. Economic integration includes but is economic communities, and monetary unions. When understood this way, 'Integration' will be deemed not limited to creation of free trade areas, customs unions, to be different from 'Cooperation'. Cooperation, then, is a much weaker and loose form of teamwork among sovereign states and it is more issue specific.

13. Which amongst the following can be said to be the most logical conclusion of the passage?
    (a) Regionalism and economic integration are concepts often used synonymously.
    (b) Regional cooperation a broader concept would invariably include economic integration.
    (c) Both (a) and (b).
    (d) Neither (a) nor (b).

**Passage 14**

Exchange of goods and services is good for the society. This fact was established by early economists such as Adam Smith (specialisation) and David Ricardo (comparative advantage). It has been firmly established that through international trade a country is able to achieve higher rates of economic growth than would be possible without trade because it can produce for a large (global) population than the population of its own nationals. It is in this context that trade is seen as the engine of growth.

14. Which amongst the following can be said to be logical corollary to what is stated in the passage?
    (a) Trade enables economies of scale in production of goods and services.
    (b) As an engine of economic growth trade has a more profound impact on economy than domestic consumption.
    (c) Both (a) and (b).
    (d) Neither (a) nor (b).

**Passage 15**

Theoretically, there are fundamental differences between the legal and regulatory framework of a command-and-control economy and a market economy. In the former, economic activity is restricted to those activities that are permitted by the state. In a market economy, the economy thrives because the state interferes only when there is 'market failure', i.e. monopoly power, asymmetric information or externalities. As a consequence, laws permit all activities, unless the state specifically restricts them in the context of market failure. The restrictions need to be part of a known and predictable regulatory regime unlike now where a lot of restrictions well intentioned as they are not part of a stable framework.

**15.** Which amongst the following is the most natural corollary of what is stated in the passage?

(a) The state should reduce the statutory compliances to be made by firms in a market economy.

(b) The state should divide different sectors of economy into large, medium and small and permit firms to operate accordingly.

(c) The state should trim its own area of economic activity.

(d) The state should restrict then negative list of sectors in which firms can-not operate to a bare minimum.

**Passage 16**

To observe morality is to attain mastery over our mind and our passions. We notice that the mind is a restless bird; the more it gets, the more it wants, and still remains unsatisfied. The more we indulge our passions the more unbridled they become. Our ancestors, therefore, set a limit to our indulgences. They saw that happiness was largely a mental condition. A man is not necessarily happy because he is rich or unhappy because he is poor. The rich are often seen to be unhappy, the poor to be happy. Millions will always remain poor. Observing all this, our ancestors dissuaded us from luxuries and pleasures.

**16.** Considering what is stated in the passage, which amongst the following corollaries can be drawn?

(1) Rich cannot be happy as they have plentiful of resources to indulge.

(2) Scarcity of resources makes the poor happy.

(3) Luxuries and pleasures do not lead to contentment.

(a) 1, 2 and 3 (b) 1 and 3

(c) 3 only (d) None of the above

**Passage 17**

They say, 'means are after all means'. I would say, 'means are after all everything'. As the means, so is the end. There is no wall of separation between the means and the end. Indeed the Creator has given us control (and that too very limited) over means, none over the end. Realisation of the goal is in exact proportion to that of the means. This is a proposition that admits of no exception.

**17.** Which of the following are not in conformity with what is stated in the passage?

(a) Ends do not justify the means.

(b) Wrong means will result in wrong ends.

(c) Means and ends are two sides of the same coin.

(d) None of the above.

**Passage 18**

Under low and predictable inflation, households and firms can make plans about the future, face reduced risk and undertake investments. The inflation uncertainty of recent years has been characterised by a surge in inflation and inflation volatility. High and unstable inflation has made it difficult to make projections about future profits from investment projects. In particular, it has an adverse effect on risk-taking by infrastructure firms, since these projects involve cash flows over multiple decades into the future.

**18.** Which amongst the following can be said to be the most rational message of the passage?

(a) Inflation is usually accompanied by volatility.

(b) Investors should be wary of economic regimes which have high and volatile inflation.

(c) Long-period projects often fail during phases of high and volatile inflation.

(d) Inflationary uncertainty adversely affects the risk-taking capacity of firms in projects involving long gestation periods.

**Passage 19**

India can make a significant contribution in addressing climate change. Unlike some countries, it has taken substantial actions to eliminate petroleum subsidies and gone beyond to impose substantial taxes on these products.

These actions have taken India from a carbon subsidisation regime to one of significant carbon taxation regime—from a negative price to an implicit positive price on carbon emissions. And the shift has been large.

**19.** What logical conclusion can be drawn from what is stated in the passage about steps taken by India for removing carbon subsidy regime?

(a) The steps taken for removal of carbon subsidies have been necessary but not sufficient.

(b) The steps taken were necessary and have been sufficient.

(c) The steps taken were neither necessary nor sufficient.

(d) Steps taken were not necessary but were sufficient.

**Passage 20**

I do not believe that the State can concern itself or cope with religious education. I believe that religious education must be the sole concern of religious associations. Do not mix up religion and ethics. I believe that fundamental ethics is common to all religions. Teaching of fundamental ethics is undoubtedly a function of the state. By religion I do not have in mind fundamental ethics but what goes by the name of denominationalism.

**20.** Which amongst the following represents a logical conclusion about the views of the author?

Conclusion 1: The author considers religious education to have a divisive or sectarian impact on the country.

Conclusion 2: The author considers ethical education to be a necessity.

(a) Only conclusion 1 can be drawn.

(b) Only conclusion 2 can be drawn.

(c) Both conclusions 1 and 2 can be drawn.

(d) Neither conclusion 1 nor 2 can be drawn.

**Passage 21**

There has been increasing concern about the difficulties faced by firms operating in India. In a purely economic sense it is easy to explain the actions of a government that restricts firms in certain ways in order to address market failures. However, the Indian landscape features numerous government interventions that are not connected to market failures. Therefore, there is immediate need to simplify processes including those relating to tax policy and administration.

**21.** Which amongst the following logical conclusions can be drawn from the passage?

(1) Government intervention, when there is no market failure, leads to fall in business confidence in the economic enterprises.

(2) The failure in tax policy and administration has led to erosion of business confidence.

(a) Only conclusion 1 can be drawn.

(b) Only conclusion 2 can be drawn.

(c) Both conclusions 1 and 2 can be drawn.

(d) Neither conclusion 1 nor 2 can be drawn.

**Passage 22**

Inclusive development incorporates social and financial inclusion and in most cases the socially excluded are also financially excluded. Many segments of the population like landless agricultural labourers, marginal farmers, scheduled castes (SCs), scheduled tribes (STs), and other backward classes (OBCs) continue to suffer social and financial exclusion. The government's policies are directed towards bringing these marginalised sections into the mainstream.

**22.** Which is the most valid assumption amongst the following which would support what is stated in the passage?

(a) For most of the sections of the society, economic wherewithal is intricately linked to social inclusion.

(b) Poverty has led to social exclusion of a vast section of society.

(c) Rural-urban divide has created financial as well as social exclusion.

(d) None of the above.

**Passage 23**

There appears to be renewed focus on controlling the rise in population, directed in particular at women, and through means that blur the lines between persuasion and coercion. Persuasion takes the form of incentives offered not just to poor couples for sterilisation but rewards to local bodies for their performance, euphemistically described as 'promotional and motivational' measures, resulting in the organisation of mass camps for female sterilisation. India's population policy seems focused on extending family planning measures, mainly contraceptives for women, leaving them with little reproductive choice or autonomy.

The negative fallouts of pursuing a population policy that largely focuses on birth control also contributes to declining child sex ratios: if every family is to have fewer children, there is a greater anxiety that at least one of them should be male. In this instance, there may be a case for the government to undo as much as to do. For example, by not setting targets (ELAs or expected levels of achievement), withdraw in incentives for female sterilisation and for mass camps.

**23.** Which amongst the following is a logical conclusion of the passage?

Conclusion 1: Population control policy is largely responsible for the declining child sex ratio.

Conclusion 2: Greater emphasis on male sterilisation would help in improving the child sex ratio.

(a) Only conclusion 1 can be drawn.

(b) Only conclusion 2 can be drawn.

(c) Both conclusions 1 and 2 can be drawn.

(d) Neither conclusion 1 nor 2 can be drawn.

**Passage 24**

Economic growth is good for the poor, both directly because it raises incomes and because it generates resources to invest in the public services and social safety nets that the poor need. Growth – and the prospects and opportunities that it brings – also encourages individuals to invest in their own human capital. A recent study found strikingly that merely informing families in villages outside Bengaluru that call centres were hiring educated women increased the likelihood that adolescent girls in those villages completed school.

**24.** Which amongst the following is a logical corollary of what is stated in the passage?

(1) Enhanced prospect for securing a job is a good incentive for certain sections of society to invest in education.

(2) Completion of school education invariably needs some form of incentive.

(a) Only 1 can be said to be a logical corollary.

(b) Only 2 can be said to be a logical corollary.

(c) Both 1 and 2 can be said to be logical corollaries.

(d) Neither 1 nor 2 can be said to be a logical corollary.

**Passage 25**

Rationalisation of subsidies and better targeting of beneficiaries through direct transfers would generate part of the resources for the public investment that is essential in research, education, extension, irrigation, water-management, soil-testing, warehousing and cold-storage. Distortions emerging from various policies, including, exempting user charges for electricity and water need to be reduced, through better targeting and eliminating leakages.

**25.** Which amongst the following statements is in logical consonance with what is stated in the passage?

(a) All subsidies are distortive and need to be done away with.

(b) Resources for agricultural investment can only be generated by rationalisation of subsidies.

(c) Subsidy distortions can be done away with better targeting of subsidies.
(d) None of the above.

**Passage 26**

The poor of India today have lost faith in God, more so than the middle classes or the rich. For a person suffering from the pangs of hunger, and desiring nothing but to fill his belly, his belly is his God. To him anyone who gives him his bread is his Master. Through him he may even see God. To give alms to such persons, who are sound in all their limbs, is to debase oneself and them. What they need is some kind of occupation.

**26.** Which amongst the following are the correct inferences which can be drawn from the passage?
(a) Giving occupation is many times more important than giving alms to a bodily sound person.
(b) Poverty tends to erode our faith in God.
(c) Both (a) & (b).
(d) Neither (a) nor (b).

**Passage 27**

As witnessed over the past two centuries, energy has been the driving force behind the process of economic development: greater access to energy has fostered economic growth as well as other indicators of human development. India has a per-capita energy consumption of only about one-third of the global average. Within this consumption, access to clean fuel is unevenly distributed spatially in rural vis-s-vis urban areas and socio-economically when seen across income groups. India, therefore, needs to quadruple its per-capita energy consumption to meet the rising aspirations of its citizens. This will also enable India to achieve the human development status of an upper-middle-income country.

**27.** In terms of what is stated in the passage, which most important inference can be drawn from it?
(a) Urban-rural divide is bound to continue till the energy consumption gap is reduced.
(b) Removal of socio-economic disparities is essential to remove the energy consumption gap.
(c) Indians economic development will hinge on its per capita energy consumption.
(d) None of the above.

**Passage 28**

Climate finance should support both the adaptation and mitigation activities of the developing countries in accordance with the country needs and priorities. The Paris Agreement gives equal weightage to adaptation mitigation. Under the UNFCCC, the intent and obligation of climate finance is unambiguous, that developed country parties shall provide financial resources to developing countries; but what constitutes of financial resources and its key elements for climate finance itself are very broadly defined. The essential elements that need to be taken up as parameters for accounting climate finance are public grants, unrequited equity and grant-equivalent values of loans. Also counting only such transfers of finance ex-post that are formalised in entry in a book of accounts as specifically climate finance and actual disbursements of such finance crossing borders in a particular year need to be ensured. Some more important parameters such as how to treat private climate finance flows that are 'mobilised' or 'leveraged', the clarity on "new and additional" also need to be understood in this context.

**28.** Which of the following can be said to be the most important messages of the passage?
(1) To highlight that the developed countries have not fulfilled their commitment of financing projects pertaining to mitigation or adoption in relation to climate change.
(2) To identify the nature of the resources which can constitute finance for climate change.
(3) To identify the scale of resources which would be required for financing climate change projects.

(a) 1, 2, 3 (b) 1, 2
(c) 2, 3 (d) 2 only

**Passage 29**

Biodegradable bioplastics that are based on renewable resources are being promoted as a climate friendly alternative to plastics, and are often referred to as zero balance alternatives. Bioplastics are produced by renewable raw materials such as wheat, sugarcane or maize. They do not contaminate the environment unlike plastics produced from non-renewable sources which provide serious environmental risks both to man and animals. The positive impact of bio plastics is that they reduce carbon footprint; do not deplete non-renewable raw materials, and are not harmful to the environment unlike non-biodegradable wastes. However, if bio plastics are produced in large amount it would mean requirement of large tracts of land to produce crops which could mean loss of forest cover. Forests it is well known act as carbon sinks absorbing CO2 from the atmosphere, and their destruction would add to global emissions.

**29.** Which of the following assumptions support what is stated in the passage?

(a) Forests as a carbon sink, absorb many more times carbon dioxide as compared to crops under cultivation.

(b) Use of biodegradable plastics is likely to reduce overall generation of plastics as it can be easily recycled as compared to non biodegradable plastics.

(c) Both (a) and (b).

(d) Neither (a) nor (b).

**Passage 30**

Princes and potentates, whether they were Indian born or foreigners, have hardly touched the vast masses except for collecting revenue. The latter in their turn seem to have rendered unto Caesar what was Caesar's and for the rest have done much as they have liked.

**30.** Identify the most valid reasons which support what is stated in the passage.

(1) The need of the masses were mostly fulfilled locally and by own self/within local community doing away with the need of intervention by a central authority.

(2) The rule of kings and potentates was accountable to only oneself.

(3) Institutions of representation of people in the administration was undeveloped.

(a) 1, 2, 3 (b) 1, 2

(c) 2, 3 (d) 2 only

**Passage 31**

Run of the river hydroelectricity plant is a type of hydroelectric generation whereby little or no water storage is provided. Run of the river power plants may either have no storage at all or limited amount of storage, in which case the storage reservoir is referred to as pondage and is, therefore, subject to seasoned river flows and may operate as an intermittent energy source. The most run of river projects, do not require a large impoundment of water, which is the key reason why such projects are often referred to as environmentally friendly or green power. It is different from other hydroelectricity projects because other hydroelectricity project is large hydropower system such as uses of dam to store river water in a reservoir and these hydropower plants range in various size from small system for a home or village to large projects producing electricity for utilities. Other hydropower plant may cause some problems to the environment and cause degradation.

**31.** In terms of what is stated in the passage which of the following conclusions can be drawn?

(a) Large reservoir based dams should be banned altogether as they are environmentally harmful.

(b) Run of the river hydroelectricity projects being intermittent would not be financially viable and hence would need external financial support.

(c) Both (a) and (b).

(d) Neither (a) nor (b).

**Passage 32**

Agriculture remains the pre-dominant occupation in India for vast sections of the population. Over the years, several new challenges have emerged before the sector. With fragmentation of agricultural holdings and depletion of water resources, the adoption of a resource-efficient, ICT based climate-smart agriculture can enhance agricultural productivity and sustainability. Smallholder farming can be a lucrative livelihood opportunity with the application of appropriate technologies and adoption of natural organic and zero budget natural farming. To transform the rural economy, greater emphasis should be given to allied sector with a major focus on dairy, poultry, fisheries and rearing of small ruminants. The rationalisation of food subsidy and greater use of technology in food management will ensure food security for all.

**32.** Which amongst the following are the most important and crucial message(s) of the passage?

(1) There is a need for rationalisation of agricultural subsidies.

(2) ICT has a critical role in resource efficient small holder farming.

(3) Microfinance is critical for small holder farming to be lucrative and sustainable.

(a) 1, 2 and 3 (b) 1 and 2

(c) 2 and 3 (d) 2 only

**Passage 33**

*Mens sana in corpore sano* is perhaps the first law for humanity. A healthy mind in a healthy body is a self-evident truth. There is an inevitable connection between mind and body. If we were in possession of healthy minds, we would shed all violence and, naturally obeying the laws of health, we would have healthy bodies without an effort.

The fundamental laws of health and hygiene are simple and easily learnt.

The difficulty is about their observance.

**33.** Identity which are the crucial influences which can be drawn from what is stated in the passage?

(1) Knowing the laws of health and hygiene is easy, following it is often difficult.

(2) Mental and physical health invariably go hand in hand.

(3) Our physical health is but a by-product of our eating habits.

(a) 1, 2 (b) 1, 3

(c) 1, 2, 3 (d) 1 only

**Passage 34**

The most effective way of providing data security is encryption. Encrypted data represents a type of code text. You must have access to a secret key or password, which can enable you to decrypt it, thus helping to read an encrypted file. On the contrary, an unencrypted data represents a plain text. It is a very effective tool for the security of important data by excluding the unauthorised access. It can be done through providing the decryption code only to the authorised persons. Military and governments have been using encryption since long, in order to facilitate secret communication. In recent times, it is more commonly used in protecting information within several kinds of civilian systems including WhatsApp, Viber, which use end-to-end encryption (E2EE). Here, except the sender and the receiver no one can decrypt the encrypted data.

**34.** Based on what is stated in the passage, which of the following conclusions can be drawn?

(a) Encryption of data ensures its complete end to end security.

(b) Data encryption had not been in vogue up till now as it was very costly and hence only used by military and governments.

(c) Both (a) and (b).

(d) Neither (a) nor (b).

**Passage 35**

I do not want my house to be walled in on all sides and my windows to be stuffed. I want the cultures of all the lands to be blown about my house as freely as possible. But I refuse to be blown of my feet by any. I refuse to live in other people's houses as in interloper, a beggar or a slave. I refuse to put the necessary strain of learning English upon my sisters for the sake of false pride or questionable social advantage. I would have our young men and young women with literary tastes to learn as much English and other worlds languages as they like, and then expect them to give the benefits of their learning to India and to the world. But I would not have a single Indian to forget, neglect or be ashamed of his mother tongue, of to feel that he or she cannot think or express the best thoughts in his or her own vernacular. Mine is not a religion of the prison-house. It has room for the least among God's creation. But it is proof against insolence, pride of race, religion or colour.

**35.** Which of the following statements best support the author's view point in the passage?

(1) Learning one's own mother tongue is the easiest for a child.

(2) Learning English opens up doors for new occupation.

(3) For enrichment of the national culture, it is essential to prevent English from being taught in schools and colleges.

(a) 1 only (b) 1, 2

(c) 1, 2, 3 (d) None of the above

**Passage 36**

Gender budgeting is a tool for gender mainstreaming. It uses the budget as an entry point to apply a gender lens to the entire policy process. The Ministry of Women and Child Development (MoWCD) as the nodal agency has adopted the mission strategy of 'Budgeting for Gender Equity' to ensure that government budgets are planned according to the differential needs of women and men and accordingly prioritised. Gender budgeting is concerned with gender-sensitive formulation of legislation, policies, plans, programmes and schemes; allocation and collection of resources; implementation and execution; monitoring, review, audit and impact assessment of programmes and schemes; and follow-up corrective action to address gender disparities. It is undertaken through several institutional mechanisms such as gender budget statement, gender budget cells, as well as various schemes/ programmes for women and girls.

**36.** Which of the following assumptions would be correct in terms of what is stated in the passage?

(1) Gender budgeting would entail specific financial allocation in policy and programmes to cater to a woman component.

(2) The Ministry of Women and Child Development as the nodal agency of gender budgeting would be the approving authority of all policies and programmes which have a gender budgeting component.

(3) Gender budgeting helps to integrate the numerous policies and pro-grammes which focus on woman and child.

(a) 1 only (b) 1 and 2

(c) 1 and 3 (d) 1, 2 and 3

**Passage 37**

Trust as public good gets enhanced with greater use. Trust can be conceptualised as a public good with the characteristics of non-excludability i.e., the citizens can enjoy its benefits at no explicit financial cost. Trust also has the characteristics of non-rival consumption i.e., the marginal cost of supplying this public good to an extra citizen is zero. It is also non rejectable i.e., collective supply for all citizens means that it cannot be rejected. Unlike other public goods, trust grows with repeated use and therefore takes time to build. Lack of trust represents an externality where decision makers are not responsible for some of the consequences of their actions.

**37.** Consider the following statements and examine as to which of them can be said to be the most important and crucial message(s) of the passage?

(1) Trust as a public good can eliminate the need for formal contracts between economic agents.

(2) An environment based on trust may face the negative externality of economic agents exploiting it.

(a) only 1 (b) only 2

(c) Both 1 and 2 (d) Neither 1 nor 2

**Passage 38**

I have repeatedly observed that no school of thought can claim a monopoly of right judgment. We are all liable to err and are often obliged to revise our judgments. In a vast country like this, there must be room for all schools of honest thought. And the least, therefore, that we owe to ourselves as to others is to try to understand the opponent's viewpoint and, if we cannot accept it, respect it as fully as we expect him to respect ours. It is one of the indispensable tests of a healthy public life.

**38.** Examine which of the following assumptions are correct in terms of the views of the author in the passage.

(1) Acceptance of the views of the majority political party should be the norm in a parliamentary democracy.

(2) Conflict of view points and interest is bound to take place in parliamentary democracy.

(3) Appropriate judgments often eludes the majority party, hence there is the need of an opposition in a parliamentary democracy.

(a) 1 only (b) 2 only
(c) 2 & 3 (d) 1, 2 and 3

**Passage 39**

Implementing 2030 sustainable Development Agenda and the Paris Agreement requires investments of scale and size which is unprecedented. This essentially means that along with domestic public budgets and international public finance, resources would have to be mobilised from a variety of sources, in particular, private sector. Currently, private sector financing has been mostly done by the banks and resides on their balance sheets. However, in future to increase the scale of sustainable investments there may be funding capacity problems for the banks if they are the primary provider of sustainable debt. Therefore, capital market products are required to free-up the banks' balance sheet capacity and allow them to underwrite loans to meet the accelerating demands for new sustainable investments. Further, by doing so institutional investors and certain retail investors can get access to sustainable debt as institutional investors are well situated to hold long term sustainable debt and they look to match long term liability funding requirements with long term assets.

**39.** In terms of what is sated in the passage, which of the following conclusion can be drawn about role of banks in financing of environmental projects?

(1) Banks should play the role of primary creditors in financing of the environmental projects.

(2) Banks should provide loans to the capital market for funding of environ-mental projects.

(3) Banks should play the role of an underwriter for the funding the environmental projects.

(a) 1, 2, 3 (b) 2, 3
(c) 3 only (d) None of the above

**Passage 40**

With an understanding of biomechanics, engineers can develop biologically inspired robots, with improved and enhanced capabilities over traditional robots, which are robotic! Biologically-inspired robots have greater mobility and flexibility than traditional robots and often possess sensory abilities. Biorobotic technologies are often utilised to provide assistance to accommodate a deficiency, either as fully-functioning robots or highly advanced prosthetics, the latter represents one area in which neural engineering and biorobotics intersect, as both disciplines are required in order to first signal and then generate movement. Such devices may also be used to measure the state of disease, track progress or offer interactive training experiences that can speed recovery from an injury or stroke.

**40.** Consider the following assumptions.

(1) The convergence of robotics and neural engineering will help in development of advanced artificial limbs and devices which can track disease progression.

(2) Biologically inspired robots will have additional abilities of artificial intelligence making them much superior to the ordinary robots.

Which of the above assumptions can be said to be correct in terms of what is stated in the passage?

(a) Only 1 (b) Only 2
(c) Both 1 and 2 (d) Neither 1 nor 2

**Passage 41**

We are all absolutely equal. But equality is of souls and not bodies. Hence, it is a mental state. We need to think of, and to assert, equality because we see great inequalities in the physical world.

**41.** Which of the following conclusions can be drawn from what is stated in the passage?

(a) The physical differences in our bodies permeate inequality in ourselves.

(b) Equality needs to be established and will not occur naturally.

(c) Both (a) & (b).

(d) Neither (a) nor (b).

**Passage 42**

For more than three-fourths of known economic history, India has been the dominant economic power globally. Such dominance was manifested by design. During much of India's economic dominance, the economy relied on the invisible hand of the market for wealth creation with the support of the hand of trust. Specifically, the invisible hand of markets, as reflected in openness in economic transactions, was combined with the hand of trust by appealing to ethical and philosophical dimensions.

**42.** Based on what is stated in the passage, which of the following conclusions can be drawn?

(1) In India's early economic history, trust was based on edicts issued by the kings and local communities.

(2) The guilds and local chiefs would control the nature of business activities so as to ensure viability of trade and economic growth.

(3) Mostly, India did not follow a command and control model of economic growth.

(a) None of the above

(b) 2 and 3

(c) 1 and 3

(d) 3 only

**Passage 43**

Today, nanotechnology has great relevance, as it has the potential to address the needs of all innovative technological solutions. Nanotechnology can be used in public health, in India, with better medical practices and affordability. With the advancement of nanomedicine, researchers have developed nano-bioceramics that repair bones and tissues and an aerosol spray that uses nanoparticles to deliver lung cancer drugs. A nanobased water filter and the 'Sens' (a sensor) are also developed in India as an affordable and user-friendly nanodiagnostic tool that anticipates heart attacks. With its vast scientific and industrial base, India can become a leader in nanoscience and nanotechnology research.

**43.** Examine the following statements and identify those which are logical and appropriate conclusion of what is stated in the passage.

(1) Nanotechnology has helped to develop drugs which offer cure for cancer.

(2) India has not invested sufficiently in research and development of nano-technology and nanosciences.

(3) Nanotechnology applications in medicine is likely to improve its efficacy and reduce its cost.

(a) 1, 2　　(b) 2 and 3

(c) 1 and 3　　(d) Only 3

**Passage 44**

Creating synthetic life is a great challenge and a complex task. It entails the creation of an artificial genetic code and an artificial DNA. It would also involve creating cellular organelles such as mitochondria, ribosome, and nucleus, completely a new. Creating a fully synthetic cell would also be expensive. These constraints can be by passed and a new organism can be created by just replacing the genome in an existing, natural cell with a different genome created by gene synthesis. This is one way around. The creation of Synthia, in 2010, marked the first instance of achieving it.

**44.** Which amongst the following are important and crucial message(s) of the passage?

(1) Despite advancement of technology, it is not possible to create synthetic life anew.

(2) It's simpler and feasible to create a new organism by replacing a genome

in existing cell with a different genome than to create the entire cell with all its components.

(3) Gene replacement technology will open the doors for treatment of a number of genetic diseases.

(a) 1, 2, 3 (b) 2 and 3
(c) 1 and 2 (d) Only 2

**Passage 45**

In adoption of 2030 global agenda, the countries are moving forward for achieving a world free from poverty, gender inequality and economic inequality and thereby ensuring a healthy planet for future generations. These goals are multi-dimensional and integrate various social, economic and environmental dimensions. India continues to target and maintain its economic growth by introducing and implementing various policies and measures relating to sustainable development, climate change, resource efficiency and air pollution. India has been progressing rapidly towards achieving the Sustainable Development Goals (SDGS). With increasing demand for resources to cater to the different developmental needs, policies need to nudge economic agents towards achieving the maximum output from the available resources. Developing countries like India need to endeavour to do the best possible within their own domestic resources, keeping in mind the sustainable development imperatives. It is time for the global community to exhibit the requisite momentum to act upon their responsibilities on establishing the enabling environment for sustainable development and climate actions.

**45.** (I) Which amongst the following socio-economic objectives are identified in the passage as a need for global and domestic agenda of countries for 2030.

(1) Elimination of poverty
(2) Sustainable development and environmental objectives
(3) Channelisation of resources from the developed to developing nations
(4) Removal of gender equality
(5) Healthcare for all

(a) 1, 2, 3, 4 and 5 (b) 1, 2, 3, 4
(c) 1, 2, 4, 5 (d) 1, 2, 4

**45.** (II) Which of the following conclusions can be drawn about India's development agenda in terms of what is stated in the passage?

(a) Policy and programmes should focus on efficient utilisation of domestic resources.
(b) Considering the environmental challenges, sustainable development and tackling our pollution needs, India's economic growth would be moderate.
(c) Both (a) and (b).
(d) Neither (a) nor (b).

**Passage 46**

Navigating in an uncertain, wobbly world requires constant monitoring of the path followed by the economy using real-time indicators. Thus, data can serve as the stones that enable one to cross the river. Concurrent with the data explosion of recent years, the marginal cost of data has declined exponentially while its marginal benefit to society has increased manifold. Therefore, society's optimal consumption of data is higher than ever. While private sector does a good job of harnessing data where it is profitable, government intervention is needed in social sectors of the country where private investment in data remains inadequate. Governments already hold a rich repository of administrative, survey institutional and transactions data about citizens, but these data are scattered across numerous government bodies. Utilising the information embedded in these distinct datasets would interalia enable government to enhance ease of living for citizens, enable truly evidence-based policy, improve targeting in welfare schemes, uncover unmet needs, integrate fragmented markets, bring greater accountability in public services, generate greater citizen participation in governance, etc. given that sophisticated technologies already exist to protect privacy and share confidential information, governments can create data as a public good within the legal framework of data privacy. In the spirit of the Constitution of India, data should be "of the people, by the people, for the people."

**46.** (I) The **most important** and **crucial message** which the author wants to convey in the passage is that:-

(a) There is need of real time indicators for shorting the economic growth path

(b) There is a need for collecting and collating date scattered or numerous government records.

(c) There is a need for utilising data as a public good.

(d) All of the above

**46.** (II) Consider the following assumptions and identify the ones which are correct in terms of what is stated in the passage:-

(1) The government may not be having the sophisticated technology to protect privacy and share data.

(2) It has become financially viable for society to consume data in large scale.

(3) Use of data by private sector for social benefits would be a failure as its efficiency lies in harnessing data that is profitable.

(a) 1, 2, 3 (b) 1, 2

(c) 2 only (d) 2, 3

**Passage 47**

While increasing access to energy is important, it is also imperative that this comes at much lower costs to the environment than it has happened historically in advanced economies. As observed above, there has been arguably a transformation in the energy mix in India. Renewable energy sources are a strategic national resource. Harnessing these resources is a part of India's vision to achieve social equity and energy transition with energy security, a stronger economy, and climate change mitigation. Government has announced zero import duty on components used in making solar panels to give a boost to domestic solar panel manufacturers. Government has also offered various financial incentives for off-grid and decentralised renewable energy systems and devices for meeting energy needs for cooking, lighting and productive purposes. Thus, progressively declining costs, improved efficiency and reliability have made renewable energy an attractive option for meeting the energy needs in a sustainable manner and helping India pursue its low carbon development pathway.

**47.** (I) Consider the following assumptions.

(1) India's transition in energy policy and reliance on renewable energy implies that soon there would be a greater percentage of renewable energy in the countries energy basket.

(2) Transition as energy policy would be sufficient for meeting the challenges of climate change mitigation.

Which assumption(s) as above can be considered to be in terms of what is stated in the passage?

(a) Only 1 (b) Only 2

(c) Both 1 and 2 (d) Neither 1 nor 2

**47.** (II) In terms of the passage, which are the benefits which are likely to accrue due to transformation of the energy mix in India.

(1) Environmental cost of energy would reduce.

(2) Energy access to under privileged section would improve.

(3) Energy consumption would improve.

(a) 1, 2, 3 (b) 1, 3

(c) 2, 3 (d) 1 only

**Passage 48**

Despite India's outstanding growth in the last two decades, low pay and wage inequality remain serious obstacles towards achieving inclusive growth. An effective minimum wage policy that targets the vulnerable bottom rung of wage earners can help in driving up aggregate demand and building and strengthening the middle class, and thus spur a phase of sustainable and inclusive growth. However, the present minimum wage system in India is extremely complex with 1,915 minimum wages defined for various scheduled job categories for unskilled works across various states. Despite its complex structure and proliferation of scheduled employments over time, the Minimum Wages Act, 1948 does not cover all wage workers. One in every three wage workers in India has fallen through the crack and is not protected by the minimum wage law.

**48.** (I) Based on what is stated in the passage which of the following conclusion(s) can be drawn?

(a) An effective minimum wage policy would also help in improving the middle class.

(b) Some states have not been able to provide for a basic minimum wage.

(c) Both (a) & (b).

(d) Neither (a) nor (b).

**48.** (II) Which amongst the following are the challenges identified in ensuring basic minimum wages in the country?

(1) Complexity in the minimum wages law and system.

(2) There being a large number of jobs in the unorganised sector.

(3) Lack of coverage of all minimum wage workers.

(4) Failure of state government machinery to ensure access to minimum wages by workers.

(a) 1, 2, 3, 4 (b) 1, 2, 3

(c) 1, 3, 4 (d) 1, 3

**Passage 49**

Coffee Board has launched blockchain based coffee e-marketplace. This is a pilot project which is likely to help integrate the farmers with markets in a transparent manner and lead to realisation of fair price for the coffee producer. It will also reduce the number of layers between coffee growers and buyers and help farmers double their income.

India is the only country where coffee is grown under shade, handpicked and sun dried. Coffee is produced in India by small coffee growers, tribal farmers adjacent to national parks and wildlife sanctuaries in Western and Eastern Ghats, which are two of the major bio-diversity hot spots in the world. India's coffee is highly valued in the world market and sold as premium coffee. However, the share of farmers in the final returns from coffee is very meagre.

Blockchain based market place app for trading of Indian coffees is intended to bring in transparency in the trade of Indian coffee, maintain the traceability of Indian coffee from bean to cup so as consumer tastes real India coffee, the grower is paid fairly for his coffee produced. This initiative will reduce grower's dependency on intermediaries by providing direct access to buyers at a fairprice for their produce. The initiative will also help coffee producers find exporters within the stipulated time to meet the growing demands and is building greater trust through increased transparency.

Coffee Board is in the process of developing blockchain based marketplace application. This platform has already registered several coffee farmers, exporters, importers and retailers are processors for coffee in the world, after France and Ethiopia.

The stakeholders like coffee farmers, traders, exporters register on platform to make trade transaction. The coffee farmers register credentials like place where coffee is grown, details of crop, elevation etc. A block is created for each lot farmer sells. The credentials of are stored on the blockchain throughout its journey and is immutable.

**49.** (I) Identify as to which of the following conclusions can be drawn in terms of what is stated in the passage?

(1) Coffee growers were unable to obtain the best price for their produce on account of existence of middlemen as well as lack of transparency in marketing of their produce.

(2) The development of blockchain based marketplace app for trading of Indian coffee will largely benefit the producers of coffee in the export segment.

(3) There is the need for use of ICT for bringing greater transparency and authentication of coffee growth/produce information, for wider marketing of Indian coffee.

(a) 1, 2 and 3 (b) 1 and 2

(c) 1 and 3 (d) 1 only

**49.** (II) Which of the following assumptions will support what is stated in the passage?

(a) There is a demand for information about production of the coffee as it would add to its verifiability of standard of quality.

(b) The introduction process being complex needs to be documented using ICT tools.

(c) Both (a) and (b).

(d) Neither (a) nor (b).

**Passage 50**

The highest form of freedom carries with it the greatest measure of discipline and humility. Freedom that comes from discipline and humility cannot be denied, unbridled licence is a sign of vulgarity injurious alike to self and one's neighbours.

There is no human institution but has its dangers. The greater the institution the greater the chances of abuse. Democracy is a great institution and therefore it is liable to be greatly abused. The remedy, therefore, is not avoidance of democracy but reduction of possibility of abuse to a minimum.

A popular State can never act in advance of public opinion. If it goes against it, it will be destroyed. Democracy disciplined and enlightened is the finest thing in the world. A democracy prejudiced, ignorant, superstitious, will land itself in chaos and may be self-destroyed.

**50.** (I) Examine which of the following assumptions are valid in terms of the passage.

(1) For democratic freedom to survive, institutional checks and balances are essential in governance.

(2) An authoritarian regime is better than a prejudiced democracy.

(3) Democracy eliminates the possibility of Institutional abuse.

(a) 1 only (b) 1, 2

(c) 1, 2, 3 (d) 1, 3

**50.** (II) Identify as to which amongst the following is the most important and crucial message which the author wants to convey.

(a) Democratic institutions are likely to be abused in any democracy.

(b) Democracy offers its citizens the maximum freedom.

(c) it is the citizens who make the democracy a success or failure.

(d) Democracy, which has disciplined and enlightened citizens, is the best form of governance.

**Passage 51**

The term culture is varyingly understood, often encompassing different manifestations of human intellectual and other expressions, particularly of ideas, beliefs, customs and social behaviour. At a more granular level, this conception incorporates different art forms, languages and literature, traditions and values and even religious norms and practices. At times, urbane lifestyles and discerning tastes of material subjects are also considered archetypal of what culture embodies.

**51.** Consider the following and determine as to which of these would fall in the description of culture as given above:-

(1) Development in the field of folk literature.

(2) Emergence of new social customs and festivals.

(3) Enactment of new civil laws.

(4) Development of new architectural styles in building construction.

(a) Only 1 and 2 (b) Only 1, 2 and 4

(c) Only 1, 3 and 4 (d) All of the above

**Passage 52**

Idealism is an ambiguous word and has been used to signify a variety of views. An "idea" is taken as a particular mental image peculiar to each individual and attempts are made in the Buddhist *Vijnanavada* (mentalism) and English empiricism to reduce all knowledge to ideas in this sense. Whatever is real in the universe is such stuff as ideas are made of. Ideas or images are regarded as self-contained existences and not as avenues of the apprehension of a world which is at once more ideal and more real than themselves. The term "idea" has also been used to signify the universal notion, which is not an existent here and now, but a quality of the existent which is shareable by other existents and knowable by other minds.

52. Consider the following statements and identify which of the following can be considered to be correct in the light of what is stated in the passage:-
   (1) The passage aims to explain the concept of idealism.
   (2) The author considers that idealism cannot be fully defined.
   (3) The author considers *Vijnanavada* to be identical to idealism.
   (4) The author considers idealism to be a quality which is shareable with and knowable to others.
   (a) 1, 2, 3 and 4 (b) 1, 2 and 3
   (c) 1 and 2 (d) 1, 2, and 4

**Passage 53**

Wealth creation happens in an economy when the right policy choices are pursued. For instance, wealth creation and economic development in several advanced economies have been guided by Adam Smith's philosophy of the invisible hand. Despite the dalliance with socialism–four decades is but an ephemeral period in the history of millennia–India has embraced the market model that represents our traditional legacy. However, scepticism about the benefits accruing from a market economy still persists. This is not an accident as our tryst with socialism for several decades makes most Indians believe that Indian economic thought conflicts with an economic model relying on the invisible hand of the market economy. However, this belief is far from the truth.

53. Which amongst the following statements can be said to be true in terms of what is stated in the passage?
   1. Socialism is a failed economic model.
   2. Indians largely continue to believe in the virtues of the socialistic economic model.
   3. A market economy is new to India.
   (a) Only statement 1
   (b) Only statements 1 and 2
   (c) Only statement 3
   (d) None of the above

**Passage 54**

There is higher biological diversity in lower latitudes as life in lower latitudes gets more sunlight and time on the evolutionary time scale in comparison to life in higher latitudes. There is a direct relationship between biological diversity and latitude. Latitudinal Diversity Gradient shows that diversity richness is more in the areas near the equator than at the poles though latitude is not the only factor responsible for the diversity of a place. There is an inverse relationship between diversity and altitude. High altitudes are less diverse than lower altitudes. With the increase in altitude, the atmosphere becomes less dense and due to the lack of oxygen, only a few species can sustain life at higher altitudes.

54. Which of the following statements would support what is stated in the passage?
   (a) Regions of more sunshine often see many organisms competing for ecological space with each other.
   (b) Higher altitudes and environmental challenges therein make organisms hardier and more likely to overcome the battle of survival of the fittest.
   (c) Both (a) and (b)
   (d) Neither (a) nor (b)

**Passage 55**

Mind is immanent in all cognitive experience as an active process which gives objective form to knowledge. It does not stand in a transcendent relation to an extraneous object which it passively contemplates.

Which of the following logical conclusions can be drawn from the passage above?
   1. Cognitive experience is the basis of all mental perceptions.
   2. Sensory perceptions are not as significant as the cognitive ability of the mind.
   3. Mind is a mere objective instrument to perceive reality.
   (a) Only conclusions 1 and 2
   (b) Only conclusion 2
   (c) Only conclusions 1 and 3
   (d) None of the above

**Passage 56**

The spirit of free inquiry and the right to think for oneself, which is not necessarily to think unlike others, have come to stay and the defenders of authority do not openly persecute the critically minded and are often anxious to appeal to reason in support of authority.

**56.** Which of the following logical conclusions can be drawn from the passage?

1. In earlier times, those critical of the social authorities were likely to face persecution at the hands of the authorities.
2. Independent thinking may or may not mean commonality of perspective.

(a) Only conclusion 1
(b) Only conclusion 2
(c) Both the conclusions 1 and 2
(d) Neither conclusion 1 nor 2

**Passage 57**

The role of local population characteristics such as population size and density is especially salient to new firms, where local markets are assumed the firm's primary product market and where most entrepreneurs are assumed to start their business in their area of residence (Dahl and Sorenson 2007). In such a case, the size of the region reflects the local market size and to some degree, the potential supply of entrepreneurs and managers. Population density also impacts other operating parameters such as competition for local resources and higher resource costs (for example wages and land rents) (Ghani et al. 2011). Some studies also link density to stronger knowledge flows, rendering its impact on entrepreneurial activity an empirical question. Researchers have also demonstrated an inverted-U relationship between regional age structure and entrepreneurship rates that underlies India's "demographic dividend", establishing this variable as an important driver of entrepreneurship.

**57.** Which of the following statements can be said to be logical corollaries of what is stated in the passage?

(a) There is an optimal age band of a society which is likely to support entrepreneurship.
(b) A positive correlation between population density and support for entrepreneurial activity cannot be said to exist.
(c) Both (a) and (b)
(d) Neither (a) nor (b)

**Passage 58**

Nature in her blind thirst for life has filled the earth with innumerable types. The offspring of living organisms are never exactly alike. They vary slightly both from the parents and from one another. Variations which help individuals to live more easily tend to survive. Those individuals which do not share these variations pass out. By a continuous piling up of small variations spread over a long time, Darwin held, a new species is produced. Though this view has suffered modifications in detail—variations are said to be discontinuous and far from gradual or by minute stages—the general theory is not much disturbed. The story of continuous development through the whole of animate nature suggests the working of an automatic mechanism. No principle outside the natural world is needed to account for it.

**58.** Which of the following statements/propositions are in logical consonance with what is stated in the passage?

1. The conception of an omnipotent God deciding the fate of man and the natural world.
2. The conception of the survival of the fittest.

(a) Only statement 1
(b) Only statement 2
(c) Both the statements 1 and 2
(d) Neither the statement 1 nor 2

**Passage 59**

The modern temper insists that the scientific attitude of veracity and self-detachment must spread to all human affairs. The assumption of religion that God, the author of the universe, is the benevolent father of us all, is an open invitation to explain away the difficulties and discomforts of life as delusions of the mind. The tendency of religion to mistake desires for facts, to take the world to be what we should like it to be, to reserve a certain part of life as falling outside the scope of ordinary knowledge is the direct opposite of empirical science.

**59.** Based on what is stated in the passage, which of the following conclusions can be drawn?

1. Religion is based on gospels.
2. Religion is based on ideals.
3. Science accepts what is a verifiable fact.

(a) 1, 2 and 3 (b) Only 1 and 2
(c) Only 1 and 3 (d) Only 2 and 3

**Passage 60**

Biodynamic agriculture is considered to be a form of alternative agriculture very similar to organic farming. It treats soil fertility, plant growth and livestock care as ecologically interrelated tasks. It also emphasizes spiritual and mystical perspectives of agriculture. It excludes the use of synthetic fertilisers, pesticides and herbicides on soil and plants. It regards animals, crops and soil as a single system. It lays stress on local production and distribution systems, use of traditional and development of new local breeds and varieties.

**60.** Which amongst the following are not one of the characteristics of biodynamic agriculture described in the passage above?

1. No use of chemical fertilisers.
2. Emphasis on ecological integration of livestock in agricultural practices.
3. Emphasis on storage and transportation of products over a long distance.
4. Use of a modern scientific variety of breeds and their import.

(a) Only statements 1, 2 and 3
(b) Only statements 2 and 3
(c) Only statements 3 and 4
(d) Only statements 2 and 4

**Passage 61**

The modern concept of a nation and nationhood is only a few centuries old. Nationhood is usually understood as a large group of people domiciled in a geographical unit and united by a common, political/administrative order, law, culture, common history, economic order and language. Other uniting characteristics could be the commonality of race, religion, ethnicity etc. The National Flag, Anthem and Emblem could be some other symbolic elements of national identity.

From the modern perspective, the intermingling of races and freedom of faith and belief has rendered race, religion and ethnicity meaningless as defining factors of nationhood. Similarly, a multitude of spoken languages in many modern nations does not make the commonality of a spoken/official language a necessary condition for nationhood. Thus, the modern-day nations can be recognised by their sovereign people domiciled out of a free will, in a geographical area, united by legal/political order, culture, history and economic activity. However, exceptions and marginal variations would exist and a watertight definition may not be possible.

**61.** Which amongst the following factors would not be considered essential as per the modern concept of nationhood enunciated in the passage?

1. Existence of sovereign law.
2. Existence of a common State language.
3. Existence of a majority ethnic group.
4. Existence of a federal government.

(a) Only 3 (b) Only 2 and 3
(c) Only 2, 3 and 4 (d) All of the above

**Passage 62**

The values for which we struggle are only a flash in the pan and will disappear sooner or later. The cosmic process is but a weaving and unweaving of forms, in which the values we cherish find precarious and brief embodiment. Ethical principles are but general rules for the guidance of human conduct and owe their significance to the developing society in which they arise. Our sense of duty is at the bottom, the "herd instinct", which is found even among animals. In obedience to this instinct, the interests of the individual are subordinated to those of the group. The authority of conscience is of purely social origin and does not require any reference to supernatural power. There is not a single human act which society has not at one time approved and at another condemned. Though standards change, life seems to be meaningless without them and so the myth of morality is invented.

**62.** Which of the following corollaries can be drawn from what is stated in the passage?

1. It is meaningless for society to believe in ethics for they are transient.
2. Ethics are changing as are the norms of society.
3. Values are a by-product of the interaction of the principles of social good vis-a-vis the individual good.

(a) 1, 2 and 3 (b) Only 1 and 3
(c) Only 3 (d) Only 2 and 3

**Passage 63**

In a market economy too, there is a need for the state to ensure a moral hand to support the invisible hand. As Sandel (2012) argues, markets are liable to debase ethics in the pursuit of profits at all costs. Trust contributes positively to the access of both formal and informal financing (Guiso et al., 2004). Ancient philosophers considered trust as an important element in society and postulated that trust can be furthered by appealing to ethical and philosophical dimensions.

**63.** Examine the following statements and ascertain as to which of these would support logically, what is stated in the passage.

(a) Market economy is based on the economic agents' pursuing individual interests.
(b) Existence of trust between economic agents helps in compliance to terms of economic transactions at lower costs without the need for legal enforcement.
(c) Both (a) and (b)
(d) Neither (a) nor (b)

**Passage 64**

Cultural units are comparable to plant growths. They pass through the stages of growth, blossoming and decay. Call it destiny or collective soul, an immutable law governs the rise and fall of races and cultures. History circles in as fixed orbits and with as predetermined a movement as the stars themselves.

**64.** Which amongst the following is/are the most crucial message of the passage?

1. Cultures are bound to pass through different phases of growth and decay.
2. History repeats itself.
3. Culture needs to be preserved.

(a) Only statement 1
(b) Only statements 1 and 3
(c) Only statements 1 and 2
(d) All the statements 1, 2 and 3

**Passage 65**

The encrypted sets of numbers showing a person's DNA makeup are called DNA profiles. It can also be used in the identification of individuals and in parental testing and investigation of criminals. In paternity cases, DNA fingerprinting technology can be used to determine persons as biological parents of a child. Although 99.9 per cent of human DNA sequences are similar in every person, only 0.1 per cent of human DNA is unique. Sir Alec Jeffreys at the University of Leicester in England first reported the DNA profiling technique in 1984. DNA fingerprinting advancement is undertaken for quicker and precise identification of criminal suspects during investigations. The DNA fingerprints of all tried and convicted criminals are stored in a database for identification.

**65.** Which amongst the following is not one of the utilities of DNA fingerprinting highlighted in the passage above?

1. It is helpful in the identification of criminals.
2. It can be applied for the verification of parentage.
3. It may be useful in the genetic and health profiling of individuals.
4. It may serve as the identity of individuals.
5. It will help in building a database of citizens.

(a) Only statement 3
(b) Only statements 4 and 5
(c) Only statements 3 and 5
(d) Only statements 3, 4 and 5

**Passage 66**

"There is a common misconception that people who are in favour of a free market are also in favour of everything that big business does. Nothing could be further from the truth," wrote Milton Friedman. The pro-crony policy supports incumbent firms but does not necessarily foster competitive markets. On the other hand, the policy that fosters competitive markets creates a level playing field for businesses to compete. It unleashes the powerful forces of creative destruction, which create wealth. Austrian economist and creator of the term, Joseph Schumpeter, described creative destruction as a "process of industrial mutation that incessantly revolutionizes the economic structure from within, incessantly destroying the old one, incessantly creating a new one."

**66.** Examine the following statements and examine as to which of these can be said to be in logical consonance with what is stated in the passage.

1. Destruction of established businesses is good for the economy.
2. Big businesses can have a detrimental effect on the market.
3. Competition amongst the businesses is essential for the markets to grow.

(a) Only statements 1 and 3
(b) Only statements 1 and 2
(c) Only statements 2 and 3
(d) All of the above

**Passage 67**

In the light of our present knowledge of man's history and the vastness of the cosmos, it seems anomalous, if not absurd, to imagine that the earth or the human species or any historic individuals in it form the centre of things. Our earth is parochial and our citizenship on it a triviality.

**67.** Examine the following statements and determine which of the following statements are logical affirmations of the author's message in the passage.

1. Rebuttal of the geocentric model of the universe.
2. Possibility of the existence of intelligent life forms in many other planets in the universe.
3. The significance of an individual's contribution to a society waning with time.

(a) Only statement 1
(b) Only statements 1 and 3
(c) Only statements 1 and 2
(d) All the statements 1, 2 and 3

**Passage 68**

Several studies from around the globe find that political connections lead to rent extraction. Faccio et al. (2006) examines politically connected firms in 47 countries and finds that around the time that a firm announces that managers or large shareholders are entering politics; there is a positive impact on the stock price. The result is consistent with the theory that markets anticipate additional sources of profit for the now politically connected firm despite no change in firm fundamentals. Faccio et al. (2006) study financial distress in politically connected firms in 35 countries and find that distressed politically connected firms are significantly more likely to be bailed out by the government than their non-connected counterparts. Claessens et al. (2008) show those Brazilian firms that provided contributions to (elected) federal deputies experienced higher stock returns than firms that did not make such contributions around the 1998 and 2002 elections. Further, contributing firms substantially increased their bank financing relative to a control group after each election, indicating that access to bank finance is an important channel through which political connections operate. They estimate the economic costs of this rent-seeking over the two election cycles to be at least 0.2 per cent of gross domestic product per annum.

**68.** Consider the following statements and examine as to which of the following conclusions do not align with what is stated in the passage?

1. Politically linked firms are more likely to have economic policies passed by the political executives which are favourable to them.

2. Markets believe that politically linked firms can give better economic returns.
3. Political linking of firms extracts an overall economic cost in economies.

(a) Only conclusion 1
(b) Only conclusion 2
(c) Only conclusion 3
(d) None of the above

**Passage 69**

The human mind is a product of the struggle for existence. It is a tool-making, food-seeking instrument which learns the right adjustment by a process of trial and error. Its working is experimental; its devices are utilitarian and its views tentative.

**69.** Consider the following statements and determine as to which corollaries are not in logical conformity with what is stated in the passage.

1. Human endeavours are often imperfect.
2. Social and human dispositions change with time.
3. Evolution and decay are laws to which all societies invariably conform.

(a) None of the above
(b) Only statement 1
(c) Only statement 2
(d) Only statement 3

**Passage 70**

As an engine of growth, technology has endless potential, which is untapped to a greater extent in the developing world. There is a lack of skilled labour and capital in underdeveloped countries. The difference in the per-capita income that is prevalent across nations is not only due to the difference in inputs but also due to the lack of ability for adoption as well as the adaption of technologies for improving productivity. For instance, computing can transform economic performance through the unlocking of infrastructure backlogs and integrated supply chain management. It enables education and healthcare services to be accessible. The human experience has been transformed with the blend of computers, the Internet, mobile handsets and the emergence of cloud computing. It empowers individuals by providing them access to knowledge and markets.

**70.** Which amongst the following are the reasons highlighted in the passage for lower economic growth in the developing world?

1. Lack of capital.
2. Poor demand for technology products.
3. Inappropriate public policies for the growth of technology and its absorption.

(a) Only 1 and 2 (b) Only 2 and 3
(c) Only 3 and 1 (d) All of the above

**Passage 71**

Comparative religion enables us to study faiths other than our own without condescension or contempt. It traces the history of our ideas of God from the simple conceptions of our remote ancestors who first formulated the experience of the great environing mystery down to the living faiths. Every mortal thing seems to have been deified. Powers of nature, sun, stars, fire, water and earth, generative energies were all made into Gods. Hero-worship and human apotheosis added to the number. Our mental pictures of God are as varied as we are.

**71.** Which of the following statements would logically support what is stated in the passage?

1. Different religious faiths believe in the existence of one and only one God.
2. Religions and society have often considered individuals with great qualities as incarnations of God.
3. Worship of elements of nature is common in many religions.

(a) All of the above
(b) Only statements 1 and 2
(c) Only statements 2 and 3
(d) Only statements 1 and 3

**Passage 72**

Pro-business policies, for example, those that make it easy to start a business, register property, enforce contracts, obtain credit, bid for natural resources, get permits, and resolve insolvency help firms to function effectively and thereby enable competitive markets. Making it easy to do business in a jurisdiction furthers the eventual goal of maximising social welfare. Reforms aimed in this direction must continue. However, catering to the needs of crony businesses alone without regard for other businesses and the remaining stakeholders in the economy may end up benefitting the preferentially treated firms at the expense of other firms, market efficiency and social welfare.

**72.** Which amongst the following can be said to be the most crucial message of the passage?

(a) It aims to identify which policies are pro-crony.

(b) It aims to identify which policies are pro-business.

(c) It aims to highlight the need for policies which are pro-business and not pro-crony.

(d) All of the above

**Passage 73**

Altering genes to enhance athletic performance is the reason behind gene doping. In the era of gene therapy, the simplest way of delivering proteins and hormones to an athlete's tissues and organs turned into reality. A substance can change the basic genetic DNA expression such that there is a large growth of muscles, quick recovery and extra forceful contracting. The muscles, which are not doped cannot be noticed by anti-doping laboratories, which would be perfect for taking advantage of competition. Gene doping is a hazard to the sports integrity and athletes' health, and as the WADA (World Anti-Doping Agency), being a worldwide organisation accountable for encouragement, coordination and monitoring the fight against doping in every form of sport, is providing vital resources and awareness to the methods for enabling the detection of gene doping.

**73.** Consider the following statements and examine as to which can be said to be correct in terms of what is stated in the passage?

(a) Current testing techniques by anti-doping laboratories cannot detect gene doping.

(b) Gene doping may not have as serious health consequences as conventional substance doping.

(c) Both (a) and (b)

(d) Neither (a) nor (b)

**Passage 74**

The burning of agricultural wastes in the fields is a practice that results in a number of environmental problems. India, being the second largest agro-based economy with year-round crop cultivation, generates a large amount of agricultural waste, including crop residues. Open burning of crop residues in the agricultural fields has become an environmental concern in India, particularly during paddy harvesting season. Varieties of surplus crop residues are burnt especially in northern states of Punjab, Haryana, UP, and Rajasthan depending on the agro-climatic region; however, about 50 per cent of all crop residue burnt in the country are residues of rice crop (TIFAC, 2018). The use of combine harvesters leaves the crop residues in the field and in order to clear the fields for the next crop in the easiest way, farmers burn the residues.

**74.** Which amongst the following are not an issue highlighted in the passage regarding the burning of crop residues?

1. There is a need for incentives to prevent the farmers from burning the crop residues.
2. The majority of the crop residues are on account of paddy cultivation.
3. Farmers who deploy combine harvesters for paddy harvesting are left with crop stubbles, burning of which is the only choice left with them.
4. The burning of crop residues is especially rampant in a specific region of the country.

(a) Only statements 1 and 2

(b) Only statements 1 and 3

(c) Only statements 2 and 3

(d) Only statements 2 and 4

**Passage 75**

Art, as the disclosure of the deeper reality of things, is a form of knowledge. It is imitation, as Aristotle said, but not of outward nature but of inner reality. Poetic objectivity is not photographic realism. Even the so-called imitative art is not mere imitation. The artist's mind is at work in it, aiming at a definite purpose. He discerns within the visible world something more real than its outward appearance, some idea or form of the true, the good or the beautiful, which is more akin to the spirit itself than to the visible things. Yet this idea or form, this meaning or value is not an added grace or refinement but the very heart of the object itself, and we cannot tear it away from it. Poetic truth is a discovery, not a creation.

**75.** Which amongst the following is the most crucial message of the author in the passage?
(a) The discovery of inner reality is the soul of creativity.
(b) Capturing the outward appearance and detail is not an essential trait of creativity.
(c) Imitation is a lesser form of creativity.
(d) All of the above.

## Answers To Exercise Set C

| | | | | | | | |
|---|---|---|---|---|---|---|---|
| **1.** (d) | **11.** (a) | **21.** (a) | **31.** (d) | **41.** (c) | **51.** (b) | **61.** (c) | **71.** (c) |
| **2.** (d) | **12.** (d) | **22.** (a) | **32.** (d) | **42.** (d) | **52.** (d) | **62.** (d) | **72.** (c) |
| **3.** (d) | **13.** (d) | **23.** (d) | **33.** (a) | **43.** (d) | **53.** (d) | **63.** (c) | **73.** (a) |
| **4.** (b) | **14.** (a) | **24.** (a) | **34.** (d) | **44.** (d) | **54.** (d) | **64.** (a) | **74.** (b) |
| **5.** (d) | **15.** (d) | **25.** (d) | **35.** (a) | **45.** I. (d) II. (a) | **55.** (d) | **65.** (c) | **75.** (a) |
| **6.** (a) | **16.** (c) | **26.** (c) | **36.** (a) | **46.** I. (c) II. (c) | **56.** (c) | **66.** (c) | |
| **7.** (a) | **17.** (d) | **27.** (c) | **37.** (d) | **47.** I. (d) II. (a) | **57.** (a) | **67.** (d) | |
| **8.** (d) | **18.** (d) | **28.** (d) | **38.** (b) | **48.** I. (a) II. (d) | **58.** (b) | **68.** (d) | |
| **9.** (b) | **19.** (a) | **29.** (a) | **39.** (c) | **49.** I. (c) II. (a) | **59.** (d) | **69.** (d) | |
| **10.** (c) | **20.** (c) | **30.** (c) | **40.** (a) | **50.** I. (a) II. (d) | **60.** (c) | **70.** (b) | |

## Exercise Set D

**1.** I do not believe that an individual may gain spiritually and those that surround him suffer. I believe in *advaita*. I believe in the essential unity of man and for that matter of all that lives. Therefore, I believe that if one man gains spiritually, the whole world gains with him and, if one man falls, the whole world falls to that extent.

There is not a single virtue, which aims at, or is content with, the welfare of the individual alone. Conversely, there is not a single moral offence, which does not, directly or indirectly, affect many others besides the actual offender. Hence, whether an individual is good or bad is not merely his own concern, but really the concern of the whole community, nay, of the whole world.

Though there is repulsion enough in Nature, she lives by attraction. Mutual love enables Nature to persist. Man does not live by destruction. Self-love compels regard for others. Nations cohere because there is mutual regard among individuals composing them. Some day we must extend the national law to the universe even as we have extended the family law to form nations—a larger family.

Mankind is one, seeing that all are equally subject to the moral law. All men are equal in God's eyes. There are, of course, differences of race and status and the like, but the higher the status of a man, the greater is his responsibility.

(i) The author states that an individual being good or bad is not only his concern but that of the whole community. Which among the following choices is **not** a logic used in the passage to emphasise this point?

(a) There is essential unity of man and for that matter of all that lives.

(b) Mutual love enables nature to persist and man does not live by destruction.

(c) There is not a single moral offence which does not affect many others.

(d) None of the above.

(ii) Which of the following best describes the concept of *advaita* as described in the passage?

(a) It means mutual love in mankind.

(b) Coexistence of the world on account of forces of attraction.

(c) It means oneness of man with all life forms.

(d) All of the above.

(iii) Which of the following assertions have been made in the passage?

1. All men are equal and have equal rights and responsibilities.
2. Spiritual upliftment of an individual has no influence on others.

(a) Only 1 (b) Only 2

(c) Both 1 and 2 (d) Neither 1 nor 2

(iv) Which amongst the following are the messages and key ideas being conveyed in the passage?

1. The law of family and universe may be extended to the nation.
2. The responsibility of the individual is in proportion to his status.
3. Spiritual gain of a man has positive influence on others also.
4. The virtues and vices of an individual affect the community and world at large.
5. There are fundamental differences between man and man.

(a) 1, 2, 3 (b) 2, 3, 4

(c) 3, 4, 5 (d) 1, 3, 5

**2.** Hard-nosed government documents usually make no mention of the role of social norms and culture in promoting development and economic efficiency. However, there is now a growing body of literature that demonstrates how certain social norms and cultural practices are vital ingredients for economic efficiency and growth. Groups and societies that are known to be honest and trustworthy tend to do better than societies that do not have this reputation. There have been broad cross-country studies and also laboratory experiments with the 'trust game' that illustrate this. More generally, what is being argued is that a nation's success depends of course on its resources, human capital and economic policies, for instance fiscal and monetary policies, but also on the cultural and social norms that permeate society. We go through life striking hundreds and thousands of minor contracts and deals. You give a person money one day and the understanding is that that person will repair your plumbing the next day or it can be the other way around (the person repairs your plumbing today and expects you to pay him the following day); you supply garments to a store and the store then pays you for it; someone gives you a hair-cut and, after that, you pay her. It is difficult to have such minor contracts enforced by a third party or some formal legal/bureaucratic machinery. If we try to do it that way, as we have on occasion in India, the result will be a cumbersome bureaucracy that is anyway unable to deliver. Societies that are endowed with personal integrity and trustworthiness have the natural advantage that no third party is required to enforce contracts. For outsiders, the mere knowledge that a particular society is trustworthy is the reason to do more business and trade with it.

(i) Which of the following can be inferred from the passage?
  (a) Government documents are silent on the role of social norms and culture in promoting economic development.
  (b) Government documents refute the role of social norms and culture in promoting economic development.
  (c) Government documents recognise the role of social norm and culture in promoting economic development.
  (d) None of the above.

(ii) Which factors according to the author affect the nation's success?
  1. Human capital
  2. Economic policies
  3. Resources
  4. Culture and social norms
  (a) 1, 2, 3 (b) 1, 2, 4
  (c) 2, 3, 4 (d) 1, 2, 3, 4

(iii) How do the social and cultural norms affect economic development?
  (a) Social and cultural norms attract more tourists.
  (b) They determine whether a society has entrepreneurial and business acumen.
  (c) Social norms of honesty and integrity bring trustworthiness encouraging others to do business and trade with such society.
  (d) All of the above.

**3.** Civilisation in the real sense of the term consists not in the multiplication but in the deliberate and voluntary reduction of wants, which promotes real happiness and contentment and increases the capacity for service. One can reduce one's wants by perseverance, and the reduction of wants makes for happiness – healthy body and a peaceful mind. The Golden rule is resolutely to refuse to have what millions cannot. This ability to refuse will not descend upon us all of a sudden. The first thing is to cultivate the mental attitude that will not have possessions or facilities denied to millions and the next immediate thing is to re-arrange our lives as fast as possible in accordance with that mentality.

Which of the following statements is a logical affirmation of what is stated in the passage?
(1) Desires lead to sorrow.
(2) Shunning of all possessions is the key to salvation.
(3) One must rule one's mind to attain contentment and peace.
  (a) 1, 2 and 3 (b) 1 and 2
  (c) 1 and 3 (d) 1 only

4. The bourgeoisie, historically, has played the most revolutionary part. The bourgeoisie, wherever it has got the upper hand, has put an end to all feudal, patriarchal, idyllic relations. It has pitilessly torn asunder the motley feudal ties that bound man to his 'natural superiors', and has left no other nexus between man and man than naked self-interest, than callous 'cash payment'. It has drowned out the most heavenly ecstasies of religious fervour, of chivalrous enthusiasm, of philistine sentimentalism, in the icy water of egotistical calculation. It has resolved personal worth into exchange value, and in place of the numberless indefeasible chartered freedoms, has set up that single, unconscionable freedom—Free Trade. In one word, for exploitation, veiled by religious and political illusions, it has substituted naked, shameless, direct, brutal exploitation.

   The bourgeoisie has stripped of its halo every occupation hitherto honoured and looked up to with reverent awe. It has converted the physician, the lawyer, the priest, the poet, the man of science, into its paid wage labourers. The bourgeoisie has torn away from the family its sentimental veil, and has reduced family relations into a mere money relation.

   The bourgeoisie cannot exist without constantly revolutionising the instruments of production, and thereby the relations of production, and with them the whole relations of society. Conservation of the old modes of production in unaltered form, was, on the contrary, the first condition of existence for all earlier industrial classes. Constant revolutionising of production, uninterrupted disturbance of all social conditions, everlasting uncertainty and agitation distinguish the bourgeoise epoch from all earlier ones. All fixed, fast frozen relations, with their train of ancient and venerable prejudices and opinions, are swept away, all new-formed ones become antiquated before they can ossify. All that is solid melts into air, all that is holy is profaned, and man is at last compelled to face with sober senses his real condition of life and his relations with his kind.

   The need of a constantly expanding market for its products chases the bourgeoisie over the entire surface of the globe. It must nestle everywhere, settle everywhere, establish connections everywhere.

   (i) Which of the assumptions are correct as per the passage?
      1. Bourgeoise (capitalist) causes a constant change in the means and processes of production.
      2. Bourgeoise has altered social relationships.

      (a) Only Assumption 1 is correct.
      (b) Only Assumption 2 is correct.
      (c) Both Assumptions 1 and 2 are correct.
      (d) Neither Assumption 1 nor 2 is correct.

   (ii) What is the revolutionary part, which the author refers to, which the bourgeoise has played?
      (a) It has transferred the social powers from the serbs to the feudal class.
      (b) It has contributed to funding of revolutions and consequent change of power.
      (c) It has made monetary interest the focal point of relationship between individuals and society.
      (d) It has brought radical change in the means of production.

   (iii) Which one of the following is correct interpretation of the views of the author?
      1. Free trade has ended the exploitation earlier carried out in the garb of religious and political beliefs.
      2. Bourgeoise has brought a degree of honour to the paid wage labourers as it has freed them from the clutches of feudalism and guildship, to earn money directly for themselves.

      (a) Only Interpretation 1 is correct.
      (b) Only Interpretation 2 is correct.
      (c) Both Interpretations 1 and 2 are correct.
      (d) Neither Interpretation 1 nor 2 is correct.

(iv) Why did the bourgeoise bring about a change in relations in the society?

1. Bourgeoise had to change the means and tools of production to cater to the rising demand of expanding market, thereby bringing in social changes.
2. Bourgeoise had to break the shackles of guilds to wrest control over means of production and the market. This brought change in social relations.
3. The bourgeoise were resentful of the old means of production, which did not have space for them.
4. The bourgeoise value only money and profit, which ushered in a culture of value of money over relationships thus changing the social relations.

(a) 1, 2, 3, 4 (b) 1, 2, 4
(c) 1, 4 (d) 4 only

**5.** This bait had this effect. I got over my dislike for bread, forswore my compassion for the goats, and became relisher of meat-dishes, if not of meat itself. This went on for about a year. But no more than half a dozen meat-feasts were enjoyed in all' because the State house was not available every day, and there was the obvious difficulty about frequently preparing expensive, savoury meat-dishes. I had no money to pay for this 'reform'. My friend had therefore always to find the wherewithal. I had no knowledge where he found it. But find it he did, because he was bent on turning me into a meat-eater. But even his means must have been limited, and hence these feasts had necessarily to be few and far between.

(i) What effect did the 'feasts' had on the author?

(1) He became more compassionate for goats.
(2) He started liking meat dishes.
(3) The feasts became a financial burden on him.
(4) He overcame aversion for bread.

(a) 1, 2, 3, 4 (b) 2, 3, 4
(c) 2, 4 (d) 1, 2, 4

(ii) Why could the author enjoy only a few 'feasts'?

(1) Meat dishes were costly.
(2) There was fear of being caught while eating.
(3) The venue where the feast was held was not easily available.
(4) There was difficulty in purchasing and smuggling the meat to the venue of its preparation.

(a) 1, 2 (b) 1, 2, 4
(c) 1, 3 (d) 1, 2, 3, 4

(iii) As per the passage which of the following two inferences can be drawn?

(1) The author's friend was more keen to make the author a meat eater than the author himself.
(2) To begin with author had aversion for meat and bread.

(a) Only inference 1 can be drawn.
(b) Only inference 2 can be drawn.
(c) Both inferences 1 & 2 can be drawn.
(d) Neither inference 1 nor 2 can be drawn.

**6.** The Oxford Advanced Learner's Dictionary defines 'Integration' as 'the act or process of combining two or more things so that they work together'. Regional integration is, however, a more complex process. It usually involves several countries, whether at the sub-regional or continental level, with different economic interest, language, administrative systems, national priorities and political and social challenges. Yet in embracing the concept of regional integration, these countries must have an appreciation of the fact that notwithstanding their many points of divergence, they have important common interest that have to be discussed and promoted, not only for the benefit of the large regional grouping or continent, but ultimately for the benefit of the individual Member States. Even though there is no exact agreement on the definition of the concept, it mostly involves developing a cooperation framework on the basis of one or more written agreements that describe the areas of cooperation in detail, as well as some coordinating bodies representing the countries involved.

Which amongst the following best describe what the author is trying to convey in the passage?

(1) The correct meaning of integration is to combine two or more things.

(2) Regional integration would necessarily involve groups identifying and promoting their common interests.

(3) Development of a cooperation framework in form of a written agreement(s) is a must for regional cooperation.

(a) 1, 2 and 3 (b) 2 and 3

(c) 1 and 2 (d) Only 2

**7.** Between two of the bookcases hung a looking-glass, presenting its high and dusty plate within a tarnished golden frame. Among many wonderful stories related of this mirror, it was believed that the spirits of all the doctor's deceased patients dwelt within its edges, and would stare him in the face whenever he looked there. The adjoining side of the chamber was ornamented with the full-length portrait of a charming young lady, dressed in the faded magnificence of silk, satin, and brocade, and with a visage as faded as her dress.

(i) Which of the two conclusions can be drawn from what is stated in the passage?

(1) The looking glass was old.

(2) The lady in the portrait had died.

(a) Only conclusion 1 can be drawn.

(b) Only conclusion 2 can be drawn.

(c) Both conclusion 1 & 2 can be drawn.

(d) Neither conclusion 1 nor 2 can be drawn.

(ii) Most likely, the paragraph gives description of a:

(a) museum

(b) study room

(c) doctors clinic

(d) none of the above

(iii) Which of the following can inferred from the expression,. "Among many wonderful stories related of this mirror…."

(a) There were many myths associated with the doctor, his activities and his life.

(b) The mirror was possessing magical powers.

(c) The person described was a witch doctor.

(d) The doctor led a life of seclusion.

**8.** By religion, I do not mean formal religion, or customary religion, but that religion, which underlies all religions, which brings us face to face with our Maker.

Let me explain what I mean by religion. It is not the Hindu religion, which I certainly prize above all other religions, but the religion that transcends Hinduism, which changes one's very nature, which binds one indissolubly to the truth within and whichever purifies. It is the permanent element in human nature, which counts no cost too great in order to find full expression and which leaves the soul utterly restless until it has found itself, known its Maker and appreciated the true correspondence between the Maker and itself. I have not seen Him, neither have I known Him. I have made the world's faith in God my own, and as my faith is ineffaceable, I regard that faith as amounting to experience. However, as it may be said that to describe faith as experience is to tamper with truth, it may perhaps be more correct to say that I have no word for characterising my belief in God.

There is an indefinable mysterious Power that pervades everything. I feel it, though I do not see it. It is this unseen power, which makes itself and yet defies all proof, because it is so unlike all that I perceive through my senses. It transcends the senses. But it is possible to reason out the existence of God to a limited extent.

I do dimly perceive that whilst everything around me is ever-changing, ever-dying there is underlying all that change a Living Power that is changeless. That informing Power or Spirit is God. And since nothing else I see merely through the senses can or will persist, He alone is.

And is this Power benevolent or malevolent? I see it as purely benevolent. For I can see that in that midst of death life persists, in the midst of untruth truth persists, in the midst of darkness light persists. Hence, I gather that God is Life, Truth, Light. He is Love. He is the Supreme God.

(i) Which of the following elements would be present in the author's concept of religion?

1. It is a reflection of the truth within.
2. It may or may not be present in human nature.
3. It transcends the customary and formal religion.
4. It seeks the maker.
5. Its characteristics undergo change with time and place.
6. It transcends Hinduism.

(a) 1, 2, 3, 4 (b) 1, 3, 5, 6
(c) 1, 3, 4, 6 (d) 2, 3, 4, 6

(ii) Which of the following can be said to be the author's view about the existence of God?

(a) It cannot be understood at all.
(b) It does not transcend the senses.
(c) It can be reasoned out to a limited extent.
(d) None of the above

(iii) The reason, the author puts forth to emphasise on the existence of God is

(a) That a Creator was necessary to create everything.
(b) That He is the unchanging and undying, underlying everything that is changing and dying.
(c) Both (a) and (b).
(d) Neither (a) nor (b).

**9.** Cultural activities are becoming increasingly important in the modern post-industrial knowledge based economy. World over, they have been recognised as an important component of growth and job creation as well as a vehicle of cultural identity. Cultural life has become an economically viable private and public service activity as well as social integrator. There is growing positive correlation between culture and employment. A large number of people are getting viable employment by engaging in cultural activities as writers, publishers, librarians, photographers, sculptors, painters, musicians, singers, choreographers, dancers and actors. Cultural activities also support other economic activities, cultural tourism being one such example. A major chunk of tourism in India, national and international, can be classified as cultural tourism because it is geared to visit monuments, museums, archaeological sites and cultural heritage including traditional fairs and festivals.

To meet the objective of preserving and promoting all forms of art and culture, a variety of activities are being undertaken by the Government of India, ranging from protecting and encouraging cultural endeavours at grassroots level to promoting cultural exchanges internationally; from programmes to preserve India's ancient heritage to encouraging an array of contemporary creative arts. A network of 41 organisations is functioning under the Ministry of Culture, for protection, development, and promotion of tangible heritage, intangible heritage, and knowledge heritage. There are also a large number of schemes and programmes to extend financial support to individuals, group of individuals, and cultural organisations engaged in performing, visual and literary arts.

Creative industry includes cultural heritage; printed matter and literature; music and performing arts; visual arts; audiovisual media including cinema, television, radio and photography, and socio-cultural activities; museum and archives.

(i) Which of the following inferences can be drawn from what is stated in the passage?

1. Cultural activities and services are helping in earning valuable foreign exchange.
2. Cultural services create a sense of national identity.

(a) Only Assertion 1 is correct.
(b) Only Assertion 2 is correct.
(c) Both Assertions 1 and 2 are correct.
(d) Neither Assertion 1 nor 2 is correct.

(ii) Which amongst the following can be said to be true about cultural services and activities?

1. They are social integrators.
2. They are job creators.
3. They are good source of entertainment.

(a) 1, 2, 3 (b) 1, 2
(c) 1, 3 (d) 2, 3

(iii) As per the passage, which amongst the following is **not** a measure undertaken by the government to promote and protect art and culture?

(a) Providing financial support to individuals engaged in cultural activities.
(b) Promoting international cultural exchanges.
(c) Assisting private organisations engaged in promoting cultural endeavours.
(d) None of the above.

(iv) Which amongst the following **cannot** be treated as cultural activity in terms of what is stated in the passage?

(a) Activity of a production house engaged in production of a dance-drama.
(b) Activity of a publishing house engaged in printing and publication of children's literature.
(c) Activity of a government organisation dealing with archiving of manuscripts.
(d) Activity of a chain of resorts operating in cities/places where world heritage sites are located.

(v) Which amongst the following does the passage highlight as the measures undertaken by the government to promote and preserve arts and culture?

1. The government has a network of organisations functioning under it which undertake the work of protection/promotion of culture.
2. The government promotes cultural activities at the grass root levels.
3. The government operates a number of guest houses/hotels through undertakings in important tourist places.
4. Government has a number of schemes to extend financial support to artists.

(a) 1, 2, 3, 4 (b) 1, 2, 3
(c) 1, 2, 4 (d) 2, 3, 4

**10.** One phase of the business cycle is the expansion phase. This phase is twofold, including recovery and prosperity. During the recovery period there is ever-growing expansion of existing facilities, and new facilities for production are created. Newer businesses are created and older ones expanded. Improvements of various kinds are made. There is an ever-increasing optimism about the future of economic growth. Much capital is invested in machinery or 'heavy' industry. More labour is employed. More raw materials are required. As one part of the economy develops, other parts are affected. For example, a great expansion in automobiles results in an expansion of the steel, glass, and rubber industries. Roads are required; thus, the cement and machinery industries are stimulated. Demand for labour and materials results in greater prosperity for workers and suppliers of raw materials, including farmers. This increases purchasing power and the volume of goods bought and sold. Thus, prosperity is diffused among the various segments of the population. This prosperity period may continue to rise and rise without an apparent end. However, a time comes when this phase reaches a peak and stops spiralling upwards. This is the end of the expansion phase.

(i) Which of the following statements is the best example of the optimism mentioned in the passage as being part of the expansion phase?

(a) Public funds are designated for the construction of new highways designed to stimulate tourism.

(b) Industrial firms allocate funds for the purchase of machine tools.

(c) The prices of agricultural commodities are increased at the producer level.

(d) Full employment is achieved at all levels of the economy.

(ii) It can be inferred from the passage that the author believes that

(a) When consumers lose their confidence in the market, a recession follows.

(b) Cyclical ends to business expansion are normal.

(c) Luxury goods such as jewellery are unaffected by industrial expansion.

(d) With sound economic policies, prosperity can become a fixed pattern.

(iii) Which of the following statements would be most likely to begin the paragraph immediately following the passage?

(a) Some industries are, by their very nature, cyclical, having regular phases of expansion and recession.

(b) Inflation is a factor that must be taken into consideration in any discussion of the expansion phase.

(c) The farmer's role during the expansion phase is of vital importance.

(d) The other phase of the business cycle is called the recession phase.

**11.** Though it appears complex, over the last 10 years, there have been dramatic improvements in the computing power, thanks to Moore's law and the use of large internet applications. Today we can do millions of matches every second. Aadhaar uses massive and modern computational technology. Aadhaar provides the facility of online authentication. By feeding any unique identification number and biometrics anywhere in the country the system through its central server would confirm instantaneously whether the person is indeed the person he/she claims to be. This kind of online ID system has not been attempted anywhere else in the world.

Which amongst the following can be said to be the key message/messages that the author wants to convey?

1. Power of computation has dramatically improved over a period of time.
2. Instantaneous online authentication facility is a unique feature of Aadhaar.
3. Aadhaar and unique ID have multifarious applications and possibilities.

(a) 1, 2 and 3 (b) 1 and 2
(c) 2 and 3 (d) 2 only

**12.** There is now overwhelming scientific evidence and growing quantitative assessment of risks to establish that human activities are changing the composition of the atmosphere and its properties. This realisation brings to the fore ways and means of addressing the challenge and associated resources, which in turn brings us to economics. Science suggests that the impacts of climate change are serious and broad ranging, with economics implying that they interact with other market failures and economic dynamics, giving rise to complex policy issues. To put it briefly, climate change is a global externality associated with the emission of Green House Gases (GHG), which has long, persistent and, beyond a level, irreversible effects. These emissions impose a cost on both the present and future generations, which are not fully recouped from the emitters of these emissions. Hence, there is need for policy intervention as markets alone fail to account for these failures.

This forms the starting point for the international climate change negotiating regime, suggesting a need for globally coordinated policy action as the incremental impact of a ton of GHG on climate change is independent of where in the world it is emitted, and because the nature of GHG emissions is such that it affects the environment with a lag. This characteristic shapes some important features of climate change policy framework, namely historical responsibilities and inter- and intra-generational equity. The requisite policy hence should balance the distribution of outcomes within and across generations. Every effort for conservation must be carried out early to protect our future generations by providing them with a better quality of life including productive resources for the future. Along with this we also have to safeguard our reasonable interests and concerns as environmental issues cannot be delinked from our efforts to provide the present generation with the basic necessities and a better quality of life. Also, there has to be a cooperative endeavour to protect the climate and environment along with development imperatives. Put together, combating climate change ultimately boils down to a complex economic policy issue with very difficult choices involving rates of economic growth, volumes of emission, probable increase in temperature, and adverse impacts and costs of addressing climate change.

(i) To address the challenge of climate change, the economics of policy making becomes important because

1. The challenge of mitigation and adaptation due to the climate change, calls for allocation of resources.
2. The world does not have sufficient resources for addressing the challenge of climate change.
3. A balance has to be struck in meeting the economic needs of present generation and protecting the interest of future generation.

(a) 1, 2, 3 (b) 1, 3
(c) 2 only (d) 3 only

(ii) Which of the following assertions can be said to be in conformity with what is stated in the passage?

1. The emission of GHGs does not show its effect on environment immediately.
2. Every unit of GHG emission affects the environment and its effect can never be reversed.

(a) Only Assertion 1 is in conformity.
(b) Only Assertion 2 is in conformity.
(c) Both Assertions 1 and 2 are in conformity.
(d) Neither Assertion 1 nor 2 is in conformity.

(iii) Which one of the following will **not** be in conformity with the principle of intra-generational equity enunciated in the passage?

(a) Excessive utilisation of earth's resources by the present generation leads to depletion of resources.
(b) High per capita GHG emissions are produced by the developed countries of the world.
(c) Both (a) and (b).
(d) Neither (a) nor (b).

(iv) As per the passage, which amongst the following features should be incorporated into an economic policy on climate change?

1. The principle of 'polluters should pay'.
2. Conservation of earth's resources to safeguard the interest of future generations.
3. Provision of basic necessity to the present generation.
4. Fairness to countries/population groups polluting, less but suffering equally or more because of global warming.

(a) 1, 2, 3, 4 (b) 1, 3, 4
(c) 2, 3, 4 (d) 1, 2, 3

**13.** She came to know the plight of heavy housework and the odious cares of the kitchen. She washed the dishes, using her delicate fingers and rosy nails on greasy pots and pans. She washed the sullied linen, the shirts and the dishcloths, which she dried upon a line; she carried the dirty water down to the street every morning and carried up the clean water, stopping for breath at every landing. And dressed terribly like a woman of the people, she went to the vegetable market, the grocery shop, the butcher, a basket on her arm, bargaining, meeting with impertinence, defending her miserable money.

(i) Which amongst the following activity has not been described in the passage to have been carried out by the women?

(1) She purchased grocery.
(2) She mopped floor.
(3) She washed dirty clothes.
(4) She collected water.
(5) She stitched clothes.

(a) 1, 3 (b) 2, 4
(c) 1, 5 (d) 2, 5

(ii) Which of the following statements would be correct in terms of what is stated in the passage?

(a) The women was born poor and was compelled to do menial work to make ends meet.
(b) The woman was not born poor but compelled by circumstances to do menial work to make ends meet.
(c) The women enjoyed menial work as she believed in dignity of labour.
(d) In terms of what is stated, no conclusion as in (a) or (b) or (c) can be drawn.

(iii) What is implied by, " … like a women of the people."?

(a) A women belonging to the common class of poor people.
(b) A women having looks of a women from middle class.
(c) A women not having a poignant look.
(d) All of the above

**14.** Indeed at the root of this doctrine of equal distribution must lie that of the trusteeship of the wealthy for superfluous wealth possessed by them. For according to the doctrine they may not possess a rupee more than their neighbours. How is this to be brought about? Non-violently? Or should the wealthy be dispossessed of their possessions? To do this we would naturally have to resort to violence. This violent action cannot benefit the society. Society will be the poorer, for it will lose the gifts of a man who knows how to accumulate wealth. Therefore, the non-violent way is evidently superior. The rich man will be left in possession of his wealth, of which he will use what he reasonably requires for his personal needs and will act as a trustee for the remainder to be used for the society. In this argument honesty on the part of the trustee is assumed. If however, in spite of the utmost effort, the rich do not become guardians of the poor in the true sense of the term and the latter are more and more crushed and die of hunger, what is to be done? In trying to find a solution to this riddle, I have lighted on non-cooperation and civil disobedience as the right and infallible means. The rich cannot accumulate wealth without the co-operation of the poor in society. If this knowledge were to penetrate to and spread amongst the poor, they would become strong and would learn how to free themselves by means of non-violence from the crushing inequalities, which have brought them to the verge of starvation.

I cannot imagine anything nobler or more nationalistic than that for, say, one hour in the day, we should all do the labour that the poor do, and thus identify ourselves with them and through them with all mankind. I cannot imagine better worship of God than that in His name I should labour for the poor even as they do.

"Earn thy bread by the sweat of thy brow" says the Bible. Sacrifices may be of many kinds. One of them may well be bread labour. If all laboured for their bread and no more, then there would be enough food and enough leisure for all. Then there would be no cry of over-population, no disease and no such misery as we see around. Such labour will be the highest form of sacrifice. Men will no doubt do many other things either through their bodies or through their minds, but all this will be labour of love for the common good. There will be no rich and no poor, none high and none low, no touchable and no untouchable.

(i) Why does the author forbid dispossession of wealth of rich by use of force?
   (a) Use of force would lead to violence.
   (b) Use of force will make society bereft of the man who has the knowledge of generating and accumulating wealth.
   (c) Use of force is against principles of democracy.
   (d) All of the above.

(ii) What remedy does the author suggest if the rich refuse to adopt the doctrine of guardianship and be guardians of poor?
   (a) The state should intervene and nationalise their wealth.
   (b) The poor may forcibly acquire what is their right.
   (c) The poor should adopt the technique of non-cooperation with the rich in matters of generation of wealth.
   (d) All of the above.

(iii) Which of the following **cannot** be said to be true about the doctrine of trusteeship as enunciated in the passage?
   (a) The wealthy are trustee of their superfluous property.
   (b) They should not possess more than what their neighbours do.
   (c) The wealth in excess of his needs is to be utilised for the benefit of society.
   (d) None of the above.

(iv) Which of the following ideas has the author tried to convey in the passage?
   1. The superfluous wealth of the rich should be nationalised by the state and used for the benefit of the poor.
   2. Everybody must labour for his bread.
   3. The rich should act as guardians of the poor.
   4. The wealthy should be dispossessed of their possession by all means.
   5. The poor should employ non-co-operation in case rich fail to act as guardians of the poor.

   (a) 1, 2, 3 (b) 1, 3, 4
   (c) 2, 3, 5 (d) 2, 3, 4

(v) Based on what has been stated in the passage examine whether the following inferences can be drawn or not.
   1. The rich should not possess superfluous wealth.
   2. Violent action to dispossess rich will not benefit society.

   (a) Only Conclusion 1 can be drawn.
   (b) Only Conclusion 2 can be drawn.
   (c) Both conclusions can be drawn.
   (d) None of the conclusions can be drawn.

**15.** Apart from being a means of entertainment, physical fitness, and development of human personality, sports have also played an important role in national identity, community bonding and international bonding. Since sports have become highly competitive, the use of modern infrastructure and equipment and advanced scientific support has changed the scenario at the international level. In view of this, the Government of India has taken several initiatives to help sportspersons with scientific and equipment support as well as providing them training and exposure in international competitions. The first National Sports Policy was unveiled in 1984 with the objective of developing an organised and systematic framework for the development and promotion of sports in the country. In 2001, another version of the Sports Policy, with the twin planks of 'broad-basing' of sports and 'achieving excellence' at national and international levels was introduced.

Though sports is a state subject under the Seventh Schedule of the Constitution of India, the central government supplements the efforts of states in the task of promotion and development of sports. Several schemes have been announced by the Government of India aiming at promotion of drug-free sports, sports infrastructure development separately for urban and rural India, promotion of excellence in sports, incentives to sportspersons, assistance to sports-support institutions, and promotion of sports among persons with disabilities. Indian athletes put up a commendable and impressive performance at the Commonwealth Games 2018 and Asian Games 2018.

Government of India's current policies also identify core areas for providing comprehensive and intensive training, both within the country and abroad, as well as competition exposure in international sports events.

(i) As per the passage, which amongst the following is a part of the government's policy for promotion of sports?

(1) Giving pecuniary assistance/stipends to sports persons.

(2) Development of sports infrastructure.

(3) Providing scientific inputs to sports person in training.

(4) Assisting sports persons in finding suitable jobs.

(5) Providing international exposure to sportspersons.

(a) 1, 2, 3, 4, 5 (b) 2, 3, 4, 5

(c) 2, 3, 5 (d) 2, 5

(ii) Examine whether the following conclusions can be drawn from what has been stated in the passage.

1. Organising sport events has emerged as a financially viable option; as such, the government has increased the spending on sports.

2. The government provides support to sportspersons either through central government's sports authorities and institutions or through state government institutions.

(a) Only Assertion 1 is correct.

(b) Only Assertion 2 is correct.

(c) Both Assertions 1 and 2 are correct.

(d) Neither Assertion 1 nor 2 is correct.

(iii) Which amongst the following is **not** highlighted in the passage as a role which sports is envisaged to play?

(a) It helps in providing entertainment to the masses.

(b) It helps in providing employment to the athletes.

(c) It helps in creating national identity and a sense of pride.

(d) It helps in peace and international brotherhood.

(iv) As per the Constitution, the primary responsibility of promotion of sports vests with

(a) State governments

(b) The Central Government

(c) Private institutions

(d) All of the above

**16.** Industrialisation on a mass scale will necessarily lead to passive or active exploitation of the villagers as the problems of competition and marketing come in. Therefore, we have to concentrate on the village being self-contained, manufacturing mainly for use.

In terms of what is stated in the passage which amongst the following can be said to be an assumption made by the author?

(a) Villagers with meagre resources cannot compete with larger industrial centres.

(b) Local consumption based manufacturing in villages can thrive despite competition from industrial centres.

(c) Both (a) and (b).

(d) Neither (a) nor (b).

**17.** Global climate change pundits have for long been blowing hot and cold over melting ice caps, rising ocean levels and unusually hot summers on the one hand and receding deserts, shrinking biodiversity and colder winters on the other. Climatologists are, however, unanimous in their opinion that, regional variations notwithstanding, the Earth as a whole is becoming warmer—and largely due to the increased human activity. And yet, as a continent, Antarctica would seem to be bucking the trend. Recent reports quoting American scientists from the South Pole say that while temperatures in every other continent have risen over the past century, Antarctica has become appreciably colder over the past 35 years and continues to cool, becoming the only one of Earth's seven continents to react differently to global warming. The world's average temperature over the last 100 years has risen by 0.06°C a decade, and the average actually went up to 0.19°C between 1979 and 1998. In the Antarctic, on the other hand, temperatures fell on an average by 0.7°C a decade. Traditional theories of climate change have held that the effects of global warming ought to be magnified at the Poles. Nonetheless, recent research points out that while the Arctic is indeed getting warmer, the Antarctic is definitely getting cooler. This will mean that previous estimates of rising sea levels that included the melting ice caps of both the North and South Poles will have to be suitably revised. So what is the mystery behind the cooling of the White continent?

Since most of the inhabited and industrialised countries are clustered close to the Arctic, polluting emissions waft across to the North Pole, creating a greenhouse effect, warming the air and loosening the ice sheets. Complex interplay of ocean currents appears to have changed temperatures, cooling the southern ocean around the Antarctica and transforming the Pole's temperature profile. Antarctica's harsh desert valleys are turning cooler, setting off a series of ecological consequences in the region. Meanwhile, here's another contradiction; reports from New Zealand describe how there is a surfeit of global warming—induced breakaway icebergs in the Southern Hemisphere.

(i) According to the passage, all of the following are **not** true, except

(a) Effect of global warming on Antarctica is on expected lines.

(b) Fall in temperatures in the Antarctic is in accordance with the traditional theories.

(c) Effect of global warming is the maximum at the Poles.

(d) Effect of global warming on Antarctica is on unexpected lines.

(ii) According to the passage, it can be said that

(a) both the Arctic and Antarctic are getting cooler with global warming.

(b) Antarctica has become warmer than the Earth over the last 35 years.

(c) the decade growth in temperature is much higher for Antarctica than the Earth itself.

(d) the average temperature rise for the decade 1979–98 was more than the average rise in temperature over the last 100 years.

(iii) Which of the following statements are correct in terms of what is stated in the passage?

1. As per empirical studies, the effect of climate change is maximum at poles.
2. The proximity of North Pole to most of the industrialised nations is the reason for abnormal rise of temperature over there.

(a) Only Statement 1 is correct.

(b) Only Statement 2 is correct.

(c) Both Statements 1 and 2 are correct.

(d) Neither Statement 1 nor 2 is correct.

**18.** In the struggle between capital and labour, it may be generally said that more often than not the capitalists are in the wrong box. But when labour comes fully to realise its strength, I know it can become more tyrannical than capital. The mill-owners will have to work on the terms dictated by labour if the latter could command intelligence of the former. It is clear, however, that labour will never attain to that intelligence;

if it does, labour will cease to be labour and become itself the master. The capitalists do not fight on the strength of money alone. They possess intelligence and tact.

Which amongst the following is a crucial message which the author wants to convey?

(a) The capitalists are always wrong.

(b) The labour class is more tyrannical than capitalists.

(c) Struggle between the labour and capitalists will always continue.

(d) None of the above.

**19.** The appointed day has come—the day appointed by destiny—as India stands forth again, after long slumber and struggle, awake, vital, free and independent. The past clings on to us still in some measure and we have to do much before we redeem the pledges we have so often taken.

Yet the turning point is past, and history begins anew for us, the history which we shall live and act and others will write about.

It is a fateful moment for us in India, for all Asia and the free world. A new star rises, the star of freedom in the East, a new hope comes into being, a vision long-cherished materialises. May the star never set and that hope never be betrayed!

We rejoice in that freedom, though clouds surround us, and many of our people are sorrow-stricken and difficult problems encompass us. But freedom brings responsibilities and burdens and we have to face them in the spirit of a free and disciplined people.

On this day our first thoughts go to the architect of this freedom, the Father of our Nation, who, embodying the old spirit of India, held aloft the torch of freedom and lighted up the darkness that surrounded us. We have often been unworthy followers of his and have strayed from his message, but not only we but succeeding generations will remember his message and bear the imprint in their hearts of this great son of India, magnificent in his faith and strength and courage and humility.

We shall never allow that torch of freedom to be blown out, however high the wind or stormy the tempest.

The future beckons to us. Whither do we go and what shall be our endeavour? To bring freedom and opportunity to the common man, to the peasants and workers of India; to fight and end poverty and ignorance and disease, to build up a prosperous, democratic and progressive nation, and to create social, economic and political institutions, which will ensure justice and fullness of life to every man and woman.

We have hard work ahead. There is no resting for any one of us till we redeem our pledge in full, till we make all the people of India what destiny intended them to be. We are citizens of a great country, on the verge of bold advance, and we have to live up to that high standard.

(i) What is the appointed day referred to in the title?

(a) It is the day when India became independent from the British Rule.

(b) It is the day when India joined the United Nations.

(c) It is the day when the Constitution of India was given to the people of India.

(d) None of the above.

(ii) What does the new star that the narrator refers to represent?

(a) It represents the freedom of India.

(b) It represents a new hope for the people this world symbolising freedom from imperialism.

(c) Both (a) and (b).

(d) Neither (a) nor (b).

(iii) The 'clouds' which 'surround us' refers to

(a) The severest monsoon clouds to have ever hit India.

(b) The cloud of imperialism and slavery.

(c) The cloud of sorrow, poverty and problems engulfing the people.

(d) The cloud of gloom on account of assassination of father of our nation.

(iv) Which amongst the following are challenges which the narrator highlights in the passage that the country has to overcome?

1. Attain freedom and opportunity for all.
2. End poverty and ignorance.
3. Provision of education and employment.
4. Creation of important institutions for nation building.

(a) 1, 2, 4 (b) 1, 2, 3
(c) 1, 2 (d) 1, 2, 3, 4

**20.** I could not be leading a religious life unless I identified myself with the whole of mankind, and that I could not do unless I took part in politics. The whole gamut of man's activities today constitutes an indivisible whole. You cannot divide social, economic, political and purely religious work into watertight compartments. I do not know any religion apart from human activity. It provides a moral basis to all other activities which they would otherwise lack, reducing life to maze of 'sound and fury signifying nothing.

(i) Why is taking part in politics essential for the author?

(a) Politics is an integral part of human activity which cannot be compartmentalised.

(b) Politics provides a moral basis for all social activities.

(c) Politics is essential for upliftment of masses and country.

(d) All of the above

(ii) What is meant here by the expression,"…. a maze of sound and fury signifying nothing"?

(a) A voluble but meaningless display of anger.

(b) A complex web of activity but which is meaningless.

(c) A complicated pathway riddled with difficulties.

(d) None of the above.

(iii) What is most important message that the author trying to convey in the passage?

(a) Politics is an integral part of human life and cannot be segregated from it.

(b) Life cannot be compartmentalised and politics and religion are reflection of the some larger whole.

(c) Human activity cannot be compartmentalised and cannot be devoid of religion.

(d) All of the above.

**21.** Low-income tax compliance is known to limit the capacity of Governments in developing countries to raise revenue for developmental purposes. Many factors have been acknowledged as contributing to this problem, such as the large informal sector, weak legal system, ambiguity in tax laws, inadequate information and accounting system, and corruption. In rectifying this problem it is important to be realistic and separate out what can be changed in the short run and what cannot. Experience from around the world shows that reforming certain aspects of the tax administration–such as increasing the number of audit officers and their supporting staff and altering procedures for grouping taxpayers into assessment units – can be implementable option for reforming the tax system for generating higher revenues for the Government. Interestingly, a detailed econometric study shows that, in India, significant compliance gains would accrue from expanded employment. With regard to increased support staff in circles, both own and cross revenue effects turn out to be statistically positive and significant. Further, issues such as taxpayers strategically selecting into wards or circles, variation in support staff or enforcement effort generating spillover effects on work-load and compliance in related units may be considered for change to increase the efficacy of tax collection. Hence, the problem is not of the size of bureaucracy. If anything, there is scope for growth. The need is for administrative reform so that the resource of bureaucratic personnel can be used more effectively in promoting individual initiative.

Research results show that consideration should be given to removing the ward/circle distinction, replacing it with random assignment rules. This will remove the strategic underfiling incentive, with beneficial compliance effects. Revenue gains may be achieved by reallocating support staff from wards to circles, where they can be more productive. Penalty and prosecution effort appears to have significant effect on compliance (though here one has to be cautious not to encourage corrupt officials to misuse the system). Encouraging efforts to improve thc quality of information available to assessing officers and including measures of penalty effort in their performance evaluation will also be helpful in reforming the tax administration.

(i) Which of the following can be said to be the most suitable caption for the passage above?

(a) Corruption in income-tax administration.

(b) Need for redistribution of resources in income-tax administration.

(c) Generating greater revenue from reforms in income-tax administration.

(d) Improvement in quality of information available with assessing officers.

(ii) Consider the following factors attributable to low tax revenues in developing countries:

1. Large informal sector
2. Weak legal system
3. Poor culture of tax compliance
4. High progressive rates of taxation
5. Corruption
6. Inadequate information

Which of the aforesaid the author considers to be the reason for low income-tax compliance in developing countries?

(a) 1, 2, 3, 4 (b) 2, 3, 4, 5

(c) 1, 3, 4, 5 (d) 1, 3, 5, 6

(iii) Which of the following suggestions has the author given to bring better tax compliance?

(a) Allocation of more economic resources for strengthening the income-tax department.

(b) Bringing administrative reforms in the income-tax department for more effective utilisation of the resource of bureaucratic personnel.

(c) Following a zero-tolerance principle for corruption in the income-tax department.

(d) All of the above.

**22** Thc first order fact about the developing world today is that this is an era of unprecedented prosperity. And that is true about India too which has been one of the most dynamic economic performers in the world. A major driver of these good times is 'economic convergence,' whereby poorer countries have grown faster than richer countries and closed the gap in standards of living. The convergence process has been broadening and accelerating for the last 20–30 years. However, while fears of a middle-income trap are over blown, there could be a slowdown in this process for lower-middle-income countries such as India. The possibility of such a 'Late Converge Stall' arises because of four possible headwinds in the post Global Financial Crisis era that were largely absent for the early converges such as Japan and Korea. These headwinds include: the backlash against globalisation which reduces exporting opportunities, the difficulties of transferring resources from low productivity to higher productivity sectors (structural transformation), the challenge of upgrading human capital to the demands of a technology-intensive workplace and coping with climate change-induced agricultural stress. India has so far defied these headwinds but can continue to do so only if the challenges are decisively addressed.

Which amongst the following measures, if taken by India, is likely to directly redress the impact of economic headwinds?

(1) Higher education and skill upgradation particularly in areas of ICT.

(2) Transfer of more capital to large scale enterprises from medium and small scale enterprises.

(3) Export-oriented policy and custom duty rationalisation.

(4) Agricultural research to develop crops with high yield and resistant to adverse weather conditions.

(a) 1, 2 and 3 (b) 2, 3 and 4
(c) 1, 3 and 4 (d) 1, 2 and 4

**23.** Equity, as far as climate change is concerned, has two dimensions—inter-generational and intra-generational. In the specific context of climate change, intergenerational refers to the spatial distribution of global green house gases (GHG) emissions budgets, GHG emissions rights, implicit costs and benefits, and impacts of climate change inflicted by each generation on its successors, across generations. Intra-generational equity relates to the allocation of utilisation of resources among members of the present generation.

Quite often, in climate change debates the emphasis is on inter-generational equity. However, we cannot overlook intra-generational equity. The stake of developing countries, in growth and poverty eradication cannot be questioned. Developed countries, being responsible for causing climate change, owing to their historical as well as current emissions should take actions as committed, to stabilise and reduce their emissions of GHGs and also provide financial and technological support to enable developing countries in addressing the challenge of climate change. The social discount rate is crucial for a cost-benefit analysis reflecting society's relative valuation on today's well-being versus well-being in the future.

(i) The principle that "polluters should pay" in deciding which countries should finance/fund the actions for addressing the challenge of climate change, can be said to be a reflection of

(a) Inter-generational equity.
(b) Intra-generational equity.
(c) Both (a) and (b).
(d) Neither (a) nor (b).

(ii) Excessive use and consequent depletion of ground water would be a violation of

(a) Inter-generational equity.
(b) Intra-generational equity.
(c) Both (a) and (b).
(d) Neither (a) nor (b).

(iii) What is meant by the 'cost benefit analysis' which is referred to in the passage?

(a) The analysis of the cost the society has to bear on account of climate change to the cost it has to bear to fight the climate change.
(b) The analysis of the need of economic development of present generation vis-à-vis the harm this economic development causes in environmental terms to the next generation.
(c) The analysis of cost, which developed countries have to bear to assist developing countries in terms of finances and technological assistance, to the cost they would have to bear due to environmental degradation if such assistance is not rendered.
(d) All of the above.

**24.** Constitution talks about India that is Bharat being a Union of States. It is not a federation of states. It is described as the Union of States and there are a number of articles in the Constitution which emphasise the overwhelming character, the unitary character of our polity. Article 3 gives the power to the Parliament of India to create a new state, to bifurcate states, to change the boundary of states, to change the name of a state. Now can you do it a federation of States? This is a power which gives pre-eminence to the Centre, to the Union, through its Parliament.

Which amongst the following are logical conclusions which can be drawn from the passage?

1. The Indian Constitution is unitary is nature.

2. A federation is essentially formed by coming together of all states which have equal power and equal division of power between the centre and the states.
   (a) Only 1 is the correct logical conclusion.
   (b) Only 2 is the correct logical conclusion.
   (c) Both 1 and 2 are the correct logical conclusions.
   (d) Neither 1 nor 2 is the correct logical conclusion.

**25.** Occasions like the present do not occur in everybody's life and but rarely in anybody's life. I want you to know and feel that there is nothing but purest *Ahimsa* in all that I am saying and doing today. The draft resolution of the Working Committee is based on *Ahimsa*, the contemplated struggle similarly has its roots in *Ahimsa*. If, therefore, there is any among you who has lost faith in *Ahimsa* or is wearied of it, let him not vote for this resolution.

Let me explain my position clearly. God has vouchsafed to me a priceless gift in the weapon of *Ahimsa*. I and my *Ahimsa* are on our trail today. If in the present crisis, when the earth is being scorched by the flames of *Himsa* and crying for deliverance, I fail to make use of the God given talent, God will not forgive me and I shall be judged unwrongly of the great gift. I must act now. I may not hesitate and merely look on, when Russia and China are threatened.

Ours is not a drive for power, but purely a non-violent fight for India's independence. In a violent struggle, a successful general has been often known to effect a military coup and to set up a dictatorship. But under the Congress scheme of things, essentially non-violent as it is, there can be no room for dictatorship. A non-violent soldier of freedom will covet nothing for himself, He fights only for the freedom of his country. The Congress is unconcerned as to who will rule, when freedom is attained. The power, when it comes, will belong to the people of India, and it will be for them to decide to whom it placed in the entrusted. May be that the reins will be placed in the hands of the Parsis, for instance—as I would love to see happen or they may be handed to some others whose names are not heard in the Congress today. It will not be for you then to object saying, "This community is microscopic. That party did not play its due part in the freedom's struggle; why should it have all the power?" Ever since its inception the Congress has kept itself meticulously free of the communal taint. It has thought always in terms of the whole nation and has acted accordingly.

I know how imperfect our *Ahimsa* is and how far away we are still from the ideal, but in *Ahimsa* there is no final failure or defeat. I have faith, therefore, that if, in spite of our shortcomings, the big thing does happen, it will be because God wanted to help us by crowning with success our silent, unremitting *Sadhana* for the last twenty two years.

(i) As per the passage what is the fallout of a violent struggle which the speaker fears?
   1. It will lead to bloodshed.
   2. It may lead to set up of dictatorship.
   (a) Both 1 and 2 are true.
   (b) Neither 1 nor 2 is true.
   (c) Only 1 is true.
   (d) Only 2 is true.

(ii) Which of the following assumptions would be correct in terms of what is stated in the passage?
   1. Speaker does not believe his brand of *Ahimsa* to be perfect.
   2. The speaker believes that in a democracy power should essentially be vested in the hands of the minority community to protect its interest.
   3. Speaker believes selflessness to be an essential trait of man believing and practising non-violence.
   (a) 1, 2, 3 (b) 1, 2
   (c) 1, 3 (d) 2, 3

(iii) What does the speaker mean by "... but in *Ahimsa* there is no final failure or defeat."?

(a) It is important to adopt the right path and *Ahimsa* being the path of righteousness is the right course to adopt if even success is not imminent.

(b) *Ahimsa* is the right course to adopt as it would never lead to failure or defeat.

(c) Despite shortcomings and being far from ideal, *Ahimsa* as a path is bound to lead to success as such any failure is only momentary.

(d) All of the above.

**26.** The three terms *administration, organisation* and *management* are used inter-changeably. However, there is a specific difference in their meanings. This distinction is made clear by William Schulze. He says, "Administration is the force which lays down the object for which an organisation and its management are to strive and the broad policies under which they are to operate. An organisation is a combination of the necessary human beings, materials, tools, equipment and working space, appurtenances brought together in systematic and effective co-relation to accomplish some desired object. Management is that which leads, guides and directs an organisation for the accomplishment of a pre-determined object." Similarly, Oliver Sheldon states, "Administration is the function in an industry in the determination of the policy. Management is the function in an industry concerned with the execution of policy within the limits set by administration and the employment of the organisation for the particular objects set before it Organisation is the formation of an effective machine, management of an effective executive, administration of an effective direction. Administration determines the organisation, management uses it. Administration defines the goal; management strives towards it. Organisation is the machine of management in its achievements of the ends determined by the administration."

Thus, administration is a broader concept and includes within itself both organisation and management.

(i) Administration as per Schulze is best described by which of the following statements?

(a) Administration is the objective for which the organisation and management are to strive.

(b) Administration is the motive power or the force which prescribes the goal which the management and the organisation are to attain.

(c) Administration is the force laying down the object of an organisation and the broad policy under which they are to operate.

(d) It is the burden which regulates the human beings material function to attain objective.

(ii) Which of the following statements about the organisation are correct?

(a) Organisation is basically formation of an effective machinery management of an effective executive and administration of an effective direction.

(b) Organisation is the force, which lays down the object that is to be attained.

(c) Organisation is what leads and guides for accomplishment of a predetermined objective.

(d) All of the above.

(iii) As per the author what is the difference between administration and management?

(a) Administration determines the objective that the management strives to attain.

(b) Administration deals with the function of determination of a policy while management is concerned with the execution of it.

(c) Both (a) and (b).

(d) None of the above.

**27.** The principal objective of development planning is human development and the attainment of higher standard of living for the people. This requires a more equitable distribution of development benefits and opportunities, better living environment and empowerment of the poor and marginalised. There is special need to empower women who can act as catalysts for change. In making the development process inclusive, the challenge is to formulate policies and programmes to bridge regional, social and economic disparities in as effective and sustainable a manner as possible. One such challenge to the process of inclusive development is the demographic dividend the country is likely to experience, which also opens doors for new opportunities.

India is passing through a phase of unprecedented demographic changes. These demographic changes are likely to contribute to a substantially increased labour force in the country. The Census projection report shows that the proportion of working age population between 15 and 59 years is likely to increase from approximately 58 per cent in 2001 to more than 64 per cent by 2021. In absolute numbers, there will be approximately 63.5 million new entrants to the working age group between 2011 and 2016. Further, it is important to note that the bulk of this increase is likely to take place in the relatively younger age group of 20–35 years. Such a trend would make India one of the youngest nations in the world. In 2020, the average Indian will be only 29 years old. Comparable figures for China and the US are 37, 45 for West Europe, and 48 for Japan. This 'demographic dividend' provides India great opportunities, but it also poses a great challenge. It will benefit India only if our population is healthy, educated, and appropriately skilled. Therefore, greater focus on human and inclusive development is necessary to best utilise the demographic dividend.

(i) Why is demographic dividend a challenge to the process of inclusive development?

(a) More people in working age group would mean need for creating more jobs.

(b) There will be need for additional resources for keeping the additional working age population, healthy, educated and appropriately skilled.

(c) Both (a) and (b).

(d) Neither (a) nor (b).

(ii) Examine whether the following assertion can be made in terms of what is stated in the passage.

1. Demographic dividend will lead to rise in the skilled man-power available for the manufacturing sector.
2. Demographic dividend will surely aid in the process of inclusive development.

(a) Only Conclusion 1 can be drawn.

(b) Only Conclusion 2 can be drawn.

(c) Both Conclusions 1 and 2 can be drawn.

(d) Neither Conclusion 1 nor 2 can be drawn.

(iii) Examine whether the following programmes and schemes of government can be said to aid inclusive development.

1. Programme for development of infrastructure in the North East region of the country.
2. Programmes for imparting higher education and reservation of jobs for members of SC and ST community.
3. Programme for providing subsidised food grains to families of those who are below poverty line (BPL).

(a) 1, 2, 3 (b) 1, 2

(c) 1, 3 (d) 2, 3

(iv) What is the most important message that the author has tried to convey in the passage?

(a) India is soon going to be the youngest country in the world and it must make use of this opportunity.

(b) The government must utilise the opportunity of demographic dividend, which the country will soon have, to surmount the larger challenges of inclusive and overall human development.

(c) To attain inclusive development, policies and programmes should be such to counter the regional, social and economic disparities existent in the country.

(d) All of the above.

**28.** To teach is to create a space in which obedience to truth is practiced. Space may sound like a vague, poetic metaphor until we realise that it describes experiences of everyday life. We know what it means to be in a green and open field; we know what it means to be on a crowded rush hour bus. These experiences of physical space have parallels in our relations with others. On our jobs, we know what it is to be pressed and crowded, our working space diminished by the urgency of deadlines and competitiveness of colleagues.

But then there are times when deadlines disappear and colleagues cooperate, when everyone has space to move, invent and produce with energy and enthusiasm. With family and friends, we know how it feels to have unreasonable demands placed upon us, to be boxed in the expectations of those nearest to us. But then there are times when we feel accepted for who we are (or forgiven for who we are not), times when a spouse or a child or a friend gives us the space both to be and to become.

Similar experiences of crowding and space are found in education. To sit in a class where the teacher stuffs our minds with information, organises it with finality, insists on having the answers while being utterly uninterested in our views, and forces us into a grim competition for grades— to sit in such a class is to experience a lack of space for learning. But to study with a teacher who not only speaks but also listens, who not only gives answers but asks questions and welcomes our insights, who provides information and theories that do not close doors but open new ones, who encourages students to help each other learn—to study with such a teacher is to know the power of a learning space.

A learning space has three essential dimensions: openness, boundaries and an air of hospitality. To create open learning space is to remove the impediments to learning that we find around and within us: we often create them ourselves to evade the challenge of truth and transformation. One source of such impediments is our fear of appearing ignorant to others or to ourselves. The openness of a space is created by the firmness of its boundaries. A learning space cannot extend indefinitely; if it did, it would not be a structure for learning but an invitation for confusion and chaos. When space boundaries are violated, the quality of space suffers. The teacher who wants to create an open learning space must define and defend its boundaries with care, because the pursuit of truth can often be painful and discomforting, the learning space must be hospitable.

(i) Which of the following is **not** an essential dimension of the learning space as per the passage?

(a) Knowledge (b) Openness

(c) Boundaries (d) Air of hospitality

(ii) Which of the following statements best describes the author's conception of learning space?

(a) Where the teacher is friendly.

(b) Where there is no grim competition for grades.

(c) Where the students are encouraged to learn about space.

(d) Where the teacher provides information and theories which open new doors and encourages students to help each other learn.

(iii) The statement "the openness of a space is created by the firmness of its boundaries" appears contradictory. Which of the following statements provides the best justification for the proposition?

(a) We cannot have a space without boundaries.

(b) Bounded space is highly structured.

(c) When space boundaries are violated, the quality of space suffers.

(d) A teacher can effectively defend a learning space without boundaries.

**29.** It was the examination day and Victor felt as if he had swallowed a frozen elephant. He went to the toilet a third time that morning, washed his face twice, drank cup after cup of coffee and basically behaved in the most illogical way imaginable. He felt he was standing at the edge of an abyss and his forehead started sweating. His stomach felt as though it were upside down, his head was being pounded regularly by a group of imaginary boxers with spiked gloves. He had not slept the previous night. His heart throbbed and throbbed, and then suddenly stopped throbbing. Victor felt a burning in his throat, and strangely, he felt as if his legs were made of cloth: he could swear they wobbled.

(i) What illogical things which Victor did, have been described in the passage?

(1) He swallowed a frozen chocolate elephant.

(2) He drank a number of cups of coffee.

(3) He stood at the edge of an abyss.

(4) He went to the toilet thrice.

(a) 1, 4 (b) 2, 4

(b) 1, 3, 4 (d) 1, 2, 3

(ii) Why was Victor behaving in an illogical manner?

(a) He was ill.

(b) He did not sleep the previous night.

(c) He was nervous because of the examination.

(d) All of the above.

(iii) Which of the following is correct?

(a) Victor had been pounded by a group of boxers.

(b) His legs were weak because of fatigue.

(c) He did not sleep the previous night.

(d) All of the above.

**30.** With the production of over 1,000 films a year, in over 20 languages, the Indian film industry is the largest in the world. The film industry is also contributing to outsourcing of services such as animation, visual effects, conversion of 3D, and post-production services, to the ICT sector, thus contributing to its growth. The Indian film industry is also generating additional revenue through collaboration with the ICT sector, such as DVDs, music CDs, mobile downloads and online gaming. High rates of entertainment tax and lack of uniformity in tax structure across states are major factors inhibiting growth of the film industry. Adoption of the goods and services tax (GST), subsuming service tax and entertainment tax, could promote growth of the film industry. Piracy is another challenge for the Indian film sector. To make it relevant to present day requirements and to check piracy, the Ministry of Information and Broadcasting is in the process of amending the Cinematograph Act 1952. India has also signed co-production agreements with six countries with a view to pooling their creative, artistic, technical, financial, and marketing resources for coproduction of films and television programmes. During 2011–12, the Ministry has accorded 20 foreign production houses shooting permission. Given the potential of this sunrise sector in India's growth and trade in services, efforts are needed to relocate the business of the Indian film industry from foreign countries to India by addressing issues like tax credit, which can increase activities in India and also generate employment.

(i) As per the passage, how is the adoption of goods and service tax (GST) likely to benefit the film industry?

1. Service and entertainment tax could become a part of GST thus unifying and simplifying diverse laws.

2. There will be uniformity of tax structure in all the states.

3. There will be reduction in entertainment tax.

(a) All 1, 2, 3 can be concluded.
(b) Only 1 and 2 can be concluded.
(c) Only 1 and 3 can be concluded.
(d) Only 2 and 3 can be concluded.

(ii) Examine whether the following inferences can be drawn in terms of what is stated in the passage.

1. Growth of films has helped in growth of ICT sector.
2. GST is likely to reduce the problem of piracy associated with film industry as uniformity of tax structure will deter sales in the black market.

(a) Only Conclusion 1 can be drawn.
(b) Only Conclusion 2 can be drawn.
(c) Both Conclusions 1 and 2 can be drawn.
(d) Neither Conclusion 1 nor 2 can be drawn.

(iii) As per the passage, which amongst the following is likely to help in relocation of Indian film business in India from foreign destinations?

(a) Investment by foreign production companies in India.
(b) Improvement of infrastructure of film business in India.
(c) Resolving issues like tax credit.
(d) All of the above.

(iv) Which amongst the following are challenges highlighted in the passage, which need to be surmounted, to help in the growth of Indian film industry?

1. Limited growth in ICT in perspective of requirement of film industry, which is necessary to meet the world standards of filming technology.
2. Uniformity and amendment of laws relating to taxation and piracy.
3. Competition from foreign film industry, which has better technology and money, which has been given permission to start production houses in India.

(a) 1, 2, 3 (b) 1 only
(c) 2 only (d) 2 and 3

**31.** What is truth? A difficult question; but I have solved it for myself by saying that it is what the voice within tells you. How then, you ask, different people think of different and contrary truths? Well, seeing that the human mind works through innumerable media and that the evolution of the human mind is not the same for all, it follows that what may be truth for one may be untruth for another, and hence those who have made these experiments have come to the conclusion that there are certain conditions to be observed in making those experiments... It is because we have at the present moment everybody claiming the right of conscience without going through any discipline whatsoever that there is so much untruth being delivered to a bewildered world. All that I can in true humility present to you is that Truth is not to be found by anybody who has not got an abundant sense of humility.

(i) As per the author why is the perception of truth different to different persons?

(a) Because truth is not uniform but different.
(b) Because human mind, its evolution and interests of people are different.
(c) Because same underlying conditions are not observed by different people in understanding truth.
(d) None of the above

(ii) Why there is so much untruth being delivered to the world?

(1) Everybody is claiming their conscience to be right.
(2) People are not observing discipline.

(a) Only 1 is the correct explanation.
(b) Only 2 is the correct explanation.
(c) Both 1 & 2 are the correct explanation.
(d) Neither 1 nor 2 is the correct explanation.

**32.** In 2002, Dr. Foster drew up his own three-part definition of grid computing. A grid, he proposed, should co-ordinate computing resources that are not centrally controlled, rely on open standards, and provide more reliability than standalone machines. Alas for Dr. Foster, his checklist immediately raised hackles within the computer industry, since much existing 'grid computing' software fails to meet these criteria. Linking many small computers together to create a more powerful machine, for example, is not new, and is usually called network. For marketing purposes, however, some firms like to call it grid instead.

Similarly, grid is often confused, sometimes deliberately, for marketing reasons, with equally nebulous terms, such as utility computing, on-demand computing, autonomic computing and datacentre virtualisation. Behind all this terminology is the idea of continuously and automatically adjusting the configuration of a corporate datacentre to meet the demands made on it. But Andrew Chien, a grid pioneer at the University of California at San Diego, notes that though useful, such approaches generally eschew the harder part of the grid vision, which requires automated sharing of computing resources between different organisations, not just within one firm.

What of those deliberately decentralised systems, peer-to-peer file-sharing networks? Some of them, at least, operate using open standards, and they are certainly robust: repeated attempts to close them down have failed. But they do not count as grid computing either, since they are mostly storage and distribution systems, and do not perform general purpose data-processing.

Grid computing is not entirely fictional; however, scientists have been building grids on a national or even global scale for several years. A good example is the LHC computing Grid, which links large clusters and storage systems in 87 computer centres around the world, for the benefit of particle physicists. Another example is Tera Grid, an American effort to link nine large supercomputing centres for scientific use. Even within the academic arena, though, convergence towards common standards is slow, partly because each grid project tends to reinvent the wheel. To tackle this problem, the European Union launched a major initiative called EGee this year, to provide a common grid infrastructure for scientists; America has a similar initiative.

It is presumed that such projects will provide the first glimpse of 'the grid', a single global computing grid that will do for data processing what the World Wide Web did for online publishing. Wolfgang Gentzsch, a former grid guru at Sun Microsystems, who is now director of MCNC, North Carolina's statewide grid initiative, says the term 'grid' really refers to this ultimate goal towards which today's systems are merely stepping stones. But it would, he admits, be more accurate to refer to them as 'grid-like' or using 'grid technology'.

Constructing a single, global grid will mean solving difficult security, privacy and billing problems. Scientists have a tradition of sharing their results and resources, but others do not. Yet the hurdles are not so much technological as political, economic and terminological. The dream of a single grid, akin to the web in its simplicity and pervasiveness, still seems a long way off—as does agreement about what 'grid' really means.

(i) According to the passage, a grid should not be mistaken as
   (a) Utility computing.
   (b) On-demand computing.
   (c) Autonomic computing.
   (d) All of the above.

(ii) According to the passage, which of the following benefit particle physicists?
   (a) LHC computing grid
   (b) United Devices
   (c) IBM
   (d) Argon National laboratory

(iii) What is the author's assertion in the passage?

(a) Grid computing's biggest problem is that nobody knows for sure, what it is.

(b) In the present scenario, it will be extremely difficult to put grid communication in practice.

(c) Grid computing is an unknown thing.

(d) All of the above.

**33.** India continues to undertake and effectively implement a large number of actions relating to energy, environment and climate, in particular, covering renewable energy, energy efficiency, sustainable agriculture, sustainable habitat, water, forestry, Himalayan ecosystem and knowledge and capacity building. These actions reflect India's commitment to meet (and reconcile) the goals of climate change, sustainable development and energy access. India also expects the international community to be ambitious and fulfil its commitments in accordance with the principles of equity and common but differentiated responsibilities.

Considering the passage above, which of the given statement can be said to be its most logical corollary?

(a) India has taken sufficient steps for meeting the goals of climate change.

(b) India has taken appropriate steps to exhort the international community to fulfil its commitments pertaining to climate change.

(c) India is committed to meet its goals pertaining to climate change.

(d) None of the above.

**34.** Non-possession is allied to non-stealing. A thing not originally stolen must nevertheless be classified stolen property, if one possesses it without needing it. Possession implies provision for the future. A seeker after Truth, a follower of the Law of Love cannot hold anything against tomorrow. God never stores for the morrow; He never creates more than what is strictly needed for the moment. If, therefore, we repose faith in His providence, we should rest assured, that He will give us everything that we require. Saints and devotees, who have lived in such faith, have always derived a justification for it from their experience. Our ignorance or negligence of the Divine Law, which gives to man from day to day his daily bread and no more, has given rise to inequalities with all the miseries attendant upon them. The rich have a superfluous store of things, which they do not need, and which are, therefore, neglected and wasted, while millions are starved to death for want of sustenance. If each retained possession only of what he needed, no one would be in want, and all would live in contentment. As it is, the rich are discontented no less than the poor. The poor man would fain become a millionaire, and the millionaire multimillionaire. The rich should take the initiative in dispossession with a view to a universal diffusion of the spirit of contentment. If only they keep their own property within moderate limits, the starving will be easily fed, and will learn the lesson of contentment along with the rich.

Economic equality is the master key to non-violent independence. Working for economic equality means abolishing the eternal conflict between capital and labour. It means the levelling down of the few rich in whose hands is concentrated the bulk of the nation's wealth on the one hand, and a levelling up of the semi-starved naked millions on the other. A non-violent system of government is clearly an impossibility so long as the wide gulf between the rich and the hungry millions persists. The contrast between the palaces of New Delhi and the miserable hovels of the poor, labouring class cannot last one day in a free India in which the poor will enjoy the same power as the richest in the land. A violent and bloody revolution is a certainty one day unless there is a voluntary abdication of the common good. I adhere to my doctrine of trusteeship in spite of the ridicule that has been poured upon it. It is true that it is difficult to reach. So is non-violence difficult to attain.

(i) Which of the following is **not** one of the reasons given by the author while advocating against excessive possession?

(a) Excessive possession is akin to stealing.

(b) God never stores for the morrow.

(c) Excessive possession leads to wasting of material products while millions suffer while millions suffer from lack of it.

(d) None of the above.

(ii) Which of the following conclusions have been drawn by the author?

1. Economic equality is essential for non-violent independence.
2. For attaining contentment it is imperative for the rich to take initiative in dispossession.

(a) Only Conclusion 1 has been drawn.

(b) Only Conclusion 2 has been drawn.

(c) Both Conclusions 1 and 2 have been drawn.

(d) Neither Conclusion 1 nor 2 have been drawn.

(iii) As per the passage what does economic equality mean?

(a) Non-possession of material things not required by the rich.

(b) Distribution of wealth concentrated in hands of few amongst the have-nots.

(c) Granting equal opportunity to all so as to secure employment/work.

(d) All of the above.

(iv) Which of the following are the messages/ key ideas conveyed by the author in the passage?

1. Possession of a thing without needing it is akin to stealing.
2. The rich should take initiative in dispossession.
3. Although economic equality has little bearing on attaining peaceful independence, it is nevertheless essential for the society to attain.
4. Peaceful governance cannot be attained until the divide between the rich and poor is bridged.

(a) 1, 2, 3 (b) 1, 2, 4

(c) 2, 3, 4 (d) 1, 2, 3, 4

(v) What, as per the author, is the root cause of inequalities?

(a) A man's tendency to possess things even if not needed by him.

(b) Lack of opportunity for work for everybody.

(c) Insufficiency of resources for everybody considering the burgeoning population.

(d) All of the above.

**35.** Mattre Saval, a notary at Vernon, was passionately fond of music. Although just thirty-five, he was already bald, and like other comparatively young bald men, he heroically shaved off whatever remained so that the nature could not abase him and fashion need not be compromised. Now our hero was somewhat corpulent, and the shape of his round stomach harmonised with the naked head. He was active, gallant and convivial at parties. In most matters that interest most men, he was dispassionate enough. But if someone mentioned Beethoven or Haydn, M. Saval lost all control of his stumpy hands; he would begin frothing at the mouth, and stammer furious words of approval.

(i) Which of the following would be a correct description of Saval?

(a) He was fat, bald and lethargic.

(b) He was fit, bald and energetic.

(c) He was fat, bald and energetic.

(d) None of the above.

(ii) Which of the following can be inferred from the passage about Saval's nature?

(a) Saval enjoyed parties.

(b) He was fond of music particularly Beethoven and Haydn.

(c) Both (a) & (b).

(d) Neither (a) nor (b).

(iii) What does the author want to convey by the expression,"... he would begin frothing at the mouth and stammer furious words of approval."

(a) Saval was a connoisseur of music.

(b) He suffered from epileptic fits.

(c) He conveyed the impression of being an ardent music lover of some music masters.

(d) He was a phoney who pretended to be a discerning music lover.

**36.** The Unique Identification (UID) System is envisioned as a means for citizens to easily establish their identity, anywhere in the country. It will be an important step towards ensuring that residents in India can access the resources and benefits they are entitled to. The resident will be able to enrol for a UID number by providing basic demographic as well as biometric details (which may include photograph, fingerprints and iris scan) to the enrolling agency. The enrolling agency will transmit these details to a central UID server. The server will then perform a de-duplication check using the resident's key demographic and biometric fields against existing UID records in the database, to ensure that she does not already have a UID number. Once the check confirms that a duplicate record does not exist, the central system will issue a UID number to the resident. The resident can then use the number with different service providers, who can verify his or her identity online. The agency has to transmit the UID number and information provided by the resident to the UID server, and the server immediately responds with a yes or a no.

The UID can have a significant impact on service delivery. The existing patchwork of multiple agency databases in India gives individuals the incentive to provide different personal information to different agencies and also impersonate someone else. In the UID infrastructure, all resident records are stored in a central database, and each new entry is de-duplicated. Consequently, residents can only have one UID number, which is mobile and can be used anywhere in the country. The lack of duplicates, and accuracy and mobility in identity verification, would reduce opportunities for fraud and enable agencies across the country to provide residents with targeted, effective services and benefits.

(i) Consider the following objectives:

1. Establish the identity of the resident.
2. Do away with the requirement of identities like PAN Card, Election Commissioner Card.
3. Residents will have easy access to resources and benefits to which they are entitled.
4. Residents have access to cheap bank loans.
5. Reduce opportunities for frauds.
6. Help in better targeting of services.

As per passage which of the aforesaid objectives does the UID strive to attain?

(a) 1, 2, 3, 4 (b) 1, 3, 5, 6
(c) 1, 3, 4, 5 (d) 2, 4, 5, 6

(ii) Why UID is likely to reduce the opportunity of frauds?

(a) It will be a smart electronic card.

(b) It will contain personal details of the resident.

(c) The entries in database will be accurate and de-duplicated making impersonation very difficult.

(d) None of the above.

(iii) Consider the following stages of enrolment of a resident for UID:

1. De-duplication check by server.
2. Providing basic demographic and biometric details by the resident to enrolling agency.
3. Issuing of a UID number to the resident.
4. Transmission of the details of the resident to the UID Central Server.

Which one of the following will be the correct sequence?

(a) 1, 2, 3, 4 (b) 3, 4, 1, 2
(c) 2, 4, 3, 1 (d) 2, 4, 1, 3

**37.** From the view of climate change negotiations at the United Nations Framework Convention on Climate Change (UNFCCC) and also in other international forums, countries often unite themselves into groups or regional bodies to represent their mutual interests and to establish common negotiating positions. With differing interests and issues faced by different countries, these groups often play a catalytic role in the dynamics of the negotiations. Hence, certain Non-Annex I countries (Annex 1-countries: Countries, which have a specific emission target relative to its emissions of GHGs in its base year 1990) form coalitions and line behind some positions, which may be unacceptable to other developing country groups. The Durban negotiations also demonstrated these dynamics and pressures. Small Island Developing Nations (SIDS) and Least Developed Countries (LDCs) are two country groups that are very proactive in the climate change negotiations since they are considered most susceptible to climate change threats. SIDS consists of small islands and low lying coastal countries that share similar sustainable development challenges related to climate change. The majority of SIDS countries are also members of the Association of Small Island States (AOSIS) and 12 are listed as LDCs as well. The 50 countries defined as LDCs by the United Nations (UN) regularly work together in the UN system. They have become increasingly active in the climate change process, usually working together to defend their particular interests. Often in the negotiations, India's position on its vulnerability has not received due attention and coverage. India is highly vulnerable to adverse impacts of climate change with its long coast-line, large number of islands, dependence on primary sectors for livelihood, etc. Since India along with Small Island Developing Nations and Least Developed Countries is vulnerable to climate change impacts and is likely to suffer from it, so it would be a good idea to see how these countries have fared against other regions of the world, on the basis of the indicators such as GDP, $CO_2$ emissions, and energy consumption.

When we compare the per capita GDP of India and SIDS against that of the world, collectively SIDS members have greater improvement with their GDP being closer to the world average. India's per capita GDP, on the other hand, is very low. Statistics also show that India and the LDCs have had lower per capita GDP as well as smaller per capita emissions than SIDS.

(i) Why SIDS and LDCs are important in UNFCCC?

1. They are able to form a homogenous negotiating group based on common environmental concerns shared by them.
2. They are propped up by developed countries to counter the collective bargaining power of the developing countries.
3. They are considered the most susceptible to climate change threats.

(a) 1, 2, 3 (b) 1, 3
(c) 2, 3 (d) 3 only

(ii) Why has India's position on climate change and its vulnerability not received due attention?

(a) India is not perceived to be among the most threatened states by the climate change.
(b) India's GDP is higher than the SIDs and LDCs.
(c) India has the technological capability to adapt and mitigate the effects of climate change.
(d) All of the above.

(iii) Which of the following assertions are correct in terms of what is stated in the passage?

1. At times, there are underlying conflicts between the positions of developing countries vis-à-vis the SIDs and LDCs on the climate change issues.
2. Per capita emission of India is lower than that of SIDs.

(a) Only Assertion 1 is correct.
(b) Only Assertion 2 is correct.
(c) Both Assertions 1 and 2 are correct.
(d) Neither Assertion 1 nor 2 is correct.

**38.** Every economy has to go for its development through exploitation of its natural and human resources. There are priorities of objectives set by the economy, which is attempted to be realised in a proper time frame. The availability and the non-availability of resources (natural as well as human) are not the only issues, which make an economy decide to declare whether it opts for agriculture or industry as its prime moving force. There are many more socio-political compulsions and objectives which play their roles in such decision-making.

The political leadership selected industry as the leading force of the economy after independence. This was already decided by the dominant group of the nationalist leaders way back in the mid-1930s when they felt the need for economic planning in India before setting up the National Planning Committee (1938). Given the available resource base it seems an illogical decision as India lacked all those pre-requisites, which could suggest the declaration of industry as its prime mover:

(i) Almost no presence of infrastructure sector, i.e., power transportation and communication.

(ii) Negligible presence of the infrastructure industries, i.e., iron and steel, cement, coal, crude oil, oil refining and electricity.

(iii) Lack of investible capital—be the case of either the government or the private sector.

(iv) Absence of the required technology to support the process of industrialisation and no research and development.

(v) Lack of skilled manpower.

(vi) Absence of entrepreneurship among the people.

(vii) Absence of the market for industrial goods.

(viii) Many other socio-psychological factors, which were negative forces for the proper industrialisation of the economy.

The obvious choice for India would have been the agriculture sector as the moving force of the economy because:

(i) The country had the natural resource of fertile land, which was fit for cultivation.

(ii) The human resource did not require any kind of higher training.

By only organising our land ownership, irrigation and other inputs to agriculture, India could have gone for better prospects of development. Once there was no crises of food, shelter, basic healthcare, etc. to the masses, one goal of development could have been realised—a general welfare of the people. Once the masses were able to achieve a level of purchasing capacity, India could have gone for the expansion of industries. India was capable of generating as much surplus income for its masses as was required by the emerging industries for a marked success. The People's Republic of China did the same in 1949. By taking a realistic evaluation of its resources it declared agriculture as its prime moving force for the economy. The surplus generated from agriculture was suitably invested to develop the pre-requisites for industrialisation and the county went for it in the 1970s.

(i) Which of the following is **not** the reason cited by the author, to justify that the agriculture sector was the ideal choice at the time of independence, as the prime mover of the economy?

(a) The country had fertile land fit for agriculture.

(b) Agriculture did not require higher training or much technical inputs.

(c) Country already had suitable irrigation facilities.

(d) It had human resource or labour to meet the requirements of agriculture.

(ii) As per the author, for which of the following reasons, the choice of the industry as the prime mover of the economy was not proper?

1. Lack of infrastructure
2. Lack of skilled human resource
3. Lack of suitable land
4. Lack of capital

(a) 1, 2, 3 (b) 1, 2, 3, 4
(c) 1, 2, 4 (d) 2, 3, 4

(iii) What as per the passage could have been the first milestone of development achieved by the nation had the choice of agriculture been made as the prime mover of economy?

(a) Availability of capital in the society.
(b) Food security, housing and health care.
(c) Social awareness, spread of education and over all development
(d) All of the above.

**39.** Here is the pathetic truth. One dollar and eighty-seven cents. That was all. And sixty cents of it was in pennies. Pennies saved one and two at a time by bullying the grocer and the vegetable man and the butcher until one's cheeks burned with the silent imputation of parsimony that such close dealing involved. Three times Della counted it. One dollar and eighty-seven cents. And the next day would be Christmas. There was clearly nothing to do but flop down on the shabby little couch and raise a hue-and-cry and blame the destiny. So Della did it. The circumstances instigated the moral reflection that life is made up of sobs, sniffles, and smiles, with sniffles dominating.

(i) What is implied by the expression, "... cheeks burned with silent imputation of parsimony."?

(a) Acute embarrassment over an unsaid charge of stinginess.
(b) Silent burning of cheeks due to misery and poverty.
(c) Embarrassment due to shortage of money faced when making a purchase.
(d) None of the above.

(ii) What is the pathetic truth referred to in the passage?

(a) The truth that she was poor.
(b) The truth that she had been a miser.
(c) The truth that she was not able to save sufficient money.
(d) All of the above.

(iii) Which of the following traits of Della's personality have been reflected in the passage?

(1) She was fatalistic.
(2) She detested her penury.

(a) Only 1
(b) Only 2
(c) Both 1 & 2
(d) Neither 1 nor 2

**40.** My notion of democracy is that under it the weakest should have the same opportunity as the strongest. That can never happen except through non-violence.

I have always held that social justice, even unto the least and lowliest, is impossible of attainment by force. I have believed that it is possible by proper training of the lowliest by non-violent means to secure the redress of the wrongs suffered by them. That means is non-co-operation. At times, non-co-operation becomes as much a duty as co-operation. No one is bound to co-operation in one's own undoing or slavery. Freedom received through the effort of others; however benevolent, cannot be retained when such effort is withdrawn. In other words, such freedom is not real freedom. But the lowliest can feel its glow, as soon as they learn the art of attaining it through non-violent non-co-operation.

Civil disobedience is the inherent right of a citizen. He dare not give it up without ceasing to be a man. Civil disobedience is never followed by anarchy. Criminal disobedience can lead to it. Every State puts down criminal disobedience by force. It perishes if it does not. But to put down civil disobedience is to attempt to imprison conscience.

True democracy or the *swaraj* of the masses can never come through untruthful and violent means, for the simple reason that the natural corollary to their use would be to remove all opposition through the suppression or extermination of the antagonists. That does not make for individual freedom. Individual freedom can have the fullest play only under a regime of unadulterated *ahimsa*.

(i) As per the author's view what is the essence of democracy?

(a) Freedom from exploitation for the weakest.

(b) Equality of opportunity for all including the weakest.

(c) Both (a) and (b).

(d) Neither (a) nor (b).

(ii) Why does the author state that the freedom obtained from the efforts of others is not real freedom?

(a) Such freedom is fraught with the possibility of violence.

(b) Such freedom does not enable development of qualities worthy of free people and hence such freedom may be lost when outside effort is withdrawn.

(c) Such freedom gets stigmatised that it is not attained by self effort and hence is not real freedom.

(d) All of the above.

(iii) Which of the following is **not** a difference between civil and criminal disobedience as per the passage?

(a) Civil Disobedience is the inherent right of a citizen while criminal disobedience is not.

(b) Civil Disobedience does not lead to anarchy while criminal disobedience may lead to.

(c) Civil Disobedience will not lead to destruction of state while criminal disobedience may lead to.

(d) None of the above.

(iv) Why does the author feel that true democracy cannot be attained through violent and untruthful means?

(a) Such means cause suppression of individual freedom.

(b) It leads to suppression or extermination of those who are opposing the seekers of democracy.

(c) Both (a) and (b).

(d) Neither (a) nor (b).

(v) Which of the following assertions have been made in the passage above?

1. Civil disobedience is the inherent right of a citizen.
2. A person who is being exploited should not co-operate with his own exploiter.
3. Equality of opportunity can never be attained through non-violence.
4. To suppress disobedience is the right of the state otherwise it may cause its own extinction.
5. Non-violence is the only path for attainment of true democracy.
6. Individual freedom blooms in a regime of non-violence.

(a) 1, 3, 4, 6 (b) 1, 2, 5, 6

(c) 1, 2, 4, 5, 6 (d) 1, 2, 4, 6

**41.** It was a dark autumn night. The old banker was walking up and down his study and remembering how, fifteen years before, he had given a party one autumn evening. There had been many clever men there, and there had been interesting conversations. Among others things they had talked of capital punishment. The majority of the guests, among whom were many journalists and intellectual men, disapproved of the death penalty. They considered that form of punishment out of date, immoral, and unsuitable for Christian States. In the opinion of some of them the death penalty ought to be replaced everywhere by imprisonment for life. "I don't agree with you," said their host the banker. "I have not tried either the death penalty or imprisonment for life, but if one may judge a priori, the death penalty is more moral and more humane than imprisonment for life. Capital punishment kills a man at once, but lifelong imprisonment kills him slowly.

(i) What was the host's view about capital punishment?

(a) He was against capital punishment as state had no right to take life as it could not restore it.

(b) Capital punishment should be replaced by imprisonment for life as the latter was more humane.

(c) Capital punishment was preferred over imprisonment for life as the latter killed slowly.

(d) Both were inhuman as state had no right to take what it could not restore.

(ii) What was the occupation of the host?

(a) A journalist

(b) A banker

(c) A lawyer

(d) Not specified in the passage

(iii) Examine which of the following assertions can be inferred from the passage?

(1) The majority of guests believed that death sentence ought to be replaced by imprisonment for life.

(2) The guests in the party had gathered to discuss the suitability of imprisonment for life vis-à-vis death sentence.

(a) Only 1 can be inferred.

(b) Only 2 can be inferred.

(c) Both 1 & 2 can be inferred.

(d) Neither 1 nor 2 can be inferred.

**42.** 'Philosophy' is a word which has been used in many ways, some wider, some narrower. I propose to use it in a very wide sense, which I will now try to explain.

Philosophy, as I shall understand the word, is something intermediate between theology and science. Like theology, it consists of speculations on matters as to which definite knowledge has, so far, been unascertainable; but like science, it appeals to human reason rather than to authority, whether that of tradition or that of revelation. All definite knowledge—so I should contend—belongs to science; all dogma as to what surpasses definite knowledge belongs to theology. But between theology and science, there is a 'No Man's Land', exposed to attack from both sides; this 'No Man's Land' is philosophy. Almost all the questions of most interest to speculative minds are such as science cannot answer, and the confident answers of theologians no longer are as convincing as they did in former centuries. Is the world divided into mind and matter, and if so, what is mind and what is matter? Is mind subject to matter, or is it possessed of independent powers? Has the universe any unity or purpose? Is it evolving towards some goal? Are there really laws of nature, or do we believe in them only because of our innate love of order? Is man what he seems to the astronomer, a tiny lump of carbon and water impotently crawling on a small and unimportant planet? Or is he what he appears to Hamlet? Is he perhaps both at once?

Ever since men became capable of free speculation, their actions in innumerable important respects, have depended upon their theories as to the world and human life, as to what is good and what is evil. This is as true in the present day as at any former time. To understand an age or a nation, we must understand its philosophy, and to understand its philosophy, we must ourselves be in some degree philosophers. There is here a reciprocal causation: the circumstances of men's lives do much to determine their philosophy, but, conversely, their philosophy does much to determine their circumstances.

There is also, however, a more personal answer. Science tells us what we can know, but what we can know is little, and if we forget how much we cannot know, we may become insensitive to many things of very great importance. Theology, on the other hand, induces a dogmatic belief that we have knowledge, where in fact, we have ignorance, and by doing so, generates a kind of impertinent insolence towards the universe. Uncertainty, in the presence of vivid hopes and fears, is painful, but must be endured if we wish to live without the support of comforting fairy tales. It is not good either to forget the questions that philosophy asks, or to persuade ourselves that we have found indubitable answers to them. To teach how to live without certainty, and yet without being paralysed by hesitation, is perhaps the chief thing that philosophy, in our age, can still do for those who study it.

(i) The purpose of philosophy is to
   (a) Reduce uncertainty and chaos.
   (b) Help us to cope with uncertainty and ambiguity.
   (c) Help us to find explanations for uncertainty.
   (d) Reduce the terror of cosmic loneliness.

(ii) Based on this passage, what can be concluded about the relation between philosophy and science?
   (a) The two are antagonistic.
   (b) The two are complementary.
   (c) There is no relation between the two.
   (d) Philosophy derives from science.

(iii) According to the author, which of the following statements about the nature of the universe must be definitely true?
   (a) The universe has unity.
   (b) The universe has a purpose.
   (c) The universe is evolving towards a goal.
   (d) None of the above.

**43.** Environmental protection and management is deservedly attracting a lot of attention these days. This is a desirable development in the face of the alarming rate of natural resource degradation, which greatly hampers their optimal utilisation. When waste waters emanating from municipal sewage, industrial effluent, agricultural and land runoffs, find their way either to ground water reservoirs or other surface water sources, the quality of water deteriorates, rendering it unfit for use. The natural balance is disturbed when concentrated discharges of waste water is not controlled. This is because the cleansing forces of nature cannot do their job in proportion to the filthy matter.

According to the National Environment Engineering and Research Institute (NEERI), a staggering 70 per cent of water available in the country is polluted. According to the Planning Commission, "From the Dal Lake in the North to the Periyar and Chaliyar rivers in the South, from Damodar and Hoogly in the East to the Thane creek in the West, the picture of water pollution is uniformly gloomy. Even our large perennial rivers, like the Ganga, are today heavily polluted."

According to one study, all the 14 major rivers of India are highly polluted. Besides Ganga, these rivers include Yamuna, Narmada, Godavari, Krishna and Cauvery. These rivers carry 85 per cent of the surface runoff and their drainage basins cover 73 per cent of the country. The pollution of the much revered Ganga is due in particular to municipal sewage that accounts for 3/4$^{th}$ of its pollution load. Despite India having legislation on water pollution, the Water [(Prevention and Control of Pollution) Act, 1974, and various water pollution control boards, rivers have today become synonymous with drains and sewers.

(i) The degradation of natural resources will necessarily lead to
   (a) Poor economic utilisation of resources.
   (b) Contamination of water from municipal sewage.
   (c) Water unfit for human consumption.
   (d) None of the above.

(ii) According to NEERI
   (a) The extent of water pollution in the Dal Lake is grim.
   (b) Seventy per cent of total water available in the country is polluted.
   (c) Only a few towns and cities have sewage treatment facilities.
   (d) All the major rivers of India are highly polluted.

(iii) Municipal sewage pollutants account for
   (a) The lowest percentage of water pollution.
   (b) Seventy-five per cent of the Ganga's water pollution load.

(c) Twice the volume of the waste water of industrial origin.

(d) Three times as much discharge from the agricultural fields.

(iv) Which of the following assumptions would be correct in terms of what has been stated in the passage?

1. All water bodies across the length and breadth of the country have become polluted.
2. Pollution caused by manufacturing units and industries is the major cause of pollution of rivers and, in particular, of Ganga.

(a) Only Assumption 1 is correct.

(b) Only Assumption 2 is correct.

(c) Both Assumptions 1 and 2 are correct.

(d) Neither Assumption 1 nor 2 is correct.

**44.** A central focus of India's economic policy is to achieve inclusive growth. However, while India's success in growth over the last two decades has been universally praised, much remains to be done on the inclusion front. Accordingly, the government is committed to making this a central tenet of policy. In doing so, it is worthwhile to be self-critical and analyse why India has not done better on this dimension despite so much energy and rhetoric directed to it. Some recent papers analysed this, by focusing on the distribution of food, and shed useful light.

It is a maintainable ethical principle that any nation that is able to provide basic food to all, it should not treat as an option or a luxury, but as a right. The Indian government's new food security bill is rooted in this fundamental ethical precept and is, as such, highly desirable. An implication of this bill is that all the poor and vulnerable must be empowered by the state to be able to get their basic food requirements.

Before commenting on this it is worth clarifying that when economists measure poverty, there are two very different motivating factors. One is to see how the level of poverty is changing over time and the other is to identify the poor in order to direct benefits. While tracking the level of poverty over time we have to hold the poverty line constant (subject to corrections for the changing value of the rupee). It is for this reason that we use the same standard over time to see if global warming is occurring. To change the standard would make inter-temporal comparison quite meaningless. However, to decide on whom to direct subsidies, we have reason to use different standards for measuring poverty. We could think of measures, which change as society becomes better off and is able to service the poor better. One criterion in this spirit is the quintile income measure, which assesses society in terms of how its poorest 20 per cent population or the bottom quintile fares. We of course know that they do not fare well. But what is more dismaying is that they do not even adequately get the benefits they are supposed to get. A study showed that the bottom quintile of rural population in Maharashtra and Andhra Pradesh got 10 per cent and 20 per cent, respectively of the foodgrain that they were supposed to get. In general, several studies confirm that our track record of delivering to the vulnerable remains highly flawed. One of the most comprehensive recent studies of this, by Swedberg, suggests that a key secret lies in giving the benefit to the poor directly. Swedberg estimates that to transfer ₹ 1 to a poor household by the current method of giving cheap food first to PDS stores and then having them transfer it to the poor, the Government of India incurs a budgetary expenditure of ₹ 9. At this rate, a large food programme becomes fiscally unviable.

Fortunately, with Aadhaar coming up, it is possible to make a cash transfer to the poor directly, which, especially if given to the female head of the household, can empower the poor and the women, and sharply cut down leakages and the costs of the programme. This in turn means that we can greatly increase the coverage of the population that gets the subsidy. Success stories with cash transfer programmes from Mexico's Oportunidades and Brazil's Bolsa Familia bolster this argument. Of course, we have to be aware that in many regions of India private markets hardly exist and so we will in these regions have to, for now, rely on actual food being delivered through the PDS system. On the other hand, it is important to recognise that one reason private markets do not exist in these areas is because the people do not have enough buying power. Once we make cash transfers to them, private markets will develop even in these areas. This is what is meant by the enabling role of government. It should create a setting where it is in the interest of private agents to deliver on what needs to be delivered.

(i) What is implied by inclusive growth in the above passage?
   (a) A growth which covers all sections of the society including the poor and vulnerable.
   (b) A growth which covers all sections of economy including agriculture and rural sector.
   (c) Both (a) and (b).
   (d) Neither (a) nor (b).

(ii) How is Aadhaar likely to help in inclusive growth?
   (a) It would help in ascertaining the base line for poverty.
   (b) It would help in identifying the poor below poverty line and enable direct transfer of cash to them.
   (c) It would help in assessing the efficacy of the schemes for benefit of the poor and enable discarding inefficient schemes.
   (d) All of the above.

(iii) As per the passage how is direct cash transfer to poor women likely to be beneficial?
   (a) It will help in empowerment of women as they would be the foremost beneficiary.
   (b) It will cut down leakages and overall cost of subsidies.
   (c) It will augment/create purchasing power for the poor, which will help in market forces to develop a distribution system.
   (d) All of the above.

(iv) Consider the following assertions in terms of what is stated in the passage.
   1. Ethically, provision of basic food to all should be a matter of right.
   2. For tracking poverty over a period of time, the poverty line would be required to be varied to account for the overall growth in GDP.
   (a) Only Assertion 1 is correct.
   (b) Only Assertion 2 is correct.
   (c) Both Assertions 1 and 2 are correct.
   (d) Neither Assertion 1 nor 2 is correct.

(v) From what has been stated in the passage, examine which of the following conclusions can be drawn.
   1. The economic growth of India in recent years cannot be said to be an inclusive one.
   2. Inclusive growth cannot be achieved by trying to deliver subsidies to the poor through the existing government PDS.
   3. Experience the world over shows that direct cash subsidies have not helped government in achieving inclusive growth.
   (a) 1, 2, 3 (b) 1, 2
   (c) 1, 3 (d) 2, 3

**45.** Climate change has enormous implications for the natural resources and livelihoods of the people. It has wide-ranging effects on the environmental and socio-economic and related sectors. Various studies indicate that the key sectors in India such as agriculture, water, natural ecosystem, biodiversity and health are vulnerable to climate change. This is happening precisely at a time when it is confronted with huge development imperatives. The Indian Network for Climate Change Assessment (INCCA) report warns of impacts such as sea-level rise, increase in cyclonic intensity, reduced crop yield in rain-fed crops, stress on livestock, reduction in milk productivity, increased flooding, and spread of malaria. These changes are likely to increase pressure on Indian agriculture, in addition to existing stresses of yield stagnation, land use, and competition for land, water and other resources. Any uncertainty in agriculture can considerably affect the food systems and thus increase the vulnerability of a large section of the resource-poor population. This calls for urgency of action in reducing vulnerability to adverse impacts of climate change and enhancing adaptive capacity through sector-specific interventions and efforts.

The food and nutritional security of India currently depends, to a great extent, on the production of wheat and rice, which together constitute around 75 per cent of total food grain production. Simulation models suggest that in the absence of adaptation and fertilizer benefits, a 1°C increase in temperature alone could lead to a 6 million tonnes drop in wheat production. Production of milk, which is increasingly becoming an important item in the food basket, may also be adversely affected by the increased heat stress associated with global climate change to dairy animals. Reduced water availability, owing to glacier retreat and decreased rainfall, and a growing population will increase water stress. India's forests are likely to experience a shift in forest type, adversely impacting associated biodiversity and regional climate dynamics as well as livelihoods based on forest products. Health is also likely to be adversely affected by climate change. Heat stress, vector-borne diseases, water contamination are some of the projected health impacts of climate change. For example, similar to other tropical countries, India is predicted to have increased susceptibility to vector-borne diseases such as malaria, which is also projected to move to higher latitudes and altitudes.

(i) As per the passage the agricultural sector is likely to be affected most by climate change because of

1. Drastic change in rain patterns and pursuant droughts and floods.
2. Yield stagnation/drop in yield of crops, due to temperature rise.
3. Stress on land available for agricultural use.

(a) 1, 2, 3 (b) 1, 2
(c) 1, 3 (d) 1 only

(ii) What makes the issue of climate change **even worse** for a country like India is

(a) That India has not agreed to binding emission cuts although in gross terms it is a large emitter of GHGs. Thus, it is facing immense international pressure.
(b) That India is extremely vulnerable to climate change because of its geographical location and susceptible ecosystem.
(c) That India is faced with the urgent need for development initiatives, which call for a delicate balance between utilisation of its natural resources and its preservation.
(d) All of the above.

(iii) Which of the following assertions are correct in terms of what is stated in the passage?

1. A 1°C increase in temperature could lead to a drop of 6 million tonnes in wheat and rice production.
2. Increase in vector borne diseases on account of rise in temperature will reduce crop yield and, production, affecting India's food security.

(a) Only Assertion 1 is correct.
(b) Only Assertion 2 is correct.
(c) Both Assertions 1 and 2 are correct.
(d) Neither Assertion 1 nor 2 is correct.

(iv) Which one of the following can be said to be the most important objective of the passage?

(a) To highlight that India is highly susceptible to climate change.

(b) To highlight the adverse impact on India of climate change and emphasise on the need of sector-wise mitigation efforts.

(c) To chalk out a strategy for countering the effects of adverse climate change.

(d) All of the above.

**46.** Modern science, exclusive of geometry, is a comparatively recent creation and can be said to have originated with Galileo and Newton. Galileo was the first scientist to recognise clearly that the only way to further our understanding of the physical world was to resort to experiment. However obvious Galileo's contention may appear in the light of our present knowledge, it remains a fact that the Greeks, in spite of their proficiency in geometry, never seem to have realised the importance of experiment. To a certain extent, this may be attributed to the crudeness of their instruments of measurement. Still, an excuse of this sort can scarcely be put forward when the elementary nature of Galileo's experiments and observations is recalled. Watching a lamp oscillate in the cathedral of Pisa, dropping bodies from the leaning tower of Pisa, rolling balls down inclined planes, noticing the magnifying effect of water in a spherical glass vase, such was the nature of Galileo's experiments and observations. As can be seen, they might just as well have been performed by the Greeks. At any rate, it was thanks to such experiments that Galileo discovered the fundamental law of dynamics, according to which the acceleration imparted to a body is proportional to the force acting upon it.

The next advance was due to Newton, the greatest scientist of all time if account be taken of his joint contributions to mathematics and physics. As a physicist, he was of course an ardent adherent of the empirical method, but his greatest title to fame lies in another direction. Prior to Newton, mathematics, chiefly in the form of geometry, had been studied as a fine art without any view to its physical applications, other than in very trivial cases. But with Newton, all the resources of mathematics were turned to advantage in the solution of physical problems. Thenceforth, mathematics appeared as an instrument of discovery, the most powerful one known to man, multiplying the power of thought just as in the mechanical domain, the lever multiplied our physical action. It is this application of mathematics to the solution of physical problems, this combination of two separate fields of investigation, which constitutes the essential characteristic of the Newtonian method. Thus, problems of physics were metamorphosed into problems of mathematics.

But in Newton's day, the mathematical instrument was still in a very backward state of development. In this field again, Newton showed the mark of genius by inventing the integral calculus. As a result of this remark-able discovery, problems, which would have baffled Archimedes, were solved with ease. We know that in Newton's hands, this new departure in scientific method led to the discovery of the law of gravitation. But here again the real significance of Newton's achievement lay not so much in the exact quantitative formulation of the law of attraction, as in his having established the presence of law and order at least in one important realm of nature, namely, in the motions of heavenly bodies. Nature thus exhibited rationality and was not mere blind chaos and uncertainty. To be sure, Newton's investigations had been concerned with but a small group of natural phenomena, but it appeared unlikely that this mathematical law and order should turn out to be restricted to certain special phenomena; and the feeling was general unfolding themselves according to rigorous mathematical laws.

(i) According to the author, why did the Greeks **not** conduct experiments to understand the physical world?

(a) Apparently they did not think it necessary to experiment.

(b) They focused exclusively on geometry.

(c) Their instruments of measurement were very crude.

(d) The Greeks considered the application of geometry to the physical world more important.

(ii) Newton may be considered as one of the greatest scientists of all time because he

(a) Discovered the law of gravitation

(b) Married physics with mathematics

(c) Invented integral calculus

(d) Started the use of the empirical method in science

(iii) The statement "nature thus exhibited rationality and was not mere blind chaos and uncertainty" suggests that

(a) Problems that had baffled scientists like Archimedes were not really problems

(b) Only a small group of natural phenomena was chaotic

(c) Physical phenomena conformed to mathematical laws

(d) Natural phenomena were evolving towards a less chaotic future

**47.** People's participation means participation of people in the administrative process. It implies citizens' control over administration or public influence on administration. It is essential for the smooth and effective performance of the administrative machinery. It makes the administration responsive to the needs of the people. It secures public support to the government policies and makes them a success. It constitutes an important means of enforcing administrative accountability.

A democratic government is based on the 'doctrine of popular sovereignty', which means that the people are supreme in a democracy, or the final authority in democracy is vested in the people. Therefore, administration in democracy is or should finally and ultimately be responsible to the people. It is in this context that the people's participation in administration assumes importance. It transfers the representative democracy into participatory democracy. It facilitates what is known as 'bottom-up rule'.

(i) Which of the following statements is **not** true in respect of people's participation in the administrative process?

(a) People's participation brings transparency and accountability in the administration.

(b) It is also referred as the bottom-up rule.

(c) It is essential for protecting all of the fundamental rights of citizens.

(d) It is people's participation, which makes them supreme in democracy.

(ii) In a democracy the doctrine of popular sovereignty means the following:

1. People have the final authority in democracy.
2. Administration should be responsible to people.
3. There should be equal protection of rights of all.
4. People should frame the policies to be implemented by administration.
5. Administration should take popular measures only in keeping with principles of sovereignty.
6. People are supreme in democracy.

Which of the options are correct?

(a) 1, 2, 6 (b) 1, 2, 4, 6

(c) 1, 2, 4, 5 (d) 2, 4, 6

**48.** "Reality is much bigger than it seems... the part we call the universe is the merest tip of the iceberg", one scientist remarked. How true. In the beginning, skeptics wouldn't accept that the earth actually moves, let alone that it revolves around the sun because of an unshaken belief that the earth was at the centre of the universe. We've come a long way. Today, scientists have spotted nearly 80 extra-solar planets using sophisticated instruments. What's more, our universe may not be the only universe in the cosmos; there could well be several parallel universes teeming with many galaxies, solar systems and planets, although none of this may be perceptible to the naked eye. Perhaps sages who say that truth is not easily perceptible, mean just this—what is evident before us is not the whole truth.

Scientists say that "everything in the tangible universe has its shadowy counterpart in other, parallel universes". In fact, it is by observing the play of cosmic light and shadow through powerful devices that scientists have been able to 'feel' shapes or 'see' shadows that indicate the existence of other heavenly bodies without actually seeing them. The international team of scientists involved in the present discovery conducted their search through telescopes in Australia, Belgium, the UK and the US. Two of the newly discovered eight planets are believed to have circular orbits very like the Earth's, while the others have well-defined elliptical orbits much like Pluto's. This is significant because a planet with a circular orbit would more likely be hospitable to life forms than would one with an elliptical orbit. In the latter, the planet experiences extreme temperatures depending on whether it is proximate to or distant from the energy-giving star it's circum-ambulating. As in the case of other recent discoveries—such as finding traces of microbes in a meteorite—this too strengthens the belief that we're not alone in the universe. So would we be exchanging inter galactic e-mails soon? Perhaps not as yet, given that our closest neighbouring galaxy is millions of light years away. What is within our immediate grasp, though, is exploring the viability of establishing human settlements in space—an endeavour that has assumed urgency what with biological terrorism and the like threatening humankind on earth. As Stephen Hawking recently said, "I don't think the human race will survive the next thousand years unless we spread into space. There are too many accidents that can befall life on a single planet".

(i) According to Dr. Hawking, there is need to spread into space because

1. Human race is going to perish in another thousand years.
2. There are possibilities of accidents on earth, which can wipe the life here and hence, the need to spread on other planets.
3. We can use the resources on other planets as the resources on earth are dwindling fast.
4. Global warming will leave the planet devoid of resources and unfit for living in another thousand years.

(a) 1 only (b) 2 only
(c) 1, 2, 3 (d) 1, 2, 3, 4

(ii) According to the passage it can be inferred that

1. A planet with a circular orbit is more likely to be hospitable to life than the one with an elliptical orbit because the latter experiences very low temperatures.
2. A planet with a circular orbit is more likely to be hospitable to life form than the one with an elliptical orbit since the latter is proximate to the energy giving star it is circum-ambulating.
3. A planet with a circular orbit is more likely to be hospitable to life forms than the one with an elliptical orbit because the latter experiences extreme temperatures.

(a) 1, 2, 3 (b) 1, 2
(c) 1, 3 (d) 2, 3

(iii) As per the passage which of the following can be inferred?

(a) Parallel universes are half truth and half truth is not perceptible.
(b) Parallel universes are not easily perceptible because they are not the whole truth.
(c) Parallel universes are not easily perceptible and what we perceive is not the whole truth.
(d) Truth is easily perceptible.

(iv) Which of the following is **not** correct in terms of what is stated in the passage?

(a) Scientists have detected presence of microbes in meteorites.

(b) Scientists have detected presence of shadow universe.

(c) Scientists have detected nearly 80 extra solar planets.

(d) None of the above.

**49.** The discussion on growth and development has shown their internal connectivity. If the quality of life in an economy is to be enhanced there is a need of conscious public policy, which can spend and invest in areas, such as food, nutrition, health, education, shelter and social security. But for such expenditures and investments the economy needs equitable level of income, too! And the income enhancement in any economy takes place via increasing the level of production in the economy, i.e., real gross national product (GNP). It means, development requires higher growth, i.e., higher levels of economic activities. With the help of suitable kind of economic policies the government of an economy keeps trying to maintain a higher level of economic activity. But, at times, economy keeps failing in this objective. And, thus economies fluctuate between the best and the worst levels of economic activities which is known in economics as boom and depression, respectively. They can be called different phases of the economic activities of the economies. In between boom and depression, there might be many other situations of the economic activities, such as stagnation, slowdown, recession and recovery. The fluctuations in the level of economic activity between the depressions and booms has been called by the economists as business cycle or trade cycle with recession and recovery as the main intermediate

(i) As per the passage the economic cycle can be divided in which four phases in order of sequence (starting from depression)?

(a) Depression, stagnation, slowdown, stagflation.

(b) Depression, recovery, boom, recession.

(c) Depression, recession, recovery, boom.

(d) Depression, slowdown, recovery, boom.

(ii) Which three among the following are factors which effect the economic cycle the most?

1. Level of production.
2. Level of economic activities.
3. Standard of education and other social factors.
4. Nature of economic policies and its implementation.
5. Size of population.

(a) 1, 2, 4 (b) 1, 2, 3

(c) 2, 3, 4 (d) 1, 3, 4

(iii) As per author which are the main intermediate stages of each economic cycle?

(a) Boom and depression.

(b) Stagnation and slowdown.

(c) Boom and recession.

(d) Recession and recovery.

**50.** The foundation of irreligious criticism is: Man makes religion, religion does not make man. Religion is, indeed, the self-consciousness and self-esteem of man who has either not yet won through to himself, or has already lost himself again. But, man is no abstract being squatting outside the world. Man is the world of man, state, society. This state and this society produce religion, which is an inverted consciousness of the world, because they are in an inverted world. Religion is the general theory of this world, its encyclopaedic compendium, its logic in popular form, its spiritual point *d'honneur*, its enthusiasm, its moral sanction, its solemn complement, and its universal basis of consolation and justification. It is the fantastic realisation of the human essence since the human essence has not acquired any true reality. The struggle against religion is, therefore, indirectly the struggle against that world whose spiritual aroma is religion.

Religious suffering is, at one and the same time, the expression of real suffering and a protest against real suffering. Religion is the sigh of the oppressed creature, the heart of a heartless world, and the soul of soul-less conditions. It is the opium of the people.

The abolition of religion as the illusory happiness of the people is the demand for their real happiness. To call on them to give up their illusions about their condition is to call on them to give up a condition that requires illusions. The criticism of religion is, therefore, in embryonic stage, the criticism of that vale of tears of which religion is the halo.

Criticism has plucked the imaginary flowers on the chain not in order that man shall continue to bear that chain without fantasy or consolation, but so that he shall throw off the chain and pluck the living flower. The criticism of religion disillusions man, so that he will think, act and fashion his reality like a man who has discarded his illusions and regained his senses, so that he will move around himself as his own true Sun. Religion is only the illusory Sun, which revolves around man as long as he does not revolve around himself.

It is, therefore, the task of history, once the other-world of truth has vanished, to establish the truth of this world. It is the immediate task of philosophy, which is in the service of history, to unmask self-estrangement in its unholy forms once the holy form of human self-estrangement has been unmasked. Thus, the criticism of Heaven turns into the criticism of Earth, the criticism of religion into the criticism of law, and the criticism of theology into the criticism of politics.

(i) Which of the following conclusions can be drawn from the passage?

1. Religion is illusory.
2. It has the effect of dulling the senses of the people.

(a) Only Assumption 1 is correct.

(b) Only Assumption 2 is correct.

(c) Both Assumptions 1 and 2 are correct.

(d) Neither Assumption 1 nor 2 is correct.

(ii) As per the author what is the ultimate object of criticism of religion?

(a) To encourage people to become atheists.

(b) To encourage people to throw away the chain of illusory religion.

(c) To encourage people to overcome the disillusion created by religion.

(d) All of the above.

(iii) Which of the following are correct reflections of the views of the author?

1. Human beings are disillusioned by the criticism of religion.
2. Religion is a remedy for the suffering of humanity.
3. The abolition of religion, which is only an illusory happiness, will eventually lead to real happiness.

(a) 1 only (b) 1 and 2 only

(c) 2 and 3 (d) 1 and 3 only

**51.** Towards inclusive development, India has been implementing programmers for social sectors like education and health to include women and the marginalised sections of the people to bridge the gaps in educational attainments, health outcomes and employment opportunities. Though macro-economic growth and efficient markets are essential, it is necessary to equally ensure that the benefit of growth is equitably accessible to all citizens to make growth broad based. To conclude, strengthening the policy and institutional ecosystem supporting inclusive growth deserves to be a top policy priority for countries, whether they are experiencing slow growth, elevated inequality, or both. This is an imperative for countries seeking to thrive in the Fourth Industrial Revolution.

What is the most logical conclusion that can be drawn from the passage is?

(a) Efficiency and equity both are essential for broad based growth.

(b) India's effort towards inclusive growth has not been sufficient.

(c) Both (a) and (b).

(d) Neither (a) nor (b).

**52.** Climate change is a complex policy issue with major implications in terms of finance. All actions to address climate change ultimately involve costs. Funding is vital in order for countries like India to design and implement adaptation and mitigation plans and projects. The problem is more severe for developing countries like India, which would be one of the hardest hit by climate change, given its need to finance development. Most countries do indeed treat climate change as a real threat and are striving to address it in a more comprehensive and integrated manner with the limited resources at their disposal. But financial ways and means must be found to enable developing countries to enhance their efforts in this direction, especially enhancing their adaptive capacity. Thus, climate change is both an environmental issue and an economic costs and development issue.

Lack of funding is a large impediment to implementing adaptation plans. The scale and magnitude of the financial support required by developing countries to enhance their domestic mitigation and adaptation actions are a matter of intense debate in the multilateral negotiations under the UNFCCC. The Convention squarely puts the responsibility for the provision of financial support on the developed countries taking into account their contribution to the stock of GHGs in the atmosphere.

Countries like India that are on the path of development would need access to finance and technology if the world is to achieve emission standards in line with the stabilisation and sustainable development goals. The funds that are currently available under the Convention and Kyoto Protocol are small compared to the magnitude of need assessed by many studies. The UNFCCC has estimated a requirement of US$ 200–210 billion as additional annual investment in 2030 to return GHG emissions to current levels. Further, additional investment needed worldwide for adaptation is estimated by the UNFCCC to be annually US$ 60–182 billion in 2030, inclusive of an expenditure of US$ 28–67 billion in developing countries. As various estimates point to the enormity of funds needed for meeting the long-term finance requirements for adaptation and mitigation, developing countries including India have been arguing that a global mechanism for generating and accounting for additional resources, mainly from public sources, is essential. There should be a multilateral financial mechanism under the Convention that is funded by developed countries on the basis of assessed contributions.

Attempts are being made to design appropriate institutions and mechanisms for this purpose at a global level. This is evident in the setting up of a GCF under the Convention, developed countries' announcement of US$ 30 billion as fast start funds, US$ 100 billion (to be mobilised) as long-term finance, etc. However, these attempts do not suffice to address the challenge. On the other hand, efforts are being made by some developed countries to shift the discussions on 'sources of long-term finance' to the G-20 forum where the emphasis is on evolving new and innovative financial instruments involving both developed and developing countries. This idea is strongly resisted by many developing countries in the multilateral negotiations. The high-level panel appointed by the UN Secretary General in 2010 had attempted to address some of these issues but its recommendations, which favour dependence on market-related instruments (not public funding) and private-sector resources have not found favour by many in the multilateral negotiations.

A major part of the adaptation and mitigation needs of developing countries can be met by accessing international finance. The mobilisation of the requisite amount of climate finance for the developing countries will be one of the biggest challenges in the times to come. Though alternative sources including the private sector can be explored to fill the gaps between the demand and supply of climate finance, public finance should be at the core to ensure predictability and reliability of flow of funds to the developing countries.

(i) Which of the following factors are identified by the passage as being most critical issues in combating the challenge of climate change?

1. The requirement of appropriate technology for reduction of green house gas (GHG) emissions.
2. The requirement of finance to fund the programmes to combat the challenge of climate change.
3. The dilemma of funding development vis-à-vis the degradation of environment and exploitation of resources resulting from developmental efforts.

(a) 1, 2, 3 (b) 1, 3
(c) 1, 2 (d) 2, 3

(ii) Examine whether the following assumptions are correct in terms of what is stated in the passage.

1. The responsibility of funding initiatives for combating climate change vests, both on the developed and the developing countries.
2. Multilateral climate change conventions like UNFCCC have been able to organise sufficient funds to finance initiatives for combating climate change.

(a) Only Assumption 1 is correct.
(b) Only Assumption 2 is correct.
(c) Both Assumptions 1 and 2 are correct.
(d) Neither Assumption 1 nor 2 is correct.

(iii) Which of the following measures is recommended by the author to finance initiatives to combat climate change?

1. G-20 as a forum should organise public finance for funding initiatives for combating climate change.
2. Developing countries should be able to access international finance to fund adaptation and mitigation efforts.
3. The bulk of funding should be done through public finances while private finances should supplement it.

(a) 1, 2, 3 (b) 1, 2
(c) 2, 3 (d) 3 only

**53.** Reason and free enquiry are the only effectual agents against error. Give a loose to them, they will support the true religion, by bringing every false one to their tribunal, to the test of their investigation. They are the natural enemies of error, and of error only. Had not the Roman government permitted free enquiry, Christianity could never have been introduced. Had not free enquiry been indulged, at the area of the reformation, the corruptions of Christianity could not have been purged away. If it be restrained now, the present corruptions will be protected, and new ones encouraged.

(i) What is meant here by, "bringing every false one to their tribunal"?

(a) Bringing every culprit to the court of law.
(b) Bringing falsehood to the test of reasoning.
(c) Removing false religion from the social purview.
(d) None of the above

(ii) What is the message conveyed in the passage?

(a) Religion has always been infested with falsehood and errors and it is necessary to purge them of it.
(b) Reason and free enquiry are the appropriate antidote for purging religion of its errors.
(c) Both (a) & (b)
(d) Neither (a) nor (b)

**54.** When the doctor's four guests heard him talk of his proposed experiment, they anticipated nothing more wonderful than the murder of a mouse in an air-pump or the examination of a cobweb by the microscope, or some similar nonsense, with which he was constantly in the habit of annoying his intimates. But without waiting for a reply, Doctor Heidegger hobbled across the chamber, and returned with the same ponderous book, bound in black leather, which common report affirmed to be a book of magic. Undoing the silver clasps, he opened the volume, and took from among its black-letter pages a rose, or what was once a rose, though now the green leaves and crimson petals had assumed one brownish hue, and the ancient flower seemed ready to crumble to dust in the doctor's fumbling hands.

(i) The initial impression of the guests about the experiment to be conducted by the doctor was that,

(a) he was about to do a silly and a futile experiment.

(b) he was about to do an experiment on a mouse.

(c) he was about to do a wonderful experiment on a rose petal.

(d) none of the above.

(ii) What is implied in the passage by the expression, ".. common report affirmed to be a book of magic…."

(a) The book was a report about common and affirmed magic.

(b) It was a book on magic which was performed by common people.

(c) The book was commonly believed by people to deal with magic.

(d) There was a confirmed report about the book dealing with magic.

(iii) Which of the following inferences can be drawn from the passage?

(1) The doctor habitually did experiments.

(2) The doctor was old.

(a) Only inference 1 can be drawn.

(b) Only inference 2 can be drawn.

(c) Both inference 1 & 2 can be drawn.

(d) Neither inference 1 nor 2 can be drawn.

**55.** Recent technological advancement in manned and unmanned undersea vehicle, overcome some of the limitations of divers equipment. Without a vehicle, divers often became sluggish and their mental concentration was limited. Because of undersea pressure that affected their mind, concentration among divers was difficult or impossible. But today, most oceanographers make observations by means of instruments that are lowered into the ocean or from samples taken from the water. Direct observations of the ocean floor are made not only by the divers, but also by deep-diving submarines. Some of these submarines can dive to depths of more than several miles and cruise at depths of 15 thousand feet. Radio equipped buoys can be operated by remote control in order to transmit information back to land-based laboratories including data about water temperature, currents and weather. Some of mankind's most serious problem, especially those concerning energy and food may be solved with the help of observations made possible by these undersea vehicles.

(i) With what topic is the passage primarily concerned?

(a) Recent technological advances.

(b) Communication among divers.

(c) Direct observation of the ocean floor.

(d) Undersea vehicles.

(ii) Divers have had problems in concentrating underwater because

(a) The pressure affected their minds.

(b) The vehicles they used have not been perfected.

(c) They did not think clearly.

(d) The pressure destroyed their mental processes.

(iii) According to the author, what are some of the problems underwater studies may eventually resolve?

1. Weather and temperature control.
2. Food and energy shortages.
3. Transportation and communication problems.
4. Resource shortages.

(a) 1, 2 (b) 2 only

(c) 1, 2, 3, 4 (d) 2 and 4

(iv) Examine whether the following assumptions are correct in terms of what is started in the passage.

1. Direct observation of the ocean floor is only possible with deep diving submarines and radio equipped buoys.
2. Unmanned sea vehicles have been able to overcome all the problems related to diver's equipment.

(a) Only Assumption 1 is correct.
(b) Only Assumption 2 is correct.
(c) Both Assumptions 1 and 2 are correct.
(d) Neither Assumption 1 nor 2 is correct.

**56.** The subsidies provided by the government to the agricultural sector (i.e., domestic support) is termed by the WTO as Aggregate Measure of Support (AMS). It is calculated in terms of *product* and *input* subsidies. The WTO argues that product subsidies like minimum support prices and input subsidies (non-product) like credit, fertilizers, irrigation and power will cut the production cost of farming and will give undue advantage to such countries in their access to world market—such subsidies are called to cause ***'distortions'*** to the world trade. Such subsidies are not permitted in one sense as they have a minimum permissible limit *de minimis* under the provisions, which is 5 per cent and 10 per cent of their total agricultural output in the case of developed and developing countries, respectively.

The agricultural subsidies, in the WTO terminology have in general been identified by 'boxes', which have been given the colours of the traffic lights—*green* (means permitted), *amber* (means slowdown, i.e., to be reduced) and *red* (means forbidden).

In the agriculture sector, as usual, things are more complicated. The WTO provisions on agriculture have nothing like *red box* subsidies, although subsidies exceeding the reduction commitment levels are prohibited in the *'amber box'*. The *'blue box'* subsidies are tied to programmes that limit the level of production. There is also a provision of some exemptions for the developing countries sometimes called the 'S and D box'.

(i) Which are the two broad categories in terms of which the Aggregate Measure of Support is calculated?
(a) Product and input subsidies.
(b) Product and output subsidies.
(c) Support price and input subsidies.
(d) Support price and credit subsidies.

(ii) Giving cheap micro credit to farmers below the market lending rate can be classified as
(a) Product subsidy
(b) Input subsidy
(c) None of the above
(d) Both (a) and (b)

(iii) As per WTO which one of the following is **not** the effect of agricultural subsidies?
(a) Subsidies cause distortion to the world trade.
(b) They give undue advantage to the countries in their access to the world market.
(c) They improve the quality of produce and hence are preferred by the world market.
(d) All of the above.

**57.** Sheepish scientists now admit that the first and most famous cloned animal, Dolly, is probably growing old before her time. It is reported that Dolly suffers from arthritis in one of her hind legs. Created from a cell taken from an adult ewe's mammary glands by Ian Wilmut and his team of scientists, Dolly created ripples in frontier biotech research. Hundreds of such cloned animal foetuses created before Dolly were found to be either abnormal or incapable of survival or both. Now, sceptics point out that Dolly's arthritis at so young an age is proof of the untenability of the cloning technique itself. Anti-cloning activists are quick to point out that the dangers of serious side-effects would be similar in human clones—making the entire technology highly questionable. Dolly's limping back into the limelight has opened up a fresh debate on the pros and cons of using cloning techniques to create new embryos, stem lines and tissues, whether animal or human.

Dolly's creator, however, is optimistic. According to him, only systematic studies could help us overcome all these difficulties as there is no way of knowing whether Dolly's arthritis is due to cloning, or whether it is an unrelated occurrence. Dr. Wilmut had earlier come out strongly against extending cloning to human embryos, as he felt that the nascent technique ought to be perfected and understood in animals before being extended to humans. Dolly's premature ageing, however, was not entirely unexpected as it was revealed—soon after her birth—that she had very short telomeres for a newborn. Produced during embryonic development, telomeres are the nubs that cap the ends of chromosomes rather like shoe-lace ends. As the cells mature and divide with growth, the telomeres crumble and eventually, when the erosion is complete, the cell dies. Dolly's shortened telomeres are attributed to the fact that she was made using genetic material taken from a six-year-old ewe, making her technically as old as her 'Mom'. As such, Dolly's ageing should not be taken as a representative example of how cloning technology can go wrong. The case should be treated as pointer to the complexities involved and could provide guidance for the future. The therapeutic value of cloning to create stem cells and tissues to treat terminally ill patients is too important to be dismissed summarily.

(i) Why Dolly created ripples in frontier of science and biotech research?
   (a) It was considered unethical to clone living beings.
   (b) This showed that technically cloning was possible.
   (c) Earlier clones were incapable of survival or were abnormal or both.
   (d) None of the above.

(ii) Which of the following sentences matches with the opinion of the scientist about the newly cloned sheep?
   (a) The cloning process is completely impeccable.
   (b) The cloning process has got many side-effects.
   (c) Medical science failed to detail any clarification with respect to the abnormalities besetting Dolly.
   (d) The cloning process is still not impeccable.

(iii) Which of these sentences relates to the opinion of Dr. Wilmut?
   (a) Dolly's premature ageing was revealed after a long time after its birth.
   (b) Cloning has to be first perfected in animals before being extended to human beings.
   (c) Dolly's premature ageing was due to short telomeres.
   (d) Both (b) and (c).

(iv) Which of the assumptions are correct in terms of what is stated in the passage?
   1. The example of Dolly and the problems faced by it shows the untenability of cloning technique.
   2. The technological challenges and ethical problems associated with genetic engineering are far too many to let it be a successful science.
   (a) Only Assumption 1 is correct.
   (b) Only Assumption 2 is correct.
   (c) Both Assumptions 1 and 2 is correct.
   (d) Neither Assumption 1 is correct.

**58.** My aunt's appearance did not invite one to open one's mouth and devour these sweets: the course of years, her loss of teeth, her eyes dimmed to an unusual degree, the sprouting of a mustache or bristles on her sunken-in mouth, which was three inches wide, dull gray locks fluttering above her sallow temples, a neck flaccid and livid as the crest of the turkey when in a good temper. She had reached that old age when one is nearer to the morgue than the natal chamber. In short, I did not take the candies. Ugh! A feeling of indignation, a manly protest rose in me, and I said forcibly: "I do not want it, I don't want it."

(i) Why did the narrator not want to have the sweets?
   (a) His aunt's appearance filled him with disgust.
   (b) He did not like the sweets she had brought.
   (c) He was too old to have sweets.
   (d) All of the above.

(ii) Which of the following is a correct inference about the narrator's aunt as per the description given by him?
   (1) She had no teeth
   (2) She had poor vision
   (a) Only 1 can be inferred.
   (b) Only 2 can be inferred.
   (c) Both 1 & 2 can be inferred.
   (d) Neither 1 nor 2 can be inferred.

**59.** Sustainable development is a difficult balancing act in countries especially with low incomes. Society has to simultaneously accomplish three things with trade-offs: improve economic well-being with social justice for the present generation, yet manage with more restrained use of land, air, forest, energy and water resources, and protect the interests of future generations. The choices are more difficult in developing countries— because they affect people's livelihoods. For such a 'stewardship' to succeed, therefore, it has to respond to people's needs, share information on choices and costs, and ensure participation and ownership.

India has done well on all these counts of stewardship over the past decades. It has followed a conscious path in response to the key environmental issues. Sustainable development in terms of environmental concerns has been a recurring theme in Indian policy and planning. Economic reforms since the 1980s have accelerated growth and incomes. Social well-being has improved broadly, as measured by gains in life-expectancy and other indicators. India has stepped up protection of its natural environment such as its forests. India's particular development path has relied on fast growing services, which has helped reduce the emissions intensity of its growth path and accelerate literacy and education. While India could have done even better, much has been accomplished. The reasons behind such progress are undoubtedly strong institutional underpinnings: democratic participation, Constitutional protection of social justice, steady accretion of environmental laws and regulations, multiple actors, markets, and expanding government programmes and policies. The challenges ahead are, nevertheless, large. The 2009 State of the Environment Report by the Ministry of Environment and Forests (MoEF) clubs the issues under five key challenges faced by India, which are climate change, food security, water security, energy security and managing urbanisation. Broad-based economic and social development is ultimately the answer for greater environmental sustainability. Economic pricing of energy and other resources will be key to switching to a more sustainable development path. Deployment of appropriate technologies is certainly going to be crucial. At the same time, stepped-up public spending on energy access and other basic necessities for the poor will be required.

(i) Why is sustainable development described as a difficult balancing act in countries with low incomes?
   (a) They do not have the resources for economic growth.
   (b) They have to strike a balance with trade-offs between; economic growth of present generation, protecting the environment and interest of future generation.

(c) They are unable to respond to people's need, share information on choices and cost and ensure participation and ownership.

(d) All of the above.

(ii) Which of the following are features of India's growth on path of sustainable development?

1. India has laid emphasis on protection of its natural environment.
2. Industrial growth has contributed significantly to its GDP.
3. Reliance on fast growing services has helped in reducing the emission intensity of its growth.
4. There has been improvement in social well being measured by parameters like life expectancy.

(a) 1, 2, 3 (b) 2, 3, 4

(c) 1, 3, 4 (d) 1, 2, 4

(iii) Which amongst the following is **not** listed in the passage as a measure for environmentally sustainable growth?

(a) Robust growth of three key sections of economy viz. agriculture industry and services.

(b) Increasing expenditure on energy access and other basic necessities for poor.

(c) Pricing of energy and other resource economically.

(d) Broad basing of economic and social development.

(iv) Consider the following assertions:

1. For any development to be sustainable there must be protection of livelihood of people, their participation and a sense of ownership in the development process.
2. Development in countries with low income cannot inherently be sustainable on account of contradictory requirements of economic growth and protecting the environment.

(a) Only Assertion 1 is true.

(b) Only Assertion 2 is true.

(c) Both Assertions 1 and 2 are true.

(d) Neither Assertion 1 nor 2 is true.

(v) As per the passage which are the five key challenges for sustainable growth before India?

1. Managing continuous growth in agriculture.
2. Achieving food security.
3. Challenge of climate change.
4. Challenge of providing basic health services.
5. Achieving water security.
6. Achieving goal of housing for everybody.
7. Managing the rapid urbanisation.
8. Achieving the energy security.

(a) 1, 2, 3, 6, 7, 8

(b) 2, 3, 4, 7, 8

(c) 1, 2, 3, 4, 5, 8

(d) 2, 3, 5, 7, 8

**60.** According to Riggs, the pace of development in any society is related mainly to the sources of change. Western societies were able to adjust their effective behaviour gradually to the evolving behaviour since they had relatively long time span for their development. Consequently, these societies experienced less heterogeneity, formalism and overlapping than the contemporary developing (transitional) societies.

In a prismatic society (i.e., a transitional or developing society), the pressure for change is external as well as internal. When it is external, it is called 'exogenous' change and when internal, it is called 'endogenous' change. Further, when the change is caused by both external and internal pressures, it is called 'equi-genetic change'.

Riggs stated that greater heterogeneity (i.e., simultaneous presence of different kinds of practices, viewpoints and systems), formalism (i.e., incongruence or divergence between the formally prescribed and effectively practiced) and overlapping (i.e., coexistence of differentiated structures of a diffracted society with undifferentiated structures of a fused society) are likely to exist in an 'exo-prismatic' society (a society where the pressure for change is primarily external) than in an 'endo-prismatic' society (a society where the pressure for change is primarily internal). The reason is that in an 'endo-genetic' change, effective behaviour precedes the establishment of new formal institutions, while in an 'exo-genetic' change the sequence is reversed. Prismatic (transitional) societies face the problems of greater heterogeneity, formalism and overlapping in their bid to absorb the externally induced change in the shortest possible time.

(i) As per Riggs, the western societies experienced less heterogeneity, formalism and overlapping than the contemporary developing societies. What was the reason for this?

(a) The change in western societies came from within, i.e., it was endogenetic change.

(b) The western societies were quickly able to adjust to change.

(c) The western societies had relatively long time span for their development and adapting to it.

(d) All of the above.

(ii) In a society where the pressure for change is external, exo-prismatic society, the following is true:

1. Heterogeneity and homogeneity both are likely to co-exist.
2. Such a society is likely to have greater formalism, heterogeneity and over lapping.
3. The change in such society precedes the establishment of formal institutions.
4. Formal institutions get established before the change.

(a) 2 and 4 (b) 2 and 3

(c) 1 and 3 (d) 1 and 4

(iii) In a prismatic society, which of the following is true?

(a) They face greater transitional problems in their effort to absorb the pressure of change at the earliest.

(b) They are not likely to face the problems of heterogeneity.

(c) They react slowly to change.

(d) All of the above.

**61.** Self-government depends entirely upon our own internal strength, upon our ability to fight against the heaviest odds. Indeed, self-government which does not require continuous striving to attain it and sustain it, is not worth the name. I have, therefore, endeavoured to show both in word and deed that political self-government—that is self-government for a large number of men and women is no better than individual self-government, and therefore, it is to be attained by precisely the same means that are required for individual self-government or self-rule. The true source of rights is duty. If we all discharge our duties, right will not be far to seek. If leaving duties unperformed we run after rights, they will escape us like a will-o'-the-wisp. The more we pursue them, the farther will they fly.

To me political power is not an end but a means of enabling people to better their condition in every sphere of life. Political power means capacity to regulate national life through national representative. If national life becomes so perfect as to become self-regulated, no representation becomes necessary, there is then a state of enlightened anarchy. In such a state, everyone is his own ruler. He rules himself in such a manner that he is never a hindrance to his neighbour. Hence, the classical statement of Thoreau that government is best, which governs the least.

I believe that true democracy can only be an outcome of non-violence. The structure of a world federation can be raised only on a foundation of non-violence, and violence will have to be totally given up in world affairs.

My idea of society is that while we are born equal, meaning that we have a right to equal opportunity, all have not the same capacity. It is, in the nature of things, impossible. For instance, all cannot have the same height, or colour or things, some will have ability to earn more and others less. People with talents will have more, and they will utilise their talents for this purpose. If they utilise kindly, they will be performing the work of the State. Such people exist as trustees, on no other terms. I would allow a man of intellect to earn more, I would not cramp his talent. But the bulk of his greater earnings must be used for the good of the State, just as the income of all earning sons of the father goes to the common family fund. They would have their earning only as trustees. It may be that I would fail miserably in this. But that is what I am sailing for.

(i) Examine whether the following inferences can be drawn from the passage or not.

1. Men though not born equal can become equal by proper governance.
2. Rights emanate from duties.

(a) Only Inference 1 can be drawn.
(b) Only Inference 2 can be drawn.
(c) Both the inferences can be drawn.
(d) Neither of the inferences can be drawn.

(ii) Which of the following **cannot** be said to be correct as per the passage?

(a) Political power is a means but not an end in itself.
(b) It is a means to uplift the condition of people.
(c) This power in democracy is to be exercised through national representatives.
(d) None of the above.

(iii) What is meant by a state of enlightened anarchy?

(a) A state where there is confusion among the enlightened masses.
(b) A state where people have awareness but are engulfed in confusion about their duties.
(c) A state which does not regulate its subjects but still they are conscious of their duties.
(d) None of the above.

(iv) Which of the following statements is correct as per the passage?

(a) All men have equal opportunity in life.
(b) All men have right to work.
(c) All men are born equal.
(d) All men should have equal capability.

(v) Examine the following statements in light of what is stated in the passage and determine which of the following are correct.

1. Rights and duties are inter-linked.
2. An ideal state is devoid of political power.
3. Democracy can only rest on the foundation of non-violence.
4. Equality of opportunity is an ideal which cannot be realised.

(a) 1, 2, 3 (b) 2, 3, 4
(c) 1, 3, 4 (d) 1, 2, 3, 4

**62.** The production of histories of India has become very frequent in recent years and may well call for some explanation. The reason is twofold: changes in the Indian scene require a reinterpretation of the facts and changes in attitudes of historians about the essential elements of Indian history. Changes in the attitudes of historians have occurred everywhere, changes in attitudes to the content of the subject as well as to particular countries, but in India, there have been some special features. Prior to the British, Indian historiographers were mostly Muslims, who relied, as in the case of Sayyid Ghulam Hussain, on their own recollection of events and on information from friends and men of affairs. Only a few like Abu'l Fazl had access to official papers. These were personal narratives of events, varying in value with the nature of the writer. The early British writers were officials. In eighteenth century, they were concerned with some aspect of company policy, or, like Robbert Orme in his Military Transactions, gave a straight narrative in what was essentially a continuation of the Muslim tradition. In the early nineteenth century, the writers were still, with two notable exceptions, officials, but they were now engaged in chronicling, in varying moods of zest, pride, and awe, the rise of the British power in India to supremacy. The two exceptions were James Mill, with his critical attitude to the Company and John Marchman, the Baptist missionary. But they, like the officials, were anglo-centric in their attitude, so that the history of modern India in their hands came to be the history of the rise of the British in India. The official school dominated the writing of Indian history until we get the first professional historian's approach, Ramsay Muir and P.E. Roberts in England and H. H. Dodwell in India. Then Indian historians trained in the English school joined in, of whom the most distinguished was Sir Jadunath Sarkar and the other notable writers: Surendranath Sen, Dr. Radhakumud Mukerji, and Professor Nilakanta Sastri. They, it may be said, restored India to Indian history, but their bias was mainly political. Finally have come the nationalists who range from those who can find nothing good or true in the British to sophisticated historical philosophers like K.M. Panikker.

Along with types of historians with their varying biases, have gone changes in the attitude to the content of Indian history. Here, Indian historians have been influenced both by their local situation and by change of thought elsewhere. It is in this field that this work can claim some attention since it seeks to break new ground, or perhaps to deepen a freshly turned furrow in the field of Indian history. The early official historians were content with the glamour and drama of political history from Plassey to the Mutiny, from Dupleix to the Sikhs. But when the *raj* settled down, glamour departed from politicians, and they turned to the less glorious but more solid ground of administration. Not how India was conquered but how it was governed became the theme of this school of historians.

(i) Which of the following may be the closest in meaning to the statement "restored India to Indian History"?

(a) Indian historians began writing Indian history.

(b) Trained historians began writing Indian history.

(c) Writing India-centric Indian history.

(d) Indian history began to be written in India.

(ii) Which of the following is the closest implication of the statement "to break new ground, or perhaps to deepen a freshly turned furrow"?

(a) Dig afresh or dig deeper

(b) Start a new stream of thought or help establish a recently emerged perspective

(c) Begin or conduct further work on existing archaeological sites to unearth new evidence

(d) Begin writing a history free of any biases

(iii) Historians moved from writing political history to writing administrative history because

(a) Attitudes of the historians changed

(b) The *raj* was settled down

(c) Politics did not retain its past glamour

(d) Administrative history was based on solid ground

**63.** The Serengeti lions have been under continuous observation for more than 35 years, beginning with George Shaller's pioneering work in the 1960s. But the lions in Tsavo, Kenya's oldest and largest protected ecosystem, have hardly been studied. Consequently, legends have grown up around them. Not only do they look different, according to the myths, they *behave* differently, displaying greater cunning and aggressiveness. "Remember too," *Kenya: The Rough Guide warms,* "Tsavo's lions have a reputation of ferocity." Their fearsome image became well known in 1898, when two males stalled construction of what is now Kenya Railways by allegedly killing and eating 135 Indian and African labourers. A British Army officer in charge of building a railroad bridge over the Tsave River, Lt. Col. J. H, Patterson, spent nine months pursuing the pair before he brought them to bay and killed them. Stuffed and mounted, they now glare at visitors to the Field Museum in Chicago. Patterson's account of the leonine reign of terror, The Man-Eaters of Tsavo, was an international bestseller when published in 1907. Still in print, the book has made Tsavo's lions notorious. That annoys some scientists. "People don't want to give up mythology," Dennis King told me one day. The zoologist has been working in Tsavo off and on for four years. "I am so sick of this man-eater business. Patterson made a helluva lot of money off that story, but Tsavo's lions are no more likely to turn man-eater than lions from elsewhere."

But tales of their savagery and wiliness don't all come from sensationalist authors looking to make a buck. Tsavo lions are generally larger than lions elsewhere, enabling them to take down the predominant prey animal in Tsavo, the Cape buffalo, one of the strongest, most aggressive animals of Earth. The buffalo don't give up easily: They often kill or severely injure an attacking lion, and a wounded lion might be more likely to turn to cattle and humans for food.

And other prey is less abundant in Tsavo than in other traditional lion haunts. A hungry lion is more likely to attack humans. Safari guides and Kenya Wildlife Service rangers tell of lions attacking Land Rovers, raiding camps, stalking tourists. Tsavo is tough neighbourhood, they say, and it breeds tougher lions.

But are they really tougher? And if so, is there any connection between their manelessness and their ferocity? An intriguing hypothesis was advanced two years ago by Gnoske and Peterhans: Tsavo lions may be similar to the unmanned cave lions of the Pleistocene. The Serengeti variety is among the most evolved of the species—the latest model, so to speak—while certain morphological differences in Tsavo lions (bigger bodies, smaller skulls, and maybe even lack of a mane) suggest that they are closer to the primitive ancestor of all lions. Craig and Peyton had serious doubts about this idea, but admitted that Tsavo lions pose a mystery to science.

(i) The book *Man-Eaters of Tsavo* annoys some scientists because
   (a) It revealed that Tsavo lions are ferocious.
   (b) Patterson made a lot of money from the book by sensationalism.
   (c) It perpetuated the bad name Tsavo lions had.
   (d) It narrated how two male Tsave lions were killed.

(ii) According to the passage, which of the following has not contributed to the popular image of Tsavo lions as savage creatures?
   (a) Tsavo lions have been observed to bring down one of the strongest and most aggressive animals—the Cape buffaloes.
   (b) In contrast to the situation in traditional lion haunts, scarcity of non-buffalo prey in the Tsavo makes the Tsavo lions more aggressive.
   (c) The Tsavo lion is considered to be less evolved than the Serengeti variety.
   (d) Tsavo lions have been observed to attack vehicles as well as humans.

(iii) Which of the following, if true, would weaken the hypothesis advanced by Gnoske and Peterhans most?
   (a) Craig and Peyton develop even more serious doubts about the idea that Tsavo lions are primitive.

(b) The maneless Tsavo East lions are shown to be closer to the cave lions.

(c) Pleistocene cave lions are shown to be far less violent than believed.

(d) The morphological variations in body and skull size between the cave and Tsavo lions are found to be insignificant.

**64.** India has an estimated 600,000 legal practitioners and is next only to the USA in terms of numbers. The service providers are individual lawyers and small or family-based firms. In India, the practice of law is governed by the Advocates Act of 1961. Under this Act, foreign law firms are not allowed to engage in practice of law in India. Many foreign legal firms have set up liaison offices (currently permitted under the law), while a few have established referral relationships with Indian firms.

India is ranked 51, with a score of 4.3, in terms of judicial independence by the Global Competitiveness Report 2011–12. As regards efficiency of the legal framework in settling disputes, India is ranked 64, with a score of 3.7. India is ranked at 51st position when it comes to the efficiency of the legal framework in challenging regulations, with a score of 3.9. This shows that India needs to improve its ranking through legal and judicial reforms and speed up disposal of cases.

Global recession has been putting pressure on companies to reduce costs and they are trying out various methods of outsourcing their non-core functions to low cost destinations. Outsourcing of legal services to low cost destinations like India is one such measure being taken by legal firms in developed countries, especially the USA and the UK. The legal systems in India, the USA, and the UK are rooted in British common law, thus making Indian lawyers competent, without much additional training, to undertake standard legal work such as vetting of contracts, patent registrations, or reviewing of documents. Besides, offshoring legal work to India saves about 80 per cent of the cost that may be incurred in a developed country like the USA.

The major challenges in the field of legal education are curriculum, skills, attitudes and ethics required of legally trained persons, and dearth of quality law teachers. The National Knowledge Commission recommended establishing a separate body to regulate legal education and setting up Centres for Advanced Legal Studies and Research. The proposal for instituting an independent body, the National Council of Legal Education and Research, is under process. The proposal for setting up four Regional Centres for Advanced Legal Studies and Research to promote advanced research on various aspects of law and academic excellence through continuing legal education is also under process.

(i) As per the passage which of the following could be said to be a challenge for India in the legal field?

1. Need of greater number of legal practitioners to cope up with the increasing number of cases being filed in the Indian courts.
2. Need to amend the Indian Advocates Act to permit foreign law firms. This would bring more investment and improve quality in the field of legal representation.
3. Need to bring judicial reforms to improve efficiency of legal framework in dispute resolution.

(a) 1 only (b) 2, 3

(c) 3 only (d) 1, 2, 3

(ii) Which amongst the following are the factors, as per the passage, which have helped in outsourcing of legal work to India?

1. Presence of a sound legal framework and skilled human resource.
2. Need for companies to reduce costs in the wake of economic recession
3. Indian legal system being based on British common law which is also the case in USA and the UK.

(a) 1, 2, 3 (b) 2, 3
(c) 3 only (d) 1, 2

(iii) Examine whether the following assertions are correct in terms of what is stated in the passage.

1. In terms of global standards, India fares better in respect of independence of the judicial set up as compared to judicial efficiency in settling disputes.
2. Indian legal education makes Indian lawyers fully competent to handle cases of all those countries in which the legal system is based on British Common Law.

(a) Only Assertion 1 is correct.
(b) Only Assertion 2 is correct.
(c) Both Assertions 1 and 2 are correct.
(d) Neither Assertion 1 nor 2 is correct.

(iv) The objective of the passage is to highlight

(a) The opportunities and challenges in the field of legal system and legal education.
(b) Need to open up the Indian legal system.
(c) The need for higher centres of legal studies.
(d) All of the above.

**65.** Our tyranny, if we impose our will on others, will be infinitely worse than that of the handful of Englishmen who form the bureaucracy. Theirs is a terrorism imposed by a minority struggling to exist in the midst of opposition. Ours will be a terrorism imposed by a majority and, therefore, worse and really more godless than the first. We must, therefore, eliminate compulsion in any shape from our struggle. If we are only a handful holding freely the doctrine of non-cooperation, we may have to die in the attempt to convert others to our view, but we shall have truly defended and represented our cause. If however, we enlist under our banner men by force, we shall be denying our cause and God, and if we seem to succeed for the moment, we shall have succeeded in establishing a worse terror. A born democrat is a born disciplinarian. Democracy comes naturally to him who is habituated normally to yield willing obedience to all laws, human or divine. I claim to be a democrat both by instinct and training. Let those who are ambitious to serve democracy qualify themselves by satisfying first this acid test of democracy. Moreover, a democrat must be utterly selfless. He must think and dream not in terms of self or party but only of democracy. Only then does he acquire the right of civil disobedience. I do not want anybody to give up his convictions or to suppress himself. I do not believe that a healthy and honest difference of opinion will injure our cause. But opportunism, camouflage or patched up compromises certainly will. If you must dissent, you should take care that your opinions voice your innermost convictions and are not intended merely as convenient party cry.

I value individual freedom but you must not forget that man is essentially a social being. He has risen to his present status by learning to adjust his individualism to the requirement of social progress. Unrestricted individualism is the law of the beast of the jungle. We have learnt to strike a mean between individual freedom and social restraint. Willing submission to social restraint for the sake of the well-being of the whole society enriches both the individual and the society of which one is a member.

(i) What does the author mean by the expression 'our tyranny'?

(a) Subjugation of the masses by minority elite and rich section of the society.
(b) The British rule on Indians by means of handful of Britishers.
(c) Compulsory enlistment of men against their will in the freedom struggle.
(d) All of the above.

(ii) Examine whether the following inferences can be drawn based on what has been stated in the passage.

1. To uphold the principles of democracy one must exercise strict discipline.

2. For the progress of society, individualism needs to be curtailed to a certain degree.

(a) Only Inference 1 can be drawn.
(b) Only Inference 2 can be drawn.
(c) Both Inferences 1 and 2 can be drawn.
(d) Neither Inference 1 nor 2 can be drawn.

(iii) Which of the following statements correctly represent the views of the author?

1. In the path of social progress a man may have to give up his individual convictions.
2. It is important to convert others to one's view but not to coerce them.
3. In case of expressing a dissenting view one must ensure that the dissenting view is a reflection of what the individual thinks is right.
4. It is better to die while trying to convince others of our views than to browbeat them to act as per it.

(a) 1, 2, 3 (b) 2, 3, 4
(c) 1, 3, 4 (d) 1, 2, 4

(iv) What is meant by the term 'acid test of democracy'?

(a) The right of a person to participate in a civil-disobedience movement.
(b) The ability to articulate innermost convictions despite pressure of peers and party.
(c) To be able to tolerate the dissenting views of others despite conviction that his own views are correct.
(d) To be disciplined, selfless and compliant of all laws.

(v) What is the most important message/idea which the author wants to convey in the above passage?

(a) Democracy can only coexist with discipline and selflessness.
(b) Tolerance of others' view is important for society to survive.
(c) Sacrifice of individualism is a sine-qua-non for social progress.
(d) None of the above.

**66.** The control exercised by the Courts over the administrative acts is called judicial control. In other words, it means the power of the courts to keep the administrative acts within the limits of law. It also implies the right of an aggrieved citizen to challenge the wrongful acts of administrators in a court of law. The primary objective of judicial control over administration is the protection of the rights and liberties of citizens by ensuring the legality of administrative act. In the words of L.D. White, "The purpose of legislative supervision is principally to control the policy and the expenditure of the executive branch, the end sought by judicial control of administrative acts is to ensure their legality and thus, protect citizens against unlawful trespass on their constitutional or other rights."

The judicial control over administration emanates from the concept of 'rule of law', which is a cardinal feature of the British Constitution as well as the Indian Constitution. A.V. Dicey, the British constitutional lawyer, in his famous book *Introduction to the Study of the Law of the Constitution* gave a classic exposition of this concept, which is as follows: "No man is punishable or can be lawfully made to suffer in body or goods except for a distinct breach of law established in the ordinary legal manner before the ordinary courts of the land... no man is above the law, but... every man, whatever be his rank or condition, is subject to the ordinary law of the realm and amenable to the jurisdiction of the ordinary tribunals... every official from the Prime Minister down to a constable or a collector of taxes, is under the same responsibility for every act done without legal justification as any other citizen... the general principles of Constitution... are with us the result of judicial decision determining the rights of private persons in particular cases brought before the courts."

(i) Which of the following statements are correct regarding the difference between the judicial control over administration and legislative supervision over the administration?

1. Both are two faces of the same coin and not much different.
2. Judicial control aims at protecting the rights and liberties of the citizens while legislative supervision aims at controlling the policy and expenditure of the executive.
3. Judicial control prevents transgression of constitutional rights while legislative supervision regulates and supervises powers, functions, policies, etc.
4. Both aim at protecting the legal rights of citizens.

(a) 1, 2, 3 and 4 (b) 1, 2, 3
(c) 2, 3, 4 (d) 2, 3

(ii) Which of the following statements about 'rule of law' is correct?

1. It emanates from judicial control.
2. It is an integral part of the Indian Constitution.
3. It controls the policy and function of executive.
4. It protects rights of every citizen against arbitrary exercise of power.
5. It applies equally to everybody.

(a) 1, 2, 3, 4 (b) 2, 4, 5
(c) 1, 2, 4, 5 (d) 2, 3,4, 5

(iii) Which of the following assumptions can be drawn based on what is stated in the passage?

1. Rule of law and judicial control are one and the same thing as both control the administrative acts.
2. Rule of law implies application of the same ordinary law to everybody.

(a) Only Assumption 1 can be drawn.
(b) Only Assumption 2 can be drawn.
(c) Both Assumptions 1 and 2 can be drawn.
(d) Neither Assumption 1 nor 2 can be drawn.

**67.** The World Trade Organisation (WTO) was created in the early 1990s as a component of the Uruguay Round negotiation. However, it could have been negotiated as part of the Tokyo Round of the 1970s, since that negotiation was an attempt at a 'constitutional reform' of the General Agreement on Tariffs and Trade (GATT). Or it could have been put off to the future, as the US government wanted. What factors led to the creation of the WTO in the early 1990s?

One factor was the pattern of multilateral bargaining that developed late in the Uruguay Round. Like all complex international agreements, the WTO was a product of a series of trade-offs between the principal actors and groups. For the United States, which did not want a new organisation, the dispute settlement part of the WTO package achieved its longstanding goal of a more effective and more legal dispute settlement system. For the Europeans, who by the 1990s had come to view GATT dispute settlement less in political terms and more regime of legal obligations, the WTO package was acceptable as a means to discipline the resort to unilateral measures by the United States. Countries like Canada and other middle and smaller trading partners were attracted by the expansion of rules-based system and by the symbolic value of a trade organisation, both of which inherently support the weak against the strong. The developing countries were attracted due to the provisions banning unilateral measures. Finally, and perhaps most important, many counties at the Uruguay Round came to put a higher priority on the export gains than on the import losses that the negotiation would produce, and they came to associate the WTO and a rule based system with those gains. This reasoning—replicated in many countries—was contained in US Ambassador Kantor's defence of the

WTO, and it amounted to a recognition that international trade and its benefits cannot be enjoyed unless trading nations accept the discipline of a negotiated rules-based environment.

(i) What could be the closest reason why WTO was not formed in the 1970s?
   (a) The US government did not like it.
   (b) Important players did not find it in their best interest to do so.
   (c) Lawyers did not work for the dispute settlement system.
   (d) The Tokyo Round negotiation was an attempt at constitutional reform.

(ii) The most likely reason for the acceptance of the WTO package by nations was that
   (a) It had the means to prevent the US from taking unilateral measures.
   (b) They recognised the need for a rule-based environment to protect the benefits of increased trade.
   (c) It settles disputes more legally and more effectively.
   (d) Its rule-based system leads to export gains.

(iii) In the statement ".... It amounted to a recognition that international trade and its benefits cannot be enjoyed unless trading nations accept the discipline of a negotiated rules-based environment.", 'it' refers to:
   (a) Ambassador Cantor's defence of the WTO.
   (b) The higher priority on export gains placed by many countries at the Uruguay Round.
   (c) The export gains many countries came to associate with a rule-based system.
   (d) The provision of a rule-based system by the WTO.

**68.** Internationally, the United Nations Framework Convention on Climate Change (UNFCCC, the Convention) was set up in 1992 and entered into force in 1994. Although global in scope, it differentiated the commitments/responsibilities of parties on the basis of respective capabilities, economic structures, and resource base and on the basis of the principle of 'equity', which is at the core of the climate change debate. The Convention lays down binding commitments for the developed countries, taking into account their historical responsibilities. It recognises that economic and social development and poverty eradication are the 'first and overriding priorities' of developing countries.

Climate change is a complex policy issue with major implications in terms of finance. All actions to address climate change ultimately involve costs. Funding is vital for countries like India to design and implement adaptation and mitigation plans and projects. Lack of funding is a large impediment to implementing adaptation plans. The scale and magnitude of the financial support required by developing countries to enhance their domestic mitigation and adaptation actions are a matter of intense debate in the multilateral negotiations under the UNFCCC. The Convention squarely puts the responsibility for provision of financial support on the developed countries, taking into account their contribution to the stock of GHGs in the atmosphere. Given the magnitude of the task and the funds required, domestic finances are likely to fall short of the current and projected needs of the developing countries. Global funding through the multilateral mechanism of the Convention will enhance domestic capacity to finance the mitigation efforts. The Durban Climate Change Conference 2011 marks an important step forward in the climate change negotiations. The Durban outcomes made significant contribution as they established the second commitment period of the Kyoto Protocol and operationalised some of the key Cancun agreements related to a Green Climate Fund (GCF), Technology Mechanism (TM), and Adaptation Framework. The Durban outcomes also opened a window for discussions on the post 2020 arrangements for the global climate change regime for which the Durban Platform has been launched.

Though India and other developing countries came under tremendous pressure at Durban, India took the lead in ensuring that the new arrangements are firmly anchored in the Convention and are based on the principles of 'common but differentiated responsibilities and equity'.

(i) In determining the responsibilities and commitments of various countries under UNFCCC which of the following factors are taken into account?

1. Status of a country as developed or developing.
2. Principle of Equity.
3. Resource base of a country.
4. Economic structure of the country.

(a) 1, 2, 3 (b) 2, 3, 4
(c) 1, 2, 4 (d) 1, 2, 3, 4

(ii) Which amongst the following has been identified in the passage as a major challenge for developing countries in addressing the issue of climate change?

(a) Need for funding to implement adaptation and mitigation plans.
(b) Lack of access to appropriate technology.
(c) Lack of unanimity of view, at the international level.
(d) All of the above.

(iii) Consider the following two assertions:

1. The UNFCCC places responsibility of binding commitments on the developed countries.
2. There is no unanimity at international level as to who is to fund the adaptation and mitigation plans.

As per the passage which of the above two assertions is correct?

(a) Only Assertion 1 is correct.
(b) Only Assertion 2 is correct.
(c) Both Assertions 1 and 2 are correct.
(d) Neither Assertion 1 nor 2 is correct.

(iv) As per the passage which amongst the following can be said to be the outcome of Durban Climate Change conference?

1. It fixed the emission cuts which developed countries have to make.
2. It established the second commitment period for Kyoto protocol.
3. It made some important agreements pertaining to Cancun round of talks operative.

(a) 1, 2, 3 (b) 1, 2
(c) 1, 3 (d) 2, 3

**69.** It is obvious today that America has defaulted on this promissory note insofar as her citizens of colour are concerned. Instead of honouring this sacred obligation, America has given the black people a bad check, a check which has come back marked "insufficient funds." But we refuse to believe that the bank of justice is bankrupt. We refuse to believe that there are insufficient funds in the great vaults of opportunity of this nation. So we have come to cash this check – a check that will give us upon demand the riches of freedom and the security of justice. We have also come to this hallowed spot to remind America of the fierce urgency of now. This is no time to engage in the luxury of cooling off or to take the tranquilising drug of gradualism. Now is the time to make real the promises of democracy.

(i) What is the 'promissory note' referred to by the speaker?

(a) A check that was promised but not eventually paid.
(b) A separate state which was promised to the black citizens but never given.
(c) The promise of freedom and justice to the black people.
(d) None of the above

(ii) What is the "tranquilising drug of gradualism" referred to in the passage?

(a) A drug which dulls ours sense to distinguish what is right and what is not.

(b) An attitude of demanding ones right gradually.

(c) An attitude of accepting things as fait-accompli.

(d) An attitude of despair where one is hardly conscious of one's political rights.

**70.** Non-violence is the greatest force at the disposal of mankind. It is mightier than the mightiest weapon of destruction devised by the ingenuity of man. Destruction is not the law of the humans. Man lives freely by his readiness to die, if need at the hands of his brother, never by killing him. Every murder or other injury, no matter for what cause, committed or inflicted on another is a crime against humanity.

The first condition of non-violence is justice all round in every department of life. Perhaps, it is too much to expect of human nature. I do not, however, think so. No one should dogmatise about the capacity of human nature for degradation or exaltation.

Just as one must learn the art of killing in the training for violence, so one must learn the art of dying in the training for non-violence. Violence does not mean emancipation from fear, but discovering the means of combating the cause of fear. Non-violence, on the other hand, has no cause for fear. The votary of non-violence has to cultivate the capacity for sacrifice of the highest type in order to be free from fear. He recks not if he should lose his land, his wealth, his life. He who has not overcome all fear cannot practice *ahimsa* to perfection. The votary of *ahimsa* has only one fear that is of God. He who seeks refuge in God ought to have a glimpse of the *Atma* that transcends the body; and the moment one has a glimpse of the imperishable *Atma* one sheds the love of the perishable body. Training in violence is thus diametrically opposed to training in violence. Violence is needed for the protection of things external, non-violence is needed for the protection of *Atma*, for the protection of one's honour.

I have found that life persists in the midst of destruction and, therefore, there must be a higher law than that of destruction. Only under that law would a well-ordered society be intelligible and life worth living. And if that is the law of life, we have to work it out in daily life. Whenever there are jars, whenever you are confronted with an opponent conquer him with love. In this crude manner I have worked it out in my life. That does not mean that all my difficulties are solved. Only I have found that the law of love has answered as the law of destruction has never done. It is not that I am incapable of anger, for instance, but I succeed on almost all occasions to keep my feelings under control. Whatever may be the result, there is always in me conscious struggle for following the law of non-violence deliberately and ceaselessly. Such a struggle leaves one stronger for it. The more I work at this law, the more I feel the delight in my life, the delight in the scheme of the universe. It gives me a meaning of the mysteries of nature that I have no power to describe.

(i) Which of the following statements as per the passage are correct?

1. Violence means overcoming the cause of fear.
2. Violence means trying to eliminate the cause of fear.
3. Non-violence means combating the source of fear.
4. Non-violence means sacrificing even self for shedding fear.

(a) 1 and 2 (b) 1, 4
(c) 2 and 3 (d) 2 and 4

(ii) What logic does the author employ to emphasise that there must be a higher law than that of destruction?

(a) Although there is destruction in this world life continues amidst it.

(b) Life and death, destruction and reconstruction go hand in hand.

(c) Destruction is essential for recreation and what is created must be destroyed.

(d) All cf the above.

(iii) Why does the author suggest that practitioners of non-violence should develop capacity for sacrifice?

(a) As practitioner of non-violence remains defenceless, sacrifice is the only available remedy.

(b) Practitioner of non-violence, by sacrificing, strikes at the root cause of violence, which is self.

(c) Sacrifice imparts the practitioner of non-violence a moral force.

(d) Sacrifice is essential for practitioner of non-violence to overcome fear and be free from it.

**71.** The Unique Identification Authority of India (UIDAI), attached to the Planning Commission, is engaged in providing residents of India a Unique Identification number (called Aadhaar) linked to the resident's demographic and biometric information. The project aims to create a platform that serves as an 'identification infrastructure' for delivery of public and private services to the residents of India. The Aadhaar project is set to become the largest biometric capture and identification project in the world. Aadhaar has huge potential for improving operations and delivery of services. Its potential applications in various significant public service delivery and social sector programs are as follows:

India's PDS with a network of 4.78 lakh fair price shops (FPS) is perhaps the largest retail system of its type in the world. The PDS is operated under the joint responsibility of the central and the state Governments. By using Aadhaar it is possible to have the subsidy go directly to the target households whc can then purchase their food from any PDS store or maybe even non-PDS shops. The PDS system stands to benefit from Aadhaar in several ways:

Integration with the UID programme will lead to better identification of individuals and families making possible better targeting and increased transparency. Further, an individual who migrates to some other part of the country can easily continue to avail his designated benefits.

The UID database will maintain details of the beneficiary that can be updated from multiple sources. The PDS system can use this database for authentication of beneficiaries.

The UIDAI will provide a detection infrastructure to the PDS programme to weed out duplicate and ghost cards.

The UID will become an important identifier in banking services. This can support PDS reform by, for example, providing the banking account number for a family to effect direct cash transfer.

Further, incorporation of the UID into the MGNREGS programme will assist in addressing some of the major challenges that impede progress:

The UID can replace the need to provide supporting documentation for the standard Know Your Customer (KYC) fields, making opening a bank account significantly simpler.

Once each citizen in a job card needs to provide his UID before claiming employment, the potential for ghost or fictitious beneficiaries is eliminated.

The UID system will provide a platform for managing citizens who relocate or migrate from one place to another and want to seamlessly enjoy benefits of the programme.

The village-level social audit committee can be selected after authentication with the UID database. The social audit reports filed by the village-level committees can be authenticated by the biometrics of the committee members and social audit coordinator.

Health, and health-related development schemes, could also benefit from the UID. Currently, infrequent national or state surveys are the major mode of capturing data on infectious disease conditions. However, chronic or lifestyle diseases are not captured in any meaningful way even through surveys. An integrated routine health system that can capture and track population-level disease conditions by linking citizen IDs with hospital or other medical facility records generated through facility visits can (1) inform the public health system of the prevalence of various routine disease conditions and (2) help prepare the health system to respond to unforeseen epidemics.

Currently, the primary education system in our country faces a serious problem of inflated enrolment at school level. Leakages occur in various areas, including mid-day meals, books, scholarships, provision of uniforms and bicycles. If UIDs are given to children, it will do away with the problems of multiple enrolments and ghosts. Provision of UIDs will ensure that there are no problems due to migration of students anywhere within the country as one would have no difficulty in establishing one's identity at the new location.

(i) Which amongst the following is **not** a benefit which the PDS will get from the 'Aadhaar'?

(a) Through Aadhaar, the PDS system can be made more robust and capable of delivering greater subsidy to a larger target population.

(b) Through Aadhaar, individuals can be better identified and subsidies directly can be transferred to beneficiaries leading to prevention of leakages.

(c) Through Aadhaar, multiple source updation of beneficiary details can be done. This will help the PDS to better identify and deliver the subsidies.

(d) None of the above.

(ii) From what is stated in the passage, examine whether the following conclusions can be drawn.

1. Aadhaar will help in identification and weeding out of ghost and duplicate PDS beneficiaries.
2. It will help in making identification and documentation process for opening a bank account much simpler.

(a) Only Conclusion 1 can be drawn.

(b) Only Conclusion 2 can be drawn.

(c) Both Conclusions 1 and 2 can be drawn.

(d) Neither Conclusion 1 nor 2 can be drawn.

(iii) How is Aadhaar likely to be helpful in improvement of health-related development schemes?

(a) The capture of biometric and demographic information of individuals will also capture health-related information, which will help in formulating health schemes for the people.

(b) Information of citizens pertaining to hospital and health services could be tagged to their unique identity thus helping in identifying prevalent diseases and helping in evolving health schemes.

(c) It will make the national/state disease survey superfluous thus saving resources, which can be channelised in health schemes.

(d) All of the above.

(iv) Which of the following **cannot** be inferred from the passage?

1. Aadhaar will help to eliminate the ghost and duplicate records of PDS.
2. Aadhaar will help to deliver only a variety of public services.
3. Aadhaar will benefit only those below the poverty line.

(a) 1 only (b) 1 and 2 only

(c) 2 and 3 only (d) 1, 2, 3

(v) Which amongst the following are the likely benefits of Aadhaar to the education system?

1. It will help in improving the quality of education as needy section of population could be identified.

2. It will help in better recording of the performance of the child as with child UID the educational performance of all children could be tagged and monitored.

(a) 1 only (b) 2 only
(c) Both 1 and 2 (d) Neither 1 nor 2

**72.** In the modern scientific story, light was created not once but twice. The first time was in the Big Bang, when the universe began its existence as a glowing, expanding fireball, which cooled off into darkness after a few million years. The second time was hundreds of millions of years later, when the cold material condensed into dense nuggets under the influence of gravity, and ignited to become the first stars.

Sir Martin Rees, Britain's astronomer royal, named the longer interval between these two enlightenments, the cosmic 'Dark Age'. The name describes not only the poorly lit conditions, but also the ignorance of astronomers about that period. Nobody knows exactly when the first stars formed, or how they organised themselves into galaxies—or even whether stars were the first luminous objects. They may have been preceded by quasars, which are mysterious, bright spots found at the centres of some galaxies.

Now, two independent groups of astronomers, one led by Robert Becker of the University of California, Davis, and the other by George Djorgovski of the Caltech, claim to have peered far enough into space with their telescope (and, therefore, backwards enough in time) to observe the closing days of the Dark Age.

The main problem that plagued previous efforts to study the Dark Age was not the lack of suitable telescopes, but rather the lack of suitable things at which to point them. Because these events took place over 13 billion years ago, if astronomers are to have any hope of unravelling them, they must study objects that are at least 13 billion light years away. The best prospectuses are quasars, because they are so bright and compact that they can be seen across vast stretches of space. The energy source that powers a quasar is unknown, although it is suspected to be the intense gravity of a giant black hole. However, at the distances required for the study of Dark Age, even quasars are extremely rare and faint. Recently, some members of Dr. Becker's team announced their discovery of the four most distant quasars known. All the new quasars are terribly faint, a challenge that both teams overcame by peering at them thorough one of the twin Keck telescopes in Hawaii. These are the world's largest, and can, therefore, collect the most light. Dr. Becker's team analysed the light from all four quasars. Three of them appeared to be similar to ordinary, less distant quasars. However, the fourth and the most distant one, unlike any other quasar ever seen, showed unmistakable signs of being shrouded in a fog of hydrogen gas. This gas is leftover material from the Big Bang that did not condense into stars or quasars. It acts like fog because new born stars and quasars emit mainly ultraviolet light. Seeing this fog had been the goal of would be Dark Age astronomers since 1965, by using quasars as backlighting beacons to observe the fog's shadow.

(i) In the passage, the Dark Age refers to
   (a) The period when the universe became cold after the Big Bang.
   (b) A period about which astronomers know very little.
   (c) The medieval period when cultural activity seemed to have come to an end.
   (d) The time that the universe took to heat up after the Bing Bang.

(ii) Astronomers find it difficult to study the Dark Age because
   (a) Suitable telescopes are few.
   (b) The associated events took place aeons ago.

(c) The energy source that powers a quasar is unknown.

(d) Their best chance is to study quasars, which are faint objects, to begin with.

(iii) Examine which of the following is not true as per the passage.

(a) Quasars offer the best prospect of looking at events 13 billion years ago.

(b) After the initial expansion in the wake of the Big Bang, the universe cooled and it became dark.

(c) Quasars' source of energy is giant black holes.

(d) None of the above.

73. As per the United Nations Development Programme (UNDP) *Human Development Report 2009* (HDR 2009), the Human Development Index (HDI) for India in 2007 was 0.612 on the basis of which India is ranked 134 out of 182 countries of the world placing it at the same rank as in 2006. The HDI is based on three indicators, namely GDP per capita (PPP US $), life expectancy at birth, and education as measured by adult literacy rate and gross enrolment ratio (combined for primary, secondary and tertiary education). The value of HDI for India gradually increased from 0.427 in 1980 to 0.556 in 2000 and went up to 0.612 in 2007. In 2016, India's HDI value of 0.624 put it at 131$^{st}$ rank. India's HDI value in 2017 is 0.640 which puts the country in Medium Human Development Category as per HDR released by UNDP. The movement of the index value in some of the comparable countries indicates that improvement in HDI in India in recent years has been better than in most of them. This trend indicating improvement in the HDI powered by per capita income growth for India is heartening though there is no room for complacency as India is still in the Medium Human Development category with even countries like China, Sri Lanka and Indonesia having better ranking.

- India's HDI rank is also lower than its per capita GDP (PPP US $) rank by six notches, indicating that our human development effort still needs to catch up with the progress made in GDP per capita.
- The existing gap between the health and education indicators of India and those in the developed world and even many developing countries needs to be bridged at a faster pace.
- According to the Report, *life expectancy* at birth in India was 63.4 years in 2007 as against 80.5 years in Norway, 81.4 years in Australia, 74.0 years in Sri Lanka and 72.9 years in China. *Adult literacy* rate (aged 15 and above) in 1999–2007 was 66.0 per cent in India as against near 100 per cent in many of the developed nations, 93.3 per cent in China and 92.0 per cent in Indonesia. Combined *gross enrollment* ratio in education in 2007 was 61 per cent in India as against 99.3 per cent in Canada, 98.6 per cent in Norway, 78.0 per cent in Thailand and 76.4 per cent in Egypt.

In terms of the *Gender Development Index (GDI)*, with an index value of 0.594, India ranks 114 out of 155 countries. When the HDI ranks used are recalculated for the countries with a GDI value, a zero count for HDI rank minus GDI rank is obtained for India, which is indicative of the same status of world ranking in terms of gender development and human development. Therefore, continued efforts are called for in the area of gender development.

(i) What conclusion can be drawn about human development progress and economic progress in India?

(a) Human Development Progress (HDP) has been less than Economic Progress (EP).

(b) HDP has been equal to EP.

(c) HDP has been more than EP.

(d) No conclusion can be drawn.

(ii) Which one of the following is **not** a parameter used to evaluate the Human Development Index of a country?

(a) GDP per capita

(b) Life expectancy at birth

(c) Sex ratio

(d) Adult literacy rate and gross enrolment ratio

(iii) As per the passage which factor has contributed most to the improvement in HDI of India?

(a) Human and social progress

(b) Progress in education and adult literacy

(c) Improvement in Gender Development Index

(d) Economic progress

**74.** A generalist civil servant is one who does not possess a specialist background but is well equipped with the administrative procedures, rules and regulations and hence can be appointed in any field of administration. He belongs to the managerial class and usually performs the POS-DCORB functions, that is, Planning, Organising, Staffing, Directing, Coordination, Reporting and Budgeting. Thus, the civil servants who make policies, coordinate, supervise and control the administration are called generalists. An IAS officer is an example of a generalist civil servant. In his professional capacity, a generalist possesses the skills and techniques of a manager and a kind of politician. As a manager, he is entrusted with the responsibility of getting things done, and as a politician, he is responsible for interpreting the public mind to the complex social, economic and even political problems of the state within the constraints of the administrative system.

A specialist civil servant, on the other hand, is one who possesses special knowledge or skill in a specific field or area of administration. He is an expert professional. Thus, like a generalist, he is not an all-rounder. Engineers, doctors, agriculturists, meteorologists, educationists and statisticians are some of the examples of specialists.

The civil services in India can be grouped into two broad categories viz. Technical services and non-technical services. The technical services are those to which recruitment is done only on the basis of specialised and professional qualifications of the candidates. These services include Indian Economic Service, Indian Statistical Service, Indian Forest Service, Central Engineering Service, Central Legal Service, Central Health Service, Indian Meteorological Service and so on. These technical services are called Specialist Services, and the members of these services are called the Specialists.

The non-technical services, on the other hand, are those to which recruitment is done on the basis of general educational qualifications and is open to all candidates who possess the minimum required educational qualification, for instance, a university degree. These services include Indian Administrative Service, Indian Police Service, Indian Revenue Services, India Foreign Service, India Audit and Accounts Service, Indian Postal Service, Central Secretariat Service and so on. These non-technical services can be further divided into two sub-categories, that is, functional services and general purpose service. The members of the functional services remain in the specific field of administration for which they are selected and appointed throughout their career. In the course of time, they acquire expert and specialised knowledge due to work experience and regular training. These functional services include all the non-technical services except the IAS. The IAS is the only general purpose service at the national level. The members of IAS occupy various positions in the administrative hierarchy in different fields of administration. There is no functional field carved out for the members of IAS. To sum up, the specialists' class includes members of the technical services and the non-technical functional services, and the generalists' class includes the members of only the IAS. Thus, the generalists' and the specialists' controversy is nothing but the controversy between the members of the IAS and the non IAS.

(i) As per the author the Indian Police Service (IPS) would be categorised as
(a) a generalist service
(b) a specialist service
(c) a non-technical functional service
(d) none of the above

(ii) Which of the following can be said to be applicable to the generalist?
1. He performs the POS-DCORB functions.
2. He is an expert professional possessing knowledge of specific field or area of administration.
3. He is not an all rounder.
4. He is like a civil servant who supervises and controls the administration and frames policies.
5. IAS and IPS officers both can be classified as generalist.
6. A generalist's role involves interpreting the public mind.

(a) 1, 2, 3 (b) 1, 4, 6
(c) 2, 4, 6 (d) 1, 2, 6

**75.** I walked quickly over the yellow plain. It was elastic, like flesh and seemed to sweat beneath my tread with a squelching sound. The sea had been there very lately. Now I perceived it at a distance, escaping out of sight, and I no longer could distinguish the line which separated the sands from ocean. I felt as though I were looking at a titanic supernatural work of enchantment. The Atlantic had just now been before me, then it had disappeared into the sands, just as scenery disappears through a trap; and I was now walking in the midst of a desert.

(i) Where was the speaker walking?
(a) on a plane
(b) on a sea beach
(c) on the sea bed where water had receded
(d) on a desert land which was once covered by sea

(ii) What is being referred to by, "a titanic supernatural work of enchantment"?
(a) A huge ship at a distance in the sea.
(b) The natural beauty of large coast and receding ocean.
(c) A huge and beautiful mountain on the coast behind the sea.
(d) Cannot be inferred based on what is given in the passage.

(iii) Which of the following can be inferred from the description given by the narrator?
(1) It was a time of high tide on the coast.
(2) The narrator could clearly see the sea and its waves.
(a) Only 1 can be inferred.
(b) Only 2 can be inferred.
(c) Both 1 & 2 can be inferred.
(d) Neither 1 nor 2 can be inferred.

**76.** The story begins as the European pioneers crossed the Alleghenies and started to settle in the Midwest. The land they found was covered with forest. With incredible effort they felled the trees, pulled the stumps and planted their crops in the rich, loamy soil. When they finally reached the western edge of the place we now call Indiana, the forest stopped and ahead lay a thousand miles of the great grass prairie. The Europeans were puzzled by this new environment. Some even called it the 'Great Desert'. It seemed untellable. The earth was often very wet and it was covered with centuries of tangled and matted grasses. With their cast iron plows, the settlers found that the prairie sod could not be cut and the wet earth stuck to their plowshares. Even a team of the best oxen bogged down after a few years of tugging. The iron plow was a useless tool to farm the prairie soil. The pioneers were stymied for nearly two decades. Their western march; was halted and they filed in the eastern regions of the Midwest.

In 1837, blacksmith in the town of Grand detour, Illinois, invented a new tool. His name was John Deere and the tool was a plow made of steel. It was sharp enough to cut through matted grasses and smooth enough to cast off the mud. It was a simple too, the 'sod buster' that took the great prairies to agricultural development.

When the European settlers arrived at the Sauk prairie in 1837, the government forced the native Sauk people west of the Mississippi River. The settlers came with John Deere's new invention and used the tool to open the area to a new kind of agriculture. They ignored the traditional ways of the Sauk Indian and used their sod-busting tool for planting wheat. Initially, the soil was generous and the farmers thrived. However, each year the soil lost more of its nurturing power. It was only thirty years after the Europeans arrived with their new technology that the land was depleted. Wheat farming became uneconomic and tens of thousands of farmers left Wisconism seeking new land with sod to bust.

It took the Europeans and their new technology just one generation to make; their homeland into a desert. The Sauk Indians who knew how to sustain themselves on the Sauk prairie land were banished to another kind of desert called a reservation. And they even forgot about the techniques and tools that had sustained them on the prairie for generations unrecorded. And that is how it was that three deserts were created—Wisconsin, the reservation and the memories of a people. A century later, the land of the Sauks is now populated by the children of a second wave of European farmers who learned to replenish the soil through the regenerative powers of dairying, ground cover crops and animal manures.

(i) The Prairie was a great puzzlement for the European pioneers because
   (a) It was covered with thick, untellable layers of grass over a vast stretch.
   (b) It was a large desert immediately next to lush forests.
   (c) It was rich cultivable land left fallow for centuries.
   (d) It could be easily tilled with iron plows.

(ii) Which of the following does the 'desert' in the passage refer to?
   (a) Prairie soil depleted by cultivation of wheat.
   (b) Reservations in which native Indians were resettled.
   (c) Absence of, and emptiness in, community kinship and relationships.
   (d) All of the above

(iii) Why was the Western March halted?
   (a) They were halted by armies of west.
   (b) Death and diseases halted them.
   (c) They could not cultivate the land.
   (d) The answer is not specified in the passage; nor can it be inferred.

**77.** Now, there were two possessions of the James Dillingham Young in which they both took a mighty pride. One was Jim's gold watch that had been his father's and his grandfather's. The other was Della's hair. Had the Queen of Sheba lived in the flat across the airshaft, Della would have let her hair hang out the window someday to dry just to depreciate Her Majesty's jewels and gifts. Had King Solomon been the gatekeeper, with all his treasures piled up in the basement, Jim would have been cavalier enough to pull out his watch every time he passed, just to see him pluck at his beard from envy.

(i) What is the writer trying to convey in the passage?
   (1) The preciousness of the possessions of the Young's.
   (2) The pride which the young's had in their possessions.
   (a) Only 1
   (b) Only 2
   (c) Both 1 & 2
   (d) Neither 1 nor 2

(ii) The Young's were extremely proud of;
   (1) Jim's Hair
   (2) Della's Jewels
   (3) Jims watch

(4) Della's Hair
(5) Jims basement treasure
(a) 1, 4 (b) 2, 3
(c) 3, 4 (d) 3, 5

(iii) Why would Della want to depreciate the jewels and gifts of the queen?
(1) To show her scorn at the riches of the queen.
(2) To show her pride and value in, her possession.
(3) To show her envy for the queens' jewels.
(a) Only1 (b) Only 2
(c) Both 1 & 2 (d) 1, 2, 3

**78.** The controversy over genetically modified food continues unabated in the West. Genetic modification (GM) is the science by which the genetic material of a plant is altered, perhaps to make it more resistant to pests or killer weeds, or to enhance its nutritional value. Many food biotechnologists claim that GM will be a major contribution of science to mankind in the 21st century. On the other hand, large numbers of opponents, mainly in Europe claim that the benefits of GM are a myth propagated by multinational corporations to increase their profits that they pose a health hazard, and have therefore, called for governments to ban the sale of genetically modified food.

The anti-GM campaign has been quite effective in Europe, with several European Union member countries imposing a virtual ban for five years over genetically modified food imports. Since the genetically modified food industry is particularly strong in the United States of America, the controversy also constitutes another chapter in the US–Europe skir-mishes, which have become particularly acerbic after the US invasion of Iraq.

To a large extent, the GM controversy has been ignored in the Indian media, although Indian biotechnologists have been quite active in GM research. Several groups of Indian biotechnologists have been working on various issues connected with crops grown in India. One concrete achievement, which has recently figured in the news is that of a team led by the former vice-chancellor of Jawaharlal Nehru University, Asis Datta—it has successfully added an extra gene to potatoes to enhance the protein content of the tuber by at least 30 per cent. Not surprisingly, the new potato has been called the "protato". The protato is now in its third year of field trials. It is quite likely that the GM controversy will soon hit the headlines in India since a spokesperson of the Indian Central government has recently announced that the government may use the potato in its midday meal programme for schools as early as next year.

Why should "scientific progress, with huge potential benefits to the poor and malnourished, be so controversial?" The anti-GM lobby contends that pernicious propaganda has vastly exaggerated the benefits of GM and completely evaded the costs, which will have to be incurred if the genetically modified food industry is allowed to grow unchecked. In particular, they allude to different types of costs.

This group contends that the most important potential cost is that the widespread distribution and growth of genetically modified food will enable the corporate world (alias the multinational corporations—MNCs) completely capture the food chain. A 'small' group of biotech companies will patent the transferred genes as well as the technology associated with them. They will then buy up the competing seed merchants and seed-breeding centres, thereby controlling the production of food at every possible level. Independent farmers, big and small, will be completely wiped out of the food industry. At best, they will be reduced to the status of being subcontractors.

This line of argument goes on to claim that the control of the food chain will be disastrous for the poor since the MNCs, guided by the profit motive, will only focus on the high-value food items demanded by the affluent in the long run, the production of basic staples, which constitute the food basket of the poor will taper.

However, this vastly overestimates the power of the MNCs. Even if the research promoted by them does focus on the high-value food items, much of biotechnology research is also funded by governments in both developing and developed countries. Indeed, the protato is a by-product of this type of research. If the protato passes the field trials, there is no reason to believe that it cannot be marketed in the global potato market. And this type of success story can be repeated with other basic food items.

(i) Using the clues in the passage, which of the following countries would you expect to be in the forefront of the anti-GM campaign?
   (a) USA and Spain
   (b) India and Iraq
   (c) Germany and France
   (d) Australia and New Zealand

(ii) The author doubts the anti-GM lobby's contention that MNC control of the food chain will be disastrous for the poor because
   (a) MNCs will focus on high-value food items.
   (b) MNCs are driven by the motive of profit maximisation.
   (c) MNCs are not the only group of actors in genetically modified food research.
   (d) Economic development will help the poor buy MNC-produced food.

(iii) Which of the following about the Indian media's coverage of scientific research does the passage seem to suggest?
   (a) Indian media generally covers a subject of scientific importance when its mass application is likely.
   (b) Indian media's coverage of scientific research is generally dependent on MNCs' interests.
   (c) Indian media, in partnership with the government, is actively involved in publicising the results of scientific research.
   (d) Indian media only highlights scientific research, which is funded by the government.

(iv) According to the passage, biotechnology research
   (a) Is of utility only for high value food items.
   (b) Is funded only by multinational corporations.
   (c) Allows multinational corporations to control the food basket of the poor.
   (d) Addresses the concerns of rich and poor countries.

**79.** India's journey on the path of sustainable development has so far been marked both by reasons for celebration and introspection. The right place to begin the story would be the 1980s and early 1990s, which mark the beginning of economic reforms, catalyst for India's phenomenally faster growth rates since, and coinciding with a time when countries around the world acknowledged and started addressing the increasing environmental concerns, such as at the Earth Summit in Rio in 1992. India's faster gross domestic product (GDP) growth over the last two decades has been unprecedented; but at the same time India's rankings in terms of the human development index (HDI) as well as indices measuring environmental sustainability are yet to fully reflect this growth. However, it would be a mistake to downplay the enormous progress made, as India has followed a much more conscious path of sustainable development with impressive results on the ground.

The key environmental challenges have become sharper in the past two decades. The 2009 State of the Environment Report by the Ministry of Environment and Forests (MOEF) clubs the issues under five key challenges faced by India, which are climate change, food security, water security, energy security and managing urbanisation. Climate change is impacting the natural ecosystems and is expected to have substantial adverse effects in India, mainly on agriculture on which around 58 per cent of the population depends for livelihood, water storage in the Himalayan glaciers, which are the source of major rivers and groundwater recharge, sea-level rise and threats to a long coastline and habitations. Climate change will also cause increased frequency of extreme events such as storms, floods and droughts. These in turn will impact India's food and water security problems. India also faces the critical challenge of meeting its rapidly growing energy demands. It currently depends on around 80 per cent imports for its crude oil requirements. A large section of the rural population is still not connected to the grid or efficient modern cooking fuel sources, and India's per capita energy consumption of 439 kg of oil equivalent is far below the world average of 1688 kg. The energy poverty of the household sector is indicated not only by the low penetration of electricity into the sector, but also by its primary dependence on traditional inefficient fuel for cooking and lighting. As per the National Sample Survey Organisation (NSSO) survey 2004–05, around 45 per cent of rural households depend on inferior fuels like kerosene or candle light for lighting and 84 per cent have to rely primarily on biomass comprising fuel wood, dung cake and agro-waste for cooking fuel. Finally, urbanisation is proceeding very rapidly, creating new issues of affordable housing, access to safe water and sanitation, solid waste disposal, transport and air quality. Prices, incentives, regulations and taxes could be designed to help respond to these areas.

(i) Which of the two assumptions are correct in terms of what is stated in the passage?

1. India's progress in terms of sustainable development does not match its economic development.
2. India fares better in the index of measuring environmentally sustainable development than on the index of human development.

(a) Only Assumption 1 is correct.
(b) Only Assumption 2 is correct.
(c) Both Assumptions 1 and 2 are correct.
(d) Neither Assumption 1 nor 2 is correct.

(ii) Which of the following is not a challenge highlighted in the passage?

(a) Provision of electricity to a large section of population.
(b) Access to modern cooking fuel.
(c) Access to basic healthcare.
(d) Access to safe water.

(iii) Which of the following conclusions can be drawn from the passage?

1. India's growth cannot be deemed to be sustainable.
2. India is not self-sufficient as far as its energy requirements are concerned.
3. The brunt of the adverse impact of climate change is likely to be borne by the agricultural sector.

(a) 1, 2 and 3 (b) 2 and 3 only
(c) 2 only (d) 3 only

(iv) India's energy poverty of household sector is reflected by

1. Excessive dependence of a large section of population on inefficient fuels.
2. Lack of access to electricity.
3. Inefficient technique of burning of conventional fuels.

(a) 1, 2 and 3 (b) 1 and 3
(c) 2 and 3 (d) 1 and 2

**80.** Interdependence is and ought to be as much the ideal of man as self-sufficiency. Man is a social being. Without interrelation with society he cannot realise his oneness with the universe or suppress his egotism. His social interdependence enables him to test his faith and to prove himself on the touchstone of reality. If man were so placed or could so place himself as to be absolutely above all dependence on his fellow-beings he would become so proud and arrogant as to be a veritable burden and nuisance to the world. Dependence on society teaches him the lesson of humanity. That a man ought to be able to satisfy most of his essential needs himself is obvious; but it is no less obvious to me that when self-sufficiency is carried to the length of isolating oneself from society it almost amounts to sin. A man cannot become self-sufficient even in respect of all various operations from the growing of the cotton to the spinning of the yarn. He has at some stage or other to take the aid of members of his family. And if one may take the help from one's own family, why not from one's neighbours? Or otherwise what is the significance of the great saying, "The world is my family"?

Duties to self, to the family, to the country and to the world are not independent of one another. One cannot do good to the country by injuring himself or his family. Similarly, one cannot serve the country by injuring the world at large. In the final analysis, we must die that the family may live, the family must die that the country may live and the country must die that the world may live. But only pure things can be offered in sacrifice. Therefore, self-purification is the first step. When the heart is pure, we at once realise what is our duty at every moment. The golden way is to be friends with the world and to regard the whole human family as one. He who distinguishes between the votaries of one's own religion and those of another mis-educates the members of his own and opens the way for discord and irreligion.

(i) Which of the two conclusions have been drawn in the passage? Conclusion 1-A man can satisfy all of his essential needs himself. Conclusion 2-Interdependence and self-sufficiency complement each other.

(a) Only Conclusion 1
(b) Only Conclusion 2
(c) Both Conclusions 1 and 2
(d) Neither of the two conclusions

(ii) Why interdependence needs to be an ideal of man?

(a) Man is a social animal.
(b) He cannot be self-sufficient in all essential matters.
(c) Dependence on others instils humility and teaches humanity.
(d) All of the above

(iii) What is the most important message/idea conveyed by the passage?

(a) An individual should sacrifice himself for the sake of family, the family for the sake of country and the country for the sake of the world.
(b) Interdependence and self sufficiency both are equal ideals for humanity and essential for society.
(c) Man cannot be self-sufficient for everything.
(d) None of the above

(iv) Which of the following assertions have been made in the passage?

1. The world is akin to a big family.
2. It is natural to distinguish between one's own and other's religion.
3. Duties to self, family, country and world are not independent of each other.
4. Self sufficiency and interdependence do not go hand in hand.
5. Purity of heart enables us to have a better understanding of our duties.

(a) 1, 2, 3 (b) 2, 3, 4
(c) 1, 3, 5 (d) 2, 3, 5

(v) Which of the following acts would be in contravention of the ideals espoused in the passage?

(a) Preparing one's own meal without assistance of others.
(b) Offering assistance to ones neighbour with the expectation of seeking his help in time of need.
(c) Emphasising superiority of one's own religion
(d) All of the above

**81.** In considering the Origin of Species, it is quite conceivable that a naturalist, reflecting on the mutual affinities of organic beings, on their embryological relations, their geographical distribution, geological succession, and other such facts, might come to the conclusion that each species had not been independently created, but had descended, like varieties, from other species. Nevertheless, such a conclusion, even if well founded, would be unsatisfactory, until it could be shown how the innumerable species inhabiting this world have been modified, so as to acquire that perfection of structure and co-adaptation, which most justly excites our admiration. Naturalists continually refer to external conditions, such as climate food, etc., as the only possible cause of variation. In one very limited sense, as we shall hereafter see, this may be true; but it is preposterous to attribute to mere external conditions, the structure, for instance, of the woodpecker, with its feet, tail, beak, and tongue, so admirably adapted to catch insects under the bark of trees. In the case of the mistletoe, which draws its nourishment from certain trees, which has seeds that must be transported by certain birds, and which has flowers with separate sexes absolutely requiring the agency of certain insects to bring pollen from one flower to the other, it is equally preposterous to account for the structure of this parasite, with its relations to several distinct organic beings, by the effects of external conditions, or of habit, or of the volition of the plant itself.

The author of the 'Vestiges of Creation' would, I presume, say that, after a certain unknown number of generations, some bird had given birth to a woodpecker, and some plant to the mistletoe, and that these had been produced perfect as we now see them; but this assumption seems to me to be no explanation, for it leaves the case of the co-adaptations of organic beings to each other and to their physical conditions of life, untouched and unexplained.

It is, therefore, of the highest importance to gain a clear insight into the means of modification and co-adaptation. At the commencement of my observations it seemed to me probable that a careful study of domesticated animals and of cultivated plants would offer the best chance of making out this obscure problem. Nor have I been disappointed; in this and in all other perplexing cases I have invariably found that our knowledge, imperfect though it be, of variation under domestication, afforded the best and safest clue. I may venture to express my conviction of the high value of such studies, although they have been very commonly neglected by naturalists.

(i) What could be the reason for the author considering it preposterous, to attribute the features of a woodpecker or a mistletoe, to mere external conditions?

(a) Because external conditions are incapable of bringing variation in species.

(b) Because the features seem almost perfect and too complex to be caused by external conditions.

(c) Because there is scientific evidence to show that genetic modification caused the unique changes.

(d) None of the above.

(ii) Which of the conclusions would be in conformity with the views of the author?

1. Species like woodpecker and mistletoe could have been produced perfect, from a different species with all its features, in a single generation.
2. External conditions would have little role in emergence of new species.

(a) Only Conclusion 1.

(b) Only Conclusion 2.

(c) Both Conclusions 1 and 2.

(d) Neither Conclusion 1 nor 2.

(iii) Examine which of the following is true as per the passage.

(a) The author concludes in the passage that each species had not been independently created but descended like varieties from other species.

(b) The author concludes that each species could not have descended from other species.

(c) The author does not draw any conclusion regarding descent of one species from the other.

(d) None of the above.

(iv) Why does the author consider the proposition not correct that plants and animals had been produced perfect with the features we see, after a generation from other plants or animals?

(a) The proposition is illogical and preposterous.

(b) The proposition would fail to explain the cases of co-adoption of living beings to each other and physical environment.

(c) The proposition would fail to explain the sudden emergence of new features in the plants and animals.

(d) All of the above.

**82.** Recently, I spent several hours sitting under a tree in my garden with the social anthropologist William Ury, a Harvard University professor who specialises in the art of negotiation and wrote the best-selling book, Getting to Yes. He captivated me with his theory that tribalism protects people from their fear of rapid change. He explained that the pillars of tribalism that humans rely on from security would always counter any significant cultural or social change. In this way, he said, change is never allowed to happen too fast.

But we have all heard that nothing is as permanent as change. Nothing is guaranteed. Pithy expressions, to be sure, but no more than cliches. Change is over-rated, anyway. Consider the automobile. It's an especially valuable example, because the auto industry has spent tens of billions of dollars on research and product development in the last 100 years. Henry Ford's first car had a metal chassis with an internal combustion, gasoline-powered engine, four wheels with rubber tyres, a foot operated clutch assembly and brake system, a steering wheel, and four seats, and it could safely do 18 miles per hour. A hundred years and tens of thousands of research hours later, we drive cars with a metal chassis with an internal combustion, gasoline-powered engine, four wheels with rubber tyres, a foot operated clutch assembly and brake system, a steering wheel, four seats—and the average speed in London in 2001 was 17.5 miles per hour! That's not a hell of a lot of return for the money. Ford evidently doesn't have much to teach us about change. The fact that they are still manufacturing cars is not proof that it takes very large companies to make cars in great quantities—making for an almost impregnable entry barrier.

Fifty years after the development of the jet engine, planes are also little changed. They've grown bigger, wider and can carry more people. But those are incremental, largely cosmetic changes.

Taken together, this lack of real change has come to mean that in travel, whether driving or flying—time and technology have not combined to make things much better. The safety and design have of course accompanied the times and the new volume of cars and flights, but nothing of any significance has changed in the basic assumptions of the final product.

At the same, moving around in cars or aeroplanes becomes less and less efficient all the time. Not only has there been no great change, but also both forms of transport have deteriorated as more people clamour to use them. The same is true for telephones, which took over hundred years to become mobile, or photographic film, which also required an entire century to change.

The only explanation for this is anthropological. Once established in calcified organisations, humans do two things: sabotage changes that might render people dispensable, and ensure industry-wide emulation. In the 1960s, German auto companies developed plans to scrap the entire combustion engine for an electrical design (The same existed in the 1970s in Japan, and in the 1980s in France.). So for 40 years, we might have been free of the wasteful and ludicrous dependence on fossil fuels. Why didn't it go anywhere? Because auto executives understood pistons and carburettors, and would be loath to cannibalise their expertise, along with most of their factories.

(i) According to the passage, which of the following statements is true?

(a) Executives of automobile companies are inefficient and ludicrous.

(b) The speed at which an automobile is driven in a city has not changed much in a century.

(c) Anthropological factors have fostered innovation in automobiles by promoting use of new technologies.

(d) Further innovation in jet engines has been more than incremental.

(ii) Which of the following views does the author fully support in the passage?

(a) Nothing is as permanent as change.

(b) Change is always rapid.

(c) More money spent on innovation leads to more rapid change.

(d) Over decades, structural change has been incremental.

(iii) Which of the following best describes one of the main ideas discussed in the passage?

(a) Rapid change is usually welcomed in the society.

(b) Industry is not as innovative as it is made out to be.

(c) We should have less change than what we have now.

(d) Competition spurs companies into radical innovation.

**83.** The country has been able to manage one of the most deficient monsoons with concerted efforts of the State Governments and the Centre. Several incentives and concessions allowed to farmers by the States and the Central Government resulted in minimising the loss in kharif production and maximising rabi production. Part of the loss in kharif production is expected to be made up in the rabi season. The sector, however, faces various challenges which need to be addressed sooner than later.

Although the yield per hectare of foodgrains has shown some improvement in recent years it is not significant enough to cater to the needs of the rising population particularly when income levels are also rising. Since farm productivity is not showing desirable growth there is urgent need to focus on research as well as better agricultural practices to ensure that productivity levels are increased in the shortest time possible. Special attention may be required for States with relatively low productivity.

Production and productivity in pulses and oilseeds are of growing concern. A sizeable proportion of these items is met through imports. The scope for import of pulses is limited due to the limited number of countries producing it. Due to this supply–demand gap domestic prices fluctuate with availability and prices in the international market apart from the impact of domestic production trends.

Consistent decline in the share of private sector investment in the agriculture sector is a matter of concern. This trend needs to be reversed through creation of a favourable policy environment and availability of credit at reasonable rates on time for the private sector to invest in agriculture.

There has been substantial increase in Minimum Support Services (MSPs) of various crops over the last few years. This is considered necessary to incentivise the farmers to increase production and productivity. At the same time, the MSP signals the floor price for the produce which, in turn, has the potential of increasing the prices. Addressing the welfare of agricultural producers and consumers simultaneously poses a challenge. Further, inability of a large number of small and marginal farmers to directly access the agri-market puts a question mark on increases in MSP actually benefiting such farmers.

Record procurement of rice and wheat in the last few years has helped to build up the buffer stock and strategic reserve of wheat and rice. There is, however, a huge cost involved in the process, which is met through budgetary sources in the form of food subsidy. This puts a lot of stress on the fiscal system. The issue of efficient food stocks management and offloading of stocks in time needs urgent attention.

Studies indicate adverse impact of climate change on agriculture. Crop improvement and research to develop drought-resistant, high-yielding varieties of seeds assumes importance with a view to combating adverse impact of drought on food production and to ensure food security.

To sum up, we need to address the challenges of the agriculture sector through comprehensive and coordinated efforts. Renewed attention needs to be paid to improving farm production and productivity, better utilisation of agricultural inputs, proper marketing infrastructure and support, stepping up investment in agriculture with due emphasis on environmental concerns and efficient food management.

(i) What is the negative fallout of increase in Minimum support Prices (MSPs)?

(a) It gives an incentive to the farmer to cultivate the crop.

(b) It has the potential of increasing the market price of the crop and contributing to inflation.

(c) It increases the overall supply of the crop in the market.

(d) All of the above.

(ii) Which of the following challenges have been highlighted in the passage above?

1. Fall in agricultural productivity
2. Deficiency in irrigation infrastructure
3. Adverse impact of climate change
4. Need for building/improving storage and distribution network
5. Need for balancing the increase in the MSPs with possible increase in inflation

(a) 1, 2, 3 (b) 1, 3, 4

(c) 1, 3, 5 (d) 2, 3, 5

(iii) Production and productivity of pulses and oilseeds is stated to be of growing concern. The reason for this concern is

(a) Pulses and oilseeds are a very important ingredient of the national food habits.

(b) They have very high nutritional and calorific value and hence very important for rural nutrition.

(c) Their productivity has been consistently falling and research has not been able to arrest the fall.

(d) Pulses and oilseeds are imported to meet the demand. Domestic prices and production often fluctuate due to fluctuation in availability and price in international market.

**84.** The e-Choupal, the first private sector initiative by the private sector in agricultural marketing, is a business platform consisting of a set of organisational subsystems and interfaces connecting farmers to global markets. This common structure can be leveraged to procure/provide a host of products and services for the farmer as a producer as well as a consumer. The e-Choupal business platform consists of three layers, each at different levels of geographic aggregation. Each of the three layers is characterised by three key elements:

(a) The infrastructure (physical or organisational) through which transactions take place

(b) The entity (person or organisation) orchestrating the transactions

(c) The geographical coverage of the layer

The first layer consists of the village-level kiosks with internet access (or e-Choupal), managed by an ITC-trained local farmer (called a Sanchalak) and within walking distance (1–5 kilometres) of each target farmer. The relatively sparse population density in rural India justified the location of one e-Choupal per cluster of five villages. The second layer consists of a bricks-and-mortar infrastructure (called hubs) managed by the traditional intermediary who has local knowledge/skills (called a Samyojak in his new role) and within tractor-able distance (25–30 kilometres) of the target farmer. The ITC chose to operate the platform on the following three business principles:

(a) Free information and knowledge, which ensures wider participation by the farmer.
(b) Freedom of choice in transactions (farmers, after accessing information at the e-Choupal, are free to transact their own way).
(c) Transaction-based income stream for the Sanchalak by tying his revenue stream to the transaction (on a commission basis).

(i) Which amongst the following can be considered as key elements of the e-Choupal?
   1. Village level kiosks with internet access.
   2. Sanchalaks or trained farmers.
   3. Samyojaks as intermediaries having local knowledge or skills.
   4. The network connectivity providing access to information.

   (a) 1 and 2 (b) 1, 2, 3
   (c) 1, 2, 3, 4 (d) None of the above

(ii) Which one is **not** a benefit which the farmer gets from the e-Choupal?
   (a) Access to the information about price of agricultural produce.
   (b) Access to agricultural credit.
   (c) Access to markets for sale of agricultural produce.
   (d) None of the above.

(iii) The e-Choupal can provide/procure a host of products and services in its capacity as
   (a) A producer
   (b) A consumer
   (c) None the above
   (d) Both (a) and (b)

**85.** Climate change has emerged as a highly debated and controversial subject in recent times. Climate change by affecting the livelihood and health of the people is intricately connected to human development and poverty issues. The United Nations Framework Convention on Climate Change (UNFCCC) 1992 and its Kyoto Protocol 1997 have laid down the existing international regime for addressing climate change. The UNFCCC requires the industrialised countries listed in Annex I of the Convention to reduce their emissions from 1990 levels. The Kyoto Protocol mandates Annex I countries to reduce their emissions by 5.6 per cent over 1990 levels by 2012. The UNFCCC also recognises that the extent to which developing country parties will take action to mitigate emissions will depend on the effective implementation by developed country parties of their commitments relating to provision of financial resources and transfer of technology. Despite the commitments made by developed countries as inscribed in the UNFCCC and its Kyoto Protocol, emissions in most of the Annex I countries, except a few European countries, have been rising since 1990. In recognition of the fact that climate change is irreversible and that the developing countries are likely to be impacted most if it is not urgently addressed, the 13th Conference of Parties (CoP) to the UNFCCC held at Bali in December 2007 adopted the Bali Action Plan (BAP) to enhance the implementation of the Convention. The BAP expected the developed countries (including the Kyoto Protocol Parties and the US) to undertake commitments to reduce emissions and encouraged the developing countries to take nationally appropriate mitigation actions as supported and enabled in terms of finance and technology provided by the developed countries. The BAP had mandated the parties to reach an agreed outcome on all its elements at the CoP 15 at Copenhagen in December 2009.

India's total $CO_2$ emissions are about 4 per cent of total global $CO_2$ emissions. India's per capita emissions, even with 8–9 per cent GDP growth every year for the next decade or two, are likely to be well below developed country averages. Its energy intensity of production has been falling with improvements in energy efficiency, autonomous technological changes and economical use of energy. Its climate modelling studies show that its per capita emissions will be around 2–2.5 tonnes of carbon dioxide equivalent by 2020 and around 3–3.5 tonnes of carbon dioxide equivalent by 2030, as compared to around 1–1.2 tonnes presently. India has conveyed that its per capita emission levels will never exceed the average levels of developed countries.

(i) Which one of the following is **not** one of the objectives of the Bali Action plan (BAP)?

(a) The BAP expects the developed countries to undertake commitments to reduce emissions.

(b) It expects developed countries to provide financial and technological assistance to developing countries.

(c) It expects developing countries to take nationally appropriate binding emission cuts.

(d) None of the above.

(ii) Consider the following statements about India?

1. India's $CO_2$ emissions are about 4% of the global $CO_2$.
2. In the next two decades with growth of 8–9% in GDP, India $CO_2$ emissions are likely to catch up with the $CO_2$ emission average of the developed countries.
3. In the present international framework for mitigating global warming, India is expected to take specific binding emission cuts as compared to the emission level in 1990.
4. Energy intensity of production has been falling in India.

(a) 1 and 2 (b) 2 and 3

(c) 1 and 4 (d) 3 and 4

(iii) Which one of the following is true about Kyoto protocol?

(a) It mandates developing countries to take emission cuts irrespective of the cuts by developed nations.

(b) It mandates developed countries to reduce their emissions by specific level.

(c) It links the aid to developing countries to their emission cut efforts.

(d) All of the above.

**86.** The fact that North Indian classical music emanates from, and evolved through, oral culture, means that this music has a significantly different aesthetic, and that this aesthetic, has a different politics, from that of Western classical music. A piece of music in the Western tradition, at least in its most characteristic and popular conception, originates in its composer, and the connection between the two, between composer and the piece of music, is relatively unambiguous precisely because the composer writes down, in notation, his composition, as a poet might write down and publish his poem. However, for the notion of property remains at the heart of the Western conception of 'genius', which derives from the Latin *gignere* or 'to beget'. The genius in Western classical music is, then, the originator, begetter and owner of his work—the printed, notated sheet testifying to his authority over his product and his power, not only of expression or imagination, but of origination. The conductor is a custodian and guardian of this property. Is it an accident that Mandelstam, in his notebooks, compares–celebratorily-the conductor's baton to a policeman's saying all the music of the orchestra lies mute within it, waiting for its first movement to release it into the auditorium. The raga-transmitted through oral means is, in a sense, no one's property; it is not easy to pin down its source, or to know exactly where its provenance or origin lies. Unlike the Western classical tradition, where the composer begets his piece, notates it and stamps it with his ownership and remains, in effect, larger than, or the father of, his work, in the North Indian classical tradition, the raga—unconfined to a single incarnation, composer or performer remains necessarily greater than the artiste who invokes it.

This leads to a very different politics of interpretation and valuation, to an aesthetic that privileges the evanescent moment of performance and invocation over the controlling authority of genius and the permanent record. It is a tradition, thus, that would appear to value the performer, as medium, more highly than the composer who presumes to originate what, effectively, could not be originated in a single person, because the raga is the inheritance of a culture.

(i) The author's contention that the notion of property lies at the western conception of genius is best indicated by which one of the following?
   (a) The creative output of a genius is invariably written down and recorded.
   (b) The link between the creator and his output is unambiguous.
   (c) The word 'genius' is derived from a Latin word, which means 'to beget'.
   (d) The music composer notates his music and thus becomes the 'father' of a particular piece of music.

(ii) According to the passage, in the North Indian classical tradition, the raga remains greater than the artiste who invokes it. This implies an aesthetic, which
   (a) Emphasises performance and invocation over the authority of genius and permanent record.
   (b) Makes the music no one's property.
   (c) Values the composer more highly than the performer.
   (d) Supports oral transmission of traditional music.

(iii) From the author's explanation of the notion that in the Western tradition, music originates in its composer, which one of the following **cannot** be inferred?
   (a) It is easy to transfer a piece of Western classical music to a distant place.
   (b) The conductor in the Western tradition, as a custodian, can modify the music, since it 'lies mute' in his baton.
   (c) The authority of the Western classical music composer over his music product is unambiguous.
   (d) The power of the Western classical music composer extends to the expression of his music.

**87.** The Group of Twenty (G-20) was established in 1999 to bring together Finance Ministers and Central Bank Governors of systemically important industrialised and developing economies to discuss key issues relating to the global economy and financial stability. By contributing to the strengthening of the international financial architecture and providing opportunities for dialogue on national policies, international co-operation, and international financial institutions, the G-20 helps to support growth, financial stability and development across the globe.

Since its inception, the G-20 has held annual Finance Ministers and Central Bank Governors' meetings and discussed measures to promote financial stability in the world and achieve sustainable economic growth and development.

In the wake of the global financial and economic crisis in 2008, the G-20 was elevated to a Leaders' Summit. It was designated as a premier forum for international economic cooperation in 2009, effectively replacing the G-8 as a forum for steering the global issues. The move was considered a milestone in reforming global governance, making it more inclusive since this forum comprises both emerging as well as industrialised economies. Several landmark reforms of international financial institutions were initiated at the behest of the G-20, which heightened the expectation for bringing about fundamental changes in the functioning of the global institutions and in the global governance structure. India as a member of the G-20 has been actively engaged in global economic governance and in shaping the world order.

The most concerted response to the global economic crisis came from the platform of the G-20 countries. G-20 Leaders' Summits have set the agenda rolling for both short and medium term actions to meet the crisis.

(i) In the year 2008, G-20 was elevated to a leaders' Summit. Which of the following best describes the reason for such a move?

(a) It is essential to make important institutions of the world more democratic.

(b) It was a part of the inceptive policy of the G-20 to make it more broad based.

(c) It was essential in the wake of the economic crisis to make it a more inclusive and premier forum for economic co-operation so as to take effective decisions to combat the crisis.

(d) All of the above.

(ii) What was the initial objective of establishing the Group of Twenty (G-20)?

1. To provide a platform for discussion of economic issues, to the industrialised and developing economies.
2. To help achieve regional economic cooperation to support growth and bring financial stability.
3. To enable the Finance Ministers and Central Bank Governors of important developing and industrialised countries to discuss critical issues pertaining to global economy development and stability.
4. To eventually replace the current economic forums like G-8 and WTO as a forum for deciding upon important emerging world economic issues.
5. To provide an opportunity for discussion on, international economic policies, national policies financial stability and international institutions.

(a) 1, 2, 3 (b) 1, 3, 5

(c) 2, 3, 5 (d) 1, 4, 5

(iii) Which of the following fact mentioned in the passage best highlights the great significance being attached to the G-20 by the world leaders in current politico-economic situation of the world?

(a) It is to effectively replace G-8.

(b) India as a member of G-20 has been actively engaged in global economic governance.

(c) Reforms of international financial institutions have been initiated at the behest of G-20.

(d) The most concerted response to global economic crisis came from the platform of the G-20 countries.

(iv) Examine whether the following inferences can be drawn on the basis of what is stated in the passage.

1. The elevation of G-20 to a leaders' summit in 2008 was a knee-jerk reaction to the global economic crisis.
2. Expectation of people from G-20 has been duly fulfilled.

(a) Only Conclusion 1 can be drawn.

(b) Only Conclusion 2 can be drawn.

(c) Both the Conclusions 1 and 2 can be drawn.

(d) Neither Conclusion 1 nor 2 can be drawn.

**88.** The ancient view of medicine was essentially a holistic one, i.e., an intimate interaction of body, mind, environment and spirit. The human being and the whole of society and nature for that matter, was viewed as being intelligent, conscious and ordered. Nature had laws and in order to stay well or to treat illness, one had to work with those laws. The physical world was believed to be underpinned by the mental world—by the spiritual. As these 'worlds,' move 'inwards' they become more subtle and difficult to measure. A lot of work has nevertheless gone into developing measurement tools for physical and psychological parameters and through their combination, we are able to test if such relationships exist. This field of study is called mind–body medicine, probably the most comprehensive and reliable scientific examination of holism.

Mind–body medicine focuses on the interactions between mind and body and the powerful ways in which emotional, mental, social and spiritual factors can directly affect health. It regards as fundamental, an approach which respects and enhances each person's capacity for self-knowledge, self-care and emphasises techniques, which are grounded in this approach. These techniques include self-awareness, relaxation, meditation, exercise, diet, biofeedback, visual imagery, self-hypnosis and group support. It explores and integrates the healing practices of other cultures, such as acupuncture and accupressure, meditation and yoga, as well as alternative Western approaches, including herbalism, massages, muscu-loskeletal manipulation and prayer. It views illness as an opportunity for personal growth and transformation and health care providers as catalysts and guides in this process. Consciousness, being primary, illuminates thoughts, desires and emotions in the mind and these in turn affect behaviour and physiology. Consciousness gives life to mind and body.

Over recent times, there has been an explosion of knowledge in the physical sciences. In medicine, the emphasis has tended to focus on the human body, but it has often ignored a holistic perspective, that is the body's interaction with mind, emotions, social environment and spirit. This more mechanistic and materialistic way of viewing the human being and illness has often times been at the expense of more traditional holistic models, which placed great emphasis on these more subtle elements of human experience. Mind–body medicine and its kindred fields of study, such as psycho-neuro-immunology and psycho-oncology, are opening our awareness and require more communication and cooperation across the scientific community than ever before. Thus, far we can say that the potential of mind–body medicine for promoting health, both physically and psychologically, seems to be great. Its costs are relatively low and the 'side-effects' seem to be generally low. It may well be that the next major breakthrough in clinical medicine will involve the re-integration of contemporary physical sciences with traditional wisdom.

(i) It can be inferred from the given passage, that

(a) Modern medicine totally rejects the need of harmonising the human body interaction with the human mind.

(b) Modern medicine does not accept the traditional holistic models.

(c) Modern medicine is more mechanistic and materialistic in its approach than that of the traditional holistic models.

(d) Modern medicine is superior to traditional holistic models.

(ii) According to the passage, mind–body medicine is the most comprehensive and scientific examination of holism because

1. It developed measurement tools for physical and psychological parameters.
2. It tests the relationships between physical and psychological parameters.
3. In it, the physical world, the mental world and the spiritual world move inwards to become one.

(a) Only 3 is correct.

(b) Only 1 and 2 are correct.

(c) 1, 2 and 3 are correct.

(d) Only 1 and 3 are correct.

(iii) According to the passage, consciousness does not affect

1. Thoughts, desires and emotions
2. Behaviour and physiology
3. Mind and body

(a) 2 and 3 only (b) 3 only
(c) 1 and 2 only (d) None of these

**89.** But the lesson of faithfulness had also an untoward effect. 'If I should be pledged to be faithful to my wife, she also should be pledged to be faithful to me.' I said to myself. The thought made me a jealous husband. Her duty was easily converted into my right to exact faithfulness from her, and if it had to be exacted. I should be watchfully tenacious of the right. I had absolutely no reason to suspect my wife's fidelity, but jealousy does not wait for reasons. I must need be forever on the lookout regarding her movements, and therefore she could not go anywhere without my permission. This sowed the seeds of a bitter quarrel between us. The restraint was virtually a sort of imprisonment. And Kasturbai was not the girl to brook any such thing. She made it a point to go out whenever and wherever she liked. More restraint on my part resulted in more liberty being taken by her, and in my getting more and more cross.

(i) What was the untoward effect of the lesson of faithfulness had on the author?

(a) He became suspicious of his wife.
(b) He expected faithfulness from his wife as a matter of right.
(c) He started to follow his wife's movements.
(d) All of the above.

(ii) What is the author trying to convey in the passage?

(1) How misconceptions arise between a husband and a wife.
(2) His futility to exact faithfulness from his wife.
(3) The reason for bitterness in his marriage.

(a) 1, 2, 3 (b) 2, 3
(c) 2 only (d) 3 only

(iii) Why did the author forbid his wife from going anywhere without his permission?

(a) He was jealous.
(b) He suspected her fidelity.
(c) His superior male ago compelled such behaviour.
(d) All of the above

**90.** That economics is untrue, which ignores or disregards moral values. The extension of the law of non-violence in the domain of economics means nothing less than the introduction of moral values as a factor to be considered in regulating international commerce.

According to me, the economic constitution of India and for that matter of the world should be such that no one under it should suffer from want of food and clothing. In other words, everybody should be able to get sufficient work to enable him to make the two ends meet. And this ideal can be universally realised only if the means of production of the elementary necessaries of life remain in the control of the masses. These should be freely available to all as God's air and water are or ought to be; they should not be made a vehicle of traffic for the exploitation of others. Their monopolisation by any country, nation or group of persons would be unjust. The neglect of this simple principle is the cause of the destitution that we witness today not only in this unhappy land but in other parts of the world too.

My ideal is equal distribution, but so far as I can see, it is not to be realised. I, therefore, work for equitable distribution.

Love and exclusive possession can never go together. Theoretically, when there is perfect love, there must be perfect non-possession. The body is our last possession. So a man can only exercise perfect love and be completely dispossessed, if he is prepared to embrace death and renounce his body for the sake of human service.

But that is true in theory only. In actual life, we can hardly exercise perfect love, for the body as a possession will always remain with us. Man will ever remain imperfect and it will always be his part to try to be perfect. So that perfection in love or non-possession will remain an unattainable ideal as long as we are alive, but towards which we must ceaselessly strive.

(i) As per the passage which of the following should **not** be one of the objectives of the economic constitution of India and the world?
   (a) There should be availability of food and clothing for everybody.
   (b) There should be availability of work for everybody.
   (c) There should be availability of education for everybody.
   (d) None of the above.

(ii) As per the author, the introduction of non-violence in the domain of economics means the same as
   (a) Introduction of non-violence in the freedom struggle.
   (b) Introduction of ethics in social life.
   (c) Introduction of moral values in international commerce.
   (d) All of the above.

(iii) Which of the following assertions have been made by the author in the passage?
   1. Economics must incorporate moral values.
   2. Fulfillment of food, clothing and employment must be the objective of the economic constitution.
   3. One must work for realisation of ideal of equal distribution of wealth.
   4. It is not necessary for means of production to be in control of masses for achieving the objectives of the economic constitution.
   5. Love and exclusive possession can never go together.

   (a) 1, 2, 3 (b) 2, 3, 4
   (c) 2, 4, 5 (d) 1, 2, 5

(iv) Which of the following is **not** the reason because of which the author wants the means of production to be in control of masses?
   (a) The resources should be freely available to all.
   (b) Control of means of production leads to monopoly.
   (c) Control of means of production is necessary for fulfillment of basic necessities of life.
   (d) None of these.

(v) Which of the following best explains the statement that love and exclusive possession can never go together?
   (a) There is nothing, which belongs exclusively to anybody.
   (b) Love said to be perfect when there is complete detachment and perfect non-possession.
   (c) Nothing is permanent. Even human body is transient. Therefore, there cannot be exclusive possession.
   (d) All of the above.

**91.** Pioneering work by agriculture scientists and the efforts of farmers had helped achieve a breakthrough in the agriculture sector in the 1960s, popularly known as the 'Green Revolution'. High agricultural production and productivity achieved in subsequent years has been the main reason for attaining food security to a large extent. The country has not witnessed any big technological breakthrough in agriculture since then. The food safety net for each and every of the over a billion citizens—a number that is growing—requires enhanced agricultural production and productivity in the form of a Second Green Revolution. Further, special attention is required for achieving higher production and productivity levels in pulses, oilseeds, fruits, and vegetables, which had remained untouched in the First Green Revolution but are essential for nutritional security. In this regard, achieving high production of poultry, meat and fisheries is also essential. The relatively weak supply responses to price hikes in agricultural commodities, especially food articles, in the recent past brings back into focus the central question of efficient supply chain management and need for sustained levels of growth in agriculture and allied sectors. The choice before the nation is clear—to invest more in agriculture and allied sectors with the right strategies, policies and interventions. This is also a 'necessary' condition for 'inclusive growth' and for ensuring that the benefits of growth reach a larger number of people.

The growth of agriculture and allied sectors is still a critical factor in the overall performance of the Indian economy. As per the 2010–11 advance estimates released by the Central Statistics Office (CSO) on 07.02.2011, the agriculture and allied sector accounted for 14.2 per cent of the gross domestic product (GDP), at constant 2004–05 prices. However, its share in GDP has thus declined rapidly in the recent past. This is explained by the fact that whereas overall GDP has grown by an average of 8.62 per cent during 2004–05 to 2010–11, agricultural sector GDP has increased by only 3.46 per cent during the same period. The role of the agriculture sector, however, remains critical as it accounts for about 58 per cent of employment in the country (as per 2001 census). Moreover, this sector is a supplier of food, fodder and raw materials for a vast segment of industry. Hence, the growth of Indian agriculture can be considered a necessary condition for 'inclusive growth'. More recently, the rural sector (including agriculture) is being seen as a potential source of domestic demand, a recognition that is even shaping the marketing strategies of entrepreneurs wishing to widen the demand for goods and services.

(i) As per the passage what would be the objective of the second green revolution?
   (a) Improving agricultural production and productivity of crops.
   (b) Enhancing the production and productivity of fruits, vegetables, oilseeds.
   (c) Both (a) and (b).
   (d) Neither (a) nor (b).

(ii) Growth in agricultural sector is important for inclusive growth of the economy. Which of the following best explains this?
   (a) Agricultural output is major contributor of the GDP and has a profound effect on the economy.
   (b) Agriculture accounts for nearly 58% of employment in the country.
   (c) Agriculture as a part of rural sector is seen as a potential source of domestic demand.
   (d) All of the above.

(iii) What suggestions are offered in the passage regarding bringing sustained levels of growth in agricultural sector?
   (a) To increase investment in agricultural and allied sector with right policies and strategies
   (b) To reduce unremunerative agricultural subsidies and channelise them in creating efficient supply chain management
   (c) To concentrate more on those areas of agriculture, which cater to industrial sector by supplying input raw material
   (d) All of the above.

(iv) Examine whether the following conclusions can be drawn from the passage.
   1. Despite the rise in prices of agricultural commodities the production/productivity of agricultural commodities has not shown substantial improvement.
   2. Share of agriculture in GDP is low and hence agricultural sectors failure does not dent the economy.
   (a) Only Conclusion 1 can be drawn.
   (b) Only Conclusion 2 can be drawn.
   (c) Both Conclusions 1 and 2 can be drawn.
   (d) Neither Conclusion 1 nor 2 can be drawn.

**92.** The role of training for civil servants was thoroughly analysed for the first time by the Assheton Committee in its report of 1944, in the UK. On the objectives of training, it stated, "In any large-scale organisation, efficiency depends on two elements, the technical efficiency of the individual to do the particular work allotted to him, and the less tangible efficiency of the organisation as a corporate body, derived from the collective spirit and outlook of the individuals of which the body is composed. Training must have regard to both elements." The five objectives of training, according to the report are:

(1) To produce a civil servant who can transact his business with precision and clarity.

(2) To attune the civil servant to the tasks he is called upon to perform in a changing world. "The civil service must continuously and boldly adjust its outlook and its methods to the new needs of new times."

(3) To make the civil servant community conscious. "There is a need to develop resistance to the danger of the civil servants becoming mechanised by the machine; whilst we must aim at the highest possible standard of efficiency, our purpose is not to produce a robot like, mechanically perfect civil service."

(4) To develop the capacity of the civil servants for higher work and greater responsibilities.

(5) To improve the morale of the civil servants.

The following can be added to the original list of the Assheton Committee Report:

(6) To make up for the deficiencies of the new entrants of the civil service.

(7) To broaden the vision and outlook of the civil servants.

(8) To promote integrity in the civil servants.

(9) To promote *espirit de corps* in the employees.

(10) To inculcate the attitude that a civil servant is not a master but a public servant.

(i) Amongst the ten desirable objective of training of a civil servant, which five amongst the following do you consider most important in today's context?

(a) (1), (2), (7), (8), (10)
(b) (1), (2), (3), (4), (5)
(c) (1), (3), (4), (8), (9)
(d) (1), (5), (7), (8), (10)

(ii) Consider the following objectives, which are proposed to be added to the aforesaid.

(1) To be adept in use of computer and information technology.

(2) To develop empathy and understanding of the problems of our nation and its people.

(3) To develop the ability to take decisions with alacrity, keeping in mind the rules and regulations and the interest of people.

(4) To develop good managerial abilities to manage subordinates superiors and political bosses.

(5) To have ability to be an innovator and overcome administrative and functional problems.

Which three amongst the aforesaid objectives would you consider as the most important in today's context?

(a) (1), (2), (3) (b) (2), (3), (4)
(c) (2), (3), (5) (d) (1), (4), (5)

**93.** Long-run institutional development co-evolves with fiscal accountability involving, perhaps requiring, a low and declining dependence on devolved resources and a high and rising share of direct taxes in total taxes. India's second and third tiers of government tend to under-perform relative to these standards. The extent of tax and functional devolution to these tiers is one possible explanation. However, one key finding is that these tiers under-collect direct taxes even relative to the powers that they have. Whether this could lead to a low-equilibrium trap of weak direct tax collection leading to inadequate service delivery provision, back to weak collection and accountability, needs to be actively discussed.

With reference to the passage above which of the following conclusions can be drawn?

(1) Lower level of direct tax collection can be partly attributed to meagre functional devolution.

(2) Fiscal accountability and institutional development generally go hand-in-hand.

(3) There is an imminent threat of low-equilibrium trap of direct tax collection vis-a-vis service delivery provision.

(a) 1, 2 and 3 (b) 1 and 2

(c) 1 and 3 (d) 2 and 3

**94.** Amidst growing concern and increasing awareness on the need for pollution control, the concept of carbon credit came into vogue as part of an international agreement, known popularly as the Kyoto Protocol. Carbon credits are certificates issued to countries that reduce their emission of GHG (green house gases), which leads to global warning. It is estimated that 60–70 per cent of the GHG emission is through fuel combustion in industries like cement, steel, textiles, and fertilizers. Some GHGs like hydro fluorocarbons, methane, and nitrous oxide are released as byproducts of certain industrial process, which adversely affect the ozone layer leading to global warming. Kyoto Protocol is a voluntary treaty signed by 141 countries including the European Union, Japan, and Canada for reducing GHG emission by 5.2 per cent below 1990 levels by 2012. However, the US, which accounts for one-third of the total GHG emission is yet to sign this treaty. The preliminary phase of Kyoto Protocol started in 2007 while the second phase starts from 2008. The penalty for non-compliance in the first phase in 40 Euro per tonne of $CO_2$ equivalent and in the second phase the penalty will be hiked to 100 Euros per tonne of $CO_2$.

The Kyoto Protocol provides for three mechanisms that enable developed countries with quantified emission limitation and reduction commitments to acquire greenhouse gas reduction credits. These mechanisms are Joint Implementation (JI), Clean Development Mechanism (CDM) and International Emission Trading (IET). Under JI, a developed country with a relatively higher cost of domestic greenhouse reduction as a whole sets up a project in another developed country, which has a relatively low cost. Under CDM, a developed country can take up a greenhouse gas reduction project activity in a developing country where the cost of GHG reduction project activities is usually much lower. The developed country would be given credits for meeting its emission reduction target, while the developing country would receive the capital and clean technology to implement the project. Under IET mechanisms, countries can trade in the international carbon credit market. Countries with surplus credits can sell the same to those with quantified emission limitation and reduction commitments under the Kyoto Protocol.

The concept of carbon credit trading seeks to encourage countries to reduce their GHG emissions, as it rewards those countries, which meet their targets and provides financial incentives to the others to do so as quickly as possible. Surplus credits (collected by overshooting the emission reducing target) can be sold in the global market. One credit is equivalent to one tonne of $CO_2$ emission reduced. Carbon Credit (CC) is available for companies engaged in developing renewable energy projects that offset the use of fossil fields. Developed countries have to spend nearly $25 billion which will be ultimately spent by developing countries. In countries like India, GHG emission is much below the target fixed by Kyoto Protocol and so, they are excluded from reduction of GHG emission.

On the contrary, they are entitled to sell surplus credits to developed countries. It is here that trading takes place. Foreign companies, who cannot fulfill the protocol norms, can buy the surplus credit from companies in other countries through trading. Thus, the stage is set for

Credit Emission Reduction (CER) trade to flourish. India is considered as the *largest* beneficiary claiming about 31 per cent of the total world carbon trade through the Clean Development Mechanism (CDM).

(i) Which of the following is **not** correct?

(a) **Joint implementation**—A developed country sets up a project in another developed country, which has a lower cost of green house emission reduction.

(b) **CDM**—A developed country takes up a green house reduction project in another developed country where the cost of GHG reduction is much lower.

(c) **IET**—A mechanism vide, which countries can trade in international carbon credit market.

(d) None of the above.

(ii) In international trade of carbon credits which country would get the Credit for Emission Reduction (CER)?

(a) Country purchasing the carbon credit.

(b) Country selling the carbon credit.

(c) Both of them.

(d) None of them.

(iii) Which of the following fact is not true about the Kyoto Protocol?

(a) It prescribes for reducing GHG emission by 5.2% below the 1990 level.

(b) The above objective is to be met by 2012.

(c) It provides for penalty for non-compliance of the emission reduction target.

(d) It is signed voluntarily by all major greenhouse gas emitting countries.

**95.** The concept of accountability connotes the obligation of the administrators to give a satisfactory account of their performance and the manner in which they have exercised powers conferred on them. Its main aim is to check wrong and arbitrary administrative actions and increase efficiency and effectiveness of administrative process.

The two terms 'administrative accountability' and 'administrative responsibility' are very often used interchangeably. Thus, L.D. White wrote, "Administrative responsibility consists of the sum total of the constitutional, statutory, administrative and judicial rules and precedents and the established practices by means of which public officials may be held accountable for their official actions." However, Pfiffner distinguished between accountability and responsibility. According to him, accountability refers to the formal and specific location of responsibility, whereas responsibility has a highly personal, moral quality and is not necessarily related to formal status or power. He further stated that responsibility refers to the public servant's responsiveness to public will, whereas accountability denotes the specific methods and procedures to enforce the public servant's responsibility. Therefore, responsibility is subjective and works from within, while accountability is objective and works from without.

In a constitutional and democratic system of government, administrative responsibility cannot be allowed to depend solely on the personal responsibility of public servants. It must be provided with a formal legal and procedural basis. This basis of enforcing responsibility is known as accountability.

(i) As per White, what does responsibility mean?

1. Responsibility means responsiveness to public will.

2. Responsibility refers to the methods and procedures by which a public servant can be enforced to do an assigned job.
3. It is a subjective trait, which works from within.
4. It is a set of rules to hold officials accountable.
5. It is a special quality not related to formal status or power.

(a) 1, 2, 5 (b) 1, 3, 5
(c) 2, 3, 5 (d) 2, 3, 4

(ii) "In a constitutional and democratic system of government the administrative responsibility cannot be allowed to depend solely on the personal responsibility of public servant."

Which of the following reasons gives the best justification for the aforesaid statement?

(a) Administrative responsibility can vary from person to person.
(b) It is imperative to have a system of governance where administrative responsibility is definite, explicit and independent of the individual.
(c) A written set of rules is likely to bring better efficiency in the system.
(d) It is important to have an institutional basis for administrative responsibility.

(iii) What is the relationship between accountability and responsibility?

(a) Both are one and the same thing.
(b) Accountability is formal while responsibility is informal.
(c) Responsibility is subjective but accountability is objective.
(d) The basis of enforcing responsibility is known as accountability.

**96.** The persistent patterns in the way nations fight reflects their cultural and historical traditions and deeply rooted attitudes that collectively make up their strategic culture. These patterns provide insights that go beyond what can be learnt just by comparing armaments and divisions. In the Vietnam War, the strategic tradition of the United States called for forcing the enemy to fight a massed battle in an open area, where superior American weapons would prevail. The United States was trying to fight World War II in the jungles of Southeast Asia, against an enemy with no intention of doing so.

Some British military historians describe the Asian way of war as one of indirect attack, avoiding frontal attack meant to overpower an opponent. This traces back to Asian history and geography: the great distances and harsh terrain have often made it difficult to execute the sort of open field clashes allowed by the flat terrain and relatively compact size of Europe. A very different strategic tradition arose in Asia.

The isolation of the US troops in Vietnam was not just a logistical detail, something that could be overcome by, for instance, bringing in reinforcements by helicopter. In a big army reinforcements are readily available. It was Napoleon who realised the extraordinary effects on morale that come from being part of a larger formation. Just the knowledge of it lowers the soldier's fear and increases his aggressiveness. In the jungle and on isolated bases, this feeling was removed. The thick vegetation slowed down the reinforcements and made it difficult to find stranded units. Soldiers felt they were on their own.

More important, by altering the way the war was fought, the Viet Cong stripped the United States of its belief in the inevitability of victory, as it had done to the French before them. Morale was high when these armies first went to Vietnam. Only after many years of debilitating and demoralising fighting did Hanoi launch its decisive attacks, at Dienbienphu in 1954 and against Saigon in 1975. It should be recalled that in the final push to victory, the North Vietnamese abandoned their entire army of twenty divisions to pushing the South Vietnamese into collapse. The final battle, with the enemy's army all in one place, was the one that the United States had desperately wanted to fight in 1965. When it did come out into the open in 1975, Washington had already withdrawn its forces and there was no possibility of re-intervention.

(i) According to the author, the main reason for the US losing the Vietnam War was
   (a) The Vietnamese understood the local terrain better.
   (b) The lack of support for the war from the American people.
   (c) The failure of the US to mobilise its military strength.
   (d) Their inability to fight a war on terms other than those they understood well.

(ii) Which of the following statements does **not** describe the 'Asian' way of war?
   (a) Indirect attacks without frontal attacks.
   (b) The swordsman charging forward to obliterate the enemy once and for all.
   (c) Manipulation of an adversary without his knowledge.
   (d) Subduing an enemy without fighting.

(iii) To the Americans, the approach of the Viet Cong seemed devious because
   (a) The Viet Cong did not fight like men out in the open.
   (b) The Viet Cong allied with America's enemies.
   (c) The Viet Cong used bows and arrows rather than conventional weapons.
   (d) None of these.

**97.** Food prices are cyclical in nature. A sharp increase in food prices during the recent period has been a cause of concern. A significant part of this inflation could be explained by supply-side bottlenecks in some of the essential commodities, precipitated by the delayed and sub-normal southwest monsoon as well as drought-like conditions in some parts of the country. However, inflation in some of the commodities, like wheat and rice, in which there is ample stock available, could have been exacerbated due to inflationary expectations. Making available adequate and timely quantities of these items and at different locations to overcome supply demand mismatches is the real challenge.

India cannot be immune to global price situations especially when a significant proportion of our requirement of edible oils, pulses and sugar (in years of shortages) is met through imports. At the same time, for a large country like India the scope for imports for many commodities is limited. Any decision to import food items raises global prices, which impacts domestic prices as well. Proper and timely assessment of the supply–demand situation and preventive action become the essence of supply-side management. The concentrated pressure on headline inflation arising from high food prices entails the risk of getting transmitted over time to other non-food items through expectations-driven wage price revisions, and thereby manifesting into a generalised inflation.

(i) What is the suggestion given in the passage to prevent inflation in commodities like wheat and rice in which there is ample stock available?
   (a) Improve the distribution system of these items to ensure adequate and timely availability in different location.
   (b) Reduce the minimum support price of these items.
   (c) Make India immune from the global price situation.
   (d) None of the above.

(ii) It is not expected that India will remain immune to global price situation. Which of the reasons mentioned below does **not** explain/justify the above statement?
   (a) A significant portion of our requirements of edible oils pulse and sugars is met through imports.
   (b) Decision to import food items raises global prices, which impact the domestic prices as well.

(c) Imports affect the balance of payment and foreign currency reserves, which lead to inflation.

(d) None of the above.

(iii) What are the factors which have been considered to be responsible for inflation in the passage?

1. Supply side bottlenecks
2. Delayed and sub normal monsoon
3. Low minimum support price for food items
4. Inflationary expcctations
5. Lack of purchasing power in vast section of society
6. Rise in global price of various commodities

(a) 1, 2, 3, 4 (b) 1, 2, 4, 6

(c) 2, 3, 5, 6 (d) 3, 4, 5, 6

**98.** People who look down on abstract art have several major arguments to support their beliefs. They feel that artists turn abstract because they are not capable of the technical drafting skills that appear in a Russell; therefore, such artists create an art form that anyone is capable of and that is less time consuming, and then parade it as artistic progress. Secondly, they feel that the purpose of art is to create something of beauty in an orderly, logical composition. Russell's compositions are balanced and rational; everything sits calmly on the canvas, leaving the viewer satisfied that he has seen all there is to see. The modern abstractionists, on the other hand, seem to compose their pieces irrationally. For example, upon seeing Picasso's Guernica, a friend of mine asked me. "What's the point?" Finally, many people feel that art should feel that art should portray the ideal and real. The exactness of detail in Charlie Russell's work is an example of this. He has been called a great historian because his pieces depict the life style, dress, and events of the times. His subject matter is derived from his own experiences on the trail, reproduced to the smallest detail. I agree in part with many of these arguments, and at one time, even endorsed them. But now, I believe differently. Firstly, I object to the argument that abstract artists are not capable of drafting. Many abstract artists, such as Picasso, are excellent draftsmen. As his work matured, Picasso became more abstract in order to increase the expressive quality of his work. Guernica was meant as a protest against the bombing of that city by the Germans. To express terror and suffering of the victims more vividly, he distorted the figures and presented them in a black and white journalistic manner. If he had used representational images and colour, much of the emotional content would have been lost and the piece would not have caused the demand for justice that it did. Secondly, I do not think that a piece must be logical and aesthetically pleasing to be art. The message it conveys to its viewers is more important. It should reflect the ideals and issues of its time and be true to itself, not just a flowery, glossy surface. For example, through his work, Mondrain was trying to present a system of simplicity, logic and rational order. As a result, his pieces did end up looking like a scrabble board. Miro created powerful, surrealistic images from his dreams and subconscious. These artists were trying to evoke a response from society through an expressionistic manner. Finally, abstract artists and representational artists maintain different ideas about 'reality'. To the abstract artist, reality is what he feels about what his eyes see. This is the reality he interprets on canvas. This can be illustrated by Mondrain's Trees series. You can actually see the progression from the early recognisable, though abstracted, Trees, to his final solution, the grid system.

(i) The author argues that many people look down upon abstract art because they feel that

(a) Modern abstract art does not portray what is ideal and real.

(b) Abstract artists are unskilled in matters of technical drafting.

(c) Abstractionists compose irrationally.

(d) All of the above.

(ii) In the author's opinion, Picasso's Guernica created a strong demand for justice since

(a) It was a protest against the German bombing of Guernica

(b) Picasso's managed to express the emotional content well with his abstract depiction.

(c) It depicts the terror and suffering of the victims in a distorted manner.

(d) It was the mature work of Picasso's, painted when the artist's drafting skills were excellent.

(iii) The author acknowledges that Mondrain's pieces may have ended up looking like a scrabble board because

(a) Many people declared the poor guy played too many scrabble games.

(b) Mondrain believed in the 'grid-work' approach to abstractionist painting.

(c) Mondrain was trying to convert the message of simplicity and rational order.

(d) Mondrain learned from his Trees series to evolve a grid system.

**99.** Studies of the factors governing reading development in young children have achieved remarkable degree of consensus over the past two decades. This consensus concerns the casual role of phonological skills in young children's reading progress. Children, who have good phonological skills, or good 'phonological awareness', become good readers and good spellers. Children with poor phonological skills progress more poorly. In particular, those who have a specific phonological deficit are likely to be classified as dyslexic by the time that they are 9 or 10 years old.

Phonological skills in young children can be measured at a number of different levels. The term phonological awareness is a global one, and refers to a deficit in recognising smaller units of sound within spoken words. Development work has shown that this deficit can be at the level of syllables, of onsets and rimes, or of phonemes. For example, a 4-year old child might have difficulty in recognising that a word like valentine has three syllables, suggesting a lack of syllabic awareness. A 5-year old might have difficulty in recognising that the odd word out in the set of words fan, cat, hat, mat is fan. This task requires an awareness of the sub-syllabic units of the onset and the rime. The onset corresponds to any initial consonants in a syllable, and the rime corresponds to the vowel and to any following consonants. Rimes correspond to rhyme in single-syllable words, and so the rime in fan differs from the rime in cat, hat and mat. In longer words, rime and rhyme may differ. The onsets in val: en: tine are/v/and/t/, and the rimes correspond to the spelling patterns 'al', 'en', and 'ine'.

A 6-year-old might have difficulty in recognising that plea and pray begin with the same initial sound. This is phonemic judgment. Although the initial phoneme/P/ is shared between the two words, in plea it part of the onset 'pl', and in pray it is part of the onset 'pr'. Until children can segment the onset (or the rime), such phonemic judgments are difficult for them to make. In fact, a recent survey of different developmental studies has shown that the different levels of phonological awareness appear to emerge sequentially. The awareness of syllables, onsets and rimes appears to emerge at around the ages of 3 and 4, long before most children go to school. The awareness of phonemes, on the other hand, usually emerges at around the age of 5 or 6, when children have been taught to read for about a year. An awareness of onsets and rimes thus appears to be precursor of reading, whereas an awareness of phonemes at every serial position in a word, only appears to develop as reading is taught. The onset-rime and phonemic levels of phonological structure, however, are not distinct. Many onsets in English are single phonemes, and so are some rimes (e.g., sea, go, zoo).

(i) From the following statements, pick out the true statement according to the passage:

(a) A mono-syllabic word can have only one onset.
(b) A mono-syllabic word can have only one rhyme but more than one rime.
(c) A mono-syllabic word can have only one phoneme.
(d) All of the above.

(ii) A phonological deficit in which of the following is likely to be classified as dyslexia?
(a) Phonemic judgment
(b) Onset judgment
(c) Rime judgment
(d) Any one or more of the above

(iii) The single-syllable words Rhyme and Rime are constituted by the exact same set of

1. Rime(s) 2. Onset(s)
3. Rhyme(s) 4. Phonemes(s)

(a) 1, 2 (b) 1, 3
(c) 1, 2, 3 (d) 2, 3, 4

**100.** The history of all hitherto existing society is the history of class struggles. Freeman and slave, patrician and plebeian's lord and serf, guild-master and journeyman, in a word, oppressor and oppressed, stood in constant opposition to one another, carried on an uninterrupted, hidden, now open fight, a fight that each time ended, either in a revolutionary reconstitution of society at large, or in the common ruin of the contending classes.

In the earlier epochs of history, we find almost everywhere a complicated arrangement of society into various orders, a manifold gradation of social rank. In ancient Rome, there were patricians, knights, plebeians, slaves; in the Middle Ages, feudal lords, vassals, guild-masters, journeymen, apprentices, serfs; in almost all of these classes, again, subordinate gradations.

The modern bourgeois society that has sprouted from the ruins of feudal society has not done away with class antagonisms. It has but established new classes, new conditions of oppression, new forms of struggle in place of the old ones.

Our epoch, the epoch of the bourgeoisie, possesses, however, this distinct feature: it has simplified class antagonisms. Society as a whole is more and more splitting up into two great hostile camps, into two great classes directly facing each other—bourgeoisie and proletariat.

From the serfs of the Middle Ages sprang the chartered burghers of the earliest towns. From these burgesses the first elements of the bourgeoisie were developed.

The discovery of America, the rounding of the Cape, opened up fresh ground for the rising bourgeoisie. The East-Indian and Chinese markets, the colonisation of America, trade with the colonies, the increase in the means of exchange and in commodities generally, gave to commerce, to navigation, to industry, an impulse never before known, and thereby, to the revolutionary element in the tottering feudal society, a rapid development.

The feudal system of industry in which industrial production was monopolised by closed guilds, now no longer suffices for the growing wants of the new markets. The manufacturing system took its place. The guild-masters were pushed aside by the manufacturing middle class; division of labour between the different corporate guilds vanished in the face of division of labour in each single workshop.

Meantime, the markets kept ever growing, the demand ever rising. Even manufacturers no longer sufficed. Thereupon, steam and machinery revolutionised industrial production. The place of manufacture was taken by the giant, 'Modern Industry; the place of the industrial middle class by industrial millionaires, the leaders of the whole industrial armies, the modern bourgeois.

(i) What does 'revolutionary reconstitution of the society' imply?

(a) Change in the ruling class by means of force with over throw of the monarch and establishment of a new people's government.

(b) Change in the administrative order by means of force, with replacement of the oppressive administration with a more pro-people administration.

(c) Change in the social order with radical shift in the distribution of power amidst the two conflicting classes.

(d) None of the above.

(ii) Examine whether the following assumptions are correct in terms of what is stated in the passage.

1. Human society has always been fragmented into different classes with conflicting interests.
2. The growth of manufacturing and industry has further aggravated the class struggle.

(a) Only Assumption 1 is correct.

(b) Only Assumption 2 is correct.

(c) Both Assumptions 1 and 2 are correct.

(d) Neither Assumption 1 nor 2 is correct.

(iii) What does the author imply by "the epoch of bourgeoisie has further simplified the class antagonism"?

(a) The epoch has reduced the hostility between the classes.

(b) It has fragmented the society into two large groups and crystallised the hostility between them.

(c) The hostility between the various classes has no more remained a complex web but has become simpler and clearly defined.

(d) None of the above.

(iv) Which of the following conclusions can be drawn from the passage?

1. Colonisation assisted in industrialisation and growth of modern bourgeoisie.
2. Industrialisation perpetuated the old feudalistic set up of the society.
3. Industrialisation further widened the class struggle.

(a) 2, 1, 3 (b) 1, 3

(c) 2, 3 (d) 1, 2

***Courtesy:*** The Economic Survey of India; some of these passages have been reproduced with permission from the Department of Economic Affairs.

## Answers to Exercise Set D

| S.No. | (i) | (ii) | (iii) | (iv) | (v) |
|---|---|---|---|---|---|
| 1. | (b) | (c) | (d) | (b) | |
| 2. | (a) | (d) | (c) | | |
| 3. | (c) | | | | |
| 4. | (c) | (c) | (d) | (c) | |
| 5. | (c) | (c) | (c) | | |
| 6. | (d) | | | | |
| 7. | (a) | (b) | (a) | | |
| 8. | (c) | (c) | (b) | | |
| 9. | (c) | (a) | (d) | (d) | (c) |
| 10. | (b) | (b) | (d) | | |
| 11. | (d) | | | | |
| 12. | (b) | (a) | (b) | (a) | |
| 13. | (d) | (b) | (a) | | |
| 14. | (b) | (c) | (d) | (c) | (b) |
| 15. | (c) | (d) | (b) | (a) | |
| 16. | (c) | | | | |
| 17. | (d) | (d) | (b) | | |
| 18. | (d) | | | | |
| 19. | (a) | (c) | (c) | (a) | |
| 20. | (a) | (b) | (c) | | |
| 21. | (c) | (d) | (b) | | |
| 22. | (c) | | | | |
| 23. | (b) | (a) | (b) | | |
| 24. | (a) | | | | |
| 25. | (d) | (c) | (a) | | |
| 26. | (c) | (a) | (c) | | |
| 27. | (c) | (d) | (a) | (b) | |
| 28. | (a) | (d) | (c) | | |
| 29. | (b) | (c) | (c) | | |
| 30. | (b) | (a) | (c) | (c) | |
| 31. | (b) | (c) | | | |
| 32. | (d) | (a) | (a) | | |

| S.No. | (i) | (ii) | (iii) | (iv) | (v) |
|---|---|---|---|---|---|
| 33. | (c) | | | | |
| 34. | (d) | (c) | (b) | (b) | (a) |
| 35. | (c) | (c) | (c) | | |
| 36. | (b) | (c) | (d) | | |
| 37. | (d) | (a) | (c) | | |
| 38. | (c) | (c) | (b) | | |
| 39. | (a) | (c) | (c) | | |
| 40. | (b) | (b) | (d) | (c) | (b) |
| 41. | (c) | (b) | (d) | | |
| 42. | (b) | (b) | (d) | | |
| 43. | (a) | (b) | (b) | (d) | |
| 44. | (a) | (b) | (d) | (a) | (b) |
| 45. | (b) | (c) | (d) | (b) | |
| 46. | (a) | (b) | (c) | | |
| 47. | (c) | (a) | | | |
| 48. | (b) | (d) | (c) | (b) | |
| 49. | (b) | (a) | (d) | | |
| 50. | (c) | (b) | (d) | | |
| 51. | (a) | | | | |
| 52. | (d) | (d) | (c) | | |
| 53. | (b) | (b) | | | |
| 54. | (a) | (c) | (a) | | |
| 55. | (d) | (a) | (b) | (d) | |
| 56. | (a) | (b) | (c) | | |
| 57. | (c) | (d) | (b) | (d) | |
| 58. | (a) | (b) | | | |
| 59. | (b) | (c) | (a) | (a) | (d) |
| 60. | (c) | (a) | (a) | | |
| 61. | (b) | (d) | (c) | (c) | (a) |
| 62. | (c) | (b) | (d) | | |
| 63. | (c) | (c) | (c) | | |
| 64. | (c) | (b) | (a) | (a) | |
| 65. | (c) | (c) | (b) | (d) | (a) |
| 66. | (d) | (b) | (b) | | |

| S.No. | (i) | (ii) | (iii) | (iv) | (v) |
|---|---|---|---|---|---|
| 67. | (b) | (b) | (c) | | |
| 68. | (d) | (a) | (a) | (d) | |
| 69. | (c) | (b) | | | |
| 70. | (d) | (a) | (d) | | |
| 71. | (a) | (c) | (b) | (c) | (d) |
| 72. | (b) | (b) | (c) | | |
| 73. | (a) | (c) | (d) | | |
| 74. | (c) | (b) | | | |
| 75. | (c) | (b) | (d) | | |
| 76. | (a) | (d) | (c) | | |
| 77. | (b) | (c) | (b) | | |
| 78. | (c) | (c) | (a) | (a) | |
| 79. | (a) | (c) | (b) | (d) | |
| 80. | (b) | (d) | (b) | (c) | (c) |
| 81. | (b) | (d) | (c) | (b) | |
| 82. | (b) | (d) | (b) | | |
| 83. | (b) | (c) | (d) | | |
| 84. | (c) | (b) | (d) | | |
| 85. | (c) | (c) | (b) | | |
| 86. | (c) | (b) | (b) | | |
| 87. | (c) | (b) | (d) | (d) | |
| 88. | (c) | (b) | (d) | | |
| 89. | (b) | (c) | (a) | | |
| 90. | (c) | (c) | (d) | (d) | (b) |
| 91. | (c) | (b) | (a) | (a) | |
| 92. | (a) | (c) | | | |
| 93. | (b) | | | | |
| 94. | (b) | (a) | (d) | | |
| 95. | (b) | (b) | (d) | | |
| 96. | (d) | (b) | (a) | | |
| 97. | (a) | (c) | (b) | | |
| 98. | (d) | (b) | (c) | | |
| 99. | (a) | (d) | (b) | | |
| 100. | (c) | (c) | (b) | (b) | |

# Literary Aptitude and Vocabulary

2

## Introduction

The test of language, besides incorporating the evaluation of the skills of comprehension, would also test the understanding of the language, literary aptitude and vocabulary. As highlighted earlier in the previous chapter, section 1A of the CUET is likely to have questions emanating from the comprehension as well as vocabulary and language sections. This is seen from the notification of the CUET examination which states as below.

*'Language to be tested through Reading Comprehension (based on different types of passages–Factual, Literary and Narrative, [Literary Aptitude and Vocabulary]'.*

Further the syllabus for the languages, as notified for sections IA and IB of the CUET, specifies as below.

*Questions from the Language Section will be from the following topics but are not limited to:*

1. *Reading Comprehension: There will be three types of passages (maximum 300-350 words): which will be: **(i) Factual, (ii) Narrative (iii) Literary***
2. *Verbal Ability*
3. *Rearranging the parts*
4. *Choosing the correct word*
5. *Synonyms and Antonyms*
6. *Vocabulary*

Thus, like most of the aptitude tests, in CUET also one can expect the language section to comprise questions emerging from comprehension, grammar and vocabulary. The latter two are a direct test of the language skills, while the former is an evaluation of the ability to understand as to what is stated. In this chapter, it is endeavoured to bring out as to what will be the nature of questions and how to go about their preparation. The chapter includes reasonable material to build on one's vocabulary, besides appropriate number of practice questions of varied categories are also included.

**The type of questions on language, literary aptitude and vocabulary**: Based on the nature of questions which have been asked in the previous papers of the CUCET examination conducted in the past by the National Testing Agency (NTA) and also considering the industry testing standards as observed in the other aptitude tests, the nature/ categories of questions likely to arise are identified as below. One can also expect around 20% to 40% of the questions in section 1A to be of this nature, while the remaining could emanate from the comprehension passages.

1. **Test of vocabulary:** A wide variety of questions arise in the aptitude tests which directly or indirectly, are a test of vocabulary. These may be structured variedly but inherently what is put to test is the understanding of the meaning of words and expressions. Some form of the questions along with illustrative examples are highlighted below.
   **(a) Words same/similar in meaning:** The question may specify a word with four given options requiring the option which is same or similar in meaning to the given word, to be identified. Thus, essentially this type of questions entail, understanding of the given words meaning as well as identification of its synonym or near synonym.

## Illustrations

***Identify as to which word is the synonym or similar in meaning to the given words in question.***

**1.1 Illustration**

Accrue

(a) To earn (b) To increase
(c) To multiply (d) To accumulate

The meaning of accrue as per the Cambridge dictionary is*: to increase over a period of time, or to get an amount of something gradually over a period of time.* Thus, option (d), *to accumulate,* is the right answer to the question.

**1.2 Illustration**

Metamorphosis

(a) Rupture of metamorphic rock

(b) Transformation

(c) Degradation

(d) None of the above

The right answer for this question is option (b), *transformation.*

**(b) Words matching a definition:** In such questions, a short definition is given, which is followed by four, word choices. The option which best suits the definition is required to be identified. In a way the questions of this category are reverse of the earlier one, where the word was specified and is single word meaning/ definition/ synonym was to be identified. The questions of this category could be as below.

***In the questions below, one definition and word options are given. Choose the appropriate word option for the definition.***

**1.3 Illustration**

To placate somebody;

(a) Appreciate (b) Criticise

(c) Idolise (d) Appease

Here, appease is the appropriate word to suit the definition.

**1.4 Illustration**

To specify as an essential condition;

(a) Incorporate (b) Integrate

(c) Stipulate (d) Apprise

Stipulate would be the right choice amongst the given options.

**(c) Effective words to fill in the blanks:** Here a sentence would be provided with a blank space and four given options. The question requires the selection of the most appropriate word to fill in the blank. Thus, what is tested here is not only the knowledge of meaning of different words, but more importantly the contextual application of the word in the given sentence. It ought to be remembered that while more than one word may fill in the blanks appropriately from the perspective of grammatical correctness, here it is the contextual correctness which is more relevant and is required to be identified. Examples of this category are as below.

*In the given questions pick out the most effective word(s) from the given words to fill in the blanks and make the sentence meaningfully complete.*

**1.5 Illustration**

The court issued a summons to him and enjoined him to _______ as a witness.

(a) speak (b) register

(c) testify (d) record

From the grammatical perspective all of the first three options are correct. But from the contextual perspective, the best options could be 'testify' or 'appear'. As the latter is not specified as one of the four options here, testify would be the correct choice.

Sometimes the questions include two blanks and different pair of words. In such questions the most suitable pair of words to fill in the blanks space is to be determined.

*There are two gaps in each of the following sentences. From the pairs of words given, choose the one that fills the gaps most appropriately. The first word in the pair should fill the first gap.*

**1.6 Illustration**

This simplified __________ to the decision-making process is a must read for anyone _________ important real estate, personal, or professional decisions.

(a) primer, maximising

(b) tract, enacting

(c) introduction, under

(d) guide, facing

Such questions can be more complicated than the single word ones and appear difficult to solve at the first instance. The best way to go about it, is to fit the words and see their suitability in the context. In the options for the first blank, primer, tract, introduction or guide all are fitting. The sentence is referring to some sort of literature on the subject of real estate, personal .... (tract can also mean a short piece of writing). Hence none of the options are eliminated by the first set of words (in some questions a single or a couple of options may get eliminated).

On fitting the second set of words, we find that 'facing' best suits the context as compared to the other words. Hence, option (d) is the correct choice.

Another variant of such question is where the question has a number of word pairs in different sentences for identification

*In each question, there are five sentences. Each has a pair of words that are italicised and highlighted. From the italicised and highlighted words, select the most appropriate words (A or B) to form correct sentences. The sentences are followed by options that indicate the words, which may be selected to correctly complete the set of sentences. From the options given, choose the most appropriate one.*

**1.7 Illustration**

(i) Anita bore a beautiful broach (A)/ brooch (B) on the lapel of her jacket.

(ii) If you want to complain about the amenities in your neighbourhood, please meet your councillors (A)/counsellors (B).

(iii) I would like your advice (A)/advise (B) on which job I should choose.

(iv) The last scene provided a climactic (A)/climatic (B) ending to the film.

(v) Jeans that flair (A)/flare (B) at the bottom are in fashion these days.

(a) BABAA (b) BABAB

(c) BAAAB (d) ABABA

For (i) the correct option is brooch (a clasp or an ornament having a pin at the back). Hence option B is correct for (i) Councillors (option A), advice (option A), climactic (option A) and flare (option B). Hence, the correct sequence would be BAAAB which is the option choice (c).

**(d) Words opposite in meaning:** Antonyms or words having the opposite meaning are another category of questions. Here we have to remember that the option may or may not have the exact opposite meaning and so, we may have to identify the option having the nearly opposite meaning.

**1.8 Illustration**

Unscrupulous

(a) Polite (b) Righteous

(c) Right (d) Reformist

Unscrupulous means, a person having or showing no moral principles or scruples. The most appropriate antonym would be scrupulous which is 'however' not a given option. Amongst the options, righteous would be the appropriate choice.

**1.9 Illustration**

Mundane

(a) Social (b) Sophisticated

(c) Special (d) Solver

Mundane means very ordinary, dull, insipid, hence special would be the appropriate antonym. Sophisticated means complex and not an appropriate choice while the other two words are no where near the meaning of dull / ordinary.

**(2) Test of grammar and syntax:** A variety of questions come up in aptitude tests which evaluate the understanding of grammar and syntax. Some questions of this category are also likely to arise in the CUET. Some of the different categories of grammar-based questions are highlighted below.

(a) **Improvement in the sentence:** The questions of this category require candidate to identify any mistake of grammar or syntax in a give part of the sentence. The options give in the question may improve the sentence if the underlined portion is replaced with the option. The option which thus improves the sentence is required to be identified. Thus, spotting of error of grammar and its correction is what the question requires the candidates to attempt. Questions of this category are as below.

*In the questions given below, a part of the sentence is underlined. Below are given alternatives to the underlined portion which may improve the sentence. Choose the correct alternative. In case no improvement is needed then select the option (d).*

**1.10 Illustration**

The rock band was playing music at the beach.

(a) on the beach.

(b) by the beach.

(c) upon the beach.

(d) No improvement can be done

The question tests the use of correct preposition. The grammatically correct choice would be option (a) 'on the beach'.

(b) **Identification of error in a sentence part**: Certain questions require the identification of the sentence part which has an error. Questions of this type can be as given below.

*In the following questions a sentence is divided into four parts (a) (b) (c) & (d). Identify which one of these parts have any error. The error will be in only one part of the sentence.*

**1.11 Illustration**

The house was at fire when the family returned home.

(a) The house was (b) at fire

(c) when the family (d) returned home.

Here the use of preposition *at* is incorrect. The correct sentence should be, 'the house was *on fire*'. Hence, the answer choice would be option (b).

**1.12 Illustration**

The task was too difficult; many a contestants failed.

(a) The task was (b) too difficult;

(c) many a contestants (d) failed.

Here the error is in part (c). Either it should be, *many a contestant* or *many contestants*.

(c) **Correct words to fill in the blanks:** The questions of filling the correct/ appropriate words in blank spaces, can also be used to test the grasp over grammar. Consider the following example.

*In the question below, choose the correct pair of option to fill in the blank spaces.*

**1.13 Illustration**

Amitabh comes to school _____ car but Sanjay likes to come ______ foot.

(a) in/at. (b) in/by.

(c) by/on. (d) at/by.

Here the right prepositions to be filled in the blank spaces are to be identified. The correct prepositions are *by* and *on* (option (c)).

3. **Test of understanding of idioms and phrases:** A category of question evaluates the understanding of the meaning of common idiom and phrases. In the question, the relevant idiom or phrase in a given sentence is underlined/ highlighted/italicised. In the options, the meaning of the idiom or phrase is given and the correct meaning is to be identified. Consider the following example.

*Choose the alternative which best express the meaning of the idiom/phrase that is italicised and underlined in the sentence.*

**1.14 Illustration**

He thought that the examination would be *a piece of cake* for him, but it did not turn out to be so.

(a) Very challenging (b) very interesting

(c) very easy (d) none of the above.

A piece of cake means something very easy, hence option(c) is the right choice.

**1.15 Illustration**

He was elated to see his uncle, who visited only *once in a blue moon.*

(a) Once in a fortnight

(b) once in a month

(c) on special occasions

(d) very rarely

The idiom once in a blue moon means very rarely, hence option (d) is the right choice.

## How to Prepare

The questions on the above subjects and others may be structured in a variety of forms but the fundamental traits required are the knowledge of grammar and a sound vocabulary. Thus, preparation for this section involves some techniques which are common/similar to the preparation for the comprehension passages. As such, while the principal activity remains the same (viz. wide reading) the focus has to be made more specific to incorporate preparation for this section. Some helpful methods and tips are highlighted below.

- **Brush up your vocabulary**: It is highly prudent and advisable to work upon your vocabulary, specially if it has not been your forte. Understandably the time available to you is short and development of vocabulary through the ordinary course of language development skills is a time-taking journey. However, here is what you could do even in a short span of time. With the annexure to this chapter, a list of nearly 400 words is provided. These words are identified from the perspective of aptitude examinations, particularly of the high school and undergraduate level. The meaning of the words their synonyms and antonyms are also given. At the outset test yourself against this list. If you are conversant with more than 90% of the words contained in it, then your vocabulary is sound enough to tackle most of the questions on vocabulary likely to appear in the CUET. If you are falling short, then identify the words which are new to you or you were not sure about. Go through them time and again. While learning these words, try to use them in a sentence. This is one of the surest ways of internalising what you learn. With each iteration and revision, keep on noting the words which are still not comprehended by you. However, learning words takes some time and your need to be patient with yourself and persistent in your effort.
- **Read good books and articles** which have fluent language, especially those which hone your language skills and enrich your vocabulary. This is to be done in the early preparation phase of CUET when you still have some time to devote to your language skills and are not hard pressed for time to revise your core subjects.
- **Identify new words:** While going through the books, newspapers, magazines or other material read by you, be conscious of the new words which you come across. Sometimes the word may not be altogether new. However, you may know of it only vaguely or know a singular contextual meaning. The exact meaning or its different contextual meanings may not be known. Note down such new words, whose meaning you are not aware of or sure about. Check it up in the dictionary, especially the usage of the word in different contexts. Always keep a good English dictionary readily available near your reading table. Do not procrastinate looking up the meaning. It's also advisable to make a note of the sentence in which you spotted the new word. If the word has different contextual meanings, then try to make a sentence (at least mentally) in different contexts in which the word can be used.
- Noting them in a file or memo page of the **mobile phone** is also a very good and handy option. You may also like to **download a dictionary application** (App) on your smart phone so that you can quickly check the word definition, meanings/synonyms and antonyms. This is the natural and more enduring way of building one's vocabulary as the contextual meaning of the word as well as its application is readily seen and understood.
- If you are unable to look up the dictionary then underline/mark the word or **jot it down in a diary or a note book.** A pocket note book which you can carry with yourself is the best form of making such notes. Look up the dictionary and note the word usage at the earliest.
- A good approach to understanding word meaning is, trying first to **guess what is the contextual meaning of the word or expression.** Then look it up the dictionary and check whether your understanding was correct or not. If you have assistance of friends or elders who can explain the meaning of the

word or expression, then do not hesitate to ask them, especially when you do not have ready access to a dictionary. Keep your shyness or ego aside. This is a useful technique to accelerate the process of learning. Scientific studies have shown that children, whose growth of vocabulary is many times more than that of elders, adopt this methodology of contextual understanding as well as seeking available assistance. However, it is also important to cross check the meaning with the dictionary to understand the entire gamut of the contextual usage of the word.

- Always revise whatever you have noted periodically and preferably daily. This steadily but surely enriches your vocabulary and understanding of the language.
- **Antonyms and synonyms** question as highlighted are also likely to arise. Candidates often face the dilemma, whether or not to use a thesaurus to work upon antonyms and synonyms. It is always advisable to work upon your vocabulary by doing a wide and extensive reading provided time permits you. However, a thesaurus can always serve as a good reference book. You need not purchase, it if you do not have one. Borrow it from a library **or download a free application** on your smartphone.
- Building your own list of words as highlighted above pay rich dividends However, it is time taking process. It would be prudent to employ both the techniques, that is jumpstart your vocabulary by learning the words given in the **annexure of this chapter** (or similar other compilation/ compilations) as well as build your vocabulary gradually by **compiling your own list of new words**.
- **Keep an eye for expressions, idioms and phrases** whose meaning you are unaware, or which you seldom or never use yourself. Make a note of these also, in your diary. A list of some common idioms and phrases along with their meaning is also provided as an annexure to this chapter.
- If you consider **grammar/syntax** to be your weak area, then it is advisable to go back to the basics. **Pick up a high school/ class X level grammar book and go through it. Peruse the portion on the 'parts of sentence'. Work upon areas such as prepositions, punctuation, articles etc.** These are the areas (apart from correction of sentence structure / spotting grammatical mistakes) from which questions are likely to emanate. The best method to work upon such areas is to solve as many exercises as possible in a **good work-book**, especially on those topics which you feel you need to improve upon.
- **Watch your punctuation**. This is an area where many falter. Do a preliminary reading of the basics of punctuation from a grammar book. Practice exercises on it from a work-book. Be conscious of the punctuation marks being used in the articles/ news items which you are reading. Make a mental note of the punctuation marks you are coming across while reading and ascertain mentally whether the usage is appropriate or not.
- **Develop selection by elimination technique:** While tackling questions in this section (say on word meaning), if we are aware of the meaning of the word, then selecting the right response becomes easier. However, where the meaning is not definitely known, or one to one identification of the word and its meaning / synonym/ antonym, is difficult then, the technique of selection by elimination is helpful. In such cases the options which are clearly not the right choice, need to be eliminated first. Many a time elimination leads to only a couple of remaining options and candidates may then make a reasoned choice. For example, in the illustration 7, where antonym is to be found of the word *mundane*, the options, *social* and *solver* can be eliminated at the very outset, as they have no closeness/connect to *mundane* (as a synonym or antonym). The choice reduces to that between *sophisticated* and *special*. A candidate may prefer then to make a reasoned guess or select a choice for which he/she has a hunch of it being the write answer. However, this is not the best technique and no substitute to the right knowledge. It is only a mechanism to be adopted in an emergency with its inherent risk of incurring negative marks.

- Make a fair assessment of your proficiency in this entire area of preparation. It is possible that English language may have been one of those subjects which you were particularly proficient in/ fond of at the middle school/ high school level. But it is also possible that post your class 10th, you have focused on the non-language/ core subjects. You may have drifted afar from the position of strength and might have some catching up to do. If it is so, then do devote some time to this area lest it becomes your waterloo.
  - Last but not the least; do not expect a dramatic or overnight improvement in your understanding of grammar or repertoire of words. Make a sincere, diligent and persistent effort. **Budget a daily 30 minutes to an hour** for this area of preparation. As mentioned earlier, **revise regularly** whatever you have noted in your diary and be eager to learn new words or expressions idioms and phrases. Rest assured that you will notice a perceptible improvement in your language and grammar skills in a matter of weeks, if not days.

## Word Meanings, Synonyms & Antonyms

**Abandon:** To leave completely; to cease to support or look after; forsake utterly; desert; to yield without restraint or moderation; to give oneself to natural impulses
**Synonym:** Spontaneity, recklessness, wantonness, uninhibitedness
**Antonyms:** Restraint

**Abash**: To destroy self-confidence, poise, or self-possession
**Synonyms**: Confuse, confound, discomfit, rattle
**Antonyms**: Calm, comfort, soothe

**Abate**: To become less strong, to decrease
**Synonyms**: Reduce, subside, decline
**Antonyms**: Accumulate, aggravate, escalate, swell

**Abdicate**: To give up a right, power or position
**Synonyms**: Resign, renounce, quit, relinquish
**Antonyms**: Accept, taken on, adopt, undertake

**Aberrant:** Deviating from what is normal or accepted standard
**Synonym:** Abnormal, anomalous freak, odd, unusual
**Antonyms:** Common customary, normal, ordinary, unexceptional

**Abeyance**: A state of temporary inactivity; temporary suppression or suspension
**Synonyms**: Discontinuation, dormancy, suspension, remission
**Antonyms**: Continuation, renewal, revival

**Abject**: Utterly hopeless or miserable, contemptible
**Synonyms**: Contemptible, despicable, wretched
**Antonyms**: Commendable, exalted, excellent, worthy

**Abjure**: to renounce upon oath; to reject solemnly
**Synonyms**: Forsake, renounce, forswear
**Antonyms**: Approve, allow, sanction

**Abound**: To exist or occur in great numbers; to be rich or well supplied
**Synonyms**: Thrive, swarm, flourish, proliferate
**Antonyms**: Decline, deficient, languish, short

**Abscond**: To depart secretly
**Synonyms**: Decamp, bolt, escape, disappear
**Antonyms**: Appear, arrive, abide

**Absolve:** to be free from guilt or blame, to set free or release
**Synonyms**: Acquit exempt, relieve pardon, forgive
**Antonyms**: Accuse, blame, censure, charge

**Abstemious:** Moderate in appetite, marked by restraint in consumption of food and drinks
**Synonyms:** Abstinent, continent, self-denying, sober, temperate
**Antonyms:** Gluttonous, greedy, Self-indulgent

**Abstinence:** Giving up of certain pleasures; any self-restraint or self-denial
**Synonyms**: Chastity, fasting, frugality, self-control
**Antonyms**: Indulgence, excess, Intemperance

**Abysmal:** Very bad, immeasurably deep or great; hopeless
**Synonyms**: Bottomless, boundless, endless, unfathomable
**Antonyms**: Even, flat, finite, measured

**Accord:** To be in agreement or harmony to make agree or correspond
**Synonyms**: Deal, pact, reconciliation, agreement, harmony
**Antonyms**: Disagreement, difference, discord

**Acrimony:** Sharpness or harshness or bitterness of speech, disposition or nature etc.
**Synonyms**: Animosity, antagonism, harshness, bitterness
**Antonyms**: Good will, love, kindness, courtesy, benevolence

**Acumen:** Shrewdness; keen insight
**Synonyms**: Ingenuity, intellect, guile, brilliance
**Antonyms**: Inability, stupidity, ignorance, obtuseness

**Adamant:** One who is utterly unyielding in attitude or opinion
**Synonyms**: Stubborn, inflexible, rigid, resolute, uncompromising
**Antonyms**: Flexible, yielding, irresolute, soft

**Adhere:** To stay attached; to cling; to stick fast
**Synonyms**: Comply, heed, obey, observe
**Antonyms**: Disobey, ignore, overlook

**Adjunct:** something added or connected to a larger or more important thing, but not essential to it
**Synonyms**: Appendix, adjutant, joined, added, supplement
**Antonyms**: Subtraction, separated, detriment

**Admonish:** To reprove or scold, to caution
**Synonyms**: Berate, censure, counsel, chide, reprove, rebuke, reprimand, upbraid
**Antonyms**: Compliment, allow, approve, applaud

**Affinity:** A habitual attraction to some activity or thing, fondness, liking
**Synonyms**: Affection, bent, disposition, proclivity, penchant
**Antonyms**: Aversion, Disinclination, detachment, apathy

**Aggrandise:** To assign a high status or value
**Synonyms**: Canonise, deify, dignify, elevate
**Antonyms**: Abase, degrade, belittle, depreciate, disparage

**Alacrity:** Cheerful readiness to do something eagerness, speed
**Synonyms**: Amenability, willingness, alertness, briskness
**Antonyms**: Apathy, dullness, indifference, slowness

**Alien:** Extra-terrestrial; one who owes allegiance to another country
**Synonyms**: Foreigner, outsider, external, non-native
**Antonyms**: Native, familiar, resident

**Allay:** To put to rest any fear, doubt or suspicion
**Synonyms**: Alleviate, assuage, pacify, soothe
**Antonyms**: Agitate, incite, aggravate, excite

**Alleviate:** To make easier to endure, to lesson, to mitigate
**Synonyms**: Assuage, allay, abate, ease, mitigate, relieve
**Antonyms**: Agitate, aggravate, enhance, increase, intensify

**Allure:** To attract or tempt by something flattering or desirable; to fascinate or to charm
**Synonyms**: Attraction, charm, enticement, fascination, temptation
**Antonyms**: Repulsion, repel

**Ambiguous:** Unclear or doubtful in meaning or veiled in meaning; open to having several possible meanings or interpretations
**Synonyms**: Cryptic, dubious, double edged, enigmatic, equivocal, nebulous, opaque, obscure
**Antonyms**: Certain, comprehensible, clear, intelligible, unequivocal

**Ambivalence:** The state of having conflicting emotional attitude; simultaneous contradicting attitude
**Synonyms**: Doubt, hesitancy, uncertainty
**Antonyms**: Certainty, sureness

**Ameliorate:** To improve, to make better
**Synonyms**: Amend, better, enhance, improve, refine
**Antonyms**: Damage, injure, blemish, worsen

**Amenable:** Ready or willing to answer, act, agree or yield; open to influence or persuasion
**Synonyms**: Agreeable, responsive, susceptible, inclined, willing
**Antonyms**: Averse, loath, reluctant, non-conforming

**Amplify:** To expand, to make larger or greater, to increase
**Synonyms**: Enlarge, augment, expand, deepen
**Antonyms**: Compress, contract, lessen

**Anarchy:** State of disorder or lawlessness; absence of government
**Synonyms**: Lawlessness, misrule
**Antonyms**: Lawfulness, harmony, orderliness

**Anomalous:** Irregular; deviating from the norm; being out of ordinary
**Synonyms**: Aberrant, abnormal, exceptional, rare, singular,
**Antonyms**: Everyday, familiar, frequent

**Antipathy:** A strong feeling of dislike, hostility
**Synonyms**: Animosity, bitterness, grudge, hostility, rancor
**Antonyms**: Amity, amiability, cordiality, goodwill, friendship, understanding

**Apathy:** Lack of feeling or emotion; lack of interest or concern
**Synonyms**: Emotionlessness, impassiveness, numbness
**Antonyms**: Sensibility, emotion, empathy, pity

**Appease:** To calm, pacify, placate, to cause to subside
**Synonyms**: Assuage, conciliate, mollify, pacify
**Antonyms**: Anger, enrage, incense, infuriate, outrage

**Apprise:** to inform; to brief
**Synonyms**: Acquaint, advise, inform, advertise, alert, notify
**Antonyms**: Misinform, mislead

**Approbation:** Approval, commendation, praise; an acceptance of something as satisfactory
**Synonyms**: Approval, praise, commendation, blessing
**Antonyms**: Refusal, rejection, repudiation

**Arduous:** Extremely difficult, labourious; hard to accomplish
**Synonyms**: Challenging, demanding, grueling, toilsome, tough
**Antonyms**: Easy, effortless, facile, simple, undemanding

**Arraign:** To call or bring before a court; a formal charge, to accuse or charge
**Synonyms**: Summon, incriminate, indict
**Antonyms**: Exonerate, exculpate, pardon

**Ascend:** To move up, climb, or go upward; to slant upward
**Synonyms**: Climb, escalate, move-up
**Antonyms**: Decrease, Descend, Decline, fall

**Aspersion:** A damaging or derogatory remark or criticism; false rumor; slander
**Synonyms**: Abuse, calumny, libel, slander, defamation
**Antonyms**: Adulation, compliment, flattery

**Assiduous:** Showing great care, attention, diligent, hardworking
**Synonyms**: Active, diligent, industrious
**Antonyms**: Inactive, unemployed, unoccupied

**Audacity:** The quality or state of being bold, or arrogant, or disregard normal restraint
**Synonyms**: Boldness, brazenness, brashness, presumptuousness, temerity
**Antonyms**: Humility, mildness, cowardice

**Austere:** Severe in manner or appearance; uncompromising, strict, severe, unadorned
**Synonyms**: Exacting, formal, rigid, strict, stringent
**Antonyms**: Flexible, indulgent, extravagant, mild

**Authentic:** Genuine; real; not false, representing true nature
**Synonyms**: Authoritative, convincing, accurate, credible
**Antonyms**: Doubtful, fictitious, unreal, untrustworthy

**Avarice:** Insatiable greed, selfish or miserly desire to gain wealth
**Synonyms**: Greediness, covetousness, stinginess
**Antonyms**: Generosity

**Aver:** To affirm or declare to be true
**Synonyms**: Affirm, assert, avouch, claim, declare proclaim
**Antonyms**: Deny, disclaim, forget, discredit

**Badmouth:** To talk ill of, to express scornfully one's low opinion of another
**Synonym:** Belittle, denigrate, run-down, trash-talk
**Antonyms:** Acclaim, applaud, glorify, laud, praise

**Baffle:** To confuse, bewilder, to frustrate
**Synonyms**: Amaze, astound, befuddle, confound, dumbfound, frustrate, perplex, puzzle
**Antonyms**: Clear-up, clarify, explain, delight

**Banal:** Devoid to freshness, common place, lacking originality
**Synonyms**: Bland, hackneyed, mundane, trite
**Antonyms**: Intelligent, new, original, uncommon

**Banter:** Playful conversation, an exchange of light teasing remarks
**Synonyms:** Chitchat, gossip, repartee, ribbing, ridicule, small talk
**Antonyms:** Flattery, praise

**Barbarous:** An uncivilised, wild or savage act
**Synonyms**: Atrocious brutal, cruel wild, uncivilised
**Antonyms**: Civilised, Compassionate, considerate

**Barren:** Sterile, not capable of reproducing, unfruitful
**Synonyms**: Arid, desolate, sterile, empty
**Antonyms**: Fruitful, productive, child bearing, fertile

**Bawdy:** Indecent, lewd or obscene talk or action
**Synonyms**: Coarse, lewd, obscene, ribald
**Antonyms**: Clean, decent, moral, proper

**Bedizen:** To dress in a vulgar, showy or tasteless manner
**Synonyms**: Attire, dope, dress-up, swaddle
**Antonyms**: Disrobe, open, unclothe

**Befog:** To envelop in fog/cloud, confuse by irrelevancies or distractions, to render unclear
**Synonyms**: Darken, dim, obscure
**Antonyms**: Clear headed, uncloud

**Belie:** To contradict or misrepresent, give a false impression
**Synonyms**: Contradict, repudiate
**Antonyms**: Approve, affirm, harmonise, help

**Benevolent:** Having sympathy or consideration for others
**Synonyms**: Beneficent, benign, compassionate, generous
**Antonyms**: merciless, ruthless, inconsiderate

**Benign:** Someone or something gentle, kind or unharmful
**Synonyms**: Favourable, friendly, kindly, warmhearted
**Antonyms**: Cruel, menacing, offensive, poisonous

**Bewitching:** Someone or something enchanting, captivating or fascinating
**Synonyms**: Alluring, captivating, charming, enchanting, fascinating, luring
**Antonyms**: Repulsive, repugnant, boring

**Bleak:** Causing or marked by an atmosphere lacking in cheer
**Synonyms**: Cheerless, cold, austere, dark
**Antonyms**: Blithe, buoyant, bright, pleasant

**Boisterous:** Being rough or noisy in a high-spirited way
**Synonyms**: Clamorous, raucous, rowdy, rambunctious
**Antonyms**: Calm, dignified, placid, sedate, sober

**Bolster:** To give a boost, to prop up, to support
**Synonyms:** Aid, boost, buoy, help, support
**Antonyms:** Block, hinder, obstruct, stop, weaken

**Boorish:** Rude or insensitive, crude
**Synonyms**: Barbaric, coarse, crude, impolite, tasteless, vulgar
**Antonyms**: Delicate, gentle, charming, cultured

**Burgeon:** To grow or develop quickly, flourish
**Synonyms**: Prosper, snow fall, sprout, flourish
**Antonyms**: Decline, decrease, fade, shrivel, wither

**Bustle:** A state of noisy, confused activity
**Synonyms**: Bluster, commotion, disturbance, hullaballoo, tumult, pandemonium
**Antonyms**: Crawl, creep, slowness, quiet

**Cacophony:** Harsh sound which is discordant, a meaningless mixture of sounds
**Synonyms:** Babel, clamor, noise, roar
**Antonyms:** Calm, lull, melody

**Calculating:** making calculations, marked by prudent analysis or shrewd consideration of self-interest
**Synonyms**: Cagey, canny, foresighted, shrewd,
**Antonyms**: Careless, candid heedless, brash, lax

**Callous:** Being hardened or thickened, feeling no emotion or sympathy for others
**Synonyms**: Compassionless, hard hearted, unsensitive, unfeeling
**Antonyms**: Compassionate, humane, merciful, sensitive, tender

**Calumny:** A misinterpretation intended to harm another's reputation, the act of uttering false charges
**Synonyms**: Aspersion, defamation, libel, slander, vilification
**Antonyms**: Adulation, commendation, esteem, flatter, praise

**Camouflage:** To disguise, concealment by means of disguise, behaviour designed to deceive or hide
**Synonyms**: Costume, cloak, disguise, guise
**Antonyms**: Display exhibit, reveal, unmask.

**Canard:** A false or deliberately misleading story, a fabricated report
**Synonyms**: Gossip, hearsay, libel, slander, whisper
**Antonyms**: Truth

**Candid:** Honest sincere expression, free from bias or prejudice
**Synonyms**: Blunt, direct, frank, forthright, honest, straight forward
**Antonyms**: Coloured, deceptive, evasive, unforthcoming, uncandid

**Capricious:** Subject to or indicative of odd notion or unpredictable change, fickle
**Synonyms**: Arbitrary, erratic, fickle, quirky, volatile
**Antonyms**: Cautious, constant, reasonable, reliable, stable

**Captivate:** To influence and dominate by some special charm, casting an irresistible appeal, to attract or delight as if by magic
**Synonyms**: Allure, bewitch, charm, fascinate, enchant
**Antonyms**: Disillusion, disgust, offend, repel

**Carnal:** Of the flesh or body, relating to passion or physical appetites
**Synonyms**: Earthly, lewd, sensuous, wanton
**Antonyms**: Chaste, clean, moral, pure, spiritual

**Cease:** To cause to come to an end, no longer continue, to become extinct
**Synonyms**: Arrest, close, discontinue, desist end, finish, terminate
**Antonyms**: Continue, persist, hang on

**Celebrated:** Renowned, well known
**Synonyms**: Acclaimed, renowned, revered
**Antonyms**: Obscure, inglorious, unknown,

**Censure:** Strong or vehement expression of disapproval
**Synonyms**: Condemnation, rebuke, reprimand
**Antonyms**: Endorsement, acceptance

**Chicanery:** Trickey or deception, a subterfuge used to trick or deceive
**Synonyms**: Dishonesty, deception, duplicity, machination, trickery,
**Antonyms**: Honesty, forthrightness, openness

**Churlish:** Boorish or rude
**Synonyms**: Rude, sullen, loutish uncivilised,
**Antonyms**: Gentle, refined, polished

**Clandestine:** Characterised by, done in, or executed with secrecy or concealment
**Synonyms**: Covert, fraudulent, furtive, hidden, illicit, surreptitious
**Antonyms**: Above board, honest, legal, open, public

**Classic:** Serving as a standard of excellence, enduring, traditional, memorable
**Synonyms**: Archetypal, exemplary, model, paradigmatic
**Antonyms**: Low-grade, poor, substandard

**Coarse:** Composed of relatively large parts of particles, lacking fineness or delicacy of texture, structure, of poor quality
**Synonyms**: Bawdy, crass, crude, obscene, rude, vulgar
**Antonyms**: Clear, refined, pure

**Cognizant:** Aware, having legal recognition
**Synonyms**: conscious, judicious, observant
**Antonyms**: Ignorant, senseless, unaware

**Commensurate:** Corresponding in amount magnitude or degree, proportionate
**Synonyms**: Comparable, consistent, proportionate
**Antonyms**: Incomparable, inappropriate, unfitting

**Complement:** Something that completes or makes up a whole
**Synonyms**: Accompaniment, augmentation, addition
**Antonyms**: Base, part, decrease

**Comprise:** To include, to consist of or be composed of, to form or constitute
**Synonyms**: Amount to, Compose, include, contain
**Antonyms**: Abandon, exclude, lack, reject

**Concede:** To acknowledge as true, just or proper, to grant as right or privileges
**Synonyms**: Accept, admit, cede, give-up, yield, relinquish
**Antonyms**: Deny, defend, dispute, hold, reject

**Conceit:** An excessively favourable opinion of one's own ability importance, wit etc.
**Synonyms**: Arrogance, egotism, immodesty, self-importance
**Antonyms**: Humility, modesty, timidity

**Concord:** Agreement between persons, groups, nations etc., concurrence in attitudes, feelings
**Synonyms**: Agreement, accord, consensus, unanimity, unison
**Antonyms**: Disagreement, discord

**Concur:** To accord in opinion, agree, to co-operate, work together
**Synonyms**: Acquiesce, approve, agree, coincide
**Antonyms**: Clash, differ, disagree, dissent

**Condemn:** To express an unfavorable or adverse judgement on, indicate strong disapproval of
**Synonyms**: Castigate, censure, criticise
**Antonyms**: Approve, compliment, laud, praise, sanction

**Condone:** To overlook voluntarily, to forgive
**Synonyms**: Excuse, forgive, ignore
**Antonyms**: Condemn, deny, forbid, refuse

**Consolidate:** To bring together into a single or unified whole, to discard the unused or unwanted items of and organise the remaining
**Synonyms**: Buildup, cement, concentrate, strengthen, reinforce
**Antonyms**: Decrease, disperse, disconnect, separate, weaken

**Conspicuous:** Easily seen or noticed, attracting special attention, readily visible
**Synonyms**: Apparent, discernible, prominent, obvious, visible
**Antonyms**: Concealed, hidden, indistinct, invisible, obscured

**Contempt:** Open dislike for someone or something, state of being despised, dishonest, disgrace
**Synonyms**: Antipathy, defiance, derision, scorn
**Antonyms**: Approval, honour, regard, praise

**Contrite:** One very sorrowful for a wrong done, showing sincere remorse
**Synonyms**: Apologetic, remorseful, sorry
**Antonyms**: Hurtful, indifferent, unrepentant

**Courtesy:** Behaviour marked by respect or consideration for others or refined manners
**Synonyms**: Benevolence, civility, deference, kindness, generosity, sympathy, respect
**Antonyms**: Discourteous, disdain, disregard, disrespect, impoliteness, rudeness, unmannerliness

**Dabble:** To play or splash in water, to work at anything in a superficial or irregular manner
**Synonyms:** Dally, flirt with, play, trifle
**Antonyms:** Drudge, labour, plod struggle, serious

**Dainty:** Something delicious to taste, of delicate beauty, something of choice and pleasing, attractively prepared and served
**Synonyms:** Cute delicate, graceful, nice, tasty
**Antonyms:** Coarse, crude, gross, unpolished, ugly, vulgar

**Daunting:** Causing fear or discouragement, intimidating
**Synonyms:** Astounding, dire, frightful, horrific, terrifying
**Antonyms:** Calming, delightful, nice, pleasant

**Dawdle:** To waste time, idle, trifle, loiter
**Synonyms:** Laze, idle, loiter, procrastinate, saunter, trifle
**Antonyms:** Hasten, rush, push

**Deceit:** The act of causing someone to accept as true or valid, what is false or invalid, the quality of being dishonest
**Synonyms**: Chicanery, cheating, crookery, deception, fraud, trickery
**Antonyms**: Forthrightness, sincerity, uprightness, veracity

**Decipher:** To make out or discover the meaning of, to interpret by using a key or code.
**Synonyms**: Analyse, decode, deduce, interpret, reveal
**Antonyms**: Conceal, confuse, distort, misinterpret, suppress

**Defile:** To make foul, dirty, to violate chastity, to make impure
**Synonyms**: Debase, desecrate, pollute
**Antonyms**: Cleanse, elevate, purify, sanctify

**Defray:** To bear or pay all or part of the cost/ expenses etc.
**Synonyms**: Finance, fund, spend, pay
**Antonyms**: Take, defund,

**Deliberate:** To think about or discuss issues and decisions carefully
**Synonyms**: Calculated, considered, cautious, measured, weighed
**Antonyms**: Casual, rash, sudden, unconsidered

**Denigrate:** To slur someone's reputation
**Synonyms**: Belittle, decry, deprecate, run-down
**Antonyms**: Acclaim, applaud, exalt, extol, laud, praise

**Denounce:** To condemn or censure openly, to make a formal accusation against, to announce or proclaim
**Synonyms**: Accuse, blame, boycott, censure, decry
**Antonyms**: Approve, defend, laud, welcome

**Deride:** To make someone or something the object of unkind laughter, to scoff or jeer
**Synonyms**: Disdain, jeer, mock, taunt, ridicule
**Antonyms**: Admire, applaud, approve, commend, compliment, endorse flatter, respect

**Derogatory:** Intended to make a person or thing, of little importance or value
**Synonyms**: Belittling, contemptuous, sarcastic
**Antonyms**: Admiring, adulatory, appreciative, laudatory

**Despair:** Loss of hope, to give up, hopelessness
**Synonyms**: Despondency, depression, gloom, misery
**Antonyms**: Cheer, contentment, faith, hope

**Diatribe:** A bitter verbal attack or criticism
**Synonyms**: Invective, denunciation, tirade
**Antonyms**: Compliment, praise

**Diffidence:** Lack of confidence, modesty or shyness resulting from lack of self confidence
**Synonyms**: Modesty, meekness, shyness, hesitation, self-consciousness
**Antonyms**: Arrogance, boldness

**Discerning:** Exhibiting keen insight and good judgement
**Synonyms**: Astute, insightful, knowledgeable
**Antonyms**: Idiotic, ignorant, negligent, stupid

**Discomfit:** To make uneasy, to confuse and deject, to disconcert
**Synonyms**: Disconcert, perplex, vex
**Antonyms**: Aid, comfort, help soothe

**Discordant:** Not in tune, being at variance, disagreeing, incongruous
**Synonyms**: Cacophony, clashing, divergent, dissonant
**Antonyms**: Agreeable, similar, harmonious

**Disdain:** To look upon or treat with contempt, to think unworthy of notice, response etc.
**Synonyms**: Antipathy, detest, despise, derision, scorn
**Antonyms**: Admiration, approval, compliment, praise

**Disparage:** To belittle, to speak or treat slightingly or to belittle
**Synonyms**: Belittle, decry, discredit, ridicule, vilify
**Antonyms**: Admire, compliment, laud, respect

**Dissuade:** To deter by adverse or persuasion, to persuade not to do something
**Synonyms**: Deter, discourage, thwart
**Antonyms**: Aid, assist, encourage, persuade

**Docile:** Easily managed or handled, readily trained or taught
**Synonyms**: Easy going, meek, pliable
**Antonyms**: Determined, headstrong, obstinate, stubborn

**Dogmatic:** Asserting opinions in an arrogant manner, without proof in an opinionated way, inclined to lay down principles as undeniably true
**Synonyms**: Arbitrary, assertive, fanatical intolerant
**Antonyms**: Equivocal, indefinite, vague, yielding

**Earthy:** Of the nature of or consisting of earth/soil, having the characteristic of earth, rough or coarse in taste, realistic or practical
**Synonyms:** Coarse, down-to-earth, matter-of-fact, simple, pragmatic, practical
**Antonyms:** Sophisticated, impractical, idealistic, utopian

**Earnest:** Characterised by an intense or serious state of mind, grave, important
**Synonyms:** Grave, no-nonsense, serious, solemn, weighty
**Antonyms:** Antic, comic, farcical, frivolous, lighthearted

**Ebb:** The flow backward or away, the decline or decay
**Synonyms:** Abatement backflow, decay, wane, withdrawal
**Antonyms:** Advance, expansion, growth, rise

**Eccentric:** Deviating from the recognised or customary character or practice, irregular
**Synonyms**: Abnormal bizarre, erratic, irregular, strange
**Antonyms**: Common, conventional, natural, normal

**Eclectic:** Selecting from various sources, not following any one system
**Synonyms**: Diverse, varied, wide ranging
**Antonyms**: Similar, narrow minded, unvaried

**Ecstasy:** A rapturous delight, an overpowering emotion exaltation, a state of sudden intense feeling
**Synonyms**: Delight, euphoria, elation, exultation, joy
**Antonyms**: Despair, depression, sorrow, woe

**Efface:** To wipe out, to do away with, to rub out, erase, or obliterate
**Synonyms**: Delete, destroy, expunge obliterate
**Antonyms**: Build, construct, retain, maintain

**Efficacy:** Capacity of producing a desired result or effect, effectiveness
**Synonyms**: Effectiveness, adequacy, potency, virtue
**Antonyms**: Ineffectiveness, inadequacy, inefficiency

**Elicit:** To provoke, to draw-out, to evoke
**Synonyms**: Bring-out, evoke, extract, obtain
**Antonyms**: Hide, ignore, suppress

**Eloquence:** The practice or art of using language with fluency and aptness
**Synonyms**: Expressiveness, fluency, poise
**Antonyms**: Dullness, inarticulateness

**Empirical:** That what is derived from observation or experiment
**Synonyms**: Experimental, factual, observational
**Antonyms**: Conjectural, hypothetical, theoretic

**Emulate:** To imitate or to copy, to try to equal, to rival with some degree of success
**Synonyms**: Follow suit, imitate, mimic
**Antonyms**: Neglect

**Encumbrance:** Something or someone creating a burden or impediment, mortgage or other claim on property a person or child dependent on someone else for support
**Synonyms**: Debt, handicap, hindrance, obstacle, obstruction
**Antonyms**: Aid, incentive, stimulant, support

**Endeavour:** To try to do some thing or an effort to attain something
**Synonyms**: Aim, effort, enterprise, undertaking, venture
**Antonyms**: Idleness, inactivity

**Endemic:** Inherent to or belonging to an area
**Synonyms**: Indigenous, local, native
**Antonyms**: Exotic, foreign, immigrant, imported

**Ephemeral:** That what is short lived or fleeting
**Synonyms**: Brief, short-lived, temporary, transient
**Antonyms**: Ceaseless, deathless, enduring, permanent

**Epitome:** A person or thing representing the features of a whole class, a condensed account especially of literacy work
**Synonyms**: Embodiment, essence, exemplar
**Antonyms**: Enlargement, expansion, increment

**Equanimity:** Evenness of mind, composure
**Synonyms**: Calmness, composure, repose, sangfroid
**Antonyms**: Anxiety, apprehension, disquiet, worry

**Equivocal:** That which is possible to have several different meanings, of doubtful nature or character
**Synonyms**: Ambiguous, ambivalent, uncertain, hazy, evasive
**Antonyms**: Certain, clear, lucid, obvious, unequivocal

**Exhort:** To urge by strong appeals, to try to persuade a person to follow a course of action
**Synonyms**: Goad, prod, prompt, urge
**Antonyms**: Deter, discourage, dissuade, restrain

**Fabricate:** To make by art or skill and labour, to make by assembling parts or sections, to devise, to fake or forge a document
**Synonyms**: Assemble, formulate, construct, produce
**Antonyms**: Destroy, Dismantle, demolish, ruin

**Facilitate:** To make less difficult, or easier
**Synonyms**: Aid, expedite, help, simplify
**Antonyms**: Block, hunder, unpede, obstruct

**Fallacy:** A deceptive or misleading or false notion or belief, a misleading argument
**Synonyms**: Deception, falsehood, untruth
**Antonyms**: Accuracy, certainty, truth, veracity

**Fanatical:** Motivated by an extreme zeal, enthusiasm as in religion or politics
**Synonyms**: Bigoted, narrow-minded, biased, rabid
**Antonyms**: Broad-minded, impartial, liberal, tolerant

**Feeble:** Physically weak or sick, frail, intellectually or morally weak, lacking in volume, lacking in force
**Synonyms**: Frail, fragile, infirm, tame, weak
**Antonyms**: Firm, healthy, strong, robust, sound

**Fervor:** Warmth or intensity of emotion or feeling
**Synonyms**: Ardor, earnestness, passion, warmth
**Antonyms**: Apathy, dullness, insincerity, lethargy

**Flout:** To treat with disdain or scorn, to show contempt
**Synonyms**: Defy, disregard, repudiate, scorn
**Antonyms**: Approve, command, praise, respect

**Foment:** To instigate or foster, to incite or to arouse, to apply warm water or medicated liquid
**Synonyms**: Arouse, agitate incite, whip-up,
**Antonyms**: Calm, deter, dampen, stop, tranquilise

**Forsake:** To quit or leave entirely, abandon, desert, to give up or renounce
**Synonyms**: Disown, forgo, desert, renounce
**Antonyms**: Allow, approve, continue, hold

**Frugality:** Quality of living prudent in saving, lack of wastefulness
**Synonyms**: Thrift, prudence, moderation
**Antonyms**: Lavishness, extravagance, wastefulness

**Futile:** Incapable of producing any result ineffective
**Synonyms**: Fruitless, ineffective, unproductive, useless
**Antonyms**: Effective, fruitful, productive

**Garner:** To gather into a storage, to deposit as if in a granary, to acquire by effort
**Synonyms:** Accumulate, collect, corral, round-up
**Antonyms:** Dispel, disperse, scatter

**Glib:** Fluent in an insincere way, superficially or thoughtlessly
**Synonyms**: Articulate, eloquent, facile, loquacious, talkative
**Antonyms**: Inarticulate, quiet, silent

**Gloomy:** Dark or dim, deeply shaded, causing sadness or depression or despair
**Synonyms**: Bleak, cloudy, dim, dismal, murky
**Antonyms**: Bright, cheerful, gay, hopeful

**Glut:** To feed or full to satisfaction or excess, to flood with a particular item, to choke-up
**Synonyms**: Oversupply, satiate, surplus, stuff,
**Antonyms**: Lack, Starve, insufficiency

**Gracious:** Pleasantly kind, benevolent and courteous, characterised by good taste comfort, ease
**Synonyms**: Affable, congenial, courteous, beneficent, polite
**Antonyms**: Cold, impolite, rude, Unforgiving

**Gregarious:** One who is sociable or fond of other's company
**Synonyms**: Affable, sociable
**Antonyms**: Unfriendly unsociable

**Grudge:** A feeling of ill will or resentment
**Synonyms**: Animosity, aversion, bad-blood, hatred, rancor, resentment
**Antonyms**: Friendliness, liking, kindness, loving

**Guile:** Insidious cunning unattaining goal, crafty or artful, deception, duplicity
**Synonyms**: Chicanery, cunning, deceit, trickery
**Antonyms**: Forthrightness, honesty, frankness

**Gullible:** One who is easily deceived or cheated
**Synonyms**: Foolish, naive, unsophisticated
**Antonyms**: Astute, discerning, unbelieving, wise

**Haggard:** Looking exhausted or wasted, an appearance as if suffering from prolonged exertion or anxiety, worn out
**Synonyms:** Exhausted, lean, tired, pale, wearied
**Antonyms:** Fresh, strong, unworn

**Hallowed:** That what is holy or sacred
**Synonyms**: Holy, revered, sacred, venerated
**Antonyms**: Ignominious, immoral, shameful

**Hamper:** To restrict the movement by bonds or obstacles, to interfere with the operations of.
**Synonyms**: Clog, fetter, hinder, obstruct, retard, prevent
**Antonyms**: Aid, assist, facilitate, promote

**Hapless:** Having no luck, helplessly caught in grip of forces.
**Synonyms**: Hard luck, unfortunate, ill-fated, unlucky
**Antonyms**: Fortunate, happy, lucky

**Harmony:** Internal calm, pleasing arrangement of parts, combination of simultaneous musical notes in a chord
**Synonyms**: Balance, coherence, consonance, symphony
**Antonyms**: Asymmetry, discordance imbalance, incoherence,

**Harrowing:** Extremely distressing or painful
**Synonyms**: Agonising, excruciating, hurtful, tormenting
**Antonyms**: Gratifying, pleasing, sweet

**Hasty:** Done or made in a hurry, rapid in action or movement, fast and typically superficial
**Synonyms**: Abrupt, careless, cursory, hurried, impetuous, rash, reckless
**Antonyms**: Careful, cautious leisurely, loitering, sluggish, unhurried

**Haughty:** Showing an attitude of superiority and contempt blatantly and disdainfully proud
**Synonyms**: Arrogant, pompous, presumptuous, pretentious, supercilious
**Antonyms**: Humble, modest, submissive, unpretentious

**Heretic:** Person differing in opinion from the established religious dogma, one who differs in opinion from an accepted belief or doctrine
**Synonyms**: Dissenter, dissident, non-conformist
**Antonyms**: Conformist

**Heterodox:** Not widely accepted, different from an acknowledged standard, a traditional form or an established religion
**Synonyms**: Dissident, unconventional, unorthodox
**Antonyms**: Conformist, conventional, orthodox

**Hideous:** Offensive to the senses, exceedingly ugly, morally offensive
**Synonyms**: Abhorrent, appalling, disgusting, repulsive
**Antonyms**: Attractive, alluring, innocuous, inoffensive

**Histrionics:** Related to exaggerated emotional behaviour, theatrical arts or performances
**Synonyms**: Melodramatic, theatrical
**Antonyms**: Non-dramatic, unpretentious, subdued

**Humility:** Quality of being humble, freedom from pride or arrogance
**Synonyms**: Humbleness, meekness, modesty
**Antonyms**: Arrogance, egoism, pride, pompousness

**Hypocrisy:** Pretending to be what one is not, behaviour that contradicts what one claims or believes
**Synonyms**: Deception, insincerity
**Antonyms**: Sincerity, frankness, genuineness

**Ideological:** Relating to or based on ideology, the set of political or economic ideas
**Synonyms**: Doctrinaire, philosophical, conceptual
**Antonyms**: Concrete, representational

**Idolatry:** The worship of idols, blind or excessive, devotion
**Synonyms**: Adoration, worship
**Antonyms**: Condemnation, disapproval

**Immaculate:** Spotlessly clean, having or containing no flaw or error
**Synonyms**: Chaste, clean, spotless, pure, unsullied
**Antonyms**: Defiled, impure, tarnished, unchaste

**Imminent:** Likely to occur at any moment, projecting or leaning forward
**Synonyms**: Forthcoming, impending, inevitable, looming
**Antonyms**: Avoidable, distant, doubtful, receding

**Impair:** To make or cause to become worse, diminish in ability, value excellence
**Synonyms**: Debilitate, diminish, deteriorate, lessen, weaken
**Antonyms**: Increase extend, restore,

**Impassive:** Without emotion, apathetic, unmoved
**Synonyms**: Emotionless, placid, unemotional
**Antonyms**: Agitated, responsive

**Impediment:** An obstruction or hindrance
**Synonyms**: Barrier, hindrance, hurdle, obstruction, obstacle
**Antonyms**: Assistance, facilitation, support

**Impenitent:** Not feeling regret about one's sins
**Synonyms**: Hardened, uncontrite
**Antonyms**: Repentant, penitent

**Implicit:** Implied, understood but not stated
**Synonyms**: Implied, contained, latent, tacit
**Antonyms**: Apparent, specific, straight forward

**Impulsive:** Swayed by emotional or involuntary impulses
**Synonyms**: Hasty, impetuous
**Antonyms**: Cautious, deliberate, headful

**Impute:** To attribute or ascribe
**Synonyms**: Attribute, ascribe, accuse, charge, indict
**Antonyms**: Absolve, exculpate, exonerate

**Inadvertent:** An act done carelessly or unintentionally
**Synonyms**: Careless, reckless, unintended, unwitting
**Antonyms**: Advertent careful, cautious, intentional,

**Incongruous:** Out of keeping or place, inappropriate, unbecoming
**Synonyms**: Incompatible, inappropriate, incoherent absurd, bizarre
**Antonyms**: Congruous, Compatible, consistent, harmonious, uniform

**Indigent:** Lacking food clothing or other necessities of life, deficient in what is requisite
**Synonyms**: Destitute, impoverished, needy, poor
**Antonyms**: Affluent, rich

**Inevitable:** Unable to be avoided or escaped, sure to happen
**Synonyms**: Imminent, impending, unavoidable
**Antonyms**: Avoidable, unlikely, doubtful

**Infernal:** An extremely troublesome, annoying, fiendish
**Synonyms**: Damned, accursed, hellish, wicked
**Antonyms**: Heavenly, angelic, godlike

**Infringe:** To commit a breach or infraction, violate or transgress
**Synonyms**: Breach, violate, encroach, trespass
**Antonyms**: Comply, concur, give, discharge, obey

**Ingenuous:** Showing innocence or childlike simplicity and candidness
**Synonyms**: Genuine, guileless, honest, naive, undisguised
**Antonyms**: Artificial, crafty, dishonest, pretentious, wily

**Insinuate:** To suggest in an artful or indirect way, to introduce something gradually
**Synonyms**: allude, hint, imply infiltrate
**Antonyms**: Eject, eliminate, withdraw

**Insipid:** Lacking in flavour or dull
**Synonyms**: Bland, banal, prosaic, plain
**Antonyms**: Pleasing, tasty, delicious, exciting

**Insolvent:** Unable to satisfy creditors or discharge liabilities
**Synonyms**: Bankrupt, broke
**Antonyms**: Solvent, wealthy

**Instill:** To infuse slowly or gradually into the mind or feelings
**Synonyms**: Engender, inculcate
**Antonyms**: Dislodge, extract, uproot

**Intangible:** Not tangible or material
**Synonyms**: Abstract, ethereal, unreal,
**Antonyms**: Real, tangible, perceptible

**Intricate:** Having many interrelated parts or facets, complicated
**Synonyms**: Complex, tangled, complicated, sophisticated
**Antonyms**: Clear, easy, uncomplicated

**Intrigue:** To arise the curiosity or interest by unusual new or fascinating qualities, to draw or capture, to accomplish by crafty plot
**Synonyms**: Complication, conspiracy, scheme, plot
**Antonyms**: Candor, sincerity, honesty

**Intrinsic:** Belonging to a thing by its very nature
**Synonyms**: Inherent, innate, underlying
**Antonyms**: Acquired, extraneous, incidental

**Invective:** Vehement or Violent denunciation, censure or reproach, an insulting or abusive word
**Synonyms**: Censure, denunciation, diatribe, tirade
**Antonyms**: Approval, praise, compliment

**Invincible:** Incapable of being conquered or subdued
**Synonyms**: impregnable, unconquerable, unsurmountable, unbeatable
**Antonyms**: Beatable, destructible

**Irrepressible:** Incapable of being restrained repressed or controlled
**Synonyms**: Irresistible, uncontainable, unrestrainable
**Antonyms**: Controllable, resistible

**Jaded:** Dulled or satiated by over indulgence, worn out or wearied as by overwork or over use
**Synonyms**: Exhausted tired, weary, worn-out
**Antonyms**: Fresh, renewed

**Jejune:** Without interest or significance, juvenile or immature
**Synonyms**: Arid, banal, childish, dull, boring, insipid, juvenile, unexciting
**Antonyms**: Interesting, exciting

**Jibe:** To be in harmony or accord, agree
**Synonym:** Conform, correspond, harmonise
**Antonym:** Clash, differ, disagree

**Jovial:** Marked by high spirits or good humour
**Synonyms**: Blithe, cheerful, frolicsome, gay
**Antonyms**: Anguished, morose, sad, solemn

**Jubilant:** Feeling or expressing great joy
**Synonyms**: Elated. Euphoric, rejoicing, triumphant
**Antonyms**: Crestfallen, depressed, defeated, melancholy

**Judicious:** Having or showing good judgement and restraint specially in conduct or speech
**Synonyms**: Intelligent thoughtful, prudent,
**Antonyms**: Careless, irrational, foolish

**Juggernaut:** Huge force destroying everything in its path
**Synonyms**: Barrage, cavalcade, steamroller
**Antonyms**: Inferior, powerlessness

**Juvenile:** Being in early stage of life, adolescent, immature
**Synonyms**: Adolescent, immature, tender, young
**Antonyms**: Aged, mature, elderly

**Juxtapose:** Place side by side or close together
**Synonyms**: Appose, pair, connect
**Antonyms**: Disconnect, separate, detach

**Kin:** A person's relatives, family relationship, a group of persons related from a common ancestor
**Synonyms:** Affinity, clan, kith, lineage, relationship, tribe
**Antonyms**: Disconnection, strangership, inaffinity, irrelation

**Kindred:** Of a similar nature or character, of same ancestry
**Synonyms**: Affiliated, associated, relation
**Antonyms**: Dissimilar, distinguishable, unrelated

**Knave:** An unprincipled, untrustworthy or dishonest person
**Synonyms**: Dishonest, fraud, lowlife, scoundrel,
**Antonyms**: Paragon, innocent

**Knotty:** having knots, intricate or difficult
**Synonyms**: Complicated difficult, perplexing
**Antonyms**: Easy, manageable, simple, uncomplicated

**Kudos:** Honour, glory, acclaim
**Synonyms**: Applause, honour, acclaim
**Antonyms**: Condemnation, dishonour, criticism

**Laconic:** Using few words
**Synonyms**: Pithy, terse, crisp
**Antonyms**: Wordy, long-winded

**Languid:** Lacking in vigour or vitality, drooping or flagging
**Synonyms**: Apathetic, lazy, lethargic, sluggish
**Antonyms**: Active, energetic, spirited

**Laud:** to praise, a song or hymn of praise
**Synonyms**: Compliment, praise, eulogise
**Antonyms**: Blame, censure, criticise

**Lethargic:** Drowsy, sluggish, affected with lethargy
**Synonyms**: Apathetic, dull, passive, lackadaisical, sleepy
**Antonyms**: Active, Alert, energetic, vivacious

**Levity:** Light manner or attitude, lack of seriousness, lightness in weight
**Synonyms:** Frivolity, hilarity, mirth, repartee
**Antonyms:** Depression, gravity, seriousness

**Lucid:** Easily understood, completely intelligible
**Synonyms**: Clear, intelligible, unambiguous
**Antonyms**: Clouded, obscure, hidden

**Lunacy:** Insanity or mental disorder
**Synonyms**: Absurdity, insanity, mania
**Antonyms**: Normalcy, sanity, sense

**Lure:** Anything that attracts or entices
**Synonyms**: Allurement, attract, enticement
**Antonyms**: Deter, dissuade, repulsion

**Luscious:** Highly pleasing to the taste or smell, very satisfying to the senses
**Synonyms**: Appetising, palatable, delicious, succulent
**Antonyms**: Bland, dull, unsavory

**Lustrous:** Having lustre, shining
**Synonyms:** Dazzling, gleaming, luminous, shimmering, shining
**Antonyms:** Dark, dim dull, unshiny

**Luxuriant:** Abundant or lush in growth, florid, fertile
**Synonyms: A**bundant, lush, opulent, profuse
**Antonyms**: Barren, meagre, scanty,

**Machinations:** Crafty schemes and plots, intrigues
**Synonyms**: Chicanery, deception, intrigues, subterfuge
**Antonyms**: Faithfullness, plainspeak

**Magnanimity:** Displaying generosity towards others, specially when undeserving
**Synonyms:** Altruism, big-heartedness, generosity, nobility,
**Antonyms:** Hard-heartedness, mercilessness, ruthlessness

**Malice:** Desire to inflict injury, harm or suffering on another
**Synonyms**: Animosity, grudge, vengefulness
**Antonyms**: Friendliness, goodwill, kindness

**Malign:** To speak evil of
**Synonyms**: Slander, defame, besmirch, denigrate, smear
**Antonyms**: Compliment, praise, honour

**Metamorphosis:** A profound change in form from one stage to another, or in character
**Synonyms**: Evolution, transmutation
**Antonyms**: Stagnation

**Meticulous:** One who is very careful, showing or involving great care and effort
**Synonyms:** Assiduous, careful, mindful
**Antonyms:** Careless, cursory, rash, reckless, undiscriminating

**Mettle:** Courage and fortitude
**Synonyms**: Bravery, courage, temperament
**Antonyms**: Cowardice, timidity, powerlessness

**Mitigate:** To lessen in force or intensity, to make less severe
**Synonyms**: Allay, alleviate, ease, relieve
**Antonyms**: Aggravate, augment, enhance, worsen

**Modest:** Having or showing a moderate or humble estimate of one's merits, importance etc.
**Synonyms**: Humble, unassuming
**Antonyms**: Arrogant, egotistical, pompous

**Mollify:** To soften in feeling or temper, to mitigate or reduce
**Synonyms**: Allay, appease, assuage, mitigate
**Antonyms**: Aggravate, irritate, infuriate

**Momentous:** Of great or far-reaching importance
**Synonyms**: Crucial, notable, eventful, far-reaching
**Antonyms**: Inconsequential insignificant, trivial

**Monotonous:** Lacking in variety, tediously unvarying
**Synonyms**: Boring, irksome, tedious, dreary
**Antonyms**: Bright exciting, Varied, pleasant

**Morbid:** An unhealthy mental state, unwholesome, gloomy
**Synonyms**: Gruesome, macabre, melancholy
**Antonyms**: Cheerful, joyful

**Motley:** Many coloured, made up of many parts, exhibiting great diversity of elements
**Synonyms**: Disparate, diverse, assorted
**Antonyms**: Single, uniform

**Mundane:** Worldly as opposed to spiritual, concerned with the ordinary
**Synonyms**: Banal, everyday, ordinary, prosaic
**Antonyms**: Abnormal, uncommon, exciting

**Munificent:** Extremely liberal in giving, very generous
**Synonyms**: Benevolent, charitable, liberal
**Antonyms**: Frugal, greedy, stingy

**Murky:** Dark, gloomy and cheerless
**Synonyms**: Cloudy, dusky, dreary, gloomy
**Antonyms**: Bright, cheerful, shining

**Nexus:** Means of connection, a connected group or series
**Synonyms**: Connection, link, tie
**Antonyms**: Outside, exterior

**Nimble:** Quick and light in movement, moving with ease
**Synonyms**: Agile, active, brisk, swift
**Antonyms**: Clumsy, slow, sluggish

**Non-plussed:** Completely puzzled or perplexedly something unexpected
**Synonyms**: Baffled, bewildered, dazed, perplexed
**Antonyms**: Clear, composed, ordered

**Non-chalant:** Coolly unconcerned,indifferentor unexcited
**Synonyms**: Casual, detached, indifferent
**Antonyms**: Attentive, concerned

**Nostalgia:** Sentimental longing for a past time
**Synonyms**: longing, sentimentality, yearning
**Antonyms**: Unsentimentality, hard-headedness

**Novice:** A person who is new to the work or circumstances
**Synonyms**: Beginner, learner, new-comer, pupil
**Antonyms**: Expert, professional, veteran

**Noxious:** Harmful or injurious to health or physical well-being
**Synonyms**: Corrupting harmful, injurious, pernicious
**Antonyms**: Harmless, healthy, helpful

**Nullify:** To render or declare legally void or inoperative, to deprive something of value or effectiveness
**Synonyms**: Abolish, abrogate, annual, cancel, quash
**Antonyms**: Allow, confirm, uphold

**Obdurate:** Unmoved by persuasion or entreaties, stubborn and unyielding
**Synonyms**: Adamant, dogged, inexorable, stubborn, unyielding, thick-skinned, obstinate
**Antonyms:** Amenable, pliable, flexible, yielding

**Obtrusive:** Thrust out or jutting out, forward in a manner of conduct
**Synonyms**: Bulging, noticeable, interferring, meddlesome, officious, presumptuous
**Antonyms**: Modest, shy, unobtrusive

**Obviate:** To make unnecessary, to anticipate and prevent
**Synonyms**: Counteract, forestall, preclude
**Antonyms**: Support, aid

**Obscure:** Not clear or plain, vague
**Synonyms**: Ambiguous, arcane, confusing, vague
**Antonyms**: Apparent, clear, obvious

**Odious:** That which is causing hatred, or is detestable, highly offensive
**Synonyms**: Abhorrent, disgusting, malevolent, obnoxious
**Antonyms**: Delightful, engaging, fascinating

**Officious:** Too helpful and meddlesome
**Synonyms**: Intrusive, meddlesome
**Antonyms**: Modest, shy

**Oligarchy:** A kind of government in which power is vested only in a few persons
**Synonyms:** Authoritarianism, autocracy, despotism, monocracy
**Antonyms:** Democracy

**Ominous:** That what is portending harm or occurrence of something evil
**Synonyms**: Foreboding, threatening
**Antonyms**: Auspicious, cheerful, joyful

**Onerous:** Burdensome or oppressive, having obligations or responsibilities
**Synonyms**: Arduous, burdensome, exhaustive, weighty
**Antonyms**: Easy, effortless, light

**Ordain:** To enact or establish by law, to endow the functions of the priest. etc
**Synonyms**: Anoint, appoint order, impose
**Antonyms**: Abolish, cancel, refuse, revoke

**Ornamental:** Used or grown for decoration or ornament (as an ornamental plant)
**Synonyms**: Decorative, exquisite, ornate, showy
**Antonyms**: Plain, ordinary,

**Ostentatious:** Trying to attract attention, showy display, pretentious
**Synonyms:** Flamboyant, flashy, showy, swanky, pretentious
**Antonyms:** Conservative, quiet, understated,

**Outrage:** An act of utter cruelty or violence, gross violation of law
**Synonyms**: Shock, maltreatment, violence
**Antonyms**: Delight, favour, praise

**Paean:** A song of praise, joy or triumph, a fervent expression of joy, a hymn or invocation of thanksgiving
**Synonyms**: Acclaimation, hymn, eulogy ode, psalm
**Antonyms**: Censure, condemnation, criticism

**Pamper:** To treat with or satisfy with indulgence
**Synonyms**: Coddle, indulge, gratify
**Antonyms**: Deny, neglect

**Paragon:** A model of excellence or perfection
**Synonyms**: Epitome, exemplar, ultimate
**Antonyms**: Flaw, imperfection

**Paramount:** Of central or chief importance, someone above in rank or authority
**Synonyms**: Pre-eminent, foremost, dominant
**Antonyms**: Insignificant, inferior, trivial, unimportant

**Paucity:** Lack of something, scarcity
**Synonyms**: Dearth, insufficiency, scarcity
**Antonyms**: Abundance, sufficiency

**Peerless:** one having no equal or a match
**Synonyms**: matchless, unrivalled, unequalled
**Antonyms**: Inferior, commonplace, mediocre,

**Peevish:** Showing annoyance or irritation, one who is cross, querulous or discontented
**Synonyms**: Angry, captious, complaining, sullen, querulous
**Antonyms**: Amiable, friendly

**Penchant:** A strong inclination or liking
**Synonyms**: Affinity, proclivity, propensity
**Antonyms**: Antipathy, indifference, dislike

**Penury:** Extreme poverty, destitution
**Synonyms**: Deprivation, scantiness, poverty
**Antonyms**: Affluence, plenty, sufficiency

**Perfunctory:** Performed superficially, not thoroughly, lacking interest
**Synonyms**: Cursory, superficial
**Antonyms**: Careful, detailed

**Perturbed:** Showing great concern or an upset emotional state, greatly disordered
**Synonyms**: Annoyed, bothered, flustered,
**Antonyms**: Calm, composed

**Pervasive:** Spread everywhere, present throughout or in all parts
**Synonym:** Common, omnipresent, widespread
**Antonym:** Rare, strange, unusual, uncommon

**Perverse:** One disposed to go against what is desired, cantankerous or wayward
**Synonyms**: Contradictory, petulant, obstinate, wicked
**Antonyms**: Agreeable, compliant, docile

**Placid:** pleasantly calm or peaceful, undisturbed
**Synonyms**: Calm, peaceful, tranquil, undisturbed
**Antonyms**: Disturbed, turbulent, violent

**Plummet:** To fall, to plunge, to go to a lower level abruptly
**Synonym:** Crash, decline, fall, plunge, tumble
**Antonym:** Burgeon, escalate, increase, swell

**Pompous:** Ostentatious and lofty, an overt show of importance and dignity
**Synonyms**: Boastful, haughty, pretentious
**Antonyms**: Humble, modest, unpretentious

**Pragmatic:** Practical, relating to practical point of view
**Synonyms**: Practical, realistic
**Antonyms**: Impractical, idealistic

**Precarious:** Depending on uncertain and insecure circumstances, or on the will of others
**Synonyms**: Dicey, doubtful, insecure, perilous, unsteady
**Antonyms**: Certain, definite, undoubted

**Predicament:** A difficult, perplexing or dangerous situation
**Synonyms**: Crisis, dilemma, plight, impasse
**Antonyms**: Agreement, solution

**Propagate:** to cause to multiply, to reproduce, to transmit
**Synonyms**: Inseminate, multiply, proliferate
**Antonyms**: Decrease, deplete, diminish, suppress

**Prudence:** Quality or fact of being prudent or wise in practical affairs, caution and discretion with respect to practical, exercise economy/frugality in in monetary matters or management of resources
**Synonyms**: Austerity, foresight, discretion, frugality, wisdom
**Antonyms**: Carelessness, indiscretion, ignorance, imprudence, rashness

**Quagmire:** Marsh, difficult situation
**Synonyms**: Dilemma, imbroglio, predicament, quandry
**Antonyms**: Agreement, ease

**Quaint:** Possessing an old-ashioned charm, strange or unusual and interesting
**Synonyms**: Antiquates, curious, queer, strange, weird
**Antonyms**: Common, modern, unsual

**Qualm:** Uneasy feeling or pans of conscience about rightness of actions
**Synonyms**: Anxiety, nervousness, misgiving, remorse
**Antonyms**: Calm, ease, unremorseful

**Quarantine:** A strict isolation placed to prevent spread of diseases
**Synonyms**: Detention, seclusion
**Antonyms**: Release, combine, socialize

**Quell:** To suppress, put an end to, extinguish
**Synonyms**: Conquer, crush, subdue, reduce, putdown
**Antonyms**: Agitate buildup, exacerbate,

**Quibble:** Argue over unsignificant detail, use of vague or irrelevant language, argument to evade a point at issue
**Synonyms**: Fuss, niggle, nitpick
**Antonyms**: Applaud, compliment, recommend, praise

**Ratify:** To confirm or express consent, approval or formal sanction
**Synonyms**: Endorse, consent, approve
**Antonyms**: Deny, contradict, dissent,

**Rampage:** Rush wildly about, a course of violent riotous action or behaviour
**Synonyms**: Agitation, frenzy, hysteria, uproar
**Antonyms**: Calmness, peacefulness, quietude, tranquility

**Recalcitrant:** Resisting authority or control
**Synonyms**: Fractious, rebellious, wayward
**Antonyms**: Agreeable, compliant, obedient

**Recant:** To retract a statement or opinion
**Synonyms**: Annul, backtrack, renege, retract
**Antonyms**: Agree, corroborate, confirm, validate

**Rectify:** To correct a thing or set right
**Synonyms**: Amend, fix, improve, remedy
**Antonyms**: Corrupt, harm, worsen

**Redeem:** To buy or pay off, clear by payment
**Synonyms**: Payoff, recover, regain, reclaim
**Antonyms**: Forefeit, hold, lose

**Refute:** To prove as false or incorrect
**Synonyms**: Contradict, rebut, repudiate
**Antonyms**: Agree, prone, ratify, sanction

**Reluctant:** Someone who is unwilling or disinclined to do something
**Synonyms**: Averse, cautious, hesitant, circumspect, wary
**Antonyms**: Certain, anxious, eager

**Remnant:** A remaining part of something, a fragment or scrap
**Synonyms**: Fragment, residue, piece
**Antonyms**: Complete, entire, whole

**Remonstrate:** To say or plead in protest, objection or disapproval
**Synonyms**: Censure dissent, protest
**Antonyms**: Accept, agree, approve laud, concede

**Remorse:** Deep or painful regret for wrong doing
**Synonyms**: Anguish, contrition, repentance, regret, penitence
**Antonyms**: Indifference, joy, remorselessness

**Renege:** To go back on one's word
**Synonyms**: Back out, default, retract
**Antonyms**: Fulfill, comply

**Reproach:** To find fault with, blame
**Synonyms**: Blame, censure, disgrace, discredit
**Antonyms**: Approval, endorsement

**Rescind:** To abrogate or annul, to invalidate (an act, measure, etc.)
**Synonyms**: Annul, abrogate, abolish, quash, repeal, set aside
**Antonyms**: Approve, permit, validate

**Resentment:** The feeling of displeasure or indignation at some act, remark person etc.
**Synonyms**: Animosity, displeasure, rage, rancor
**Antonyms**: Content, cheer, delight, friendliness

**Restrain:** To hold back from action, keep in check or under control, to deprive of liberty
**Synonyms**: Constrain, confine, detain, restrict, suppress
**Antonyms**: Allow, free liberate, let go, set free

**Reticent:** Not speaking freely, reserved
**Synonyms**: Hesitant, reluctant, reserved, restrained
**Antonyms**: Communicative, outgoing, unrestrained

**Retract:** To draw back in, to draw back within one self
**Synonyms**: Back off, reverse, recant, withdraw,
**Antonyms**: Advance, go forward

**Reverence:** A feeling of deep respect, awe and veneration
**Synonyms**: Admiration, awe, esteem, respect, veneration,
**Antonyms**: Disregard, disrespect, censure, scorn

**Rout:** An overwhelming defeat, a defeat accompanied with disorderly flight
**Synonyms**: Debacle, disaster, vanquish
**Antonyms**: Triumph, victory, win,

**Salutary:** Producing an improvement, promoting health
**Synonyms**: beneficent, curative, favourable, helpful
**Antonyms**: Bad, disadvantageous, harmful, unfavourable

**Sarcastic:** Having the character of sarcasm, a sharp and satirical or ironic utterance
**Synonyms**: Acerbic, derisive, ironical
**Antonyms**: Amusing, gracious, sportive

**Satiate:** To satisfy to the full
**Synonyms**: Content, gratify, satisfy,
**Antonyms**: Disappoint, deprive, dissatisfy

**Savage:** A mean, evil or unprincipled person
**Synonyms**: Brute, devil, villain
**Antonyms**: Angel, civilised, innocent,

**Savor:** To enjoy, a distinct flavour or smell
**Synonyms**: Odour, relish, scent
**Antonyms**: Blandness

**Scanty:** Limited or less than sufficient in degree quantity or extent
**Synonyms**: Meagre, scarce, insufficient, sparse
**Antonyms**: Adequate, lavish, luxuriant

**Sensual:** Relating to the senses, gratifying physical senses, particularly sexual, desire
**Synonyms**: Exciting, sensuous, bodily, sexual
**Antonyms**: Abstemious, chaste

**Servile:** Expressing a spirit of humility or submissiveness
**Synonyms**: Humble, docile slavish
**Antonyms**: Arrogant, aggressive, dominant

**Shabby:** Clothed with worn or seedy garments, showing signs of advanced wear and tear and neglect
**Synonyms**: Beatup, dilapidated, impoverished, motheaten, miserable, tatty,
**Antonyms**: Fresh, new, maintained, prosperous, thriving

**Shrewd:** Showing or having practical cleverness or judgement
**Synonyms**: Astute, canny, cunning, crafty
**Antonyms**: Artless, gullible, imbecile, naïve, simple

**Slander:** To make a false statement that damages another's reputation
**Synonyms**: Aspersion, defame, malign, libel
**Antonyms**: Applaud, approve, exalt, glorify, honor

**Sneer:** To express scornful amusement
**Synonyms**: mock, smirk, scorn, taunt
**Antonyms**: Applause, appreciation, praise

**Solicit:** To approach with a request, to make a petition, to urge strongly
**Synonyms**: Canvass, entreat, implore, seek
**Antonyms**: Answer, give, reject

**Solicitous:** Anxious or concerned for a person or a thing, desirous
**Synonyms**: Anxious, desirous, mindful, apprehensive
**Antonyms**: Heedless, inattentive, easygoing

**Sporadic:** Appearing or happening at irregular intervals
**Synonyms**: Infrequent, intermittent, occasional, scattered
**Antonyms**: Abundant, common, frequent, incessant

**Spurious:** Not genuine, authentic or true
**Synonyms**: Bogus, counterfeit, fake
**Antonyms**: Authentic, genuine, true, real

**Squalid:** Foul and repulsive, as from lack of care or cleanliness
**Synonyms**: Dingy, dirty, filthy, sordid
**Antonyms**: Clean, clear tidy

**Startled:** Disturbed or agitated suddenly, expressing surprise or alarm
**Synonyms**: Frightened, scared, shocked, stunned
**Antonyms**: Disinterested, unimpressed, bored

**Stigma:** A mark of disgrace or inferiority
**Synonyms**: Blemish, disgrace, stain
**Antonyms**: Esteem, honour, respect

**Stipulate:** To specify as an essential condition
**Synonyms**: Designate, impose, lay down, specify
**Antonyms**: Imply confuse, muddle, unsettle

**Stupor:** Physical or mental inertness
**Synonyms**: Languor, lethargy, torpor
**Antonyms**: Eagerness, keenness, spiritedness

**Sublime:** Causing wonder or astonishment
**Synonyms**: Astounding, eminent, magnificent
**Antonyms**: Jaded, monotonous, unimpressive

**Subsume:** To include or in corporate
**Synonyms**: Contain, include, incorporate, involve
**Antonyms**: Exclude

**Subterfuge:** Deceit used to achieve ones goal, a trick or dishonest way of achieving something
**Synonyms**: Bluff, deceit, stratagem, ploy
**Antonyms**: Frankness, honesty, openness

**Subvert:** To cause downfall of, to overthrow, to undermine the principles of
**Synonyms**: Demolish, overthrow, sabotage
**Antonyms**: Aid, build, create, uphold

**Succinct:** expressed in few words, precise and clear
**Synonyms**: Concise, curt, terse, pithy
**Antonyms**: Lengthy, wordy, longwinded

**Sycophant:** A servile self-seeking flatterer
**Synonyms**: Freeloader, flatterer, leech, parasite
**Antonyms**: Benefactor, loyal, philanthropist

**Tabernacle:** A house of worship, a temporary shelter or place of dwelling
**Synonyms**: Abbey, cathedral, sanctuary, shrine
**Antonyms**: Unholy place

**Taboo:** Banned or forbidden, on grounds of morality taste, or due to it posing a risk
**Synonyms**: Banned, forbidden, impermissible, proscribed, prohibited
**Antonyms**: Accepable, allowable, permissible

**Tacit:** Silently understood or implied
**Synonyms**: Implicit, implied, unspoken
**Antonyms**: Explicit, stated

**Taciturn:** Tending not to speak frequently
**Synonyms**: Laconic, reserved, silent, tight-lipped
**Antonyms**: Extrovert, talkative, outspoken, vocal

**Tedious:** causing weariness, restlessness or lack of interest
**Synonyms**: Boring, drab, drudging, wearisome, tiresome
**Antonyms**: Energising, exhilarating, lively, sensational

**Tenacious:** Continuing despite difficulties, opposition or discouragement
**Synonyms**: Dogged, insistent, stubborn, patient
**Antonyms**: Quitting, yielding, faltering

**Tenet:** An opinion, belief, doctrine or dogma, held as true
**Synonyms**: Doctrine, dogma, faith, teaching
**Antonyms**: Disbelief, doubt, reality

**Tenuous:** Lacking a sound basis as reasoning, unsubstantiated or weak
**Synonyms**: Dubious, flimsy, insubstantial, nebulous
**Antonyms**: Certain, definite, substantial, significant

**Terse:** Marked by use of few words to convey the meaning or information
**Synonyms**: Brief concise, incisive, succinct
**Antonyms**: Long winded, repetitious, verbose, wordy

**Tractable:** Easily managed and controlled
**Synonyms**: Amenable, complaint, obedient
**Antonyms**: Intractable, obstinate, stubborn

**Travesty:** A parody or caricature or likeness or imitation
**Synonyms**: Caricature, distortion, exaggeration, imitation, mockery
**Antonyms**: Homage, seriousness, tribute

**Trepidation:** Emotion in the face of threat or danger
**Synonyms**: Anxiety, dread, fear, panic, terror
**Antonyms**: Aplomb, assurance, courage, valour

**Tryst:** Agreement between lovers to meet
**Synonyms**: Appointment, date, rendezvous
**Antonyms**: Division, non-engagement, non-involvement

**Thrifty:** Given to or marked by economy and frugality
**Synonyms**: Economical, frugal, prudent,
**Antonyms**: Extravagant, thriftless, spendthrift, unthrifty

**Throng:** A multitude of assembled persons or crowding together of persons, a pressing increase of activity
**Synonyms**: Crowd, herd, congregation, swarm, mob, rout
**Antonyms**: Scattering, dispersion, sparsing

**Timid:** Lacking in courage bravery or self-assurance, one who is easily alarmed, shy
**Synonyms**: Demure, diffident, feeble, coward, weak
**Antonyms**: Bold, courageous, brave, strong, unabashed

**Tranquil:** Free from commotion or tumult, peaceful
**Synonyms**: Calm, peaceful, placid, quiet, serene, sober
**Antonyms**: Agitated, chaotic, excitable, fierce, rough, stormy, violent

**Transient:** That which is not lasting or enduring, short and temporary
**Synonyms**: Ephemeral, fleeting, temporal, transitory, evanescent
**Antonyms**: Enduring, lasting, permanent, perpetual

**Treacherous:** That what is dangerous, deceptive, untrustworthy and likely to betray
**Synonyms**: Dangerous, deceptive, deceitful, dishonest, duplicitous, slippery, tricky, unreliable
**Antonyms**: Honest, forthright, harmless, reliable, untreacherous

**Tremble:** To shake involuntarily as with fear or cold, to be affected with great fear
**Synonyms**: Quiver, shiver, shudder, shake
**Antonyms**: Steady, still, calm

**Trenchant:** Having keenness and forcefulness and penetration in thought expression or intellect, incisiveness of language
**Synonyms**: Acerbic, caustic, incisive, forceful, sharp, severe
**Antonyms**: Ambiguous, bland, blunt, feeble, ineffective, ineffectual

**Trivial:** Of little importance, value or significance
**Synonyms**: Commonplace, frivolous, insignificant, paltry, petty, trifling
**Antonyms**: Consequential, essential, important, pertinent, significant

**Tumultuous:** Marked by disturbance, full of tumult or riotousness
**Synonyms**: Boisterous, raucous, riotous, turbulent, violent
**Antonyms**: Calm, harmonious, moderate, peaceful, quiet

**Umbrage:** Offence, annoyance, displeasure
**Synonyms**: Annoyance, displeasure, indignation, offense
**Antonyms**: Calmness, peace, pleasure

**Uncanny:** Having or seeming to have a supernatural or inexplicable basis, mysterious
**Synonyms**: Astonishing, eerie, mysterious, spooky
**Antonyms**: Boring, commonplace, normal, ordinary, unremarkable, usual

**Uncouth:** Awkward, clumsy or unmannerly
**Synonyms**: Awkward, boorish, cheap, crass, clumsy, unmannerly, ungraceful
**Antonyms**: Cultivated, couth, refined, sophisticated, elegant

**Untenable:** Incapable of being defended, indefensible
**Synonyms**: Illogical, indefensible, unsound
**Antonyms:** Logical, rational, commonsensical, real, clear, cogent, reasonable

**Untoward:** Unfavourable, unfortunate or improper
**Synonyms**: Adverse, perverse, unfavourable, unfortunate
**Antonyms:** Fortunate, proper, suitable

**Urchin:** A mischievous or a small boy, a young child poorly dressed
**Synonyms**: Brat, cub, waif, rascal
**Antonyms**: Adult, cherub, dearie, major,

**Urge:** To try to persuade through earnest appeals
**Synonyms**: Exhort, goad, implore, prod
**Antonyms**: Deter, discourage, dissuade

**Utterly:** To a full extent or degree
**Synonyms**: Altogether, completely, entirely fully, thoroughly
**Antonyms**: Barely, hardly, scarcely, slightly,

**Vacillate:** To waiver in mind or opinion, to be indecisive or irresolute
**Synonyms**: Dither, oscillate, waver
**Antonyms:** Persist, stay, continue

**Vacuous:** Without contents, empty lacking intelligence, purposeless
**Synonyms**: Dull, emptied, shallow, superficial, vacant, void
**Antonyms:** Aware, intelligent, filled

**Vagary:** An erratic or unpredictable action occurrence or course
**Synonyms**: Caprice, fancy, quirk, whim
**Antonyms**: Actuality, certainty, consistency, fact

**Vagrant:** One who has no established residence and wanders idly
**Synonyms**: Ambulant, nomad, vagabond, wanderer, rover
**Antonyms**: Immobile, steady, settled, stationery

**Vain:** Having a too high opinion of oneself, showing or having excessive pride
**Synonyms**: Arrogant, egoistic, conceited, pompous, prideful, smug
**Antonyms**: egoless, humble, modest

**Valour:** Strength of mind or spirit to carry on in spite of danger
**Synonyms**: Bravery, courage, dauntlessness, gutsiness, prowess
**Antonyms**: Fear, cowardice, spinelessness, timidity

**Vanity:** Inflated pride in oneself or one's appearance, something that is vain, empty or valueless
**Synonyms**: Conceit, egotism, pride, pretension
**Antonyms**: Humbleness, humility, modesty

**Vapid:** Without liveliness or spirit, dull or tedious
**Synonyms**: Boring, insipid, stale, uninspiring, tedious
**Antonyms:** Exciting, interesting

**Vaunt:** To boast of, brag
**Synonyms**: Boast, brag
**Antonyms:** Modest, conceal, hide

**Verbose:** Characterised by use of many or too many words
**Synonyms**: Bombastic, flowery, rhetorical, wordy
**Antonyms:** Concise

**Venerable:** Deserving respect by age or character
**Synonyms**: Esteemed, honoured, reputable, respectable
**Antonyms**: Disgraceful, ignominious, immature, unworthy

**Vexation:** The state of being vexed, irritation, annoyance
**Synonyms**: Aggravation, annoyance, irritation, chagrin
**Antonyms:** Calmness, contentment

**Viable:** Capable of developing or living, practicable
**Synonyms**: Feasible, practicable, possible
**Antonyms:** Unfeasible, impracticable, impossible, unlikely

**Vigilant:** One who is alert and watchful to avoid danger
**Synonyms**: Alert, awake, cautious, observant, watchful
**Antonyms**: Asleep, careless, negligent

**Vilify:** To utter slanderous or abusive statement against somebody or to lower in estimation or importance
**Synonyms**: Malign, slander, slur, defame, denigrate, smear
**Antonyms**: Approve, cherish, commend, compliment, exalt, flatter

**Virtue:** Moral excellence, goodness, righteousness
**Synonyms**: Ethic, morality, quality
**Antonyms**: Dishonesty, evil imperfection, immorality, vice

**Virtuoso:** Someone with masterly skills or knowledge of a field, expert musician
**Synonyms**: Musician, prodigy, celebrity
**Antonyms:** Amateur, greenhorn

**Vivacious:** Lively, animated, spirited
**Synonyms**: Active, animated, effervescent, spirited, energetic
**Antonyms**: Boring, dispirited, dull

**Vivid:** Strikingly bright or intense as colour or light, lively, presenting an appearance of freshness
**Synonyms**: Animated, bright, colourful, eloquent, lucid, sharp, telling
**Antonyms**: Bland, boring, dull, dim, lifeless, tasteless, undramatic

**Vogue:** The prevailing fashion or practice
**Synonyms**: Fashionable, happening, popular
**Antonyms:** Unfashionable, unpopular

**Vortex:** A whirlpool, a whirlwind, centre of turbulence
**Synonyms**: Whirlpool, awhirlwind, malestorm
**Antonyms:** Motionless, standstill

**Vouch:** To support as true, to attest, to guarantee
**Synonyms**: Affirm, attest, certify, confirm, declare, vow, warrant
**Antonyms**: Deny, disapprove, oppose, repudiate, reject

**Waft:** To carry lightly over air/water, to float
**Synonyms**: Drift, float
**Antonyms**: Hold, keep

**Waive:** To refrain from claiming or insisting on, give up
**Synonyms**: Forgo, relinquish, put off, renounce, surrender
**Antonyms**: Claim, carry out, impose, retain

**Wane:** To diminish in phases or intensity, to become less brilliant or powerful
**Synonyms**: Abate, decline, decrease, ease, fade, relent, taper
**Antonyms**: Appear, accumulate, escalate, increase, intensify, soar, swell, wax

**Wanton:** Deliberate and without motive or provocation, maliciously or unjustifiably, without regard, extravagant or luxuriously, sportive or frolicsome
**Synonyms**: Lewd, shameless, carefree, abandoned
**Antonyms**: Decent, gentle, responsible

**Wary:** Marked by caution, watchfulness, cunning
**Synonyms**: Alert, cautious, circumspect, guarded, heedful
**Antonyms**: Careless, heedless, negligent, unmindful

**Whimsical:** Resulting from whim, fanciful, subject to erratic behaviour
**Synonym:** Capricious, freakish, unpredictable
**Antonym:** Levelheaded, commonsensical, pragmatic, grounded

**Wield:** To exercise power or authority, to exert one's authority, to handle something as a tool or weapon
**Synonyms**: Apply, exert, employ, utilise
**Antonyms**: Ignore, neglect, fail, forgo, avoid

**Wile:** A tick or a stratagem to fool, trap or entice, trickery
**Synonyms**: Guile, stratagem, trickery, chicanery, deceit, subterfuge
**Antonyms**: Fairness, honesty, naivety, honour, openness

**Wilt:** To become limp or droop, to lose strength or vigour
**Synonyms**: Droop, dwindle, fade, perish shrivel, wane, wither
**Antonyms**: Grow, revive, bloom, develop, enlarge

**Winsome:** Sweetly or innocently charming, showing a good mood or disposition
**Synonyms**: Alluring, blithe, captivating, cute, delightful, engaging
**Antonyms**: Dour, gloomy, glum, morose, sulky, sullen

**Wistful:** Vague longing for a past, sadly thoughtful,
**Synonym:** Forlorn, melancholy, mournful, nostalgic, thoughtful
**Antonym:** Cheerful, happy, joyful

**Yap:** To talk noisily, shrilly or foolishly
**Synonyms**: Babble, chit-chat, ramble, yelp
**Antonyms**: Whisper

**Yearn:** To long for something persistently, wistfully or sadly, to feel tenderness for,
**Synonyms**: Long, languish, crave, yearn, pine, hunger
**Antonyms**: Abjure, dislike, hate, despise

**Yield:** To give forth or to produce by a natural process, to give up as to a superior power or authority.
**Synonyms**: Harvest, earnings, income, output, give-up, surrender,
**Antonyms**: Deny, resist, hold, refuse, withstand,

**Yoke:** A device for joining a pair of draft animals, an emblem of subjugation or servitude
**Synonyms**: Burden, connect, chain, enslavement, harness, tie
**Antonyms**: Detach, disjoin, loosen, liberate, release

**Zap:** To kill or shot, to attack and destroy with sudden force or jolt
**Synonyms**: Exterminate, jolt, kill
**Antonyms**: Create, start

**Zeal:** Eagerness or ardent interest in pursuit of something
**Synonyms**: Ardor, eagerness, fervor, passion, zest
**Antonyms**: Apathy, disinterest, indifference, indolence, lethargy, torpidity, sluggishness

**Zealot:** One who is fanatically devoted to a cause
**Synonym:** Crusader, fanatic, ideologue, radical
**Antonym:** Conservative

**Zenith:** The highest part or point
**Synonyms**: Acme, apex, apogee, climax, crescendo, summit, pinnacle
**Antonyms**: Abyss, base, nadir

**Zest:** The quality or state of being stimulating to mind or senses
**Synonyms**: Enthusiasm, tang, zing
**Antonyms**: Flatness, passiveness, tastelessness

## IDIOMS

1. **Back up:** To help or support

   **Sentence:** Nobody believed him as he couldn't back up his claim with evidence.

2. **Blow over:** To fade away or pass off

   **Sentence:** Let's hope that this crisis soon blows over.

3. **Bear out:** Confirm or substantiate

   **Sentence:** The document produced by him did not bear out the veracity of his statement.

4. **Clear up:** Solve or explain something

   **Sentence:** The differences between the two have been cleared up.

5. **Hear me out:** To listen to, to hear me to the end

   **Sentence:** Please hear me out before you take any adverse view.

6. **Hit upon:** To discover or to find

   **Sentence:** The new employee hit upon an excellent idea to solve the marketing problem.

7. **Hang about:** Spend time aimlessly

   **Sentence:** The headmaster forbade the students from hanging about in the school corridors.

8. **Prevail on:** To ask or to persuade

   **Sentence:** The kids could eventually prevail on their parents to take them to a foreign holiday.

9. **Bear down:** To exert full strength, to overthrow, to crush

   **Sentence:** The young king could soon bear down all the rebel generals with the help of his loyalists.

10. **Bear out:** To substantiate or to confirms

    **Sentence:** The court held that the documentary evidence bears out the testimony of the accused.

11. **Bear up:** to support, to withstand

    **Sentence:** As the witness had turned hostile, his statement did not bear up in the proceedings.

12. **Break down:** To fail, to cry

    **Sentence (a):** We did not expect the new machinery to break down so soon.

    **Sentence (b):** The speaker was so touched by the occasion that he broke down in the middle of his speech.

13. **Break into :** Entered or open by force

    **Sentence:** The police found that the thief could have broken into the house through the unguarded back door.

14. **Broke off:** To stop abruptly or suddenly

    **Sentence:** They broke off their business relationship with the sister company.

15. **Break with:** To have quarrel with or end relationship with someone

    **Sentence:** The two friends had a break with each other over a petty issue.

16. **Bring about:** Cause something to happen

    **Sentence:** Gaming and digital addiction has brought about ruin of the health of many teenagers.

17. **Bring forth:** produce or give rise to, cause

    **Sentence:** Unhygienic conditions bring forth many diseases.

18. **Bring forward:** adduce or to move to an earlier time

    **Sentence:** The management asked him to bring forward more reasons to support the project.

19. **Bring out:** to produce or to publish

    **Sentence:** The government brings out an annual report on the economic situation in the country.

20. **Called for:** Demanded or required

    **Sentence:** An explanation was called for from the employee for his rude behaviour.

21. **Call in:** Enlist someones help or services, send for someone

    **Sentence:** Considering the disaster, experts were called in to handle the situation.

22. **Called on:** To pay a visit

    **Sentence:** The new set of employees called on the divisional heads of the company.

23. **Carry out:** To perform or execute a task

    **Sentence:** The king selected his most trusted and able general to carry out the plans of invasion in the enemy territory.

24. **Carried away:** Deprive of self control

    **Sentence:** In the heat of moment many get carried away and say things which they regret later.

25. **Carried on:** To continue doing an activity or task

    **Sentence:** Despite the death of the chairman of the company, the team led by his young son carried on the business well.

26. **Cast away:** Some body shipwrecked and stranded in an isolated place

    **Sentence:** The cast away of the shipwreck survived on the island for over a month before they were spotted and rescued.

27. **Cast down:** To feel depressed

    **Sentence:** His friends were trying to cheer him up as he was cast down after the poor performance in the examination.

28. **Come about:** To take place/happen

    **Sentence:** No body knew as to how the unfortunate turn of events came about.

29. **Come out:** Emerge (of facts)/become known

    **Sentence:** Everybody was surprised when the reality came out from the police investigations.

30. **Come to:** Reach to/amount to

    **Sentence:** If you follow the rules, then you will come to no harm while operating the machine.

31. **Came up:** To come near/to raise for discussion/ to rise in rank or status

    **Sentence:** Though the issue came up for discussion before the committee, there was hardly any time left for deliberations.

32. **Done for:** To suffer defeat/ruined/about to die

    **Sentence:** As the company suffered losses and his business closed, he knew that he was done for.

33. **Fall back:** Move or turn back/retreat

    **Sentence:** Considering the heavy attack of the enemy, the general ordered his troops to fall back.

34. **Get off:** To escape a punishment/be acquitted

    Due to his good past records, he could get off with only with a reprimand.

35. **Get on with:** Perform or make progress in a specified way

    **Sentence:** Despite the adversities of life, one has to get on with it.

36. **Given himself up:** Surrender, to be fully affected or controlled by something

    **Sentence:** Owing to the police investigation and all-round pressure, the criminals eventually gave themselves up.

37. **Give in:** Submit, yield

    **Sentence:** She is not the one who gives in to adversities so easily.

38. **Give away:** To give as gift/donation

    **Sentence:** Emperor Harsha would occasionally give away all his material possession in charity.

39. **Go by:** To be known by / judged / pass by

    **Sentence:** Don't go by my judgment on the issue, think and act on your own.

    **Sentence:** Don't let the opportunities go by so easily.

40. **Go through:** Experience/suffer

    **Sentence:** We can understand what you have gone through during your illness.

41. **Hold out:** Survive or resist in difficult circumstances

    **Sentence:** The small group of warriors held out against the enemy till reinforcement arrived.

42. **Lay down:** To give up/ surrender

    **Sentence:** Surrounded by enemy they had no choice but to lay down their arms.

43. **Lay out:** To open or spread out/to arrange something

    **Sentence:** She laid out the map to explain the plan to his team mates.

44. **Make out:** To hear or see something/discover, to deal with a situation

    **Sentence:** Despite the darkness, she could make out as to who the thief was

45. **Pass by:** To go past or near something

    **Sentence:** I notice that the door was open when I passed by the house of Mr. Sharma.

46. **Pull together:** Help/co-operate, work together

**Sentence:** Challenges require that members of the team pull together to tide over them.

47. **Pull through:** To get through difficulty or dangerous situation

**Sentence:** With the help of best medical care, he could pull through the dreaded disease.

48. **Pull up:** To scold or rebuke

**Sentence:** He was pulled up by his teacher for the errant behaviour.

49. **Put up with:** Tolerate or endure something

**Sentence:** The family was finding very difficult to put up with the loss of job of its sole bread earner.

50. **Run through:** spend recklessly/ squandered away

Despite the rich legacy, he ran through the fortune only in a few years.

51. **Run into:** Incur expense, collide with someone or something

**Sentence:** He ran into huge debts

**Sentence:** He ran into the stationary car

52. **Run up:** Increase, allow a debt or bill to accumulate, the period of time before an important event

**Sentence:** The electricity bill has run up to several lakhs.

**Sentence:** The party had to make several arrangements in the run up to the elections.

53. **Set about:** To start to do something with vigour or determination/take steps towards something

**Sentence:** He is unstoppable, when he sets about to achieve any target.

54. **Set off:** Start/ begin a journey

**Sentence:** With some money and handful of possessions, he set off for the long journey.

55. **Set up:** Place or erect something

**Sentence:** After meeting many challenges, he could eventually set up the new business.

56. **Speak of:** Mention or discuss something in speech or writing

**Sentence:** There was hardly any issue to speak off, yet he continued to lecture his employees.

57. **Speak out:** Express ones feeling or opinion freely

**Sentence:** Very few are able to speak out about their difficulties in front of their superiors.

58. **Struck down with:** Annul/declare invalid

**Sentence:** The Supreme Court struck down the law as it ultra vires the Constitution.

59. **Take up:** Occupy time or space, become interested in a pursuit

**Sentence:** Her clothes took up a lot of space of the suitcase.

**Sentence:** She took up painting as a hobby very recently.

60. **Talk over:** To discuss

**Sentence:** She wanted to talk over with her parents about her future career plan.

61. **Throw away:** To squander/ waste

**Sentence:** Opportunities in life need to be availed of, they can't simply be thrown away.

62. **Turn out:** Prove to be the case

**Sentence:** The decision turned out to be profitable for the business in the long run.

63. **Turn against:** Yo stop liking or supporting/ became hostile to

**Sentence:** In adversity, even the so called friends turn against each other.

64. **Worked out:** Plan or devise something/solve

**Sentence:** We need to work out as to how to make the business profitable.

65. **Work up:** To get to a state of anger, excitement, anxiety

**Sentence:** He has a tendency to get worked up even at a smallest of problems.

66. **Eat humble pie:** To apologize humbly, to face humiliation

**Sentence:** As he had boasted of great success to his superiors in the company, the poor financial results made him eat humble pie before them.

67. **Meet half-way:** To come to an agreement or compromise

**Sentence:** Both the parties to the dispute agreed to meet half way and strike a compromise.

68. **Not worth one's salt:** Worth the pay or its monetary value, quite worthless

    **Sentence:** A professional who isn't able to solve his client's problems, is not worth his salt.

69. **Win laurels:** To acquire honour, achievements, distinction or glory.

    **Sentence:** Indian athletes won laurels for the country in the Olympics.

70. **Play fast and loose:** Says one thing and do the other

    **Sentence:** No one can trust a person who plays fast and lose.

71. **Take to task:** Admonish/rebuke someone

    **Sentence:** For the mischiefs of the boy, the parents took him to task.

72. **Turn a deaf ear to:** Ignore/disregard

    **Sentence:** All his entreaties were turned a deaf ear to and no help was provided at all.

73. **Hold water:** A statement/theory to be sound or reasonable

    **Sentence:** Postulations and theories are meaningless unless they hold water and stand the scrutiny of logic and reasoning.

74. **By hook or by crook:** By any means fair or foul

    **Sentence:** Victory, by hook or by crook, should not be the objective of sports.

75. **To all intent and purposes:** In all important respects, practically, virtually

    **Sentence:** Although he has not been removed from the job, to all intent and purposes he is not handling any work now.

76. **Take exception to:** Object strongly to

    **Sentence:** All in the meeting took exception to his rude behaviour.

77. **To settle old scores:** To take revenge

    **Sentence:** Positions of public responsibility and authority, should never be misused to settle old scores.

78. **Put a spoke in wheel:** To deliberately make difficult the executions of someone's plans.

    **Sentence:** Although he claims to be a friend, he has always attempted to put a spoke in the wheel of all my business ventures.

79. **Make one's mark:** Attain distinction or recognition

    **Sentence:** Although the career of acting appears glamourous, but its not easy to make one's mark in this field.

80. **To have at one's fingers end:** Within the range of one's skill or knowledge, to know it thoroughly

    **Sentence:** Only the very few, who have the subject at their finger's end, will eventually be successful in the tough competition.

81. **Fall flat:** Fail to produce the desires or expected response

    **Sentence:** It is a nightmare for a comedian whose jokes fall flat in a performance.

82. **Put one's foot down:** To adopt a firm policy special in face of opposition or disobedience, take a firm stand

    **Sentence:** The new supervisor put his foot down on the reckless expenditure in the office.

83. **Turn over a new leaf:** Start to act in a better or more responsible way

    **Sentence:** Given his reckless attitude, one can only hope that he turns over a new leaf and assumes responsibilities of life.

84. **Make up one's mind:** To make a decision, to resolve firmly

    **Sentence:** The parents made up their mind not to yield to their son's spendthrift demands anymore.

85. **No love lost:** Do not like each other, not on good terms.

    **Sentence:** Although they were once friends, there is no love lost between the two now.

86. **From hand to mouth:** To have barely sufficient resources or money to live, extreme poverty

    **Sentence:** Owing to the job loss, many erstwhile workers of the factory faced, from hand to mouth existence.

87. **Nick of time:** Just at the last or the right moment

    **Sentence:** For the starving families, the aid arrived just at the nick of time.

88. **Through thick and thin:** Under all circumstance,

**Sentence:** One would expect friends to help through thick and thin, but that may not happen in real life.

89. **Throw cold water/Pour cold water:** Discourage any proposal or be indifferent to

**Sentence:** The management tried to revive the sick factory, but a group of vested workers, threw cold water on the plan.

90. **Hand in glove:** Extremely close, close collusion or association

**Sentence:** In a large project like this, all the constituent teams have to work hand in glove, for the project to be successful.

91. **To hold a candle to:** To be comparable to

**Sentence:** The authors present novel cannot hold a candle to her earlier Booker prize winning novel.

92. **To burn one's fingers:** To harm oneself or to face the consequences of one's actions got himself into trouble

**Sentence:** Having burnt his fingers once at the stock market, he is very hesitant in investing now.

93. **Sixes and sevens:** Condition of confusion or disarray

**Sentence:** Although the kids were left home alone just for a few hours, the entire house was at sixes and sevens when the parents returned home.

94. **Wash one's hands of:** To disclaim responsibility for

**Sentence:** After their son was charged for fraud, the parents have washed their hands of, all their son's deeds.

95. **Have a finger in the pie:** To be involved with something, to be mixed up in the affairs.

**Sentence:** Being the trusted relative of the owner of business, it is believed that he has a finger in the pie in all the ventures of the business.

96. **Hit the nail on the head:** To find exactly the right answer

**Sentence:** In any complex situation, one can expect him to **hit the nail on the head** and find the way out of it.

97. **Out of spirits:** Despondent, gloomy, sad

**Sentence:** Owing to the poor performance in the examination, she was out of spirits, when her friends visited her.

98. **An axe to grind:** To have a selfish reason, to serve one's own ends

**Sentence:** Nobody blamed him for the fiasco as everybody knew that he has no axe to grind.

99. **Spread like wild fire:** To spread very rapidly

**Sentence:** The news of the death of the leader spread like wildfire in the organisation.

100. **Take to heart:** To be deeply hurt or affected

**Sentence:** Don't ever take to heart hardships and failures in your life.

101. **To have heart in the right place:** To mean well

**Sentence:** Don't be put off by his plain speak, he has his heart in the right place.

102. **Gift of the gab:** Ability to speak with eloquence and fluency

**Sentence:** Knowing Geetanjali's gift of the gab, her friends often turn to her on social occasions and functions.

103. **In good books of:** To be in favour with somebody

**Sentence:** By working overtime, he is now trying to be in the good books of the new management.

104. **Behind the scenes:** To work out of public view or in the secret, to be in possession of facts not generally known

**Sentence:** He is shy by nature and likes to work behind the scenes.

**Sentence:** He is the person who knows, as to what is going on behind the scenes.

105. **Foot the bill:** Pay the cost of

**Sentence:** One may tend to splurge if it is known that somebody else is to foot the bill.

106. **Tooth and nail:** To engage with all one's might

**Sentence:** The army fought tooth and nail to defend its position against the enemy forces.

107. **Within a stone's throw:** Very close to or at a short distance from someone or something

**Sentence:** His new office is within a stone's throw from his residence.

108. **Make a clean breast of:** To speak openly and honestly/to confess

**Sentence:** Gripped by a feeling of guilt, he made a clean breast of his mistakes before his family.

109. **Where the shoe pinches:** To know the source of trouble or difficulty etc.

**Sentence:** I can sympathise with your situation, as I am aware of where the shoe pinches.

110. **At wit's end:** Completely puzzled and perplexed.

**Sentence:** Having failed even after trying everything to make the car start, he was at his wit's end as what to do next.

111. **Go back on:** To fail to keep a promise or to change an agreement.

**Sentence:** One expects governments not to go back on their election promises, but now it happens often.

112. **Put their head together:** To plan together/ consult one another

**Sentence:** All the division heads of the company put their heads together to find the reason for sudden slump in their sales.

113. **Create bad blood:** Animosity, ill-feeling, bitterness

**Sentence:** Property disputes often create bad blood amongst the family members.

114. **Read between the lines:** To look at/gather the implied or hidden meaning rather than what is stated or expressed.

**Sentence:** It makes sense to read between the lines before signing any legal document.

115. **In cold blood:** Without feeling, not in the heat of passion but deliberately

**Sentence:** The judge awarded the highest possible sentence to the accused as the murder was done in cold blood.

116. **Thorn in his side:** A source of constant problems or annoyance

**Sentence:** The recalcitrant employees were always a thorn in the side of the management.

117. **Smell a rat:** To suspect trickery or deception

**Sentence:** Seeing the abnormal behaviour of their family members, I could immediately smell a rat.

118. **Nip in the bud:** To stop something immediately before it worsens.

**Sentence:** Certain diseases if not nipped in the bud can become life threatening.

119. **Long and the short of it:** The sum and substance of, explain in a few words

**Sentence:** As the report was quite voluminous, the minister asked about the long and short of its recommendations.

120. **To take stock of:** To make an overall assessment of a situation

**Sentence:** The losses incurred in the pandemic, compelled the company to take stock of its financial viability.

121. **Man of straw:** A person of no substance or integrity

**Sentence:** Knowing that he is a man of straw, his words were given little credence by others.

122. **Born with a silver spoon in one's mouth:** born in a family of wealth and luxury

**Sentence:** Those who are born with a silver spoon in their mouth, hardly understand struggle and hardship of ordinary people.

123. **Stand in good stead:** To be useful or helpful

**Sentence:** His understanding of human psychology will stand him in good stead in dealing with people.

124. **Take to task:** To call someone to account for/ to admonish or reprove

**Sentence:** The government took to task the errant official for making irresponsible comments before the court.

125. **Payback in one's own coin:** to treat another person in the same way as he had treated you

**Sentence:** He refused to help me earlier, now I paid back in his own coin when he asked me for help.

# Exercise on General English

## Exercise 1

**Which of the following options has meaning same/similar to the given word?**

1. Impede
   (a) Ill humoured (b) Stop
   (c) Hinder (d) Improve
2. Spendthrift
   (a) A person who spends on self
   (b) A miserly person
   (c) A person who spends recklessly
   (d) None of the above
3. Gullible
   (a) Soft person
   (b) Believer in many Gods
   (c) One who exploits others
   (d) None of the above
4. Vaunt
   (a) To raise (b) To grant
   (c) To brag (d) None of the above
5. Recalcitrant
   (a) Resisting authority
   (b) Indignant
   (c) Haughty
   (d) Stupid
6. Viable
   (a) Ideal (b) Practicable
   (c) Visible (d) Verifiable
7. Paragon
   (a) Model of excellence
   (b) Leader of masses
   (c) Ideological state
   (d) None of the above
8. Squalor
   (a) Square object (b) Pitiful condition
   (c) filthy state (d) Helplessness
9. Sanction
   (a) Approval (b) Penalty
   (c) Request (d) Prohibition
10. Paleontology
    (a) Study of plants
    (b) Study of old fossils
    (c) Study of sea surfaces & beds
    (d) Study of native species
11. Tacit
    (a) Latent (b) Ignorant
    (c) Obvious (d) Implied
12. Arduous
    (a) Laborious (b) Treacherous
    (c) Risky (d) Time consuming
13. Sensation
    (a) Fame (b) Creation
    (c) Pain (d) Feeling
14. Canard
    (a) Pack of worms (b) cantankerous
    (c) Lies (d) difficult
15. Rescind
    (a) Revise (b) Improve
    (c) Cancel (d) Postpone
16. Satiate
    (a) Integrate (b) Include
    (c) Satisfy (d) Exemplify
17. Alacrity
    (a) Stupidity (b) Happiness
    (c) Eagerness (d) Resistance
18. Plummet
    (a) Summit (b) Rise
    (c) Fall (d) Base
19. Imbroglio
    (a) Complicated situation
    (b) Hardship
    (c) Conflict
    (d) None of the above
20. Rationale
    (a) An exercise of arithmetic
    (b) Primary reason

(c) Main objective
(d) Key agreement

21. Penury
(a) Collection of pennies
(b) Art of prophecy
(c) State of difficulty
(d) Extreme poverty

22. Idolatry
(a) An art of false praise
(b) Following ideals
(c) Hero worship
(d) Idol worship

23. Verbose
(a) Wordy (b) To speak
(c) Argument (d) Pertaining to a verb

24. Succinct
(a) Successful (b) Sharp
(c) Distinct (d) Visible

25. Aggregate
(a) To create (b) Total
(c) Appreciate (d) Improve

## Exercise 2

**In the questions below one definition and word options are given, choose the word option which best suits/is most appropriate for the definition.**

26. Very talkative
(a) Sombre (b) Meticulous
(c) Garrulous (d) None of the above

27. A huge force destroying everything in its path
(a) Titan (b) Juggernaut
(c) Colossal (d) Atlas

28. Sentimental longing for an event from past
(a) Imagery (b) Nostalgia
(c) Recapitulation (d) Reverie

29. Showy and trying to attract attention
(a) Ostentatious (b) Extravagant
(c) Superfluous (d) Intermittent

30. Great emotion and passion
(a) Inspiration (b) Ardor
(c) Affinity (d) Inclination

31. To disturb greatly
(a) Probe (b) Prod
(c) Prick (d) Perturb

32. A fraud or a trickery
(a) Chicanery (b) Phishing
(c) scam (d) Hacking

33. To lack in flavour or be dull
(a) Ordinary (b) Insipid
(c) Mundane (d) Tangy

34. To divide into two parts
(a) Intersect (b) Replicate
(c) Bifurcate (d) Brood

35. That which varies frequently
(a) Violate (b) Viable
(c) Volatile (d) Motile

36. Pertaining to an exaggerated emotional behaviour
(a) Histrionics (b) Emote
(c) Act (d) Mime

37. Acceptance of something as true;
(a) Credibility (b) Credence
(c) Faith (d) Hope

38. To cover with water
(a) Irrigate (b) Drain
(c) Inundate (d) None of the above

39. Delusion of power or importance
(a) Arrogance (b) Ego
(c) Insolence (d) Megalomania

40. To appease
(a) Appreciate (b) Acknowledge
(c) Propitiate (d) Prefer

41. To desire something owned by other
(a) Attract (b) Design
(c) Aspire (d) Covet

42. Showing no emotion
(a) Resolute (b) Impassive
(c) Impervious (d) Brave

43. Occurring twice in a year
(a) Biennial (b) Annual
(c) Quarterly (d) Biannual

44. Something small or insignificant
(a) Trifle (b) Negligent
(c) Worthwhile (d) Neglect

45. Something which is harmless
(a) Petty (b) Mundane
(c) Innocuous (d) Impertinent

46. Route of the journey of a traveller
(a) Plan (b) Itinerary
(c) Brochure (d) Map

47. That which can be shaped by pounding
(a) Ductile (b) Pervious
(c) Soft (d) Malleable

48. To lessen other's anger
(a) Please (b) Agree
(c) Placate (d) Comply

49. Deep and not superficial
(a) Profuse (b) Profound
(c) Progressive (d) Supercilious

50. To damage or to corrupt morally
(a) Vitiate (b) Vicious
(c) Violate (d) Vex

## Exercise 3

**Pick out the most effective word(s) from the given words to fill in the blanks to make the sentence meaningfully complete.**

51. The doctor.................. the patient against having sugar, as he was suffering from diabetes.
(a) Proclaimed (b) Prohibited
(c) Advised (d) Allowed

52. Mumbai is famous .................. its film Industry, Bollywood.
(a) For (b) Of
(c) About (d) Through

53. Since he had worked earlier in the Income-tax Department, he was well................. with the provisions of taxation.
(a) Viable (b) Versed
(c) Known (d) Touch

54. Lions are now ...................... only to Gujarat in India.
(a) Confounded (b) Confined
(c) contained (d) Compounded

55. The .................... in New Delhi, in July is very hot and humid.
(a) Climate (b) Season
(c) Weather (d) Atmosphere

56. Camels are often referred to as the ship ............ the desert.
(a) For (b) Through
(c) In (d) Of

57. Those who are ............. to hard work seldom attain success.
(a) Avoid (b) Attuned
(c) Averse (d) Akin

58. A circle when divided ..................... four equal parts gives four quarter circles.
(a) Into (b) Upto
(c) In (d) Upon

59. As the terrorists attacked the hotel, the whole area around it was cordoned..................
(a) With (b) Of
(c) Out (d) Off

60. The mill owners, after two months of strike of the workers.................... to their demand so as to end the strike.
(a) Confronted (b) Conceded
(c) Confounded (d) Condescended

61. Freedom ............... desire is the basis of salvation, as per the teachings of Buddhism.
(a) With (b) Of
(c) Through (d) From

62. He claimed that the negative statement was wrongly................. to him.
(a) Ascribed (b) Prescribed
(c) Blamed (d) Claimed

63. Once the *Devas* had the nectar of immortality, they became ............... in any war.
(a) Immoral (b) Invincible
(c) Strong (d) Irreproachable

64. Parity............... their male counterparts in pay and other emoluments, has been a constant demand of all female employees.

(a) From (b) like
(c) Through (d) With

65. The contrabands were ............. by the customs authorities at the airport.
(a) Impounded (b) Confiscated
(c) Prohibited (d) Removed

66. After years of meditation and penance, Gautama .............. true knowledge and became Buddha.
(a) Attained (b) Arrived
(c) Absolved (d) Accrued

67. Smoking is truly ............... to a person's health.
(a) Suicidal (b) Acceptable
(c) Bad (d) Detrimental

68. Till the case was decided, the court................ the accused from leaving the country.
(a) Pardoned (b) Prohibited
(c) Cordoned (d) Contained

69. Yoga aims at .................. body, mind & soul.
(a) Increasing (b) Including
(c) Integrating (d) Inciting

70. The hotel was adjacent .................... the railway station.
(a) Of (b) To
(c) From (d) None of the above

71. The act of ............ on part of criminals, make the crime an even more serious offence.
(a) Cohesion (b) Consonance
(c) Collusion (d) Coalition

72. On the occasion of several national festivals, prominent monuments are ..................... by the Department of Tourism.
(a) Illuminated (b) Lightened
(c) Glowed (d) None of the above

73. The plane stopped.............. Delhi on way to Dubai.
(a) In (b) On
(c) At (d) Over

74. The shop was ................. with rats.
(a) Crowded (b) Brimming
(c) Filled (d) Infested

## Exercise 4

**Chose the alternative which best expresses the meaning of the idiom/phrase that is underlined in the sentence.**

75. Nowadays playing videogames is <u>all the rage</u> in kids.
(a) Cause of violence
(b) Raging bull
(c) Very popular
(d) Very harmful

76. One must be wary of those, who are <u>wolf in sheep's clothing</u>.
(a) Wily (b) Hypocrite
(c) Dangerous (d) Slimy

77. He claims to <u>rub shoulders</u> with the who's who of the company.
(a) In close contact with
(b) Playing golf with
(c) Related with
(d) None of the above

78. The news of the film star's death <u>spread like wild fire</u>.
(a) Caused fire in social media
(b) Caused concern in public
(c) Spread rapidly
(d) Caused much sorrow

79. I could put <u>two and two together</u>.
(a) Calculate the right answer
(b) Come to the right conclusion
(c) Overcome the problem
(d) Determine the root cause of problem

80. The family was not getting even <u>one square meal</u>.
(a) A complete meal
(b) A nutritious meal
(c) A traditional meal
(d) A desired meal

81. He is under the thumb of his lover.
    (a) Under legal obligation
    (b) Under social obligation
    (c) Under complete influence of
    (d) Under psychological pressure of
82. After many days in ICU the patient turned the corner.
    (a) Passed away (b) Passed in coma
    (c) Passed the crisis (d) None of the above
83. The deal is now a dead letter.
    (a) No longer valid
    (b) No longer legal
    (c) Not clear
    (d) An old understanding
84. The lesson was all Greek to me.
    (a) A foreign language
    (b) Not understandable
    (c) Not interesting
    (d) Not pertinent
85. The couple were invariably at cross-purposes.
    (a) In love with
    (b) Fighting with
    (c) Misunderstanding
    (d) Sloop with
86. He always tried to lord it over his juniors.
    (a) Domineer over (b) Show off
    (c) Abuse (d) Exploit
87. The advice has stood me in good stead invariably in difficult situations.
    (a) Proven costly
    (b) Proved useful
    (c) Shown no good result
    (d) Helped to stand up to the situation
88. These days he is in the bad books of the professor.
    (a) Not attending class
    (b) Not having an account
    (c) Not in good terms
    (d) Not in the same course
89. I have no axe to grind.
    (a) No work to do
    (b) No instruments to do the job
    (c) No personal interest
    (d) No authority
90. Professionals must be up-to-date with their areas of competency.
    (a) Concurrent (b) Contextual
    (c) Correct (d) None of the above
91. Do not go back on your word.
    (a) Disagree with
    (b) Fail to keep a promise
    (c) Partly comply with the promise
    (d) Review what was said
92. These is no point in dealing with a man of straw.
    (a) Financially broke person
    (b) Cruel person
    (c) Person of bad repute
    (d) A person of no substance
93. She takes after her mother.
    (a) To care for
    (b) To love
    (c) To resemble
    (d) To have differences with
94. Subordinates are expected to carry out their bosses orders.
    (a) Implement (b) Promote
    (c) Accept (d) Criticise
95. The help arrived in the nick of time.
    (a) A bit late (b) At the right moment
    (c) Before time (d) Much late

## Exercise 5

**Choose the alternative which means the opposite of the given words.**

96. Create
    (a) Uncreate (b) Recreate
    (c) Destroy (d) Reduce
97. Affirm
    (a) Confirm (b) Conclude
    (c) Deny (d) Unaffirm

98. Curiosity
(a) Inquisitiveness (b) Indifference
(c) Inertness (d) Impassionlessness

99. Authority
(a) Inability (b) Indifference
(c) Ignorance (d) None of the above

100. Approbation
(a) Approval (b) Disregard
(c) Confirmation (d) Criticism

101. Hearsay
(a) Gossip (b) Scandal
(c) Truth (d) Report

102. Amenable
(a) Uncooperative (b) Guilty
(c) Friendly (d) Indifferent

103. Sinister
(a) Propitious (b) Deceitful
(c) Dangerous (d) Uneventful

104. Virtual
(a) Digital (b) Assumed
(c) Apparent (d) Real

105. Capricious
(a) Stable (b) Arbitrary
(c) Capable (d) Competent

106. Conundrum
(a) Enigma (b) Solution
(c) Inspiration (d) Vision

107. Delusion
(a) Illusion (b) Fallacy
(c) Actuality (d) Aspiration

108. Forensic
(a) Investigation (b) Theoretical
(c) Procedural (d) None of the above

109. Garrulous
(a) Talkative (b) Hesitant
(c) Expressive (d) Reticent

110. Enigma
(a) Solution (b) Riddle
(c) Perpleseity (d) Hesitancy

111. Horrendous
(a) Delightful (b) Disturbing
(c) Illuminating (d) Artistic

112. Limpid
(a) Firm (b) Clear
(c) Obscure (d) Novice

113. Mourn
(a) Love (b) Rejoice
(c) Anguish (d) Hurt

114. Nostalgic
(a) Reminiscent (b) Unsentimental
(c) Charismatic (d) Clear headed

115. Omnipotent
(a) Omniscient (b) Heedless
(c) Harmless (d) Helpless

116. Probationary
(a) Unconditional (b) Doubtful
(c) Unimportant (d) Patent

117. Influx
(a) Input (b) Increase
(c) Flux (d) Outgo

118. Sombre
(a) Sleepy (b) Solemn
(c) Calm (d) Cheerful

119. Trivial
(a) Significant (b) Secret
(c) General (d) Ordinary

120. Vague
(a) Clear (b) Composed
(c) Confident (d) Candid

## Exercise 6

**In the questions given below, a part of the sentence is underlined. Below are given alternatives to the underlined portion which may improve the sentence. Choose the correct alternative. In case no improvement is needed then select the option (d).**

121. The boy <u>ran through the road</u> without caring for the traffic.
(a) ran on the road (b) ran across the road
(c) ran by the road (d) No improvement

122. I will be thankful if you can help me with the upcoming project.
(a) may help (b) would help
(c) could help (d) No improvement

123. The mother was looking for the child, who stood beside the curtain.
(a) Behind the curtain
(b) aside the curtain
(c) beyond the curtain
(d) No improvement

124. Though I called to the police station several times, I did not get any response on their phone.
(a) called for (b) called on
(c) called (d) No improvement

125. Could you buy some apples for the festival?
(a) any apple (b) apples
(c) many (d) No improvement

126. Medicines are now having some effect. Now there is a little hope of recovery.
(a) Little (b) More than a little
(c) hardly a little (d) No improvement

127. The king could not nominate a heir to the throne
(a) an heir (b) some heir
(c) heirs (d) No improvement

128. He travelled by a train for the entire journey.
(a) on a train (b) by the train
(c) by train (d) No improvement

129. We all travelled in my car to Shimla.
(a) by my car (b) Through my car
(c) above my car (d) No improvement

130. I recommend you reduce your expenditure.
(a) recommend to you
(b) recommend that you
(c) recommend
(d) No improvement

131. Why are you raking old issues?
(a) raking on (b) raking up
(c) raking for (d) No improvement

132. Had I been richer I would have purchased a new car.
(a) If I had been richer
(b) If I was richer
(c) If I was rich
(d) No improvement

133. The wooden broken house was demolished.
(a) Wooden house broken
(b) house wooden and broken
(c) house broken and wooden
(d) broken wooden house

134. He directed to remove the steel rusty Almirah.
(a) rusty steel almirah
(b) steel and rusty almirah
(c) rusty and steel almirah
(d) No improvement

135. I, you and Shyama, would be going to the market.
(a) I, Shyama and you
(b) You, Shyama and I
(c) You, I and Shyama
(d) No improvement

136. Any body was not there to do the work.
(a) Nobody was there
(b) Somebody was not there
(c) Everybody was not there
(d) No improvement

137. It is very impolite to laugh on others
(a) laugh behind (b) laugh about
(c) Laugh at (d) No improvement

138. The thief was thoroughly searched but there was no money on him.
(a) Money with (b) money inside
(c) money over (d) No improvement

139. The bank charges interest of 10%.
(a) Interest at (b) Interest with
(c) Interest on (d) No improvement

140. I don't think I should be able to go.
(a) can (b) would
(c) shall be able to (d) No improvement

141. I could have come from the market, you would not have waited for me.
   (a) Could not have (b) Should not have
   (c) Need not have (d) No improvement
142. I could not go to college as it was heavily raining.
   (a) heavy raining (b) heavy rain
   (c) raining heavily (d) No improvement
143. The teacher remarked, 'You have again come late'.
   (a) come again late (b) come late again
   (c) late again come (d) No improvement
144. Dont let your dreams perish, he said.
   (a) Don't let your dreams perish,
   (b) "Don't let your dreams perish",
   (c) "Don't let your dreams perish,"
   (d) No improvement
145. Lets eat grandmother.
   (a) Let's eat (b) Let's eat
   (c) lets eat, (d) No improvement
146. Are you coming home today, she asked.
   (a) Are you coming home today?
   (b) "Are you coming home today,"
   (c) "Are you coming home today?"
   (d) No improvement
147. A decent acommodation is all what I need.
   (a) accomodation (b) acommodation
   (c) accommodation (d) No improvement

## Exercise 7

**In the following questions, a sentence is divided into four parts (a) (b) (c) & (d). Identify which one of these parts have an error. The error will be in only one part of the sentence.**

148. Sentence: Many a man have succumbed to lust.
   (a) Many (b) a man
   (c) have succumbed (d) to lust
149. Sentence: There is a buffalo grazing on the field.
   (a) There is (b) a buffalo
   (c) grazing on (d) the field
150. Sentence: You and I are the only batsmen left to defend the score.
   (a) you and I (b) are the only
   (c) batsmen left (d) to defend the score
151. Sentence: He has not come to office from Friday.
   (a) He has (b) not come
   (c) to office (d) from Friday
152. Sentence: If I was the king of the land, I would build a huge palace.
   (a) If I was the king (b) of the land
   (c) I would build (d) A huge palace.
153. Sentence: Could you possibly lend me any money?
   (a) Could (b) you possibly
   (c) lend me (d) any money?
154. Sentence: An one rupee note is no more in circulation.
   (a) An one (b) rupee note
   (c) is no more (d) in circulation.
155. Sentence: A thousand metre make a kilometre.
   (a) A (b) thousand metre
   (c) make a (d) kilometre

## Exercise 8

**In questions 156-170 in each sentences, a word is underlined. From the given options pick up the one which is nearest in meaning to the underlined word and can replace it without altering the meaning of the sentence.**

156. The whole family cloistered in the basement of the house as a typhoon was raging.
   (a) Confined (b) Prayed
   (c) Slept (d) None of the above
157. The virus remains dormant in the body for long after exposure.
   (a) Dead (b) Weakened
   (c) Inactive (d) Hibernating
158. The new fund house duped him of all his investments.
   (a) Damaged (b) Developed
   (c) Depreciated (d) Deceived

159. The efficacy of the drug is being evaluated.
   (a) Economic value
   (b) Effectiveness
   (c) Ethical suitability
   (d) None of the above
160. Considering the exigency of the situation, the company allowed him an additional leave of a month.
   (a) Urgency (b) Nature
   (c) Requirement (d) Helplessness
161. The soldiers who returned after the war, were received with great fervor.
   (a) Fear (b) Warmth
   (c) Sincerity (d) Felicitation
162. The parents goaded their child to work hard.
   (a) Guided (b) Disciplined
   (c) Admonished (d) Proded
163. After the harrowing journey, everybody was speechless.
   (a) Enjoyable (b) Difficult
   (c) Distressing (d) Arduous
164. Soul is immutable while the body perishes.
   (a) Omnipressent (b) Unchangable
   (c) Immortal (d) Pure
165. The levity of his remarks was liked by all.
   (a) Light mannered (b) laughter
   (c) Rationale (d) Meaningfulness
166. He did not know that his own partner was maligning him.
   (a) Deceiving (b) Speaking evil of
   (c) reprimanding (d) None of the above
167. Because of his obdurate nature, his friends do not like him.
   (a) Irritable (b) Stubborn
   (c) Angry (d) Selfish
168. His petulant remark was taken note of by one and all.
   (a) Rude (b) Angry
   (c) Insincere (d) Partisan
169. Rain in this reason is sporadic.
   (a) Irregular (b) Heavy
   (c) Moderate (d) Low
170. With great trepidation he approached his boss for leave.
   (a) Hope (b) Anxiety
   (c) Anger (d) None of the above

## Exercise 9

**Choose the alternative which best express the meaning of the idiom/phrase that is italicised in the sentence.**

171. He stated that of late he has been *under the weather.*
   (a) Troubled by the weather
   (b) Not very well
   (c) Not taking care of self
   (d) None of the above
172. I could *smell a rat.*
   (a) Find a dead rat
   (b) Catch smell of a rat
   (c) Have a reason to suspect
   (d) Have a reason to fear
173. The problem was *nipped in the bud.*
   (a) Made to fail before it could mature
   (b) to be able to control a pest
   (c) To be able to create a problem
   (d) To identify deceitful behaviour.
174. Despite being an underdog, he *stood his ground* in the contest.
   (a) Maintain one's position
   (b) Stand firmly on ground
   (c) Cover a lot of ground
   (d) Marginally retreat from ones position
175. He could not make *both ends meet.*
   (a) To bend a rod at both ends
   (b) Live within income
   (c) Save money
   (d) Earn well

## Exercise 10

**In the questions below a sentence is given in which a word has been underlined. In the answer options, four word choices are provided, select the word which is closest in meaning to the underlined word.**

**176.** I wish you all the success in your new endeavour.

(a) journey (b) business
(c) thought (d) enterprise

177. His parents are simply fed up with his wanton approach in life.

(a) dangerous (b) reckless
(c) stupid (d) restrained

178. Nobody is so naive to believe his cooked-up story.

(a) friendly (b) cunning
(c) immature (d) sophisticated

## Exercise 11

**There are two gaps in each of the following sentences. From the pairs of words given, choose the one that fills the gaps most appropriately. The first word in the pair should fill the first gap.**

179. The best punctuation is that of which the reader is least conscious; for when punctuation, or lack of it,________ itself, it is usually because it __________,

(a) obtrudes, offends
(b) enjoins, fails
(c) conceals, recedes
(d) effaces, counts

180. The argument, that the need for a looser fiscal policy to __________ demand, outweighs the need to __________ budget deficits, is persuasive.

(a) asses, minimise
(b) outstrip, eliminate
(c) stimulate, control
(d) restrain, control

181. The Athenians on the whole were peaceful and prosperous; they had ________ to sit at home and think about the universe and dispute with Socrates, or to travel abroad and _________ the world.

(a) leisure, explore (b) time, ignore
(c) ability, suffer (d) temerity, understand

182. Their achievement in the field of literature is described as ________; sometimes it is even called ________.

(a) magnificent, irresponsible
(b) insignificant, influential
(c) significant, paltry
(d) unimportant, trivial

183. _______makes a man perfect, goes the saying. One should_____ as much as possible before any examination.

(a) Practice, practice (b) Practise, practise
(c) Practise, practice (d) Practice, practise

## Exercise 12

**In each question, the word at the top of the table is used in four different ways, numbered 1 to 4. Choose the option in which the usage of the word is incorrect or inappropriate.**

184. Near

(a) I got there just after you left; a near miss!
(b) She and her near friend left early.
(c) The war led to a near doubling of oil prices.
(d) They came near to tears seeing the plight of the victims.

185. Hand

(a) I have my hand full, I cannot do it today.
(b) The minister visited the jail to see the breach at first hand.
(c) The situation is getting out of hand here!
(d) When the roof of my house was blown away, he was willing to lend me a hand.

## Exercise 13

**The question consists of four sentences on a topic. Some sentences are grammatically incorrect or inappropriate. Select the option that indicates the grammatically correct and appropriate sentence(s).**

186. A. When virtuoso teams begin their work, individuals are in and group consensus is out.

B. As project progresses, however, the individual stars harness themselves to the product of the group.

C. Sooner or later, the members break through their own egocentrism and become a plurality with single-minded focus on the goal.

D. In short, they morph into a powerful team with a shared identity.

(a) A & C (b) A & D
(c) B & D (d) A, C & D

## Exercise 14

**Each of the following questions has a sentence with two blanks. Given below each question are five pairs of words. Choose the pair that best completes the sentence.**

187. As navigators, calendar markers, and other ___________of the night sky accumulated evidence to the contrary, ancient astronomers were forced to________ that certain heavenly bodies might move in circles about points, which in turn moved in circles about the earth.
(a) scrutinizers; believe
(b) observers; agree
(c) observers; concede
(d) students; conclude

188. Every human being, after the first few days of his life, is a product of two factors; on the one hand, there is his_________ endowment; and on the other hand, there is the affect of environment, including_________.
(a) constitutional; weather
(b) congenital; education
(c) personal; climate
(d) economic; learning

## Exercise 15

**In each of the questions, a word has been used in sentences in four different ways. Choose the option corresponding to the sentence in which the usage of the word is incorrect or inappropriate.**

189. **Round**
(a) The police fired a round of tear gas shells.
(b) The shop is located round the corner
(c) We took a round on merry-go-round.
(d) I shall proceed further only after you come round to admitting it.

190. **Buckle**
(a) After the long hike our knees were beginning to buckle.
(b) The horse suddenly broke into a buckle.
(c) The accused did not buckle under the police interrogation.
(d) Sometimes, an earthquake can make a bridge buckle.

191. **File**
(a) You will find the paper in the file under C.
(b) I need to file an insurance claim.
(c) The cadets were marching in a single file.
(d) When the parade was on, a soldier broke the file.

## Exercise 16

**In each question, there are five sentences. Each has a pair of words that are italicised and highlighted. From the italicised and highlighted words, select the most appropriate words (A or (B) to form correct sentences. The sentences are followed by options that indicate the words, which may be selected to correctly complete the set of sentences. From the options given, choose the most appropriate one.**

192. The bill received the *assent (A) / ascent (B)* of the Parliament.
The management agreed to *accept (A) / except (B)* all the demands of the trade union.
All the political parties wanted to *canvass (A) / canvas (B)* for the polls at the earliest.
It was alleged that the team won by adopting *foul(A) / fowl (B)* means.
It is not safe to venture out of house in rain and *lightening (A)/lightning(b)*.
(a) BABAA (b) AABAB
(c) BAAAB (d) ABABA

193. The cake had lots of *currents (A) / currants (B)* and nuts in it.
If you engage in such *exceptional (A) / exceptionable (B)* behaviour, I will be forced to punish you.

He has the same capacity as an adult to *consent (A) / assent (B)* to surgical treatment.

The minister is *obliged (A) /compelled (b)* to report regularly to a parliament board.

His analysis of the situation is far too *sanguine (a) genuine (b).*

(a) BBABA (b) BBAAA
(c) BBBBA (d) ABBAB

194. She managed to bite back the *ironic (A) / caustic (B)* retort on the tip of her tongue.

He gave an impassioned and *valid (A) / cogent (B)* plea for judicial reform.

I am not *adverse (A) / averse (B)* to helping out.

The *coupe (A) / coup (B)* broke away as the train climbed the hill.

They heard the bells *peeling (a) pealing (B)* far and wide.

(a) BBABA (b) BBBAB
(c) BAABB (d) BBBBA

## Exercise 17

**The questions given below, comprise, a sentence a portion of which is underlined and four options. Select the option which if substituted in place of the underlined portion, improves the sentence/ makes it grammatically correct.**

195. Although I could not give my best performance, still I am hopeful about success.
(a) hopeful of success
(b) hopeful on success
(c) hopeful to success
(d) hopeful as success

196. Please drop the parcel when you pass from my house.
(a) pass upon
(b) pass by
(c) pass behind
(d) no improvement can be done

197. He had to wait for an hour on the bus stop.
(a) at the bus stop.
(b) by the bus stop.
(c) under the bus stop.
(d) no improvement can be done.

198. Do not let the glass jar fall from the chair.
(a) fall by
(b) fall beside
(c) fall off
(d) no improvement can be done.

199. It was extremely cold and everybody wanted to sit by the fire.
(a) sit at
(b) sit about
(c) sit on
(d) no improvement can be done

200. The important matter was brought in the notice of the District Collector.
(a) to the notice
(b) of the notice
(c) on the notice
(d) no improvement can be done

201. The child is in bed and is asleep.
(a) on bed
(b) at bed
(c) over bed
(d) no improvement can be done

202. Ramesh spend a long time at the phone.
(a) on the phone
(b) in the phone
(c) by the phone
(d) no improvement can be done

203. Harish was getting on the train.
(a) on to
(b) over
(c) in
(d) no improvement can be done

204. The directions required him to go on the stairs.
(a) over
(b) up
(c) in
(d) no improvement can be done

205. There was an interesting programme about global warming <u>on</u> the television.
(a) in
(b) over
(c) at
(d) no improvement can be done

206. Poverty drove him to seek work <u>on</u> the age of fifteen.
(a) in
(b) up
(c) at
(d) no improvement can be done

207. Harish was standing <u>at the window</u> when someone through a stone at him
(a) beside the window
(b) in the window
(c) on the window
(d) no improvement can be done

208. The building was <u>on</u> fire, they had to call the fire brigade.
(a) in
(b) at
(c) into
(a) no improvement can be done

209. <u>Each soap</u> costs Rs ten.
(a) Each piece of soap
(b) Each cake of soap
(c) Each of soap.
(d) no improvement can be done

210. Please add a <u>piece of salt</u> to the curry.
(a) a pinch of salt
(b) a speck of salt
(c) a lump of salt
(d) no improvement can be done

211. The teacher was annoyed as there was not even a <u>chalk</u> in the class room.
(a) speck of chalk
(b) bit of chalk
(c) piece of chalk
(d) no improvement can be done

## Exercise 18

**In the questions below, choose the correct pair of options to fill in the blank spaces.**

212. He lives ___New Delhi ___Nivedita Kunj colony.
(a) in/in (b) at/in
(c) in/at (d) at/at

213. The dog jumped ______ the wall ______ the garden
(a) on/over (b) over/into
(c) at/over (d) into/over

214. The drunk man was driving the car _____ 100 kilometres per hour when he crashed ____ the standing truck.
(a) on/with (b) in/with
(c) on/by (d) at/into

215. The school is _____ the Merchant Street _____ the temple
(a) in/next to (b) on/at
(c) at/in (d) none of the above

216. The police officer ran _____ the corridor and _____ the stairs to catch the thief.
(a) on/into (b) along/up
(c) into/on (d) upto/on

## Exercise 19

**In the questions below, a sentence is given in which a word has been underlined. In the answer options, four word choices are provided, select the word which is closest in meaning to the underlined word.**

217. The preacher asked his disciples to <u>abjure</u> violence.
(a) renounce (b) practice
(c) criticize (d) none of the above

218. His <u>haughty</u> attitude immediately puts off the person to whom he is talking to.
(a) insipid (b) arrogant
(c) garrulous (d) rigid

219. He received unanimous acclaim for his work.
    (a) criticism (b) support
    (c) praise (d) none of the above

220. One could easily detect malice in his statement.
    (a) generosity (b) kindness
    (c) interest (d) wickedness

221. His innovative approach helped them to complete the project even in a limited budget.
    (a) novel (b) thrifty
    (c) meticulous (d) imaginative

222. We could easily gauge from his demeanour that he was not interested in the partnership.
    (a) voice (b) behaviour
    (c) anxiety (d) none of above

223. Investigation has to be based on hard facts and not on conjectures.
    (a) speculation (b) myth
    (c) lies (d) anger

***For each of the words below a context is provided. From the given alternatives, pick the word or phrase that is closest in meaning in the given context.***

224. *Portend:* It appears to many that the US "war on terrorism" portends trouble in the Gulf.
    (a) Introduces (b) Evokes
    (c) Spells (d) Bodes

225. *Prevaricate:* When a videotape of her meeting was played back to her and she was asked to explain her presence there, she started prevaricating.
    (a) Speaking evasively
    (b) Speaking violently
    (c) Lying furiously
    (d) Throwing a tantrum

## Answers of Exercise on General English

| 1. (c) | 26. (c) | 51. (c) | 76. (b) | 101. (c) | 126. (d) | 151. (d) | 176. (d) | 201. (d) |
|---|---|---|---|---|---|---|---|---|
| 2. (c) | 27. (b) | 52. (a) | 77. (a) | 102. (a) | 127. (a) | 152. (a) | 177. (b) | 202. (a) |
| 3. (d) | 28. (b) | 53. (b) | 78. (c) | 103. (a) | 128. (c) | 153. (d) | 178. (c) | 203. (a) |
| 4. (c) | 29. (a) | 54. (b) | 79. (b) | 104. (d) | 129. (d) | 154. (a) | 179. (a) | 204. (b) |
| 5. (a) | 30. (b) | 55. (c) | 80. (a) | 105. (a) | 130. (b) | 155. (b) | 180. (c) | 205. (d) |
| 6. (b) | 31. (d) | 56. (d) | 81. (c) | 106. (b) | 131. (b) | 156. (a) | 181. (a) | 206. (c) |
| 7. (a) | 32. (a) | 57. (c) | 82. (c) | 107. (c) | 132. (d) | 157. (c) | 182. (d) | 207. (a) |
| 8. (c) | 33. (b) | 58. (a) | 83. (a) | 108. (b) | 133. (d) | 158. (d) | 183. (d) | 208. (d) |
| 9. (a) | 34. (c) | 59. (d) | 84. (b) | 109. (d) | 134. (a) | 159. (b) | 184. (b) | 209. (b) |
| 10. (b) | 35. (c) | 60. (b) | 85. (c) | 110. (a) | 135. (b) | 160. (a) | 185. (a) | 210. (a) |
| 11. (d) | 36. (a) | 61. (d) | 86. (a) | 111. (a) | 136. (a) | 161. (b) | 186. (b) | 211. (c) |
| 12. (a) | 37. (b) | 62. (a) | 87. (b) | 112. (c) | 137. (c) | 162. (d) | 187. (d) | 212. (c) |
| 13. (d) | 38. (c) | 63. (b) | 88. (c) | 113. (b) | 138. (d) | 163. (c) | 188. (b) | 213. (b) |
| 14. (c) | 39. (d) | 64. (d) | 89. (c) | 114. (b) | 139. (a) | 164. (b) | 189. (d) | 214. (d) |
| 15. (c) | 40. (c) | 65. (b) | 90. (a) | 115. (d) | 140. (c) | 165. (a) | 190. (b) | 215. (a) |
| 16. (c) | 41. (d) | 66. (a) | 91. (b) | 116. (a) | 141. (c) | 166. (b) | 191. (d) | 216. (b) |
| 17. (c) | 42. (b) | 67. (d) | 92. (d) | 117. (d) | 142. (c) | 167. (b) | 192. (c) | 217. (a) |
| 18. (c) | 43. (d) | 68. (b) | 93. (c) | 118. (d) | 143. (b) | 168. (a) | 193. (b) | 218. (b) |
| 19. (a) | 44. (a) | 69. (c) | 94. (a) | 119. (a) | 144. (b) | 169. (a) | 194. (b) | 219. (c) |
| 20. (b) | 45. (c) | 70. (b) | 95. (b) | 120. (a) | 145. (b) | 170. (b) | 195. (a) | 220. (d) |
| 21. (d) | 46. (b) | 71. (c) | 96. (c) | 121. (b) | 146. (c) | 171. (b) | 196. (b) | 221. (a) |
| 22. (d) | 47. (d) | 72. (a) | 97. (c) | 122. (c) | 147. (c) | 172. (c) | 197. (a) | 222. (b) |
| 23. (a) | 48. (c) | 73. (c) | 98. (b) | 123. (a) | 148. (c) | 173. (a) | 198. (c) | 223. (a) |
| 24. (c) | 49. (b) | 74. (d) | 99. (a) | 124. (c) | 149. (c) | 174. (a) | 199. (d) | 224. (d) |
| 25. (b) | 50. (a) | 75. (c) | 100. (d) | 125. (a) | 150. (a) | 175. (b) | 200. (a) | 225. (a) |

## HINTS AND SOLUTIONS TO SELECTED QUESTIONS

**148.** Many a man has succumbed to lust.

**149.** There is a buffalo grazing in the field.

**150.** You and me are the only batsmen left to defend the score.

**151.** He has not come to office since Friday.

**152.** If I were the king of the land, I would build a huge palace.

**153.** Could you possibly lend me some money?

**154.** A one rupee note is no more in circulation.

**155.** A thousand metres make a kilometre.

# Practice Question Papers for Section 1: General Test

*"An ounce of practice is worth more than tons of preaching."*

**—Mahatma Gandhi**

*"Practice as if you are the worst, perform as if you are the best."*

**—Anonymous**

This section consists of 10 Practice question papers. These have been set as per the prescribed syllabus of the CUET and the previous years' questions asked in CUCET.

The objective of these practice question papers is to provide an opportunity to assess your standing, *vis-à-vis* the complexity of questions as well as constraint of time. It is advised that you attempt these papers only after you have gone through the preceding chapters and acquired a fair degree of proficiency over the subject. Besides, you should attempt each paper in a single sitting in a time bound fashion so as to simulate an examination-like environment.

The notification of CUET specifies that section-1A would entail the test of language by means of reading comprehension. These would be of different types. It will also incorporate the test of literary aptitude and vocabulary. Accordingly, in the practice test papers a variety of passages, of different categories, including literary, factual, narrative etc. are incorporated. Besides, there are questions which test the vocabulary and literary aptitude. The notification also specifies that the section would have 50 questions out of which 40 would be required to be attempted. As such in each of the papers 50 practice questions are provided.

This section of the paper is to be attempted in just 45 minutes. Therefore, it will be prudent to time yourself. This will give you a fair idea as to in which category of questions you are overshooting the permissible time and in which you are saving some. This helps in time management during the examination. Use this idea while solving the subsequent practice question papers and analyse how your performance has changed.

Make the best use of the practice question papers.

# Practice Question Paper 1

**(A) Read the following passage and answer the questions that follow. The answers should be based on the passage only.**

**(I)**

Once upon a time there was a bird. It was ignorant. It sang all right, but never recited scriptures. It hopped pretty frequently, but lacked manners.

Said the Raja to himself, 'Ignorance is costly in the long run. For fools consume as much food as their betters, and yet give nothing in return.'

He called his nephews to his presence and told them that the bird must have a sound schooling.

The pundits were summoned, and at once went to the root of the matter.

They decided that the ignorance of birds was due to their natural habit of living in poor nests. Therefore, according to the pundits, the first thing necessary for this bird's education was a suitable cage.

The pundits had their rewards and went home happy.

A golden cage was built with gorgeous decorations. Crowds came to see it from all parts of the world. 'Culture, captured and caged!' exclaimed some, in a rapture of ecstasy, and burst into tears. Others remarked, 'Even if culture be missed, the cage will remain, to the end, a substantial fact. How fortunate for the bird!'

The goldsmith filled his bag with money and lost no time in sailing homewards.

The pundit sat down to educate the bird. With proper deliberation he took his pinch of snuff, as he said: 'Text-books can never be too many for our purpose!'

The nephews brought together an enormous crowd of scribes. They copied from books, and copied from copies, till the manuscripts were piled up to an unreachable height. Men murmured in amazement: 'Oh, the tower of culture, egregiously high! The end of it lost in the clouds!'

The scribes, with light hearts, hurried home, their pockets heavily laden.

The nephews were furiously busy keeping the cage in proper trim. As their constant scrubbing and polishing went on, the people said with satisfaction: 'This is progress indeed!'

1. The king decided to give a good schooling to the parrot as it was ______
   (a) Untamed (b) Ignorant
   (c) Inactive (d) All of the above
2. The pundits examined the ________ of the ignorance of the parrot.
   (a) The fundamental reason
   (b) The apparent cause
   (c) The effect
   (d) All of the above
3. The golden cage had ______ decorations.
   (a) Mundane (b) Unique
   (c) Exquisite (d) All of the above
4. Men remarked in amazement that the tower of culture was _______ high.
   (a) Impractically (b) meaninglessly
   (c) Extraordinarily (d) All of the above

**(II)**

Means and end are convertible terms in my philosophy of life.

They say 'means are after all means'. I would say 'means are after all everything'. As the means so the end. There is no wall of separation between means end. Indeed the Creator has given us control (and that too very limited) over means, none over the end. Realisation of the goal is in exact proportion to that of the means. This is a proposition that admits of no exception.

*Ahimsa* and Truth are so intertwined that it is practically impossible to disentangle and separate them. They are like the two sides of a coin, or rather a smooth unstamped metallic disc. Who can say, which is the obverse, and which the reverse? Nevertheless, *ahimsa* is the means; Truth is the end. Means to be means must always be within our reach, and so *ahimsa* is our supreme duty. If we take care of the means, we are bound to reach the end sooner or later. When once we have grasped this, final victory is beyond question. Whatever difficulties we encounter, whatever apparent reverses we sustain, we may not give up the quest for truth which alone is, being God himself.

I do not believe in short-violent-cuts to success. However, much I may sympathise with and admire worthy motives, I am an uncompromising opponent of violent methods even to serve the noblest of causes. There is, therefore, really no meeting-ground between the school of violence and myself. But my creed of non-violence not only does not preclude me but compels me even to associate with anarchists and all those who believe in violence. But that association is always with the sole object of weaning them from what appears to me their error. For experience convinces me that permanent good can never be the outcome of untruth and violence. Even if my belief is a fond delusion, it will be admitted that it is a fascinating delusion.

5. As per the passage which of the following is **not** true about 'means' and 'ends'?
   (a) As the means so are the ends.
   (b) One has little control over means and ends.
   (c) Means and ends cannot be separated.
   (d) Realisation of ends is dependent on the means.
6. Which of the following statements best justifies the author's statement, 'Permanent good can never be the outcome of untruth and violence'?
   (a) Ends justify the means.
   (b) Ends do not justify means.
   (c) As the means so the end.
   (d) All of the above.
7. Examine which of the following conclusions can be drawn from the passage.
   (i) *Ahimsa* and Truth are one and the same thing.
   (ii) Short but violent cuts to success are not justified.
   (a) Only Conclusion (i) can be drawn.
   (b) Only Conclusion (ii) can be drawn.
   (c) Both Conclusions (i) and (ii) can be drawn.
   (d) Neither Conclusion (i) nor (ii) can be drawn.
8. Which of the following statements about '*Ahimsa* and Truth' can be said to be correct?
   (i) *Ahimsa* is the means, Truth is the end.
   (ii) *Ahimsa* and Truth are inseparable from each other.
   (iii) To attain the truth the path of *Ahimsa* is one amongst many.
   (iv) Quest of truth should not be given up despite reverses.
   (v) Truth is sacred, *Ahimsa* is not.
   (vi) *Ahimsa* and truth are like two sides of a coin.
   (a) (i), (ii), (iv), (vi) (b) (i), (ii), (iii), (vi)
   (c) (i), (ii), (v), (vi) (d) (ii), (iii), (iv), (vi)
9. Which of the following can be said to be the author's views about violence?
   (i) Violence is not justified even where the cause is noble.
   (ii) There should be no association with the believers of violence.
   (iii) Permanent good has to be based on the bedrock of non-violence and truth.
   (a) (i), (ii), (iii) (b) (ii), (iii)
   (c) (i), (iii) (d) (i), (ii)

**(B) Read the following passage and answer the questions that follow. The answers should be based on the passage only.**

While India has diversified its export basket as well as export markets over the years, substantial diversification in tune with world demand has not taken place. This can be seen by matching India's exports with the top 100 imports of the world at the six-digit HS level. The exercise shows that India's presence in these top items of world demand is negligible except for a few items such as diamonds and jewellery, oil cakes, T-shirts, men/boys' trousers, flat rolled iron products and maize (corn). There are many electronic, electrical, and engineering items (the three Es) in the top 100 imports of the world where India's presence is negligible.

India has been progressively lowering peak customs duty. The fall in peak duty has not led to the feared collapse in revenue collections. The duty cuts have neither wiped out the domestic manufacturing sector nor resulted in large-scale unemployment as forecasted by many. The data show that progressive peak duty cuts have been accompanied by rise in customs duty collections. However, further bold tariff reforms with minimum revenue loss are needed to reach levels comparable to those in ASEAN both for peak rate as well as total duty.

10. As a result of the lowering of the peak customs duty which of the following, feared to have happened, has not occurred?
    (i) The revenue collections have not risen.
    (ii) The unemployment has not risen.
    (iii) Domestic manufacturing sector has not been wiped out.
    (a) (i), (ii), (iii) (b) (i), (ii)
    (c) (ii), (iii) (d) (i), (iii)
11. The passage cites the need for substantial diversification of India's export basket. Which of the following would best explain this need?
    (a) Diversification of exports will bring valuable foreign exchange to India.
    (b) Diversification of exports will help in arresting the slide in Indian rupee.
    (c) Diversification is essential to bring competitiveness in trade and parity with major international players such as China and the USA.
    (d) Diversification will help in increasing overall exports, strengthening large sections of economy and buffering exports from decline in one or few sectors of exports.
12. What is the most important thing the author is trying to convey in the above passage?
    (a) Highlight the need for diversification in trade.
    (b) Bring out the challenges before Indian trade and suggest possible areas of reforms.
    (c) Emphasise on the Indian growth in exports which has taken place *vis-a-vis* the world export growth.
    (d) All of the above.
13. Examine whether the following conclusions can be drawn from the passage.
    (i) Further reforms and duty cuts will be helpful in making our export more competitive.
    (ii) India has made reasonable improvement in export of electronic, electrical and engineering products.
    (a) Only Conclusion (i) can be drawn.
    (b) Only Conclusion (ii) can be drawn.
    (c) Both the Conclusions (i) and (ii) can be drawn.
    (d) Neither Conclusion (i) nor (ii) can be drawn.

**(C) Read the following passage and answer the questions that follow. The answers should be based on the passage only.**

Economic development without environmental considerations can cause serious environmental damage, in turn impairing the quality of life of present and future generations. Such environmental degradation imposes a cost on the society and needs to be explicitly factored into economic planning, with necessary remedial measures incorporated. The challenge of sustainable development thus requires integration of the country's quest for economic development with its environmental concerns. Environment management in India has, over the years, recognised these sustainable development concerns. The National Environment Policy 2006 has attempted to mainstream environmental concerns in all our developmental activities. It underlines that 'while conservation of environmental resources is necessary to secure livelihoods and well-being of all, the most secure basis for conservation is to ensure that people, dependent on particular resources, obtain better livelihoods from the fact of conservation, than from degradation of the resource.' The Government of India, through its various policies, has been factoring ecological concerns into the development process so that economic development can be achieved without critically damaging the environment. The strong sustainable development agenda followed by India incorporates rigorous environmental safeguards for infrastructure projects, strengthening of the environmental governance system, revitalising of regulatory institutions, focusing on river conservation, and efforts for improvements in air and water quality, on a continuous basis.

Our environmental standards are set through government policies which are aimed at a development process that is environmentally sustainable and foregrounds well-being of the people. The broad objectives of our environmental policies and programmes are:

- Conservation of flora, fauna, forests, and wildlife;
- Prevention and control of pollution;
- Afforestation and regeneration of degraded areas; and
- Protection of the environment.

As a country, India has been at the forefront of preserving biodiversity, sustainable management of forests, reducing emissions intensity of the economy, and following sustainable consumption and production patterns. Specifically, India has been following a development path that takes into consideration the needs of the present generation without compromising the ability of future generations to meet their needs. Suitable attention has been given to protecting and conserving critical ecological systems and resources and invaluable natural and man-made heritage, which are essential for life-support, livelihoods, economic growth, and a broad conception of human well-being. Moreover, the effort has been to ensure equitable access to environmental resources and quality for all sections of society, in particular to ensure that poor communities which are most dependent on environmental resources for their livelihoods are assured secure access to these resources.

14. In the context of the passage above what would sustainable development mean?
    (a) A development model which causes no damage to the environment.
    (b) A development model which integrates the need for economic development with environmental concerns.
    (c) A development model which does not contribute to global warming.
    (d) All of the above.

15. What underlying principle does the passage enunciate to strike harmony between environmental conservation and securing the livelihood of people?
    (a) To provide better livelihood to people by conserving the environment than degrading.
    (b) To permit only those activities, which do not lead to green house gas emissions.
    (c) To ensure that emission intensity of the new activities do not exceed the prescribed level.
    (d) No such principle has been enunciated in the passage.

16. As per the passage which of the following are a part of India's policy regarding environmental conservation and sustainable development?
    (i) Reduction of emission intensity.
    (ii) Reduction of global green house gas (GHG) emission to below 1990 levels by the year 2020.
    (iii) Control of pollution.
    (iv) Afforestation and regeneration of degraded areas.

    (a) (i), (ii), (iii) (b) (ii), (iii), (iv)
    (c) (i), (iii), (iv) (d) (i), (ii), (iv)

17. Which of the following conclusions can be drawn from what has been stated in the passage above?
    (i) The developmental policies and programmes of government of India are such that they do not cause any damage to the environment.
    (ii) The endeavour of the policies and programmes is to provide all sections of society equitable access to environmental resources.

(a) Only Conclusion (i) can be drawn.
(b) Only Conclusion (ii) can be drawn.
(c) Both the Conclusions (i) and (ii) can be drawn.
(d) Neither Conclusion (i) nor (ii) can be drawn.

**(D)** ***Read the following passage and answer the questions that follow. The answers should be based on the passage only.***

In many poor nations the government takes the stance that, when in doubt about the goodness or badness of two or more adults voluntarily conducting an exchange, stop them. An enabling state, on the contrary, takes the view that, when in doubt, do not interfere. There are, of course, many actions of individuals and groups that will need to be stopped for the welfare of society at large. But the default option of an enabling state is to allow rather than stop, to permit instead of prevent. This altered conception of the state can have dramatic effect on the functioning of an economy, in general by promoting greater efficiency and higher productivity. A concrete example can help clarify this. One repeated question that comes up in policy discussions concerns future trades. Should we allow traders to strike advance deals about buying and selling wheat or rice or pulses in the future? Since for vital goods such as these, a natural concern of every government is to adopt policies that do not lead to inflationary pressures. Our policy stance on future markets depend on what we expect them to do to spot the prices. In other words, it depends on our view of what the existence of future markets does to the level of prices in today's market. An enabling government takes the view that if we cannot establish a connection between the existence of future trading and inflation in spot prices, we should allow future's trade. This is in contrast to what an intrusive government tends to do. In the event of finding no firm connection between the two markets, it takes the stance that it will not give individuals the freedom to conduct future trades. In fact, it is true that the theoretical literature maintains a somewhat ambivalent position on this. While allowing future trade does take us towards a more complete market system, it is not true that allowing each additional market always leads to greater efficiency. However, the converse of these claims is not true either. What is being argued here is that, under these circumstances, government should, ideally, desist from imposing an outright ban on future trades and, instead, provide it with a regulatory structure to promote transparency and to discourage collusion.

18. Which of the following best summarises what this passage intends to convey?
    (a) The difference in approach of an enabling government *vis-à-vis* an intrusive government with respect to those exchanges about whose goodness or badness there is doubt.
    (b) What should be the governing principle to allow or not to allow the existence of future market?
    (c) India's stand *vis-à-vis* the futures trading in food.
    (d) A correlation between 'futures trading' in food grains and between food inflation cannot be established.

19. As per discussion in the passage what would 'futures trading' mean?
    (a) Trading in financial instruments called 'futures'
    (b) Striking advance deals about buying or selling of commodities in future.
    (a) Both (a) and (b).
    (b) Neither (a) nor (b).

20. Consider the following two conclusions based on what is stated in the passage.
    (i) The default option of an enabling state is to permit rather than stop an act of individual or a group.
    (ii) Futures trading brings greater efficiency in the market system. Which of the two conclusions can be drawn?
    (a) Only Conclusion (i) can be drawn.
    (b) Only Conclusion (ii) can be drawn.
    (c) Both Conclusions (i) and (ii) can be drawn.
    (d) Neither Conclusion (i) nor (ii) can be drawn.

21. When in doubt about the goodness or badness of two adults conducting two voluntary exchange what will be the response of different governments?
    (i) Enabling government to permit.
    (ii) Interfering government to permit.
    (iii) Enabling government to prohibit.
    (iv) Interfering government to prohibit.
    (a) (i) and (ii) (b) (i) and (iii)
    (c) (iii) and (iv) (d) (i) and (iv)

**(E) Read the following passage and answer the questions that follow. The answers should be based on the passage only.**

Civilisation, in the real sense of the term, consists not in multiplication but in the deliberate voluntary restriction of wants. This alone promotes real happiness and contentment, and increases the capacity for service.

A certain degree of physical harmony and comfort is necessary, but above that level, it becomes a hindrance instead of a help. Therefore, the ideal of creating an unlimited number of wants and satisfying them seems to be delusional and a snare. The satisfaction of one's physical needs, even the intellectual needs of one's narrow self, must meet at a point, a dead stop, before it degenerates into physical and intellectual voluptuousness. A man must arrange his physical and cultural circumstances so that they may not hinder him in his service of humanity, on which all his energies should be concentrated.

The relations between the body and the mind is so intimate that if either of them got out of order, the whole system would suffer. Hence it follows that a pure character is the foundation of health in the real sense of the term; and we may say that all evil thought and evil passions are but different forms of disease.

I have learnt through bitter experience one supreme lesson to conserve my anger, and as heat conserved is transmuted into energy, even our controlled anger can be transmuted into a power which can move the world.

It is not that I do not get angry. I don't give vent to anger. I cultivate the quality of patience as angerlessness, and generally speaking, I succeed. But I only control my anger when it comes. How I find it possible to control it would be a useless question, or it is a habit that everyone must cultivate and must succeed in forming by constant practice.

22. Which of the following is the main issue the author wants to communicate in the passage?
    (a) The wants of a human being are unlimited.
    (b) Harmony and comfort are essential for life.
    (c) Human needs need to be limited at a particular level.
    (d) All of the above.

23. As per the passage, restriction of wants is essential because
    (a) All wants cannot be satisfied.
    (b) Restriction of wants promotes happiness and contentment.
    (c) Desire needs to be eliminated as it leads to degeneration of self.
    (d) All of the above.

24. Consider whether the following inferences can be drawn from the passage or not?
    (i) Desires lead to degeneration.
    (ii) Health is affected by character.
    (a) Only Inference (i) can be drawn.
    (b) Only Inference (ii) can be drawn.
    (c) Both inferences can be drawn.
    (d) Neither of the above inferences can be drawn.

**(F) Read the following passage and answer the questions that follow. The answers should be based on the passage only.**

There is a growing literature in economics arguing that pro-social behaviour, which includes altruism and trustworthiness, is innate to human beings and, moreover, forms an essential ingredient for the efficient functioning of economies. In other words, human beings have a natural ability to forgo personal gains for the sake of other people or because that is what is required because of a promise the person had made. This trait may well have evolutionary roots but its existence is now well demonstrated in laboratory tests. The broad idea behind these laboratory experiments is as follows. The experimenter pairs up all the subjects in a laboratory and then asks each pair to have the following interaction. One of the two persons, call him A, is asked to hand over if he wishes a certain amount of money (which may be called A's investment) to B. If A refuses to invest anything, their interaction is over, A and his partner, B get nothing and they go home. If A invests a certain amount of money and gives that money to B, then the experimenter also adds some more money and lets B have it all. B is then asked whether B wants to hand a part of the total money she received back to A. In other words, B is given an opportunity to pay back to A some of B's gains, since B would have got nothing if A had not made the first move. In the Trust Game, once B decides how much to give A, that is given to A, and that is the end of the interaction. (The Hold-up game is a variant of this with a slightly different closure rule.)

In a totally selfish world, we would expect B to offer nothing to A and for A, anticipating this, not to give any money to B to start with. However, experiments conducted all over the world with this or related games demonstrated that in a large number of cases, the first player does give money to the second player and the second player does give back a part of her income to the first player. Moreover, there are conditions which lead to a higher propensity among the players for this kind of cooperative behaviour.

25. What can be said to be the objective of the passage above?
    (a) To shed light on significance of game theories on economic models.
    (b) To highlight significance of economic research.
    (c) To highlight significance of trust and social behaviour in economic modelling and development.
    (d) All of the above.

26. What is the conclusion which has been drawn in the passage from the laboratory experiments?
    (a) People can forgo personal gains because human beings are altruistic by nature.
    (b) People do not forego their gains but want returns for the efforts put in by them.
    (c) Altruism and the desire for gains are opposite and not linked to each other.
    (d) People have the ability to forgo personal gains either for the sake of others or because of the promise the other person has made.

27. As per the passage what would be the outcome if the world were totally selfish?
    (a) A would give money to B without expecting any return.
    (b) A would not give any money to B expecting B not to return.
    (c) A would give money to B and expect him to return.
    (d) None of the above.

**(G) Read the following passage and answer the questions that follow. The answers should be based on the passage only.**

I must confess that I do not draw a sharp line or any distinction between economics and ethics. Economics that hurt the moral well-being of an individual or a nation are immoral and, therefore, sinful. Thus, the economics that permit one country to prey upon another are immoral.

The end to be sought is human happiness combined with full mental and moral growth. I use the adjective moral as it is synonymous with spirituality. This end can be achieved under decentralisation. Centralisation as a system is inconsistent with a non-violent structure of society.

I would categorically state my conviction that the mania for mass production is responsible for the world crisis. Granting for the moment that the machinery may supply all the needs of humanity, still, it would concentrate production in particular areas, so that you would have to go about in a roundabout way to regulate distribution, whereas, if there is production and distribution both in the respective areas where things are required, it is automatically regulated, and there is less chance for fraud, none for speculation.

Mass production takes no note of the real requirement of the consumer. If mass production were in itself a virtue, it should be capable of indefinite multiplication. But it can be definitely shown that mass production carries within its own limitations. If all countries adopted the system of mass production there would not be a big enough market for their products. Mass production must then come to a stop.

28. Which of the following conclusions can be drawn from the passage?
    (i) There are inherent contradictions between economics and ethics.
    (ii) System of centralisation can disturb peaceful and non-violent structure of the society.
    (a) Only Conclusion (i) can be drawn.
    (b) Only Conclusion (ii) can be drawn.
    (c) Both Conclusions (i) and (ii) can be drawn.
    (d) Neither (i) nor (ii) can be drawn.

29. What is the most important logic the author employs to criticise mass production?
    (a) Mass production leads to moral degeneration of society.
    (b) Mass production is unethical.
    (c) Mass production is not based on principles of demand and supply.
    (d) Mass production leads to concentration of means of production and distribution in the hands of a few.

30. The author states that he does not draw a sharp line of distinction between economics and ethics. Which amongst the following can be the reason for the aforesaid?
    (i) Economics is inherently based on greed and profiteering motive.
    (ii) At times economics can instigate an entity to exploit another.
    (iii) Economics may hurt the well-being of an individual or a nation and in such instance are unethical.
    (a) (i) and (ii) (b) (ii) and (iii)
    (c) (i) and (iii) (d) (i), (ii) and (iii)

31. What remedy does the author suggest as an alternative to mass production?
    (a) Produce only as per actual requirement of consumer.
    (b) Decentralise production and distribution in areas of actual requirement.
    (c) Both (a) and (b).
    (d) Neither (a) nor (b).

**(H)** ***Read the passages below and answer the questions that follow. Your answer to these items should be based on the passages only.***

32. Maintaining sustainable growth in agriculture requires continual research in developing innovative technologies for conservation and management of limited natural resources. The ICAR has developed new crop varieties with specific traits that improve yield and nutritional quality along with tolerance/resistance to various biotic and abiotic stresses besides matching crop production and protection technologies for target agro ecologies. For different agro-ecological niches, 104 varieties of various crops were released.

    Which amongst the following are specific traits developed in the new crop varieties?
    1. Higher yield
    2. Resistance to adverse weather
    3. Improvement in nutritional value
    4. Agro-ecology specific traits
    (a) 1,2 and 3 (b) 1,3 and 4
    (c) 1,2 and 4 (d) 1,2,3 and 4

33. Woman has been suppressed under custom and law for which man was responsible and in the shaping of which she had no hand. In a plan of life based on nonviolence, women have as much right to shape her own destiny as man has to shape his. But as every rights in a non-violent society proceed from the precious performance of a duty, it follows that rules of the social conduct must be framed by mutual co-operation and consultation. They can never be imposed from outside. Men have not realized this truth in its fullness in their behaviour towards women.

    Which amongst the following can be said to be the logical inference of the passage?
    (a) Along with men, women too should have the right to decide the rules of social conduct.

(b) Denial of rights of women may eventually lead to violence in society.

(c) Custom and law have been solely responsible for suppression of women.

(d) All of the above

34. What does communism mean in the last analysis? It means a classless society—an ideal that is worth striving for. However, I part company with it when force is called to aid for achieving it. We are all born equal, but we have all these centuries resisted the will of God. The idea of inequality, of 'high and low', is an evil, but I do not believe in eradicating evil from the human breast at the point of the bayonet. The human breast does not lend itself to that means.

Which amongst the following can be said to be a logical conclusion about the views of the author?

Conclusion 1: The author does not believe in the ideal of a classless society as the same is a utopian concept which the human society has failed to achieve.

Conclusion 2: The author does not believe in eradicating the evil of inequality as that can only be done by means of force.

(a) Only conclusion 1 can be drawn.

(b) Only conclusion 2 can be drawn.

(c) Both conclusion 1 and 2 can be drawn.

(d) Neither conclusion 1 not 2 can be drawn.

35. While the debate goes on, India like many developing nations, has not even utilized its fair share of the earth's carbon space, nor has it achieved basic minimum standards of living for its entire population. On average, per capita energy use in developing countries is only about 25 per cent of that in developed economies. Besides, there is the issue of access to clean fuels for a sizeable proportion of the rural population. About 400 million Indians still do not have electricity in their homes and about 800 million use some form of biomass as their primary or only energy source for cooking, which is worrisome.

The passage above aims to highlight:

1. The large divide in per capita energy consumption between the developing and the developed countries.

2. Limited or no access to clean energy to a large percentage of Indian population.

(a) Only statement (1) above

(b) Only statement (2) above

(c) Both the statements (1) and (2) above

(d) Neither statement (1) nor (2) above

**(I) Which word is the synonym or similar in meaning to the given words in the questions below.**

36. Abate

(a) Lose (b) Appreciate

(c) Neglect (d) Reduce

37. Quagmire

(a) Marsh (b) Mountain

(c) Desert (d) Riverbed

38. Banter

(a) Hateful speech

(b) Teasing conversation

(c) Vile remark

(d) Sarcastic comment

39. Laconic

(a) Lacking in substance

(b) Sad

(c) Using few words

(d) Insipid

40. Grouse

(a) Grease (b) Appreciate

(c) Complain (d) Backbite

**(J) In the given questions pick out the most effective word(s) from the given words to fill in the blanks and make the sentence meaningfully complete.**

41. The provision of an/a .................................. judiciary is essential the principle of rule of law.

(a) efficient (b) vibrant

(c) independent (d) interdependent

42. The office of the Chief Election Commissioner is located ................ New Delhi.
    (a) around (b) inside
    (c) at (d) in
43. The case was lost in the court as the three independent witness did not ...................... before the court.
    (a) approve (b) speak
    (c) agree (d) testify
44. The Professor was unable to respond to the calls as his mobile phone was missing......... yesterday.
    (a) since
    (b) from
    (c) around
    (d) None of the above
45. The contract was required to be signed by all the parties ................ the agreement.
    (a) of (b) to
    (c) in (d) from

**(K) In the following questions choose the word that means the exact opposite of the word given.**

46. Harsh
    (a) Strict (b) Fair
    (c) Flat (d) Soft
47. Prohibit
    (a) Uphold (b) Permit
    (c) Promote (d) Protect

**(L) In the questions given below a part of the sentence has been underlined. Below are given alternatives to underlined part which may improve the sentence. In case no improvement is possible then chose the option (d).**

48. The sun was so bright that I could not <u>look up</u> the flying plane.
    (a) Look to
    (b) Look at
    (c) See
    (d) No improvement
49. The student asked the teacher, 'Sir <u>can</u> I go to the rest room'.
    (a) Will
    (b) May
    (c) If
    (d) No improvement
50. I have not met him <u>till</u> last month.
    (a) Since
    (b) From
    (c) Around
    (d) No Improvement

## Answers of Practice Question Paper-1

| | | | | |
|---|---|---|---|---|
| **1.** (b) | **11.** (d) | **21.** (d) | **31.** (b) | **41.** (c) |
| **2.** (a) | **12.** (b) | **22.** (c) | **32.** (d) | **42.** (d) |
| **3.** (c) | **13.** (a) | **23.** (b) | **33.** (a) | **43.** (d) |
| **4.** (c) | **14.** (b) | **24.** (b) | **34.** (d) | **44.** (a) |
| **5.** (b) | **15.** (a) | **25.** (c) | **35.** (c) | **45.** (b) |
| **6.** (c) | **16.** (c) | **26.** (d) | **36.** (d) | **46.** (d) |
| **7.** (b) | **17.** (b) | **27.** (b) | **37.** (a) | **47.** (b) |
| **8.** (a) | **18.** (a) | **28.** (b) | **38.** (b) | **48.** (b) |
| **9.** (b) | **19.** (b) | **29.** (d) | **39.** (c) | **49.** (b) |
| **10.** (c) | **20.** (a) | **30.** (b) | **40.** (c) | **50.** (a) |

# Practice Question Paper 2

**(A) Read the following passage and answer the questions that follow. The answers should be based on the passage only.**

**(I)**

She was Princess Ajita. And the court poet of King Narayan had never seen her. On the day he recited a new poem to the king, he would raise his voice just to that pitch which could be heard by unseen hearers in the screened balcony high above the hall. He sent up his song towards the star-land out of his reach, where, circled with light, the planet who ruled his destiny shone unknown and out of ken.

He would espy some shadow moving behind the veil. A tinkling sound would come to his ear from afar, and would set him dreaming of the ankles whose tiny golden bells sang at each step. Ah, the rosy red tender feet that walked the dust of the earth like God's mercy on the fallen! The poet had placed them on the altar of his heart, where he wove his songs to the tune of those golden bells. Doubt never arose in his mind as to whose shadow it was that moved behind the screen, and whose anklets they were that sang to the time of his beating heart.

1. The poet would raise the pitch of his voice while reciting new poems to _________
   (a) impress the king with the range of his creativity and elocution skills.
   (b) be heard by all in the hall and the balcony.
   (c) be specifically heard by the unseen princess behind the veil in the upper balcony.
   (d) All of the above
2. The poet believed that his poems were heard by the princess as______
   (i) he could see the movement of a shadow behind the veils.
   (ii) he could hear the tinkling of anklets with each steps taken by the person.
   (iii) he could occasionally catch a glimpse of the person from behind the veils.

   Which amongst the above are the correct reasons?
   (a) (i), (ii), & (iii)
   (b) (i) & (ii)
   (c) (i) & (iii)
   (d) (i) only

**(II)**

I cannot picture to myself a time when no man shall be richer than another. But I do picture to myself a time when the rich will spurn to enrich themselves at the expense of the poor and the poor will cease to envy the rich. Even in a most perfect world, we shall fail to avoid inequalities, but we can and must avoid strife and bitterness. There are numerous examples extant of the rich and the poor living in perfect friendliness. We have but to multiply such instances.

I do not believe that the capitalists and the landlords are all exploiters by an inherent necessity, or that there is a basic or irreconcilable antagonism between their interests and those of the masses. All exploitation is based on co-operation, willing or forced, of the exploited. However, much we may detest admitting it, the fact remains that there would be no exploitation if people refused to obey the exploiter. But self comes in and we hug the chains that bind us. This must cease. What is needed is not the extinction of landlords and capitalists, but a transformation of the existing relationship between them and the masses into something healthier and purer.

The idea of class war does not appeal to me. In India a class war is not only not inevitable, but it is avoidable if we have understood the message of non-violence. Those who talk about class war as being inevitable have not understood the implications of non-violence or have understood them only skin-deep.

Exploitation of the poor can be extinguished not by effecting the destruction of a few millionaires, but by removing the ignorance of the poor and teaching them to non-co-operate with their exploiters. That will convert the exploiters also. I have even suggested that ultimately it will lead to both being equal partners. Capital as such is not evil; it is its wrong use that is evil. Capital in some form or other will always be needed.

**3.** Examine whether the following two assertions have been made by the author in the passage.

(i) Exploitation of the masses cannot happen without the co-operation of those who are exploited.

(ii) It is possible to create a society where all are equal and no one is richer than another.

(a) Only Assertion (i) is true.
(b) Only Assertion (ii) is true.
(c) Both Assertions (i) and (ii) are true.
(d) Neither Assertion (i) nor (ii) is true.

**4.** What is the reason, as per the author that the exploited continue to bear the exploitation?

(a) They do not have means to fight against exploitation.
(b) It is their self, which prohibits them from breaking the shackles of exploitation.
(c) Often the exploited ones are ignorant about the fact that they are actually being exploited.
(d) All of the above

5. What remedy does the author suggest to end the exploitation in society?

(a) Replace capitalism with socialism.
(b) Eradicate capitalist from society.
(c) Permit a class war in society.
(d) Educate the exploited not to co-operate with the exploiters.

**6.** Which of the following statements can be said to be correct?

(i) Capital is not evil but its wrong use is.
(ii) By very nature of their work capitalist and landlord become exploiters.
(iii) Complete elimination of inequality is an impossibility.
(iv) Class war is inevitable.

(a) (i), (ii) (b) (i), (iii)
(c) (ii), (iii) (d) (ii), (iv)

**7.** Which of the following can be said to be the most important core message of the passage?

(a) Capitalists and landlords are not exploiters but circumstances make them so, and the exploited ones are themselves responsible for it.
(b) Perfect equality may not be possible but strife between rich and poor can be avoided, not by eliminating the capitalist but by teaching the poor non-co-operation with their exploiters.
(c) Capital is not an evil nor is the capitalist. Rich are as much needed in the society as much the poor are needed.
(d) All of the above Ans-b

**(B) Read the following passage and answer the questions that follow. The answers should be based on the passage only.**

The issue of climate change is now placed firmly on national and international agendas, subject to scrutiny by public and media and is even shaping the strategies of a number of businesses. Internationally, the United Nations Framework Convention on Climate Change (the Convention) was set up in 1992 and came into force in 1994. This was a crucial step in putting in place the institutions and processes for the world's governments to take coordinated and effective action. The Convention enjoins near universal membership.

As on date, 194 countries are part of the Convention. The ultimate objective of the Convention is to stabilise the concentration of GHGs in the atmosphere at a level that would prevent dangerous anthropogenic interference with the climate system. Such a level should be achieved within a time frame sufficient to allow ecosystems to adapt naturally to climate change, to ensure that food production is not threatened and to enable economic development to proceed in a sustainable manner. Although global in scope, it differentiates the commitments/ responsibilities of the Parties on the basis of their respective capabilities, economic structures, and resource bases and on the basis of the principle of equity, which is the core of the climate change debate. Hence, any discussion on stabilisation of the concentration of GHGs in the atmosphere should be preceded by a paradigm for equitable access to global atmospheric resources that determines the development space of nations. The Convention lays down legally binding commitments for the developed countries, taking into account their historical responsibilities. These commitments are to be implemented in the form of reduction of GHG emissions by the developed countries with reference to 1990 levels and provision of support to developing countries in terms of finance and technology so as to enable them to take voluntary mitigation and adaptation measures. The Convention recognises that economic and social development and poverty eradication are the first and the overriding priorities of the developing countries.

**8.** As per the passage, what is the ultimate objective of UN Framework Convention on Climate Change?

(i) Stabilising the emission of greenhouse gases.

(ii) Doing (i) above in a time frame which is sufficient to allow ecosystems to adapt to the climate change.

(iii) Doing (i) above so as to prevent dangerous changes in climate which are generated by human activity.

(iv) Taking measures to mitigate the effect of climate change.

(v) Doing (i) above so as to prevent food production from being adversely affected

(vi) Doing (i) above to prevent melting of glaciers.

(a) (i), (ii), (iii), (iv), (v), (vi)

(b) (i), (ii), (iii), (v)

(c) (i), (ii), (iii), (iv)

(d) (i), (iii), (iv), (v)

**9.** Which one of the following is not true about UNFCCC?

(a) It is based on the principle of equality.

(b) It differentiates the commitments and responsibilities of various parties.

(c) It takes into consideration the economic capabilities, resources and capabilities of different countries.

(d) None of the above

10. Is the principle, "polluters should pay", implied in the framework of convention?

(a) It is implied in the mandatory cuts prescribed for the developed countries.

(b) It is implied as only voluntary mitigation and adaptation measures are prescribed for developing countries, that too with financial and technological assistance of developed countries.

(c) It is implied in both (a) and (b).

(d) It is not implied in the framework.

11. Which of the following conclusions can be drawn from the passage?

(i) It recognises the historical responsibility of the developed nations in environmental degradation.

(ii) It recognises that for developing nations, economic and social progress and eliminating poverty are the topmost priorities.

(a) Only Conclusion (i) can be drawn.

(b) Only Conclusion (ii) can be drawn.

(c) Both Conclusions (i) and (ii) can be drawn.

(d) Neither Conclusion (i) nor (ii) can be drawn.

**(C) Read the following passage and answer the questions that follow. The answers should be based on the passage only.**

Given the advantage of young population, the realisation of the democratic dividend is another factor that calls for some more reforms in the education system and health sector. While a skilled, trained and healthy young population with the right education, unskilled, less healthy, and unemployed population could lead to a demographic disaster. Reaping the demographic dividend needs a vision, a long-term plan, and bold decisions. While the National Skill Development Mission is a step in the right direction, much more is required, both in terms of achievements and speed. The RTE Act must face no implementation deficit for it to work towards realising the demographic dividend. Similar reforms are needed in university and higher education and the demand-supply mismatch in the job market needs to be corrected. Mobilisation of funds for higher education is indeed a challenge for the Government. The gap in the available resources could possibly be met by a tailor-made Public—Private—Partnership (PPP) mode of funding without diluting the regulatory oversight of the Government. Private- sector participation on social sectors, such as health and education, sometimes referred to as public—social—private—partnership (PSPP), could be one of the possible alternatives for supplementing the ongoing efforts of the Government. However, in order to put in place such mechanisms, crucial issues such as risks and returns associated with such high-cost projects need to be suitably addressed to ensure that there are enough takers for such PSPP projects in the market on a self-sustainable basis. While the potential of the demographic dividend is high, the effort to realise it also has to be in similar proportions.

12. What is implied above by "reaping the demographic dividend"?
    (a) Economic benefit accrued by the society due to rise in the working age population.
    (b) Economic benefit arising in the society on account of a large section of the society falling in the middle class category.
    (c) Economic benefit arising on account of the emergence of an educated middle class.
    (d) All of the above.
13. Which of the following input is **not** required for reaping the demographic dividend?
    (a) Vision and long-term plans.
    (b) Reforms in primary, secondary and higher education.
    (c) A skill development mission.
    (d) None of the above.
14. Examine which of the following statements are correct.
    (i) The government should play the role of regulator in PPP mode of project finding.
    (ii) Reforms in the education system are critical to reaping the demographic dividend.
    (iii) PSPP model of project finding and implementation remains the only viable alternative if the demographic dividend is to be reaped.
    (a) (i), (ii), (iii) (b) (i), (ii)
    (c) (i), (iii) (d) (ii), (iii)
15. Which one of the following would **not** qualify as public–social–private–partnership (PSPP)?
    (a) Investment by PSU in a hospital in rural area.
    (b) Development of a private university as per government norms.
    (c) Construction of a national highway by a private sector company which employs unemployed youth of the nearby villages.
    (d) None of the above.

**(D) Read the following passage and answer the questions that follow. The answers should be based on the passage only.**

Those who claim to lead the masses must resolutely refuse Those who claim to lead the masses must resolutely refuse to be led by them, if we want to avoid mob law and desire ordered progress for the country. I believe that mere protestation of one's opinion and surrender to the mass opinion is not only not enough, but in matters of vital importance, leaders must act contrary to the mass of opinion if it does not commend itself to their reason.

A leader is useless when he acts against the prompting of his own conscience, surrounded as he must be by people holding all kinds of views. He will drift like an anchorless ship, if he has not the inner voice to hold him firm and guide him.

While admitting that man actually lives by habit, I hold that it is better for him to live by the exercise of will. I also believe that men are capable of developing their will to an extent that will reduce the exploitation to minimum. I look upon an increase in the power of the State with the greatest fear because, although, while apparently doing good by minimising exploitation, it does the greatest harm to mankind by destroying individuality which lies at the root of all progress. We know of so many cases where men have adopted trusteeship, but none where the State has really lived for the poor.

16. Why does the author look upon the rise in the power of state with greatest fear?
    (a) The rise in power of state leads to exploitation of the masses rather than curbing exploitation.
    (b) It destroys individual freedom which is fundamental to social progress.
    (c) It leads to concentration of power in hands of the ruling elite which often corrupts them.
    (d) All of the above.
17. As per the passage, what should be the correct conduct of a leader in a democracy?
    (a) To lead by his own conviction and opinion if it is in consonance with logic and reason.
    (b) To accommodate the opinion of the masses, which is contrary to his opinion despite firmly believing in appropriateness of his own opinion.
    (c) To protest against the mass opinion if it is not in conformity with his own, but to act as per the mass opinion.
    (d) None of the above.
18. Examine whether the following inferences can be drawn from the passage.
    (i) Instead of acting upon as per force of habit, one must act upon by consciously exercising one's will.
    (ii) Growth of state is inimical to the growth of individuality.
    (a) Only Inference (i) can be drawn
    (b) Only Inference (ii) can be drawn
    (c) Both Inferences (i) and (ii) can be drawn
    (d) Neither Inference (i) nor (ii) can be drawn

**(E) Read the following passages and answer the questions that follow. The answers should be based on the passage only.**

**(I)**

Among the new forces that have made our world so different from what it was earlier, the most important is natural science, which has imposed its methods and conclusions on us and altered the very atmosphere in which we live, move and think. The strict method of science requires us to believe a proposition only when we are in a position to prove it. Whenever statements are made, we must find out whether they are capable of verification by those who will take the trouble to investigate them.

19. Which is the most rational and crucial message of the passage?
    1. Science has significantly affected the world and our lives.
    2. Science considers a proposition to be established only if it has been proven to be correct.
    (a) Only statement 1
    (b) Only statement 2
    (c) Both the statements 1 and 2
    (d) Neither the statement 1 nor 2

**(II)**

The history of humanity measured against the inconceivably long vista of time is but the twinkling of an eye. Human beings confined to an infinitesimal part of space seem so far removed from the main plan of the universe. We cannot be certain that man is the last and the supreme utterance of life. The chain may well extend to other links which may be as different from him as he is different from the amoeba. Man is a relatively recent arrival on the earth. He has possessed and governed it for less than a thousandth part of its existence. Gigantic reptiles and dinosaurs ruled it for millions of years and might have thought that they would continue forever. Man today regards himself as the final triumph of biological evolution and has come to stay!

20. Consider what is stated in the passage to be correct and examine which of the following conclusions can be drawn from it.
    1. Man has not reached the apex of evolution.
    2. Dinosaurs can be said to be more evolved than men.
    (a) Only conclusion 1
    (b) Only conclusion 2

(c) Both the conclusions 1 and 2
(d) Neither conclusion 1 nor 2

**(III)**

Trust is the glue that has traditionally bound our economy and is an important ingredient in our recipe of economic well-being. Trust is a vital ingredient in the functioning of the banking and financial markets as well. If there is high trust, economic activity can flourish despite the increased potential for opportunism. However, just because trust is functionally useful to an economy does not mean that it will necessarily arise. We need to identify the factors that underlie opportunistic behaviour and consider processes that facilitate trust creation since there has been a market failure of this public good.

21. Which of the following conclusions can be drawn from the passage?
    1. There exists a certain degree of trust deficit in the market today.
    2. Opportunism is always inimical to trust and bears a negative correlation to it.
    3. Traditionally Indian economy valued trusts and their creation.

    (a) Only conclusions 2 and 3
    (b) Only conclusions 1 and 2
    (c) Only conclusions 1 and 3
    (d) All of the above

**(IV)**

Creative destruction brings innovations into the market that serve people better than the old technologies they displace. It brings new firms into the markets, which compete with existing firms and lower prices for consumers. It brings dynamism to the marketplace that keeps firms on their toes, always on the lookout for the next big way to serve consumers. It has only one prerequisite—a pro-business policy stance that fosters competitive, unfettered markets. When creative destruction is fostered, sectors as a whole will always outperform individual companies within the sector in creating wealth and maximizing welfare. Therein lies the motivation for India to pursue pro-business, rather than pro-crony, growth.

22. Examine as to which of the following logical conclusions can be drawn from the passage?
    1. Innovation is a key factor in economic growth.
    2. The threat to profit and existence is the key motivation for firms for innovation and better service.
    4. Innovation comes at a certain cost to individual enterprises.
    3. Innovation helps the sectors to grow rather than just the individual companies.

    (a) Only statements 1, 2 and 3
    (b) Only statements 1, 2 and 4
    (c) Only statements 1and 2
    (d) All of the above

**(F) Read the following passage and answer the questions that follow. The answers should be based on the passage only.**

The ultimate objective of development planning is human development or increased social welfare and well-being of the people of a nation. This goal is also important because the sustainability of the development process hinges upon the quality of life enjoyed by the people. A healthy and educated population leads to increased productivity which, in turn, can contribute effectively to output growth. Development strategy, therefore, needs to continuously strive for broad-based improvement in standards of living. High growth is essential to generate resources for social spending. However, the fruits of growth need to be shared equitably among all sections of society. Especially, it needs to be ensured that the weaker and disadvantaged sections are not left out of the benefits of growth. The inclusive growth strategy being pursued in the Eleventh Plan has this very objective as it aims to ensure that higher growth of the economy helps overcome the problems of chronic poverty, ignorance and disease.

As per the United Nations Development Programme (UNDP) Human Development Report 2019, the Human Development Index (HDI) for India was 0.647 on the basis of which India is ranked 129 out of 189 countries of the world placing it one rank higher than in 2018. The HDI is based on three indicators, namely GDP per capita (PPP USD), life expectancy at birth, and education as measured by adult literacy rate and gross enrolment ratio (combined for primary, secondary and tertiary education). The value of HDI for India gradually increased from 0.427 in 1980 to 0.556 in 2000 and went up to 0.612 in 2007 and further to 0.647 in 2019. The movement of the index value in some of the comparable countries indicates that improvement in HDI in India in recent years has been better than in most of them.

This trend, indicating improvement in the HDI powered by per capita income growth for India, is heartening though there is no room for complacency as India is still in the Medium Human Development category with even countries like China, Sri Lanka and Indonesia having better ranking. India's HDI rank is also lower than its per capita GDP (PPP USD) rank by three notches, indicating that our human development effort still needs to catch up with the Human Development, Poverty and Public Programmes progress made in GDP per capita. The existing gap between the health and education indicators of India and those in the developed world and even many developing countries needs to be bridged at a faster pace.

23. Which one of the following is **not** one of the factors which are considered for determining the Human Development Index (HDI)?
    (a) Infant mortality rate.
    (b) GDP per capita.
    (c) Life expectancy at birth.
    (d) Education as measured by adult literacy rate and gross enrolment ratio.

24. Why does the sustainability of development hinges upon the quality of life enjoyed by the people?
    (a) Human development is the ultimate aim of any society.
    (b) Fruits of development need to be shared equally amongst all, otherwise it creates social disharmony and affects progress.
    (c) A healthy and educated population has higher productivity and contributes more effectively to growth.
    (d) All of the above.

25. What is meant by 'inclusive growth strategy' in the passage above?
    (a) It is a strategy of growth, which includes the interest of weaker and disadvantaged sections of the society.
    (b) It is a strategy, which aims to achieve higher rate of economic growth so as to eliminate poverty, ignorance and diseases
    (c) Neither (a) nor (b)
    (d) Both (a) and (b)

26. Which of the following conclusions can be drawn from what is stated in the passage?
    (i) Any strategy for development should be such that it should aim at bringing broad based improvement in standard of living.
    (ii) Though improvement in India's HDI has been continuous over the past 30 years, it is not as good as that of some other comparable countries.
    (iii) In next 10 years, India's HDI is likely to move from the medium category to high category.
    (a) (i) and (ii) (b) (i) only
    (c) (i) and (iii) (d) (i), (ii) and (iii)

**(G) Read the following passage and answer the questions that follow. The answers should be based on the passage only.**

Whenever I had occasion to indulge in these surreptitious feasts, dinner at home was out of the question. My mother would naturally ask me to come and take my food and want to know the reason why I did not wish to eat. I would say to her, "I have no appetite today; there is something wrong with my digestion." I knew I was lying, and lying to my mother. I also knew that, if my mother and father came to know of me having become a meat eater, they would be deeply shocked. This knowledge was gnawing at my heart.

27. What does the author mean by surreptitious feast?
    (a) Feasts the author and friends had at school.
    (b) Occasions of eating meat.
    (c) Occasions when author had food outside in a restaurant.
    (d) None of the above.

28. Which of the following can be inferred from the passage?
    (i) The author had no remorse in lying to his mother.
    (ii) He enjoyed eating meat as he did not like home food.
    (a) Only Statement (i) can be inferred.
    (b) Only Statement (ii) can be inferred.
    (c) Both Statements (i) and (ii) can be inferred.
    (d) Neither Statement (i) nor (ii) can be inferred.
29. Which thought was eating up the author from within?
    (a) The fear of being caught on having become a meat eater.
    (b) The shock which his parents would undergo on coming to know that their son had become a meat eater.
    (c) The sadness parents and mother in particular would experience on coming to know that their son preferred meat to home cooked food.
    (d) All of the above.

**(H) Read the passages below and answer the questions that follow. Your answer to these items should be based on the passages only.**

30. All exploitation is based on cooperation, willing or forced, of the exploited. However much we may detest admitting it, the fact remains that there would be no exploitation if people refused to obey the exploiter. But self comes in and we hug the chains that bind us. This must cease.

    What is the most logical corollary of the message of the author in the passage?
    (1) Revolution is necessary to end exploitation and servitude.
    (2) The exploited do not want to admit that they are being exploited as the chain of bondage prevents them from doing so.
    (a) Only statement 1 is a logical corollary.
    (b) Only statement 2 is a logical corollary.
    (c) Both statements 1 and 2 are logical corollaries.
    (d) Neither statement 1 nor 2 is a logical corollary.
31. Developing countries including India have been stressing that Common but Differentiated Responsibilities (CBDR) and equity must continue to be the bedrock of ongoing and future sustainable development financing. Subsequently, the financial flows and the means of implementation thus strategist for pursuing a sustainable development trajectory must ensure that the provisions with regard to new and additional resources are both adequate and predictable.

    Which of the following statements can be said to be logically in consonance with what is stated in the passage?
    (1) It can be inferred from the passage that there are substantial differences between the developing countries and the developed countries over the principles governing the future sustainable development financing.
    (2) The developing countries are of the view that financing should be such that additional resources are adequate and predictable.
    (a) Only statement (1) above is correct.
    (b) Only statement (2) above is correct.
    (c) Both statements (1) and (2) above are correct.
    (d) Neither statement (1) nor (2) is correct.
32. The defining challenge in India today is that of generating employment and growth. Jobs are created by firms when firms invest and grow. Hence it is important to create an environment that is conducive for firms to invest. The recent business cycle downturn has seen a sharp decline in investment. Reviving investment is, therefore, on top of the government's priorities.

    Investments are made on the basis of long-term growth prospects. The key to reviving investment in India lies in reviving the trend growth rate of the Indian economy. Reforms are needed on three fronts: creating a framework for sustained low and stable inflation, setting public finances on a sustainable path by tax and expenditure reform, and creating the legal and regulatory framework for a well-functioning market economy.

Which amongst the following can be said to be the most logical and crucial message of the passage?

(a) Business cycle downturn has had an adverse impact on the investment.

(b) Creation of jobs in economy can only happen when there is investment by firms and growth.

(c) The key to investment is the long-term growth prospects of an economy which is not bright in the current scenario.

(d) For growth and investment there is a need for reforms relating to, controlling of inflation, tax and expenditure and creation of legal and regulatory framework for an efficient market economy.

33. The problem is not to set class against class, but to educate labour to a sense of its dignity. Moneyed men after all form microscopic minority in the world. They will act on the square, immediately labour realizes its power and yet acts on the square. To inflame labour against moneyed men is to perpetuate class hatred and all the evil consequences flowing from it. The strife is a vicious circle to be avoided at any cost. It is an admission of weakness, a sign of inferiority complex. The moment labour recognizes its own dignity, money will find its rightful place, i.e. it will be held in trust for labour. For labour is more than money.

Which amongst the following is the crux of the passage?

(a) Moneyed men are less important than labour as they are a microscopic minority.

(b) The rights of labour will emanate not from violence and protest, but from understanding of its own dignity.

(c) Through class conflict, the labour cannot gain upper hand as the money class has wealth and power.

(d) All of the above.

34. If instead of insisting on rights everyone does his duty, there will immediately be the rule of order established among mankind. There is no such thing as the divine right of kings to rule and the humble duty of the ryots to pay respectful obedience to their masters. Whilst it is true that these hereditary inequalities must go as being injurious to the well-being of the society, the unabashed assertion of rights of the hitherto downtrodden millions is equally injurious, if not more so to the same well-being. The latter behaviour is probably calculated to injure the millions rather than the few claimants of divine rights. They could but die a brave or cowardly death but those few would not bring in the orderly life blissful contentment. It is, therefore, necessary to understand the correlation of the rights and duties. I venture to suggest that rights that do not flow directly from duty performed well are not worth having. They will be usurpations, the sooner they are discarded the better it will be.

Which amongst the following is the appropriate logical expression of the author's view point?

(a) Rights and duties are correlated and proportionate. Rights in excess of duties would be detrimental.

(b) Assertion of rights by down trodden is less injurious than that by the priviledged.

(c) Nobody should assert his right and thus everybody should be denied rights. Only, there should be a right to perform one's duty.

(d) All of the above.

35. According to projections of the model, pursuit of low carbon strategies will bring down the average GDP growth rate by 0.15 percentage point, while per capita CO2 emissions (in 2030) will fall from 3.6 tonnes per person in the BIG (baseline, inclusive growth) scenario to 2.6 tonnes per person in the LCIG (low carbon, inclusive growth) scenario.

However, in both scenarios, total carbon emissions will continue to rise up to the year 2030. The cumulative costs of low carbon strategies between 2010 and 2030 have been estimated at around US$ 834 billion at 2011 prices. This will divert resources from other needs and may not be possible to sustain if growth is not fast enough. The total GDP loss caused by the additional energy investment in the LCIG scenario has been quantified at US$ 1344 billion at 2011 prices. International support, in both finance and technology, would therefore be critical.

Which of the following conclusions can be drawn as per what is stated in the passage?

**Conclusion 1:** Despite the adoption of low carbon strategies, there will be no reduction in the total carbon emissions till 2030.

**Conclusion 2:** As a result of diversion of resources on adoption of low carbon strategies, it will not be possible to sustain the growth of GDP.

(a) Only conclusion 1 can be drawn.
(b) Only conclusion 2 can be drawn.
(c) Both conclusions 1 and 2 can be drawn.
(d) Neither conclusion 1 nor conclusion 2 can be drawn.

**(I) Which word is the synonym or similar in meaning to the given words in question.**

36. Abeyance
(a) distance (b) hate
(c) suspension (d) grievance

37. Mendicant
(a) man of medicine (b) dishonest
(c) meticulous (d) beggar

38. Sage
(a) silent
(b) wise
(c) solitary
(d) none of the above

39. Behemoth
(a) very large (b) very ugly
(c) very old (d) very bold

40. Laud
(a) to praise (b) to dominate
(c) to explain (d) to explain

**(J) In the questions below one definition and word options are given. Choose the appropriate word option for the definition.**

41. Present throughout the year
(a) annual (b) perennial
(c) biennial (d) biannual

42. Use of agreeable or inoffensive language in place of what may be unpleasant
(a) melifluous (b) euphoria
(c) euphemism (d) eulogy

43. To grow by additions
(a) accumulate
(b) integration
(c) appreciation
(d) None of the above

**(K) In the given questions pick out the most effective word(s) from the given words to fill in the blanks and make the sentence meaningfully complete**

44. The artist was profusely .............. by the media on the excellent live performance.
(a) commented (b) criticized
(c) complimented (d) covered

45. The Judge................ himself from the case as he personally knew one of the parties us to the litigation.
(a) refused (b) abstained
(c) recused (d) separated

46. The distribution of wealth in society should be done taking into account the principle of ...................
(a) equality (b) law
(c) jurisprudence (d) equity

47. The coach............. all the players to give their best performance in the final match.
(a) made (b) exhorted
(c) reprimanded (d) pleaded

48. Despite Ravi's excellent performance in the examination, his father advised him not be ............... in the subsequent semester, as the course would get tougher.
(a) complacent (b) lazy
(c) arrogant (d) cool

**(L) In the following questions choose the word that means the exact opposite of the word given.**

49. Stale
    (a) new (b) bright
    (c) fresh (d) old

50. Pertinent
    (a) inappropriate (b) impertinent
    (c) impolite (d) incomplete

## Answers of Practice Question Paper-2

| | | | | |
|---|---|---|---|---|
| **1.** (c) | **11.** (c) | **21.** (c) | **31.** (b) | **41.** (b) |
| **2.** (b) | **12.** (a) | **22.** (b) | **32.** (d) | **42.** (c) |
| **3.** (a) | **13.** (d) | **23.** (a) | **33.** (b) | **43.** (a) |
| **4.** (b) | **14.** (b) | **24.** (c) | **34.** (a) | **44.** (c) |
| **5.** (d) | **15.** (c) | **25.** (d) | **35.** (a) | **45.** (c) |
| **6.** (b) | **16.** (b) | **26.** (b) | **36.** (c) | **46.** (d) |
| **7.** (b) | **17.** (a) | **27.** (b) | **37.** (d) | **47.** (b) |
| **8.** (b) | **18.** (c) | **28.** (d) | **38.** (b) | **48.** (a) |
| **9.** (a) | **19.** (b) | **29.** (b) | **39.** (a) | **49.** (c) |
| **10.** (c) | **20.** (d) | **30.** (d) | **40.** (a) | **50.** (a) |

# Practice Question Paper 3

**(A) Read the following passage and answer the questions that follow. The answers should be based on the passage only.**

This belief in God has to be based on faith which transcends reason. Indeed, even the so-called realisation has, at bottom, an element of faith without which it cannot be sustained. In the very nature of things it must be so. Who can transgress the limitations of his being? I hold that complete realisation is impossible in this embodied life. Nor is it necessary. A living immovable faith is all that is required for reaching the full spiritual height attainable by human beings. God is not outside this earthly case of ours. Therefore, exterior proof is not of much avail, if any at all. We must ever fail to perceive Him through the senses because He is beyond them. We can feel Him, if we will but withdraw ourselves from the senses. The divine music is incessantly going on within ourselves, but the loud senses drown the delicate music, which is unlike and infinitely superior to anything we can perceive or hear with our senses.

But he is not God who merely satisfies the intellect, if he ever does.

God to be God must rule the heart and transform it. He must express Himself in every smallest act of His votary. This can only be done through a definite realisation more real than the five senses can ever produce. Sense perceptions can be, often are, false and deceptive, however real they may appear to us. Where there is realisation outside the senses it is infallible. It is proved not by extraneous evidence but in the transformed conduct and character of those who have felt the real presence of God within. Such testimony is to be found in the experiences of an unbroken line of prophets and sages in all countries and climes. To reject this evidence is to deny oneself.

1. Which of the two conclusions can be drawn from what is stated in the passage?
   (i) Realisation of God is not possible without faith.
   (ii) Complete realisation of God is not possible in this bodily existence.
   (a) Only Conclusion (i) can be drawn.
   (b) Only Conclusion (ii) can be drawn.
   (c) Both Conclusions (i) and (ii) can be drawn.
   (d) Neither Conclusion (i) nor (ii) can be drawn.
2. "The loud senses drown the delicate music." What does the author mean by this statement?
   (a) Human senses are not sharp enough to capture the subtle sounds of nature.
   (b) Our senses are too blunt to understand divine music.
   (c) We are so much involved in our sensory perceptions that we fail to notice the continuous presence of God within us.
   (d) All of the above.
3. Which of the following qualities of God does the author refer to in the passage?
   (i) God is omnipresent and omnipotent.
   (ii) God must be capable of transforming the being of man.
   (iii) God must express Himself even in the smallest act of his believer.
   (iv) God should be capable of being perceived through faith and reason.
   (a) (i), (ii) (b) (ii), (iii)
   (c) (iii), (iv) (d) (i), (iv)
4. Which one of the following is **not** correct as per the passage?
   (a) Realisation of God, which is extrasensory, cannot fail.

(b) Realisation of God is to be established by the transformed conduct and character of those who have realised God.

(c) The realisation of God is more real than the sensory perceptions.

(d) None of the above.

**(B) Read the following passage and answer the questions that follow. The answers should be based on the passage only.**

Four score and seven years ago our fathers brought forth on this continent, a new nation, conceived in liberty, and dedicated to the proposition that all men are created equal.

Now we are engaged in a great civil war, testing whether that nation, or any nation so conceived and so dedicated, can long endure. We are met on a great battle field of that war. We have come to dedicate a portion of that field, as a final resting place for those who here gave their lives that that nation might live. It is altogether fitting and proper that we should do this.

But, in the larger sense, we cannot dedicate, we cannot consecrate, we cannot hallow, this ground. The brave men, living or dead, who struggled here, have consecrated it, far above our poor power to add or detract. The world will little note, nor long remember what we say here, but it can never forget what they did here. It is for us the living, rather, to be dedicated here to the unfinished work which they who fought here have thus far so nobly advanced. It is rather for us to be here dedicated to the great task remaining before us—that from these honoured dead we take increased devotion to that cause for which they gave the last full measure of devotion—that we here highly resolve that these dead shall not have died in vain—that this nation, under God, shall have a new birth of freedom—and that government of the people, by the people, for the people, shall not perish from the earth.

5. Which are founding principles of nationhood which have been referred to in the passage?
   (a) Liberty and fraternity
   (b) Sovereignty and equality
   (c) Justice and freedom
   (d) Liberty and equality

6. What does the speaker mean by the sentence, "But in a larger sense we cannot dedicate…"?
   (a) Since the brave men who laid their lives are already dead, it is pointless to felicitate them.
   (b) The task for which the brave men laid their lives is unfinished hence felicitation is meaningless.
   (c) The act of bravery was of such an immense nature that no degree of felicitation would be fitting for it.
   (d) All of the above.

7. What, as per the speaker, the great civil war is putting to test?
   (a) The fortitude and bravery of people.
   (b) Whether a nation based on principles of liberty and equality is sustainable or not.
   (c) Whether the people have conviction to fulfil the dream of their forefathers of independent state.
   (d) All of the above.

**(C) Read the following passage and answer the questions that follow. The answers should be based on the passage only.**

Climate change, as a global environmental problem has been receiving intense political attention at domestic and international levels. Climate change means a change in climate which is attributed directly or indirectly to human activity that alters the composition of the global atmosphere and which in addition to natural climate variability is observed over comparable time periods. Increasing levels of fossil fuel burning and land use changes have emitted, and are continuing to emit, greenhouse gases (mainly carbon dioxide [CO2], methane, and nitrous oxide) into the earth's atmosphere. This increasing level of emissions of greenhouse gases have caused a rise in the amount of heat from the sun trapped in earth's atmosphere, heat that would normally be radiated back into space. This has led to the greenhouse effect, resulting in climate change. The major characteristics of climate change are rise in average global temperature, ice cap melting, changes in precipitation and increase in ocean temperature. The efforts needed to address the climate change problem include mitigation of greenhouse gas emissions on the one hand and building of capacities to cope with the adverse impacts of climate change on various sectors of the society and economy on the other hand.

8. What are the features of definition of climate change given in the passage?
   (i) A change in climate attributable to human activity directly or indirectly.
   (ii) A change as in (i) above, which is in addition to natural climate variability.
   (iii) A change as in (i) above, which alters the composition of world atmosphere over comparable time periods.
   (iv) A change as in (i) above, which has adverse ecological impact.
   (a) (i), (ii), (iii), (iv) (b) (i), (iii), (iv)
   (c) (i), (ii), (iii) (d) (i), (ii), (iv)
9. Which of the following is not a factor referred to in the passage for bringing climate change?
   (a) Burning of fossil fuel in increasingly high quantities.
   (b) Changes in land use.
   (c) Deforestation of large forest areas.
   (d) None of the above.
10. Identify the characteristics of climate change recounted in the passage.
   (i) Destruction of habitat of flora and fauna.
   (ii) Melting of ice caps.
   (iii) Increase in ocean temperature.
   (iv) Rise in average global temperature.
   (v) Rise in mean sea level.
   (vi) Changes in precipitation.
   (a) (i), (iii), (iv), (vi)
   (b) (i), (ii), (iii), (iv), (v), (vi)
   (c) (ii), (iii), (iv), (v)
   (d) (ii), (iii), (iv), (vi)
11. What measures have been mentioned in the passage to address the challenges of climate change?
   (i) Mitigation of green-house gas emission.
   (ii) Protection of the endangered species of flora and fauna.
   (iii) Trading in carbon credits to encourage green-house gas emission reduction technology.
   (iv) Building capacities to cope up with adverse impact of climate change.
   (a) (i), (iv) (b) (i), (iii), (iv)
   (c) (i), (ii), (iii), (iv) (d) (ii), (iii), (iv)

**(D) Read the following passages and answer the questions that follow. The answers should be based on the passage only.**

**(I)**

Our scientific theories which supersede earlier ones are only links in a long chain of progressive advances likely in time to be themselves transcended. Their only justification is their adequacy for the relevant facts. They are temporary resting places in the search for truth and there is nothing absolute about them. Religion on the other hand claims to be absolutistic. Its truths are said to be unalterable and our only duty is to defend them. Such truths, if any, belong to heaven; our truths are always provisional and tentative.

12. Consider the following statements and determine as to which statement(s) if correct would support the crucial message of the passage.
   1. Religion is based on faith and transcends reasoning and inquiry.
   2. Scientific inquiry has substantially been strengthened due to the growth of physical sciences.
   (a) Only statement 1
   (b) Only statement 2
   (c) Both the statements 1 and 2
   (d) Neither the statement 1 nor 2

**(II)**

Morality is a working arrangement and its sanction is a social necessity. As morality is a matter of convention, society has a right to alter or amend it, if it judges such modifications in line with its interests. No God is commanding us into a prescribed mode of behaviour. Ethical rules are objective only in the sense that they are independent of this or that individual and not in the sense that they are unconditional commands or that they assume that "good" is an unanalysable and ultimate quality.

13. Consider the following statements and examine as to which support the crucial message of the passage
    1. Polygamy and polyandry, accepted norms in society at some point of time, do not enjoy a positive social sanction now.
    2. Society is becoming less God-fearing and more immoral.

    (a) Only statement 1
    (b) Only statement 2
    (c) Both the statements 1 and 2
    (d) Neither statement 1 nor 2

**(III)**

Although the primary tenet of any investment is that high expected rewards come with high risk, many Indian firms have found a peculiar way to reap rewards without commensurate risk. Many firms enjoy profits in good times but often rely on the state or their financiers to bail them out in bad times. A particularly egregious form of such riskless return is the phenomenon of wilful default—a classic case of a one way gamble in which "heads, the promoter wins; tails, the lender loses". Wilful default occurs when firms take loans, divert the proceeds out of the firm for the personal benefit of owners, default on loans and declare bankruptcy, thereby expropriating a range of stakeholders—lenders, minority shareholders, employees, regulators and state coffers.

14. Examine as to which of the following inferences are implied by the passage?
    (a) Promoters' greed is often the cause of the bankruptcy of firms in modern times.
    (b) There is a strong need for statutory auditing of firms' accounts, to oversee that the funds' transfer out of the firms is bona fide.
    (c) Both (a) and (b)
    (d) Neither (a) nor (b)

**(IV)**

By postulating a perfect God who is responsible for the government of the universe, religion seems to take away the edge from ethical striving. For Plato, the Good who is the Truth and Real, shines everlastingly like the sun in the high heaven. Man, dwelling in the cave of his ignorance, bound in the chains of his stupidity and selfishness, takes the shadows thrown upon the farthest walls by the light of his own passions as realities, knows not that the Good is there, the eternal source of all light and life. If his eyes are cleared up, he will see the Real. There is nothing to fight against except the doubts in his mind and the shadows of his errors.

15. Which of the following conclusions can be drawn from what is stated in the passage?
    1. The postulation of a perfect God is a fallacy.
    2. Man pursues untruth as reality owing to his own weaknesses.
    3. Goodness within is the ultimate Truth.

    (a) All conclusions 1, 2 and 3
    (b) Only conclusion 2, and 3
    (c) Only conclusions 1 and 2
    (d) Only conclusion 1 and 3

**(E) Read the following passage and answer the questions that follow. The answers should be based on the passage only.**

To see the universal and all-pervading Spirit of Truth face-to-face one must be able to love the meanest of creation as oneself. And a man who aspires after that cannot afford to keep out of any field of life. That is why my devotion to truth has drawn me into the field of politics; and I can say without the slightest hesitation, and yet in all humility, that those who say that religion has nothing to do with politics do not know what religion means.

Identification with everything that lives is impossible without self-purification; without self-purification the observance of the law of *ahimsa* must remain an empty dream; God can never be realised by one who is not pure of heart. Self-purification, therefore, must mean purification in all walks of life.

And purification being highly infectious, purification of oneself necessarily leads to the purification of one's surroundings.

But the path of self-purification is hard and steep. To attain to perfect purity one has to become absolutely passion-free in thought, speech and action; to rise above the opposing currents of love and hatred, attachment and repulsion. I know that I have not in me as yet that triple purity, in spite of constantly striving for it. That is why the world's praise fails to move me, indeed it very often stings me. To conquer the subtle passions seems to me to be far harder than the physical conquest of the world by the force of arms.

16. What is the reason the author cites for his joining politics?
    (a) He is a seeker of Truth, which he seeks in politics also.
    (b) For him Religion and Truth are one and the same thing.
    (c) He believes that his entering politics is essential for national salvation.
    (d) All of the above.

17. Which of the following conclusions can be drawn from what is stated in the passage?
    (i) To realise God and Truth, one must be able to see oneself even in the tiniest of living being.
    (ii) Purity cannot be attained without overcoming passion.
    (a) Only Conclusion (i) can be drawn.
    (b) Only Conclusion (ii) can be drawn.
    (c) Both Conclusions (i) and (ii) can be drawn.
    (d) Neither Conclusion (i) nor (ii) can be drawn.

18. Which one of the following is **not** implied by what is stated in the passage?
    (a) Purifying oneself from within is essential to be a practitioner of non-violence.
    (b) Purity of oneself leads to purity of one's surroundings and others.
    (c) A man who sees himself in all creation cannot distance himself from any field of life.
    (d) None of the above.

19. To attain perfect purity, which of the following is essential as per the author?
    (i) Control of passion in thought, speech and action.
    (ii) Practising Ahimsa in all walks of life.
    (iii) Overcoming love and hatred.
    (iv) Rising above attachment and repulsion.
    (a) (i), (ii), (iii), (iv) (b) (i), (iii), (iv)
    (c) (ii), (iii), (iv) (d) (i), (ii), (iii)

20. Amongst the following which are the most important messages that the author wants to convey in the passage?
    (i) To realise God one must be able to identify himself with the tiniest of the creation and love it as one loves oneself.
    (ii) Politics and religion both are reflections of same truth.
    (iii) Self-purification in all walks of life is essential.
    (iv) To attain perfect purity, it is essential to overcome passion in thought, speech and action, hatred, attachment, love and repulsion.
    (v) Identification with all creation is impossible without self-purification.
    (vi) The path of self-purification is hard and steep.
    (a) (i), (iii), (vi) (b) (ii), (iii), (vi)
    (c) (i), (iv), (v) (d) (ii), (iv), (v)

**(F) Read the following passage and answer the questions that follow. The answers should be based on the passage only.**

When in the course of human events, it becomes necessary for one people to dissolve the political bonds which have connected them with another, and to assume among the powers of the earth, the separate and equal station to which the Laws of Nature and of Nature's God entitle them, a decent respect to the opinions of mankind requires that they should declare the causes which impel them to the separation.

We hold these truths to be self-evident, that all men are created equal, that they are endowed by their Creator with certain unalienable rights, that among these are life, liberty and the pursuit of happiness. That to secure these rights, governments are instituted among men, deriving their just powers from the consent of the governed. That whenever any form of government becomes destructive of these ends, it is the right of the people to alter or to abolish it, and to institute new government, laying its foundation on such principles and organising its powers in such form, as to them shall seem most likely to affect their safety and happiness. Prudence, indeed, will dictate that governments long established should not be changed for light and transient causes; and accordingly all experience hath shewn, that mankind are more disposed to suffer, while evils are sufferable, than to right themselves by abolishing the forms to which they are accustomed. But when a long train of abuses and usurpations, pursuing invariably the same object evinces a design to reduce them under absolute despotism, it is their right, it is their duty, to throw off such government, and to provide new guards for their future security. Such has been the patient sufferance of these colonies; and such is now the necessity which constrains them to alter their former Systems of government. The history of the present King of Great Britain is a history of repeated injuries and usurpations, all having in direct object the establishment of an absolute tyranny over these States. To prove this, let facts be submitted to a candid world.

21. Which amongst the following is not one of the rights which have been referred to in the passage?
   (a) Right of pursuit of happiness
   (b) Right of justice
   (c) Right of liberty
   (d) None of the above

22. As per the passage, where are the governments to derive their power from?
   (a) The sovereign king.
   (b) The laws of the land.
   (c) The people; through their consent.
   (d) All of the above.

23. Which of the following assertions have been made in the passage?
   (i) People tend to suffer evils till they can, than to change or abolish its cause.
   (ii) It is imprudent to call for a change of government which is long established.
   (a) Only Assertion (i) has been made.
   (b) Only Assertion (ii) has been made.
   (c) Both Assertions (i) and (ii) have been made.
   (d) Neither Assertion (i) nor (ii) has been made.

24. As per the passage what is the objective of instituting a government?
   (a) To maintain law and order amongst its citizens.
   (b) To prevent despotism and anarchy from gripping the state.
   (c) To provide the citizens certain basic rights.
   (d) All of the above.

25. As per the passage when are the people entitled to change the government?
   (a) When a government becomes destructive of the rights of people.
   (b) When it becomes abusive of people and usurper of their rights.
   (c) When its objective is despotic.
   (d) All of the above.

26. Which of the following can be said to be part of the core theme of the passage?
   (i) Men should not change a government for light and transient causes.
   (ii) Men are created equal and have certain unalienable rights.
   (iii) A government derives its authority from the consent of the people it governs.
   (a) (i), (ii), (iii)    (b) (i), (ii)
   (c) (i), (iii)    (d) (ii), (iii)

**(G) Read the following passage and answer the questions that fellow. The answers should be based on the passage only.**

As I searched myself deeper, the necessity for changes both internal and external began to grow upon me. As soon as, or even before, I made alterations in my expenses and my way of living, I began to make changes in my diet. I saw that the writers on vegetarianism had examined the question very minutely, attacking it in its religious, scientific, practical and medical aspects. Ethically, they had arrived at the conclusion that the man's supremacy over the lower animals meant not that the former should prey upon the latter, but that the higher should protect the lower, and that there should be mutual aid between the two as between man and man. They had also brought out the truth that man eats not for enjoyment but to live.

27. As per the passage which of the following is **not** a conclusion about relationship of man and lower animals?
    (a) Man could prey on some animals for survival.
    (b) Relationship between the two should be of mutual aid.
    (c) Man should be a protector of lower animals.
    (d) None of the above.
28. What does the author mean by, "the necessity for changes … began to grow upon me"?
    (a) He felt that there was need to cut expenses.
    (b) He began to realise the need for change in his diet and lifestyle.
    (c) He started to dislike the non-vegetarian food.
    (d) All of the above.
29. Which of the two can be said to be a corollary of the assertions made by the author?
    (i) Co-existence of all living beings is only ethical possible solution for this world.
    (ii) Food habit should be governed by need and desire.
    (a) Only (i) can be said to be right corollary.
    (b) Only (ii) can be said to be right corollary.
    (c) Both (i) and (ii) can be said to be right corollaries.
    (d) Neither (i) nor (ii) can be said to be right corollary.

**(H) Read the passages below and answer the questions that follow. Your answer to these items should be based on the passages only.**

**(I)**

Woman is the companion of man, gifted with equal mental capacities. She has the right to participate in every minute detail in the activities of man and she has an equal right of freedom and liberty with him. She is entitled to a supreme place in her own sphere of activity as man is in his. This ought to be the natural condition of things and not as a result only of learning to read and write. By sheer force of a vicious custom, even the most ignorant and worthless men have been enjoying a superiority over women which they do not deserve and ought not to have. Many of our movements stop half way because of the conditions of our women. Much of our work done does not yield appropriate results; our lot is like that of the penny-wise and pound-foolish trader who does not employ enough capital in his business.

30. In terms of what is stated in the passage, which of the following statements reflect correctly, the views of the author?
    (i) Men have enjoyed superiority over women because of physical might although women have equal mental capacities.
    (ii) Women have a right to enjoy a supreme place in their own realm of work
    (a) Only (i)
    (b) Only (ii)
    (c) Both (i) & (ii)
    (d) Neither (i) nor (ii)

**(II)**

Divorce between intelligence and labour has resulted in criminal negligence of the villages. And so, instead of having graceful hamlets dotting the land, we have dung-heaps. The approach to many villages is not a refreshing experience. Often one would like to shut one's eyes and stuff one's nose; such is the surrounding dirt and offending smell. If the majority of political leaders were derived from our villages, as they should be, they should be able to make our villages models of cleanliness in every sense of the word. But they have never considered it their duty to identify themselves with the villagers in their daily lives. A sense of national or social sanitation is not a virtue among us. We may take a kind of a bath, but we do not mind dirtying the well or the tank or the river by whose side or in which we perform ablutions. I regard this defect as a great vice which is responsible for the disgraceful state of our villages and the sacred banks of the sacred rivers and for the diseases that spring form insanitation.

31. Identify, which amongst the following is/are the reasons which the author ascribes for neglect of the villages.
    (i) Lack of emergence of any political leadership from our villages.

(ii) Lack of sense of sanitation amongst the people.

(iii) Use of cow dung as a manure for agriculture.

(a) (i), (ii), (iii)

(b) (i), (ii)

(c) Only (ii)

(d) None of the above

**(III)**

The greatest service we can render society is to free ourselves and it from the superstitious regard we have learnt to pay to the learning of the English language. It is the medium of instruction in our schools and colleges. It is becoming the *lingua franca* of the country. Our best thoughts are expressed in it. This belief in the necessity of English training has enslaved us. It has unfitted us for true national service. Were it not for force of habit, we could not fail to see that by reason of English being the medium of instruction, our intellect has been segregated, we have been isolated from the masses, the best mind of the nation has become gagged and the masses have not received the benefit of the new ideas we have received.

32. Which amongst the following as per the author is/are the reasons for English increasingly becoming a medium of instruction of schools and colleges?

(i) English connects various parts of the country.

(ii) It is easy for students to learn English as compared to the vernacular languages.

(iii) Expression of thoughts and ideas in English is better.

(a) (i), (ii), (iii)

(b) (i), (ii)

(c) (i), (iii)

(d) None of the above

**(IV)**

Nothing can be further from my thought than that we should become exclusive or erect barriers. But I do respectfully contend that an appreciation of other cultures can fitly follow, never precede, an appreciation and assimilation of our own. It is my firm opinion that no culture has treasures so rich as ours has. We have not known it, we have been made even to deprecate its study and depreciate its value. We have almost ceased to live it. An academic grasp without practice behind it is like an embalmed corpse, perhaps lovely to look at but nothing to inspire or ennoble. My religion forbids me to belittle or disregard other cultures, as it insists under pain of civil suicide upon imbibing and living my own.

It stands for synthesis of the different cultures that have come to stay in India, what have influenced Indian life, and that, in their turn, have been themselves been influenced by the spirit of the soil. This synthesis will naturally be of the Swadeshi type, where each culture is assured its legitimate place, and not of the American pattern, where on dominant culture absorbs the rest, and where the aim is not towards harmony, but towards an artificial and forced unity.

The India culture of our times is in the making. Many of us are striving to produce a blend of all the cultures which seem today to be in clash with one another. No culture can live, if it attempts to be exclusive. There is no such thing as pure Aryan culture in existence today in India. Whether the Aryans were indigenous to India or were unwelcome intruders, does not interest me much. What does interest me is the fact that my remote ancestors blended with one another with the utmost freedom and we of the present generation are a result of that blend. Whether, we are doing any good to the country of our birth and the tiny globe which sustains us or whether we are burden, the future alone will show.

**Choose the correct option as per the passage:**

33. The harmony of cultures which the author believes in, would allow;

(i) free intermingling of different cultures.

(ii) a dominant culture to subsume the other.

(iii) a constitutional promotion of minority cultures.

(a) (i), (ii), (iii)  (b) (i), (ii)

(c) (i), (iii)  (d) only (i)

34. In terms of what is stated in the passage, which among the following can be said to correctly reflect authors view about Indian culture?

(i) Every individual must believe in the supremacy of one's own culture.

(ii) Academic knowledge of culture without its actual practice is infructuous.

(iii) It is impossible to create barriers and to make cultures exclusive.

(a) (i), (ii), (iii) (b) (ii), (iii)

(c) (i) & (ii) (d) only (ii)

35. Which amongst the following statements would correctly describe the reason for the author's belief that appreciation of other cultures can follow but never precede appreciation and assimilation of our own?

(a) Indigenous culture should be the dominant culture.

(b) Indian culture being a synthesis of different cultures over a long period of time is essential to understand the more recent and exclusive cultures.

(c) Both (a) & (b)

(d) Neither (a) nor (b)

**(I) Which word is the synonym or similar in meaning to the given words in question.**

36. Abscond

(a) to depart secretly (b) to defy

(c) to spy (d) to grief

37. Bawdy

(a) Bold (b) Boastful

(c) Obscene (d) Strange

38. Facilitate

(a) To lessent difficulty (b) To grow

(c) To impede (d) To cut

39. Quibble

(a) To argue over petty

(b) To respond quickly

(c) To doubt

(d) To criticize

40. Rescind

(a) To review (b) To refute

(c) To rebuke (d) To cancel

**(J) In the given questions pick out the most effective word(s) from the given words to fill in the blanks and make the sentence meaningfully complete**

41. As the train was scheduled to be late, there was no point in reaching the railway station.......................... 6:30 PM.

(a) after

(b) around

(c) before

(d) None of the above

42. The case accused the dependent of .......... communal hatred.

(a) Fomenting (b) forming

(c) inspiring (d) gathering

43. The hunter clamed to have killed two birds ........... on shot.

(a) by (b) from

(c) at (d) with

44. Rama and Krishna are considered a/an .............. of Lord Vishnu as per the Puranas.

(a) imagery (b) incanation

(c) incarnation (d) intonation

45. Considering the wide spread protests on increase of taxes, the Finance Minister tried to............. the angry masses by offering some food subsidy.

(a) please (b) placate

(c) mislead (d) cuddle

**(K) Choose the alternative which best express the meaning of the idiom/phrase that is italicised and underlined in the sentence**

46. The family *disposed of* the old car for a meagre sum.

(a) Threw away (b) Renovate

(c) Sold (d) Scrapped

47. Although it was his second offence, he was likely to *get off* with only a reprimand.

(a) Move away (b) Escape

(c) Pay cost of (d) Go down

48. Although I have differences with you I am ready to *meet you half way.*
    (a) Travel half the journey
    (b) Pay half the expenses
    (c) Solve half the problem
    (d) come to a compromise
49. Through on most points we differ, on the issue of how to raise funds for the company, *we are at one.*
    (a) On the same place
    (b) of the same opinion
    (c) At the same time
    (d) None of the above
50. They were office colleagues ones but now there is no *love lost between them.*
    (a) No decrease in friendship
    (b) Development of another relationship
    (c) Not at good terms
    (d) Sworn enemies

## Answers of Practice Question Paper-3

| | | | | |
|---|---|---|---|---|
| **1.** (c) | **11.** (a) | **21.** (b) | **31.** (c) | **41.** (c) |
| **2.** (c) | **12.** (a) | **22.** (c) | **32.** (d) | **42.** (a) |
| **3.** (b) | **13.** (a) | **23.** (a) | **33.** (d) | **43.** (d) |
| **4.** (d) | **14.** (d) | **24.** (c) | **34.** (d) | **44.** (c) |
| **5.** (d) | **15.** (b) | **25.** (d) | **35.** (d) | **45.** (b) |
| **6.** (c) | **16.** (a) | **26.** (d) | **36.** (a) | **46.** (c) |
| **7.** (b) | **17.** (c) | **27.** (a) | **37.** (c) | **47.** (b) |
| **8.** (c) | **18.** (d) | **28.** (b) | **38.** (a) | **48.** (d) |
| **9.** (c) | **19.** (b) | **29.** (a) | **39.** (a) | **49.** (b) |
| **10.** (d) | **20.** (c) | **30.** (b) | **40.** (d) | **50.** (c) |

# Practice Question Paper 4

**(A) Read the passage and answer the questions that follow. Your answer should be based on the passage only.**

**(I)**

At ten minutes before five in the evening the office doors of the Florida and Key West Railway Company flew open and a young man emerged in a hurry. Suitcase in one hand, umbrella in the other, he sped along the corridor to the elevator-shaft, arriving in time to catch a glimpse of the lighted roof of the cage sliding into depths below.

"Down!" he shouted, but the glimmering cage disappeared, descending until darkness enveloped it.

Then the young man jammed his hat on his head, seized the suitcase and umbrella and ran down the steps. The spiral marble staircase echoed his clattering flight; scrub-women heard him coming and fled; he leaped a pail of water and a mop; several old gentlemen flattened themselves against the wall to give him room; and a blond young person with pencils in her hair exclaimed "Gee!" as he whizzed past and plunged through the doors, which swung back, closing behind him with a dour whack.

1. In the passage 'the lighted roof of the cage' refers to
   (a) The roof of the grilled room of the floor below.
   (b) The animal's cage the top of which was lighted.
   (c) The top of the elevator going down.
   (d) None of the above.

2. Which of the two items mentioned below did the young man had in hand while climbing down the stairs?

| | |
|---|---|
| (1) Suitcase | (2) Cap |
| (3) Stick | (4) Umbrella |
| (a) 1, 2 | (b) 2, 3 |
| (c) 1, 4 | (d) 2, 4 |

3. With reference to the passage consider the following inferences which are being made
   (1) The man was in a hurry as he had to catch a train.
   (2) Several persons gave way to him as he ran downstairs to prevent colliding with him.

   Based on the passage;
   (a) Only inference (1) can be drawn.
   (b) Only inference (2) can be drawn.
   (c) Both inferences (1) & (2) can be drawn.
   (d) Neither inference (1) nor (2) can be drawn.

4. Chose the expression which best fits in the description given in the passage, and highlighted below.

   "*The* __________ *cage disappeared, descending until darkness enveloped it.*"

| | |
|---|---|
| (a) faintly shining | (b) brightly shining |
| (c) slowly moving | (d) jerkily moving |

**(II)**

The norm of anonymity means that the civil servants must work from behind the curtain, without praise or blame. In the words of Mohit Bhattacharya, "Anonymity meant that the civil servant would merely advise the politician from behind and would be protected from being exposed to the din and fury of politics."

The norm of anonymity requires that the minister has to answer for the actions of the civil servants working under him in the Parliament and thus, protect them from the criticism of the Parliamentarians. This implies that the minister assumes total responsibility for the commissions and omissions of the civil servants working under him.

The minister runs his department/ministry and is politically responsible for its activities. He is mainly concerned with policy and consults his secretary on policy decisions. It is the minister who decides which course of action to adopt. He alone would be answerable in the Parliament for good or bad results of the policy, not the secretary.

Therefore, the norm of anonymity is the counterpart of the principle of ministerial responsibility. In other words, the principle of anonymity goes hand-in-hand with the principle of ministerial responsibility.

India has adopted the Parliamentary form of government. The bedrock principle of this system of government is the principle of collective responsibility. This principle states that the executives shall be responsible to the Parliament for their actions and policies. Thus, the principle of ministerial responsibility ensures that for every act or wrong act in his ministry/department, the minister has to answer in the Parliament and protect the civil servants working under him from criticism of the Parliament.

It must be mentioned here that the norm of anonymity operates only in the case of legal and proper acts of the civil servants, not in the case of illegal and improper acts. In other words, the minister has to protect the civil servant who has implemented his definite order or who has acted in accordance with the policy adopted by him. But he need not assume responsibility for the actions of the civil servant who is guilty of abuse of authority for personal ends or criminal acts or any other improper and illegal act. In all such cases, the civil servant is personally responsible and can be held guilty under the law.

As the civil service is governed by the norm of anonymity, it is not accountable to the Parliament. However, it is accountable to the political executive (i.e., minister). That the minister is answerable to parliament causes him to insist that the civil servants shall be answerable to him. The scheme of accountability is so distributed that while the minister is solely accountable to the Parliament, the civil servant is accountable to the minister.

5. Which among the following is not implied by anonymity in the passage above?
   (a) That the civil servant should work from behind the curtain, hidden from public eye.
   (b) That the civil servant should work from behind the curtain without praise or blame.
   (c) That the civil servant should work from behind the curtain and not have a direct responsibility *vis-à-vis* the Parliament.
   (d) That the minister has to answer the Parliament for actions of the civil servants acting under his orders.

6. What does collective responsibility mean as per the passage above?
   (a) The minister is not answerable for illegal deeds of the civil servants.
   (b) The civil servant is responsible and accountable for his legal and illegal deeds to the Parliament.
   (c) The civil servant along with the minister is responsible directly to the Parliament for all executive acts.
   (d) The executive is responsible to the Parliament for all its actions and policies.

7. What, as per the passage, can be said to be the relationship between "anonymity" and "ministerial responsibility"?
   (a) Anonymity is just opposite of ministerial responsibility.
   (b) Anonymity and responsibility are applicable *vis-à-vis* the public.
   (c) Anonymity applies to the civil servant while ministerial responsibility is that of political executive to the Parliament.
   (d) Both (b) and (c)

8. The minister is responsible to the Parliament for
   (a) Only the policy decisions taken by him.
   (b) All acts of the ministry under him.
   (c) All acts of the ministry except illegal and improper acts of the civil servants.
   (d) Only policy decisions taken by the ministry concerned.

9. The civil servant is responsible for his *bona fide* act and implementation of policy to
   (i) the Parliament
   (ii) to the minister
   (a) (i) only
   (b) (ii) only
   (c) Both (i) and (ii)
   (d) Neither (i) nor (ii)

**(B) Read the passage given below and answer the questions pertaining to it.**

The economic profile of India was in complete distress at the time of independence. Being a typical case of colonial economy India was serving a purpose of development not for herself but a foreign land—the United Kingdom (UK). Both agriculture and industry had structural distortions while the state was playing not even a marginal role. During the half century, before India became independent, the world was having accelerated development and expansion in its agriculture and industry on the shoulders of the active role being played by the states, with the same happening in the UK itself.

There was not only the unilateral transfer of investible capital to Britain by the colonial state (the drain of wealth) but the unequal exchange was day-by-day crippling India's commerce, trade and the thriving handloom industries, too. The colonial state practiced policies which were great impediments in the process of development in the country. Throughout the colonial rule, the economic vision the state had was to increase India's capacity to export primary products, and increase the purchase/ import of the British manufactured goods and raise revenues to meet the drain of capital as well as meet the revenue requirements of the imperial defence.

The social sector was a neglected area for the British rulers which had a negative impact on the production and productivity of the economy. India remained a continent of illiterate peasants under British rule. At the time of independence, its literacy was only 17 per cent with 32.5 years of life expectancy at birth.

Industrialisation in India was also neglected by the colonisers—the infrastructure was not built to industrialise India but to exploit its raw materials. Indian capitalists who did emerge were highly dependent on British commercial capital and many sectors of industry were dominanted by British firms (for example shipping, banking, insurance, coal, plantation crops and jute).

The pre-independence period was altogether a period of near stagnation showing almost no change in the structure of production or in the levels of productivity—the aggregate real output during the first half of the 20th century estimated at less than 2 percent a year or less.

10. As per the passage what were the main reasons for the complete distress of the Indian economy before and at the time of independence?
    (i) Structural distortions in agriculture and industry.
    (ii) Lack of Indian capitalists.
    (iii) Unilateral transfer of investible capital to Britain.
    (iv) Low literacy and life expectance of Indians.
    (v) Neglect of the social sector by the British rulers.
    (vi) Policy of exploitation of the raw materials and resources of India while turning it into a market for British goods.
    (a) (i), (ii), (iii) (b) (ii), (iii), (iv), (vi)
    (c) (i), (iii), (vi) (d) (i), (iii), (v), (vi)
11. What does the author mean by "drain of wealth"?
    (a) Crippling of Indian agriculture and industry by the British.
    (b) Establishment of administrative and legal control over the country.
    (c) Unilateral transfer of investible capital to Britain.
    (d) Thwarting of Indian capitalist's aspirations.
12. Due to which of the following reasons could the Indian capitalists not make much of a difference in the economic scenario in the pre-independence period?
    (a) They were highly dependent on British commercial capital.
    (b) Many sectors of industry were dominated by the British.
    (c) The laws did not permit Indian capitalists to invest.
    (d) Both (a) and (b).
13. As per the passage the purpose of development of infrastructure in India during British Rule was
    (i) To build basic framework of setting up of British industry
    (ii) To help in exploitation of India's raw materials

(iii) To enable British rulers to establish administration control over India

(a) (i), (ii) and (iii) (b) (ii), (iii)
(c) (ii) only (d) (iii) only

**(C) Read the passages and answer the questions that follow. Your answer should be based on the passage only.**

Since World War II, the nation–state has been regarded with approval by every political system and every ideology. In the name of modernisation in the west, of socialism in the Eastern Bloc, and of development in the Third World, it was expected to guarantee the happiness of individuals as citizens and of people as societies. However, the state today appears to have broken down in many parts of the world. It has failed to guarantee either security or social justice, and has been unable to prevent either international wars or civil wars. Disturbed by the claims of communities within it, the nation–state tries to repress their demands and to proclaim itself as the only guarantor of security of all. In the name of national unity, territorial integrity, equality of all its citizens and non-partisan secularism, the state can use its powerful resources to reject the demands of the communities; it may even go so far as genocide to ensure that order prevails.

As one observes the awakening of communities in different parts of the world, one cannot ignore the context in which identity issues arise. It is no longer a context of sealed frontiers and isolated regions, but is one of integrated global systems. In a reaction to this trend towards globalisation, individuals and communities everywhere are voicing their desire to exist, to use their power of creation and to play an active part in national and international life. There are two ways in which the current upsurge in demands for the recognition of identities can be looked at. On the positive side, the efforts by certain population groups to assert their identity can be regarded as "liberation movements", challenging oppression and injustice. What these groups are doing—proclaiming that they are different, rediscovering the roots of their culture or strengthening group solidarity—may accordingly be seen as legitimate attempts to escape from their state of subjugation and enjoy a certain measure of dignity. On the downside, however, militant action for recognition tends to make such groups more deeply entrenched in their attitude and to make their cultural compartments even more watertight. The assertion of identity then starts turning into self-absorption and isolation, and is liable to slide into intolerance of others and towards ideas of "ethnic cleansing", xenophobia, and violence.

14. Demands for recognition of identities can be viewed
    (a) Positively and negatively.
    (b) As liberation movements and militant action.
    (c) As efforts to rediscover cultural roots which can slide towards intolerance of others.
    (d) All of the above.
15. According to the author, the nation-state
    (a) Has fulfilled its potential.
    (b) Is willing to do anything to preserve order.
    (c) Generates security for all its citizens.
    (d) Has been a major force in preventing civil and international wars.
16. According to the author, happiness of individuals was expected to be guaranteed in the name of
    (a) Development in the Third World.
    (b) Socialism in the Third World.
    (c) Development in the west.
    (d) Modernisation in the Eastern Bloc.
17. As per the passage the rise of identity issues is
    (i) A reaction towards globalisation and domination
    (ii) A reaction towards isolation
    (a) (i) only
    (b) (ii) only
    (c) Both (i) and (ii)
    (d) Neither (i) nor (ii)
18. What reason is given for the apparent view that state has failed/broken down?
    (i) It has failed to provide basic necessities of life to its citizens.
    (ii) It has failed to provide security or social justice.

(iii) It has turned repressive in certain instances.

(a) (i), (ii), (iii) (b) (i), (ii)

(c) (ii), (iii) (d) (i), (iii)

**(D) Read the passage carefully and answer the questions related to it.**

Right through history, imperial powers have clung to their possessions to death. Why, then, did Britain in 1947, gave up the jewel in its crown, India? For many reasons. The independence struggle exposed the hollowness of the white man's burden. Provincial self-rule since 1935 paved the way for full Self-rule. Churchill resisted independence, but the Labour government of Atlee was anti-imperialist by ideology. Finally, the Royal Indian Navy mutiny in 1946 raised fears of a second Seapoy Mutiny, and convinced British waverers that it was safer to withdraw gracefully. But politico-military explanations are not enough. The basis of empire was always money.

The end of empire had much to do with the fact that British imperialism had ceased to be profitable. World War II left Britain victorious but deeply indebted, needing Marshall Aid and loans from the World Bank. This constituted a strong financial case for ending the no-longer profitable empire.

Historically, conquered nations paid taxes to finance fresh wars of the conqueror. India itself was asked to pay a large sum at the end of World War I to help repair Britain's finances. But, as shown by historian Indivar Kamtekar, the independence movement led by Gandhiji changed the political landscape, and made mass taxation of India increasingly difficult. By World War II, this had become politically impossible. Far from taxing India to pay for World War II, Britain actually began paying India for its contribution of men and goods. Troops from white dominions such as Australia, Canada and New Zealand were paid for entirely by these countries, but Indian costs were shared by the British government. Britain paid in the form of non-convertible sterling balances, which mounted swiftly. The conqueror was paying the conquered, undercutting the profitability on which all empire was funded. Churchill opposed this, and wanted to tax India rather than owe it money. But he was overruled by India, hands who said India would resist payment, and paralyse the war effort. Leo Amery, Secretary of State for India, said that when you are driving in a taxi to the station to catch a life-or-death train, you do not loudly announce that you have doubts whether to pay the fare. Thus, World War II converted India from a debtor to a creditor with over one billion pounds in sterling balances. Britain, meanwhile, became the biggest debtor in the world. It's not worth ruling over people you are afraid to tax.

19. Which one of the following best expresses the main theme which the author is trying to express?
    - (a) To present the various reasons that lead to the collapse of an empire and the granting of independence to the subjects of an empire.
    - (b) To point out the critical role played by the 'white man's burden' in making a colonising power give up its claims to native possessions.
    - (c) To highlight the contradictory impulse underpinning empire building which was a costly business but very attractive at the same time
    - (d) To illustrate how erosion of the financial basis of an empire supported the granting of independence to an empire's constituents.
20. Why didn't Britain tax India to finance its World War II efforts?
    - (a) Australia, Canada, and New Zealand had offered to pay for Indian troops.
    - (b) India had already paid a sufficiently large sum during World War I.
    - (c) Britain was afraid that if India refused to pay, it's war efforts would be jeopardised.
    - (d) The British empire was built on the premise that the conqueror pays the conquered.
21. Which of the following best captures the meaning of the "white man's burden", as it is used by the author?
    - (a) British claim to a civilising mission directed at ensuring the good of the natives.
    - (b) Inspiration for the French and American revolutions.

(c) Resource drain that had to be borne by the home country's white population.

(d) Justification given for open looting of resources.

**(E) Read the passages and answer the questions which follow. Your answer should be based on the passage only.**

I decided at last to write out the confession, to submit it to my father and ask his forgiveness. I wrote it on a slip of paper and handed it to him myself. In this note not only did I confess my guilt, but I asked adequate punishment for it, and closed with a request to him not to punish himself for my offence. I also pledged myself never to steal in future.

I was trembling as I handed the confession to my father. He was then suffering from a fistula and was confined to bed. His bed was a plain wooden plank. I handed him the note and sat on the opposite plank.

He read it through, and pearldrops trickled down his cheeks, wetting the paper. For a moment he closed his eyes in thought and then tore up the note. He had sat up to read it. He again lay down. I also cried. I could see my father's agony.

22. Why did the narrator's father cry after reading the note?
    (a) He was shocked and deeply agonised by the guilt of the narrator.
    (b) He was in physical pain due to the disease he was suffering from.
    (c) Though he was agonised by the narrator's guilt, he was moved by his repentance, seeking of forgiveness and punishment.
    (d) All of the above.

23. As per the passage, why did the narrator write the note to his father?
    (i) To confess his guilt.
    (ii) To seek forgiveness.
    (iii) To get rid of the guilty conscience within him.

    (a) (i) only　　(b) (i) and (ii)
    (c) (i) and (iii)　　(d) (i), (ii) and (iii)

**(F) Read the passage and answer the questions:**

The climbing really started now in earnest. Steep rock pitches were interspersed with narrow snow arêtes, and in places we moved one at a time. We made a labourious two hundred feet and then reached a steep rock face which looked too formidable to tackle directly, scrambled down into a snow gully on the right, and cut steps up it for a hundred feet, to emerge once more on the ridge, above the obstacle. The snow was firm and safe where it lay in any depth, but crumbled easily when there were only a few inches of it on the slabs. We crossed carefully over another stretch of rock and then I cut a few more steps up some snow to bring us to the foot of the great rock buttress.

24. What does the author mean by "the climbing really started now in earnest"?
    (i) The climbers now became serious about the mountain climb.
    (ii) The mountain climb now became steep and challenging.

    (a) Only (i)
    (b) Only (ii)
    (c) Both (i) and (ii)
    (d) Neither (i) nor (ii)

25. Why did the climbers cut steps in the snow gully and climb through it?
    (i) They could not climb the steep rock face.
    (ii) Climbing through snow gully by cutting steps was a safer and secure way of climbing.
    (iii) Climbing through the snow gully by cutting steps was much quicker than climbing the rock face.

    (a) (i), (ii) and (iii)　　(b) (i) and (ii)
    (c) (i) and (iii)　　(d) Only (iii)

26. What is the 'obstacle' which the narrator refers to in the passage?
    (a) The deep gully of snow.
    (b) The steep climb on the mountain.
    (c) The steep rock face, which was too formidable to climb directly.
    (d) None of the above.

**(G) Read the passage and answer the questions that follow based on what is written in the passage.**

India has engaged in the WTO negotiations to ensure that its core concerns and interests continue to be adequately addressed as negotiations proceed from one stage to the next. The Minister of Commerce and Industry had participated in a number of Mini-Ministerial Meetings as well as meetings of G-20, G-3(iii), FIPS (Five Interested Parties) to move the negotiations forward. India's approach to the negotiations has always been dictated by its national interests, especially its concerns for millions of farmers who are dependent for their livelihood on agriculture as also its objective of stimulating economic growth and development through trade.

At Hong Kong, India was proactive in articulating its position on issues of concern to it and other developing countries and played a key role in further strengthening the developing country coalitions by bringing together G-20, G-33 and G-90 groups of countries in a broad alliance to reinforce each other's positions on issues of mutual interest. The Hong Kong Ministerial Declaration, as finally agreed upon, had addressed India's core concerns and interests, with sufficient negotiating space for future work leading to modalities for negotiations in the coming months.

27. Which one of the following has not been an area of concern for India?
    (a) Interest of farmers
    (b) Trade and development
    (c) Stimulus to economic growth
    (d) None of the above
28. As per the passage, what has dictated India's approach to negotiations in WTO?
    (i) India's national interest
    (ii) Issues of concern to other developing countries
    (iii) Larger interest of the world economy
    (a) (i) only (b) (i) and (ii)
    (c) (i) and (iii) only (d) (i), (ii), (iii)

**(H) Read the passages and answer the questions that follow.**

**(I)**

We cannot be sure that species move on to higher stages of development in orderly sequence. Ever so many degenerate and some die out altogether. No sooner has some form of existence perfected itself than it proceeds to decay. The progress we have achieved is the result of the terrible method of trial and error. Struggle and suffering, disease and death are such pregnant facts that if there is any ruling power in the universe, it may be fate or chance or careless gods, but in no case a beneficent providence. Man is nothing more than the latest of a long series of living creatures, and he did not arrive on this planet faultless and finished but is being slowly ground into shape by the shocks of circumstance.

29. Which of the following is the most important message of the passage?
    (a) There is no controlling force in the universe. The latter is governed by physical laws.
    (b) Many species have not survived, despite a high level of evolution achieved by them.
    (c) Man's evolution is shaped by adaptation to the circumstances.
    (d) All of the above.

**(II)**

Many surprises lay in store for an academic who strays in the real world. The first such surprise to come my way during a stint as a university administrator was related to the photocopying machines within my jurisdiction. I discovered that paper for the machines plus contractual maintenance, costed substantially more than photocopies available in the private market. This took no account of the other costs such as photocopiers ink, spare part, the space occupied by the machine, the interest and depreciation on it, the wages of the machine operator, the loss of time when the machine broke down or the operator absented himself.

30. What is the surprise which has been referred to in the passage?
    (a) The author was surprised to have become a university administrator.

(b) He was surprised to find out that the photocopying cost in private sector worked out cheaper than that in the university.

(c) He was surprised that the university continued to use such photocopying machines whose running and maintenance cost was substantially more than the cost of photocopying in private sector.

(d) All of the above.

31. What does the expression 'strays into the real word' mean here?

(a) Real word can be confusing and one can lose way.

(b) It is difficult to find ones way in the real world.

(c) Real world can be harsh as compared to the academic environment.

(d) It implies unsuspectingly stepping in the harsh real world from the theoretical academic environment.

**(I) Read the passages below and answer the questions that follow. Your answer to these items should be based on the passages only.**

**(I)**

I am uncompromising in the matter of women's rights. In my opinion she should labour under no legal disability not suffered by men. I should treat the daughter and sons on a footing of perfect equality.

Equality of sexes does not mean equality of occupations. There may be no legal bar against a woman hunting or wielding a lance. But she instinctively recoils from a function that belongs to man. Nature has created sexes as complements of each other. Their functions are defined as are their forms.

32. Which of the following statements are a natural corollary of author's statement, "*equality of sexes does not mean equality of occupations*":

(a) Women may not have right of equal pay for equal work.

(b) Certain occupations should be legally banned for women.

(c) Both (a) and (b)

(d) Neither (a) nor (b)

Today pure water, good and earth, fresh air are unknown to us. We do not know the inestimable value of either and the sun. If we make use of these five powers and if we eat the proper and balanced diet, we shall have done the work of ages. For acknowledging this knowledge, we need neither degrees nor crores of money. What we need are, a living faith in God, a zeal for service, an acquaintance with the five powers of nature and a knowledge of dietetics. All this can be acquired without wasting time in schools and colleges.

Disease springs from wilful or ignorant breach of the laws of nature. It allows, therefore, that timely return to those laws should mean restoration. A person who has tried beyond endurance, must either suffer the punishment inflicted by nature or in order to avoid it, seek the assistance of the physician or the surgeon as the case may be. Every submission to merited punishment strengthens the mind of man, every avoidance saps it.

33. Which amongst the following statements, if true, are a natural corollary of the message which the author wants to convey in the passage?

(a) Diabetes, hypertension and heart diseases which are the major lifestyle diseases, are outcome of human prosperity and indiscipline.

(b) The development of antibiotics and some other life saving drugs have added nearly 15 years to human life span.

(c) Both (a) & (b)

(d) Neither (a) nor (b)

**(II)**

Chastity is not a hot-house growth. It cannot be protected by the surrounding wall of the *purdah*. It must grow from within, and to be worth anything it must be capable of withstanding every unsought temptation. And why is there all this morbid anxiety about female purity? Have women any say in the matter of male purity? We hear nothing of women's anxiety about men's chastity. Why should men arrogate to themselves the right regulate female purity? It cannot be superimposed from without. It is a matter of evolution from within and therefore of individual self-effort.

34. Which of the following statement(s) correctly reflect author's view?
    (i) Chastity of women should be a non / issue in a modern society.
    (ii) Chastity cannot be imposed on women by men.
    (iii) Women should also be allowed to question men's chastity.
    (a) (i), (ii), (iii) (b) (i), (ii)
    (c) only (ii) (d) (ii) & (iii)

**(III)**

While the debate goes on, India like many developing nations has not even utilized its fair share of the earth's carbon space, nor has it achieved basic minimum standards of living for its entire population. On average, per capita energy use in developing countries is only about 25 per cent of that in developed economies. Besides, there is the issue of access to clean fuels for a sizeable proportion of the rural population. About 400 million Indians still do not have electricity in their homes and about 800 million use some form of biomass as their primary or only energy source for cooking, which is worrisome.

35. The passage above aims to highlight:
    (1) The large divide in per capita energy consumption between the developing and the developed countries.
    (2) Limited or no access to clean energy to a large percentage of Indian population.
    (a) Only statement 1 above
    (b) Only statement 2 above
    (c) Both the statements 1 and 2 above
    (d) Neither statement 1 nor 2 above

**(J) Which word is the synonym or similar in meaning to the given words in question**

36. Abstinence
    (a) To fast
    (b) To give up certain pleasure
    (c) To avoid
    (d) None of the above

37. Morose
    (a) Sullen (b) Laughable
    (c) Sleepy (d) Dead

38. Savor
    (a) Suave (b) To increase
    (c) To enjoy (d) To breed

39. Belie
    (a) Deceive
    (b) give false impression
    (c) defeat
    (d) Boast

40. Paucity
    (a) Pausing (b) Scarcity
    (c) Break (d) Incomplete

**(K) In the questions given below a part of the sentence has been underlined. Below are given alternatives to underlined part which may improve the sentence. In case no improvement is possible then chose the option (d)**

41. The earth <u>revolved</u> around the sun.
    (a) Revolving (b) Rotates
    (c) Revolves (d) No Improvement

42. When I <u>had</u> my breakfast, I go to office.
    (a) have had (b) had had
    (c) has had (d) No improvement

43. I will let you know when he <u>called</u> back.
    (a) is calling (b) has called
    (c) calls (d) No improvement

44. <u>Could you</u> complete the job by tonight?
    (a) Would it be possible for you to
    (b) Could you possibly
    (c) Can you possibly
    (d) No improvement

45. When the passengers <u>had seated</u>, the bus started.
    (a) had sat
    (b) had taken the seats
    (c) were seating
    (d) No improvement

**(L) In the questions below one definition and word options are given. Choose the appropriate word option for the definition.**

46. Irritation or annoyance
    (a) Vertigo (b) Acrid
    (c) Insipid (d) Vexation
47. Spread throughout
    (a) Pervasive (b) Integrated
    (c) Permeable (d) Inclusive
48. A unified whole
    (a) Monotheism (b) Monogamous
    (c) Monotonic (d) Monolithic
49. A burdensome task
    (a) Onerous (b) Vigorous
    (c) Meticulous (d) strenuous
50. Medication that eliminates or reduces pain
    (a) Drug (b) Placebo
    (c) Antibiotic (d) Analgesic

## Answers of Practice Question Paper-4

| | | | | |
|---|---|---|---|---|
| **1.** (c) | **11.** (c) | **21.** (d) | **31.** (d) | **41.** (c) |
| **2.** (c) | **12.** (d) | **22.** (c) | **32.** (d) | **42.** (a) |
| **3.** (b) | **13.** (c) | **23.** (b) | **33.** (a) | **43.** (c) |
| **4.** (a) | **14.** (d) | **24.** (b) | **34.** (c) | **44.** (a) |
| **5.** (a) | **15.** (b) | **25.** (b) | **35.** (c) | **45.** (b) |
| **6.** (d) | **16.** (a) | **26.** (c) | **36.** (b) | **46.** (d) |
| **7.** (c) | **17.** (a) | **27.** (d) | **37.** (a) | **47.** (a) |
| **8.** (c) | **18.** (c) | **28.** (b) | **38.** (c) | **48.** (d) |
| **9.** (b) | **19.** (d) | **29.** (c) | **39.** (b) | **49.** (a) |
| **10.** (c) | **20.** (c) | **30.** (c) | **40.** (b) | **50.** (d) |

# Practice Question Paper 5

**(A) Read the following passages and answer the questions that follow. Your answer to these items should be based on the passages only.**

The "state *versus* market debate" is a debate about the respective roles of the state and the market in the society and the economy. Historically, this debate is as old as Adam Smith, the Father of Economics. Recently, this debate has once again assumed importance in the context of liberalisation, privatisation, and globalisation. These economic reforms and structural adjustments are currently underway in many countries, both developed and developing. Moreover, the World Bank's World Development Reports of 1991, 1997 and 2000–2001 had suggested a reappraisal of the respective roles of the state and the market in the contemporary developmental process world-wide.

The theoretical base for the rise of state versus market debate lies in the public choice approach of the 1960s and 1970s. This approach to public administration argued for the institutional pluralism (plurality of agencies) in the provision of public goods and services to promote the consumers' preferences. It stated that the administrators and the politicians are concerned with the self-interest rather than public interest. It questioned the central role of the state and the very basis of the government. Hence, it recommended for minimising the role of the state, curbing the functions of government agencies, and transferring various functions of the government to the market.

The public choice approach has given rise to a new paradigm in public administration called "New Public Management" or "Entrepreneurial Government", with a dominant market-orientation. This new paradigm calls upon the government to play a more and more "enabling" role rather than the traditional "doing" role. In other words, the government should change from a "doer" of public activities to a "distributor" of public benefits and "facilitator", and "promoter" of change in society and economy. Thus, the new paradigm emphasises the vital role of the market as against the state as the key regulator of society and economy.

**1.** What does the author mean by "institutional pluralism"?

(a) A system of administration where goods and services are not to be provided by the government agencies.

(b) A system of administration where there is multiplicity of agencies, which provide public goods and services because of which consumers have preferences.

(c) A system of administration where only the private sector is to provide goods and services but multiple preferences are available to the consumers.

(d) A system of administration, which minimises and eventually eliminates the role of states in provision of public goods and services.

**2.** The references to the new paradigm in public administration called "New Public Management" or "Entrepreneurial Government" refers to which of the following?

(i) The government should play a more enabling role rather than the traditional doing role.

(ii) The government should change from a doer of public activities to a distributor of public benefits.

(iii) The government role should be that of a controller regarding provision of goods and public services.

(iii) The market should play a vital role of provider of goods and services.

(iv) The state should concentrate only on key functions of governance leaving the rest totally to the market.

Which are the most appropriate choices?

(a) (i), (ii), (iii) (b) (ii), (iii), (v)

(c) (i), (ii), (iv) (d) (iii), (iv), (v)

**3.** As per the author, the "state *versus* market" debate is significant today. Which of the following is the most important reason, which makes this debate pertinent and significant today?

(a) The communist model has been found not to be economically sustainable.

(b) This debate is as old as Adam Smith, the Father of Economics.

(c) Liberalisation, privatisation and globalisation are the slogans of today.

(d) The economic reform and structural adjustments are currently being undertaken in many countries, both developed and developing.

**4.** As per the passage the theoretical base for "state *versus* market" debate lies in

(i) Giving a wider choice to the public.

(ii) Promoting the more efficient among the state and the market.

(a) Only (i)

(b) Only (ii)

(c) Both (i) and (ii)

(d) Neither (i) nor (ii)

**5.** Which of the following is **not** a reason cited in the passage for recommending institutional pluralism?

(a) Administrators and politicians are concerned with self interest only.

(b) There is need for minimising the role of state.

(c) The market has a greater reach *vis-à-vis* the state.

(d) There is need for transferring functions from state to market.

**(B) Read the following passages and answer the questions based on it.**

**(I)**

Beyond the threshold of consciousness, we have the store of facts and impressions from which we can select any at our pleasure. Some parts of this are more easily accessible than others but with effort, even the most concealed can be revived. This is called the fore-conscious region as distinct from the first, which is the conscious. There is also a third region of the mind, called the unconscious, where the apparently lost experiences of our lives, the impressions received in our childhood and infancy, are stored up. Though we cannot lift them into the region of the conscious by any effort of ordinary thinking, they yet profoundly modify our behaviour.

**6.** Consider what is stated in the passage as correct and examine as to which of the following assumptions can be said to be logically correct in terms of what is stated in the passage.

(a) The human mind has several domains of which we normally do not know.

(b) What we do not actively recollect, can play a profound role in shaping our personality.

(c) Both (a) and (b).

(d) Neither (a) nor (b).

**(II)**

No God seems to be final and no religion perfect. There was a time when vast temples were built for Moloch and Baal, mighty in their own day with crowds of worshippers; Gods who uttered commands and prohibitions, interpreting which numerous priests spent their long lives. To doubt their power and presence was to be condemned as a heretic and thousands suffered death and persecution, but who is so poor today as to recognise them, much less do they revere? What has happened to the Egyptian Ra and the Babylonian Shamash, to Isis and Ashtoreth, Zeus and Athene, Janus and Vesta who ranked a few millenniums back with Yahveh himself; Gods mentioned with fear and trembling and believed in by millions? Their day is done and their altars smoke no more. We can only smile at the naivete of those who assume that while all other gods will pass away their own will abide forever. The broken idols of the past seem to have no lessons for them. The history of religion is the record of the conflicts of contradictory systems, each of them claiming dogmatic finality and absolute truth, a claim made absurd by the plurality of claimants.

**7.** Which of the following statements best explains the key message of the passage?
   (a) Humans tend to worship false gods.
   (b) Humans have not been able to discover and understand the absolute truth as yet.
   (c) Both (a) and (b).
   (d) Neither (a) nor (b).

**8.** Which amongst the following are logical corollaries of the passage?
   (a) The belief in specific gods is transitory; it prospers and decays with time.
   (b) It's the humans who have created gods and not vice-versa.
   (c) Both (a) and (b).
   (d) Neither (a) nor (b).

**(III)**

Launched in 2008, India's National Action Plan on Climate Change (NAPCC) identifies a number of measures that simultaneously advance the country's development and climate change-related objectives of adaptation and mitigation through focused National Missions. It was also meant to focus on key adaptation requirements and the creation of scientific knowledge and preparedness as climate change acts as a "risk multiplier" for the vulnerable groups, worsening existing social, economic and environmental stresses.

**9.** Which of the following conclusions can be drawn from what is stated in the passage?
   1. Climate change creates multiple vulnerabilities and risks for India.
   2. Adequate measures for adaptation to climate have been taken in India's NAPCC.
   3. The need for meeting the financial requirements for tackling climate change is a key focus area of India's efforts.

   (a) Only conclusion 1
   (b) Only conclusions 1 and 2
   (c) Only conclusions 1 and 3
   (d) All of the above

**(C) Read the passages and answer the questions that follow. Your answers to the questions should be based on the passages only.**

Meanwhile India was celebrating its success of the first phase, a new challenge confronted India—achieving economic access to food. The situation went on worsening and by early 2000 there was a paradoxical situation in the country when it had more than three times buffer stocks of food grains in the central pool but in several states people were dying due to lack of food—a complete mockery of the logic behind maintaining buffer stock, success of green revolution and the concept of India being a welfare state! The Supreme Court intervened after a PIL was filed by the People's Union for Civil Liberties (PUCL) and a national level Food for Work Programme came up (to be merged with the National Rural Employment Guarantee scheme now). As the court had ruled to take the governments on task if foodgrains rot either in godowns or destroyed in oceans to manage market price for the foodgrains, or if the centre had to go for exporting wheat at very low price. In this process India emerged as the seventh largest exporter of wheat (2002)! Basically, we were exporting the share of wheat which was not consumed by many Indians due to lack of economic reach to the food. As the inputs of the Green Revolution were costlier, its output naturally was to be costlier. To fight the situation there should have been a time-bound and target-oriented macro-economic policy support which could deliver comparative increase in the purchasing capacity of the masses to make the food affordable for them. India badly failed in it. The crisis was managed by throwing higher and higher subsidies ultimately affecting government expenditure on the infrastructural shortcomings in the agriculture sector. Even after providing higher food subsidies some people failed to purchase food and they were left with no option but to die of hunger!

India is still in this phase and trying to solve the crisis through twin approach. Firstly, by creating maximum number of gainful employment and secondly by cutting cost of the food grains (via the second green revolution based on the biotechnology).

**10.** What is the paradoxical situation referred to in the passage?

(i) India was exporting wheat despite domestic demand.

(ii) India was facing starvation deaths despite large buffer stock.

(a) Only (i)

(b) Only (ii)

(c) Both (i) and (ii)

(d) Neither (i) nor (ii)

**11.** As per the author what was the most important reason for death due to lack of food in several states?

(a) Deficiency in public distribution system.

(b) Shortage of food production.

(c) Lack of economic reach of food due to poverty.

(d) Poor food subsidies.

**12.** How did the government, as per the passage, try to fight the situation of starvation deaths?

(a) By decreasing the support price of crops.

(b) Increasing the food subsidies.

(c) Improving the public distribution system.

(d) All of the above.

**13.** What remedy does the author suggest in the passage, to the problem of starvation deaths due to poverty?

(a) Increase in the purchasing capacity of masses by means of specific macro-economic policies and programmes.

(b) Reduction in food subsidies.

(c) Improving the public distribution system.

(d) All of the above.

**14.** How has India been trying to mitigate the crisis?

(i) By cutting the cost of food grains

(ii) By exporting the excess produce

(iii) By creating gainful employment

(a) (i), (ii), (iii) (b) (i), (ii)

(c) (i), (iii) (d) (ii), (iii)

**(D) Read the passage carefully and answer the questions based on it.**

Throughout human history, the leading causes of death have been infection and trauma. Modern medicine has scored significant victories against both, and the major causes of ill health and death are now the chronic degenerative diseases, such as coronary artery disease, arthritis, osteoporosis, Alzheimer's, macular degeneration, cataract and cancer. These have a long latency period before symptoms appear and a diagnosis is made. It follows that the majority of apparently healthy people are pre-ill.

But are these conditions inevitably degenerative? A truly preventive medicine that focused on the pre-ill, analysing the metabolic errors which lead to clinical illness, might be able to correct them before the first symptom. Genetic risk factors are known for all the chronic degenerative diseases, and are important to the individuals who possess them. At the population level, however, migration studies confirm that these illnesses are linked, for the most part, to lifestyle factors—exercise, smoking and nutrition. Nutrition is the easiest of these to change, and the most versatile tool for affecting the metabolic changes needed to tilt the balance away from disease. Many national surveys reveal that malnutrition is common in developed countries. This is not the calorie and/or micronutrient deficiency associated with developing nations (Type-A malnutrition); but multiple micronutrient depletion, usually combined with calorific balance or excess (Type-B malnutrition). The incidence and severity of Type-B malnutrition will be shown to be worse if newer micronutrient groups such as the essential fatty acids, xanthophylls and flavonoids are included in the surveys. Commonly ingested levels of these micronutrients seem to be far too low in many developed countries.

There is now considerable evidence that Type-B malnutrition is a major cause of chronic degenerative diseases. If this is the case, then it is logical to treat such diseases not with drugs but with multiple micronutrient repletion, or "pharmaconutrition". This can take the form of pills and capsules—"nutraceuticals", or food formats known as "functional foods". This approach has been neglected hitherto because it is relatively unprofitable for drug companies—the products are hard to patent—and it is a strategy which does not sit easily with modern medical interventionism.

**15.** Which of the following inferences can be drawn from what is stated in the passage?

(i) Modern medicine has substantially reduced deaths due to infection and trauma.

(ii) Modern medicine has not been equally effective against chronic degenerative diseases.

(a) Only Inference (i) can be drawn.

(b) Only Inference (ii) can be drawn.

(c) Both Inferences (i) and (ii) can be drawn.

(d) Neither Inference (i) nor (ii) can be drawn.

**16.** Type-B malnutrition is a serious concern in developed countries because

(a) developing countries mainly suffer from Type-A malnutrition.

(b) it is a major contributor of illness and death.

(c) pharmaceutical companies are not producing drugs to treat this condition.

(d) national surveys on malnutrition do not include newer micronutrient groups.

**17.** Why are a large number of apparently healthy people deemed pre-ill?

(a) They may have chronic degenerative diseases.

(b) They do not know their own genetic risk factors which predispose them to diseases.

(c) They suffer from Type-B malnutrition.

(d) There is a lengthy latency period associated with chronically degenerative diseases.

**18.** Why does the author emphasise on nutrition amongst the lifestyle factors to combat the chronic degenerative diseases?

(i) It is the most important amongst all the factors causing chronic degenerative diseases.

(ii) It is the easiest amongst the factors to change.

(iii) It is very effective in bringing the metabolic changes required to combat the chronic degenerative diseases.

(a) (i), (ii), (iii) (b) (i), (ii)

(c) (i), (iii) (d) (ii), (iii)

**19.** The author recommends micronutrient-repletion for large-scale treatment of chronic degenerative diseases because

(a) it is relatively easy to manage.

(b) micronutrient deficiency is the cause of these diseases.

(c) it can overcome genetic risk factors.

(d) it can compensate for other lifestyle factors.

**(E) Read the passage and answer the questions pertaining to it.**

When you work, you are a flute through whose heart the whispering of the hours turns to music. Which of you would be a reed, dumb and silent, when all else sing together in unison? Always you have been told that work is a curse and labour a misfortune. But I say to you that when you work, you fulfil a part of earth's furthest dream, assigned to you when that dream was born. And in keeping yourself with labour you are in truth, loving life, and to love life through labour is to be intimate with life's inmost secret.

But if you in your pain, call birth an affliction and support of the flesh a curse written upon your brow, then I answer that naught but the sweat of your brow shall wash away that which is written. You have been told also that life is darkness, and in your weariness you echo what was said by the weary. And I say that life is indeed darkness save when there is urge, and all urge is blind save when there is knowledge, and all knowledge is vain save when there is work, and all work is empty save when there is love, and when you work with love, you bind yourself to yourself, and to one another, and to God. And what is it to work with love? It is to weave the cloth with threads drawn from your heart, even as if your beloved were to wear that cloth. It is to build a house with affection, even as if your beloved were to dwell in that house. It is to sow seeds with tenderness and reap the harvest with joy, even as if your beloved were to eat the fruit. It is to charge all things your fashion with a breath of your own spirit, and to know that all the blessed dead are standing about you and watching. Often have I heard you say, as if speaking in sleep, "He who works in marble, and finds the shape of his own soul in the stone, is nobler than he who ploughs the soil. And he who seizes the rainbow to lay it on a cloth in the likeness of man is more than he who makes the sandals for our feet." But I say, not in sleep, but in the over-wakefulness of noontide, that the wind speaks not more sweetly to the giant oaks than to the least of all the blades of grass; and he alone is great who turns the voice of the wind into a song made sweeter by his own loving.

**20.** Which amongst the following is **not** a message which the speaker is emphasising upon in the passage?
(a) The significance of hardships in life.
(b) The significance of hard work in life.
(c) The significance of loving one's work.
(d) The significance of pride and dignity in ones work.

**21.** For what purpose has the author used the analogy of the *wind* and the *oak*?
(a) He has used it to differentiate between the mighty oak and the lowly blade of grass, where the oak is much more powerful.
(b) He has tried to show that the oak, due to its sheer size, gets the maximum share of the wind in comparison to others.
(c) He has tried to show the non-partisan and the impartial character of nature and that all are equal in the eyes of nature.
(d) He has tried to explain how the wind which has the strength to blow away the giant oak, does not even harm the lowly blade of grass.

**22.** What can be understood by the line in the passage, "curse written upon your brow"?
(a) It refers to our destiny that we have been born with—to toil and support our mortal flesh.
(b) It refers to our past sins which are the reason why we have been born as mortal humans.
(c) It refers to the curse of God on all mankind.
(d) It refers to the misfortunes that we will have to endure as we have been cursed.

**23.** Which of the following is correct according to the passage?
(a) That life is full of darkness.
(b) Work is duty.
(c) A ploughman is inferior to the one who works in marble.
(d) If you love what you do, then you have the key to real happiness in life.

**24.** Sentences given in the following question, when properly sequenced, form a coherent paragraph. The first and last sentences are labelled (i) and (vi), and the four in between are labelled as ABCD. Choose the most logical order of these four sentences from among the given choices to construct a coherent paragraph.
(i) The concept of a nation-state assumes a complete correspondence between the boundaries of the nation and the boundaries of those who live in a specific state.
A. Then there are members of national collectivities who live in other countries, making a mockery of the concept.
B. There are always people living in particular states who are not considered to be (and often do not consider themselves to be) members of the hegemonic nation.
C. Even worse, there are nations which never had a state or which are divided across several states.
D. This of course has been subject to severe criticism and is virtually everywhere a fiction.
(vi) However, the fiction has been, and continues to be, at the basis of nationalist ideologies.
(a) DBAC (b) ABCD
(c) BACD (d) DACB

**(F) Read the passage below and answer the questions that follow. Your answer to these items should be based on the passages only.**

The viability of the multinational corporate system depends upon the degree to which people will tolerate the unevenness it creates. It is well to remember that the "New Imperialism" which began after 1870 in the spirit of Capitalism Triumphant, soon became seriously troubled and after 191(iv), was characterised by war, depression, breakdown of the international economic system and war again, rather than Free Trade, Pax Britannica, and Material Improvement. A major reason was Britain's inability to cope with the by-products of its own rapid accumulation of capital, i.e., a class-conscious labour force at home; a middle class in the hinterland; and rival centres of capital on the Continent and in America. Britain's policy tended to be atavistic and defensive rather than progressive – more concerned with warding off new threats than creating new areas of expansion.

**25.** What does the author say was the major reason for the failure of "New Imperialism"?

(a) Britain failed to capture major capital markets.

(b) It was unable to cope with the by-products of accumulation of capital.

(c) Colonial expansion of Britain was badly affected by depression and war.

(d) There was serious rivalry between Britain and other capitalist powers.

**26.** Which one of the following options would be closest in meaning to the term "atavistic" as used in the context above?

(a) Backward looking (b) Faulty

(c) Self-centred (d) Impractical

**27.** Which of the following has been suggested in the passage?

(i) The multinational corporate system is unviable.

(ii) The capitalist policies tend to be defensive and backward looking.

(a) Only (i)

(b) Only (ii)

(c) Both (i) and (ii)

(d) Neither (i) nor (ii)

**(G) Read the passage and answer the questions related to it.**

The teaching and transmission of north Indian classical music is, and long has been, achieved by largely oral means. The *raga* and its structure, the often breathtaking intricacies of *tala* or rhythm, and the incarnation of raga and *tala* as *bandish* or composition, are passed thus, between *guru* and *shishya* by word of mouth and direct demonstration, with no printed sheet of notated music, as it were, acting as a go between. Saussure's conception of language as a communication between addresser and addressee is given, in this model, a further instance, and a new, exotic complexity and glamour.

**28.** What are the important features of north Indian Classical music which have been highlighted in the foresaid passage?

(i) Oral tradition of teaching.

(ii) *Guru–shishya* tradition.

(iii) Offering of *dakshina* to the guru.

(iv) No written musical notations.

(v) *Shishya* living with his *guru* while learning.

(vi) Learning by direct demonstration.

(a) (i), (ii), (iii), (iv) (b) (ii), (iii), (iv), (vi)

(c) (i), (ii), (v), (vi) (d) (i), (ii), (iv), (vi)

**29.** What does breath-taking intricacy mean here?

(a) Musical composition demanding breath control

(b) Impressive musical complexity

(c) Complex breathing steps

(d) None of the above

**30.** The passage draws a parallel between Saussure's conception of language and north Indian classical music because

(i) Both are oral

(ii) Both involve communication between addresser and addressee

(a) Because of (i) only (b) Because of (ii) only

(c) Because of both (i) and (ii) (d) Because of neither (i) nor (ii)

**(H) Read the passages below and answer the questions that follow. Your answer to these items should be based on the passages only.**

Man is neither mere intellect, nor the gross animal body, not the heart or soul alone. A proper and harmonious combination of all three is required for the making of the whole man and constitutes the true economics of education.

By education I mean an all-round drawing out of the best in child and man – body, mind and spirit. Literacy is not the end of education nor even the beginning. It is only one of the means whereby man and women can be educated. Literacy in itself is no education. I would therefore begin the child's education by teaching it a useful handicraft and enabling it to produce from the moment it begins its training. I hold that the highest development of the mind and the soul is possible under such a system of education. Only every handicraft has to be taught not merely mechanically as is done today but scientifically, *i.e.* the child should know the why and the wherefore of every process.

In my scheme of things the hand will handle tools before it draws or traces the writing. The eyes will read the pictures of letters and words as they will know other things in life, the ears will catch the names and meanings of things and sentences. The whole training will be natural, responsive and, therefore, the quickest and the cheapest in the world.

Manual work will have to be the very centre of the whole thing. The manual training will not consist in producing articles for a school museum, or toys which have no value. It should produce marketable articles. The children will not do this as children used to do under the whip in the early days of the factories. They will do it because it entertains them and stimulates their intellect.

I am a firm believer in the principle of free and compulsory Primary Education for India. I also hold that we shall realize this only by teaching the children a useful vocation and utilizing it as a means for cultivating their mental, physical and spiritual faculties. It will check the progressive decay of our villages and lay the foundation of a juster social order in which there is no unnatural division between the 'haves' and the 'have-nots' and everybody is assured of a living wage and the rights to freedom.

**(I) Choose the correct option as per the passage:**

**31.** The author believes in manual training for producing marketable articles, as the centre of children's education, primarily because,

(a) it's essential to stimulate the intellect of every child.

(b) it is essential to provide physical sustenance to impoverished masses

(c) Both (a) & (b)

(d) Neither (a) nor (b)

**32.** Which amongst the following are in consonance with authors view about education?

(i) Education must cater to body mind & soul.

(ii) Vocational education is essential for children.

(iii) Literacy in itself is not complete education.

(a) (i), (ii), (iii) (b) (i), (iii)

(c) (ii), (iii) (d) (i), (ii)

**33.** The author believes in training of handicrafts to be a key aspect of education because,

(i) it stimulates children's intellect.

(ii) it is natural for children to learn by doing things.

(iii) education through literacy is a burden on child.

(a) (i), (ii), (iii) (b) (i), (ii)

(c) (i), (iii) (d) only (i)

All exploitation is based on cooperation, willing or forced, of the exploited. However much we may detest admitting it, the fact remains that there would be no exploitation if people refused to obey the exploiter. But self comes in and we hug the chains that bind us. This must cease.

**34.** What is the most logical corollary of the message of the author in the passage?

(i) Revolution is necessary to end exploitation and servitude.

(ii) The exploited do not want to admit that they are being exploited as the chain of bondage prevents them from doing so.

(a) Only statement 1 is a logical corollary.

(b) Only statement 2 is a logical corollary.

(c) Both statements 1 and 2 are logical corollaries.

(d) Neither statement 1 nor 2 is a logical corollary.

**(J) In the questions below one definition and word options are given. Choose the appropriate word option for the definition.**

35. One who is bewildered
    (a) Fatigued (b) Nonplussed
    (c) Frustrated (d) Bewitched
36. To shut or to block
    (a) Reject (b) Obviate
    (c) Exterminate (d) Occlude
37. Something that increases comfort
    (a) Aid (b) Perquisite
    (c) Amenity (d) Allowance

**(K) In the following questions choose the word that means the exact opposite of the word given.**

38. Stale
    (a) New (b) Bright
    (c) Fresh (d) Old
39. Pertinent
    (a) Inappropriate (b) Impertinent
    (c) Impolite (d) Incomplete
40. Frugal
    (a) Miser (b) Generous
    (c) Pompous (d) Extravagant

**(L) In the questions given below a part of the sentence has been underlined. Below are given alternatives to underlined part which may improve the sentence. In case no improvement is possible then chose the option (d).**

41. <u>Despite of</u> his ill health, he took the examination.
    (a) In spite (b) Despite
    (c) Inspite off (d) No improvement
42. He has <u>said to</u> complete the task by Friday.
    (a) said (b) told
    (c) told to (d) No improvement
43. Owing to the traffic jam, he could not attend the meeting <u>timely</u>.
    (a) Within time (b) In time
    (c) As per time (d) No improvement
44. Considering his superb performance in the interview he is confident <u>to get</u> the job.
    (a) of getting (b) in getting
    (c) about getting (d) No improvement
45. <u>Powerful desire</u> corrupts a person.
    (a) Desiring power (b) Desire of power
    (c) Desire for power (d) No Improvement

**(M) Which word is the synonym or similar in meaning to the given words in question.**

46. Gullible
    (a) Easily deceived (b) Foolish
    (c) Snooty (d) Insolent
47. Abject
    (a) Object (b) Miserable
    (c) Abandon (d) Suspension
48. Partisan
    (a) One sided (b) Impartial
    (c) Parted (d) Polite
49. Boorish
    (a) Stupid (b) Boastful
    (c) Rude (d) Callous
50. Sedition
    (a) State of being sad
    (b) behaviour prompting rebellion
    (c) Drive of cleanliness
    (d) advice of carefulness

## Answers of Practice Question Paper-5

| | | | | |
|---|---|---|---|---|
| **1.** (b) | **11.** (c) | **21.** (c) | **31.** (a) | **41.** (b) |
| **2.** (c) | **12.** (b) | **22.** (a) | **32.** (a) | **42.** (c) |
| **3.** (d) | **13.** (a) | **23.** (d) | **33.** (b) | **43.** (b) |
| **4.** (a) | **14.** (c) | **24.** (a) | **34.** (d) | **44.** (a) |
| **5.** (c) | **15.** (c) | **25.** (b) | **35.** (b) | **45.** (c) |
| **6.** (c) | **16.** (b) | **26.** (a) | **36.** (d) | **46.** (a) |
| **7.** (d) | **17.** (d) | **27.** (d) | **37.** (c) | **47.** (b) |
| **8.** (a) | **18.** (d) | **28.** (d) | **38.** (c) | **48.** (a) |
| **9.** (a) | **19.** (b) | **29.** (b) | **39.** (a) | **49.** (c) |
| **10.** (b) | **20.** (a) | **30.** (b) | **40.** (d) | **50.** (b) |

# Practice Question Paper 6

**(A) Read each of the following passages and answer the questions that follow. Your answer to these questions should be based on the passage only.**

**(I)**

I am sure that Chitragupta, who keeps strict record at the Gate of Death, must have noted down in big letters accusations against me, which had escaped my attention altogether. On the other hand, many of my sins, that have passed unnoticed by others, loom large in my own memory. The story of my transgression, that I am going to relate, belongs to the latter kind, and I hope that a frank confession of it, before it is finally entered in the Book of Doom, may lessen its culpability.

Which of the given option best fits in the blank space, in the context of what is stated in the passage?

1. The sins of the author, which have past unnoticed by others, ________ in his own memory.
   (a) have faded
   (b) recollect vaguely
   (c) appear as big
   (d) cause contriteness
2. The author hopes that a frank confession of his guilt would lessen its ________.
   (a) punishment
   (b) feeling of guilt
   (c) responsibility of wrong doing
   (d) all of the above

**(II)**

The cow mooed and Mary wished for the hundredth time that all the vociferous cows in the planet would go mute. She was exasperated. She was sick of her husband, that cow, this farm, that wheezing old farmer, the television. She was so sick that she almost wanted to give that cow a kick, but resisted. That inchoate mass of blood and moos, she thought. Mary looked out of the window of the old farmhouse. The view was insipid enough—hill and field and woodland, bare, colorless and mist-covered—with no other house in sight. She had never been a woman to yearn for company. She liked sewing. She was passionately fond of reading. She was not fond of talking. Probably she could have been very happy at the farm if she were alone. But then, if she were not married she wouldn't have been here in the first place!

3. Where did Mary live?
   (a) In a solitary house near a forest.
   (b) In a solitary house near a village.
   (c) In a solitary farm house.
   (d) None of the above.
4. Which amongst the following Mary was fond of?
   (1) Sewing (2) Talking
   (3) Company (4) Reading
   (a) 123 (b) 124
   (c) 1, 4 (d) 2, 4
5. Which of the two conclusions can be drawn based on the passage?
   (1) Marry was not happy with the life at the farm.
   (2) She did not like solitude.
   (a) Only conclusion 1 can be drawn.
   (b) Only conclusion 2 can be drawn.
   (c) Both conclusions (1) or (2) can be drawn.
   (d) Neither conclusion (1) nor (2) can be drawn.
6. The passage given below consists of sentences. The first and sixth sentences in order of chronology are given first and last. The chronology of the remaining four sentences is jumbled. These are shown as PQRS. Find the proper sequence of the four sentences.

(1) Administrative ethics denote the professional code of morality in civil services and constitute the moral fibre of civil servants.

(p) The civil service, being a profession in the modern state, has developed a code of morality for its members.

(q) They regulate the conduct and behaviour of different categories of civil servants and thus, they provide "rules of the game".

(r) The civil servants are expected to set-up high moral standards not only for themselves but also for the community at large.

(s) This code consists of traditions, precedents, and standards which have to be kept up by the civil servants.

This is more so in the context of the growing size and role of administration and its impact on the society.

(a) pqrs (b) qpsr
(c) qprs (d) pqsr

**(B) Read each of the following passages and answer the questions that follow. Your answer to these questions should be based on the passage only.**

Economic growth though important cannot be an end in itself. Higher standards of living as well as of development opportunities for all, stemming from the greater resources generated by economic growth, are the ultimate aim of development policy. This implies the need to bridge regional, social and economic disparities, as well as the empowerment of the poor and marginalised, especially women, to make the entire development process more inclusive.

The global economic and financial crisis, not only exposed the vulnerability of almost all the countries over the globe to external shocks, but also has lessons for development planning. Countries need to have inbuilt social safety nets for facing such eventualities, which affect the weak and vulnerable the most, and wipe out the fruits of growth for years. India with its focus on inclusive development and timely interventions has, however, been able to weather the crisis better than many other countries.

India is on the brink of a demographic revolution with the proportion of working-age population between 15 to 59 years likely to increase from approximately 58 per cent in 2001 to more than 64 per cent by 2021, the bulk of whom will be in the relatively younger age group of 20-35 years. Given that it is one of the youngest large nations in the world, human development assumes great economic significance for it as the demographic dividend can be reaped only if this young population is healthy, educated, and skilled. The emphasis on human development also gains significance in the light of our major social indicators in the recent past being less encouraging than those of our neighbours such as Bangladesh and Sri Lanka. Therefore, policy planners in India have, over the years, engaged themselves in making more inclusive growth and development policies, focusing on human development.

7. As per the passage, what are the reasons that India was able to withstand and overcome the economic crisis better than other countries?
   (i) Indian economy was secluded from external economic shocks because of its isolatory economic policies.
   (ii) It made timely economic policy interventions to overcome the economic shock.
   (iii) Its inclusive policies acted as safety net for the ones likely to be worst affected.
   (iv) Its large working age population, i.e., the demographic dividend enabled it to generate greater GDP and withstand the economic shock.

   (a) (i), (ii), (iii), (iv) (b) (ii), (iii), (iv)
   (c) (ii), (iii) (d) (ii), (iv)

8. Why is there a need for emphasis on human development?
   (a) To take advantage of the large working age population.
   (b) To improve the poor social indicators.
   (c) Both (a) and (b).
   (d) Neither (a) nor (b)

9. Why the passage does not envisage, the economic growth to be an end in itself?
   (a) Economic growth often leads to exploitation of the environment and is not sustainable.
   (b) It is inclusive of human growth based on economic and overall development which is the ultimate objective of growth.
   (c) Economic growth tends to be short lived and exploitative of the lower most strata of society.
   (d) All of the above.
10. Which amongst the following is correct as per the passage?
   (i) Economic crises worst affects the weak and vulnerable.
   (ii) India has shown good progress in the field of human development by international standards.
   (iii) There is a need to bridge regional and social gaps and overcome economic disparities to make the growth inclusive.
   (a) (i), (ii), (iii) (b) (i), (ii)
   (c) (i) only (d) (i) and (iii)

**(C) Read the passage carefully and answer the questions.**

Democracy rests on a tension between two different principles. There is, on one hand, the principle of equality before the law, or, more generally, of equality, and, on the other, what may be described as the leadership principle. The first gives priority to rules and the second to persons. No matter how skillfully we contrive our schemes; there is a point beyond which one principle cannot be promoted without some sacrifice of the other.

Alexis de Tocqueville, the great nineteenth century writer on democracy, maintained that the age of democracy, whose birth he was witnessing, would be the age of mediocrity: in saying this he was thinking primarily of a regime of equality governed by impersonal rules. Despite his strong attachment to democracy, he took great pains to point out what he believed to be its negative side: a dead level plane of achievement in practically every sphere of life. The age of democracy would, in his view, be an unheroic age; there would not be room in it for either heroes or hero-worshippers.

But modern democracies have not been able to do without heroes: this too was foreseen, with much misgiving because he believed, rightly or wrongly, that unlike in aristocratic societies, there was no proper place in a democracy for heroes and, hence, when they arose, they require heroes or not, democracies certainly require leaders, and, in the contemporary age, breed them in great profusion; the problem is to know what to do with them.

In a world preoccupied with scientific rationality, the advantages of a system based on an impersonal rule of law should be a recommendation with everybody. There is something orderly and predictable about such system. When life is lived mainly in small, self-contained communities, men are able to take finer personal distinctions into account in dealing with their fellow men. They're unable to do this in a large and amorphous society, and organised living would be impossible here without a system of impersonal rules. Above all, such a system guarantees a kind of equality to the extent that everybody, no matter in what station of life, is bound by the same explicit, often written, rules, and nobody is above them. But a system governed solely by impersonal rules can at best ensure order and stability; it cannot create any shining vision of a future in which mere formal equality will be replaced by real equality and fellowship. A world governed by impersonal rules cannot easily change itself, or when it does, the change is so gradual as to make the basic and fundamental feature of society appear unchanged. For any kind of basic or fundamental change, a push is needed from within, a kind of individual initiative which will create new rules, new terms and conditions of life.

11. Which of the following four statements can be inferred from the above passage?
   (i) Scientific rationality is an essential feature of modernity.
   (ii) Scientific rationality results in the development of impersonal rules.
   (iii) Modernisation and development have been chosen over traditional music, dance and drama.

(iv) Democracies aspire to achieve substantive equality.

(a) (i), (ii), (iii) and (iv)

(b) (i), (iv) but not (ii), (iii)

(c) (i), (ii) but not (iii), (iv)

(d) (i), (ii), (iii) but not (iv)

12. Tocqueville believed that the age of democracy would be an unheroic age because:

(a) Democratic principles do not encourage heroes.

(b) There is no urgency of development in democratic countries.

(c) Heroes that emerged in democracies would become despots.

(d) Aristocratic society has a greater ability to produce heroes.

13. A key argument that the author is making is:

(a) in the context of extreme inequality, the issue of leadership has limited significance.

(b) democracy is incapable of eradicating inequality.

(c) formal equality facilitates development and change.

(d) Impersonal rules are good for avoiding instability but fall short of achieving real equality.

**(D) Read each of the following passages and answer the questions that follow. Your answer to these questions should be based on the passage only.**

The bourgeoisie, wherever it has got the upper hand, has put an end to all feudal, patriarchal, idyllic relations. It has pitilessly torn asunder the motley feudal ties that bound man to his "natural superiors", and has left no other nexus between man and man than naked self interest, than callous "cash payment". It has drowned out the most heavenly ecstacies of religious fervor, of chivalrous enthusiasm, of philistine sentimentalism, in the icy water of egotistical calculation.

It has resolved personal worth into exchange value, and in place of the numberless indefeasible chartered freedoms, has set up that single, unconscionable freedom—Free Trade. In one word, for exploitation, veiled by religious and political illusions, it has substituted naked, shameless, direct, brutal exploitation.

The bourgeoisie has stripped off its halo every occupation hitherto honored and looked up to with reverent awe. It has converted the physician, the lawyer, the priest, the poet, the man of science, into its paid wage labourers.

The bourgeoisie has torn away from the family its sentimental veil and has reduced the family relation into a mere money relation.

The bourgeoisie cannot exist without constantly revolutionising the instruments of production and thereby the relations of production, and with them the whole relations of society. Conservation of the old modes of production in unaltered form, was, on the contrary, the first condition of existence for all earlier industrial classes. Constant revolutionising of production, uninterrupted disturbance of all social conditions, everlasting uncertainty and agitation distinguish the bourgeois epoch from all earlier ones. All fixed, fast frozen relations, with their train of ancient and venerable prejudices and opinions, are swept away, all new-formed ones become antiquated before they can ossify. All that is solid melts into air, all that is holy is profaned, and man is at last compelled to face with sober senses his real condition of life and his relations with his kind.

The need of a constantly expanding market for its products chases the bourgeoisie over the entire surface of the globe. It must nestle everywhere, settle everywhere, establish connections everywhere.

14. As per the passage, which amongst the following is not what the bourgeoisie has destroyed?

(a) The feudalties

(b) The family relationship

(c) The respect for various occupations

(d) None of the above

15. As per the author why has bourgeoisie brought a radical change in the social relationship?

(i) Bourgeoisie revolutionises the means of production and hence the whole relation of the society.

(ii) Bourgeoisie values only money.

(a) Only (i) is the correct reason.
(b) Only (ii) is the correct reason.
(c) Both (i) and (ii) are the correct reasons.
(d) Neither (i) nor (ii) is the correct reason.

16. Which of the following is not the character of bourgeoisie?
    (a) Exploitation of the masses.
    (b) Preserving earlier order and means of production.
    (c) Weighing every relationship in monetary terms.
    (d) None of the above.

17. Why does the bourgeoisie seek new markets for its products?
    (i) It is the egotistical character of the bourgeoisie to seek new markets, destroy the existing setup and establish a new order.
    (ii) New markets bring greater profits
    (iii) After some time the existing markets understand the exploitative character of the bourgeoisie, hence it is compelled to search for new markets.
    (a) (i) only (b) (ii) only
    (c) (ii) and (iii) only (d) (i), (ii) and (iii)

18. Which one of the following is the outcome of the bourgeoisie system?
    (i) Free trade
    (ii) Chartered freedoms
    (iii) More employments
    (a) (i) only (b) (i) and (ii) only
    (c) (i) and (iii) only (d) (i), (ii) and (iii)

**(E) Read the passage carefully. Answer the questions based on it from the passage itself.**

**Read each of the following passages and answer the questions that follow. Your answer to these questions should be based on the passage only.**

Civilisation cannot merely be a growing totality of happenings that by chance have assumed a particular shape and tendency which we consider to be excellent. It must be the expression of some guiding moral force which we have evolved in our society for the object of attaining perfection. The word *perfection* has a simple and definite meaning when applied to an inanimate thing, or even to a creature whose life has principally a biological significance. But man being complex and always on the path of transcending himself, the meaning of the word *perfection* as applied to him, cannot be crystallised into an inflexible idea. This has made it possible for different races to have different shades of definition for this term.

The Sanskrit word '*dharma*' is the nearest synonym in our own language, that occurs to me, for the word 'civilisation'. In fact, we have no other word except perhaps some newly coined one, lifeless and devoid of atmosphere. The specific meaning of dharma is that principle which holds us firm together and leads us to our best welfare. The radical meaning of this word is the essential quality of a thing.

We have, for over a century, been dragged by the prosperous West behind its chariot, choked by the dust, deafened by the noise, humbled by our own helplessness, and overwhelmed by the speed. We agreed to acknowledge that this chariot-drive was progress, and that progress was civilisation. If we ever ventured to ask, "Progress towards what, and progress for whom?"—it was considered to be peculiarly and ridiculously oriental to entertain such doubts about the absoluteness of progress. Of late, a voice has come to us bidding us to take count not only of the scientific perfection of the chariot but of the depth of the ditches lying across its path.

In India, we have a species of Sanskrit poem in which all the complex grammatical rules are deliberately illustrated. This produces continual sparks of delight in the minds of some readers, who, even in a work of art, seek some tangible proof of power, almost physical in its manifestation. This shows that by special cultivation, a kind of mentality can be produced which is capable of taking delight in the mere spectacle of power, manipulating materials, forgetting that materials have no value of their own. We see the same thing in the modern Western world where progress is measured by the speed with which materials are multiplying. Their measure by horse-power is one before which spirit-power has made itself humble. Horse-power drives, spirit-power sustains. That which drives is called the principle of progress, that which sustains we call *dharma*; and this word '*dharma*' I believe should be translated as civilisation.

19. Why does the author say that perfection cannot be defined for man?
    (a) Because man is not inanimate.
    (b) Because perfection is different for different races.
    (c) Because man has kept surpassing his ideal all the time.
    (d) Because man cannot be perfect.
20. Which of the following can be said to be the meaning of dharma according to the passage?
    (i) Dharma is the closest in meaning to the word civilisation.
    (ii) Dharma is that which leads to our betterment.
    (iii) Dharma is the inherent quality of a thing.
    (a) Both (i) and (ii) (b) Only (iii)
    (c) All three (d) (ii) and (iii) only
21. What is understood by the phrase in the passage—"lifeless and devoid of atmosphere"?
    (a) A word without a cultural and historical background.
    (b) A senseless word.
    (c) A new word in a language.
    (d) Something incoherent and difficult.

**(F) Read each of the following passages and answer the questions that follow. Your answer to these questions should be based on the passage only.**

Deep in our hearts, we have an intense desire to be loved. Yet, just as deeply, we know no one really understands us, and that we are separated from those around us by differences we don't fully comprehend. The 'Family of Man' we long to share and belong to does not exist. We are just a bunch of desperate, lonely orphans. We would give anything to know how to be lovable. Yet, now more than ever, seemingly caring guides want to help us in our quest. A flurry of books and lectures tell us that change is mandatory for survival. While the recipes for harmony sometimes strike chords in our hearts it is not enough to read the books or say the phrases. Only if the tools offered are actually used and do indeed make our lives better will we know that the message was correct and we understood. The majority of self-help books agree on one thing: Change is necessary for a more fulfilling life. Some say that the answers lie in justifying fear, anger and emotional suffering by holding someone else—usually a parent or spouse—responsible. Often, another race or some other force at work in our life gets the blame for the mess in which we find ourselves. But one thing is for sure: We are not responsible. "They" are. How many books, tapes and seminars does it take before the average hurting human being becomes so frustrated that he or she cries, "The true path must exist because all the wise people say so, but I'll never find it." Life must have more to offer, something most of us are missing. Otherwise, God has a stranger sense of humour than any comedian working today. Here's the bad news. We can all agree that this thing we call our self, our ego, our personality, is somehow the cause of all our conflicts and negative emotions. This is the cold, hard truth: The self has no idea how to fix itself or it already would have. But no one else can fix our self. We must do it—on our own. You would have probably always suspected this—but no one would prove it because it appears to become a problem with no solution. This realisation is extremely threatening, especially to those who have tried so hard to change in the past and have been unable to do so. But the good news is that you can learn to fix the self by understanding four basic principles: (1) What the self is; (2) How the self works; (3) How the self got broken; and (4) How you can fix the self. Each of us made our self and only we can fix it. Real changes begin to happen as soon as repair begins and, as you become a better mechanic, the changes will be greater and come easier.

22. What is the central idea of the passage?
    (a) Flurry of books and lectures guide us to become loveable.
    (b) Our personality is the cause of negative emotions and conflicts and knowing how to fix it is crucial.
    (c) Change is mandatory for survival.
    (d) The root cause for all our troubles are "others".

23. For what does the author bestow the responsibility to other people?
    (a) For justifying human sufferings.
    (b) For bringing us into intricate situations.
    (c) For not showing the true path.
    (d) None of these.
24. What is the cause behind all our conflicts and negative emotions?
    (a) Our self (b) Our personality
    (c) Our ego (d) All of above

**(G) Read the passage carefully and answer the questions based on it.**

Investments in education contribute, both to aggregate economic growth as well as enable citizens to broadly participate in the growth process through improved productivity, employment, and wages, and are therefore a critical component of the inclusive growth' agenda of the Government of India. The past decade has seen substantial increase in education investments under the Sarva Shiksha Abhiyan (SSA), and this additional spending has led to considerable progress in improving primary school access, infrastructure, pupil-teacher ratios, teacher salaries, and student enrollment. Nevertheless, student learning levels and trajectories are disturbingly low, with nationally representative studies showing that over 60 percent of children aged 6-14 are unable to read at second-grade level. Further, these figures have shown no sign of improving over time (and may even be deteriorating).

The past decade has also seen a number of high-quality empirical studies on the causes and correlates of better learning outcomes based on large samples of data and careful attention paid to identification of causal relationships. This research has identified interventions/inputs that do not appear to contribute meaningfully to improved education outcomes, as well as interventions that are highly effective. In particular, the research over the past decade suggests that increasing inputs to primary education in a "business-as-usual" way is unlikely to improve student learning meaningfully unless accompanied by significant changes in pedagogy and/or improvements in school governance. It is therefore imperative that education policy shifts its emphasis from simply providing more school inputs in a 'business-as-usual' way and focuses on improving education outcomes.

Analysis of both, administrative and survey data, show considerable improvements in most input-based measures of schooling quality. But there is very little impact of these improvements in school facilities on learning outcomes. This is not to suggest that school infrastructure does not matter for improving learning outcomes (they may be necessary but not sufficient), but the results highlight that infrastructure by itself is unlikely to have a significant impact on improving learning levels and trajectories. Similarly, while there may be good social and humanitarian reasons for mid-day meal programmes (including nutrition and child welfare), there is no evidence to suggest that they improve learning outcomes.

Even more striking is the fact that no credible study on education in India has found any significant positive relationship between teachers possessing formal teacher training credentials and their effectiveness for improving student learning. Similarly, there is no correlation between teacher salary and its effectiveness for improving student learning, and at best there are very modest positive effects of reducing pupil-teacher ratios on learning outcomes. As discussed further, these very stark findings most likely reflect weaknesses in pedagogy and governance which are key barriers in translating increased spending into better outcomes.

25. Amongst which of the following factors, increased spending in the educational sector, has brought a measurable improvement?
    (i) School access of students.
    (ii) Student enrolment.
    Ratio of retention of students in secondary level of education as compared to primary.
    (a) (i), (ii), (iii) (b) (i), (ii)
    (c) (i), (iii) (d) (ii) and (iii)

26. Investment in education from economic perspective is important because:
    (a) It improves the human development index which is an important measure of economic growth.
    (b) It enables creation of entrepreneurs who do value addition to the society thus contributing to economic growth
    (c) It improves the productivity of the citizens and enables them to participate better in the economic growth.
    (d) All of the above.
27. Which of the following is implied by the passage?
    (i) Improving school facilities has no bearing on learning outcomes.
    (ii) Increased educational spending has brought little improvement in input based measures of schooling quality.
    (a) Only (i) is implied
    (b) Only (ii) is implied
    (c) Both (i) and (ii) is implied
    (d) Neither (i) nor (ii) is implied
28. Consider the following factors and their effect in bringing improvement in learning levels of students in schools.
    (i) Mid day meal programme
    (ii) Pupil-teacher ratio
    (iii) Improvement in school governance and pedagogy

    Which amongst the above are likely to affect the most the learning levels of students
    (a) Only (i) (b) Only (ii)
    (c) Only (iii) (d) All of the above
29. The objective of the above passage is to highlight,
    (a) The impact of the spending on educational sector on the quality of education.
    (b) The factors which contribute most in improving the learning outcomes and those which contribute the least/ do not contribute.
    (c) The ineffectiveness of school input factors in improving the education outcomes.
    (d) The expenditure on schemes such as Sarva Shiksha Abhiyan has been a waste of money.

**(H) Read the passages given below carefully. Answer the questions related to it.**

In a modern computer, electronic and magnetic storage technologies play complementary roles. Electronic memory chips are fast but volatile (their contents are lost when the computer is unplugged). Magnetic tapes and hard disks are slower; but have the advantage that they are non-volatile, so that they can be used to store software and documents even when the power is off. In laboratories around the world, however; researchers are hoping to achieve best of both the worlds. They are trying to build magnetic memory chips that could be used in place of today's electronic ones. These magnetic memories would be nonvolatile; but they would also be faster, would consume less power, and would be able to stand up to hazardous environments more easily.

30. The passage mentions that researchers are hoping to achieve the best of both the worlds. What are the researchers trying to achieve?
    (a) Develop faster and less volatile electronic chips.
    (b) Develop large magnetic memory chips.
    (c) Develop cheaper and hardy electronic chips.
    (d) Develop faster magnetic memories, which would be non volatile.
31. Which one of the following is not a quality mentioned, which newly developed magnetic memories would have.
    (b) Faster
    (b) Cheaper
    (c) Non volatile
    (d) Less power consuming

**(I) Answer the questions related to the passage given below.**

**(I)**

At the time of writing I never think of what I have said before. My aim is not to be consistent with my previous statements on a given question, but to be consistent with truth, as it may present itself to me at a given moment. The result has been that I have grown from truth to truth; I have saved my memory an undue strain; and what is more, whenever I have been obliged to compare my writing even of fifty years ago with the latest, I have discovered no inconsistency between the two. But friends who observe inconsistency will do well to take the meaning that my latest writings may yield unless of course they prefer the old. But before making the choice, they should try to see if there is not an underlying and abiding consistency between the two seeming inconsistencies.

32. Why does the narrator, not think of what he has said before, when he is writing something?
    (i) He does not keep a record of his previous statement/ writings
    (ii) Inconsistency does not matter to him
    (iii) He wants to write in perspective of what is the truth
    (a) (i), (ii), (iii) (b) (ii), (iii)
    (c) (i), (iii) (d) only (iii)

33. What does the narrator mean by, "I have saved my memory an undue strain."?
    (a) He has to put pressure on his mind to examine the consistency of his present writings with previous ones.
    (b) He does not have to bother too much about consistency in his statements.
    (c) As he knows that his statements are always consistent he does not have to worry about it.
    (d) None of the above.

34. Why do you think there is no inconsistency in the narrator's statements/ writings even if there has been a gap of 50 years between them?
    (a) The narrator always endeavours to align his statements with truth.
    (b) The narrator has avoided speaking/writing anything which could be controversial.
    (c) Consistency is a result of his phenomenal memory.
    (d) None of the above.

**(II)**

Competitive markets are effective in allocating resources in an economy. However, while the idea of a completely efficient market is rare, the costs of Government intervention may outweigh the benefits when "market failures"—a term that economists use to denote situations where markets may not work very well in allocating resources—are not severe. Of course, governments play a crucial role by intervening in situations where "market failures" are acute.

35. Examine which of the following ideas are not conveyed by the passage.
    1. There is a need for government intervention when market failure is acute.
    2. Perfect markets are rare.
    3. Government intervention may have economic costs.
    4. Market failure leads to inefficiency in resource allocation.
    (a) Only statements 2
    (b) Only statements 4
    (c) Only statements 1 and 3
    (d) None of the above

**(III)**

Civilisation is indeed a milestone of human evolution. At times used synonymously with culture, the word civilisation is said to have its origin in the Latin word *Civitas*, meaning a city. Thus, it was originally meant to distinguish the human settlements particularly the more complex urban settlements from the nomadic, transitory or rootless people or those with a rudimentary society and negligible form of institutional governance. In the modern context, civilisation refers to a fairly advanced stage of human development of people, which encompasses social, urban, technological as well as cultural development.

36. In terms of what is stated in the passage which amongst the following activities can be said to be an essential element of civilisation.
    1. Development of laws of governance
    2. Development of trade and commerce

3. Development of a space programme
4. Development of a film industry

(a) Only 1 and 2 (b) Only 1, 2 and 3
(c) Only 1, 2 and 4 (d) All of the above

**(J) In the questions below one definition and word options are given. Choose the appropriate word option for the definition.**

37. A branch of philosophy that inquiries into the nature of reality
(a) Materialism (b) Metaphysics
(c) Epistemology (d) Metalogic

38. A long adventurous voyage
(a) Odyssey (b) Fantasy
(c) Sojourn (d) Adieu

39. A song of joy or triumph
(a) Ballad (b) Sonnet
(c) Symphony (d) Paean

40. A beginner or a novice
(a) Fledgling (b) Unicorn
(c) Upstart (d) Pilot

**(K) Which word is the synonym or similar in meaning to the given words in question.**

41. Cantankerous
(a) Adamant
(b) Irritable
(c) Deceitful
(d) None of the above

42. Bovine
(a) Bold
(b) Cow like
(c) Shameful
(d) pertaining to animals

43. Adamant
(a) Unyielding (b) Hateful
(c) Stupid (d) Insolent

44. Pristine
(a) Ancient (b) Bright
(c) Rare (d) Uncorrupted

45. Talisman
(a) Charismatic person (b) Trailor
(c) Good luck charm (d) Auspicious ritual

**(L) In the given questions pick out the most effective word(s) from the given words to fill in the blanks and make the sentence meaningfully complete.**

46. The citizen wrote an angry mail to the secretary of the government ................. his grievance on denial of his rights.
(a) expressing (b) exhorting
(c) pleading (d) confirming

47. He could not cotch his 5 AM flight as he slept ........... 5 AM.
(a) to (b) about
(c) till (d) from

48. The organizers asked the artist to ................. the tentative dates for the concert.
(a) express (b) involve
(c) predict (d) indicate

49. The poor man's wages of a few thousand rupees was insufficient to meet the expenses of his family ................. that of his deceased brother.
(a) asides (b) since
(c) moreover (d) besides

50. The Judge admonished the witness and asked him to give reply which was ..................... to the questions asked.
(a) pertinent
(b) particular
(c) referring
(d) None of the above

## Answers of Practice Question Paper-6

| | | | | |
|---|---|---|---|---|
| **1.** (c) | **11.** (c) | **21.** (a) | **31.** (b) | **41.** (b) |
| **2.** (c) | **12.** (a) | **22.** (b) | **32.** (d) | **42.** (b) |
| **3.** (c) | **13.** (d) | **23.** (d) | **33.** (b) | **43.** (a) |
| **4.** (c) | **14.** (d) | **24.** (d) | **34.** (a) | **44.** (d) |
| **5.** (a) | **15.** (c) | **25.** (b) | **35.** (d) | **45.** (c) |
| **6.** (b) | **16.** (b) | **26.** (c) | **36.** (a) | **46.** (a) |
| **7.** (c) | **17.** (b) | **27.** (d) | **37.** (b) | **47.** (c) |
| **8.** (c) | **18.** (a) | **28.** (c) | **38.** (a) | **48.** (d) |
| **9.** (b) | **19.** (c) | **29.** (b) | **39.** (d) | **49.** (d) |
| **10.** (d) | **20.** (c) | **30.** (d) | **40.** (a) | **50.** (a) |

# Practice Question Paper 7

**(A) Read the passages given below and answer the questions based on it.**

**(I)**

Manjari, the maid of the princess, passed by the poet's house on her way to the river, and she never missed a day to have a few words with him on the sly. When she found the road deserted, and the shadow of dusk on the land, she would boldly enter his room, and sit at the corner of his carpet. There was a suspicion of an added care in the choice of the colour of her veil, in the setting of the flower in her hair.

1. At what time of the day would Manjari usually visit the house of the poet?
   (a) During night hours
   (b) In the early morning hours
   (c) In the evening hours
   (d) Cannot be determined from the passage
2. Which of the following option would best fit in the sentence below?
   *Manjari never missed to have a few words with the poet* ________
   (a) hurriedly (b) secretly
   (c) lovingly (d) cunningly

**(II)**

It was Christmas Eve. They were in the kitchen of her uncle's farmhouse. The deaf old woman sat in her chair by the fire knitting. On her sunken face and in her eyes, a curious sardonic smile that was her habitual expression played with discreet sportiveness. The two men stood in the doorway. Mary sat at the table looking aimlessly out of the window. Outside, the snow fell in blinding showers. Inside, the fire brilliantly gleamed on to the copper pots and pans, the crockery on the old oak dresser, the hams hanging from the ceiling.

3. How many persons have been referred to in the present scene in the passage?
   (a) 1 (b) 2
   (c) 3 (d) 4
4. The expression *snow fell in blinding showers*, implies:
   (a) Occasional fall of snow
   (b) Snow with intermittent rain
   (c) Snow, rain and lightning
   (d) Very heavy snow disrupting visibility
5. Which of the following is true as per the passage?
   (1) Members of a family had gathered in a farm house.
   (2) They were huddled together near the fire place.
   (a) Only statement (1) is true.
   (b) Only statement (2) is true.
   (c) Both statements (1) & (2) are true.
   (d) Neither statements 1 nor 2 is true.
6. The smile on the face of the deaf old woman was _____
   (a) warm and pleasant
   (b) mocking and cynical
   (c) gentle and sincere
   (d) hateful and vicious

**(III)**

I look upon an increases in the power of the state with the greatest fear, because although while apparently doing good by minimizing exploitation it does the greatest harm to mankind by destroying individuality which lies at the root of all progress.

The state represents violence in a concentrated and organized form. The individual has a soul, but as the state is a soulless machine, it can never be weaned from violence to which it owes its very existence. What I disapprove of is an organization based on force which what a state is. Voluntary organization there must be.

7. Which of the following assumptions are in consonance with the views of the author expressed in the passage?
   (1) A powerful state tends to impede individual progress.
   (2) State should be made powerless and a country should function based an individual cooperation.
   (3) A state tends be violent although it suppresses exploitation.
   (a) 1, 2, 3
   (b) 1, 2
   (c) 1, 3
   (d) None of the above

8. Why does the author consider that the state destroys individuality?
   (a) The sate cannot be perfect
   (b) The concept of state is based on force
   (c) Both (a) and (b)
   (d) neither (a) nor (b)

**(IV)**

I hold the opinion firmly that civil disobedience is the purest type of constitutional agitation. Of course, it becomes degrading and despicable, if its civil, *i.e.* non-violent character, is a mere camouflage.

Disobedience to be civil must be sincere, respectful, restrained, never defiant, must be based upon some well understood principle, must not be capricious and above all must have no ill-will or hatred behind it.

Those only can take up civil disobedience, who believe in willing obedience even to irksome laws imposed by the State so long as they do not hurt their conscience or religion, and are prepared equally willingly to suffer the penalty of civil disobedience. Disobedience to be civil has to be absolutely non-violent, the underlying principle being the winning over of the opponent by suffering, *i.e.* love.

9. As per the author, which amongst the following are **not** qualities suitable for people practicing civil disobedience?
   (1) Such people should be meek and submissive.
   (2) Such people should be respectful and bear no ill will to the law makers.
   (3) Such people should mask appropriately their motive of violence.
   (4) Such people should be ready to suffer the consequences of non-violently disobeying the law.
   (a) 1, 3
   (b) 2, 4
   (c) 1, 2, 3
   (d) None of the above

10. Why does the author believe that a mere show or a camouflage of non-violence degrades the civil disobedience movement
    (a) Civil disobenience movement has to be based on the principal of love and not hatred
    (b) A camouflage of non violence may fall through
    (c) both (a) and (b)
    (d) neither (a) nor (b)

**(V)**

We must identify ourselves with the villagers who toil under the hot sun beating on their bent backs and see how we would like to drink water from the pool in which the villagers bathe, wash their clothes and pots, in which their cattle drink and roll. Then and not till then shall we truly represent the masses and they will, as surely as I am writing this, respond to every call.

11. Consider the following statements and identify the ones which are a logical corollary of the authors most important view being expressed in the passage.
    (a) The plight of villagers needs an early remedy.
    (b) Villagers will respond to leaders who have experienced and understood their plight.
    (c) Both (a) & (b)
    (d) Neither (a) nor (b)

12. What is meant here by the expression, *'respond to every call'*
    (a) reply to the queries raised by the leader
    (b) engage with the leader
    (c) comply to the command of the leader
    (d) All of the above

**(VI)**

My hope lies in the youth of the country. Such of them as are prey to vice are not vicious by nature. They are helplessly and thoughtlessly drawn to it. They must realize the harm that it has done them and society. They must understand too that nothing but a rigorously disciplined life will save them and the country form utter ruin.

Above all, unless they visualize God seek His aid in keeping them from temptation, no amount of dry discipline will do them much good. Seeing God face to face is to feel that he is enthroned in our hearts even as a child feels a mother's affection without needing any demonstration. Young men, claiming to be the fathers of tomorrow, should be the salt of the nation. If the salt loses its flavour where with shall it be salted?

13. Which amongst the following is/are the important messages which the passage conveys?
    1. Discipline as well as faith in divine are essential for amelioration of those caught in vices.
    2. Youth are the leaders of tomorrow.
    3. Moral education of youth is essential for saving them from numerous vices.

    (a) 1, 2, 3 (b) 1, 2
    (c) 1, 3 (d) 1 only
14. In the context of the passage which of the following best explains the meaning of the phrase, *"If the salt loses its flavour where with shall it be salted"*.
    (a) Youth have to toil hard
    (b) Youth are the future of a country
    (c) If the youth lose their character, how would the nation find its character.
    (d) All of the above

**(B) Read the passage. Answer the questions based on the passages.**

Socialism is a beautiful word and so far as I am aware in socialism all the members of society are equal—none low, none high. In the individual body, the head is not high because it is the top of the body, nor are the soles of the feet low because they touch the earth. Even as members of the individual body are equal, so are the members of society. This is socialism.

In it the prince and the peasant, the wealthy and the poor, the employer and employee are all on the same level. In terms of religion there is no duality in socialism. It is all unity. Looking at society all the world over there is a nothing but duality or plurality. Unity is conspicuous by its absence. This man is high, that one is low, that is a Hindu, that a Muslim, third a Christian, fourth a Parsi, fifth a Sikh, sixth a Jew. Even among these there are sub-divisions. In the unity of my conception there is perfect unity in the plurality of designs.

In order to reach this state we may not look on things philosophically and say that we need not make a move until all are converted to socialism. Without changing our life we may go on giving addresses, forming parties and hawk-like seize the game when it comes our way. This is no socialism. The more we treat it as game to be seized, the farther it recedes from us.

Socialism begins with the first convert. If there is one such, you can add zeroes to the one and the first zero will count for ten and every addition will count for ten times the previous number. If however, the beginner is a zero, in other words, no one makes the beginning, multiplicity of zeroes well also produce zero value. Time and paper occupied in writing zeros will be so much waste.

This socialism is as pure as crystal. It, therefore, requires crystal-like means to achieve it. Impure means result in an impure end. Hence the prince and the peasant will not be equalised by cutting off the prince's head, nor can the process of cutting off equalise the employer and the employed.

15. As per the author what is the essence of socialism?
    (i) Equality of all men
    (ii) Equal opportunity for all
    (iii) Belief of all in the principal of socialism

    (a) (i), (ii), (iii) (b) (i), (ii)
    (c) Only (i) (d) Only (ii)
16. Which amongst the following is/are implied by the author's concept of socialism?
    (a) Socialism cannot be achieved by eliminating the capitalist.

(b) Socialism implicitly implies a oneness in the seeming diverseness.
(c) Both (a) and (b) are implied
(d) Neither (a) nor (b) is implied.

17. Which amongst the following is not correct, in terms of what is stated in the passage?
(a) Pure means are required to attain socialism.
(b) The nature of work we discharge does not make us high or low in the society.
(c) Perfect unity is essential to attain socialism.
(d) None of the above.

**(C) Read the passage and answer the questions pertaining to it.**

Equipping the labour force with productive skills lies at the heart of tapping the demographic dividend. Apprenticeships are an effective way of ensuring that entry-level workers have the skills required to join the formal workforce by "learning on the job" and even earning while learning. It has been amongst the oldest social institutions in India. However, it needs to be formalised and scaled up.

In the current environment, India's educational system is overburdened by sheer demand for quality education. According to Team Lease, 80 percent of India's higher education system of 2030 is yet to be built and is grappling with the threefold problem of cost, quality, and scale. This is compounded by the inability of much of the current education system to produce "work-ready" labour. In fact, the disconnect between the formal educational system and the requirements of the employers have become even more acute in times of rapid structural and technological change.

In this environment, company-led apprenticeship programmes, that place employers at the heart of education, can play a powerful role in imparting job-relevant skills and also repairing, preparing, and upgrading the labour force. They can aid five important transitions that the labour force is currently making—from agriculture to non-agriculture, from rural to urban, from the unorganised sector to the organized, from school to work, and from subsistence self-employment to wage employment.

Several countries have benefited greatly from focused programmes on skilling the workforce on the job including Japan, US, UK, and Germany. Germany, in particular, has a well-known dual education system that combines classroom/online courses at a vocational school with workplace experience at a company. School authorities are responsible for the former while the company is responsible for the latter. More than 75 percent of Germans below the age of 22 have attended an apprenticeship programme.

Training apprentices also benefits corporates. A 2005 Task Force Report on Apprentices in the UK, demonstrated that the benefits of apprenticeships were numerous, including increased productivity, lower net costs of training (versus training non apprentices), greater staff retention, and a more highly motivated workforce.

Apprenticeship programmes in India are governed by the Apprentice Act 1961 and the Apprenticeship Rules 1992. The organisational structure and rules and regulations overseeing it are complex and burdensome. The Ministry of Labour and Employment oversees trade apprentices through six regional offices. The Ministry of Human Resource Development oversees 'graduate, technician, and technician (vocational) apprentices through four boards located in different cities. There are strict norms on permissions, trades permitted, training duration, stipend levels, apprentice/employee ratio, and training facilities. It is onerous to create new apprenticeship positions, and there are several vacancies even in positions that have already been created. As a consequence, India only has under 3,00,000 formal apprentices.

One of the reasons for tightly regulating apprenticeships was to prevent companies from hiring cheap labour under the guise of an apprenticeship programme. A simpler set of provisions to streamline regulation and incentivise corporates while protecting the interest and well-being of apprentices may now be needed.

18. Which amongst the following is a shortcoming in the current educational system which necessitates introduction of formal apprenticeship programmes?

(a) The current educational system is too costly for poor to afford.
(b) It does not lead to the creation of a work ready labour force.
(c) It lays too much emphasis on higher education and acquiring of degrees.
(d) All of the above.

19. Why has "apprenticeship" not been popular in India?
(a) Companies do not want to recruit apprentices as their skill levels are poor.
(b) Companies are thwarted by a plethora of controlling and regulating laws governing apprenticeship.
(c) Companies do not have financial wherewithal to launch apprenticeship schemes as many are facing stiff competition.
(d) All of the above.

20. What are the advantages of apprenticeship, highlighted in the passage?
It helps in instilling job relevant skills in the work force.
(i) It helps the workforce to earn while it learns.
(ii) It helps the companies to get cheap labour and cut costs.
(a) (i), (ii), (iii) (b) (i), (ii)
(c) (i), (iii) (d) (ii), (iii)

21. How can the apprenticeship programme be revatilised?
(i) By simplifying the numerous rules and regulations that control/govern apprenticeship today.
(ii) By suitable legislations to make apprenticeship program compulsory as in many developed countries.
(iii) By giving special incentives such as tax deductions to the corporates implementing apprenticeship scheme.
(a) (i), (ii), (iii) (b) (ii), (iii)
(c) (i), (ii) (d) (i), (iii)

22. As per the passage which among the following is **not** a benefit likely to arise for the corporates by the apprenticeship scheme?
(a) Ease of picking trained work force who have worked as apprentice from a rival corporate entity.
(b) Reduction of net training cost on the workforce.
(c) Increase in labour productivity.
(d) None of the above.

23. Why it is important to revitalise apprenticeship programme in India?
(i) India's current educational system is not likely to deliver the quality work force that is needed in the future.
(ii) Apprenticeship has been a successful model of education and for instilling job skills in many developed countries.
(iii) It is known to increase productivity, improve retention and offer other benefits to the industry.
(iv) India's economic growth, current legal framework and environment is suited for apprenticeship programme to take off.
(a) (i), (ii), (iii), (iv) (b) (i), (ii), (iii)
(c) (i), (ii) (d) (i), (iii)

**(D) Read the passages and answer the questions that follow. The answers should be based on what is stated in the passage.**

Policymakers are usually focused on short-run economic management issues. But the short run has to be a bridge to the long run. The central long-run question facing India is where will good jobs come from! Productive jobs are vital for growth. And a good job is the best form of inclusion. More than half our population depends on agriculture, but the experience of other countries suggests that the number of people dependent on agriculture will have to shrink if per capita incomes in agriculture are to go up substantially. While industry is creating jobs, too many such jobs are low productivity non-contractual jobs in the unorganised sector, offering low incomes, little protection, and no benefits. Service jobs are relatively high productivity, but employment growth in services has been slow in recent years. India's challenge is to create the conditions for faster growth of productive jobs outside of agriculture, especially in organised manufacturing and in services, even while improving productivity in agriculture. The benefit of rising to the challenge is decades of strong inclusive growth.

24. Which amongst the following would be the best form of "inclusion" for the people of backward region thriving mainly on subsistence agriculture?
   (a) Offering of food and agricultural subsidies by the government.
   (b) Offering a minimum number of days of wage employment by the government.
   (c) Set up of an industrial zone primarily of agro-based industries.
   (d) All of the above.

25. As per the passage the shortcoming(s) of the industrial jobs being created is/are that:
   (i) they are largely in unorgainsed sector.
   (ii) their productivity is low.
   (iii) the duration of time for which these jobs is created is less.

   (a) (i), (ii) (b) (i), (iii)
   (c) (ii), (iii) (d) (i), (ii), (iii)

26. The objective of the passage is to highlight:
   (a) The shortcoming of policy makers in focusing only on short term goals.
   (b) The need for improving per capita income in agriculture.
   (c) The need for creating productive jobs in manufacturing and services sector as best panacea for achieving inclusive growth.
   (d) All of the above.

**(E) Read the passage given below. Answer the questions based on this passage.**

Everything in India attracts me. It has everything that a human being with the highest possible aspirations can want.

India is essentially 'Karmabhumi' (land of duty) in contradistinction to 'bhogabhumi' (land of enjoyment).

India is one of the few nations on the earth which have retained some of their ancient institutions although they have been overlaid with superstition and error. But she has hitherto shown an inherent capacity for purging herself of error and superstition. My faith in her ability to solve the economic problems that face her millions has never been so bright as it is today.

I feel that India's mission is different from that of others. India is fitted for the religious supremacy of the world. There is no parallel in the world for the process of purification that this country has voluntarily undergone. India is less in need of steel weapons, it has fought with divine weapons, it can still do so.

Other nations have been votaries of brute force. India can win all by soul force. History supplies numerous instances to prove that brute force is nothing before soul force. Poets have sung about it and seers have described their experiences.

If India takes up the doctrine of the sword, she may gain momentary victory. Then India will cease to be the pride of my heart. I am wedded to India because I owe my all to her. I believe absolutely that she has a mission for all the world. She does not copy Europe blindly. India's acceptance of the sword will be the hour of my trial. I hope I shall not be found wanting. My religion has no geographical limits. If I have a living faith in it, it will transcend my love for India herself. My life is dedicated in the service of India through the religion of non-violence.

If India makes violence her creed, and I have survived, I would not care to live in India. She will cease to evoke any pride in me. My patriotism is subservient to my religion. I cling to India like a child to its mother's breast, because I feel that she gives me the spiritual nourishment I need. She has the environment that responds to my highest aspirations. When that faith is gone, I shall feel like an orphan without hope of ever finding a guardian.

27. Why is the author very hopeful about India, despite the ancient institutions of the country being overlaid with superstitions and errors?
   (a) India and Indians have been believers of truth and non violence.

(b) India and Indians have guided the world in past.

(c) India and Indians have the ability to correct their mistakes and eliminate them from their ethos.

(d) All of the above.

28. Why would the author not choose to live in India, if India were to select the path of violence?

(i) The author believes non violence to be primary and love for country to be secondary.

(ii) The author believes that his country should inspire him spiritually also and when it fails to do so, he cannot help but be forced to disown it.

(a) Only (i) is the correct reason.

(b) Only (ii) is the correct reason.

(c) Both (i) and (ii) are the correct reasons.

(d) Neither (i) and (ii) are the correct reasons.

29. Why does the author feel that India does not need conventional weapons?

(a) India already has sufficient conventional weapons and does not need any more.

(b) India's traditional weapons of warfare are sufficient for its defence.

(c) India has been gifted with celestial weapons and does not need conventional weapons.

(d) Truth and non violence are India's weapons.

**(F) Read the passages and answer the questions that follow. The answers should be based on what is stated in the passage.**

It is possible for a teacher situated miles away to affect the spirit of the pupils by his way of living. It would be idle for me, if I were a liar, to teach boys to tell the truth. A cowardly teacher would never succeed in making his boys valiant, and a stranger to self-restraint could never teach his pupils the value of self-restraint. I saw, therefore, that I must be an eternal object lesson to the boys and girls living with me. They thus became my teachers, and I learnt I must be good and live straight, if only for their sakes. I may say that the increasing discipline and restraint I imposed on myself was mostly due to those wards of mine.

30. What does the author mean by being an "eternal object lesson"?

(a) Being an enduring role model for wards.

(b) Creating a perpetual lesson for wards.

(c) Being a person who could always teach his wards.

(d) All of the above.

31. As per the author, how is it possible for a teacher situated miles away, to affect the spirit of the pupils?

(a) By setting a task for them which they have to follow in his absence.

(b) By deploying suitable teachers whose directions they should follow.

(c) By being an ideal example which they have to follow.

(d) None of the above.

32. Why does the author say that his wards became his teacher?

(a) The author learnt values of discipline and restraint from his wards.

(b) The author had to inculcate discipline and restraint in himself for the sake of his wards.

(c) The author started delivering lectures on discipline and self restraint to his wards which also taught him the value of discipline and self restraint.

(d) Some wards showing exemplary self restraint and discipline became a model for the author as well as others.

**(G) Read the passages and answer the questions that follow. The answers should be based on what is stated in the passage.**

**(I)**

The roots of all great thinking and noble living, lie deep in life itself and not in the dry light of mere reasoning. All creative work in science and philosophy, in art and life, is inspired by the intuitive experience. While we all possess intuitive perception, and exercise it to some extent, in exceptional minds it is well developed. Intuitive life, spiritual wisdom at its highest, is a type of achievement that belongs only to the highest range of mental life. The great scientific discoveries are due to the inventive genius of creative thinkers and not the plodding processes of the intellect. The latter might give us more precise measurements, more detailed demonstrations of well-established theories, but they cannot by themselves yield the great discoveries which have made science so wonderful.

33. Examine as to which of the following statements are not in consonance with what the author implies in the passage.
    1. Creative artists often have high IQs.
    2. Creativity and intuitiveness have a strong positive correlation.
    3. Logic and reasoning are the fundamental basis of great inventions and discoveries.

    (a) Only statement 1
    (b) Only statements 1 and 2
    (c) Only statement 3
    (d) None of the above

**(II)**

Synthetic life is referred to as creating artificial life in vitro from bio-chemicals and their component materials. It is usually distinguished from mechanical life that usually belongs to the discipline of robotics. Creating synthetic life is a great challenge and a complex task. It entails the creation of an artificial genetic code and artificial DNA. It would also involve creating cellular organelles such as mitochondria, ribosome, and nucleus, completely anew. Creating a fully synthetic cell would also be expensive. These constraints can be bypassed and a new organism can be created by just replacing the genome in an existing, natural cell with a different genome created by gene synthesis.

34. Which of the following logical conclusions can be drawn from the passage?

    Technological challenges make the creation of synthetic life only a possibility in the future.
    1. Creating synthetic life is fraught with legal and ethical challenges.
    2. Gene synthesis can be equated to creating synthetic life.

    (a) Only 1 (b) Only 1 and 2
    (c) 1, 2, and 3 (d) None of the above

**(III)**

Any substance such as an element, isotope, molecule, or phenomenon providing scientific proof of past or present life is known as a bio-signature. These are frequently used to determine the presence of living organisms in a sample. Bio-signatures, which are produced from life processes, are nucleic acids, lipids, proteins, amino acids, kerogen-like material and different morphological features. Microbes that participate in the geochemical processes leave some features in the rock record, indicative as bio-signatures. A potential bio-signature is a phenomenon, which can be produced from living sources, but it can also be originated from abiotic sources.

35. Which of the following logical inferences can be drawn from the passage?
    (a) The presence of bio-signatures is necessary and sufficient for establishing past or present life.
    (b) The presence of bio-signatures is necessary but not sufficient for establishing past or present life.
    (c) The presence of bio-signatures is not necessary and/but sufficient for establishing past or present life.
    (d) The presence of bio-signatures is neither necessary nor sufficient for establishing past or present life.

**(H) In the following questions choose the word that means the exact opposite of the word given.**

36. Enduring
    (a) Ephemeral (b) Everlasting
    (c) Worldly (d) Erring
37. Favourable
    (a) Neutral (b) Unforeseen
    (c) Adverse (d) Biased
38. Immigration
    (a) Import (b) Exit
    (c) Exodus (d) Emigration
39. Fraudulent
    (a) Reasonable (b) Geniune
    (c) Plain (d) Direct
40. Empathy
    (a) Clemency (b) Indifference
    (c) Interest (d) Difference

**(I) In the questions given below a part of the sentence has been underlined. Below are given alternatives to underlined part which may improve the sentence. In case no improvement is possible then chose the option (d).**

41. He asked for a more clearer copy of the document as it was not legible.
    (a) More clear (b) Most clear
    (c) Clearer (d) No improvement
42. I was wondering if you could guide me with the exercise.
    (a) You could (b) Could you
    (c) You would (d) No improvement
43. The employer explained that because of these problems, the project was unsuccessful.
    (a) Due to (b) Owing
    (c) Because (d) No improvement
44. The CEO was not sure if the employee was enough experienced to lead the new project.
    (a) Experienced
    (b) Fully experienced
    (c) Experienced enough
    (d) No improvement
45. Modern science explains as to why it's important being positive.
    (a) Importance of positive
    (b) Important to be positive
    (c) Positive is important
    (d) No improvement

**(J) In the questions below one definition and word options are given. Choose the appropriate word option for the definition**

46. That which deviates from the norm
    (a) Rebel (b) Innovation
    (c) Ambivalent (d) Anomalous
47. To Include
    (a) Gather (b) Subsume
    (c) Annual (d) Capture
48. A government by priests representing a god
    (a) Democracy (b) Mobocracy
    (c) Theocray (d) Plutarchy
49. To give a boost to
    (a) Launch (b) Aggregate
    (c) Bolster (d) Elevate
50. Violent speech or verbal assault
    (a) Soliloquy (b) Tirade
    (c) Torment (d) Eulogy

## Answers of Practice Question Paper-7

| | | | | |
|---|---|---|---|---|
| **1.** (c) | **11.** (b) | **21.** (d) | **31.** (c) | **41.** (c) |
| **2.** (b) | **12.** (c) | **22.** (a) | **32.** (b) | **42.** (d) |
| **3.** (d) | **13.** (b) | **23.** (b) | **33.** (c) | **43.** (a) |
| **4.** (d) | **14.** (c) | **24.** (c) | **34.** (d) | **44.** (c) |
| **5.** (a) | **15.** (c) | **25.** (a) | **35.** (b) | **45.** (b) |
| **6.** (b) | **16.** (c) | **26.** (c) | **36.** (a) | **46.** (d) |
| **7.** (c) | **17.** (c) | **27.** (c) | **37.** (c) | **47.** (b) |
| **8.** (b) | **18.** (b) | **28.** (c) | **38.** (d) | **48.** (c) |
| **9.** (a) | **19.** (b) | **29.** (d) | **39.** (b) | **49.** (c) |
| **10.** (a) | **20.** (b) | **30.** (a) | **40.** (b) | **50.** (b) |

# Practice Question Paper 8

**(A) Read each of the following passages and answer the questions that follow. Your answer to these questions should be based on the passage only.**

**(I)**

There is a dangerous fascination to be leaders of men, to which many strong minds have succumbed. To be accepted as the leader of a small circle of sycophants, in his own parlour, has the same fearful attraction for a man who suffers from a scarcity of brains and character. Gopinath assumed the part of a hero among his friends and acquaintances, and tried daily to invent new wonders in all manner of extravagance. He won a reputation among his followers for his audacity of excesses, which goaded him not only to keep up his fame, but to surpass himself at all costs.

Find the suitable option to fill in the blank. The answer should be in the context of the passage.

1. Many have ______ to the dangerous fascination of being the leaders of men.
   - (a) accepted the challenge
   - (b) toiled hard
   - (c) fallen prey to the temptation
   - (d) all of the above
2. As per the passage Gopinath was surrounded by a circle of ___________
   - (a) close friends
   - (b) crafty deceivers
   - (c) well wishers and relatives
   - (d) false flatterers

**(II)**

Some days afterwards he came to my place in the evening. He had sold his house, and taken a small cottage in the country, a few miles from town. He had been busied all day in selling all that furniture. The new house required few items, and those of the simplest kind. All the splendid furniture of his late residence had been sold, excepting his wife's piano. That, he said, was too closely associated with the idea of herself; it belonged to the little story of their love; for some of the sweetest moments of their courtship were those when he had leaned over that instrument, and listened to the melting tones of her voice. I could not but smile at this instance of romantic gallantry in a doting husband as I am a skeptic myself."

3. As per the passage why did the person described in the passage sell his splendid furniture?
   - (a) He had fallen on hard times and needed money.
   - (b) His new cottage was small and he did not need all the furniture there.
   - (c) His wife was dead and he was full of remorse.
   - (d) All of the above.
4. Which of the two conclusions can be arrived at from what is stated in the passage?
   - (1) The person described in the passage loved his wife very much.
   - (2) The person described in the passage had been rich.
   - (a) Only statement 1 can be drawn.
   - (b) Only statement 2 can be drawn.
   - (c) Both statements 1 & 2 can be drawn.
   - (d) Neither statements 1 nor 2 can be drawn.
5. Where was the new house of the person described in the passage located?
   - (a) Near a forest.
   - (b) Near a big city.
   - (c) In a village.
   - (d) Outside a town.
6. The narrator describes the person in the passage as a _________ husband.
   - (a) faithful
   - (b) meticulous
   - (c) caring and truthful
   - (d) fond and adoring

**(B) Read each of the following passages and answer the questions that follow. Your answer to these questions should be based on the passage only.**

Ever since the industrial revolution happened, man-made activities have added significant quantities of GHGs into the atmosphere. Climate change is a global negative externality primarily caused by the building up of GHG emissions in the atmosphere. The efforts needed to address the climate change include mitigation of GHG emissions on the one hand and building of adaptive capacities to cope with the adverse impacts of climate change on the other. From a developing country perspective, adaptation is of utmost importance as they are the ones who are most vulnerable to the adverse impacts of climate change.

The incremental impact of a ton of GHG on climate change is independent of where in the world it is emitted. These emissions impose a cost on both the present and future generations, which are not fully recouped from the emitters of these emissions. This formed the starting point for a globally coordinated policy action and the need for an international climate change negotiating regime.

UNFCCC, set up in 199(ii), although global in scope, differentiates the commitments/responsibilities of Parties on the basis of historic responsibilities, economic structures, and on the basis of the principle of 'equity' and CBDR which is at the core of the climate change debate. The largest share of historical and current global emissions of GHGs has originated in developed countries. Scientists attribute the global problem of climate change not to the current GHG emissions but to the stock of historical GHG emissions. Most of the countries, particularly the industrialised countries, having large current emissions are also the largest historic emitters and the principal contributors to climate change. The Convention therefore lays down legally binding commitments for the developed countries, taking into account their historical responsibilities and also squarely puts the responsibilities on developed countries for providing financial resources, including for the transfer of technology, needed by the developing countries. The Convention also acknowledges that climate change actions taken by developing countries are contingent on the resources made available to them.

7. From the perspective of a developing country which of the following is most important?
   - (i) Bringing reduction in the emission of the green house gases.
   - (ii) Building capacity to cope with the harmful impact/threat change in climate would bring.
   - (a) Course (i) is the most important.
   - (b) Course (ii) is the most important.
   - (c) Both courses are equally important.
   - (d) Neither course (i) nor course (ii) is actionable by a developing country.
8. Which of the following is **not** correct with reference to the issue of climate change?
   - (a) Adverse impact of climate change would be borne equally by all.
   - (b) Mitigation and adaptation are not the only two broad measures for tackling climate change.
   - (c) Under UNFCC the developing countries need to take binding cuts of GHG emissions.
   - (d) All of the above.
9. Why the cost of GHG emission is not fully recouped from the emitters?
   - (i) Emitters do not own up the emission caused by them.
   - (ii) The effect of emission is distributed throughout irrespective of its origin.
   - (iii) Adverse impact is not limited to the present generation but to the future generations also.
   - (iv) Comprehensive mechanism for assessment of environmental impact of emissions and for recoupment of the cost from the emitter has not been put up in place in the past.
   - (a) (i), (ii), (iii), (iv) (b) (ii), (iii), (iv)
   - (c) (iii), (iv) (d) (ii), (iii)
10. The adverse impact of climate change is caused due to the:
    - (a) build up of GHG emissions from the past.
    - (b) current stock of GHG emissions particularly from developed countries.

(c) Because of (a) and (b) both
(d) Neither because of (a) nor (b)

11. Which of the following inference is correct in terms of what is stated in the passage?
    (i) The actions regarding reduction of GHG emissions, which developing countries need to take, depends on how much finance and technology is made available to them by the developed countries.
    (ii) It is too late for mitigation efforts to tackle the problem of climate change, hence focus has to be on adaptation.
    (iii) As per UNFCC the developed countries are bound to cut their GHG emissions.
    (a) (i), (ii) (b) (i), (iii)
    (c) (ii), (iii) (d) (i), (ii)

**(C) Read the passage carefully and answers the questions based on it.**

**(I)**

It is perfectly possible for an individual to adopt this way of life without having to wait for others to so. And if an individual can observe a certain rule of conduct, it follows that a group of individuals can do likewise. It is necessary for me to emphasize that fact that no one need wait for anyone else in order to adopt a right course. Men generally hesitate to make a beginning if they feel that the objective cannot be had in its entirety. Such an attitude of mind is in reality a bar to progress.

12. Which of the following statement can be said to be a logical corollary of what the author wants to convey in the passage?
    (a) People should follow what others are doing.
    (b) Assessment of achieving the objective should be the most important criteria in the decision to whether to embark upon the activity or not.
    (c) Both (a) & (b)
    (d) Neither (a) nor (b)
13. Which of the following is correct in terms of what is stated in the passage?
    (a) men need not wait for a precedence if they think a course of action is correct.
    (b) A group can observe a rule of conduct which has been observed by an individual.
    (c) Both (a) & (b)
    (d) Neither (a) nor (b)

**(II)**

As to whether in an ideal society, there should be any or no government, I do not think, we need worry ourselves about this at the moment. If we continue to work for such a society, it will slowly come into being to an extent, such that the people can benefit by it. Euclid's line is one without breadth but no one has so far been able to draw it and never will. All the same it is only by keeping the ideal line in mind that we have made progress in geometry. What is true here is true of every ideal. It must be remembered that nowhere in the world, does a State without government exist.

14. Consider the following statements and identify the ones which are **not** a logical conclusion of what has been stated in the passage?
    (a) An ideal which is presently non-realizable is nonetheless relevant to the society.
    (b) A state without government cannot exist
    (c) Both (a) and (b)
    (d) Neither (a) nor (b)
15. What does the author mean by the statement, "*What is true here is true of every ideal*"?
    (a) Ideal has to be kept in one's view to achieve it.
    (b) Ideals always bring out the best in humanity.
    (c) Both (a) and (b)
    (d) Neither (a) nor (b)

**(III)**

The idea behind the village industries scheme is that we should look to the villages for the supply of our daily needs and that, when we find that some needs are not so supplied, we should see whether with a little trouble and organization they cannot be profitably supplied by the villagers. In estimating the profit, we should think of the villager, not of ourselves. It may be that in the initial stages we might have to pay a little more than the ordinary prices and get an inferior article in the bargain. Things will improve, if we will interest ourselves in the supplier of our needs and insist on his doing better and take the trouble of helping him to do better.

16. The most important and crucial message which the author wants to convey in the passage is,
    (a) to point that the village industry is bound to be costly and inferior to begin with.
    (b) to create a demand for the village industry despite the cost and quality consideration at the outset.
    (c) Both (a) & (b)
    (d) Neither (a) nor (b)

**(D) Read the passages and answer the questions given below:**

In the democracy which I have envisaged, a democracy established by non-violence, there will be equal freedom for all. Everybody will be his own master. It is to join a struggle for such democracy that I invite you today. Once you realise this you will forget the differences between the Hindus and Muslims, and think of yourselves as Indians only, engaged in the common struggle for independence. Then, there is the question of your attitude towards the British.

I have noticed that there is hatred towards the British among the people. The people say they are disgusted with their behaviour. The people make no distinction between British imperialism and the British people. To them, the two are one. We must get rid of this feeling. Our quarrel is not with the British people, we fight their imperialism. The proposal for the withdrawal of British power did not come out of anger. It came to enable India to play its due part at the present critical juncture. It is not a happy position for a big country like India to be merely helping with money and material obtained willy-nilly from her while the United Nations are conducting the war. We cannot evoke the true spirit of sacrifice and valour, so long as we are not free. I know the British Government will not be able to withhold freedom from us, when we have made enough self-sacrifice. We must, therefore, purge ourselves of hatred. Speaking for myself, I can say that I have never felt any hatred. As a matter of fact, I feel myself to be a greater friend of the British now than ever before. One reason is that they are today in distress. My very friendship, therefore, demands that I should try to save them from their mistakes. As I view the situation, they are on the brink of an abyss. It, therefore, becomes my duty to warn them of their danger even though it may, for the time being, anger them to the point of cutting off the friendly hand that is stretched out to help them. People may laugh, nevertheless that is my claim. At a time when I may have to launch the biggest struggle of my life, I may not harbour hatred against anybody.

17. Which amongst the following has **not** been narrated as one of attributes of the envisaged democracy?
    (a) It will have communal harmony.
    (b) It will be free from discriminations based on caste and creed.
    (c) It will be established by non violence.
    (d) It will provide equal freedom to all.

18. Why does the narrator call for purging hatred from themselves?
    (i) To distinguish that their struggle is towards British imperialism and not towards Britishers, as such their hatred is unjustified.
    (ii) To imbue themselves with a fervour of self sacrifice, they must purge themselves of hatred.
    (a) The valid reason is only (i).
    (b) The valid reason is only (ii).
    (c) Both (i) and (ii) are valid reasons.
    (d) Neither (i) not (ii) are valid reasons.

19. For what reason does the narrator consider himself to be a greater friend of British than ever previously?
    (i) A friendly overture was more likely to end the British rule in India.
    (ii) It was a time of distress and need for the British.
    (iii) Before launching the biggest struggle against the British the narrator wanted to make a friendly overture.
    (a) Only (i) (b) Only (ii)
    (c) (ii) and (iii) (d) (i), (ii), and (iii)

**(E) Read the passages and answer its questions from the passage itself.**

Indian agriculture is broadly a story of success. It has done remarkably well in terms of output growth, despite weather and price shocks in the past few years. India is the first in the world in the production of milk, pulses, jute and jute-like fibres, second in rice, wheat, sugarcane, groundnut, vegetables, fruits and cotton production, and is a leading producer of spices and plantation crops as well as livestock, fisheries and poultry. While it may appear that the performance of the agriculture and allied sector has fallen short of the target, production has improved remarkably, growing twice as fast as the population. India's agricultural exports are improving at a time when many other leading producers are experiencing difficulties. The better agricultural performance is a result of: a) farmers' response to better prices; b) continued technology gains; and c) appropriate and timely policies coming together. Yet India is at a juncture where further reforms are urgently required to achieve greater efficiency and productivity in agriculture for sustaining growth. There is a need to have stable and consistent policies where markets play a deserving role and private investment in infrastructure is stepped up. An efficient supply chain that firmly establishes the linkage between retail demand and the farmer will be important. Rationalization of agricultural incentives and strengthening of food price management will also help, together with a predictable trade policy for agriculture.

These initiatives need to be coupled with skill development and better research and development in this sector along with improved delivery of credit, seeds, risk management tools, and other inputs ensuring sustainable and climate-resilient agricultural practices. Finally, while the sharp increase in prices of food articles, especially proteins, fruits and vegetables, and the growing food grains stocks in public sector continue to be subjects of debate, these may be the pointers towards the need for both relative price shifts responding to shifts in demand and reconsidering traditional instruments of food management.

20. Which amongst the following is **not** cited as a reason for improvement of agricultural performance in India?
    (a) Better agricultural credit facilities.
    (b) Better prices for agricultural produce.
    (c) Improved agricultural technology.
    (d) Appropriate agricultural policies.
21. Why can India's agriculture growth said to be satisfactory?
    (a) India is the leading producer of many food crops.
    (b) India has reached self sufficiency in food gain production.
    (c) Agricultural growth rate is nearly twice the growth rate of population.
    (d) All of the above.
22. Which amongst the following are measures suggested for bringing further improvement and growth in agriculture?
    (i) Strengthening of food prices
    (ii) Improving irrigation facilities.
    (iii) Developing an efficient supply chain.
    (iv) Waiver of loans in areas of subsistence agriculture.
    (v) Research in field of agriculture and allied technology.
    (a) (i), (ii), (iii), (iv), (v)
    (b) (i), (ii), (iii), (v)
    (c) (i), (ii), (v)
    (d) (i), (iii), (v)
23. Examine whether the following statements are correct in terms of what is stated in the passage?
    (a) India is self sufficient in production of pulses.
    (b) The growth in agriculture has helped in maintaining relatively stable food prices.
    (c) Both (a) and (b) are correct.
    (d) Neither (a) nor (b)

**(F) Read each of the following passages and answer the questions that follow. Your answer to these questions should be based on the passage only**

Children inherit the qualities of the parents, no less than their physical features. Environment does play an important part, but the original capital on which a child starts life is inherited from its ancestors. I have always seen children successfully surmounting the effects of evil inheritance. That is due to purity being an inherent attribute of the soul.

The real property that a parent can transmit to all equally is his or her character and educational facilities. Parents should seek to make their sons and daughters self-reliant, well able to earn an honest livelihood by the sweat of the brow.

I believe implicitly that the child is not born mischievous in the bad sense of the term. If parents would behave themselves whilst the child is growing, before it is born and after, it is a well-known fact that the child would instinctively obey the Law of Truth and the Law of Love...And believe me, from my experience of hundreds—I was going to say thousands—of children, I know that they have perhaps a finer sense of honour than you or I have. The greatest lessons of life, if we would but stoop and humble ourselves, we would learn not from grownup learned men, but from the so-called ignorant children. Jesus never uttered a loftier or a grander truth than when he said that wisdom cometh out of the mouth of babes. I believe it. I have noticed it in my own experience that if we would approach babes in humility and innocence, we would learn wisdom from them, I have learned this one lesson-that what is impossible with man is child's play with God and if we have faith in that Divinity which presides on the destiny of the meanest of his creation, I have no doubt that all things are possible and in that final hope, I believe and pass my time and endeavour to obey His will. If we are to reach real peace in this world and if we are to carry on a real war against war, we shall have to begin with children; and if they will grow up in their natural innocence, we won't have to struggle, we won't have to pass fruitless, idle resolutions, but we shall go from love to love and peace to peace until at last all the corners of the world are covered with that peace and love for which, consciously or unconsciously, the whole world is hungering.

24. Which amongst the following is correct in terms of what is stated in the passage?
    (i) Evil effects of inheritance cannot be surmounted by a child.
    (ii) The capital of life is inherited by the child from its ancestors.
    (a) Only (i) is correct.
    (b) Only (ii) is correct
    (c) Both (i) and (ii) are correct.
    (d) Neither (i) nor (ii) is correct
25. Why does the author believe that the greatest lessons of life can be learnt not from grown up adults but from so called ignorant children?
    (a) Because children are wise.
    (b) Because children are innocent and truthful.
    (c) Both (a) and (b) are valid reasons.
    (d) Neither (a) nor (b) is the valid reason.
26. Why does the author feel that the harmful effects of inheritance can be overcome by children?
    (i) It can be overcome because of the inherent purity of soul.
    (ii) It can be overcome because children are corrupted by environment and not by inheritance.
    (iii) It can be overcome because children are not born mischievous.
    (a) (i), (ii), (iii) all are valid reasons.
    (b) Only (i) and (ii) are valid reasons.
    (c) Only (i) is the valid reason.
    (d) Only (ii) is the valid reason.

**(G) Read each of the following passages and answer the questions that follow. Your answer to these questions should be based on the passage only.**

The result, I think, cannot be said to have been bad. I do not consider my sons were any the worse for the experiment. On the contrary I can see that they gained something. If there was the slightest trace of superiority in them, it was destroyed and they learnt to mix with all kinds of children. They were tested and disciplined.

This and similar experiments have shown me that, if good children are taught together with bad ones and thrown into their company, they will lose nothing, provided the experiment is conducted under the watchful care of their parents and guardians.

Children wrapped up in cotton wool are not always proof against all temptation or contamination. It is true, however, that when boys and girls of all kinds of upbringing are kept and taught together, the parents and the teachers are put to the severest test. They have constantly to be on the alert.

27. What is the conclusion which the author has drawn from his experiments?
    (a) Good children are impervious to the influence of bad children.
    (b) As a result of the company of the good children, it is the bad children, who end up gaining more and good children lose less.
    (c) In company of bad children good children may not be adversely affected provided the guardians are watchful.
    (d) All of the above.
28. What does the author imply when he says, children wrapped up in cotton wool?
    (a) He refers to those children who are fully concealed in cotton clothes.
    (b) He refers to those children who are protected but succumb to temptation.
    (c) He refers to those children who are isolated from environments of harmful influences.
    (d) None of the above.
29. What is the "severest test" being referred to which parents and teachers have to undergo?
    (a) It is the test of alertness and carefulness in preventing the negative influence of bad children from affecting the good.
    (b) It is the test of character of the parents and teachers in setting an example which all children can look up to.
    (c) It is test of being able to handle all children appropriately, as per the children's character.
    (d) None of the above.

**(H) Read the given passage carefully. Answer the questions that follow based on the passage.**

The approach was through a narrow and slippery lane. Quiet there was none. The swarming flies and the noise made by the shopkeepers and pilgrims were perfectly insufferable. Where one expected an atmosphere of meditation and communion it was conspicuous by its absence. One had to seek that atmosphere in oneself. I did observe devout sisters, who were absorbed in meditation, entirely unconscious of the environment. But for this the authorities of the temple could scarcely claim any credit. The authorities should be responsible for creating and maintaining about the temple a pure, sweet and serene atmosphere, physical as well as moral. Instead of this I found a bazaar where cunning shopkeepers were selling sweets and toys of the latest fashion.

When I reached the temple, I was greeted at the entrance by a stinking mass of rotten flowers. The floor was paved with fine marble, which was, however, broken by some devotee innocent of aesthetic taste, who had set it with rupees serving as an excellent receptacle for dirt.

If any one doubts the infinite mercy of God, let him have a look at these sacred places. How much hypocrisy and irreligion does the Prince of Yogis suffer to be perpetrated in His holy name? He proclaimed long ago. 'Whatever a man sows, that shall he reap.' The Law of Karma is inexorable and impossible of evasion. There is thus hardly any need for God to interfere. He laid down the law and, as it were retired.

30. Why does the author believe God to be of infinite mercy?
    (a) God is merciful despite many human beings not believing in him.
    (b) God is merciful despite irreligious practices and intolerance perpetuated by human beings.
    (c) God is merciful despite corrupt and double faced behavior practiced in the temples in the name of religion and God.
    (d) All of the above.
31. What does the author mean by the expression, *the law of Karma is inexorable*?
    (a) The law is impartial and fair to all.
    (b) The law is unyielding and unalterable.
    (c) Both (a) and (b).
    (d) Neither (a) nor (b).

32. Why does the author believe that there is hardly any need for God to interfere?
    (i) God is merciful and therefore excuses the mistakes of human beings. As such need for divine retribution seldom arises.
    (ii) God laid the Law of Karma. According to which a man meets the fate that his actions deserve. As such there is little need for him to interfere.
    (a) Only (i) is the correct reason.
    (b) Only (ii) is the correct reason.
    (c) Both (i) and (ii) are the correct reasons.
    (d) Neither (i) nor (ii) is the correct reason.

**(I) Read the passages given below and answer the questions which follow based on what is written in the passages.**

**(I)**

Habitat destruction greatly increases an area's vulnerability to natural disasters like floods, drought, crop failure, water contamination and spread of disease. Conversely, a healthy ecosystem with good management will reduce the chance of these events or at least mitigate adverse impacts. The most profound effect that habitat destruction has on people is the loss of many valuable ecosystem services. Habitat destruction has changed nitrogen, phosphorous, sulphur and carbon cycles which in turn has increased the frequency and intensity of acid rain, algal blooms and fish death in rivers and oceans. The loss of trees from tropical rain forests represents a substantial decline in the earth's ability to produce $O_2$ and use up carbon dioxide. This assumes greater importance as increasing $CO_2$ levels is one of the chief contributors to global climate change.

33. Which of the following presumptions would be correct in terms of what is stated in the passage?
    (a) Human activity has been the chief cause of habitat destruction.
    (b) Habitat destruction is the chief cause of numerous ecological disasters occurring in recent times.
    (c) Both (a) and (b)
    (d) Neither (a) nor (b)

The shift of major landmasses (continental drift) in the past seems to explain the climatic changes in the geological past. Crustal movements as suggested by the theory of plate tectonics and changes in elevation due to mountain building and other movements must also have caused changes in the climates of different parts of the world. Structural warping of ocean basins alters sea level and oceanic circulation, thereby affecting the transport of heat and moisture. There is evidence pointing to a link between climatic fluctuations and the oceanic circulatory system. However, the relation is rather reciprocal. Changing climate affects ocean temperature and circulation patterns which, in turn, affect climate. Such results of the interaction of elements within the earth's climatic system are called auto-variation.

34. Consider the following statements and examine as to which are correct in terms of what is stated in the passage.
    1. The constant and automatic change in the climatic conditions in the different parts of the world can be said to be auto-variation.
    2. Geological changes such as the crustal movement have a profound impact on the local and world climate.
    3. Climatic changes influence the ocean currents and conditions which in turn affects the climatic conditions.

    (a) Only 1 and 2 (b) only 2 and 3
    (c) only 3 (d) 1, 2 and 3

**(II)**

Forests are important carbon sinks or stores. However, in most mature forests, the rate of production of biomass tends to be balanced by the decomposition of biomass. Hence, a more effective means of using forests as carbon sinks is to harvest mature forests and use the timber to manufacture products that have a long life. Using timber in construction is one example of such uses of wood.

35. Which of the following can be said to be a logical explanation to what is stated in the passage?
    1. Mature forests are much easier to harvest hence much lesser amount of energy is consumed in obtaining forest produce.

2. Use of wood in construction implies that the wood would remain employed for a longer period than its other conventional use and quicker demand for its replacement may not arise.
3. Younger and developing forests have lesser decomposition and more growth of carbon-absorbing plants and trees, hence their utilisation for economic purposes can be counterproductive as a carbon storehouse.

(a) Only 1 and 3 (b) only 2 and 3
(c) only 3 (d) 1, 2 and 3

**(J) In the given questions pick out the most effective word(s) from the given words to fill in the blanks and make the sentence meaningfully complete.**

36. The growing influence of western culture has led to ........... of fast food restaurants in India.
(a) Progress (b) proliferation
(c) prescription (d) proscription

37. He undertook a journey of 1000 kms across three continents .............. bus.
(a) on (b) of
(c) from (d) by

38. Heavy weight lifting exercises .............. his existing shoulder pain.
(a) appreciated (b) promoted
(c) aggravated (d) enabled

39. The burglar was hiding .............. the curtain when the police arrived.
(a) besides (b) behind
(c) beneath (d) beyond

40. It is predicted that in the coming decade sales of electronic books will .............. the sales of paper books.
(a) supersede (b) subside
(c) proceed (d) promote

**(K) In the following questions choose the word that means the exact opposite of the word given**

41. Contract
(a) Extract (b) Exhale
(c) Expand (d) Export

42. Conceal
(a) Reveal (b) Review
(c) Revamp (d) Hide

43. Apogee
(a) Zenith (b) Apex
(c) Perigee (d) Neap

44. Conservative
(a) Unprogressive (b) Radical
(c) Regressive (d) Statusquoist

45. Insolent
(a) Solvent (b) Solicitous
(c) Modern (d) Modest

**(L) Choose the alternative which best express the meaning of the idiom/phrase that is italicised and underlined in the sentence.**

46. When police entered the house, everything was at *sixes and sevens*.
(a) At six or seven places
(b) Arranged in groups of six or seven
(c) In a disorder
(d) In one big heap

47. He failed to launch the business as his partner *threw cold water* on his plans.
(a) Deceived (b) Discouraged
(c) Agreed (d) Fooled

48. I *take exception* to your rude behaviour.
(a) Note off (b) Regret deeply
(c) Disagree with (d) Object to

49. Though he is a professional comedian, the joke *fell flat*.
(a) Caused anger
(b) Caused humour
(c) Caused no amusement
(d) caused pain

50. The jury came to the conclusion that the victim was murdered *in cold blood*.
(a) Planned & deliberate manner
(b) Accidently
(c) Frozen to death
(d) None of the above

## Answers of Practice Question Paper-8

| | | | | |
|---|---|---|---|---|
| **1.** (c) | **11.** (b) | **21.** (c) | **31.** (b) | **41.** (c) |
| **2.** (d) | **12.** (d) | **22.** (d) | **32.** (b) | **42.** (a) |
| **3.** (b) | **13.** (c) | **23.** (d) | **33.** (d) | **43.** (c) |
| **4.** (c) | **14.** (d) | **24.** (b) | **34.** (b) | **44.** (b) |
| **5.** (d) | **15.** (a) | **25.** (b) | **35.** (b) | **45.** (d) |
| **6.** (d) | **16.** (b) | **26.** (c) | **36.** (b) | **46.** (c) |
| **7.** (b) | **17.** (b) | **27.** (c) | **37.** (d) | **47.** (b) |
| **8.** (d) | **18.** (c) | **28.** (c) | **38.** (c) | **48.** (d) |
| **9.** (c) | **19.** (b) | **29.** (a) | **39.** (b) | **49.** (c) |
| **10.** (a) | **20.** (a) | **30.** (c) | **40.** (a) | **50.** (a) |

# Practice Question Paper 9

**(A) Read the passages below and answer the questions which follow. Your answer should be based on what is stated in the passage.**

**(I)**

Only those were pure truths which were sung by the poet. The theme was Krishna, the Lover God, and Radha, the beloved, the Eternal Man and the Eternal Woman,. the sorrow that comes from the beginning of time, and the joy without end. The truth of these songs was tested in his inmost heart by everybody from the beggar to the king himself. The poet's songs were on the lips of all. At the merest glimmer of the moon and the faintest whisper of the summer breeze his songs would break forth in the land from windows and courtyards, from sailing-boats, from shadows of the wayside trees, in numberless voices.

1. Which of the following can be considered as true in light of the passage?
   1. The poet's songs were considered as the anthem of the kingdom.
   2. The poets song were sung by all.

   (a) only 1 (b) only 2
   (c) Both 1 and 2 (d) neither 1 nor 2
2. What was sung by the poet, only that was considered as_______.
   (a) law of the land
   (b) worthy of emulation
   (c) untainted reality
   (d) all of the above

**(II)**

The light astounded me by its power. I could clearly distinguish objects at a distance of a hundred and fifty yards. We were walking on fine, even sand, not wrinkled, as on a flat shore. It repelled the rays of the sun with great intensity. I felt as if I was in broad daylight. I recognized magnificent rocks, hung with a tapestry of zoophytes of the most beautiful kind.

It was then ten in the morning; the rays of the sun struck the surface of the waves. At the touch of light, decomposed by refraction as through a prism, flowers, rocks, plants, shells, and polypus were shaded at the edges by the seven rainbow colours. It was marvellous, a feast for the eyes.

Soon we were at a depth of a hundred and five yards and twenty inches, undergoing a pressure of six atmospheres. At this depth I could still see the feeble rays of the sun.

3. Which one of the following is implied as per the passage?
   (a) The narrator was surprised by the presence of light.
   (b) The narrator was surprised by the intensity of life.
   (c) The narrator was surprised by the colour of light.
   (d) None of the above.
4. The paragraph describes:
   (a) an underwater scene.
   (b) a scene by the sea shore.
   (c) a scene on a mountain range.
   (d) a desert scene.
5. The sand, reflected the sun rays brightly, because,
   (a) the particles of the sand were glass like.
   (b) the sand was absolutely white in colour.
   (c) the surface of the sand was smooth without any creases or folds.
   (d) All of the above
6. A the depth of nearly 105 yards the narrator could still see thȩ ___________ rays of the sun
   (a) bright (b) yellow
   (c) intense (d) weak

### (III)

It was an idyllic and balmy day. The sun shone beyond the orchard and the shade was cool inside. A light breeze stirred the branches of the old apple-tree under which the philosopher sat. None of these things did the philosopher notice, unless it might be when the wind blew about the leaves of the large volume on his knees and he had to find his place again. Then he would exclaim against the wind, shuffle the leaves till he got the right page, and settle to his reading. The book was a treatise on metaphysics; it was written by another philosopher, a friend of this philosopher's; it bristled with fallacies and this philosopher was discovering them all and noting them on the fly-leaf at the end. He was not going to review the book (as some might have thought from his behaviour), or even to answer it in his own opus. It was just that he found a pleasure in stripping any poor fallacy naked and crucifying it.

7. What is implied by the expression 'it bristled with fallacies'?
   (a) It had too many noticeable false notions and inferences.
   (b) It had a number of interesting facts.
   (c) It had a large number of new philosophies'.
   (d) It had many poignant grammatical mistakes.
8. Why was the professor making notes on the fly-leaf at the end?
   (a) He was to write a review of the book.
   (b) He had to find the mistakes in the book so it could be corrected later.
   (c) He enjoyed critcising and finding fault with incorrect propositions.
   (d) All of the above
9. Why did the professor not take note of the weather and the surroundings?
   (a) He had to cover his face because of the strong wind.
   (b) He was engrossed in reading the book.
   (c) His face was towards the tree and he sat in its shadow making it difficult to notice things.
   (d) The large numbers of leaves bellowing in the wind made it difficult to notice the general ambience blowing.

### (IV)

*Cleanliness is next to godliness.* We can no more gain God's blessing with an unclean body than with unclean mind. A clean body cannot reside in an unclean city.

No municipality can cope with insanitation and congestion by the simple process of taxation and paid services. This vital reform is possible only by wholesale and voluntary co-operation of the people, both rich and poor.

It is not enough that we clean the villages which are occupied by our pariah brethren. They are amenable to reason and persuasion. Shall we have to say that the so-called higher classes are not equally amendable to reason and persuasion and to hygienic laws which are indispensable in order to live a city-life? In a village we may do many things with impunity but immediately we transfer ourselves to crowded streets where we have hardly air to breathe, life becomes changed, and we have to obey another set of laws which immediately come into being. Do we do that? It is no use saddling the municipality with the responsibilities for the condition in which we find the central parts of every city in India, and I feel no municipality in the world will be able to over-ride the habits of a class people handed to them from generation to generation … I, therefore, suggest that it is a question of sanitary reform in these big cities, which will be a hopeless task if we expect our municipalities to do this unaided by voluntary work. Far be it from me to absolve the municipalities from their responsibilities.

I consider myself a lover of municipal life. I think that it is a rare privilege for a person to find himself in the position of a municipal councilor but let me note down for you as a man with some experience in public life that one indispensable condition of that privilege is that the municipal councilors dare not approach their office from interest or selfish motives. They must approach their sacred task in a spirit of service. They should pride themselves upon calling themselves scavengers. There is a significant expression for municipal corporation in my mother tongue—*Kachrapatti*, which means literally scavenging department, and a municipality is nothing if it is not a premier scavenging department embracing all spheres of public and social life of a city and if it is not saturated with the spirit of scavenging, scavenging not merely by way of looking after the physical sanitation of a city, but also the internal sanitation of its citizens.

If I were a taxpayer within the jurisdiction of a local board or a municipality,

I would refuse to pay a single pie by way of additional taxation and advise others to do likewise unless the money we pay is retuned four-fold. Those who enter local boards and municipalities as representatives go there not to seek honour or to indulge in mutual rivalries, but to render a service of love and that does not depend upon money. Ours is a pauper country. If our municipal councilors are imbued with a real spirit of service, they will convert themselves into unpaid sweepers, bhangis and road-makers, and take pride in doing so. They will invite their fellow councilors, to join them and if they have faith in themselves and their mission, their example will not fail to evoke response. This means that a municipal councilor has to be a whole-timer. He should have no axe of his own to grind.

10. Why does the author feel municipal work cannot be successful on the model of taxation and paid services?
    (i) Voluntary co-operation of people is essential for the success of a municipality.
    (ii) Taxes and earning from paid services cannot be sufficient to meet all municipal expenses.
    (a) Both (i) and (ii) together is this write answer.
    (b) Only (i) is the right answer.
    (c) Only (ii) is the right answer.
    (d) Neither (i) nor (ii) is the right answer.
11. What does the author feel is the biggest challenge before the municipalities of the big cities?
    (a) Overcoming the inherited habits of city dwellers regarding sanitation and following of municipal laws.
    (b) Surmounting the huge municipal challenge which big congested cities with its burgeoning population face.
    (c) Collection of sufficient revenue to keep the municipalities functional.
    (d) All of the above.
12. Which of the following is **not** implied by what is stated in the passage?
    (a) Taxes and payments for services may be necessary but not sufficient for successful functioning of a municipality.
    (b) People should refuse to pay any additional municipal taxes unless they get value for the taxes being paid.
    (c) Municipal councilors should approach their municipal work as a public duty and not as a social privilege.
    (d) None of the above.

**(B) Read the passage carefully. Answer the questions based on it from within.**

**(I)**

The real implication of equal distribution is that each man shall have the wherewithal to supply all his natural needs and no more. For example, if one man has a weak digestion and requires only a quarter of a pound of flour for his bread and another needs a pound, both should be in a position to satisfy their wants. To bring this ideal into being the entire social order has got to be reconstructed.

13. As per the views of the author, which of the following situations would represent equal distribution?
    (a) Where all citizens are able to access equal resources in society
    (b) Where all citizens have some surplus of resources after consumption
    (c) Both (a) and (b)
    (d) Neither (a) nor (b)

**(II)**

The decline in marginal cost of data clubbed with an increase in marginal benefit means that the optimal quantum of data that society should consume is much higher than before. If so, economic theory predicts that the economy should have, by now, seen a surge in efforts to harness and use data. This has indeed happened, but only partially.

14. Which of the following assumptions can be made in terms of what is stated in the passage?
    (a) As per the economic theory there should be a further increase in data consumption.
    (b) Data privacy and security concerns remain the chief reasons for suboptimal data consumption.
    (c) Both (a) & (b)

**(III)**

Energy is an integral component of the growth process for any economy. The present day developed countries pursued a path of energy-intensive industrial growth to reach the standards of living witnessed by them today. The upper-middle-income countries have also seen per capita energy consumption rise with their rise in per capita incomes. Though India accounts for around 18 percent of world's population, it uses only around 6 percent of the world's primary energy. India's per capita energy consumption equals 0.6 tonnes of oil equivalent (toe) as compared to the global per capita average of 1.8 toe. India's per capita primary energy consumption lags that of the upper-middle-income countries by a considerable margin.

15. Based on what is stated in passage, which of the following conclusions can be drawn?
    (1) India does not fall in the category of upper-middle income country.
    (2) A high energy intensive industrial growth like that of the developed countries would mean for India, sacrificing its self determined environmental commitments.
    (3) Poor per capita energy consumption of India is attributable to the high population density of India.
    (a) 1 only
    (b) 1, 2
    (c) 1, 2, 3
    (d) None of the above

**(C) Read the passages below and answer the questions which follow. Your answer should be based on what is stated in the passage.**

I am afraid that for years to come India would be engaged in passing legislation in order to raise the down-trodden, the fallen, from the mire into which they have been pushed by the capitalists, by the landlords, by the so-called higher classes, and then, subsequently and scientifically, by the British ruler. If we are to lift these people from the mire, then it would be the bounded duty of the National Government of India, in order to set its house in order, continually to give preference to these people and even free them from the burdens under which they are being crushed. And, if the landlords, zamindars, moneyed men and those who are today enjoying privileges—I do not care whether they are

Europeans or Indians—If they find that they are discriminated against, I shall sympathise with them, but I will not be able to help them, even if I could possibly do so, because I would seek their assistance in that process, and without their assistance it would not be possible to raise these people out of the mire.

It will, therefore, be a battle between the haves and the have-nots: and if that is what is feared, I am afraid the National Government will not be able to come into being if all the classes hold the pistols at the head of the dumb millions and say: "You shall not have a Government of your own unless you guarantee our possessions and our rights".

Much as I would like to spare every pice of the public treasury, it would be bad economy to do away with provincial Governors and regard Chief Ministers as a perfect equivalent. Whilst I would resent much power of interference to be given to Governors, I do not think that they should be mere figure-heads. They should have enough power enabling them to influence ministerial policy for the better. In their detached position they would be able to see things in their proper perspective and thus prevent mistakes by their cabinets. Theirs must be an all-pervasive moral influence in their provinces.

This office holding is a step towards either greater prestige or its total loss. If it is not to be a total loss, the ministers and the legislators have to be watchful of their own personal and public conduct. They have to be, like Caesar's wife, above suspicion in everything. They may not make private gains either for themselves or for their relatives or friends. If the relatives or friends get any appointment, it must be only because they are the best among the candidates, and their market value is always greater than what they get under the government. The ministers and the legislators have to be fearless in the performance of their duty. They must always be ready to risk the loss of their seats of offices.

A popular ministry is responsible to the legislatures and cannot do anything without their consent. Every elected member in a popular legislature is responsible to his voters. Therefore, the voter who represents the public should ponder well before embarking on any criticism of the government of his creation. Moreover, one bad habit of the people should be borne in mind. They do not like any tax whatsoever. Where there is good government, the tax-prayer gets full return for his money as, for example, the water tax in cities. No tax-payer could get water on his own for the same payment. But even so, and in spite of the fact that the tax is levied by the popular will, tax payers always resent even paying such taxes. It is, of course, true that one cannot prove the benefit of all taxes as easily as the one I have cited as an example. But as society grows, it is difficult to explain to the individual tax payer, how he gets his return for any particular tax. This much, however, is clear that taxes as a whole should stand for the general benefit of society. If this were not so, the argument that the taxes were levied by popular will would not hold.

16. The role of the governors, envisaged by the author in administration is that of,
    (i) A titular figure head.
    (ii) A moral influence on polices.
    (iii) An active politician.
    (iv) A detached but guiding statesman.
    (a) (i), (ii), (iii), (iv)
    (b) (ii), (iii), (iv)
    (c) (ii), (iv)
    (d) (i), (ii), (iv)
17. Why does the author feel that it is difficult to explain the role of taxes to the tax payers?
    (a) The role of taxes is not always easy to elucidate.
    (b) People have inherent resentment towards payment of taxes.
    (c) Both (a) and (b) are the correct reasons.
    (d) Neither (a) nor (b) is the correct reason.
18. Why does the author feel that holding a public office can be a matter of a greater prestige or its total loss?
    (i) People are likely to be either genuine public servants or usurpers of power.
    (ii) Work and policy of the public office holders will either endear them to the masses or draw their resentment.
    (iii) By being impartial and fearless they may either be seen as champions of masses or as villains.
    (a) (i), (ii) and (iii) all are the correct reasons.
    (b) Only (ii) and (iii) are the correct reasons.
    (b) Only (iii) is correct reason.
    (c) Only (ii) is the correct reason.
19. Why would the author sympathise with the "haves" who are discriminated but would not be able to help them?
    (a) Laws would prevent the author from assisting the haves.
    (b) There would be class conflict if he were to try to help the haves.
    (c) The have-nots would be required to be emancipated even at the cost of and with the assistance of the haves.
    (d) For all of the above reasons.

**(D) Read the passage carefully. Understand and answer them after reading the passage.**

The absence of quality infrastructure—roads, utilities, real estate, logistics— increases transaction costs disproportionately for Micro, Small and Medium Enterprises MSMEs which typically cannot create customised alternatives such as access roads and captive power plants which larger firms can. Lack of this supporting infrastructure causes greater cash burn and distraction of management from core business operations. One constraint in creating infrastructure or setting up businesses is land acquisition. A number of reforms are needed on the anvil to ensure that land is less of an impediment to growth. Going forward there is hope that massive infrastructure projects such as the Delhi-Mumbai Industrial Corridor (DMIC) will provide relatively light regulation, and heavy infrastructure, where businesses have easy access to the land they need and workers can live in a safe healthy township.

We have described the major non-labour impediments for a small business to become formal and grow large, as well as some steps the government is taking. There is evidence that these constraints affect industrial performance. On classifying industries according to their intensity of use of infrastructure, or dependence on external finance, it is noted that post de-licensing, industries more dependent on infrastructure grew less as compared to industries which are not as dependent on infrastructure; and the gain in manufacturing-sector output in these industries has been especially small in states with inferior infrastructure. They further show that industries more dependent on external finance have witnessed slower growth as opposed to those less dependent on external finance, and have fared much worse in terms of new factories, employment generation, as well as new investment. There is therefore need to take steps for improving infrastructure, access to finance, as well as the overall business environment.

20. Prior development of infrastructure, is very important for the growth of MSMEs because:
    (a) MSMEs cannot create infrastructure on their own.
    (b) Infrastructure constraint increases operation costs, or hampers business operations.
    (c) For reasons both (a) and (b)
    (d) For reasons neither (a) nor (b).
21. Which amongst the following are factors emphasised in the passage, as important for the growth of the MSMEs?
    (i) Easy availability of finance and credit for MSMEs.
    (ii) Easy availability of land for MSME.
    (iii) Simplified labour laws for MSMEs.
    (iv) Development of infrastructure for MSMEs.
    (a) (i), (ii), (iii), (iv) (b) (i), (ii), (iii)
    (c) (i), (ii), (iv) (d) (ii), (iii), (iv)
22. Which amongst the following is correct in terms of what is stated in the passage?
    (a) Larger enterprises are less likely to be affected by infrastructural constraints as compared to MSMEs, as the former are in a position to develop some infrastructure on their own.
    (b) Empirical data indicates that the enterprises more dependent on infrastructure and external finance have fared almost as well as those which are less dependent on those.
    (c) Both (a) and (b) are correct
    (d) Neither (a) nor (b) is correct

**(E) Read the passage carefully. Answer the questions pertaining to it.**

Strikes are the order of the day. They are a symptom of the existing unrest. All kinds of vague ideas are floating in the air. A vague hope inspires all, and great will be the disappointment if that vague hope does not take definite shape. The labour world in India, as elsewhere, is at the mercy of those who have become as advisers and guides. The latter are not always scrupulous, and not always wise even when they are scrupulous. The labourers are dissatisfied with their lot. They have every reason for dissatisfaction. They are being taught, and justly, to regard themselves as being chiefly instrumental in enriching their employees. And so it requires little effort to make them lay down their tools. The political situation too is beginning to affect the labourers of India. And there are not wanting labour leaders who consider that strikes may be engineered for political purpose.

In my opinion, it will be a most serious mistake to make use of labour strikes for such a purpose. I don't deny that such strikes can serve political ends. But they do not fall within the plan of non-violent non-co-operation. It does not require much effort of the intellect to perceive that is a most dangerous thing to make political use of labour until labourers understand the political condition of the country and are prepared to work for the common good. This is hardly to be expected of them all of a sudden and until they have bettered their own condition so as to enable them to keep body and soul together in a decent manner.

The greatest political contribution that labourers can make is to improve their own conditions, to become better informed, to insist on their rights, and even to demand proper use by their employers of the manufactures in which they have had such an important hand. The proper evolution, therefore, would be for the labourers to raise themselves to the status of part proprietors.

Strikes, therefore, for the present should only take place for the direct betterment of the labourers' lot, and when they have acquired the spirit of patriotism, for the regulation of prices of the manufactures.

23. Which of the following correctly reflect the view of the author regarding why the labour resorts to strikes?
    - (i) They are instigated to strike for political reasons.
    - (ii) The advisers of labourers are not scrupulous, or wise, or both.
    - (iii) The labour harbour the notion that they are largely instrumental in enriching their employers, as such they have right to stop work if there demands are not met.
    - (iv) The pitiful conditions of the labourers and exploitation by the employees is causing them to strike.

    (a) (i), (ii), (iii), (iv) (b) (i), (ii), (iv)
    (c) (i), (ii), (iii) (d) (i), (iii)

24. Why does the author feel that labour strikes should not be used for political purposes?
    - (a) The strikes ultimately fail to attain political ends.
    - (b) The labour does not fully comprehend the political situation of the country nor is ready to work for the common good.
    - (c) Such strikes usually take violent shapes.
    - (d) All of the above.

25. Which amongst the following is **not** a suggestion of the author for improving the lot of the labourers?
    - (a) They should strike for part ownership in the production.
    - (b) They should strike for being better informed.
    - (c) They should demand better use of the products manufactured by them, by their employees.
    - (d) They should strike for a stake in the entire management of the production.

26. When does the author feel that the strike would be justifiable and proper?
    - (a) When it directly benefits and improves the conditions of labourers.
    - (b) When it is not instigated by some labour leader.
    - (c) When the labourers have become part proprietors of the production.
    - (d) All of the above.

**(F) The two passages given below consists of six sentences. The first and sixth sentences in order of chronology, are given first and last, respectively. The chronology of the remaining four sentences is jumbled. These are written as PQRS. Determine the proper sequence of the four sentences.**

1. Perform Achieve and Trade (PAT) is a scheme for trading energy-efficiency certificates.

(P) At the same time this mechanism facilitates efficient industries to trade their additional certified energy savings that go beyond the assigned target.

(Q) Identified industries are required to improve their specific energy consumption (SEC) within the specified period of three years or face penalty provisions.

(R) This scheme is applicable in large energy-intensive industries under the National Mission for Enhanced Energy Efficiency.

(S) This can be traded with other designated consumers who could use these certificates to comply with their SEC-reduction targets.

6. The PAT scheme is likely to achieve about 15 million tonnes oil equivalent of annual savings in coal, oil, gas, and electricity.

27. Which is the correct chronological order?

    (a) PQRS (b) QSRP
    (c) RQSP (d) RQPS

1. Corporate borrowers in India and other emerging economies are keen to borrow foreign currency.
(p) But there are good times, when the domestic borrowers could enjoy triple benefits
(q) They want to borrow as they stand to benefit from lower interest and longer terms of credit.
(r) This is especially so in times of high currency volatility
(s) However, such borrowings however, are not always helpful.
6. These triple benefits are (i) lower interest rates, (ii) longer maturity and (iii) capital gains due to domestic currency appreciation.

28. Which is the correct chronological order?
    (a) PQRS (b) QSRP
    (c) QRSP (d) PRQS

**(G) The questions given below comprise a sentence, a portion of which is underlined and has four options. Select the option which if substituted in place of the underlined portion, improves the sentence/ makes it grammatically correct. In case no improvement is possible then chose the option (d).**

29. May I come to your house today? The boy asked his friend.
    (a) Could I come
    (b) Can I come
    (c) Would I come
    (d) No improvement can be done
30. As he dusted the old book rack, a puff of dust blew.
    (a) a pool of dust
    (b) a lump of dust
    (c) a cloud of dust
    (d) no improvement can be done
31. It is not clear as to why you leave the job.
    (a) Why left (b) Why you left
    (c) You left why (d) No improvement
32. He is so stubborn that it is difficult explaining him the problem.
    (a) to explain him the problem.
    (b) Explaining to him the problem.
    (c) to explain the problem to him.
    (d) No improvement

**(H) Which word is the synonym or similar in meaning to the given words in question.**

33. Kudos
    (a) Praise for achievement
    (b) Criticism
    (c) Key to success
    (d) Work of great relevance
34. Brazen
    (a) Shameless (b) Sharp
    (c) Stupid (d) Suave
35. Premonition
    (a) To get promoted
    (b) Forewarning
    (c) News of danger
    (d) None of the above
36. Admonish
    (a) Defeat (b) Appreciate
    (c) Reprimand (d) Suspend
37. Capricious
    (a) Willy (b) Edgy
    (c) Smiteful (d) Fickle
38. Bard
    (a) Doctor (b) Singer
    (c) Solder (d) Poet
39. Precarious
    (a) Sharp (b) Problematic
    (c) Uncertain (d) Clear
40. Fallow
    (a) Hollow (b) Empty
    (c) Unsowed (d) false

**(I) Choose the alternative which best express the meaning of the idiom/phrase that is italicised and underlined in the sentence.**

41. He has *made up his mind* to donate his property.
    (a) Agreed (b) Decided
    (c) Shown interest (d) Imagined

42. He is <u>done for</u>.
    (a) Completed (b) Successful
    (c) remorseful (d) Ruined
43. He <u>turned a deaf year</u> to the advice of his father.
    (a) Heeded (b) Disregarded
    (c) Acted upon (d) Could not hear
44. The investigator was <u>at his wits end</u> in the case.
    (a) End of understanding
    (b) Successful in understanding
    (c) At his witiful best
    (d) Puzzled
45. Nobody can trust a person who <u>plays fast and lose</u>.
    (a) Says one thing and does another
    (b) Does not help others
    (c) Is insensitive to another
    (d) Only cares for himself

**(J) In the following questions, choose the word that means the exact opposite of the word given.**

46. Unscrupulous
    (a) Polite (b) Righteous
    (c) Right (d) Reformist
47. Mundane
    (a) Social (b) Sophisticated
    (c) Special (d) Solver
48. Able
    (a) Fool (b) Disable
    (c) Enable (d) Unable
49. Perfunctory
    (a) Careless (b) Ceaseless
    (c) Careful (d) Competent
50. Dubious
    (a) Trustworthy (b) Equivocal
    (c) Calm (d) Competent

## Answers of Practice Question Paper-9

| | | | | |
|---|---|---|---|---|
| **1.** (b) | **11** (a) | **21.** (c) | **31.** (b) | **41.** (b) |
| **2.** (c) | **12** (d) | **22.** (a) | **32.** (c) | **42.** (d) |
| **3.** (b) | **13** (d) | **23.** (c) | **33.** (a) | **43.** (b) |
| **4.** (a) | **14** (a) | **24.** (b) | **34.** (a) | **44.** (d) |
| **5.** (c) | **15** (a) | **25.** (d) | **35.** (b) | **45.** (a) |
| **6.** (d) | **16** (c) | **26.** (a) | **36.** (c) | **46.** (b) |
| **7.** (a) | **17** (a) | **27.** (d) | **37.** (d) | **47.** (c) |
| **8.** (c) | **18** (b) | **28.** (b) | **38.** (d) | **48.** (d) |
| **9.** (b) | **19** (c) | **29.** (d) | **39.** (c) | **49.** (c) |
| **10** (b) | **20** (c) | **30.** (c) | **40.** (c) | **50.** (a) |

# Practice Question Paper 10

**(A) Read the passages below and answer the question which follow. Your answer should be based on what is stated in the passage.**

**(I)**

Pundarik stood up and the vast hall becamc still. With his head raised high and chest expanded, he began in his thundering voice to recite the praise of King Narayan. His words burst upon the walls of the hall like breakers of the sea, and seemed to rattle against the ribs of the listening crowd. The skill with which he gave varied meanings to the name Narayan, and wove each letter of it through the web of his verses in all manner of combinations, took away the breath of his amazed hearers.

For some minutes after he took his seat his voice continued to vibrate among the numberless pillars of the king's court and in thousands of speechless hearts. The learned professors who had come from distant lands raised their right hands, and cried, Bravo!

1. On hearing the rendition of poetry by Pundarik, the learned professors of distant land _______
   (a) declared the poet as the winner of contest
   (b) exclaimed in approval
   (c) exclaimed with surprise
   (d) All of the above
2. Which of the following would best describe the effect of the rendition of the poetry on the listeners in the court of the king?
   1. They were struck with fear at the loud rendition.
   2. They were amazed at the dexterity of the wordplay.
   3. They were speechless at the thundering rendition.

   (a) 1, 2, 3 (b) 2, 3
   (c) Only 2 (d) only 3

**(II)**

It was the examination day and Victor felt as if he had swallowed a frozen elephant. He went to the toilet for the third time that morning, washed his face twicc, drank cup after cup of coffee and basically behaved in the most illogical way imaginable. He felt he was standing at the edge of an abyss and his forehead started sweating. His stomach felt as though it were upside down, his head was being pounded regularly by a group of imaginary boxers with spiked gloves. He had not slept the previous night. His heart throbbed and throbbed, and then suddenly stopped throbbing. Victor felt a burning in his throat, and strangely, he felt as if his legs were made of cloth: he could swear they wobbled.

3. What illogical things which Victor did, have been described in the passage?
   (1) He swallowed a frozen chocolate elephant.
   (2) He drank a number of cups of coffee.
   (3) He stood at the edge of an abyss.
   (4) He went to the toilet thrice.

   (a) 1, 4 (b) 2, 4
   (b) 1, 3, 4 (d) 1, 2, 3
4. Why was Victor behaving in an illogical manner?
   (a) He was ill.
   (b) He did not sleep the previous night.
   (c) He was nervous because of the examination.
   (d) All of the above.
5. Which of the following is correct?
   (a) Victor had been pounded by a group of boxers.
   (b) His legs were weak because of fatigue.
   (c) He did not sleep the previous night.
   (d) All of the above.

### (III)

The Government of India is promoting Public Private Parnership (PPPs) as an effective tool for bringing private-sector efficiencies in creation of economic and social infrastructure assets and for delivery of quality public services. India, in recent years, has emerged as one of the leading PPP markets in the world because of several policy and institutional initiatives taken by the central government.

Following the recommendations of the Committee on Public Procurement, the Prime Minister's announcement regarding transparency and accountability in procurement and preparation of the Public Procurement Bill, and to ensure that PPP projects are procured and implemented by following laid down processes and observing principles of transparency, competitive bid process, affordability and value for money, the draft PPP Rules and PPP Policy have been prepared. These have undergone extensive consultation process at central and state government levels for finalisation.

Global experience indicates that PPPs work well when they combine the efficiency and risk assessment of the private sector with the public purpose of the government sector. They work poorly when they rely on the efficiency and risk assessment of the government sector and the public purpose of the private sector. India should be careful not to undertake PPPs that do not apportion risks and responsibilities sensibly. Moreover flexibility needs to be built into arrangements so that the contract can be withdrawn and put up for rebid when the private party underperforms. The government needs to study the PPP experience and build some central capacity to help ministries, authorities, and states structure contracts and renegotiate troubled ones.

6. Which of the following were the input factors while preparing the draft PPP Rules and PPP Policy?
   (i) Principles of transparency.
   (ii) Scarcity of resources and investible capital available with the government sector.
   (iii) Need for bringing efficiency and value for money in economic and social infrastructure.
   (a) (i), (ii), (iii) (b) (i) and (ii)
   (c) (i), (iii) (d) (ii) and [illegible]

7. As per the passage, which are the areas in which PPP will be particularly useful?
   (a) In projects involving delivery of public services.
   (b) In infrastructure projects.
   (c) In projects envisaging to create socio-economic assets.
   (d) All of the above.

8. Which of the following is the correct match for the PPP model to work properly?
   It should have the efficiency of government sector and risk assessment of private sector.
   (a) It should have the public purpose of private sector and risk assessment of government sector.
   (b) It should have efficiency of private sector and risk assessment of the government sector.
   (c) It should have public purpose of government sector, efficiency and risk assessment of private sector.

9. Which of the following about PPP models is correct as per the passage?
   (i) There should be proper distribution of risk and responsibilities between the government and the private partner.
   (ii) Terms of the contract should be such once the PPP contract has been awarded, the government would have to go ahead with the same private partner.
   (a) Only (i) is correct
   (b) Only (ii) is correct.
   (c) Neither (i) nor (ii) is correct.
   (d) Both (i) and (ii) are correct.

**(B) Read the passage carefully and answer the questions pertaining to it.**

The struggle for existence amongst all organic beings throughout the world inevitably follows from their high geometrical powers of increase. This is the Doctrine of Malthus applied to the whole animal and vegetable kingdoms. As many more individuals of each species are born than can possibly survive; and as, consequently, there is a frequently recurring struggle for existence, it follows that any being, if it vary, however slightly, in any manner profitable to itself, under the complex and sometimes varying conditions of life, will have a better chance of surviving, and thus be naturally selected. From the strong principle of inheritance, any selected variety will tend to propagate its new and modified form. When we look at the individuals of the same variety or sub-variety of our older cultivated plants and animals, one of the first points which strikes us, is, that they generally differ much more from each other, than do the individuals of any one species or variety in a state of nature. When we reflect on the vast diversity of the plants and animals which have been cultivated, and which have varied during all ages under the most different climates and treatment, I think we are driven to conclude that this greater variability is simply due to our domestic productions having been raised under conditions of life not so uniform as, and somewhat different from, those to which the parent-species have been exposed under nature. There is, also, I think, some probability in the view propounded by Andrew Knight, that this variability may be partly connected with excess of food. It seems pretty clear that organic beings must be exposed during several generations to the new conditions of life to cause any appreciable amount of variation; and that when the organisation has once begun to vary, it generally continues to vary for many generations.

10. As per the author, why would natural selection take place?
    (a) Natural selection is essential as there is always pressure on the organic resources in an eco-system.
    (b) Those species, which evolved or changed to suit and survive better, naturally got selected by the eco-system and propagated more.
    (c) Both (a) and (b) are correct reasons.
    (d) Neither (a) nor (b) is the correct reason.

11. As per the author, what is the cause of great variation among the individuals of the same variety/sub variety amongst domesticated/ cultivated animals and plants, than those found in nature?
    (i) Domestication/human cultivation exposed them to varying conditions than what would naturally happen.
    (ii) Domestication/human cultivation enabled greater possibility of cross breading, leading to greater variation of individuals.
    (a) Only (i) is the correct reason.
    (b) Only (ii) is the correct reason.
    (c) Both (i) and (ii) are the correct reasons.
    (d) Neither (i) nor (ii) is the correct reason.

12. Which one of the following is implied by the doctrine of Malthus as narrated in the passage above?
    (i) Over a period of time the geometrical powers of increase of organic beings would stabilise or diminish.
    (ii) Over a period of time organic beings would have to adapt to changes and evolve.
    (iii) There would invariably be a struggle for existence between organic beings as their geometrically increasing numbers would be sharing the same ecological space.
    (a) (i), (ii), (iii) (b) (ii), (iii)
    (c) Only (ii) (d) Only (iii)

**(C) Read the passages given below. Answer the following questions.**

**(I)**

Private Sector Investment in data-related endeavours is higher than even before. The trend holds across industries as disparate as healthcare and financial services, and across geographies and company. Infact, in the last two decades, the world has witnessed the emergence of companies, such as Facebook, Amazon, Instagram, etc., who earn revenue exclusively from people's data. But there are several areas where data is not as ubiquitously harnessed and used. Consider, for example, the agriculture market. If the marginal benefit to a farmer of acquiring price information is higher than the marginal cost of that information, he would pay for that information. Consequently, the private sector would cater to his need by gathering and selling him the information he wants. This would eventually lead to a nationally integrated agriculture market, which should have happened if the marginal benefit of data today is indeed higher than the cost. Why has the corporate sector's data wave not found a parallel in the agriculture sector?

13. Which of the following explanations, would support what is stated in the passage about suboptimal investment by private sector in agricultural market data related endeavours?
    (a) Privacy and security threats have reduced possible data utilization in agricultural sector.
    (b) Marginal benefits of data in agriculture is distributed amongst many agents and not alone to the farmer from whom the private sector can collect data revenue.
    (c) Agriculture sector has poor application of accumulated data.
    (d) All of the above

**(II)**

When people come into possession of political power, the interference with the freedom of the people is reduced to a minimum. In other words, a nation that runs its affairs smoothly and effectively without much State interference is truly democratic. Where such a condition is absent, the form of government is democratic in name.

Democracy and violence can hardly go together. The states that are today nominally democratic have either to become frankly totalitarian or, if they are to become truly democratic, they must become courageously non-violent. It is a blasphemy to say that non-violence can only be practiced by individuals and never by nations which are composed of individuals.

The very essence of democracy is that every person represents all the varied interests which compose the nation. It is true that it does not exclude and should not exclude special representation of special interest, but such representation is not its test. It is a sign of its imperfection.

14. Consider the following assumptions and examine which of them are valid in terms of what is stated in the passage.
    (a) Democracy by its very nature ensures upholding the freedom of its citizens.
    (b) Democracy without exception endows to its every citizen all rights which it endows to every citizen.
    (c) Both (a) & (b)
    (d) Neither (a) nor (b)

**(D) Read the passage carefully. Answer the questions based on it. Answer should be given from the passage itself.**

The sole aim of journalism should be service. The newspaper press is a great power, but just as an unchained torrent of water submerges whole countryside and devastates crops, even so an uncontrolled preserves but to destroy. If the control is from without, it proves more poisonous than want of control. It can be profitable only when exercised from within. If this line of reasoning is correct, how many of the journals in the world would stand the test? But who would stop those that are useless? And who should be the judge? The useful and the useless must, like good and evil, go on together and people must make their choice.

The superficiality, the one-sidedness, the inaccuracy and often even dishonesty that have crept into modern journalism, continuously mislead honest men who want to see nothing but justice done.

I have before me extracts from journals containing some gruesome things. There is communal incitement, gross misrepresentation and incitement to political violence bordering on murder. It is of course easy enough for the government to launch out prosecutions or to pass repressive ordinances. These fail to serve the purpose intended except very temporarily, and in no case do they convert the writers, who often take to secret propaganda, when the open forum of the press is denied to them.

The real remedy is healthy public opinion that will refuse to patronise poisonous journals. We have our journalists associations. Why should it not create a department whose business it would be to study the various journals and find objectionable articles and bring them to the notice of the respective editors? The function of the department will be confided to the establishment of contact with the offending journals and public criticism of offending articles where the contact fails to bring about the desired reform. Freedom of the press is a precious privilege that no country can forego. But if there is, as there should be, no legislative check save that of the mildest character, an internal check, such as I have suggested should not be impossible and ought not to be resented? I hold that it is wrong to conduct newspapers by the aid of ... immoral advertisements. I do believe that if advertisements should be taken at all there should be a rigid censorship instituted by newspaper proprietors and editors themselves and that only healthy advertisement should be taken. The evil of immoral advertisements is overtaking even what are known as the most respectable newspapers and magazines. That evil has to be combated by refining the conscience of the newspapers proprietors and editors. That refinement can come not through the influence of an amateur editor like myself but it will come when their own conscience is roused to recognition of the growing evil or when it is superimposed upon them by a government representing the people and caring for the people's morals.

15. Which of the following is correct in terms of what is stated in the passage?
    (i) External control of press is more dangerous than a press without any checks and control.
    (ii) Legislative checks are an important means for governing the conduct of press.
    (a) Only (i) is correct
    (b) Only (ii) is correct
    (c) Both (i) and (ii) is correct
    (d) Neither (i) nor (ii) is correct
16. What measure is suggested by the author for regulating the standard of advertisement in newspapers?
    (a) Development of a healthy public opinion against them.
    (b) Regulation by journalist association.
    (c) Censorship instituted from within by the newspapers proprietors and editors.
    (d) All of the above.
17. The author laments that most of the journals and newspapers would fail the "test". Which test is being referred to here?
    (i) The test of accurate reporting.
    (ii) The test of control from within.
    (iii) The test meeting the standards laid by legislative provisions.
    (a) (i) and (ii) and (iii) all are correct.
    (b) Only (i) and (ii) are correct.
    (c) Only (i) is correct.
    (d) Only (ii) is correct.
18. What is the view of the author about regulation of press by means of ordinances?
    (a) Ordinances and legislative checks are necessary for regulating the press.
    (b) Ordinances and legislative check should be mild and of regulatory nature only.
    (c) Both (a) and (b)
    (d) Neither (a) nor (b)

**(E) Read the passage carefully. Answers the questions pertaining to it.**

Another challenge is how to maximise agricultural income while adopting a more sustainable agricultural strategy. The concerns here are land and water degradation due to soil erosion, soil salinity, water logging, and excessive application of nutrients. There are concerns arising also from over-exploitation of water resources, especially in the Green Revolution belt. Better management practices for rehabilitation of degraded land and water resources hold the key. Measures must be taken to promote use of quality seeds, cultivation of drought resistant varieties of crops, judicious use of available water, balanced use of fertilizers, farm mechanization to improve efficiency levels, and wider use of irrigation facilities. Expenditure on agricultural research also needs to be stepped up substantially.

Climate change and extreme weather events with greater intensity and frequency can have serious implications for our agriculture sector and create greater instability in food production and thereby farmers' livelihood. The current crop insurance system also needs to be further refined in order to cater to the unavoidable climatic conditions or pest epidemics.

Declining per capita availability of foodgrains has been a major concern in India. For ensuring nutritional security, it is not only important to increase per capita availability of foodgrains but also to ensure the right amounts of food items in the food basket of the common man. A thrust on horticulture products and protein-rich items is required for enhancing per capita availability of food items as well as ensuring nutritional security.

The pace of agricultural growth in the eastern and north-eastern regions has been slower than in the rest of the country. The good prospects of production of many crops in these parts of the country should quickly be taken advantage of in the years to come. Hence a strategy for agricultural development in eastern and north-eastern India comprising multiple livelihood opportunities, sustainable agricultural development through a farming systems approach, efficient national resources management, eco-regional technology missions, and rice-based farming systems needs to be put in place.

Another critical issue is supply chain management in agricultural marketing in India. Farmers' access to markets is hampered by poor roads, rudimentary market infrastructure, and excessive regulation. Many agricultural crops are perishable in nature and post-harvest handling issues and marketing problems affect the farm incomes. It is necessary that we evolve mechanisms for linking wholesale processing, logistics and retailing with farm-production activities so as to generate enhanced efficiency, better farm prices, etc. The private sector should be allowed to operate in developing these market linkages for which suitable reforms will help. Recently the government allowed foreign direct investment (FDI) in retail, which has been supported by many farmer organizations as well, and it can pave the way for investment in new technology and marketing of agricultural produce in India. There has been substantial increase in the MSPs of various crops over the last few years. Though considered necessary for incentivising farmers, the MSP signals the floor price for the produce. There is a huge cost involved in the process, in the form of food subsidy. Further, this policy of stocking food grains well above the buffer norms comes under criticism on the grounds of hoarding and creating artificial shortages in the market, thereby jacking up the prices of essential commodities. Urgent attention needs to be accorded to efficient food stocks management, timely offloading of stocks, and a stable and predictable trade policy. Strengthening agricultural statistics with reliable and timely availability of forecasts of agricultural crops is also an immediate need as the gaps in agricultural statistics will hamper agricultural development planning and policymaking.

19. As per the passage, which amongst the following factors are likely to adversely affect agricultural sector in the future?
    (i) FDI in retail sector.
    (ii) Increased frequency and intensity of adverse weather events.
    (iii) Subsidy on diesel and fertilizers.
    (a) (i), (ii), (iii) (b) (ii) and (iii)
    (c) Only (ii) (d) Only (iii)
20. To tap the agricultural growth potential of eastern and north-eastern sector, which amongst the following is not a measure suggested in the passage?
    (a) Rice based farming
    (b) Efficient management of the available resources.
    (c) Formulation of appropriate agricultural development strategy.
    (d) Prevention of degradation of soil due to water logging and salinity.
21. Which of the following are the concerns / impediments to the challenge of a sustainable agricultural growth strategy?
    (i) Over exploitation of water resources specially in green revolution area.
    (ii) Non judicious use of agricultural subsidies.
    (iii) Degradation of land due to soil erosion.
    (a) (i), (ii), (iii) (b) (i), (ii)
    (c) (i), (iii) (d) (ii), (iii)
22. The shortcoming in the current crop insurance scheme is that:
    (a) it does not cover subsistence type of farmers.
    (b) it has limited access in terms of regions as well as social strata.
    (c) it needs to be improved to cater to damage caused due to unavoidable climate conditions or pest epidemics.
    (d) All of the above.

23. Which among the following is correct in terms of what is stated in the passage?
    (i) The minimum support prices need to be further increased so as to incentivise the farmers.
    (ii) FDI in retail is likely to improve marketing of agricultural produce in India.
    (a) Only (i) is correct.
    (b) Only (ii) is correct.
    (c) Both (i) and (ii) are correct.
    (d) Neither (i) nor (ii) is correct.
24. Which amongst the following is implied by what is stated in the passage?
    (i) Stocking of food grains leads to artificial shortages and price rise of food grains.
    (ii) Present agricultural research is insufficient to cater to agricultural needs.
    (iii) Change, in type of crops being grown/ promoted needs to be done, to meet the nutritional needs of the population.
    (a) (i), (ii), (iii) (b) (i), (ii)
    (c) (i), (iii) (d) (ii), (iii)

**(F) Read the passages below and answer the question which follow. Your answer should be based on what is stated in the passage.**

The key environmental challenges in India have been sharper in the past two decades. The State of the Environment Report by the Ministry of Environment and Forests (MoEF) clubs the issues under five key challenges faced by India, which are climate change, food security, water security, energy security and managing urbanization. Climate change is impacting the natural ecosystems and is expected to have substantial adverse effects in India, mainly on agriculture on which 58 percent of the population still depends for livelihood, water storage in the Himalayan glaciers which are the source of major rivers and groundwater recharge, sea level rise, and threats to a long coastline and habitations. Climate change will also cause increased frequency of extreme events such as floods, and droughts. These in turn will impact India's food security problems and water security. As per the Second National Communication submitted by India to the UNFCCC, it is projected that the annual mean surface air temperature rise by the end of the century ranges from 3.5°C to 4.3°C whereas the sea level along the Indian coast has been rising at the rate of about 1.3 mm/year on an average. These climate change projections are likely to impact human health, agriculture, water resources, natural ecosystems, and biodiversity.

Wary of the threats imposed by climate change and pressures on natural resources, sustain ability and environment are increasingly taking centre stage in the Indian policy domain. India has been part of 94 multilateral environmental agreements. India has also voluntarily agreed to reduce its emission intensity of its GDP by 20–25 percent over 2005 levels by 2020 and emissions from the agriculture sector would not form part of the assessment of its emissions intensity. Indian economy is already moving along a lower carbon and sustainable path in terms of declining carbon intensity of its GDP which is expected to fall further through lower carbon strategies. It is estimated that India's per capita emission in 2031 will still be lower than the global per capita emission in 2005 (in 2031, India's per capita GHG emissions will be under 4 tonnes of carbon dioxide equivalent ($CO_2$eq.), which is lower than the global per capita emissions of 4.22 tonnes of $CO_2$eq. in 2005)

25. Which amongst the following is correct in terms of what is stated in the passage?
    (i) India would be reducing its carbon intensity by 20–25% over 2005 levels by 2020.
    (ii) By 2031 India's per capita emission is likely to by same as the global per capita emission of the world in 2005.
    (a) Only (i) is correct.
    (b) Only (ii) is correct.
    (c) Both (i) and (ii) are correct.
    (d) Neither (i) nor (ii) is correct.
26. Why have the other four challenges as specified in the passage clubbed along with the challenge of climate change in the MOEF report?
    (i) All the other challenges are also likely to be adversely affected by climate change and thus are linked to it.

(ii) Common action to meet all the challenges would be called for.

(iii) The action for all the challenges would be required to be taken by a common ministry andclubbingthemwouldbeadministratively efficacious.

(a) For reasons (i), (ii) and (iii)

(b) For reasons (i) and (ii) only

(c) For reasons (i) and (iii) only

(d) For reason (i) only

27. Which amongst the following is correct in terms of what is stated in the passage?

(a) Considering that by 2031 India's GHGs emission is going to be under 4 tonnes of $CO_2$ which is less than the global for capita emission of 2005, India is not likely to be much adversely effected by climate change.

(b) Adverse impact of climate change on agriculture is likely to cause movement of people to other forms of livelihood.

(c) Both (a) and (b) are correct.

(d) Neither (a) nor (b) is correct.

**(G) Read the passages below and answer the question which follow. Your answer should be based on what is stated in the passage.**

The ultimate goal of economic policy is to create a sustained renaissance of high growth in which hundreds of millions of good quality jobs are created. Good quality jobs are created by high productivity firms, so this agenda is critically about how firms are created, how firms grow, and how firms achieve high productivity.

Labour laws create strong incentives for firms to avoid hiring a large number of low skill workers. An array of problems holds back the entry and maturation of new firms. This protects existing businesses, even if inefficient, and limits entry and competition. It is imperative to use India's unique demographic moment wisely and unleash the second generation of reforms.

The pursuit of long-term initiatives will feed back into the economy in the short term, with a rise in consumption and investment. In India today, there is a coincidence between the priorities for the long term and the priorities for the short term. At the same time, the deeper impact of these policy initiatives will kick in with a lag. When there is an open array of opportunities for individuals and firms, it will take some time for economic agents to understand the new landscape and how they should optimally act in it. Firms will require time and commitment in order to build up organizational capital. Hence we may envision a five year period within which the reforms are put in place, followed by a period within which the economy has fully absorbed the new environment and achieved a higher trend growth rate.

28. Which factors amongst the following would limit competition and allow inefficient existing businesses to survive?

(i) Requirement of approval of multiple government agencies for starting a business.

(ii) Easement of labour laws.

(iii) Availability of good quality manpower and demographic dividend.

(a) Only factor (i) would limit competition.

(b) Only factors (i) and (ii) would limit competition.

(c) All factors (i), (ii) and (iii) would limit competition.

(d) None of the factors would limit competition.

29. As per the passage, why is it important to understand as to what factors lead to creations and growth of high productivity firms?

(i) High productivity firms help in creation of good quality jobs.

(ii) High productivity firms are significant contributors to the exchequer as they are important centres of generation of tax revenues.

(a) Both (i) and (ii) are the correct reasons.

(b) Neither (i) nor (ii) is the correct reason.

(c) Only (i) is the correct reason.

(d) Only (ii) is the correct reason.

30. Which amongst the following is not correct in terms of what is stated in the passage?

(i) Economic policy should strive to create high growth and good quality jobs.

(ii) Strong labour laws act as a deterrence for entry of labour intensive business firms.

(iii) Firms and business take some time to understand and act as per new economic factors in an era of reforms.

(a) Only (ii) is not correct.
(b) (i) and (iii) are not correct.
(c) Only (iii) is not correct.
(d) All statements above are correct.

31. As per the passage how are long term initiatives likely to bring benefits even in the short term in the economy?

(i) They will improve the market sentiments and improve the outlook of shares in the Capital market.
(ii) They will lead to rise in consumption in the short term.
(iii) They will attract greater investment.
(iv) They will reduce the entry level problems for new firms.

(a) (i), (ii) (b) (ii) and (iii)
(c) (ii), (iii) and (iv) (d) (i), (ii), (iii), (iv)

**(H) The passage given below consists of six sentences. The first and sixth sentences in order of chronology, are given first and last. The chronology of the remaining four sentences is jumbled. These are shown as PQRS. Find the proper sequence of the four sentences.**

1. Foreign Direct Investment (FDI) is preferred to the foreign portfolio investments.
(P) As a result, only a handful of sensitive sectors now fall in the prohibited zone.
(Q) Besides it also brings in, managerial practices and is a long-term investment in nature
(R) This is primarily because FDI is expected to bring modern technology.
(S) The Government has liberalised FDI norms overtime.
6. Now FDI is allowed fully or partially in the rest of the sectors.

32. Which is the correct chronological order?

(a) QSRP (b) PQRS
(c) RQSP (d) RQPS

1. It was a hot summer afternoon.
(P) The sweltering heat combined with the hot gushing winds was taking a heavy toll on all.
(Q) This was the point where the cars would stop at the traffic light and he could hope to get a few coins from the windows of the halting cars.
(R) A beggar was seated at the corner of the street bearing the heat without any shade.
(S) The beggar would make a heart-rending crying asking for alms.
6. If he was lucky a few coins would be thrown out.

33. Which is the correct chronological order?

(a) QSRP (b) PQRS
(c) PRQS (d) RQPS

**(I) Which word is the synonym or similar in meaning to the given words in question.**

34. Tenet
(a) Ten Commandments
(b) Doctrine
(c) Rightful conduct
(d) None of the above

35. Adulterate
(a) To make impure (b) To reduce
(c) To corrupt (d) To become adult

36. Gregarious
(a) Great (b) Garrulous
(c) Sociable (d) Foolish

37. Cardinal
(a) of foremost importance
(b) of macro view
(c) of no significance
(d) of ordinary matter

38. Affinity
(a) Relativeness (b) Ability
(c) Similarity (d) love

39. Obdurate
(a) Hardy (b) Stubborn
(c) Stupid (d) Hurtful

40. Penchant
   (a) Praise for somebody
   (b) Playfulness
   (c) Something which is pursued
   (d) Inclination

**(J) Choose the alternative which best express the meaning of the idiom/phrase that is italicised and underlined in the sentence.**

41. He could render *yeoman's service* in the pandemic.
   (a) Excellent work (b) Legal work
   (c) Police work (d) called for work
42. Due to his dress sense, he *cut a poor figure* in the interview.
   (a) Score less marks
   (b) Wear ill fitting clothes
   (c) Form poor impression
   (d) Get a reprimand
43. Those who *rise to the occasion* are sucessful.
   (a) Grab the opportunity
   (b) Avoid the situation of challenge
   (c) Take due risk
   (d) Perform as per the demand of challenge
44. His friend seemed to be *out of spirits*.
   (a) Cured from fear of ghosts
   (b) Out of habit of taking alcohol
   (c) Out of the practice of spiritual pursuits
   (d) Gloomy
45. I am not expected to be *at your beck and call*.
   (a) At receiving end
   (b) Under your control
   (c) Under employment
   (d) Under tutelage

**(K) In the questions below one definition and word options are given. Choose the appropriate word option for the definition.**

46. Harsh unpleasant noise
   (a) Discordant (b) Strident
   (c) Melifluous (d) Clamorous
47. To placate somebody
   (a) Appreciate (b) Criticise
   (c) Idolise (d) Appease
48. To specify as an essential condition
   (a) Incorporate (b) Integrate
   (c) Stipulate (d) Apprise
49. To mention for the first time
   (a) Broach (b) Boast
   (c) Introduce (d) Invent
50. To dull the senses of
   (a) Stupefy (b) Nonsense
   (c) Unemotional (d) None of the above

## Answers of Practice Question Paper-10

| | | | | |
|---|---|---|---|---|
| **1.** (b) | **11.** (a) | **21.** (c) | **31.** (b) | **41.** (a) |
| **2.** (b) | **12.** (d) | **22.** (c) | **32.** (c) | **42.** (c) |
| **3.** (b) | **13.** (b) | **23.** (b) | **33.** (c) | **43.** (d) |
| **4.** (b) | **14.** (d) | **24.** (a) | **34.** (b) | **44.** (d) |
| **5.** (b) | **15.** (a) | **25.** (a) | **35.** (a) | **45.** (b) |
| **6.** (c) | **16.** (c) | **26.** (d) | **36.** (c) | **46.** (b) |
| **7.** (d) | **17.** (d) | **27.** (d) | **37.** (a) | **47.** (d) |
| **8.** (d) | **18.** (b) | **28.** (a) | **38.** (c) | **48.** (c) |
| **9.** (a) | **19.** (c) | **29.** (c) | **39.** (b) | **49.** (a) |
| **10.** (b) | **20.** (d) | **30.** (d) | **40.** (d) | **50.** (a) |

# Part-II

## General Test

## (Section III of CUET)

# General Knowledge and Current Affairs

# 4

## Introduction

The topic of 'General Knowledge and Current Affairs' is among the five broad areas which are included in the Section 3 (General Test) of the CUET. From the perspective of the examination, it is a significant area of the examination and indeed a challenging one. The ambit of both the topics, general knowledge as well as current affairs, is very vast and its expanse cannot be encapsulated in the few pages of a chapter or a or even a singular book. It is also understandable that the time of the aspirants for the preparation of CUET is limited and the effort and time which may be needed to master this area, would be considerably demanding. As such aspirants are besieged with many apprehensions and some genuine doubts, as to the approach to be adopted regarding the preparation for this topic. These include: **how many of questions** will emanate from this area, what are the **nature of the questions** from this section, how should one go about its **preparation**, does one need to **revise from the books of standard 9th and 10th** for its preparation, how should one **prepare for the current affairs** etc. This chapter endeavours to answer all these queries, give inputs to areas of preparation as well as offer lots of practice questions.

As to the **number of questions arising from general knowledge and current affairs,** one can say that around 15% to 20% of questions are likely to arise from this area. This would be in proportion to the number of the broad areas of preparation included in Section 3 of the CUET. Further, the CUET notification states that the Section 3, General Test will have 75 questions, from which 60 would be required to be answered. In these 60 questions, one can expect around 8 to 12 questions to figure from general knowledge and current affairs. From the perspective of the CUET, this is not a topic to be ignored.

The **nature of questions** can be broadly divided into those related to current affairs and others which fall within the ambit of general knowledge. The latter can again be further broken up into those which relate to the study of social sciences and general sciences and those which are outside the domain of formal studies. The last ones come in the purview of general awareness. Before one embarks on the topic of how to go about one's preparation', it is pertinent to further understand the broad areas from which the questions are likely to emanate.

**Likely Areas of Questions:** Based on the questions which have figured in the previous year papers of CUCET and aptitude tests of similar standard, one can identify the following specific areas which need the attention of the candidates and ought to be revised. These can be divided into areas of **general studies** viz. those emanating from social sciences and general sciences and those of **general awareness** which would entail reading of newspaper, magazines and keeping a tab on the current affairs. The topics enumerated here are not exhaustive, however they may offer a reasonable catchment area of the possible questions of CUET. Further, details of some chapters of the NCERT books from which some of the significant topics can be covered, is also being provided.

### 1. Topics of General Studies (General Knowledge)

#### (a) Indian History –

- Important historical events since ancient age,
- Important wars/battles and outcomes,

- Indian religions, founders and core philosophies,
- Medieval saints and reforms,
- Ancient and medieval religious and literary treatises, significant achievements in the fields of culture, arts and sciences.
- Indian national independence movement,
- Reforms and personalities in modern history
- Significant movements in freedom struggle and national leaders

**Reference books to study: NCERT**

**(i) Our Past III** class 8th NCERT textbook
- Chapter 2: From Trade to Territory
- Chapter 5: When People Rebel; 1857 and After
- Chapter 8: Women Caste and Reform
- Chapter 9: The Making of the National Movement: 1870s-1947

**(ii) Our Past II;** class 7th NCERT textbook
- Chapter 8: Devotional Paths to the Divine
- Chapter 9: The Making of Regional Cultures
- Chapter 10: Eighteenth Century Political Formations

## (b) Indian Polity

- Indian Constitution and its important features, parts of the Indian Constitution
- Sources of Indian Constitution
- Fundamental rights
- Fundamental duties
- Directive Principles of State Policy
- Important features of the role of judiciary, legislature and executive,
- Duties and functions of President, Prime Minister and Supreme Court
- Presidents and Prime Ministers of India
- Emergency provisions and features
- Amendment procedures and significant amendments
- Types of Bills and fundamentals of parliamentary process
- Languages in the Indian Constitution and relevant states

**Reference books to study: NCERT**

(i) **Social Science – Class IX** NCERT textbook**; Democratic Politics-1**

Important Chapters
- Chapter 2: Constitutional Design
- Chapter 4: Working of Institutions
- Chapter 5: Democratic Rights

(ii) **Social Science – Class X** NCERT textbook**; Democratic Politics-2**

Important Chapters
- Chapter 2: Federalism
- Chapter 6: Political Parties

(iii) **Indian Constitution at Work; Class XI** NCERT textbook;

Important chapters
- Chapter 2: Rights in the Indian Constitution
- Chapter 4: Executive
- Chapter 5: Legislature
- Chapter 6: Judiciary
- Chapter 9: Constitution as a Living Document

## (c) Geography

- Fundamentals of physical geography
- Important mountains oceans, seas, rivers and their specific features (highest, biggest, deepest etc.)
- Solar system, planets
- Country, capital and currencies, their parliaments
- India and its geographical location, geographical facts
- Important rivers, sources, confluences and other salient physical features
- National parks, wildlife sanctuaries, biosphere reserves, significant flora and fauna associated

- Agriculture, crops and agricultural revolutions in India
- Most important industries and power plants in India

**Reference books to study: NCERT**

(i) **Social Science – Class IX** NCERT textbook; **Contemporary India-1**

Important chapters

- Chapter 1: India Size and Location
- Chapter 2: Physical Features of India
- Chapter 3: Drainage
- Chapter 4: Climate
- Chapter 5: Natural Vegetation and Wildlife

(ii) **Social Science – Class X** NCERT textbook; **Contemporary India-2**

Important chapters

- Chapter 2: Forest and Wildlife Resources
- Chapter 3: Water Resources
- Chapter 4: Agriculture
- Chapter 5: Minerals and Energy Resources

## (d) General Sciences

- Discoveries – discoverers, scientific inventions and inventors
- Branches of sciences
- Human body organs and functions
- Diseases, deficiencies, vitamins, enzymes, drugs
- Scientific instruments and functions
- Environment, global warming, pollution and challenges,
- International environmental summits and outcomes

**Reference books to study: NCERT**

Class IX Science NCERT textbook

- Chapter 13: Why do We Fall Ill (XII) Class XI Biology
- Chapter 16: Digestion and absorption
- Chapter 17 Breathing and Exchange of Gases
- Chapter 18: Body Fluids and Circulation
- Chapter 19: Excretory Products and Their Elimination

## (e) Economy

- State of Indian Economy
- Important policies and programmes of the Government of India
- Statutory bodies and financial institutions of India in economic policy making and implementation.
- Significant items of goods and services of export and import in India.
- World bodies concerned with international diplomacy, world order, economic policy formulation, international trade, international finance and credit, arts and environment etc. (e.g. UNO UNESCO, WHO, World bank, IMF ADB, ICJ, UNDP, UNFCCC etc).

**Reference books to study: NCERT**

**(i) Social Science – Class X** NCERT textbook; **Understanding Economic Development-**

Important chapters

- Chapter 2: Sectors of the Indian Economy
- Chapter 4: Globalisation and Indian Economy
- Chapter 4: Agriculture
- Chapter 5: Minerals and Energy Resources

**(ii) Indian Economic Development, Class XI** NCERT textbook

- Chapter 4: Poverty
- Chapter 9: Environment and Sustainable Development

Reference to NCERT books upto that of std. 12th may be made for other topics/chapters as well not indicated above. The above recommendation of chapters from the NCERT books is not exhaustive but only indicative and are some topics of high probability from which questions are likely to emanate. The recommended books are also available online on the website of NCERT https://ncertbooks.ncert.gov.in/ and pdf copies of these books or e-books can also be downloaded.

## 2. Topics of Current Affairs and General Awareness

- **Sports**
  - International sporting events, venues/host countries, winners etc.
  - India's performance at different international events viz. Olympics, Asian Games, Common Wealth games etc.
  - Indian Sports persons and international and national achievements
- International and national days (viz. Earth-day, National youth day etc.)
- Books and authors especially those in recent news
- Indian Culture
  - Festivals and fairs
  - Folk songs and dances
  - Arts and folk theaters
  - Regional languages and dialects
- Indian space, defence, nuclear and other programmes
- Awards and awardees, viz. Bharat Ratna, Padma Vibhushan, arts, sports, films and awards for valour and defence services.
- Famous monuments and structures of the world and India (e.g. wonders of the world and monuments recognised as UNESCO World Heritage sites and those in news)
- Important acronyms

## 3. Preparing for Current Affairs: Salient Points for Preparation

**Newspapers** are the most important resource material for current affairs preparation. Read a national daily, at least a few months prior to the CUET examination. If you have not been in the habit of newspaper reading then do so at least in the last couple of months. Not all news items are important from the perspective of the CUET but look out for the topics of national and international significance. Also try to identify those issues of current affairs which are connected to the topics specified in the list above viz, sports, international events, culture, fairs and festivals, space programme nuclear programme defence issues, awards, etc. A candidate should also be on look out as to what are the current issues which are sharply in focus or have been in news for long.

Similarly, **magazines** are a good source of information as the important issues are identified and complied. Not all articles therein are relevant but be selective and identify articles on issues as mentioned above. Look out for sections on news capsules which provide a summary of the important news events. **Radio & television** news are also an aid to current affairs but focus on news capsules rather than the panel discussions or debates. Besides reference may also be made to **websites** offering such news capsules. Exclusive books on current affairs may also be useful provided these are crisp and related to the issues as highlighted. Thick voluminous guide books specifically dealing with current affairs may not be helpful and rather be a heavy draw on the limited time.

In this chapter a brief compilation information pertinent from the perspective of the examination is being given. Besides an exercise set containing nearly 200 questions from a vast range of issues is being provided. The questions are not exhaustive but surely indicative of as to what to be expected in the examination.

## 4. Compilation of Relevant Events, Facts and Other Information

**Table 1 Important Wars and Battles in Indian History**

| Date | Battle its Outcome/Significance |
|---|---|
| 326 BCE | War between Alexander and Porus at Hydaspas resulting in the defeat of the latter |
| 261 BCE | The Kalinga war in which Ashoka defeated the Kalinga forces |
| 712 CE | Invasion of Sindh by Muhammad bin Qasim |
| 1054 CE | Battle of Koppam, between the Chalukyas and the Cholas, won by the latter |
| 1191 CE | First battle of Tarain between Prithviraj Chauhan and Mohammad Ghori in which the former defeated Mohammad Ghori. |
| 1192 CE | Second battle of Tarain between Prithviraj Chauhan and Mohammad Ghori in which Prithviraj Chauhan was defeated. |
| 1526 CE | First battle of Panipat in which Babar defeated Ibrahim Lodi |
| 1527 CE | Battle of Khanwa in which Babar defeated Rana Sanga |
| 1539 CE | Battle of Chausa in which Sher Shah Suri defeated Humayun |
| 1540 CE | Battle of Kannauj in which Sher Shah Suri defeated Humayun causing his exile from India |
| 1556 CE | Second battle of Panipat in which the Mughal forces under Bairam Khan (representing Akbar) defeated Hemu |
| 1565 CE | Battle of Talikota in which the in which the combined forces of the Deccan Sultanates defeated the Vijaynagar empire |
| 1576 CE | Battle of Haldighati in which Akbar defeated Maharana Pratap |
| 1657 CE | Defeat of Dara Shikoh at the hands of Aurangzeb |
| 1665 CE | Raja Jai Singh defeated Shivaji leading to the signing of treaty of Purandar |
| 1739 CE | Nadir Shah defeated Muhammad Shah |
| 1757 CE | Battle of Plassey in which English forces defeated the Nawab of Bengal (Siraj-ud-Daula) |
| 1760 CE | Battle of Wandiwash; English forces defeated the French forces |
| 1761 CE | Third battle of Panipat, Ahmad Shah Abdali defeated the Marathas |
| 1764 CE | Battle of Buxar, English forces defeated the combined forces of, Nawab of Bengal (Mir Qasim), Nawab of Awadh (Shuja-ud-Daula) and Mughal emperor (Shah Alam) |
| 1767–69 CE | First Anglo Mysore war in which Hyder Ali defeated the British forces (East India Company) |
| 1775–82 CE | First Anglo Maratha war. The Maratha defeated the British forces. |
| 1780-84 CE | Second Anglo Mysore war. Hyder Ali died while fighting the British forces. Treaty of Mangalore signed between the British and Tipu Sultan. |
| 1790–92 CE | Third Anglo Mysore war. Tipu Sultan was defeated treaty of Seringapatam was signed. |
| 1798–99 CE | Fourth Anglo Mysore war. Tipu Sultan was defeated and killed |
| 1803–05 CE | 2nd Anglo Maratha war, British defeated the Marathas |
| 1817–18 CE | 3rd Anglo Maratha war, British defeated the Marathas convincingly |

**Table 2 Important Events in the Indian National Movement**

| Year | Event and significance |
|---|---|
| 1857 CE | Indian revolt/sepoy mutiny which takes shape of the **First War of Independence** |
| 1858 CE | Suppression of the revolt by the British |
| 1861 CE | Transfer of power to the British crown from the East India Company, passing of the **Government of India Act of 1858** for this purpose |
| 1885 CE | Establishment of the Indian National Congress |
| 1905 CE | **Partition of Bengal** |
| 1909 CE | **Morley-Minto reforms**<br>Indian Councils Act of 1909 passed, bringing a limited involvement of Indians in the governance |
| 1911CE | Annulment of the partition of Bengal |
| 1911 CE | Shifting of capital from Calcutta to Delhi |
| 1917 CE | **Champaran Satyagraha** (agrarian movement against forced indigo cultivation) bringing Mahatma Gandhi to the national scene |
| 1918 CE | **Kheda Satyagraha** launched by Mahatma Gandhi, an agrarian movement against taxation (land revenue) on account of famine |
| 1919 CE | **Rowlatt Act** passed giving the authorities power to arrest without trials.<br>**Jallianwala Bagh massacre** on 13th of April on the day of Baisakhi<br>Montagu-Chelmsford reforms<br>Government of India Act 1919 introducing diarchy |
| 1920 CE | **Non-cooperation movement** launched by Mahatma Gandhi |
| 1922 CE | ■ **Chauri Chaura Incident**<br>■ Withdrawal of non-cooperation movement by Mahatma Gandhi post Chauri Chaura incident |
| 1927 CE | Simon Commission established to study the effect of reforms introduced in 1919. Opposed by national leaders as the commission was having no Indian representation. |
| 1928 CE | Bardoli Satyagraha, an agragarian movement led by Sardar Vallabh Bhai Patel, against taxation of farmers facing natural calamities |
| 1929 CE | **Demand of Poorna Swaraj** made in the Lahore Congress session as the objective of the national movement |
| 1930 CE | ■ Launch of **Salt satyagraha** and beginning of the **Dandi March** on the 12th of March 1930. Civil Disobedience movement launched with it.<br>■ First Round Table conference |
| 1931 CE | **Gandhi Irwin pact** |
| 1935 CE | **Government of India Act of 1935**, provided for provincial autonomy to some extent and devolution of powers to the provinces |
| 1937 CE | Indian Provincial elections |
| 1942 CE | On the 6th of August 1942, the **Quit India movement** was launched<br>Cripps mission; a failed mission to secure Indian co-operation in the 2nd World War |

| Year | Event and significance |
|---|---|
| 1945 CE | **Wavell Plan** and Shimla conference to discuss transfer of power, not successful as Indian National Congress and Indian Muslim league did not agree. |
| 1946 CE | Naval mutiny |
| 1947 CE | On 15th of August India gains **independence** |
| 1948 CE | On 30th January **assassination of Mahatma Gandhi** |
| 1949 CE | Constituent assembly **adopts the Indian Constitution** of the 26th November |
| 1950 CE | India becomes a **Republic** |

**Table 3 Some Important Articles of the Indian Constitution**

| Article | Description |
|---|---|
| **Fundamental Rights** | |
| Article 14–18 | Right to Equality |
| Article 19–22 | Right to Freedom |
| Article 23–24 | Right Against Exploitation |
| Article 25–28 | Right to Freedom of Religion |
| Article 29–30 | Cultural and Educational Rights |
| Article 32 | Right to Constitutional Remedies |
| **Other Important Features** | |
| Article 36–51 | Directive Principles of State Policy |
| Article 51 A | Fundamental Duties |
| Article 53 | Vesting of the executive power of the union in the President of India and exercise of this power directly or through officer's subordinate to him |
| Article 54–61 | Manner of election of president, term of office, impeachment of the President etc. |
| Article 73 | Extent of the executive power of the Union |
| Article 74–75 | Provisions pertaining to appointment of Prime Minister and Council of Ministers, aid and advice to the President in discharge of executive functions |
| Article 79–123 | Constitution of Parliament, officers of Parliament, conduct of business, disqualification of members, legislative procedure in financial matters etc. (Article 110–111 pertaining to Money Bill) |
| Article 124–147 | Provisions pertaining to establishment of Union judiciary, the Supreme Court of India its powers and functions |
| Article 352 | Imposition of national emergency by the President of India when security threatened by external aggression or armed rebellion, other provisions as to the ministers. |
| Article 356 | Imposition of President's rule in a state on breakdown of Constitutional machinery |
| Article 360 | Imposition of Financial emergency |
| Article 368 | Powers of Parliament to amend the Constitution |
| Article 370 | Special provision of the State of Jammu and Kashmir which now stands abrogated |

**Table 4 Presidents of India**

| S. No. | Name | From | To |
|---|---|---|---|
| 1. | Dr. Rajendra Prasad | January 26th, 1950 | May 13th, 1962 |
| 2. | Dr Sarvepalli Radhakrishnan | May 13th, 1962 | May 13th, 1967 |
| 3. | Dr Zakir Hussain | May 13th, 1967 | May 3rd, 1969 |
| 4. | Varahagiri Venkata Giri | May 3rd, 1969 | July 20th, 1969 |
| 5. | Mohammad Hidayatullah | July 20th, 1969 | August 24th, 1969 |
| 6. | Varahagiri Venkata Giri | August 24th, 1969 | August 24th, 1974 |
| 7. | Fakhruddin Ali Ahmed | August 24th, 1974 | February 11th, 1977 |
| 8. | Basappa Danappa Jatti | February 11th, 1977 | July 25th, 1977 |
| 9. | Neelam Sanjiva Reddy | July 25th, 1977 | July 25th, 1982 |
| 10. | Giani Zail Singh | July 25th, 1982 | July 25th, 1987 |
| 11. | Ramaswamy Venkataraman | July 25th, 1987 | July 25th, 1992 |
| 12. | Shankar Dayal Sharma | July 25th, 1992 | July 25th, 1997 |
| 13. | Kocheril Raman Narayanan | July 25th, 1997 | July 25th, 2002 |
| 14. | Dr. A.P.J. Abdul Kalam | July 25th, 2002 | July 25th, 2007 |
| 15. | Pratibha Patil | July 25th, 2007 | July 25th, 2012 |
| 16. | Pranab Mukherjee | July 25th, 2012 | July 25th, 2017 |
| 17. | Ram Nath Kovind | July 25th, 2017 | Till date |

**Table 5 Prime Ministers of India**

| S. No. | Name | Term of Office |
|---|---|---|
| 1. | Jawahar Lal Nehru (1889–1964) | August 15th, 1947 to May 27th, 1964 |
| 2. | Gulzarilal Nanda(1898–1998) | May 27th, 1964 to June 9th 1964 |
| 3. | Lal Bahadur Shastri (1904–1966) | June 9th, 1964 to January 11th,1966 |
| 4. | Gulzarilal Nanda (1898–1998) | January 11th, 1966, January 24th |
| 5. | Indira Gandhi (1917–1984) | January 24th, 1966 to March 24th |
| 6. | Morarji Desai (1896–1995) | March 24th, 1977–July 28th 1979 |
| 7. | Charan Singh (1902–1987) | July 28th, 1979 to January 14th, 1980 |
| 8. | Indira Gandhi (1917–1984) | Januaary 14th, 1980 to Oct 31st, 1984 |
| 9. | Rajiv Gandhi (1944–1991) | Oct 31st, 1984 to Dec 2nd, 1989 |
| 10. | V. P. Singh (1931–2008) | Dec 2nd, 1989 to Nov 10th, 1990 |
| 11. | Chandra Shekhar (1927–2007) | Nov 10th, 1990 to June 21st, 1991 |
| 12. | P. V. Narasimha Rao (1921–2004) | June 21st, 1991 to May 16th, 1996 |
| 13. | Atal Bihari Vajpayee (1924-2018) | May 16th, 1996 to June 1st, 1996 |
| 14. | H. D. Deve Gowda (1933–) | June 1st, 1996 to April 21st, 1997 |
| 15. | Inder Kumar Gujral (1919–2012) | April 21st, 1997 to March 19th, 1998 |
| 16. | Atal Bihari Vajpayee (1924–2018) | March 19th 1998 to May 22nd, 2004 |
| 17. | Manmohan Singh (1932–) | May 22nd, 2004 to May 26th, 2014 |
| 18. | Narendra Modi (1950–) | 2014–Present |

**Table 6 Country, Capital & Currency**

| Country Name | Capital | Currency |
|---|---|---|
| Afghanistan | Kabul | Afghani |
| Albania | Tirana | Lek |
| Algeria | Algiers | Dinar |
| Angola | Luanda | New Kwanza |
| Antigua and Barbuda | Saint John's | East Caribbean Dollar |
| Argentina | Buenos Aires | Peso |
| Armenia | Yerevan | Dram |
| Australia | Canberra | Australian dollar |
| Austria | Vienna | Euro (formerly Schilling) |
| Azerbaijan | Baku | Manat |
| The Bahamas | Nassau | Bahamian dollar |
| Bahrain | Manama | Bahrain dinar |
| Bangladesh | Dhaka | Taka |
| Barbados | Bridgetown | Barbados dollar |
| Belarus | Minsk | Belarusian ruble |
| Belgium | Brussels | Euro (formerly Belgian Franc) |
| Bhutan | Thimphu | Ngultrum |
| Bolivia | La Paz (administrative); Sucre (judicial) | Boliviano |
| Bosnia and Herzegovina | Sarajevo | Convertible Mark |
| Botswana | Gaborone | Pula |
| Brazil | Brasilia | Real |
| Bulgaria | Sofia | Lev |
| Cambodia | Phnom Penh | Riel |
| Cameroon | Yaounde | CFA Franc |
| Canada | Ottawa | Canadian Dollar |
| Chile | Santiago | Chilean Peso |
| China | Beijing | Chinese Yuan |
| Colombia | Bogota | Colombian Peso |
| Republic of the Congo | Brazzaville | CFA Franc |
| Zimbabwe | Harare | U.S. Dollar |
| Costa Rica | San Jose | Colón |
| Croatia | Zagreb | Croatian |
| Cuba | Havana | Cuban Peso |
| Cyprus | Nicosia | Euro |
| Czech Republic | Prague | Koruna |
| Denmark | Copenhagen | Danish Krone |

| Country Name | Capital | Currency |
|---|---|---|
| Djibouti | Djibouti | Djiboutian Franc |
| Dominican Republic | Santo Domingo | Dominican Peso |
| Ecuador | Quito | U.S. Dollar |
| Egypt | Cairo | Egyptian Pound |
| El Salvador | San Salvador | Colón; U.S. Dollar |
| Estonia | Tallinn | Estonia Kroon; Euro |
| Ethiopia | Addis Ababa | Birr |
| Fiji | Suva | Fiji Dollar |
| Finland | Helsinki | Euro (formerly Markka) |
| France | Paris | Euro (formerly French Franc) |
| Georgia | Tbilisi | Lari |
| Germany | Berlin | Euro (formerly Deutsche Mark) |
| Ghana | Accra | Cedi |
| Greece | Athens | Euro (formerly Drachma) |
| Grenada | Saint George's | East Caribbean Dollar |
| Guatemala | Guatemala City | Quetzal |
| Guinea | Conakry | Guinean Franc |
| Guyana | Georgetown | Guyanese Dollar |
| Haiti | Port-au-Prince | Gourde |
| Honduras | Tegucigalpa | Lempira |
| Hungary | Budapest | Forint |
| Iceland | Reykjavik | Icelandic Króna |
| India | New Delhi | Indian Rupee |
| Indonesia | Jakarta | Rupiah |
| Iran | Tehran | Rial |
| Iraq | Baghdad | Iraqi Dinar |
| Ireland | Dublin | Euro (formerly Irish Pound [Punt]) |
| Israel | Jerusalem* | Shekel |
| Italy | Rome | Euro (formerly Lira) |
| Jamaica | Kingston | Jamaican Dollar |
| Japan | Tokyo | Yen |
| Jordan | Amman | Jordanian Dinar |
| Kazakhstan | Nur Sultan | Tenge |
| Kenya | Nairobi | Kenya Shilling |
| North Korea | Pyongyang | Won |
| South Korea | Seoul | Won |
| Kuwait | Kuwait City | Kuwaiti Dinar |

| Country Name | Capital | Currency |
|---|---|---|
| Kyrgyzstan | Bishkek | Som |
| Laos | Vientiane | New Kip |
| Latvia | Riga | Lats |
| Lebanon | Beirut | Lebanese Pound |
| Lesotho | Maseru | Maluti |
| Liberia | Monrovia | Liberian Dollar |
| Libya | Tripoli | Libyan Dinar |
| Liechtenstein | Vaduz | Swiss Franc |
| Lithuania | Vilnius | Litas |
| Luxembourg | Luxembourg | Euro (formerly Luxembourg Franc) |
| Madagascar | Antananarivo | Malagasy Ariary |
| Malaysia | Kuala Lumpur | Ringgit |
| Maldives | Male | Rufiyaa |
| Mali | Bamako | CFA Franc |
| Malta | Valletta | Euro |
| Mauritius | Port Louis | Mauritian Rupee |
| Mexico | Mexico City | Mexican Peso |
| Moldova | Chisinau | Leu |
| Monaco | Monte Carlo | Euro |
| Mongolia | Ulaanbaatar | Togrog |
| Morocco | Rabat | Dirham |
| Mozambique | Maputo | Metical |
| Myanmar (Burma) | Nay Pyi Taw | Kyat |
| Namibia | Windhoek | Namibian Dollar |
| Nepal | Kathmandu | Nepalese Rupee |
| Netherlands | Amsterdam; The Hague (seat of government) | Euro (formerly Guilder) |
| New Zealand | Wellington | New Zealand Dollar |
| Nicaragua | Managua | Gold Cordoba |
| Niger | Niamey | CFA Franc |
| Nigeria | Abuja | Naira |
| Norway | Oslo | Norwegian Krone |
| Oman | Muscat | Omani Rial |
| Pakistan | Islamabad | Pakistani Rupee |
| Palestine | Ramallah, East Jerusalem | Palestine Pound |
| Panama | Panama City | Balboa; U.S. Dollar |
| Papua New Guinea | Port Moresby | Kina |

| Country Name | Capital | Currency |
|---|---|---|
| Peru | Lima | Nuevo Sol (1991) |
| Philippines | Manila | Peso |
| Poland | Warsaw | Zloty |
| Portugal | Lisbon | Euro (formerly Escudo) |
| Qatar | Doha | Qatari Riyal |
| Romania | Bucharest | Romanian Rupee |
| Russia | Moscow | Ruble |
| Rwanda | Kigali | Rwandan Franc |
| San Marino | San Marino | Euro |
| Saudi Arabia | Riyadh | Riyal |
| Senegal | Dakar | CFA Franc |
| Serbia | Belgrade | Serbian Dinar |
| Seychelles | Victoria | Seychelles Rupee |
| Sierra Leone | Freetown | Leone |
| Singapore | Singapore | Singapore Dollar |
| Slovakia | Bratislava | Euro |
| Solomon Islands | Honiara | Solomon Islands Dollar |
| Somalia | Mogadishu | Somali Shilling |
| South Africa | Pretoria (administrative); Cape Town (legislative); Bloemfontein (judiciary) | Rand |
| South Sudan | Juba | Sudanese Pound |
| Spain | Madrid | Euro (formerly Peseta) |
| Sri Lanka | Colombo; Sri Jayewardenepura Kotte (legislative) | Sri Lankan Rupee |
| Sudan | Khartoum | Sudanese Pound |
| Suriname | Paramaribo | Surinamese Dollar |
| Sweden | Stockholm | Krona |
| Switzerland | Berne | Swiss Franc |
| Syria | Damascus | Syrian Pound |
| Taiwan | Taipei | Taiwan Dollar |
| Tajikistan | Dushanbe | somoni |
| Tanzania | Dar es Salaam; Dodoma (legislative) | Tanzanian Shilling |
| Thailand | Bangkok | Baht |
| Trinidad and Tobago | Port-of-Spain | Trinidad and Tobago Dollar |
| Tunisia | Tunis | Tunisian Dinar |
| Turkey | Ankara | Turkish Lira (YTL) |
| Turkmenistan | Ashgabat | Manat |

| Country Name | Capital | Currency |
|---|---|---|
| Uganda | Kampala | Ugandan new Shilling |
| Ukraine | Kiev | Hryvnia |
| United Arab Emirates | Abu Dhabi | U.A.E. Dirham |
| United Kingdom | London | Pound Sterling |
| United States of America | Washington D.C. | Dollar |
| Uruguay | Montevideo | Uruguay Peso |
| Uzbekistan | Tashkent | Uzbekistani Sum |
| Vatican City (Holy See) | Vatican City | Euro |
| Venezuela | Caracas | Bolivar |
| Vietnam | Hanoi | Dong |
| Yemen | Sanaa | Rial |
| Zambia | Lusaka | Kwacha |

**Table 7 Important National Parks of India:**

| Name | State | Fauna |
|---|---|---|
| Anamudi Shola National Park | Kerala | Elephant, Tiger, Nilgiri tahr, Gaur, Spotted Deer, Sambar, Grizzled Giant Squirrel, Hanuman Langur, Sloth Bear, Flying Squirrels |
| Bandhavgarh National Park | Madhya Pradesh | **Bengal tiger**, striped hyena, caracal, gaur, sambar deer, nilgai, barking deer, chital, |
| Bandipur National Park | Karnataka | Chital, **Bengal tiger**, gray langurs, Indian giant squirrel, gaur, leopard, sambar deer, Indian elephants, honey buzzard, red-headed vulture |
| Bannerghatta National Park | Karnataka | **Tiger**, sloth bear, peacock, elephant, sambar deer, mouse deer |
| Betla National Park | Jharkhand | **Tiger**, Indian bison, elephant, hyenas, monkey, leopard |
| Bhitarkanika National Park | Odisha | Mangroves, **saltwater crocodile**, white crocodile, Indian python, black ibis, wild pigs, rhesus monkeys, olive ridley sea turtle, chital |
| Bison (Rajbari) National Park | Tripura | **Bisons** |
| Blackbuck National Park, Velavadar | Gujarat | **Blackbucks**, the endangered Indian grey wolf, the nocturnal striped hyena, Indian fox, golden jackal, jungle cat and many small mammals like hare, gerbil, field mice, mongoose and hedgehog. |

| Name | State | Fauna |
|---|---|---|
| Buxa Tiger Reserve | West Bengal | Indian leopard, Bengal tiger, giant squirrel, gaur, chital and wild boar Eurasian griffon, Amur falcon<br>Endangered species include leopard cat, Bengal florican, regal python, Chinese pangolin etc. |
| Campbell Bay National Park | Andaman and Nicobar Islands | Crab-eating Macaque, the Megapode, the Giant Robber crab, the Nicobar pigeon, Olive Ridley turtles as well as Leatherback turtles, Wild Boar, deer and Civet cats. |
| Dachigam National Park | Jammu and Kashmir | Hangul or Kashmir stag, musk deer, snow leopard, Himalayan serow, long-tailed marmot, Kashmir grey langur, etc. |
| Desert National Park | Rajasthan | **Great Indian bustard** |
| Dudhwa National Park | Uttar Pradesh | **Tiger**, Sambar deer, hog deer |
| Gangotri National Park | Uttarakhand | Gaumukh Glacier |
| Gir Forest National Park | Gujarat | **Asiatic lion** |
| Great Himalayan National Park | Himachal Pradesh | **UNESCO World Heritage Site** |
| Guindy National Park | Tamil Nadu | Chitals, blackbucks, jackals |
| Gulf of Mannar Marine National Park | Tamil Nadu | has 8 species of whales and 21 small coral islands |
| Kanha National Park | Madhya Pradesh | Barasingha or swamp deer |
| Kanger Ghati National Park | Chhattisgarh | Tigers, leopards, mouse deer, wild cat, chital, sambar, barking deer, jackals, langurs, rhesus macaque, sloth bear, flying squirrel, wild boar, striped hyena, rabbits, pythons, cobra, crocodiles, monitor lizards and snakes |
| Kaziranga National Park | Assam | **Indian rhinoceros,Royal Bengal Tiger**, Asiatic Water Buffalo, Asian Elephant, Eastern Swamp Deer |
| Keoladeo National Park | Rajasthan | More than 350 species of birds, 27 species of mammals, 13 species of reptiles, 7 amphibians and 43 fish |
| Kudremukh National Park | Karnataka | Leaping leopard, tiger, the endangered lion-tailed macaque, langur, spotted deer, barking deer, sloth bear, gaur, sambar, giant flying squirrels, etc. |
| Kuno National Park | Madhya Pradesh | **Asiatic Lion Reintroduction Project**, India's first cheetah sanctuary |
| Mahatma Gandhi Marine National Park | Andaman and Nicobar Islands | Corals, sea turtles, etc. |
| Manas National Park | Assam | Assam roofed turtle, hispid hare, golden langur and pygmy hog |
| Mandla Plant Fossils National Park | Madhya Pradesh | Tiger, leopard, wild dog, gaur, chinkara, hyena, jackal, sloth bear, Nilgai, Chausingha, etc. |

| Name | State | Fauna |
|---|---|---|
| Marine National Park, Gulf of Kutch | Gujarat | **Corals, sponges, jellyfish**, endangered sea turtles such as green sea turtles, olive ridleys and leatherbacks, dugongs, Indo-Pacific humpback dolphins, blue whales |
| Mount Harriet National Park | Andaman and Nicobar Islands | Important bird area as attributed by Bird Life International<br>Andaman wild pigs (an endangered species), saltwater crocodiles, turtles and robber crabs. The park is also a butterfly hotspot. |
| Nagarhole National Park | Karnataka | **Bengal tiger**, Indian leopard, dhole, sloth bear and the striped hyena.<br>Chital, sambar deer, barking deer, four-horned antelope, gaur, wild boar, and **Indian elephant**.<br>Other mammals-gray langur, bonnet macaque, jungle cat, leopard cat, **slender loris**, small Indian civet and Asian palm civet, Indian brown mongoose. |
| Nanda Devi National Park | Uttarakhand | **UNESCO World Heritage Site, UNESCO World Biosphere Reserve** |
| Panna National Park | Madhya Pradesh | Tiger, leopard, sloth bear; a number of cat species – including jungle, rusty-spotted, desert, toddy, and civet; spotted deer, nilgai, four-horned antelope, hyena, crocodiles, etc. |
| Pench National Park | Madhya Pradesh | Rudyard Kipling's 'Jungle Book' was set in this NP. |
| Periyar National Park | Kerala | Malabar parakeet, Malabar grey hornbill, Nilgiri laughing thrush, Nilgiri blue robin, great hornbill, Malabar pied hornbill, lion-tailed macaque, hairy-winged bat |
| Rajaji National Park | Uttarakhand | Mainly known for **elephants**, **tigers**, leopards and several species of birds, reptiles and mammals. |
| Ranthambore National Park | Rajasthan | **Tiger Reserve** |
| Sariska Tiger Reserve | Rajasthan | **Tiger** |
| Satpura National Park | Madhya Pradesh | Leopard, sambar, chital, Indian muntjac, nilgai, four-horned antelope, Chinkara, wild boar, bear, black buck, fox, porcupine, flying squirrel, mouse deer, and Indian giant squirrel |
| Silent Valley National Park | Kerala | **Indian bison**, Travancore flying squirrel, Salim Ali's fruit bat, Stripe-necked mongoose, Blue-winged parakeet, Crimson-backed sunbird |
| Simlipal National Park | Odisha | **Tiger**, leopard, Asian elephant, sambar, barking deer, gaur, jungle cat, wild boar |
| Sundarbans National Park | West Bengal | **UNESCO World Heritage Site** |
| Tadoba National Park | Maharashtra | **Tiger** |
| Valley of Flowers National Park | Uttarakhand | **UNESCO World Heritage Site**, Most beautiful national park in the world |
| Valmiki National Park | Bihar | **Tiger Reserve** |

**Table 8 Biosphere Reserves**

Twelve of the eighteen biosphere reserves which are a part of the World Network of Biosphere Reserves, based on the UNESCO Man and the Biosphere (MAB) Programme list, are:

| S. No. | Name | States/UT | Year |
|---|---|---|---|
| 1 | Nilgiri Biosphere Reserve | Tamil Nadu, Kerala and Karnataka | 2000 |
| 2 | Gulf of Mannar Biosphere Reserve | Tamil Nadu | 2001 |
| 3 | Sundarbans Biosphere Reserve | West Bengal | 2001 |
| 4 | Nanda Devi Biosphere Reserve | Uttarakhand | 2004 |
| 5 | Nokrek Biosphere Reserve | Meghalaya | 2009 |
| 6 | Pachmarhi Biosphere Reserve | Madhya Pradesh | 2009 |
| 7 | Simlipal Biosphere Reserve | Odisha | 2009 |
| 8 | Great Nicobar Biosphere Reserve | Andaman & Nicobar Islands | 2013 |
| 9 | Achanakmar-Amarkantak Biosphere Reserve | Chhattisgarh, Madhya Pradesh | 2012 |
| 10 | Agasthyamalai Biosphere Reserve | Kerala and Tamil Nadu | 2016 |
| 11 | Khangchendzonga National Park | Sikkim | 2018 |
| 12 | Panna Biosphere Reserve | Madhya Pradesh | 2020 |

## Important Discoveries & Inventions

**Table 9 Inventions and Discoveries of Subjects Related to Physical Sciences**

| Invention/discovery | Inventor/Discoverer |
|---|---|
| Aeroplane | Wright brothers |
| Air Brake | Westinghouse |
| Air conditioner | Willis Carrier |
| Anemometer(wind speed) | Leon Battista Alberti |
| Atomic bomb | Robert Oppenheimer, Edward Teller, Hans Bethe, Enrico Fermi, Richard Feynman and other scientist involved in the Manhattan project |
| Automobile | Karl Benz |
| Barometer | Evangelista Torricelli |
| Battery | Alessandro Volta |
| Bicycle | K Macmillan |
| Cathode Ray Tube | Ferdinand Braun |
| Centigrade scale | Anders Celsius |
| Computer | Charles Babbage |
| Diesel Engine | Rudolf Diesel |
| Dynamite | Alfred Nobel |
| Electric Bulb | Thomas Edison |
| Electricity | Benjamin Franklin |
| Electromagnetic induction | Michael Faraday |

| Invention/discovery | Inventor/Discoverer |
|---|---|
| Gravity | Isaac Newton |
| Gramophone | Thomas Alva Edison |
| Induction motor | Nikola Tesla |
| Laser | Theodore H. Maiman, Charles Hard Townes |
| LED | Oleg Losev, Nick Holonyak |
| Lift | Elisha Otis |
| Liquid Crystal Displays(LCD) | George H. Heilmeier |
| Mobile Phone | John F. Mitchell & Martin Cooper (Motorola), Eric Tigerstedt (Finnish inventor), |
| Microscope | Z. Hansen |
| Nuclear Reactor | Enrico Fermi |
| Printing Press | Johannes Gutenberg |
| Radio | Guglielmo Giovanni Marconi |
| Railway Engine | George Stephenson |
| Refrigerator | William Cullen |
| Rocket Engine, | Robert Goddard, Fritz Van Opel |
| Seismograph | John Milne |
| Steam engine | Thomas Newcomen (early steam engine), James Watt (later steam engine) |
| Telegraph | Samuel Morse |
| Telephone | Alexander Graham Bell |
| Telescope | Hans Lippershey and Zacharias Janssen; later Galileo |
| Television | John Logie Baird |
| Thermometer | Gabriel Farenheit |
| Transistor | William Shockley, John Bardeen &Walter Brattain |
| Typewriter | Christopher Latham Sholes |
| Watch | Peter Henlein |
| **Inventions and Discoveries of Subjects Related to Medical Science** | |
| Anesthesia | William Morton |
| Anthrax Vaccine | Louis Pasteur |
| Aspirin | Felix Hofmann |
| Blood Group | Karl Landsteiner |
| Cell | Robert Hooke |
| Cholera Vaccine | Waldemar Haffkine |
| DNA sequencer | Lloyd M. Smith |
| Homeopathy | Samuel Hahnemann |
| Nucleus | Robert Brown |

| Invention/discovery | Inventor/Discoverer |
|---|---|
| Pasteurisation | Louis Pasteur |
| Penicillin | Alexander Fleming |
| Polio Vaccine | Jonas Edward Stalk |
| Rubella Vaccine | Maurice Hilleman |
| Vitamins | Casimir Funk |
| **Inventions and Discoveries of Subjects Related to Chemical Science** | |
| Atoms | John Dalton |
| Electrons | J.J. Thompson |
| Hydrogen | Henry Cavendish |
| Inert Gases | Sir William Ramsay |
| Oxygen | Carl Wilhelm Scheele |
| Periodic Table | Dmitri Mendeleev |
| Protons | Ernest Rutherford |
| Radioactivity | Henri Becquerel |
| Radium | Marie and Pierre Curie |
| X-Ray | William Rontgen |

**Table 10 Important Inventions in the Field of Computers, Internet & Communication Technology**

| Invention | Inventor |
|---|---|
| C Language | Dennis Ritchie |
| C++ | Bjarne Stroustrup |
| Cable modem | Rouzbeh Yassini |
| Computer | Charles Babbage |
| Email | Ray Tomlinson |
| GPS | Ivan A.,Getting Roger L Easton, Bradford Parkinson |
| JAVA | James Gosling |
| Laptop | Adam Osborne |
| Mobile Phone | John F. Mitchell &Martin Cooper (Motorola), Eric Tigerstedt (Finnish inventor), |
| Python | Guido Van Rossum |
| Search Engine | Alan Emtage |
| Smartphone | IBM |
| Surface Computing | Microsoft |
| TCP/IP | Bob Kahn, Vint Cerf & Ray Tomlinson |
| Webcam | Quentin Straford Fraser and Paul Jardetzky |
| World Wide Web | Tim Berners and Robert Cailliau |

**Table 11 United Nations & Other Important International Organisations**

| International organisations | Headquarters | Main Functions/Objective |
|---|---|---|
| United Nations Organisation | New York, USA | Promotion of **International peace and security** |
| United Nations Children's Emergency Fund (UNICEF) | New York, USA | Advocates the protection of **children rights,** help meet their basic needs expand their opportunities to reach their full potential |
| United Nations Population Fund (UNFPA) | New York, USA | It is the **sexual and reproductive health** agency of United Nations looking after issues like **safe pregnancy, safe childbirth,** etc. |
| UN Women | New York, USA | The United Nations entity for **gender equality and empowerment of women**. |
| United Nations Security Council (UNSC) | New York, USA | One of the six principal organs of the United Nations charged with ensuring **international peace and security.** |
| International Monetary Fund (IMF) | Washington DC, United States | International organisation charged with surveillance, financial assistance and technical assistance to promote the **stability of the International Monetary and financial system**. Also called Bretton woods organisation. |
| World Bank Group (WBG) | Washington DC, United States | International organisation dedicated to providing **financing, advice and research to developing nations**, to get their economic advancement. It acts as an organisation that attempts to **fight poverty** and offers **developmental assistance** to middle and low-income countries. Also called Bretton woods organisation. |
| World Health Organisation (WHO) | Geneva, Switzerland | International organisation responsible for providing leadership on **global health** matters, shaping the health research agenda, setting norms and standards, articulating evidence-based policy options, providing technical support to countries and monitoring and assessing health trends. |
| International Labour Organisation | Geneva, Switzerland | Aims to promote **rights at work**, encourage decent **employment opportunities**, enhance **social protection** and strengthen dialogue on work related issues. |
| International Committee of the Red Cross | Geneva, Switzerland | Its an exclusive **humanitarian assistance** to protect the **lives and dignity of the victims of war** and internal violence and to provide them assistance. |
| World Trade Organisation | Geneva, Switzerland | An international organisation administering **trade agreements,** handling trade disputes, monitoring trade policies etc. |

| International organisations | Headquarters | Main Functions/Objective |
|---|---|---|
| UNAIDS | Geneva, Switzerland | An organisation aiming to **end AIDs** as a public health threat by 2030 |
| United Nations Educational Scientific and Cultural Organisation (UNESCO) | Paris, France | To promote collaboration amongst nations through **education, science, culture** and communication and enhance universal respect for justice for rule of law, human rights, fundamental freedom, etc. |
| Organisation for Economic Cooperation and Development (OECD) | Paris, France | To achieve the highest **sustainable economic growth** and a rising standard of living to contribute to the **development of the world economy**. |
| United Nations Industrial Development Organisation (UNIDO) | Vienna, Austria | Assists countries in **economic and industrial** development |
| International Atomic Energy Agency (IAEA) | Vienna, Austria | International body under the UN which functions as the global focal point for **international nuclear cooperation** |
| Organisation of Petroleum Exporting Countries (OPEC) | Vienna, Austria | International **organisation of petroleum producing countries** to unify and coordinate petroleum policies amongst the member countries. |
| Commonwealth of Nations | London, United Kingdom | Association of 54 sovereign nations earlier called the British Commnon Wealth of Nations, working towards shared goals of prosperity, democracy and peace. |
| Amnesty International | London, United Kingdom | International non-governmental organisation which seeks to publicise violations of human rights by governments and other entities. |
| Food and Agricultural Organisation (FAO) | Rome, Italy | Help eliminate **hunger, food insecurity** and **malnutrition**. Make agriculture, forestry and fisheries more prodective and sustainable to reduce rural poverty. |
| Association of Southeast Asian Nations (ASEAN) | Jakarta, Indonesia | To promote the **economic growth, social progress and cultural development** in the region and to promote regional peace and stability. |
| Asia-Pacific Economic Cooperation (APEC) | Queenstown, Singapore | To promote and **facilitate economic growth** and the **improvement of living standards** of the member countries in the Asia-Pacific region. |
| International Renewable Energy Agency | Abu Dhabi (UAE) | An intergovernmental organisation which is mandated to facilitate, advance knowledge and promote the adoption and use of **renewable energy** |

| International organisations | Headquarters | Main Functions/Objective |
|---|---|---|
| South Asian Association for Regional Cooperation | Kathmandu, Nepal | Promote the **welfare** of the peoples of South Asia and improve the quality of life |
| Indian Ocean Rim Association for Regional Cooperation | Ebene, Mauritius | To promote **sustainable growth** and **balanced development** of the region and the member states |
| Worldwide Fund for Nature | Gland, Switzerland | An international organisation to help local communities conserve the natural resources they depend upon, transform markets and policies towards sustainability and protect and restore species and their habitats. |
| World Economic Forum | Cologny-Geneva, Switzerland | An international organisation(not for profit foundation) for public-private cooperation, funded by 1000 member companies to engage business, political academic and other leaders to shape **global regional** and **industry agendas.** |
| United Nations Environment Programme (UNEP) | Nairobi, Kenya | A UN body which aims at providing leadership for caring for the **environment** and enable nations and peoples to **improve their quality of life** without compromising that of the future generations. |
| United Nations High Commission for Refugees (UNHCR) | Geneva, Switzerland | UN agency mandated to aid and protect the refugees forcibly displaced people and stateless people and to assist in their repatriation, local integration or resettlement in a third country. |
| International Court of Justice (ICJ) | The Hague, Netherlands | A principal judicial organ of the UN to **settle** in accordance with the **international law, legal disputes** submitted by the states and to give advisory opinions on legal questions referred to it by the authorised UN organs and specialised agencies. |
| International Solar Alliance | Gurugram, Haryana, India | A group of 105 **sunshine countries**, lying completely or partly within the tropics with the objective of efficient consumption of **solar energy**, reduce dependence on fossil fuels. |
| UN-Habitat | Nairobi, Kenya | A UN agency for human settlement, to **promote environmentally sustainable towns and cities** with the goal of providing adequate shelter for all |
| United Nations Conference on Trade and Development (UNCTAD) | Geneva, Switzerland | Apart of UN secretariat dealing with trade **development and investment issues** with the goals to maximise trade investment and development opportunities of the developing countries and assist them in their effort to integrate into the world economy on an equitable basis. |

| International organisations | Headquarters | Main Functions/Objective |
|---|---|---|
| United Nations Development Programme (UNDP) | New York, USA | A UN institution mandated to **end poverty**, build democratic governance, rule of law and inclusive institutions. |
| World Food Programme (WFP) | Rome, Italy | A **food assistance** branch of the United Nations focussing on hunger and food security. Its objective include, saving lives, protecting livelihoods in emergencies, support or re-store food security and nutrition and rebuild livelihoods in fragile settings. |

**Table 12 Some Important National & International Days as Observed in India**

| Date/Period | Important Day/Event |
|---|---|
| **January** | |
| 4th – 10th | Oil Conservation Week |
| 10th – 16th | Road Safety Week |
| 12th | National Youth Day |
| 15th | Army Day |
| 15th – 21st | Pin Code Week |
| 23rd | Netaji Subhas Chandra's Birthday Ann./National Day of Patriotism/ Desh Prem Divas |
| 25th | India Tourism Day |
| 26th | Republic Day |
| 26th | International Customs Day |
| 30th | Martyrs Day(Mahatma Gandhi's Death Anniversary) |
| 30th | National Cleanliness Day |
| **February** | |
| 24th | Excise Day |
| **March** | |
| 4th – 10th | National Safety Week |
| 8th | International Women's Day |
| 12th | Dandi March Day |
| 15th | Consumers Day |
| 16th | Immunisation Day |
| 21st | World Forestry Day |
| 21st | International Day for the Elimination of Racial Discrimination |
| 22nd | World Day for Water |

| Date/Period | Important Day/Event |
|---|---|
| 23rd | Martyrdom Day of Bhagat Singh |
| 23rd | World Meteorological Day |
| 24th | World TB Day |
| **April** | |
| 1st – 7th | Prevention of Blindness Week |
| 7th | World Health Day |
| 7th – 14th | Handloom Week |
| 13th | Jallianwala Bagh Massacre/Baisakhi |
| 14th | Birth Anniversary of Dr. Ambedkar |
| 14th | Customs Day |
| 14th – 20th | Fire Service Week |
| 22nd | World Earth Day |
| 23rd | World Book Day |
| **May** | |
| 1st | International Labour Day/May Day |
| 3rd | World Press Freedom Day |
| 5th | National Labour Day |
| 8th | World Red Cross Day |
| 11th | Technology Day |
| 15th | International Day of The Family |
| 17th | World Telecommunications Day |
| 24th | Common-Wealth Day |
| 31st | No Tobacco Day |
| **June** | |
| 4th | International Day of Innocent Children Victims of Aggression |
| 5th | World Environment Day |
| 26th | International Dayagainst Drug Abuse & Illicit Trafficking |
| **July** | |
| 11th | World Population Day |
| **August** | |
| 1st – 7th | World Breast-Feeding Week |
| 9th | Quit India Movement |
| 15th | Independence Day |
| 20th | Rajiv Gandhi's Birth Anniversary (Sadbhavana Diwas) |
| 23rd Aug.- 6th Sept | National Fortnight on Eye Donation |

| Date/Period | Important Day/Event |
|---|---|
| | **September** |
| $1^{st}$ – $7^{th}$ | National Nutrition Week |
| $5^{th}$ | Teacher's Day |
| $8^{th}$ | International Literacy Day |
| $14^{th}$ | Sanchayika Day |
| $14^{th}$ | Hindi Divas |
| $23^{rd}$ | World Deaf Day |
| $27^{th}$ | World Tourism Day |
| | **October** |
| $1^{st}$ | National Voluntary Blood Donation Day |
| $1^{st}$ | International Day For Elderly People |
| $1^{st}$ – $7^{th}$ | Wild Life Week |
| 1st – $10^{th}$ | International Film Festival of India |
| $2^{nd}$ | Mahatma Gandhi's Birthday |
| $2^{nd}$ | Anti-Leprosy Day |
| $2^{nd}$ – $8^{th}$ | Prevention of Blindness Week |
| $2^{nd}$ – $8^{th}$ | Anti-UN-Touchability Week |
| $6^{th}$ | World Habitat Day (Housing) |
| $8^{th}$ | Air Force Day |
| $9^{th}$ | World Post Day |
| $10^{th}$ | National Post Day |
| $11^{th}$ – $25^{th}$ | Family Welfare Fortnight |
| $13^{th}$ | International Day For Natural Disaster Reduction (IDNDR) |
| $14^{th}$ | World Standards Day |
| $16^{th}$ | World Food Day |
| $21^{st}$ | Azad Hind Day |
| $21^{st}$ | Global Iodine Deficiency Disorder(IDD) Day |
| $24^{th}$ | UN Day |
| $24^{th}$ | World Development Information Day |
| $24^{th}$ – $30^{th}$ | Disarmament And Development Week |
| $28^{th}$ | World Thrift Day |
| $31^{st}$ | Indira Gandhi's Death Anniversary (Anti-Terrorism Day) |
| | **November** |
| $2^{nd}$ | All Saints Day |
| $9^{th}$ | Legal Services Day |
| $9^{th}$ – $14^{th}$ | International Week of Science |

| Date/Period | Important Day/Event |
|---|---|
| $14^{th}$ | Nehru's Birthday-Children's Day |
| $14^{th} – 20^{th}$ | World Heritage Week |
| $15^{th} – 21^{st}$ | National Cooperative Week |
| $16^{th}$ | International Day For Tolerance and Peace |
| $19^{th}$ | National Integration Day (Indira Gandhi's Birthday) |
| $19^{th}$ Nov.-$18^{th}$ Dec | Environment Month |
| $19^{th} – 26^{th}$ | Quami Ekta Week |
| $20^{th}$ | Child Rights Day |
| $26^{th}$ | Constitution Day |
| **December** | |
| $1^{st}$ | World Aids Day |
| $2^{nd}$ | National Pollution Control Day |
| $3^{rd}$ | International Day of Disabled Persons |
| $3^{rd}$ | National Conservation Day |
| $3^{rd}$ | Bhopal Gas Tragedy Day |
| $4^{th}$ | Naval Day |
| $5^{th}$ | International Volunteer Day For Economic And Social Development |
| $6^{th}$ | Dr. Ambedkar's Mahaparinirvan Divas |
| $7^{th}$ | Flag Day |
| $8^{th}$ | Girl Child Day-Decade (1990–2000) |
| 8th | SAARC Charter Day |
| $8^{th} – 14^{th}$ | All India Handicrafts Week |
| $10^{th}$ | Human Rights Day |
| $14^{th}$ | National Energy Conservation Day |

### Important International Days as Observed by the UN in the Year 2022

| | | |
|---|---|---|
| 4 Jan | Tuesday | World Braille Day |
| 24 Jan | Monday | International Day of Education |
| 4 Feb | Friday | International Day of Human Fraternity |
| 10 Feb | Thursday | World Pulses Day |
| 11 Feb | Friday | International Day of Women and Girls in Science |
| 20 Feb | Sunday | World Day of Social Justice |
| 21 Feb | Monday | International Mother Language Day |
| 1 Mar | Tuesday | Zero Discrimination Day |
| 3 Mar | Thursday | World Wildlife Day |
| 8 Mar | Tuesday | International Women's Day |

| | | |
|---|---|---|
| 20 Mar | Sunday | International Day of Happiness |
| 21 Mar | Monday | International Day for the Elimination of Racial Discrimination |
| 21 Mar | Monday | International Day of Forests |
| 22 Mar | Tuesday | World Water Day |
| 23 Mar | Wednesday | World Meteorological Day |
| 24 Mar | Thursday | World Tuberculosis Day |
| 24 Mar | Thursday | International Day for the Right to the Truth concerning Gross Human Rights Violations and for the Dignity of Victims |
| 5 Apr | Tuesday | International Day of Conscience |
| 6 Apr | Wednesday | International Day of Sport for Development and Peace |
| 7 Apr | Thursday | United Nations' World Health Day |
| 12 Apr | Tuesday | International Day of Human Space Flight |
| 22 Apr | Friday | Earth Day |
| 23 Apr | Saturday | World Book and Copyright Day |
| 24 Apr | Sunday | International Day of Multilateralism and Diplomacy for Peace |
| 25 Apr | Monday | World Malaria Day |
| 26 Apr | Tuesday | World Intellectual Property Day |
| 28 Apr | Thursday | World Day for Safety and Health at Work |
| 3 May | Tuesday | World Press Freedom Day |
| 8 May | Sunday | Time of Remembrance and Reconciliation for Those Who Lost Their Lives during the Second World War/World Red Cross day |
| 14 May | Saturday | World Migratory Bird Day |
| 15 May | Sunday | International Day of Families |
| 16 May | Monday | International Day of Living Together in Peace |
| 21 May | Saturday | World Day for Cultural Diversity for Dialogue and Development |
| 21 May | Saturday | International Tea Day |
| 22 May | Sunday | International Day for Biological Diversity |
| 29 May | Sunday | International Day of United Nations Peacekeepers |
| 31 May | Tuesday | World No Tobacco Day |
| 1 June | Wednesday | Global Day of Parents |
| 4 June | Saturday | International Day of Innocent Children Victims of Aggression |
| 5 June | Sunday | World Environment Day |
| 7 June | Tuesday | World Food Safety Day |
| 8 June | Wednesday | World Oceans Day |
| 12 June | Sunday | World Day Against Child Labour |

| | | |
|---|---|---|
| 14 June | Tuesday | World Blood Donor Day |
| 17 June | Friday | World Day to Combat Desertification and Drought |
| 19 June | Sunday | International Day for the Elimination of Sexual Violence in Conflict |
| 20 June | Monday | World Refugee Day |
| 21 June | Tuesday | International Day of Yoga |
| 26 June | Sunday | International Day against Drug Abuse and Illicit Trafficking |
| 30 June | Thursday | International Day of Parliamentarism |
| 11 July | Monday | World Population Day |
| 15 July | Friday | World Youth Skills Day |
| 28 July | Thursday | World Hepatitis Day |
| 30 July | Saturday | International Day of Friendship |
| 30 July | Saturday | World Day against Trafficking in Persons |
| 9 Aug | Tuesday | International Day of the World's Indigenous People |
| 12 Aug | Friday | International Youth Day |
| 19 Aug | Friday | World Humanitarian Day |
| 21 Aug | Sunday | International Day of Remembrance of and Tribute to the Victims of Terrorism |
| 29 Aug | Monday | International Day against Nuclear Tests |
| 8 Sep | Thursday | International Literacy Day |
| 15 Sep | Thursday | International Day of Democracy |
| 16 Sep | Friday | International Day for the Preservation of the Ozone Layer |
| 21 Sep | Wednesday | International Day of Peace |
| 22 Sep | Thursday | World Maritime Day |
| 26 Sep | Monday | International Day for the Total Elimination of Nuclear Weapons |
| 27 Sep | Tuesday | World Tourism Day |
| 29 Sep | Thursday | International Day of Awareness of Food Loss and Waste |
| 1 Oct | Saturday | International Day of Older Persons |
| 2 Oct | Sunday | International Day of Non-Violence |
| 3 Oct | Monday | World Habitat Day |
| 5 Oct | Wednesday | World Teachers' Day |
| 9 Oct | Sunday | World Post Day |
| 10 Oct | Monday | World Mental Health Day |
| 11 Oct | Tuesday | International Day of the Girl Child |
| 12 Oct | Wednesday | International Day for Natural Disaster Reduction |
| 16 Oct | Sunday | World Food Day |
| 17 Oct | Monday | International Day for the Eradication of Poverty |

| 24 Oct | Monday | United Nations Day |
|---|---|---|
| 10 Nov | Thursday | World Science Day for Peace and Development |
| 14 Nov | Monday | World Diabetes Day |
| 16 Nov | Wednesday | International Day for Tolerance |
| 19 Nov | Saturday | World Toilet Day |
| 20 Nov | Sunday | Universal Children's Day |
| 25 Nov | Friday | International Day for the Elimination of Violence against Women |
| 1 Dec | Thursday | World AIDS Day |
| 2 Dec | Friday | International Day for the Abolition of Slavery |
| 3 Dec | Saturday | International Day of Persons with Disabilities |
| 5 Dec | Monday | International Volunteer Day for Economic and Social Development |
| 5 Dec | Monday | World Soil Day |
| 9 Dec | Friday | International Anti-Corruption Day |
| 10 Dec | Saturday | Human Rights Day |
| 12 Dec | Monday | International Universal Health Coverage Day |
| 18 Dec | Sunday | International Migrants Day |
| 20 Dec | Tuesday | International Human Solidarity Day |
| 27 Dec | Tuesday | International Day of Epidemic Preparedness |

**Table 13 Bharat Ratna Recipients**

| S. No. | Name | Awarded In |
|---|---|---|
| 1. | Shri Chakravarti Rajagopalachari (1878–1972) | 1954 |
| 2. | Dr. Sarvapalli Radhakrishnan (1888–1975) | 1954 |
| 3. | Dr. ChandrasekharaVenkata Raman (1888–1970) | 1954 |
| 4. | Dr. Bhagwan Das (1869–1958) | 1955 |
| 5. | Dr. Mokshagundam Visvesvaraya (1861–1962) | 1955 |
| 6. | Pt. Jawaharlal Nehru (1889–1964) | 1955 |
| 7. | Pt. Govind Ballabh Pant (1887–1961) | 1957 |
| 8. | Dr. Dhondo Keshav Karve (1858–1962) | 1958 |
| 9. | Dr. Bidhan Chandra Roy (1882–1962) | 1961 |
| 10. | Shri Purushottam Das Tandon (1882–1962) | 1961 |
| 11. | Dr. Rajendra Prasad (1884–1963) | 1962 |
| 12. | Dr. Zakir Husain (1897–1969) | 1963 |
| 13. | Dr. Pandurang Vaman Kane (1880–1972) | 1963 |
| 14. | Shri Lal Bahadur Shastri (Posthumous) (1904–1966) | 1966 |
| 15. | Smt. Indira Gandhi (1917–1984) | 1971 |
| 16. | Shri Varahagiri Venkata Giri (1894–1980) | 1975 |

| S. No. | Name | Awarded In |
|---|---|---|
| 17. | Shri Kumaraswamy Kamraj (Posthumous) (1903–1975) | 1976 |
| 18. | Mother Mary Teresa Bojaxhiu (Mother Teresa) (1910– 1997) | 1980 |
| 19. | Shri Acharya Vinoba Bhave (Posthumous) (1895–1982) | 1983 |
| 20. | Khan Abdul Ghaffar Khan (1890–1988) | 1987 |
| 21. | Shri Marudur Gopalan Ramachandran (Posthumous) (1917–1987) | 1988 |
| 22. | Dr. Bhim Rao Ramji Ambedkar (Posthumous) (1891–1956) | 1990 |
| 23. | Dr. Nelson Rolihlahla Mandela (1918–2013) | 1990 |
| 24. | Shri Rajiv Gandhi (Posthumous) (1944–1991) | 1991 |
| 25. | Sardar Vallabhbhai Patel (Posthumous) (1875–1950) | 1991 |
| 26. | Shri Morarji Ranchhodji Desai (1896–1995) | 1991 |
| 27. | Maulana Abul Kalam Azad (Posthumous) (1888–1958) | 1992 |
| 28. | Shri Jehangir Ratanji Dadabhai Tata (1904–1993) | 1992 |
| 29. | Shri Satyajit Ray (1922–1992) | 1992 |
| 30. | Shri Gulzarilal Nanda (1898–1998) | 1997 |
| 31. | Smt. Aruna Asaf Ali (Posthumous) (1909–1996) | 1997 |
| 32. | Dr. A.P.J. Abdul Kalam (1931–2015) | 1997 |
| 33. | Smt. Madurai Shanmukhavadivu Subbulakshmi (1916– 2005) | 1998 |
| 34. | Shri Chidambaram Subramaniam (1910–2000) | 1998 |
| 35. | Shri Jayaprakash Narayan (Posthumous) (1902–1979) | 1999 |
| 36. | Professor Amartya Sen (b–1933) | 1999 |
| 37. | Lokpriya Gopinath Bordoloi (Posthumous) (1890–1950) | 1999 |
| 38. | Pandit Ravi Shankar (1920–2012) | 1999 |
| 39. | Sushri Lata Dinanath Mangeshkar (b–1929) | 2001 |
| 40. | Ustad Bismillah Khan (1916–2006) | 2001 |
| 41. | Pandit Bhimsen Gururaj Joshi (1922–2011) | 2009 |
| 42. | Prof. C. N. R. Rao (b–1934) | 2014 |
| 43. | Shri Sachin Ramesh Tendulkar(b–1973) | 2014 |
| 44. | Shri Atal Bihari Vajpayee (1924–2018) | 2015 |
| 45. | Pandit Madan Mohan Malaviya (Posthumous)(1861–1946) | 2015 |
| 46. | Shri Nanaji Deshmukh (Posthumous)(1916–2010) | 2019 |
| 47. | Dr. Bhupendra Kumar Hazarika (Posthumous)(1926–2011) | 2019 |
| 48. | Shri Pranab Mukherjee (1935–2020) | 2019 |

## Exercise set on General knowledge & Current Affairs

1. The evacuation of Indian citizens from Ukraine, post invasion by Russia in 2022, was known as;
   (a) Operation Devi Shakti
   (b) Operation Maitri
   (c) Operation Rahat
   (d) Operation Ganga
2. Which of the following features are associated with the Indian Constitution?
   (1) Lengthiest written Constitution
   (2) Single citizenship
   (3) Three tier government
   (4) Emergency powers
   (a) 1, 2, 3, 4 (b) 1, 2, 4
   (c) 2, 3, 4 (d) 1, 2, 3
3. On which of the following days; 'International Mother Language day' is celebrated?
   (a) 21st February (b) 8th March
   (c) 21st June (d) 1st December
4. Where was the Winter Olympics 2022 held?
   (a) Beijing (China)
   (b) Sochi (Russia)
   (c) Pyeongchang (South Korea)
   (d) Vancouver (Canada)
5. With which of the following schools of medieval painting is the famous painting Bani-Thani associated with?
   (a) Mughal School (b) Kishangarh School
   (c) Kangra School (d) Deccan School
6. The team SEZ refers to
   (a) Socio-Economic Zones
   (b) Special Economic Zones
   (c) Special Electrical Zones
   (d) None of the above
7. Which of the following is the home of the Asiatic Lion?
   (a) Kanha National park
   (b) Gir National Park
   (c) Bandipur National Park
   (d) Jim Corbett National Park
8. The parliament of which country is known as the National Diet?
   (a) Japan (b) South Korea
   (c) Denmark (d) Austria
9. When did the Indian National Congress make 'Poorna Swaraj' (complete independence) as the goal of Indian National movement?
   (a) In 1922 with the launch of Khilafat movement
   (b) In 1929 Lahore Congress session
   (c) In 1942 Quit India Movement
   (d) In 1946
10. The 101st Constitutional Amendment dealt with which of the following significant economic measure?
    (a) Introduction of demonitisation
    (b) Introduction of Goods and Service tax
    (c) Introduction of new rates of Direct taxes
    (d) None of the above
11. Which amongst the following is an anti-tank missile indigenously developed by India?
    (a) Nag (b) Trishul
    (c) Prithvi (d) Aakash
12. Kumbh Mela is held on the banks of a river every three years in rotation in a cycle of 12 years. Which city is not associated with holding of this event?
    (a) Prayagraj (b) Varanasi
    (c) Nashik (d) Ujjain
13. Teacher's day in India celebrated on 5th of September, which day is recognized as World's Teachers' Day by UNESCO?
    (a) 5th September (b) 5th October
    (c) 20th November (d) 14th November
14. If a person is suffering from CAD, then it has affected his/her;
    (a) Coronary artery (b) Carotid artery
    (c) Colon area (d) None of the above

**15.** Which statesman/international personality among the following has been awarded a Bharat Ratna?

(a) Nelson Mandela
(b) Barack Obama
(c) Martin Luther King Jr.
(d) None of the above

**16.** Which amongst the following capital cities, is located on the bank of river Siene?

(a) Berlin (b) Paris
(c) Luxembourg (d) Vienna

**17.** On which of the following rivers is located Shivsamudram falls?

(a) Kaveri (b) Godavari
(c) Krishna (d) Tapti

**18.** By which of the following Acts did the power transfer to the British Crown from the East India Company, take place?

(a) Charter Act 1853
(b) Government of India Act 1858
(c) Indian Councils Act 1861
(d) Indian Councils Act 1892

**19.** Raja Ram Mohan Roy was associated with which of the following societies of reform in the 19th Century?

(a) Arya Samaj
(b) Brahmo Samaj
(c) Prarthna Samaj
(d) Young Bengal Movement

**20.** Which of the following days is celebrated as Hindi Divas in India?

(a) 14th November (b) 14th September
(c) 14th August (d) 14th April

**21.** The concept of 'Directive Principles of the State Policy', was incorporated in the Indian Constitution from the constitution of:

(a) Germany (b) Canada
(c) Ireland (d) Australia

**22.** *Kashida* is a form of embroidery associated with

(a) Himachal (b) Chhattisgarh
(c) Kashmir (d) Karnataka

**23.** The Natraja statue of lord Shiva, showing him performing the Rudra Tandava, also shows him suppressing a demon symbolizing ignorance. This demon is:

(a) Bhasmasura (b) Ravana
(c) Apasmara (d) Mara

**24.** Which type of soil is suitable for cultivation of cotton?

(a) Black regur soil
(b) Red soil
(c) Alluvial Soil
(d) All soil types

**25.** Which amongst the following is a nuclear power station?

(a) Neyveli Power Plant- Tamil Nadu
(b) Singrauli Power Plant- Uttar Pradesh
(c) Kundakulam Power Plant-Tamil Nadu
(d) Farraka Power Plant-West Bengal

**26.** A pyrometer would be used to measure:

(a) High pressure
(b) High temperature
(c) High radiation
(d) High altitude

**27.** 8th of March is celebrated world over as:

(a) International Sports Day
(b) International Women's Day
(c) International Day of Girl Child
(d) World Wildlife Day

**28.** Ravi Kumar Dahiya who won a bronze medal at the 2021 olympics (held in 2021) is associated with:

(a) Boxing
(b) Shooting
(c) Weight lifting
(d) Wrestling

**29.** Which of the vaccines and discoverer are correctly matched?

(1) Small Pox- Edward Jenner
(2) Polio – Jonas E. Salk
(3) Tuberculosis- Albert Calmette

(a) 1, 2, 3 (b) 1, 2
(c) 1, 3 (d) 2, 3

30. The Manipur Sankirtana recognized as 'UNESCO Intangible Cultural Heritage of Humanity' is:
   (a) a ritual singing, drumming and dancing
   (b) a tribal folk dance
   (c) a modern musical performance of the state
   (d) one of the classical forms of singing

31. If a disease is endemic, it implies:
   (1) Its regular occurrence in certain people or certain area
   (2) constant flow of infected people from outside to that area
   (a) Both (1) & (2) (b) Only (1)
   (c) Only (2) (d) Neither (1) Nor (2)

32. A person having blood type $A^{-}$ is called
   (a) Universal donor (b) Universal recipient
   (c) Partial donor (d) None of the above

33. Which of the following can be said to be correct about the fundamental duties enshrined in the Indian Constitution?
   (1) They were introduced by the 42nd Amendment
   (2) They override the Fundamental Rights
   (a) Both (1) & (2) (b) Only (1)
   (c) Only (2) (d) Neither (1) Nor (2)

34. Renminbi (abbreviation RMB) is the official currency of which of the following countries?
   (a) Ireland
   (b) Peoples Republic of China
   (c) Taiwan
   (d) Argentina

35. Which amongst the following is not a crypto-currency?
   (a) Bit Coin (b) Ripple
   (c) Rand (d) Lite Coin

36. Which amongst the following is a function of the world body OECD?
   (a) Lending of funds to member countries
   (b) Policy advice to control banks of different countries
   (c) Foster International Cooperation for economic progress & world trade
   (d) All of the above

37. What was India's position in the voting in UN General assembly in April 2022 to suspend Russia from UN Human Rights Council?
   (a) It voted in favour of suspension
   (b) It abstained from voting
   (c) It voted against suspension
   (d) It had no voting rights

38. The Indian Wild Ass sanctuary is located in
   (a) Kaziranga, Assam
   (b) Little Rann of Kutch, Gujarat
   (c) Bandipur, Karnataka
   (d) Dachigam, Kashmir

39. Which of the following are correct about corticosteroid drugs?
   (1) They are used to treat inflammation in the body
   (2) They suppress the immune response
   (3) They are antipyretic
   (a) 1, 2, 3 (b) 1, 2
   (c) 1, 3 (d) 2, 3

40. Maithali, a language recognized in the 8th Schedule of the Constitution, is popular in which of the following states?
   (a) Chhattisgarh (b) Uttar Pradesh
   (c) West Bengal (d) Bihar

41. World Water day is celebrated on:
   (a) 3rd March (b) 22nd March
   (c) 22nd May (d) 5th June

42. Chhau dance, a form of folk dance is associated with which Indian state?
   (a) Andhra Pradesh
   (b) Tamil Nadu
   (c) Arunachal Pradesh
   (d) Odisha

43. In 1922 which event caused Mahatma Gandhi to suspend the Non-Cooperation movement ?
   (a) Jallianwala Bagh Incident
   (b) Chauri Chaura incident

(c) The Parliament bombing incident
(d) None of the above

**44.** On which of the following issues the meeting of Committee of Parties (COP-26) took place in Glasgow in Oct-Nov-2021?
(a) Discuss ban on biological weapons
(b) Discuss spread and control of the pandemic-Covid-19
(c) Discuss emerging economic issues post Covid pandemic
(d) Discuss global climate policy & commitment of countries under UNFCCC

**45.** The community of Manganiyars in Rajasthan and adjoining regions are associated with:
(a) Folk music
(b) Puppetry
(c) Pottery making
(d) Making of leather products

**46.** Central Excise Duty is a form of:
(a) Direct tax (b) Indirect tax
(c) Service tax (d) Property tax

**47.** He was an Indian freedom fighter popularly known as *Deshbandhu*. Who was he?
(a) C.F. Andrews
(b) Chittaranjan Dash
(c) Aurobindo Ghosh
(d) Bankim Chandra Chatterjee

**48.** The Novel Coronavirus (CoVID-19) is said to have been first noticed in a:
(a) Seafood market of Wuhan, China
(b) Infectious disease hospital at Wuhan China
(c) Caves in Xin Jiang province China
(d) Wet markets of Yanghou China

**49.** *Dhuandhar falls* is associated with which Indian river?
(a) Narmada (b) Ganaga
(c) Brahmaputra (d) Tapti

**50.** Which of the following was the outcome of the third battle of Panipat?
(a) English forces defeated Nawab of Bengal
(b) Ahmad Shah Abdali defeated the Marathas
(c) The Marathas defeated the English forces
(d) None of the above

**51.** Which of the following fundamental rights is provided by the Article 32 of the Indian Constitution?
(a) Right to Life
(b) Right to Equality
(c) Right to Freedom of Speech and Expression
(d) Right to Constitutional Remedies

**52.** A country suffering from balance of payment problem and ensuring economic crisis, is likely to approach which amongst the following international organisations for assistance?
(a) IMF (b) OECD
(c) UNESCO (d) UNHRC

**53.** If a physician wants to measure blood pressure of a patient, he would use:
(a) Glucometer
(b) ECG
(c) Sphygmomanometer
(d) All of the above

**54.** Which amongst the following world organisation's objective is reduction of global poverty?
(a) World Bank (b) OECD
(c) WTO (d) Global poverty

**55.** Children's Day in India celebrated on 14$^{th}$ of November, when is the World Children's Day celebrated?
(a) 20$^{th}$ October
(b) 20$^{th}$ November
(c) 8$^{th}$ March
(d) Not celebrated as a day

**56.** Which country won the 1$^{st}$ ICC Test Championship in June 2021?
(a) India (b) Australia
(c) England (d) New Zealand

**57.** Where is the famous statue of 'Christ the Redeemer' located?
(a) Rio de Janeiro (b) Buenos Aires
(c) Pisa (d) Bolivia

**58.** Which of the following would fall within the domain of the Reserve Bank of India?
(a) Monetary policy
(b) Tax policy
(c) Both (a) & (b)
(d) Neither (a) nor (b)

**59.** Which amongst the following pairing of books is correct?
(1) Dreams from My father- Barack Obama
(2) Turning Point –A Journey Through Challenges- Dr. A P J Abdul Kalam
(3) Beyond Survival, Emerging dimension of Indian Economy – Sh. Pranab Mukherjee
(a) 1, 2, 3 (b) 1, 2
(c) 2, 3 (d) only 1

**60.** Consider the following martial arts forms and the states. Find the correct match.
(1) Kalaripayattu (A) Punjab
(2) Silambam (B) Kerala
(3) Gatka (C) Manipur
(4) Thanga Ta (D) Tamil Nadu
(a) 1-A, 2-B, 3-C, 4-D
(b) 1-B, 2-D, 3-A, 4-C
(c) 1-B, 2-C, 3-A, 4-D
(d) 1-C, 2-B, 3-D, 4-A

**61.** 1st to 7th October is celebrated in India as:
(a) Wildlife week
(b) Anti untouchability week
(c) National Safety week
(d) Oil Conservation week

**62.** Which amongst the following fairs and states matching is correct?
1. Ganga Sagar Mela A Rajasthan
2. Pushkar Mela B West Bengal
3. Suraj Kund Mela C Haryana
(a) 1-A, 2-B, 3-C (b) 1-B, 2-A, 3-C
(c) 1-C, 2-B, 3-A (d) 1-C, 2-A, 3-B

**63.** Rupay is a payment service system launched by:
(a) State Bank of India
(b) National Payments Corporation of India
(c) Reserve bank of India
(d) Ministry of Finance, India

**64.** The national calendar of India follows,
(a) Vikram Samvat
(b) Saka Samvat
(c) Gregorian Calendar System
(d) None of the above

**65.** Which of the following sites were included as a UNESCO World Heritage site, in 2021?
(a) Kakatiya Rudreshwara (Ramappa) temple
(b) Dholavira: A Harappan city
(c) Both (a) & (b)
(d) Neither (a) Nor (b)

**66.** Consider the following cities and the colour with which they are identified/nick named? Which of the pairing are correct?
(I) Blue city-Jodhpur
(II) Pink city-Jaipur
(III) White city-Udaipur
(a) (I) (II) (III) (b) Only (II)
(c) (I) & (II) (d) (II) & (III)

**67.** In computer terminology, cache memory implies:
(a) The memory space of the installed hard disk.
(b) The memory space of the C drive as reduced by the space of system files.
(c) The temporary memory space available in the CPU.
(d) Additional memory or extendible memory of the CPU.

**68.** Which of the protocols on environment led to the banning of the use of chloroflurocarbons to prevent ozone depletion?
(a) Montreal Protocol
(b) Kyoto Protocol
(c) Rio-earth summit
(d) Paris agreement

**69.** If a person is suffering from Glaucoma, then he would be seeking treatment of his:
(a) Ears (b) Throat
(c) Eyes (d) Kidneys

**70.** UIDAI stands for:
(a) Universal Identification Authority of India
(b) Universal Identification & Development Authority of India
(c) Uniform Identification Authority of India
(d) Unique Identification Authority of India

**71.** Which Indian artists amongst the following have been awarded Bharat Ratna?
(1) Lata Mangeshkar
(2) M S Subbatakshmi
(3) Mukesh
(4) Mohammad Rafi
(a) 1, 2, 3, 4 (b) 1, 2, 3
(c) 1, 2 (d) 1

**72.** Which country won the highest number of medals in 2020 Olympics (held in 2021)?
(a) China
(b) United Kingdom
(c) Japan
(d) United States of America

**73.** Which of the following writs will a court issue to direct a public authority which is failing to perform its official duty?
(a) Habeas Corpus (b) Quo Warrants
(c) Certiorari (d) Mandamus

**74.** If a person is suffering Hepatitis B, then the likely cause of the disease is:
(a) a bacterial infection
(b) hormonal imbalance
(c) extreme iron deficiency
(d) viral infection

**75.** The Paris Agreement (COP-21) is concerned with which of the following?
(a) Elimination restriction of the use of percistent organic pollutants
(b) Protection of biological diversity
(c) Reduction in greenhouse gas emission below 2005-levels
(d) All of the above

**76.** Dada Sahab Phalke award is given for
(a) Best acting in any Indian film
(b) Best story line in a film reflecting national interest
(c) Outstanding contribution to Indian films
(d) All of the above

**77.** The 19$^{th}$ Asian Games to be held in September 2022 is scheduled to be hosted in:
(a) Hangzhou in China
(b) Doha in Qatar
(c) Aaichi-Nayoga in Japan
(d) Riyadh in Saudi Arabia

**78.** With which civilisation is the UNESCO World Heritage site of Machu Pichhu associated?
(a) Mayas (b) Aztecs
(c) Mesopotamians (d) Incas

**79.** GSTN stands for
(a) Government Security Trans-state Network
(b) Government Service Tax Network
(c) Goods Sourcing Trans-state Network
(d) Goods and Service Tax Network

**80.** The year 2013 was recognized as international year of soils by UN General assembly. It also adopted .............. as the World Soil Day
(a) 5$^{th}$ December (b) 2$^{nd}$ February
(c) 22$^{nd}$ March (d) 22$^{nd}$ May

**81.** Consider the following list of books and authors. Choose the correct pairing.

| | | | |
|---|---|---|---|
| A. | Nelson Mandela | (I) | Matter of Discretion: an autobiography |
| B. | Manmohan Singh | (II) | Long Walk to Freedom |
| C. | I.K. Gujral | (III) | My Unforgettable Memories |
| D. | Mamata Banerjee | (IV) | Changing India |

(a) A-I, B-II, C-III, D-IV
(b) A-II, B-IV, C-I, D-III
(c) A-II, B-III, C-IV, D-I
(d) A-II, B-III, C-I, D-IV

**82.** Which female playback singer has won the National Film Award for best female playback singer, the maximum numbers of times?

(a) K.S. Chitra (b) Lata Mangeshkar
(c) P. Susheela (d) Shreya Ghoshal

**83.** Which of the following are the correct description of the acronyms given;

(1) WWW-World Wide Web
(2) HTTP-Hyper test Transfer Process

(a) Both (1) & (2) (b) Only 1
(c) Only 2 (d) Neither 1 nor 2

**84.** 21st of June is recognized by UN and celebrated world over as,

(a) International Yoga Day
(b) International day of Indigenous people
(c) World Health Day
(d) World Sports day

**85.** Which of the following statements is correct with respect to Dhrupad?

(a) It is a folk dance tradition of Rajasthan
(b) It is a Vedantic system of worship
(c) It is a collection of medieval literature
(d) None of the above

**86.** In which of the following cities you would find a Jantar-Mantar?

(1) Jaipur (2) New Delhi
(3) Ujjain (4) Indore

(a) 1, 2, 3, 4 (b) 1, 2, 3
(c) 1, 2 (d) 2

**87.** The five rings of Olympics, which symbolise the five continents are in which of the following colours?

(1) Red (2) Blue
(3) Yellow (4) Orange
(5) Green (6) Black

(a) 1, 2, 3, 4, 5 (b) 1, 2, 3, 5, 6
(c) 1, 2, 4, 5, 6 (d) 1, 2, 3, 4, 6

**88.** Which of the following is correct about Mission Karmayogi launched by Government of India in September 2020?

(a) It's a programme to promote entrepreneurship.
(b) It's a programme to develop ethical leadership.
(c) It is a programme of reforms & capacity building in the civil services
(d) None of the above

**89.** A deficiency of Vitamin K can be overcome by having more of:

(a) Milk (b) Green Vegetable
(c) Citrus fruit (d) Animal protein

**90.** Which Sikh Guru founded Amrit Sarovar in the famous Golden Temple and also founded Amritsar?

(a) Guru Nanak (b) Guru Ramdas
(c) Guru Arjandev (d) Guru Govind Singh

**91.** Taking Permanent Account Number (PAN) would be essential for;

(a) Filing Income-tax Returns
(b) Applying for Aadhaar
(c) Obtaining Passport
(d) Enrolling in the Electoral rolls

**92.** Which of the following religious festivals has been included in the year 2021 in the list of UNESCO Intangible Cultural Heritage of Humanity.

(a) Durga Puja in Kolkata
(b) Chath Puja in Bihar
(c) Both (a) & (b)
(d) Neither (a) nor (b)

**93.** In which of the following monuments one would find Diwan-e-Aam?

(a) Taj Mahal
(b) Lal Quila
(c) Gol Gumbaj-Bijapur
(d) Charminar Hyderabad

**94.** Which of the following presidents of India have also been honoured with Bharat Ratna?

(1) Rajendra Prasad
(2) Dr. S. Radhakrishnan
(3) Pranab Mukherjee
(4) APJ Abdul Kalam

(a) 1, 2, 3, 4 (b) 2, 3, 4
(c) 3, 4 (d) 4 only

**95.** Which country stood at the top of the medals tally tables in the 2022 Winter Olympics?

(a) Norway (b) China
(c) USA (d) Germany

**96.** The three farm laws repealed by Government in 2021 were:

(1) The Farmers Produce Trade and Commerce (Promotion and Facilitation) Act
(2) The Farmers (Empowerment & Protection) Agreement of Price assurance and Farm Services Act
(3) The Essential Commodities (Amendment) Act

(a) 1, 2 & 3 (b) 1, 2 but not 3
(c) 1, 3 but not 2 (d) Only 1

**97.** By which of the following Acts, during the British Period, for the first time, the subjects of legislation, were divided between the central and Provincial Legislative Councils?

(a) Morley Minto Reforms 1909
(b) Govt. of India Act 1919
(c) Government of India Act-1935
(d) Indian Independence Act-1847

**98.** The currency of Thailand is:

(a) Ringet (b) Lira
(c) Baht (d) Thai-dollar

**99.** UNESCO recognized which of the followings as the International Literacy Day?

(a) 15$^{th}$ of March (b) 8$^{th}$ of September
(c) 12$^{th}$ of August (d) 30$^{th}$ of June

**100.** What position was secured by the Indian Womens' hockey team in 2020 Olympics (held in 2021)?

(a) 1$^{st}$ Position (b) 3$^{rd}$ Position
(c) 4$^{th}$ Position (d) None of the above

**101.** Which Indian actor has won the National Film award for best actor the maximum number of times?

(a) Amitabh Bachchan
(b) Kamal Hasan
(c) Naseeruddin Shah
(d) Amir Khan

**102.** GUI in computer terminology stands for,

(a) Graphical Uniform Icon
(b) Graphical User Icon
(c) Graphical User Interface
(d) Graphical Uniform Interface

**103.** In which of the Indian States is the festival of Rangoli Bihu celebrated?

(a) Odisha
(b) Assam
(c) Arunachal Pradesh
(d) West Bengal

**104.** For a person suffering from scurvy which of the following food items would be beneficial?

(a) Oranges (b) Eggs
(c) Carrot (d) Milk

**105.** Which of the following acronyms of computer terminology and full forms are correct?

(i) HDD-Hard Disk Drive
(ii) BIOS-Basic Information Output System
(iii) CPU-Core Performance Unit

(a) I,II, III (b) I,II
(c) I (d) None of the above

**106.** The team SARS relating to the spread of the viral disease stands for;

(a) Severe Acute Respiratory Syndrome
(b) Severe Antibody Respiratory Syndrome
(c) South Asian Respiratory Syndrome
(d) None of the above

**107.** Which one of the following was India's' first indigenously built satellite?

(a) Bhaskar (b) IRS-I
(c) Rohini (d) Aryabhata

**108.** Which of the allowing is true about Pradhan Mantri Jan Dhan Yojana launched in August 2014.

(a) It aims to provide affordable financial services including credit, insurance, banking savings and deposit etc.
(b) It's a scheme for investment in SME and MSME sector
(c) It provides medical insurance & health benefits
(d) None of the above

**109.** Sonepur Mela is a/an:
(a) cattle fair held in Sonepur Bihar
(b) arts and crafts fair festival of Sonepur in Eastern Uttar Pradesh
(c) traditional fair of Sonepur in Rajasthan
(d) None of the above

**110.** If there is a dispute pertaining to dumping of goods or levy of antidumping duties, then which of the following world organisations, the members countries likely to approach?
(a) WTO
(b) International Court of Justice
(c) IMF
(d) World Bank

**111.** Brahmos is a type of:
(a) Advanced super computer
(b) A subsonic intercontinental missile
(c) A cyber space defense system
(d) A supersonic cruise missile

**112.** UEFA Champions league is a:
(a) Club cricket competition in Europe
(b) North and South American Soccer competition played amidst different countries
(c) Continental club soccer (football) competition popular in Europe
(d) None of the above

**113.** *Kantha* is a form of
(a) Embroidery of West Bengal
(b) Zari work of Uttar Pardesh
(c) Handicraft of Karnataka
(d) None of the above

**114.** The Fragile Planet, a book on ethical approach dealing with the issue of climate change, published in 2021, is written by,
(a) Dalai Lama
(b) Sri Sri Ravishankar
(c) Sadguru Jaggi Vasudev
(d) Baba Ramdev

**115.** Used in launch of satellites, GSLV stands for:
(a) Geological satellite location vehicle
(b) Geosynchronous satellite location vehicle
(c) Geostationery satellite launch vehicle
(d) Geosynchronous satellite launch vehicle

**116.** Which of the following is not a viral disease?
(a) Covid-19 (b) AIDS
(c) Malaria (d) Chickenpox

**117.** Rock shelters at Bhimbetka, recognised as a UNESCO World Heritage site, is located in which of the Indian states?
(a) Bihar (b) Uttar Pradesh
(c) Chattisgarh (d) Madhya Pradesh

**118.** Bommalattam, Putul Naach & Gombeyatta are;
(a) Different forms of folk song from different states.
(b) Different forms of puppetry from different states.
(c) Different forms of folk dances from different states.
(d) None of the above

**119.** Zend-Avesta is the holy book in
(a) Sikhism (b) Zoroastrianism
(c) Judaism (d) Sufism

**120.** Jnanpith award is conferred for,
(a) Contribution in the field of music
(b) Contribution in the field of dramaturgy
(c) Contribution for social work
(d) Contribution in field of literature

**121.** The 'Ayushman Bharat' scheme of Government of India deals with,
(a) Funding of healthcare programs
(b) Creation of corpus fund for education for all
(c) Creation of job opportunities in rural sector
(d) None of the above

**122.** Which day is recognised by the United Nations and celebrated as International Mother Earth Day or the World Earth Day?
(a) 1$^{st}$ January (b) 23$^{rd}$ March
(c) 22$^{nd}$ April (d) 5$^{th}$ June

**123.** Which amongst the following books and authors are correctly matched?

(1) I do what I do- Raghuram Rajan

(2) Philosophers Stone- J K Rowling

(3) Pyjamas are Forgiving- Twinkle Khanna

(a) 1, 2, 3 (b) 1, 2

(c) Only 1 (d) 1, 3

**124.** Which amongst the following is recognised as a classical language of India?

(1) Hindi (2) Sanskrit

(3) Tamil (4) Awadhi

(5) Odia (6) Malayalam

(a) 1, 2, 3, 4, 5, 6 (b) 2, 3, 4, 5, 6

(c) 2, 3, 5, 6 (d) 3, 4, 6

**125.** In computer terminology 'boot' refers to

(a) The process of loading or initiating an operating system

(b) The process of virus scan of all the drives while initiating the computer operating system

(c) The process of activation of the backup files in HDD

(d) None of the above

**126.** The confluence of the rivers Alaknanda and Bhagirathi is known as

(a) Rudra prayag (b) Vishnu prayag

(c) Karna prayag (d) Dev prayag

**127.** Who is credited with the invention of air conditioner?

(a) Carrier (b) Voltas

(c) Lloyd (d) Fermi

**128.** Who was the first woman Finance Minister of India?

(a) Indira Gandhi

(b) Sushma Swaraj

(c) Rajkumari Amrit Kaur

(d) Nirmala Sitharaman

**129.** With which sport/game is Manika Batra associated?

(a) Tennis (b) Badminton

(c) Squash (d) None of the above

**130.** Which amongst the following is correct about Swang?

(a) It's a popular folk theatre of Haryana & Western U. P.

(b) It's a folk art involving woodwork of Kashmir

(c) Its folk music popular in Kathiawar

(d) None of the above

**131.** Pietra dura work seen in Taj Mahal refers to:

(a) Inlay of semiprecious stones in walls and flat surfaces

(b) Jali work in marble

(c) Calligraphy work on stone surfaces

(d) None of the above

**132.** Who is the only Indian sports person to be awarded Bharat Ratna?

(a) Milkha Singh (b) Dhyan Chand

(c) Kapil Dev (d) Sachin Tendulkar

**133.** Param Siddhi-AI is a ...................... developed in India

(a) Super Computer

(b) Micro processor

(c) Cyber Defence system

(d) Operating system

**134.** Which amongst the following are recognised among the eight classical dances of India?

(1) Bharatnatyam

(2) Kuchipudi

(3) Odissi

(4) Sattariya

(5) Ghoomar

(6) Garba

(a) 1, 2, 3, 4, 5, 6 (b) 1, 2, 3, 4, 5

(c) 1, 2, 3, 4 (d) 1, 2, 3

**135.** Which of the following Indian river has origin at Amarkantak?

(a) Godavari (b) Cauvery

(c) Tapti (d) Narmada

**136.** Malus Domestic is the scientific name of which fruit?

(a) Mango (b) Apple

(c) Orange (d) Guava

**137.** Pepsin a digestive enzyme is likely to be found in:

(a) Mouth (b) Stomach

(c) Upper Intestine (d) Lower Intestine

**138.** Rebels Against the Raj: Western Fighters for India's Freedom; A book published in 2022 is authored by:

(a) Dominique Lapierre

(b) Shashi Tharoor

(c) Christopher Snedden

(d) Ramchandra Guha

**139.** In which of the Olympics did India win the maximum number of medals?

(a) 2020- Tokyo Olympics

(b) 2016- Rio Olympics

(c) 2012-London Olympics

(d) 2000- Sydney Olympics

**140.** Arogya Setu launched in 2020 is a:

(a) Government of India medical insurance scheme

(b) Government of India free medical provision scheme

(c) Government of India, digital app for spread of awareness about Covid-19

(d) All of the above

**141.** Sadbhavana Divas celebrated on 20th of August, marks the birth anniversary of:

(a) Lal Bahadur Shastri

(b) Rajiv Gandhi

(c) Indira Gandhi

(d) Atal Bihari Vajpayee

**142.** Which of the works of Classical Sanskrit Literature are correctly matched?

| | |
|---|---|
| (1) Kalidasa | (A) Mricchakatika |
| (2) Bhasa | (B) Vikramorvasiya |
| (3) Sudraka | (C) Mudraraksha |
| (4) Vishakadutta | (D) Swapnavasvadatta |

(a) 1-A, 2-B, 3-C, 4-D

(b) 1-B, 2-D, 3-A, 4-C

(c) 1-C, 2-D, 3-A, 4-B

(d) 1-B, 2-A, 3-D, 4-C

**143.** Which company is credited with developing the world's first smart phone?

(a) Nokia (b) Microsoft

(c) IBM (d) Blackberry

**144.** The captain of the Indian Women's ODI cricket team which participated in the ODI World Cup 2022 was?

(a) Mithali Raj (b) Harmanpreet Kaur

(c) Jhulan Goswami (d) Smriti Mandhana

**145.** Which amongst the following UN bodies has the object of helping countries eliminate poverty and achieve sustainable economic growth?

(a) World Bank

(b) Food and Agricultural Organisation (FAO)

(c) United Nations Development Programme (UNDP)

(d) UNFCCC

**146.** Consider the following works of medieval Bhakti saints. Identify which are correctly matched.

| | |
|---|---|
| A Siksastakam | 1. Chaitanya |
| B Sur Sagar | 2. Soordas |
| C Kirtan Ghosha | 3. Shankardeva |

(a) A-1, B-2, C-3 (b) A-1, B-3, C-2

(c) A-2, B-1, C-3 (d) A-3, B-1,C-2

**147.** What does URL refer to in computer technology?

(a) Uniform Resource Locator

(b) Uniform Reference Location

(c) Uniform Resource License

(d) None of the above

**148.** Vikram-the lander and Pragyan-the rover, are associated with which Indian space mission?

(a) Chandrayaan-1 (b) Chandrayaan-2

(c) Mangalyaan-1 (d) Mangalyaan-2

**149.** Who amongst the following was the recipient of last Bharat Ratna Award given in 2019?

(a) Bhupen Hazarika

(b) Pandit Ravishankar

(c) Dr. APJ Abdul Kalam

(d) None of the above

**150.** PMJAY, a scheme of Government of India stands for;
(a) Pradhan Mantri Jan Awas Yojana
(b) Pradhan Mantri Jal Abhiyaan or Yojana
(c) Pradhan Mantri Jeevan Arogya Yojana
(d) Pradhan Mantri Jan Arogya Yojana

**151.** Besides the Sun, which is the nearest star to earth?
(a) Proxima Centauri
(b) North Star
(c) Barnard's Star
(d) Alpha Majoris

**152.** Who amongst the following were given Major Dhyan Chand Khel Ratna Award (earlier known as Rajiv Gandhi Khel ratna Award) in the year 2021?
(1) Neeraj Chopra
(2) Ravi Kumar Dahiya
(3) Lovlina Borgohian
(4) P R Rajesh
(a) 1, 2, 3, 4 (b) 1, 2, 3
(c) 1, 2 (d) 1

**153.** Consider the following sports persons & disciplines. Identify which are matched correctly.
(1) Deepika Kumar- Archery
(2) Manpreet Singh- Hockey
(a) Both (1) & (2) are correctly matched
(b) (1) is correctly matched but not (2)
(c) (2) is correctly matched but not (1)
(d) Both (1) & (2) are not correctly matched

**154.** Who among the following is credited with laying the foundation of World Wide Web (www)?
(a) Tim Berners Lee
(b) Bill gates
(c) Charles Babbage
(d) None of the above

**155.** Which of the following has been included in 2020 in UNESCO list of biosphere reserve in India?
(a) Panna Tiger Reserve
(b) Kanha Tiger Reserve
(c) Bandhavgarh National park
(d) Periyar National Park

**156.** Dronacharya award is given for:
(a) getting medals at Olympics.
(b) to coaches for producing medal winners at International events.
(c) support & training staff associated with successful athletes.
(d) All of the above

**157.** Satish Dhawan Space Centre at Sriharikota is a:
(a) satellite launch station
(b) master control facility of satellite.
(c) research and development centre
(d) All of the above

**158.** Who amongst the following is the Governor of Reserve Bank of India?
(a) Shaktikanta Das (b) Urjit patel
(c) Raghuram Rajan (d) D. Subbarao

**159.** Odentology is the science pertaining to the study of:
(a) Teeth (b) dragonflies
(c) Bones (d) Small insects

**160.** Jatakas refer to:
(a) collection of folk stories of Northern India
(b) collection of stories from previous births of Buddha.
(c) Jain stories on ethics & morality
(d) rules of conduct of Buddhist monks

**161.** Which amongst the following Indian athletes has won medals in individual events at more than one Olympic?
(a) Abhinav Bindra
(b) Mary Kom
(c) Rajyavardhan Singh Rathore
(d) P.V. Sindhu

**162.** Shukrayaan-1, an Indian space mission proposed for 2023, aims to study:
(a) The corona emanating from Sun
(b) atmosphere of Venus
(c) Gravitational waves between Sun & Venus
(d) All of the above

**163.** To focus on the growing challenges due to world population, which day is recognised by UN as the World Population day?
(a) $21^{st}$ March (b) $5^{th}$ June
(c) $12^{th}$ August (d) $11^{th}$ July

**164.** Saraswati Samman is conferred for contribution to:
(a) Spread of education in rural India
(b) Written journalism
(c) Poetry or prose writing in any of the languages of Eighth schedule of Constitution
(d) Education in weaker section.

**165.** Which of the following statements are correct about the Rajya Sabha?
(1) Rajya Sabha is not dissolved.
(2) Members of the Rajya Sabha are elected by the members of the state legislatures.
(3) Term of a Rajya Sabha Member is 5 years.
(a) 1, 2, 3 (b) 1, 2
(c) 1, 3 (d) 2, 3

**166.** Colosseum, a large amphitheater, famous for holding gladiator fights in ancient times was located in:
(a) Memphis (b) Alexandria
(c) Rome (d) Ephesus

**167.** Paracetamol is a .................. category of drug
(a) Corticosteroid (b) Antibiotic
(c) Antipyretic (d) All of the above

**168.** Rani Rampal is associated with which Indian sports/games?
(a) Weightlifting (b) Cricket
(c) Shooting (d) Hockey

**169.** ECG is used to measure:
(a) Abnormalities in brainwaves
(b) Abnormalities of heart waves
(c) Nervous System disorder
(d) All of the above

**170.** Jatra, popular in West Bengal is a form of:
(a) Folk Song
(b) Cultural festival
(c) Folk theatre
(d) Compendium of folk literature

**171.** Ficus Religiosa refers to which Indian tree?
(a) Banyan tree (b) Ashok tree
(c) Neem tree (d) Peepul tree

**172.** e Sanjeevani, a Government of India programme launched in November 2019, deals with:
(a) provision of online OPD doctor's consultation to citizens
(b) Provision of online medicines
(c) Provision of online health insurance
(d) All of the above

**173.** Which amongst the following is celebrated as anti-terrorism day?
(a) $31^{st}$ October- Indira Gandhi's birthday
(b) $2^{nd}$ October Mahatma Gandhi's Birthday
(c) $14^{th}$ November Pt. Nehru's birthday
(d) $23^{rd}$ January, birthday of Subhas Chandra Bose

**174.** The drug chloromycetin is used for which of the following diseases?
(a) Covid-19 (b) Typhoid
(c) Malaria (d) Arthritis

**175.** Which of the following planets, has the maximum surface temperature?
(a) Mercury (b) Venus
(c) Earth (d) Mars

**176.** The objective of "Stand Up India" scheme is:
(a) to provide loan to SCs, STs and Women through a bank for a greenfield enterprise.
(b) to provide loan for medical treatment of handicapped/differently abled persons.

(c) to provide funding for new projects of entrepreneurship launched by students.

(d) None of the above

**177.** Consider the following pairs of festivals and states in which they are celebrated.

1. Pongal- Tamil Nadu
2. Onam- Kerala
3. Baisakhi- Punjab

Which of the pairs are correct?

(a) 1, 2, 3 (b) 1 & 2

(c) 1 & 3 (d) 2 & 3

**178.** Consider the following pairs of books and authors and identify which are correctly matched?

1. The Third Pillar- Raghuram Rajan
2. An Era of Darkness; The British Empire- Shashi Tharoor

(a) Both 1 & 2 (b) Only 1

(c) Only 2 (d) Neither 1 nor 2

**179.** GSAT-20 proposed to be launched in 2022, is a type of

(a) Remote sensing satellite

(b) Earth observation satellite

(c) Multispectral Imaging satellite

(d) Communication satellite

**180.** Which amongst the following athletes/sports persons are associated with wrestling?

(1) Vinesh Phogat

(2) Bajrang Punia

(3) Mirabai Chanu

(4) Deepa Malik

(5) Avani Lekhara

(a) 1, 2, 3, 4, 5 (b) 1, 2, 3, 4

(c) 1, 2, 3 (d) 1 & 2

**181.** Cartography refers to:

(a) study and science of making carts & chariots

(b) science of making maps and globes

(c) science of study of cold temperatures

(d) study of sound and echoes

**182.** What is Dhruv MK-III MR?

(a) An Advanced light helicopter developed by HAL.

(b) Next generation of surface to air missile launched by DRDO.

(c) Latest satellite surveillance camera launched by ISRO

(d) None of the above

**183.** AFSPA which has been partly or substantially removed in April 2022 from several districts of North Eastern states, stands for:

(a) Army Families Special Privileges Act

(b) Armed forces Special Formation Alliance

(c) Armed Forces Special Privileges Act

(d) Armed Forced Special Powers Act

**184.** Which country amongst the following is not a part of the Quad group?

(a) India (b) Japan

(c) USA (d) Singapore

**185.** Which of the following countries and currencies are correctly matched?

(1) South Africa- Rand

(2) Russia-Rouble

(3) United Kingdom-Euro

(a) 1, 2, 3 (b) 1 and 3

(c) 1 & 2 (d) 2 & 3

**186.** Which of the following fort in India is popularly known as the Golden Fort?

(a) Jodhpur fort (b) Chittorgarh Fort

(c) Junagarh Fort (d) Jaisalmer fort

**187.** Which of the following historical works and their authors are correctly matched?

(1) Akbarnama- Abul Fazal

(2) Padmavat- Malik Muhammad Jayasi

(3) Prithviraj Raso- Chand Bardai

(a) 1, 2, 3 (b) 1 & 2

(c) 1 & 3 (d) Only 1

**188.** In the 2020 summer Olympics (held in 2021) in which event India won more than one medal

(a) Badminton (b) Hockey

(c) Wrestling (d) Boxing

**189.** Kalbelia, recognized by UNESCO as Intangible Cultural Heritage, is a:

(a) Folksong & dance of Rajasthan
(b) Folk painting of Himachal Pradesh
(c) Folk theatre of Rajasthan
(d) Tribal dance of Chhattisgarh

**190.** Which of the following rivers drain in the Bay of Bengal?

(1) Brahmaputra
(2) Godavari
(3) Cauvery
(4) Narmada

(a) 1, 2, 3, 4 (b) 1, 2, 3
(c) 1 & 2 (d) 1 only

**191.** With which Indian game/sports is Sunil Chetri associated?

(a) Cricket (b) Gymnastics
(c) Boxing (d) Football

**192.** Pinaka MK-I (Enhanced), successfully tested in April 2022 by DRDO is a:

(a) Combat helicopter
(b) Rocket system
(c) Airborne radar
(d) Light tank system

**193.** Which of the following Indian Prime ministers have been awarded Bharat Ratna?

(1) Narendra Modi
(2) Atal Bihari Vajpayee
(3) Rajeev Gandhi
(4) Manmohan Singh

(a) 1, 2, 3, 4 (b) 2, 3, 4
(c) 1, 2, 3 (d) 2, 3

**194.** ........................ is often considered the father of Indian statistics.

(a) Vishweshwariya (b) P C Mahalanobis
(c) C V Raman (d) Ramanujam

**195.** The study of soils is referred as;

(a) Terrology (b) Edaphology
(c) Eidology (d) Ecology

**196.** Chichen Itza, considered a wonder of the world, built in the 9th–10th centuries CE is;

(a) a Mayan City with pyramids
(b) a portion of the Great Wall of China
(c) an Incan site in Peru
(d) structures in the ancient city of Petra in Jordan

**197.** Consider the following books & authors. Which are correct matches?

| | |
|---|---|
| 1. Chetan Bhagat | A. Immortals of Meluha |
| 2. Amish Tripathi | B. One Indian Girl |
| 3. Jhumpa Lahiri | C. Namesake |

(a) 1-A, 2-B, 3-C (b) 1-B, 2-A, 3-C
(c) 1-B, 2-C, 3-A (d) 1-C, 2-A, 3-B

**198.** The Prime Minister of which country was removed through a no confidence vote in its parliament in April 2022?

(a) Afghanistan (b) Pakistan
(c) Bangladesh (d) Egypt

**199.** Which country is to host the Asian Games of 2026.

(a) China (b) Japan
(c) India (d) Qatar

**200.** Which of the following is true about a Money Bill?

(1) It can only be introduced in Lok Sabha
(2) It can be amended both by the Lok Sabha & the Rajya Sabha
(3) The Speaker of Lok Sabha has to certify it as a Money bill

(a) 1, 2, 3 (b) 1, 2
(c) 1, 3 (d) 2, 3

## Answers of General Knowledge & Current Affairs

| **1.** (d) | **21.** (c) | **41.** (b) | **61.** (a) | **81.** (b) | **101.** (a) | **121.** (a) | **141.** (b) | **161.** (d) | **181.** (b) |
|---|---|---|---|---|---|---|---|---|---|
| **2.** (a) | **22.** (c) | **42.** (d) | **62.** (b) | **82.** (a) | **102.** (d) | **122.** (c) | **142.** (b) | **162.** (b) | **182.** (a) |
| **3.** (a) | **23.** (c) | **43.** (b) | **63.** (b) | **83.** (b) | **103.** (b) | **123.** (a) | **143.** (c) | **163.** (d) | **183.** (d) |
| **4.** (a) | **24.** (a) | **44.** (d) | **64.** (b) | **84.** (a) | **104.** (a) | **124.** (c) | **144.** (a) | **164.** (c) | **184.** (d) |
| **5.** (b) | **25.** (c) | **45.** (a) | **65.** (c) | **85.** (d) | **105.** (c) | **125.** (a) | **145.** (c) | **165.** (b) | **185.** (c) |
| **6.** (b) | **26.** (b) | **46.** (b) | **66.** (a) | **86.** (b) | **106.** (a) | **126.** (d) | **146.** (a) | **166.** (c) | **186.** (d) |
| **7.** (b) | **27.** (b) | **47.** (b) | **67.** (c) | **87.** (b) | **107.** (d) | **127.** (a) | **147.** (a) | **167.** (c) | **187.** (a) |
| **8.** (a) | **28.** (d) | **48.** (a) | **68.** (a) | **88.** (c) | **108.** (a) | **128.** (d) | **148.** (b) | **168.** (d) | **188.** (c) |
| **9.** (b) | **29.** (a) | **49.** (a) | **69.** (c) | **89.** (b) | **109.** (a) | **129.** (d) | **149.** (a) | **169.** (b) | **189.** (a) |
| **10.** (b) | **30.** (b) | **50.** (b) | **70.** (d) | **90.** (b) | **110.** (a) | **130.** (a) | **150.** (d) | **170.** (c) | **190.** (b) |
| **11.** (a) | **31.** (b) | **51.** (d) | **71.** (c) | **91.** (a) | **111.** (d) | **131.** (a) | **151.** (a) | **171.** (d) | **191.** (d) |
| **12.** (b) | **32.** (d) | **52.** (a) | **72.** (d) | **92.** (a) | **112.** (c) | **132.** (d) | **152.** (a) | **172.** (a) | **192.** (b) |
| **13.** (b) | **33.** (b) | **53.** (c) | **73.** (d) | **93.** (b) | **113.** (a) | **133.** (a) | **153.** (a) | **173.** (a) | **193.** (d) |
| **14.** (a) | **34.** (b) | **54.** (a) | **74.** (d) | **94.** (a) | **114.** (a) | **134.** (c) | **154.** (a) | **174.** (b) | **194.** (b) |
| **15.** (a) | **35.** (c) | **55.** (b) | **75.** (c) | **95.** (a) | **115.** (d) | **135.** (d) | **155.** (a) | **175.** (b) | **195.** (b) |
| **16.** (b) | **36.** (c) | **56.** (d) | **76.** (c) | **96.** (a) | **116.** (c) | **136.** (b) | **156.** (b) | **176.** (a) | **196.** (a) |
| **17.** (a) | **37.** (b) | **57.** (a) | **77.** (a) | **97.** (b) | **117.** (d) | **137.** (b) | **157.** (a) | **177.** (a) | **197.** (b) |
| **18.** (b) | **38.** (b) | **58.** (a) | **78.** (d) | **98.** (c) | **118.** (b) | **138.** (d) | **158.** (a) | **178.** (a) | **198.** (b) |
| **19.** (b) | **39.** (b) | **59.** (a) | **79.** (d) | **99.** (b) | **119.** (b) | **139.** (a) | **159.** (a) | **179.** (d) | **199.** (b) |
| **20.** (b) | **40.** (d) | **60.** (b) | **80.** (a) | **100.** (c) | **120.** (d) | **140.** (c) | **160.** (b) | **180.** (d) | **200.** (c) |

# General Mental Ability

# 5

*"All that we are is the result of what we have thought. The mind is everything. What we think we become."*

—Gautam Buddha

## 1. Introduction

'Mental ability' usually refers to a variety of attributes, which include verbal/linguistic aptitude, facility with numbers, abstract thinking, logic and reasoning, spatial–visual aptitude, intrapersonal and interpersonal skills, sense of rhythm and kinesthetic abilities. Many of these abilities are a part of tests, which have already been dealt with, in other sections. The traits, which are to be assessed here, form a part of the following three abilities:

- Visuo-spatial ability
- Verbal ability
- Numerical ability

What these abilities entail and the type of question to expect is briefly described here.

### 1.1 Visuo-Spatial Ability

This refers to the capacity to visually perceive the spatial relationship between different objects. The questions testing this ability, usually comprise geometric figures of different shapes and patterns. The candidates are expected to understand the relationship between the figures to find the odd one out or to predict the figure coming next in the sequence. Consider the following example.

**1.1 Illustration**

Question Figures

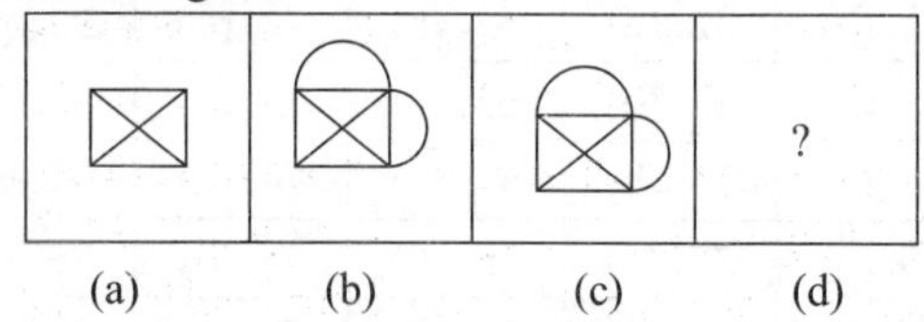


Answer Figures

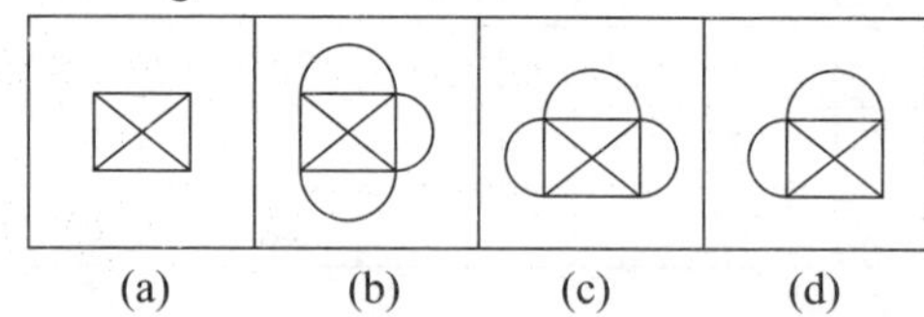


In the question above, one has to find which figure from the answer options provided, follows the first three figures in the question. The answer is Option (b), as in each subsequent figure in the question, a semicircle is getting added. Consider another example.

**1.2 Illustration**

Question Figures

Answer Figures

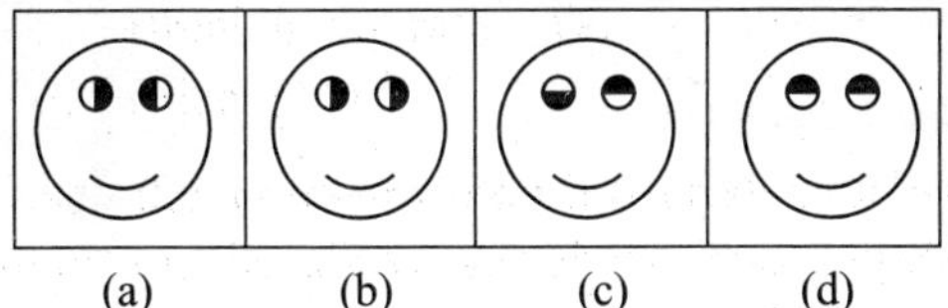

Here the right option would be Option (d) as the eyes of the face in the question figure is seen to be moving in the opposite direction.

While solving such questions, the following tips will be helpful:

- Observe the figures very carefully and understand what the question wants you to do, viz.
  - (a) Find out the odd one.
  - (b) Find the figure coming next in sequence.
  - (c) Find the figure which bears the same relationship as that given in the question.
- If the figures are changing, identify the change. This helps in predicting the next figure in the sequence.
- In case the question asks you to find out the odd figure then observe the common features of all figures very carefully. Also identify the pattern of change.
- Question as in Category (c) will also require one to understand the relationship between the figures. This can be done by observing the common features of the figures and understanding the pattern of change.

## 1.2 Verbal Ability

Verbal ability encompasses a wide variety of traits, such as linguistic intelligence, facility with words and comprehension aptitude. But the ability to be tested in this section is largely the logical understanding of words and their context of use.

Consider the examples given here.

**1.3 Illustration**

*Choose the odd one.*

(a) *House* (b) *Apartment*

(c) *Building* (d) *Society*

The answer here is, 'society', Option (d), as the other words are synonymous with and used for the purpose of dwelling.

Thus, it can be seen that what the question expects of the candidate is contextual understanding of the words and a sense of logic to appreciate the underlying relationship between them, or to distinguish between them. Consider another example.

**1.4 Illustration**

*Which one of the following responses would be a meaningful order of the following activities?*

1. *Sowing* 2. *Ploughing*

3. *Harvesting* 4. *Irrigation*

(a) 1, 2, 3, 4 (b) 2, 1, 4, 3

(c) 3, 2, 1, 4 (d) 4, 3, 2, 1

The above represents the various activities associated with agriculture and their chronological sequence would be 2, 1, 4, 3. Thus, the correct choice would be Option (b).

## 1.3 Numerical Ability

In the context of this section, numerical ability refers to a logical understanding of the relationship between numbers in a given set or matrix of numbers. Here, the ability to perform mathematical operations and understand basic mathematical concepts is not what the question aims to assess. These attributes are to be tested in the section on Numerical ability and quantitative reasoning.

The questions here are likely to be of the following types:

(a) Predicting the next number in a series

(b) Finding the missing number in a given set or matrix of number

(c) Identifying the relationship between numbers to break a code, etc. Consider the following illustrations:

**1.5 Illustration**

### Numbers Series

*Find the next number in the series.*

I. 1, 4, 7, 10 ........,

II. 1, 2, 4, 7, 11, 16 ........,

III. 1, 4, 9, 16, 25 ........,

IV. 3, 5, 6, 10, 9, 15, 12........, ........,

- The first example is that of a simple difference series, where the difference between successive numbers is constant. In Example (I), this difference is 3. Therefore, the next number in the series is 13.
- In Series (II), the difference between successive numbers is increasing. The differences are 1, 2, 3, 4, 5. The difference forms a simple series and the next difference should be 6 and the number to follow should be 22.
- The next illustration is not based on the difference but is based on the square of numbers $1^2 = 1, 2^2 = 4, 3^2 = 9, 4^2 = 16, 5^2 = 25$. As such, the next number in the series is 36 ($6^2$). A number of such series questions can be based on square or cube of numbers.
- In the last set of numbers, there are two series present. The alternate numbers 3, 6, 9, 12 form a series. The next number in sequence would be 15. The other set of alternate numbers are 5, 10, 15 and the number next to follow will be 20. Therefore, in Series (IV) the given set of numbers will be followed by 15 and 20.

**1.6 Illustration**

### Matrix of Numbers

*Find the missing number.*

| | | |
|---|---|---|
| 1 | 2 | 2 |
| 2 | 3 | 6 |
| 3 | 4 | 12 |
| 4 | 5 | ? |

In case of matrix of numbers, the pattern of matrix and the relationship between the numbers has to be understood. In the given example, the third number in each row is the product of the first and second number. As such, the missing number should be 20.

**1.7 Illustration**

### Code Breaking

In code breaking, often letters of English alphabet are represented by a separate number, which has to be identified. The numbering of alphabets may be based on chronological order of alphabets, e.g., A is 1, B is 2, C is 3 and so on, or it may have to be derived from the examples given in the question itself.

**1.8 Illustration**

*If MASK is coded as 2 4 9 8 and ICE is coded as 1 3 7 then CAKE will be coded as?* From the examples of MASK and ICE, it is seen that C is coded as 3, A as 4, K as 8 and E as 7. Thus, code for cake is 3 4 8 7.

**1.9 Illustration**

*If CAM is coded as 4, 2, 14 and BIG is coded as 3, 10, 8 then what is the code for HEAD?*

The examples show that code for each alphabet is the chronological position of the alphabet +1. Thus, A is 2, B is 3, C is 4 and so on. Therefore, HEAD will be coded as 9, 6, 2, 5.

**1.10 Illustration**

In a certain code, ABILITY is coded as PSGHGUV and WHEAT is coded as AKRPU. How would HABITAT be coded?

On analysing the codes, we see that there exists one to one relationship between the letters and their corresponding codes. Viz A is written as P and W as A. Further the letters which are common in both the words, have the same code. Viz. A has code P and T has code U in both the words. The word whose code is to be worked out is HABITAT. All the letters of the word are contained in the two words whose codes are provided. Based on that the word HABITAT is decoded as KPSGUPU.

Blood-relationships based questions are also at times considered a part of general mental ability. However, as they require logical deductions of the relationship of the parties based on the specified facts, in this book its covered under the topic of 'analytical reasoning'.

## Exercise 1 on General Mental Ability

**Directions:** Select the appreciate letter/word/ number/figure from the given alternatives.

**1.** Book: Publisher :: Film: ?

(a) Writer (b) Editor
(c) Director (d) Producer

**2.** Which one set of letters when sequentially placed at the gaps in the given letter series shall complete it?

a_n_b__ncb__ncb

(a) bcabab (b) bacbab
(c) abcbcb (d) abbbcc

**Directions:** In the given question, a series is given with one term/figure missing. Choose the correct alternative from the given ones that will complete the series.

**3.** Question Figures

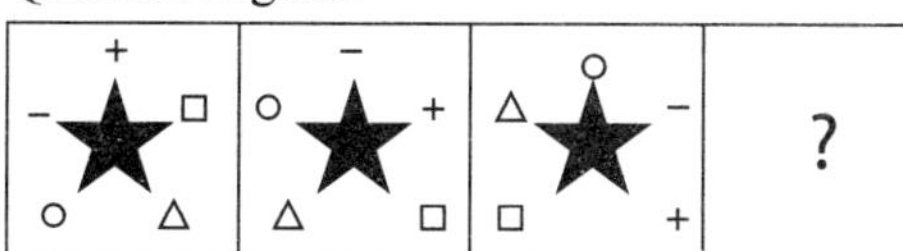

Answer Figures

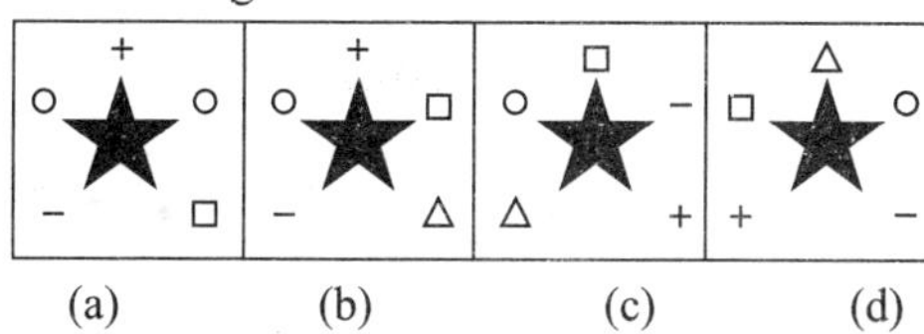

**4.** In a coding system, PEN is written as NZO and BARK as CTSL. How can we write PRANK in that coding system?

(a) NZTOL (b) CSTZN
(c) NSTOL (d) NTSLO

**5.** From the words given in the answer choices, select the word, which cannot be formed using the letters of the given word PRESIDENTIAL.

(a) SLEEP (b) DENTAL
(c) ARDENT (d) DIGITAL

**6.** How many triangles are there in the following figure?

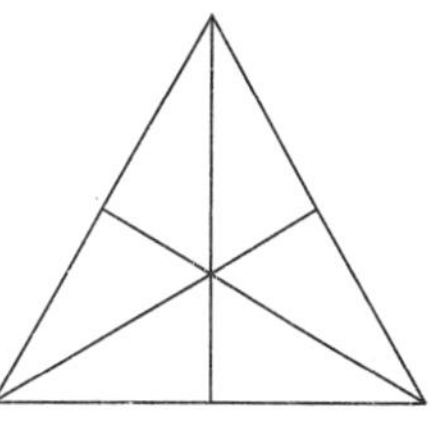

(a) 16 (b) 13
(c) 9 (d) 7

**7.** Which one of the given responses would be a meaningful order of the following words?

1. Rain 2. Monsoon
3. Rescue 4. Flood
5. Shelter 6. Relief

(a) 1, 5, 4, 5, 3, 6 (b) 1, 2, 3, 4, 5, 6
(c) 2, 1, 4, 3, 5, 6 (d) 4, 1, 2, 3, 6, 5

**8.** Find the missing number/letters/figure from the given responses 3, 10, 20, 33, 49, 68, ?

(a) 75 (b) 85
(c) 90 (d) 91

**9.** Select the missing number from the given responses.

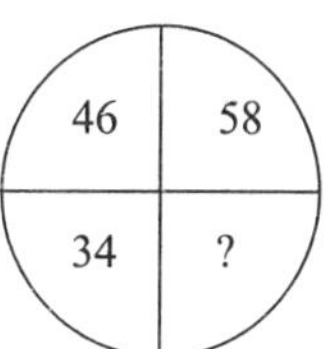


(a) 92 (b) 72
(c) 22 (d) 68

**10.** Rohan walks a distance of 3 km towards North, then turns to his left and walks for 2 km. He again turns left and walks for 3 km. At this point, he turns to his left and walks for 3 km. How many km is he from the starting point?

(a) 5 km (b) 3 km
(c) 2 km (d) 1 km

**11.** In a joint family, the members of the family are: father, mother, 3 married sons and one unmarried daughter. Of the sons, 2 have 2 daughters each, and one has a son. How many female members are there in the family?

(a) 2 (b) 3

(c) 6 (d) 9

**12.** Which one of the answer figures shall complete the given question figure?

Question Figure

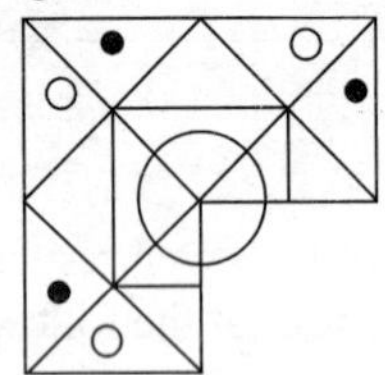

Answer Figures

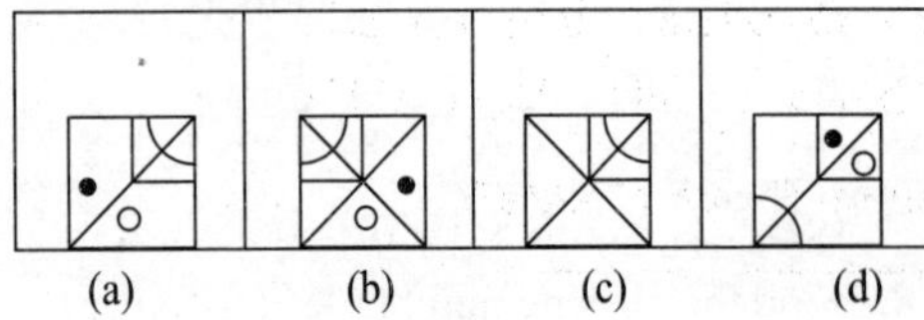

(a) (b) (c) (d)

**13.** Find the odd word/letters/number/figures from the given responses.

(a) Analysis (b) Search

(c) Conclusion (d) Investigation

**14.** Arrange the following words according to the dictionary.

1. Scenery 2. Science
3. Scandal 4. School
5. Scatter

(a) 3, 5, 1, 4, 2 (b) 3, 5, 4, 1, 2

(c) 5, 3, 4, 2, 1 (d) 5, 3, 2, 1, 4

**15.** Find the missing number/letters/figure from the given alternatives. DAB, IFG, NKL, .........?

(a) SPQ (b) SOP

(c) SPO (d) RSQ

**16.** In a certain code, the following numbers are coded in a certain way by assigning signs.

| 1 | 2 | 3 | 4 | 5 | 6 | 7 | 8 | 9 |
|---|---|---|---|---|---|---|---|---|
| > | < | ∧ | + | ◊ | ∨ | ÷ | × | – |

Which number can be decoded from the following?

∨ < – ∧ ◊

(a) 62953 (b) 62935

(c) 62593 (d) 62539

**17.** A word given in capital letters is followed by four words. Out of these only one word cannot be formed by using the letters of the given word. Find that word.

EXEMPLIFICATION

(a) FIXATION (b) EXAMPLE

(c) AXE (d) EXTRA

**18.** Given below are four views of a cube. Each face is marked with certain symbols. In Figure 3, which symbol will appear on the face opposite the face having concentric circles symbol?

Question Figures

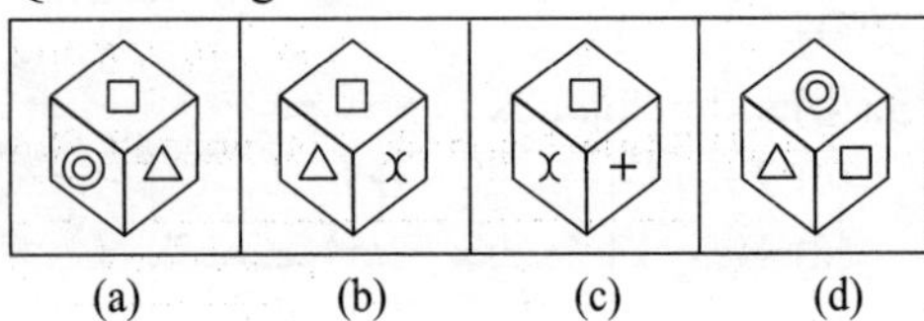

(a) (b) (c) (d)

Answer Figures

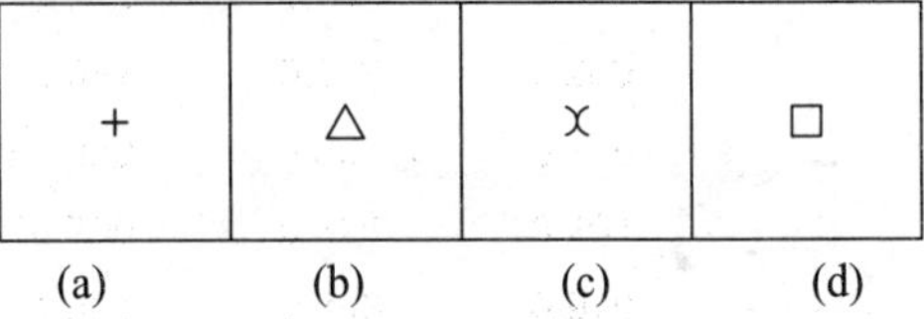

(a) (b) (c) (d)

**19.** A piece of paper is folded and punched as shown here. From the given responses, indicate how it will appear when opened.

Question Figures

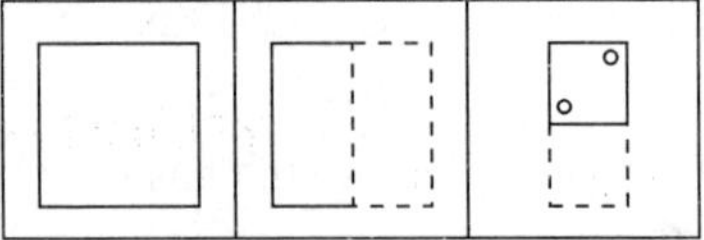

Answer Figures

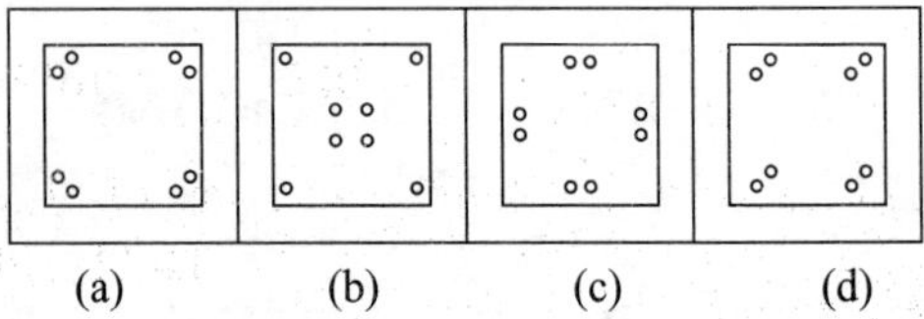

(a) (b) (c) (d)

**20.** Arun started from point A and walked 10 km east to point B, then turned North and walked 3 km to point C, and then turned West and walked 12 km to point D, then again turned South and walked 3 km to point E. In which direction is he from his starting point?

(a) East (b) South

(c) West (d) North

**21.** In an organisation of pollution control board, engineers are represented by a circle, legal experts by a square and environmentalists by a triangle. Who is most represented in the board as shown in the following figure?

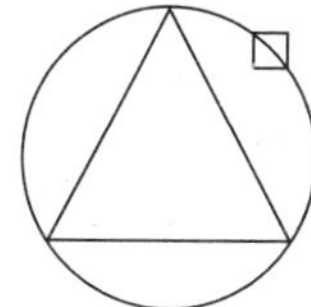

(a) Environmentalists

(b) Legal experts

(c) Engineers with legal background

(d) Environmentalists with engineering background

**22.** Select the related letters/word/number/figure from the given alternatives. REASON : SFBTPO : : THINK :?

(a) SGHMJ (b) UIJOL

(c) UHNKI (d) UJKPM

Question Figures

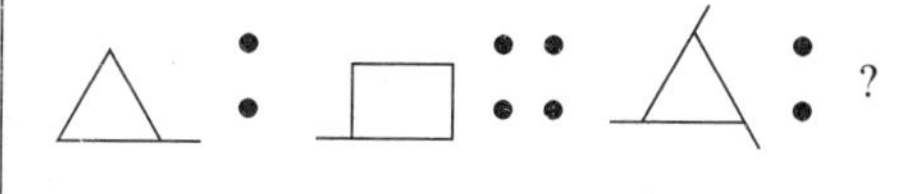

Answer Figures

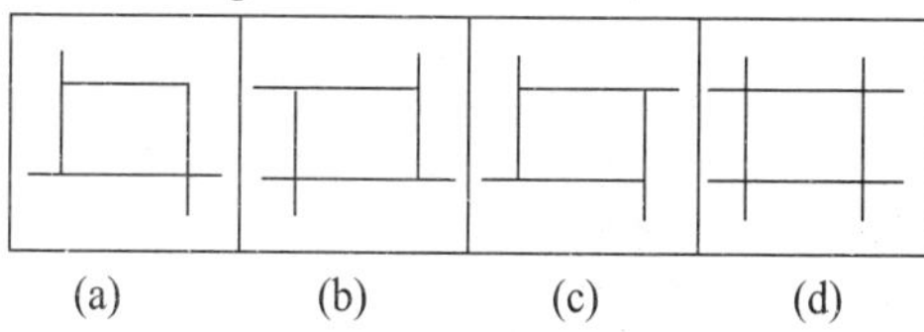

(a) (b) (c) (d)

**24.** Question Figures

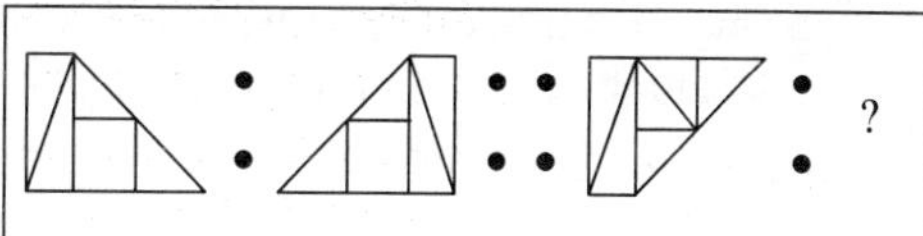

Answer Figures

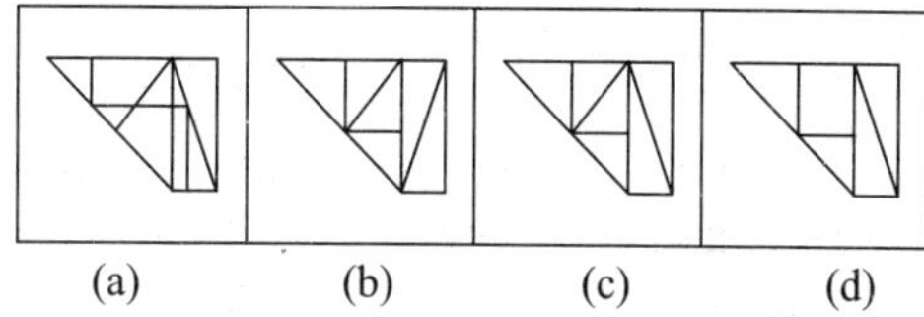

(a) (b) (c) (d)

**25.** Which one set of letters when sequentially placed at the gaps in the given letter series shall complete it?

l - n - m l l m - n – l

(a) mnmn (b) mnnm

(c) mnmm (d) nmmn

**26.** Question Figures

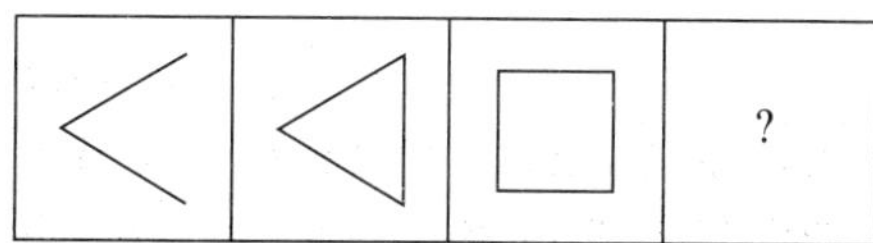

Answer Figures

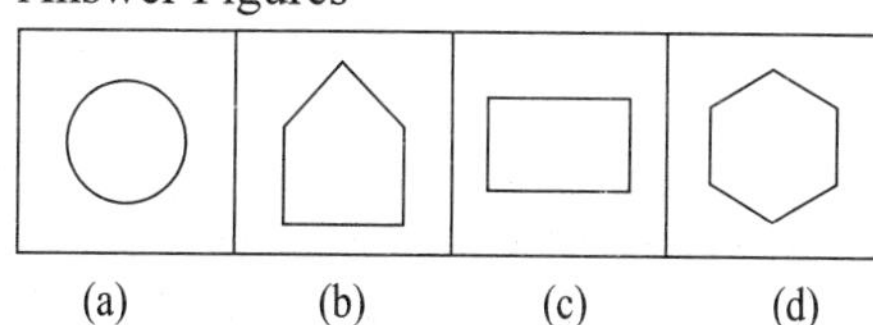

(a) (b) (c) (d)

**27.** Question Figures

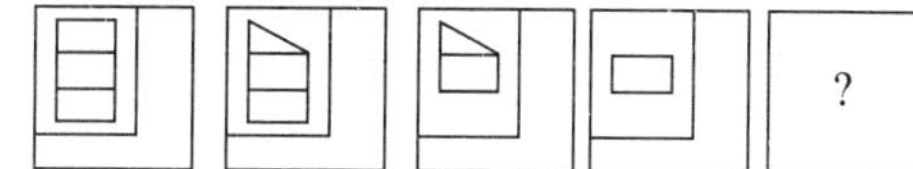

Answer Figures

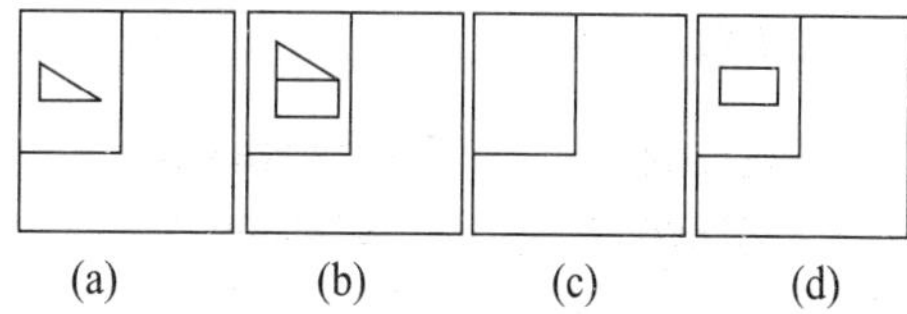

(a) (b) (c) (d)

**28.** From among the given alternatives, select the one in which the set of numbers is most like the set of numbers given in the question.

Given set: (3, 9, 11)

(a) 5, 25, 20 (b) 6, 36, 38

(c) 7, 49, 45 (d) 8, 16, 24

**29.** From among the given alternatives, select the one in which the set of numbers is most like the set of numbers given in the question.

Given set: (8, 40, 56)

(a) (3, 15, 21) (b) (7, 28, 49)
(c) (5, 20, 45) (d) (6, 24, 36)

**30.** If '–' stands for division, '÷' stands for multiplication, '+' stands for subtraction and '×' for addition then which of the following equations is correct?

(a) $20 + 8 - 7 \div 6 \times 4 = 25$
(b) $20 - 5 \div 4 + 6 \times 5 = 15$
(c) $20 \times 5 - 6 \div 7 + 4 = 28$
(d) $20 \div 4 - 8 \times 10 + 6 = 36$

**31.** Select the one which is different from the other three.

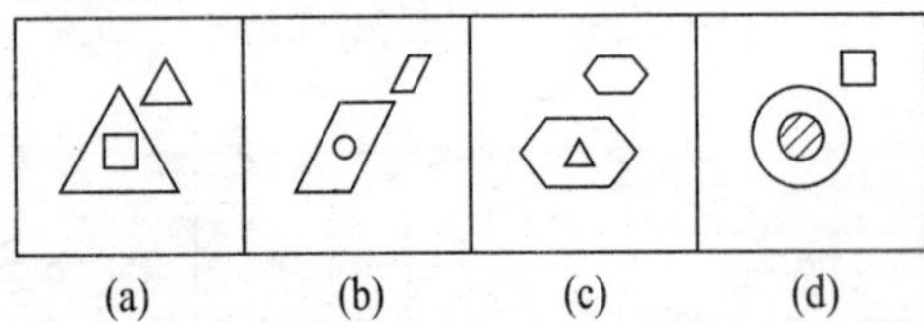

(a) (b) (c) (d)

**32.** The word given in capital letters is followed by four words, which form the answer choices. Out of these only one can be formed by using the letters of the given word. Find that word.

ENVIRONMENT

(a) EMINENT (b) ENTRANCE
(c) ENTERTAIN (d) MOVEMENT

**33.** In the accounts department of a company, there are some who are only chartered accountants and some who are only cost accountants. A few hold both chartered and cost accountancy qualifications. Besides these there are others who hold management accountancy qualifications. Some of these management accountants have also done either chartered or cost accountancy or both. Which of the following figures represents these facts?

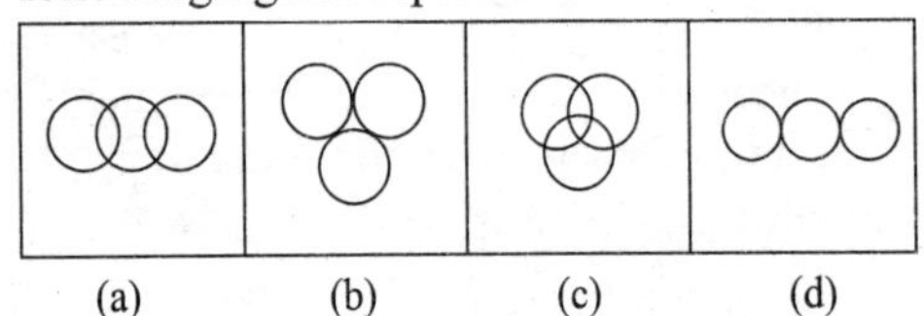

(a) (b) (c) (d)

**34.** Which one of the answer figures shall complete the given question figure?

Question Figure

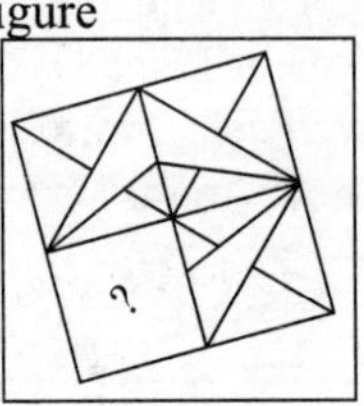


Answer Figures

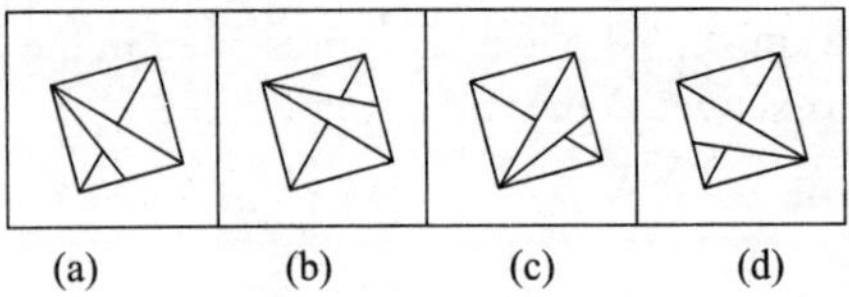

(a) (b) (c) (d)

**35.** In which answer figure is the question figure embedded?

Question Figure

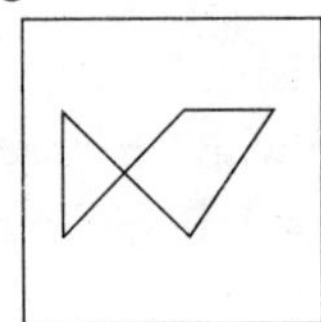

Answer Figures

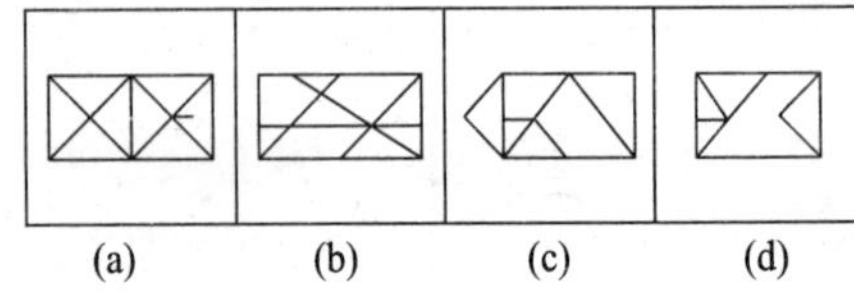

(a) (b) (c) (d)

**36.** Ice : Coldness : : Earth :?

(a) Weight (b) Gravitation
(c) Jungle (d) Sea

**37.** How many rectangles are there in the given figure?

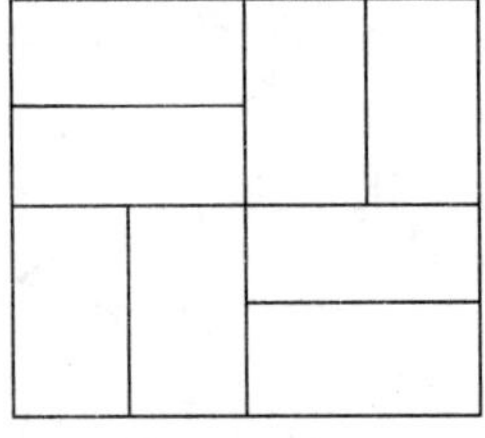

(a) 24 (b) 16
(c) 22 (d) 14

**38.** In the following figure, the boys who are athletic and disciplined are indicated by which number?

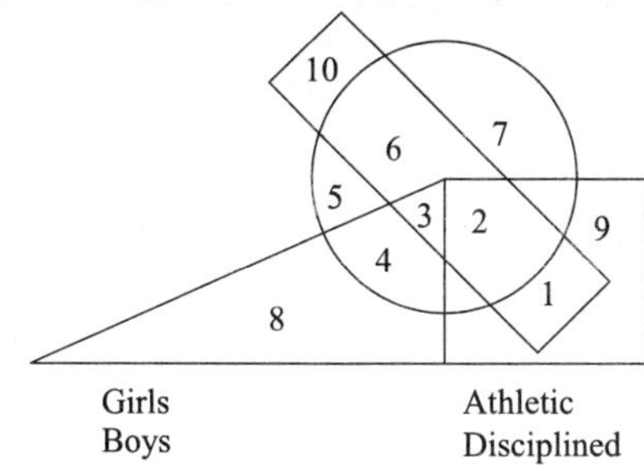


(a) 1 (b) 2
(c) 6 (d) 10

**39.** In which answer figure is the question figure embedded?

Question Figure

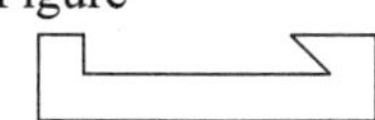

Answer Figures

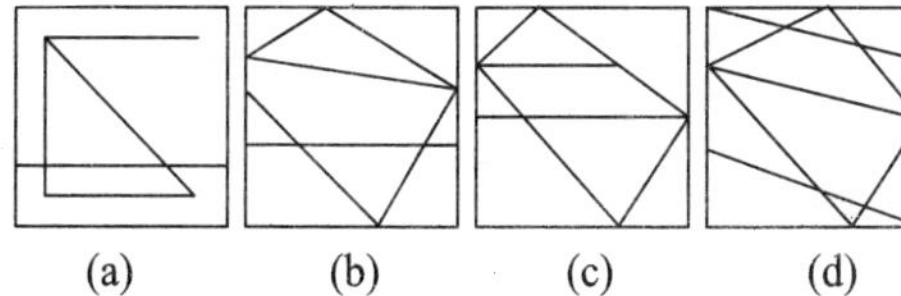

(a) (b) (c) (d)

**40.** Select the related letters/word/number/figure from the given alternatives. Safe : Secure :: Protect :?

(a) Guard (b) Lock
(c) Sure (d) Conserve

**41.** Select the related letters/word/number/figure from the given alternatives. MASTER : OCUVGT :: LABOUR :?

(a) NCDQWT (b) NDERWT
(c) NBECRWT (d) NEDRWT

**42.** M × N : 13 × 14 : : F × R :?

(a) 14 × 15 (b) 5 × 17
(c) 6 × 18 (d) 7 × 19

**43.** Question Figures

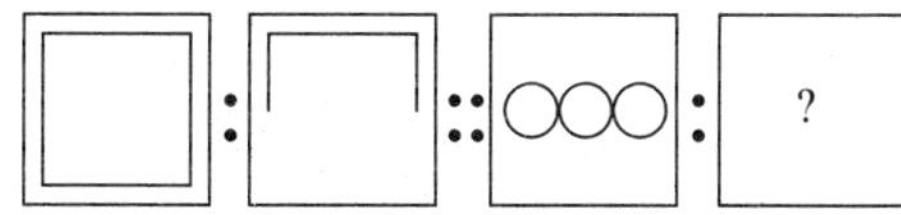

Answer Figures

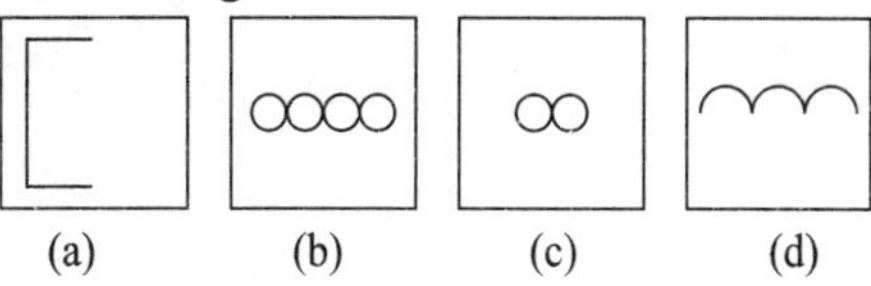

(a) (b) (c) (d)

**44.** Find the odd one from the given responses.

(a) Reward – Punishment
(b) Object – Permit
(c) Sharp – Blunt
(d) Cold – Cool

**45.** Find the odd one from the given responses.

(a) ZVRN (b) UQMJ
(c) SOKG (d) TPLH

**46.** Find the odd one from the given figures:

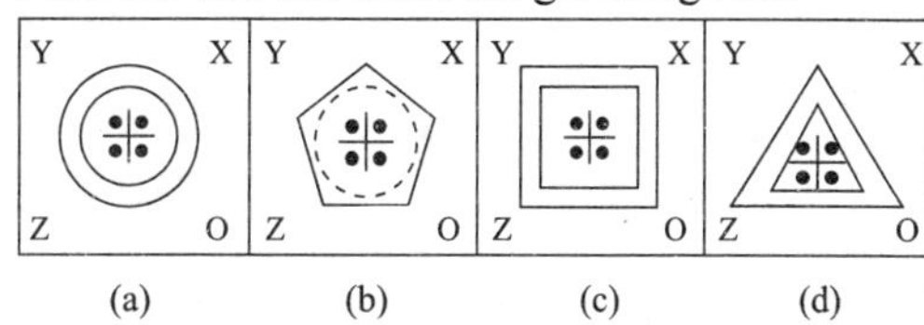


(a) (b) (c) (d)

**47.** Which one of the given responses would be a meaningful order of the following words?

1. Wall 2. Clay
3. House 4. Room
5. Bricks

(a) 5, 2, 1, 4, 3 (b) 2, 5, 4, 1, 3
(c) 2, 5, 1, 4, 3 (d) 1, 2, 3, 4, 5

**Directions:** Find out the missing numbers/letters in the given series.

**48** 1, 2, 2, 4, 8, 32, (....)

(a) 246 (b) 256
(c) 266 (d) 276

**49.** 6, 5, 12, 10, 18, (....), 24, 20

(a) 15 (2) 18
(b) 21 (4) 24

**50.** BD, FH, JL, NP, ?

(a) SV (b) SU
(c) RT (d) QS

## Answers of Exercise 1 on General Mental Ability

| | | | | |
|---|---|---|---|---|
| **1.** (d) | **11.** (d) | **21.** (d) | **31.** (d) | **41.** (a) |
| **2.** (a) | **12.** (b) | **22.** (b) | **32.** (a) | **42.** (c) |
| **3.** (d) | **13.** (c) | **23.** (b) | **33.** (c) | **43.** (d) |
| **4.** (c) | **14.** (a) | **24.** (c) | **34.** (b) | **44.** (d) |
| **5.** (d) | **15.** (a) | **25.** (b) | **35.** (a) | **45.** (b) |
| **6.** (a) | **16.** (b) | **26.** (b) | **36.** (b) | **46.** (b) |
| **7.** (c) | **17.** (d) | **27.** (c) | **37.** (b) | **47.** (c) |
| **8.** (c) | **18.** (c) | **28.** (b) | **38.** (b) | **48.** (b) |
| **9.** (c) | **19.** (c) | **29.** (a) | **39.** (a) | **49.** (a) |
| **10.** (d) | **20.** (c) | **30.** (b) | **40.** (a) | **50.** (c) |

## Exercise 2 on General Mental Ability

**1.** Consider the following matrices:

| 3 | 8 | 10 | 2 | ? | 1 |
|---|---|---|---|---|---|
| 6 | 56 | 90 | 2 | 20 | 0 |

What is the missing number at '?' in the matrix?

(a) 5 (b) 0

(c) 7 (d) 3

**2.** What is the missing number "X' of the series 7, X, 21, 31, 43?

(a) 11 (b) 12

(c) 13 (d) 14

**3.** Four cardboard pieces of specific shapes are shown in the following figure:

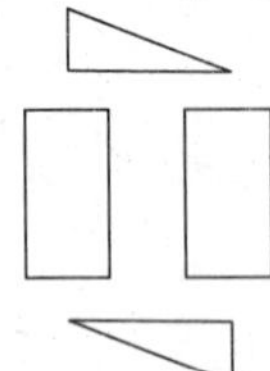

Which one of the following figures given can be formed by joining these pieces together?

(a)  (b) 

(c) 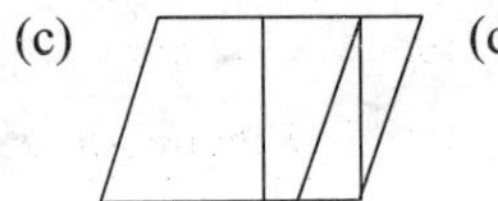 (d) 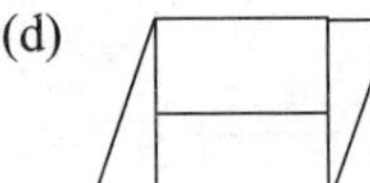

**4.** If LSJXVC is the code for MUMBAI, the code for DELHI is

(a) CCIDD (b) CDKGH

(c) CCJFG (d) CCIFE

**5.** If RAMON is written as 12345 and DINESH as 675849, then HAMAM will be written as

(a) 92233 (b) 92323

(c) 93322 (d) 93232

**6.** For a sports meet, a winner's stand comprising three wooden blocks is in the following form:

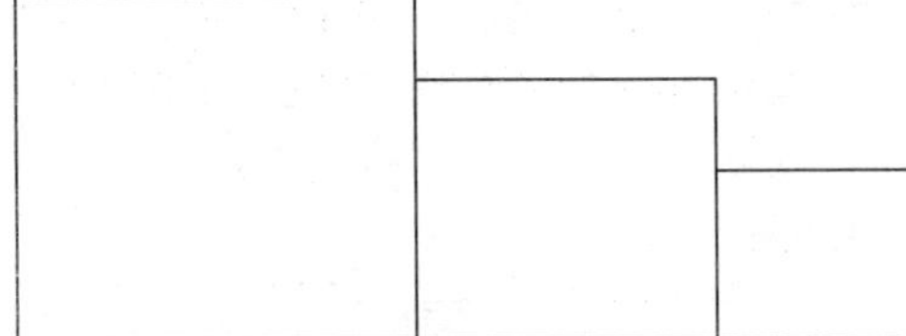

There are six different colours available to choose from. Each of the three wooden blocks is to be painted such that no two of them has the same colour. In how many different ways can the winners' stand be painted?

(a) 120 (b) 81
(c) 66 (d) 36

**7.** Consider the figures given below:

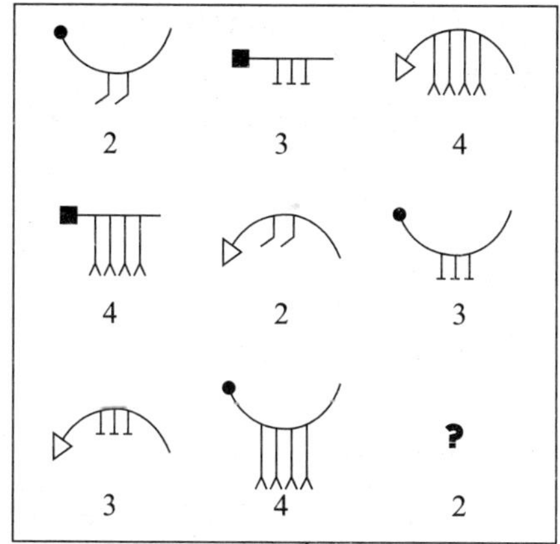


To fit the question mark, the correct answer is

(a)  (b) 
(c) 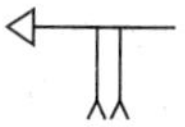 (d)

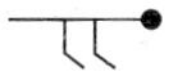

**8.** Consider the following figures:

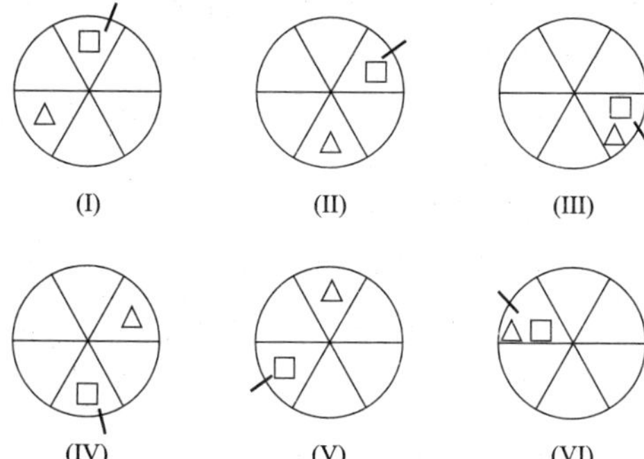


In the figures (I) to (VI) above, some parts are shown to change their positions in regular directions. Following the same sequence, which of the figures give below will appear at (VI) stage?

(a)  (b) 
(c)  (d)

**9.** There are 24 equally spaced points lying on the circumference of a circle. What is the maximum number of equilateral triangles that can be drawn by taking sets of three points as the vertices?

(a) 4 (b) 6
(c) 8 (d) 12

**10.** Consider the sequence given below: 4/12/95, 1/1/96, 29/1/96, 26/2/96, ........

What is the next term of the series?

(a) 24/3/96 (b) 25/3/96
(c) 26/3/96 (d) 27/3/96

**Directions for the following 3 (three) items:** Rotated positions of a single solid are shown below. The various faces of the solid are marked with different symbols like dots, cross and line. Answer the three items that follow the given figures.

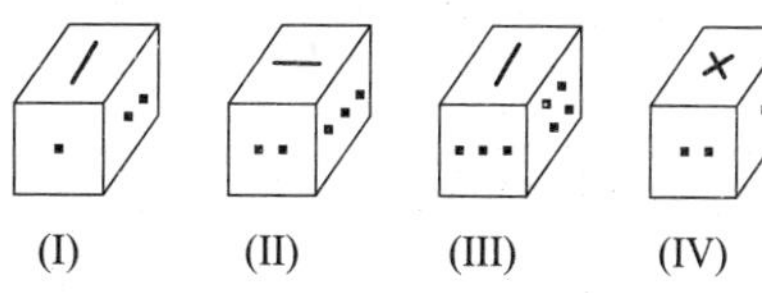


**11.** What is the symbol on the face opposite to that containing a single dot?

(a) Four dots (b) Three dots
(c) Two dots (d) Cross

**12.** What is the symbol on the face opposite to that containing two dots?

(a) Single dot (b) Three dots
(c) Four dots (d) Line

**13.** What is the symbol on the face opposite to that containing the cross?

(a) Single dot (b) Two dots
(c) Line (d) Four dots

**14.** Consider the following three-dimensional figure:

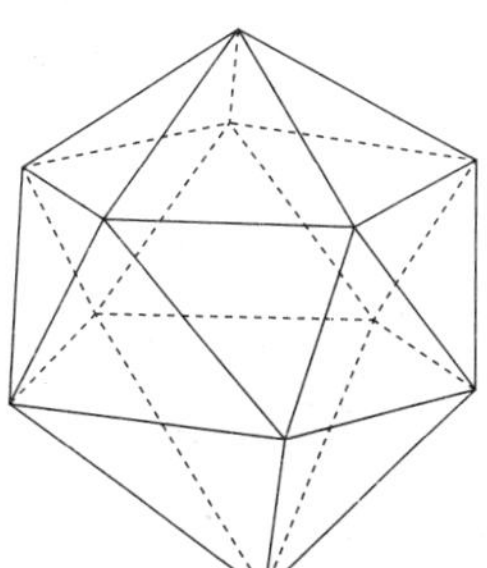

How many triangles does the above figure have?

(a) 18 (b) 20
(c) 22 (d) 24

15. Consider the following pattern of numbers:

| 8 | 10 | 15 | 13 |
|---|---|---|---|
| 6 | 5 | 7 | 4 |
| 4 | 6 | 8 | 8 |
| 6 | 11 | 16 | ? |

What is the number at '?' in the above pattern?

(a) 17 (b) 19
(c) 21 (d) 23

16. How many diagonals can be drawn by joining the vertices of an octagon?

(a) 20 (b) 24
(c) 28 (d) 64

17. If every alternative letter of the English alphabet from B onwards (including B) is written in lower case (small letters) and the remaining letters are capitalized, then how is the first month of the second half of the year written?

(a) JuLY (b) jULy
(c) jUly (d) jUlY

18. In the sequence 1, 5, 7, 3, 5, 7, 4, 3, 5, 7, how many such 5s are there which are not immediately preceded by 3 but are immediately followed by 7?

(a) 1 (b) 2
(c) 3 (d) None

19. If $ means 'divided by', @ means 'multiplied by' and # means 'minus', then the value of 10#5@1$5 is

(a) 0 (b) 1
(c) 2 (d) 9

20. What is 'X' in the sequence 132, 129, 124, 117, 106, 93, X?

(a) 74 (b) 75
(c) 76 (d) 77

21. What is 'X' in the sequence 4, 196, 16, 144, 36, 100, 64, X?

(a) 48 (b) 64
(c) 125 (d) 256

22. Consider the following sequence that follows some arrangement:

c_accaa_aa_bc_b

The letters that appear in the gaps are

(a) abba (b) cbbb
(c) bbbb (d) cccc

23. Which year has the same calendar as that of 2009?

(a) 2018 (b) 2017
(c) 2016 (d) 2015

24. Mr 'X' has three children. The birthday of the first child falls on the 5th Monday of April, that of the second one falls on the 5th Thursday of November. On which day is the birthday of his third child, which falls on 20th December?

(a) Monday (b) Thursday
(c) Saturday (d) Sunday

25. The number of parallelograms that can be formed from a set of four parallel lines intersecting another set of four parallel lines, is

(a) 18 (b) 24
(c) 32 (d) 36

26. If in a particular year 12th January is a Sunday, then which one of the following is correct?

(a) 15th July is a Sunday if the year is a leap year.
(b) 15th July is a Sunday if the year is not a leap year.
(c) 12th July is a Sunday if the year is a leap year.
(d) 12th July is not a Sunday if the year is a leap year.

27. Consider the following sequence of numbers:

5 1 4 7 3 9 8 5 7 2 6 3 1 5
8 6 3 8 5 2 2 4 3 4 9 6

How many odd numbers are followed by the odd number in the above sequence?

(a) 5 (b) 6
(c) 7 (d) 8

**28.** What is the missing term @ in the following?
ACPQ : BESU:: MNGI: @
(a) NPJL (b) NOJM
(c) NPIL (d) NPJM

**29.** Consider the following statements:
The minimum number of points of intersection of a square and a circle is 2.
The maximum number of points of intersection of a square and a circle is 8.
Which of the above statements is/are correct?
(a) 1 only (b) 2 only
(c) Both 1 and 2 (d) Neither 1 nor 2

**30.** A cube has all its faces painted with different colours. It is cut into smaller cubes of equal sizes such that the side of the small cube is one-fourth the big cube. The number of small cubes with only one of the sides painted is:
(a) 32 (b) 24
(c) 16 (d) 8

**31.** A military code writes STSTEM as SYSMET and NEARER as AENRER. Using the same code FRACTION can be written as:
(a) CARFTION (b) FRACNOIT
(c) NOITCARF (d) CARFNOIT

**32.** There are 4 horizontal and 4 vertical lines, parallel and equidistant to one another on a board. What is the maximum number of rectangles and squares that can be formed?
(a) 16 (b) 24
(c) 36 (d) 42

**33.** The outer surface of a 4 cm × 4 cm × 4 cm cube is painted completely in red. It is sliced parallel to the faces to yield 64, 1cm × 1 cm × 1 cm small cubes. How many small cubes do not have painted faces?
(a) 8 (b) 10
(c) 24 (d) 36

**34.** In a certain code, '256' means 'red colour chalk', '589' means 'green colour flower' and '254' means 'white colour chalk'. The digit in the code that indicates 'white' is
(a) 2 (b) 4
(c) 5 (d) 8

**35.** Consider the word CLEARLY. Can by using the 5th, 6th, 1st, and the 4th letters of this word, another word be formed? If yes, then which of the following could be its first letter. If no word is possible then chose option (d).
(a) C
(b) A
(c) Y
(d) No word is possible with the four letters

**36.** If the letters of the word CLARITY are arranged in the reverse alphabetic order, then which letter would be falling in the middle?
(a) L (b) I
(c) R (d) T

**37.** Find the odd one out.
(a) 4 (b) 25
(c) 125 (d) 256

**38.** Find the value of 320 + 8 – 40 + 10 where '+' means subtraction and '–' means multiplication
(a) 0
(b) –10
(c) +10
(d) None of the above

**39.** In certain word CRY is coded as 'XIB', then what is the code of DOG?
(a) WLU (b) WLT
(c) WMT (d) VLT

**40.** Find the number next in series: 2, 5, 10, 17, 26 ____
(a) 37 (b) 39
(c) 50 (d) 65

Read the following statements carefully and answer the four statements that follow.

A solid sphere which is painted red, is cut into two equal hemispheres. The new surfaces which emerge, are then painted green. After that each hemisphere is cut into four equal parts by cutting along the two perpendicular diameters of the flat surface. Thus, eight equal parts are generated from the sphere.

**41.** How many surfaces are there now in all the parts taken together?
(a) 8 (b) 16
(c) 32 (d) cannot be determined

**42.** How many surfaces are painted red?
(a) 4 (b) 8
(c) 16 (d) 32

**43.** How many flat surfaces are there in all the parts taken together?
(a) 8 (b) 12
(c) 16 (d) 24

**44.** How many surfaces are painted green?
(a) 8 (b) 12
(c) 16 (d) 24

**45.** Which of the following options does not bear the same relationship to the item given here?

Square : Cube

1. Circle : Sphere
2. Rectangle : Cuboid
3. Quadrilateral : Cuboid
4. Circle : Cone

(a) 2, 3, 4 (b) 1, 3, 4
(c) 3, 4 (d) 4

**46.** Identify which one of the following is not a part of the given series.

AE, FI, JL, MN, OP

(a) FI (b) JL
(c) MN (d) OP

**47.** Find the odd one out
(a) Hectare (b) Yard
(c) Metre (d) Inch

**48.** Find the missing term in the series.

1/2, 3/5, 5/9, 7/14,……, 11/27

(a) 9/20 (b) 9/19
(c) 8/20 (d) 8/19

**49.** Find the missing term in the figure.

| 1 | 1 | 0 |
|---|---|---|
| 2 | 8 | 6 |
| 3 | 27 | |

(a) 12 (b) 24
(c) 30 (d) None of the above

**50.** A clock is set at 12 PM 1st April. It gains 2 minute in every 3 hours. What is the right time when it shows 00:24 AM on the on 3rd April?
(a) 11 PM on 2nd April
(b) 11:36 PM on 2nd April
(c) 00:00 AM on 3rd April
(d) 00:48 AM on 3rd April

## Answers of Exercise 2 on General Mental Ability

| | | | | |
|---|---|---|---|---|
| **1.** (a) | **11.** (b) | **21.** (b) | **31.** (d) | **41.** (c) |
| **2.** (c) | **12.** (c) | **22.** (b) | **32.** (c) | **42.** (b) |
| **3.** (d) | **13.** (c) | **23.** (d) | **33.** (a) | **43.** (d) |
| **4.** (a) | **14.** (b) | **24.** (b) | **34.** (b) | **44.** (a) |
| **5.** (b) | **15.** (a) | **25.** (d) | **35.** (a) | **45.** (c) |
| **6.** (a) | **16.** (a) | **26.** (b) | **36.** (a) | **46.** (d) |
| **7.** (a) | **17.** (d) | **27.** (b) | **37.** (c) | **47.** (a) |
| **8.** (b) | **18.** (a) | **28.** (d) | **38.** (b) | **48.** (a) |
| **9.** (c) | **19.** (d) | **29.** (c) | **39.** (b) | **49.** (b) |
| **10.** (b) | **20.** (c) | **30.** (b) | **40.** (a) | **50.** (c) |

## HINTS AND SOLUTIONS

1. In every vertical column, the lower number is always a multiple of the number on the top. Hence, the only feasible value for the number in place of the question mark is 5. Hence, option (a) is correct.
2. The value of the increments in the series form an Arithmetic Progression if we place the number 13 in place of X. Thus, Option (c) is correct.
3. Only the figure in option (d) contains two rectangles with 90 degree angles. Hence, option (d) is correct.
4. Since MUMBAI is coded as LSJXVC, we realize that for the first letter of the word, the logic is to go (–1) in the alphabet, for the second letter of the word we use the logic of (–2), for the third letter the logic is (–3) and so on. Hence, DELHI would start with CC (as D would become C and E would also become C). The L in DELHI would get replaced by a letter that is 3 places before it in the alphabet – viz: I. Thus, at this point we are between options (a) and (d) as the correct answer. Also, we realize that H should be replaced by a letter, which is 4 places before it in the alphabet. Hence, H gets replaced by D and the correct option is CCIDD. Option (a) is correct.
5. For this question, we need to work out from RAMON = 12345 and DINESH = 675849 codes, which letter is represented by which alphabet. Thus, we have, by looking at both the codes that N is common to both the codes. Also, we see that N should be 5 and that logic also confirms that the number digit is in the same place as the letter it represents. Hence, for finding out the code for HAMAM, we need the codes for H, A and M. From DINESH = 675849, H = 9 and from RAMON = 12345 we get A = 2 and M = 3. Hence, HAMAM = 92323. Option (b) is the correct answer.
6. The first block can have any of the 6 colours, the second can use any of the remaining 5, while 4 colour are left to chose from in the third block. Hence the total number of combinations are $6 \times 5 \times 4 = 120$
7. It can be seen from the patterns of the figures in each row, that the figure given in option (a) should be correct.
8. Look at the movement of the square and the triangle inside the areas depicted in the circle. The square is moving clockwise, while the triangle is moving anti-clockwise. Going by this, we can easily spot that the figure given in option (b) is correct for the next figure.
9. Lets imagine a circle which has 24 equidistant points on its surface. This is similar to a clock which has the hour divisions and one division each between them.

   If we chose a vertice at the 12 O' clock position, then to form an equilateral triangle the other two vertices will be at 4 O' clock and 8 O' clock positions respectively. After 12 O' clock position the next vertice position is at 12:30 and then at 1 O' clock position. Likewise if we take the vertices from twelve of clock to 3:30 positions there are 8 vertices. Each will give a unique equilateral triangle with the other corresponding vertices at 4 O' clock and 8 O'clock positions and beyond it.

   Beyond the 4 O' clock the same positions which are already considered in the previous equilateral triangles start emerging. Hence, a total of 8 unique equilateral triangles are possible.
10. The dates are each 27 days apart. The year 1996 is a leap year.
11. From the position of figures it is apparent that in the successive figures, the dice is getting rotated along a vertical axis and new faces are emerging. The figure of a dash continues to remain on the top while its orientation changes with each turn of 90 degrees. Two dots are seen adjacent to the single dot and three dots are seen adjacent to the double dot. Hence, triple dot figure is opposite to the single dot figure.
12. As in the other question, four dot and two dot figures are adjacent to the three dot figure and hence both are opposite to each other. Answer option (c) is, therefore, correct.

**13.** As the figures at the four positions have been worked out, the remaining two figures are opposite to each other.

**14.** If you look at the front of the figure (the solid lines), you can see two triangles at the bottom, five in the middle and three at the top. On the back surface (the dotted lines) there are three at the bottom, five in the middle and two 2 at the top. Clearly, there are 20 triangles in the figure.

**15.** In each column the 1st (top number) + the 3rd number – the 2nd number is the last number.

**16.** The formula for the diagonals of a *n* sided figure is given by $^nC_{2-n}$.

Here this is $^8C_2 - 8 = 56/2 - 8 = 20$

**17.** The alphabet would look like: bCdEfGhIjKlMnOpQrStUvWxYz.

Hence, July would be written as: jUlY. Option (d) is correct.

**18.** The sequence 1, 5, 7, 3, 5, 7, 4, 3, 5, 7 has only one such 5 (the first one.) Hence, option (a) is correct.

**19.** The expression can be written as

$10 - 5 \times 1 \div 5 = 10 - 1 = 9$

**20.** It is a decreasing sequence with the difference increasing. The first difference is 3, the next is 5, then 7, 11 and then 13. The differences are prime numbers hence the next difference should be 17 and answer be 76.

**21.** There are two sequences. The 1st, 3rd and 5th terms are in one sequence. These are squares and are increasing. The 2nd, 4th and 6th are another sequence of decreasing squares of 14, 12 and 10. Hence the missing term is the square of 8.

**22.** The correct answer would be option (b) here as if we use the letters cbbb in the gaps, we get the sequence:

c c a c c a a b a a b b c b b. This sequence can be read as:

ccacc; aabaa;bbcbb. Hence, option (b) is correct.

**23.** Let 2009 – Sunday

2010 – Monday

2011 – Tuesday

2012 – Thursday ( leap year, one extra day)

2013 – Friday

2014 – Saturday

2015 – Sunday

**24.** Since there is a 5th Monday in April, it means that 29th and 30th April would either be Sunday and Monday or Monday and Tuesday. If 30th April is a Monday, it means that the following Mondays would occur in May – 7th, 14, 21, 28; June:4, 11, 18, 25; July: 2, 9, 16, 23, 30; August: 6, 13, 20, 27; September:3, 10, 17, 24; October:1, 8, 15, 22, 29; November:5, 12, 19, 26. Thus, in this case 29th would be a Thursday – which means that the Thursdays in November would be 1, 8, 15, 22 and 29 (and thus November would have 5 Mondays). Alternately, if we consider 30th April as a Tuesday, 26th November would also be a Tuesday and hence the 4th Thursday of November would occur on 28th November. In this case, there would be only 4 Thursdays in November, which contradicts the information in the question. This means that 30th April was a Monday and hence 26th November would be a Monday. Taking the calendar forward to 20th December, we can think as follows: 26th November Monday. Next Monday, 3rd, 10th and 17th December. Hence, 20th December would be a Thursday. Therefore, option (b) is correct.

**25.** For forming a parallelogram, two horizontal and two vertical lines would be needed. From each set of four given lines, two lines can be selected by the formula $^4c_2 = 6$. Hence the total no. of parallelograms are $6 \times 6 = 36$.

**26.** The number of days between 12th January and 12th July (for a non-leap year) = 19 + 28 + 31 + 30 + 31 + 30 + 12 = 181 days. For a leap year it would be 182 days. If 12th January is a Sunday, then every 7th day after that would be a Sunday. 182 is divisible by 7, hence we can conclude that in a leap year 12th July will be a Sunday. Therefore, option (c) is correct.

**27.** 51 (one case); 7, 3, 9 (2 cases); 5, 7 (one case) and 3, 1, 5 (two cases). There are a total of 6 odd numbers that are followed by an odd number in the series. Hence, option (b) is correct.

**28.** The first pair in the analogy is using a + 1, + 2, + 3 and + 4 structure between ACPQ to BESU. Thus, in the second pair, MNGI would become NPJM. Hence, option (d) is correct.

**29.** For minimum intersection, a single line (side) of the square will intersect at two points or two lines will intersect at one point each. For maximum intersections, each line of the square will intersect the circle at two points.

**30.** When the cube is cut into smaller cubes whose sides are 1/4th the side of the original cube, it means that we are going to have 64 smaller cubes formed. The cubes with single side painted would always be seen on each of the six surfaces. If you were to visualise any of the six sides of the cube, you would realise that it would have 16 smaller cubes that would be visible on it (as shown). Out of these 16, 12 cubes would be on its edges and hence those 12 would have at least 2 sides painted. The cubes having only a single side painted would be those numbered 13 to 16 in the figure. Hence, we would have 4 cubes on each side, which would have only one of their sides painted. Thus, the required answer is $4 \times 6 = 24$ such cubes.

| 1 | 2 | 3 | 4 |
|---|---|---|---|
| 12 | 13 | 14 | 5 |
| 11 | 15 | 16 | 6 |
| 10 | 9 | 8 | 7 |

**31.** The code can be understood as one where the word is broken into two equal parts and the letters of each of the parts are reversed.

Hence, FRACTION would become CARFNOIT.

**32.** The maximum number of rectangles and squares that can be formed.

$= (1^3 + 2^3 + 3^3) = 1 + 8 + 27 = 36$

**33.** No. of having no painted surfaces.

No. of having no painted surfaces.

$$= \left[\frac{L}{l} - 2\right]^3 = \left[\frac{4}{1} - 2\right]^3 = 2^3 = 8$$

Where $L$ = edge of larger cube

$l$ = edge of smaller cube.

**34.** From the first and the second clue, we have that 5 = colour. Then from 256 and 254, we can see that 2 = chalk and hence from 254, we can conclude that 4 = white. Hence, option (b) is correct.

**35.** Four letters are L,Y,C and A. Two words CLAY and LACY are possible using these letters. So, the words may begin with C or L. Among the four options given option of letter C exists and not of letter L hence the that is chosen.

**36.** The letters arranged in the reverse alphabetic order are YTRLICA. The letter L falls in the middle.

**37.** 4, 25 and 256 are squares of 2, 5, and 16, respectively while 125 is not a perfect square. Hence option (c).

**38.** As per the meaning of the operation we get $320 - 8 \times 40 - 10 = -10$

**39.** The coding is in the reverse alphabetical order of the arrangement of letters, i.e., the first letter is coded as Z and B is coded as Y.

**40.** Every number in the series is one more than the square of the natural numbers. Thus, the last given number $26 = 5^2 + 1$. Hence the next number would $36 + 1 + 37$. Alternatively, the problem can also be solved by working out the difference between the numbers which in turn form a series. The differences are 3, 5, 7, and 9. Hence the next difference would be 11 and therefore the next number in the series would be 37.

**41.** There are 8 parts of the sphere after cutting. Each part has 1 curved surface (corresponding to the outer surface of the sphere) and 3 flat surfaces (which are generated on cutting the sphere. Thus 32 surfaces are generated.

**42.** The curved surfaces are painted red. Each of the 8 parts has 1 curved surface, hence the answer is option (b).

**43.** Each part has 3 flat surface. Therefore, a total of 24 flat surfaces are there.

**44.** The 2 flat surfaces of the hemisphere are painted green. Each of these is then cut in 4 parts. Thus 8 surfaces would be painted green.

45. Cube is a three-dimensional figure corresponding to the two-dimensional square. Similar relationship exists between rectangle and cuboid and a circle and sphere. However, same is not true for the other two options.

46. In first term of the series, A and E are given. There is a gap of three letters between A and E. In the second term FI, there is a gap of two letters between F and I. One would expect the third term to have a gap of only one alphabet. In JL there is indeed gap of one letter and in MN there is no missing letter thus the gap reduces. By the same logic the next term in series should be OO instead of OP.

47. Hectare is a measure of area while the other three are measures of length.

48. The numerators are in a series where the successive numerators are increasing by 2. Thus, the numerators are 1, 3, 5, 7, 9, 11. The denominators are in another series where the difference in the denominators is increasing by 1. The first difference between 2 and 5 is 3. The 2nd difference between 5 and 9 is 4. the third difference would be 5 and the denominator accordingly is 14. The next difference should be 6 and the denominator should be 20.

49. The terms in the 2nd columns are the cubes of the terms in the first column. The third columns figures are the difference of the 2nd and first column figures.

50. The time passed as per the clock is 36 hours and 24 minutes. Since the clock gains time, therefore, the actual time would be less than this. In 36 hours, the clock would gain 24 minute (that is, 2/3rd of a minute in every hour). Hence the actual time which has passed is 36 hours. Therefore, the actual time would be 00:00 AM on 3rd April.

# Numerical Ability and Quantitative Reasoning

# 6

*"The White Queen: Can you do addition? What's one and one and one and one and one and one and one and one and one and one?*
*Alice: I don't know. I lost count."*

—In Alice in Wonderland

*"Pure mathematics is, in its way, the poetry of logical ideas."*

—Albert Einstein

*"If there is a God, he's a great mathematician."*

—Paul Dirac

## 1. Introduction

The test of **Numerical Ability and Quantitative Reasoning** forms a salient part of every aptitude assessment. Such tests are usually designed to gauge the candidate's comprehension of various numerical relations and operations and also the ability to understand and interpret data, represented in form of charts, graphs, tables, etc. The scheme of the CUET clearly specifies that the level of expectation from the candidates is that equivalent to the standard of questions of grade $8^{th}$. Thus, instead of coping with complex mathematical theories and performing tedious calculations, the candidate will be expected to have a basic idea of a subject to which they already have a prior exposure.

From the perspective of the examination, this section presents a challenge as well as an opportunity. The speed and accuracy demanded by the numerical ability questions may be a challenge to some. But these questions also present the right opportunity to grab some good marks, and thus catapult your score to a higher level.

**Scheme of the examination and significance of the topic**

The scheme of examination specifies that the candidates are to have understanding of the simple application of basic mathematical concepts arithmetic/algebra/ geometry/mensuration/statisitics etc.' Though a detailed description of topics has not been given, questions are likely to figure from topics, such as **number system, average, percentage, ratio and proportion, H.C.F. and L.C.M., Profit – loss discount, basic mensuration (area, perimeters), time, distance and speed, time and work, probability, data handling and statistics** etc. Finding solution to this may entail knowledge of allied topics like **algebra, geometry** as well.

As the questions are objective type with multiple choices, a step by step working or procedural accuracy would not be put to test like in the Board examination. Further the understanding of these topics in itself may not be a challenge for most. However, if you are among those who were out of touch with such questions after completing your $X^{th}$ grade, then it will be a good idea to practice very well in this section. Taking a note of the time being required by you to solve these questions is very important. In the section 3 of the CUET paper of which quantitative reasoning would be a sub-part, 60 questions out of 75 would be required to be solved in just 60 minutes. Thus, the average time available for each question would be a meagre one minute. Thus, adequate practice to timely and accurately solve the questions of numerical ability and quantitative reasoning, would be absolutely essential. This would also enable the aspirants cover a good ground in the paper as well as save time for other questions in this section.

The following pages covers the various types of questions which may be expected from numerical ability and quantitative reasoning. Solved examples as well as a variety of practice questions which are based on the pattern of previous CUCET papers are also provided.

## Solved Examples

(a) **Percentage**: Percentage refers to a fraction the denominator of which is 100. Problems involve determination of what percentage is a number of the other. Or a percentage may be given and the numerator or denominator needs to be determined.

### Solved examples 1

**Question:** What percentage is $\frac{3}{5}$ of $\frac{2}{3}$ ?

**Solution:** Let it be $x\%$

Then $\frac{3}{5} \div \frac{2}{3} \times 100 = x$

or $\frac{3}{5} \times \frac{3}{2} \times 100 = x$

$x = 90\%$

### Solved example 2

**Question:** The sides of a rectangle are increased by 10% each. By what percentage has the area of the rectangle increased?

**Solution:** Let length & breadth of rectangle be $l \times b$ respectively

Area $= l \times b = l\,b$

$\therefore$ New area $= 1.1\,l \times 1.1b = 1.21\,lb$

$\therefore$ Percentage increase in area $= \frac{1.21lb - lb}{lb} \times 100$

$= 21\%$

### Solved example 3

**Question:** The price of gold falls by 20%. How much gold can be bought from the same money that was used to buy 10 gms. of gold earlier?

**Solution:** Let price of gold earlier be ₹ $x$ /gm

$\therefore$ Price for 10 gms $= 10x$

$\therefore$ New price of gold $= 0.8x$/gm.

$\therefore$ quantity which can be purchased in ₹ $10x$

$= \frac{10x}{0.8x} = 12.5$ gms

### Solved example 4

**Question:** The income of a family has increased by 20% but inflation has increased by 10%. Considering that the consumption level remains the same, by what percentage has the savings increased or decreased? Is the data sufficient?

**Solution:**

Let earlier income of family be $= x$

Earlier Consumption $= y$

Earlier saving be $z_1 = x - y$

New income increased by 20% $= 1.2x$

New consumption expenditure increased by 10% $= 1.1y$

New savings $= 1.2x - 1.1y$

$= z_2$

Percentage change on savings $= \frac{z_2 - z_1}{z_1} \times 100$

$$= \frac{(1.2x - 1.1y) - (x - y)}{x - y} \times 100$$

$$= \frac{0.2x - 0.1y}{x - y}$$

As the value of $x$ & $y$ are not given the problem cannot be fully solved and the data is insufficient.

**(b) Average**

### Solved example 5

**Question:** The average of 20 numbers is 25. The average of the 1st 10 numbers is 20. The average of the last 9 numbers is 31. What is the 11th number?

**Solution:** Sum of all 20 numbers $= 20 \times 25 = 500$

Sum of $1^{st}$ 10 numbers $= 10 \times 20 = 200$

Sum of last 10 numbers $= 500 - 200 = 300$

Sum of last 9 numbers $= 9 \times 31 = 279$

$\therefore$ The $11^{th}$ number $= 300 - 279 = 21$

### Solved example 6

**Question:** The average weight of a class of 50 boys and girls is 38 kg. The average weight of 25 boys is 40 kg. What is the average weight of a girl?

**Solution:**

Sum of weights of all boys & girls $= 38 \times 50 = 1900$ kg

Sum of weights of 25 boys $= 25 \times 40 = 1000$ kg

Sum of weights of 25 girls $= 1900 - 1000 = 900$ kg.

Average weight of 25 girls $= \frac{900}{25} = 36$ kg

**(c) Ratio & proportion:** In this type of problems, usually the ratio of two or more constituents in a product are given. The question may require, the determination of new ratio where the quantity of one or more of the constituents is changed.

### Solved example 7

**Question:** In a 20 kg mixture of sand and cement, the ratio of the two is 7:1. Which item and what quantity should be added to make this ratio 8:1?

**Solution:** The item to added is sand as the ratio has to increase.

Let the quantity of sand in the mixture be $s$ and of cement be $c$

Ratio of sand in the mixture $= \frac{s}{(s+c)}$ & ratio of cement in the mixture $= \frac{c}{(s+c)}$

Current quantity of sand in the mixture $\left(\frac{7}{8}\right) \times 20 = 17.5$kg.

Current quantity of cement = 2.5 kg.

Let $x$ kg of sand be added

New ratio of sand $= \frac{17.5 + x}{(17.5 + x) + 2.5} = \frac{8}{8+1} = \frac{8}{9}$

or $(17.5 + x) \times 9 = (20 + x) \times 8$

Solving for $x$ we get $x = 2.5$ kg.

### Solved example 8

**Question:** A bag contains coins of ₹ 1, ₹ 2 & ₹ 5 in the ratio of 5:2:1. if the total value of the coins in the bag is ₹ 84 then how many coins of ₹ 2 are present in the bag?

**Solution**

Let the no. of coins of ₹ 5 be $= x$

$\therefore$ The number of coins of ₹ 2 is $2x$ and number of coins of ₹1 is $5x$

The total value of coins

$= 5 \times x + 2 \times 2x + 1 \times 5x = 84$

or $14x = 84$

$\therefore$ $x = 6$

$\therefore$ Number of coins of ₹ 2 = 12.

### Solved example 9

**Question:** A mixture of ethyl and methyl alcohol is in a ratio of 1:2. A volume of 9 litres of this mixture is mixed with another 10 litres of a mixture in which the two liquids are present in the ratio 2:3. What is the ratio of liquids in the final mixture?

**Solution:**

Total Volume of ethyl alcohol in the final mixture $\left(\frac{1}{3}\right)\times 9+\left(\frac{2}{5}\right)\times 10=7$

Total volume of methyl alcohol in the final mixture $=\left(\frac{2}{3}\right)\times 9+\left(\frac{3}{5}\right)\times 10=12$

$\therefore$ The final ratio = 7:12

**(d) Time & work :** Problems in this category specify the rate of work done by two or more entities. The problem often requires the determination of the time take for same or enhanced work's completion, when two or more such entities are combined to do the work. In such problems determination of work done by a single entity or in one unit of time (also referred as the unitary method) is a good starting point.

### Solved example 10

**Question:** 5 men can build a wall in 10 days. While 10 boys take 20 days to do the same work. In how many days 5 men and 10 boys put together do the work?

**Solution:**

Fraction of work done by 5 men in a day $=\frac{1}{10}$

Fraction of work done by 10 boys in a day $=\frac{1}{20}$

Total fraction of work done in a day by 5 men and 10 boys $=\frac{1}{10}+\frac{1}{20}=\frac{3}{20}$

$\therefore$ No. of days to complete the work $=\frac{20}{3}=6\frac{2}{3}$ days

### Solved example 11

**Question:** A tank is filled by tap 1 in 4 hours, while tap 2 and tap 3 take 6 and 8 hours respectively. How much time will it take to fill a tank which is seven times its volume and when tap 1 and tap 2 are operating at half and 1/4th of their original capacity?

**Solution:**

Fraction of tank filled by tap-1 in 1 hour $=\frac{1}{4}$

Fraction of tank filled by tap-2 in 1 hour $=\frac{1}{6}$

Fraction of tank filled by tap-3 in 1 hour $=\frac{1}{8}$

Fraction of tank filled by the three taps per hour with tap 1 at half and tap-2 at $\frac{1}{4}$th Capacity

$=\frac{1}{4}\times\frac{1}{2}+\frac{1}{6}\times\frac{1}{4}+\frac{1}{8}=\frac{3+1+3}{24}=\frac{7}{24}$

No. of hours to fill the tank of 7 times capacity

$=\frac{7}{(7/24)}=24$ hrs.

**(e) Profit & Loss:** The problems of profit and loss entail three elements. The cost price, the profit and the selling price. These are related as below.

Selling Price (SP) = Cost Price ( CP) + Profit ( P)

The problems usually involve determination of the third entity when two elements of this relationship are specified. However, the absolute value of these may or may not be specified or their relationship may be given in form of a percentage or a fraction. Based on the specified conditions, a linear equation is formed and solved to determine the variable.

### Solved example 12

**Question:** The sale price of 12 television sets is same as the cost price of 15 television sets. What is the percentage of profit on sale of one television set?

**Solution:** Let the cost price of one television set be CP, profit be P and selling price be SP

The selling Price (SP) = CP + P

12 × SP = 12 (CP + P) = 15 CP

$\therefore$ 12P = 3 CP

or P $=\frac{3}{12}$ CP $=\frac{1}{4}$ CP

Profit percentage = 25%

### Solved Example 13

**Question:** A shopkeeper purchase two watches for a total sum of ₹ 10000. He sells the first at a loss of 25% while sells the other at a profit of 25%. His net profit on the entire transaction is ₹ 1000. What is the cost price of the 2nd watch?

**Solution:**

Let the cost price (CP) of 2nd watch = $x$

∴ Its selling price = $1.25x$

The CP of 1st watch = $(10000 - x)$

∴ $0.75\,(10000 - x) + 1.25\,x = 11000$

or $7500 + 0.5x = 11000$

or $x = 7000$

## Solved example 14

**Question:** A retailer sells a shirt at a markup of 40%. He offers 30% discount in off-season on the selling price. What is the final profit or loss percentage?

**Solution:** Let the cost price = $x$

∴ Selling price = $1.4x$

∴ Discount = $1.4 \times \dfrac{30}{100} = 0.42x$

∴ Final price = $1.4x - 0.42x = 0.98x$

$$\text{Loss \%} = \frac{x - 0.98x}{x} \times 100 = 2\%$$

(f) **Time, Distance & Speed:** The problems in this category also require, the determination of the third factor when two factors are specified. The relationship between time distance and speed is as below.

(a) Distance ($d$) = Speed ($s$) × Time ($t$)

(b) Time ($t$) = $\dfrac{\text{Distance (d)}}{\text{Speed (s)}}$

(c) Speed ($s$) = $\dfrac{\text{Distance (d)}}{\text{Time (t)}}$

While solving the problems, the homogeneity of unit must be maintained. For, instance where the speed is in metres/second and the distance is in kilometre then either of the speed may be converted in terms kilometres/hour or distance in metres as required by the problem.

## Solved example 15

**Question:** A girl goes to her school on foot. If she walks at 2/3rd of her normal speed, she reaches 10 minutes later than when walking at the normal speed. In what time she normally reaches her school?

**Solution:**

Let the distance to school be $d$ and her normal walking speed = $s_1$

∴ Normal time ($t_1$) = $\dfrac{d}{s_1}$

When she walks at slower speed $s_2$, she would take time $t_2$

$$= \frac{d}{(2/3s_1)} = \left(\frac{3}{2}\right)\left(\frac{d}{s_1}\right)$$

∴ Extra time taken = $\dfrac{3}{2}\dfrac{d}{s_1} - \dfrac{d}{s_1} = \dfrac{d}{2s_1} = 10$ minutes

∴ Normal time ($t_1$) = $\dfrac{d}{s_1} = 2 \times 10 = 20$ Minutes

## Solved example 16

**Question:** A train 180 metre long moves at a speed of 20 metre/s. A man is walking at a speed of 2 metre/s in the same direction as the train. From the moment the locomotive reaches the man to the moment the last coach crosses the man how much time will be taken?

**Solution:** Let the time taken be $t$

In time t, the distance man has walked = $2t$

Distance covered by train is, the length of the train and the distance covered by train = $180 + 2t$

∴ Time taken by train to cover this distance

$$= \frac{180 + 2t}{20} = t$$

or $180 = 18t$

or $t = 10$ seconds

## Solved example 17

**Question:** A boat is able to travel upstream at a speed $a$ and downstream at a speed $b$. What will be the speed of the boat if the water is still?

**Solution:** Let speed of boat in still water be $x$ & speed of stream be $y$

∴ Speed of boat downstream = $x + y = b$ (1)

∴ Speed upstream = $x - y = a$ (2)

∴ Adding (1) & (2) we get

$2x = a + b$ or $x = \dfrac{a+b}{2}$

(g) **Principal & Interest:** Principal and interest problems also involve working out one of the three factors in Principal, Interest and Time where two of the factors are specified in the problem. These factors are governed by the relationship a below.

$$I = \frac{PRT}{100}$$

where I = Interest, P = Principal, R = Rate and T = Time

### Solved example 18

**Question:** A bank $B_1$ offers interest @10% per annum. Another bank $B_2$ offers interest @5% every six months. If ₹ 100 is invested in bank $B_1$ how much more or lesser interest is earned in bank $B_1$ as compared to bank $B_2$?

**Solution:**

$$\text{Interest} = \text{Principal} \times \text{Rate} \times \frac{\text{Time}}{100};\ I = \frac{PRT}{100}$$

$$\text{Interest earned in bank } B_1 = 100 \times \left(\frac{10}{100}\right) \times 1$$

$$= ₹\ 10$$

Interest earned in bank $B_2$ in first 6 months

$$= 100 \times \left(\frac{5}{100}\right) = ₹\ 5$$

Principal available in bank $B_2$ for second 6 months = (100 + 5) = 105

∴ Interest in the 2nd 6 months in bank

$$B_2 = 105 \times \left(\frac{5}{100}\right) = ₹\ 5.25$$

∴ Total interest earned = 5 + 5.25 = 10.25

∴ The second bank gives extra interest of ₹ 0.25

(h) **Mensuration:** The problems in mensuration require the determination of the perimeter/ circumference, area, volume of a variety of figures. The formulas governing these are specified below for ready reference.

(i) **Perimeter of rectangle** = $2(l + b)$

where $l$ = length, $b$ = breadth of rectangle

(ii) **Area of rectangle** = $l \times b$

(iii) **Area of Triangle**

$$= \left(\frac{1}{2}\right) \times \text{base} \times \text{perpendicular} = \left(\frac{1}{2}\right) b \times l$$

(iv) **Circumference of Circle** = $2\pi r$

where $r$ = radius

(v) **Area of a circle** = $\pi r^2$

(vi) **Surface area of cuboid**

$$= 2(l \times b + l + h + b \times h)$$

where $l$ = length, $b$ = breadth & $h$ = height

(vii) **Volume of Cuboid** = $l \times b \times h$

(viii) **Outer Surface area of open cylinder**

$$= 2\pi rh$$

where $r$ = radius & $h$ = height

(ix) **Outer Surface area of closed cylinder**

$$= 2\pi rh + 2\pi r^2$$

(x) **Area of sphere** = $4\pi r^2$

where $r$ = radius

(xi) **Volume of sphere** = $\left(\frac{4}{3}\right) \pi r^3$

### Solved example 19

**Question:** A cube of side $x$ is melted and from the material, a solid cylinder of radius $r$ is formed. What would be the length of the cylinder?

**Solution:** Volume of cube = $x^3$

Let the length of solid cylinder = $l$

∴ its volume = $\pi r^2 l$

∴ $x^3 = \pi r^2 l$

or $l = \dfrac{x^3}{\pi r^2}$

### Solved example 20

**Question:** The four walls and the ceiling of a room are to be painted. The walls have to be painted red. The cost of painting & labour is ₹ 50/Sq. metre. While ceiling is to be painted white and cost of which is ₹ 42/Sq. metre. If the room is of dimension 4m × 3m × 3m how much is the cost of painting?

**Solution:**

Area of ceiling = 4m × 3m = 12m²

∴ Cost of painting ceiling = 42 × 12 = 504

Area of four walls = $2(l\,h + b\,h)$

$= 2(4 + 3) \times 3 = 42$ Sq. metre

∴ Cost of painting the four walls = $42 \times 50 = 2100$

Total cost = 2100 + 504 = ₹ 2604

**(i) Age problems**: The problems of age, involve the principles of algebra and solving of linear equations in one variable. Usually, the problem entails the description of the age of two or more individuals at two different points of time. Using the conditions specified, linear equations are required to be constructed and the variable is required to be solved for, as seen in the examples below.

### Solved Example 21

**Question:** The ratio of the age of two sisters, Anita and Binita is 3 : 2. Four years ago the difference in their ages was four. Find the age of Binita now.

**Solution:** Let the age of Binita now be $x$

∴ The age of Anita now = $1.5\,x$

Four years ago their ages were $(x - 4)$ and $(1.5\,x - 4)$ respectively

∴ $(x - 4) + 4 = 1.5x - 4$

∴ $0.5\,x = 4$ or $x = 8$

Binita's age is 8 years now

### Solved Example 22

**Question:** A father has two sons $b$ and $c$. The father's age is twice that of $b$ while $b$ is 5 years elder to $c$. If 10 years ago the age of the father was thrice that of $b$, find the age of $c$.

**Solution:** Let the current age of $b$ be $x$

∴ The age of father = $2x$

The age of father and $b$, 10 years ago were $(2x - 10)$ and $(x - 10)$ respectively.

∴ $2x - 10 = 3(x - 10)$

or $3x - 2x = 30 - 10$

or $x = 20$

∴ The current age of $c = 20 - 5 = 15$

**(j) Problems on probability:** Probability of an event or its occurrence is defined as the ratio of the desired outcome to the total possible outcomes. Say, the questions requires to find out the possibility of a number coming up in a dice or a card being drawn from a deck etc. In the entire event the total number of times the desired outcomes can arise and the total number of possible outcomes are to be first determined and hence the probability of the desired outcome is to worked out. For instance, the probability of any number coming up in an unbiased dice having 6 sides, is 1 out of 6. Here the desired events frequency is 1, while the possible events which can arise on roll of dice is 6. Similarly the probability of drawing an ace in a deck of card can be worked as below.

No. of aces in a deck which can be possibly be drawn = 4

No. of cards in a deck = 52

The probability of drawing an ace = $\frac{4}{52} = 1$ out of 13

Where the probability of, simultaneous occurrence of two events, is to be determined, then the probability of individual occurrence of these events get multiplied. If $p(a)$ and $p(b)$ are the probability of individual occurrence of the events $a$ and $b$ respectively, then the probability of their simultaneous occurrence is $p(a) \times p(b)$.

### Solved example 23

**Question:** Determine the probability of a player getting two sixes in two simultaneous rolls of dice.

**Solution:** The probability of getting a six in the 1st roll = $\frac{1}{6}$

The probability of getting a six in 2nd roll $= \frac{1}{6}$

∴ The probability of getting two sixes in two simultaneous rolls of dice $= \left(\frac{1}{6}\right) \times \left(\frac{1}{6}\right) = \frac{1}{36}$

Where the probability of either of the two possible events $a$ and $b$ is to be calculated then the individual probability of occurrence of the event gets added up.

### Solved example 24

**Question:** What is the probability of a person getting 1 or 4 in a roll of dice.

**Solution:** Probability of rolling $1 = \frac{1}{6}$

Probability of rolling $4 = \frac{1}{6}$

$\therefore$ Probability of rolling either 1 or 4 is $\frac{1}{6} + \frac{1}{6} = \frac{1}{3}$

### Solved example 25

**Question:** A bag contains 2 red balls, 3 white balls, 4 yellow balls and 1 black ball. What is the probability of the ball being red or black if only one ball is drawn randomly?

**Solution:** No. of red balls in the bag = 2

No. of black balls in the bag = 1

No. of favourable balls to be drawn = 2 + 1 = 3

Total no. of balls which are there in the bag to be drawn from = 1 + 2 + 3 + 4 = 10

The probability of a red or black ball being drawn $= \frac{3}{10}$

**(k) Geometry and applications:** The question of geometry are likely to be more on the application of the geometrical knowledge rather than on any practical construction of geometrical figures or measurement of angles as in conventional exams. Particularly likely to arise are the problems associated with directions and movement from point A to point B. Further such problems may also require knowledge of the Pythagoras theorem.

The theorem states that in a right angle triangle where the base perpendicular and hypotenuse are of the lengths *l*, *b*, and *h* respectively, there relationship is governed by the formula;

$l^2 + b^2 = h^2$

### Solved example 26

**Question:** Raman walks from his house to his school. He walks 2 km east and then 3 km south. At this point he turns towards left and walks again 2 km to reach his school. What would be the shortest possible distance from his home to school if it were to be connected with a straight line?

(a) 7 km (b) 6 km

(c) 5 km (d) cannot be determined

**Solution:** The path taken by Raman is as below

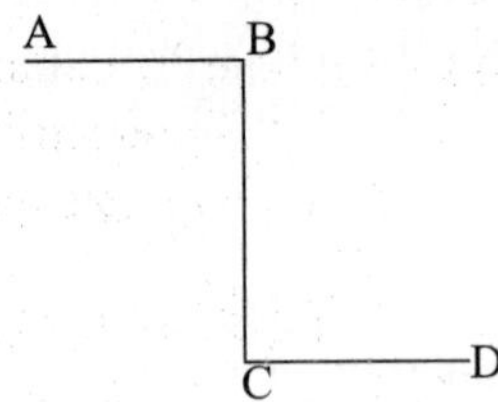


Where AB and CD are 2 kms each while BC is 3 km. The shortest distance AD can be calculated as per figure below

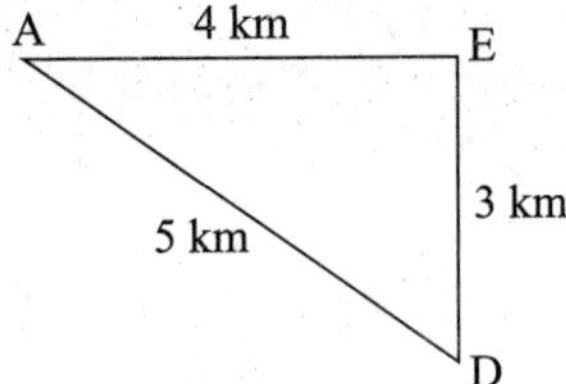


The straight line between points A and D can be calculated by applying Pythagoras theorem. As $3^2 + 4^2 = 5^2$, the distance AD is hence determined to be 5 km.

**Ans (c)**

### Solved example 27

**Question:** The clock is showing 2 pm. What will be the increase in angle between the minute and hour hands after half an hour?

(a) 45 degrees (b) 60 degrees

(c) 90 degrees (d) 105 degrees

**Solution:** The angle between any two consecutive hours on a clock is 30 degrees. $\left(\frac{360}{12}\right)$ The angle between the hands at 2 pm is 60 degrees as the minute hand is at 12 and hour hand is at 2. After half an hour, at 2:30 pm, the minute hand is at 6 and the hour hand is exactly in between 2 and 3. Thus, the angle between them now is, 105 degrees. Therefore the increase in angle is 45 degrees.

### Solved Example 28

**Question:** A circle of diametre 10 cm, as shown in the figure has a tangent AB of length 12 cm. O is the centre of the circle. If OB intersects the circle at C, then find the length BC.

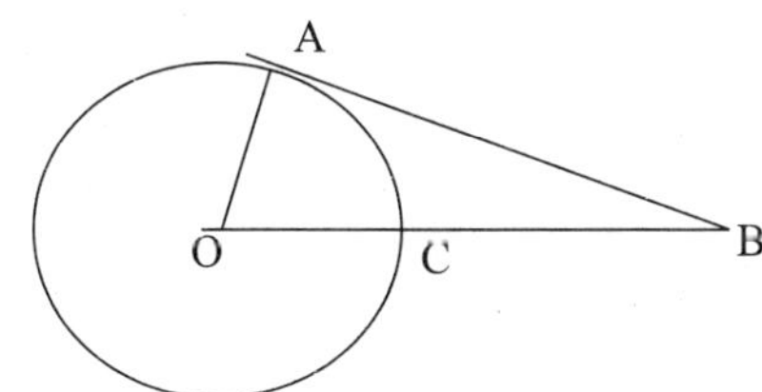


(a) 6 cm (b) 7 cm
(c) 8 cm (d) 9 cm

**Solution:** We use the property that the tangent to the circle and the radius to the point of contact of the tangent, are perpendicular to each other. Hence angle OAB is 90 degree and triangle OAB is a right angle triangle with OB as the hypotenuse.

Therefore applying Pythagoras theorem we get

$$OA^2 + AB^2 = OB^2 \qquad (1)$$

As diametre of circle is 10 cm, its radius OA is 5 cm. Therefore we get;

$5^2 + 12^2 = OB^2$

or $OB^2 = 169$

Solving, we get OB = 13

As OC = OA (radius) = 5

Hence, BC = 8 cm

**(L) Algebraic identities:** The portion on algebra may have some questions related to algebraic identities. The algebraic expressions, which are expressed as an equality and are true for every value of the variable in it, are called an identity. For example the expression, $(x + 1)(x + 2) = x^2 + 3x + 2$; can be said to be an algebraic identity. Of relevance to us are the standard algebraic identities of 2nd degree. These are;

$$(x + y)^2 = x^2 + 2xy + y^2$$
$$(x - y)^2 = x^2 - 2xy + y^2$$
$$(x + y)(x - y) = x^2 - y^2$$

### Solved Example 29

**Question:** If $(a - b)^2 = 25$ and $ab = 14$, Find the value of $a + b$.

(a) 7 (b) 8
(c) 9 (d) 10

**Solution:** $(a - b)^2 = a^2 - 2ab + b^2$

Adding $4ab$ on both the sides we get

$$(a - b)^2 + 4ab = a^2 - 2ab + b^2 + 4ab$$
$$= a^2 + 2ab + b^2 = (a + b)^2$$

Therefore, we get

$$(a + b)^2 = 25 + 4 \times 14 = 81$$

or $(a + b) = 9$

### Solved Example 30

**Question:** If $\left(3x - \frac{2}{x}\right) = 5$, find the value of $\left(9x^2 - \frac{4}{x^2}\right)$

(a) 35 (b) 14
(c) 49 (d) none of the above

**Solution:** Let $3x = a$ and $\frac{2}{x} = b$

$$(a - b) = 5 \text{ and } ab = (3x)\left(\frac{2}{x}\right) = 6$$

As $(a - b)^2 + 4ab = a^2 - 2ab + b^2 + 4ab$
$$= a^2 + 2ab + b^2 = (a + b)^2$$

We get $(a + b)^2 = 25 + 4 \times 6 = 49$

or $(a + b) = 7$

Therefore $\left(9x^2 - \frac{4}{x^2}\right) = a^2 - b^2 = (a + b)(a - b)$
$$= 7 \times 5 = 35$$

## 2. Data Interpretation And Statistics

A number of questions in the aptitude tests entail interpretation/ handling of the data and statistics. This section deals with solving those problems which are based on information or data furnished in form tables, bar charts, pie charts, graphs, etc. Most of us would have basic familiarity with these forms of data presentation. However, to refresh a brief description of the salient aspects of the aforesaid is being given here. Besides some of the central tendencies such as mean, median, mode and their determination in ungrouped or grouped data is also being described.

### Forms of data presentation

(a) **Tables:** These are the simplest of data presentation formats. They consist of vertical columns and horizontal rows containing figures or quantitative data. Tables are versatile form of presentation of data as a large amount of information can be put in them. However, from the analytical perspective and visual representation point of view, tabular data has a weak impact, as the trend analysis or forecasting becomes difficult.

Consider the following distribution of marks and students in a class:

**Distribution of students of Class X of ABC school in various marks brackets**

| Marks brackets | Less than 40 | 40 – 60 | 60 – 80 | 80 – 100 |
|---|---|---|---|---|
| English | 20 | 42 | 39 | 19 |
| Hindi | 19 | 45 | 41 | 15 |
| Soc. Science | 10 | 45 | 44 | 21 |
| Science | 12 | 24 | 48 | 36 |
| Mathematics | 15 | 25 | 50 | 30 |

### Solved example 31

**Question:** If marks below 40 are treated as grade F and above 80 are A, then what is the difference in percentage of students who have got A and F in Mathematics?

**Solution:** Total no. of students in class = 120

Percentage of students getting less than 40 in mathematics = $\left(\frac{15}{120}\right)\times 100 = 12.5\%$

Percentage of students getting more than 80 in mathematics = $\left(\frac{30}{120}\right)\times 100 = 25\%$

The difference in percentage is 25% – 12.5% = 12.5%

**Bar Charts:** Bar charts offer a better visual representation of numerical data than the tables. The statistical information is visually presented in form of horizontal or vertical axis. The length of each bar represents the value of data (while the breadth is of no quantitative significance but for a better visual presentation). Depending on how many variables the information contains the bar chart can be a simple bar chart or a composite/multiple bar chart. For example, for the information in the table above a multiple bar chart as given hereunder can be drawn. More examples of such charts are given in the exercise set on data handling and statistics.

**Distribution of students in various marks brackets**

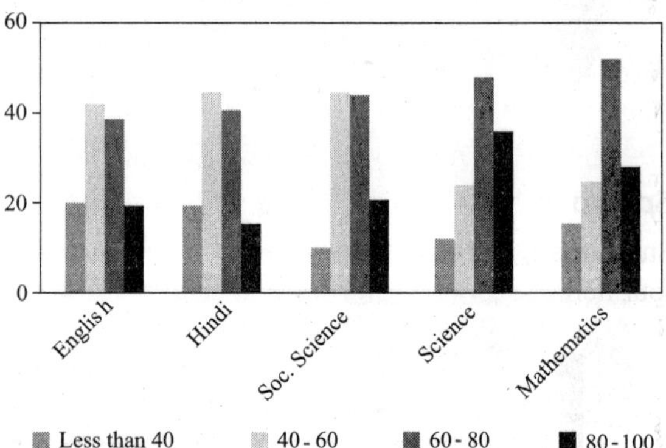


### Solved example 32

**Question:** The bar chart above, depicts distribution of students of Class X$^{th}$ of ABC school, in various marks brackets for the subjects as shown. If the pass marks is 40, then in which subject the least number of students have failed?

(a) Mathematics (b) English
(c) Social science (d) Hindi

**Solution:** In the above question, based on observation, one can see that the bar of marks below 40, is the smallest for social science, hence the right answer is option (c).

**(b) Pie Charts:** Pie diagrams or charts entail representation of data in form of circles, with the circle divided into several sector or segments. Each sector represents the value of a particular variable. The angle of each sector representing a variable is calculated in proportion to the value of the variable. Pie diagrams give an excellent visual representation of proportional / fractional value of a single variable data. For example, in chart above, if the distribution of students in various marks brackets is considered for the English subject then the pie chart will be as shown here.

However, where the variables become many, a number of Pie charts will be required and visual correlation between them becomes difficult.

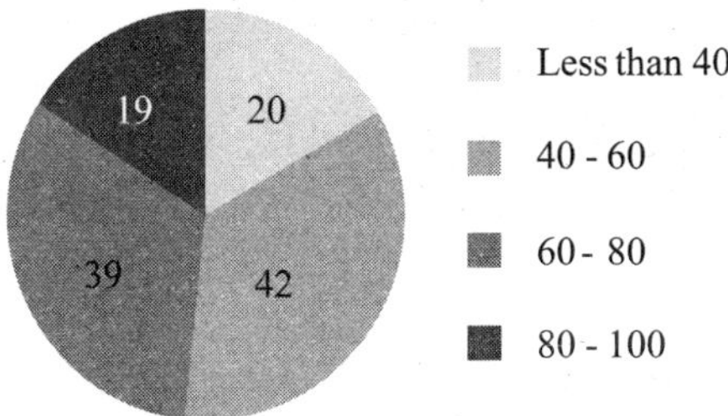


### Solved examples 33–36

Study the two figures given below and answer the four items that, follow:

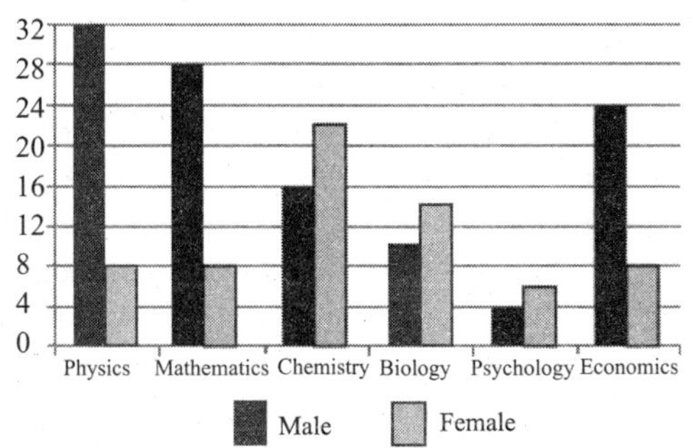


Figure 1: Number of professors in selected subjects in a University by sex (males and females)

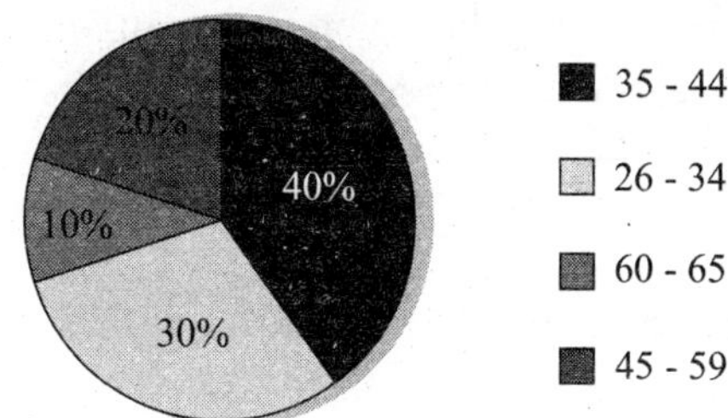


Figure 2: Age of Physics Professors

### Solved example 33

**Question:** How many Physics professors belong to the age group 35 - 44?

(a) 18 (b) 16

(c) 14 (d) 12

**Solution:** From the bar chart for physics, it can be seen that there 32 and 8 professors of physics or total 40 professors of physics. From the pie chart it is seen that 40% of the physics professors are in the age group of 35 - 44.

Hence the correct answer is $\left(\frac{40}{100}\right) \times 40 = 16$

### Solved example 34

**Question:** Which one of the following disciplines has the highest ratio of males to females?

(a) Physics (b) Mathematics

(c) Chemistry (d) Economics

**Solution:** From the bar charts it is seen that the ratio of male is to female is the highest for physics and is 32 : 8 or 4 : 1

### Solved example 35

**Question:** What percentage of all Psychology professors are females?

(a) 40% (b) 50%

(c) 60% (d) 70%

**Solution:** From the bar chart it is seen that;

No. of male psychology professors = 4

No. of female psychology professors = 6

Total no. of psychology professors = 10

Percentage of female psychology professors =

$$\left(\frac{6}{10}\right)\times 100 = 60\%$$

## Solved example 36

**Question:** If the Psychology professors in the University constitute 2% of all the professors in the University, then what is the number of professors in the University?

(a) 400 (b) 500

(c) 600 (d) 700

**Solution:** From the bar chart the total no. of psychology professors = 10

The total no. of professors in the university

$$= \left(\frac{10}{2}\right)\times 100 = 500$$

**(c) Graphs or X-Y charts:** These represent data along two axes—the horizontal or X axis and vertical or Y axis. This is one of the most versatile forms of representation of data. While bar charts are used to represent discrete data, such as distribution of marks of students, a graph can be used to represent a continuous variable data, such as variation of NSE Sensex with time and day or temperature variation during a day or month. A simple graph of monthly variation of sales figures of a magazine is shown here.

**Circulation Figures of magazine ABC for the various months of the Year 2019–20**

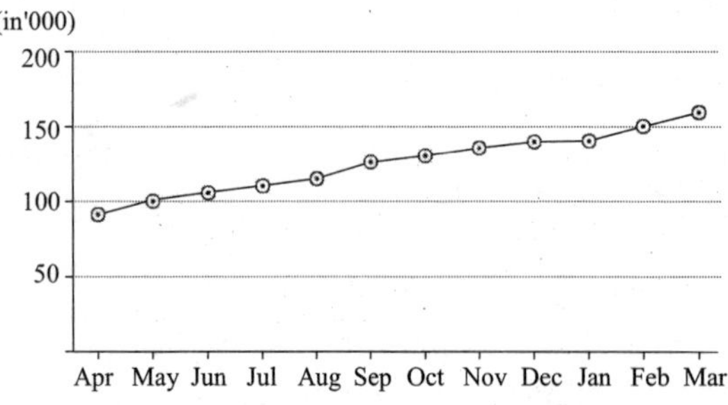


## Solved example 37

**Question:** Study the graph above. Which of the following conclusions can be drawn form the graph?

(a) The figures of newspapers circulation have increased in all of the months.

(b) The figures of newspapers circulation have decreased in some of the months as compared to the previous one.

(c) The figures of newspapers circulation have increased exponentially

(d) None of the above

**Solution:**

- From the graph it is seen that the figure of circulation have remained stagnant in the Dec-Jan phase. Hence option (a) is not correct.
- No month has shown a decline over previous month. Hence option (b) is not correct.
- The figure of growth is almost like a straight inclined line and not an exponential curve. Hence option (c) is not correct.

## Certain tips to answer data handling questions

- Understand properly and then analyse the data/graphs. Most questions in data handling/statistics are likely to test, your understanding of data, its analysis and interpretation. They are not likely to involve complex numerical calculations although elementary computation may be involved. As such while preparation emphasis should be on exposing yourself to a variety of graphs bar charts, pie charts tables and understanding their import rather than being bogged by speed calculation.
- Read the question carefully. A minor oversight or misunderstanding of the question may mean arriving at the wrong analysis or conclusion. This may imply loss of marks or loss of time in having to work out all over again. This also means that while reading the question do not lose a grasp over it. If you have not understood a part of the question, read and understand it before proceeding to the remaining portion of the question.

- In data handling / statistics questions, go through the data provided and the questions once and then begin analysis of data as per the question. Do not start analysing the data even before reading what you are required to do, lest you waste your time in frivolous and fruitless analysis.
- Always use the proper Units. Be cautious in those questions where non-uniform or a mix of units has been used. For example, a part of the data may be in metres while another part may be in centimetres. Similarly, be cautious where the data is in percentage while the answer expected of you is in absolute value.
- In questions where there are more than one graph charts or tables used, understand properly the correlation between them.

## Mean, Median and Mode

Mean, median, and mode are the measures of central tendency in statistics. These concepts are used to examine & analyse the characteristics of a given data set and have application in different places

**Mean:** Arithmetic mean is the most common representative value of a group of data and is denoted by the symbol $\bar{x}$. For any data set **arithmetic mean is the sum of all observations divided by the total number of observations.**

### Solved Example 38

**Question:** The marks scored by a student in five subjects are as follows; 52, 38, 55, 60, 45. What is his average marks?

**Solution:** His average marks can be determined through an arithmetic mean using the formula of mean:

$$\text{Means} = \frac{\text{Sum of all observations}}{\text{Number of observations}}$$

$$\text{Mean} = 52 + 38 + 55 + 60 + 45 = \frac{250}{5} = 50$$

**Types of data and determination of mean:** Statistical data can be in **raw form** or **tabular form**. Raw data implies where each value of data is individually given in a random manner and not as groups.

**Determination of mean in a raw data set:** Let $x_1$, $x_2, x_3, \ldots, x_n$ be $n$ observations. Arithmetic mean of this distribution is given as below.

$$\text{Mean, } \bar{x} = \frac{x_1 + x_2 + \ldots x_n}{n}$$

### Solved Example 39

**Question:** If the weight of 5 people are: 68 kg, 72 kg, 80 kg, 40 kg & 50 kg, then find the mean weight.

$$\text{Mean weight, } \bar{x} = \frac{(68+72+80+40+50)}{5}$$

$$= \frac{310}{5} = 62$$

or Mean, $x = 62$ kg

**Determination of mean in frequency distribution (Tabular) form of data:** Data may be present in a tabular form where the frequency of occurrence of each individual data is described. When the data is present in tabular form, then the following formula is used for determination of mean;

$$\text{Mean, } \bar{x} = \frac{(x_1 f_1 + x_2 f_2 + \ldots + x_n f_n)}{(f_1 + f_2 + \ldots + f_n)}$$

Where $x$ **is the data value** and **f** represents the **frequency of distribution** of each individual data.

### Solved Example 40

**Question:** Find the mean of the following distribution of data of age of the students in a class-

| X (age) | 13 | 14 | 15 | 16 | 17 |
|---|---|---|---|---|---|
| F (frequency) | 3 | 12 | 15 | 10 | 10 |

**Solution:** We first prepare a table for calculation of the arithmetic mean by determining the product of $x_i$ and $f_i$

| $x_i$ | $f_i$ | $x_i f_i$ |
|---|---|---|
| 13 | 3 | 39 |
| 14 | 12 | 168 |
| 15 | 15 | 225 |
| 16 | 10 | 160 |
| 17 | 10 | 17 |
| | $\sum f_i = 50$ | $\sum x_i f_i = 762$ |

Mean, $\overline{x} = \frac{\sum x_i f_i}{\sum f_i}$

$= \frac{762}{50}$

$= 15.24$

Thus, Mean = 15.24

**Determination of mean for data presented in groups:** Data may be given in groups called class. In such situation for determination of the mean first the mid value of each class has to be determined. This is taken as $x_i$. The product of this value and the frequency of the class is then to be taken ($x_i f_i$). The sum of all $x_i f_i$ ($\sum x_i f_i$) **is then divided by the total number of data** ($\sum f_i$)

### Solved Example 41

**Question:** The data of the marks scored (out of total marks of 50) by students of 12th grade in Mathematics, is given as below. What is the mean marks of the students?

| Marks range | Number of students |
|---|---|
| 0–10 | 1 |
| 10–20 | 9 |
| 20–30 | 15 |
| 30–40 | 15 |
| 40–50 | 10 |

**Solution:** In this case, first the midpoint of the class interval for each class is to be determined. This is also called the class mark. This is given as;

**Class mark** = (lower limit of interval + upper limit of interval)/2

| Marks range | Class mark ($x_i$) | Frequency ($f_i$) | $x_i f_i$ |
|---|---|---|---|
| 0 – 10 | 5 | 1 | 5 |
| 10 – 20 | 15 | 9 | 135 |
| 20 – 30 | 25 | 15 | 375 |
| 30 – 40 | 35 | 15 | 525 |
| 40 – 50 | 45 | 10 | 450 |
| | | $\sum f_i = 50$ | $\sum f_i x_i = 1490$ |

Mean, $\overline{x} = \frac{\sum x_i f_i}{\sum f_i}$

$= \frac{1490}{50} = 29.8$

or $\overline{x} = 29.8$

## Median

The value of the **middlemost observation**, obtained after arranging the data in a specific order ascending or descending, is called the **median** of the data. This data divides the entire data into two equal parts (usually).

For example, consider the data: 5,8,4,6,7. On arranging this data in ascending order we can write the data as : 3,4,5,6,7.There are 5 data values in this set. Hence the 3rd data is the middlemost one. Here the median is 3rd data value i.e. 5.

**Determination of median in ungrouped data**: To determine the median of an ungrouped data, the data is first arranged in ascending or descending order and then the total number of observations (say) $n$ is determined. Based on whether this $n$ (total no. of data) is odd or even different formulas are used.

If **n is odd**, then we use the formula: Median

$$= \left(\frac{n+1}{2}\right)^{\text{th}} \text{ observation}$$

### Solved Example 42

**Question:** Given below is the data of marks of 9 students. The total marks in the subject is 20. Find the median.

Marks distribution : 12,18,19,15,17,13,16,14,15.

**Solution:** The data is arranged in ascending order, as below;

12,13,14,15,15,16,17,18,19.

Here, $n$ (number of observations) = 9. So, $\frac{(9+1)}{2} = 5$.

Hence the median would be the 5th observation.

∴ Median = 5th observation which is 15

If ***n* is even**, then the formula for determination of median is:

$$\text{Median} = \frac{(n/2)^{\text{th}} \text{ observation} + (n/2+1)^{\text{th}} \text{ observation}}{2}$$

### Solved Example 43

**Question:** Given below is the data of marks of 10 students. The total marks in the subject is 20. Find the median.

Marks distribution: 12,18,19,15,17,13,16,14,15,18.

**Solution:** The data is arranged in ascending order, as below: 12,13,14,15,15,16,17,18,18,19

Here, $n$ (no. of observations) = 10

Using the median formula,

Median = $\dfrac{(5^{th}\text{ observation} + 6^{th}\text{ observation})}{2}$. In the present data set the 5th and 6th observations are 15 and 16 respectively.

Hence median = $\dfrac{(15+16)}{2}$ or Median = 15.5

### Determination of median in case of grouped data:

In case of a continuous data, the median is found as shown below. First the median class is to be determined. This is the class in which the middle most data would lie. If there are 100 data in a set, then the class in which the 50th data lies is determined as median class. Then we need to determine as to how far the median data is in that particular class from the lower end of the class. The determination is explained through the following steps and formula.

**Step 1:** Find the median class.

Let $n$ = total number of observations i.e. $\sum f_i = n$ then the median class is that class where $\left(\dfrac{n}{2}\right)$th data lies.

**Step 2:** formula to find the median.

$$\text{Median} = 1 + \left[\frac{\frac{n}{2} - C_f}{f}\right]h$$

where,

- $l$ = Lower limit of median class
- $C_f$ = cumulative frequency of the class which precedes the median class
- $f$ = frequency of the median class
- $h$ = class size

### Solved Example 44

Question: The following is the distribution of marks of a set of students in mathematics. The total marks in the subject is 50. Find the median marks.

| Classes | 0–10 | 10–20 | 20–30 | 30–40 | 40–50 |
|---|---|---|---|---|---|
| Frequency | 1 | 10 | 15 | 15 | 9 |

**Solution:** We calculate the cumulative frequencies to find the median as per table below.

| Classes | Number of students | Cumulative frequency |
|---|---|---|
| 0 – 10 | 1 | 1 |
| 10 – 20 | 10 | 11 |
| 20 – 30 | 15 | 26 |
| 30 – 40 | 15 | 41 |
| 40 – 50 | 9 | 50 |

Median Class is the class of 20 to 30

N = 50.

$\dfrac{N}{2} = \dfrac{50}{2} = 25$

$l = 20$,

$f = 15$,

$C_f = 11$

$h = 10$

Using Median formula:

$$\text{Median} = 1 + \left[\frac{\left(\frac{n}{2} - C_f\right)}{f}\right]h$$

$$= 20 + \frac{(25-11)}{15} \times 10$$

$$= 20 + \left(\frac{14}{15}\right) \times 10$$

$= 20 + 9.33 = 29.33$

∴ Median = 29.33

### Mode

Mode refers to the value which appears most often in a given data or the observation which has the highest frequency in the data set.

**Determination of mode for ungrouped data**

For ungrouped data, observation which occurs maximum number of times is the mode, or **Mode = Observation with maximum frequency**

**Example**: Given below is the data set of marks scored by a student in class quiz in different subjects. the total marks in each quiz is 10. find the mode

Data set: 8,9,9,8,7,6,8,5,4,8,

In the above data set, the value 8 appears four times and is the data appearing the most. Thus, mode = 8.

When the data is continuous, the mode can be found using the specific formula for it. However, questions requiring mode data determination in grouped data are less likely to arise on account of such questions not squarely falling in the 8th grade standard of mathematics of NCERT.

### Relation Between Mean, Median and Mode

The three measures of central values i.e. mean, median, and mode are closely connected by the following relations (called **empirical relationship**). 2 Mean + Mode = 3 Median

## Data Sufficiency

Certain aptitude tests also contain the problems of data sufficiency. These questions test the ability of the candidates to find out whether a given set of data is sufficient or not to answer the question asked without there being a need to actually solve a problem.

Questions on data sufficiency are usually of two types which are explained here.

### (ii) Questions of 1st Type

Such questions may be followed by two statements, A and B, in which certain data are given. Using the given data of these two statements and the basic knowledge (rules and formula) of mathematics, one has to choose the answer as in the following.

Answer choices may be ;

(a) If the data in Statement A alone are sufficient to answer the question asked, while the data in Statement B alone are not sufficient to answer the question

(b) If the data in Statement B alone are sufficient to answer the question asked, while the data in Statement A alone are not sufficient to answer the question

(c) If the data either in Statement A alone or in Statement B alone are sufficient to answer the question

(d) If the data even in both the Statements A and B together are not sufficient to answer the question

(e) If the data in both the Statements A and B together are necessary to answer the question

**Solved Example 45**

**Question:** Is $x$ an integer?

(a) $3x$ is an integer

(b) $\frac{x}{3}$ is an integer

**Solution:** The answer here is (b) as the data in Statement B alone is sufficient to answer the question while that in Statement A is not sufficient.

(**Justification:** From (a), $3x$ = integer;

hence $x = \frac{\text{integer}}{3}$; hence $x$ can be integer or fraction.

So no conclusion can be drawn. Thus (a) is insufficient.

From (b) $\frac{x}{3}$ = integer hence $x = 3$ times an integer; hence $x$ is always integer.

Thus only (b) is sufficient.

### (iii) Questions of 2nd Type

Under this type of data sufficiency test, each question is followed by three statements I, II and III, in which certain data are given. The candidate is asked to decide which of the statement or statements are necessary to answer the question asked.

Questions from any of this type may be asked from topics, such as Number System, Average, Percentage, Time and Work, Time and Distance, Profit and Loss, Compound Interest, Age Problems, Simple Application of Algebra, Mensuration etc. But they are not asked in the conventional form.

### Solved Example 46

**Directions:** In each of the following questions, a question is asked followed by three statements. While answering the question, you may or may not require the data provided in all the statements. You have read the question and the three statements and then decide upon whether the question can be answered with any one or two of the statements or all the three statements are required to answer the question. The answer number bearing the statements which are required to answer the question is your answer.

1. How much vote did the winner get in the election of 16 lakh electorates?

   (i) He defeated his rival by 2.5 lakh votes.
   (ii) He got 150% more than his rival.
   (iii) Of the 71% votes polled the runner got only 25%.

   (a) Only (i) and (ii)
   (b) Only (i) and (iii)
   (c) (i), (ii) and (iii)
   (d) (ii) and either (i) or (iii)
   (e) Any two of the three

**Solution:** From (i), the difference of votes of winner and runner is obtained and by using (ii), the no. of votes got by winner can be found out, similarly, using (ii) with (iii) together, the no. of votes of winner can be obtained.

## Exercise Set A

**1.** The greatest 5-digit number that is exactly divisible by 100 is
(a) 99899 (b) 99800
(c) 99900 (d) 99889

**2.** Which of the following numbers is a prime number?
(a) 541 (b) 323
(c) 217 (d) 551

**3.** Which is the least 7-digit number that leaves a remainder of 3 when divided by 7?
(a) 1000003 (b) 1000010
(c) 1000005 (d) 1000002

**4.** A number when divided by 627 leaves a remainder 43. By dividing the same number by 19, the remainder will be
(a) 19 (b) 24
(c) 43 (d) 5

**5.** The sum of all odd numbers from 1 to 41 is
(a) 372 (b) 505
(c) 441 (d) 398

**6.** In a division, a student took 63 as divisor instead of 36. His answer was 24. The correct answer is
(a) 42 (b) 32
(c) 48 (d) 28

**7.** How many numbers are there between 500 and 600 in which 9 occurs only once?
(a) 18 (b) 19
(c) 20 (d) 21

**8.** The value of $101 + 102 + 103 + \ldots + 200$ is
(a) 15050 (b) 20200
(c) 10909 (d) 16500

**9.** The four integers consecutively lower than 81, and the four consecutively higher than 81, are added together. This sum is divisible by
(a) 7 (b) 9
(c) 11 (d) 13

**10.** A number when divided by a divisor, leaves a remainder of 63. If the remainder is 55 when twice the number is divided by the same divisor then the divisor is

(a) 21 (b) 37
(c) 16 (d) None of these

**11.** How many digits are required to number a book containing 200 pages?
(a) 200 (b) 600
(c) 492 (d) 372

**12.** A number is multiplied by 5 and 25 is added to it. The result is divided by 5 and the original number is subtracted from the same. The remainder will be
(a) 0 (b) 1
(c) 2 (d) 3

**13.** The LCM of two numbers is 1296 and HCF is 96. If one of the numbers is 864 then the other is
(a) 72 (b) 64
(c) 144 (d) 11,664

**14.** How many times is the HCF of 48, 36, 72 and 24 contained in their LCM?
(a) 10 (b) 12
(c) 120 (d) 2

**15.** Which is the smallest number that can be subtracted from 1936 so that on being divided by 9, 10, 15, the remainder is 7 every time?
(a) 93 (b) 46
(c) 76 (d) 39

**16.** The smallest number from which if 4000 subtracted, is exactly divisible by 7, 11 and 13, is
(a) 5001 (b) 2999
(c) 1000 (d) 6303

**17.** The HCF of two numbers is 12 and their difference is also 12. The numbers are
(a) 12, 84 (b) 100, 112
(c) 40, 52 (d) 84, 96

**18.** The least number by which 825 must be multiplied in order to produce a multiple of 715 is
(a) 11 (b) 5
(c) 13 (d) 17

**19.** The least number which is a multiple of 31 and when divided by 15, 24 and 32 leaves the remainders 2, 11, 19, respectively is
(a) 2356 (b) 2387
(c) 2325 (d) 2418

**20.** Three men start together to travel the same way around a circular track of 11 km. Their speeds are 4, 5.5 and 8 km per hour, respectively. When will they meet at the starting point?
(a) 22 hr (b) 12 hr
(c) 11 hr (d) 44 hr

**21.** In a seminar, the number of participants in Physics, Chemistry and Mathematics are 96, 36 and 180, respectively. Find the minimum number of rooms required if in each room the same number of participants are to be seated and all of them being in the same subject.
(a) 12 (b) 21
(c) 36 (d) 26

**22.** The greatest number of three digits which when added to 45 is exactly divisible by 6, 8, 12 is
(a) 963 (b) 987
(c) 984 (d) 980

**23.** A number when divided by 10 leaves a remainder 9, when divided by 9 leaves a remainder of 8, when divided by 8 leaves a remainder of 7...... when divided by 2 leaves a remainder of 1. Determine the number.
(a) 31 (b) 1029
(c) 2519 (d) 1679

**24.** The LCM of two numbers is 2900% more than their HCF and the sum of LCM and HCF of two numbers is 310. If one of the numbers is 20, find the other number.
(a) 290 (b) 150
(c) 75 (d) 58

**25.** A man spends 1/7 of his salary on food and 1/2 of the remaining on clothing and 1/3 of the remaining on entertainment. He is still left with ₹ 600. How much does he spend on entertainment?
(a) ₹ 600 (b) ₹ 450
(c) ₹ 300 (d) ₹ 700

**26.** A man left 1/7 of his property to his daughter and the remaining to his sons to be equally divided among them. If the share of the each son be double of that of the daughter, find the number of sons.

(a) 2 (b) 3
(c) 6 (d) 4

**27.** A scooter before overhauling requires 2/3 hour service time every 45 days, while after overhauling it requires 2/3 hour service time every 60 days. What fraction of pre-overhauling service time is saved in the latter case?

(a) 4/3 (b) 1/3
(c) 3/4 (d) 1/4

**28.** Sundari, Kusu and Jyoti took two tests each. Sundari secured 24/60 marks in the first test and 32/40 marks in the second test. Kusu secured 35/70 marks in the first test and 54/60 marks in the second test. Jyoti secured 27/90 marks in the first test and 45/50 marks in the second test. Who among them did register maximum progress?

(a) Only Sundari
(b) Only Kusu
(c) Only Jyoti
(d) Both Sundari and Kusu

**29.** *A* has twice as much money as *B*. They play together, and at the end of the first game, *B* wins one third of *A*'s money from *A*; what fraction of the sum that *B* now has, must *A* win back in the second game so that they may have exactly equal money?

(a) 1/3 (b) 1/5
(c) 1/4 (d) 1/10

**30.** If the price of sugar is increased by 7% then by how much per cent should a housewife reduce her consumption of sugar, to have no extra expenditure?

(a) 7 over 107% (b) 107 over 100%
(c) 100 over 107% (d) 7%

**31.** If of 1/8 of 2/3 of 0.8 of a number is 12 then 30 per cent of the number will be

(a) 48 (b) 64
(c) 54 (d) 42

**32.** The percentage by which 120 is to be diminished to get 90 is

(a) 30 (b) 25
(c) 20 (d) 33

**33.** If the length of a rectangle is increased by 20% and the breadth is reduced by 20%, what will be the effect on its area?

(a) 4% increase (b) 6% increase
(c) 4% decrease (d) No change

**34.** In measuring the side of a square, an error of 5% in excess is made. The error percentage in the calculated area is

(a) 10.25 (b) 10.75
(c) 1.75 (d) 25

**35.** In a class of 52 students, 25% are rich and others are poor. There are 20 females in the class, of whom 55% are poor. How many rich males are there in the class?

(a) 13 (b) 4
(c) 39 (d) 2

**36.** Naresh's monthly income is 30% more than that of Raghu. Raghu's monthly income is 20% less than that of Vishal. If the difference between the monthly incomes of Naresh and Vishal is ₹ 800, what is the monthly income of Raghu?

(a) ₹ 16,000 (b) ₹ 20,000
(c) ₹ 12,000 (d) Data inadequate

**37.** The rate for admission to an exhibition was ₹ 5 and was later reduced by 20%. As a result, the sale proceeds increased by 44%. The percentage increase in attendance was

(a) 80 (b) 24
(c) 64 (d) 20

**38.** In an examination in which maximum marks are 500, *A* got 10% less than *B*, *B* got 25% more than *C*, *C* got 20% less than *D*. If *A* got 360 marks, what percentage of marks was obtained by *D*?

(a) 60 (b) 72
(c) 55 (d) 80

**39.** There are Indians and Europeans in an army of 12,000. The average height of Europeans is

5'10" and that of Indians is 5'9" and the average height of the entire army is 5'9.75". Find out the number of Indians in the army.

(a) 2500 (b) 3000
(c) 2800 (d) 2200

**40.** Among three numbers, the first is twice the second and thrice the third. If the average of three numbers is 49.50 then what is the difference between the first and the third number?

(a) 54 (b) 28
(c) 39.50 (d) 41.50

**41.** The average of Suresh's marks in English and History is 55. His average marks in English and Science is 65. What is the difference between the marks that he obtained in History and Science?

(a) 40 (b) 60
(c) 20 (d) Data inadequate

**42.** The captain of a cricket team of 11 players is 25 years and the wicket keeper is 3 years older. If the ages of these two are excluded, the average age of the remaining players is 1 year less than the average age of the whole team. The average age of the whole team is

(a) 24 years (b) 21 years
(c) 26 years (d) 22 years

**43.** The average of '$n$' numbers is $A$. If the number $Y$ is replaced by the number $Y^0$ then the average becomes $A^0$. Which of the following equations is true?

(a) $A = A^0 (Y-Y^0)/n$
(b) $A = A^0 + n (Y-Y^0)$
(c) $A^0 = y/n + y^0/A$
(d) $A^0 + y/n = A + y^0/n$

**44.** Two numbers are in the ratio of 3 : 5. If 9 be subtracted from each, they are in the ratio of 12 : 23. The first number is

(a) 27 (b) 33
(c) 55 (d) 49

**45.** If the ratio of boys to girls in a class is B, and the ratio of girls to boys is G then B + G is

(a) Equal to 1
(b) Greater than 1
(c) Less than 1
(d) Greater than or equal to 1

**46.** There is a ratio of 5:4 between two numbers. If 40 per cent of the first number is 12 then what would be 50 per cent of the second number?

(a) 12 (b) 24
(c) 18 (d) Data inadequate

**47.** The income of A and B are in the ratio 3:2 and expenses are in the ratio 5:3. If both save ₹ 200 then the income of A is

(a) ₹ 800 (b) ₹ 1,500
(c) ₹ 1,000 (d) ₹ 1,200

**48.** If 8 men or 17 boys can do a piece of work in 26 days, how many days will it take for 4 men and 24 boys to a piece of work $50 \times 0.9$ times as great?

(a) 680 days (b) 612 days
(c) 61 days (d) 68 days

**49.** Jeetendra can wire '$x$' radios in 3/4 minutes. At this rate, how many radios can he wire in 3/4 of an hour?

(a) $40/x$ (b) $4x/3$
(c) $9x/16$ (d) $60\,x$

**50.** 'M' men agreed to purchase a gift for ₹ D. If 3 men drop out, how much more will each have to contribute towards the purchase of the gift?

(a) (D – 3)/M (b) D/($M^2$ – 3)
(c) 3 D/(M – 3) (d) 3 D/($M^2$ – 3M)

**51.** Rajesh and Ajay can complete a job in 16 days. Rajesh alone can do it in 24 days. How long will Ajay alone take to finish the whole work?

(a) 20 days (b) 48 days
(c) 30 days (d) 36 days

**52.** Xavier can do a job in 40 days. He worked on it for 5 days and then Paes finished it in 21 days.

In how many days Xavier and Paes can finish the work?

(a) 10 (b) 15
(c) 20 (d) 24

**53.** A shopkeeper sells almonds at the rate ₹ 114 a kg and bears a loss of 5%. If he sells it at ₹ 126 per kg, what will be the result?

(a) 15% gain (b) 5% loss
(c) 5% gain (d) 15% loss

**54.** A man sold his book for ₹ 891, thereby gaining 1/10 of its cost price. The cost price is

(a) ₹ 850 (b) ₹ 810
(c) ₹ 851 (d) ₹ 840

**55.** A shopkeeper, by selling 44 calculators, earns a profit of equal to the selling price of 11 calculators. His profit percentage is

(a) $33^1/_3$ (b) 20
(c) 25 (d) 30

**56.** A sells a watch to B at a gain of 20% and B sells it to C at a loss of 10%. If C pays ₹ 216, what had it cost A?

(a) ₹ 200 (b) ₹ 216
(c) ₹ 100 (d) ₹ 250

**57.** A man pays 40 times the annual rent to purchase a building. The rate % p.a. he derives from his investment is

(a) 25% (b) 2.5%
(c) 5% (d) 40%

**58.** If x is the simple interest on $y$ and $y$ is the simple interest on $z$, the rate % and the time being the same in both cases, what is the relation between $x$, $y$ and $z$?

(a) $x^2 = yz$ (b) $y^2 = xz$
(c) $z^2 = xy$ (d) $xyz = 1$

**59.** The interest on a sum of money at the end of 2.5 years is 0.8 of the sum (at simple interest). The rate per cent per year is

(a) 10% (b) 20%
(c) 16% (d) 32%

**60.** A certain sum of money amounts to 5/4 of itself in 5 years. The rate per cent p.a. is

(a) 10% (b) 5%
(c) 7% (d) 11%

**61.** Namrata deposited ₹ 8,000 which amounted to ₹ 9,200 after 3 years at simple interest. Had the interest been 2% more, she would get how much?

(a) ₹ 1,680 (b) ₹ 9,860
(c) ₹ 9,980 (d) ₹ 9,680

**62.** A car travels from A to B at $V_1$ km/h and travels back from B to A at $V_2$ km/h. The average speed of the car is

(a) $(V_1 + V_2) / 2V_1 V_2$
(b) $(1/V_1 + 1/V_2) / 2$
(c) $(V_1 + V_2) / 2$
(d) $2V_1 V_2 / (V_1 + V_2)$

**63.** A man walks $a$ km in $b$ hours. The time taken to walk 200 metres is

(a) $ab/200$ hours (b) $200b/a$ hours
(c) $b/5a$ hours (d) $b/5b$ hours

**64.** A man travels at the rate of '$x$' cm per minute, how many km does he travel in '$y$' hours?

(a) $2xy/5{,}000$ km (b) $y/1{,}000x$ km
(c) $xy/60{,}000$ km (d) $3xy/5{,}000$ km

**65.** A train does a journey without stoppage in 8 hours, if it had travelled 5 km/h faster, it would have done the journey in 6 hours 40 min. Find its original speed.

(a) 25 km/h (b) 40 km/h
(c) 45 km/h (d) 36.5 km/h

**66.** The distance between two cities is 800 km. A motor car starts from the first city at the speed of 30 km/hr. At the same time, another car starts from the second city towards the first at the speed of 50 km/hr. The distance of the point from the first city where both the cars meet is

(a) 200 km (b) 300 km
(c) 400 km (d) 500 km

**67.** A hare pursued by a greyhound, is 50 of her own leaps ahead of him. While the hare takes 4 leaps, the greyhound takes 3 leaps. In one leap, the hare goes 1.75 metres and the greyhound 2.75 metres. In how many leaps will the greyhound overtake the hare?

(a) 210 leaps (b) 180 leaps
(c) 200 leaps (d) 224 leaps

**68.** A train 110 metres long passes a telegraph pole in 3 seconds. How long will it take to cross a railway platform 165 metres long?

(a) 4 s (b) 10 s
(c) 5 s (d) 7½ s

**69.** A train of unknown length crosses a platform $L_1$ metres in $t_1$ seconds and also crosses a telegraph post in $t_0$ seconds. Then speed of train Vt is

(a) $L_1 (t_1 - t_0)$ (b) $L_1/(t_1 - t_0)$
(c) $(L_1 t_1)/t^2_0$ (d) $(L_1 t_1)/(t_1 + t_0)$

**70.** A train crosses two platforms of $L_1$ metres and $L_2$ metres in $t_1$ seconds and $t_2$ seconds, respectively. If the length of train is Lt then

(a) $Lt/(L_1 + L_2) = t_1 + t_2$
(b) $Lt (L_1 - L_2) = t_1 \times t_2$
(c) $(Lt + L_1)/t_1 = (Lt + L_2)/t_2$
(d) $Lt\, L_1\, L_2 = t_1 - t_2$

**71.** A train of length Lt crosses a man moving in opposite direction at Vm metre/s in $t_m$ seconds. If the speed of train is Vt m/s then

(a) $t_m = Lt/(V_t + V_m)$
(b) $t_m = Lt/ (Vt - V_m)$
(c) $V_t V_m = L_t/T_m$
(d) $V_t = L_t/T_m + V_m V_t$

**72.** The driver of a Maruti car driving at the speed of 68 km/h locates a bus 40 metres ahead of him. After 10 seconds, the bus is 60 metres behind. The speed of the bus is

(a) 30 km/h (b) 32 km/h
(c) 25 km/h (d) 38 km/h

**73.** A passenger in train 'P' travelling at 1 km/min uses his stop watch and finds that another train 'Q' travelling in the opposite direction, completely passed his windows in 3 seconds. If the length of the train 'Q' is 87.50 m. Find its speed (km/hr).

(a) 36 (b) 54
(c) 48 (d) 45

**74.** In a flat race of L metres, A beats B by $x_1$ metres, and beats C by $x_3$ metres; then C will beat B if

(a) $x_1 = x_3$ (b) $x_1 > x_3$
(c) $x_3 > x_1$ (d) $x_1 x_3 = 1$

**75.** In a 500 metres race, A beats B by 50 metres or 8 seconds. Find A's time over the course.

(a) 2 minutes
(b) 1 minutes 12 seconds
(c) 2 minutes 35 seconds
(d) 1 minute

**76.** In a 500 metres race, the ratio of speeds of two contestants A and B is 3:4. A has a start of 140 metres then

(a) B wins by 20 metres
(b) A wins by 20 metres
(c) B wins by 40 metres
(d) B wins by 25 metres

**77.** If A can run a kilometre in $3\frac{1}{6}$ minutes and B in $3\frac{1}{3}$ minutes, by what distance can A beat B?

(a) 100 metres (b) 75 metres
(c) 60 metres (d) 50 metres

**78.** The radius of a sphere is increased 50%. The increase in the surface area of sphere is

(a) 100% (b) 125%
(c) 150% (d) 200%

**79.** The diagonal of a square is doubled to make another square. The area of the new square will

(a) Become four-fold
(b) Become two-fold
(c) Become three-fold
(d) Remains the same

**80.** A wire of length $y$ cm is bent to form a rectangle of area 13½ cm². If one side of this rectangle measures $x$ cm then

(a) $2y = x + 27/x$ (b) $y = 2x + 27/2x$
(c) $y = x + 27/2x$ (d) $y = 2x + 27/x$

**81.** If the ratio of the area of two squares is 2 : 1 then the ratio of the perimeters of the square is

(a) 1 : 2 (b) 1 : √2
(c) √2 : 1 (d) 2 : 1

**82.** The area of a rectangular field is 144 m². If the length had been 6 metres more, the area would have been 54 $m^2$ more. The original length of the field is

(a) 22 metres (b) 18 metres
(c) 16 metres (d) 24 metres

**83.** It costs ₹ 0.3 per square centimetre to carpet a room. The cost of carpeting a room $x/100$ metres long and half as broad is

(a) ₹ $3x^2/100$ (b) ₹ $3x^2/20$
(c) ₹ $3x/50$ (d) ₹ $9x^2/100$

**84.** A typist uses a paper 12" by 5" length wise and leaves a margin of 1" at the top and the bottom and a margin of 1/2" on either side. What fractional part of the paper is available to him for typing?

(a) 2/3 (b) 1/2
(c) 1/3 (d) 5/7

**85.** If the area of a circle is $A$ sq. metres, radius of the circle is $r$ metres, and circumference of it is $C$ metres then

(a) $rC = 2A$ (b) $C/A = r/2$
(c) $AC = r^2/4$ (d) $A/r = C$

**86.** Two squares $A$ and $B$ have each side as 10 and 24 metres, respectively. Find the side of another square $C$ whose area is equal to the sum of area of $A$ and $B$

(a) 34 m (b) 14 m
(c) 26 m (d) $\sqrt{14} \times 34$

**87.** A cube of 1 cc volume will have surface area equal to

(a) $\frac{1}{12}$ sq.cm (b) $\frac{1}{24}$ sq.cm
(c) 6 sq.cm (d) $\frac{1}{36}$ sq.cm

**88.** A rectangular tank can hold K litres of water. How many litres of water can a tank with all its dimensions double that of the first one hold?

(a) 2 K litres (b) 8 K litres
(c) 4 K litres (d) 6 K litres

**89.** The height and the radius of the base of a cone each are increased by 100%. The volume of the cone then increases by

(a) 8 times (b) 6 times
(c) 4 times (d) 3 times

***Directions:*** In each of the following questions, a question is asked followed by three statements. While answering the question, you may or may not require the data provided in all the statements. You have to read the question and the three statements and then decide upon whether the question can be answered with any one or two of the statements or all the three statements are required to answer the question. The answer number bearing the statements which are required to answer the question is your answer.

**90.** What is the average marks obtained by Ram in three subjects?

(i) He gets 137 in Physics and English.
(ii) He gets 160 in English and Maths.
(iii) He gets 158 in Maths and Chemistry.

(a) Only (i) and (ii)
(b) Only (ii) and (iii)
(c) All three
(d) None

**91.** A trader sells a homogenous mixture of A and B at the rate of 32 per kg. What is the profit percentage of the trader?

(i) He bought B at the rate of ₹ 29 per kg.
(ii) He bought A at ₹ 8 higher than the rate of B per kg.
(iii) He bought A at the rate of ₹ 34 per kg.

(a) Only (i) and (ii)
(b) Only (i) and (iii)
(c) (i), (ii) and (iii) together not sufficient
(d) either (i) or (ii)

**92.** What is the difference between the two numbers?

(i) 80% of the greater number is equal to the smaller number.
(ii) Half of the greater number is 18 less than the smaller number.
(iii) 60% of the greater number is equal to 2/3rd of the smaller number.

(a) Only (i) and (ii) together
(b) Only (ii) and (iii) together
(c) Any two of the three above
(d) Only (i)

93. In how many minutes the 300 m long train crosses the man?
    (i) The man is standing.
    (ii) The train is running at 60 km per hour.
    (iii) The man is running at 60 metres per minute.

    Which of the above statements is redundant?
    (a) Only (i)
    (b) Only (iii)
    (c) Only (i) or (iii)
    (d) Only (ii) or (iii)

***Directions:*** Each question given here is followed by two statements:

**Mark**

**(a)** If Statement (i) alone, but not Statement (ii) alone, is sufficient to answer the question.

**(b)** If Statement (ii) alone, but not Statement (ii) alone, is sufficient to answer the question.

**(c)** If the question can be answered with the help of both statements together, but not with the help of either statement alone.

**(d)** If the question cannot be answered unless more information is provided.

94. is $x = y$?
    **(i)** $x$ is average of $p$ and $q$
    **(ii)** $y$ is the average of $x$, $p$ and $q$

95. What is the value of m?
    (i) $m + n = 12$
    (ii) $m$, $n$ are integers, $mn = 35$

96. How many members are there in committee A?
    (i) All the members of committee B are in A.
    (ii) The number of members of committee B is 15.

97. A number is a product of three successive prime numbers. What is the number?
    (i) The number is less than 200.
    (ii) The difference between the first two numbers in the ascending order is 1.

98. What is difference between x and y?
    (i) $x$ is 80% of A
    (ii) $y$ is 70% of A

99. Which of the two has a larger area—the rectangle or the square?
    (i) The width of the rectangle is equal to the side of the square.
    (ii) The length of the rectangle is numerically equal to the area of the square.

100. What is the speed of a running train?
    (i) Length of the train is 200 m.
    (ii) The train crosses another train of length 150 m in 10 secs.

## Answers of Exercise Set A

| | | | | | | | | | |
|---|---|---|---|---|---|---|---|---|---|
| **1.** (c) | **11.** (c) | **21.** (d) | **31.** (c) | **41.** (c) | **51.** (b) | **61.** (d) | **71.** (a) | **81.** (c) | **91.** (c) |
| **2.** (a) | **12.** (a) | **22.** (b) | **32.** (b) | **42.** (d) | **52.** (b) | **62.** (d) | **72.** (b) | **82.** (c) | **92.** (c) |
| **3.** (d) | **13.** (c) | **23.** (c) | **33.** (c) | **43.** (d) | **53.** (c) | **63.** (c) | **73.** (d) | **83.** (b) | **93.** (b) |
| **4.** (d) | **14.** (b) | **24.** (b) | **34.** (a) | **44.** (b) | **54.** (b) | **64.** (d) | **74.** (b) | **84.** (a) | **94.** (c) |
| **5.** (c) | **15.** (d) | **25.** (c) | **35.** (b) | **45.** (b) | **55.** (a) | **65.** (a) | **75.** (b) | **85.** (a) | **95.** (d) |
| **6.** (a) | **16.** (a) | **26.** (b) | **36.** (a) | **46.** (a) | **56.** (a) | **66.** (b) | **76.** (b) | **86.** (c) | **96.** (d) |
| **7.** (a) | **17.** (d) | **27.** (d) | **37.** (a) | **47.** (d) | **57.** (b) | **67.** (a) | **77.** (d) | **87.** (c) | **97.** (b) |
| **8.** (a) | **18.** (c) | **28.** (c) | **38.** (d) | **48.** (b) | **58.** (b) | **68.** (d) | **78.** (b) | **88.** (b) | **98.** (d) |
| **9.** (b) | **19.** (b) | **29.** (d) | **39.** (b) | **49.** (d) | **59.** (d) | **69.** (b) | **79.** (a) | **89.** (a) | **99.** (a) |
| **10.** (d) | **20.** (a) | **30.** (a) | **40.** (a) | **50.** (d) | **60.** (b) | **70.** (c) | **80.** (d) | **90.** (d) | **100.** (d) |

## Exercise Set B

**1.** Four teams A, B, C and D participate in a car race. The velocity–time graph of the car of each team is shown here. The race ends at time T4 when one of the cars crosses the winning post and till time T4 the velocity–time graph of all the cars is plotted. Point T2 is the half time while time T1 and T3 indicate the first and third quarter time marks.

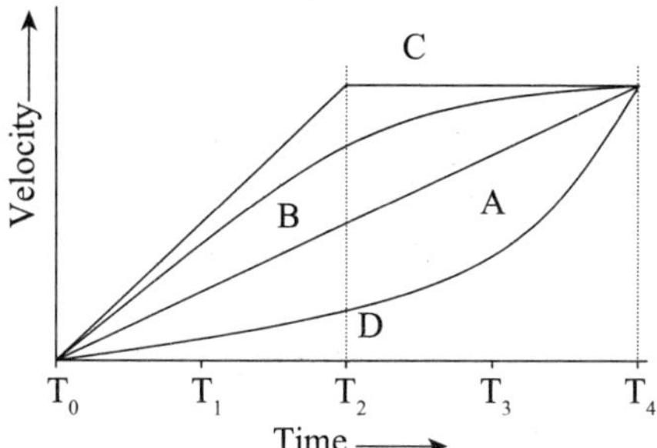


(i) Which of the following statements are correct?

1. All cars had travelled equal distance till time $T_2$.
2. Velocity of all cars has always been different.
3. Car A was not accelerating.

(a) 123
(b) 23
(c) 2 only
(d) None of the above

(ii) Which car showed maximum acceleration at any given time during the entire course of race till time $T_4$?

(a) A (b) B
(c) C (d) D

(iii) Which team's car won the race?

(a) A
(b) B
(c) C
(d) Cannot be determined

(iv) Which car covered the least distance when the race ended at time $T_4$?

(a) B
(b) C
(c) D
(d) Cannot be determined

**2.** Nagesh scores the following marks in his Class X^th Board examination. Along with his marks the average marks and the range of marks of 5000 students of the particular city is also displayed.

| Subject | Ramesh's Marks Out of 100 | Average Marks Out of 100 | Range of Marks |
|---|---|---|---|
| English | 70 | 65 | 30–96 |
| Hindi | 70 | 68 | 35–98 |
| Science | 75 | 70 | 20–100 |
| Mathematics | 74 | 60 | 10–100 |
| Social Science | 56 | 70 | 15–90 |

(i) In which subject is his performance best comparatively?

(a) English
(b) Hindi
(c) Science
(d) Mathematics

(ii) If the average marks in mathematics of the students of the city were to be 70 instead of 60 then how would the overall performance of Nagesh compare with the average performance of the city students?

(a) Substantially better than others
(b) Marginally better than others
(c) Substantially poorer than others
(d) Marginally poorer than others

3. The market capture by various mobile operators of cities P and Q is depicted by the two pie charts as shown here.

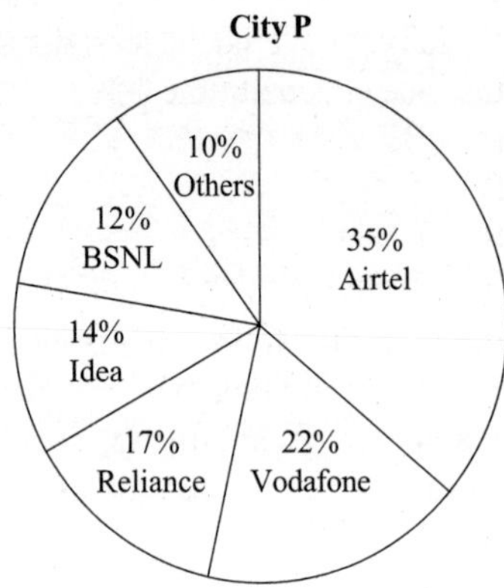


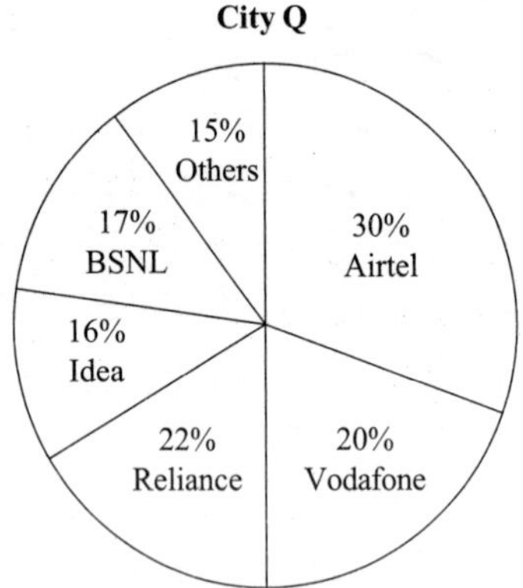


(i) Which of the cities has more number of Idea customers?
   (a) City P
   (b) City Q
   (c) Equal number in both cities
   (d) Data insufficient

(ii) In which of the two cities there are customers, which have mobiles of more than one mobile operator?
   (a) Only City P
   (b) Only City Q
   (c) Both cities P and Q
   (d) Data insufficient

(iii) The data given above pertains to year 2010 when the market size of mobile phones customers of city P was 20 lakh and of City Q was 25 lakh (i.e., 100% corresponds to 20 lakh in City P and 25 lakh in city Q).

In two years time the market size in city P increases by 10% while of city Q increases by 8%. In 2012, the market share of Airtel in city P drops to 30%. While in City Q it increases to 25%. In which city does Airtel have more customers in terms of absolute numbers in 2012?
   (a) City P
   (b) City Q
   (c) Equal on both cities
   (d) Data insufficient

4. The following bar chart depicts the figures of the number of deaths caused due to various diseases in a country in the years 2010 and 2011. Examine the data and answer the questions that follow.

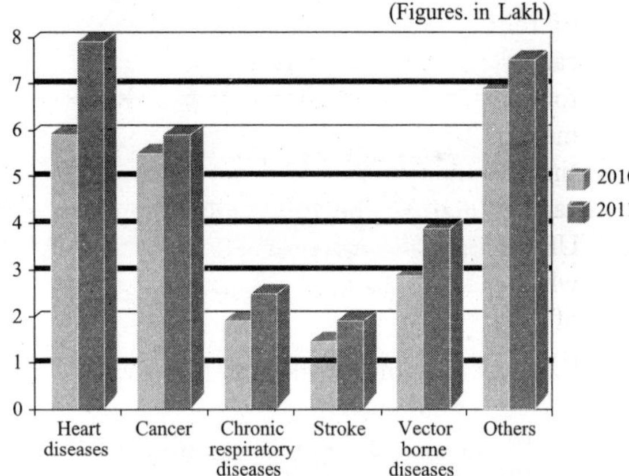


(i) The percentage of deaths due to cancer (out of total deaths due to various diseases) in 2011 is
   (a) Less than that in 2010
   (b) Equal to that in 2010
   (c) More than that in 2010
   (d) Data insufficient to draw such inference

(ii) For which disease there has been maximum increase in the deaths in the year 2011?

Consider this increase as a percentage of deaths which took place in 2010.

1. Heart diseases
2. Cancer
3. Stroke
4. Vector borne diseases

(a) 1, 2, 3 (b) 1, 3, 4
(c) 2, 3, 4 (d) 1, 2, 4

(iii) What is the percentage increase in the total number of deaths due to various diseases in 2011 as compared to 2010?
(a) 16.66%
(b) 20%
(c) 25%
(d) Data insufficient

**5.** A team of psephologists conduct an exit poll on a sample of 1000 voters for election of a Lok Sabha constituency. The candidates for purposes of the poll were classified in four categories 'UPA candidate', 'NDA candidate', 'other party candidates' and 'Independent candidates'.

The exit poll data showed that 50% of the males had voted for the UPA candidate, while of the females, 35% had voted for NDA candidate. 30 persons were found to have voted for independents, two thirds of which were males. Equal number of females had voted for 'independent candidates' as for 'other party candidates'. The number of males who voted for UPA is ten times more than the number of males who voted for 'other party candidates'. The ratio of male to female voters in the exit poll was 3:2.

(i) How many females voted for NDA?
(a) 200
(b) 180
(c) 140
(d) Data insufficient

(ii) Which one of the following statements is correct?
1. 250 males voted for NDA.
2. 250 males voted for UPA.
(a) Only 1 is correct.
(b) Only 2 is correct.
(c) Both 1 and 2 are correct.
(d) Neither 1 nor 2 is correct.

(iii) What percentage of females who participated in the exit poll, had voted for UPA?
(a) 40%
(b) 50%
(c) 60%
(d) Data insufficient

(iv) The per cent of votes polled by NDA was
(a) 39%
(b) 40%
(c) 45%
(d) Data insufficient

(v) The number of exit poll voters who had voted for UPA is
(a) 500 (b) 520
(c) 540 (d) 560

**6.** The figures in the table here represent the number of cases of dengue detected/treated in hospitals of Delhi over a period of seven years and the number of persons out of the above who died due to dengue.

| Year | 2005 | 2006 | 2007 | 2008 | 2009 | 2010 | 2011 | 2012 |
|---|---|---|---|---|---|---|---|---|
| Number of cases of dengue detected | 55 | 70 | 105 | 120 | 155 | 175 | 250 | 255 |
| Number of patients which died out of above | 8 | 7 | 15 | 12 | 14 | 12 | 10 | 9 |

(i) Which of the following conclusions can be drawn from the figures given above?
1. The measure to control the spread of disease has not been very effective over the years.
2. From 2005 to 2009 the percentage of patients who died due to dengue is erratic/shows no clear trend.
3. The percentage of patients who died due to dengue can be said to have stabilised in the latter years.
(a) 1, 2, 3 (b) 1, 2
(c) 1, 3 (d) 2, 3

(ii) Which year comparatively can be said to be worst in terms of deaths resulting from dengue?
(a) Year 2007
(b) Year 2009
(c) Both 2007 and 2009
(d) No such inference can be drawn.

(iii) Examine which of the following graphs would best represent the percentage of dengue deaths over the year.

(a)

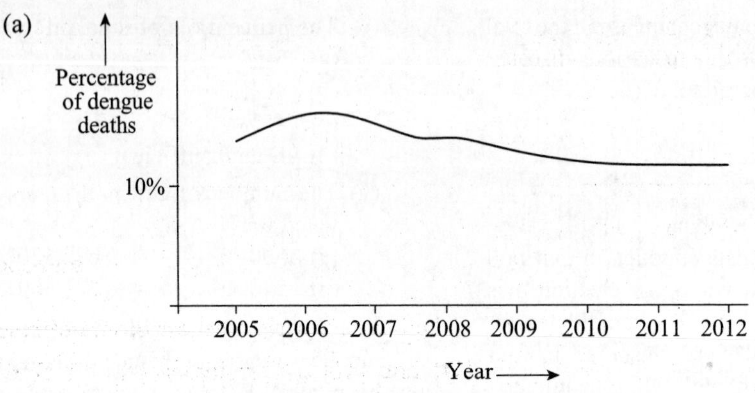
Percentage of dengue deaths
10%
2005 2006 2007 2008 2009 2010 2011 2012
Year

(b)

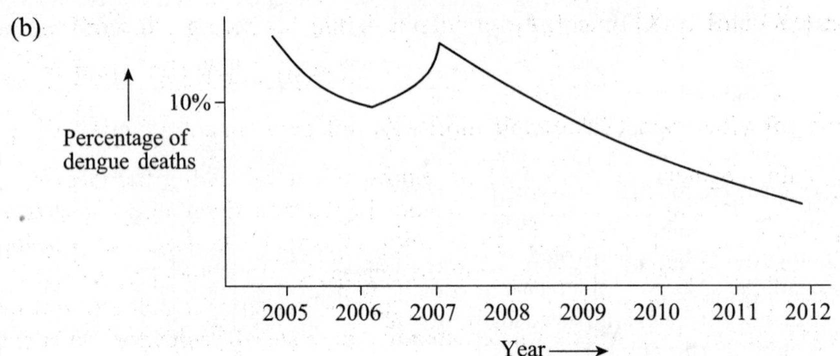
10%
Percentage of dengue deaths
2005 2006 2007 2008 2009 2010 2011 2012
Year

(c)

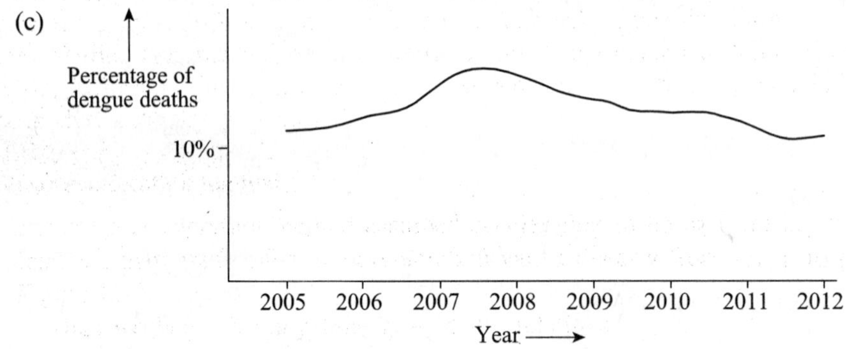
Percentage of dengue deaths
10%
2005 2006 2007 2008 2009 2010 2011 2012
Year

(d)

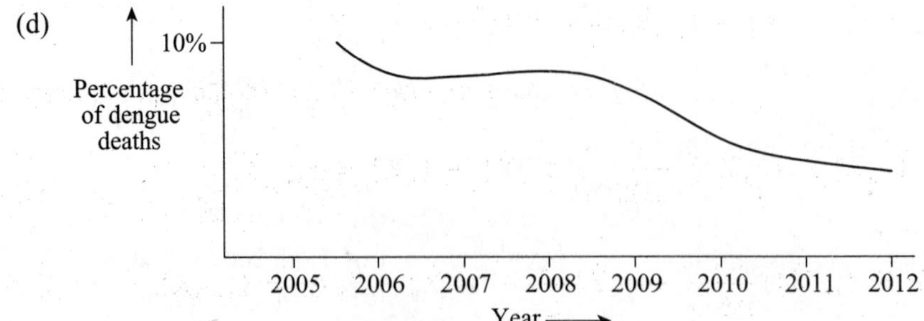
10%
Percentage of dengue deaths
2005 2006 2007 2008 2009 2010 2011 2012
Year

7. The following graph indicates the population growth rate characteristics of four different countries over a period of 30 years from time $T_0$ to $T_3$, each phase of a decade. Presume no change in population due to migration.

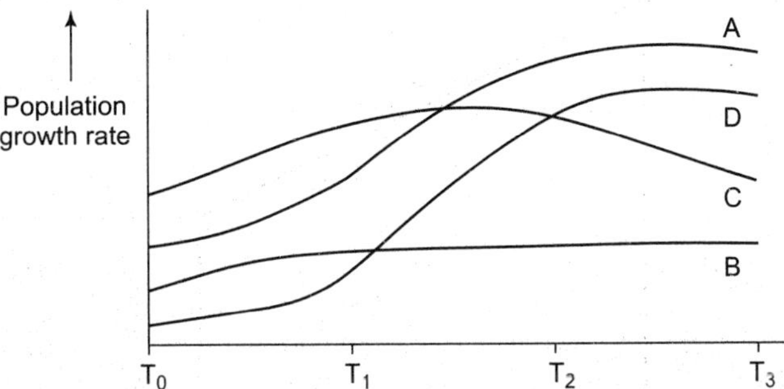


(i) Which graph best displays the population growth characteristic of a developed country?

(a) A (b) B
(c) C (d) D

(ii) Which one of the following can be said to be true about country D?

(a) It represents the population growth characteristics of an under-developed country at point $T_0$ which enters a development phase at point $T_1$.
(b) It represents population growth of a developing country the population growth of which is stabilising got point $T_3$.
(c) It represents the population growth characteristic of a developed country since time $T_0$.
(d) No such conclusion can be drawn.

(iii) Which country has shown a decline in population in absolute terms?

(a) A
(b) B
(c) C
(d) None of the above

8. The pie charts of market share of sales in India of leading brand of air conditioners, for three years is as shown here. Examine the figures and answer the questions that follow.

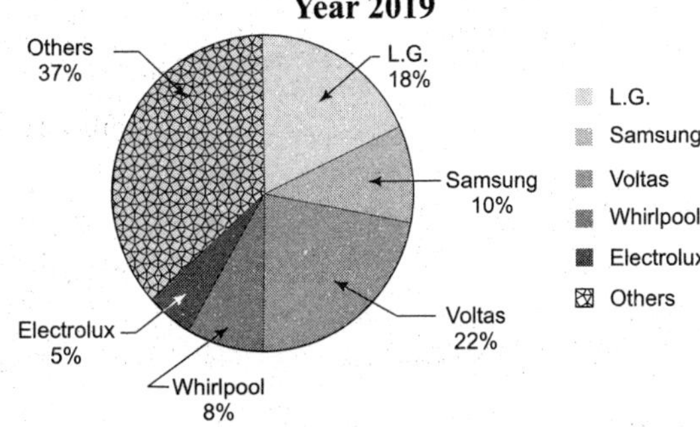


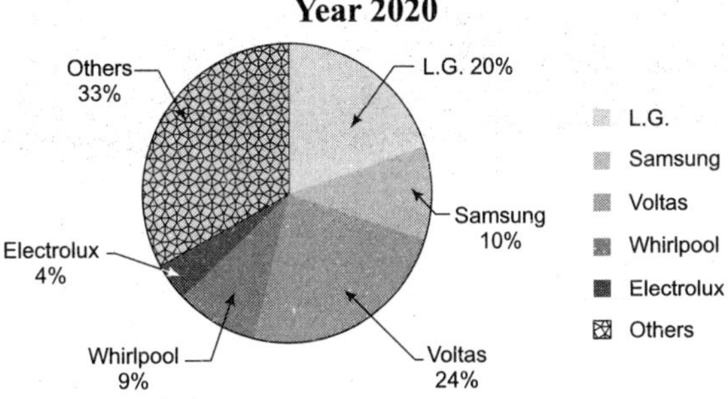


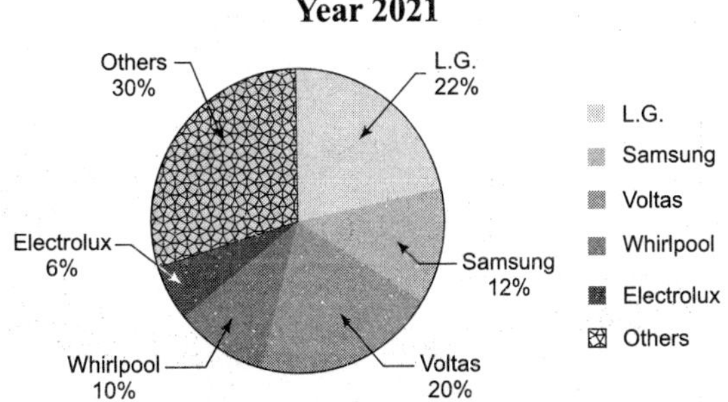

The sales volume of all air conditioners is 2.5 million units for 2019, 3.3 million units for 2020 and 3.0 million units for 2021.

(i) How has the sale of L.G. air conditioners changed from 2020 to 2021 in absolute numbers?
(a) It has increased.
(b) It has decreased.
(c) It has remained constant.
(d) Data insufficient to draw any conclusion

(ii) What is the increase in number of air conditioners sold by Whirlpool, from 2019 to 2021 (in percentage terms)?
(a) 25%
(b) 50%
(c) 20%
(d) Data insufficient

(iii) Which of the following conclusions can be drawn from the figures given above?
1. The number of AC units of L.G. sold has increased from year to year.
2. The number of AC units of Samsung sold, has remained same from 2019 to 2020 but increased in 2021.
3. The number of units of Electrolux ACs sold has increased in each successive year.
(a) 1, 2, 3
(b) 2, 3
(c) 2 only
(d) 3 only

**9.** The bar/charts here reflect the percentage of various items of revenue expenditure for the financial years 2004–05 to 2011–12. Study the data and answer the questions that follow.

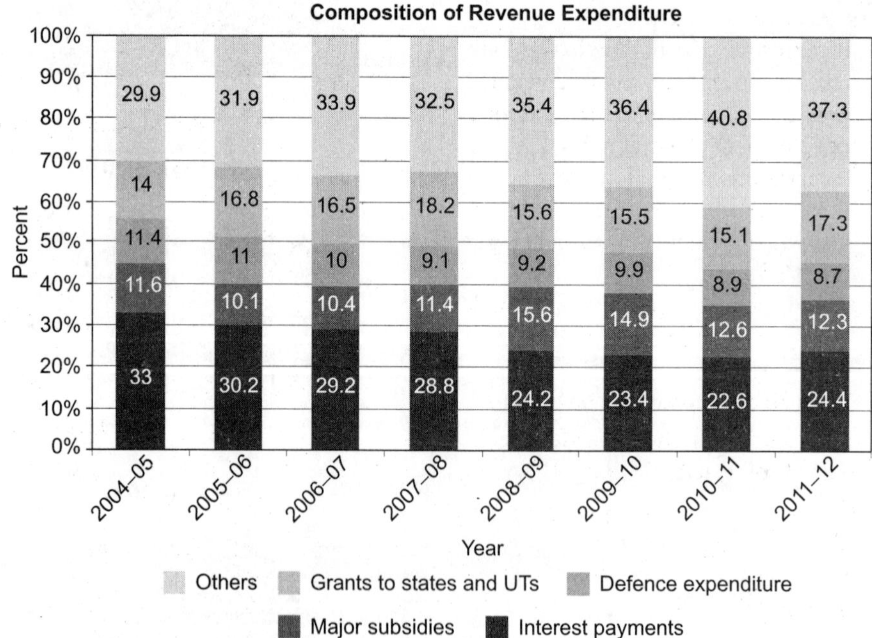


(i) As a percentage of revenue expenditure which amongst expenditure, which amongst the following items has always shown a decline over the years?
(a) Interest payments
(b) Major subsidies
(c) Defence expenditure
(d) None of the above

(ii) Which of the following is true?

1. The quantum of major subsidies has decreased from FY 2010–11 to FY 2011–12.
2. The quantum of interest payments has increased from FY 2010–11 to FY 2011–12.

(a) Only 1 is true.
(b) Only 2 is true.
(c) Both 1 and 2 are true.
(d) None of the above conclusions can be drawn.

(iii) Which of the following is sufficient to find the quantum of change in defence expenditure from 2010–11 to 2011–12?

1. The quantum of major subsides in FY 2010–11.
2. The quantum of interest payments in FY 2011–12.
3. The quantum of revenue expenditure in FY 2011–11 and FY 2010–12.

(a) 1 and 2 together or 1 and 3 together.
(b) 1 and 2 together or only 3.
(c) 1 and 3 together or 2 and 3 together.
(d) Only 3

**10.** Four cyclists participate in a race over a distance $d_2$. The time distance graph is as shown here. The distance $d_1$ is the half-way mark.

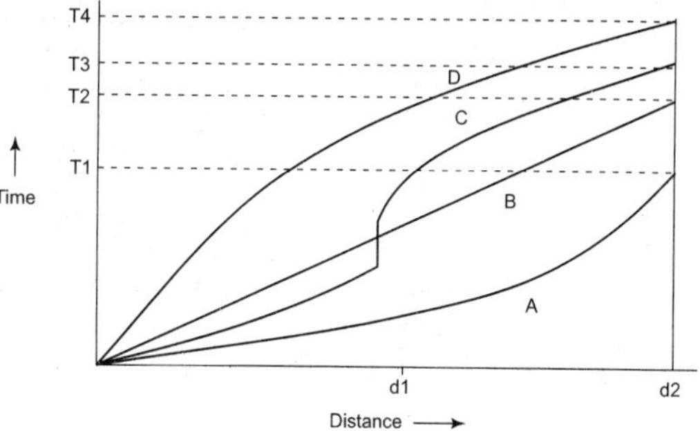


(i) Which cyclist won the race?
(a) A (b) B
(c) C (d) D

(ii) A cyclist had minor break down in his bike. He had to halt for a while repair his bike and then continue the race. Which cyclist was this?
(a) A (b) B
(c) C (d) D

(iii) Which cyclist was slowing down towards the end of the race?
(a) A (b) B
(c) C (d) D

**11.** A cricket association of a state awards two cricketers annually for their performance. The first award is for being the most prolific run scorer while the second award is for being the most consistent player. Four players are shortlisted. Their batting scores of their last 10 innings are evaluated for this purpose and it is as shown here.

| Batting scorer of last 10 innings | Inning 1 | Inning 2 | Inning 3 | Inning 4 | Inning 5 | Inning 6 | Inning 7 | Inning 8 | Inning 9 | Inning 10 |
|---|---|---|---|---|---|---|---|---|---|---|
| Player A | 105 | 90 | 25 | 5 | 0 | 60 | 30 | 28 | 22 | 150 |
| Player B | 65 | 70 | 45 | 52 | 48 | 80 | 48 | 112 | 35 | 85 |
| Player C | 77 | 22 | 73 | 45 | 160 | 0 | 170 | 5 | 23 | 155 |
| Player D | 62 | 5 | 35 | 50 | 0 | 130 | 115 | 95 | 140 | 88 |

(i) Which amongst the above will get the award for most prolific run scorer (best batting average)?
(a) A (b) B
(c) C (d) D

(ii) Which amongst the four is the most consistent player over the last ten test innings?
(a) A (b) B
(c) C (d) D

(iii) Amongst the four players one player is to be recommended for playing for the national team. This recommendation is to be based on; overall run scored in the last 10 innings, and the recent form (which is performance in the last five innings, i.e., innings 6 to 10). Which player should be recommended?
(a) A (b) B
(c) C (d) D

(iv) Which form of data representation would be best suited to represent the above data?
(a) Bar chart
(b) Graph
(c) Pie chart
(d) None of the above

**12.** Given here are graphs showing amount of subsidies given by the government from the year 2004–05 to the year 2011–12. The figures of subsidies as a per cent of GDP is also depicted in the graphs. Study the graphs and answer the questions that follow.

(a)

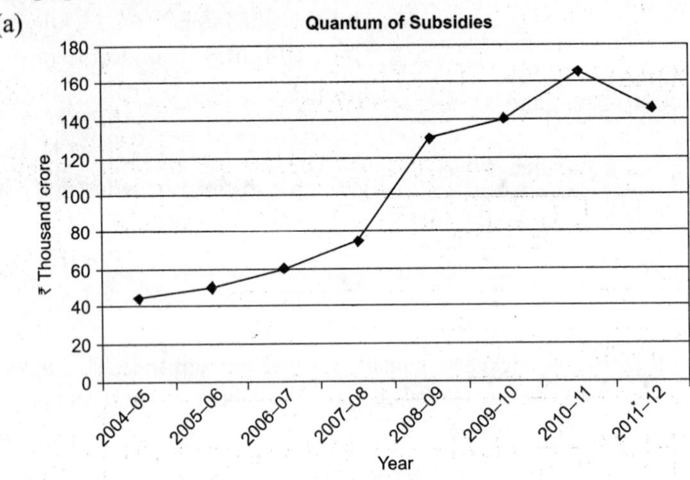


(b)

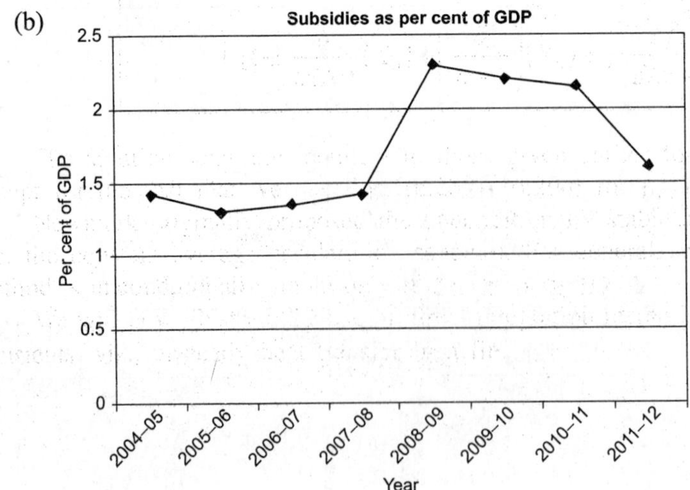

(i) From the FY 2008–09 till FY 2010–11, which of the following can be drawn about the subsidies and the GDP?
   (a) Subsidies are rising and GDP is rising at nearly the same rate.
   (b) Subsidies are falling but GDP is rising.
   (c) Subsidies are rising but GDP is rising at a higher rate.
   (d) Subsidies are rising but GDP is rising at a lower rate.

(ii) What can be said to the approximate GDP for the year 2011–12?
   (a) ₹ 70 lakh crore
   (b) ₹ 80 lakh crore
   (c) ₹ 90 lakh crore
   (d) Data insufficient to draw such conclusion

(iii) If in the FY 2012–13, the GDP were to grow by 10% and the quantum of subsidies were to fall by 10% then approximately what per cent of GDP the subsidies would be?
   (a) 1.3% (b) 1.4%
   (c) 1.2% (d) Data insufficient

**13.** The bar chart below shows the per capita $CO_2$ emissions (in metric tons), of countries which are major contributors to Green House Gas (GHG) emissions, for the years 1992 and 2007. Examine the data and answer the questions that follow.

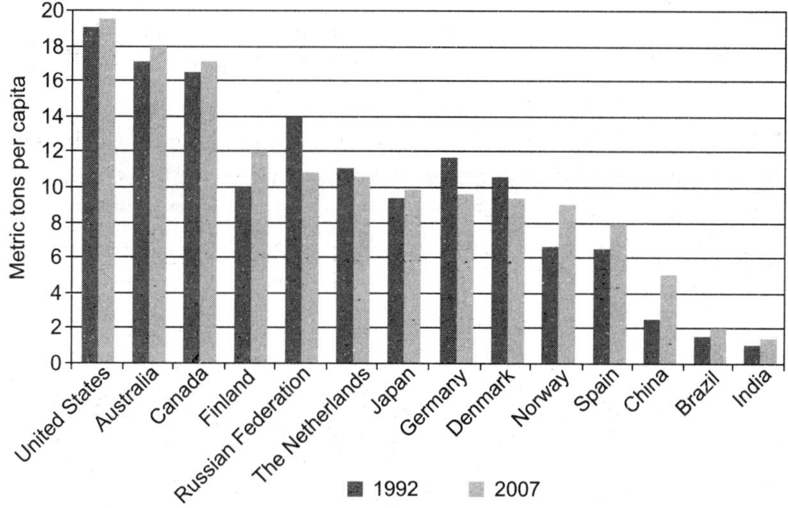


(i) For which country the per capita emission has shown maximum change (increase/decrease) from 1992 to 2007?
   (a) Finland
   (b) Russian Federation
   (c) China
   (d) Norway

(ii) In terms of absolute quantum of Green House Gases emitted, which country can be said to be the least contributor of GHGs, in 2007?
   (a) India
   (b) Brazil
   (c) China
   (d) Data insufficient to draw such conclusion

(iii) For which of the following countries, there has been more than 25% increase in per capita $CO_2$ emissions from 1992 to 2007?
   1. Russian Federation
   2. Norway
   3. Australia
   4. China

   (a) 1, 2, 3, 4 (b) 1, 2, 4
   (c) 2, 4 (d) 2, 3

**14.** A Delhi to Lucknow flight takes an hour. The velocity of the aeroplane is as shown in the time–velocity graph at different stages of flight.

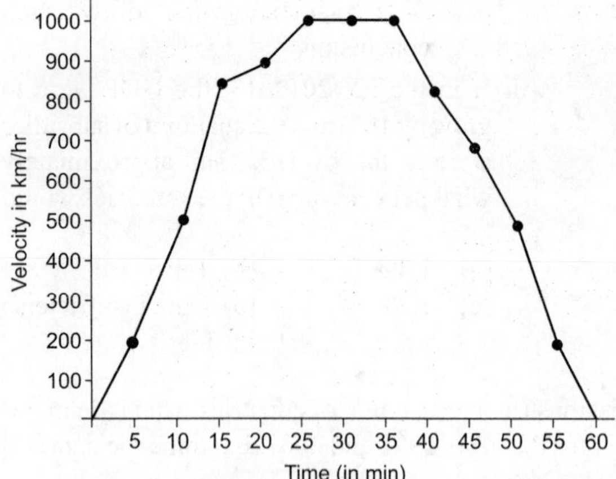


**(where the dot indicating the velocity data is between two marks of 100s, presume it to be at value of 50 viz. at 40 minutes, the velocity is = 850 ms$^{-1}$)**

(i) In which stage of flight does the aircraft has maximum acceleration?
   (a) 0–5 min
   (b) 5–10 min
   (c) 10–15 min
   (d) None of the above

(ii) Examine the following statements:
   1. The aircraft travels more distance in the time interval 10–15 minutes than in the interval 40 – 45 minutes.
   2. The aircraft travels a distance of 50 km in the time interval 45–50 minutes.

   (a) Only 1 is correct.
   (b) Only 2 is correct.
   (c) Both 1 and 2 are correct.
   (d) Neither 1 nor 2 is correct.

**15.** The following graph shows the level of charge of a mobile battery over a period of seven hours. Study the graph carefully and answer the questions.

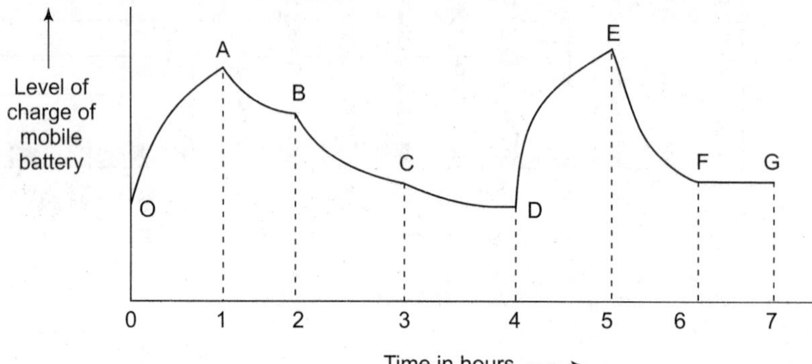


(i) Which parts of the curve represents the time when mobile is being charged?
   (a) OA
   (b) FG
   (c) DE
   (d) Both OA and DE

(ii) In which phase is the mobile switched off?
   (a) BC
   (b) CD
   (c) FG
   (d) Never switched off

(iii) In which hour/phase is the usage of mobile maximum?
   (a) AB (b) BC
   (c) CD (d) EF

(iv) In which phase mobile is not switched off but mobile usage is least?
   (a) AB (b) BC
   (c) CD (d) FG

**16.** In a school, the percentage of students which play different games in two different sections of Class 10 is depicted by the stacked bar charts shown here.

(i) From the bar charts which of the following conclusions can be drawn?

1. The data given is erroneous.
2. Some students in both the sections are not playing any game.
3. Some students in both the sections are playing more than one game.

(a) 1, 2, 3 (b) 2, 3
(c) 2 only (d) 3 only

(ii) In which section, more number of students are playing table tennis?

(a) Sec A
(b) Sec B
(c) Equal in both sections
(d) Data insufficient

(iii) If there are 60 students in Sec A and 50 in Sec B then which of the following is correct (assume all students play at least one game and no student plays three different games)?

(a) Sec A has more number of students than Sec B who play two games.
(b) Sec B has more number of students than Sec A who play two games.
(c) Both sections have equal number of students playing two games.
(d) Data is insufficient to draw any such conclusion.

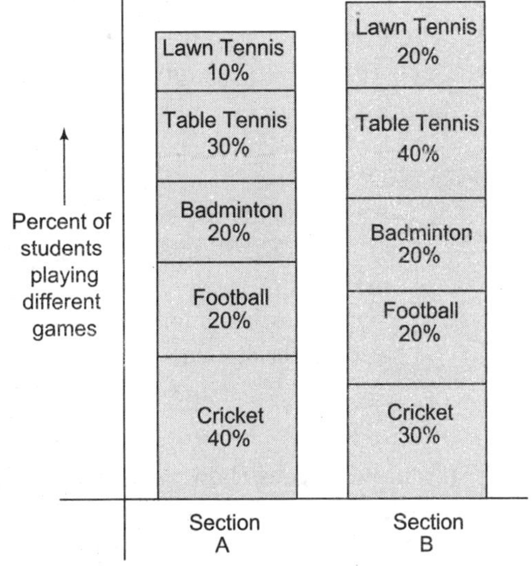


**17.** The data in the table here shows the figures of growth in sales and expenditure of listed public limited manufacturing companies in the private sector for the financial years 2008–09 and 2009–10. Study the data and answer the questions that follow.

**Year-on-Year Growth in Sales and Expenditure of listed public limited manufacturing companies in the private sector**

| Items | 2008–09 | | | | 2009–10 | | | |
|---|---|---|---|---|---|---|---|---|
| | Q1 | Q2 | Q3 | Q4 | Q1 | Q2 | Q3 | Q4 |
| No. of companies | 1926 | 1837 | 1849 | 1901 | 1885 | 1876 | 1901 | 1912 |
| **Growth Rates in per cent** | | | | | | | | |
| Sales | 30.1 | 32.1 | 6.3 | 0.1 | –2.7 | –0.4 | 28.7 | 34.9 |
| Change in stock-in-trade | 131.9 | 230.1 | a | a | –79.5 | 0.1 | b | b |
| Expenditure | 34.3 | 38.8 | 9.3 | –2.9 | –6.6 | –3.4 | 26.6 | 37.5 |
| Consumption of Raw Materials | 38.1 | 44 | 4 | –9.6 | –14.5 | –4.7 | 35.5 | 46.6 |
| Staff Cost | 19.3 | 17 | 12.4 | 7.9 | 9.9 | 9.1 | 12 | 18.1 |
| Power and Fuel | 28.8 | 37.8 | 21.7 | 3.1 | –1.4 | –5.7 | 1.7 | 10.6 |
| Other income | –9.5 | 2.7 | 14.9 | 26.8 | 62.7 | 10 | 12.3 | 42.4 |
| Interest Costs | 52 | 69.9 | 60.5 | 43.3 | 8.3 | –2.1 | –5 | 1.1 |
| Profits after Tax (PAT) | 6.9 | –4.2 | –66.4 | –28.3 | 3.2 | 17.6 | 178 | 69.4 |
| **Ratio in per cent** | | | | | | | | |
| PAT to Sales | 8.7 | 7.6 | 3.6 | 6.7 | 9.2 | 9 | 8 | 8.6 |

Note: a: Numerator is negative; b: Denominator is negative

(i) The profit after tax figures in $Q_2$ and $Q_3$ of FY 2008–09 are negative. What could be the reason for it?
1. Recession in a particular trade/sector
2. Recession/ contraction of the economy in general
3. Statistical error in computation of profit after tax

(a) 1, 2, 3 (b) 1, 2
(c) 1 only (d) 2 only

(ii) During the second half of 2008–09 the figures of growth of 'stock in trade', is in negative. Which of the following conclusions can be drawn?
1. The accumulated 'stock in trade' in Q1 and Q2 of 2008–09 is depleted in $Q_3$ and $Q_4$.
2. Manufacturing is falling.
3. Demand has fallen.

(a) 1 only (b) 1 and 2
(c) 1, 2 and 3 (d) 2 and 3

(iii) From the figures shown above, in which quarter can the economy be said to have come out of recession?
(a) In $Q_2$ of 2009–10
(b) In $Q_3$ of 2009–10
(c) In $Q_4$ of 2009–10
(d) No such conclusions can be drawn.

**18.** A culture of bacteria is allowed to develop in a petridish in a laboratory. Its growth follows the formula $B = B_0 2^t$ where $B_0$ is the initial number of bacteria introduced in the culture, t is the time in minutes and B is the number of bacteria after time t.

(i) Which of the following graphs best represent the growth of bacteria in culture?

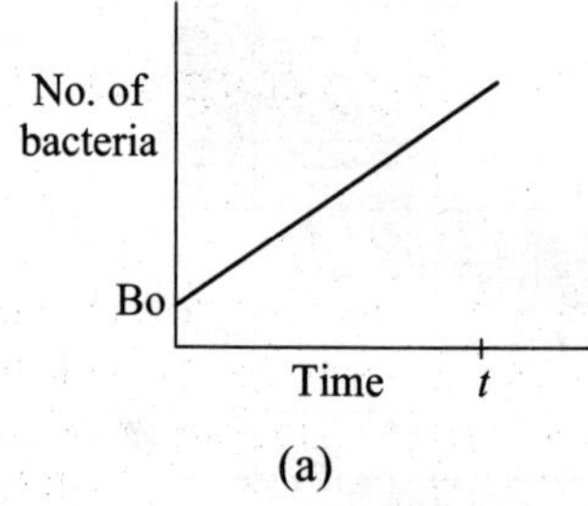

(a)

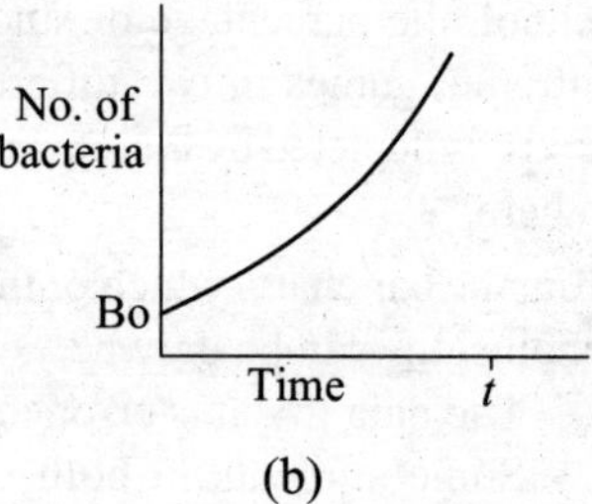

(b)

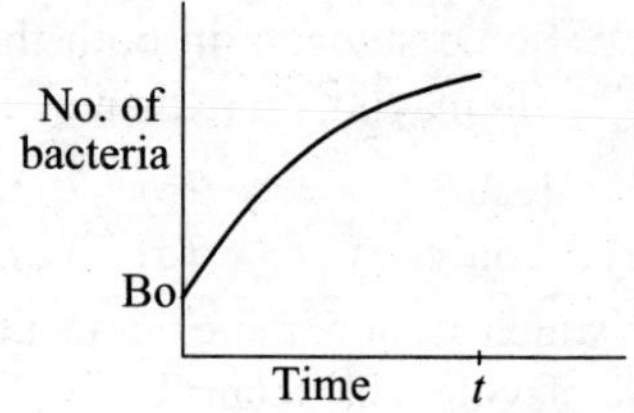

(c)

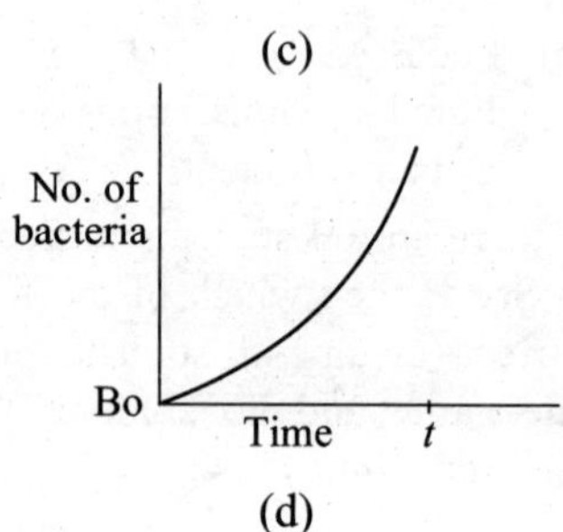

(d)

(ii) After time interval $t_1$ a culture of Bacteriophage virus is introduced in the culture of the bacteria. The Bacteriophage virus is able to kill the bacteria. The growth of virus follows the formula $V = V_0, 2^t$ where $V_0$ is the initial number of virus introduced in the culture, t is time in minutes and V is number of virus after time t.

Which of the following graphs best represents the number of bacteria in the culture at time $t_2$? Presume each virus is able to grow (as per above formula) as well as kill many bacteria and $v_0$ is less than B the number of bacteria in culture at time $t_1$.

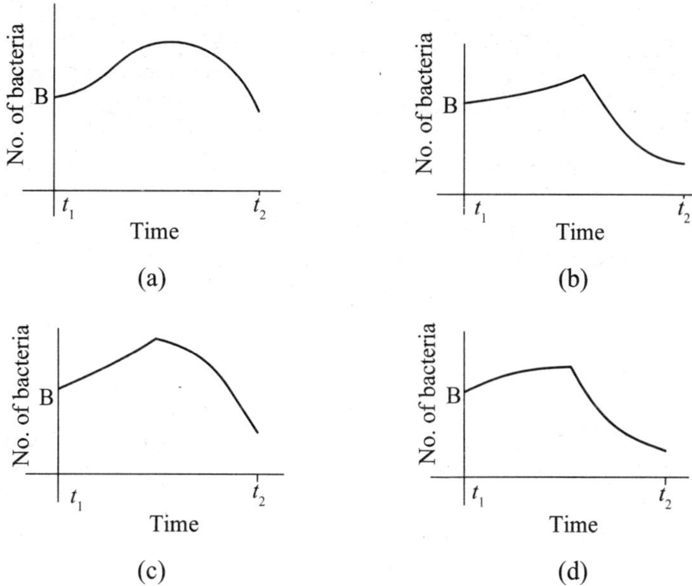


**19.** The age-wise population distribution graph of a country is as shown here. Study the data and answer the questions that follow.

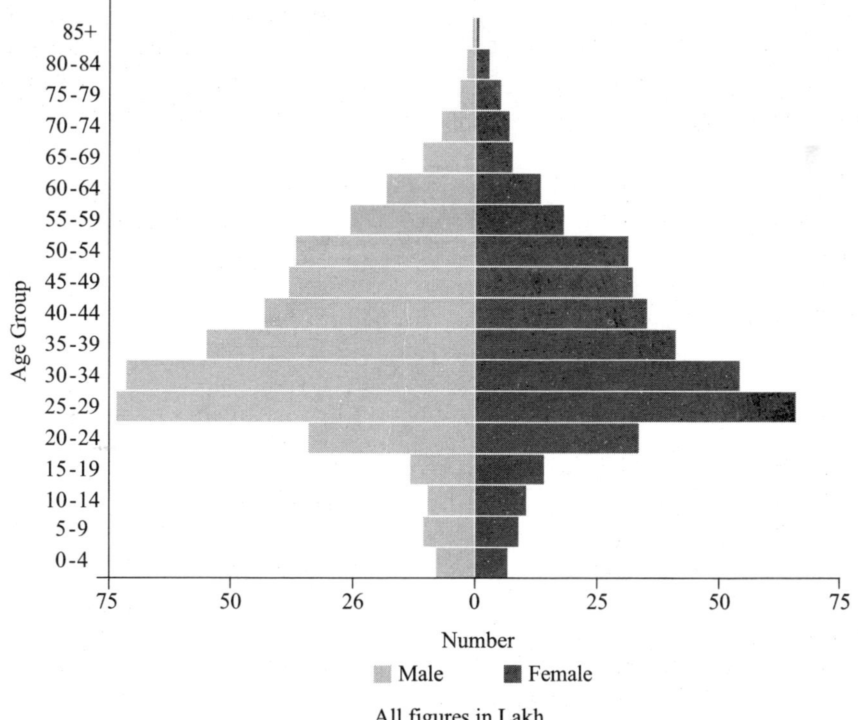


All figures in Lakh

(i) On the basis of the population distribution, it can be inferred that the country is most likely
   (a) a developing country with growing population
   (b) a developed country with stabilising/ declining population
   (c) an under developed country with high population growth rate
   (d) a developed country with growing population

(ii) The country had launched a nation-wide population control programme which yielded very good results in less than five years of it being launched. When was the programme launched?
   (a) 20–24 years ago
   (b) 25–29 years ago
   (c) 30–34 years ago
   (d) No such conclusion can be drawn from the given graph.

(iii) Which of the following conclusions can be drawn?
   1. The life expectancy of the people of the country is 75 years.
   2. The majority of the population is in the working age group (i.e., 20–60 years)

   (a) Only Conclusion 1 can be drawn.
   (b) Only Conclusion 2 can be drawn.
   (c) Both Conclusions 1 and 2 can be drawn.
   (d) Neither Conclusion 1 nor 2 can be drawn.

**20.** In a particular year, 800 candidates are successful for the Civil-Services examination conducted by the UPSC, of which 25% are females. The successful candidates are classified in three broad categories based on their educational background. These are 'humanities', 'sciences' and 'other streams'. The candidates are also categorised into three classes, i.e., General, OBC and SC/ST. The following information is known:

- 52.5% candidates have 'humanities' background while 130 are from 'other streams'.
- Overall amongst all educational backgrounds 50% of candidates are from 'general category'. Amongst males as well as females 'general category' candidates constitute 50% in all educational background.
- Amongst males, from 'humanities' and 'sciences' the representation of OBCs is 30%.
- From 'humanities', 90 female candidates are successful while from sciences only 70 are successful.
- Amongst female candidates, who are from 'humanities' background, 30% are OBCs. 15 female OBC candidates are from science background and 10 female OBC candidates are from 'other streams'.

(i) How many general category males are from humanities background?
   (a) 165 (b) 90
   (c) 45 (d) Data insufficient

(ii) What is the total number of female candidates who have come from 'other streams'?
   (a) 130 (b) 40
   (c) 90 (d) Data insufficient

(iii) Among the candidates from 'sciences' background, how many female candidates are from general category?
   (a) 35 (b) 40
   (c) 15 (d) Data insufficient

(iv) Among the candidates from 'other streams', the male candidates who fall in the OBC category are
   (a) 45 (b) 30
   (c) 15 (d) Data insufficient

(v) The number of SC/ST category students who are from 'sciences' background is
   (a) 84 (b) 69
   (c) 56 (d) Data insufficient

(vi) Which of the following data is sufficient to know the total number of OBC candidates from other streams?
   1. Total number of SC/ST candidates from 'other streams'
   2. Total number of male OBC candidates from 'other streams'

   (a) Only 1 is sufficient.
   (b) Only 2 is sufficient.
   (c) Both 1 and 2 independently are sufficient.
   (d) Both 1 and 2 together are sufficient.

## Answers of Exercise Set B

| S.No. | (i) | (ii) | (iii) | (iv) | (v) | (vi) |
|---|---|---|---|---|---|---|
| 1. | (d) | (d) | (c) | (c) | | |
| 2. | (d) | (b) | | | | |
| 3. | (d) | (c) | (b) | | | |
| 4. | (a) | (b) | (b) | | | |
| 5. | (c) | (a) | (c) | (a) | (c) | |
| 6. | (a) | (a) | (b) | | | |
| 7. | (b) | (a) | (d) | | | |
| 8. | (c) | (b) | (c) | | | |
| 9. | (d) | (d) | (b) | | | |
| 10. | (a) | (c) | (a) | | | |
| 11. | (c) | (b) | (d) | (a) | | |
| 12. | (c) | (c) | (a) | | | |
| 13. | (b) | (d) | (c) | | | |
| 14. | (c) | (b) | | | | |
| 15. | (d) | (c) | (d) | (c) | | |
| 16. | (d) | (d) | (b) | | | |
| 17. | (d) | (c) | (b) | | | |
| 18. | (b) | (a) | | | | |
| 19. | (b) | (b) | (b) | | | |
| 20. | (a) | (b) | (a) | (d) | (c) | (c) |

## Exercise Set C

1. A contract on construction job specifies a penalty for delay in completion of the work beyond a certain date is as follows: ₹ 200/- for the first day, ₹ 250/- for the second day, ₹ 300/- for the third day etc., the penalty for each succeeding day being ₹ 50/- more than that of the preceding day. How much penalty should the contractor pay if he delays the work by 10 days?
   (a) ₹ 4950/- (b) ₹ 4250/-
   (c) ₹ 3600/- (d) ₹ 650/-

2. Consider the following figure and answer the item that follows:

   15

   48

   A square is divided into four rectangles as shown above. The lengths of the sides of rectangles are natural numbers. The areas of two rectangles are indicated in the figure. What is the length of each side of the square?
   (a) 10
   (b) 11
   (c) 15
   (d) Cannot be determined as the given data are insufficient

3. A person has only ₹ 1/- and ₹ 2/- coins with her. If the total number of coins that she has is 50 and the amount of money with her is ₹ 75/-, then the number of ₹ 1 and ₹ 2 coins are, respectively
   (a) 15 and 35 (b) 35 and 15
   (c) 30 and 20 (d) 25 and 25

4. Three persons start walking together and their steps measure 40 cm, 42 cm and 45 cm respectively. What is the minimum distance each should walk so that each can cover the same distance in complete steps?
   (a) 25 m 20 cm (b) 50 m 40 cm
   (c) 75 m 60 cm (d) 100 m 80 cm

5. If a bus travels 160 km in 4 hours and a train travels 320 km in 5 hours at uniform speeds, then what is the ratio of distances travelled by them in one hour?
   (a) 8 : 5 (b) 5 : 8
   (c) 4 : 5 (d) 1 : 2

6. There are 100 students in a particular class. 60% students play cricket, 30% students play football and 10% students play both the games. What is the number of students who play neither cricket nor football?
   (a) 25 (b) 20
   (c) 18 (d) 15

7. A village having a population of 4000 requires 150 litres of water per head per day. It has a tank measuring 20 m by 15 m by 6 m. The water of this tank will last for
   (a) 2 days (b) 3 days
   (c) 4 days (d) 5 days

8. Mr. Kumar drives to work at an average speed of 48 km per hour. The time taken to cover the first-60% of the distance is 10 minutes more than the time taken to cover the remaining distance. How far is his office?
   (a) 30 km (b) 40 km
   (c) 45 km (d) 48 km

9. In a rare coin collection, there is one gold coin for every three non-gold coins. 10 more gold coins are added to the collection and the ratio of gold coins to non-gold coins would be 1: 2. Based on the information, the total number of coins in the collection now becomes.
   (a) 90 (b) 80
   (c) 60 (d) 50

**10.** A gardener has 1000 plants. He wants to plant them in such a way that the number of rows and the number of columns remains the same. What is the minimum number of plants that he needs more for this purpose?

(a) 14 (b) 24
(c) 32 (d) 34

**11.** A sum of ₹ 700/- has to be used to give seven cash prizes to the students of a school for their overall academic performance. If each prize is ₹ 20/- less than its preceding prize, what is the least value of the prize?

(a) ₹ 30 (b) ₹ 40
(c) ₹ 60 (d) ₹ 80

**12.** Out of 120 applications for a post, 70 are male and 80 have a driver's license. What is the ratio between the minimum to maximum number of males having driver's license?

(a) 1 to 2 (b) 2 to 3
(c) 3 to 7 (d) 5 to 7

**13.** In a garrison, there was food for 1000 soldiers for one month. After 10 days, 1000 more soldiers joined the garrison. How long would the soldiers be able to carry on with the remaining food?

(a) 25 days (b) 20 days
(c) 15 days (d) 10 days

**14.** The tank-full petrol in Arun's motorcycle lasts for 10 days. If he starts using 25% more every day, how many days will the tank-full petrol last?

(a) 5 (b) 6
(c) 7 (d) 8

**15.** A person can walk a certain distance and drive back in six hours. He can also walk both ways in 10 hours. How much time will he take to drive both ways?

(a) Two hours
(b) Two and a half hours
(c) Five and a half hours
(d) Four hours

**16.** Four friends, A, B, C and D distribute some money among themselves in such a manner that A gets one less than B, C gets 5 more than D, D gets 3 more than B. Who gets the smallest amount?

(a) A (b) B
(c) C (d) D

**17.** There are five hobby clubs in a college viz., photography, yachting, chess, electronics and gardening. The gardening group meets every second day, the electronics group meets every third day, the chess group meets every fourth day, the yachting group meets every fifth day and the photograph group meets every sixth day. How many times do all the five groups meet on the same day within 180 days?

(a) 3 (b) 5
(c) 10 (d) 18

**18.** In a class of 45 students, a boy is ranked 20. When two boys joined, his rank dropped by one. What is his new rank from the end?

(a) 25$^{th}$ (b) 26$^{th}$
(c) 27$^{th}$ (d) 28$^{th}$

**19.** A thief running at 8 km/hr. is chased by a policeman whose speed is 10 km/hr. If the thief is 100 m ahead of the policeman, then the time required for the policeman to catch the thief will be

(a) 2 min (b) 3 min
(c) 4 min (d) 6 min

**20.** A train travels at a certain average speed for a distance of 63 km and then travels a distance of 72 km at an average speed of 6 km/hr. more than its original speed. If it takes 3 hours to complete the total journey, what is the original speed of the train in km/hr.?

(a) 24 (b) 33
(c) 42 (d) 66

**21.** In a row 'A' is in the 11$^{th}$ position from the left and 'B' is in the 10$^{th}$ position from the right. If 'A' and 'B' interchange, then 'A' becomes 18$^{th}$ from the left. How many persons are there in the row other than 'A' and 'B'?

(a) 27 (b) 26
(c) 25 (d) 24

22. Location of B is north of A and location of C is east of A. The distances AB and AC are 5 km and 12 km respectively. The shortest distance (in km) between the locations B and C is
(a) 60 (b) 13
(c) 17 (d) 7

23. Two cars start towards each other, from two places A and B which are at a distance of 160 km. They start at the same time 08:10 am. If the speeds of the cars are 50 km and 30 km per hour respectively, they will meet each other at
(a) 10:10 am (b) 10:30 am
(c) 11:10 am (d) 11:20 am

24. If the 3rd day of a month is Monday, which one of the following will be the fifth day from 21st of this month?
(a) Monday (b) Tuesday
(c) Wednesday (d) Friday

25. For a charity show, the total tickets sold were 420. Half of these tickets were sold at the rate of ₹ 5 each, one-third at the rate of ₹ 3 each and the rest for ₹ 2 each. What was the total amount received?
(a) ₹ 900 (b) ₹ 1,540
(c) ₹ 1,610 (d) ₹ 2,000

26. There are 50 students admitted to a nursery class. Same students can speak only English and some can speak only Hindi. 10 students can speak both English and Hindi. If the number of students who can speak English is 21, then how many students can speak Hindi, how many can speak only Hindi and how many can speak only English 1
(a) 21, 11 and 29 respectively
(b) 28, 18 and 22 respectively
(c) 37, 27 and 13 respectively
(d) 39, 29 and 11 respectively

27. A gardener increased the area of his rectangular garden by increasing its length by 40% and decreasing its width by 20%. The area of the new garden
(a) has increased by 20%.
(b) has increased by 12%.
(c) has increased by 8%,
(d) is exactly the same as the old area?

28. A straight line segment is 36 cm long. Points are to be marked on the line from both the end points. From each end, the first point is at a distance of 1 cm from the end, the second point is at a distance of 2 cm from the first point and the third point is at a distance of 3 cm from the second point and so on. If the points on the ends are not counted and the common points are counted as one, what is the number of points?
(a) 10 (b) 12
(c) 14 (d) 16

29. If Sohan, while selling two goats the same price, makes a profit of 10% on one goat and suffers a loss of 10% on the other
(a) he makes no profit and no loss.
(b) he makes a profit of 1%.
(c) he suffers a loss of 1%.
(d) he suffers a loss of 2%.

30. Out of a total of 120 musicians in a club, 5% can play all the three instruments, guitar, violin and flute. It so happens that the number of musicians who can play any two and only two of the above instruments is 30. The number of musicians who can play the guitar alone is 40. What is the total number of those who can play violin alone or flute alone?
(a) 45 (b) 44
(c) 38 (d) 30

31. Six identical cards are placed on a table. Each card has number '1' marked on one side and number '2' marked on its other side. All the six cards are placed in such a manner that the number '1' is on the upper side. In one try, exactly four (neither more nor less) cards are turned upside down. In how many least number of tries can the cards be turned upside down such that all the six cards show number '2' on the upper side?
(a) 3
(b) 5
(c) 7
(d) This cannot be achieved

32. Five persons fire bullets at a target at an interval of 6, 7, 8, 9 and 12 seconds respectively. The

number of times they would fire the bullets together at the target in an hour is

(a) 6 (b) 7
(c) 8 (d) 9

**33.** A group of 630 children is seated in rows for a group photo session. Each row contains three less children than the row in front of it. Which one of the following number of rows is not possible?

(a) 3 (b) 4
(c) 5 (d) 6

**34.** Assume that

1. the hour and minute hands of a clock move without jerking.
2. the clock shows a time between 8 o'clock and 9 o'clock.
3. the two hands of the clock are one above the other.

After how many minutes (nearest integer) will the two hands be again lying one above the other?

(a) 60 (b) 62
(c) 65 (d) 67

**35.** A bell rings every 18 minutes. A second bell rings every 24 minutes. A third bell rings every 32 minutes. If all the three bells ring at the same time at 8 o'clock in the morning, at what other time will they all ring together?

(a) 12:40 hrs (b) 12:48 hrs
(c) 12:56 hrs (d) 13:04 hrs

**36.** Between 6 PM and 7 PM the minute hand of a clock will be ahead of the hour hand by 3 minutes at

(a) 6:15 PM (b) 6:18 PM
(c) 6:36 PM (d) 6:48 PM

**37.** The monthly incomes of Peter and Paul are in the ratio of 4 : 3. Their expenses are in the ratio of 3 : 2. If each saves ₹ 6,000 at the end of the month, their monthly incomes respectively are

(a) 24,000 and 18,000
(b) 28,000 and 21,000
(c) 32,000 and 24,000
(d) 34,000 and 26,000

**38.** Two cities A and B are 360 km apart. A car goes from A to B with a speed of 40 km/hr. and returns to A with a speed of 60 km/hr. What is the average speed of the car?

(a) 45 km/hr. (b) 48 km/hr.
(c) 50 km/hr. (d) 55 km/hr.

**39.** In a box of marbles, there are three less white marbles than the red ones and five more white marbles than the green ones. If there are a total of 10 white marbles, how many marbles are there in the box?

(a) 26 (b) 28
(c) 32 (d) 36

**40.** Candidates in a competitive examination consisted of 60% men, and 40% women 70% men and 75% women cleared the qualifying test and entered the final test. 80% men and 70% women were successful.

Which of the following statements is correct?

(a) Success rate is higher for women,
(b) Overall success rate is below 50%.
(c) More men cleared the examination than women.
(d) Both (a) and (b) above are correct.

**41.** A selection is to be made for one post of Principal and two posts of Vice-Principal. Amongst the six candidates called for the interview, only two are eligible for the post of Principal while they all are eligible for the post of Vice-Principal. The number of possible combinations of selectees is;

(a) 4 (b) 12
(c) 18 (d) None of the above

**42.** A student has to opt for 2 subjects out of 5 subjects for a course, namely, Commerce, Economics, Statistics, Mathematics I and Mathematics II. Mathematics II can be offered only if Mathematics I is also opted. The number of different combinations of two subjects which can be opted is;

(a) 5 (b) 6
(c) 7 (d) 8

**43.** A person ordered 5 pairs of black socks and some pairs of brown socks. The price of a black pair was thrice that of a brown pair. While preparing the bill, the bill clerk interchanged the number of black and brown pairs by mistake which increased the bill by 100%. What was the number of pairs of brown socks in the original order?

(a) 10 (b) 15
(c) 20 (d) 25

**44.** The number of persons who read magazine X only is thrice the number of persons who read magazine Y. The number of persons who read magazine Y only is thrice the number of persons who read magazine X, Then, which of the following conclusions can be drawn?

1. The number of persons who read both the magazines is twice the number of persons who read only magazine X.
2. The total number of persons who read either one magazine or both the magazines is twice the number of persons who read both the magazines.

Select the correct answer using the code given below:

(a) 1 only (b) 2 only
(c) Both 1 and 2 (d) Neither 1 nor

**45.** Two pipes A and B can independently fill a tank completely in 20 and 30 minutes respectively. If both the pipes are opened simultaneously, how much time will they take to fill the tank completely?

(a) 10 minutes (b) 12 minutes
(c) 15 minutes (d) 25 minutes

**46.** If ABC × DEED = ABCABC; where A, B, C, D and E are different digits, what are the values of D and E?

(a) D = 2, E = 0 (b) D = 0, E = 1
(c) D = 1, E = 0 (d) D = 1, E = 2

**47.** Twelve people form a club. By picking lots, one of them will host a dinner for all once in a month. The number of dinners a particular member has to host in one year is,

(a) One
(b) Zero
(c) Three
(d) Cannot be predicted

**48.** In a test, a candidate attempted only 8 questions and secured 50% marks in each of the questions. If he obtained a total of 40% in the test and all questions in the test carried equal marks, how many questions were there in the test?

(a) 8 (b) 10
(c) 15 (d) 16

**49.** A father is nine times as old as his son and the mother is eight times as old as the son. The sum of the father's and the mother's age is 51 years. What is the age of the son?

(a) 7 years (b) 5 years
(c) 4 years (d) 3 years

**50.** Shahid and Rohit start from the same point in opposite directions. After each 1 km, Shahid always turns left and Rohit always turns right. Which of the following statements is correct?

(a) After both have travelled 2 km, the distance between them is 4 km,
(b) They meet after each has travelled 3 km.
(c) They meet for the first time after each has travelled 4 km.
(d) They go on without ever meeting again.

**51.** In a 500 metres race, B starts 45 metres ahead of A, but A wins the race while B is still 35 metres behind. What is the ratio of the speeds of A to B assuming that both start at the same time?

(a) 25: 21 (b) 25: 20
(c) 5: 3 (d) 5:7

**52.** In a group of persons travelling in a bus, 6 persons can speak Tamil, 15 can speak Hindi and 6 can speak Gujarati. In that group none can speak any other language. If 2 persons in the group can speak two languages only and one person can speak all the three languages, then how many persons are there in the group?

(a) 21 (b) 22
(c) 23 (d) 24

**53.** In a parking area, the total number of wheels of all the cars (four-wheelers) and scooters/ motorbikes (two-wheelers) is 100 more than twice the number of parked vehicles. The number of cars parked is

(a) 35 (b) 45
(c) 50 (d) 55

**54.** A lift has the capacity of 18 adults or 30 children. How many children can board the lift with 12 adults?

(a) 6 (b) 10
(c) 12 (d) 15

**55.** A person bought a refrigerator worth ₹ 22,800/- with 12.5% interest compounded yearly. At the end of first year he paid ₹ 8,650/- and at the end of second year ₹ 9,125/-. How much will he have to pay at the end of third year to clear the debt?

(a) ₹ 9,900/- (b) ₹ 10,000/-
(c) ₹ 10,590/- (d) ₹ 11,250/-

**56.** If $x - y = 8$, then which of the following must be true?

(1) Both $x$ and $y$ must be positive for any value of $x$ and $y$.

(2) If $x$ is positive, $y$ must be negative for any value of $x$ and $y$.

(3) If $x$ is negative, $y$ must be positive for any value of $x$ and $y$. Select the correct answer using the code give below.

(a) 1 only (b) 2 only
(c) Both 1 and 2 (d) Neither 1 nor 2 nor 3

**57.** A number consists of three digits of which the middle one is zero and their sum is 4. If the number formed by interchanging the first and last digits is greater that the number itself by 198, then the difference between the first and last digits is

(a) 1 (b) 2
(c) 3 (d) 4

**58.** A solid cube of 3 cm side, painted on all its faces, is cut up into small cubes of 1 cm side. How many of the small cubes will have exactly two painted faces?

(a) 12 (b) 8
(c) 6 (d) 4

**59.** While writing all the numbers from 700 to 1000, how many numbers occur in which the digit at hundred's place is greater than the digit at ten's place and the digit at ten's place is greater than the digit at unit's place?

(a) 61 (b) 64
(c) 85 (d) 91

**60.** A bookseller sold '$a$' number of Geography textbooks at the rate of ₹ $x$ per book, '$a + 2$' number of History textbooks at the rate of ₹ $(x + 2)$/ per book and '$a - 2$' number of Mathematics textbooks at the rate of ₹ $(x - 2)$/ per book. What is the total sale in ₹ ?

(a) $3x + 3a$ (b) $3ax + 8$
(c) $9ax$ (d) $x^3a^3$

**61.** A bag contains 15 red balls and 20 black balls. Each ball is numbered either 1 or 2 or 3.20% of the red balls are numbered 1 and 40% of them are numbered 3. Similarly, among the black balls, 45% are numbered 2 and 30% are numbered 3. A boy picks a ball at random. He wins if the ball is red and numbered 3 or if it is black and numbered 1 or 2.

What are the chances of his winning?

(a) $\frac{1}{2}$ (b) $\frac{4}{7}$
(c) $\frac{2}{5}$ (d) $\frac{12}{13}$

**62.** Two persons, A and B are running on a circular track. At the start, B is ahead of A and their positions make an angle of 30° at the centre of the circle. When A reaches the point diametrically opposite to his starting point, he meets B. What is the ratio of speeds of A and B, if they are running with uniform speeds?

(a) 6 : 5 (b) 4 : 3
(c) 6 : 1 (d) 4 : 2

**63.** A student has to get 40% marks to pass in an examination. Suppose he gets 30 marks and fails by 30 marks, then what are the maximum marks in the examination?

(a) 100 (b) 120
(c) 150 (d) 300

64. 19 boys turn out for playing hockey. Of these, 11 are wearing hockey shirts and 14 are wearing hockey shirts and 14 are wearing hockey pants. There are no boys without shirts and/or pants. What is the number of boys wearing full uniform?

(a) 3 (b) 5
(c) 6 (d) 8

65. A shopkeeper sells an article at ₹ 40 and gets X% profit. However, when he sells it at ₹ 20/-, he faces same percentage of loss. What is the original cost of the article?

(a) ₹ 10 (b) ₹ 20
(c) ₹ 30 (d) ₹ 40

66. Twelve equal squares are placed to fit in a rectangle of diagonal 5 cm. There are three rows containing four squares each. No gaps are left between adjacent squares. What is the area of each square?

(a) 5/7 sq cm (b) 7/5 sq cm
(c) 1 sq cm (d) 7/5 sq cm

67. A train 200 metres long is moving at the rate of 40 kmph. In how many seconds will it cross a man standing near the railway line?

(a) 12 (b) 15
(c) 16 (d) 18

68. An 8-digit number 4252746B leaves remainder 0 when divided by 3. How many values of B are possible?

(a) 2 (b) 3
(c) 4 (d) 6

69. A wall clock moves 10 minutes fast in every 24 hours. The clock was set right to show the correct time at 8:00 a.m. on Monday. When the clock shows the time 6:00 p.m. on Wednesday, what is the correct time ?

(a) 5:36 p.m. (b) 5:30 p.m.
(c) 5:24 p.m. (d) 5:18 p.m.

70. If the numerator and denominator of a proper fraction are increased by the same positive quantity which is greater than zero, the resulting fraction is

(a) always less than the original fraction
(b) always greater than the original fraction
(c) always equal to the original fraction
(d) such that nothing can be claimed definitely

71. In a group of 15 people; 7 can read French, 8 can read English while 3 of them can read neither of these two languages. The number of people who can read exactly one language is

(a) 10 (b) 9
(c) 5 (d) 4

72. A printer numbers the pages of a book starting with 1 and uses 3089 digits in all. How many pages does the book have?

(a) 1040 (b) 1048
(c) 1049 (d) 1050

73. A family has two children along with their parents. The average of the weights of the children and their mother is 50 kg. The average of the weights of the children and their father is 52 kg. If the weight of the father is 60 kg, then what is the weight of the mother?

(a) 48 kg (b) 50 kg
(c) 52 kg (d) 54 kg

74. Suppose you have sufficient amount of rupee currency in three denominations: ₹ 1, ₹ 10 and ₹ 50. In how many different ways can you pay a bill of ₹ 107?

(a) 16 (b) 17
(c) 18 (d) 19

75. 'A' started from his house and walked 20 m towards East, where his friend B' joined him. They together walked 10 m in the same direction. Then 'A' turned left while 'B' turned right and travelled 2 m and 8 m respectively. Again 'B' turned left to travel 4 m followed by 5 m to his right to reach his office. 'A' turned right and travelled 12 m to reach his office. What is the shortest distance between the two offices?

(a) 15 m (b) 17 m
(c) 19 m (d) 20 m

76. Consider two statements $S_1$ and $S_2$ followed by a question: $S_1$: p and q both are prime numbers. $S_2$: p + q is an odd integer. Question: Is pq an odd integer?

Which one of the following is correct?

(a) $S_1$ alone is sufficient to answer the question
(b) $S_2$ alone is sufficient to answer the question
(c) Both $S_1$ and $S_2$ taken together are not sufficient to answer the question
(d) Both $S_1$ and $S_2$ are necessary to answer the question

77. Number 136 is added to 5B7 and the sum obtained is 7A3, where A and B are integers. It is given that 7A3 is exactly divisible by 3. The only possible value of B is

(a) 2 (b) 5
(c) 7 (d) 8

78. The number of times the digit 5 will appear while writing the integersfrom 1 to 1000 is

(a) 269 (b) 271
(c) 300 (d) 302

79. A solid cube is painted yellow, blue and black such that opposite faces are of same colour. The cube is then cut into 36 cubes of two different sizes such that 32 cubes are small and the other four cubes are big. None of the faces of the bigger cubes is painted blue. How many cubes have only one face painted?

(a) 4 (b) 6
(c) 8 (d) 10

80. A and B are two heavy steel blocks. If B is placed on the top of A, the weight increases by 60%. How much weight will reduce with respect to the total weight of A and B, if B is removed from the top of A?

(a) 60% (b) 45.5%
(c) 40% (d) 37.5%

81. In a school every student is assigned a unique identification number. A student is a football player if and only if the identification number is divisible by 4, whereas a student is a cricketer if and only if the identification number is divisible by 6. If every number from 1 to 100 is assigned to a student, then how many of them play cricket as well as football?

(a) 4 (b) 8
(c) 10 (d) 12

82. When a runner was crossing the 12 km mark, she was informed that she had completed only 80% of the race. How many kilometres was the runner supposed to run in this event?

(a) 14 (b) 15
(c) 16 (d) 16.5

83. Raju has ₹ 9000/- with him and he wants to buy a mobile handset; but he finds that he has only 75% of the amount required to buy the handset. Therefore, he borrows ₹ 2000 from a friend. Then,

(a) Raju still does not have enough amount to buy the handset.
(b) Raju has exactly the same amount as required to buy the handset.
(c) Raju has enough amount to buy the handset and he will have 500 with him after buying the handset.
(d) Raju has enough amount to buy the handset and he will have 1000 with him after buying the handset.

84. In 2002, Meenu's age was one-third of the age of Meera, whereas in 2010, Meenu's age was half the age of Meera. What is Meenu's year of birth?

(a) 1992 (b) 1994
(c) 1996 (d) 1998

85. Rakesh and Rajesh together bought 10 balls and 10 rackets. Rakesh spent ₹ 1300 and Rajesh spent ₹ 1500. If each racket costs three times a ball does, then what is the price of a racket?

(a) ₹ 70 (b) ₹ 90
(c) ₹ 210 (d) ₹ 240

86. In a conference, out of a total 100 participants, 70 are Indians. If 60 of the total participants are vegetarian, then which of the following statements is/are correct?

1. At least 30 Indian participants are vegetarian.
2. At least 10 Indian participants are non-vegetarian. Select the correct answer using the codes given below:

(a) 1 only (b) 2 only
(c) Both 1 and 2 (d) Neither 1 nor 2

**87.** P, Q and R are three towns. The distance between P and Q is 60 km, whereas the distance between P and R is 80 km. Q is in the West of P and R is in the South of P. What is the distance between Q and R?

(a) 140 km (b) 130 km
(c) 10 km (d) 100 km

**88.** All members of a club went to Mumbai and stayed in a hotel. On the first day, 80% went for shopping and 50% went for sightseeing, whereas 10% took rest in the hotel. Which of the following conclusion(s) can be drawn from the above data?

1. 40% members went for shopping as well as sightseeing.
2. 20% members went for only shopping.

Select the correct answer using the code given below:

(a) 1 only (b) 2 only
(c) Both 1 and 2 (d) Neither 1 nor 2

**89.** In a school, 60% students play cricket. A student who does not play cricket, plays football. Every football player has got a two-wheeler. Which of the following conclusions cannot be drawn from the above data?

1. 60% of the students do not have two-wheelers.
2. No cricketer has a two-wheeler.
3. Cricket players do not play football.

Select the correct answer using the code given below:

(a) 1 and 2 only (b) 2 and 3 only
(c) 1 and 3 only (d) 1, 2 and 3

**90.** In an examination, A has scored 20 marks more than B. If B has scored 5% less marks than A, how much has B scored?

(a) 360 (b) 380
(c) 400 (d) 420

**91.** Seeta and Geeta go for a swim after a gap of every 2 days and every3 days respectively. If on 1st January both of them went for a swim together, when will they go together next?

(a) 7th January (b) 8th January
(c) 12th January (d) 13th January

**92.** X, Y and Z are three contestants in a race of 1000 m. Assume that all run with different uniform speeds. X gives Y a start of 40 m and X gives Z a start of 64 m. If Y and Z were to compete in a race of 1000 m, how many metres start will Y give to Z?

(a) 20 (b) 25
(c) 30 (d) 35

**93.** Ena was born 4 years after her parents' marriage. Her mother is three years younger than her father and 24 years older than Ena, who is 13 years old. At what age did Ena's father get married?

(a) 22 years (b) 23 years
(c) 24 years (d) 25 years

**94.** Rakesh had money to buy 8 mobile handsets of a specific company. But the retailer offered very good discount on that particular handset. Rakesh could buy 10 mobile handsets with the amount he had. What was the discount the retailer offered?

(a) 15% (b) 20%
(c) 25% (d) 30%

**95.** The average marks of 100 students are given to be 40. It was found later that marks of one student were 53 which were misread as 83. The corrected mean marks are

(a) 39 (b) 39.7
(c) 40 (d) 40.3

**96.** Let $XYZ$ be a three-digit number, where $(X + Y + Z)$ is not a multiple of 3. Then $(XYZ + YZX + ZXY)$ is not divisible by

(a) 3 (b) 9
(c) 37 (d) $(X + Y + Z)$

**97.** Let $p$, $q$, $r$ and $s$ be natural numbers such that $p - 2016 = q + 2017 = r - 2018 = s + 2019$ which one of the following is the largest natural number?

(a) $p$ (b) $q$
(c) $r$ (d) $s$

**98.** How many five-digit prime numbers can be obtained by using all the digits 1, 2, 3, 4 and 5 without repetition of digits?

(a) Zero (b) One
(c) Nine (d) Ten

**99.** In the sum ⊗ +1 ⊗ + 5 ⊗ + ⊗ ⊗ + ⊗ 1 =1 ⊗ ⊗ for which digit does the symbol ⊗ stand?

(a) 2 (b) 3
(c) 4 (d) 5

**100.** If you have two straight sticks of length 7.5 feet and 3.25 feet, what is the minimum length can you measure?

(a 0.05 foot (b) 0.25 foot
(c) 1 foot (d) 3.25 feet

**101.** A simple mathematical operation in each number of the sequence 14, 18,20, 24, 30, 32, results in a sequence with respect to prime numbers.

Which one of the following is the next number in the sequence?

(a) 34 (b) 36
(c) 38 (d) 40

**102.** One page is torn from a booklet whose pages are numbered in the usual manner starting from the first page as 1. The sum of the numbers on the remaining pages is 195. The torn page contains which of the following numbers?

(a) 5, 6 (b) 7, 8
(c) 9, 10 (d) 11, 12

**103.** Let *A3BC* and *DE2F* be four-digit numbers where each letter represents a different digit greater than 3. If the sum of the numbers is 15902, then what is the difference between the values of *A* and *D*?

(a) 1 (b) 2
(c) 3 (d) 4

**104.** Two Statements $S_1$ and $S_2$ are given below followed by a Question:

$S_1$: $n$ is a prime number.

$S_2$: $n$ leaves a remainder of 1 when divided by 4.

Question: If n is a unique natural number between 10 and 20, thenwhat is n?

Which one of the following is correct in respect of the above Statements and the Question?

(a) $S_1$ alone is sufficient to answer the Question.

(b) $S_2$ alone is sufficient to answer the Question.

(c) $S_1$ and $S_2$ together are sufficient to answer the Question, but neither $S_1$ alone nor $S_2$ alone is sufficient to answer the Question.

(d) $S_1$ and $S_2$ together are not sufficient to answer the Question.

**105.** Two Statements $S_1$ and $S_2$ are given below with regard to two numbersfollowed by a Question:

$S_1$: Their product is 21. $S_2$: Their sum is 10.

Question: What are the two numbers?

Which one of the following is correct in respect of the above Statements and the Question?

(a) $S_1$ alone is sufficient to answer the Question.

(b) $S_2$ alone is sufficient to answer the Question.

(c) $S_1$ and $S_2$ together are sufficient to answer the Question, but neither $S_1$ alone nor $S_2$ alone is sufficient to answer the Question.

(d) $S_1$ and $S_2$ together are not sufficient to answer the Question.

**106.** A man walks down the backside of his house straight 25 meters, then turns to the right and walks 50 meters again; then he turns towards left and again walks 25 meters. If his house faces to the East, what is his direction from the starting point?

(a) South-East (b) South-West
(c) North-East (d) North-West

**107.** Two Statements are given followed by two Conclusions:

Statements:

All numbers are divisible by 2.

All numbers are divisible by 3.

Conclusion-I

All numbers are divisible by 6.

Conclusion-II

All numbers are divisible by 4.

Which of the above Conclusions logically follows/follow from the two given Statements?

(a) Only Conclusion-I
(b) Only Conclusion-II
(c) Neither Conclusion-I nor Conclusion-II
(d) Both Conclusions-I and Conclusion-II

**108.** How many integers are there between 1 and 100 which have 4 as a digit but are not divisible by 4?

(a) 5 (b) 11
(c) 12 (d) 13

**109.** Let *x, y* be the volumes; *m, n* be the masses of two metallic cubes *P* and *Q* respectively. Each side of *Q* is two times that of *P* and mass of *Q* is two times that of *P*. Let $u = m/x$ and $v = n/y$. which one or the following is correct?

(a) $u = 4v$ (b) $u = 2v$
(c) $v = u$ (d) $v = 4u$

**110.** A person bought a car and sold it for ₹ 3,00,000. If he incurred a loss of 20%, then how much did he spend to buy the car?

(a) ₹ 3,60,000 (b) ₹ 3,65,000
(c) ₹ 3,70,000 (d) ₹ 3,75,000

**111.** A shop owner offers the following discount options on an article to acustomer:

1. Successive discounts or 10% and 20%, and then pay a service tax of 10%
2. Successive discounts of 20% and 10%, and then pay a service tax of 10%
3. Pay a service tax or 10% first, then successive discounts of 20% and 10%

Which one of the following is correct?

(a) 1 only is the best option for the customer.
(b) 2 only is the best option for the customer.
(c) 3 only is the best option for the customer.
(d) All the options are equally good for the customer.

**112.** What is the greatest length *x* such that 3½ m and 8¾ m are integral multiples of *x*?

(a) $1\frac{1}{2}$m b) $1\frac{1}{3}$ m
(c) $1\frac{1}{4}$m (d) $1\frac{3}{4}$ m

**113.** The recurring decimal representation 1.272727... is equivalent to

(a) 13/11 (b) 14/11
(c) 127/99 (d) 137/99

**114.** What is the least four-digit number when divided by 3, 4, 5 and 6 leaves a remainder 2 in each case?

(a) 1012 (b) 1022
(c) 1122 (d) 1222

**115.** In adult population of a city, 40% men and 30% women are married. What is the percentage of married adult population if no man marries more than one woman and no woman marries more than one man; and there are no widows and widowers?

(a) $33\frac{1}{7}$% (b) 34%
(c) $34\frac{2}{7}$% (d) 35%

**116.** What is the remainder when $51 \times 27 \times 35 \times 62 \times 75$ is divided by 100?

(a) 50 (b) 25
(c) 5 (d) 1

**117.** A sum of ₹ 2,500 is distributed among *X, Y* and *Z* in the ratio $\frac{1}{2} : \frac{3}{4} : \frac{5}{6}$.
What is the difference between the maximum share and the minimum share?

(a) ₹ 300 (b) ₹ 350
(c) ₹ 400 (d) ₹ 450

**118.** For what value of *n*, the sum of digits in the number $(10n + 1)$ is 2?

(a) For $n = 0$ only
(b) For any whole number *n*
(c) For any positive integer *n* only
(d) For any read number *n*

**119.** In a class, there are three groups $A$, $B$ and $C$. If one student from group $A$ and two students from group $B$ are shifted to group $C$, then what happens to the average weight of the students of the class?

(a) It increases.

(b) It decreases.

(c) It remains the same.

(d) No conclusion can be drawn due to insufficient data.

**120.** How many different sums can be formed with the denominations ₹ 50, ₹100, ₹200, ₹500 and ₹ 2,000 taking at least three denominations at a time?

(a) 16 (b) 15

(c) 14 (d) 10

**121.** How many different 5-letter words (with or without meaning) can be constructed using all the letters of the word 'DELHI' so that each word has to start with D and end with I?

(a) 24 (b) 18

(c) 12 (d) 6

**122.** A bottle contains 20 litres of liquid $A$. 4 litres of liquid $A$ is taken out of it d replaced by same quantity of liquid $B$. Again 4 litre of the mixture is taken out and replaced by same quantity of liquid $B$. What is the ratio of quantity of liquid $A$ to that of liquid $B$ in the final mixture?

(a) 4 : 1 (b) 5 : 1

(c) 16 : 9 (d) 17 : 8

**123.** The average score of a batsman after his 50th innings was 46.4. After 60th innings, his average score increases by 2.6. What was his average score in the last ten innings?

(a) 122 (b) 91

(c) 62 (d) 49

**124.** As a result of 25% hike in the price of rice per kg, a person is able to purchase 6 kg less rice for ₹ 1,200. What was the original price of rice per kg?

(a) ₹ 30 (b) ₹ 40

(c) ₹ 50 (d) ₹ 60

**125.** A person $X$ can complete 20% of work in 8 days and another person $Y$ can complete 25% of the same work in 6 days. If they work together, in how many days will 40% of the work be completed?

(a) 6 (b) 8

(c) 10 (d) 12

**126.** A car travels from a place $X$ to place $Y$ at an average speed of $V$ km/hr from $Y$ to $X$ at an average speed of $2v$ km/hr, again from $X$ to $Y$ at an average speed of $3v$ km/hr and again from $Y$ to $X$ at an average speed of $4v$ km/hr. Then the average speed of the car for the entire journey

(a) is less than $v$ km/hr

(b) lies between $v$ and $2v$ km/hr

(c) lies between $2v$ and $3v$ km/hr

(d) lies between $3v$ and $4v$ km/hr

**127.** A man takes half time in rowing a certain distance downstream than upstream. What is the ratio or the speed in still water to the speed of current?

(a) 1 : 2 (b) 2 : 1

(c) 1 : 3 (d) 3 : 1

**128.** How many pairs of natural numbers are there such that the difference of whose squares is 63?

(a) 3 (b) 4

(c) 5 (d) 2

**129.** Which one of the following will have minimum change in its value if 5 is added to both numerator and the denominator of the fractions 2/3, 3/4, 4/5 and 5/6?

(a) 2/3 (b) 3/4

(c) 4/5 (d) 5/6

**130.** A digit $> 3$ is divisible by 3 but not divisible by 6. Which one of the following is divisible by 4?

(a) $2n$ (b) $3n$

(c) $2n + 4$ (d) $3n + 1$

**131.** If 1 litre of water weighs 1 kg, then how many cubic millimeters of water will weigh 0.1 gm?

(a) 1 (b) 10

(c) 100 (d) 1000

132. A vessel full of water weighs 40 kg. If it is one-third filled, its weight becomes 20 kg. What is the weight of the empty vessel?
(a) 10 kg (b) 15 kg
(c) 20 kg (d) 25 kg

133. A frog tries to come out of a dried well 4.5 m deep with slippery walls. Every time the frog jumps 30 cm, slides down 15 cm. What is the number of jumps required for the frog to come out of the well?
(a) 28 (b) 29
(c) 30 (d) 31

134. In a garrison, there was provision of food for 42 days. After 10 days, 300 more soldiers joined the garrison,as result of which the food lasted only 24 more days. The number of soldiers originally in the garrison were;
(a) 600 (b) 700
(c) 900 (d) 800

135. A Shopkeeper increases the price of his product by 40% and later on he reduces the price by 40%. The shopkeeper is
(a) gains 20% (b) loses 20%
(c) gains 16% (d) loses 16%

136. Two stations Patna and Kolkata are 600 km apart. One train starts at 9 AM from Patna and travels at a speed of 60 km/h. Another train starts from Kolkata at 11AM to Patna and it travels a speed of 100 km/h. They meet each other and then they start returning to their respective stations. What will be the distance between the two trains at 4:30 PM?
(a) 300 km (b) 240 km
(c) 400 km (d) 480 km

137. If number $x$ is 50% of number $y$ and the sum of their squares is 500, then the number $x$ is;
(a) 8 (b) 12
(c) 10 (d) 20

138. If $\frac{x}{5} = \frac{y}{9}$, then what is $(x + 5) : (y + 9)$ ?
(a) 9 : 5 (b) 5 : 9
(c) 4 : 9 (d) 5 : 4

139. Aman undertakes to dig a trench in 150 days. He employs 200 men. He finds that only a quarter of work is done in 50 days. How many additional men must be employed so that the work may be finished on time?
(a) 100 men (b) 300 men
(c) 150 men (d) 175 men

140. Nikhil bought a mobile phone and sold it to Prateek at 10% profit. Then Prateek wanted to sell it back to Nikhil at 10% loss. What will be Nikhil's position if he were to agree?
(a) Neither loss nor gain
(b) Loss 1%
(c) Gain 1%
(d) Gain 0.5%

141. A train 300 m long is running at a speed of 90 km/h in what time will it pass a tunnel of 150 m long?
(a) 18 sec (b) 10 sec
(c) 15 sec (d) 16 sec

142. If the length and breadth of a rectangular piece of paper is decreased by cutting it, the area decreases by 19 %. If the length was decreased by 10%, by what percentage was its breadth decreased?
(a) 10 (b) 9
(c) 5 (d) 8

143. There is a milk sample with 50% water in it, if 1/3rd of this milk is added to equal amount of pure milk,then water in the new mixture will fall down to
(a) 25% (b) 30%
(c) 35% (d) 40%

144. A cistern can be filled by a tap in 6 hrs and emptied by an outlet pipe in 8 hrs. How long will it take to fill if both the tap and the pipe are opened simultaneously?
(a) 18 hrs (b) 20 hrs
(c) 24 hrs (d) Never

145. Kabir sells his property worth ₹ 1 crore to Jain at a loss of 10%. Later Jain sells it back to Kabir at 10% profit. What will be the result after the two transactions?

(a) Kabir neither loses nor gains
(b) Kabir loses ₹ 9 lakhs
(c) Kabir loses ₹ 1 lakh
(d) Jain gains ₹ 11 lakhs

**146.** Between 6 PM and 7 PM the minute hand of a clock will overlap with of the hour hand or be nearest to it at what time?

(a) 6:15 PM (b) 6:30 PM
(c) 6:33 PM (d) 6:36 PM

**147.** A ladder is resting against the wall in an inclined position. The base of the ladder is 3 metres from the wall. The ladder slips and falls on the ground with the upper end now touching the base of the wall. The other end is now 2 metres further away from the position it was, when it was standing at an inclined position. At white height against the wall was the ladder initially resting?

(a) 4 metre
(b) 3 metre
(c) 5 metre
(d) data not sufficient

**148.** A clock shows a time of 630pm. After one hour and 30 minutes, what will be the angle between the minute and hour hands of the clock?

(a) 30 degrees (b) 60 degrees
(c) 90 degrees (d) 120 degrees

**149.** The angle between the minute and hour hand of the clock is 15 degrees at a given time. What will be the angle between them after one hour?

(a) 15 degrees
(b) will always be more than 15 degrees
(c) will always be less than 15 degrees
(d) Will depend on the initial time in the clock

**150.** A person travels east for a distance of 5 kilometres. He turns right and travels 3 kilometres. After which he travels in western direction for another 2 kilometres. If the final destination was to be connected from the initial point by a straight line then what will be the angle of the line from the eastern direction?

(a) 45 degree south of east
(b) 30 degree south of east
(c) 45 degree north of east
(d) 30 degree north of east

## Answers of Exercise Set C

| | | | | | | | | | |
|---|---|---|---|---|---|---|---|---|---|
| 1. (b) | 16. (a) | 31. (a) | 46. (c) | 61. (b) | 76. (b) | 91. (a) | 106. (d) | 121. (d) | 136. (c) |
| 2. (b) | 17. (a) | 32. (b) | 47. (d) | 62. (a) | 77. (d) | 92. (b) | 107. (a) | 122. (c) | 137. (c) |
| 3. (d) | 18. (c) | 33. (d) | 48. (b) | 63. (c) | 78. (c) | 93. (b) | 108. (c) | 123. (c) | 138. (b) |
| 4. (a) | 19. (b) | 34. (c) | 49. (d) | 64. (c) | 79. (c) | 94. (b) | 109. (a) | 124. (b) | 139. (a) |
| 5. (b) | 20. (c) | 35. (b) | 50. (b) | 65. (c) | 80. (d) | 95. (b) | 110. (d) | 125. (a) | 140. (c) |
| 6. (b) | 21. (c) | 36. (c) | 51. (a) | 66. (c) | 81. (b) | 96. (b) | 111. (d) | 126. (b) | 141. (a) |
| 7. (b) | 22. (b) | 37. (a) | 52. (c) | 67. (d) | 82. (b) | 97. (c) | 112. (d) | 127. (d) | 142. (a) |
| 8. (b) | 23. (a) | 38. (b) | 53. (c) | 68. (c) | 83. (a) | 98. (a) | 113. (b) | 128. (d) | 143. (a) |
| 9. (a) | 24. (c) | 39. (b) | 54. (b) | 69. (a) | 84. (b) | 99. (b) | 114. (b) | 129. (d) | 144. (c) |
| 10. (b) | 25. (c) | 40. (c) | 55. (d) | 70. (b) | 85. (c) | 100. (b) | 115. (c) | 130. (d) | 145. (b) |
| 11. (b) | 26. (d) | 41. (b) | 56. (d) | 71. (b) | 86. (c) | 101. (c) | 116. (a) | 131. (c) | 146. (c) |
| 12. (c) | 27. (b) | 42. (c) | 57. (b) | 72. (c) | 87. (d) | 102. (b) | 117. (c) | 132. (a) | 147. (a) |
| 13. (d) | 28. (b) | 43. (d) | 58. (a) | 73. (d) | 88. (d) | 103. (c) | 118. (b) | 133. (b) | 148. (d) |
| 14. (d) | 29. (c) | 44. (d) | 59. (c) | 74. (c) | 89. (d) | 104. (d) | 119. (c) | 134. (c) | 149. (d) |
| 15. (a) | 30. (b) | 45. (b) | 60. (b) | 75. (b) | 90. (c) | 105. (c) | 120. (a) | 135. (d) | 150. (a) |

## HINTS AND SOLUTIONS TO SELECTED PROBLEMS

1. Penalty on first day = ₹ 200

   Subsequent increment = ₹ 50

   Total penalty for 10 days

   $= 200 \times 10 + 50\,(1 + 2 + \text{---}\; 9)$

   $=$ ₹ 4250

   So the correct answer is (b).

2. Try with integers for finding the sides out of the given area.

   15 = 3 × 5     3 × 5

   48 = 6 × 8     12 × 4

   Since the sides of the square are equal, so, we find that 3 + 8 = 6 + 5 = 11 = side of the square. So correct answer – (b).

3. Each option has no. of options as 50.

   So, only to check if the amount is ₹75.

   $25 \times 1 + 25 \times 2 = 75$. So (d) is the correct answer.

4. (a) is the correct answer because the easiest method is to divide the option by 40, 42 and 45. The lowest option, divisible by all three, will be the minimum distance.

5. $\frac{160}{4} = 40$

   $\frac{320}{5} = 64 \qquad \frac{40}{64} = 5:8.$

6. Only cricket = 60 – 10 = 50.

   Only football = 30 – 10 = 20.

   Neither = 100 – (50 + 10 + 20) = 20. Hence answer is (b).

7. Number of days $= \frac{\text{volume of tank}}{\text{quantity of water required}}$

   $= \frac{20 \times 15 \times 6}{4000 \times 150} \times 10^3 = 3.$

   So the correct answer is (b).

8. Let the distance to the office be $x$ km.

   using, time $= \frac{\text{speed}}{\text{distance}}$

   $\frac{1}{48} \times \frac{3x}{5} \times \frac{1}{48} \times \frac{2x}{5} = \frac{1}{6} \quad (\because 10 \text{ min} = \frac{10}{60})$

   $\Rightarrow \frac{x}{5} = \frac{48}{6} \qquad \Rightarrow x = 40 \text{ km}$

9. $\frac{\text{Gold}}{\text{Non-Gold}} = \frac{1}{3} = \frac{G}{N}$, at the start ...(i)

   After adding 10 gold coins,

   $\frac{G+10}{N} = \frac{1}{2}$ ...(ii)

   From (i) and (ii)

   $\frac{G+10}{3G} = \frac{1}{2}$ & G = 20; so N = 60

   Total no. of coins = 20 + 60 + 10 = 90. Hence, answer is (a).

10. Since, the number of rows = number of columns, so, number of plants must be perfect square.

    1024 is a perfect square nearest to 1000

    ⇒ 24 more plants are to be added. Hence, answer is (b).

11. Let the least value of prize = $x$, then

    as per question,

    $7x + 20\,(1 + 2 + 3 + 4 + 5 + 6) = 700$

    $7x + 420 = 700$

    $\Rightarrow x = 40$. Hence, answer is (b).

12. Number of females = 120 – 70 = 50

    Minimum number of males having driver's licence = 80 – 50 = 30

    Maximum number of males having driver's licence = 70

    Reqd. ratio $= \frac{30}{70} = \frac{3}{7}$.

    Hence, answer is (c).

13. Let us assume the food will last for $x$ days, then

    $1000 \times (30 - 10) = (1000 + 1000) \times x$

    $\Rightarrow x = 10$ days. Hence, answer is (d).

**14.** No. of days petrol will last $= \frac{10}{1.25} = 8$. Hence, answer is (d).

**15.** He walks 2 ways in 10 hrs.

$\Rightarrow$ He walks one way in 5 hrs.

Drive 1 way + walk 1 way = 6 hr.

$\Rightarrow$ drive 1 way = 6 – 5 = 1 hr.

$\Rightarrow$ drive 2 ways = 2 × 1 = 2 hrs.

Hence, answer is (a).

**16.** Assume B gets ₹ $x$, then

A gets $x - 1$

D gets $x + 3$

C gets $x + 8$

$\Rightarrow$ A gets the smallest amount.

Hence, answer is (a).

**17.** The LCM of 2,3,4,5 and 6 is 60. Hence in 180 days they would meet 3 times. Hence answer is (a)

**18.** His new rank is 21 from the start

New rank from the end will be (47 – 21) + 1 = 27th.

Hence, answer is (c).

**19.** Using time $= \frac{\text{distance}}{\text{relative speed}}$

$$= \frac{100}{\frac{100-8}{60} \times 1000}$$

$$= \frac{100 \times 60}{2 \times 1000}$$

= 3 minutes.

Hence, answer is (b).

**20.** Let the original speed be $x$ km/h, then

$$\frac{63}{x} + \frac{72}{x+6} = 3$$

On solving, $x = 42$. Hence, answer is (c).

**21.** Since A becomes 18th from the left when he interchanges his position with B, and we also know that B is in the tenth position from the right – it means that there are 17 people to B's left and 9 people to B's right initially- a total of 26 people. However, one of these 26 people would be A himself. Hence, there are 25 people apart from A and B in the row. Option (c) is correct.

**22.**

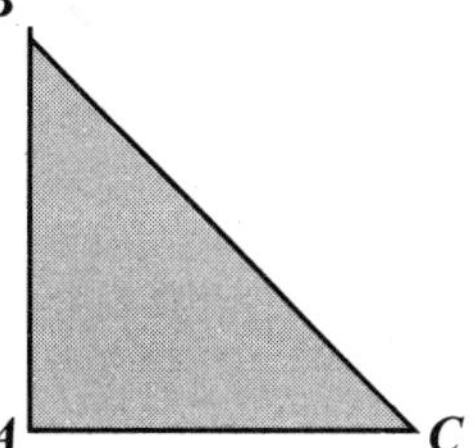


B is north of A and C is east of A

Shortest distance $CB = \sqrt{5^2 + 12^2} = 13$

**23.** Time $= \frac{\text{distance}}{\text{relative speed}} = \frac{160}{50+30} = 2$ hours.

They will meet at 10.10 A.M.

**24.** 3rd day is Monday so, 3rd +21 = 24th day will be Monday.

So, 21+5th = 26th day will be

= 24+2 = Monday + 2 = Wednesday

**25.** Total amount received

$$\frac{420}{2} \times 5 + \frac{420}{3} \times 3 + \left(1 - \frac{1}{2} - \frac{1}{3}\right) \times 420 \times 2$$

= 1610

**26.** Only English = English – both (Eng +Hin)

= 21+10=11

Only Hindi = Total – Eng = 50 – 21 = 29

Hindi = Only Hindi + both (Eng + Hin)

= 29+10 = 39

**27.** Let the initial area = 100

100... +40% .... ....140.... ....(–)20% ..........112

Of 100 = +40 of 140 = –28

So, net 112 – 100 = +12% => 12% increase in area.

**28.**

| | 8 | | 28 | |
|---|---|---|---|---|
| 0 1 3 6 | | 10 15 21 26 | | 30 33 35 36 |

Make the scale from 0 to 36, then

Start numbering from both end by increasing as per given problem . From left the point after

15 will come to 15+6 = at 21 and from right end the point after 21 will come to 21 – 6 = 15. So at 15 and at 21, there will be 2 common points. Next point from left will be at 21 + 7 = at 28 and from right will be at 15 – 7 = at 8. Similarly the next points will be at 28 + 8 =36 and 8 – 8 at 0, both of these are end points and not to be counted.

Hence total number of points = 6+6 =12

**29.** 10% profit $\Rightarrow$ SP = 1.1 CP and 10% loss $\Rightarrow$ SP = 0.9 CP

Net loss or profit = $(1.1 \times .9 - 1) \times 100 = -1$

$\Rightarrow$ 1% loss.

**30.** Only flute or only violin = total – (only guitar + any two + all three ) = 120 – (40 + 30 + 6) = 44

**31.** After the first iteration there will be four 2's and two 1's. Next turn around three 2's and one 1 to get two 2's and four 1's. Next turn around the four 1's to get all six 2's. Hence, this can be achieved in three iterations. Option (a) is correct.

**32.** LCM of 6,7,8 9 and 12 = 504 seconds. Hence all 5 persons will fire together after every 504 seconds. In one hour (=3600 seconds), they fire together $\frac{3600}{4} = 7$ times

**33.** Assuming no. of children in first row = $x$, then in the subsequent rows no. of children will be $x - 3, x - 6, x - 9, x - 12, x - 15$ and so on.

Now check each option one by one.

(a) no. of rows = 3, so, $x + x - 3 + x - 6 = 630$

$\Rightarrow x = \frac{639}{9}$ is divisible so $x$ is possible.

(b) no. of rows = 4, so, $x + x - 3 + x - 6 + x - 9 = 630 \Rightarrow x = \frac{648}{4}$ is divisible, so $x$ is possible

(c ) no. of rows = 5, so, $x + x - 3 + x - 6 + x - 9 + x - 12 = 630 \Rightarrow x = \frac{660}{5}$ is divisible so $x$ is possible

(d) no. of rows = 6, so $x + x - 3 + x - 6 + x - 9 + x - 12 + - 15 = 630 \Rightarrow x = \frac{675}{6}$ is not divisible, so $x$ is not possible, Hence no. of rows = 6 is not possible.

In other way , after checking first 3 options we can conclude the answer is (d)

**34.** The hour and minute hands over lap at nearly 8:44 and then at nearly 9:49. Hence after 65 minutes. By the time the minute hand completes one revolution of 60 minutes hour hand moves ahead (by 1 hour). Hence to again overlap the minute hand has to move further ahead by 5 minutes

**35.** LCM of 18, 24, 32 = 288 minutes = $\frac{288}{60} = 4$ hours 48 minutes

Hence , the bells will ring together again at 8 + 4h 48 min. = 12 hr 48 min.

**36.** 3 minutes = $3 \times 6^\circ = 18^\circ = A$

Required time = $\frac{2}{11}(H \times 30 + A)$ minutes past H

here, $A = 18^\circ$, $H = 6$

$= \frac{2}{11}(6 \times 30 + 18)$ minutes past 6

= 36 minutes past 6 = 6.36 PM

**37.** Let the incomes of Peter & Paul be $4x$, $3x$.

Expenses of Peter & Paul be $3y$, $2y$

$\therefore 4x = 3y + 6000 \times 2$

$\underline{3x = 2y + 600 \times 3}$

$8x = 6y + 1200$

$\underline{9x = 6y + 18000}$

$x = 6000$

**38.** Average speed = $\frac{2V_1V_2}{V_1 + V_2} = \frac{2 \times 60 \times 40}{60 + 40}$

= 48 km/h

**39.** Number of White Marbles = 10, Number of Red Marbles= 13 and Number of green Marbles = 5. Total number of marbles = 10 + 13 + 5 = 28. Option (b) is correct.

**40.** Let total candidates = 100

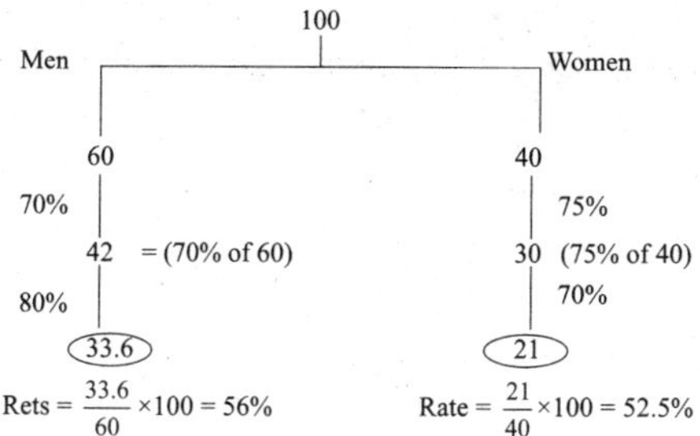


Overall = 33.6 + 21 = 54.6%

Hence option (c) is correct

**41.** $\frac{\text{2 for Principal}}{2_4 \times {}^4c_2} = \frac{\text{4 for Vice Principal}}{2 \times 6 = 12}$

**42. Case 1**

| | No. of ways |
|---|---|
| Maths 1 opted, then Maths 2 | $1 \times 1 = 1$ |
| **Case 2** | |
| Maths 1 opted, but not Maths 2 | $1 \times {}^3C_1 = 3$ |
| **Case 3** | |
| Maths I not opted, so maths II also not opted – | |
| | ${}^3C_2 = \frac{3}{7}$Ways |

**43.** Black Brown, Assume cost of brown = ₹ 1

| | Black | Brown | Assume cost of brown = ₹1 |
|---|---|---|---|
| No. of Pain | –5 | $x$ | |
| Cost/ Unit | –3 | –1 | |
| Total cost | 5×3 = 15 | $x$ | |

Now after inter changing the cost

| Black | Brown |
|---|---|
| 5 | $x$ |
| 1 | 3 |

Total cost = $5 + 3x$

As per question, $3x + 5 = 2\,(15 + x)$

$x = 25$

**44.** If the number of people who read Only magazine X is '$x$' and the number of people who read magazine Y is '$n$', then we have $x = 3n$ from the first statement given.

Also, if the number of people who read magazine Y alone is '$y$' and the number of people who read magazine X is 'm', then we have $y = 3m$ from the first statement given.

However, both of these cannot be simultaneously true as $x$ is a part of m, while $y$ is a part of $n$. So if a part of $m$, is greater than $n$, then simultaneously a part of $n$ cannot be greater than $m$.

Hence, we cannot draw any of the conclusions.

Option (d) is the correct answer

**45.** Time reqd. $= \frac{t_1t_2}{t_1 + t_2} = \frac{20 \times 30}{20 + 30} = 12$ minutes

**46.** In general, when we multiply a three digit number with 1001, we get a six digit number that is written by writing the three digit number twice consecutively. This can be confirmed for instance when we do 234 × 1001 = 234234. Hence, DEED must be 1001. Hence, Option (c) is correct.

**47.** Since the host is decided by picking lots, it is like deciding the host on a random basis. Hence, we cannot predict who would be the host how many times. Hence, option (d) is the correct answer.

**48.** Say each question carries = 10 marks

then 8 ×5 = 40

How, it is 40%, so total marks = 100

$\therefore$ No. of question $= \frac{100}{10} = 10$

**49.** Let Son's age = $x$, then

$9x + 8x = 51 \Rightarrow x = 3$

**50.** Option (b) is correct .The picture of their movements would naturally see them separating by a total of 2 kms (when each of them travels 1 km each in the opposite direction. Next, Shahid turns left while Rohit turns right means that they would move in parallel directions (as shown in the figure below. Note this figure is one of the two figures possible, since the question just starts by telling us that they move in the opposite directions. In the figure drawn here, we have considered that Shahid starts going towards the right, while Rohit walks in the opposite direction to start off)

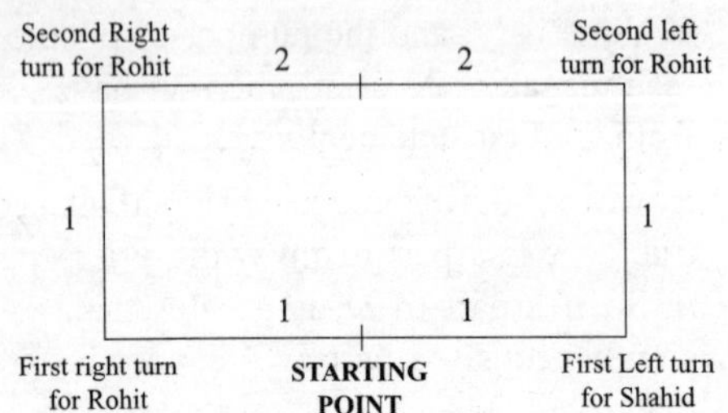


It is evident from the figure that option (b) is correct.

**51.** B Covers (500 – 45 – 35) = 420 mts in 't' see

A Cover = 500 units in time t see.

$$\frac{\text{A's Speed}}{\text{B's Speed}} = \frac{500/t}{420/t} = \frac{25}{21}$$

**52.** Option (c) is correct .There are a total of 27 people who have been talked about in the group: viz: 6 speaking Tamil, 15 speaking Hindi and 6 speaking Gujarati. Since, two people speak two languages, in this 27 people there is a double count of two people – i.e. two people are counted twice each for reaching the figure of 27. Further, since one person can speak all the languages, it means that, one person is counted three times. Thus, there is a total of 1 + 1 + 2 = 4 extra counts in the group. Thus, there must be 23 people in the group. Hence, option (c) is correct.

**53.** Let no. of Cars = $x$, no of scooters = $y$

then $4x + 2y = 100 + 2(x + y)$

$\Rightarrow x = 50$

**54.** Twelve adults would occupy 2/3rd of the lift's capacity. In the remaining 1/3rd of the lift, there would be 10 children who could board the lift.

**55.**

| | | |
|---|---|---|
| Cost – | ₹ 22,800 | |
| Interest 12.5% | + 2850 | (12.5% of 22800 = 2850) |
| | 25650 | |
| Paid after First Year | – 8650 | |
| | 170000 | |
| Interest @ 12.5% | 2125 | (12.5% of 17000 = 2125) |
| | 19125 | |
| Paid after Second Year | 9125 | |
| | 10000 | |
| Interest @ 12.5% | 1250 | |
| | 11250 | |

**56.** The first statement is false since, $x$ and $y$ can have values that are both negative (like –11 and –19). Also, it is possible that $x$ is positive and $y$ negative (like 3 and –5). The second statement is false because it is not necessary that if $x$ is positive, $y$ would be necessarily negative (like 20 and 12, where $x$ is positive and $y$ is also positive). The third statement is also false, since if $x$ is negative, $y$ being lower than $x$, would need to be negative and cannot be positive.

Hence, option (d) is correct.

**57.** Let the number be YOX and XOY then as per problem $(100y + x) - (100x + y) = 198$

$y - x = 2$

**58.** On the top and bottom surfaces, there would be 4 cubes each that would be painted on two sides (the middle cube on each side). On the middle line the corner pieces (four of them) would be painted on two surfaces. Hence, the correct answer is 4 + 4 + 4 = 12. Option (a) is correct.

**59.** Here digit at hundred places is greater than ten's place. So, for 700 – 799, we can use 1, 2, 3, 4, 5, 6

Sum = 1 + 2 + 3 + 3 + 4 + 5 + 6 = 21

For 800 – 899, we can use 1, 2, 3, 4, 5, 6, 7.

Sum = 1 + 2 + 3 + 4 + 5 + 6 + 7 = 28

For 900 – 999, we can use 1, 2, 3, 4, 5, 6, 7, 8

Sum = 1 + 2 + 3 + 4 + 5 + 6 + 7 + 8 = 36

Total = 85

**60.** His total sale would be:

$a \times x + (a + 2)(x + 2) + (a - 2)(x - 2)$

$ax + ax + 2a + 2x + 4 + ax - 2a - 2x + 4 = 3ax + 8$

Option (b) is correct.

**61.** Reqd. Chance = P (red and 3) OR P (black and 1 or )

$$= \frac{40}{100} \times \frac{15}{35} + \frac{75}{100} \times \frac{20}{35} = \frac{4}{7}$$

**62.** A reaches diametrically opposite, so,

A covers 180°.

B is 30° ahead of A,

So B covers $180° - 30° = 150°$

Ratio of speeds = A : B = 180 : 150 = 6 : 5

**63.** Pass marks = 30 + 30 = 60

Now 40% of maximum marks = 60

Maximum marks = $\frac{60}{40} \times 100 = 150$

**64.** Let no. of boys with shirt = 11 = $n(s)$

No. of boys with pants = 14 = $n(p)$

$n(s \cup p) = n(s) + n(p) - n(s \cup p)$

$19 = 11 + 14 - x \Rightarrow x = 6$

**65.** The same percentage profit or loss means the same absolute profit or loss. Hence, the profit = loss. Since, the two selling prices mentioned in the question are ₹ 40 and ₹ 20, the original cost of the article must be ₹ 30 (Halfway between 20 and 40). Option (c) is correct.

**66.** Diagonals = 5

Area of rectangle = $2 \times \frac{1}{2} \times 3 \times 4 = 12$ cm$^2$

Area of each square = $\frac{12}{12} = 1$ cm$^2$

**67.** The speed of the train in m/s would be $40 \times \frac{5}{18} = \frac{200}{18}$.

Also, we know that: speed × time = distance

Thus: $\frac{200}{18} \times$ time = 200 $\Rightarrow$ time = 18 seconds.

**68.** Sum of the digits = 4 + 2 + 5 + 2 + 7 + 4 + 6 + B = 30 + B

For the number to be divisible by 3, sum is to be divisible by 3.

So B can take the values as 0 ,3, 6, and 9 = 4 possible values

**69.** At 8 AM on Wednesday, the clock would show 8:20 AM (20 minutes ahead). At 8 AM on Thursday it would be 30 minutes ahead. Hence, between the actual time of 8 AM on Wednesday and on Thursday the clock would be between 20-30 minutes ahead (more than 20 but less than 30). Looking at the options it is clear that the only possible value of the actual time would be 5:36 PM (since only in that case would we get the clock to be fast by more than 20 minutes but less than 30 minutes). Hence, option (a) is correct.

**70.** $\frac{1}{2} < \frac{1+2}{2+3} = \frac{3}{3}$. Fraction is more than the original

**71.** 3 persons belong to neither;

Hence 15 – 3 = 12 belong to either

Now number of persons belong to both

= 7 + 8 – 12 = 3

3 7 8

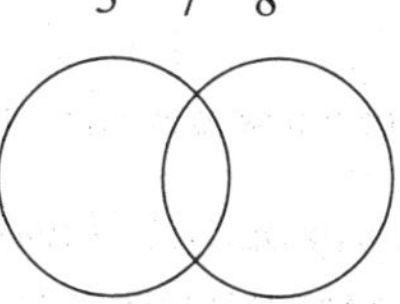

Number of persons to exactly one = ( 7 – 3 ) + ( 8 – 3) = 4 + 5 = 9

**72.**

| Number of pages | Number of digits used |
|---|---|
| 1 – 9 | 9 |
| 10 – 99 | 2 × 90 = 180 ( 2 -digits) |
| 100 – 999 | 3 × 900 = 2700 ( 3- digits) |
| 1 – 999 | 2889 digits |

Number of digits remaining 3089 – 2889 = 200

Number of 4 -digit pages = $\frac{200}{3} = 50$

Total number of pages = 999 + 50 = 1049

**73.** 2C + M = 150

2C + F = 156

Subtracting, F – M = 6

60 – M = 6

M = 60 – 6 = 54

**74.** With two 50 rupee currencies, we can pay in only one way: 50+50 + 1×7; With one fifty rupee currency, we can pay using 50 + 10s + 1s in 6 different ways (as we could use between 0 tens to 5 tens). With No 50 rupee currency, we can pay in 11 ways (as we could use between 0 tens to 10 tens), Thus, the total number of ways is 1+6+11=18.

Option (c) is correct.

**75.** The following figure would represent the situation. Hence the correct answer is got by visualizing the Pythagoras triplet of 8, 15, 17. Hence, option (b) is correct.

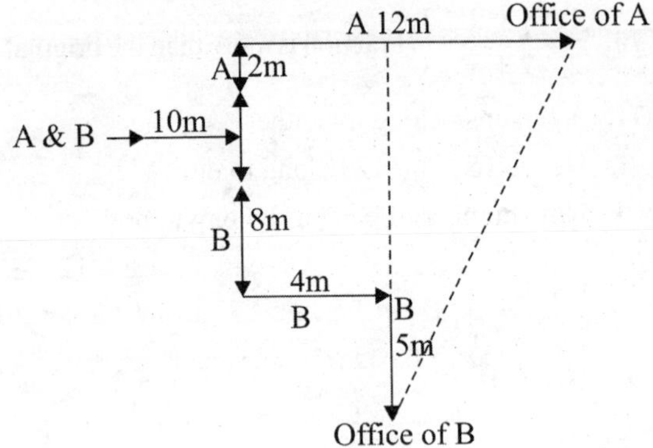


**76.** $S_2 - p + q$ is an odd integer

Assume 3 + 4 = 7 an odd

Hence one must be even .

pq must be even × odd = even

Hence $S_2$ alone is sufficient.

**78.**

| Interval | No, of 5 's |
|---|---|
| 1–10 | 1 |
| 11–20 | 1 |
| 41–50 | 2 |
| 51–60 | 10 |
| 91–100 | 1 |
| 1–100 | 20 |

In between 1–1000 there will be 10 sets, number of 5's = 20 × 10 =200

There will be 5's in between 501 – 600 = 100

Total 5's = 200 + 100 =300

**79.** The given image shows how to cut this cube:

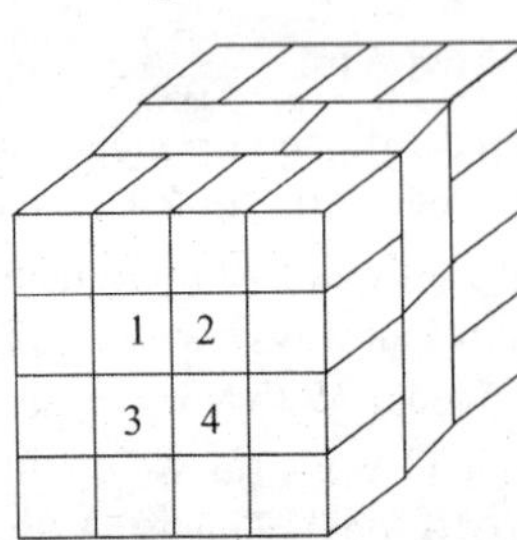


As you can see on the front surface and the back surface the cubes are smaller (and 16 each). The middle part of the cube has 4 larger cubes which are not painted blue. Hence, the blue colors should be on the front and the back side. In this cutting situation, there would be 4 small cubes on the front surface that would be colored only on one surface. Likewise, there would be 4 on the back surface. Hence, there would be 8 cubes with only 1 side painted. Option (c) is correct.

**80.** $\frac{B}{A} = \frac{60}{100} = \frac{6}{10}$

$\frac{B}{(B+A)} = \frac{6}{(6+10)} \times 100\% = 37.5\%$

**81.** LCM ( 4, 6 ) =12

Different combinations of 12 in between 1 – 100 are 12, 24, 36, 48, 60, 72, 84, 96 = 8

**82.** 80% → 12 km

100% → $\frac{12}{80} \times 100 = 15$ km

**83.** 75% → ₹ 9000

100% → $\frac{9000}{75} \times 100 = 12000$ = cost of the mobile hand set

Raju borrows ₹ 2000.

Total amount available = 9000 = 2000 =11000 which is less than the cost of the handset.

**84.** In 2002, let Meenu's age = $x$ then Meera's age = $3x$

In 2012 , Meenu's age = $x + 8$ and Meera's age = $3x + 8$

Given that $2(x + 8) = 3x + 8$

$x = 8$

Meenu's age = 8 years in 2002

Meenu's year of birth = 2002 – 8 =1994

**85.** Let the cost of one ball = $x$

Cost of one racket = $3x$

$10x + 10(3x) = 2800$

$x = 70$

Cost of racket = $3x = 3 \times 70 =$ ₹210

**86.** Number of Indians = 70

∴ Number of Foreigners = 30

Let vegetarian Indians = $x$

∴ Number of non-vegetarian Indians = $70 - x$

Let the number of vegetarian foreigners be = $y$

∴ Number of non-vegetarian foreigners = $30 - y$

Here, $y$ cannot exceed 30

Total no. of vegetarians = $x + y = 60$

When $y$ is maximum then $x$ is minimum

Maximum $y = 30$

∴ Minimum $x = 60 - 30 = 30$

Hence, condition 1 is correct

When $y$ is minimum $x$ is maximum

Minimum $y$ is 0 (no foreign vegetarian)

Hence, maximum $x$ is 60

∴ Maximum Indian vegetarian is 60 this corresponds to minimum Indian non-vegetarians = 10

Hence, condition 2 is also correct.

**87.** Using Pythagoras

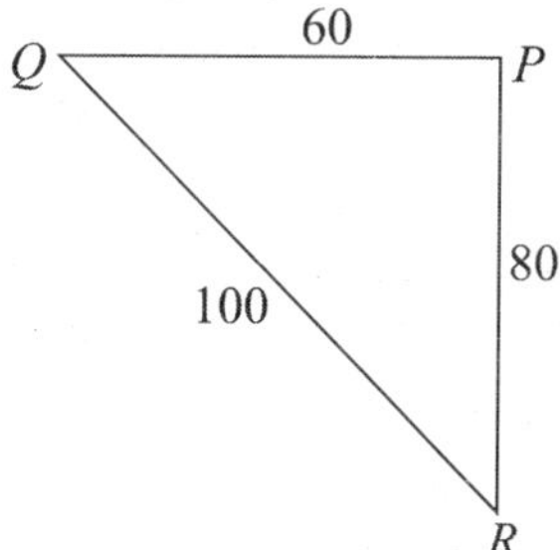


$$QR = \sqrt{PQ^2 + PR^2}$$

$$= \sqrt{60^2 + 80^2}$$

$$= 100$$

The figure representing the placement of the towns would be:

The distance between Q and R can be seen to be 100 kms (using the 6,8,10 Pythagoras triplet). Option (d) is correct.

**88.** Suppose there are 100 members in total.

Let the number of those who did only shopping be = $x$

Let the number of those who did sightseeing and shopping be = y

Let the number of those who did only sight seeing be = z (eqn. 3)

The number of those who did neither = 10 (given)

$x + y + z + 10 = 100$ (eqn. 1)

∴ $x + y + z = 90$ (eqn. 2)

Total who went for shopping = $x + y = 80$ (eqn. 3)

Total who went for sightseeing = $y + z = 50$ (eqn. 4)

Solving above, we get $x = 40$ (eqn. 1– eqn. 3); $z = 10$ (eqn. 1 – eqn. 2); hence, $y = 40$

Hence only condition 1 is correct.

**89.** Conclusion 1 is not valid. Question states every football player has a two-wheeler. 40% players do not play cricket and at least 40% players foot ball . However, there could be more than 40% football players including those who play cricket as well as football. Hence the no. of football players could be more than 40%.

Conclusion 2 is not valid. Question only states that every football player has a two wheeler but it does state that cricket players do not have two wheelers.

Conclusion 3 is not correct as no such assertion is made in the question. Hence the right option is (d)

**90.** Let B scored = 400

A scored 5% more than B

B scored = 400 + 5% of 400 = 420

Hence option C is correct.

**91.** Sita will swim on 1st 3rd 5th 7th

Gita will swim on 1st 4th 7th

Hence they will swim together again on 7th January

**92.** X + 40 Y + 24 Z

Remaining race for Y and Z = 1000 – 40 = 960 m

For 960 m head start given 24 m

For 1000 m head start given 24/960 × 1000 = 25 m

**93.** Mother's age = 13 + 24 =37

Father' s age = 37 + 3 = 40

Ena is 13 years now , born 4 years after marriage

They are married = 13 + 4 =17 years back

Father's age at marriage = 40 – 17 = 23 years

Ena's father must have been 27 when she was born (as her mother was 24 and her father is three years older than her mother). Since, she was born 4 years after their marriage, her father would have been 23 years at the time of his marriage. Option (b) is correct.

**94.** Let each mobile cost = ₹ 100

8 mobiles cost = 8 × 100 = ₹ 800

Now after discount 10 mobiles cost ₹ 800

1 mobile cost after discount cost ₹ 800 /10 = 80

$\text{Discount \%} = \frac{(100 - 80)}{100} \times 100 = 20\%$

**95.** Total marks = 40 × 100 = 4000

$\text{Corrected mean} = \frac{(4000 - 83 + 53}{100} = 39.7$

**96.** Given X+Y+Z is not divisible by 3

Hence XYZ is not divisible by 3

Given XYZ + YZX + ZYX = 3XYZ is divisible by 3 but as XYZ is not divisible by 3, so 3XYZ is not divisible by 9.

**97.** As $q$ and $s$, when added become equal, so $q$ and $s$ are the smallest and eliminated.

Out of $p$ and $r$, it is clear that $r - p = 2$. Hence it cannot be a prime number.

**98.** Adding the digits, sum = 1 + 2 + 3 + 4 + 5 = 15 which is divisible by 3, hence it cannot be a prime number.

**99.** Solve it by options. Put 2 for x and check

2 + 12 + 52 + 22 + 21 = 122, not true

Put 3 for x and check

3 + 13 + 53 + 33 + 31 = 133, true.

**100.** 3.25 if taken twice will measure 6.5 out of given 7.5 will give a balance of 1 feet.

Further this 1 feet if taken for 3 times will measure upto 3 feet which will give a balance of 0.25 feet it is the minimum length that can be measured.

**101.** 13 + 1 = 14, 17 + 1 = 18, 19 + 1 = 20, 23 + 1 = 24, 29 + 1 = 30, 31 + 1 = 32, 37 + 1 =38

**102.** Assume there are 20 pages. Then

1 + 2 + 3 +... = 20 (20 + 1)/2 = 210

210 – 195 = 15 = sum of 2 torn pages

Option (b), 7 + 8 = 15

**103.**

```
  A 3 B C
+ D E 2 F
---------
 1 5 9 0 2
```

Think of the question using the figure above. Since each of A, B, C, D, E and F are distinct greater than 3, they would use digits from 4, 5, 6, 7, 8, 9. From the addition of the units digit we see that C + F = 2 (can only happen if C + F = 12 and 1 gets carried over the tens place). This means that C, F would be using the digits (7, 5) or (8, 4) in any order. From the second column, we have B + 2 + 1(Carryover from units place) = 10 B = 7. This means that C + F = 8 + 4 or 4 + 8. From the hundreds column we see that 3 + E + 1= 9 E = 5. This can only mean that A+ D = 15 with them sharing the digits 6 and 9 in any order. The difference between A and D would be 3.

**104.** Even after using both the statements together we can see that we have two possible values of the number $n$ i.e. 13 and 17, which satisfy both the conditions of S1 and S2. Hence, option (d) is correct.

**105.** Both the statements are required to answer the question – as a product of 21 by itself does not tell you whether it is 7 × 3 or 21 × 1. Hence, option (c) is correct.

**106.** From the following figure ends up North-West of his original position. Hence, option (d) is correct.

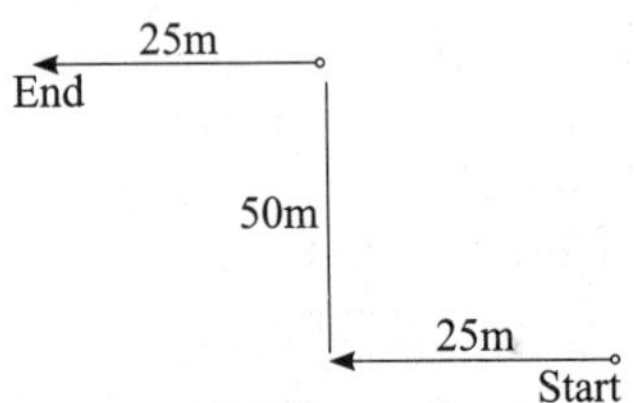

**107.** If all numbers are divisible by 2 and 3 (as given in the statement) it must follow that all numbers must be divisible by 6. They may or may not be divisible by 4. Hence, the first conclusion can be drawn but the second one cannot be. Option (a) is the correct answer.

**108.** Such integers are 14, 34, 41, 42, 43, 45, 46, 47, 49, 54, 74, 94 = 12

**109.** Given $u = m/x$ and $v = nly$

Mass $Q = 2x$ (mass P), $n = 2m$

Side of $Q = 2x$ (side of P),

Volume of Q = $8x$ (volume of P)

$y = 8x$

$u = m/x$, $v = n/y = 2m/8x = m/4x = u/4$ or $u = 4v$

**110.** Let he bought at ₹C, then

300000 = (100 – 20)% of C

300000 = (80)% of C

C = 5 × 30000/4 = 375000

**111.** Equivalent discount = 10 + 20 + (10 x 20) /100 =32%

Effective% = (100 – 32) × (100 + 10)

= 68% × 110%

Effective% = 68% × 110%

Effective% = 110% × 68%

**112.** Greatest length $x$ = HCF of (3 1/2, 8 3/4)

= HCF of (7/ 2, 35 /4)

= HCF (7, 35) / LCM (2, 4) = 7 /4 = 1 3/4

**113.** 1.27 =(127 – 1)/ 99 = 126/99 =14 /11

**114.** Number divisible by 3, 4, 5, 6 = LCM (3, 4, 5, 6) = 60

Subtract 2 from each choice and check which one is divisible by 60

(a) 1010 not divisible by 60 (b) 1020 is divisible by 60

**115.** Let the number of men in the population be = m
Let the number of women in the population be = w
Given the condition of one man marries not more than one women and one woman marries only one man and no widows or widowers, we get the number married men will be equal to the number of married women.

Married men = 0.4 m

Married women = 0.3 w

We get 0.4 m = 0.3 w or m = 0.75 w

Ratio of married people to adult population is ( 0.4 m + 0.3 w)/(m + w)

= (0.6/1.75) = 34.28%

**116.** Product = 51 × 27 × 35 × 62 × 75

Remainder when divided by 100 = last two digit of product

= last two digit of (product of last digits)

= (7 × 5 × 2 × 5)

= last two digit (350)

= 50

**117.** Ratio of X : Y: Z = 1/2 : 3/4 : 5/6

LCM (2, 4, 6) = 12, multiply each fraction by 12

= 6 : 9 :10

6 + 9 + 10 = 25 parts = 2500

So, difference = 10 – 6 = 4 parts = 400.

**118.** In 10^$n$ + 1

Put $n$ = 0, 10″0 + 1 = 1 + 1 = 2

Put $n$ = 1, 10'1 + 1 = 11 = 1 + 1 = 2

Put $n$ = 2 10^2 + 1 = 101 = 1 + 1 = 2

**119.** Shifting is within the class. Hence average remains the same.

**120.** Out of 5 denominations, we have to take at least 3

number of ways = ways to take 3 + ways to take 4 + ways to take 5

$= {}^5C_3 + {}^5C_4 + {}^5C_5 = 10 + 5 + 1 = 16$

**121.** Starting with D and ending with I, we are left with E, L, H

Number of ways = 3 × 2 × 1= 6

**122.** Bottle has 20 litres of A.

| | A | B |
|---|---|---|
| after 1st draw | 16 | 0 |
| adding 41 of B | 16 | 4 |

In 2nd draw of 4L mixture results a draw of B = (1/ 1 + 4) × 4 = 4/5L of B Again adding 4L of B, total mixture = 20L

A B

$4 - 4/5 + 4 = 36/5$

$(20 - 36/5)$

Required ratio $= (20 - 36/5) : 36/5$

$= 64/36 = 16/9$

**123.** Total score after 50 innings $= 50 \times 46.4$

Total score after 60 innings $= 60 \times (46.4 + 2.6)$

$= 60 \times 49$

Total score in last 10 innings

$= 60 \times 49 - 50 \times 46.4$

$= 50 \times 49 + 10 \times 49 - 50 \times 46.4$

$= 50\,(49 - 46.4) = 10 \times 49$

$=130 + 490 = 620$

Average score in last 10 innings $= 620/10 = 62$

**124.** 25% hike gives 6 kg less for 120

Originally 6 kg costs 25% of 1200 (= 300)

1 kg costs now 300/6 = 50/kg

Original price per kg = 50/1.25 = ₹ 40

**125.** X can do 20% in 8 days

X can 100% in $8 \times 5 = 40$ days

Y can do 25% in 6 days

Y can do 100% in $6 \times 4 = 24$ days

X + Y can do it in $= (24 \times 40)/24 + 40$

$= 24 \times 40/64 = 15$ days.

X + Y can do 40% of it in 40% of 15 = 6 days.

**126.** Let the speeds be 10, 20, 30 and 40

Distance from X to Y= LCM of 10, 20, 30 40) = 120

Time taken will be

$= 120/10 + 120/20 + 120/30 + 120/40 = 25$

average speed = distance / time

$= 120 + 120 + 120 + 120/25 = 480/25 = 19.2$

Hence average speed lies between 10 and 20 that is between $v$ and $2v$.

**127.** $x + y = d/t$

$x - y = d/2t$

$x + y/x - y = 2/1 = x/y = 3 : 1$

**128.** $64 - 1 = 63\ 8^2 - 2^2$

$144 - 81 = 63\ 12^2 - 9^2$

**129.** The largest fraction will have minimum change

**130.** Assume $n = 9$, now check each option.

(a) $2n = 2 \times 9 = 18$ not divisible

(b) $3n = 3 \times 9 = 27$, not divisible

(c) $2n + 4 = 2 \times 9 + 4 = 22$ not divisible by 4

(d) $3n + 1 = 3 \times 9 + 1 = 28$

**131.** 1000 gm = 1 litre of water

1000 gm = 1000 cubic centimeter

1 gm = 1 cubic centimeters

1 gm = 1000 cubic milimetres

0.1 gm = $1000 \times 0.1$ cubic millimeters

= 100 cubic millimeter

**132.** It can be solved by options.

Let weight of empty vessel = 10 kg

1/3 water + empty = 20

1/3 of water = 20 – 10 = 10

Full water $= 10 \times 3 = 30$

then full water + empty = 30 + empty = 40 (given)

empty = 40 – 30 = 10

**133.** Number of jumps $= [4.5 \times 100/(30 - 15) - 1]$

$= 30 - 1 = 29$

**134.** $x$ = number of persons originally, then after 10 days, remaining food provision

$= x \times 32$

Since 300 more persons join, so last for 24 days,

$N_1D_1 = N_2D_2$

$\Rightarrow (x + 300) \times 24 = x \times 32 \Rightarrow x = 900$

**135.** Since % increase = % decrease, so

there will be net loss% $= \left(\frac{40}{10}\right)^2 = 16\%$

**136.** By 11 AM the train from Patna has travelled towards Kolkata a distance of 120 km and is now 480 km from Kolkata.

The two trains cover this distance of 480 km in another 3 hrs. (relative speed = 160 kmph). Hence, they meet at 2 pm.

The trains return and travel for a further time of 2 and a half hours (till 4:30 pm).

In two and half hours the train returning towards Patna covers 150 km.

While the train returning to Kolkata cover 250 kms in this time.

The combined distance covered is 400 km

**137.** $x = y/2$ or $2x = y$

$x^2 + (2x)^2 = 500$

or $x^2 + 4x^2 = 500$

or $5x^2 = 500$

or $x^2 = 100x = 10$

**138.** Given $\frac{x}{5} = \frac{y}{9}, \frac{x}{y} = \frac{5}{9}$

$$\frac{x+5}{y+9} = \frac{5+5}{9+9} = \frac{5}{9}$$

**139.** Fraction of work done by 200 men in 50 days = 1/4

Fraction of work done by one man in one day

$= \frac{1}{4} \times \frac{1}{200} \times \frac{1}{50} = \frac{1}{40000}$

Fraction of work left $= \frac{3}{4}$

Time left = 100 days

Fraction of work to be done per day

$= \frac{3}{4} \times \frac{1}{100} = \frac{3}{400}$

No. of men required to complete this work

$$= \frac{\frac{3}{400}}{\frac{1}{40000}} = 300$$

Addition no. of men required = 100

**140.** Let the cost price to Nikhil = ₹100,

with 10% profit, Selling price by Nikhil

= 1.1 × 100 = ₹110 = Cost price to Prateek

Selling price by Prateek $= 110 \times \frac{90}{100}$ = ₹99

Savings of Nikhil = 100 – 99 = ₹ 1

% profit $= \frac{1}{100} \times 100 = 1\%$

**141.** 90 km/h = 90 (5/18) = 25 m /sec

Time to cross = distance/speed

= (300 + 150)/25

= 450/25 = 18 sec

**142.** Let original length and breadth be $l$ and $b$ respectively

Original area= $l \times b$

Length after cutting = 0.9 l

New area after cutting = 0.81 lb ( given)

Hence the new breadth after cutting

$= (0.81lb)/0.9l = 0.9b$

Therefore, reduction in breadth

$= (b - 0.9b)/b = 0.1$ or 10%

**143.** Let the milk sample = 30 litre,

then 1/3 of it $= \frac{1}{3} \times 30 = 10$ litres

10 litres has 50% water, quantity of water = 5 litres

Now this 10 litres of milk sample + 10 litres of pure milk has 5 litres of water

Required percentage of water $= \left(\frac{5}{10+10}\right) \times 100$

= 25%

**144.** Fraction of cistern filled in one hour = 1/6

Fraction of cistern getting emptied in one hour = 1/8

Net filling in one hour $= \left(\frac{1}{4} - \frac{1}{6}\right) = \frac{1}{12}$ 1/6 - 1/8=1/24

Time taken to fill whole cistern = 24 hours

(Tap + Pipe outlet) together can fill the tank in 24 hrs.

**145.** Let the property of Kabir be worth ₹ 100, then selling price to Jain is ₹ 90. Jain sells it at 90 + 9 = 99 to Kabir.

Hence, Kabir has loss = 100 – 99 = ₹ 1,

that is Kabir's loss % = 1%.

Kabir's loss = 1% of 1 crore = 1 lakh

**146** 3 minutes = 3 × 6° = 18° = A

Required time $= \frac{2}{11}$ (H × 30 + A)

$= \frac{2}{11}$ (6 × 30 + 18) minutes past 6

= 36 minutes past 6 = 6.36 PM

**147.** In inclined position the ladder is 3 metres from the wall

In fallen position, the base of the ladder further slips by 2 metres

In fallen position the base is 3 + 2 = 5 metre away from the wall

Hence, length of ladder = 5 m

When ladder is in incline position it becomes the hypotenuse of a right angle triangle whose base is 3 m and the length of whose vertical side is to be determined.

Using Pythagoras theorem, we get vertical = 4 metre

**148.** Current time is 6:30 pm and after 1.5 hours the time is 8 pm

At 8 pm the minute hand is at 12 and the hour hand is at 8

The angle between the hands = 30 × 4
= 120 degrees

**149.** The angle between the minute and hour hand is 15 degrees. This means that the hands are half of a division away between two numbers, viz. as in 5:30 pm, where minute hand is at 6 and hour hand is between 5 and 6 .

However, there are many positions in which such an angle is possible. In some the minute hand can be ahead of the hour hand and vice versa. Depending on the positions the angle may increase or decrease after one hour and the change will also depend on the initial position. Hence option (d) is correct.

**150.** The net/resultant travel of the person is 3 km to east and 3 km to south. Therefore. The final direction from initial point is 45 degree south of east.

## Exercise Set D

*Read the following passage and answer the 3 (three) items that follow:*

In a survey regarding a proposed measure to be introduced, 2878 persons took part of which 1652 were males. 1226 persons voted against the proposal of which 796 were male. 1425 persons voted for the proposal. 196 females were undecided.

1. How many females voted for the proposal?
(a) 430 (b) 600
(c) 624 (d) 640

2. How many males were undecided?
(a) 31 (b) 227
(c) 426 (d) 581

3. How many females were not in favour of the proposal?
(a) 430 (b) 496
(c) 586 (d) 1226

4. Consider the following distance – time graph. The graph shows three athletes *A*, *B* and *C* running side for a 30 km race.

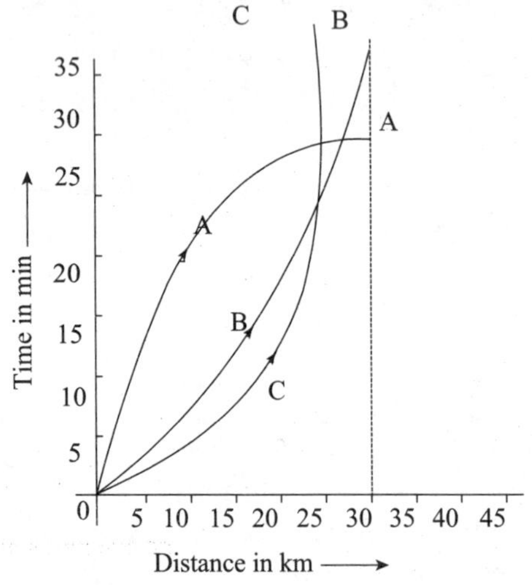


With reference to the above graph, consider the following statements:

1. The race was won by *A*.
2. B was ahead of A up to 25 km mark.
3. C ran very slowly from the beginning.

Which of the statements given above is/are correct?

(a) 1 only (b) 1 and 2 only
(c) 2 and 3 only (d) 1, 2 and 3

**5.** Consider the following information regarding the performance of a class of 1000 students in four different tests:

| Test | I | II | III | IV |
|---|---|---|---|---|
| Average marks | 60 | 60 | 70 | 80 |
| Range of marks | 39 to 90 | 45 to 75 | 20 to 100 | 0 to 100 |

If a student scores 74 marks in each of the four tests, in which one of the following tests in her performance the best comparativly?

(a) Test I (b) Test II
(c) Test III (d) Test IV

**6.** Consider the following diagrams:

x men, working at constant speed, do a certain job in y days. Which one of these diagrams shows the relation between x and y?

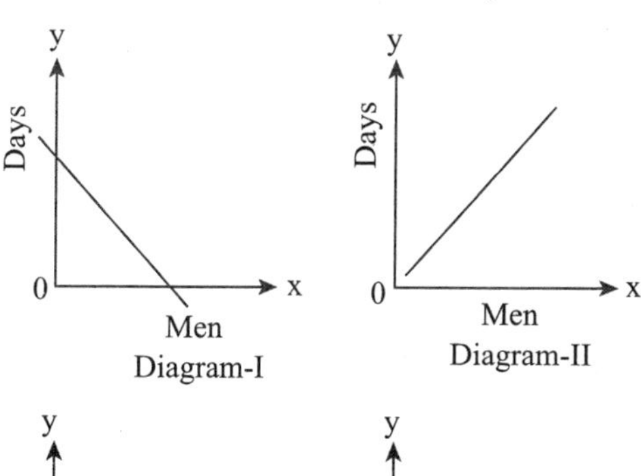

Diagram-I

Diagram-II

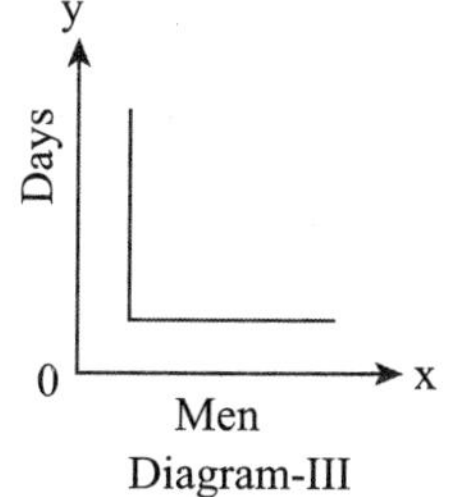

Diagram-III

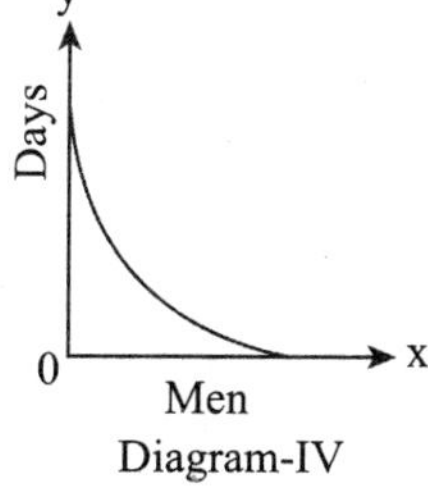

Diagram-IV

(a) diagram I (b) diagram II
(c) diagram III (d) diagram IV

**7.** Four cars are hired at the rate of ₹6 per km plus the cost of diesel at ₹40 a litre. In this context, consider the details given in the following table:

| *Car* | *Mileage (Km/l)* | *Hours* | *Total Payment (₹)* |
|---|---|---|---|
| A | 8 | 20 | 2120 |
| B | 10 | 25 | 1950 |
| C | 9 | 24 | 2064 |
| D | 11 | 22 | 1812 |

Which car maintained the maximum average speed?

(a) Car A (b) Car B
(c) Car C (d) Car D

**Directions for the following 4 (four) items**

*The following graph shows the average profit of two fruit-sellers A and B in thousands (₹) per year from the year 1995 to 2000. Consider the graph and answer the 4 (four) items that follow:*

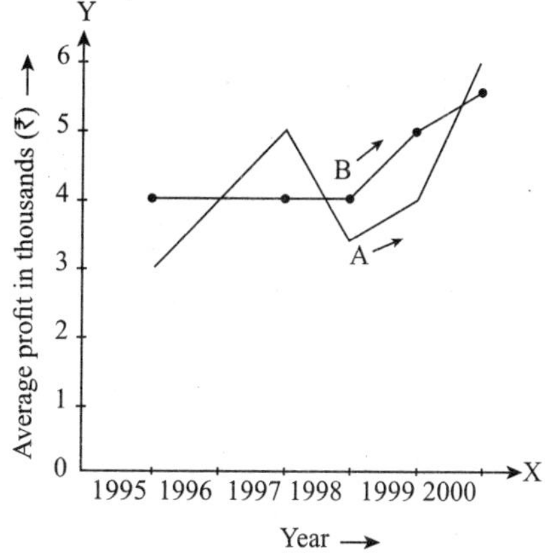


**8.** In which year is the average profit of A and B same?

(a) 1995 (b) 1996
(c) 1997 (d) 1998

**9.** What is the difference between the average profit of B and A in the year 1998?

(a) – ₹100 (b) – ₹1,000
(c) + ₹600 (d) –₹300

**10.** How much more average profit did A make in the year 2000 than in the year 1999?

(a) ₹200 (b) ₹1,000
(c) ₹1,500 (d) ₹2,000

11. What is the trend of the average profit of B from the year 1997 to the year 2000?
(a) Non-increasing, (b) Non-decreasing
(c) Steady, (d) Fluctuating

12. The following table shows the marks obtained by two students in different, subjects:

| | Student A | Maximum Marks | Student B | Maximum Marks |
|---|---|---|---|---|
| English | 60 | 100 | 80 | 150 |
| Psychology | 70 | 100 | 70 | 100 |
| History | 50 | 100 | 60 | 100 |
| Sanskrit | 30 | 50 | 15 | 25 |

The difference in the mean aggregate percentage marks of the students is
(a) 2.5% (b) 13.75%
(c) 1.25% (d) Zero

13. The following table gives population and total income of a city for four years:

| Year | 1992 | 1993 | 1994 | 1995 |
|---|---|---|---|---|
| *Population in lakh* | 20 | 21 | 22 | 23 |
| *Income in crores (Rs.)* | 1010 | 1111 | 1225 | 1345 |

Which one of the fallowing statements is correct in respect of the above data?
(a) Population increased by 5% or more every year.
(b) Income increased by 10% or more every year.
(c) Per capita income was always above ₹5,000.
(d) Per capita income was highest in 1994.

14. The graph below depicts the earnings of A and B over the period 2000 to 2010:

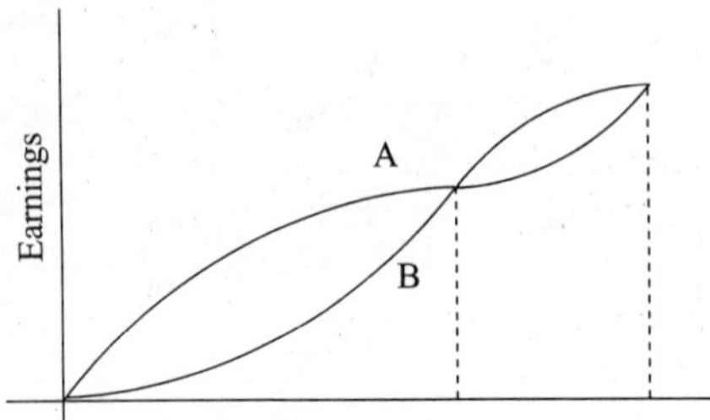


From the graph, which one of the following can be concluded?
(a) On the average A earned more than B during this period.
(b) On the average B earned more than A during this period.
(c) The earnings of A and B were equal during this period.
(d) The earnings of A were less as compared to B during this period.

15. Year-wise variation of the price of a certain commodity is shown in the following graph:

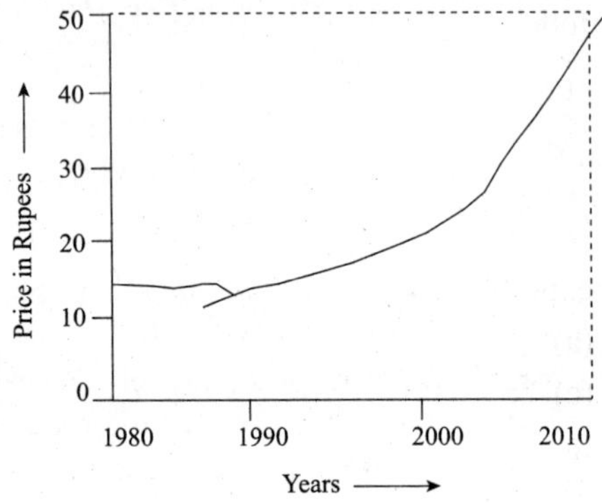


The price of the commodity in the year 1990
(a) must have been ₹10/-
(b) must have been ₹12/-
(c) must have been anywhere between ₹10/- and Rs.20/-
(d) is higher than that in the year 1991

16. The proportion of expenditure on various items by two families A and B are represented in the following Bar Charts:

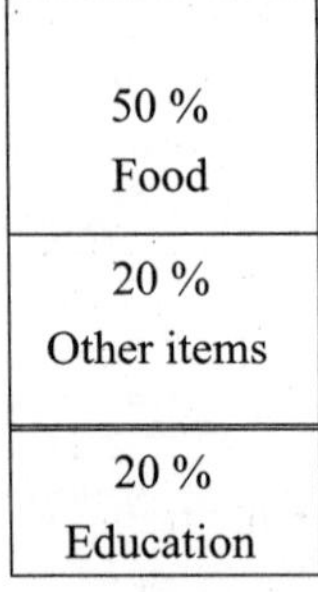


Family A
Total expenditure : ₹20,000 per month

10 % Food
60 % Other items
30 % Education

Family B
Total expenditure: ₹1,00,000 per month

From these charts, we can conclude that

(a) Family A spent more money on food than Family B.

(b) Family B spent more money on food than Family A.

(c) Family A and Family B spent the same amount on food.

(d) The expenditure on food by Family A and Family B cannot be compared.

**17.** An automobile owner reduced his monthly petrol consumption when the prices went up. The price-consumption relationship is as follows:

| Price (in ₹ per litre) | 40 | 50 | 60 | 75 |
|---|---|---|---|---|
| Monthly consumption (in litres) | 60 | 43 | 40 | 32 |

If the price goes up to ₹ 80 per litre, his expected consumption (in litres) will be

(a) 30 (b) 28
(c) 26 (d) 24

**18.** In a town, 45% population read magazine A, 55% read magazine B, 40% read magazine C, 30% read magazines A and B, 15% read magazines B and C, 25% read magazines A and C; and 10% read all the three magazines. What percentage do not read any magazine?

(a) 10% (b) 15%
(c) 20% (d) 25%

**19.** Consider the following graph:

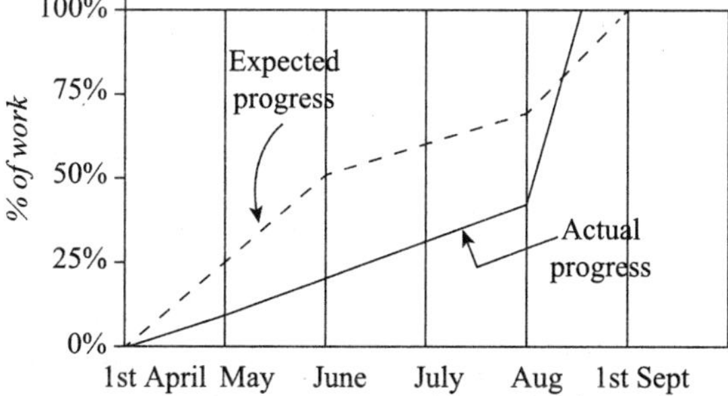


Which one of the following statements is not correct with reference to the graph given above?

(a) On 1st June, the actual progress of work was less than expected.

(b) The actual rate of progress of work was the greatest during the month of August.

(c) The work was actually completed before the expected time.

(d) During the period from 1st April to 1st September, at no time was the actual progress more than the expected progress.

***Directions for the following 2 (two) items:*** Consider the following graph in which the birth rate and death rate of a country are given, and answer the two items that follow:

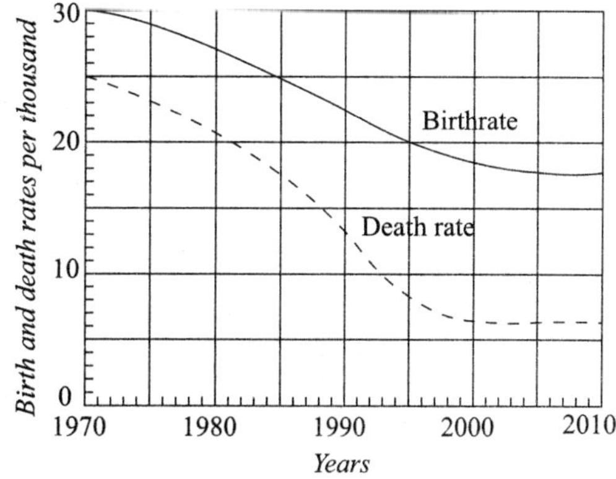


**20.** Looking at the graph, it can be inferred that from 1990 to 2010

(a) population growth rate has increased

(b) population growth rate has decreased

(c) growth rate of population has remained stable

(d) population growth rate shows no trend.

**21.** With reference to the above graph, consider the following statements considering 1970 as base year:

1. Population has stabilized after 35 years
2. Population growth rate has stabilized after 35 years.
3. Death rate has fallen by 10% in the first 10 years
4. Birth rate has stabilized after 35 years

Which of the above are the ***most logical and rational statements*** that can be made from the above graph?

(a) 1 and 2 only (b) 1, 2 and 3
(c) 3 and 4 (d) 2 and 4

22. Average hourly earnings per year (E) of the workers in a firm are represented in figures A and B as follows:

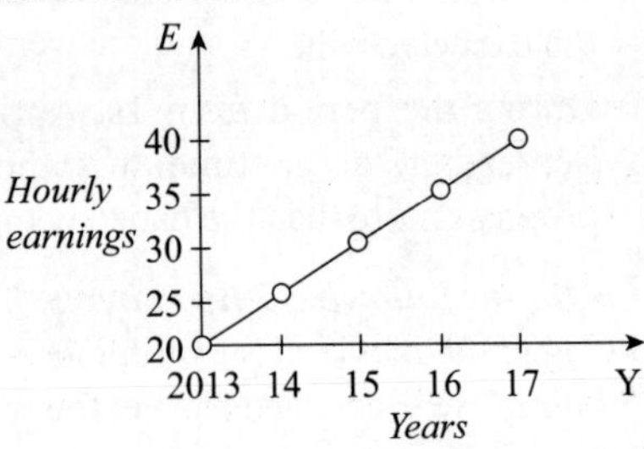


**Fig. A**

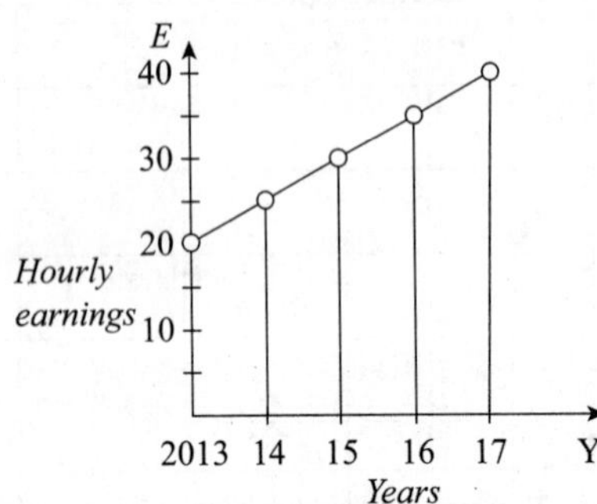


**Fig. B**

From the figure, it is observed that the

(a) values of E are different

(b) range (i.e., the difference between the maximum and the minimum) of E are different.

(c) slopes of the graphs are same

(d) rates of increase of E are different.

23. Consider the following figures A and B:

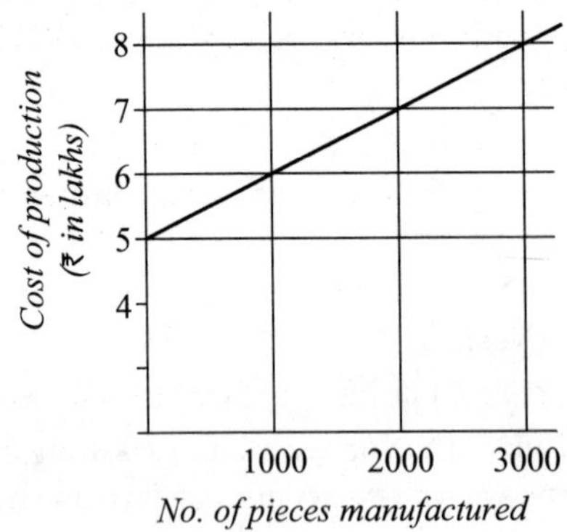


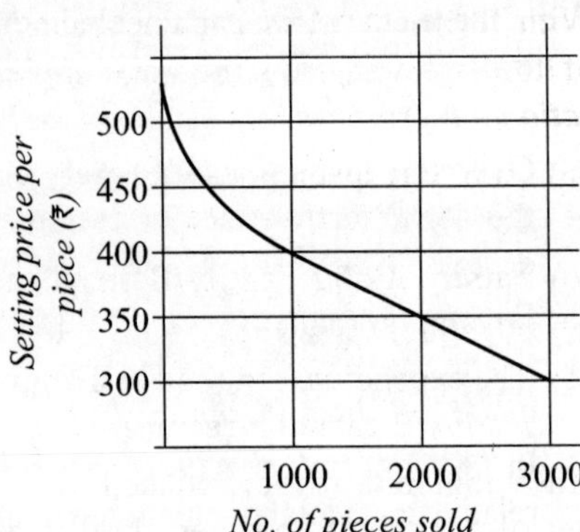


The manufacturing cost and projected sales for a product are shown in the above figures A and B respectively. What is the minimum number of pieces that should be manufactured to avoid a loss?

(a) 2000 (b) 2500

(c) 3000 (d) 3500

24. Consider the following graphs. The curves in the graphs indicate different age groups in the population of two countries A and B over a period of few decades:

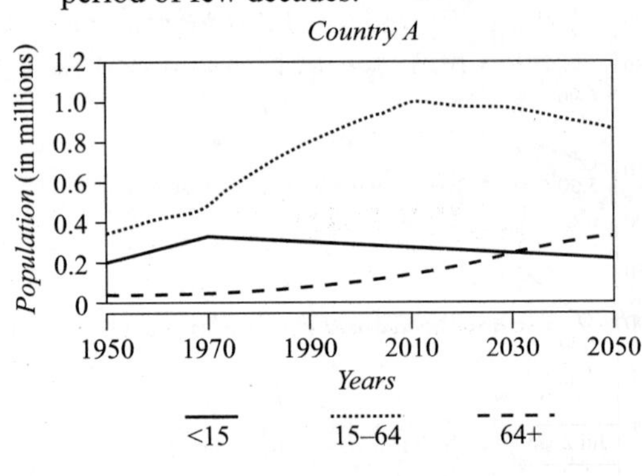


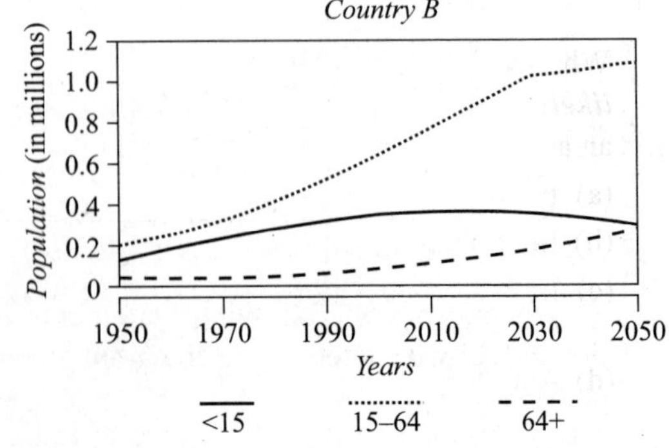

With reference to the above graphs, which of the following are the ***most logical and rational inferences*** that can be made?

1. Over the last two and a half decades, the dependency ratio for country B has decreased.
2. By the end of next two and a half decades, the dependency ratio of country A will be much less that of country B.
3. In the next two decades, the work-force relative to its total population will increase in country B as compared to country A.

Select the correct answer using the code given below:

(a) 1 and 2 only (b) 2 and 3 only
(c) 1 and 3 only (d) 1, 2 and 3

**25.** The graph given below indicates the changes in key policy rates made by the Central Bank several times in a year.

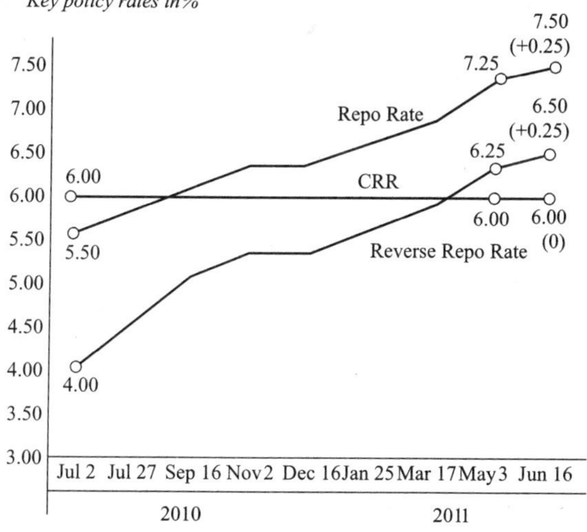


Which one of the following can be the ***most likely reason*** for the Central Bank for such an action?

(a) Encouraging foreign investment
(b) Increasing the liquidity
(c) Encouraging both public and private savings
(d) Anti-inflationary stance

***Directions for the following 2 (two) items:*** The following table gives the GDP growth rate and Tele-density data of different States of a country in a particular year. Study the table and answer the two items that follow.

**26.** With reference to the above table, which of the following is/are the ***most logical and rational inference/inferences*** that can be made?

1. Higher per capita income is generally associated with higher Tele-density.
2. Higher GDP growth rate always ensures higher per capita income.
3. Higher GDP growth rate does not necessarily ensure higher Tele-density.

Select the correct answer using the code given below.

(a) 1 only (b) 2 and 3
(c) 1 and 3 (d) 3 only

27. With reference to the above table, the following assumptions have been made:
    1. Nowadays, prosperity of an already high performing State cannot be sustained without making further large investments in its telecom infrastructure.
    2. Nowadays, a very high Tele-density is the most essential condition for promoting the business and economic growth in a State.

    Which of the above assumptions is/are valid?

    (a) 1 only (b) 2 only
    (c) Both 1 and 2 (d) Neither 1 nor 2

28. The following graph indicates the composition of our tax revenue for a period of two decades:

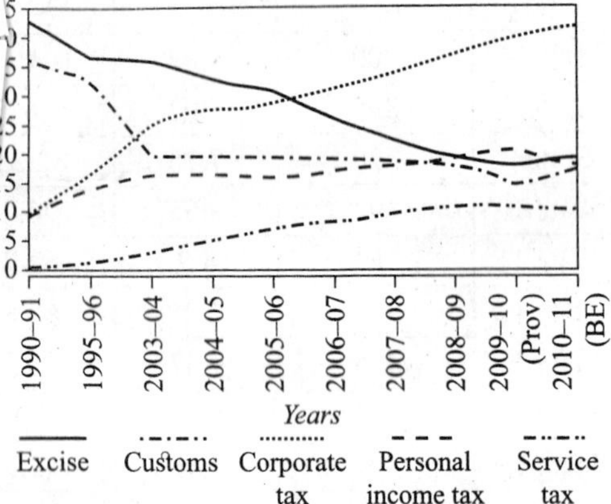


With reference to the above graph, which of the following is/are the ***most logical and rational inference/inferences*** that can be made?

1. During the given period, the revenue from Direct Taxes as percentage of gross tax revenue has increased while that of Indirect Taxes decreased.
2. The trend in the revenue from Excise Duty demonstrates that the growth of manufacturing sector has been negative during the given period.

Select the correct answer using the code given below.

(a) 1 only (b) 2 only
(c) Both 1 and 2 (d) Neither 1 nor 2

***Directions for the following 3 (three) items:*** The following three items are based on the graph given below which shows imports of three different types of steel over a period of six months of a year. Study the graph and answer the three items that follow.

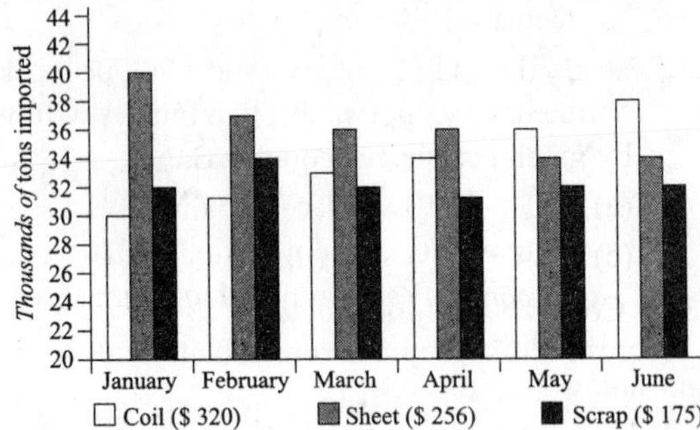


The figures in the brackets indicates the average cost per ton over six months period.

29. By how much (measured in thousands of tons) did the import of sheet steel exceed the import of coil steel in the first three months of the year?

    (a) 11 (b) 15
    (c) 19 (d) 23

30. What was the approximate total value (in $) of sheet steel imported over the six months period?

    (a) 45,555 (b) 50,555
    (c) 55,550 (d) 65,750

31. What was the approximate ratio of sheet steel and scrap steel imports in the first three months of the year?

    (a) 1 : 1 (b) 1 : 2 : 1
    (c) 1 : 4 : 1 (d) 1 : 6 : 1

32. The figure drawn blow gives the velocity graphs of two vehicles A and B. The straight line OKP represents the velocity of vehicle A at any instant, whereas the horizontal straight line CKD represents the velocity of vehicle B at any instant. In the figure, D is the point where perpendicular from

    P meets the horizontal line CKD such that PD = 2 LD:

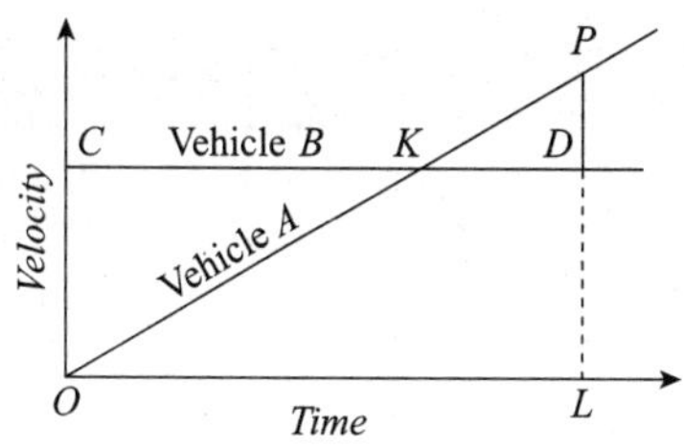


What is the ratio between the distances covered by vehicles A and B in the time interval OL?

(a) 1 : 2 (b) 2 : 3
(c) 3 : 4 (d) 1 : 1

**33.** Consider the following data:

| | Average marks in English | Average marks in Hindi |
|---|---|---|
| Girls | 9 | 8 |
| Boys | 8 | 7 |
| Overall average marks | 8.8 | $x$ |

What is the value of $x$ in the above table?

(a) 7.8 (b) 7.6
(c) 7.4 (d) 7.2

**34.** Consider the following data:

| *Year* | *Birth rate* | | *Death rate* |
|---|---|---|---|
| 1911–1921 | 48.1 | | 35.5 |
| 1921–1931 | 46.4 | | 36.3 |
| 1931–1941 | 45.2 | | 31.2 |
| 1941–1951 | 39.9 | | 27.4 |
| 1951–1961 | 41.7 | | 22.8 |
| 1961–1971 | 41.1 | | 18.9 |
| 1971–1998 | 37.1 | | 14.8 |

For which period was the natural growth rate maximum?

(a) 1911–1921 (b) 1941–1951
(c) 1961–1971 (d) 1971–1981

**35.** If for a sample data

Mean < Median < Mode then the distribution is

(a) symmetric
(b) skewed to the right
(c) neither symmetric nor skewed
(d) skewed to the left

## Answers of Exercise Set D

| | | | | | | |
|---|---|---|---|---|---|---|
| **1.** (b) | **6.** (d) | **11.** (b) | **16.** (c) | **21.** (d) | **26.** (d) | **31.** (b) |
| **2.** (a) | **7.** (a) | **12.** (d) | **17.** (a) | **22.** (c) | **27.** (d) | **32.** (c) |
| **3.** (a) | **8.** (b) | **13.** (c) | **18.** (c) | **23.** (a) | **28.** (a) | **33.** (a) |
| **4.** (b) | **9.** (c) | **14.** (a) | **19.** (d) | **24.** (c) | **29.** (c) | **34.** (d) |
| **5.** (b) | **10.** (d) | **15.** (c) | **20.** (a) | **25.** (c) | **30.** (c) | **35.** (d) |

## HINTS AND SOLUTIONS

***Solutions to Questions 1 to 3:***

The following table would emerge in this situation:

| | Total | Male | Female |
|---|---|---|---|
| Overall | 2878 | 1652 | 1226 |
| Voted Against | 1226 | 796 | 430 |
| Voted For | 1425 | 825 | 600 |
| Undecided | 227 | 31 | 196 |

Based on this the answers are:

1. Option (b). 600
2. Option (a). 31
3. Option (a). 430
4. It can be seen that A is winning the race because his distance (seen on the x-axis) reaches 30 km in least time. It can also be seen that initially B is ahead of A and gets overtaken by A at the 25 km mark. Thus both statements 1 and 2 are correct. Option (b) is the right answer.
5. In Test II, the average marks is 60 and range of marks is 45–75, so his 74 marks is nearly the best in Test II.
6. The graph depends on the expression $xy$ = constant and hence option (d) is correct.
7. Car A maintains the highest speed. The cost per km of hiring would be calculated as 6 + 40/(fuel consumption per liter). Thus, for Car A, the cost per km of travel is 6 +40/8 = 11. With this cost per km of travel you would need to divide the total cost (as per the amount paid) in order to calculate the number of kms traveled by car A. Thus, Car A travels 2120/11 = 192.7 kms approx. Since, this travel has been done by Car A in 20 hours, it would mean car A's average speed is 192.7/20 = 9.6 kmph approximately. If you go through the same calculations for Cars B,C and D you would realise that the average speeds for these cars come out as lower than 9 for each of B,C and D. Hence, car A had the highest average speed.
8. In 1996 , the average profit of A and B is same.
9. In 1998 , average profit of A = 3400 and average profit of B = 4000

   Difference = 4000 – 3400 = +600
10. In 2000, average profit of A = ₹6000

    In 1999, average profit of A = ₹4000

    => required difference = ₹2000
11. Non–decreasing
12. Mean aggregate of A = $\frac{\text{total marks obtained}}{\text{maximum marks}} \times 100\% = \frac{210}{350} \times 100\% = 60\%$

    Mean aggregate of B = $\frac{\text{total marks obtained}}{\text{maximum marks}} \times 100 = \frac{225}{375} = 60\%$

    Required difference = 0
13. Consider each option and check with given data,

    (a) 20 + 5% = 21.5

    (b) 1010 + 10% =1111 ---- +10% = 1222 ≠ 1225 (as given)

    (c) $\frac{1010}{20}, \frac{1111}{21}, \frac{1225}{22}, \frac{1345}{23}$

    are all greater than 50, so it is true.
14. Visually you can interpret this as the average earnings of A are greater than the average earnings of B. Hence, option (a) is correct.
15. As is seen from the graph in the question, the only conclusion which is possible is that the price was between 10 and 20 in the year 1990
16. A = 50% of 20,000 = ₹10,000

    B = 10% of 1,00,000 = ₹10,000
17. Price increases by $x$% , then

    Consumption deceases by $\times \frac{x}{100+x}$ 100%

    So, Price increases from 40 to ₹80/litre

    i.e. increases by 100%

Consumption deceases by

$$\frac{100}{100+100}\times 100\% = 50\%$$

Consumption decreases from 60 litres to 30 litres

**18.** (c)

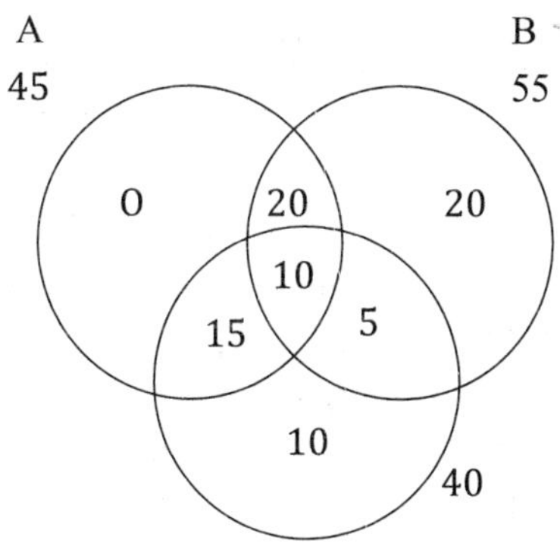


Total = 45 + 20 + 5 + 10 = 80% Not reading any magazine = 100 – 80 = 20

**19.** It can be clearly seen that for the month of September, the actual progress graph is showing a much higher progress percentage than the expected progress graph. Hence, Option (d) is clearly the correct answer.

**20.** Death rate is steeper than birth rate. So, population growth rate has increased.

**21.** Looking at the two graphs it can be made out, that statement 1 is incorrect – since, there is a difference in birth rate and death rate – hence, the population could not have stabilized from 2005 onwards (it would continue to grow). Since, the difference between birth rate and death rate has stabilized in the graph from 2005 onwards – the population growth rate would have stabilized. Hence, the statement 2 is correct. Statement 3 is incorrect – as the drop we see in the death rate in the first 10 years (1970–1980) is clearly not a 10% drop. Statement 4 is correct –as the birthrate is seen to be constant after 2005. Hence, option (d) is correct.

**22.** Option (c) is correct here, since the two graphs are exhibiting the same numbers.

**23.** From the given graphs it can be seen that when the number of pieces sold is 2000, the selling price per piece is 350, a revenue of 7 lakhs. The cost of production of 2000 pieces is also 7 lakhs. Hence, the correct answer is option (a) – 2000 pieces.

**24.** Dependency ratio can be seen by looking at the ratio of the dependents (who comprise of the <15 and the 64+ year olds in any country) to the people who fall in the 15–64 year bracket. We can consider current year as 2022. Based on this, we can see that statement (1) and (3) are correct, while statement (2) is incorrect. Hence, the correct answer would be option (c).

**25.** Raising of interest rates is a direct policy intervention in order to encourage public and private savings. Hence, option (c) is correct.

**26.** There is no co-relation between higher per capita income and higher Tele-density. Hence, the first statement is false. Similarly, the second statement is also false, as we can see cases where the GDP growth rate is lower, yet the per capita income is higher (For instance, State 7 versus State 13). Also, we can clearly see that a higher GDP growth rate does not necessarily mean a higher Tele-density. Hence, statement 3 is correct and we choose option (d) as the correct answer.

**27.** From the table it can be seen that none of the two assumptions is borne out. Hence, option (d) is correct.

**28.** The inference in statement (1) is correct, since it is quite evident that the direct taxes (corporate tax and personal income tax) combined have increased their percentage share of total tax revenue. The inference in statement (2) cannot be made, since a lower percentage collected as tax revenue doesn't necessarily mean that the value of the excise duty collected has come down. Hence, only (1) is correct and option (a) is the correct answer.

**29.** In January, the difference between Sheet steel and Coil steel is 10 (thousand tons), in February this difference is 6 and in March it is 3. Thus, the total difference (in thousand tons) = 10 + 6 + 3 = 19. Option (c)

**30.** Total imports of Sheet steel = 40 + 37 + 36 + 36 + 34 + 34 = 217000 tons. Total cost = 217 × 256 = 55552. Option (c) is closest and hence would be correct.

***Note:*** The actual answer is in thousands of dollars – while the options fail to mention the same – clearly an error in the paper. However, you should still mark option (c) since, its an obvious oversight.

**31.** The ratio is 113:97 – which is closest to 1.2:1. Option (b) is correct.

**32.** In the figure it can be seen that the vehicle B is traveling at a constant speed. If we assume that speed to be 60 kmph, then the speed of Vehicle A would have gone up from 0 to 90 (Since, $\frac{1}{12}$, if LD = 60, PD = 30 and LP = 90) A's average speed for the time would be $\frac{0+90}{2} = 45$.

Since, the speed ratio would be 3 : 4, the distance ratio would also be 3 : 4 (since the time is constant. Option (c) is correct.

**33.** Using weighted averages and the concept of alligations, we can make out from the marks in English, that the number of students would be 4 : 1 (girls to boys). The required average for Hindi (given as $x$) in the table, would be the weighted average of 7 and 8, in the ratio 1 : 4.

The answer would be got by: $\frac{4 \times 8 + 1 \times 7}{4+1} =$ 7.8. Option (a) is correct.

**34.** The natural growth rate can be seen as the difference between the birth rate and the death rate. It is maximum for 1971-1981. Option (d) is correct.

**35.** In a perfectly symmetric data distribution the mean= median = mode . This is represented by a perfect bell shaped curve .

Mean represents the average value , median the value dividing the data range into two equal parts and mode the peak value of the graph .

Where the mean is less than the median which is less than the mode, then the peak is towards the higher value side of the graph or towards the right side, while a longer tail is there towards the lower side or the left side. Hence the graph would be skewed towards left .

To summarize, generally if the distribution of data is skewed to the left, the mean is less than the median, which is often less than the mode. If the distribution of data is skewed to the right, the mode is often less than the median, which is less than the mean.

## Exercise Set E

**1.** A person climbs a hill in a straight path from point '$O$' on the ground in the direction of north-east and reaches a point '$A$' after travelling a distance of 5 km. Then, from the point '$A$' he moves to point '$B$' in the direction of north-west. Let the distance $AB$ be 12 km. Now, how far is the person away from the starting point '$O$'?

(a) 7 km (b) 13 km
(c) 17 km (d) 11 km

**2.** An agricultural field is in the forms of a rectangle having length $X_1$ meters and breadth $X_2$ meters ($X_1$ and $X_2$ are variable). If $X_1 + X_2 =$ 40 meters, then the area of the agricultural field will not exceed which one of the following values?

(a) 400 sq m (b) 300 sq m
(c) 200 sq m (d) 80 sq m

**3.** The sum of the ages of 5 members comprising a family, 3 years ago was 80 years. The average age of the family today is the same as it was 3 years ago, because of an addition of a baby during the intervening period. How old is the baby?

(a) 6 months
(b) 1 year
(c) 2 years
(d) 2 years and 6 months

**4.** The total emoluments of two persons are the same, but one gets allowances to the extent of 65% of his basic pay and the other gets allowances to the extent of extent of 80% of his basic pay. The ratio of the basic pay of the former to the basic pay of the latter is:

(a) 16 : 13 (b) 5 : 4
(c) 7 : 5 (d) 12 : 11

**5.** A person is standing on the first step from the bottom of a ladder. If he has to climb 4 more steps to reach exactly the middle step, how many steps does the ladder have?

(a) 8 (b) 9
(c) 10 (d) 11

**6.** AB is a vertical trunk of a huge tree with A being the point where the base of the trunk touches the ground. Due to a cyclone, the trunk has been broken at C which is at a height of 12 meters, broken part is partially attached to the vertical portion of the trunk at C. If the end of the broken part B touches the ground at D which is at a distance of 5 meters from A, then the original height of the trunk is:

(a) 20 m (b) 25 m
(c) 30 m (d) 35 m

**7.** A person walks 12 km due north, then 15 km due east, after that 19 km due west and then 15 km due south. How far is he from the starting point?

(a) 5 km (b) 9 km
(c) 37 km (d) 61 km

**8.** Ram and Shyam work on a job together for four days and complete 60% of it. Ram takes leave then and Shyam works for eight more days to complete the job. How long would Ram take to complete the entire job alone?

(a) 6 days (b) 8 days
(c) 10 days (d) 11 days

**9.** If R and S are different integers both divisible by 5, then which of the following is ***not necessarily true***?

(a) R – S is divisible by 5
(b) R + S is divisible by 10
(c) R × S is divisible by 25
(d) $R^2 + S^2$ is divisible by 5

**10.** How many numbers are there between 100 and 300 which either begin with or end with 2?

(a) 110 (b) 111
(c) 112 (d) None of the above

**11.** Four-digit numbers are to be formed using the digits 1, 2, 3 and 4; and none of these four digits are repeated in any manner. Further,

1. 2 and 3 are not to immediately follow each other
2. 1 is not to be immediately followed by 3

3. 4 is not to appear at the last place
4. I is not to appear at the first place

How many different numbers can be formed?

(a) 6 (b) 8
(c) 9 (d) None of the above

**12.** A cylindrical overhead tank of radius 2 m and height 7 m is to be filled from an underground tank of size 5.5 m × 4 m × 6 m. How much portion of the underground tank is still filled with water after filling the overhead tank completely?

(a) $\frac{1}{3}$ (b) $\frac{1}{2}$
(c) $\frac{1}{4}$ (d) $\frac{1}{6}$

**13.** In a class of 60 students, where the number of girls is twice that of boys, Kamal, a boy, ranked seventeenth from the top. If there are 9 girls ahead of Kamal, the number of boys in rank after him is:

(a) 13 (b) 12
(c) 7 (d) 3

**14.** *A* and *B* walk around a circular park. They start at 8 a.m. from the same point in the opposite directions. *A* and *B* walk at a speed of 2 rounds per hour and 3 rounds per hour respectively. How many times shall they cross each other after 8.00 a.m. and before 9.30. a.m.?

(a) 7 (b) 6
(c) 5 (d) 8

**15.** W can do 25% of a work in 30 days, X can do $\frac{1}{4}$ of the work in 10 days, Y can do 40% of the work in 40 days and *Z* can do $\frac{1}{3}$ of the work in 13 days. Who will complete the work first?

(a) *W* (b) *X*
(c) *Y* (d) *Z*

**16.** The average monthly income of a person in a certain family of 5 is ₹10,000. What will be the average monthly income of a person in the same family if the income of one person increased by ₹1,20,000 per year?

(a) ₹12,000 (b) ₹16,000
(c) ₹20,000 (d) ₹34,000

**17.** In a race, a competitor has to collect 6 apples which are kept in a straight line on a track and a bucket is placed at the beginning of the track which is a starting point. The condition is that the competitor can pick only one apple at a time, run back with it and drop it in the bucket. If he has to drop all the apples in the bucket, how much total distance he has to run if the bucket is 5 meters from the first apple and all other apples are placed 3 meters apart?

(a) 40 m (b) 50 m
(c) 75 m (d) 150 m

**18.** A round archery target of diameter 1 m is marked with four scoring regions from the centre outwards as red, blue, yellow and white. The radius of the red band is 0.20 m. The width of all the remaining bands is equal. If archers throw arrows towards the target, what is the probability that the arrows fall in the red region of the archery target?

(a) 0.40 (b) 0.20
(c) 0.16 (d) 0.04

**19.** A person allows a 10% discount for cash payment from the marked price of a toy and still be makes a 10% gain. What is the cost price of the toy which is marked ₹770?

(a) ₹610 (b) ₹620
(c) ₹630 (d) ₹640

**20.** A person *X* was driving in a place where all roads ran either north-south or east-west, forming a grid. Roads are at a distance of 1 km from each other in a parallel. He started at the intersection of two roads, drove 3 km north, 3 km west and 4 km south. Which further route could bring him back to his starting point, if the same is not repeated?

(a) 3 km east, then 2 km south
(b) 3 km east, then 1 km north
(c) 1 km north, then 2 km west
(d) 3 km south, then 1 km north

**21.** There are some nectar-filled flowers on a tree and some bees are hovering on it. If one bee lands on each flower, one bee will be left out. It two bees land on each flower, one flower will be left out. The number of flowers and bees respectively are:

(a) 2 and 4 (b) 3 and 2
(c) 3 and 4 (d) 4 and 3

**22.** There is an order of 19000 quantity of a particular product from a customer. The firm produces 1000 quantity of the product per day out of which 5% are unfit for sale. In how many days will the order be completed?

(a) 18 (b) 19
(c) 20 (d) 22

**23.** A class starts at 11:00 am and lasts till 2:27 pm. Four periods of equal duration are held during this interval. After every period, a rest of 5 minutes is given to the students. The exact duration of each period is:

(a) 48 minutes (b) 50 minutes
(c) 51 minutes (d) 53 minutes

**24.** Four friends *A*, *B*, *C* and *D* need to cross a bridge. A maximum of two persons can cross it at a time. It is night and they just have one lamp. Persons that cross the bridge must carry the lamp to find the way. A pair must walk together at the speed of slower person. After crossing the bridge, the person having faster speed in the pair will return with the lamp each time to accompany another person in the group. Finally, the lamp has to be returned at the original place and the person who returns the lamp has to cross the bridge again without lamp. To cross the bridge, the time taken by them is as follows: A: 1 minute, B: 2 minutes, C: 7 minutes and D: 10 minutes. What is the total minimum time required by all the friends to cross the bridge?

(a) 23 minutes (b) 22 minutes
(c) 21 minutes (d) 20 Minutes

**25.** 30 g of sugar was mixed in 180 ml water in a vessel *A*, 40 g of sugar was mixed in 280 ml of water in vessel *B* and 20 g of sugar was mixed in 100 ml of water in vessel *C*. The solution in vessel *B* is:

(a) sweeter than that in *C*
(b) sweeter than that in *A*
(c) as sweet as that in *C*
(d) less sweet than that in *C*

**26.** In aid of charity, every student in a class contributes as many rupees as the number of students in that class. With the additional contribution of ₹2 by one student only, the total collection is ₹443. Then how many students are there in the class ?

(a) 12 (b) 21
(c) 43 (d) 45

**27.** Anita's mathematics test had 70 problems carrying equal marks i.e., 10 arithmetic, 30 algebra and 30 geometry. Although she answered 70% of the arithmetic, 40% of the algebra and 60% of the geometry problems correctly, she did not pass the test because she got less than 60% marks. The number of more questions she would have to answer correctly to earn a 60% passing marks is:

(a) 1 (b) 5
(c) 7 (d) 9

**28.** In a class, there are 18 very tall boys. If these constitute three-fourths of the boys and the total number of boys is two-thirds of the total number of students in the class, what is the number of girls in the class?

(a) 6 (b) 12
(c) 18 (d) 21

**29.** The monthly average salary paid to all the employees of a company was ₹5000. The monthly average salary paid to male and female employees was ₹5200 and ₹4200 respectively. Then the percentage of males employed in the company is:

(a) 75% (b) 80%
(c) 85% (d) 90%

**30.** Two numbers X and Y are respectively 20% and 28% less than a third number Z. By what percentage is the number Y less than the number X?

(a) 12% (b) 10%
(c) 9% (d) 8%

31. A daily train is to be introduced between station *A* and station *B* starting from each end at 6 AM and the journey is to be completed in 42 hours. What is the number of trains needed in order to maintain the shuttle service?
(a) 2 (b) 3
(c) 4 (d) 7

32. A piece of tin is in the from of a rectangle having length 12 cm and width 8 cm. This is used to construct a closed cube. The side of the cube is:
(a) 2 cm (b) 3 cm
(c) 4 cm (d) 6 cm

33. In a question paper there are five questions to be attempted and answer to each question has two choices – True (T) or False (F). It is given that no two candidates have given the answers to the five questions in an identical sequence. For this to happen the maximum number of candidates is:
(a) 10 (b) 18
(c) 26 (d) 32

34. If second and fourth Saturdays and all the Sundays are taken as only holidays for an office, what would be the minimum number of possible working days of any month of any year?
(a) 23 (b) 22
(c) 21 (d) 20

35. If there is a policy that 1/3rd of a population of a community has migrated every year from one place to some other place, what is the leftover population of that community after the sixth year, if there is no further growth in the population during this period?
(a) 16/243$^{rd}$ part of the population
(b) 32/243$^{rd}$ part of the population
(c) 32/729$^{th}$ part of the population
(d) 64/ 729$^{th}$ part of the population

36. The sum of income of A and B is more than that of C and D taken together. The sum of income of A and C is the same as that of B and D taken together. Moreover, A earns half as much as the sum of the income of B and D. Whose income is the highest?
(a) A (b) B
(c) C (d) D

37. There are three pillars X, Y and Z of different heights. Three spiders A, D and C start to climb on these pillars simultaneously. In one chance, A climbs on X by 6 cm but slips down 1 cm. B climbs on Y by 7 cm but slips down 3 cm. C climbs on Z by 6.5 cm but slips down 2 cm. If each of them requires 40 chances to reach the top of the pillars, what is the height of the shortest pillar?
(a) 161 cm (b) 163 cm
(c) 182 cm (d) 210 cm

38. 15 students failed in a class of 52. After removing the names of failed students, a merit order list has been prepared in which the position of Ramesh is 22$^{nd}$ from the top. What is his position from the bottom?
(a) 18$^{th}$ (b) 17$^{th}$
(c) 16$^{th}$ (d) 15$^{th}$

39. Gopal bought a cell phone and sold it to Ram at 10% profit. Then Ram wanted to sell it back to Gopal at 10% loss. What will be Gopal's position if he agreed?
(a) Neither loss nor gain
(b) Loss 1%
(c) Gain 1%
(d) Gain 0.5%

40. Suppose the average weight of 9 persons is 50 kg. The average weight of the first 5 persons is 45 kg, whereas the average weight of the last 5 persons is 55 kg. Then the weight of the 5th person will be
(a) 45 kg (b) 47.5 kg
(c) 50 kg (d) 52.5 kg

41. P = (40% of A) + (65% of B) and Q = (50% of A) + (50% of B), where A is greater than B.
In this context, which of the following statements is correct?
(a) P is greater than Q.
(b) Q is greater than P.
(c) P is equal to Q.
(d) None of the above can be concluded with certainty.

**42.** A watch loses 2 minutes in every 24 hours while another watch gains 2 minutes in every 24 hours. At a particular instant, the two watches showed an identical time. Which of the following statements is correct if 24-hour clock is followed?

(a) The two watches show the identical time again on completion of 30 days.

(b) The two watches show the identical time again on completion of 90 days.

(c) The two watches show the identical time again on completion of 120 days.

(d) None of the above statements is correct.

**43.** In a city, 12% of households earn less than ₹30,000 per year, 6% households earn more than. ₹2,00,000 per year, 22% households earn more than ₹1,00,000 per year and 990 households earn between ₹30,000 and ₹1,00,000 per year. How many households earn between ₹1,00,000 and ₹2,00,000 per year?

(a) 250 (b) 240

(c) 230 (d) 225

**44.** A clock strikes once at 1 o'clock, twice at 2 o'clock and thrice at 3 o'clock, and so on. If it takes 12 seconds to strike at 5 o'clock, what is the time taken by it to strike at 10 o'clock?

(a) 20 seconds (b) 27 seconds

(c) 28 seconds (d) 30 seconds

**45.** There are thirteen 2-digit consecutive odd numbers. If 39 is the mean of the first five such numbers, then what is the mean of all the thirteen numbers?

(a) 47 (b) 49

(c) 51 (d) 45

**46.** Six boys A, B, C, D, E and F play a game of cards. Each has a pack of 10 cards. F borrows 2 cards from A and gives away 5 to C who in turn gives 3 to B while B gives 6 to D who passes on 1 to E. Then the number of cards possessed by D and E is equal to the number of cards possessed by

(a) A, B and C (b) B, C and F

(c) A, B and F (d) A, C and F

**47.** There is a milk sample with 50% water in it. If 1/3rd of this milk is added to equal amount of pure milk, then water in the new mixture will fall down to

(a) 25% (b) 30%

(c) 35% (d) 40%

**48.** A freight train left Delhi for Mumbai at an average speed of 40 km/hr. Two hours later, an express train left Delhi for Mumbai, following the freight train on a parallel track at an average speed of 60 km/hr. How far from Delhi would the express train meet the freight train?

(a) 480 km (b) 260 km

(c) 240 km (d) 120 km

**49.** In a test, Randhir obtained more marks than the total marks obtained by Kunal and Debu. The total marks obtained by Kunal and Shankar are more than those of Randhir. Sonal obtained more marks than Shankar. Neha obtained more marks than Randhir. Who amongst them obtained highest marks?

(a) Randhir (b) Neha

(c) Sonal (d) Data are inadequate

**50.** Certain 3-digit numbers have the following characteristics:

1. All the three digits are different.
2. The number is divisible by 7.
3. The number 611 reversing the digits is also divisible by 7.

How many such 3-digit numbers are there?

(a) 2 (b) 4

(c) 6 (d) 8

**51.** How many numbers are there between 99 and 1000 such that the digit 8 occupies the units place?

(a) 64 (b) 80

(c) 90 (d) 104

**52.** The age of Mr. X last year was the square of a number and it would be the cube of a number next year. What is the least number of years he must wait for his age to become the cube of a number again?

(a) 42 (b) 38

(c) 25 (d) 16

**53.** P works thrice as fast as Q, whereas P and Q together can work four times as fast as R. If P, Q and R together work on a job, in what ratio should they share the earnings?

(a) 3 : 1 : 1 (b) 3 : 2 : 4
(c) 4 : 3 : 4 (d) 3 : 1 : 4

**54.** A bag contains 20 balls. 8 balls are green, 7 are white and 5 are red. What is the minimum number of balls that must be picked up from the bag blindfolded (without replacing any of it) to be assured of picking at least one ball of each colour?

(a) 17 (b) 16
(c) 13 (d) 11

**55.** If 2 boys and 2 girls are to be arranged in a row so that the girls are not next to each other, how many possible arrangements are there?

(a) 3 (b) 6
(c) 12 (d) 24

**56.** A 2-digit number is reversed. The larger of the two numbers is divided by the smaller one. What is the largest possible remainder?

(a) 9 (b) 27
(c) 36 (d) 45

**57.** The monthly incomes of X and Y are in the ratio of 4 : 3 and their monthly expenses are in the ratio of 3 : 2. However, each saves ₹6,000 per month. What is their total monthly income?

(a) ₹28,000 (b) ₹42,000
(c) ₹56,000 (d) ₹84,000

**58.** Two walls and a ceiling of a room meet at right angles at a point P. A fly is in the air 1 m from one wall, 8 m from the other wall and 9 m from the point P. How many meters is the fly from the ceiling?

(a) 4 (b) 6
(c) 12 (d) 15

**59.** There are certain 2-digit numbers. The difference between the number and the one obtained on revers- ing it is always 27. How many such maximum 2-digit numbers are there?

(a) 3 (b) 4
(c) 5 (d) None of the above

**60.** What is the total number of digits printed, if a book containing 150 pages is to be numbered from 1 to 150?

(a) 262 (b) 342
(c) 360 (d) 450

## Answers of Exercise Set E

| | | | | | |
|---|---|---|---|---|---|
| **1.** (b) | **11.** (a) | **21.** (c) | **31.** (c) | **41.** (d) | **51.** (c) |
| **2.** (a) | **12.** (a) | **22.** (c) | **32.** (c) | **42.** (d) | **52.** (b) |
| **3.** (b) | **13.** (b) | **23.** (a) | **33.** (d) | **43.** (b) | **53.** (a) |
| **4.** (d) | **14.** (a) | **24.** (a) | **34.** (b) | **44.** (b) | **54.** (b) |
| **5.** (b) | **15.** (d) | **25.** (d) | **35.** (d) | **45.** (a) | **55.** (c) |
| **6.** (b) | **16.** (c) | **26.** (b) | **36.** (b) | **46.** (b) | **56.** (d) |
| **7.** (a) | **17.** (d) | **27.** (b) | **37.** (b) | **47.** (a) | **57.** (b) |
| **8.** (c) | **18.** (c) | **28.** (b) | **38.** (c) | **48.** (c) | **58.** (a) |
| **9.** (b) | **19.** (c) | **29.** (b) | **39.** (c) | **49.** (d) | **59.** (d) |
| **10.** (a) | **20.** (b) | **30.** (b) | **40.** (c) | **50.** (b) | **60.** (b) |

## HINTS AND SOLUTIONS

1. The required solution is based on the Pythagoras theorem as can be seen in the figure below: When he goes North-East (O to A) and then turns to North-West (A-B), he will make a 90 degree angle. The required answer is 13.

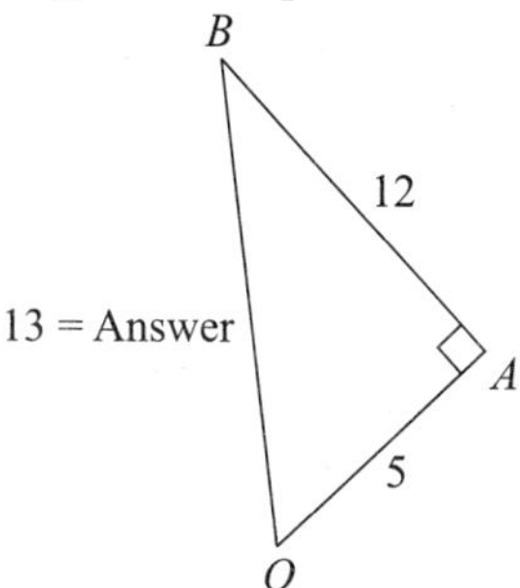


2. Given length = $x_1$ m and breadth = $x_2$ m and $x_1 + x_2 = 40$, where $x_1$ and $x_2$ are variables. It is known that of all the rectangles, a square has the largest area. So, $x_1 = x_2$.

   Since $x_1 + x_2 = 40$, so $x_1 = x_2 = 20$ m.

   Maximum area of the rectangle = $x_1 x_2 = 20 \times 20 = 400$

3. Let $a_1$, $a_2$, $a_3$, $a_4$ and $a_5$ be the present ages of the family comprising 5 members, then 3 years ago,

   $(a_1 + a_2 + a_3 + a_4 + a_5) - 3 \times 5 = 80 \qquad (1)$

   Let the age of new born baby be $a_6$, then, given that average age of family 3 years ago = average age of family today

$$\Rightarrow \frac{(a_1 + a_2 + a_3 + a_4 + a_5) - 15}{5}$$

$$= \frac{a_1 + a_2 + a_3 + a_4 + a_5 + a_6}{6}$$

   $\Rightarrow a_6 = 1$ $\qquad \therefore$ Baby's age = 1 year.

4. Let the basic pay of the first person be ₹$x$ and that of the second person be ₹$y$, then emolument of first person = emolument of second person.

$$x + 0.65\,x = y + 0.8\,y.$$

$$\frac{x}{y} = \frac{1.8}{1.65} = \frac{12}{11}$$

5. The information provided in the question tells us that he will need to take 4 more steps to get to the middle rung of the ladder. This means that he would be on the middle rung when he reaches the fifth step. If the fifth step is the middle step, it means that there would be 9 steps on the ladder.

**Solutions to 6 to 8:**

Based on the information in the question, we can make the following starting table for the solution.

| Person | A | B | C |
|---|---|---|---|
| Garment | Tie/Jacket/ Sweater | Tie/Jacket/ Sweater | Tie/Jacket/ Sweater |
| Colour | Blue/White/ Black | Blue/White/ Black | Blue/White/ Black |
| Surname | Ribeiro/ Kumar/ Singh | Ribeiro/ Kumar/ Singh | Ribeiro/ Kumar/ Singh |

We now start to use the clues in order to start deducing the reactions.

Using the first and second clue we know that:

C wore a tie;

The sweater was white &

Ribiero did not wear a white sweater

B did not wear a white sweater

We can use this information to modify our table

| Person | A | B | C |
|---|---|---|---|
| Garment | Jacket/ Sweater | Jacket/ Sweater | Tie |
| Colour | Blue/White/ Black | Blue/White/ Black | Blue/White/ Black |
| Surname | Ribiero/ Kumar/ Singh | Ribiero/ Kumar/ Singh | Ribiero/ Kumar/ Singh |

The following deductions have not been used on the table till now:

[The sweater was white; Ribeiro did not wear a white sweater → Ribeiro Black or Blue; B did not wear a white sweater]

But we do know that Sweater and White have to go together to either A or B. When we add the information from clues 3 to 5, we can see that:

Singh is not wearing the white sweater → So Singh is Jacket or tie → Also Singh = Blue or Black Kumar doesn't wear a jacket → Kumar = Sweater or Tie

Ribeiro does not like to wear black → Ribeiro = Blue & Since Ribeiro is Blue we can modify Singh to Black. This also means that Kumar wears white.

The table transforms to:

| Person | A | B | C |
|---|---|---|---|
| Garment | Sweater | Jacket | Tie |
| Surname & Colour | Kumar – White | Ribeiro- Blue OR Singh- Black | Singh- Black OR Ribeiro- Blue |

We can then try to answer the questions:

6. Truck $AB$ is broken at $C$ and $CD$ is the broken part touching the ground at $D$,

$\therefore$ $AB = AC + CD$.

$ACD$ is a right triangle, so using Pythagoras theorems

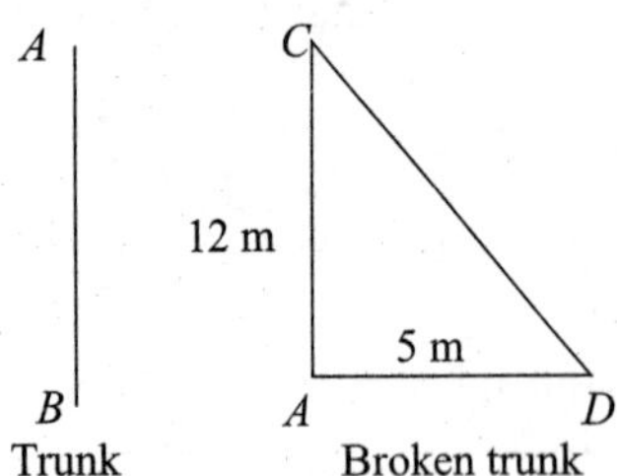


$$CD^2 = AC^2 + AD^2 = 12^2 + 5^2 = 169.$$

$$\therefore\ CD = \sqrt{169} = 13 \text{ m}.$$

$$\therefore\ AB = AC + CD = 12 + 13 = 25 \text{ m}.$$

7. Going 15 km east followed by 19 km west, would mean a net of 4 km west. The figure for the movement would look like what is shown here and hence the required distance = 5 km (Using the Pythagoras triplet of 3,4,5):

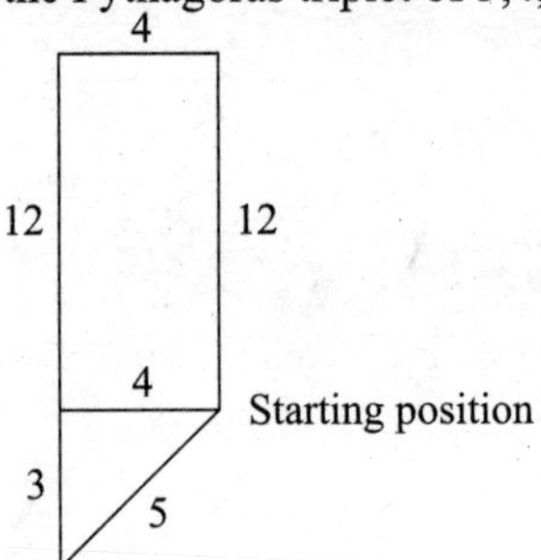


8. Let Ram and Shyam can complete the work alone in '$r$' days and '$s$' days respectively then Ram's 1 day work

$= \frac{1}{r}$, Shyam's 1 day work $= \frac{1}{5}$

So, in 4 days, $\frac{4}{r} + \frac{4}{s} = \frac{60}{100}$ (given).

$$\frac{4}{r} + \frac{4}{s} = \frac{3}{5} \quad (1)$$

For 8 days. Shyam finishes the rest 40% $= \frac{3}{5}$ of work so,

$\frac{8}{s} = \frac{2}{5} \Rightarrow s = 20.$

Putting this value in equation (1)

$\frac{4}{r} + \frac{4}{20} = \frac{3}{5} \Rightarrow r = 10$ days.

9. It is known that a number is divisible by 10 if and only if it has '0' at the unit's place.

Now, if $R = 25$, $S = 30$, $R + S$ is not divisible by 10 Hence (b) is not necessarily true.

10. From 100 – 199, there are 10 numbers ending with 2 102, 112, 122 … 192 From 200 – 300, there are 100 numbers beginning with 2, 200, 201, … 299.

Hence total required numbers = 10 + 100 = 110.

11. Meeting the constraints, the possible numbers are 2142, 2413, 3412, 3421, 4213 and 4312.

**12.** Volume of cylindrical overhead tank

$= \pi r^2 h = \frac{22}{7}(2)^2 \times 7 = 88\ m^2.$

Volume of underground tank = $(5.5 \times 4 \times 6)\ m^3$ = $132\ m^3$.

Required part of underground tank filled with water after filling overhead tank

$$= \frac{\text{vol. of underground tank} - \text{vol. of overhead tank}}{\text{volume of underground tank}}$$

$$= \frac{132 - 88}{132} = \frac{44}{132} = \frac{1}{3}$$

**13.** Let the number of boys be $x$, no. of girls = $2x$.

$\therefore$ $x + 2x = 60 \Rightarrow x = 20$.

So, no. of boys = 20 and no. of girls = 40.

No. of students behind Kamal in rank = 60 – 17 = 43.

No of girls ahead of Kamal in rank = 9.

$\therefore$ No. of boys behind Kamal in rank = (43 – 31) = 12.

**14.** Here, $A$ and $B$ are walking in opposite directions. So, relative speed = 2 + 3 = 5 rounds/hour. So, they cross each other 5 times in an hour i.e. once in 12 min so, 2 times in half an hour. Hence in between 8 am – 9.30 am i.e.

in $1\frac{1}{2}$ hr.

they cross 5 + 2 = 7 times.

**15.** $w$ can do 25% of work in 30 days

$\Rightarrow$ $w$ can do 100% work in $30 \times \frac{100}{25} = 120$ days.

$X$ can do $\frac{1}{4}$ work in 10 days

$\Rightarrow$ $X$ can do 1 work in $10 \times 4 = 40$ days.

$Y$ can do 40% of work in 40 days

$\Rightarrow$ $Y$ can do 100% work in $40 \times \frac{100}{40} = 100$ days

$Z$ can do $\frac{1}{3}$ work in 13 days

$Z$ can do 1 work in $13 \times 3 = 39$ days.

So, $Z$ will complete the work first.

**16.** Average monthly income of a person in family of 5 = ₹10,000

$\therefore$ Monthly income of the family = 5 × 10,000 = ₹50,000

After increment,

Increase in monthly income of one person

$= \frac{1,20,000}{12} = 10,000$

Now, Average monthly income of a person in family of 5

= 10,000 + 10,000 = 20,000

**17.**

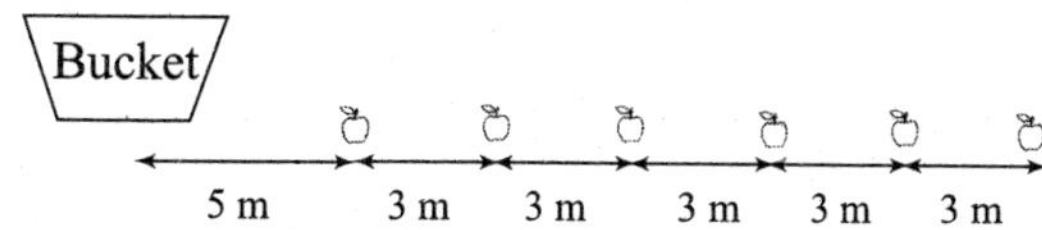


Distances covered by the competitor while collecting

I[st] apple: 2 (5) = 10 m.

2[nd] apple: 2 (5 + 3) = 16 m.

3[rd] apple: 2 (5 + 2 × 3) = 22 m.

4[th] apple: 2 (5 + 3 × 3) = 28 m.

5[th] apple: 2 (5 + 4 × 3) = 34 m.

6[th] apple: 2 (5 + 5 × 3) = 40 m.

Total distance covered = 10 + 16 + 22 + 28 + 34 + 40 = 150 m.

**18.** Area of a circle = $\pi r^2$

Red band area = $\pi(0.2)^2 = 0.04\pi$

Except Red, all the bands are rings.

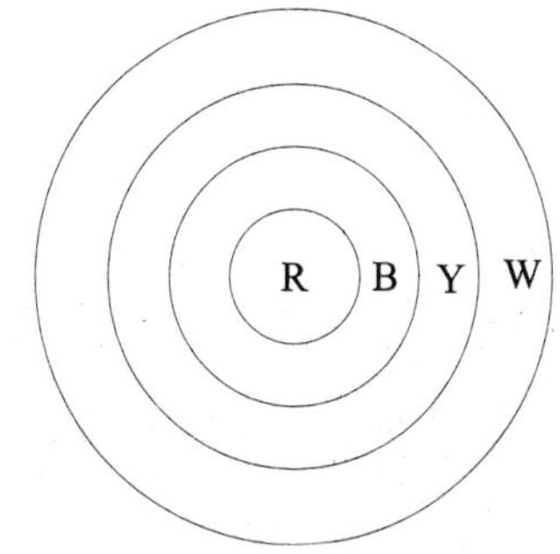

Area of ring = $\pi(R^2 - r^2)$

Blue band area = $\pi\,[(.3)^2 - (0.2)^2] = 0.05\pi$

Yellow band area = $0.07\pi$.

White band area = $0.09\pi$.

Required probability

$$= \frac{0.04\pi}{(0.04+0.05+0.07+0.09)\pi} = 0.16.$$

**19.** Marked price (MP) of toy = ₹770

Discount = 10% of MP = $\frac{10}{100} \times 770 = 77$

Price after discount = (770 – 77) = 693

Let CP of toy be ₹$x$; then, as per question

$693 - x = \frac{10}{100}$ of $x \Rightarrow x = 630$.

∴ cost price of the toy = ₹630

**20.** Option (b) can be seen to be clearly correct from the figure.

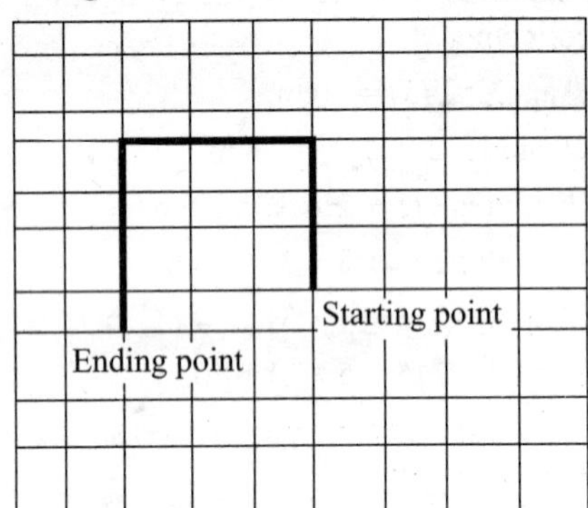


**21.** Let the number of flowers = $f$ and the number of bees = $b$

from given conditions we get-

$b = f + 1$

$(b/2) + 1 = f$

Solving we get $f = 3$; $b = 4$

**22.** Everyday a firm produces 1000 products of which 50 are unfit and 950 are fit.

To complete order the firm will take 19000/950 = 20 days

**23.** Class starts at 11.00 am and ends at 2.27 pm.

Duration of class = 2.27 pm – 11 am = 3 hr 27 min = 207 min.

There will be 4 periods. After every period, there will be a 5 min. break. Hence there will be 3 breaks in between.

Duration of periods = 207 – (3 × 5) = 192 min

Time for each period = $\frac{192}{4}$ = 48 min.

**24.** Here, $A$ takes the shortest time to cross the bridge i.e. 1 min and $D$ takes 10 min. $C$ takes 7 min. and $B$ takes 2 min. to cross the bridge.

All 4 friends, $A$, $B$, $C$ and $D$ can cross the bridge in minimum time in the following ways.

(a) $A + B$ crossing and $A$ returning – (2 + 1) min = 3 min

(b) $A + C$ crossing and $A$ returning – (7 + 1) min = 8 min

(c) $A + D$ crossing and $A$ returning – (10 + 1) min = 11 min

(d) A crossing the bridge for the last time – 1 min = 1 min

Hence total minimum time = 3 + 8 + 11 + 1 = 23 min.

**25.** Here sugar (in gm.) is mixed in water (in ml.).

So, sweetness-concentration of sugar = $\frac{\text{gm}}{\text{ml}}$

| Vessel A | Vessel B | Vessel C |
|---|---|---|
| conc. of sugar | conc. of sugar | conc. of sugar |
| $= \frac{30}{180} = \frac{1}{6}$ g/ml | $= \frac{40}{280} = \frac{1}{7}$ gm/ml | $= \frac{20}{100} = \frac{1}{5}$ gm/ml |

More the conc., more the sweetness. So, in terms of sweetness, $C > A > B$.

**26.** Let the no. of students = $x$.

Total collection (without considering the dl. contribution)

= 443 – 2 = 441.

$\Rightarrow x \times x = 441 \Rightarrow x = 21$.

**27.** No. of questions answered correctly by Anita is

Arithmetic = 70% of 10 = 7.

Algebra = 40% of 30 = 12.

Geometry = 60% of 30 = 18.

∴ Total questions correctly answered = 7 + 12 + 18 = 37

Anita had to attempt 60% of 70 questions i.e. 42 questions correctly to pass the test.

Reqd. no. of more questions = 42 – 37 = 5

**28.** Here, $\frac{3}{4} \times x = 18 \Rightarrow x = 24.$, Boys = 24.

and $\frac{2}{3} \times y = 24 \Rightarrow y = 36$, total students = 36.

No. of girls = 36 – 24 = 12.

**29.** Let the number of employees = 100. and no. of male employees = $x$.

∴ no. of female employees = $100 - x$.

$$\frac{5200x + 4200(100 - x)}{100} = 5000$$

$\Rightarrow x = 80$

So, there are 80% male employees.

**30.** Let the third number be $z = 100$.

So, $x = 80$, $y = 72$.

% by which $y$ is less than $x = \frac{80 - 72}{80} \times 100$

= 10%

**31.** (c)

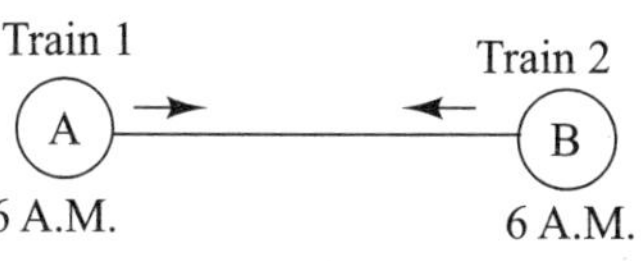


Ist day

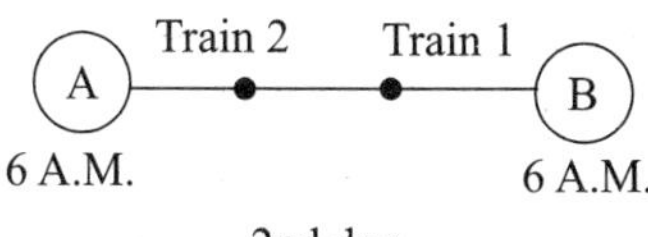


2nd day

As given in figure, train 1 leaves station $A$ at 6 AM on 1st day and train 2 leaves station B at 6 AM. Both the trains do not reach their destination on 2nd day after 24 hrs. as journey completes in 42 hrs. So, one additional train from each station $A$ and $B$ are to start at 6 AM on 2nd day.

Hence total 4 trains are needed.

**32.** Area of rectangle = 12 × 8 = 96 cm$^2$.

Rectangle is used to construct a closed cube.

Surface area of cube formed = Area of given rectangle

$6(\text{side})^2 = 96 \Rightarrow$ side = 4 cm.

**33.** There are 5 questions and each question has two options—True or False.

| 2 | 2 | 2 | 2 | 2 |
|---|---|---|---|---|

Hence each question can be filled with 2 choices.

Reqd no. of candidates = 2 × 2 × 2 × 2 × 2 = 32

**34.** If we consider the month of February, having either 28 or 29 days with the 1[st] of the month being a Sunday, we would get 28 – 4 – 2 = 22 or 29 –5 – 2 = 22 working days. This is the minimum possible.

**35.** Population after 6 years

$$= \frac{2}{3} \times \frac{2}{3} \times \frac{2}{3} \times \frac{2}{3} \times \frac{2}{3} \times \frac{2}{3} = \frac{64}{729}$$

of the population

**36.** A + B > C + D, A + C = B + D

and $A = \frac{B + D}{2}$ => B + D = 2A

∴ A + C = 2A => A = C

Since A + B > C + D => B > D

**37.** The total height of the three pillars can be estimated as follows:

Pillar X = In one chance, total height gained = 6–1 = 5 cm. In 40 chances, the total height gained would have been 40 × 5 = 200. But in the last chance, the spider would climb up 6 cm and reach the top and hence, it would not slip down. Hence, the height of Pillar X = 39 × 5 + 6 = 201. Similarly the height of Pillar 2 = 4 × 39 + 7 = 163 cm (and is shorter than Pillar Z too). Hence, the height of the shortest pillar = 163 cm. Hence, option (b) is correct.

**38.** L + R – 1 = total

=> 22 + R – 1 = 37 => R = 38 – 22 = 16

**39.** Let, CP of Gopal = ₹100

with 10% profit, SP of Gopal = 1.1 × 100 = ₹110 = CP of Ram

SP of Ram = $110 \times \frac{90}{100}$ = ₹99 = CP of Gopal

Savings of Gopal = 100 – 99 = ₹1

% profit = $\frac{1}{100} \times 1 = 1\%$

**40.** Total wt. of 9 persons = 9 × 50 = 450 kg

Sum wt. of first 5 persons = 5 × 45 = 225 kg

Sum wt. of second 5 person = 5 × 55 = 275 kg

**41.** Given A > B

P – Q = ( 0.4A + 0.65B) – (0.5A +0.5 B)

= 0.15B – 0.1A

Determination of whether P-Q is > or < or = 0 we need to know as to by how much A is greater than B. As this not given, the required determination is not possible.

**42.** The two watches have a time gap of 4 min in 1 day

=> 60 mins gap in 15 days

=> 24 has gap in 15 × 24 = 360 days

**43.** Tabulating the data, we get

| Income | % | *No. of households* |
|---|---|---|
| Less than ₹30,000 | 6% | |
| 30,000–100000 | 66% | 990 |
| 100000–200000 | 16% | $x$ |
| Above 20000 | 6% | |

66 : 990 = 16 : $x$

=> $x$ = ₹240

**44.** There are 4 gaps in 5 strikes at 5'o clock. This takes 12 seconds. Therefore, each gap is of 3 seconds. At 10'o clock there are 9 gaps hence, 27 seconds would be taken.

**45.** Since the 13 numbers would form an Arithmetic Progression, it is quite clear that their mean would be the 7th number. Also, since 39 is the mean of the first five numbers, the list of the 13 consecutive odd numbers would start from 35. The list would be 35,37,39,41,43,45,47,49,51, 53,55,57,59. The mean of the thirteen numbers is 47. Hence, option (a) is correct.

**46.** The number of cards after the exchange would be as follows:
A = 10 – 2 = 8; B = 10 + 3 – 6 = 7;
C = 10 + 5 – 3 = 12; D = 10 + 6 – 1 = 15;
E = 10 + 1 = 11; F = 10 + 2 – 5 = 7. It can be seen that the number of cards possessed by D and E = 15 + 11 = 26 is the same as the number of cards possessed by B + C + F = 7 + 12 + 7 = 26. Hence, option (b) is correct.

**47.** Let part of water in new mixture = $x$

Part of water in given sample = $\frac{1}{2}$

Part of water in pure milk = 0

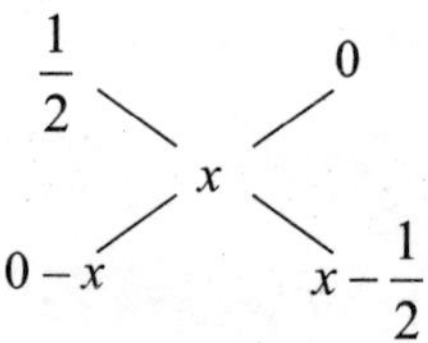

Applying, rule of alligation,

$$\frac{0-x}{x-\frac{1}{2}} = \frac{\text{quantity of sample}}{\text{quantity of pure milk}} = \frac{1}{1}$$

=> $-x = x - \frac{1}{2}$

=> $x = \frac{1}{4} = 25\%$

**48.** Let after $t$ has express trains meet the freight to distance covered by express train in $t$ hrs = distance covered by freight trains in $(t + 2)$

$t \times 60 = (t + 2) \times 40$ => $t = 4$ hr

Distance (of meet) covered by express train in 4 hr = 4 × 60 = 240 km

**49.** The data is clearly inadequate here because, we cannot determine the order of ages in this question. Hence, option (d) is correct.

**50.** 168 – 861, 259 – 952

**51.** Hundred place can be filled in 9 ways

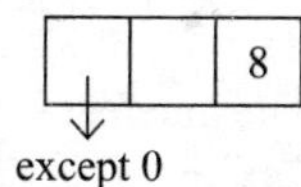


Tens place can be filled in 10 ways

**52.** Present age of Mr. X = 26 years

So, 1 years before 25 yrs and 1 vr later 27 years $= (3)^3$

Next curve years $= 4^3 = 64$

$\therefore$ No. of years to wait = 64 – 26 = 38 years

**53.** Let $Q$ does it in $x$ days.

$P$ does it in $\frac{x}{3}$ days.

$(P + Q)$'s 1 day work $= \frac{1}{x} + \frac{3}{4} = \frac{4}{x}$

R's 1 day work $= \frac{1}{4} \times \frac{4}{x} = \frac{1}{x}$

Efficiency of P : Q : R $= \frac{3}{x} : \frac{1}{x} : \frac{1}{x} = 3 : 1 : 1$

**54.** Least no. of balls to be picked = 20 – 5 + 1 = 16

**55.** 2 boys can sit in $\lfloor 2 [* B * B *]$ and 2 girls can sit in (*) in ${}^3p_2 = \lfloor 3 = 6$ ways

Required of arrangements $= \lfloor 2 \times 6 = 12$ ways

**56.** Considering 94 and 49, remainder = 45

**57.**

| | A | B |
|---|---|---|
| Income | $4x$ | $3x$ |
| Expenditure | $3y$ | $2y$ |

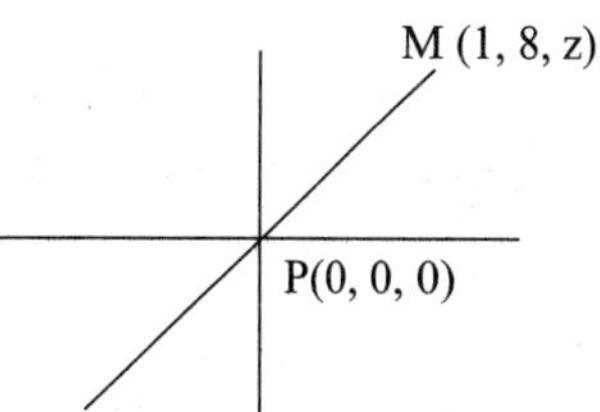


$4x - 3y = 3x \quad 2y \Rightarrow x - y$

Now, $4x - 3x = 6000 \Rightarrow x = 6000$

Total income $= 4x + 3x = 7x =$ ₹42000

**58.** As per co-ordinate axes, distance

$(PM)^2 = x^2 + y^2 + z^2$

$9^2 = 1^2 + 8^2 + 2^2$

$2^2 = 16 \Rightarrow z = 4$ m

**59.** There are more than 5 such numbers viz: 14, 41, 25, 52, 36, 63, 47, 74, 58, 85 and 69, 96. Hence, option (d) is correct.

**60.**

1 to 9 = 1 × 9 = 9

10 – 99 = 2 × 90 = 180

100 – 150 = 3 × 51 = 153

On adding these 3, we will get the total number of digits printed, which is 342.

# Logical and Analytical Reasoning

# 7

*"Reason is the life of the law."*

**—Edward Coke**

*"Genius is nothing but a greater aptitude for patience."*

**—Benjamin Franklin**

## 1. Introduction

The test of reasoning is an important part of CUET and every aptitude test. The purpose of incorporating this test in an examination is to gauge a person's intrinsic ability to understand the inherent logic in a given statement and aptitude for analysing a complex situation.

From the perspective of the examination, the questions on logical reasoning and analytical reasoning are not one and the same thing. They are distinct and separate in terms of the nature of questions, abilities and time required to tackle them. As such, separate and distinct sections have been devoted to each one of them explaining in depth the type of questions, preparation required and answering tips along with a comprehensive set of exercises. A brief idea is being given here about the nature of these questions and what to expect in the test.

### 1.1 Test of Logical Reasoning

The test of logical reasoning (argument type questions) entails **application of logic to a given statement or a 'logic stimulus' to arrive at a conclusion. The question may also require you to examine, whether the drawn conclusion stands the test of logical reasoning or not.** For instance, consider the following statement and the conclusion drawn.

*A patriot is not a coward. Hari is a patriot. As such, he is not a coward.*

The statements have two assertions: (a) A patriot is not a coward and (b) *Hari* is a patriot. This is followed by the conclusion, "*Hari* is not a coward", which is in logical consonance with the two assertions. Let us consider another example.

*Some men are brave. Ram is a man. As such, Ram is brave.*

The conclusion drawn here is clearly not in logical consonance with the statements. The statement mentions "Some men are brave and Ram is a man." Ram may fall in the category of the brave men or he may not. As such, it is not logically correct to draw a conclusion that Ram indeed is brave. Thus, questions of this section primarily test the understanding of logic although the way in which it will be tested will vary from question to question.

### 1.2 Questions on Analytical Reasoning

**The questions on analytical reasoning on the other hand entail a given matrix of conditions or constraints, to which, by means of deductions and analytical reasoning, the desired solution is to be arrived at.** These are at times also referred as analytical reasoning game questions. Consider the following example:

*Four friends, A, B, C, D, participated in a race. A did not come first. B did not come last. C was ahead of D and D was not last. Who came last?*

The question contains certain given conditions. These provide the rules governing the question. Analytical reasoning has to be applied to the given conditions. The question itself says that B and D were not last. Therefore, we deduce that either A or C would be last. It also says that C was ahead of D who was not last. Therefore, C could not have been last. As such, we infer that only A can be last.

### 1.3 What to Expect in the Examination

The logical reasoning questions should typically take around a minute and a half to two minutes to solve. The analytical reasoning questions on the other hand are more time consuming. Each question has a constraint matrix—a statement of a few lines—which describes the conditions or constraints. This is followed by one or more questions items, i.e., questions requiring to deduce certain things. Each of these questions has four choices. Whole question may have 3–6 sub-parts.

One can expect questions 5 to 10 questions each from both the topics in the 75 questions which are prescribed for the section 3 or the General test.

## 2. Test of Logical Reasoning

### 2.1 Abilities to be Tested

The questions on logical reasoning (LR), test the ability of the reader to fully comprehend the import of a given statement or a concise passage. It may further require one to be a critique of the conclusion drawn, by applying the touchstone of logic and argument. This means that one has to test the logical consonance of statements and the conclusion drawn. But not necessarily all questions of 'logical reasoning' are statements and conclusion type. As seen in the illustration given earlier, some may require the reader to determine as to which statement is the logical conclusion of the others. While in certain questions there may not be any conclusion at all but may require one to examine the logical sequence of certain jumbled up statements. In some other questions, certain presumptions may be provided and a logical conclusion may be required to be drawn from them. But irrespective of the format of the question, they quintessentially test the reasoning and logical comprehension of a candidate.

### 2.2 Nature and Type of Questions

The questions on LR usually consist of three parts, a logic stimulus, a question stem and the answer choices. The logic stimulus is a statement or a concise passage, the underlying logic in which has to be comprehended. The question stem indicates what is expected of the candidate and how the logic has to be applied. In fact, the question stem specifies what the candidate is supposed to do, based on which he selects the right option from the answer choices.

There can be several types of questions depending on, whether the conclusion is a part of the logic stimulus, or it is contained in the question stem or has to be picked out from answer choices. Some of the more common question types likely to figure in the examination, are described here.

(i) **Questions where Statement and Conclusion are a Part of the Logic Stimulus**

The statement and conclusion both may be contained in the passage (i.e., the logic stimulus). In such cases, one is required to ascertain, whether the conclusion/conclusions (as more than one conclusion may be provided) is/are correct or not. Consider the following example.

**2.1 Illustration**

*Statement: All students are chemistry scholars. Some chemistry scholars are pianists.*

Conclusion: 1 *All pianists are students.*

2 *Some pianists may be chemistry scholars.*

The aforesaid statements and conclusions are both a part of the logic stimulus.

*Question stem – Which of the following option is correct about the* conclusions?

(a) *Only Conclusion 1 is correct.*

(b) *Only Conclusion 2 is correct.*

(c) *Both Conclusions 1 and 2 are correct.*

(d) *None of them is correct.*

The solution to the aforesaid question is easy to gauge. It is given that only some chemistry scholars are pianists. Therefore, all pianists cannot be chemistry scholars nor can they be students. Hence, Conclusion 1 is incorrect. Regarding Conclusion 2, it has to be understood that here the pianists form a larger set, of which some chemistry scholars are a sub-set. Hence, some pianists may be chemistry scholars. As such, Conclusion 2 is correct and the right answer would be option (b).

(ii) **Where Conclusion is a Part of the Question Stem or of the Answer Choices.**

Some questions may be such that the logic stimulus only contains a statement but no conclusion, which is either a part of the question stem or the answer choices. Consider the following example.

**2.2 Illustration**

*Statement: Statistics reveal that diseases spread by mosquito bites cause hundreds of times more deaths than what snake bites do. But we have mortal fear of snakes and not of mosquitoes.*

*Question: Which of the following conclusions is logical?*

(a) *Mosquito bite is more poisonous than snake bite.*

(b) *Mosquitoes are hundred times more in number than snakes.*

(c) *Mosquitoes on a whole are a greater hazard for humanity than snakes.*

(d) *None of the above*

Here the obvious choice is (c). The statement is neither comparing the poison in the bite of a mosquito *vis-a-vis* in that of a snake, nor is it trying to compare their absolute numbers. It is only trying to convey that which one should be treated as a greater threat to humanity.

(iii) **Finding the Correct Assumption**

There are certain questions,? which contain the statement and a conclusion but a vital assumption is missing, which is essential for the conclusion to be drawn properly. The answer choices contain the possible assumptions, the right one of which is to be picked.

**2.3 Illustration**

*Statement: Ganesh is a student of Unity International School of Laxmi Bai Nagar, New Delhi. He is in the school's basketball team, which won the inter school basketball tournament.*

*Conclusion: As such, Ganesh is more than six feet tall.*

*Question: Which is the missing assumption that enables the conclusion to be drawn properly from the statement?*

*Answer Choices:*

(a) *All members of Ganesh's family are tall.*

(b) *All students of Unity International School are tall.*

(c) *Only a student above six feet is admitted in the school's basketball team.*

(d) *Basketball requires tall players.*

The choice which best explains the conclusion is obviously (c). Although other choices too help in showing that Ganesh should be a tall boy; however, the conclusion specifies that he is more than six feet tall, which is best explained if Assumption (c) is true.

(iv) **Strengthening or Weakening of Argument**

In some LR questions, the statement and the conclusion are both contained in the logic stimulus. The question asks you to identify those assumptions from the answer choices, which strengthens/weakens the conclusion or the argument, the most. Consider the following illustration.

**2.4 Illustration**

***Logic stimulus:*** *Media report suggests that the reason for the dip in international performance of the Indian cricket team is that it is playing too much of international cricket in three different formats of the game—test cricket, ODI and T-20.*

*Question: Which of the following assumptions if true, most weakens the conclusion drawn in the statement above?*

*Answer Choices:*

(a) *The cricket team is being paid very well, which makes up for the lack of rest.*

(b) *They are getting a number of commercial endorsements.*

(c) *Expectation from the cricketers has considerably increased.*

(d) *The selectors follow a policy of rotation where the players are rested and different players are selected for the three different formats of the game.*

It is seen that Choice (a) is ineffective in weakening the conclusion. Money paid to the cricketers cannot compensate for the rest they need. Choice (b) is also not weakening the argument; rather it is providing another explanation for the poor performance. Choice (c) attacks the statement by presuming that the expectation from them has increased and the performance has not actually fallen. Option (d) is the most appropriate one. If the players are rotated, then they are getting adequate rest and the lack of it cannot, therefore, be the reason for poor performance.

(v) **Ascertaining the Logical Compatibility of Statements**

In certain questions, the logic stimulus may contain a number of statements. The question stem requires those statements to be examined and to ascertain, as to which of those statements are logically compatible or coherent with each other. Illustration of this type of question is given here:

**2.5 Illustration**

*Consider the following statements:*

1. *A cow is cattle.*
2. *No sheep is cattle.*
3. *Some cattle are goat.*
4. *No sheep is a cow.*
5. *All cattle are sheep.*

*Which of the statements mentioned above are logically compatible?*

(a) *1,2,3* (b) *1,3,4*

(c) *2,3,5* (d) *3,4,5*

Such questions are initially a bit confusing to read. But once you understand the chain of logic connecting them, you will figure out the correct choice easily. Generally, such questions incorporate a set of objects and things and its sub-sets or sub-groups. Here the question mentions about cattle and the various kinds, which comprise the larger set. This includes cows, sheep, goats, etc. The first statement, "Cow is cattle," fits in this logic. But Option (2), "No sheep is cattle" and Option (5), "All cattle are sheep" are obviously incorrect. Sheep are cattle but all cattle are not sheep. Choice (3), "Some cattle are goat" and Choice (4), "No sheep is a cow", are correct and logically compatible. As such, the correct answer would be Option (b).

(vi) **Arranging Statements in a Logical Sequence**

Some questions contain a number of statements, which are not in a chronological order. The question requires one to figure out the underlying logic and arrange the statements in a chronological order to form a logically correct concise passage. In a different question format, a concise passage followed by various choices of statements is given. One has to ascertain as to which statement should precede/succeed the paragraph in a logical manner. Consider the following example:

**2.6 Illustration**

*Sentences given in each question, when arranged in a proper sequence, form a coherent paragraph. Each sentence is labelled with a letter. Choose the most logical order of sentences from among the four given choices to construct a coherent paragraph.*

A. *In rejecting the functionalism in positivist organisation theory, either wholly or partially, there is often a move towards a political model of organisation theory.*

B. *Thus, the analysis would shift to the power resources possessed by different groups in the organisation and the way they use these resources in actual power play to shape the organisational structure.*

C. *At the extreme, in one set of writings, the growth of administrators in the organisation is held to be completely unrelated to the work to be done and to be caused totally by the political pursuit of self-interest.*

D. *The political model holds that individual interests are pursued in organisational life through the exercise of power and influence.*

*Answer Choices:*

(a) ADBC (b) CBAD

(c) DBCA (d) ABDC

Such questions require one to try the various permutations of the answer sequence to arrive at a logical and correct sequence. A shorter method is to examine the answer choices given. In the present question there are two choices beginning with part A. As such, the probability of the correct sequence beginning with part A is more. However, the other options should also be considered. The other options begin with part C and part D. However, it is noted that if the passage were to start with part C or D, then it would become abrupt and incoherent. Thus, it should begin with part A only. The only thing to be worked out is whether part D or part B should follow part A. On reading part A followed by part D and then B and C, the passage appears to be coherent and logical. As such, the right answer should be Choice (a).

Besides, the question formats illustrated above, there may be some other types of LR questions, which have a format similar to the ones discussed above or slightly different. But the thing common to all, is the requirement of **comprehension of underlying logic.**

**Syllogism and logical deductions:** Some of the question of logical reasoning can also be solved by understanding the concept of syllogism and relationship theories. Syllogisms are a kind of deductive reasoning which enable to arrive at a conclusion based on two propositions, which are asserted or are presumed to be correct. Consider the statements in the illustration below.

**2.7 Illustration**

*All test aspirants are students.*

*Raghav is a test aspirant.*

*Raghav is a student.*

The above statements are a part of syllogism where there are two assertions or premises and a conclusion. The conclusion may or may not be valid in terms of the assertions and the questions in the examination may require one to evaluate whether the conclusion flows from the statements/ assertions given. In the present example, the conclusion can rightly be drawn. Consider another example.

**2.8 Illustration**

*Some test aspirants are students.*

*Raghav is a test aspirant*

*Raghav is a student*

In this example, the conclusion being drawn **may or may not be true** in terms of the statements or assertions. Only some test aspirants are students and not all. Hence Raghav may be a student or may not be and the conclusion cannot be drawn.

**Parts of Syllogism:** Broadly the syllogisms are said to have three parts, which are the two premise and a conclusion.

*All test aspirants are students.* **Major premise**

*Raghav is a test aspirant.* **Minor Premise**

*Raghav is a student.* **Conclusion**

Each of the statement is further divided into certain distinct parts. Consider the statement. *All test aspirants are students.* The different parts of this statement are:

(a) **All:** This is referred to as to the quantifier which gives an idea of the quantity of the subject (here test aspirants) which are being described. The quantifier is usually of three types ***All, Some*** or ***No.***

(b) **Test Aspirants:** This is the subject whose quality/ features etc are being described here.

(c) **Connector/Copula**: This is the copula or the connecting word which is connecting the subject (test aspirants) and the complement/ predicate (student). The copula can be of type, **is/ are** or **is not / are not.**

(d) **Predicate**: Student is the predicate here and gives a description of the subject.

Depending on the above structure of the syllogism, there can be four broad types of syllogisms as shown in the table below.

| Type | Illustration | Quantifier | Subject | Connector | Predicate | Extent &Type |
|---|---|---|---|---|---|---|
| 1 | *All test aspirants are students* | All | test aspirants | are | Students | Universal affirmative |
| 2 | *No test aspirants are students* | No | test aspirants | are | Students | Universal negative |
| 3 | *Some test aspirants are students* | Some | test aspirants | are | Students | Particular affirmative |
| 4 | *Some test aspirants are not students* | Some | test aspirants | Are not | Students | Particular negative |

**Deduction and relationships through Venn diagrams.** The relationships described above can also be represented through diagrams where, the subjects and the predicates are represented through specific figures such as circles, triangles, rectangles etc. These diagrams are called Venn diagrams and are illustrated below.

1. ***All test aspirants are students.*** The relationship of **'universal affirmative'** is best represented by the diagram below. The outer circle represents the universal set of students and the inner circle represents the set of test aspirants which are a sub-set of the universal set. Thus, one set ( test aspirant ) is **completely inclusive** in the other set (students).

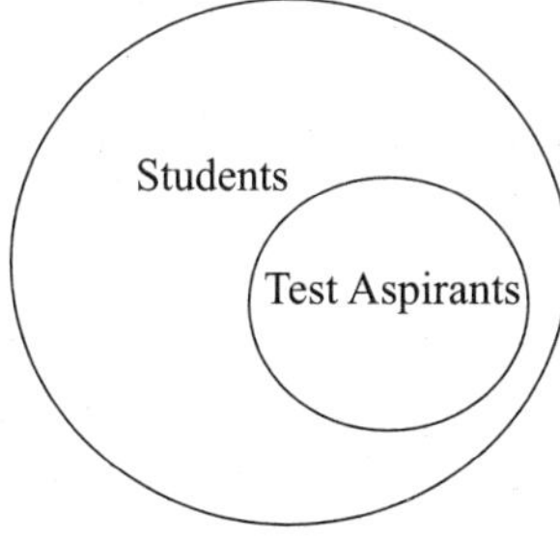


2. ***No test aspirants are students:*** This is the relationship of **'universal negative'**. The test aspirants are not falling at all in the universal set of students as shown in the diagram below. Thus, the two sets of subjects are **mutually exclusive**.

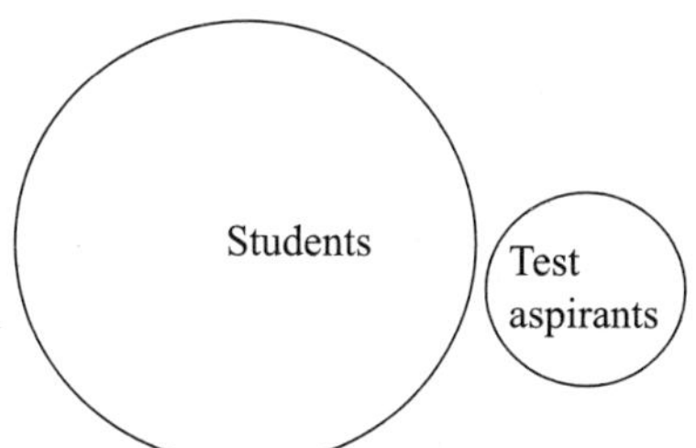


3. ***Some-test aspirants are students:*** This relationship of **'particular affirmative'**, is described through two overlapping sets where one is **neither fully inclusive** in the other (as in example 1) **nor** both are **mutually exclusive** ( as in example 2.

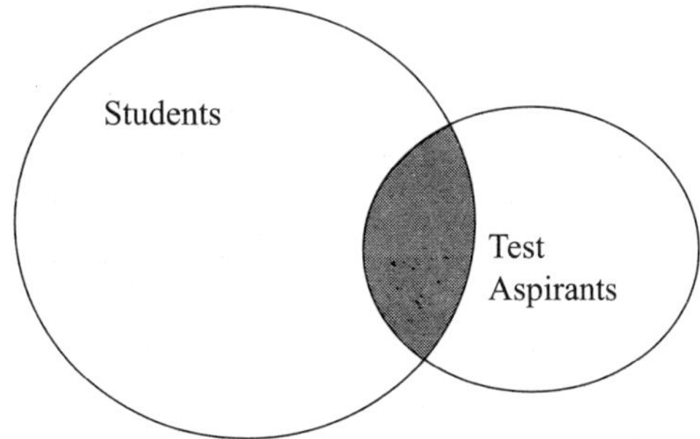


The above circles show a part overlap, hence represent the relationship of some elements of both the sets being common. The common elements are those which fall in the region of overlap. Thus the area of overlap, shown in grey, represents the test aspirants who are students.

4. ***Some test aspirants are not students:*** The diagrammatic representation of this relationship is analogous to that in the earlier example. However, the area which represents this relationship is completely different from the above example. The portion of the circle shown in grey, represents the test aspirants which are outside /not overlapping with the circle representing the students. Hence the shaded area represents the test aspirants which are not students.

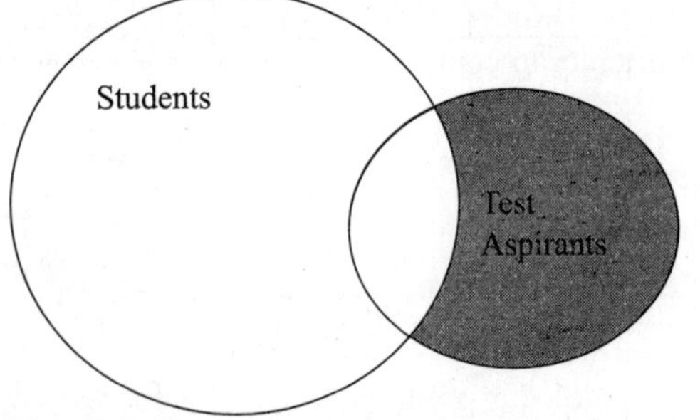


**2.9 Illustration**

Now let us consider the example given at 2.7 again

*All test aspirants are students.* **Major premise**

*Raghav is a test aspirant.* **Minor Premise**

*Raghav is a student.* **Conclusion**

**The relationship in the major and minor premises are given by the Venn diagram below.**

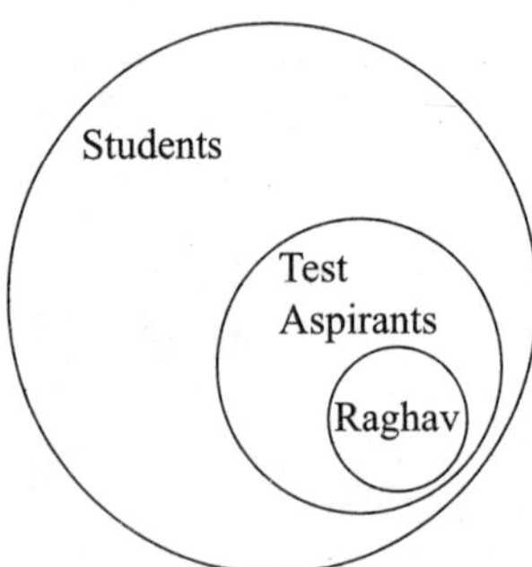


From the figures above we can see that Raghav falls within the universal set of students. Hence the conclusion in the example can be drawn.

**2.10 Illustration**

Let us consider the example at 2.8 and understand it through Venn diagram

*Some test aspirants are students.* **Major premise**

*Raghav is a test aspirant.* **Minor Premise**

*Raghav is a student.* **Conclusion**

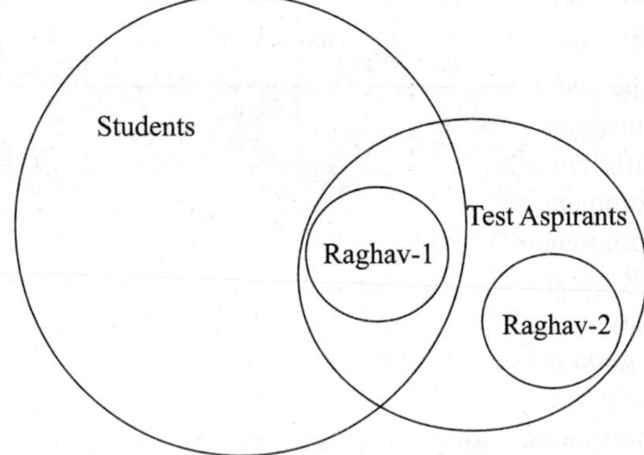


The relationship is represented by the Venn diagram as above where two broad positions are possible for Raghav. These are indicated by Raghav–1 falling within the circle of students and other Raghav-2 falling outside it. However, both are falling within the circle of 'test aspirants' and hence fully conform to the minor premise. Thus, the conclusion, Raghav is a student, may or may not be correct and hence cannot be drawn.

## 1.3 How to Prepare: Charting the Road Ahead

This section contains some suggestions and tips, which will be helpful in acquiring proficiency in solving the LR questions. Read them carefully and make earnest effort to incorporate them in your practice.

**(i) Practice and more Practice**

Practicing is the only way of being able to solve LR questions. Unlike other sections of aptitude test paper, where certain acquired skills are essential, to be proficient in solving the question (viz. linguistic ability for comprehension, quantitative abilities for numericals), the only ability essential is an innate sense of logical comprehension. As one practices more, the intrinsic abilities become active and surface to the fore of our personality. Thus, while other sections may require you to hone certain basic abilities before you become proficient in solving the questions, in the LR section, solving more and more questions sharpens your ability of logical thinking more and more, enabling you to become proficient. Besides, practice also brings confidence, speed and accuracy.

**(ii) Solve a Variety of Questions**

The test of logical reasoning comprises a variety of questions as discussed earlier. It is essential to solve different types of questions to acquire a good command over the subject. Although logical comprehension is the common denominator of all LR questions, yet a change in format of the question may pose difficulty to some of the aspirants. To get a good grasp over the subject, around 50 questions have been provided in the five exercise sets, while the practice question papers further contain many such questions. While solving them, always identify and mark those questions that you found difficult to understand and solve, or where you could not work out the right answer. As your learning of LR questions progresses, come back to these questions to assess whether you have been able to get a hang of these questions or not. There may be specific types of LR questions, where despite your best efforts your success rate is low. It is advisable to steer clear of such question types in the examination, or come back to them only if time permits.

**(iii) Is Speed Essential?**

The answer to this question is, yes. Speed is essential for the timely completion of the questions in this section. As mentioned earlier, one can expect 5–10 questions of LR with each question required to be completed within a minute. Reading the entire question, the answer choices, grasping what is to be done and ascertaining the right choice that too in merely 60 seconds, appears to be a daunting task. This can only be accomplished with good speed and accuracy, which in turn develops with practice. But while attempting the initial exercise set, your objective should be to develop a knack for solving such problems and not be bogged down by the constraint of time. Start timing yourself when you have advanced to the fourth exercise set where you should strive to solve these problems within the average time of one and a half to two minutes (at the most).

**(iv) Paraphrase What you have Read**

Paraphrase means restatement of a text or a passage in a simple form to clarify the meaning. Once you have read the question, paraphrase to yourself what you have understood. Initially it may appear a bit peculiar, as to how can one explain to oneself. If it is so then visualise that a young student has approached you seeking your help to understand the question. Picturise the mental image of you explaining to him what the question means. This is a psychological ploy where you make yourself believe in your own abilities. Besides, this way you give yourself an opportunity to comprehend the question rather than getting bogged down by its complexities at the very outset.

Paraphrasing is not a difficult technique to learn. To some it may come naturally while others may have to practice a bit. But one thing is for sure, **it is effective.**

**(v) Visualising What is Stated**

Many a time, questions contain subjects or issues, which can be visualised. Creating mental images of objects or things and then trying to figure out what the question means, makes the entire exercise simpler and brings clarity. Consider the following example:

*Statement: All tables are chairs. Some chairs are stools. Conclusion – All stools are tables.*

*Is the conclusion valid?*

Here visualising the subjects, which are tables, chairs and stools, makes comprehension easier, and helps you to generate a mental picture of what is happening and what the question means. Besides it also aids understanding of the fact as to which is a larger set and which is the sub-set.

**Preparing Venn diagrams and representing the relationships** through circles/ diagram etc., is a quick and effective way of visual representation of the relationship. This also integrates expression of what one has understood.

**(vi) Converse Should not be Presumed to be True**

While reading the statements and conclusions one must always be careful that the converse of what is stated may not always be true. In the aforesaid example, it is stated, "All tables are chairs". Although this can be taken as true, its converse, "All chairs are tables", has not been stated and should not be presumed to be true.

**(vii) Take the Facts Stated to be Correct**

Always take the facts stated in the question to be correct, even though they may appear to be different from or contrary to the commonly known facts. Besides, do not presume anything, which is not stated in the question.

## Exercise Set-1 on Logical Reasoning

**In the following two questions, there are two statements and two conclusions numbered 1 and 2. Take the given two statements as true even if they appear to be in variance from commonly known facts. Read the conclusions and then decide which of the given conclusions follow the two given statements.**

1. Statement: Some men are married. All married men are educated. Conclusion: 1. Some married men are educated. 2. Some educated men are married.
   (a) Only Conclusion 1 is correct.
   (b) Only Conclusion 2 is correct.
   (c) Both the conclusions are correct.
   (d) None is correct.
2. Statement: Some drivers are dancers. All dancers are stout. Conclusion: 1. Some drivers are stout. 2. All drivers are stout.
   (a) Only Conclusion 1 is correct.
   (b) Only Conclusion 2 is correct.
   (c) Both the conclusions are not correct.
   (d) No conclusion can be drawn.
3. While giving evidence before the Indian Parliamentary Committee examining the allegation that the Association of Cigarette Manufacturers of India had altered the quantity of nicotine in cigarettes in order to addict consumers, the Association of Cigarette Manufacturers claimed that cigarette smoking is not addictive. They argued that the quantity of nicotine in cigarette was not regulated by the Tobacco Products (Prohibition of Advertisement and Regulation of Trade and Commerce, Production, Supply and Distribution) Act, 2003.

   For the Association of Cigarette Manufacturers of India's claim to be logically correct, which of the following must be assumed?
   (a) Products that are not regulated by the law are not addictive.
   (b) Products that are not addictive are not regulated by the law.
   (c) Some addictive products are not regulated by the law.
   (d) There is no scientific proof that cigarette smoking is addictive.
4. Various studies have shown that our forested and hilly regions and, in general, areas where biodiversity—as reflected in the variety of flora—is high, are the places where poverty also appears to be high. And these same areas are also the ones where educational performance seems to be poor. Therefore, it may be surmised that, even disregarding poverty status, richness in biodiversity goes hand in hand with educational backwardness.

   Which one of the following statements, if true, can be said to best provide supporting evidence for the surmise mentioned in the passage?
   (a) In regions where there is little variety in flora, educational performance is seen to be as good as in regions with high variety in flora, when poverty levels are high.
   (b) Regions, which show high biodiversity also exhibit poor educational performance, at low levels of poverty.
   (c) Regions, which show high biodiversity, reveal high levels of poverty and poor educational performance.

(d) In regions where there is low biodiversity, at all levels of poverty, educational performance is seen to be good.

**5.** Cigarettes constitute a mere 20 per cent of tobacco consumption in India, and fewer than 15 per cent of the 200 million tobacco users consume cigarettes. Yet these 15 per cent contribute nearly 90 per cent of the tax revenues to the Exchequer from the tobacco sector. The punitive cigarette taxation regime has kept the tax base narrow and reducing taxes will expand this base.

Which one of the following best bolsters the conclusion?

(a) The cigarette manufacturers' association has decided to indulge in aggressive promotion.

(b) There is a likelihood that tobacco consumers will shift to cigarette smoking, if cigarette prices were to reduce.

(c) The cigarette manufacturers are lobbying for a reduction on duties.

(d) An increase in duties on non-cigarette tobacco may lead to a shift in favour of cigarette smoking.

**6.** Animals in general are shrewd in proportion as they cultivate society. Elephants and beavers show the greatest signs of this sagacity when they are together in large numbers, but when man invades their communities they lose all their spirit of industry.

Among insects, the labours of the bee and the ant have attracted the attention and admiration of naturalists, but all their sagacity seems to be lost upon separation and a single bee or ant seems destitute of every degree of industry. It becomes the most stupid insect imaginable, and it languishes and soon dies.

Which of the following can be inferred from the above passage?

(a) Humankind is responsible for the destruction of the natural habitat of animals and insects.

(b) Animals, in general, are unable to function effectively outside their normal social environment.

(c) Naturalists have great admiration for bees and ants, despite their lack of industry upon separation.

(d) Elephants and beavers are smarter than bees and ants than human beings.

**7.** Amongst the following statements, which would be logically compatible?

1. A shoe is a footwear.
2. No sandal is a shoe.
3. A shoe is a slipper.
4. All footwear are shoes.
5. A sandal is a footwear.

(a) 1, 2, 3 (b) 2, 3, 5
(c) 1, 2, 5 (d) 2, 4, 5

**8.** Amongst the following statements, which would be logically compatible?

1. A cart is not a car.
2. A car is not a vehicle.
3. A cart is a vehicle.
4. All vehicles are not cars.
5. A car is a vehicle.

(a) 1, 2, 3, 4. (b) 2, 3, 5
(c) 1, 2, 5 (d) 1, 3, 4, 5

**Sentences given in each of the following two questions, when properly sequenced, form a coherent paragraph. Each sentence is labelled with a letter. Choose the most logical order of sentences from among the four given choices to construct a coherent paragraph.**

**9.** A. Group decision-making, however, does not necessarily fully guard against arbitrariness and anarchy, for individual capriciousness can get substituted by collusion of group members.

B. Nature itself is an intricate system of checks and balances, meant to preserve the delicate balance between various environmental factors that affect our ecology.

C. In institutions also, there is a need to have in place a system of checks and balances, which inhibits the concentration of power in only some individuals.

D. When human interventions alter this delicate balance, the outcomes have been seen to be disastrous.

(a) CDAB (b) BCAD

(c) CABD (d) BDCA

**10.** A. He was bone-weary and soul-weary, and found himself muttering, "Either I can't manage this place, or it's unmanageable."

B. To his horror, he realised that he had become the victim of an amorphous, unwitting, unconscious conspiracy to immerse him in routine work that had no significance.

C. It was one of those nights in the office when the office clock was moving towards four in the morning and Bennis was still not through with the incredible mass of paper stacked before him.

D. He reached for his calendar and ran his eyes down each hour, half hour and quarter hour, to see where his time had gone that day, the day before, the month before.

(a) ABCD (b) CADB

(c) BDCA (d) DCBA

**In the following two questions, there are two statements and two conclusions numbered 1 and 2. Take the given two statements as true even if they appear to be in variance from commonly known facts. Read the conclusions and then decide which of the given conclusions follows the two given statements.**

**11.** Statements: All puppets are dolls. All dolls are toys. Conclusion:

1. Some toys are puppets.
2. All toys are puppets.

(a) Only Conclusion 1 is correct.

(b) Only Conclusion 2 is correct.

(c) Both the conclusions are correct.

(d) None is correct.

**12.** Statement: All leaves are stems. All stems are branches. Conclusion:

1. All branches are leaves.
2. All stems are leaves.

(a) Only Conclusion 1 is correct.

(b) Only Conclusion 2 is correct.

(c) Both the conclusions are correct.

(d) None is correct.

**13.** Thomas Malthus, the British clergyman turned economist, predicted that the planet would not be able to support the human population for long. His explanation was that human population grows at a geometric rate while the food supply grows only at an arithmetic rate. Which one of the following, if true, would not undermine the thesis offered by Malthus?

(a) Population growth can be slowed down by the voluntary choices of individuals and not just by natural disasters.

(b) The capacity of the planet to feed a growing human population can be enhanced through biotechnological means.

(c) Human systems, and natural systems like food supply, follow natural laws of growth which have remained constant, and will remain unchanged.

(d) Human beings can colonise other planetary systems on a regular and on-going basis to accommodate a growing population.

**14.** The company's coffee crop for 2008–09 totalled 8079 tonnes, an all time record. The increase over the previous year's production of 5830 tonnes was 38.58 per cent. The previous highest crop was 6089 tonnes in 1980–81. The company had fixed a target of 8000 tonnes to be realised by the year 2010–11, and this has been achieved two years earlier, thanks to the emphasis laid on the key areas of irrigation, replacement of unproductive coffee bushes, intensive refilling and improved agricultural practices. It is now our endeavour to reach the target of 10000 tonnes in, the year 2011–12. Which one of the following would contribute most to making the target of 10,000 tonnes in 2011–12 unrealistic?

(a) The potential of the productivity enhancing measures implemented up to now has been exhausted.

(b) The total company land under coffee has remained constant since 1979 when an estate in the Nilgiri Hills was acquired.

(c) The sensitivity of the crop to climatic factors makes prediction about production uncertain.

(d) The target-setting procedures in the company have been proved to be sound by the achievement of the 8000 tonne target.

**15.** Amongst the following statements, which would be logically compatible?

1. A puppet is a toy.
2. Some dolls are puppets.
3. No puppet is a doll.
4. All dolls are toys.
5. Some dolls are not toys.

(a) 1, 2, 4 (b) 2, 3, 5
(c) 1, 3, 4 (d) 3, 4, 5

**16.** Amongst the following statements, which would be logically compatible?

1. A tree is a shrub.
2. Some plants are shrubs.
3. No plants are shrubs.
4. A bush is always a plant.
5. A shrub is a bush.

(a) 1, 2, 4 (b) 2, 3, 4
(c) 1, 2, 5 (d) 2, 4, 5

**Sentences given in each of the following two questions, when properly sequenced, form a coherent paragraph. Each sentence is labelled with a letter. Choose the most logical order of sentences from among the four given choices to construct a coherent paragraph.**

**17.** A. With that, I swallowed the shampoo, and obtained most realistic results almost on the spot.

B. The man shuffled away into the back regions to make up a prescription, and after a moment I got through on the shop telephone to the Consulate, intimating my location.

C. Then, while the pharmacist was wrapping up a six-ounce bottle of the mixture, I groaned and inquired whether he could give me something for acute gastric cramp.

D. I intended to stage a sharp gastric attack, and entering an old-fashioned pharmacy I asked for a popular shampoo mixture, consisting of olive oil and flaked soap.

(a) DCBA (b) DACB
(c) BDAC (d) BCDA

**18.** A. Since then, intelligence tests have been mostly used to separate dull children in school from average or bright children, so that special education can be provided to the dull ones.

B. In other words, intelligence tests give us a norm for each age.

C. Intelligence is expressed as intelligence quotient, and tests are developed to indicate what an average child of a certain age can do—what a five-year-old can answer, but a four-year-old cannot, for instance.

D. Binet developed the first set of such tests in the early 1900s to find out which children in school needed special attention.

E. Intelligence can be measured by tests.

(a) CDABE (b) DECAB
(c) EDACB (d) CBADE

**For each of the two questions indicate which of the statements given with that particular question is consistent with the description of the unreasonable man in the following passage. Unreasonableness is a tendency to do socially permissible things at the wrong time. The unreasonable man is the sort of person who comes to confide in you when you are busy. He asks a man who has just lost money by paying a bill for a friend to pay a bill for him. He invites a friend to go for a ride just after the friend has finished a long car trip. He is eager to offer services, which are not wanted but which cannot**

**be politely refused. If he is present at arbitration, he stirs up dissension between the two parties, who were really anxious to agree. Such is the unreasonable man.**

19. He tends to
    (a) Entertain women
    (b) Be a successful arbitrator when dissenting parties are anxious to agree
    (c) Tell a long story to people who have heard it many times before
    (d) Be helpful when solicited
20. He tends to
    (a) Bring a higher bidder to a salesman who has just closed a deal
    (b) Disclose confidential information to others
    (c) Sing the praises of the bride when he goes to a wedding
    (d) Sleep late and rise early

**In the following two questions, there are two statements and two conclusions numbered 1 and 2. Take the given two statements as true even if they appear to be in variance from commonly known facts. Read the conclusions and then decide which of the given conclusions follows the two given statements.**

21. Statement: All watermelons are guavas. Some guavas are grapes.
    Conclusion: 1. Some watermelons are grapes.
    Conclusion: 2. Some grapes are watermelons.
    (a) Only Conclusion 1 is correct.
    (b) Only Conclusion 2 is correct.
    (c) Both the conclusions are correct.
    (d) None is correct.
22. Statement: Law and order is a subject of State List. But the States at times have to take the assistance of forces under the Central Government to maintain the law and order situation.
    Conclusion 1: Maintenance of law and order should be a subject of the Union List.
    Conclusion 2: The Constitution permits the States to take the assistance of the Union Government in maintenance of law and order.
    (a) Only Conclusion 1 is valid.
    (b) Only Conclusion 2 is valid.
    (c) Both Conclusions 1 and 2 are valid.
    (d) Both Conclusions 1 and 2 are not valid.
23. Road vehicles are safer than trains. 7 per cent of train accidents result in death, while only 2 per cent of road vehicles accidents result in death. Which of the following, if true, would most seriously weaken the argument above?
    (a) Train drivers are well trained road vehicle drivers may not be.
    (b) Trains are better maintained than road vehicles.
    (c) The number of road vehicles accidents is thousands of times more than the number of train accidents.
    (d) Trains transport more passengers than road vehicles do.
24. Mr. X is the President of an India based multinational company that produces 3% of the world's total annual production of metal Y. The sales head Mr. Z wants to increase the turnover and profit by increasing sales. Mr. X, however, believes that increased production would only reduce the world price of metal Y and lower the companies' turnover.

    Which amongst the following statements brings out the logical flaw in Mr. X's assumption?
    (a) He believes that production eventually materialise into sales.
    (b) He believes that the increased production by his company can largely influence and change the aggregate supply for the market.
    (c) He believes that on increasing production his competitors will also increase production.
    (d) None of the above

**Each of the following two questions consists of five statements followed by options consisting of three statements put together in a specific order. Choose the option, which indicates a valid argument, that is, where the third statement is a conclusion drawn from the preceding two**

**statements. ABC is a valid option, where Statement C can be concluded from Statements A and B.**

**25.** A. All software companies employ intelligent workers.
B. Softlogic employs intelligent workers.
C. Softlogic is a software company.
D. Some software companies employ intelligent workers.
E. Softlogic employs only intelligent workers.

(a) ABC (b) ACB
(c) CDB (d) ACE

**26.** A. Traffic congestion increases carbon monoxide in the environment.
B. Increase in carbon monoxide is hazardous to health.
C. Traffic congestion is hazardous to health.
D. Some traffic congestion does not cause increased carbon monoxide.
E. Some traffic congestion is not hazardous to health.

(a) CBA (b) BDE
(c) CDE (d) BAC

**Each of the following two questions has four statements and each statement has three segments. Choose the alternative where the third segment in the statement can be logically deduced using both the preceding two but not just from one of them.**

**27.** A. Sona is an actor. Some actors are pretty. Sona is pretty.
B. Some men are cops. Some men are brave. Some brave people are cops.
C. All cops are brave. Some men are cops. Some men are brave.
D. All actors are pretty; Sona is not an actor; Sona is not pretty.

(a) D only (b) C only
(c) A only (d) B and C

**28.** A. All IITs are in India. No MITs are in India. No IITs are MITs.
B. All IITs are in India. No MITs are in India. No MITs are IITs.
C. Some IITs are not in India. Some MITs are not in India. Some IITs are MITs.
D. Some IITs are not in India. Some MITs are not in India. Some MITs are IITs.

(a) A and B (b) C and D
(c) A only (d) B only

**Each of the following two questions has a set of four sequentially ordered statements. Each statement can be classified as one of the following:**
**Facts, which deal with pieces of information that one has heard, seen or read, and which are open to discovery or verification (the answer option indicates such a statement with an 'F').**
**Inferences, which are conclusions drawn about the unknown, on the basis of the known (the answer option indicates such a statement with an 'I').**
**Judgments, which are opinions that imply approval or disapproval of persons, objects, situations and occurrences in the past, the present or the future (the answer option indicates such a statement with a 'J').**
**Select the answer option that best describes the set of four statements.**

**29.** 1. So much of our day-to-day focus seems to be on getting things done, trudging our way through the tasks of living—it can feel like a treadmill that gets you nowhere; where is the childlike joy?
2. We are not doing the things that make us happy; that which brings us joy; the things that we cannot wait to do because we enjoy them so much.
3. This is the stuff that joyful living is made of— identifying your calling and committing yourself wholeheartedly to it.
4. When this happens, each moment becomes a celebration of you; there is a rush of energy that comes with feeling completely immersed in doing what you love most.

(a) IIIJ (b) IFIJ
(c) JFJJ (d) JJJJ

30. 1. Given the poor quality of service in the public sector, the HIV/AIDS affected should be switching to private initiatives that supply anti-retroviral drugs (ARVs) at a low cost.

2. The government has been supplying free drugs since 2004, and 35,000 have benefitted up to now—though the size of the affected population is 150 times this number.

3. The recent initiatives of networks and companies, such as AIDSC are Network, Emcure and Reliance-Cipla-CII, would lead to availability of much-needed drugs to a larger number of affected people.

4. But how ironic it is that we should face a perennial shortage of drugs when India is one of the world's largest suppliers of generic drugs to the developing world.

(a) JFIJ (b) JIIJ
(c) IFIJ (d) IFFJ

31. Statement: The collection of direct taxes in the recent years has increased manifold.

Which of the two assumptions could be valid?

Assumption: 1. The increase in the Direct Tax collection is due to increase in the number of tax payers.

Assumption: 2. The increase in the Direct Tax collection is due to better compliance of the tax laws by the tax payers.

(a) Only Assumption 1 is valid.
(b) Only Assumption 2 is valid.
(c) Both the assumptions are valid.
(d) None of the assumption is valid.

32. Statement: The government proposes to bring about a new law to bring in transparency in the functioning of bureaucracy.

Which of the two assumptions are surely valid?

Assumption: 1. There is need for greater transparency in the functioning of bureaucracy.

Assumption: 2. Only way of bringing in transparency is by enactment of law.

(a) Only Assumption 1 is valid.
(b) Only Assumption 2 is valid.
(c) Both the assumptions are valid.
(d) None of the assumptions is valid.

33. The Luxury Cars magazine conducted a poll of its readers regarding the increase in the Road Tax paid on C and D segment vehicles in the State of Delhi. More than 80% of the readers opposed the increase in tax. The magazine announced that the majority of Delhiites opposed the increase in the Road Tax on luxury vehicles.

Which one of the following statements, if true, would most weaken the magazines conclusion?

(a) Some readers of the magazine were not contacted, thus the poll does not reflect their views.
(b) Some readers of Luxury Cars magazine are residing outside Delhi.
(c) Road Tax laws are modified by the Delhi Government; readers play no role in it.
(d) The poll result of the readers of Luxury Cars magazine differ from the views of most Delhiites.

34. Judges of Courts and Tribunals do not have expertise in computer technology and information technology. As such, it is unethical for them to decide cases involving such matters.

Which of the following, if it was true, would weaken the aforesaid argument, most?

(a) There is shortage of experts of both the fields as such the judicial system has to depend only on legal experts.
(b) Technical experts do not have legal knowledge. They cannot be expected to sit in judgment in such cases.
(c) Legal experts cannot be imparted technical knowledge.
(d) Most cases require only the understanding of the law and public policy. They do not require the understanding of technical aspects beyond the level of a layman.

**Each of the following two questions consists of five statements followed by options consisting of three statements put together in a specific order. Choose the option, which indicates a valid**

**argument, that is, where the third statement is a conclusion drawn from the preceding two statements. ABC is a valid option, where Statement C can be concluded from Statements A and B.**

**35.** A. Apples are not sweets.
B. Some apples are sweet.
C. All sweets are tasty.
D. Some apples are not tasty.
E. No apple is tasty.
(a) CEA (b) BDC
(c) CBD (d) EAC

**36.** A. Some towns in India are polluted.
B. All polluted towns should be destroyed.
C. Town Hira should be destroyed.
D. Town Hira is polluted.
E. Some towns in India should be destroyed.
(a) BDE (b) BDC
(c) ADE (d) CDB

**Each of the following two questions has four statements and each statement has three segments. Choose the alternative where the third segment in the statement can be logically deduced using both the preceding two but not just from one of them.**

**37.** A. Citizens of Dreamland speak only the truth. Citizens of Dreamland are young people. Young people speak only the truth.
B. Citizens of Dreamland speak only the truth. Some Dreamlands are in the Pacific. Some citizens of Dreamland are in the Pacific.
C. Citizens of Dreamland speak only the truth. Some young people are citizens of Dreamland. Some young people speak only the truth.
D. Some people speak only the truth. Some citizens of Dreamland speak only the truth. Some people who speak only the truth are citizens of Dreamland.
(a) A only (b) B only
(c) C only (d) D only

**38.** A. All mammals are viviparous. Some fish are viviparous. Some fish are mammals.
B. All birds are oviparous. Some fish are not oviparous. Some fish are birds.
C. No mammal is oviparous. Some creatures are oviparous and some are not. Some creatures are not mammals.
D. Some creatures are mammals some creatures are viviparous. Some mammals are viviparous.
(a) A only (b) B only
(c) C only (d) D only

**Each of the following two questions has a main statement followed by four statements labelled A, B, C and D. Choose the ordered pair of statements where the first statement implies the second, and the two statements are logically consistent with the main statement.**

**39.** Either the orangutan is not angry, or he frowns upon the world.
A. The orangutan frowns upon the world.
B. The orangutan is not angry.
C. The orangutan does not frown upon the world.
D. The orangutan is angry.
(a) CB only (b) DA only
(c) AB only (d) CB and DA

**40.** If I talk to my professors, then I do not need to take a pill for headache.
A. I talked to my professors.
B. I did not need to take a pill for headache.
C. I needed to take a pill for headache.
D. I did not talk to my professors.
(a) AB only (b) DC only
(c) CD only (d) AB and CD

**41.** Statement: The United Nations was formed to settle the international disputes between the member nations. However, in recent times very few international disputes eventually got settled under the aegis of the UN.

Which of the two conclusions can be drawn?

Conclusion: 1. The authority of UN has eroded in the recent times. Conclusion: 2. Few member nations are approaching the UN for settlement of disputes.

(a) Only Conclusion 1 can be drawn.
(b) Only Conclusion 2 can be drawn.
(c) Both the conclusions can be drawn.
(d) None of the conclusions can be drawn.

42. Statement: India has become the 4th largest economy of the world. In the past decade, India's economic progress has surpassed that of many developed countries.

Which of the two conclusions can be drawn?

Conclusion: 1. India has become a developed country as its growth has surpassed that of the developed countries.

Conclusion: 2. The level of poverty in India has become lower than those countries, which it has surpassed in economic growth.

(a) Only Conclusion 1 can be drawn.
(b) Only Conclusion 2 can be drawn.
(c) Both the conclusions can be drawn.
(d) None of the conclusions can be drawn.

43. Washing powder X claims to be the most effective detergent. Its advertisement shows around 15 housewives vouching for its effectiveness in removing the toughest of stains. They would not exchange a kilogram of brand X detergent for 2 kilograms of any other detergent.

Which one amongst the following statements, if true, would weaken the claim of the advertisement most?

(a) The housewives in the advertisement were all from the same neighbourhood.
(b) They were given a sample of the detergent free of cost.
(c) The housewives were loyal to the brand for many years accordingly they had been chosen.
(d) The housewives were paid professional actors.

44. The piracy of movies and music video is rampant in our country today. Even before the movie or the music album has been released, the black market is flooded with its pirated CDs, or it is being downloaded through the internet. Strict anti-piracy laws are needed to protect the industry and encourage the investors and producers to produce better quality movies and music.

Which amongst the following best explains the concluding line of the aforesaid statement?

(a) Strict anti-piracy laws prevent the wider dissemination of movies and videos; hence, the genuine purchasers have to pay higher price.
(b) Strict anti-piracy laws are needed because it is unethical to sell products without copyright.
(c) Strict anti-piracy laws shrink the black market.
(d) Strict anti-piracy laws prevent the leakage of revenue, thus improving the commercial viability of a product, encouraging investment and manufacture of quality products.

**Each of the following four questions has four statements and each statement has three segments. Choose the alternative where the third segment in the statement can be logically deduced using both the preceding two but not just from one of them.**

45. A. All earthquakes cause havoc. Some landslides cause havoc. Some earthquakes cause landslides.
B. All glass things are transparent. Some curios are glass things. Some curios are transparent.
C. All clay objects are brittle. All XY are clay objects. All XY are brittle.
D. No criminal is a patriot. Ram is a criminal. Ram is a patriot.

(a) C and D (b) B and C
(c) A only (d) C only

**46.** A. A few farmers are rocket scientists. Some rocket scientists catch snakes. A few farmers catch snakes.

B. Poonam is a kangaroo. Some kangaroos are made of teak. Poonam is made of teak.

C. No bull eats grass. All matadors eat grass. No matador is a bull.

D. Some skunks drive Cadillacs. All skunks are polar bears. Some polar bears drive Cadillacs.

(a) B only (b) A and C
(c) C only (d) C and D

**47.** A. All good people are knights. All warriors are good people. All knights are warriors.

B. No footballers are ministers. All footballers are tough. Some ministers are players.

C. All pizzas are snacks. Some meals are pizzas. Some meals are snacks.

D. Some barkers are musk-deer. All barkers are sloth bears. Some sloth bears are musk-deer.

(a) C and D (b) B and C
(c) A only (d) C only

**48.** A. Dinosaurs are prehistoric creatures. Water-buffaloes are not dinosaurs. Water-buffaloes are not pre-historic creatures.

B. All politicians are frank. No frank people are crocodiles. No crocodiles are politicians.

C. No diamond is quartz. No opal is quartz. Diamonds are opals.

D. All monkeys like bananas. Some commandos like bananas. Some commandos are monkeys.

(a) C only (b) B only
(c) A and D (d) B and C

**Each of the following two questions has a set of four sequentially ordered statements. Each statement can be classified as one of the following:**

**Facts, which deal with pieces of information that one has heard, seen or read, and which are open to discovery or verification (the answer option indicates such a statement with an 'F').**

**Inferences, which are conclusions drawn about the unknown, on the basis of the known (the answer option indicates such a statement with an 'I').**

**Judgments, which are opinions that imply approval or disapproval of persons, objects, situations and occurrences in the past, the present or the future (the answer option indicates such a statement with a 'J').**

**Select the answer option that best describes the set of four statements.**

**49.** 1. According to all statistical indications, the Sarva Shiksha Abhiyan has managed to keep pace with its ambitious goals.

2. The Mid-Day Meal Scheme has been a significant incentive for the poor to send their little ones to school, thus establishing the vital link between healthy bodies and healthy minds.

3. Only about 13 million children in the age group of 6 to 14 years are out of school.

4. The goal of universalisation of elementary education has to be a pre-requisite for the evolution and development of our country.

(a) IIFJ (b) JIIJ
(c) IJFJ (d) IJFI

**50.** 1. We should not be hopelessly addicted to an erroneous belief that corruption in India is caused by the crookedness of Indians.

2. The truth is that we have more red tape—we take days to start a small business, Australians take two.

3. Red tape leads to corruption and distorts a people's character.

4. Every red tape procedure is a point of contact with an official, and such contacts have the potential to become opportunities for money to change hands.

(a) JFIF (b) JFJJ
(c) JIJF (d) JFJI

## Answers of Exercise Set-1 on Logical Reasoning

| | | | | |
|---|---|---|---|---|
| **1.** (b) | **11.** (a) | **21.** (a) | **31.** (c) | **41.** (c) |
| **2.** (a) | **12.** (d) | **22.** (b) | **32.** (a) | **42.** (d) |
| **3.** (a) | **13.** (c) | **23.** (c) | **33.** (d) | **43.** (d) |
| **4.** (d) | **14.** (a) | **24.** (b) | **34.** (d) | **44.** (d) |
| **5.** (b) | **15.** (a) | **25.** (b) | **35.** (a) | **45.** (b) |
| **6.** (b) | **16.** (d) | **26.** (d) | **36.** (b) | **46.** (d) |
| **7.** (c) | **17.** (a) | **27.** (b) | **37.** (c) | **47.** (a) |
| **8.** (d) | **18.** (c) | **28.** (a) | **38.** (c) | **48.** (b) |
| **9.** (d) | **19.** (c) | **29.** (d) | **39.** (d) | **49.** (c) |
| **10.** (b) | **20.** (a) | **30.** (a) | **40.** (d) | **50.** (d) |

## Exercise Set-2 on Logical Reasoning

**1.** "By liberty I mean the eager maintenance of that atmosphere in which men have the opportunity to be their best selves," Which one of the following expresses the implied in the above statement?

(a) Liberty is the absence of restraint on human action.

(b) Liberty is what law permits people to perform.

(c) Liberty is the ability to do what one desires.

(d) Liberty is the maintenance of conditions for the growth of human personality.

**2.** If Pen < Pencil, Pencil < Book and Book > Cap, then which one of the following is always true?

(a) Pen > Cap (b) Pen < Book

(c) Pencil = Cap (d) Pencil > Cap

***Directions for the following 2 (two) items:*** Read the following statements SI and S2 and answer the two items that follow:

S1: Twice the weight of Sohan is less than the weight of Mohan or that of Rohan.

S2: Twice the weight of Rohan is greater than the weight of Mohan or that of Sohan.

**3.** Which one of the following statements is correct?

(a) Weight of Mohan is greatest

(b) Weight of Sohan is greatest

(c) Weight of Rohan is greatest

(d) 'Whose weight is greatest' cannot be determined

**4.** Which one of the following statements is correct?

(a) Weight of Mohan is least

(b) Weight of Sohan is least

(c) Weight of Rohan is least

(d) 'Whose weight is least' cannot be determined

**5.** Consider the following Statements and Conclusions:

*Statements:*

1. Some rats are cats.
2. Some cats are dogs.
3. No dog is a cow.

*Conclusions:*

I. No cow is a cat.

II. No dog is a rat.

III. Some cats are rats.

Which of the above conclusions is/are drawn from the statements?

(a) I, II and III (b) Only I and II
(c) Only III (d) Only II and III

**6.** If $x$ is greater than or equal to 25 and $y$ is less than or equal to 40, then which one of the following is always correct?

(a) $x$ is greater than y
(b) $(y - x)$ is greater than 15
(c) $(y - x)$ is less than or equal to 15
(d) $(x - y)$ is greater than or equal to 65

**7.** Two statements S1 and S2 are given below followed by a Question:

S1: There are not more than two figures on any page of a 51-page book.

S2: There is at least one figure on every page.
Question: Are there more than 100 figures in that book?

Which one of the following is correct in respect of the above Statements and the Question?

(a) Both S1 and S2 are sufficient to answer the Question, but neither S1 alone nor S2 alone is sufficient to answer the Question.
(b) S1 alone is sufficient to answer the Question.
(c) S1 and S2 together are not sufficient to answer the Question.
(d) S2 alone is sufficient to answer the Question.

**8.** Two Statements S1 and S2 are given below with regard to four numbers

*P, Q, R* and *S* followed by a Question:

S1: *R* is greater-than *P* as well as *Q*. S2: *S* is not the largest one.

Question: Among four numbers *P, Q, R* and *S* which one is the largest?

Which one of the following is correct in respect of the above Statements and the Question?

(a) S1 alone is sufficient to answer the Question.
(b) S2 alone is sufficient to answer the Question.
(c) S1 and S2 together are sufficient to answer the Question, but neither S1 alone nor S2 alone is sufficient to answer the Question.
(d) S1 and S2 together are not sufficient to answer the Question.

**9.** Two Statements are given followed by two Conclusions:

Statements:

All cats are dogs.

All cats are black.

Conclusion-I:

All dogs are black.

Conclusion-II:

Some dogs are not black.

Which of the above Conclusions logically follows/follow from the two given Statements disregarding commonly known facts?

(a) Only Conclusion-I
(b) Only Conclusion-II
(c) Neither Conclusion-I nor Conclusion-II
(d) Both Conclusions-I and Conclusion-II

**10.** Three Statements S1, S2 and S3 are given below followed by a Question:

S1: *C* is younger than *D*, but older than *A* and *B*. S2: *D* is the oldest.

S3: *A* is older than *B*.

Question: Who among *A, B, C* and *D* is the youngest?

Which one of the following is correct in respect of the above Statements and the Question?

(a) S1 alone is sufficient to answer the Question.
(b) S1 and S2 together are sufficient to answer the Question.
(c) S2 and S3 together are sufficient to answer the Question.
(d) S1 and S3 together are sufficient to answer the Question.

**11.** Consider the following statements:

1. The rate of population growth is increasing in the country

2. The death rate is declining faster in the country compared to birth rate
3. The birth rate is declining faster in the country compared to death rate
4. Rural-urban migration is taking place regularly in the country

Which one of the following conclusions may be true in the light of the above facts?

(a) The rate of population growth is increasing due to rural-urban migration
(b) The rate of population growth is increasing due to decline in death rate only
(c) The rate of population growth is increasing due to increase in birth rate only
(d) The rate of population growth is increasing due to faster decline in death rate than in birth rate

**12.** Consider the following statement:

"We shall go either for a picnic or for trekking". Which of the following, if true, would falsify this claim?

(a) We go for a picnic but not for trekking
(b) Activities such as picnic and trekking are encouraged by the health authorities
(c) We go for trekking and not for picnic
(d) We do not go either for picnic or for trekking

**13.** There were 50 faculty members comprising 30 males and the rest females. No male faculty member knew music, but many of the female faculty members did. The Head of the institution invited six faculty members to a tea party by draw of lots. At the party it was discovered that no member knew music. The conclusion is that:

(a) the party comprised male faculty members only
(b) the party comprised only those female faculty members who could not give renderings in music
(c) the party comprised both male and female faculty members
(d) nothing can be said about the gender composition of the party

**14.** Consider the following statements:

1. Either A and B are of the same age of A is older than B
2. Either C and D of the same age or D is older than C
3. B is older than *C*

Which of the following conclusions can be drawn from the above statements?

(a) A is older than B
(b) B and D are of the same age
(c) D is older than C
(d) A is older than C

***Directions for the following 2 (two) items:*** Consider the given information and answer the two items that follow.

No supporters of 'party X', who knew Z and supported his campaign strategy, agreed for the alliance with 'party Y'; but some of them had friends in 'party Y'.

**15.** With reference to the above information, which one among the following statements must be true?

(a) Some supporters of 'party Y' did not agree for the alliance with the 'party X'.
(b) There is at least one supporter of 'party Y' who knew some supporters of 'party X' as a friend.
(c) No supporters of 'party X' supported Z's campaign strategy.
(d) No supporters of 'party X' knew Z.

**16.** With reference to the above information, consider the following statements:

1. Some supporters of 'party X' knew Z.
2. Some supporters of 'party X', who opposed Z's campaign strategy, knew Z.
3. No supporters of 'party. X' supported Z's campaign strategy.

Which of the statements given above is/are not correct?

(a) 1 only (b) 2 and 3 only
(c) 3 only (d) 1, 2 and 3

**17.** Consider the following Statement:

Good voice is a natural gift but one has to keep practising to improve and excel well in the field of music.

*Conclusions:*

I. Natural gifts need nurturing and care,

II. Even though one's voice is not good, one can keep practising.

Which one of the following is correct in respect of the above statement and conclusions?

(a) Only conclusion I follows from the statement.

(b) Only conclusion II follows from the statement.

(c) Either conclusion I or conclusion II follows from the statement.

(d) Neither conclusion I nor conclusion II follows from the statement.

**18.** "Rights are certain advantageous conditions of social well-being indispensable to the true development of the citizen."

In the light of this statement, which one of the following is the correct understanding of rights?

(a) Rights aim at individual good only.

(b) Rights aim at social good only.

(c) Rights aim at both individual and social good.

(d) Rights aim at individual good devoid of social well-being.

**19.** Consider the following:

A + B means A is the son of B.

A – B means A is the wife of D.

What does the expression P + R – Q mean?

(a) Q is the son of P.

(b) Q is the wife of P.

(c) Q is the father of P.

(d) None of the above

**20.** Consider the given statement and the two conclusions that follow :

*Statement:*

Morning walk is good for health.

*Conclusions:*

1. All healthy people go for morning walk.
2. Morning walk is essential for maintaining good health.

What is/are the valid conclusion/conclusions?

(a) 1 only (b) 2 only

(c) Both 1 and 2 (d) Neither 1 nor 2

## Answers to Exercise Set-2 on Logical Reasoning

| | | | | | | | | | |
|---|---|---|---|---|---|---|---|---|---|
| **1.** (d) | **2.** (b) | **3.** (d) | **4.** (b) | **5.** (c) | **6.** (c) | **7.** (c) | **8.** (c) | **9.** (c) | **10.** (d) |
| **11.** (d) | **12.** (d) | **13.** (d) | **14.** (d) | **15.** (b) | **16.** (b) | **17.** (d) | **18.** (c) | **19.** (c) | **20.** (d) |

## HINTS AND SOLUTIONS TO EXERCISE SET-2 ON LOGICAL REASONING

**1.** As given in the statement, liberty implies that atmosphere where the inidividual has the opportunity to be their best. This is possible where the atmosphere permits the growth of human personality. Hence, option (d) is the answer.

**2.** We have two definite inequalities in the question:

Pen<Pencil<Book. Also, Cap<Book. But we are not sure where cap figures in the first inequality. Hence, no conclusion about Cap with respect to pen or pencil is possible. From Pen<Pencil<Book, we know that Pen<Book. Hence, option (b) is correct.

**Question 3 to 4:** Since twice the weight of Sohan is less than Mohan and Rohan's weight, it means clearly that Sohan weighs the least. However, between Rohan and Mohan we cannot determine who is weighing more – since the second statement does not tell us a clear relationship between them.

(Note: Twice Rohan being greater than Mohan can mean

Rohan > Mohan as well as Mohan > Rohan.)

Hence, the answers are:

3. We cannot determine who weighs maximum. Option (d)
4. Sohan weighs the least. Option (b)
5. We cannot draw any definite conclusions between cow and cat or for that matter between dogs and rats. However, conclusion III is self evident as when some rats are cats, then it must follow that some cats are rats. Hence, option (c) is correct.
6. $x \geq 25$ and $y \leq 40$

   Minimum of $x = 25$ and Maximum of $y = 40$

   $y - x = 40 - 25 = 15$ or less
7. In this case, we can see that the answer to the question can be yes or no, even after using both the statements together. Hence, Option (c) is correct.
8. In this question, you require both the statements together to identify that R is the largest – the second statement alone obviously is not sufficient and likewise, the first statement only shows us that P and Q are not the largest – so the largest could be R or S (if we consider S1 alone). Hence, option (c) is correct.
9. There can be many relationships between dogs and black, including all dogs are black as well as some dogs are not black as shown in the diagrams below. Hence, we can neither draw conclusion 1 or conclusion 2. Hence, option (c) is correct.

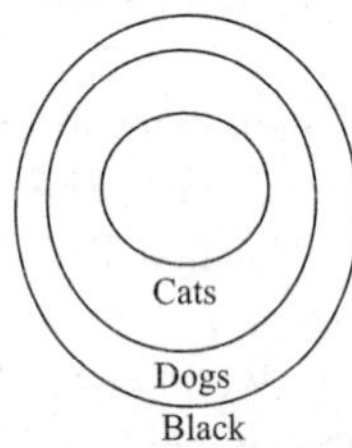

Relationship 1:
All dogs are black

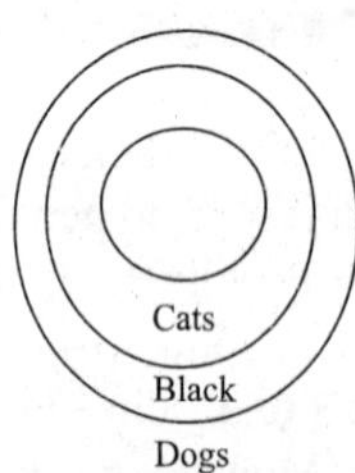

Relationship 2:
Some dogs are not black

10. From Statement 1 we get that the youngest has to be amongst A and B. S3 confirms for us that B is the youngest. Hence, option (d) is the correct answer.
11. Clearly option (d) is the reason for the faster rate of population growth.
12. The statement claims that we would go for 'either picnic or trekking'. Clearly one of them is compulsory. Hence, if we do not go for either of the two, we would have made a false claim. Hence, option (d) is correct.
13. We cannot conclude that there were only male faculty members at the party – since there could easily be some female faculty members who did not know music. So we reject option (a). We also cannot definitely conclude that the party had both male and female faculty members. Hence, we reject option (c) too. Option (b) is also not a conclusion we can reach. Hence, option (d) is the correct answer.
14. As per the question we know,

    A > or = B

    D > or = C

    B > C

    Hence we get, A > C
15. It is quite clear that since some supporters in Party X had friends in Party Y, it follows that at least one supporter of Party Y would know some supporters of Party X as a friend. Hence, option (b) is correct.
16. The third statement is clearly incorrect here - as it contradicts the fact that there are some people in Party X who supported Z's campaign strategy. Also, the second statement is not correct too, because it is not certain that there would be some supporters of Party X, who opposed Z's campaign strategy, Knew Z. Hence, option (b) is correct.
17. Neither of the two given conclusions can be concluded from the given statement. Hence, option (d) is correct.
18. It is clearly stated in the question statement that rights are conditions of 'social well being' as also that they have an indispensable role in the 'true development of the citizen'. Hence, they aim at both individual and social good. Option (c) is correct.
19. The statement P + R – Q means that P is the son of R & R is the wife of Q. Hence, Q must be the father of P. Hence, option (c) is correct.

**20.** Just because a morning walk is good for health, it doesn't mean that all healthy people go for morning walk - as there might be some people who are healthy and yet they do not go for morning walks. Likewise, the second conclusion can also be rejected - as one could maintain good health even without a morning walk. Hence, option (d) is correct.

# 3. Analytical Reasoning

## 3.1 Abilities to be Tested

The section on analytical reasoning (AR) comprises questions, which assess a candidate's ability to identify and process relationship between different set of subjects, (which may be persons or things) and to make further analytical inferences from the information furnished.

Thus, AR tests the skills of analogical deductions within a matrix of rules and conditions. But besides the key ability mentioned above, skills of logical comprehension and quick and accurate processing of information are also put to test.

## 3.2 Structure of AR Questions

The AR questions usually consist of three parts. The first part introduces the players or the subjects, which are either persons or things. The second one provides the set of conditions, which govern the relationship between the various subjects, which are like a matrix of constraints or the rules of the game. The third part is the actual query, which specifies what the reader is to do or find out. However, the first and second part may not be fully compartmentalised or separate from each other. Many a time players and rules may be introduced together in a concise passage.

## 3.3 Nature and Categories of Questions

The questions on AR can broadly be classified into four categories, depending on the nature of question and what the question requires the candidate to do. The question categories along with relevant illustrations are being discussed here.

### (a) Ordering or Linear Arrangement Type Questions

In this category of AR questions, the subjects of the questions (i.e., persons and things) are required to be placed in a specific order. The question stipulates the rules, which govern the linear arrangement or sequence in which players are to be placed. Consider the following illustration.

#### 3.1 Illustration

*In a parade five friends A, B, C, D, E participate. They are placed next to each other but not in this specific order. B is just behind A, D is in the middle E is not last and C is not amongst the first two. Find the order in which they are standing.*

The problem requires one to ascertain the order in which the five persons are standing. The rules, which govern the placement, are specified in the question. Though the problem may in the first reading, appear to be complicated but on carefully reading what is stated and inferring from it step by step, it becomes clear and the following points emerge.

- A and B are standing next to each other. A is ahead of B (stated in the question). However, the exact position is not known
- D is in middle (stated in the question). As such in a sequential representation, we place D at position 3

  1 2 3 4 5
  D
- C is stated to be not amongst first two. Therefore, C cannot occupy position 1 or 2 and has to be at position 4 or 5, as position 3 is already occupied by D (inference drawn).
- If C is going to occupy position 4 or 5 then A and B cannot be placed there, that is behind D, as at the positions 4 and 5 only one position will be vacant after placing C (both A and B have to be placed together). As such, A and B have to be placed at no. 1 and 2 position (inference). As A is ahead of B, he occupies the first position (inference). The possible arrangement is

| 1 | 2 | 3 | 4 | 5 |
|---|---|---|---|---|
| A | B | D | E or C | E or C |

- The last step is to infer the position of E and C. The question states that E is not last (i.e., no. 5) Thus, the only position for E is number 4. As such, C gets to occupy no. 5 position. Therefore, the order in which they are standing is

| 1 | 2 | 3 | 4 | 5 |
|---|---|---|---|---|
| A | B | D | E | C |

(b) **Choosing or Selecting the Right Player**

In this category of problem (also referred as selection problem), a set of conditions is specified and one or more players fulfilling those conditions is to be selected. Thus, within a set of subjects, a smaller set of subjects has to be chosen.

**3.2 Illustration**

*In an inter college festival X is to be represented by a team of two students. In the initial selection trial five students, A, B, C, D, E were shortlisted. A, C and E are males, while B, D are females. The team representing the college should not be an all-male team. A and D both would not want to be in the same team as they do not like each other. Band E are both singers and cannot be sent together. A, B and D are in Commerce stream, C and E are in Arts stream. The final team should not consist of both the participants from the same stream. Which are the pair of students who can be sent?*

The problem can be solved in many ways. A simple yet comprehensive method is, to try the various possible pairs and eliminate those, which the given conditions rule out. This is worked out in the following:

| Possible Pairs | Those which are Ruled Out and Reasons for it |
|---|---|
| AB | Both in Commerce Stream |
| AC | Both males |
| AD | Do not like each other and in same stream |
| AE | Both males |
| BC | |
| BD | Both in commerce stream |
| BE | Both singers |
| CD | |
| CE | Both in Arts and both males |
| DE | |

From the analysis, it is apparent that out of ten possible pairs, the given conditions eliminate seven and allow only three pairs, which are BC, CD and DE In the examination, the question may have more sub-parts, which may ask further questions based on the above analysis. For instance, the question may say, "*if one of the participants is B, who is the other?*" The analysis shows that the answer is participant C.

(c) **Allocation or Matching of Players**

In some AR questions, the subjects or the players may be required to be matched with another set of subjects. Sometimes they may be required to be placed in smaller groups. Some 'allocation type' problems have elements of similarity with the 'selection type' problems. However, unlike the latter, 'allocation type' problems require all the players/subjects to be placed in sub-groups and not just a few. Consider the following example:

**3.3 Illustration**

*Five friends A, B, C, D and E are studying in XYZ college the following subjects (but not in the same order)—Physics, Chemistry, Botany, Zoology and Maths.*

*A is not studying Chemistry. C likes Maths and took this subject. B opted neither for Chemistry nor for Physics, while E was the Botany topper of the 1st semester examination. Find out who studied which subject.*

- Careful reading of the question reveals that the following two subjects are read by C and E. C-Maths E-Botany (Topper in exam).
- Three subjects remain to be allocated, i.e., Physics, Chemistry and Zoology, amongst the remaining three students who are A, B and D. The question states that B does not study Physics or Chemistry. Therefore, the only subject remaining is Zoology. Thus, the new allocation of subjects is C-Maths, E-Botany B-Zoology.
- Now only two students A and D and two subjects, Physics and Chemistry remain. The question states that A is not studying Chemistry. Thus, he would be in Physics stream while the only remaining student D

should be allocated Chemistry. The final allocation would be as follows:

C-Maths

E-Botany

B-Zoology

A-Physics

D-Chemistry

(d) **Reasoning and Quantitative Application Questions**

Some questions in AR besides involving reasoning and deduction abilities, also entail quantitative reasoning skills. Such questions require basic understanding of mathematical operations, such as percentage, ratio and proportions, and averages. Besides, features of ordering or matching or allocation will also be incorporated in the problem.

**3.4 Illustration**

*Five friends A, B, C, D and E appear in Civil Services Preliminary examination. The relationship between their scores (in percentage) is as follows.*

*D scored twice as much marks as E. The marks of C was the average of A and B. A scored 23 more marks than E, while B scored 5 marks less than D. If E scored 42 then how much was scored by C.*

- The marks of E is given as 42.
- D scored twice as much as E, as such he scored 84.
- B scored 5 less than D, therefore he scored 79.
- A scored 23 marks more than E, as such his score will be 65.
- Score of C is average of B and A= (79+65)/2 =144/2 = 72.

  Besides the basic question formats specified above, AR questions may be of some other types also. But those are either derived from the formats specified above or at times are a mix of them.

(e) **Relationship questions**

Certain question of AR require to deduce the relationship between two persons say A and B. The question describes as to how each may be related to intermediary persons such as C, D and E. Hence the question requires a sequential analysis and building of the relationship between the parties.

**3.5 Illustration**

*Hariharan's father is the nephew of Radhika' mother. What is the relationship between Hariharan and Radhika?*

Such problems are complicated to begin with. The best way to solve them is to build a rough diagram showing the relationships and the family tree. While doing so, parties may be named with initial's/abbreviations to save time. A higher level just above a person is used to indicate a father or mother while a sideways connect may show a brother or sister. A connection vertically below usually represents a daughter or a son. There is no hard and fast rule and developing once own technique is the best. For example, above the family tree could look like as given below. From there it is clearly visible that father of Hariharan and Radhika are cousins and hence Radhika is the aunt of Hariharan.

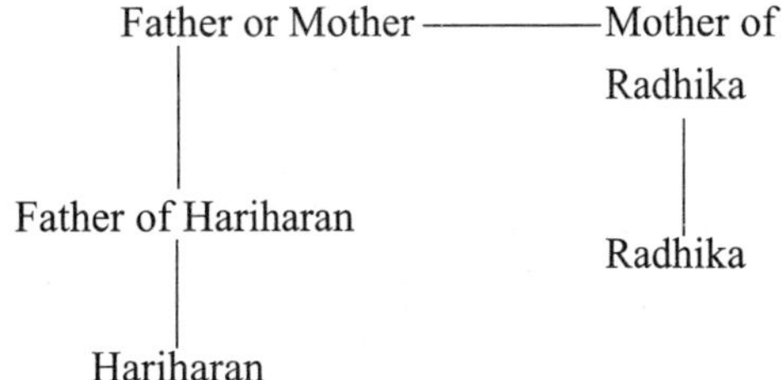


## 3.4 How to Prepare and Answer: Survival Tips

- **Read carefully.** While preparing for AR questions as well as while answering them in the examination, read them very carefully and with complete concentration. Casual reading of AR questions is meaningless and sheer waste of time. The questions are such, that mere cursory reading offers you little insight or understanding.
- **Do not presume anything, which is not stated** in the question. Rely totally on the information provided.
- **Always keep a pen and paper handy** while solving these questions. Unlike questions on 'comprehension ability' and 'logical reasoning', where the information of the question can be processed mentally and solution picked without the need of a pen and paper, in AR questions you need to jot down

the information provided, in a logical manner. Doing the entire exercise mentally will be extremely challenging and time consuming.

- **Use symbols, short forms and line diagrams to represent relationships,** sequences, chronology, etc. This is of utmost importance as this is what gives a quicker and better grasp over the question.

  Some examples can be

  A>B: A is greater than/elder to/taller than B.

  $B_A$: A is son of B/daughter of B.

  Ax Chemistry: A did not take Chemistry as a subject.

  There is no standard set of symbols. It is best to device your own symbols as you practice. Remembering symbols developed yourself, will be much easier and you are more likely to make use of them while solving problems.

- **Read every word meticulously** Pay special heed to words like exactly, always, only, never, not, etc. Improper understanding or missing out even a single such word can change the meaning of the question.

- **As you continue to read,** simultaneously **keep on deducing** what the information further implies. This can be done by jotting the information symbolically and diagrammatically and side by side noting down your own conclusions.

- Once you have gone through the problem and noted your inferences, **go through the problem once again, to make sure that you have used all of the information provided and your inferences are in consonance with the rules** and restrictions specified.

- **Do not remain stuck in a question.** If you cannot fathom how to solve a problem, it is better to press the mental 'skip button' and move on to the next one. With more practice and better understanding, you will be able to identify which are the problems which are beyond you, which ones are within your reach and which ones will take disproportionately long time to solve.

- **Selection by elimination does not work** in AR questions. So do not waste time in using this technique to arrive at a solution or to narrow down the choices. The answers in AR questions have to be worked out. Besides each question will have only one unique answer and not more than one partly correct choice, as in comprehension ability questions. So, if you have logically worked out an answer, which is given in the choice, you do not have to waste time in considering the other choices.

- **Practice and Practice more.** Exercise set given herewith includes a variety of questions, to help you grasp, the basics of the problem and the approach to attack them. Practice brings confidence, speed and accuracy, apart from understanding of the subject.

## Exercise Set-1 on Analytical Reasoning

1. In a student's union election of a college, three parties have been formed—Progressive Thoughts Party, Discipline and Progress Party and Cultural Awakening Party. Three students Kabir, Raju and Srestha are heading the parties (not in the given order). Following further information is known.

   The party, which Srestha is heading, has the symbol of violin. Football is the symbol of 'Discipline and Progress' party. The third party's symbol is a computer. Srestha had refused membership of the Discipline and Progress party. Raju is heading the Progressive Thoughts party.

   (i) With which party is Srestha associated?

   (a) Progressive Thoughts Party
   (b) Cultural Awakening Party
   (c) Discipline and Progress
   (d) Data insufficient

   (ii) What is the symbol of the party headed by Raju?

   (a) Computer (b) Football
   (c) Violin (d) Data insufficient

(iii) Kabir is heading
   (a) Progressive Thoughts Party
   (b) Cultural Awakening Party
   (c) Discipline and Progress Party
   (d) Data insufficient

**2.** V. Anand and B. Gelfand are playing a chess tournament. This is the last game and whosoever wins the game wins the tournament. In the previous game, which ended in a draw, Anand had black pieces.

After the 35th move, both players have equal number of pieces on board. There is at least one piece of a kind on board between the two players (viz. king, queen, rook, bishop, knight and pawn). The black wants to attack the opponent's rook but it is supported by the opponent's queen. No player has two pieces of the same kind. Between the two players, there are two kings and two pawns but all other pieces on board are single.

(i) How many pieces are there on board between the two players?
   (a) 10
   (b) 9
   (c) 8
   (d) Cannot be determined

(ii) Which combination of player, colour and pieces would be correct?
   (a) Anand-Black-Rook, Knight, King, Pawn
   (b) Anand-White-Rook, Queen, King, Pawn
   (c) Gelfand-White-Bishop, Queen, King, Pawn
   (d) Gelfand-Black-Bishop, Rook, King, Pawn

**3.** Nidhi and Sonali (two girls) and Saurabh and Prashant (two boys) are participating in a college bridge tournament. The teams have to be of a boy and a girl. A fifth person who is watching them play, deciphers the following information about the distribution of the four aces and four kings (of spades, hearts, diamonds and clubs) from their conversation and bidding.

- The aces of spades and hearts are with one person and that person's partner has the ace of diamonds.
- Sonali is not Prashant's partner and she has no aces, but has two kings.
- Saurabh has a king of hearts and an ace.
- Nidhi has no kings but her partner has a king of spade.
- Amongst the eight kings and aces, Prashant has three.

(i) Who is Saurabh's partner?
   (a) Sonali (b) Nidhi
   (c) Prashant (d) Data insufficient

(ii) Who has ace of clubs?
   (a) Prashant (b) Saurabh
   (c) Sonali (d) Nidhi

(iii) Sonali has
   (a) King of hearts and king of clubs
   (b) King of hearts and king of diamonds
   (c) King of diamonds and king of clubs
   (d) King of diamonds and king of spades

(iv) Which king does Prashant have?
   (a) Heart (b) Spade
   (c) Diamond (d) Club

**4.** The following information is known about the income of a team of employees in a manufacturing unit.

- B earns less than C.
- A's income is four times D.
- D earns 50% of what C earns.

(i) Which of the following conclusion can be arrived at?
   (a) B earns more than D.
   (b) B earns equal to what D earns.
   (c) B earns less than D.
   (d) No conclusion can be drawn about comparative earnings of B and D.

(ii) Who earns the least among all the four?
   (a) B
   (b) C
   (c) D
   (d) No conclusion can be drawn.

(iii) Which amongst the following information would be sufficient to establish their income in descending order?

1. B's income is 30% of what A's is.
2. If C were to give 20% of his income to B then income of both would be equal.

(a) Only 1 is sufficient.
(b) Only 2 is sufficient.
(c) Both 1 and 2 are individually sufficient.
(d) Even 1 and 2 together are not sufficient.

**5.** In a family, the following relations are given:

- U is R's son.
- P is Q's father.
- S is U's mother.
- R is Q's brother.
- T is R's mother.

(i) Who is the father of U?

(a) P (b) R
(c) C (d) Data not sufficient

(ii) What is the relationship between Q and T?

(a) Q is T's son.
(b) Q is T's daughter.
(c) Q is T's son or daughter.
(d) Q is T's mother.

(iii) T is P's

(a) sister (b) daughter
(c) mother (d) wife

**6.** After the success of a film, the actor, the director and the producer of the film get together for a private party. An attendant of the party gathers the following information about them. Aamir is richer than the director. Akshay has lesser money than the producer and Farhan is not the producer.

(i) Who is the richest?

(a) Farhan (b) Aamir
(c) Akshay (d) Data insufficient

(ii) Akshay is

(a) actor (b) director
(c) producer (d) data insufficient

(iii) Who is the producer?

(a) Farhan (b) Aamir
(c) Akshay (d) Data insufficient

**7.** Six girls A, B, C, D, E and F are very good friends and sit together in two consecutive rows of a class. Each row has three seats only, as shown in the following figure.

| | | |
|---|---|---|
| | | |

| | | |
|---|---|---|
| | | |

A is not in the front row and seats of B and C are diagonal to her in the opposite row, to her right and left, respectively. D is not adjacent to A and F is not to the left of A.

(i) Who sits to the left of A in the same row?

(a) E (b) F
(c) D (d) Data insufficient

(ii) Who sits to the right of B?

(a) Nobody (b) Either E or F
(c) D (d) C

(iii) Who is/are neighbour(s) of D?

(a) B and C (b) B only
(c) E and F (d) F only

**8.** A girl rolls a dice. Number 6 comes on the top most face of the dice. NS. 1 and 3 are seen opposite to each other. 5 is not opposite to 4, 6 is not opposite to 2 and 4 is not opposite to 6.

(i) Which number is at the bottom of the dice?

(a) 1 (b) 3
(c) 5 (d) Data insufficient

(ii) Which number is opposite to 2?

(a) 4 (b) 5
(c) 6 (d) Data insufficient

**9.** Six friends are sitting in a park facing one another. They have formed a circle and one person sits exactly opposite to the other. Tanay is sitting exactly opposite to Amar and on his left is Hari. Mahesh is between Amar and Hari and exactly opposite to Chetan. The sixth friend is Eesh.

(i) Who is sitting opposite to Hari?

(a) Tanay (b) Eesh
(c) Amar (d) Chetan

(ii) Amar is sitting between which of the following persons?
(a) Hari and Eesh
(b) Chetan and Tanay
(c) Mahesh and Eesh
(d) Hari and Tanay

(iii) If Hari and Tanay were to inter-change their positions then who would be sitting opposite to Hari?
(a) Chetan (b) Amar
(c) Eesh (d) Mahesh

**10.** Vaibhav has scored 85% in class XII[th] Board examination in which he took examination in five subjects. He scored 95 in Physics, which was his highest score. He scores more in Mathematics than in Chemistry and English. His marks in English was not the least in the five subjects. The average of his Mathematics and English scores is equal to that of Chemistry. The sum of his Chemistry and Economics marks is twice that of his English marks. He was satisfied with his score in English of 80.

(i) Which subject he scores the least?
(a) English (b) Chemistry
(c) Economics (d) Data insufficient

(ii) His score in Mathematics is
(a) 90 (b) 85
(c) 82 (d) Data insufficient

(iii) In which subject he scores exactly equal to his overall average marks?
(a) English (b) Chemistry
(c) Mathematics (d) Data not sufficient

**11.** A family of four comprises Sunita—mother, Ravi—father and two children, Rashmi and Rohan. They decide that once a week a dinner of each person's choice would be prepared. While on remaining three days regular meals (including chapatti, vegetable, dal, etc.) would be served. The dishes of choice are pizza, chowmein, paratha and pulao.

Rohan's favourite is pizza. Ravi's favourite dish is prepared on Sunday. On Tuesday night, the parents keep a fast and for children regular meal is served. Sunita does not like pulao and her favourite dish is prepared on Thursday. On Wednesday, chowmein is prepared. While on Fridays and Saturdays, regular meals are served.

(i) Whose favourite dish is Paratha?
(a) Sunita (b) Rashmi
(c) Ravi (d) Rohan

(ii) On which day Rashmi's favourite dish is prepared?
(a) Monday (b) Wednesday
(c) Thursday (d) Data insufficient

(iii) Which amongst the following is a correct matching?
(a) Sunita-Monday-Paratha
(b) Rohan-Wednesday-Pizza
(c) Rashmi-Wednesday-Pulao
(d) Ravi-Sunday-Pulao

**12.** A, B, C, D, E, F, G and H are eight friends who are sitting along the sides of a square to play a game. There are three persons on each side of the square and everybody is facing the centre of the square and is able to see each other. The following information is known.

- G and H are not adjacent to A.
- E is to the immediate right of D.
- A and C are in opposite rows and also in the centre of their respective rows.
- F and H are on the opposite end of one of the diagonals of the square.
- B and D are not in corners.
- C is in the row to the right of B.

(i) Who is to the left of B?
(a) F (b) G
(c) E (d) H

(ii) Apart from A and C, which two persons are in the centre of their respective sides?
(a) E and H (b) E and D
(c) B and D (d) H and B

(iii) Who is to the right of G?
(a) A (b) B
(c) C (d) D

(iv) Apart from F and H, which two other persons are on the opposite sides of the diagonal of the square?

(a) E and A (b) E and B

(c) B and G (d) G and E

**13.** An award function to felicitate a scientist, a poet, a writer and a social worker is organised. The function is presided over by a Minister while the local MP and a Secretary of the organising Department are also present. The seven persons are seated on a stage. No two awardees are to be seated adjacent to each other and the protocol demands that the Minister be seated in the centre.

The Secretary has to announce awards and he wants to sit as much towards the left of Minister as possible. The scientist and the writer are quite senior and cannot be seated on the end. The poet is known to the secretary and wants to sit next to him. The social worker has a train to catch he cannot sit for the whole function and wants to be on end of the row to facilitate his leaving early.

(i) Who is seated on the end of the row to the right of the Minister?

(a) Social worker

(b) Secretary

(c) Scientist

(d) Poet

(ii) What is the position of the Secretary from the Minister?

(a) 1st position to the left of Minister

(b) 2nd position to the left of Minister

(c) 3rd position to the left of Minister

(d) Data insufficient

(iii) Where is the scientist seated?

(a) 1st position to the left of Minister

(b) 2nd position to the left of Minister

(c) 1st position to the right of Minister

(d) Data insufficient

**14.** A group of eight college students decide to form a college rock band. Two of them sing, three of them play drums while another three of them play guitar (of different types).

All of the students are of different age. The youngest does not play guitar while the eldest does not sing. Manish does not play guitar, he is elder to Mahesh and he is also the second oldest. Mridul is elder to Manav and Mayank but Manan and Mahesh are elder to Mridul. Mayank is elder to Mohit and Manav is younger to Mohit. In terms of age, the position of Manan is fourth eldest and he plays drums, so does Mayank. Mohit neither sings nor plays guitar. Mahesh does not sing. The last person in this group is Mrigank.

(i) What does Mrigank do in the band?

(a) Plays guitar (b) Sings

(c) Plays drums (d) Data insufficient

(ii) Who is the youngest person in the band?

(a) Mohit (b) Manav

(c) Mayank (d) Mrigank

(iii) Who is/are elder to Manish?

(a) Manan and Mridul

(b) Mrigank and Mahesh

(c) Mohit only

(d) Mrigank only

(iv) Which two persons sing in the band?

(a) Manish and Mrigank

(b) Manav and Mahesh

(c) Manav and Mrigank

(d) Manish and Manav

**15.** Five employees of a company named A, B, C, D and E wear shirts of different colours— Yellow, Brown, Black, Grey and Orange (not necessarily in the same order). They come to office by five different types of car, an SX4, a Santro, a Nano, an Indigo and a Dzire. B owns an Indigo and does not wear a yellow shirt. C wears a brown shirt and does not have an SX4 or a Dzire. E has Santro and does not wear a black or yellow shirt. A has a Dzire and D does not wear a yellow or grey shirt.

(i) Which car is owned by C?

(a) Nano (b) Santro

(c) Dzire (d) Data insufficient

(ii) What is the colour of B's shirt?

(a) Black (b) Grey

(c) Yellow (d) Data insufficient

(iii) What does the owner of Santro wear?

(a) Black or Orange shirt

(b) Orange or Grey shirt

(c) Orange shirt

(d) Grey shirt

(iv) What does the owner of Dzire wear?

(a) Yellow shirt (b) Brown shirt

(c) Grey shirt (d) Data insufficient

**16.** Mr. X is murdered. He is discovered unconscious by his wife in the morning who also calls the police. The police discovers that he was hit in the night by a heavy object and it records the statement of all the persons in the house. Their statements are given here:

Wife — I don't know who did it. I did not do it. I was sleeping in another room as I was having severe headache and my husband wanted to watch TV.

Watchman — I was outside the house and did not even enter it during the night.

Cook — The wife must have done it as I heard her having a quarrel with her husband.

Gardener — The cook must have done it as a few days ago he was rebuked by Mr. X for stealing some money.

Amongst all four, only one person told the truth while others were lying. Who amongst the four murdered Mr. X?

(a) Wife (b) Watchman

(c) Cook (d) Gardener

**17.** In a family the following relationships are given:

- P is sister of M (not a cousin).
- K is daughter of O.
- N is son of P.
- J is mother of M.
- N is brother of K (not a cousin).

(i) Who is the father of N?

(a) O (b) P

(c) J (d) Data insufficient

(ii) What is the relationship between K and M?

(a) M is an aunt of K.

(b) M is an uncle of K.

(c) M can be either an aunt or an uncle of K.

(d) Data not given to establish relationship.

(iii) O is ________ of P.

(a) brother (b) sister

(c) father (d) husband

**18.** Puja and Nira are playing a game. Puja writes a four digit number and Nira has to guess it. As clues Puja can tell whether any of the digits and their positions are correct. Nira has to guess the number correctly in four attempts.

Nira – Is the no. 1234?

Puja – All digits are wrong.

Nira – Is it 5789?

Puja – Two digits are right but their position is wrong.

Nira – Is it 1854?

Puja – Two digits are right and their positions are also right.

Nira guesses the number in 4th attempt rightly.

(i) Are 7 and 8 contained in the number?

(a) Only 7 is contained in the number.

(b) Only 8 is contained in the number.

(c) Both 7 and 8 are contained in the number.

(d) Neither 7 nor 8 is contained in the number.

(ii) The correct number is;

(a) 5708 (b) 6580

(c) 5860 (d) 6850

**19.** Four friends Amit, Mayank, Vijay and Pradeep are discussing the runs scored by the top four batsmen of the Indian side in the world cup cricket tournament. As per Amit, Gambhir scored the 2nd highest runs while Sachin scored the 4th highest runs. Mayank recollects that Sachin was the top scorer while Yuvraj had scored the 4th highest runs. Pradeep interjects that Yuvraj was the 3rd highest run scorer and Sehwag's aggregate was the 2nd highest. Vijay is in conformity with Mayank regarding Sachin being the top scorer but as per him Gambhir was the 3rd highest scorer. When they check the runs scored on internet, they find that one statement of each friend was right while one statement of each was wrong.

(i) Which player was the highest runs scorer?
  (a) Sachin (b) Sehwag
  (c) Gambhir (d) Yuvraj

(ii) Which player scored the least runs amongst the four players?
  (a) Sachin (b) Sehwag
  (c) Gambhir (d) Yuvraj

(iii) Which, in descending order, is the correct order in which the players scored runs?
  (a) Sachin, Sehwag, Gambhir, Yuvraj
  (b) Sehwag, Gambhir, Sachin, Yuvraj
  (c) Sachin, Gambhir, Sehwag, Yuvraj
  (d) Sachin, Gambhir, Yuvraj, Sehwag

**20.** Five friends Ajay, Chandan, Dinesh, Joy and Mukesh who were taking coaching in a cricket academy, are picked up by five separate cricket clubs for playing a cricket tournament. The clubs are P, Q, R, S and T (not in the given order). The clubs have jerseys of separate colours, which are green, blue, yellow, orange and red (not in the given order).

Ajay does not wear orange or blue jersey. Mukesh wears red jersey and is not in club Q. Chandan always wanted to play for Club T and manages to get selected for it. Dinesh is picked by Club R, which has yellow jersey as dress. The players of club P wear orange jersey.

(i) Which colour jersey does Ajay wear?
  (a) Green (b) Blue
  (c) Orange (d) Red

(ii) For which club does Joy play?
  (a) P (b) Q
  (c) R (d) S or T

(iii) Which of the following combinations is right?
  (a) Ajay-Q-Blue
  (b) Chandan-Q-Blue
  (c) Dinesh-R-Orange
  (d) Mukesh-S-Red

(iv) Chandan wears jersey of which colour?
  (a) Red (b) Blue
  (c) Yellow (d) Green

**21.** Four friends purchase a shop each on different floors of a mall, which has ground and five floors. Tina runs a leather bags shop. Reena's shop is immediately above that of Asha's and no other two shops are on consecutive floors. On the ground floor, there is a cosmetics shop of one of the friends. Bina's shop is not on the topmost floor. Reena's shop is not on the 1st floor or the topmost floor. The two other shops are of jewellery and garments. Reena wanted to start a jewellery shop but did not have enough capital for it.

(i) Who has a shop on the ground floor?
  (a) Asha (b) Bina
  (c) Reena (d) Tina

(ii) Who runs the jewellery shop?
  (a) Asha (b) Bina
  (c) Reena (d) Tina

(iii) Where is Tina's shop located?
  (a) Ground Floor
  (b) Third Floor
  (c) Fifth Floor
  (d) Data insufficient

(iv) Which shop does Reena own?
  (a) Jewellery shop
  (b) Leather bags shop
  (c) Garments shop
  (d) Cosmetics shop

**22.** A family, consisting of six members A, B, C, D, E and F goes from New Delhi to Howrah on Rajdhani Express. The family comprises the father, his two sons, the wife and two children (a boy and a girl) of the elder married son. The other son is unmarried. They are allotted 6 berths in AC III tier coach having numbers 1 to 6. 1 and 4 are lower berths of the coupe, 2 and 5 are middle berths while 3 and 6 are top berths. The berths 1, 2 and 3 are on one side and the rest opposite to them.

- B is the only senior citizen of the group and he is allotted a lower berth.
- The wife of elder son sleeps on berth no. 1.
- The girl child sleeps on a middle berth.
- A sleeps on the berth just above his wife's.
- On berth no. 3 is E who sleeps just above his father.
- C is not a female.
- E is brother of F.

(i) Who is wife of A?

(a) B (b) C

(c) D (d) Data not sufficient

(ii) On which berth F sleeps?

(a) No. 2 (b) No. 3

(c) No. 5 (d) No. 6

(iii) On which berth is the unmarried son sleeping?

(a) No. 2 (b) No. 3

(c) No. 5 (d) No. 6

(iv) What is the relationship between C and D?

(a) D is wife of C.

(b) C is brother of D.

(c) C is son of D.

(d) C is brother in law of D.

**23.** In a coaching institute, five courses Mathematics, Biology, Chemistry, Physics and English are taught. Each subject is taught on a different day from Monday to Friday (not in the given order). Five visiting lecturers teach these subjects who are Arora, Bajaj, Roy, Sarkar and Garg (not in the same order). No two subjects are taught on the same day.

Arora teaches Biology but not on Thursday or Friday. Bajaj teaches Mathematics on Wednesday. Roy teaches on Monday but does not teach Chemistry or Physics.

(i) Which lecturer's course immediately follows after Biology?

(a) Bajaj (b) Arora

(c) Sarkar (d) Garg

(ii) Which course is taught by Sarkar?

(a) Either Chemistry or Physics

(b) Either Biology or Mathematics

(c) English

(d) Mathematics

(iii) Which course is taught on Thursday?

(a) Mathematics (b) English

(c) Biology (d) Data inadequate

(iv) Which course is taught on Monday?

(a) English (b) Biology

(c) Chemistry (d) Data inadequate

**24.** Ramesh and his wife invite four of their friends for dinner at their new house at Laxmi Bai Nagar, New Delhi. The friends are Suresh, Mahesh, Umesh and Dinesh and their wives (not in order) are Seema, Maya, Uma and Diya. One of the couples has two children a boy and a girl while one has none and one couple did not bring their children.

- Mahesh is the first to arrive with his family and is greeted at the house by Rama. Suresh is not the last to arrive and on his arrival, he was greeted by Umesh.
- Uma on her arrival with her husband was greeted by the two ladies present till then, they were Maya and Rama.
- Diya has a daughter Rita, aged 12 and Diya is not the wife of Dinesh.
- In all there are four children at the gathering. Joy and Jyoti are children of Maya. Seema regrets not bringing her children. Mohit plays a good host to the children and shows all his games and story books, which he has at the house.

(i) Who arrives last at the party?

(a) Dinesh (b) Umesh

(c) Mahesh (d) Suresh

(ii) How many people including children were present at the gathering?

(a) 12 (b) 13
(c) 14 (d) Data not sufficient

(iii) Who is the father of Rita?
(a) Ramesh (b) Dinesh
(c) Mahesh (d) Suresh

(iv) Which lady arrived second for the dinner?
(a) Rama (b) Maya
(c) Diya (d) Uma

(v) Who is Ramesh's child?
(a) Joy (b) Mohit
(c) Rita (d) Data insufficient

(vi) Which couple does not have any child?
(a) Umesh–Uma
(b) Ramesh–Rama
(c) Dinesh–Diya
(d) Data not sufficient

**25.** In a video game race course, the following types of signals for the player motorcyclist is provided.

White light = start
Blue light = turn left
Red light = turn right
Yellow light = stop
Green light = drive at speed of 5 m/s
Pink light = drive at speed of 2 m/s
Brown light = drive at speed of 1 m/s

A motorcyclist at the start point is facing east on the video game map. He receives the following signals during the course, which he exactly complies with.

- Starting Point – white light and brown light
- After 20 seconds, 1st signal – blue light and pink light
- After 15 seconds, 2nd signal –red light
- After 20 seconds, 3rd signal –red and green lights
- After 10 seconds, 4th signal – blue and pink lights
- After 15 seconds, 5th signal – yellow light

(i) What is the distance travelled by the motorcyclist from the starting point till the last signal?
(a) 150 m
(b) 180 m
(c) 170 m
(d) Distance cannot be determined

(ii) If at the starting point, motorcyclist was heading towards north instead of east, what would be the final position of the motor-cyclist?
(a) 90 m to the east and 20 m to the south
(b) 80 m to the east and 40 m to the south
(c) 90 m to the north and 20 m to the east
(d) 80 m to the west and 30 m to the north

**26.** A group of ten students A, B, C, D, E, F, G, H, I and J are staging a play. B, D and E are girls. The play has five characters P, Q, R, S and T. P is the male lead character while Q is the female lead character. R and T are male characters. C would only act if A is in the play, as A is his best friend. Because of certain differences, E does not want to be in the play with F nor does A want to be with H. D and J are sister and brother and one would be in the play only if the other is there. B would only act in the play if H is also there. C is the best actor among males and E amongst the females. The director of the play strongly wants them to take the respective lead roles. A is too tall for character T. Fulfilling all of the aforesaid conditions, the Director selects the actors and assigns a character to them.

(i) Which of the following are true?
1. A is not selected in the play.
2. B is not selected in the play.
(a) Only 1 is true.
(b) Only 2 is true.
(c) Both 1 and 2 are true.
(d) Neither 1 nor 2 is true.

(ii) Who from amongst B, D and E are selected?
(a) B and D (b) B and E
(c) D and E (d) All of the above

(iii) Who plays the character 'R'?
(a) A (b) F
(c) C (d) None of the above

(iv) Who plays the character 'S'?

(a) D (b) B

(c) E (d) Data insufficient

(v) Which amongst the following is the correct set of persons acting in the play?

(a) A, C, E, H, J

(b) A, B,C, E, H

(c) A, C, D, E, I

(d) A, C, D, E, J

**27.** Ten members of a family A, B, C, D, E, F, G, H, I and J go for a picnic. A is the head of the family and is 70 years old. Only his wife, their off-springs and their families live with him. The family stretches across three generations and has equal number of males and females. The family has three sons and three daughters. No two members are of the same age.

- A has 3 grandchildren. H, who is 12 years old, is the eldest grand-child of A (from paternal side).
- A's wife loves her maternal granddaughter J the most as she is only two years old and the youngest.
- D is a doctor and not married and takes care of his mother B's health.
- C's wife is not working now. She left her job after the birth of her second child, I a daughter. Her first child is now aged 12 years.
- J's father is a businessman and lives with his in-laws.
- E is sister of D and C is brother of D.
- F is not a male.

(i) Who is A's wife?

(a) E (b) B

(c) F (d) Data insufficient

(ii) Who is J's father?

(a) G (b) C

(c) A (d) D

(iii) What is the relationship between G and E?

(a) G is the father of E.

(b) G is the son of E.

(c) G is the brother of E

(d) G is the husband of E.

(iv) Who are A's granddaughters?

(a) H and I (b) H only

(c) J only (d) I and J

(v) Who is C's wife?

(a) D (b) E

(c) F (d) G

(vi) What is the relation between E and F?

(a) E is the sister of F.

(b) E is sister in law of F.

(c) E is brother of F.

(d) E is brother in law of F.

**28.** In an engineering college's placement, five friends Ramesh, Ravi, Ram, Rohan and Rohit are selected by five different I.T. companies A, B, C, D and E (not in the specific order). These companies have their offices in different cities—Ahmedabad, Bengaluru, Delhi, Hyderabad and Mumbai (not in the specific order).

- Ravi was not selected by either company, A or C.
- Ramesh did not want to go to Bengaluru where company C's office is located and did not apply for it.
- Company B is not located either at Delhi or Mumbai.
- Rohan was selected by company D and got posted at Ahmedabad.
- Rohit was selected by company E.

(i) Where did Ramesh get posted?

(a) Delhi (b) Delhi or Mumbai

(c) Hyderabad (d) Data insufficient

(ii) Who was posted at Bengaluru?

(a) Ram (b) Rohan

(c) Ravi (d) Rohit

(iii) Which of the following combination of person, company and posting is correct?

(a) Ramesh-A-Mumbai

(b) Rohit-D-Mumbai

(c) Ram-C-Ahmedabad

(d) Ravi-B-Hyderabad

(iv) Which company has its office in Mumbai?

(a) A (b) B

(c) E (d) Data insufficient

(v) Who was posted in company A?
(a) Ravi (b) Ram
(c) Rohan (d) Ramesh

**29.** Ten students A, B, C, D, E, F, G, H, I and J are going to a college fest from Delhi to Jaipur. Students A, B, C and D are females. Two females are participating in Hindi duet. Two males are singing an English duet. J is performing a mono-acting, while the remaining five students are staging a play.

In the Jaipur college hostel, the students are allocated rooms numbering. 11 to 18. Rooms 11 and 17 are double-bedded while the rest are single ones. The rooms are arranged in a sequential order as per their respective numbers. Girls and boys cannot share a room. The ladies' toilet is located next to room no. 11 and all girls want to be as near it as possible.

- D who is participating in the play is superstitious about room no. 13 and does not want to stay there.
- The male student performing monoacting wants to take a single-seater room at either end so that he can practice in solitude.
- C does not have any specific choice of a room and she is not singing the duet.
- E and F are singing the English duet and would like to stay together, so would the two girls singing Hindi duet.

(i) The two girls who are singing Hindi duet are
(a) A and D (b) B and D
(c) A and B (d) Data insufficient

(ii) Which room is allotted to I?
(a) 18 (b) 17
(c) 16 (d) Data insufficient

(iii) Which is the right combination of people participating in the play?
(a) A, B, C, G, H
(b) B, C, D, H, I
(c) C, D, G, H, J
(d) C, D, G, H, I

(iv) Which of the following statements are correct?
(a) E and F are doubling and I is in a single-seater room.
(b) G and H are doubling and I is in a single-seater room.
(c) H and I are doubling and J is in a single-seater room.
(d) None of the above

(v) Who stays in room no. 13?
(a) A (b) B
(c) C (d) Data insufficient

**30.** Five relatives, all males gather to settle a family property dispute. They are Sohan, Mohan, Rohan, Ram and Shyam. The following information about them is known.

- Sohan is a farmer.
- Ram's uncle addresses Shyam's uncle, as uncle.
- Rohan has no children and he retired as teacher.
- Mohan is Sohan's son.
- Ram is the doctor's only son and he is the youngest in the entire family.
- The difference in Shyam's and Mohan's age is two years only.
- Ram's uncle is an engineer.
- One amongst the five does business.
- There are two set of brothers amongst the five.
- Shyam is not Ram's uncle.
- Everybody follows Shyam's father's advice to settle the dispute.

(i) Who is Ram's father?
(a) Sohan (b) Mohan
(c) Rohan (d) Shyam

(ii) Who's occupation is business?
(a) Ram (b) Shyam
(c) Mohan (d) Rohan

(iii) What is the relationship between the doctor and the engineer?

(a) The doctor is engineer's father.

(b) The doctor is engineer's son.

(c) The doctor is engineer's uncle.

(d) The doctor is engineer's brother.

(iv) Who is Shyam's uncle?

(a) Sohan (b) Mohan

(c) Rohan (d) Data insufficient

(v) How many sons does Sohan have?

(a) One

(b) Two

(c) Three

(d) Data insufficient

(vi) What is Mohan's occupation?

(a) Doctor (b) Engineer

(c) Business (d) Data insufficient

## Answers of Exercise Set-1 on Analytical Reasoning

| S.No. | (i) | (ii) | (iii) | (iv) | (v) | (vi) |
|---|---|---|---|---|---|---|
| 1. | (b) | (a) | (c) | | | |
| 2. | (c) | (b) | | | | |
| 3. | (a) | (b) | (c) | (b) | | |
| 4. | (d) | (d) | (c) | | | |
| 5. | (b) | (c) | (d) | | | |
| 6. | (a) | (b) | (b) | | | |
| 7. | (a) | (a) | (a) | | | |
| 8. | (c) | (a) | | | | |
| 9. | (b) | (c) | (b) | | | |
| 10. | (c) | (a) | (b) | | | |
| 11. | (a) | (b) | (d) | | | |
| 12. | (a) | (c) | (c) | (d) | | |
| 13. | (a) | (b) | (d) | | | |
| 14. | (a) | (b) | (c) | (d) | | |
| 15. | (a) | (d) | (b) | (a) | | |
| 16. | (b) | | | | | |
| 17. | (a) | (c) | (d) | | | |
| 18. | (b) | (d) | | | | |
| 19. | (a) | (b) | (d) | | | |
| 20. | (a) | (a) | (d) | (b) | | |
| 21. | (b) | (a) | (c) | (c) | | |
| 22. | (c) | (c) | (d) | (d) | | |

| S.No. | (i) | (ii) | (iii) | (iv) | (v) | (vi) |
|---|---|---|---|---|---|---|
| 23. | (a) | (a) | (d) | (a) | | |
| 24. | (a) | (c) | (d) | (d) | (b) | (a) |
| 25. | (c) | (c) | | | | |
| 26. | (b) | (c) | (a) | (a) | (d) | |
| 27. | (b) | (a) | (d) | (d) | (c) | (b) |
| 28. | (b) | (a) | (d) | (d) | (d) | |
| 29. | (c) | (d) | (d) | (a) | (c) | |
| 30. | (d) | (a) | (d) | (c) | (b) | (b) |

## Exercise Set-2 on Analytical Reasoning

**1.** Ten new TV shows started in January – 5 sitcoms, 3 drama and 2 news magazines. By April, only seven of the new shows were still on, five of them being sitcoms.

Based on the above information, four conclusions, as given below, have been made. Which one of these logically follows from the information given above?

(a) Only one news magazine show is still on.
(b) Only one of the drama shows is still on.
(c) At least one discontinued show was a drama.
(d) Viewers prefer sitcoms over drama.

**2.** Read the passage given below and the two statements that follow (given on the basis of the passage):

Four men are waiting at Delhi airport for a Mumbai flight. Two are doctors and the other two are businessmen. Two speak Gujarati and two speak Tamil. No two of the same profession speak the same language. Two are Muslims and two are Christians. No two of the same religion are of the same profession, nor do they speak the same language. The Tamil-speaking doctor is a Christian.

1. The Christian-businessman speaks Gujarati.
2. The Gujarati-speaking doctor is a Muslim.

Which of the above statements is/are correct conclusion/conclusions?

(a) 1 only (b) 2 only
(c) Both 1 and 2 (d) Neither 1 nor 2

***Directions for the following 5 (five) items:***

*Examine the information given in the following paragraph and answer the items that follow:*

Guest lectures on five subjects viz., Economics, History, Statistics, English and Mathematics have to be arranged in a week from Monday to Friday. Only one lecture can be arranged on each day. Economics cannot be scheduled on Tuesday. Guest faculty for History is available only on Tuesday. Mathematics lecture has to be scheduled immediately after the day of Economics lecture. English lecture has to be scheduled immediately before the day of Economics lecture.

**3.** Which lecture is scheduled on Monday?

(a) History (b) Economics
(c) Mathematics (d) Statistics

**4.** Which lecture is scheduled between Statistics and English?

(a) Economics (b) History
(c) Mathematics (d) No lecture

5. Which lecture is the last one in the week?
   (a) History (b) English
   (c) Mathematics (d) Economics

6. Which lecture is scheduled on Wednesday?
   (a) Statistics (b) Economics
   (c) English (d) History

7. Which lecture is scheduled before the Mathematics lecture?
   (a) Economics (b) History
   (c) Statistics (d) English

8. Two glasses of equal volume are respectively half and three-fourths filled with milk. They are then filled to the brim by adding water. Their contents are then poured into another vessel. What will be the ratio of milk to water in this vessel?
   (a) 1 : 3 (b) 2 : 3
   (c) 3 : 2 (d) 5 : 3

9. In five flats, one above the other, live five professionals. The professor has to go up to meet his IAS officer friend. The doctor is equally friendly to all, and has to go up as frequently as go down. The engineer has to go up to meet his MLA friend above whose flat lives the professor's friend.

   From the ground floor to the top floor, in what order do the five professionals live?
   (a) Engineer, Professor, Doctor, IAS officer, MLA
   (b) Professor, Engineer, Doctor, IAS officer, MLA
   (c) IAS officer, Engineer, Doctor, Professor, MLA
   (d) Professor, Engineer, Doctor, MLA, IAS officer

10. Only six roads A, B, C, P, Q and R connect a military camp to the rest of the country. Only one out of A, P and R is open at any one time. If B is closed, so is Q. Only one of A and B is open during storms. P is closed during floods. In this context, which one of the following statements is correct?
   (a) Under normal conditions only three roads are open.
   (b) During storms at least one road is open.
   (c) During floods only three roads are open.
   (d) During calamities all roads are closed.

11. Four political parties W, X, Y and Z decided to set up a joint candidate for the coming parliamentary elections. The formula agreed by them was the acceptance of a candidate by most of the parties. Four aspiring candidates, A, B, C and D approached the parties for their tickets.

   A was acceptable to W but not to Z.

   B was acceptable to Y but not to X.

   C was acceptable to W and Y.

   D was acceptable to W and X.

   When candidate B was preferred by W and Z, candidate C was preferred by X and Z, and candidate A was acceptable to X but not to Y who got the ticket?
   (a) A (b) B
   (c) C (d) D

***Direction for the following 4 (four) items***

*Read the following statements and answer the four items that follow:*

Five, cities P, Q, R, S and T are connected by different modes of transport as follows:

P and Q are connected by boat as well as rail. S and R are connected by bus and boat.

Q and T are connected by air only. P and R are connected by boat only.

T and R are connected by rail and bus.

12. Which mode of transport would help one to reach R starting from Q, but without changing the mode of transport?
   (a) Boat (b) Rail
   (c) Bus (d) Air

13. If a person visits each of the places starting from P and gets back to P, which of the following places must he visit twice?
   (a) Q (b) R
   (c) S (d) T

**14.** Which one of the following pairs of cities is connected by any of the routes directly, without going to any other city?

(a) P and T (b) T and S
(c) Q and R (d) None of these

**15.** Between which two cities among the pairs of cities given below are there maximum travel options available?

(a) Q and S (b) P and R
(c) P and T (d) Q and R

***Directions for the following 3 (three) items***

*Read the following passage and answer the three items that follow:*

A tennis coach is trying to put together a team of four players for the forthcoming tournament. For this 7 players are available: males A, B and C; and females W, X, Y and Z. All players have equal capability and at least 2 males will be there in the team. For a team of four, all players must be able to play with each other. But, B cannot play with W, C cannot play with Z and W cannot play with Y.

**16.** If Y is selected and B is rejected, the team will consist of which one of the following groups?

(a) A, C, W and Y (b) A, C, X and Y
(c) A, C, Y and Z (d) A, W, Y and Z

**17.** If B is selected and Y is rejected, the team will consist of which one of the following groups?

(a) A, B, C and W (b) A, B, C and Z
(c) A, B, C and X (d) A, W, Y and Z

**18.** If all the three males are selected, then how many combinations of four member teams are possible?

(a) 1 (b) 2
(c) 3 (d) 4

**19.** The music director of a film wants to select four persons to work on different aspects of the composition of a piece of music. Seven persons are available for this work; they are Rohit, Tanya, Shobha, Kaushal, Kunal, Mukesh and Jaswant. Rohit and Tanya will not work together. Kunal and Shobha will not work together. Mukesh and Kunal want to work together.

Which of the following is the most acceptable group of people that can be selected by the music director?

(a) Rohit, Shobha, Kunal and Kaushal
(b) Tanya, Kaushal, Shobha and Rohit
(c) Tanya, Mukesh, Kunal and Jaswant
(d) Shobha, Tanya, Rohit and Mukesh

**20.** Five people A, B, C, D and E are seated about a round table. Every chair is spaced equidistant from adjacent chairs.

(i) C is seated next to A.
(ii) A is seated two seats from D.
(iii) B is not seated next to A. Which of the following must be true?

(I) D is seated next to B.
(II) E is seated next to A.

Select the correct answer from the codes given below:

(a) I only (b) II only
(c) Both I and II (d) Neither I nor II

**Directions for the following 3 (three) items**

*Examine carefully the following statements and answer the three items that follow:*

Out of four friends A, B, C and D, A and B play football and cricket, B arid C play cricket and hockey, A and D play basketball and football, C and D play hockey and basketball.

**21.** Who does not play hockey?

(a) D (b) C
(c) B (d) A

**22.** Who plays football, basketball and hockey?

(a) D (b) C
(c) B (d) A

**23.** Which game do B, C and D play?

(a) Basketball (b) Hockey
(c) Cricket (d) Football

**24.** A, B, C, D and E belong to five different cities P, Q, R, S and T (not necessarily in that order). Each one of them comes from a different city. Further it is given that:

1. B and C do not belong to Q.
2. B and E do not belong to P and R.

3. A and C do not belong to R, S and T.
4. D and E do not belong to Q and T.

Which one of the following statements is not correct?

(a) C belongs to P (b) D belongs to R
(c) A belongs to Q (d) B belongs to S

**25.** Seven men, A, B, C, D, E, P and G are standing in a queue in that order. Each one is wearing a cap of a different colour like violet, indigo, blue, green, yellow, orange and red. D is able to see in front of him green and blue, but not violet. E can see violet and yellow, but not red. G can see caps of all colours other than orange. If E is wearing an indigo coloured cap, then the colour of the cap worn by F is

(a) Blue (b) Violet
(c) Red (d) Orange

**26.** A question paper must have a question on one of the eight poets: A, B, C, D, E, F, G or H. The first four belong to the medieval period while the rest are considered modern poets. Generally, modern poets figure in the question paper in alternate years. Generally, those who life H like G also; and those who like F like E also. The paper-setter does not like to ask about F as he has written a book on F, but he likes F. Last year, the paper contained a question on A. On the basis of the information given, this year's paper is most likely to contain a question on

(a) C (b) E
(c) F (d) H

**27.** In a group of six women there are four dancers, fear vocal magicians, one actress and three violinists. Girija and Vanaja are among the violinists while Jalaja and Shailaja do not know how to play on the violin. Shailaja and Tanuja are among the dancers. Jalaja, Vanaja, Shailaja and Tanuja are all vocal musicians and two of them are also violinists. If Pooja is an actress, who among the following is certainly a dancer and a violinist?

(a) Jalaja (b) Pooja
(c) Shailaja (d) Tanuja

**28.** The letters L, M, N, O, P, Q, R, S and T in their order are substituted by nine integers 1 to 9 but not in that order. 4 is assigned to P. The difference between P and T is 5. The difference between N and T is 8. What is the integer assigned to N?

(a) 7 (b) 5
(c) 4 (d) 6

**29.** Examine the following statements:

1. George attends Music classes on Monday.
2. He attends Mathematics classes on Wednesday.
3. His Literature classes are not on Friday.
4. He attends History classes on the day following the day of his Mathematics classes.
5. On Tuesday, fee attends his Sports classes.

If he attends just one subject in a day and his Sunday is free, then he is also free on

(a) Monday (b) Thursday
(c) Saturday (d) Friday

**30.** Six books are labelled A, B, C, D, E and F and are placed side by side. Books B, C, E and F have green covers while others have yellow covers. Books A, B and D are new while fee rest are old volumes. Books A, B and C are law reports while the rest are medical extracts. Which two books are old medical extracts and have green covers?

(a) B and C (b) E and F
(c) C and E (d) C and F

**31.** There are seven persons up on a ladder, A, B, C, D, E, F and G (not in that order). A is further up than E but is lower than C. B is in the middle. G is between A and B. E is between E and F. If F is between E and D, the person on the bottom step of the ladder will be

(a) B (b) F
(c) D (d) E

**32.** Consider that:

1. A is taller than B.
2. C is taller than A.

3. D is taller than C.
4. E is the tallest of all.

If they are made to sit in the above order of their height, who will occupy the mid position?

(a) A (b) B
(c) C (d) D

**33.** Consider the following statements:

There are six villages A, B, C, D, E and F.

F is 1 km to the west of D.

B is 1 km to the east of E.

A is 2 km to the north of E.

C is 1 km to the east of A.

D is 1 km to the south of A.

Which three villages are in a line?

(a) A, C, B (b) A, D, E
(c) C, B, F (d) E, B, D

**34.** Four children are sitting in a row. A is occupying the seat next to B but not next to C. If C is not sitting next to D, who is/are occupying seat/ seats adjacent to D?

(a) B (b) A
(c) B and A (d) Impossible to tell

**35.** There are 5 tasks and 5 persons. Task-1 cannot be assigned to either person-1 or person-2. Task-2 must be assigned to either person-3 or person-4. Every person is to be assigned one task. In how many ways can the assignment be done?

(a) 6 (b) 12
(c) 24 (d) 144

***Directions for the following 2 (two) items***

***Read the following passage and answer the 2 (two) items that follow:***

A, B, C, D, E and F are cousins. No two cousins are of the same age, but all have birthdays on the same day of the same month. The youngest is 17 years old and the oldest E is 22 years old. F is somewhere between B and D in age. A is older than B, C is older than D* A is one year older than C.

**36.** Which one of the following is possible?

(a) D is 20 years old
(b) F is 18 years old
(c) F is 19 years old
(d) F is 20 years old

**37.** What is the number of logically possible orders of all six cousins in terms of increasing age?

(a) 1 (b) 2
(c) 3 (d) 4

**38.** In a society it is customary for friends of the same sex to hug and for friends of opposite sex to shake hands when they meet. A group of friends met in a party and there were 24 handshakes.

Which one among the following numbers indicates the possible number of hugs?

(a) 39 (b) 30
(c) 21 (d) 20

**39.** Two men, Anil and David, and two women, Shabnam and Rekha are in a sales group. Only two speak Tamil. The other two speak Marathi. Only one man and one woman can drive a car. Shabnam speaks Marathi, Anil speaks Tamil. Both Rekha and David can drive.

Which of the following statements is true?

(a) Both the Tamil speakers can drive a car.
(b) Both the Marathi speakers can drive a car.
(c) Both of those who can drive a car speak Marathi.
(d) One of those who can drive a car speaks Tamil.

**40.** Four persons A, B, C and D consisting of two married couples are in a group. Both the women are shorter than their respective husbands. A is the tallest among the four, C is taller than B, D is B's brother. In this context, which one of the following statements is not correct?

(a) All four have family ties,
(b) B is the shortest among the four.
(c) C is taller than D,
(d) A is B's husband.

**41.** Consider the following statements:

1. A man had a wife, two sons and two daughters in his family.
2. The daughters were invited to a feast and the male members of the family went out to take part in a picnic.

3. The man's father did not return from his work. Which of the following statements is true?

(a) Only the man's wife was left at home.

(b) It is likely that the man's wife was left at home.

(c) None was left at home.

(d) More than one person was left at home.

***Directions for the following 2 (two) items:*** Read the following information and answer the two items that follow.

The plan of an office block for six officers A, B, C, D, E and F is as follows: Both B and C occupy offices to the right of the corridor (as one enters the office block) and A occupies on the left of the corridor. E and F occupy offices on opposite sides of the corridor but their offices do not face each other. The offices of C and D face each other. E does not have a corner office. F's offices is further down the corridor than A's, but on the same side.

**42.** If E sits is his office and faces the corridor, whose office is to his left?

(a) A (b) B

(c) C (d) D

**43.** Lakshmi, her brother, her daughter and her son are badminton players. A game of doubles is about to begin:

(1) Lakshmi's brother is directly across the net from her daughter.

(2) Her son is diagonally across the net from the worst player's sibling.

(3) The best player and the worst player are on the same side of the net. Who is the best player?

(a) Her brother (b) Her daughter

(c) Her son (d) Lakshmi

***Directions for the following 6 (six) items:*** Read the information given below and answer the six items that follows:

A, B, C and D are students. They are studying in four different cities, viz. P, Q, R and S (not necessarily in that order). They are studying in Science college, Arts college, Commerce college and Engineering college (Not necessarily in that order), which are situated in four different States, viz. Gujarat, Rajasthan, Assam and Kerala (not necessarily in that order). Further, it is given that—

(1) D is studying in Assam

(2) Arts college is located in city S which is in Rajasthan

(3) A is studying in Commerce College

(4) B is studying in City Q

(5) Science college is located in Kerala.

**44.** A is studying in

(a) Rajasthan (b) Gujarat

(c) City Q (d) Kerala

**45.** Science college is located in

(a) City Q (b) City S

(c) City R (d) City P

**46.** C is studying in

(a) Science college (b) Rajasthan

(c) Gujarat (d) City Q

**47.** Which one of the following statements is correct?

(a) D is not studying in city S.

(b) A is studying in Science college

(c) A is studying in Kerala

(d) Engineering college is located in Gujarat.

**48.** Which one of the following statements is correct regarding Engineering college?

(a) C is studying there.

(b) B is studying there.

(c) It is located in Gujarat.

(d) D is studying there.

**49.** Which one of the following statements is correct?

(a) Engineering college is located in Assam.

(b) City Q is situated in Assam.

(c) C is studying in Kerala.

(d) B is studying in Gujarat.

**50.** A joint family consists of seven members A, B, C, D, E, F and G with three females. G is a widow and sister-in-law of D's father F. B and D are siblings and A is daughter of B. C is cousin of B. Who is E?

1. Wife of F
2. Grandmother of A
3. Aunt of C

Select the correct answer using the code given below:

(a) 1 and 2 only (b) 2 and 3 only
(c) 1 and 3 only (d) 1, 2 and 3

***Directions for the following 3 (three) items:*** Read the following information and answer the three items that follow:

Six students A, B, C, D, E and F appeared in several tests. Either C or F scores the highest. Whenever C scores the highest, then E scores the least. Whenever F scores the highest, B scores the least. In all the tests they got different marks; D scores higher than A, but they are close competitors; A scores higher than B; C scores higher than A.

**51.** If F stands second in the ranking, then the position of B is
(a) Third (b) Fourth
(c) Fifth (d) Sixth

**52.** If B scores the least, the rank of C will be
(a) Second (b) Third
(c) Fourth (d) Second or third

**53.** If E is ranked third, then which one of the following is correct?
(a) E gets more marks than C
(b) C gets more marks than E
(c) A is ranked fourth
(d) D is ranked fifth

**54.** A five-storeyed building with floors from I to V is painted using four different colours and only one colour is used to paint a floor.
Consider the following statements:
1. The middle three floors are painted in different colours.
2. The second (II) and the fourth (IV) floors are painted in different colours.
3. The first (I) and the fifth (V) floors are painted red.

To ensure that any two consecutive floors have different colours
(a) Only statement 2 is sufficient
(b) Only statement 3 is sufficient
(c) Statement 1 is not sufficient, but statement 1 along with statement 2 is sufficient
(d) Statement 3 is not sufficient, but statement 3 along with statement 2 is sufficient

**55.** A family of two generations consisting of six members *P, Q, R, S, T* and *U* has three males and three females. There are two married couples and two unmarried siblings. *U* is *P*'s daughter and *Q* is *R*'s mother-in-law. *T* is an unmarried male and *S* is a male. Which one of the following is correct?
(a) *R* is *U*'s husband.
(b) *R* is *S*'s wife.
(c) *S* is unmarried.
(d) None of the above

**56.** *A* is 16th from the left end in a row of boys and *V* is 18th from the right end. *Q* is 11th from *A* towards the right and 3rd from *V* towards the right end. How many boys are there in the row?
(a) 40
(b) 41
(c) 42
(d) Cannot be determined due to insufficient data

***Direction for the following 3 (three) items:*** Consider the given information and answer the three items that follow.

When three friends A, B and C met, it was found that each of them wore an outer garment of a different colour. In random order, the garments are: jacket, sweater and tie: and the colours are: blue, white and black. Their surnames in random order are: Ribeiro, Kumar and Singh. Further, we know that:

1. Neither B nor Ribeiro wore a white sweater
2. C wore a tie
3. Singh's garment was not white
4. Kumar does not wear a jacket
5. Ribeiro does not like to wear the black colour
6. Each of the friends wore only one outer garment of only one colour

**57.** What is C's surname?
(a) Ribeiro
(b) Kumar
(c) Singh
(d) Cannot be determined

**58.** What is the colour of the tie?
(a) Black
(b) Blue
(c) White
(d) Cannot be determined

**59.** Who wore the sweater?
(a) A
(b) B
(c) C
(d) Cannot be determined

**60.** *A* ate grapes and pineapple; B ate grapes and oranges; *C* ate oranges, pineapple and apple; *D* ate grapes, apple and pineapple. After taking fruits, *B* and *C* fell sick. In the light of the above facts, it can be said that the cause of sickness was:
(a) Apple (b) Pineapple
(c) Grapes (d) Oranges

**61.** Five people *A*, *B*, *C*, *D* and *E* are seated about a round table. Every chair is spaced equidistant from adjacent chairs.
(i) *C* is seated next to *A*
(ii) *A* is seated two seats from *D*
(iii) *B* is not seated next to *A*

On the basis of above information, which of the following must be true?
1. *D* is seated next to *B*
2. *E* is seated next to *A*
3. *D* and *C* are separated by two seats

Select the correct answer using the code given below:
(a) 1 only
(b) 1 and 2 only
(c) 3 only
(d) Neither 1 nor 2 nor 3

**62.** There are five hobby clubs in a college — photography, yachting, chess, electronics and gardening. The gardening group meets every second day, the electronics group meets every third day, the chess group meets every fourth day, the yachting group meets every fifth day and the photography group meets every sixth day. How many times do all the five groups meet on the same day within 180 days?
(a) 5 (b) 18
(c) 10 (d) 3

***Directions for the following 5 (five) items:*** Consider the following information and answer the five items that follow:

There are five persons in a group – *P*, *Q*, *R*, *S* and *T*. The group has one doctor, one lawyer and one artist. P and S are unmarried students. T is a man married to one of the group members. *Q* is the brother of *P* and is neither doctor nor artist. *R* is not doctor.

**63.** Who is the doctor?
(a) T (b) P
(c) Q (d) R

**64.** Who is the artist?
(a) P (b) Q
(c) R (d) T

**65.** Who is the spouse of R?
(a) P (b) T
(c) Q (d) S

**66.** Who is the lawyer?
(a) P (b) Q
(c) R (d) S

**67.** Who of the following is definitely a man?
(a) P (b) S
(c) Q (d) None of the above

***Direction for the following 3 (three) items:*** Consider the given information and answer the three items that follow.

Six boxes *A*, *B*, *C*, *D*, *E* and *F* have been painted with six different colours viz., violet, indigo, blue, green, yellow and orange and arranged from left to right (not necessarily either kept or painted with the colours in the same order). Each box contains a ball of any one of the following six games: cricket, hockey, tennis, golf, football and volleyball (not necessarily in the same order). The golf ball is in violet box and is not in box *D*. The box *A* which contains tennis ball is orange in colour and is at the extreme right. The hockey ball is neither in box *D* nor in box *E*. The box *C* having cricket ball is painted green. The hockey ball is neither in the box painted blue nor in the box painted yellow. The box *C* is fifth from right and next to box B. The box B contains volleyball. The box containing the hockey ball is between the boxes containing golf ball and volleyball.

**68.** Which one of the following boxes contains the golf ball?
(a) F (b) E
(c) D (d) None of the above

**69.** Which of the following statements is/are correct?
(a) D is painted yellow
(b) F is painted indigo
(c) B is painted blue
(d) All of the above

**70.** The football is in the box of which colour?
(a) Yellow
(b) Indigo
(c) Cannot be determined as data are inadequate
(d) Blue

**71.** Four tests–Physics, Chemistry, Mathematics and Biology–are to be conducted on four consecutive days, not necessarily in the same order. The Physics test is held before the test which is conducted after Biology. Chemistry is conducted exactly after two tests are held. Which is the last test held?
(a) Physics (b) Biology
(c) Mathematics (d) Chemistry

**72.** In a group of six women, there are four tennis players, four postgraduates in Sociology, one postgraduate in Commerce and three bank employees. Vimala and Kamla are the bank employees while Amala and Komala are unemployed. Komala and Nirmala are among the tennis players. Amala, Kamla, Komala and Nirmala are postgraduates in Sociology of whom two are bank employees. If Shyamala is a postgraduate in Commerce, who among the following is both a tennis player and a bank employee?
(a) Amala (b) Komala
(c) Nirmala (d) Shyamala

**73.** Consider the following relationships among members of a family of six persons A, B, C, D, E and F :
1. The number of males equals that of females.
2. A and E are sons of F.
3. D is the mother of two, one boy and one girl.
4. B is the son of A.
5. There is only one married couple in the family at present.

Which one of the following inferences can be drawn from the above?
(a) A, B and C are all females.
(b) A is the husband of D.
(c) E and F are children of D.
(d) D is the daughter of F.

**74.** Consider the following :
A, B, C, D, E, F, G and H are standing in a row facing north.
B is not neighbour of G.
F is to the immediate right of G and neighbour of E. G is not at the extreme end.
A is sixth to the left of E. H is sixth to the right of C.
Which one of the following is correct in respect of the above?
(a) C is to the immediate left of A.
(b) D is immediate neighbour of B and F.
(c) G is to the immediate right of D.
(d) A and E are at the extreme ends.

***Directions for the following 3 (three) items:*** Consider the given information and answer the three items that follow.

A, B, C, D, E, F and G are Lecturers from different cities-Hyderabad, Delhi, Shillong, Kanpur, Chennai, Mumbai and Srinagar (not necessarily in the same order) who participated in—a conference. Each one of them is specialized in a different subject, viz., Economics, Commerce, History, Sociology, Geography, Mathematics and Statistics (not necessarily in the same order). Further

1. Lecturer from Kanpur is specialized in Geography
2. Lecturer D is from Shillong
3. Lecturer C from Delhi is specialized in Sociology
4. Lecturer B is specialized in neither History nor Mathematics
5. Lecturer A who is specialized in Economics does not belong to Hyderabad
6. Lecturer F who is specialized in Commerce belongs to Srinagar
7. Lecturer G who is specialized in Statistics belongs to Chennai

**75.** Who is specialized in Geography?

(a) B
(b) D
(c) E
(d) Cannot be determined as data are inadequate

**76.** To which city does the lecturer specialized in Economics belong?

(a) Hyderabad
(b) Mumbai
(c) Neither Hyderabad nor Mumbai
(d) Cannot be determined as data are inadequate

**77.** Who of the following belongs to Hyderabad?

(a) B
(b) E
(c) Neither B nor E
(d) Cannot be determined as data are inadequate

***Directions for the following 3 (three) Items:*** Consider the given information and answer the three items that follow.

Eight railway stations A, B, C, D, E, F, G and H are connected either by two-way passages or one-way passages. One-way are from C to A, E to G, B to F, D to H, G to C, E to C and H to G. Two-way passages are between A and E, G and B, F and D, and E and D.

**78.** While travelling from C to H, which one of the following stations must be passed through?

(a) G (b) E
(c) D (d) F

**79.** In how many different ways can a train travel from F to A without passing through any station more than once?

(a) 1 (b) 2
(c) 3 (d) 4

**80.** If the route between G and C is closed, which one of the following stations need not be passed through while travelling from H to C?

(a) E (b) D
(c) A (d) B

## Answers of Exercise Set-2 on Analytical Reasoning

| | | | | | | | |
|---|---|---|---|---|---|---|---|
| **1.** (c) | **11.** (c) | **21.** (d) | **31.** (c) | **41.** (d) | **51.** (c) | **61.** (b) | **71.** (c) |
| **2.** (c) | **12.** (a) | **22.** (a) | **32.** (c) | **42.** (c) | **52.** (d) | **62.** (c) | **72.** (c) |
| **3.** (d) | **13.** (b) | **23.** (b) | **33.** (b) | **43.** (a) | **53.** (b) | **63.** (a) | **73.** (b) |
| **4.** (b) | **14.** (d) | **24.** (d) | **34.** (b) | **44.** (b) | **54.** (b) | **64.** (c) | **74.** (c) |
| **5.** (c) | **15.** (a) | **25.** (c) | **35.** (c) | **45.** (a) | **55.** (b) | **65.** (b) | **75.** (a) |
| **6.** (c) | **16.** (b) | **26.** (b) | **36.** (b) | **46.** (b) | **56.** (b) | **66.** (b) | **76.** (b) |
| **7.** (a) | **17.** (c) | **27.** (d) | **37.** (b) | **47.** (a) | **57.** (d) | **67.** (c) | **77.** (d) |
| **8.** (d) | **18.** (b) | **28.** (d) | **38.** (c) | **48.** (d) | **58.** (d) | **68.** (b) | **78.** (b) |
| **9.** (d) | **19.** (c) | **29.** (d) | **39.** (d) | **49.** (a) | **59.** (a) | **69.** (b) | **79.** (d) |
| **10.** (b) | **20.** (c) | **30.** (b) | **40.** (c) | **50.** (d) | **60.** (d) | **70.** (c) | **80.** (c) |

## HINTS AND SOLUTIONS TO SOME SELECTED QUESTIONS IN EXERCISE SET 2 ON ANALYTICAL REASONING

1. Since all the five sitcoms are still on, it leaves us with only 2 more shows to fit into the shows that continue running. This would necessarily mean that at least one of the shows that was discontinued was a drama show. Hence, option (c) is correct.

2.

| | Doctor 1 | Doctor 2 | Business-man 1 | Business-man 2 |
|---|---|---|---|---|
| Language | Tamil | Gujarati | Tamil | Gujarati |
| Religion | Christian | | | |

Since the question talks about a Tamil speaking Christian doctor, the other doctor must be a Gujarati while the two businessmen must also be one Tamil and one Gujarati. From the above table we can move to the final structure with the following deductions:

1. Doctor 2 is a Muslim – as no two of the same religion are of the same profession.
2. The Gujarati businessman should be a Christian – as no two of the same religion speak the same language.

The final table would look as follows:

| | Doctor 1 | Doctor 2 | Business-man 1 | Business-man 2 |
|---|---|---|---|---|
| Language | Tamil | Gujarati | Tamil | Gujarati |
| Religion | Christian | Muslim (1) | Muslim (3) | Christian (2) |

From the above table, it is clear that both the statements are true.

Option (c) is correct.

3. Statistics is scheduled on Monday. Option (d) is correct.

4. The History lecture is scheduled between Statistics and English. Option (b) is correct.

5. Mathematics is the last lecture of the week. Option (c) is correct.

6. English is scheduled on Wednesday. Option (c) is correct.

7. Economics is scheduled before the Mathematics lecture. Option (a) is correct.

8. In glass 1, $\frac{\text{milk}}{\text{water}} = \frac{1}{1}$; glass 2, $\frac{\text{milk}}{\text{water}} = \frac{3}{1}$

when mixed, $\frac{\text{milk}}{\text{water}} = \frac{\frac{1}{2}+\frac{3}{4}}{\frac{1}{2}+\frac{1}{4}} = \frac{5}{3}$

9. The flats and their vertical order with the person living in each would be as follows:

| Floor | Person | Described as |
|---|---|---|
| 5 | IAS officer | Professor's friend |
| 4 | MLA | |
| 3 | Doctor | |
| 2 | Professor/Engineer | |
| 1 | Engineer/Professor | |

Only option (d) gives us a possible solution to the given situation. Hence, option (d) is correct.

10. Obviously option (b) is the correct answer because in storm, at least one of A or B is open. Thus, it follows that at least one road is open during storms.

11. We can form a grid about the acceptance or lack of acceptance of each of the four candidates based on the initial conditions:

| Candidate | A | B | C | D |
|---|---|---|---|---|
| Acceptable to | W | Y | W,Y | W,X |
| Not acceptable to | Z | X | | |
| Decision pending | X,Y | W,Z | X,Z | Y,Z |

Based on the information that when

W, Z preferred B, then X, Z also preferred C it is evident that C is preferred by all the four parties – W, Y, X and Z. Hence, Candidate C would be getting the ticket. Option (c) is correct.

24. The correct allocations according to the statements is: P-C; Q-A; R-D, S-E, T- B. Thus, the statement in option (d) which says that B belongs to S is not correct. Since, we are looking at which of the options does not give us the correct association, option (d) is correct.

**26.** Since last year the paper contained a question on A, it contained a question on a poet from the medieval period. Hence, this year the paper would contain a question on a poet from the modern period. Since the paper setter likes F, he would also like E. Also, since he does not like to ask a question about F, he would most likely ask a question on E. Option (b) is correct.

**27.** You can make the following table:

| Girija | Vanaja | Jalaja | Shailaja | Tanuja | Pooja |
|---|---|---|---|---|---|
| Violinist | Violinist | Not Violinist | Not Violinist | Violinist | Violinist |
| | Musician | Musician | Musician | Musician | Actress |
| | | | Dancer | Dancer | |

Tanuja is a dancer and a violinist. Option (d) is correct.

**28.** Since P = 4, T will be 9. Hence, N would be 9 – 3 = 6. Option (d) is correct.

**29.** George's schedule for the week is:

| Monday | Tuesday | Wednesday | Thursday | Friday | Saturday | Sunday |
|---|---|---|---|---|---|---|
| Music | Sports | Mathematics | History | Free | Literature | Free |

He is free on Fridays. Option (d) is correct.

**30.** The following encapsulation of the information is possible:

| | | | |
|---|---|---|---|
| A | Yellow cover | New | Law report |
| B | Green cover | New | Law report |
| C | Green cover | Old | Law report |
| D | Yellow cover | New | Medical Extract |
| E | Green cover | Old | Medical Extract |
| F | Green cover | Old | Medical Extract |

E and F are old medical extracts with green covers.

**31.** The correct order from top to bottom is C-A-G-B-E-F-D. Hence, D is at the bottom rung. Hence, option (c) is correct.

**32.** The correct order of heights is E-D-C-A-B. Hence, if they sit in the order of their heights, C will be in the middle. Option (c) is correct.

**33.** The correct order of the villages would be (with 1 row & 1 column representing a distance of 1 km):

| | | |
|---|---|---|
| | A | C |
| F | D | |
| | E | B |

Option (b) is correct.

**34.** The 24 possibilities of seating A,B,C and D in a row can be first listed down as:

If A is in the first seat: ABCD; ABDC; ACBD; ACDB; ADBC; ADCB;

If B is in the first seat: BACD; BADC; BCAD; BCDA; BDAC; BDCA;

If C is in the first seat: CABD; CADB; CBAD; CBDA; CDAB; CDBA;

If D is in the first seat: DABC; DACB; DBAC; DBCA; DCAB; DCBA.

If you us, the first condition "A is occupying the seat next to B, but not next to C" you reject a few of the above possibilities and come up with a shortened list of only nine possibilities as follows:

If A is in the first seat: ABCD; ABDC;

If B is in the first seat: BACD; BADC;

If C is in the first seat: CBAD; CDAB; CDBA;

If D is in the first seat: DABC; DCBA.

If we now add the condition that C is not sitting next to D, we get two possibilities left from these nine:

CBAD and DABC. In both the cases A is next to D and hence option (b) is correct.

**35.**

| | Persons | | | | | | | No. of ways |
|---|---|---|---|---|---|---|---|---|
| | 1 | | 2 | 3 | | 4 | 5 | |
| Task – 1 | ✓ | or | ✓ | | | | | 2 |
| Task – 2 | | | | ✓ | or | ✓ | | 2 |
| Task – 3 | ✓ | or | ✓ | ✓ | or | ✓ | ✓ | 3 |
| Task – 4 | | Rest 2 | | | | | | 2 |

Reqd. No. of ways = $2 \times 2 \times 3 \times 2 = 24$

**36.** The information given to us tells us the following:

$A = C + 1$; $C > D$; $A > B$; F between B and D.

Situation 1: C = 17. From the above, the first deduction we can make is that C cannot be 17, because if we put C as 17, A would need to be 18 and then since $A > B$, we cannot put an age for B. So, we reject the case of C as 17.

Situation 2: If we try C as 18, we would get B = 17, C = 18, A = 19, F = 20 and D = 21.

However, this solution contravenes the need to put $C > D$.

Situation 3: C = 19 means A = 20. However, in this case, we would need to put B and D amongst 17 and 18. This is not possible since it gives us no scope to put F between B and D.

Situation 4: C = 20, A = 21. Then 17,18 and 19 have to be shared between B, F and D. This can be done in two orders: $B > F > D$ or $D > F > B$. Hence, we get the list of possibilities as given in the table below:

| Possibility 1 | Possibility 2 | |
|---|---|---|
| E | E | 22 years old |
| A | A | 21 |
| C | C | 20 |
| B | D | 19 |
| F | F | 18 |
| D | B | 17 |

The answer to question 12, then is that F is 18 years old is the only possibility.

Also, for question 13, we know that there are two logically possible orders of the cousins in terms of their ages.

Hence, option (b) is correct.

**37.** Option (b) is correct.

**38.** If there are 'm' men and 'w' women in the party, there would be ${}^{m}C_1 \times {}^{w}C_1 = m \times w$ handshakes in the party. Since it is given that there are 24 handshakes, the number of people of the same sex could either be: 24 & 1; 12 and 2; 8 & 3; 6 & 4. These are the factor pairs of 24.

Also, for m men and w women, the number of handshakes would be:

${}^{m}C_2 + {}^{w}C_2$. The possible values of these are:

${}^{24}C_2 = 276$

${}^{12}C_2 + {}^{2}C_2 = 67$

${}^{8}C_2 + {}^{3}C_2 = 31$

${}^{6}C_2 + {}^{4}C_2 = 21$.

If we match with the possibilities given in the options, we can see that only 21 is a possibility for the same.

Hence, Option (c) is the correct answer

**39.** From the information given in the question, we can create the following table:

| Men | A (Tamil) | David (Drives) |
|---|---|---|
| Women | S (Marathi) | Rekha (Drives) |

Only option (d) is valid once you match the information with the above table.

Hence, option (d) is correct.

**40.** The relationships of the four would be:

A & B are one husband wife couple, while D& C are another husband wife couple. Also D is B's brother. So all of them have family ties. Also, since C is taller than B, B must be the shortest. Likewise, A is B's husband. It is obvious also, that C is shorter than D, as she is his wife. The option (c) is giving us the opposite of this truth. Since we are looking for the 'not correct' conclusion, option (c) is the correct answer.

**42.** Option (c) is correct.

**43.** From the first sentence, we have, that Lakshmi's daughter and her brother must be opposite each other. This gives rise to two placements for Lakshmi and her son as shown in the figure:

**Possibility 1**

| Son | Brother | |
|---|---|---|
| Lakshmi | Daughter | NET |

**Possibility 2**

| Lakshmi | Brother | |
|---|---|---|
| Son | Daughter | NET |

Analysis of Possibility 1 using the statement: "Her son is diagonally across the net from the worst player's sibling." = "Her son is diagonally across the net from her daughter." Thus, the daughter is the worst player's sibling. In such a case, the son must be the worst player. Also, since the best player and the worst player are on the same side of the net, we get that the brother must be the best player.

Analysis of Possibility 2 using the statement: "Her son is diagonally across the net from the worst player's sibling." = "Her son is diagonally across the net from her brother." Thus, the brother is the worst player's sibling. In such a case, the Lakshmi must be the worst player. Also, since the best player and the worst player are on the same side of the net, we get that the brother must be the best player.

Since, the brother is the best player in both possibilities, we can conclude that option (a) is correct.

***Solutions 44 to 49: Putting the direct information into a tabular form gives us:***

| Student | A | B | C | D |
|---|---|---|---|---|
| State | | | | Assam |
| College | Commerce | | | |
| City | | Q | | |

We also know from (ii) that Arts –City S – Rajasthan should be in one column. They can only be attributed to student C, in the solution table. Then, Science college and Kerala can only be allocated to student B.

The table becomes:

| Student | A | B | C | D |
|---|---|---|---|---|
| State | Gujarat | Kerala | Rajasthan | Assam |
| College | Commerce | Science | Arts | Engg |
| City | | Q | S | |

From the table, the answers can be read off:

44. Gujarat. Option (b)
45. City Q. Option (a)
46. Rajasthan. Option (b)
47. Option (a) is correct as it can be seen that D is not studying in city S.
48. D is studying in the Engineering college. Hence, option (d) is correct.
49. The engineering college is in Assam. Option (a) is correct.
50. The family structure would be as follows:

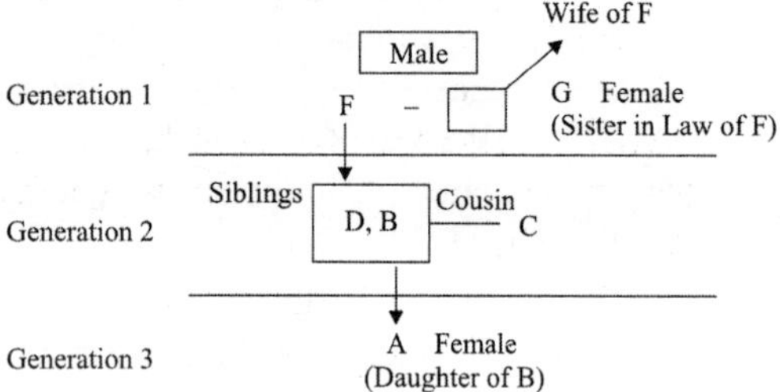


From the figure it is clear that the only missing person in the family should be the wife of F. Since, E is the only person who has not been talked about in the question, she must be F's wife, A's grand mother and Aunt of C.

Hence, option (d) is correct.

**Questions 51 to 53:** The questions solution is based on analyzing the two cases the question has set out: These look as follows:

| | Case 1 | Case 2 |
|---|---|---|
| First | C | F |
| Second | | |
| Third | | |
| Fourth | | |
| Fifth | | |
| Sixth | E | B |

We also know that: D > A > B and Also that C > A. Also, since A and D are close competitors, it means that there is nobody between A and D.

51. If F stands second, we are referring to case 1. D > A > B can then only be placed with B in the 5th place. Hence, option (c) is correct.
52. If B score the least, we are referring to Case 2. In this case, D and A can only occupy 4th–5th or 3rd–4th. In either case, C can only be 2nd or 3rd. Option (d) is correct.
53. If E is third, we are referring to Case 2. In this case, D and A can only be 4th & 5th. C would be 2nd then and hence C would get more marks than E. Option (b) is correct.
55. We can make the following 2 generation family tree based on the clues. We can see directly that Q is a female, U is a female while T and S are males. Also, P and Q belong to the first generation since P has a daughter and Q is R's Mother in law. Thus, they must be one of the two married couples with P as the husband and Q as the wife. At this point we realise that P, T and S are the three males and hence Q, R and U must be the three females. Since, T is unmarried male, it follows that R must be married to S.

    Generation 1 [P – Q′]

    Generation 2 U′ T [S – R′]

    The correct answer would be option (b) i.e. R is S's wife.

56 If we try to arrange people from the left hand side, we get that A is 16th from the left (given), while it can be deduced that G is 27th from the left and V is 24th from the left (since G is third from V, towards the right). Also, since we know that V is 18th from the right end, it means that there must be 41 people in the row. (***Note:*** It would not be 42, since if there were 42 people in the row, the 18th from right end would be at 25th position and not at the 24th position). Option (b) is correct.

**Solutions to 57 to 59:**

Based on the information in the question, we can make the following starting table for the solution.

| Person | A | B | C |
|---|---|---|---|
| Garment | Tie/Jacket/Sweater | Tie/Jacket/Sweater | Tie/Jacket/Sweater |
| Colour | Blue/White/Black | Blue/White/Black | Blue/White/Black |
| Surname | Ribeiro/Kumar/Singh | Ribeiro/Kumar/Singh | Ribeiro/Kumar/Singh |

We now start to use the clues in order to start deducing the reactions.

Using the first and second clue we know that:

C wore a tie;

The sweater was white &

Ribiero did not wear a white sweater

B did not wear a white sweater

We can use this information to modify our table

| Person | A | B | C |
|---|---|---|---|
| Garment | Jacket/Sweater | Jacket/Sweater | Tie |
| Colour | Blue/White/Black | Blue/White/Black | Blue/White/Black |
| Surname | Ribiero/Kumar/Singh | Ribiero/Kumar/Singh | Ribiero/Kumar/Singh |

The following deductions have not been used on the table till now:

[The sweater was white; Ribeiro did not wear a white sweater → Ribeiro Black or Blue;

B did not wear a white sweater]

But we do know that Sweater and White have to go together to either A or B.

When we add the information from clues 3 to 5, we can see that:

Singh is not wearing the white sweater → So Singh is Jacket or tie → Also Singh = Blue or Black

Kumar doesn't wear a jacket → Kumar = Sweater or Tie

Ribeiro does not like to wear black → Ribeiro = Blue

& Since Ribeiro is Blue we can modify Singh to Black.

This also means that Kumar wears white.

The table transforms to:

| Person | A | B | C |
|---|---|---|---|
| Garment | Sweater | Jacket | Tie |
| Surname & Colour | Kumar – White | Ribeiro- Blue OR Singh- Black | Singh- Black OR<br>Ribeiro- Blue |

We can then try to answer the questions:

**57.** Cannot be determined as it could be either Singh or Ribeiro

**58.** Cannot be determined as it could be either Blue or Black

**59.** A (Kumar) wore the sweater.

**60.** B and C both ate oranges and hence it is the oranges that would be the cause of sickness

61. There are two possible reactions to the given information in statements (i) and (iii). These can be seen in the figures below:

Possibility 1

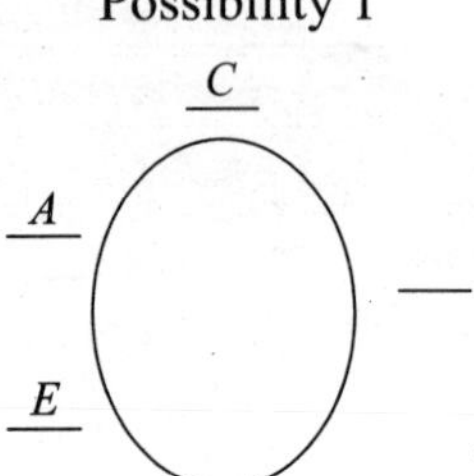


Possibility 2

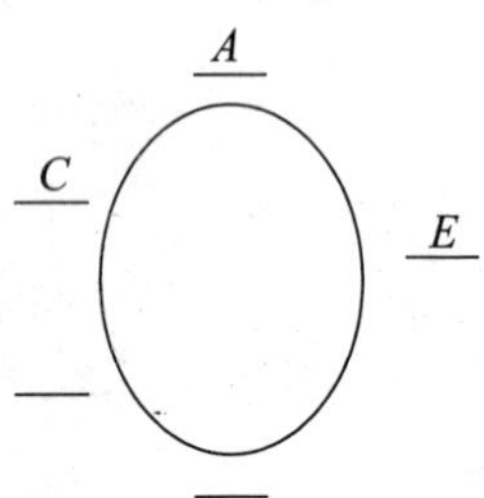


71. It is clear from the question that the Chemistry test is held on the third day. Also, Biology cannot be last (since there is a test after it) and so also Physics cannot be last, since it is held before Biology. Clearly, only Mathematics must be last. Hence, option (c) is correct.
72. Amongst the four Sociology Post graduates (viz: Amala, Kamla, Komala and Nirmala we know that Amala and Komala are not employed. Hence, the two bank employees amongst these 4 would be Kamla and Nirmala. We are also given that Nirmala is one of the 4 tennis players. Clearly, then Nirmala is both a tennis player and a bank employee. Hence, option (c) is correct.
73. A must be the husband of D, since both A and D have children (and their children would be B- son and C -daughter). None of the other options fits in the conditions of the problem. Hence, option (b) is correct.
74. The correct arrangement would be: A-C-B-D-G-F -E-H. Hence, option (c) is correct as we can see that G is to the immediate right of D.

**Solutions for 75 to 77:**

| Name | A | B | C | D | E | F | G |
|---|---|---|---|---|---|---|---|
| City | Not Hyderabad | | Delhi | Shillong | | Srinagar | Chennai |
| Subject | Economics | Not History or Mathematics | Sociology | | | Commerce | Stats |

At this stage, we have only three subjects to place – viz: History, Mathematics and Geography. Since B is not specialized in History or Mathematics - he must be specialized in Geography. Hence, he must be from Kanpur. This leaves only Mumbai and Hyderabad to be placed in the row for cities. Since A is not from Hyderabad, he must be from Mumbai and E must be from Hyderabad.

| Name | A | B | C | D | E | F | G |
|---|---|---|---|---|---|---|---|
| City | Mumbai | Kanpur | Delhi | Shillong | Hyderabad | Srinagar | Chennai |
| Subject | Economics | Geography | Sociology | History or | | | |
| Mathematics | Mathematics or History | Commerce | Stats | | | | |

The answers can then be read off this table:

78. The route from C to H involves going through C-A-E-D-H.
From the given options Station E would have to be passed. Hence, option (b) is correct.
79. The available routes are: F-D-E-A; F-D-E-C-A; F-D-E-G-C-A; F-D-H-G-C-A. Thus, there are a total of 4 routes. Hence, option (d) is correct.
80. The route from H to C would be through: H-G-B-F-D-E-C. Station A doesn't come on this route. Hence, option (c) is correct.

Practice Question Paper 1

Practice Question Paper 2

Practice Question Paper 3

Practice Question Paper 4

Practice Question Paper 5

Practice Question Paper 6

Practice Question Paper 7

Practice Question Paper 8

Practice Question Paper 9

Practice Question Paper 10

# Practice Question Papers for Section 3: General Test

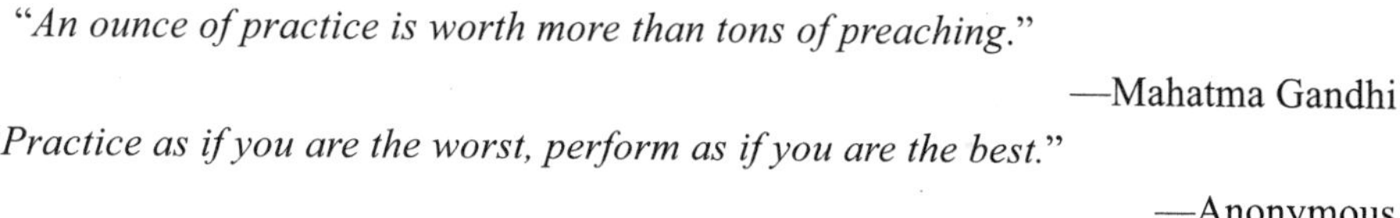

"*An ounce of practice is worth more than tons of preaching.*"

—Mahatma Gandhi

"*Practice as if you are the worst, perform as if you are the best.*"

—Anonymous

This section consists of 10 practice question papers pertaining to Section 3–General Test of the CUET paper. These have been set as per the prescribed syllabus of the CUET.

The objective of these practice question papers is to provide an opportunity to assess your standing, vis-à-vis the complexity of questions as well as the constraint of time. It is advised that you attempt these papers only after you have gone through the preceding chapters and acquired a fair degree of proficiency over the subject. Besides you should attempt each paper in a single sitting in a time bound fashion, so as to simulate an examination-like environment.

It should be remembered that in Section 3, there would be 75 questions out of which 60 are to be attempted. However, for attempting these 60 questions, a time of only 60 minutes has been given. This works out to only a minute for each question. As such, it will be prudent to time yourself, question-wise, while attempting these set of papers. This will give you a fair idea as to in which category of questions you are overshooting the permissible time and in which you are saving some. This helps in time management during the examination. Besides this also gives a good idea of the type of questions you need to work upon and in which you can speed up. Use this idea while solving the subsequent practice question papers and analyse how your performance has changed.

So make the best use of the practice question papers

# Practice Question Paper

**(A) Consider the graph here which shows growth of various financial elements from FY 1997–98 to FY 2009–10.**

(i) Direct tax– GDP ratio

(ii) GDP growth rate

(iii) Direct tax growth rate

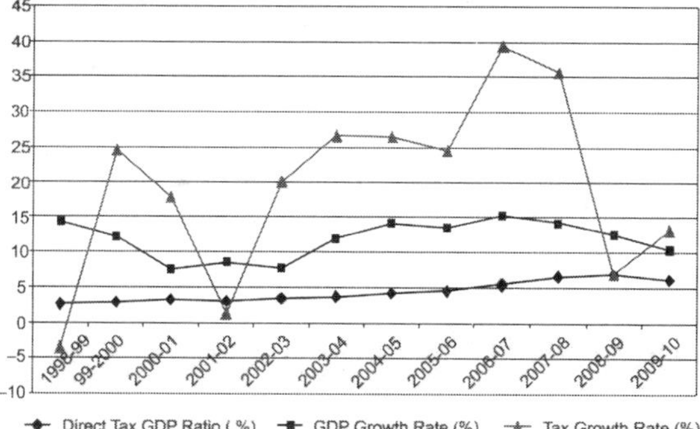


**Answer the following questions:**

1. Which of the following statement is correct?
   (a) Tax growth rate has always shown an increasing trend.
   (b) Direct tax to GDP ratio has always been increasing.
   (c) The graph above does not indicate whether collection of direct tax has been increasing or decreasing over the years.
   (d) None of above.

2. Which of the following conclusions can be drawn from the graph?
   (i) In FY 2008–09, the direct tax collection was less than what it was in FY 2007–08.
   (ii) In FY 2008–09, the ratio of direct tax to GDP was maximum in the past 10 years.
   (iii) The GDP growth rate has shown a declining trend since FY 2006–07.
   (iv) After 2006–07, the economy is shrinking.
   (a) (i), (ii) (b) (ii), (iii)
   (c) (iii), (iv) (d) (ii), (iv)

**(B) Study the graph here and answer the questions that follow.**

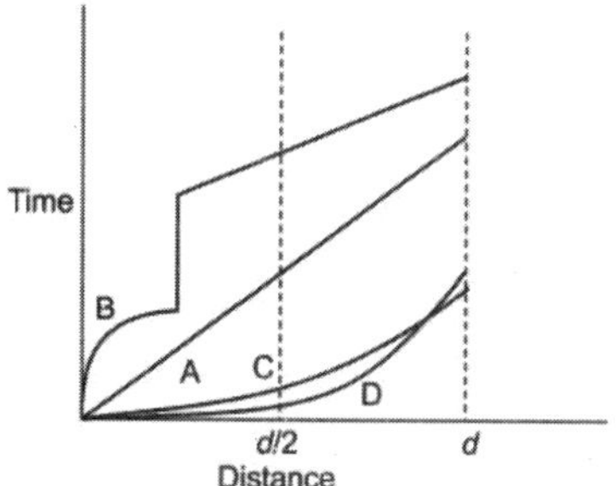


Four cyclists participate in a race where they have to cover a distance *d*. Their time-distance graph is given above.

3. Which cyclist was leading the race till half the distance?
   (a) A (b) B
   (c) C (d) D

4. One of the cyclists had a breakdown. He had to halt to repair his vehicle. Which one was that?
   (a) A (b) B
   (c) C (d) D

5. Which of the cyclists did not slow down as he neared the end of the race?
   (a) A only (b) B only
   (c) A and B (d) B and D

**(C) For the next two questions, study the conditions specified and based on it, answer the questions that follow.**

In a conference, a group of eight doctors A, B, C, D, E, F, G and H participated. Two groups are formed using them. Put them into either of the two groups based on the following conditions:

(i) Group (i) could accommodate at the most five doctors and at least four doctors.

(ii) A and C being best friends would be in the same group.

(iii) A and H are bitter rivals and are never in the same group.

(iv) B and F are not selected along with C.

(v) E will be selected with A and D only, but not with G.

6. If G and H are selected in Group (i) who are in Group (ii)?
   (a) A, C, E and D
   (b) F, B, A and D
   (c) A, E, F and D
   (d) E, D, C and B

7. If A and D are in the same group which of the following statements is true?
   (a) One of the groups has five people.
   (b) B is in the same group.
   (c) E is in the other group.
   (d) G is not in the same group.

8. A book has 400 pages. How many digits are used to print the page numbers of the book?
   (a) 400 (b) 863
   (c) 1092 (d) 1243

9. The age of a man is the same as his son's age when the digits of his age are reversed. The man is 27 years older than his son. How old is his son if the father is in his fifties?
   (a) 32 (b) 27
   (c) 42 (d) 25

10. If the following number pattern is extended, in which row would 2010 be?

1
2 3
4 5 6
7 8 9 10
11 12 13 14 15

   (a) 40 (b) 51
   (c) 59 (d) 63

**(D) Based on the data given below answer the following questions:**

A survey is conducted in an MNC about the preference of employees of tea and coffee. The employees had to indicate their preference in any of the following four categories:

(a) Prefer tea
(b) Prefer coffee
(c) Prefer both
(d) No preference of either tea or coffee

Out of 200 employees 60% of employees prefer tea while only 30% prefer coffee. While 24 women prefer coffee, 72 men prefer tea. 6 men and 6 women preferred both tea and coffee. The office has 80 female employees.

11. How many men prefer neither tea nor coffee?
   (a) 6 (b) 8
   (c) 10 (d) 12

12. Consider the two pie charts shown here. Which one represents the aforesaid data correctly?

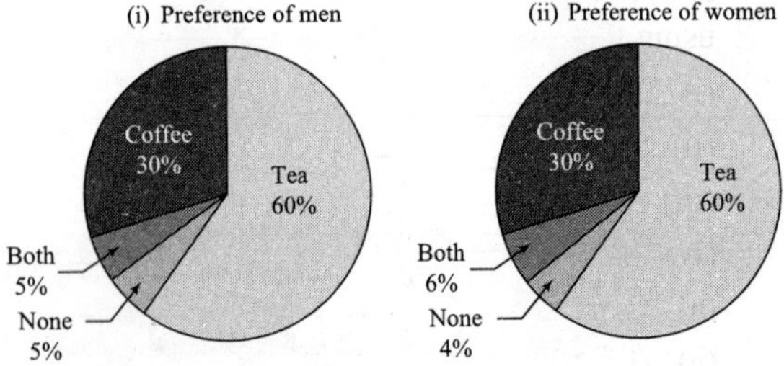


   (a) Pie chart (i) only
   (b) Pie chart (ii) only
   (c) Both pie charts
   (d) None of the pie charts

13. A subsequent survey was conducted after three months on same set of employees. The data of men remained the same. Following conclusions were given regarding the data of women.
   (i) Percentage of women coffee drinkers has increased by 1/3rd.
   (ii) Number of women tea drinkers remained same.
   (iii) Number of women preferring coffee and tea both, decreased by 6.

   Which of the aforesaid is sufficient to find the number of women who preferred neither tea nor coffee?
   (a) All of (i), (ii) and (iii)
   (b) Only (i) and (ii)
   (c) Only (i) and (iii)
   (d) Data insufficient

14. Consider the following argument:

    To be a civil servant, one must be a graduate. All graduates are intellectuals. Some politicians are graduates.

    Which one of the following is true?

    (a) Some civil servants are graduates.
    (b) All politicians are intellectuals.
    (c) Some civil servants are politicians.
    (d) Some politicians are intellectuals.

15. The following question consists of four statements two of which cannot be true simultaneously. But they can be false at the same time. Study the statements carefully and identify which pair of statements fulfill the above conditions. Select the correct answer using the codes below the statements.

    (i) Some men are vegetarian.
    (ii) Some men are non-vegetarian.
    (iii) All men are non-vegetarian.
    (iv) All men are vegetarian.

    (a) (i) and (iii) (b) (ii) and (iv)
    (c) (iii) and (iv) (d) (i) and (iv)

**(E) Choose the correct option for the questions given below**

16. Find the possible values of 'a' in 444444a222222 so that the number is divisible by 7.

    (a) 1, 8
    (b) 0, 7
    (c) 2, 9
    (d) the number will never be divisible by 7

17. A plot of rectangular land is divided into four smaller plots of rectangular land. Find the perimeter of the plot of land if sides of all rectangles are natural numbers. (The figure is not to scale.)

    | $14\ m^2$ | |
    |---|---|
    | | $30\ m^2$ |

    (a) 24 m (b) 36 m
    (c) 44 m (d) 58 m

18. How many squares are there in the given figure?

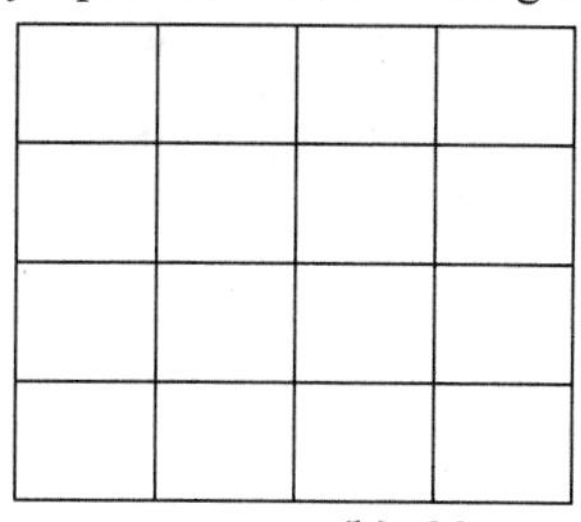

    (a) 25 (b) 29
    (c) 30 (d) 32

19. A person goes from A to Z always moving to the right or downwards along the lines. How many different routes can he or she adopt?

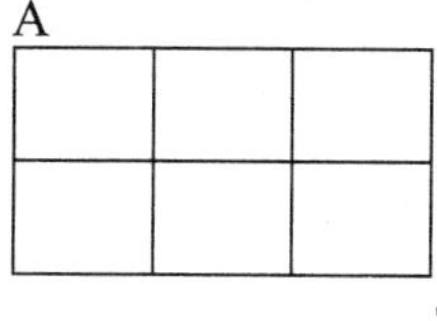


    (a) 12 (b) 11
    (c) 10 (d) 9

**(F) Read the pie chart and answer the questions pertaining to it.**

The average annual expenditure of Mr. Malhotra's family is depicted in the pie chart here.

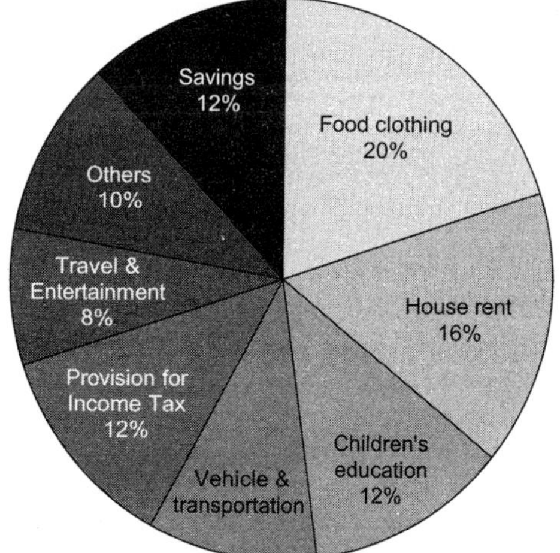


20. In the next financial year, Mr. Malhotra expects to get a promotion. His salary will increase by 18%. Food and clothing expenses are likely to increase by 25% over previous year owing to

inflation. He proposes to cut down on travel and entertainment by 25%. Consider that all other expenses and provision for income tax increase by 20%, what will be the effect on his net saving?

(a) Increases by 25%

(b) Increases by 20%

(c) Decreases by 20%

(d) Data insufficient

21. If Mr. Malhotra has no increase in the salary but the expenses were to increase as mentioned above. How much decrease in travel and entertainment expenses would need to be done to maintain the same level of savings?

(a) 25% decrease in travel and entertainment expenses.

(b) No decrease in travel and entertainment expenses.

(c) Decrease in travel and entertainment expenses would not compensate for increase in all other expenses put together.

(d) His salary will not be sufficient to meet increase in expenses even if his savings, travel and entertainment expenses are nil.

22. In a rain water harvesting system, water from a roof which is 22 m × 7 m falls into a cylindrical container of radius 50 cm. To what height the water will rise in the cylinder if there is 10 mm of rainfall?

(a) 156 cm (b) 196 cm

(c) 235 cm (d) 324 cm

23. In the following question, two statements are given followed by two conclusions. Take the statements to be true even if it is in variance with commonly accepted facts. Determine which of the two conclusions can be drawn from the statements.

Statement 1—All bureaucrats are graduates.

Statement 2—Some bureaucrats are of doubtful integrity. Conclusion 1—All graduates are bureaucrats.

Conclusion 2—Some graduates are of doubtful integrity.

(a) Only Conclusion (i) can be drawn.

(b) Only Conclusion (ii) can be drawn.

(c) Both Conclusions (i) and (ii) can be drawn.

(d) Neither Conclusion (i) nor (ii) can be drawn.

24. The following questions consist of five statements followed by options consisting of three statements put together in a specific order. Choose the option which indicates a valid argument that is where the third statement is conclusion drawn from preceding two statements. ABC is a valid option where C can be concluded from statement A and B.

(i) Smoking is a costly habit.

(ii) Smoking should be banned in public places.

(iii) Cigarettes emit passive smoke.

(iv) Smoking causes cancer.

(v) Passive smoke is injurious to health.

(a) (ii), (i), (iv) (b) (iv), (i), (iii)

(c) (ii), (iii), (iv) (d) (iii), (v), (ii)

25. Find the missing number in the block given below.

| 4 | 10 |
|---|---|
| 64 | 16 |

| 10 | |
|---|---|
| 1000 | 100 |

(a) 20 (b) 25

(c) 30 (d) 35

26. A boy folds a square piece of paper four times, each time in equal halves. He unfolds the paper and colours the square boxes formed because of the folding marks. He does not colour the adjacent square boxes with the same colour but wants to use minimum number of different colours to colour all the boxes. How many different colours would be used?

(a) 2 (b) 3

(c) 4 (d) 8

27. The digit in the one's/unit's place in the number $9^{19}$ is

(a) 1 (b) 9

(c) 3 (d) 7

28. Find the biggest number which when divides 954 leaves a remainder 4, when divides 763 leaves a remainder 3, when divides 572 leaves a remainder 2 and when divides 381 leaves a remainder 1.

(a) 19 (b) 95
(c) 190 (d) 380

29. A car travels a distance $d_1$ at speed $s_1$ then travels distance $d_2$ at speed $s_2$ then travels distance $d_3$ at speed $s_3$. What is the car's average speed?
(a) $(d_1 + d_2 + d_3)/(d_1/s_1 + d_2/s_2 + d_3/s_3)$
(b) $d_1/s_1 + d_2/s_2 + d_3/s_3$
(c) $(d_1/s_1 + d_2/s_2 + d_3/s_3)/ (d_1 + d_2 + d_3)$
(d) $(d_1 + d_2 + d_3)/(s_1 + s_2 + s_3)$

**(G) Based on the graph, answer the following questions.**

The figures of circulation of four major national dailies in the NCR are represented by the following graph.

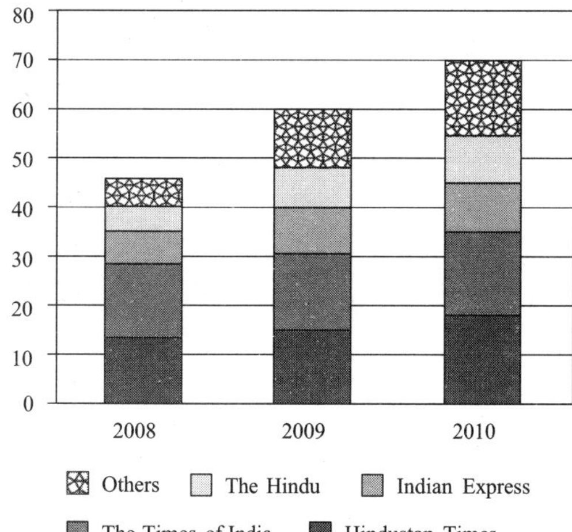


30. Which one of the following conclusions can be drawn?
(i) The Times of India has shown the maximum growth in circulation from 2008 to 2010 in terms of volume.
(ii) Hindustan Times has always remained the market leader.
(a) Only Conclusion (i) can be drawn.
(b) Only Conclusion (ii) can be drawn.
(c) Both the conclusions can be drawn.
(d) Neither Conclusion (i) nor (ii) can be drawn.

31. Examine whether in terms of percentage of overall sales of all the news papers taken together, the market share of Indian Express increased/decreased during 2009–10.
(a) increased (b) Remained same
(c) decreased (d) Data insufficient

30. Which newspaper has recorded the maximum growth both in volume and percentage over the years?
(a) The Times of India (b) Indian Express
(c) The Hindu (d) Others

**(H) Read the information given in passage below and answer the questions that follow.**

Five friends Dinesh, Eeshwar, Girish, Jitender and Manoj are working in a company in the same work team. They want to take fortnight holiday. Each wants to go to a separate destination Shimla, Goa, Darjeeling, Mandi and Andamans. Their group leader allows them holidays in different months so that work is not hampered. They take vacations in month of April June, August, November and December (Not in the given order).

- Jitender took a holiday in December but did not go to Mandi or Darjeeling.
- Eeshwar went to Shimla in June.
- Dinesh took vacation in Goa but not in April or August.
- Manoj got leave in April, he had already gone to Mandi and did not go there.

33. Who went to Mandi?
(a) Eeshwar
(b) Girish
(c) Jitender
(d) Data not sufficient

34. Where did Jitender go?
(a) Andamans
(b) Goa
(c) Shimla
(d) Data not sufficient

35. Who took a holiday in November?
    (a) Eeshwar
    (b) Dinesh
    (c) Manoj
    (d) Data not sufficient

36. Two friends A and B move towards each other from their respective houses. They travel with the same speed and meet each other midway 30 minutes after they have left their houses. If A was to travel at double the speed at what he was earlier travelling and B travels at the same speed at which he was earlier travelling, then after how much time would they meet each other?
    (a) 10 minutes (b) 15 minutes
    (c) 20 minutes (d) 26.5 minutes

37. Find the missing number in the matrix below.

| 3 | 27 | 30 |
|---|---|---|
| 5 | 125 | 130 |
|  | 343 | 350 |

(a) 4 (b) 6
(c) 7 (d) 9

38. A shopkeeper has 25 television sets. Out of these he is able to sell 10 pieces at a profit of 10% (on each piece); 8 pieces at a loss of 8% and 6 pieces at a loss of 6% on each television set. The last one set he is able to set at a profit of 25%. Take that the cost price of each television set was the same, then what is the overall profit or loss percent?
    (a) No profit or loss (b) Profit of 1%
    (c) Profit of 0.1% (d) loss of 1%

39. A bus company prints tickets for passengers. There are separate tickets for each starting and ending bus stops. A particular bus route has 10 stops in its entire route. If a passenger can travel from any stop to any other stop, how many different types of tickets the bus company will have to print?
    (a) 100 (b) 90
    (c) 50 (d) 60

40. 4 men, 4 women and 12 children are required to do a given work in one day. To find out how many children will be required to complete the work in one day which of the following information would be sufficient?
    (i) 5 men and 10 women complete the work in one day.
    (ii) 6 men and 8 women complete the work in one day.
    (a) Statement (i) alone is sufficient.
    (b) Statement (ii) alone is sufficient.
    (c) Both statements are required to solve the problem.
    (d) Even with both the statements the problem cannot be solved.

41. Ramesh and Shyam are two friends whose houses face each other and are on opposite sides of School Street. One day Ramesh comes out of his house and moves towards right hand side for 3 km. He takes a left turn and again moves ahead for 3 km. He again takes a right turn moves 3 km and again a left turn and reaches his destination after 3 km. At the end point on the road where he halts his vehicle, he is facing the direction 45° North of West. Which direction does Shyam's house face?
    (a) East
    (b) 45° South of East
    (c) 45° West of South
    (d) 45° North of West

42. If Fig. (1) was to cut out from Fig. (2) then what would be left?

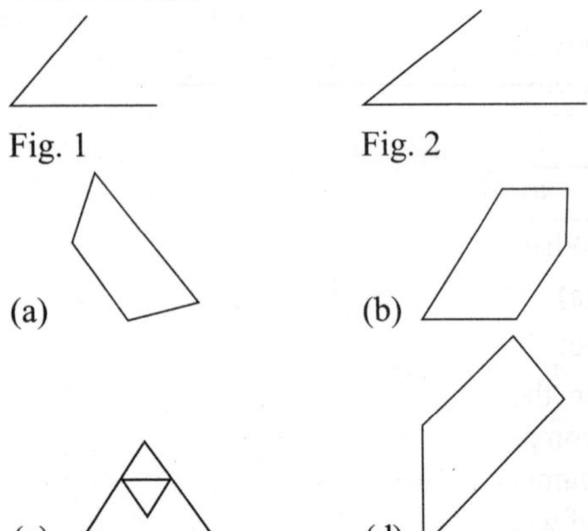

43. Consider the figure given below and answer the item that follows :

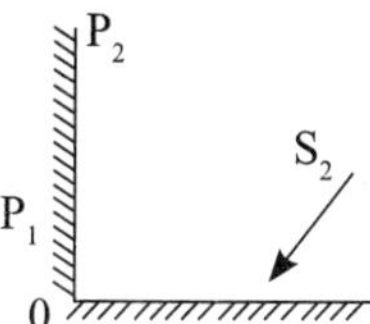


In the figure shown above, $OP_1$ and $OP_2$ are two plane mirrors kept perpendicular to each other. S is the direction of the beam of light falling on the mirror $OP_1$. The direction of the reflected beam of light from the mirror $OP_2$ will be

(a) Perpendicular to the direction S.
(b) At 45° to the direction S.
(c) Opposite and parallel to the direction S.
(d) At 60° to the direction S.

44. Consider the following figure and answer the item that follows :

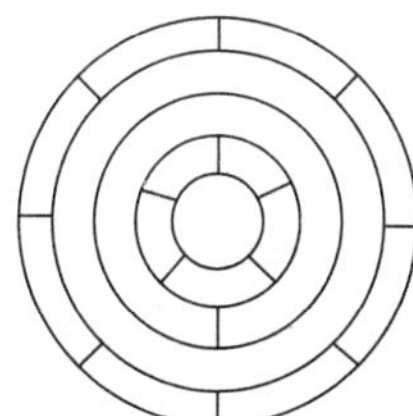

What is the minimum number of different colours required to paint the figure given above such that no two adjacent regions have the same colour?

(a) 3 (b) 4
(c) 5 (d) 6

45. Consider the following figures:

| 2 | 6 |
|---|---|
| 80 | 24 |

| 3 | ? |
|---|---|
| 120 | 36 |

What is the missing number?

(a) 7 (b) 8
(c) 9 (d) 10

46. In the city of Unnao, 50% of the population comprise men and 40% are women. If the number of children are 75000, then the number of women is:

(a) 3,50,000 (b) 3,75,000
(c) 3,00,000 (d) 4,00,000

47. The average of seven consecutive numbers is 91. The numbers in middle is;

(a) 10 (b) 15
(c) 14 (d) 13

48. In 2022 the number of candidates appearing for CUET in Science and Arts streams are in the ratio 3 : 4 respectively. If in the following year, the candidates in Science stream and Arts stream increases by 10000 and 11000 respectively, the respective ratio becomes 4 : 5. What was the total number of candidates in Science and Arts together ?

(a) 30000 (b) 42000
(c) 22000 (d) 28000

49. M can do 25 % of a work in 30 days, N can do 1/4 of work in 10 days, P can do 40 % of the work in 40 days and Q can do 1/3 of the work in 13 days. Who will complete the work first?

(a) M (b) N
(c) P (d) Q

50. A bus without stoppage travels at 90 km/h and with stoppages it travels at 84 km/h. How many minutes does the bus stop in one hour of travel?

(a) 3 mins (b) 4 min
(c) $3\frac{1}{2}$ mins (d) 2 mins

51. Two numbers $n_1$ and $n_2$ are respectively 25 % and 40 % less than a third number $n_3$. By what percentage is the number $n_1$ more than $n_2$?

(a) 10% (b) 20%
(c) 25% (d) 15%

52. The average age of 25 boys in a class is 14. If the teacher is included and one boy is excluded from the group, the average increases by one. The age of the teacher is:

(a) 41 (b) 32
(c) 45 (d) data insufficient

53. Ten years hence, Kangana will be three times as old as she was 10 years ago. Her present age is:

(a) 20 (b) 35
(c) 30 (d) 45

54. The Dachigam National Park famous for Hangul, is located in which of the following state/Union territory?
   (a) Jammu and Kashmir
   (b) Himachal Pradesh
   (c) Assam
   (d) Kerala
55. Who among the following was not awarded the Bharat Ratna in 2019?
   (a) Pranab Mukherjee
   (b) Bhupen Hazarika
   (c) Sachin Tendulkar
   (d) Nanaji Deshmukh
56. World Earth Day is celebrated on
   (a) $1^{st}$ of April (b) $22^{nd}$ of April
   (c) $22^{nd}$ of May (d) $1^{st}$ of May
57. Who amongst the following won a gold medal in 2021 Olympics?
   (a) Abhinav Bindra (b) Neeraj Chopra
   (c) Mary Kom (d) P.V. Sindhu
58. The Securities and Exchange Board of India, deals with which of the following?
   (a) Determination of the monetary policy of the Government of India.
   (b) Determination of the policy framework of the capital markets.
   (c) Regulation of the security markets and stock exchanges.
   (d) All of the above
59. The Quit India movement was launched on;
   (a) $13^{th}$ March 1930
   (b) $13^{th}$ march 1942
   (c) $8^{th}$ August 1942
   (d) $8^{th}$ August 1945
60. The malfunctioning of which of the organs is likely to result in the disease of diabetes?
   (a) The liver
   (b) The islets of langerhans in the pancreas
   (c) The thyroid glands in the throat
   (d) The left kidneys

## Answers of Practice Question Paper-1

| | | | | | |
|---|---|---|---|---|---|
| **1.** (d) | **11.** (a) | **21.** (c) | **31.** (c) | **41.** (b) | **51.** (c) |
| **2.** (b) | **12.** (a) | **22.** (b) | **32.** (d) | **42.** (a) | **52.** (d) |
| **3.** (d) | **13.** (b) | **23.** (b) | **33.** (b) | **43.** (c) | **53.** (a) |
| **4.** (b) | **14.** (d) | **24.** (d) | **34.** (a) | **44.** (a) | **54.** (a) |
| **5.** (c) | **15.** (c) | **25.** (b) | **35.** (b) | **45.** (c) | **55.** (c) |
| **6.** (a) | **16.** (b) | **26.** (a) | **36.** (c) | **46.** (c) | **56.** (b) |
| **7.** (d) | **17.** (c) | **27.** (b) | **37.** (c) | **47.** (d) | **57.** (b) |
| **8.** (c) | **18.** (c) | **28.** (c) | **38.** (b) | **48.** (b) | **58.** (c) |
| **9.** (d) | **19.** (c) | **29.** (a) | **39.** (b) | **49.** (d) | **59.** (c) |
| **10.** (d) | **20.** (a) | **30.** (d) | **40.** (c) | **50.** (b) | **60.** (b) |

# Practice Question Paper 2

1. If $2315x$ is divisible by 3, find the possible values of $x$.
   (a) 2, 5, 8
   (b) 1, 3, 6
   (c) 1, 4, 7
   (d) Data is insufficient

2. There are two squares in the figure here. The length of the side of each square is a natural number. The area of the unshaded region is 32 cm$^2$. Find the perimeter of the unshaded region. (The figure is not to scale.)

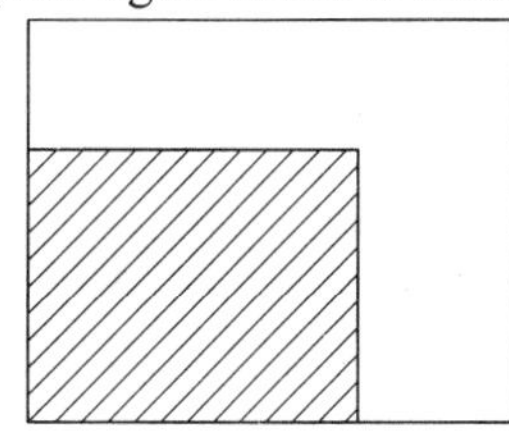

   (a) 26 (b) 30
   (c) 32 (d) 36

3. Find the value of 6 + 13 + 20 + 27 + … + 685 + 692 + 699
   (a) 36,250 (b) 34,250
   (c) 35,250 (d) 38,250

**(A) Study the graph here and answer the questions that follow.**

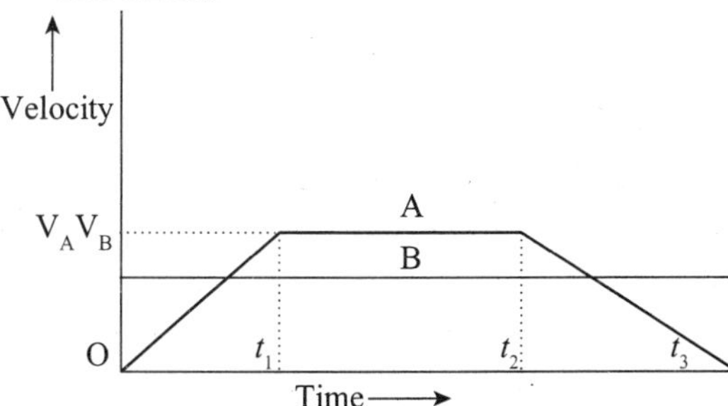


The graph shows the velocity of two cars A and B for time period up till $t_3$. Based on the information, answer the following questions:

4. Which of the following statements is **not** true?
   (i) Cars A and B do not start together.
   (ii) Car A shows greater acceleration than Car B during time period $t_1$ to $t_2$.
   (iii) Car A covers greater distance than Car B during the period $t_1$ to $t_2$
   (a) (i) only (b) (ii) only
   (c) (i) and (iii) (d) (ii) and (iii)

5. In the time period 0 to $t_3$, which car travels greater distance?
   (a) Car A
   (b) Car B
   (c) Both travel equal distance.
   (d) Cannot be determined as data is not sufficient

6. In total time $t_3$, the distance travelled by car A will be
   (a) $V_a \times t_3$
   (b) $V_a(-t_1 + t_2 + t_3)$
   (c) $V_a(t_1/2 + (t_2 - t_1) + \frac{1}{2}(t_3 - t_2))$
   (d) Cannot be determined

**(B) Read the information given and answer the two questions that follow.**

There are four relatives A, B, C and D. A is three times older than B, C half the age of D. B is older than C.

7. Which of the following can be inferred?
   (a) B is older than D.
   (b) A is older than D.
   (c) A may be younger than D.
   (d) None of the above

8. Which of the following information will be sufficient to estimate A's age?
   (a) C is 20 years old.
   (b) Both B and D are older than C by the same number of years.
   (c) Both 1 and 2 above
   (d) None of the above
9. Consider the following statements.
   (i) Only graduates can appear in the civil services examination.
   (ii) Some candidates in the examination are girls.
   (iii) All girl candidates are invited for free coaching by ABCD Classes.
   Which amongst the following conclusions can be drawn?
   (a) All students get free coaching in ABCD classes.
   (b) All students in ABCD classes are girls.
   (c) All graduates appear in the civil services examination.
   (d) None of the above.

**(C) Answer the questions after reading carefully.**

10. The following question consists of four statements, two of which cannot be true simultaneously. But they can be false at the same time. Study the statements carefully and identify which pair of statements fulfil the above conditions. Select the correct answer using the codes following the statements.
    (i) All buses in New Delhi run on CNG.
    (ii) Some buses in New Delhi do not run on CNG.
    (iii) Some buses in New Delhi run on CNG.
    (iv) No bus in New Delhi runs on CNG.
    (a) (iii) and (iv) (b) (i) and (iii)
    (c) (i) and (ii) (d) (i) and (iv)
11. How many rectangles of different sizes can be formed by using 24 squares which are identical?
    (a) 10 (b) 8
    (c) 6 (d) 4
12. Sita and Gita start walking together on a circular track whose radius is 140 m. When they are walking in the same direction they meet each other after an interval of 22 minutes. If they walk in opposite direction they meet each other after 4 minutes. If Sita is walking faster than Gita, then her speed is
    (a) 90 m/min
    (b) 260 m/min
    (c) 130 m/min
    (d) data is insufficient
13. In a school of 500 students, 10% do not play cricket, 20% do not play football and 4% neither play cricket nor football. How many students play football but do not play cricket?
    (a) 80 (b) 50
    (c) 30 (d) Data insufficient
14. In the question above how many students play both games?
    (a) 370 (b) 390
    (c) 450 (d) Data insufficient
15. How many triangles are there in the figure here?

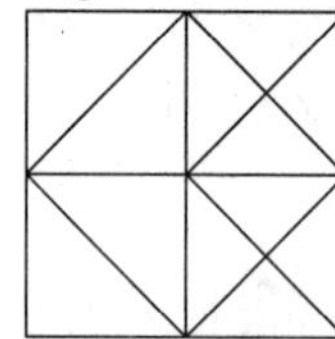

    (a) 27 (b) 25
    (c) 24 (d) 20
16. How many minimum numbers of different colours must a painter use to paint the figure given here so that no two adjacent regions have the same colour?

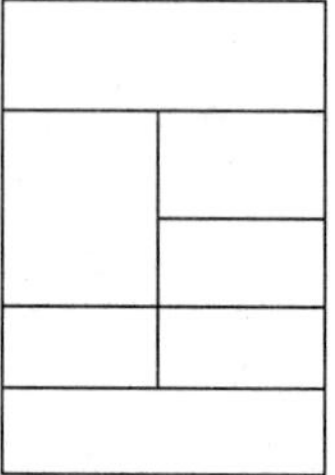

    (a) 2 (b) 3
    (c) 4 (d) 5

**(D) Study the graphs here and answer the questions that follow.**

A survey of different type of car owners was conducted in two towns, X and Y. The result of survey is indicated in the pie chart shown here.

**Town X**

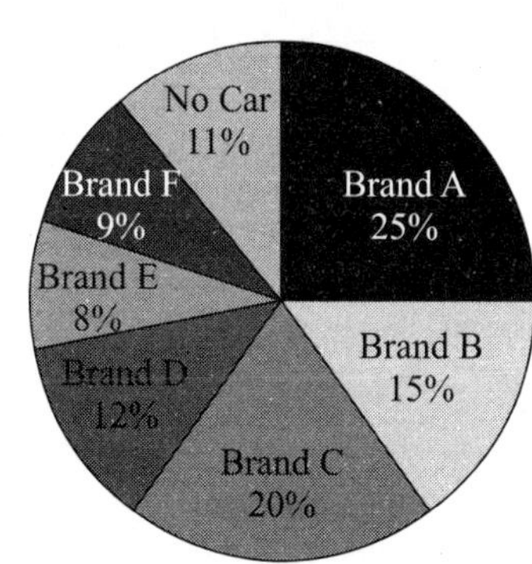


**Town Y**

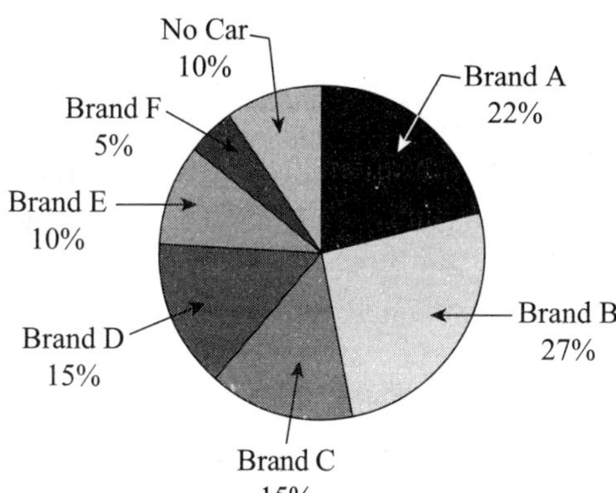


17. Citizens of which town are likely to own more than one car as per the data given?
    (a) Town X
    (b) Town Y
    (c) Both of Town Y and Town X
    (d) Cannot be determined
18. Which car has maximum sales in terms of volume if both towns taken together?
    (a) Brand A
    (b) Brand B
    (c) Brand C
    (d) Cannot be determined
19. In Question Number 17, what percentage of population is likely to have more than one car?
    (a) 4%
    (b) 10%
    (c) 14%
    (d) Cannot be determined

**(E) Read the following passage and answer the questions that follow. The answers should be based on the passage only.**

Six girls, Abha, Vidushi, Chetna, Garima, Deepa and Manisha sit in a circle facing one another to play the game of the Chinese Whisper (not in the given order). Abha is sitting opposite to Manisha and to left of Chetna. Deepa is not adjacent to either Garima or Vidushi. Vidushi is not adjacentto Abha.

20. If every player has to say the message in the ear of the person sitting to her right then in whose ear will Garima speak?
    (a) Abha
    (b) Vidushi
    (c) Chetna
    (d) Data not sufficient
21. Who is sitting in between Manisha and Chetna?
    (a) Vidushi (b) Garima
    (c) Deepa (d) Abha
22. If Vidushi is the first person to say the message and speaks in the ear of person on her right than who will be the last player to receive the message?
    (a) Garima (b) Manisha
    (c) Chetna (d) Data insufficient

**(F) Read the information and data given here and answer the questionsthat follow.**

People of Town X are gripped by a communicable disease of unknown nature. The disease spreads in a large section of society before the health experts are able to find a cure and begin administering the medicine. This chart shows the percentage of population gripped by the disease for various days. Presume that people get cured by the effect of medicine and not by natural immunity.

| Day | 1 | 2 | 3 | 4 | 5 | 6 | 7 | 8 | 9 | 10 | 11 | 12 | 13 | 14 | 15 |
|---|---|---|---|---|---|---|---|---|---|---|---|---|---|---|---|
| Percentage of population affected by disease | 1 | 3 | 7 | 15 | 25 | 30 | 34 | 37 | 39 | 41 | 42 | 42 | 41 | 40 | 38 |

| Day | 16 | 17 | 18 | 19 | 20 | 21 | 22 | 23 | 24 | 25 |
|---|---|---|---|---|---|---|---|---|---|---|
| Percentage of population affected by disease | 35 | 30 | 24 | 17 | 9 | 1 | 0.5 | 0.25 | 0.1 | 0.05 |

Answer the following questions:

23. Which of the following graphs best represents the spread and then the cure of the disease?

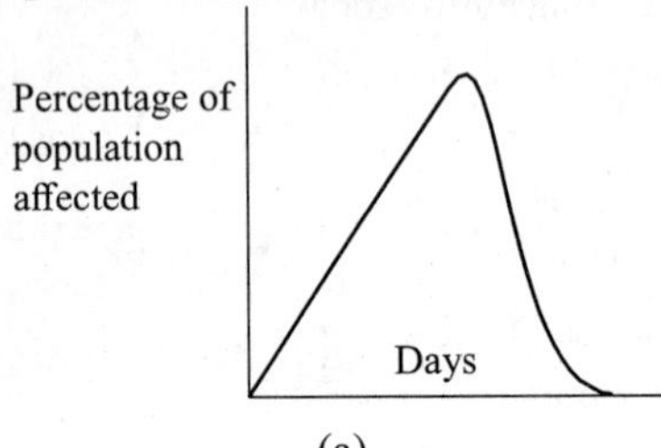

(a)

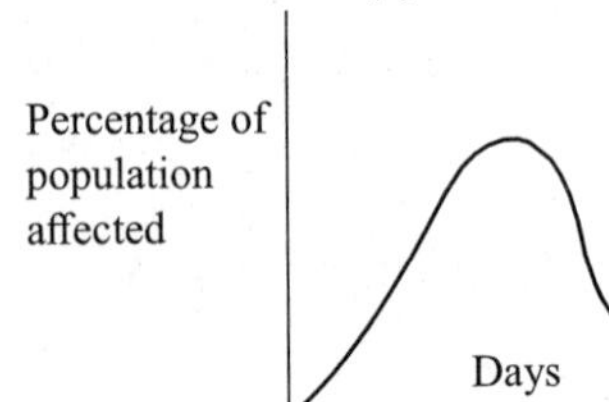

(b)

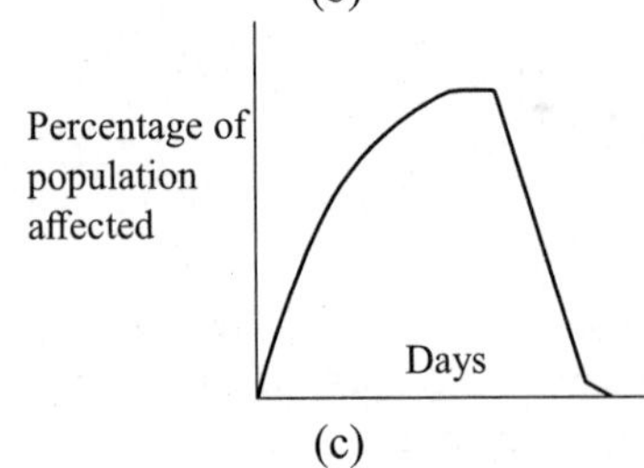

(c)

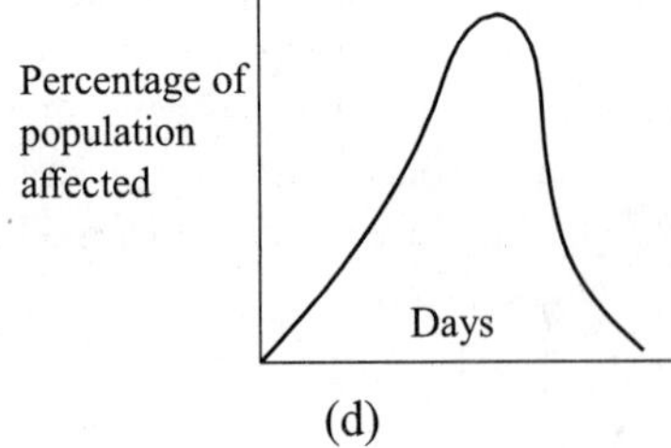

(d)

24. If the drug was very quick acting and starts curing the infected people from the very first day it is administered, then from which day can the drugs administration be said to have begun?
    (a) 3rd to 4th day
    (b) 5th to 6th day
    (c) 10th to 11th day
    (d) Cannot be determined

**(G) Read the information and data given here and answer the questions that follow.**

The radioactive decay of radium is represented by the formula $A = Ao\ e^{-kt}$, where *A0* is the number of radioactive atoms of radium present initially, *t* is the time (in years) and *k* is a constant. A represents the number of atoms leftafter time *t*. Study the following graphs.

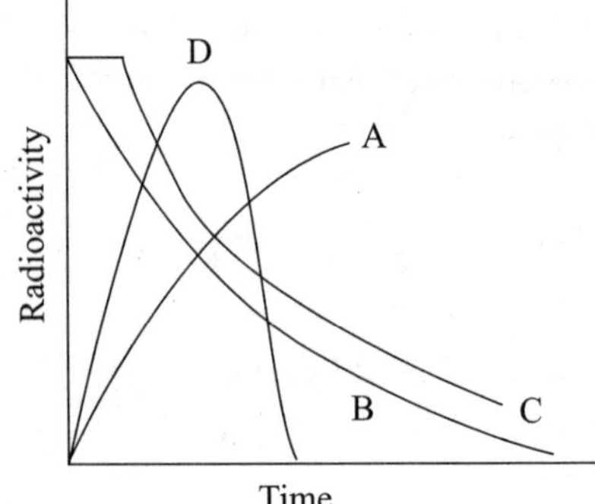


25. Which of the graphs best represents radioactive decay?
    (a) A
    (b) B
    (c) C
    (d) D

26. Half life is that time period in which half of the radioactive atoms decay. If half life of Radium is nearly 1600 years when will the full decay take place?
    (a) 3200 years
    (b) 2400 years
    (c) Value of k in the formula is required.
    (d) Full decay will take infinite time.
27. In the above question, when will 75% of decay take place?
    (a) 2000 years
    (b) 2400 years
    (c) 3200 years
    (d) Value of k in above formula required
28. A boy was asked to find the LCM of 3, 5, 12 and an another number. But while calculating he wrote 21 instead of 12 and yet came up with the right answer. What could be the fourth number?
    (a) 15 (b) 18
    (c) 24 (d) 28
29. There are five friends who have three fruits, an apple, an orange and a banana. In how many ways can the fruits be distributed so that nobody gets all the three fruits?
    (a) 120 (b) 125
    (c) 75 (d) 20

**(H) Read the questions carefully and answer them**

30. A hollow metal cylinder having external radius $r_1$, inner radius $r_2$ and length $l$ is molten and cast into a solid cylinder with length $L$. Find its new radius.
    (a) $[(r_1^2 - r_2^2)1/L]1/2$
    (b) $[L/(r_1^2 - r_2^2)1/L]1/2$
    (c) $[(r_1^2 - r_2^2)1/L]$
    (d) $[L\,(r_1^2 - r_2^2)1/]$
31. A large roll of cloth is of size 1000 m ¥1 m. Small pieces of cloth each of size 1.5 m ¥1 m are to be cut leaving minimum amount of wastage. What fraction of cloth will get wasted in each roll?
    (a) $\frac{1}{1000}$ (b) $\frac{2}{1000}$
    (c) $\frac{3}{1000}$ (d) $\frac{3}{1000}$

32 In a game of chance, two dices are rolled together. If the sum of the numbers which appear on both the dices is the same as the number which has been bet upon then the player wins. A person bets on number 7. What is the chance that he will win?
    (a) $\frac{1}{5}$ th (b) $\frac{1}{6}$ th
    (c) $\frac{1}{7}$ th (d) $\frac{1}{8}$ th
33. In the following questions, two statements are given followed by two conclusions. Take the statements to be true even if they are in variance with commonly accepted facts. Determine which of the two conclusions can be drawn from the statements. Choose option as follows:
    (a) If only Conclusion 1 can be drawn
    (b) If only Conclusion 2 can be drawn
    (c) If only Conclusions 1 and 2 both can be drawn
    (d) If neither Conclusion 1 nor 2 can be drawn

    Statement-1: Some cups are broken.
    Statement-2: All cups are utensils.
    Conclusion-1: All utensils are cups.
    Conclusion-2: All utensils are broken.
34. Amongst the statements given here which of these would be logically compatible?
    (i) A ship is a canoe.
    (ii) A canoe is a boat.
    (iii) All boats are yachts.
    (iv) A yacht is a boat.
    (v) No canoe is a yacht.
    (a) (ii), (i), (v) (b) (ii), (iv), (v)
    (c) (iii), (iv), (v) (d) (i), (iii), (iv)
35. A study on quantum of pollution caused by various class of vehicles on the roads of Delhi, reveals that the private four wheeler vehicles

cause the maximum pollution, this is followed by the pollution caused by buses, the trucks and finally the two wheelers. Based on this information which of the following conclusions can be drawn?

(i) The number of two wheelers is less than the number of trucks plying on Delhi roads.

(ii) Pollution caused by a single private vehicle would be more than the pollution caused by a single bus.

(a) Only conclusion (i) can be drawn.
(b) Only conclusion (ii) can be drawn.
(c) Both conclusions (i) and (ii) can be drawn.
(d) Neither conclusion (i) nor (ii) can be drawn.

36. A recent study reveals that female foeticide is more rampant in towns and cities where greater economic development has taken place as compared to rural areas and suburban pockets. Which amongst the following could explain the reason behind the above observation?

(i) Law enforcement agencies are unable to detect centres commit- ting female foeticide as these cities and towns have large physical spread. Besides, their focus is more on pressing and urgent issues/ crimes plaguing the cities/town.

(ii) Economic prosperity has led to growth of medical centres which have facility to detect female foetus and carry such foeticide safely. Besides, people here have the money to afford the cost of such medical centres.

(a) Only statement (i) is logically explains the reason.

(b) Only statement (ii) is logically explains the reason.

(c) Both the statements (i) and (ii) logically explain the reason.

(d) Neither statement (i) nor statement (ii) are the logically explain the reason.

37. Madan's brother's uncle is Karan's father's brother. What is the relationship between Madan and Karan?

(a) Madan is Karan's father.
(b) Madan is Karan's uncle.
(c) Madan is Karan's son.
(d) Madan is Karan's brother.

**(I) Answer the questions given below.**

38. Find the missing number in the figure given here.

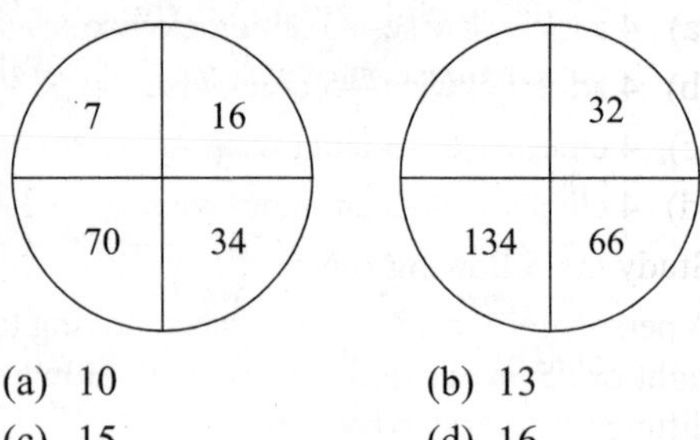


(a) 10 (b) 13
(c) 15 (d) 16

39. In a cycle race, the cyclists have to travel on streets which are perpendicular to each other. The cyclists start off and move north for a km then turn towards east and cycle for 2 km. They then travel 3 km towards south and finally turn towards west and travel 4 km.

Examine the following statements in light of what is given above.

(i) The final destination is less than 3 km from the starting point.

(ii) The cyclists take 4 turns in the entire race.

(iii) The match officials, who are standing on the street facing the cyclists and who are to decide which cyclists came first, second, etc., would be facing west.

(iv) The cyclists travel a distance of 10 km. Which of the aforesaid are true?

(a) (i), (ii), (iii), (iv) (b) (ii), (iii), (iv)
(c) (i) and (iv) (d) (iii) and (iv)

40. In a transmission system, five wheels which are touching each other are used for transmission of power (see the following figure). The motion in Wheel 1 sets in motion the other wheels all of which are of different sizes. If Wheel 1 is rotating clockwise then in which direction Wheel 4 and Wheel 5 rotate?

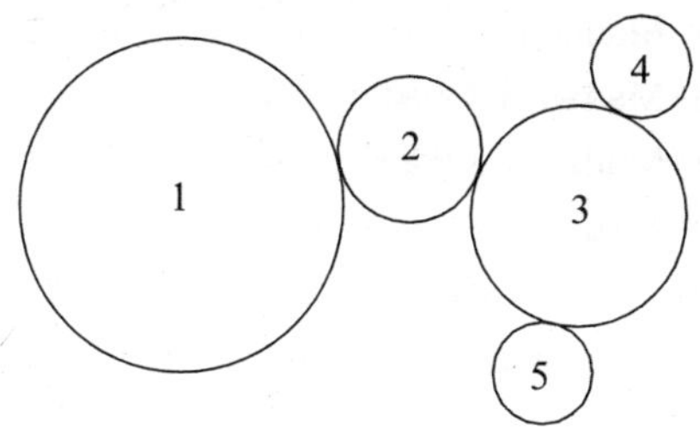


(a) 4 anticlockwise—5 anticlockwise
(b) 4 anticlockwise—5 clockwise
(c) 4 clockwise—5 clockwise
(d) 4 clockwise—5 anticlockwise

41. Study the following figure:

A person goes from *A* to *B* always moving to the right or downwards along the lines. How many different routes can he adopt?

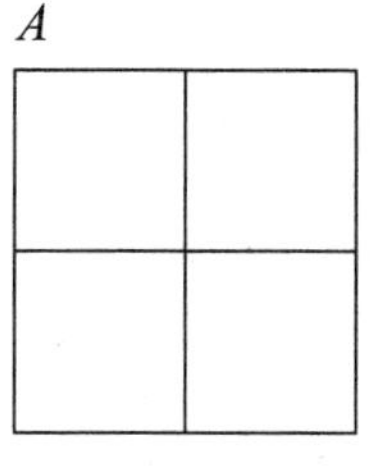


Select the correct answer from the codes given below:

(a) 4 (b) 5
(c) 6 (d) 7

42. Consider the following figure and answer the item that follows:

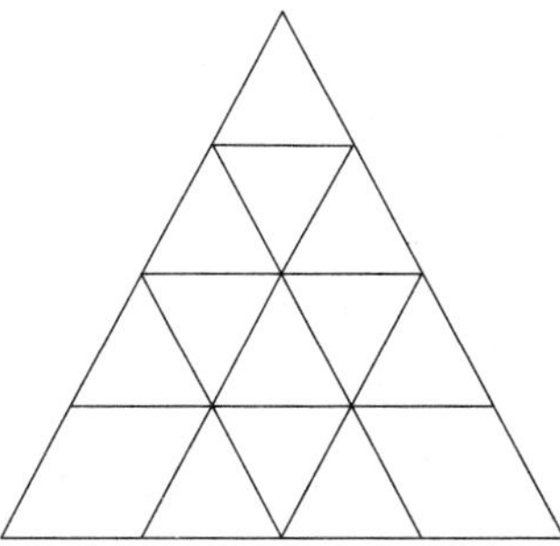

What is the total number of triangles in the above grid?

(a) 27 (b) 26
(c) 23 (d) 22

43. The elements of the problem figures given below are changing with a certain rule as we observe them from left to right:

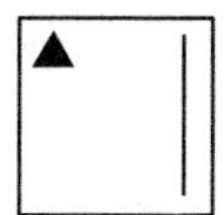 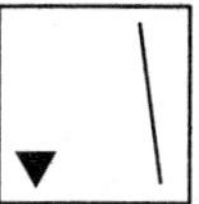 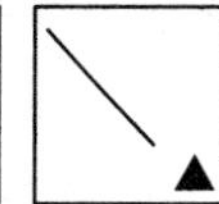 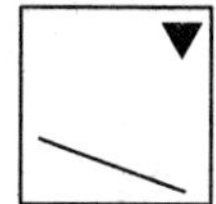

According to this rule, which of the following would be the next figure if the changes were continued with the same rule.

(a) 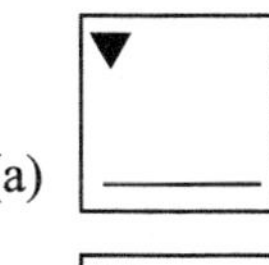 (b) 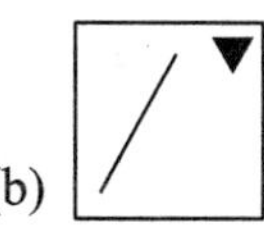

(c) 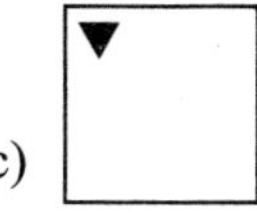 (d) 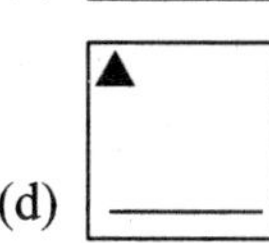

44. Six squares are coloured, front and back, red (R), blue (B), yellow (Y), green (G), white (W) and orange (O) and are hinged together as shown in the figure given below. If they are folded to form a cube, what would be the face opposite the white face?

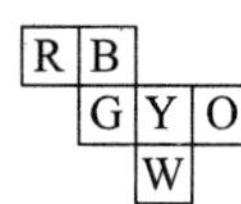


(a) R (b) G
(c) B (d) O

45. 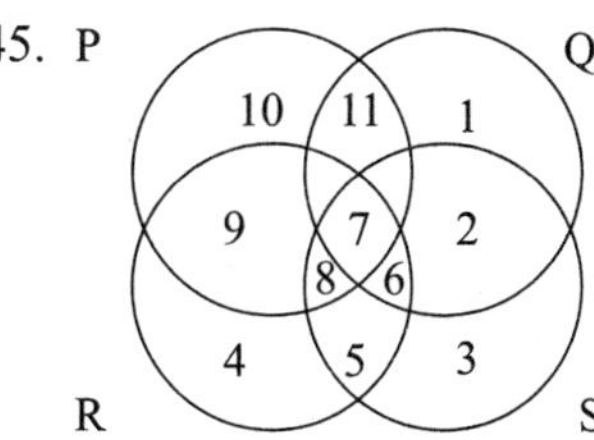


In the above figure, circle P represents hardworking people, circle Q represents intelligent people, circle R represents truthful people, and circle S represents honest people. Which region represents the people who are intelligent, honest and truthful but not hardworking?

(a) 6 (b) 7
(c) 8 (d) 11

46. Three views of a cube following a particular motion are given below:

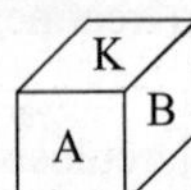

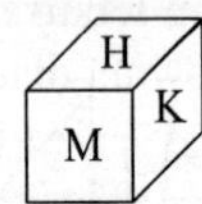

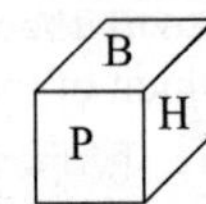


What is the letter opposite to A?

(a) H (b) P

(c) B (d) M

47. 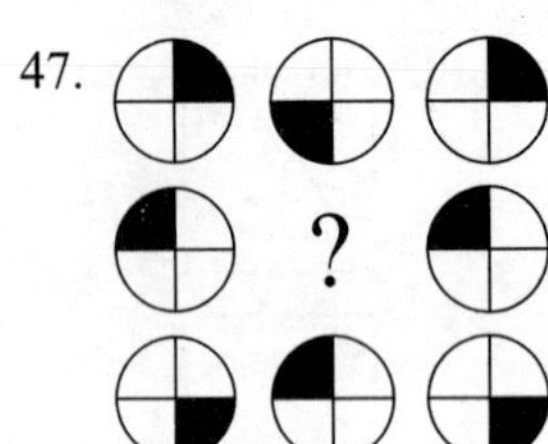


Which one of the figures shown below occupies the blank space (?) in the matrix given above?

(a) (b)

(c) (d)

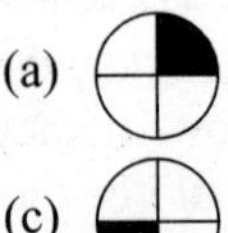
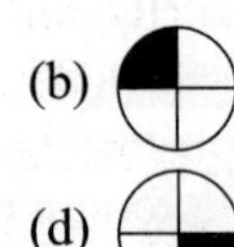

48. Raman can finish a piece of work in 20 days. He worked alone for 5 days and then Urmila joined him. Together they could finish the remaining work in 5 days. In how many days can Urmila alone finish the same work?

(a) 10 (b) 15

(c) 20 (d) 5

49. A person on a bike covers a distance in 45 minute at an average speed of 80 km/h. Then he increase the speed of bike by $x$ km/h to complete his return journey in 40 minute. The value of $x$ is;

(a) 10 (b) 15

(c) 6 (d) 12

50. A student has to get 40 % marks to pass in an examination. Suppose he gets 25 marks and fails by 25 marks, then what are the maximum marks in the examination?

(a) 100 (b) 120

(c) 150 (d) 125

51. Of the three numbers, the first is two times the second and three times the third. If the product of all the three numbers is 36, then the second number is:

(a) 1 (b) 2

(c) 3 (d) 4

52. In a class, there are certain number of desktop computers. If 6 students are to share one desktop, then to accommodate all of them, one more desktop computer is required. However, if 8 students are made to sit on a desktop computer after accommodating all of them, space for 4 students is still left. What is the total number of students in the class?

(a) 31 (b) 28

(c) 43 (d) None

53. Raghunathan sold a car to Jyothi for ₹2,40,000 losing 20%, Jyothi sells it to Ramesh at a price which would have given Raghunathan a profit of 15%. What is Jyothi's gain ?

(a) ₹1,00,000 (b) ₹1,05,000

(c) ₹1,10,000 (d) ₹80,000

54. Alam is thrice as fast as Benoy and Benoy is twice as fast as Chitra. How much time will Alam take to cover the distance covered by Chitra in 48 minutes?

(a) 8 min (b) 12 min

(c) 16 min (d) 6 min

55. Which of the following day is celebrated on the 5th of June ?

(a) World Environment Day

(b) World Ozone Day

(c) World Food Day

(d) World Aids Day

56. Mirabai Chanu is associated with which sporting discipline?

(a) Weight lifting (b) Archery

(c) Boxing (d) Gymnastics

57. National Assests & Reconstruction Company Limited, the creation of which was announced in the budget of 2021-22, is to discharge which of the following functions?

(a) An institution to take over the bad assets of other institutions and to undertake their resolution.

(b) An institution to provide judicial orders for settlement of disputes pertaining to the bad assets of other banks.

(c) An institution to enable the reconstruction and finance of the loss-making government PSUs.

(d) None of the above

58. The languages of Nepali, Bhutia and Lepcha are associated with which Indian state ?

(a) Manipur (b) Assam

(c) Sikkim (d) West Bengal

59. Hydroxy Chloroquine(HCQ) controversially used in some places for prevention/ treatment of Covid-19, is used medically for treatment of which of the following disease?

(a) Typhoid (b) Tuberculosis

(c) Malaria (d) Whooping cough

60. In which country the 2024 Olympics is to be held?

(a) Paris (b) New York

(c) London (d) Berlin

## Answers of Practice Question Paper-2

| | | | | | |
|---|---|---|---|---|---|
| **1.** (c) | **11.** (d) | **21.** (c) | **31.** (a) | **41.** (c) | **51.** (c) |
| **2.** (d) | **12.** (c) | **22.** (b) | **32.** (b) | **42.** (c) | **52.** (d) |
| **3.** (c) | **13.** (c) | **23.** (b) | **33.** (d) | **43.** (d) | **53.** (b) |
| **4.** (b) | **14.** (a) | **24.** (b) | **34.** (b) | **44.** (c) | **54.** (a) |
| **5.** (d) | **15.** (b) | **25.** (b) | **35.** (d) | **45.** (a) | **55.** (a) |
| **6.** (c) | **16.** (b) | **26.** (d) | **36.** (b) | **46.** (b) | **56.** (a) |
| **7.** (b) | **17.** (b) | **27.** (c) | **37.** (d) | **47.** (d) | **57.** (a) |
| **8.** (c) | **18.** (d) | **28.** (d) | **38.** (c) | **48.** (a) | **58.** (c) |
| **9.** (d) | **19.** (a) | **29.** (a) | **39.** (c) | **49.** (a) | **59.** (c) |
| **10.** (d) | **20.** (a) | **30.** (a) | **40.** (a) | **50.** (d) | **60.** (a) |

# Practice Question Paper 3

**(A) Study the graph and answer the questions that follow.**

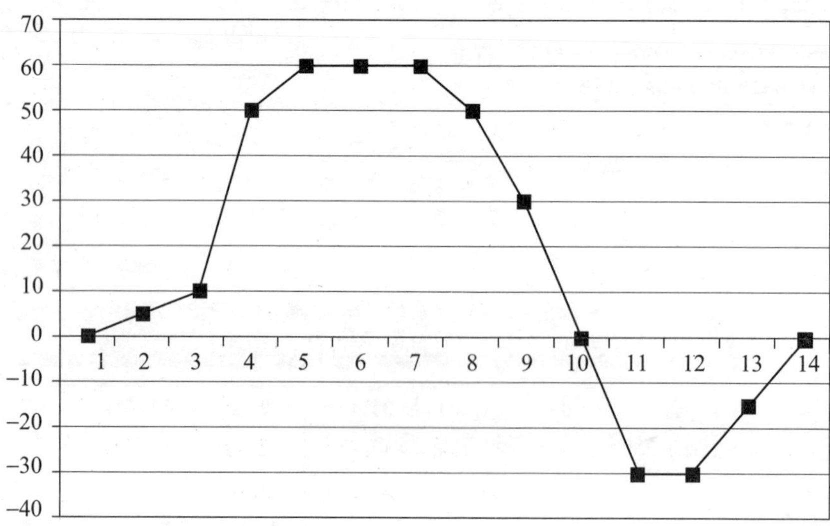


**(x-axis-time in seconds; y-axis-velocity in metres/sec.)**

The graph represents the flight of an experimental rocket, which has the following stages. **Lift off-powered ascent coasting phase-reaching apogee-ejection, which brings out parachute and slows the descent.**

Answer the following questions:

1. After what time does the rocket reach the maximum height?

   (a) 9 seconds  (b) 10 seconds
   (c) 12 seconds  (d) 14 seconds

2. Which phase would correspond to powered ascent?

   (a) 0–2 second(s)  (b) 2–5 seconds
   (c) 5–7 seconds  (d) 8–10 seconds

3. Which phase corresponds to coasting flight in above question?

   (a) 0–2 second(s)  (b) 2–5 seconds
   (c) 5–7 seconds  (d) 8–10 seconds

4. What is the maximum height attained by the rocket?

   (a) 305 m  (b) 325 m
   (c) 345 m  (d) 405 m

5. Neena has some pebbles. When she divides all the pebbles into 3 equal groups, 1 pebble is left. She divides one such group into 3 equal groups again; the remainder will still be 1. She splits one of such groups into 1 equal groups again,

the remainder is still 1. What is the minimum number of pebbles she has?

(a) 22 (b) 34
(c) 40 (d) 50

6. Four rectangles of different sizes are shown here. The sides of each triangle measures with a natural number. The respective areas of the three rectangles are indicated in the figure in $cm^2$. Find the area of the fourth rectangle. (Figure not to scale)

| 15 | 45 |
|---|---|
| 20 | |

(a) 80 (b) 70
(c) 50 (d) 60

7. There are 21 rows of seats in an amphitheatre. Each row has 4 seats more than the row in front. The last row has 100 seats. Altogether how many seats are there in the amphitheatre?

(a) 1260 (b) 1200
(c) 1140 (d) 1080

K, L, M, N, P, Q, R, S, U and W are the only ten members in a department. There is a proposal to form a team from within the members of the department, subject to the following conditions:

- A team must include exactly one among P, R, and S.
- A team must include either M or Q, but not both.
- If a team includes K then it must also include L and vice versa.
- If a team includes one among S, U and W then it must also include the other two.
- L and N cannot be members of the same team.
- L and U cannot be members of the same team.

The size of a team is defined as the number of members in the team.

8. What could be the size of a team that includes K?

(a) 2 or 3 (b) 2 or 4
(c) 3 or 4 (d) Only 4

9. In how many ways a team can be constituted so that the team includes N?

(a) 2 (b) 3
(c) 4 (d) 6

10. What would be the size of the largest possible team?

(a) 8 (b) 7
(c) 6 (d) 5

**(B) Answer questions based on the following pie charts.**

The pie charts given here provide the break-up of total government receipts in the years 2008–09 and 2009–10.

**2008–09**

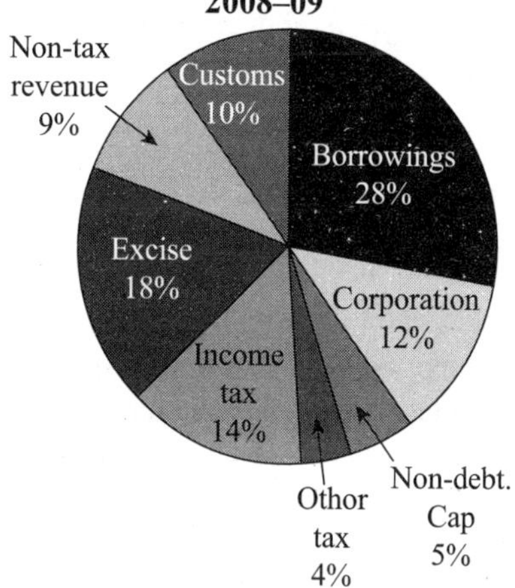


**FY 2009–10**

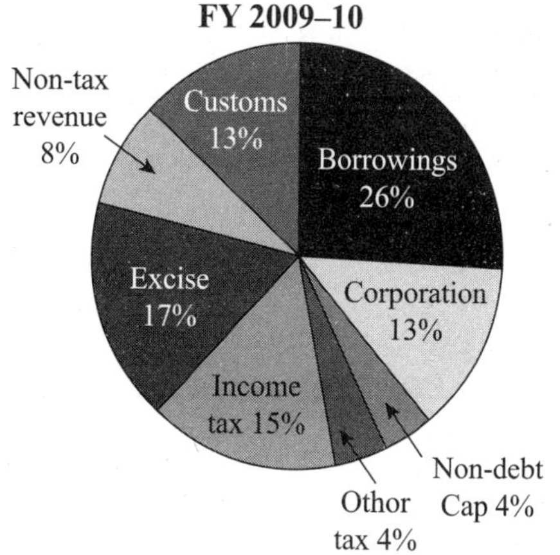

11. How many receipts recorded an absolute increase in quantum from FY 2008–09 to FY 2009–10?
    (a) 3
    (b) 2
    (c) 0
    (d) Cannot be determined
12. If the total government receipts increased by 20% from FY 2008–09 to FY 2009–10, what was the growth in revenues from Customs?
    (a) 46%
    (b) 30%
    (c) 56%
    (d) Cannot be determined
13. In the question above, what would be the increase in the receipts of Excise?
    (a) –5.55%
    (b) 13.33%
    (c) 21.25%
    (d) Cannot be determined.
14. Consider the following three statements.
    (i) Only persons above the age of 25 can contest Lok Sabha elections.
    (ii) Some contestants are members of Congress party.
    (iii) All Congress party candidates are fully funded by the party.

    Based on the three statements, which of the following conclusions can be drawn?
    (a) All candidates are funded by the Congress party.
    (b) All candidates funded by the party are Congress candidates.
    (c) All persons contesting on party funds are above 25 years of age.
    (d) All Lok Sabha contestants are funded by the Congress.

**(C) Answer the following questions.**

15. In the following questions, two statements are given followed by two conclusions. Take the statements to be true even if it is in variance with commonly accepted facts. Determine which of the two conclusions can be drawn from the statements. Choose the option as follows.

    Option (a) – If only Conclusion (i) can be drawn.

    Option (b) – If only Conclusion (ii) can be drawn.

    Option (c) – If both Conclusions (i) and Conclusion (ii) can be drawn.

    Option (d) – If neither Conclusion (i) nor Conclusion (ii) can be drawn.

    Statement – 1: All children are naughty.
    Statement–2: Some children are intelligent.
    Conclusion – 1: Some naughty children are intelligent.

    Conclusion – 2: Some intelligent children are not naughty.
16. What should be the smallest number with which 999 be multiplied so that the product is the square of a natural number?
    (a) 77 (b) 99
    (c) 111 (d) 132
17. In an examination the average of marks of Ramesh and Suresh is $x$, average of marks of Suresh and Ganesh is $y$ and average of marks of Ganesh and Ramesh is $z$. What are the marks Ramesh scored?
    (a) $x-y+z$
    (b) $x+y-z$
    (c) $y+z-x$
    (d) Cannot be determined
18. A box contains oranges. When they are counted in twos, it leaves 1 orange extra. When it is counted in threes it leaves 2 oranges extra; when it is counted in fours it leaves 3 extra, while on counting in fives it leaves 4 extra and on counting in sixes leaves 5 extra. But on counting in sevens there were no extra. What was the minimum number of oranges in the box?
    (a) 49 (b) 91
    (c) 119 (d) 189
19. Two trains are at a distance of 300 km from each other on a long railway track. Each is travelling at a speed of 75 km/hr towards the other. A bird flies from 1st train to the 2nd train, flies back to

the 1st train and then back to the second train and so forth. The bird flies at a constant speed of 100 km/ hr without stopping. By the time trains meet each other how much distance the bird would have flown?

(a) 100 km (b) 200 km
(c) 300 km (d) 400 km

20. How many rectangles are there in the figure here?

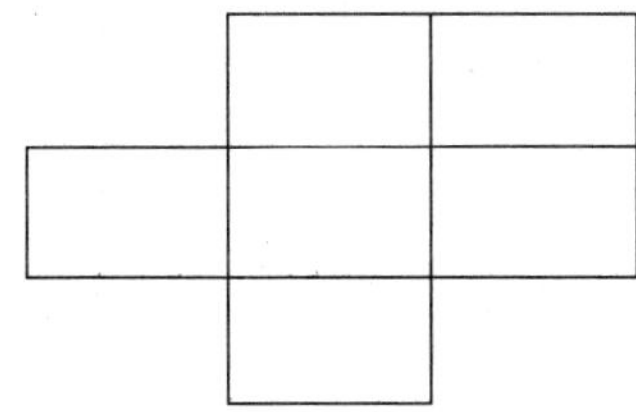

(a) 15 (b) 14
(c) 12 (d) 16

21. A box has 2 marbles each of red, blue, yellow and green colours. The box is kept in a darkroom where the colours of the marble cannot be distinguished. A boy wants 2 marbles of the same colour. How many minimum numbers of marbles he must draw from the box so that he is sure that he has got two marbles of the same colour?

(a) 5 (b) 4
(c) 3 (d) 6

22. Find the number coming next in the series. 1, 4, 8, 32, 36, …

(a) 40 (b) 140
(c) 144 (d) 48

**(D) Read the information given here and answer the questions that follow.**

Five students Rohit, Kumar, Vikram, Simran and Vivek are preparing for an engineering competition. The tutor sets papers for Maths and Physics. Amongst the five students the following is the inter se ranking.

- Vivek was the topper in one subject but had the last rank in other.
- Simran stood just above Vikram in Maths but below him in Physics.
- Rohit was last in Maths but scored more than Simran in Physics.
- Kumar was topper in one subject and had number two rank in another.

**(E) Answer the following questions:**

23. What was Simran's rank in Physics?

(a) $2^{nd}$ (b) $3^{rd}$
(c) $4^{th}$ (d) Data insufficient

24. Who was the topper in Maths?

(a) Vivek (b) Kumar
(c) Simran (d) Data insufficient

25. Who scored the 2nd rank in Physics?

(a) Kumar (b) Rohit
(c) Simran (d) Data insufficient

**(F) Read the information and answer the questions that follow.**

In a culture, the growth of bacteria follows the formula $n = K2^t$ where $n$ is total number of bacteria, $t$ is time in hours for which culture has been allowed to grow and $K$ is the number of bacteria initially introduced in the culture. Answer the following questions.

26. Which of the following graphs best represents the growth of bacteria in the culture?

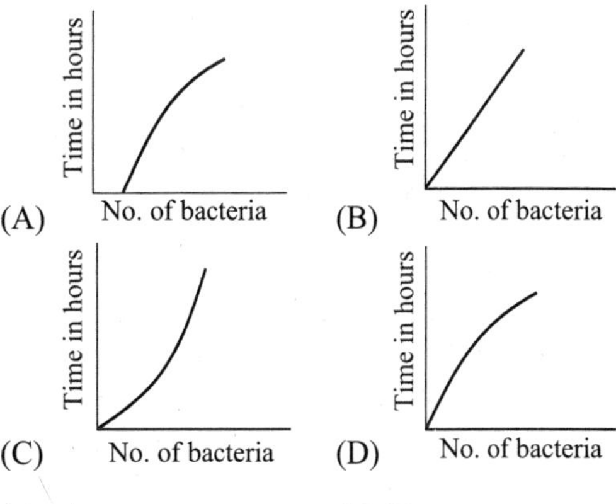


(a) A (b) B
(c) C (d) D

27. In the culture above, $x$ number of bacteria is introduced. After half an hour a sample of $2x$ bacteria is again introduced in the culture. After an hour (from the beginning) what would be the total number of bacteria in the culture.

(a) $4x$ (b) $2\sqrt{2}\,x$

(c) $2(1+\sqrt{2})x$ (d) $x.2^{3/2}$

28. A sample culture is allowed to develop for an hour after which it is stored at –20° C for one hour. At this temperature the bacteria do not multiply and remain in a dormant state. After this the sample is taken out and thawed to normal temperature, and allowed to develop for another hour. Presuming that thawing takes less than a minute, which graph would best represent the growth of bacteria in the culture.

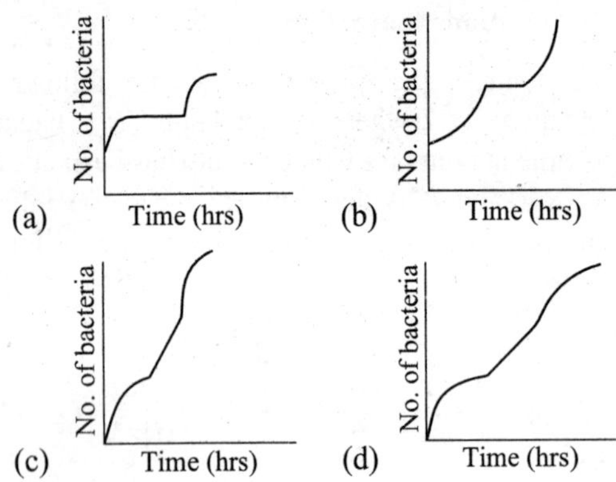


29. The following questions consist of five statements followed by options consisting of three statements put together in a specific order. Choose the option which indicates a valid argument, that is, where the third statement is conclusion drawn from preceding two statements. ABC is a valid option where C can be concluded from statements A and B.

(i) Some vehicular traffic is not hazardous to environment.

(ii) Vehicular traffic leads to emission of carbon dioxide and other greenhouse gases.

(iii) Carbon dioxide and green-house gases are hazardous to the environment.

(iv) Some vehicular traffic does not emit carbon dioxide and other green-house gases.

(v) Vehicular traffic is hazardous to the environment.

(a) (ii), (v), (iii) (b) (iii), (i), (vi)
(c) (ii), (iv), (i) (d) (iii), (ii), (v)

30. Amongst the statements given here which would be logically compatible?

(i) No suit is a dress.
(ii) A jacket is not a suit.
(iii) All shirts are dresses.
(iv) No trouser is a dress.
(v) A jacket is always a dress.

(a) (i), (iv), (v) (b) (ii), (iii), (iv)
(c) (ii), (iii), (v) (d) (i), (iii), (v)

31. Three boys are coming down a staircase. One boy climbs down two steps in one go, another climbs down 3 steps in one go, while the third boy climbs down 4 steps in one go. They start together leaving their footmarks on each staircase and end together at the bottom of the staircase. If the number of steps in the staircase is the minimum for which the above synchronisation is possible, then how many steps are there where no footmarks have been left by any of the three boys?

(a) 4 (b) 3
(c) 2 (d) 1

32. A sphere has volume $V$ and surface area $S$. If its volume is doubled then the new surface area would be

(a) $2S$ (b) $2^{1}/_{3}\,S$
(c) $2^{2}/_{3}\,S$ (d) $S$

**(G) Read the information here and answer the questions that follow.**

In a gathering of alumni of a college, it was noted that 54 persons were professionals (self-employed), 60 were in business while 78 were in government jobs. 40% of men were employed in private sector job. 320 alumni had gathered for the meet. The ratio of men to women was 5:3. The number of men who were in business was twice that of women in business and 28 women were in government sector.

33. What percentage of women were professionals?
    (a) 20% (b) 30%
    (c) 35% (d) Data insufficient
34. What percentage of professionals were women?
    (a) 22.2% (b) 44.4%
    (c) 55.6% (d) Data insufficient
35. Examine whether the following stacked bar charts are correct.

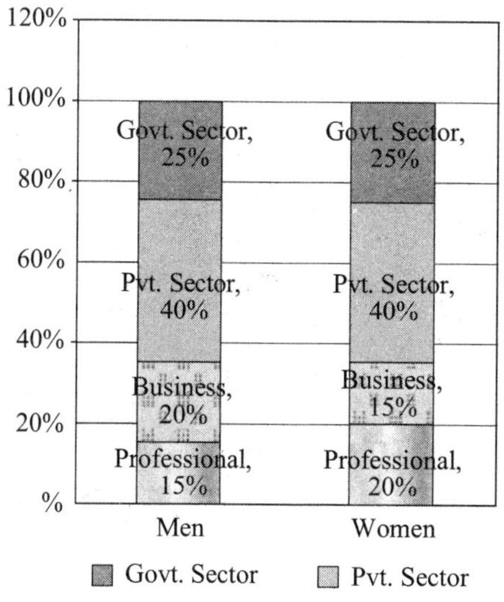


    (a) Data representation of only Men is correct.
    (b) Data representation of only Women is correct.
    (c) Data representation of both is correct.
    (d) Data representation of neither Men nor Women is correct.

**(H) Read the information given below and answer the questions which follow:**

Four persons get inside a lift of an apartment which has ground and seven floors. Each person lives on a separate floor. The ground floor has only parking and no flats. The four persons are Ms. Susan, Ravi, Mr. Verma, and Mr. Bajaj. Each person is wearing a dress of separate colour and has a different occupation, i.e., a bureaucrat, a teacher, a scientist, and a student (not in any specific order). Following information is also known.

- Ravi lives on the 6th floor, he is neither a teacher nor a student.
- Susan is wearing a pink saree and she is not a student. She did not get off at the 1st floor.
- None of the four live on the 7th or the 4th floor.
- The scientist is wearing a grey shirt and lives on the 3rd floor.
- The person in red T-Shirt lives on the 2nd floor.
- One person is wearing a white shirt.
- Mr. Verma is not a scientist and he does not live on the first floor.

36. What is the occupation of Mr. Verma?
    (a) Bureaucrat
    (b) Student
    (c) Teacher
    (d) Data is insufficient
37. On which floor does the teacher live?
    (a) 2nd (b) 3rd
    (c) 5th (d) 1st
38. Who is the scientist?
    (a) Mr. Bajaj
    (b) Mr. Ravi
    (c) Ms. Susan
    (d) Data is insufficient
39. Who amongst the four lives on the 1st Floor?
    (a) Ms. Susan (b) Mr. Bajaj
    (c) Mr. Verma (d) No body
40. Ravi is wearing a
    (a) white shirt
    (b) red T-Shirt
    (c) grey shirt
    (d) data is insufficient
41. Red T-Shirt is worn by
    (a) Ravi (b) Mr. Bajaj
    (c) Mr. Verma (d) Data insufficient
42. In a school of 1200 students, 66% of students use school bus while the rest use private vehicles. If 60% of students are boys and 480 boys use school bus then how many girls come to school by private vehicles?
    (a) 240 (b) 168
    (c) 312 (d) Data insufficient

43. Which one of the following number is the biggest?

(a) $2^{1/2}$ (b) $5^{1/5}$

(c) $10^{1/10}$ (d) $20^{1/20}$

44. Which is the odd one out?

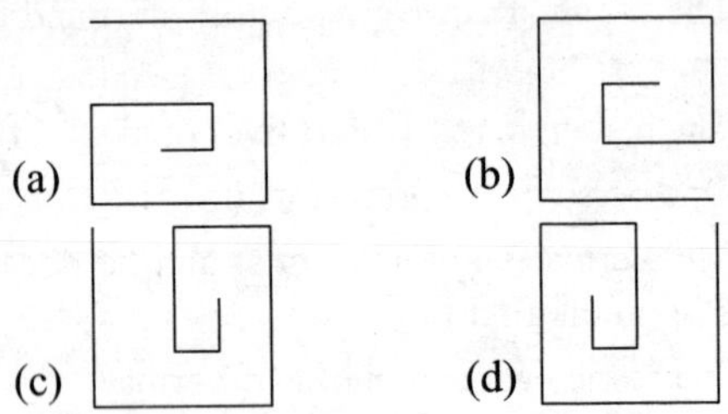


45. A square piece of paper is folded along the dotted lines as shown in Fig. 1. Two holes are then punched in it as shown in Fig. 2. The paper is then opened. Which figure will it look like?

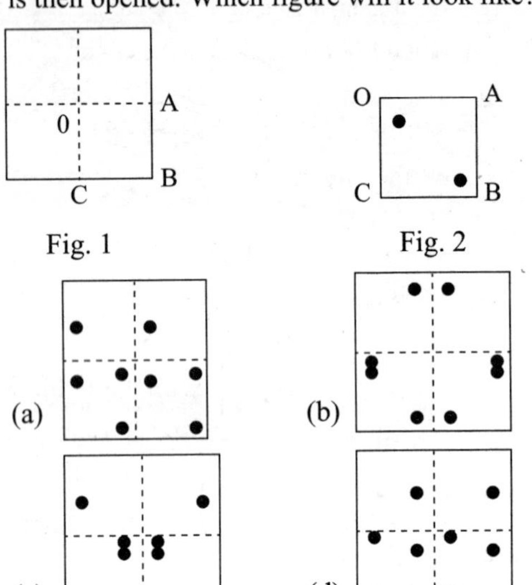


46. Consider the following figures 1, 2, 3 and 4:

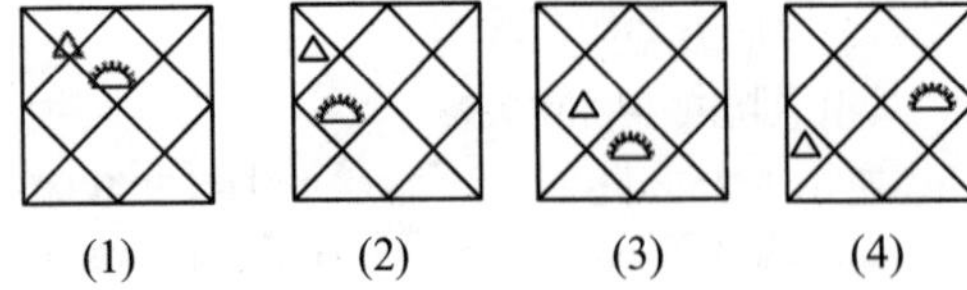


In the figures from 1 to 4 above, two symbols are shown to change their position in a regular direction. Following the same sequence, which one of the following will appear at the fifth stage?

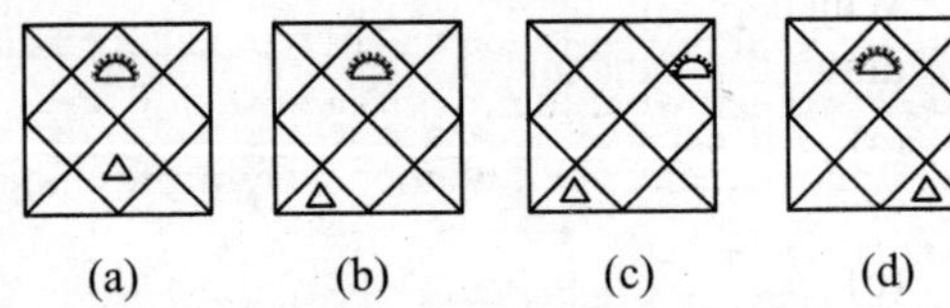


**(I) Directions for the following 2 (two) items**

In each item, there are two sets of figures; first four figures named Problem Figures and next four figures named Answer Figures indicated as (a), (b), (c) and (d). The problem figures follow a particular sequence. In accordance with the name, which one of the four figures should appear as the fifth figure?

47. Problem figures:

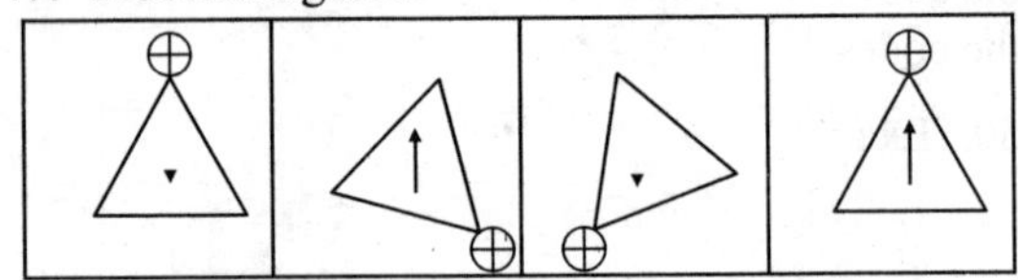

Answer figures:

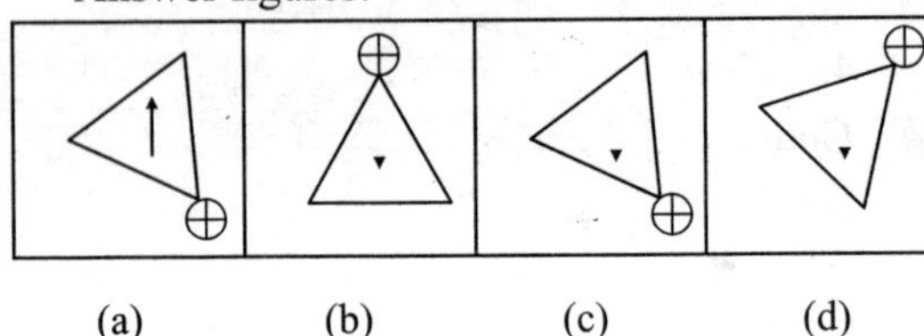


48. Problem figures:

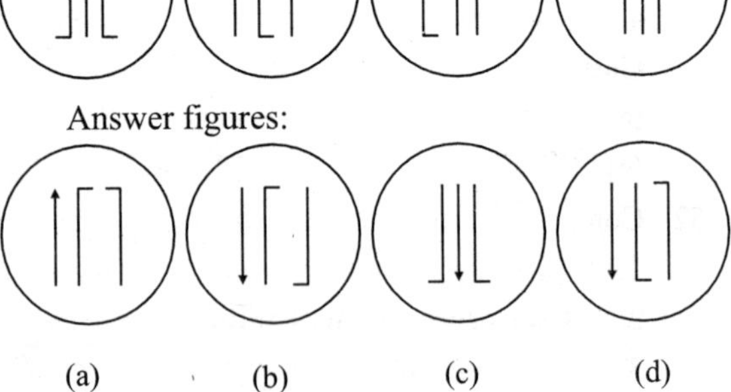


49. Consider the following three statements:

a. Only students can participate in the race.

b. Some participants in the race are girls.

c. All girl participants in the race are invited for coaching.

Which one of the following conclusions can be drawn from the above statements?

(a) All participants in the race are invited for coaching.

(b) All students are invited for coaching.

(c) All participants in the race are students.

(d) None of the statements (a), (b) and (c) given above is correct.

**(J) Directions for the following 2 (two) items:**

Each of the following two items consists of four statements. Of these four statements, two cannot both be true, but both can be false. Study the statements carefully and identify the two that satisfy the above condition. Select the correct answer using the codes given below each set of statements:

50. Examine the following statements:
   1. All animals are carnivorous.
   2. Some animals are not carnivorous.
   3. Animals are not carnivorous.
   4. Some animals are carnivorous.

   **Codes:**

   (a) 1 and 3 (b) 1 and 2
   (c) 2 and 3 (d) 3 and 4

51. Examine the following statements:
   1. All trains are run by diesel engine.
   2. Some trains are run by diesel engine.
   3. No train is run by diesel engine.
   4. Some trains are not run by diesel engine.

   **Codes:**

   (a) 1 and 2 (b) 2 and 3
   (c) 1 and 3 (d) 1 and 4

52. Consider the following statements:
   1. All artists are whimsical.
   2. Some artists are drug addicts.
   3. Frustrated people are prone to become drug addicts.

   From the above three statements it may be concluded that

   (a) Artists are frustrated.
   (b) Some drug addicts are whimsical.
   (c) All frustrated people are drug addicts.
   (d) Whimsical people are generally frustrated.

53. Examine the following statements:
   1. Either A and B are of the same age or A is older than B.
   2. Either C and D are of the same age or D is older than C.
   3. B is older than C.

   Which one of the following conclusions can be drawn from the above statements?

   (a) A is older than B
   (b) B and D are of the same age
   (c) D is older than C
   (d) A is older than C

54. Examine the following statements:
   1. Only those who have a pair of binoculars can become the members of the birdwatcher's club.
   2. Some members of the birdwatcher's club have cameras.
   3. Those members who have cameras can take part in photo contests.

   Which of the following conclusions can be drawn from the above statements?

   (a) All those who have a pair of binoculars are members of the birdwatcher's club.
   (b) All members of the birdwatcher's club have a pair of binoculars.
   (c) All those who take part in photo contests are members of the birdwatcher's club.
   (d) No conclusion can be drawn.

55. Which of the following European country does not recognise Euro as its official currency?
   (a) Germany
   (b) Austria
   (c) Spain
   (d) United Kingdom

56. The Great Himalayan National Park, recognised as a UNESCO World Heritage Site in 2014 is located in which of the following state/union territory?
   (a) Jammu and Kashmir
   (b) Himachal Pradesh
   (c) Assam
   (d) Uttarakhand

57. Which of the following Harappan settlements in India, was included in the list of UNESCO World Heritage sites in the year 2021?
   (a) Lothal (b) Rakhigarhi
   (c) Dholavira (d) Sinauli
58. Lovlina Borgohain, who won a Bronze in 2021 Olympics is associated with which sport?
   (a) Weight lifting (b) Table tennis
   (c) Gymnastics (d) Boxing
59. Which of the following Bhakti saints was associated with the Krishna Bhakti movement and Gaudiya Vaishnavism in the 15th century Bengal?
   (a) Mira (b) Sankardeva
   (c) Chaitanya (d) Dadudayal
60. The Reserve Bank of India is charged with which of the following functions?
   (a) Determining and implementing the monetary policy.
   (b) Determining and implementing the taxation policy.
   (c) Determining and implementing the capital markets policy.
   (d) All of the above

## Answers of Practice Question Paper-3

| | | | | | |
|---|---|---|---|---|---|
| **1.** (b) | **11.** (d) | **21.** (a) | **31.** (a) | **41.** (c) | **51.** (c) |
| **2.** (b) | **12.** (c) | **22.** (c) | **32.** (c) | **42.** (b) | **52.** (b) |
| **3.** (c) | **13.** (b) | **23.** (c) | **33.** (a) | **43.** (a) | **53.** (d) |
| **4.** (b) | **14.** (c) | **24.** (a) | **34.** (b) | **44.** (c) | **54.** (b) |
| **5.** (c) | **15.** (a) | **25.** (d) | **35.** (a) | **45.** (c) | **55.** (d) |
| **6.** (d) | **16.** (c) | **26.** (a) | **36.** (b) | **46.** (b) | **56.** (b) |
| **7.** (a) | **17.** (a) | **27.** (c) | **37.** (c) | **47.** (c) | **57.** (c) |
| **8.** (d) | **18.** (c) | **28.** (b) | **38.** (a) | **48.** (a) | **58.** (d) |
| **9.** (d) | **19.** (b) | **29.** (d) | **39.** (d) | **49.** (c) | **59.** (c) |
| **10.** (d) | **20.** (a) | **30.** (c) | **40.** (a) | **50.** (a) | **60.** (a) |

# Practice Question Paper 4

**(A) Read the question statements and answer the questions that follow.**

1. **Statement**: The Indian states which have shown higher rate of economic growth have also been seen to have made greater progress in the field of attaining higher literacy.

   Which of the two conclusions can be drawn from the above statement?

   **Conclusion-1**. All states which have high percentage of literacy are sure to have high economic growth.

   **Conclusion-2**. Literacy plays an important role even in the economic growth of a state.

   (a) Only Conclusion 1 can be drawn.
   (b) Only Conclusion 2 can be drawn.
   (c) Both the conclusions can be drawn.
   (d) None of the conclusions can be drawn.

2. **Statement:** *Legislation of strict laws has not led to the reduction of crime.*

   Which out of the two conclusions is correct?

   **Conclusion-1**. Strictness of law has no bearing at all on the incidence of crime.

   **Conclusion-2**. Effective implementation of the law is the only factor which can have an impact on crime reduction efforts.

   (a) Only Conclusion 1 is correct.
   (b) Only Conclusion 2 is correct.
   (c) Both the conclusions are correct.
   (d) None is correct.

3. **Statement:** *All of the Indian scientists at CERN, except for Ramesh are physicists.*

   Which of the statement mentioned here leads to the aforesaid inference?

   (a) Ramesh is not a physicist.
   (b) Except for Ramesh at CERN, all scientists are not physicists.
   (c) Besides the scientist Ramesh, if someone is an Indian at CERN, then he is a physicist.
   (d) Ramesh is the only non-Indian scientist who is a physicist.

**(B) Study the information and answer the questions that follow.**

Four couples go to a restaurant which has a variety of food items. Each one of them orders a different kind of food item but only one item. The wives are Vani, Sheela, Homi, and Romi and the husbands are Rajiv, Hari, Varun, and Sumit (not in the correct order of relationship).

- Vani orders dosa and her husband orders a pizza.
- Romi is not Sumit's wife and she wants chaat.
- Varun is Sheela's husband and only wanted idli.
- Sumit wanted light refreshment he placed order for lassi while his wife had kulfi.
- Hari wanted burger.

Apart from the items specified above the waiter also brought chowmein ordered by one of them.

4. Who orders chowmein?
   (a) Sheela
   (b) Homi
   (c) Romi
   (d) Data not sufficient

5. Homi is ________ wife.
   (a) Rajiv's
   (b) Hari's
   (c) Sumit's
   (d) Data not sufficient

6. Romi and her husband had
   (a) *Chaat* and *lassi* (b) *Kulfi* and burger
   (c) *Chaat* and *idli* (d) *Chaat* and burger

7. Who ordered *kulfi*?
   (a) Romi
   (b) Homi
   (c) Sheela
   (d) Data not sufficient

8. Who is Vani's husband?
   (a) Hari
   (b) Rajiv
   (c) Sumit
   (d) Data not sufficient

**(C) Read the graphs and answer the questions**

The following graphs give the production and consumption of coal in certain countries of the world, as well as their reserves. Shortfall/excess between production and consumption is met by imports/exports.

**Coal Production and Consumption of Select Countries**
**(Fig. in million tonnes)**

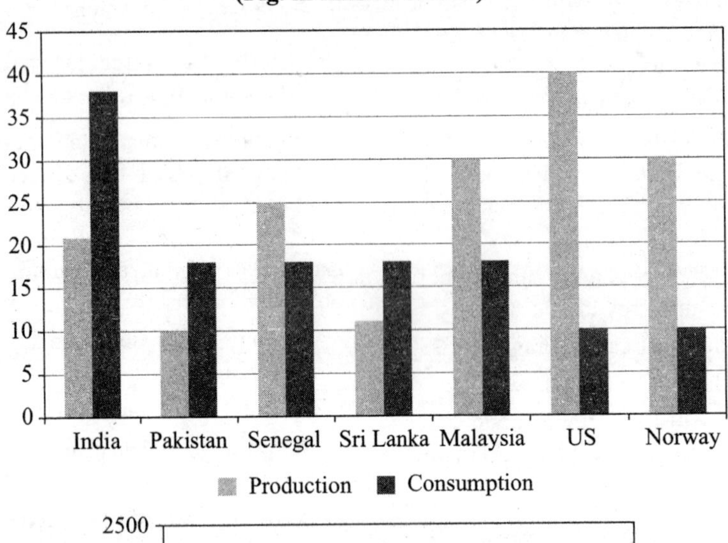


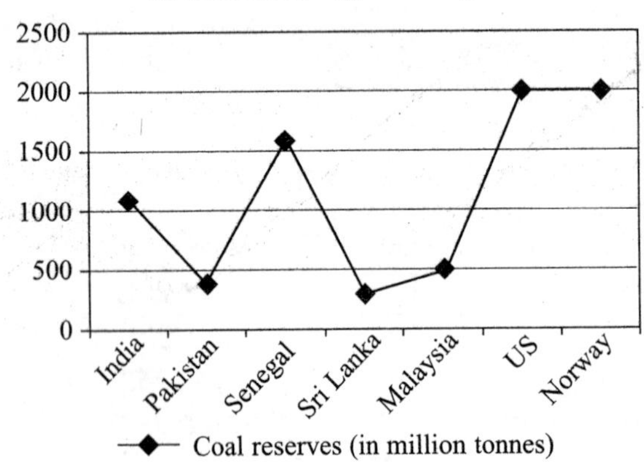


9. In the beginning of the year, Malaysia had coal stock of 3 million tonnes, which rose to 5 million tonnes by the end of the year. Approximately, what percentage of its production is exported?
   (a) 50%
   (b) 44.44%
   (c) 33.33%
   (d) 30%

10. If India imports its entire coal shortfall from Norway, what percentage of Norway's exports is not directed towards India? (Assume there is no change in coal stocks.)
   (a) 30
   (b) 50
   (c) 40
   (d) 20

11. If the US produces 5% of the world coal production, what is the percentage share of Pakistan?
 (a) 1.25 (b) 2
 (c) 2.5 (d) 3
12. If all the countries, which have shortfall, of coal want to import from only one country, among the given countries which one can export coal to all countries?
 (a) Norway (b) USA
 (c) Malaysia (d) Senegal
13. If coal requirement of the given set of countries is met by production within the set, approximately how long would the reserves last? (Assume that they do not conduct trade with countries other than specified, their requirements are constant and no new reserves are discovered during this time.)
 (a) 80 years (b) 70 years
 (c) 60 years (d) 50 years

**(D) Choose the correct option for the questions given below:**

14. What are the values of '*a*' and '*b*', if 4266 *ab* is divisible by 45?
 (a) 4 and 5 (b) 1 and 7
 (c) 9 and 0 (d) Either (a) or (c)
15. Three men start together to walk along a road at the same rate. The lengths of their strides are 68 cm, 51 cm, and 85 cm, respectively. How far will they go before they will be 'in step' again?
 (a) 102 m (b) 1020 m
 (c) 10.2 m (d) 150 m
16. The price of an article is cut by 10%; to restore to its original value, the new price must be increased by
 (a) 10% (b) 9%
 (c) 11.2% (d) 11.11%

**(E)** ***Each of the following two questions consist of five statements followed by options consisting of three statements put together in a specific order. Choose the option which indicates a valid argument, that is, where the third statement is a conclusion drawn from the preceding two statements.***

***ABC is a valid option, where statement C can be concluded from statements A and B.***

17. A. Modern industry is research-driven.
 B. ABC is a modern industry.
 C. ABC is research-driven.
 D. ABC may be research-driven.
 E. Research-driven industry is modern.
 (a) ECB (b) EBC
 (c) BCE (d) DEB
18. A. Graduates are in great demand.
 B. Harish and Rani are in great demand.
 C. Harish is in great demand.
 D. Rani is in great demand.
 E. Harish and Rani are graduates.
 (a) ABE (b) ECD
 (c) AEB (d) EBA
19. Which of the following options should come in place of the question mark? Menu : Food :: Catalogue : ?
 (a) Books (b) Library
 (c) Newspaper (d) Rack
20. Which figure should come in place of the question mark?

**Questions Figures**

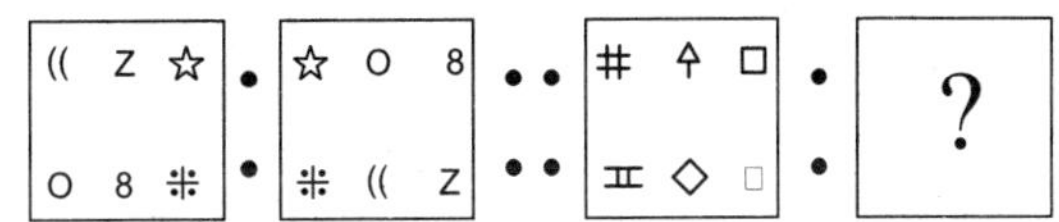

**Answer Figures**

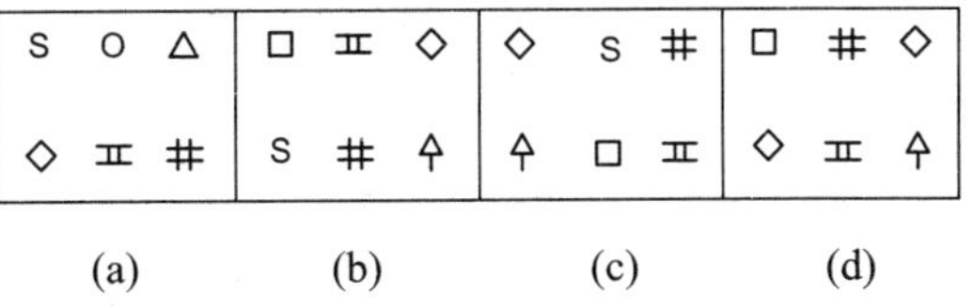

(a) (b) (c) (d)

21. Select the missing number from the given responses.

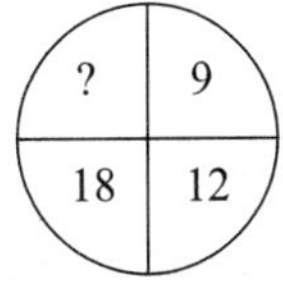


 (a) 11 (b) 25
 (c) 10 (d) 27

**(F) Read the questions carefully and answer them correctly.**

22. If $a$, $b$, $c$, $d$ and $e$ are five consecutive odd numbers, their average is

(a) $5(a+4)$ (b) $\frac{(abcd)}{5}$

(c) $5(a+b+c+d+e)$ (d) $a+4$

23. If $\frac{a}{b}=\frac{2}{3}$ and $\frac{b}{c}=\frac{4}{5}$, then $\frac{(a+b)}{(b+c)}$ is equal to

(a) 8 : 15 (b) 20 : 27

(c) 3 : 4 (d) 27 : 20

24. If $M$ men can complete a job in $H$ hours, then in how many hours will 5 men complete the job?

(a) $\frac{H}{5}$ (b) $\frac{M}{5H}$

(c) $\frac{MH}{5}$ (d) $MH$

25. Two trains move from station A and station B towards each other at the speed of 50 km/hr and 60 km/hr. At the meeting point, the driver of the second train felt that the train has covered 120 km more. What is the distance between A and B?

(a) 1,320 km (b) 1,200 km

(c) 1,100 km (d) 960 km

26. If BROTHER is coded as 2456784 and sister is coded as 91968(iv), what is the code for ROBBERS?

(a) 18, 15, 2(ii), 5, 18, 19

(b) 4562684

(c) 9245784

(d) 4522849

27. Three positions of a cube are given below. Based on them, find out which number is found opposite the number 2 in the given cube?

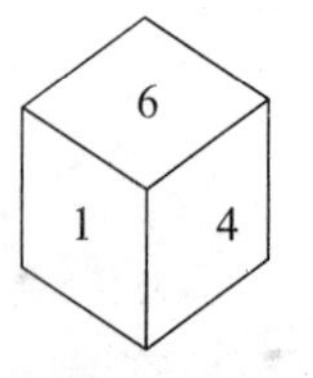


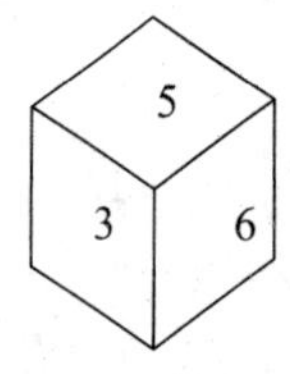


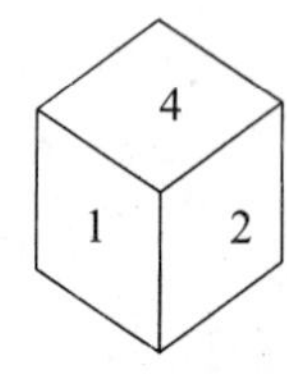


(a) 3 (b) 5

(c) 1 (d) 6

28. Find the missing number in the series. 4, 28, 8, 21, 12, 14, (...), 7

(a) 12 (b) 14

(c) 16 (d) 18

29. Find the odd one out.

(a) ABTEL (b) RAHCI

(c) LOOTS (d) LPATN

**(G) Study the information and answer the questions that follow.**

A manager of a production unit company has to manage the inventory level of three important components A, B and C. On a particular day he receives the news that the delivery van which was scheduled to deliver the three components to the workshop from the main unit, which is in a different city,has broken down. It may take a few days to send a fresh consignment of components from the main unit. Meanwhile, he has to purchase these three components from the local market and run the production. He has ₹25,000 in cash to make these purchases from the local market. The current level of inventory, daily consumption of components, and cost of each component is given in the following table.

| Component | Current inventory level | Consumption per day | Cost of each component |
|---|---|---|---|
| A | 150 | 100 | ₹50 |
| B | 180 | 90 | ₹40 |
| C | 160 | 80 | ₹30 |

30. For how many days the Work Manager can run the production by purchasing components A, B, and C from local market by using the entire ₹25,000?

(a) 2 days (b) 3 days

(c) 4 days (d) Data insufficient

31. If he were to have ₹35,000 instead of ₹25,000 as cash, then how many additional days (in compared to when he had ₹25,000) will he be able to run the production?

(a) No additional day (b) 1 additional day

(c) 2 additional days (d) Data insufficient

32. How much minimum amount of money should the manager have had if he were to run production for a week without the replenishment from the main unit?
    (a) 46,000
    (b) 46,500
    (c) 57,500
    (d) None of the above
33. A train of unknown length crosses two platforms of $L_1$ metres and $L_2$ metres in $t_1$ seconds and $t_2$ seconds, respectively. Then the speed of the train ($Vt$) is
    (a) $L_1 L_2/Vt = t_1 + t_2$
    (b) $1/L_1 + 1/L_2 = [1/t_1 + 1/t_2]\ V_t$
    (c) $L_1 t_1 + L_2 t_2 = Vt$
    (d) $Vt = (L_1 - L_2) / (t_1 - t_2)$
34. $J$ is 1⅜ times as fast as $k$. If $J$ gives $k$ a start of 150 metres, how far must be the winning post so that the race ends in a dead heat (both finish together)?
    (a) 100 metres (b) 440 metres
    (c) 200 metres (d) 550 metres
35. If it costs ₹$y$ to whitewash the 4 walls of a room, how much it would cost if all the dimensions were to be 5 times more?
    (a) ₹5$y$ (b) ₹25$y$
    (c) ₹25$y^2$ (d) ₹20$y$
36. In an office 40% workers take hot beverages (tea or coffee) 48 workers prefer to take only cold beverages. If 10% workers take both hot as well as cold beverage, then how many workers are there in the office? Presume that all workers take either hot beverages or cold beverages or both.
    (a) 100 workers (b) 72 workers
    (c) 80 workers (d) Data insufficient
37. Examine the following statement and answer the question that follows.

    It is paradoxical that despite having poor access to healthcare people of rural area have a higher life span than that of people in big cities.

    Which amongst the following statement could offer the best explanation for the above paradox?
    (a) People in cities are afflicted by lifestyle diseases.
    (b) Health-care system is costly in cities.
    (c) Life span of a population is not dependent on access to health care.
    (d) People in cities have a higher per capita income.
38. Gaurav's uncle is married to Richa's aunt. What can be the possible relationship between Gaurav and Richa?
    (i) Siblings (ii) Cousins
    (iii) Mother and son (iv) Uncle and niece

    Which among the aforesaid are the possible options.
    (a) (i), (ii), (iii), (iv) (b) (i), (ii), (iii)
    (c) (i), (ii) (d) (ii) only

**(H) Read the information given and answer the questions that follow.**

In a university, an inter-college fest was organised which included six different programmes—monoacting, singing, instrumental, elocution, debate and dance-drama. These items were performed by six different students Manoj, Nitin, Rupak, Tanmay, Vijay and Yogesh, not necessarily in the same order. The programme begins with a song which is not sung by Nitin and ends with a dance-drama. Rupak performs instrumental immediately after the elocution. Vijay performs monoacting just before the dance-drama. Tanmay's or Yogesh's name is available for the last performance. Manoj does not participate in elocution. There is a break after instrumental with three more items remaining to be performed. Tanmay performs immediately after the break.

39. Who performed the dance-drama?
    (a) Manoj
    (b) Nitin
    (c) Either Manoj or Nitin
    (d) Yogesh
40. Which item is performed by Yogesh?
    (a) Song (b) Dance-drama
    (c) Elocution (d) Data inadequate

41. Who was the first performer?
(a) Tanmay (b) Vijay
(c) Manoj (d) Data inadequate

42. Which item is performed by Tanmay?
(a) Debate (b) Song
(c) Instrumental (d) Data inadequate

43. Select the correct matching of person item number-performance.
(a) Manoj—Item 1 – Song
(b) Yogesh—Item 2 – Elocution
(c) Rupak—Item 3 – Instrumental
(d) Vijay—Item 4 – Debate

**(I) Read the statements and answer the questions that follow.**

A recent survey has revealed that the percentage of youth unemployed are more in the category of graduates and postgraduates rather than in the category of undergraduates. As such the government should not invest money in higher education in the entire country, as it is not materialising in employment of the youth.

Which of the following statements, if true, would weaken the conclusion drawn above, most?

(a) The survey of the entire population was not conducted.
(b) The survey was conducted in rural pockets where undergraduates were employed as agrarian labour and the region did not have jobs in the secondary and tertiary sectors.
(c) The survey took nearly six months to be completed and a large population sample was considered.
(d) The survey was conducted by a media group.

45. Equity in personal taxation demands that the rate of personal income tax payable by an individual should reduce as the income reduces and should be nil below a specific limit.

Which of the following choices would best explain the aforesaid taxation philosophy?

(a) The principal of equality incorporated in the Indian constitution calls for such a taxation structure.
(b) The disposable income of the poor is less than that of the rich. As such the rate of taxation should progressively increase with the income.
(c) It is easier to collect taxes where the rates are progressive than to collect taxes where the rates are flat and same for all.
(d) Taxation of only rich should be done as it is easier to collect taxes from them.

46. Find the total number of customers in a shop if on a Sunday, 40% of them purchase on credit, and the number of those who do cash purchase exceeds the number of credit purchases by 220?
(a) 1000 (b) 725
(c) 1100 (d) 1200

47. If $a$, $b$, $c$, $d$, $e$ and $f$ are six consecutive even numbers, their average is:
(a) $6(a + 5)$
(b) $\frac{abcdef}{5}$
(c) $6(a + b + c + d + e + f)$
(d) $a + 15$

48. A number when $\frac{1}{5}$ of it is subtracted from itself gives 160. How much is $\frac{6}{5}$ of this number?
(a) 240 (b) 200
(c) 160 (d) 180

49. Karthik bought a toy after 20 % discount and it is sold at 25 % profit. What is the label price if the price he sells it is ₹ 5,000?
(a) ₹5000 (b) ₹4200
(c) ₹4500 (d) ₹4000

50. A Rajdhani Express train crosses a stationery Shatabdi Express train in 50 seconds and a pole in 20 seconds. with the same speed. The length of the Rajdhani Express train is 240 metre. What is the length of the Shatabdi Express train?
(a) 300m (b) 360m
(c) 320m (d) 400m

51. The radius of a circle is increased by 15%, then the percentage increase in area is?
    (a) 30% (b) 32.55%
    (c) 22.5% (d) 32.25%
52. The sum of the ages of 5 members of a family, 3 years ago was 80 years. The average age of the family today is the same as it was 3 years ago, because of an addition of a baby during the intervening period. How old is the baby?
    (a) 6 months
    (b) 1 year
    (c) 2 years
    (d) 2 years and 6 months
53. The sum of five numbers is 250. The average of the first two number is 51 and the average of last two numbers is 52. What is the third number?
    (a) 48 (b) 54
    (c) 50 (d) 44
54. Lemons are bought at 4 for ₹3 and sold at 3 for ₹4.
    The gain per cent is;
    (a) 25% (b) 66.66%
    (c) 125% (d) 77.77%
55. Ranganathan and Shyam start walking towards each other at 11 AM at speeds of 4km/h and 5km/h respectively. They were initially 15 km apart. At what time do they meet?
    (a) 11:30 AM (b) 12:30 PM
    (c) 12:40 PM (d) 12:45 PM
56. June 21st is celebrated every year as
    (a) International Yoga day
    (b) International Day of the World's Indigenous Peoples
    (c) International Day of Ayurveda and traditional remedies
    (d) None of the above
57. Who amongst the following has won two Olympic medals for India?
    (a) Neeraj Chopra
    (b) Saina Nehwal
    (c) P.V. Sindhu
    (d) Ravi Dahiya
58. Which important national movement was launched on the 12th March 1930?
    (a) Poorna Swaraja movement
    (b) Salt Satyagraha movement
    (c) Non cooperation movement
    (d) Quit India movement
59. Who among the following is a Bharat Ratna Awardee?
    (a) Homi Jahangir Bhabha
    (b) A.P.J. Abdul Kalam
    (c) Vikram Sarabhai
    (d) Satyendra Nath Bose
60. NPCI stands for
    (a) National Poultry Council of India
    (b) National Payments Corporation of India
    (c) National Police Co-operation India
    (d) National Corporate Payment Institute

## Answers of Practice Question Paper-4

| | | | | | |
|---|---|---|---|---|---|
| **1.** (b) | **11.** (a) | **21.** (d) | **31.** (a) | **41.** (d) | **51.** (d) |
| **2.** (d) | **12.** (b) | **22.** (d) | **32.** (c) | **42.** (a) | **52.** (b) |
| **3.** (c) | **13.** (c) | **23.** (b) | **33.** (d) | **43.** (c) | **53.** (d) |
| **4.** (a) | **14.** (d) | **24.** (c) | **34.** (d) | **44.** (b) | **54.** (d) |
| **5.** (c) | **15.** (c) | **25.** (a) | **35.** (b) | **45.** (b) | **55.** (c) |
| **6.** (d) | **16.** (d) | **26.** (d) | **36.** (c) | **46.** (c) | **56.** (a) |
| **7.** (b) | **17.** (a) | **27.** (d) | **37.** (a) | **47.** (a) | **57.** (c) |
| **8.** (b) | **18.** (c) | **28.** (c) | **38.** (c) | **48.** (a) | **58.** (b) |
| **9.** (c) | **19.** (a) | **29.** (d) | **39.** (c) | **49.** (a) | **59.** (b) |
| **10.** (d) | **20.** (b) | **30.** (c) | **40.** (d) | **50.** (b) | **60.** (b) |

# Practice Question Paper 5

**(A) Read the statements and answer the questions that follow.**

1. **Statement:** Though democracy has been stated to be the best form of governance, it has not always materialised into quick economic progress.

   Which of the two conclusions can be drawn?

   Conclusion 1—Democracy has no bearing on economic progress.

   Conclusion 2—Democracy is not the best form of governance.

   (a) Only Conclusion 1 is correct.
   (b) Only Conclusion 2 is correct.
   (c) Both the conclusions are correct.
   (d) None is correct.

2. **Statement:** In states showing greater economic progress, law and order is seen to be better.

   Which of the two conclusions can be drawn?

   Conclusion 1—States with low incidence of crime will always be economically progressive.

   Conclusion 2—There is no co-relation between economic progress and the law and order situation.

   (a) Only Conclusion 1 can be drawn.
   (b) Only Conclusion 2 can be drawn.
   (c) Both the conclusions can be drawn.
   (d) None of the conclusions can be drawn.

3. Amar earns more money than Ajay. But since Aditya earns more money than Abhay, it follows that Amar earns more money than Abhay.

   Which one of the following, when introduced into the argument does **not** make the argument above logically correct?

   (a) Ajay and Aditya earn the same amount of money.
   (b) Ajay earns more money than Abhay.
   (c) Ajay earns more money than Aditya.
   (d) Aditya earns more money than Amar.

4. Research has shown that people who have acquired higher educational degrees such as a post graduation or a doctorate degree have a lower incidence of brain related ailments such as Alzheimer's disease and Parkinson disease.

   What could be the most logical explanation for it amongst the following?

   (a) Higher educational degree means a better and healthier lifestyle.
   (b) People with higher educational degree would be more prone to hiding their ailment and would not reveal the truth in the research.
   (c) Higher educational degrees mean that people continue to study and do brain related work till higher age, thus delaying the onset and reducing the incidence of such diseases.
   (d) It is merely a propaganda by research institutions to entice more students in research work.

5. Statement 1: A says I am brother of B. Statement 2: B says I am not brother of A.

   In light of the above what can be concluded about the statements?

   (a) If Statement 1 is correct then Statement 2 cannot be correct.
   (b) If Statement 2 is correct then Statement 1 cannot be correct.
   (c) Both the statements can be correct simultaneously.
   (d) No co-relation between the two statements can be drawn.

**(B) Study the graph and answer the questions given in the following.**

Population Trends and Cycle Usage Trends in a Village over the Period 1994–95

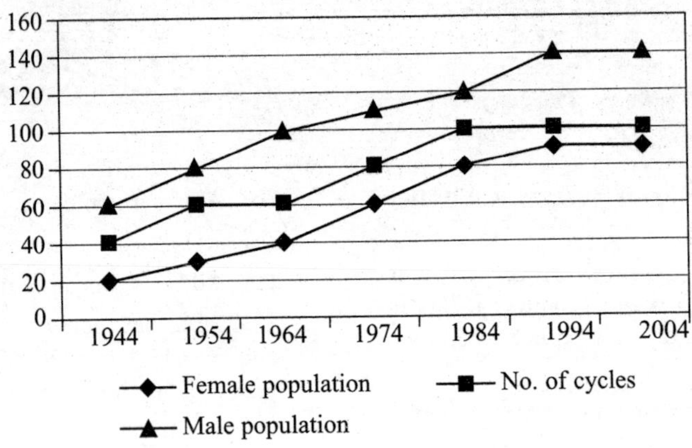


(Population in '000s and cycles in '00s)

6. What is the average ten year percentage increase in the number of cycles over the period 1944 to 1994?
   (a) 25% (b) 15%
   (c) 20% (d) None of these
7. In 199(iv), if females used 40% of the total number of cycles used, then what is the per capita usage of cycles by females in 1994?
   (a) 0.0444 (b) 0.04888
   (c) 0.05 (d) 0.055
8. In which one of the following years was the ratio of male population to female population the lowest?
   (a) 1964 (b) 1974
   (c) 1984 (d) 1994
9. The highest percentage increase in the total population has been shown by the decade ended
   (a) 1954 (b) 1964
   (c) 1974 (d) 1994

**(C) Study the information and answer the questions that follow.**

Pranav, Manav, Mini, Joy, and Tarun have books of five different subjects, i.e., Physics, Chemistry, Maths, Biology and English. These books have been written by authors A, B, C, D and E. Everyone has a book of one of the five subjects only. Mini has the Maths book. Tarun has the English book and B is not its author. The Biology book is authored by D. The author of the Physics book is A which is not owned by Pranav. Joy has the book which has been written by E.

10. The Chemistry book has been penned by whom?
    (a) A (b) E
    (c) C (d) Data inadequate
11. Who is the owner of the book written by C?
    (a) Manav (b) Tarun
    (c) Pranav (d) Joy
12. Who wrote the Maths book?
    (a) A (b) B
    (c) C (d) D
13. Manav owns the book written by
    (a) A (b) B
    (c) C (d) D
14. Which of the following is the correct combination of subject, student and author?
    (a) Maths–Mini–C
    (b) Physics–Joy–A
    (c) English–Tarun–E
    (d) Biology–Pranav–D

15. The sum of two numbers is $s$ and their quotient is $p/q$. The numbers are

(a) $\frac{ps}{q}, \frac{qs}{p}$ (b) $\frac{s}{p}, \frac{s}{q}$

(c) $\frac{(s-p)}{q}, \frac{(s-q)}{p}$ (d) $\frac{ps}{(p+q)}, \frac{qs}{(p+q)}$

16. Three stringed instruments vibrate 6, 8 and 12 times a second, respectively. If all the three begin to vibrate simultaneously, find the shortest time interval before all three vibrate together again.

(a) 2 sec (b) 48 sec

(c) $\frac{1}{2}$ sec (d) $\frac{1}{24}$ sec

17. When 30 percent of a number is added to another number the second number increases to its 140 percent. The second number = $x$% of the first number.

The value of $x$ is

(a) 130 (b) 75

(c) 133.33 (d) 33.33

18. A mathematics teacher tabulated the marks secured by 35 students of 8th class. The average of their marks was 72. If the marks secured by Reema was written as 36 instead of 86 then find the correct average marks up to two decimal places.

(a) 73.41 (b) 74.31

(c) 72.43 (d) 73.43

**(D) Each of the following two questions consist of five statements followed by options consisting of three statements put together in a specific order. Choose the option, which indicates a valid argument, i.e., where the third statement is a conclusion drawn from the preceding two statements.**

ABC is a valid option, where Statement C can be concluded from Statements A and B.

19. A. No patriot is a criminal.
B. is not a criminal.
C. A is a patriot.
D. B is not a patriot.
E. B is a criminal.

(a) ACB (b) ADC

(c) ADE (d) ABE

20. A. Ant eaters like ants.
B. Parrots are ant eaters.
C. Chimp is an ant eater.
D. Chimp likes ants.
E. Chimp may eat ants.

(a) DCA (b) ADC

(c) ABE (d) ACD

21. If 10 men weave 10 mats in 10 days, how many men will be required to weave 100 mats in 100 days?

(a) 100 (b) 1000

(c) 10 (d) 1

22. A lamp is bought for ₹850 and sold at a gain of $x$%. The selling price of the lamp is

(a) ₹$\frac{85x}{100}$ (b) ₹$\frac{(850+x)}{100}$

(c) ₹$\frac{8500x}{1000}$ (d) ₹$850+\frac{17x}{2}$

23. A man travels 300 kilometres in 13 hours, partly by rail and partly by steamer. If he had gone all the way by rail he would have ended his journey 8 hours sooner, and saved $\frac{4}{5}$ of the time he was on steamer. How far did he go by rail?

(a) 150 km (b) 130 km

(c) 180 km (d) 205 km

**(E) Read the following information and answer the questions that follow.**

- A student 'A' is enrolled in a college 'B' affiliated to university 'C'.
- He has opted for a 3-year graduation course 'X' in which subjects P, Q, R, S, T have to be studied.
- To be a graduate, the following conditions must be fulfilled:

(i) The average score of all the 3 years should be 60% or more.

(ii) The average score of all five subjects for each year should be at least 50%.

(iii) The score in any single subject in any year should be at least 40%.

(iv) He should score 60% or more in the project report to be submitted at the end of the 3rd year. This marks is not to be taken into account for calculating average of the subjects.

(v) He should have attendance of at least 75% in the college.

- If in one subject only he has scored marks ranging from 35–39 then grace marks up to 5 can be awarded by examiner to pass him in that subject.
- If in one subject he has scored 30–34 marks then grace marks of up to 10 marks can be awarded by the 'Controller of Examination' so as to pass him in the subject.
- If average of all subjects in a year is less than 50% but overall-average of the 3 years—taken together—is 60% or more, then approval of the Vice Chancellor is required to pass him.
- College can condone attendance shortage up to 20% on medical grounds.
- The marks of student 'A' are as follows:

| Subject | P | Q | R | S | T | Total |
|---|---|---|---|---|---|---|
| 1st year | 65 | 42 | 85 | 69 | 89 | 350 |
| 2nd year | 67 | 40 | 83 | 59 | 71 | 320 |
| 3rd year | 48 | 32 | 63 | 42 | 50 | 235 |

(Marks in each subject are out of 100)

- He got 65% in project report.
- His attendance was 82%.

24. Which of the following options regarding his graduation is correct?
    (a) He will require only to be awarded grace marks by the Controller of Examination.
    (b) He will require grace marks as in option (a) above, as well as approval of the Vice Chancellor.
    (c) He will pass without any approval or grace marks.
    (d) He will not pass.

25. If he got 57 marks in subject 'S' in 3rd year instead of 4(ii), then which option out of (a), (b), (c), (d) mentioned above would be correct?

26. If in the marks shown above the student gets 40 instead of 32 in subject Q in the 3rd year while all other marks remain the same, then which of the following options regarding graduation would he correct?
    (a) He would only require to be awarded grace marks by Controller of Examination.
    (b) He would only require the approval of Vice Chancellor.
    (c) He would require grace marks as in (a) as well as approval as in (b).
    (d) He would pass without any grace marks or approval.

27. Which one of the answer figures shall complete the given question figure?

**Question Figure**

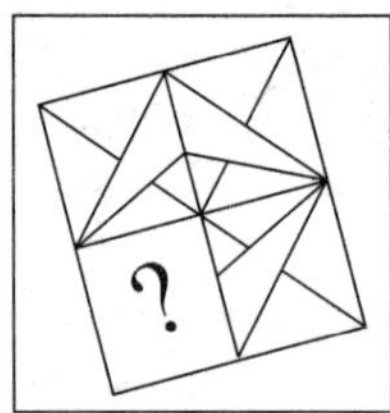

**Answer Figures**

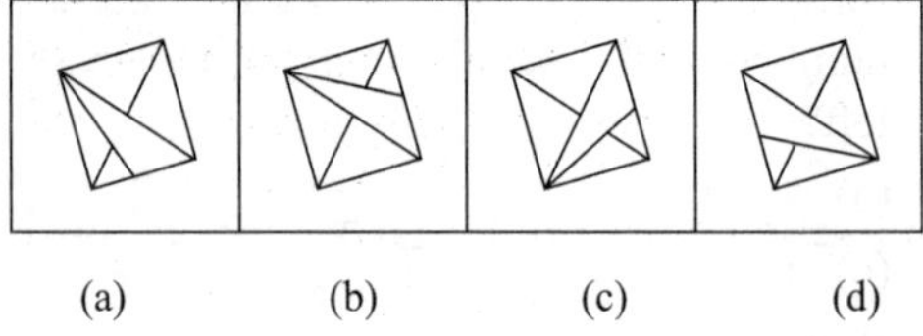

(a) (b) (c) (d)

28. Select the appropriate number/figure from the given alternatives. 24 : 60 : : 120:?
    (a) 160 (b) 220
    (c) 300 (d) 108

29. Find the missing number/letters/figure from the given responses. NOA, PQB, RSC, ?
    (a) TUD (b) DTU
    (c) ENO (d) FNQ

30. If GARDEN is coded as 325764 and WATER as 92165, how can we code the word WARDEN in the same way?
   (a) 925764 (b) 295764
   (c) 952764 (d) 957264

**(F) Study the following information and answer the questions given here.**

There are six members in a family. They are mother, father, son, daughter, grandfather and grandmother. In their house, on a shelf, six files are kept which are named A, B, C, D, E and F and have different colours, red blue, yellow, green, orange and maroon (not in the order of names of the files). The files contain health related documents of the above-mentioned persons and are arranged on the shelf from left to right.

- The documents of the grandfather is in the blue colour file which is not marked either D or A.
- The file marked A is of the mother and it is of orange colour and is placed to the extreme right.
- The file of the daughter is neither marked D nor marked E and is not of yellow or green colour.
- The file marked C contains documents of the father, it is of maroon colour and it is fifth from right and next to file B which has the documents of the son.

31. If the daughter's file is immediately between the files of the grandfather and the son, then at what number is the grandmother's file placed from left?
   (a) Fifth (b) Second
   (c) First (d) Data inadequate
32. Which is the correct combination of file names and their colours?
   (a) E-Yellow (b) F-Red
   (c) B-Green (d) Data inadequate
33. The file of the grandmother is of which colour?
   (a) Yellow (b) Green
   (c) Blue (d) Data inadequate
34. The documents of the grandfather are in which file?
   (a) D (b) E
   (c) F (d) None of these
35. If the file covers of the son and grandmother are interchanged, then the colour of file cover of the son is
   (a) Green (b) Yellow
   (c) Blue (d) Data inadequate
36. Two trains running at $V_1$ m/s and $V_2$ m/s crosses the same tunnel in $t_1$ seconds and $t_2$ seconds, respectively. If the difference of lengths of two trains is $x$ metres then
   (a) $x = V_1 t_1 - V_2 t_2$
   (b) $1/x = 1/V_1 t_1 + 1/V_2 t_2$
   (c) $x = V_1 t_1 + V_2 t_2$
   (d) $x/V_1 t_1 = V_2 t_2 + 1$
37. Which of the information statements (i), (ii) and (iii) are required to solve the question mentioned here?
   How many students failed in subject $X$?
   (i) 12 students have passed in subject $Y$.
   (ii) No. of students failed in $X$ is 3 more than $Y$.
   (iii) 22 students appeared in subject $Y$.
   (a) (ii) and (iii) (b) All three
   (c) Any two (d) Only (i) and (iii)
38. Rajdhani Express travelling at a uniform speed clears a platform 200 metres long in 10 seconds and passes a telegraph post in 6 seconds. The speed of train is
   (a) 150 km/h (b) 180 km/h
   (c) 200 km/h (d) 175 km/h
39. Which number is next in the series? 1, 4, 10, 22, 46, ?
   (a) 68 (b) 48
   (c) 12 (d) 94
40. Find the odd one out.
   (a) BLOW (b) NOPOS
   (c) LETAP (d) DHATUMB

41. Find the missing number in the figure given here.

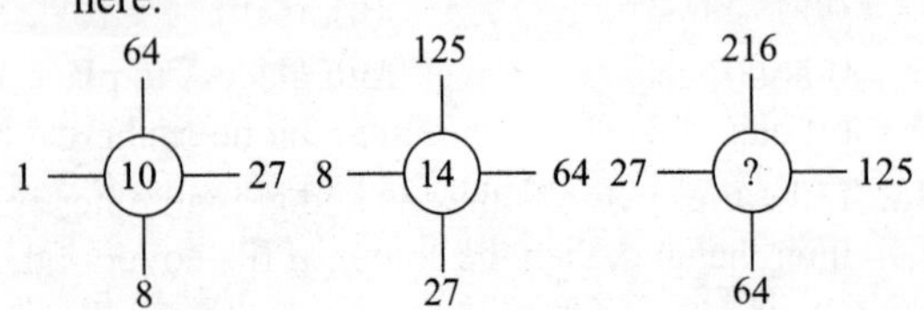


(a) 17 (b) 9
(c) 2 (d) 18

42. Consider the following matrix:

| 3 | 370 | 7 |
|---|---|---|
| 2 | 224 | 6 |
| 1 | 730 | X |

What is the number of 'X' in the above matrix:

(a) 5 (b) 8
(c) 9 (d) 11

43. Examine the following three figures in which the numbers follows a specific pattern:

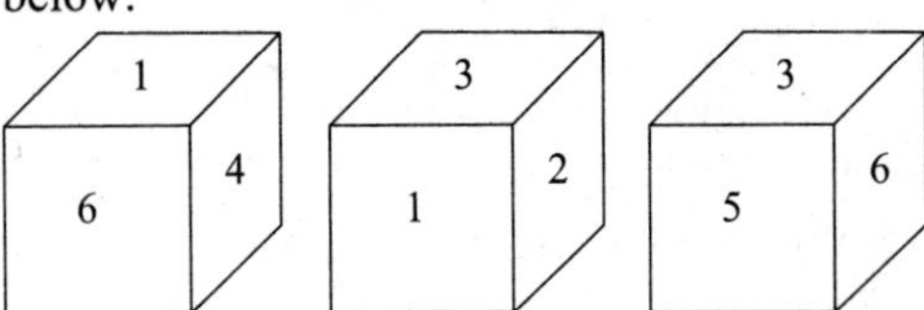


This missing number (?) in the third figure above is:

(a) 7 (b) 16
(c) 21 (d) 28

44. A cube has six numbers marked 1, 2, 3/4, 5 and 6 on its faces. Three views of the cube are shown below:

| 1 / 6 / 4 | 3 / 1 / 2 | 3 / 5 / 6 |
|---|---|---|

What possible numbers can exist on the two faces marked (A) and (B), respectively on the cube?

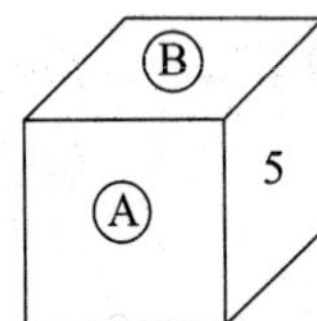


(a) 2 and 3 (b) 6 and 1
(c) 1 and 4 (d) 3 and 1

45. Consider the following figures:

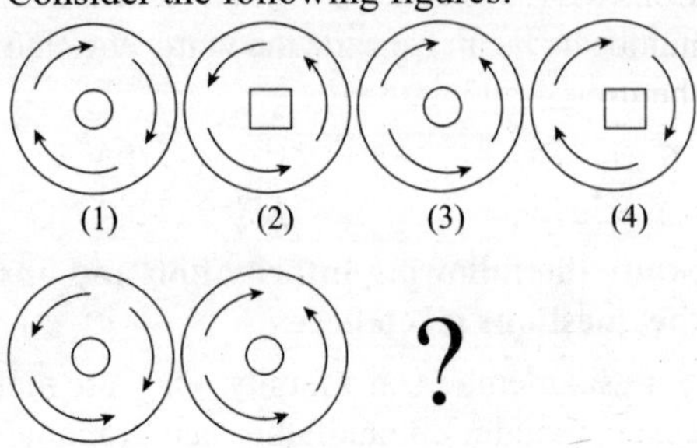


Which one of the following figures would logically come in the 7th position indicated above by a question mark?

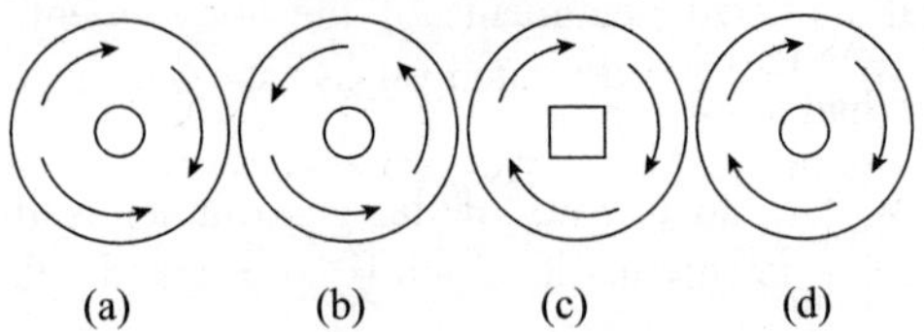


46. Examine the following figure:

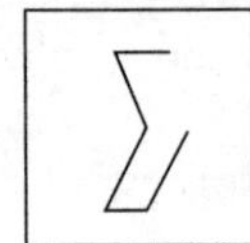

Which one of the following figures has the above figure embedded in it?

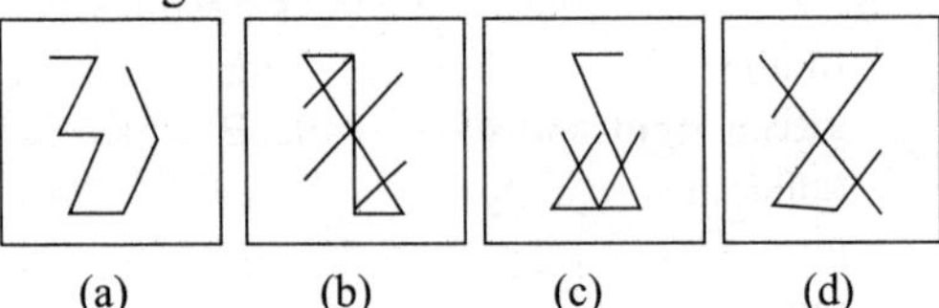


47. Consider the following matrix:

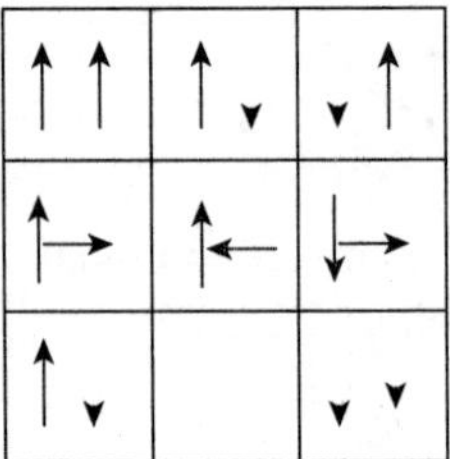

Which one of the following figures fits into the blank part of the above matrix?

(a) 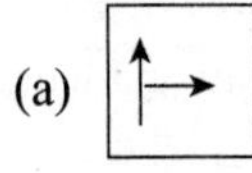

(b) 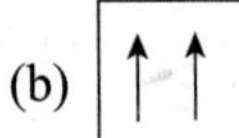

(c) 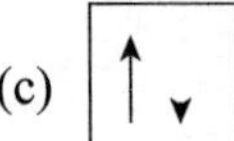

(d) 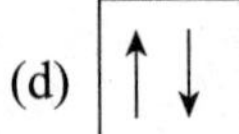

48. Consider the table given below in which the numbers bear certain relation- ship among themselves along the rows:

| 29 | 13 | 18 |
|---|---|---|
| 33 | X | 19 |
| 30 | 27 | 3 |

Which one of the following numbers is the missing number indicated above by X?

(a) 19 (b) 15
(c) 14 (d) 8

49. As per agreement with a bank, a businessman had to refund a loan in some equal installments without interest. After paying 18 installments he found that 60% of his loan was refunded. How many installments were there in the agreement?

(a) 22 (b) 24
(c) 30 (d) 33

50. The ages of Lalitha and Perumal are in the ratio of 4 :3. After 6 years the ratio of their ages will be 5:4. What is the difference of their ages?

(a) 5 (b) 7
(c) 9 (d) 6

51. In a class of 60 students, where the number of girls is twice that of boys, Srinivas, a boy is ranked seventeenth from the top. If there are 9 girls ahead of Srinivas, the number of boys in rank after him is;

(a) 13 (b) 12
(c) 7 (d) 3

52. Pradeep bought an old mobile phone for ₹7000 and spent ₹500 on its repairs. Then, he sold it for ₹7125. He incurs

(a) 5% loss (b) 4% loss
(c) 4% gain (d) 5% gain

53. John walk from his house and reaches his factory 3 minutes late if his speed from his house to the factory is 5 km/hr. If he walks at a speed of 6 km/hr, then he reaches the factory 7 minutes early. The distance of the factory from his house is;

(a) 3 km (b) 4 km
(c) 5 km (d) 6 km

54. *A* and *B* decide to travel from place *X* to place *Y* by bus. *A* has ₹ 10 with him and he finds that it is 80% of the bus fare for two persons. *B* finds that he has ₹ 3 with him and hands it over to *A*. In this context, which one of the following statements is correct?

(a) Now the money *A* has is just enough to buy two tickets.
(b) *A* still needs ₹2 for buying the tickets.
(c) After buying the two tickets *A* will be left with 50 paise.
(d) The money *A* now has is still not sufficient to buy two tickets.

55. In 1954 the Bharat Ratna was awarded for the first time to three Indians. Who among the following was not awarded the Bharat Ratna in this year ?

(a) S. Radhakrishnan
(b) C.V. Raman
(c) C. Rajagopalachari
(d) Rajendra Prasad

56. The Silent Valley National Park forming a part of Nilgiri Biosphere reserve, is located in which of the following state/union territory ?

(a) Karnataka (b) Tamil Nadu
(c) Andhra Pradesh (d) Kerala

57. International Women's Day is celebrated on

(a) 1st January (b) 1st March
(c) 8th March (d) 22nd March

58. The world body IMF deals with which of the following important functions ?

(a) Fostering monetary cooperation and securing financial stability amidst member countries.
(b) Prevention of nuclear proliferation in the world.
(c) Providing financial advice and aid to developing economies.
(d) Providing a just international order.

59. Which country won the FIFA World Cup in 2018?
(a) France
(b) Croatia
(c) Brazil
(d) Belgium

60. Azithromycin and erythromycin are which type of drugs?
(a) Cortico-steroids
(b) Antipyretics
(c) Anti-inflammatory
(d) Antibiotics

## Answers of Practice Question Paper-5

| | | | | | |
|---|---|---|---|---|---|
| **1.** (d) | **11.** (b) | **21.** (c) | **31.** (c) | **41.** (d) | **51.** (b) |
| **2.** (d) | **12.** (b) | **22.** (d) | **32.** (b) | **42.** (c) | **52.** (a) |
| **3.** (d) | **13.** (a) | **23.** (c) | **33.** (d) | **43.** (b) | **53.** (c) |
| **4.** (c) | **14.** (d) | **24.** (b) | **34.** (b) | **44.** (a) | **54.** (c) |
| **5.** (c) | **15.** (d) | **25.** (a) | **35.** (d) | **45.** (c) | **55.** (d) |
| **6.** (d) | **16.** (c) | **26.** (b) | **36.** (a) | **46.** (c) | **56.** (d) |
| **7.** (a) | **17.** (b) | **27.** (b) | **37.** (b) | **47.** (b) | **57.** (c) |
| **8.** (c) | **18.** (d) | **28.** (c) | **38.** (b) | **48.** (d) | **58.** (a) |
| **9.** (a) | **19.** (a) | **29.** (a) | **39.** (d) | **49.** (c) | **59.** (a) |
| **10.** (b) | **20.** (d) | **30.** (a) | **40.** (d) | **50.** (d) | **60.** (d) |

# Practice Question Paper 6

**(A) Read each of the following statements/passages and answer the questions that follow. Your answer to these questions should be based on the statements/passages only.**

1. **Statement:** The Indian states which have shown higher rate of economic growth have also been seen to have made greater progress in the field of attaining higher literacy.

   Which of the two conclusions can be drawn from the above statement?

   **Conclusion-1**: All states which have high percentage of literacy are sure to have high economic growth.

   **Conclusion-2**: Literacy plays an important role even in the economic growth of a state.

   (a) Only conclusion 1can be drawn.
   (b) Only conclusion 2 can be drawn.
   (c) Both the conclusions can be drawn.
   (d) None of the conclusions can be drawn.

2. Statement: Bipin is elder to Bansal and Brajesh is younger to Bomkesh. This implies that Bomkesh is the eldest.

   Which of the following should be true for this implication to be correct?

   (a) Bomkesh is elder to Bipin.
   (b) Bomkęsh is elder to Bansal.
   (c) Bipin is elder to Brajesh.
   (d) In none of the above case.

3. Three airlines—IA, JA and KA—operate on the Delhi-Mumbai route. To increase the number of seats sold, KA reduced its fares and this was emulated by IA and JA immediately. The general belief was that the volume of air travel between Delhi and Mumbai would increase as a result.

   Which of the following, if true, would add credence to the general belief?

   (a) There is increase in profitability of the three airlines.
   (b) There is extension of the discount scheme to other routes.
   (c) A study has been done that shows that air travellers in India are price-conscious.
   (d) A study has been done that shows that as much as 80 percent of air travels in India are company-sponsored.

4. Developed countries have made adequate provisions for social security for senior citizens. State insurers (as well as private ones) offer medicare and pension benefits to people who can no longer earn. In India, with the collapse of the joint family system, the traditional shelter of the elderly has disappeared. A state faced with a financial crunch is not in a position to provide social security to the elderly. So, it is advisable that the working population give serious thought to building a financial base for itself.

   Which one of the following, if it were to happen, weakens the conclusion drawn in the above passage the most?

   (a) The investible income of the working population, as a proportion of its total income, will grow in the future.
   (b) The insurance sector is underdeveloped and trends indicate that it will be extensively privatised in the future.
   (c) India is on the path of development that will take it towards the status of a developed country, with all its positive and negative implications.
   (d) If the working population builds a stronger financial base, there will be a revival of the joint family system.

5. Amongst the statements given below which ones would be logically compatible?
   (i) A car is not a truck.
   (ii) Some cars are vans.
   (iii) No van is a car.
   (iv) A van is always a truck.
   (v) A van is car.
   (a) (i), (ii), (iv) (b) (ii), (iii), (iv)
   (c) (i), (ii), (v) (d) (iii), (iv), (v)

**(B) Read the information given below and answer the questions which follow**

A group has six members A, B, C, X, Y and Z. There are three male members. The females work in three departments—Marketing, Sales and HR, and sit on three different floors — ground, second and fourth. Persons working in the same department are not on the same floor. Two persons work on each floor.

No two females work in the same department or on the same floor. B and Y work in the same department but not in HR. X works in Sales. Y and A are on the ground and fourth floors respectively and work in the same department. X, a female, does not work on the second floor. C, a male, works on ground floor.

6. Which of the following groups of persons are females?
   (a) XYZ (b) XAZ
   (c) XCZ (d) Data inadequate
7. Which of the following pairs of persons work in administration?
   (a) XC (b) XB
   (c) YC (d) Data inadequate
8. Which of the following pairs work on the second floor?
   (a) CZ (b) YAA
   (c) XB (d) BZ
9. If T is transferred to accounts and S is transferred to administration, who is to be transferred to personnel to maintain the original distribution of females on each floor?
   (a) C (b) B
   (c) X (d) Data inadequate

**(C) Read each of the following passages and answer the questions that follow. Your answer to these questions should be based on the passage only.**

In a company, a project group has seven persons. Among the seven, two are women, Sheela and Rani, and five men: Anil, Bikram, Chetan, Dharam and Eesh. For field study three or four persons have to be nominated. Anil would not like to be in the group if Bikram is also selected. Bikram and Eesh want to be nominated together in the group. Rani would like to be in the group only if Chetan is also there. Chetan, if nominated, would not like Dharam in the group. Anil would like to be in the group only if Dharam is also there. Chetan insists that Sheela be nominated in case he is there in the group.

10. Which of the following statements is true?
    (a) Rani and Anil can be part of a group of four.
    (b) A group of four can have two women.
    (c) A group of four can have all four men.
    (d) None of the above.
11. Which of the following is feasible group of four?
    (a) Anil, Dharam, Sheela, Eesh
    (b) Bikram, Eesh, Rani, Chetan
    (c) Bikram, Eesh, Sheela, Chetan
    (d) Sheela, Chetan, Anil, Dharam
12. Which of the following is a feasible group of three?
    (a) Chetan, Anil, Eesh
    (b) Dharam, Shyam, Eesh
    (c) Ram, Chetan, Bikram
    (d) Sheela, Chetan, Anil

**(D) On the basis of information available in the graphs given below, answer the question that follows:**

The graphs below give the GDP and the percentage of GDP in education, for the given years.

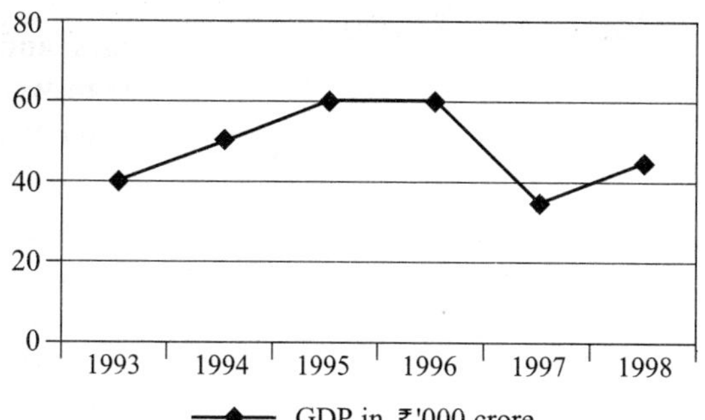


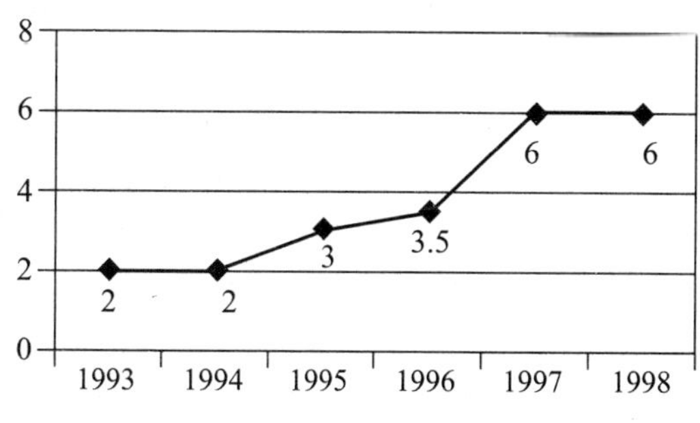


13. In how many years has actual educational spending reduced as compared to that of the previous year?

(a) 0 (b) 1
(c) 2 (d) 4

14. Between the given years, both inclusive, what percentage of the country's total GDP has gone into education?

(a) 4.3% (b) 3.6%
(c) 3.4% (d) 3.1%

15. The total amount given to education would be how many times that of the total amount given to defence, if every year 2 percent of the GDP is given to defence (for the entire period)?

(a) 2.15 times (b) 1.55 times
(c) 1.7 times (d) 1.8 times

16. If due to an HR Ministry report, it is obligatory for the government to allocate at least ₹3,200 crore for education in 1999, provided educational spending as a percentage of the GDP does not exceed 6.5 percent then what is the least desirable GDP for 1999 (in ₹'000 crore)?

(a) 51.52 (b) 48.24
(c) 49.23 (d) 42.72

17. In which year was the spending on education the lowest?

(a) 1996 (b) 1995
(c) 1994 (d) 1993

18. If percentage of GDP allocated to education in 1999 increases by twice as much percent from 1998 allocation as the 1995 increase over 1994, what is the increase likely to be in percentage terms?

(a) 2%
(b) 33.33%
(c) 6.48%
(d) Cannot be determined

**(E) Answer the questions carefully.**

19. A number when divided by 5 leaves a remainder 3. What is the remainder when the square of the same number is divided by 5?

(a) 9 (b) 3
(c) 0 (d) 4

20. Traffic lights at three different points are changing respectively at 24, 48 and 72 seconds. If all the three change together at 9 : 10 : 24 hours, then when will the next change take place together?

(a) 9 : 12 : 25 hrs (b) 9 : 10 : 48 hrs
(c) 9 : 12 : 48 hrs (d) 9 : 10 : 50 hrs

21. If the height of a triangle is decreased by 40% and its base is increased by 40%, what will be the effect on its area?

(a) No change (b) 16% increase
(c) 8% decrease (d) 16% decrease

22. If two numbers are respectively 20% and 50% of the third number, then what percentage is the first number of the second?

(a) 30 (b) 70
(c) 40 (d) 30

23. A contractor undertakes to build a house in 8 months. He plans to complete the work in time with 210 men working 20 days in a month for 6 hours a day. However, he manages to get only

140 men and is allowed 12 months to complete the work. If his men worked for 24 days a month, how many hours a day should they work to complete the work?

(a) 6 (b) 5
(c) 8 (d) 4

24. Which one of the following represents the relationship between men, rodents and living beings?

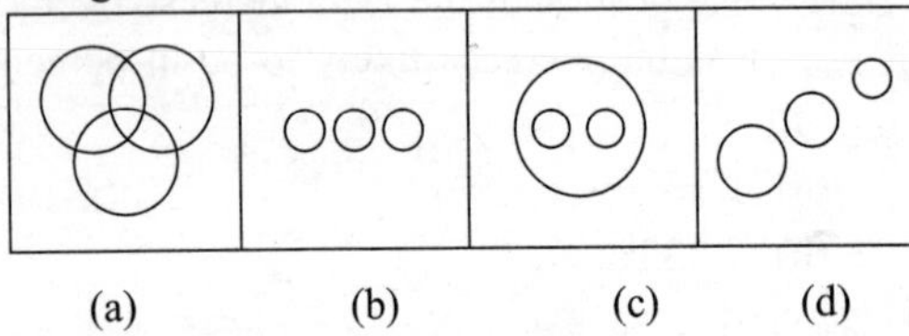

(a) (b) (c) (d)

25. Which one of the answer figures shall complete the given question figure?

Question figure

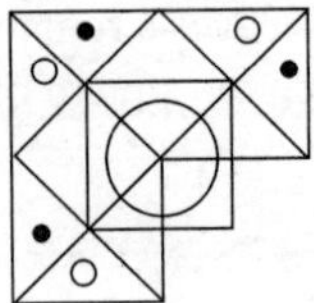

Answer figures

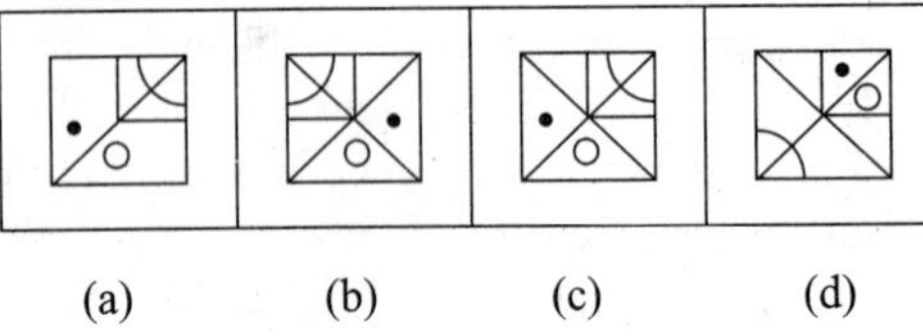

(a) (b) (c) (d)

26. Find the odd one out.

(a) Analysis (b) Search
(c) Conclusion (d) Investigation

27. Find the missing number/letters/figure from the given alternatives.

DAB, IFG, NKL, ____?___

(a) SPQ (b) SOP
(c) SPO (d) RSQ

28. Find the missing number from the given responses.

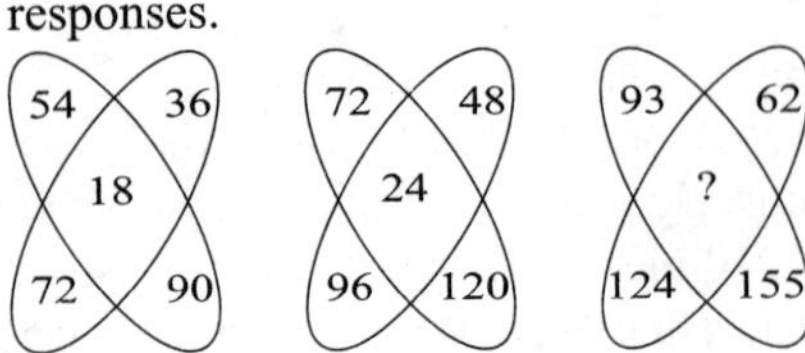


(a) 30 (b) 12
(c) 31 (d) 42

29. Find out the correct alternative to replace the question mark.

| 1 | 7 | 9 |
|---|---|---|
| 2 | 14 | ? |
| 3 | 105 | 117 |

(a) 20 (b) 16
(c) 12 (d) 26

30. Find the odd one out.

(a) GABER (b) YRFRE
(c) NUKKS (d) THACY

31. The first third of a 75 km trip took twice as long as the rest of the trip. If the first third took '$h$' hours, then the average speed for the whole trip was:

(a) 50/h (b) 75/2h
(c) 25/2h (d) 225/2h

32. The distance from P to Q is 25 km, 6 km of which is uphills, 12 km downhill and the rest 7 km in level ground. The time in which a man would go from P to Q and back again, supposing his speed uphill is 2 km, downhill 3 km and on the level ground 3.5 km per hour is:

(a) 9 hours (b) 15 hours
(c) 18 hours (d) 19 hours

33. A train running at a speed of 84 km/h crosses a man running at a speed of 6 km/h in the opposite direction in 4 seconds. The length of the train in metres is

(a) 180 (b) 75
(c) 200 (d) None of these

34. If the ratio of areas of two circles is 16 : 25, the ratio of their circumference is

(a) 25 : 16 (b) 5 : 4
(c) 4 : 5 (d) 3 : 5

35. Which of the statement in the question given below is redundant?

How much time will a boat take to cross the river against the stream of the river?

(i) In still water the speed of the boat is 15 km/hr

(ii) The width of the river is 8 km

(iii) The speed of the stream is 2 km/hr

(a) Only (i) (b) Only (ii)

(c) Only (iii) (d) Insufficient data

**(F) On the basis of information given below, answer the questions that follow.**

Mr Kunal Dwivedi wants to buy a motorbike which is priced at ₹45,500/-. The bike is also available at ₹25,000/- down payment and monthly installments of ₹1000 per month for 2 years or ₹18,000/- down payment and monthly installment of ₹1000/- per month for 3 years. Mr Kunal has with him only ₹12,000/-. He wants to borrow the balance money of the down payment from a private lender whose terms are:

If ₹6000/- is borrowed for 12 months, the rate of interest is 20 percent. The interest will be calculated on the whole amount for the whole year, even thought the repayment has to be done in 12 equal monthly installments starting from the first month itself. Thus he will have to repay an amount of ₹600/- per month for 12 months to repay ₹6000/- (Principal) + ₹1200/- (Interest @ 20 percent).

If ₹10,000/- upwards is borrowed for one year, the rate of interest is 30 percent and is calculated at exactly the same manner as above.

36. If Mr. Kunal is ready to pay either of the down payments, then which of the installment schemes is the better option of the two? (Assume that Mr. Kunal will pay the installments out of his own earnings and he keeps his savings with himself and earns no interest on the same.) Also assume that instead of borrowing the remaining money for the down payment, he saves the balance before purchase.

(a) ₹1000/- for 2 years

(b) ₹2000/- for 3 years

(c) Either of two

(d) None of these

37. If Kunal can spare only a total of ₹2000 to be paid to the bike dealer and the money lender from his monthly earnings starting from the first month onwards which scheme should he choose?

(a) ₹1000 for 2 years (b) ₹1000 for 3 years

(c) Either of two (d) Data inadequate

38. *A* travels at a speed which is 20% more than of *B*. A travels from points *X* towards point *Y* and *B* travels from point *Y* towards point

*X*. The distance between point *X* and point *Y* is 11 km. How far from point *X* will they meet? Take that they both start simultaneously.

(a) 5 kms (b) 6 kms

(c) 4 kms (d) 7 kms

39. A cube is made up of soft metal. The cube is stretched in one direction to increase its length by 10%. The cube is compressed in another perpendicular direction to decease its dimension by 10%. If the third side has the same dimension as that of the original cube than what is the percentage change in the volume of the cube?

(a) No change in volume

(b) Increase in volume by 1%

(c) Decrease in volume by 1%

(d) Data is insufficient to compute the change in volume

40. A manufacturer of shirt sells each of his shirt at a profit of 25%. The whole seller also sells at a profit of 25%. The retailer sells the shirt in a clearance sale at ₹1000 thereby incurring a loss of 20%. What was the cost to the manufacturer?

(a) ₹1000/- (b) ₹1200/-

(c) ₹900/- (d) ₹800/-

41. Two equal glasses of same type are respectively $\frac{1}{2}$ and $\frac{1}{3}$ of milk. They are then filled up with water and the contents are mixed in a tumbler. What is the ratio of milk and water in the tumbler?

(a) 5 : 7 (b) 3 : 2

(c) 1: 6 (d) 7 : 5

42. In a High school some sweets were to be distributed among 525 children on the occasion

of sports day. But 175 children remained absent on that particular day and hence each child got one sweat extra. How many sweats were planned for each child?

(a) 2 (b) 3
(c) 6 (d) 1

43. A man purchased some eggs at 4 for ₹15 and sold them at 2 for ₹8. Thus he gained ₹55 in all. The number of eggs he bought is

(a) 210 (b) 200
(c) 220 (d) 225

44. A goods train left Delhi for Mumbai at an average speed of 40 km/hr. Two hours later, a Rajdhani express train left Delhi for Mumbai, following the freight train on a parallel track at an average speed of 60 km /hr. how far from Delhi would the Rajdhani express train meet the freight train?

(a) 480 km (b) 260 km
(c) 240 km (d) 120 km

45. In a class, 60% of the students pass in History and 45% fail in English. If 35% of them pass in both subjects, What percentage of students in the class fails in both subjects?

(a) 10 (b) 20
(c) 30 (d) 40

46. $x$ and $y$ are two alloys made of zinc and copper the proportion 5:3 and 5:7, respectively. If 2kg of $x$ and 1 kg of $y$ are melt to form a third alloy $z$ then the proportion of zinc and copper in alloy $z$ is

(a) 5:4 (b) 16:25
(c) 10:7 (d) 15:10

47. During the last summer vacation, Ankit went to a summer camp where he took part in biking swimming and boating. This summer, he is looking forward to a music camp where he hopes to sing, dance and learn to play the guitar.

Based on the above information, four conclusions, as given below, have been made. Which one of these logically follows from the information given above?

(a) Ankit's parents want him, to play the guitar.
(b) Ankit prefers music to outdoor activities.
(c) Ankit goes to some type of camp every summer.
(d) Ankit likes to sing and dance.

48. Consider the following statement:

*"Though quite expensive, television is not a luxury item, as one can learn many things through television."*

Which one of the following is a valid inference from the above statement?

(a) All expensive things are regarded as luxury.
(b) All essential things for learning are not luxury.
(c) Television is essential for learning.
(d) Television is not a luxury item.

49. Gita is prettier than Sita but not as pretty as Rita. Then,

(a) Sita is not as pretty as Gita.
(b) Sita is prettier than Rita.
(c) Rita is not as pretty as Gita.
(d) Gita is prettier than Rita.

50. Given that,

1. A is the brother of B.
2. C is the father of A.
3. D is the brother of E.
4. E is the daughter of B.

Then, the uncle of D is

(a) A (b) B
(c) C (d) E

51. Examine the following statements:

1. Rama scored more than Rani.
2. Rani scored less than Ratna.
3. Ratna scored more than Rama.
4. Padma scored more than Rama but less than Ratna.

Who scored the highest?

(a) Rama (b) Padma
(c) Rani (d) Ratna

52. Consider the following statements:

1. All machines consume energy.
2. Electricity provides energy.

3. Electrically operated machines are cheap to maintain.
4. Electrically operated machines do not cause pollution.

Which one of the following inferences can be drawn from the above statements?

(a) All machines are run by electric energy.
(b) There is no form of energy other than electricity.
(c) Most machines are operated on electric energy.
(d) Electrically operated machines are preferable to use.

53. Examine the following statements:

1. None but the rich can afford air-travel.
2. Some of those who travel by air become sick.
3. Some of those who become sick require treatment.

Which one of the following conclusions can be drawn from the above statements?

(a) All the rich persons travel by air.
(b) Those who travel by air become sick.
(c) All the rich persons become sick.
(d) All those who travel by air are rich.

54. Who among the following has won the maximum number of Grand Slam tournaments in tennis?

(a) Roger Federer (b) Novak Djokovic
(c) Rafael Nadal (d) Pete Sampras

55. Which among the following temples has been included in the UNESCO World Heritage site in 2021?

(a) Kakatiya Rudreshwara (Ramappa)
(b) Kashi Vishwanath Temple
(c) Mahabodhi Temple, Bodhgaya
(d) None of the above

56. Under the United Nations Framework Conventions on Climate Change (UNFCCC), in which of the following cities, was the 26th Conference of the Parties (COP) held in 2021?

(a) Paris (b) Montreal
(c) Glasgow (d) Geneva

57. Which amongst the following countries was the largest supplier of crude oil to India in 2021?

(a) Iraq (b) UAE
(c) USA (d) Russia

58. TRAI refers to

(a) Tourism Reforms Authority of India
(b) Trade Regulation Authority of India
(c) Telecom Regulatory Authority of India
(d) none of the above

59. In case a person has suffered from myocardial ischemia, then which organ of the body is likely to have been affected?

(a) Brain (b) Heart
(c) Lungs (d) All of the above

60. In which of the significant battles did the army of East India Company defeat the combined armies of nawab of Bengal, Nawab of Awadh and the Mughal Emperor Shah Alam?

(a) Battle of Plassey
(b) Battle of Buxar
(c) 3rd battle of Panipat
(d) None of the above

## Answers of Practice Question Paper-6

| | | | | | |
|---|---|---|---|---|---|
| 1. (b) | 11. (c) | 21. (d) | 31. (a) | 41. (a) | 51. (d) |
| 2. (a) | 12. (b) | 22. (c) | 32. (d) | 42. (a) | 52. (d) |
| 3. (c) | 13. (a) | 23. (b) | 33. (d) | 43. (c) | 53. (d) |
| 4. (c) | 14. (b) | 24. (c) | 34. (c) | 44. (c) | 54. (c) |
| 5. (c) | 15. (d) | 25. (b) | 35. (d) | 45. (b) | 55. (a) |
| 6. (a) | 16. (c) | 26. (c) | 36. (a) | 46. (a) | 56. (c) |
| 7. (d) | 17. (d) | 27. (a) | 37. (b) | 47. (c) | 57. (a) |
| 8. (d) | 18. (b) | 28. (c) | 38. (b) | 48. (d) | 58. (c) |
| 9. (c) | 19. (d) | 29. (c) | 39. (c) | 49. (a) | 59. (b) |
| 10. (d) | 20. (c) | 30. (c) | 40. (d) | 50. (a) | 60. (b) |

# Practice Question Paper 7

**(A) Read the questions carefully and then answer them correctly.**

1. Rohan asks his grandmother about her age. She replies that if you subtract 20 from my age, divide the sum by 5, subtract 10 from the quotient and multiply the difference by 5 you will get 10. What is Rohan's grandmother's age?

   (a) 50 (b) 75

   (c) 80 (d) 95

2. A wall clock takes 4 seconds to chime twice at 2 pm. How long does the clock take to chime 4 times at 4 pm?

   (a) 8 second (b) 6 second

   (c) 10 second (d) 12 second

3. Mahesh goes to his office walking. If he walks at a speed of 60 metres per minute, he will be 6 minutes late. If he walks at a speed of 80 metres per minute, he will reach the office 3 minutes earlier than the scheduled office time. What is the distance of Mahesh's office from his home?

   (a) 2100 m (b) 2160 m

   (c) 2200 m (d) 2220 m

4. The product of $x$ and 2320 is a square of a natural number. Find the least possible value of $x$.

   (a) 16 (b) 4640

   (c) 145 (c) 2320

5. A bottle is filled with liquid A. Half of the content is poured out and filled with liquid B. One third of the new mixture was then poured away and filled with liquid B. Finally one fourth of the mixture was poured away and filled with liquid B. What is the final ratio of liquid A and liquid B in the mixture?

   (a) 1:1 (b) 1:2

   (c) 1:3 (d) 1:4

**(B) Read the information given below and answer the questions that follow.**

Five erstwhile college friends now live at five different places while A,B,C and D reside in four different metros cities E lives in a remote village. Each friend now is in contact with two other friends only. A is in contact with B and C. C is in contact with A and E while D is in contact with B and E only.

They contact each other either through a mobile phone or via an e-mail or through postal mail. Following information is known about their choice of communication.

- B uses all the three forms of communication.
- E communicates only through postal mail.
- C uses mobile phone and postal mail.
- D does not use a mobile phone limit other two forms of communication.
- A does not communicate via postal mail but uses other two forms of communications.

Based on the above information answer the following questions.

6. If A has to send some information to E then how many different combinations of modes of communication is possible? (Message from one person to another via any of the three forms of communication is to be taken as a combination.)

   (a) 2 (b) 4

   (c) 5 (d) 6

7. Take that any communication via a postal mail takes 5 days and a message sent via e-mail is usually seen by friends in a day's time, while communication via mobile is instantaneous or takes 0 days time. How much minimum time it will take for A to receive a response from E if A sends a message to him?

   (a) 5 days (b) 6 days

   (c) 10 days (d) 14 days

8. If C were to send a message to D, then how much minimum time it would take?

(a) 0 days (b) 1 days

(c) 3 days (d) 10 days

9. B wants to send all his friends a message for a get together and also wants to receive a reply from them. How many minimum number of days it will take for this process to be over?

(a) 10 days (b) 12 days

(c) 8 days (d) 6 days

**(C) Read the information given below and answer the related questions.**

A four member inter-ministerial team is to be selected for an international conference. The members will be from the Ministries of Commerce, Environment and Defence. The names which have been proposed to be considered are: Abhinav, Girish, Jai and Sanjay from the Environment Ministry, Sheela, Rohini, Kartik and Mohan from Commerce and Asim, Sunita and Chetan from Defence.

The final team of four must have at least one female member and one member from each ministry. Besides, there are other constraints and conditions in the team selection as mentioned below:

- Asim and Chetan if selected must be selected together as both have been working together on all important projects and complement each other.
- Sheela and Rohini both cannot be spared simultaneously by the Commerce ministry.
- Girish and Jai are from the same specialisation and same rank, as such sending them together will be improper.
- All proposed names of a particular ministry should not be selected together.

10. If Chetan has been selected in the team and Rohini has not been selected then how many different combinations of team are possible?

(a) 1 (b) 2

(c) 3 (d) 4

11. In the above question which amongst the following can be an appropriate team?

(a) Chetan, Asim, Sheela, Mohan

(b) Chetan, Asim, Sheela, Jai

(c) Chetan, Rohoni, Sheela, Jai

(d) Chetan, Asim, Sunita, Sheela

12. If in the final team, Abhinav, Sanjay and Sunita were not to be selected, then how many combination of teams would be possible?

(a) 4 (b) 5

(c) 3 (d) 6

13. A team was being selected with conditions as specified in question 12, but the ministry withdrew the name of Jai at the last moment. Which amongst the following could then be an appropriate team?

(a) Girish, Sheela, Asim, Chetan

(b) Girish, Rohini, Karik, Chetan

(c) Girish, Sheela, Rohini, Asim

(d) Girish, Sheela, Mohan, Sunita

14. In a team if Girish was to be selected and Asim was not to be selected, then who can be the other team members?

(i) Sanjay, Sheela and Sunita

(ii) Jai, Rohini and Sunita

(a) Only option (i) is possible

(b) Only option (ii) is possible.

(c) Both options (i) and (ii) are possible.

(d) Neither option (i) nor (ii) is possible

15. Examine the following statements: Arun is heavier than Binay. Charu is taller than Dinesh. Binay is of same height as Dinesh but heavier than him. Dinesh is taller than Arun.

Which amongst the following conclusions can be drawn from the above statements?

(a) Arun is the heaviest and shortest of all.

(b) Charu is the heaviest and Arun is the shortest of all.

(c) Charu is the heaviest but no conclusion can be drawn about who is the shortest.

(d) No conclusion can be drawn about who is the heaviest but Arun is the shortest.

16. Examine the following statements.

(i) Only these who are science graduates can become members of the Illuminati society.

(ii) Some members of Illuminati are also engineers.

(iii) The engineers of Illuminati live in the same apartment called Technology Apartments.

Based on the above which of the following conclusion can be drawn?

(a) All residents of Technology Apartment are engineers.

(b) All engineers are members of "Illuminati".

(c) All engineers who are members of "Illuminati" are also science graduates.

(d) No such conclusion can be drawn.

17. Read the following statements.

(i) Use of fossil fuels such as petrol, diesel and CNG causes pollution.

(ii) CNG vehicles are costlier than petrol vehicles.

(iii) Vehicles running on battery do not cause pollution.

(iv) Use of CNG causes less pollution than petrol.

Based on the above, which of the following inferences can be drawn?

(a) CNG vehicles do not cause pollution.

(b) Diesel vehicles are costlier than petrol vehicles.

(c) Battery operated vehicles are the costliest.

(d) None of the above.

18. Consider the following statements.

Controlled nuclear fusion, if successful, would reduce the cost of each unit of electricity to its fifth of present value. This would end poverty as energy would become very cheap. Heavy investment and continuous research is required for controlled nuclear fusion to be successful. Oil rich economies are likely to be most affected as their natural resources would become too costly and redundant.

Which amongst the following inference are logical in terms of the stated facts?

(i) Controlled nuclear fusion is not likely to be achieved in near future.

(ii) Controlled nuclear fusion will change the world economy forever.

(iii) Oil rich economics will not invest in researches pertaining to controlled nuclear fusion.

(a) Only (ii) (b) (ii) and (iii)

(c) Only (iii) (d) (i), (ii), and (iii)

19. Following information is known about the marks scored by four friends in an examination.

(i) Lalit scored more than Chetan.

(ii) Chetan scored less than or equal to the marks scored by Mridul.

(iii) Jack scored more than or equal to the marks scored by Lalit.

Based on the above facts which of the following conclusion can be drawn?

(a) Jack scored more marks than Mridul.

(b) Chetan scored less marks than Jack.

(c) Mridul scored marks equal to Lalit or more than Lalit.

(d) None of the above.

20. Examine the following three statements.

(i) Only those shooting underwater scenes with underwater camera can upload the underwater pictures on Facebook.

(ii) Those who have to go for scuba diving need scuba diving gear.

(iii) Some scuba divers carry underwater cameras.

Which amongst the following conclusion is not valid?

(a) Only persons with scuba diving gear can upload underwater photos on Facebook.

(b) All persons with underwater cameras can upload underwater photos on Facebook.

(c) Underwater cameras is not carried by all scuba divers.

(d) Those scuba divers who carry underwater cameras can shoot under water pictures.

**(D) Carefully read the information given below. Answer the questions pertaining to it.**

In a university there are 10,000 students. The distribution of students in various streams of education are given as per bar chart below. The students are in the age group of 20–40. The age-wise distribution is given as per the following pie chart.

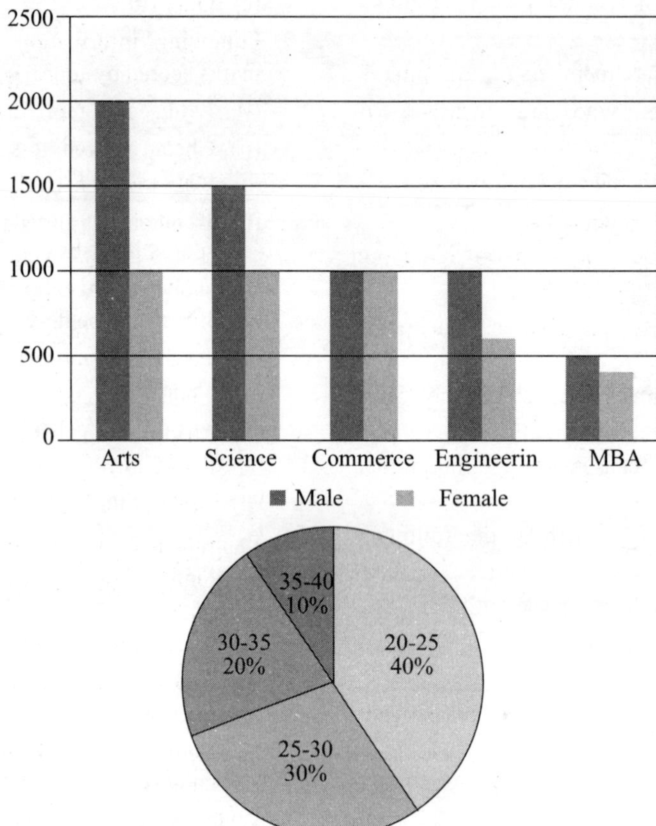


21. Which stream has the lowest ratio of male is to female?
    (a) Arts (b) Commerce
    (c) Engineering (d) MBA
22. What is the overall ratio of male is to female in the university?
    (a) 3:2 (b) 2:1
    (c) 7:3 (d) Data insufficient
23. If out of total students in the age group 20–25, 35% have taken arts, out of which 400 are females, then how many males have taken arts in the age group of 20–25?
    (a) 800 (b) 900
    (c) 1000 (d) 1400
24. If 40% of commerce students are in the age group of 25–30, then how many non-commerce students are there in the age group of 25–30.
    (a) 2000 (b) 2200
    (c) 2400 (d) Data insufficient
25. Examine the two statements.
    (i) In the age group of 35–40, 80% students are MBAs.
    (ii) In the MBA stream 80% students are in the age group of 35–40.

    Which of the following is correct about the above two statements?
    (a) Statement (i) can be correct but statement (ii) cannot be correct.

(b) Statement (ii) can be correct but statement (i) cannot be correct.

(c) Both statements cannot be correct simultaneously.

(d) Both statements are correct simultaneously.

26. A piece of paper, as shown in figure below, is folded to form a cube. Which number would be on the face opposite to the face on which 6 is written?

(a) 1 (b) 2

(c) 3 (d) 4

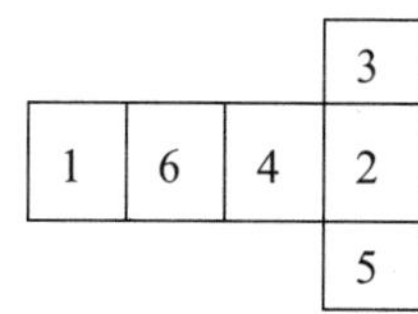


27. Find the possible values of $x$ and $y$ in the series.
3, 4, 5, 8, 7, 16, 9, 32, $x$, $y$

(a) 11, 22 (b) 10, 40

(c) 22, 60 (d) 11, 64

28. Which of the following sequence is different from the others?

(a) 1, 1, 2, 3, 5, 8, 13

(b) 1, 2, 3, 6, 11, 20, 37

(c) 1, 3, 4, 7, 11, 18, 29

(d) 1, 4, 5, 9, 14, 23, 37

29. Find the missing number in the following matrix of numbers.

| 15 | |
|---|---|
| 90 | 12 |

| 14 | |
|---|---|
| 98 | |

| 13 | |
|---|---|
| 65 | 10 |

(a) 14 (b) 11

(c) 13 (d) 15

30. How many squares are there in the figure?

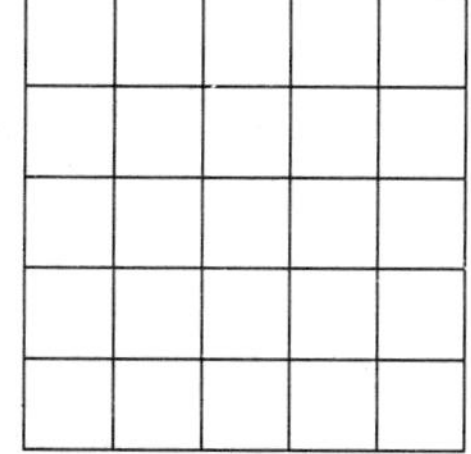

(a) 55 (b) 50

(c) 46 (d) 41

31. A shopkeeper sells two different models of cars at the same price. He earns a profit of 50% on the sale of one car and a loss of 25 % on the sale of other car. How much was his total profit or loss percentage on the sale of both cars taken together?

(a) 25% profit (b) 15 % profit

(c) No profit or loss (d) 10% loss

32. A box contains cards of different colours. There are 6 red, 5 green, 4 yellow and 2 blue coloured cards. How many minimum number of cards must be drawn from the box so that there will be 3 cards of the same colour?

(a) 8 (b) 7

(c) 9 (d) 12

33. In a survey of 700 persons, 75% stated that they take tea. 225 persons confirmed having coffee. If 25 persons neither take tea nor coffee, then what is the ratio of persons taking only tea to those taking only coffee?

(a) 1:1 (b) 2:1

(c) 3:1 (d) Data insufficient

34. A square of side 12 cm is divided into two smaller squares of different sizes and two rectangles of equal size as shown below. If the area of the larger square is 9 times than that of the smaller square then what is the area of each rectangle? Take the length of sides of each square, to be a natural number.

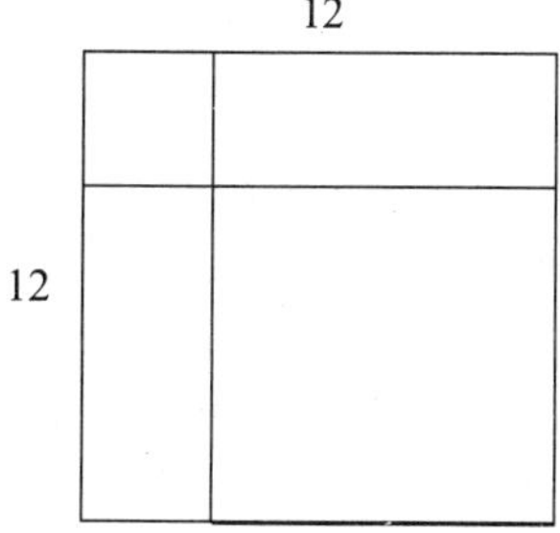


(a) 36 cm$^2$ (b) 27 cm$^2$

(c) 15 cm$^2$ (d) Data insufficient

**(E) Read the information given below and answer the questions that follow.**

Five friends are appearing for the Civil Services Main examination. Each one has a different optional subject viz geography, mathematics, public administration, physics and history. Amongst them, they read four different newspapers. None of them reads two newspapers. The Hindu is the only newspaper which is read by Ashok and another aspirant. The other newspapers subscribed to by the group of friends are The Times of India, The Indian Express and Dainik Jagran. The following information is known.

- Bani reads The Times of India and mathematics is not her optional subject.
- Eela has taken history as an optional subject and she does not read The Hindu or The Indian Express.
- One of the aspirant who reads The Hindu has geography as the optional subject.
- Deepak has taken physics. He does not read The Hindu and Chetna has not taken geography as an optional subject.

Answer the following queries:

35. Who has taken mathematics as an optional subject ?
(a) Ashok (b) Bani
(c) Chetna (d) Data insufficient

36. Which newspaper does Eela read?
(a) The Times of India (b) Dainik Jagran
(c) The Indian Express (d) Data insufficient

37. Which optional subject has Ashok taken?
(a) Geography
(b) Public Administration
(c) Mathematics
(d) Physics

38. Who is the second person reading The Hindu?
(a) Bani (b) Chetna
(c) Deepak (d) Data insufficient

39. Who reads the newspaper The Indian Express?
(a) Eela (b) Deepak
(c) Ashok (d) Chetna

40. Study the figure shown below.

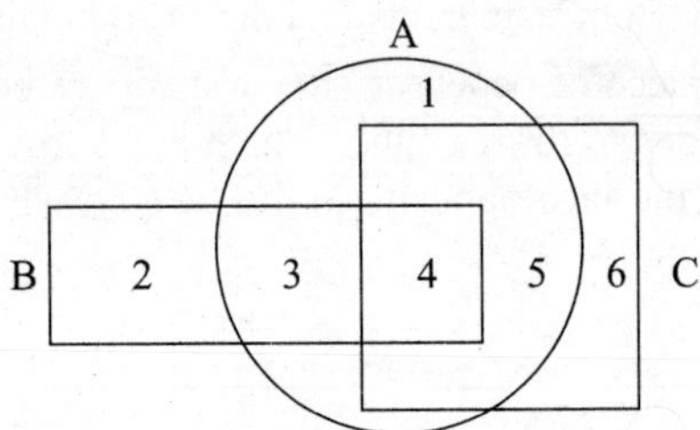


If circle A represents predators, rectangle B represents birds and rectangle C represents nocturnal creatures, then a tiger which hunts by the day time, will fall in which part of the figure?
(a) 1 (b) 3
(c) 4 (d) 6

41. Three plane mirrors are placed perpendicular to each other as shown in the figure below. If a ray of light *I* is falling on mirror 1 at an angle of 45 degree from the mirror then the ray coming out after reflection from the mirror 3 will be;

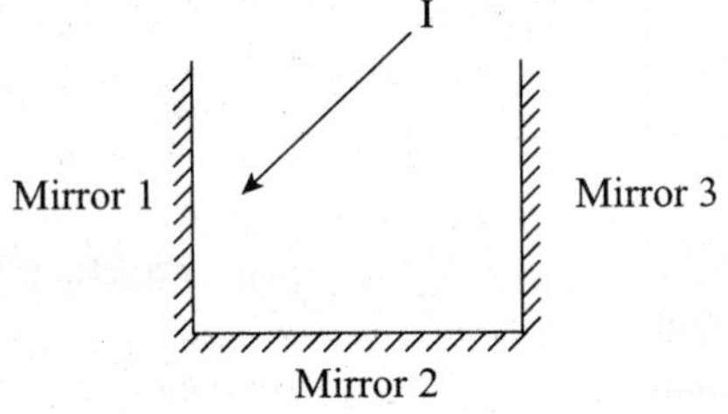


(a) Perpendicular to *I* (b) Parallel to *I*
(c) At 45 degree to *I* (d) At 60 degree to *I*

42. Find the figure coming next in the series.

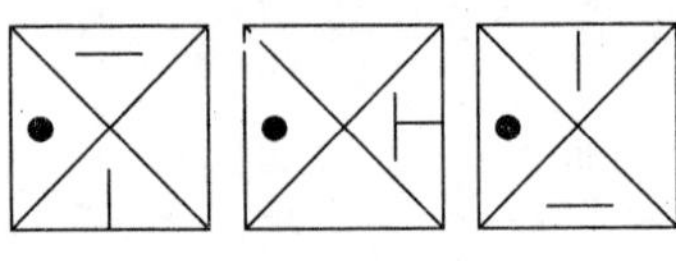

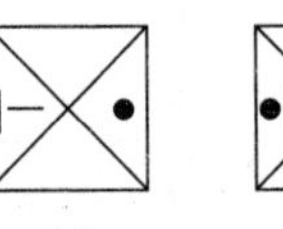 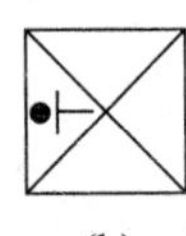 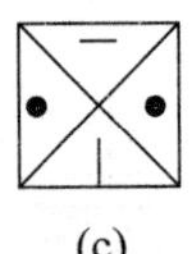 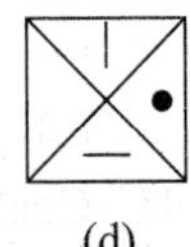

(a) (b) (c) (d)

43. Consider the following matrix with one empty block in the lower extreme corner:

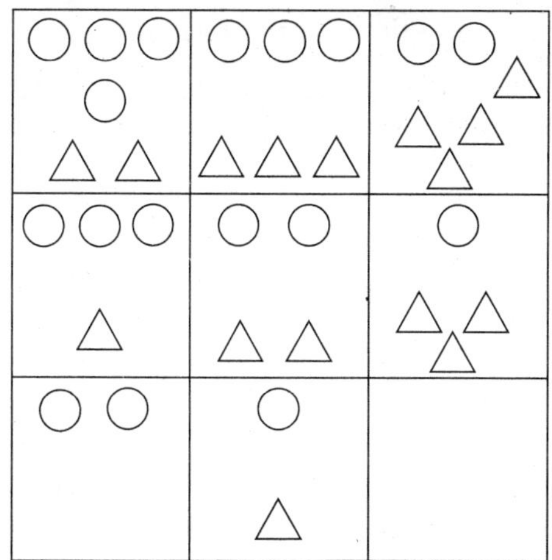

Which of the following figures could fit in the empty block and thus complete the matrix?

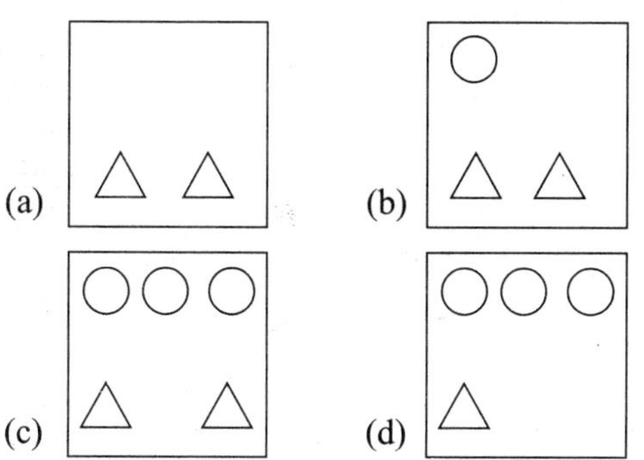


44. With reference to the figure given below, the number of different routes from S to T without retracing from U and/or V, is

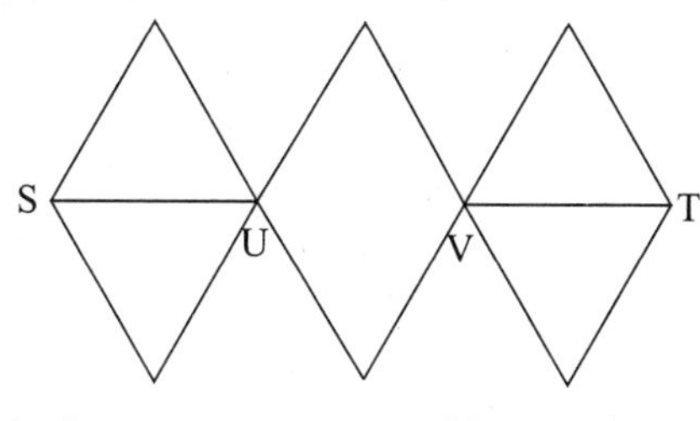


(a) 3 (b) 6
(c) 9 (d) 18

45. Consider the following figures:

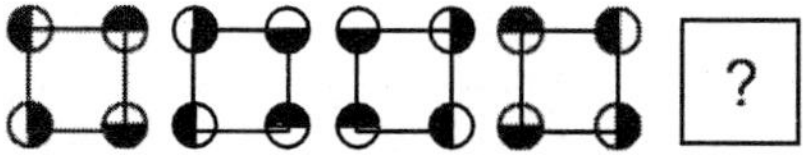


Change in positions of beads in the four figures above follows a sequence. Following the same sequence, which of the figures below should appear as the fifth figure above?

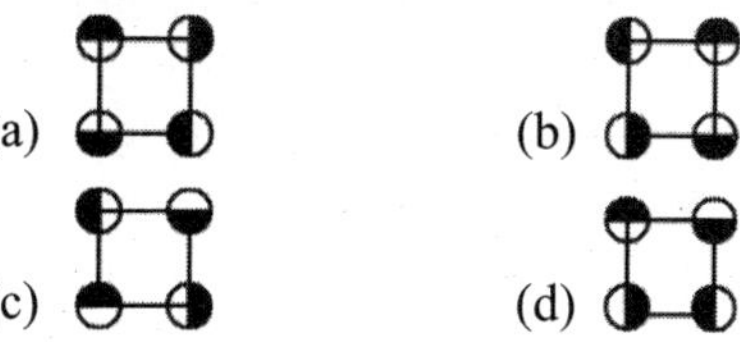


46. Each of the six different faces of a cube has been coated with a different colour, i.e., V, I, B, G, Y and O. Following information is given ;
   1. Colours Y, O and B are on adjacent faces,
   2. Colours I, G and Y are on adjacent faces,
   3. Colours B, G and Y are on adjacent faces.
   4. Colours O, V and B are on adjacent faces.

   Which is the colour of the face opposite to the face coloured with O?

   (a) B (b) V
   (c) G (d) I

47. Consider the figures given below:

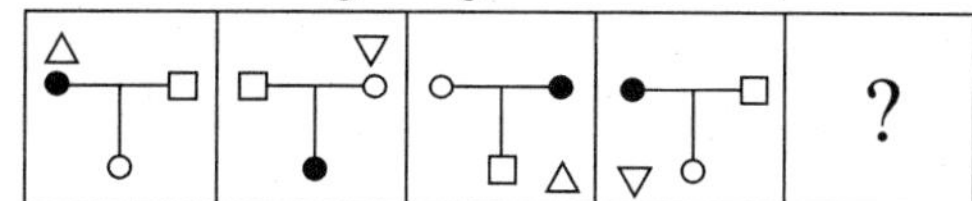


To fit the question mark, the correct answer

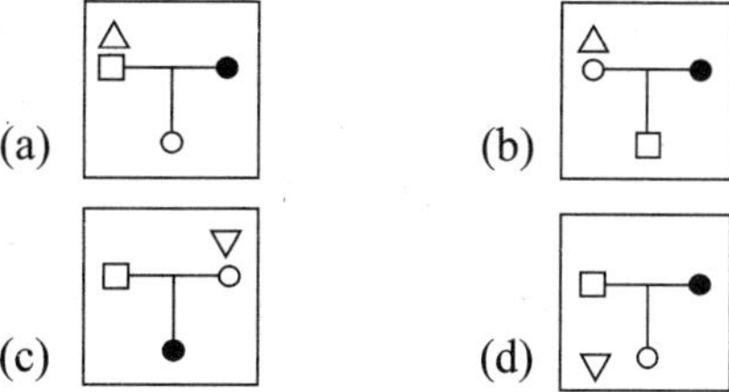


48. Examine the following statements:
   1. I watch TV only if I am bored.
   2. I am never bored when I have my brother's company.
   3. Whenever I go to the theatre 1 take my brother along.

   Which one of the following conclusions is valid in the context of the above statements?

   (a) If I am bored, I watch TV.
   (b) If I am bored, I seek my brother's company.

(c) If I am not with my brother, then I watch TV.

(d) If I am not bored. I do not watch TV.

49. Examine the following statements:

1. None but students are members of the club.
2. Some members of the club are married persons.
3. All married persons are invited for dance.

Which one of the following conclusions can be drawn from the above statements?

(a) All students are invited for dance.

(b) All married students of the club are invited for dance.

(c) All members of the club are married persons.

(d) None of the above conclusions can be drawn.

50. Consider the following statement:

1. All X-brand cars parked here are white.
2. Some of them have radial tyres.
3. All X-brand cars manufactured after 1986 have radial tyres.
4. All cars are not X-brand.

Which one of the following conclusions can be drawn from the above statements?

(a) Only white cars are parked here.

(b) Some white X-brand cars with radial tyres are parked here.

(c) Cars other than X-brand cannot have radial tyres.

(d) Most of the X-brand cars are manufactured before 1986.

51. Consider the following statement:

The Third World War, if it ever starts, will end very quickly with the possible end of civilization. It is only the misuse of nuclear power which will trigger it. Based on the above statement, which one of the following inferences is correct?

(a) Nuclear power will be used in the Third World War.

(b) There will be no civilization left after the Third World War.

(c) The growth of nuclear power will destroy civilization in the long run.

(d) The Third World War will not take place.

52. Geeta is older than her cousin Meena. Meena's brother Bipin is older than Geeta. When Meena and Bipin visit Geeta, they like to play chess. Meena wins the game more often than Geeta.

Based on the above information, four conclusions, as given below, have been made. Which one of these logically follows from the information given above?

(a) While playing chess with Geeta and Meena, Bipin often loses.

(b) Geeta is the oldest among the three.

(c) Geeta hates to lose the game.

(d) Meena is the youngest of the three.

53. There are some balls of red, green and yellow colour lying on a table. There are as many red balls as there are yellow balls. There are twice as many yellow balls as there are green ones. The number of red balls

(a) is equal to the sum of yellow and green balls.

(b) is double the number of green balls.

(c) is equal to yellow balls minus green balls.

(d) cannot be ascertained.

54. The number of deaths among the army personnel is 8 in 1000, but among the civilian population it is 20 per 1000. Which one of the following inferences can be drawn from this statement?

(a) It is better to join the army.

(b) The relationship is fortuitous.

(c) Quality of Life Index is very high within the armed forces.

(d) The groups cannot be compared due to their heterogeneity.

55. The Asian Development Bank has headquarters in

(a) New Delhi (b) Manila

(c) Tokyo (d) Singapore

56. OPEC stands for
    (a) Oil Producing Economies and Countries
    (b) Organisation of Petroleum Exporting Countries
    (c) Organisation for Policy on Export Commodities
    (d) Oil and Petrochemical Exporting Countries
57. Whose birth day on the 12th January is celebrated as National Youth Day?
    (a) Subhash Chandra Bose
    (b) Bhagat Singh
    (c) Swami Vivekananda
    (d) Madan Mohan Malviya
58. Who among the following Indians is currently elected as a Judge of the International Court of Justice?
    (a) Amartya Sen (b) Dalveer Bhandari
    (c) R.S. Pathak (d) Raghuram Rajan
59. Which amongst the following countries won the Cricket ODI World Cup in 2019?
    (a) England
    (b) New Zealand
    (c) Australia
    (d) India
60. From which International company did India purchase the multi role fighter aircraft Rafale?
    (a) Dassault Aviation S.A.
    (b) Boeing Aerospace Company
    (c) Lockheed Martin
    (d) Airbus and BAE systems

## Answers of Practice Question Paper-7

| | | | | | |
|---|---|---|---|---|---|
| **1.** (c) | **11.** (b) | **21.** (b) | **31.** (c) | **41.** (a) | **51.** (b) |
| **2.** (d) | **12.** (a) | **22.** (a) | **32.** (c) | **42.** (b) | **52.** (d) |
| **3.** (b) | **13.** (a) | **23.** (c) | **33.** (c) | **43.** (a) | **53.** (b) |
| **4.** (c) | **14.** (a) | **24.** (b) | **34.** (b) | **44.** (d) | **54.** (d) |
| **5.** (c) | **15.** (d) | **25.** (c) | **35.** (c) | **45.** (b) | **55.** (b) |
| **6.** (c) | **16.** (c) | **26.** (b) | **36.** (b) | **46.** (c) | **56.** (b) |
| **7.** (c) | **17.** (d) | **27.** (d) | **37.** (a) | **47.** (a) | **57.** (c) |
| **8.** (b) | **18.** (a) | **28.** (b) | **38.** (b) | **48.** (d) | **58.** (b) |
| **9.** (a) | **19.** (b) | **29.** (a) | **39.** (b) | **49.** (b) | **59.** (a) |
| **10.** (d) | **20.** (b) | **30.** (a) | **40.** (a) | **50.** (b) | **60.** (a) |

# Practice Question Paper 8

**(A) Read the statements carefully. Answer the questions pertaining to it.**

1. Consider the following statements.
   (i) Reasoning is the heart of law.
   (ii) Some lawyers have a sharp sense of reasoning.
   (iii) All lawyers must have a degree in law.
   In the light of the above statements, which amongst the following conclusions can be drawn?
   (i) All persons with a sharp sense of reasoning can be lawyers.
   (ii) All lawyers would have a sharp sense of reasoning.
   (iii) All lawyers would have a degree in law.
   (a) (i), (ii), (iii) (b) (i), (iii)
   (c) Only (i) (d) Only (iii)
2. In an office, the following is known about the seniority of four officers.
   (i) Mahesh is senior to or equal to Nitin in rank.
   (ii) Raman is junior to or equal to Shiv in rank.
   (iii) Nitin is senior to Shiv in rank.
   Based on the above facts which of the following conclusion can be drawn?
   (a) Shiv is senior to Raman.
   (b) Nitin is junior to Mahesh.
   (c) Mahesh is senior to Raman.
   (d) No such conclusion can be drawn.
3. Consider the following statements.
   (i) I eat pizza only when I go to a mall.
   (ii) I do not go to a mall on a weekday.
   (iii) Whenever I go to a mall, I take my wife with me.
   Which of the following conclusions can be drawn based on the aforesaid statements?
   (a) Whenever I go to a mall, I eat a pizza.
   (b) On a weekend I always go to a mall.
   (c) I do not go to a mall without my wife.
   (d) My wife and I eat pizza together in a mall.
4. Examine the following statements.
   In order to be a minister one must be an MP No business man is poor. Some politicians run a business. All ministers are politicians.
   Which amongst the following is a valid conclusion based on the above statements?
   (a) Some ministers are not poor.
   (b) Some ministers are politicians.
   (c) All MPs run business.
   (d) All MPs are ministers.
5. Consider the following statements.
   (i) The cost of transportation of goods by trains is ₹ 1000 per ton/km as compared to ₹ 1100 per ton/km by trucks ₹ 3000 per ton/km by airplanes.
   (ii) Trains are the cheapest means of transportation of goods.
   Which amongst the following statements, if taken to be true, weakens the conclusion drawn in (ii) above?
   (a) Trains are run by the government of India, as such are subsidised and cannot be compared to other means of transport.
   (b) Trains take much more time as compared to transportation by air or even when compared to trucks, as such the comparison is improper.

(c) Trains only take goods from a railway station to another railway station and do not provide door to door service as trucks.

(d) Volume of goods carried by the three modes is totally different and cannot be compared.

6. Read the information given below.

Pranshu goes to a library only on weekends. He usually borrows books on science or fiction. His parents encourage him to read mathematics books. Sometimes he delays the return of books.

Which amongst the following inference can be conclusively drawn from the above information?

(i) Pranshu does not go to library on Wednesday.

(ii) Pranshu likes science and fiction.

(iii) Pranshu does not like mathematics.

(a) All conclusions (i), (ii) and (iii) can be drawn.

(b) Only conclusion (i) and (ii) can be drawn.

(c) Only conclusion (i) and (iii) only can be drawn.

(d) Only conclusion (i) only be drawn.

**(B) Each question has four options. Understand the question and choose the correct option.**

7. A wooden pole was cut into half. Half of the pole was cut into half again. After four such cuts, the length of one such portion was 2 m. What was the original length of the pole?

(a) 8 m (b) 16 m
(c) 32 m (d) 69 m

8. The circumference of a circular park is 500 m. Trees are planted at regular intervals of 10 m round the lake. How many trees are planted a round the park?

(a) 49 (b) 50
(c) 51 (d) 52

9. Ranjana drives to a neighbouring town in her new car. If she drives at a speed of 40 km/hr, she would have arrived at 10 am. If she travelled at 60 km/hr she would have arrived at 9 am. At what speed should she drive if she has to reach the town at 9.30 am?

(a) 50 kmph (b) 45 kmph
(c) 48 kmph (d) 40 kmph

10. Find the values of $X$ and $Y$ if $X431Y$ is divisible by 8 and 9.

(a) (iii), 7 (b) (ii), 8
(c) 6, 2 (d) 8, 2

11. Two tanks of different heights and different diameters are filled with water. The shorter tank has a greater diameter. The first tank which is of greater height takes 12 hours to empty while the second takes 18 hours. The two tanks after filling were allowed to empty at the same time and after 6 hours the level of water in both the tanks was the same. What was the ratio of the heights of the tanks?

(a) 4:3 (b) 5:3
(c) 2:1 (d) 8:3

12. Lalit does a work for 3 hours. After that Leena works alone and completes the remaining work in 4 hours. If Lalit works for 4.5 hours then Leena alone would take 2 hours to complete the remaining work. How much time Leena would take to complete the whole work?

(a) 2 hrs (b) 5 hrs
(c) 6 hrs (d) 8 hrs

13. A pack of 52 cards has 13 cards each of one of the suits, i.e., heart, spade, diamond and club. How many minimum number of cards must be drawn from the pack so that there are 4 cards of the same suit?

(a) 16 (b) 17
(c) 12 (d) 13

14. How many digits does a book use for printing its page numbers if the book has 300 pages?

(a) 790 (b) 789
(c) 792 (d) 788

**(C) Read the information given below and answer the questions that follow.**

A family of five persons is travelling in a five seater car which has two seats in the front and three back seats. The members of the family are, father. mother, son, daughter and grandfather. The following information is known.

- The father is not driving the car.
- Nayna is not sitting on the rear seat.

- Vasudha, the other female member, is sitting directly behind her grandfather.
- Abhi does not have a window seat.
- The mother is not driving the car.
- Kamal is the grandfather and the last person is Raj who is not the son.

Based on above information, answer the following questions.

15. Who is driving the car?
    (a) Father (b) Mother
    (c) Grandfather (d) Son
16. Where is Abhi sitting?
    (a) At driver's seat.
    (b) In front but not on driver's seat.
    (c) Left window seat of back side.
    (d) Middle seat of back side.
17. Who is sitting directly in front of Raj?
    (a) Nayna (b) Kamal
    (c) Abhi (d) Vasudha
18. Who is the father?
    (a) Kamal (b) Abhi
    (c) Raj (d) Data insufficient
19. Who is to the right of Abhi?
    (a) Raj (b) Nayna
    (c) Vasudha (d) Kamal
20. If Abhi was to exchange the seat with Nayna, then who would be seated to her left?
    (a) Raj (b) Vashudha
    (c) Abhi (d) Kamal
21. Four friends Prem, Qasim, Suresh and Ravi, went to a Chinese restaurant. One of them accidentally tripped over a costly flower vase and broke it. When the manager came and asked who broke it, there reply was as follows:

    Prem- I did not break it. By the time I entered the restaurant the vase had already fallen down.

    Qasim- Suresh broke it.

    Suresh- Qasim is lying, I did not break it.

    Ravi- Qasim is telling the truth.

    If only one of them told the truth, then who broke the vase?

    (a) Prem (b) Qasim
    (c) Suresh (d) Ravi
22. Which of the following piece of paper if folded along the marked lines will not form a complete closed cube?

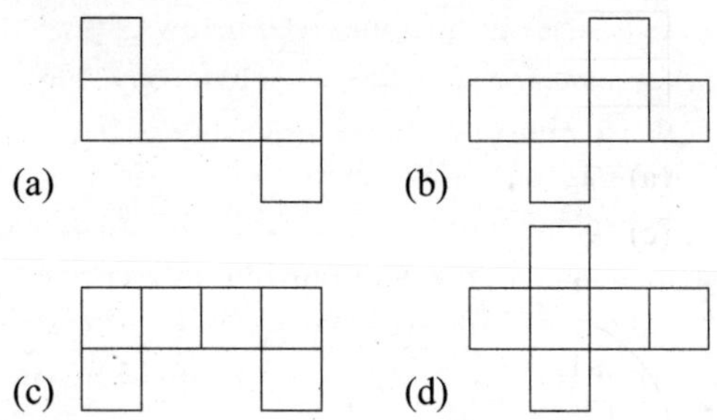


23. Find the missing number in the series. 7, 11, 19, ? , 67,.......
    (a) 30 (b) 32
    (c) 33 (d) 35
24. Find the missing number.

| 16 | 4 |
|---|---|
| 1 | 3 |

| 15 | 3 |
|---|---|
| 1 | 4 |

| 24 | 4 |
|---|---|
| 1 | ? |

    (a) 5 (b) 4
    (c) 6 (d) 3
25. A dice has six numbers 1, 2, 3, 4, 5 and 6 on its faces. The cube is so placed that number 1 is seen on the top face, number 2 on the front face, and number 6 on the right face, as shown in the figure below:

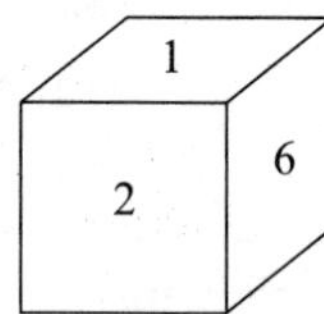


Number 3 is not opposite to either 1 or 6 and number 6 is not opposite to 4. If the dice is rotated so that number 1 remains on the top face while number 6 comes on the front face (which is the present position of number 2 in the figure) then which number would come at the right face? (At the position of number 6 presently shown in the figure.)

(a) 3 (b) 4
(c) 5 (d) 2

26. In the figure given below, in how many ways a person can move from point A to point B, if one cannot move upwards or leftwards and cannot pass through point C?

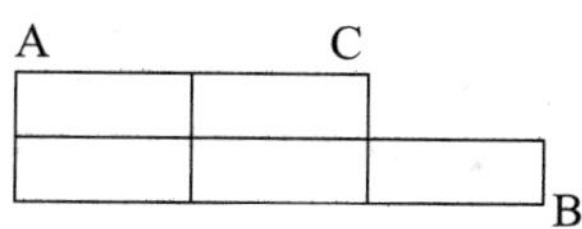


(a) 7 (b) 8
(c) 9 (d) 10

27.

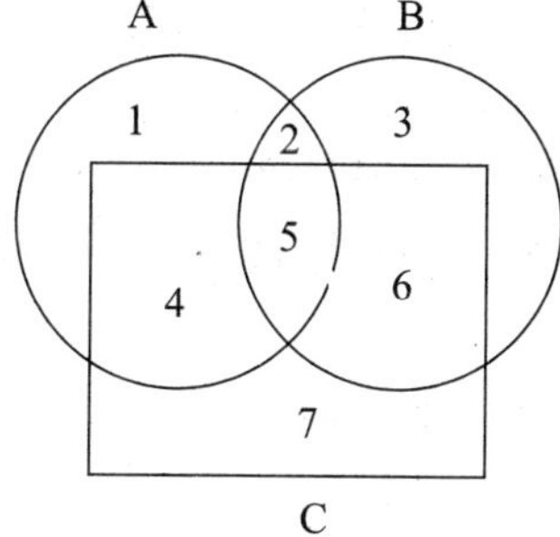


In the figure above, circle A represents musicians, circle B represents members of philanthropic society, while rectangle C represents administrators.

Which region represents musicians and administrators but not members of the philanthropic society.

(a) 5 (b) 4
(c) 6 (d) 7

28. If Figure 1 is cut from figure 2 which figure would be left?

Figure 1

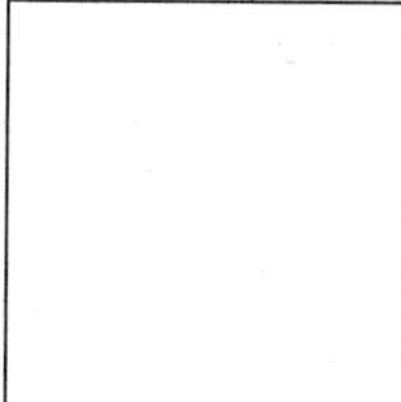
Figure 2

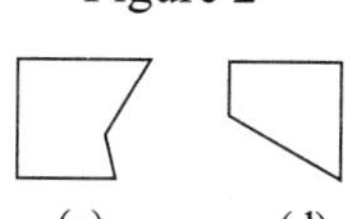


29. Which group of letters would follow the series given below?

B 28 H, G 713 M, L 1218 R

(a) Q 1721 V (b) P 1622 V
(c) Q 1723 W (d) R 1823 W

30. Find the figure coming next in the series?

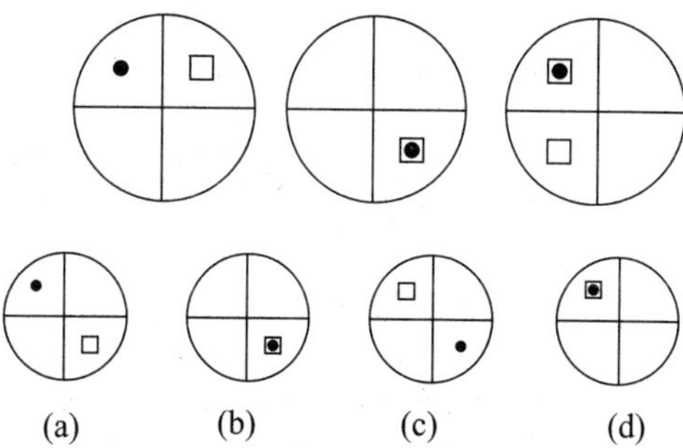


31. Two cylinders, A and B are placed side by side and connected via pipe at the bottom (of both the cylinders). Cylinder A is filled with water till a height of 10 meters. It has a diameter that is half of the diameter of cylinder B. Water is allowed to flow from cylinder A to cylinder B and continues to flow till the level of water in both the cylinder is equal. If the level of water in cylinder A is plotted along $y$-axis and that of cylinder B plotted along $x$-axis of a graph, then which among the following graphs would represent correctly the levels of water in cylinders A and B at various points of time during flow from the cylinder A to B?

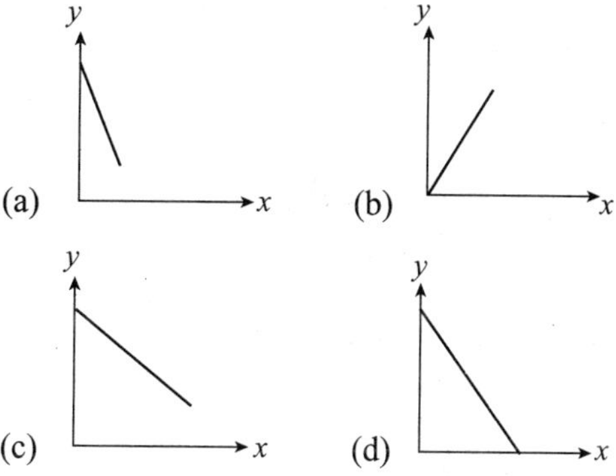

**(D) Read the information given below and answer the questions that follow.**

A survey was conducted amongst 2000 men, women and children to determine their preferred past time activity. The activities were categorised broadly as (a) surfing on internet/social media (b) watching television (c) playing games. 50% of participants in the survey were men.

The following other information is also known.

- There were 1000 persons who preferred watching television over other activities.
- Twice the numbers of men preferred watching internet as compared to women.
- The ratio of women to children in the survey was 3:2.
- As many men preferred watching television as women and children put together.
- 350 respondents liked playing games, out of which 150 were children. Only 50 children preferred internet surfing.
- Only 100 men like playing games.

32. How many children prefer watching TV?
    (a) 200 (b) 150
    (c) 100 (d) Data insufficient
33. What percentage of respondents who watch TV are women?
    (a) 20% (b) 30%
    (c) 40% (d) 50%
34. What percentage of men prefer surfing on the internet?
    (a) 20% (b) 30%
    (c) 40% (d) 50%
35. The percentage of respondents preferring to play games is the least for,
    (a) men
    (b) women
    (c) children
    (d) cannot be determined
36. How many triangles are there in the figures given below?

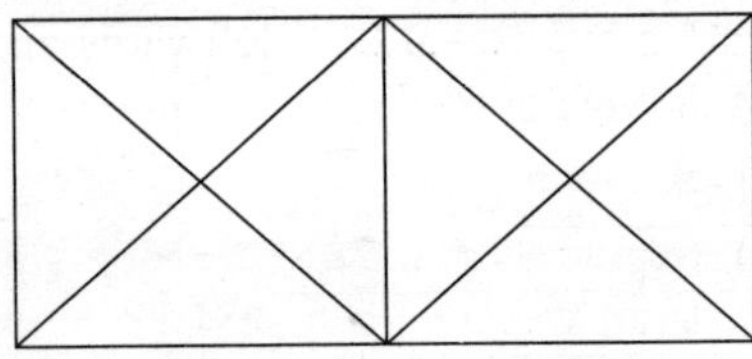

    (a) 8 (b) 16
    (c) 18 (d) 20
37. Manoj goes to a temple every third day. He goes to a library every seventh day. He visits one of his friends every alternate day. If on the 1st of January of a year all the three occurrences coincide, then on which day again they will fall together?
    (a) On the 12th February.
    (b) On the 11th February.
    (c) On the 13th February.
    (d) On none of the above days.
38. In a sale, a shop keeper sells two different quality television sets at the same price. On the first television set he earns a profit of 20%. On the second he incurs a loss of 20%. What is the overall profit or loss percent?
    (a) Profit of 8%
    (b) Loss of 4%
    (c) Profit of 4%
    (d) No profit and no loss
39. Two statements S1 and S2 are given below followed by a question.

    **S1:** If the numbers written on each page of the book are added then the total of all the numbers is 5500.

    **S2:** The number of pages in the book is more than 50.

    **Question:** What is the total number of pages in the book?

    Which of the following are correct in respect of the above statements and the question?

(a) Both S1 and S2 are sufficient to answer the question but neither S1 alone nor S2 alone is sufficient to answer the question.
(b) S1 alone is sufficient to answer the question.
(c) S2 alone is sufficient to answer the question.
(d) S1 and S2 alone together are not sufficient to answer the question.

40. Two statements S1 and S2 are given below about the age of four friends, Ajay, Bibek, Chetan and Dev. They are followed by a question.

**S1:** Ajay is not the oldest although he is elder to Bibek and Chetan.

**S2:** Dev is not the youngest.

**Question:** Who is the oldest amongst the four?

Which of the following are correct in respect of the above statements and the question?
(a) S1 alone is sufficient to answer the question.
(b) S2 alone is sufficient to answer the question.
(c) Both S1 and S2 are sufficient to answer the question but neither S1 alone nor S2 alone is sufficient to answer the question.
(d) S1 and S2 alone together are not sufficient to answer the question.

41. Two statements S1 and S2 are given below about a set of numbers followed by two inferences and a question.

**S1:** The set comprises natural numbers which are having 0 or 5 in the unitary place.

**S2:** The set of numbers are not multiples of 3.

**Inference-1:** All numbers in the set are multiples of 5

**Inference-2:** 150 is not a number in the set

**Question:**

Which of the following are correct in respect of the above statements and the question?
(a) Both, Inference-1 and Inference-2 are correct.
(b) Only Inference-1 is correct.
(c) Only Inference-2 is correct.
(d) Neither Inference-1 nor Inference-2 is correct.

**(E) Read the passage given below, study the graph that follows and answer the three items given below the figure.**

During a party, a person was exposed to contaminated water. A few days later, he developed fever and loose motions. He suffered for some days before going to a doctor for treatment. On starting the treatment, he soon became better and recovered completely a few days later. The following graph shows different phases of the person's disease condition as regions A, B, C, D and E of the curve.

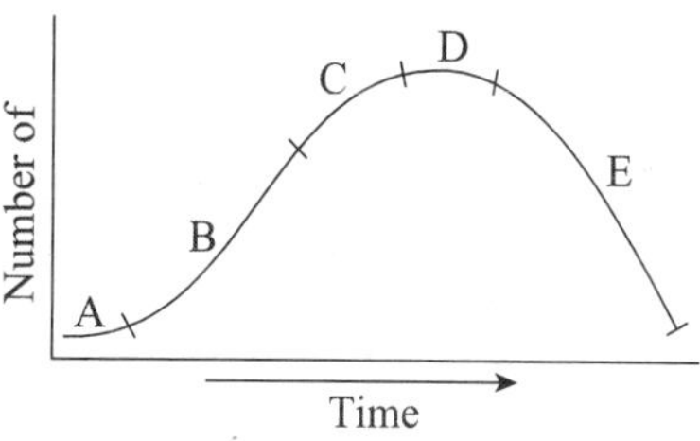


42. Which region/regions of the curve corresponds/correspond to incubation phase of the infection?
(a) A only
(b) B only
(c) B and C
(d) No part of the curve indicates the incubation phase

43. Which region of the curve indicates that the person began showing the symptoms of infection?
(a) A (b) B
(c) C (d) D

44. Which region of the curve indicates that the treatment yielded effective relief?
(a) C
(b) D
(c) E
(d) The curve does not indicate the treatment

45. There are four routes to travel from city A to city B and six routes from city B to city C. How many routes are possible to travel from the city A to city C?
(a) 24 (b) 12
(c) 10 (d) 8

46. The following figure has four curves namely A, B, C and D. Study the figure and answer the item that follows.

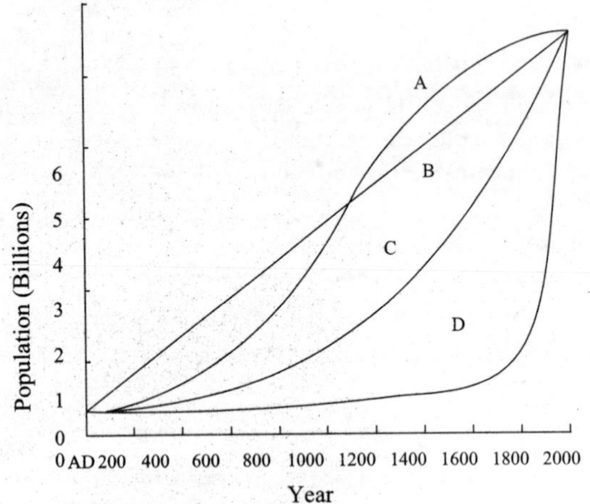


Which curve indicates exponential growth?

(a) A (b) B

(c) C (d) D

47. Given the statement: "Buses are the cause of more accidents than cars, and trucks cause fewer accidents than buses", which of the following conclusions can we draw?

(a) There are more buses on the road than trucks.

(b) Car drivers are more careful than bus drivers.

(c) Truck drivers are more skilled than either car or bus drivers.

(d) None of the above

48. "If political leadership fails to emerge, there is likelihood of military taking over power in developing countries. Radical student groups or labour may try to raise revolution but they are not likely to compete with the military. Military intervention, rule, and withdrawal from politics is closely related to a society's level of political development."

In the context, of political development, the assumption, in the above passage is that

(a) political leadership is not an effective installment.

(b) military fills in political vacuum.

(c) military intervention is inevitable for development.

(d) None of the above.

49. Four persons, Alok, Bhupesh, Chander and Dinesh have a total of ₹100 among themselves. Alok and Bhupesh between them have as much money as Chander and Dinesh between them, but Alok has more money than Bhupesh; and Chander has only half the money that Dinesh has. Alok has in fact ₹5 more than Dinesh has. Who has the maximum amount of money?

(a) Alok (b) Bhupesh

(c) Chander (d) Dinesh

50. In a plane, line X is perpendicular to line Y and parallel to line Z; line U is perpendicular to both lines V and W; line X is perpendicular to line V.

Which one of the following statements is correct?

(a) Z, U and W are parallel

(b) X, V and Y are parallel

(c) Z, V and U are all perpendicular to W

(d) Y, V and W are parallel

51. A cow costs more than 4 goats but less than 5 goats. If a goat costs between ₹600 and ₹800, which of the following is a most valid conclusion?

(a) A cow costs more than ₹2,500.

(b) A cow costs less than ₹3,600.

(c) A cow costs between ₹2,600 and 3,800.

(d) A cow costs between ₹2,400 and 4,000.

52. A society consists of only two types of people—fighters and cowards. Two cowards are always friends. A fighter and a coward are always enemies. Fighters are indifferent to one another. A and B are enemies, C and D are friends, E and F are indifferent to each other, A and E are not enemies, while B and F are enemies.

Which of the following statements is correct?

(a) B, C and F are cowards.

(b) A, E and F are fighters,

(c) B and E are in the same category.

(d) A and F are in different categories.

53. International Solar Alliance, an alliance of 102 solar countries working for the efficient utilisation of the solar energy, is headquartered at
(a) New Delhi (b) Gurugram
(c) Greater Noida (d) Bengaluru

54. Who amongst the following won the Australian Open tennis men's title in 2022?
(a) Novak Djokovic
(b) Rafale Nadal
(c) Daniil Medvedev
(d) None of the above

55. Hepatitis disease cause the inflammation of which of the following organs of human body?
(a) Kidneys (b) Heart
(c) Liver (d) Pancreas

56. The Aditya L1 mission of ISRO is to be associated with which of the following objectives?
(a) Mapping of the hilly terrains of Himalayas in Northern India.
(b) Mapping of the solar intensity and potential of solar energy in different parts of India.
(c) Study of the dark side of the moon.
(d) Study of the corona and chromosphere etc. of the sun.

57. Who was the first Chief of the Defence Staff of India?
(a) General Manekshaw
(b) General Bipin Rawat
(c) General Manoj Mukund Navarane
(d) None of the above

58. The folk art of Madhubani painting is associated with which Indian state?
(a) Uttar Pradesh (b) West Bengal
(c) Jharkhand (d) Bihar

59. Which of the following river, is **not** included in the 'river rejuvenation through forestry project', of government of India, proposed in March 2022?
(a) Ganga (b) Brahmaputra
(c) Yamuna (d) Narmada

60. Which of the following was one of the reasons for the launch of non- cooperation movement by Mahatma Gandhi in 1920?
(a) India's forced participation in the first world war.
(b) Opposition to the Rowlatt Act of 1919.
(c) Levy of heavy taxes on the Indian textiles.
(d) Opposition to the practice of indigo plantation and heavy taxation of the Indian farmers.

## Answers of Practice Question Paper-8

| | | | | | |
|---|---|---|---|---|---|
| **1.** (d) | **11.** (a) | **21.** (a) | **31.** (a) | **41.** (a) | **51.** (d) |
| **2.** (c) | **12.** (d) | **22.** (c) | **32.** (a) | **42.** (a) | **52.** (b) |
| **3.** (c) | **13.** (d) | **23.** (d) | **33.** (b) | **43.** (b) | **53.** (b) |
| **4.** (a) | **14.** (c) | **24.** (a) | **34.** (c) | **44.** (c) | **54.** (b) |
| **5.** (c) | **15.** (c) | **25.** (a) | **35.** (a) | **45.** (a) | **55.** (c) |
| **6.** (d) | **16.** (d) | **26.** (a) | **36.** (c) | **46.** (c) | **56.** (d) |
| **7.** (c) | **17.** (a) | **27.** (b) | **37.** (a) | **47.** (d) | **57.** (b) |
| **8.** (b) | **18.** (c) | **28.** (b) | **38.** (b) | **48.** (c) | **58.** (d) |
| **9.** (c) | **19.** (c) | **29.** (c) | **39.** (b) | **49.** (a) | **59.** (a) |
| **10.** (d) | **20.** (a) | **30.** (c) | **40.** (a) | **50.** (d) | **60.** (b) |

# Practice Question Paper 9

**(A) Read the conditions given below in each questions. Answer them correctly.**

1. Mansi is the elder sister of Mehul. Ravi is a good friend of Mehul and of the same age as him. All of them play several rounds of a card game. The fourth player is Ravi's younger brother Suraj, who comes first in 60% of the games. In the remaining games it is Mansi who stands first. Mehul is second in all the games.

   Which of the two conclusions can be drawn from the stated facts?

   (i) Ravi comes last in all the games.
   (ii) Suraj is the youngest of all.

   (a) Only conclusion (i) can be drawn.
   (b) Only conclusion (ii) can be drawn.
   (c) Both the conclusions (i) and (ii) can be drawn.
   (d) Neither conclusion (i) nor (ii) can be drawn.

2. A school is to select some students from the classes 7, 8 and 9 for an inter-school play competition. In the first round of audition ten students are selected from class 9, five from class 8 and the remaining three from class 7. However in the second round of audition, only 10 students are shortlisted of which six are from class 9.

   Which of the following conclusion can be said to logically flow from the information given above?

   (a) All students of class 7 have been dropped from the auditions.
   (b) At least one student from class 8 remains in the audition.
   (c) Two students each from class 7 and class 8 remain in the audition.
   (d) No such conclusion can be drawn.

3. Examine the following statements.

   (i) The students of class 10th who have topped in their respective sections are members of the student's council.
   (ii) Some members of the student's council are also the members of the school magazine editorial board.
   (iii) The school principal nominates some members in student's council who have exceptional proficiency in sports, arts or other activities.
   (iv) Only the members of student council are invited for its bimonthly meeting.

   Based on the above facts, which amongst the following conclusions can be drawn?

   **Conclusion** (I): Only section toppers participate in the student's council meetings.

   **Conclusion** (II): All students proficient in either sports or arts or other activities are invited in student council meetings.

   (a) Only conclusion I can be drawn.
   (b) Only conclusion II can be drawn.
   (c) Both conclusions I and II can be drawn.
   (d) Neither conclusion I nor II can be drawn.

4. Consider the following statements.

   (i) Family relationship is an inherent character of all mammals.
   (ii) Orangutans are mammals which have long forearms.
   (iii) Intimacy between individuals may be displayed between family members of mammals.
   (iv) Very few apes have as long forearms as Orangutans.

Based on the above statements which of the following conclusions can be drawn?

I. All apes with long forearms are Orangutans.

II. All mammals displaying intimacy between family members are Orangutans.

III. All mammals display family relationship.

(a) Only conclusion I and III are correct.

(b) Conclusion I, II, and III all are correct.

(c) Only conclusion III is correct.

(d) Only conclusion II and III are correct.

5. Examine the statements given below and determine whether the two conclusions given below can be drawn from them?

**Statement (1)**: All books are furniture.

**Statement (2)**: Some furniture are jewellery.

**Conclusion (I)**: Some books are jewellery.

**Conclusion (II)**: All jewellery are books.

(a) Only conclusion (I) can be drawn.

(b) Only conclusion (II) can be drawn.

(c) Both conclusion (I) and (II) can be drawn.

(d) Neither conclusion (I) nor (II) can be drawn.

6. Consider the following sentences.

(i) I go to temple only on Saturday.

(ii) I do not go to a temple when I am ill.

(iii) Whenever I feel ill, I drink two glasses of water in one go.

Which of the following conclusions can be drawn from the statements?

I. If I have drunk two glasses of water in one go, I will not go to a temple even on a Saturday.

II. If not ill, I will always go to a temple on a Saturday.

(a) Only conclusion I can be drawn.

(b) Only conclusion II can be drawn.

(c) Both the conclusions I and II can be drawn.

(d) Neither conclusion I nor II can be drawn.

**(B) Read the information given below and answer the questions which follow**

Five friends gather for a reunion after 10 years of completion of their college education. Each of them has joined a different profession. Amongst them there is a doctor, a lawyer, an engineer, a bureaucrat and a journalist.

The doctor has come from Ahmadabad. The lawyer and the bureaucrat, both are from Delhi. One of the friends is Kamini. She was the last to arrive as her flight from Chennai got delayed. She is not an engineer.

Vinod is a doctor and was the first to arrive. While Ganesh is not from Delhi, the other two friends are Dinkar and Shekhar, one friend has come from Mumbai.

7. Which amongst the following is from Delhi?

(a) Vinod (b) Ganesh

(c) Shekhar (d) Data insufficient

8. What is the profession of Kamini?

(a) Journalist (b) Doctor

(c) Lawyer (d) data insufficient

9. Who is the engineer?

(a) Dinkar (b) Shekhar

(c) Vinod (d) Ganesh

10. What is the profession of Dinkar?

(a) Bureaucrat (b) Engineer

(c) Lawyer (d) Data insufficient

11. Shekhar is a lawyer then what can be said about Dinkar?

(a) He is a doctor.

(b) He is a engineer.

(c) He is a bureaucrat.

(d) No conclusion can be drawn

**(C) Read the conditions given below and answer the question pertaining to it.**

A meeting of a particular department of the government is being attended by six officials. These are the Secretary, the Additional Secretary, the Joint Secretary, the Director, the Under Secretary and the Section Officer (in decreasing order of seniority). The names of officers (not in order) are A. Wilson, H. Khan, M.P. Verma, Naresh Kumar, P. Kashyap and Sohan Singh. They are sitting around a round table facing each other. The following information is known.

- Naresh Kumar is senior to the under secretary and is sitting adjacent to the Addl. Secretary and the Joint Secretary.
- The Director is not sitting adjacent to the Joint secretary.
- H. Khan is sitting to the immediate left of the Director and is diametrically opposite to the Joint Secretary.
- Sri P. Kashyap has recently taken over as the under secretary, to his left, the Director is sitting and to his right is Sohan Singh.

Based on the information above answer the following questions.

12. Who is the secretary?
    (a) Naresh Kumar (b) A. Wilson
    (c) M.P. Verma (d) Sohan Singh
13. Who is sitting to the right of the Addl. Secretary?
    (a) Secretary (b) Joint Secretary
    (c) Under Secretary (d) Section Officer
14. What is the designation of Sohan Singh?
    (b) Secretary (b) Joint Secretary
    (c) Director (d) Data insufficient
15. A. Wilson is,
    (a) Addl. Secretary
    (b) Section Officer
    (c) Director
    (d) Either a Director or Addl. Secretary
16. If the Secretary and the Director were to interchange their seats, who would be sitting to the left of the secretary?
    (a) Section Officer (b) Under Secretary
    (c) Joint Secretary (d) Data insufficient
17. What is the angle formed between hour and minute hands of clock at 10:10 am?
    (a) 120 (b) 115
    (c) 110 (d) 90
18. A shopkeeper sells two products at the same price. On one he earns profit of 10% and on the other he incurs a loss of 10%. What is the overall profit/loss percentage?
    (a) 1% profit (b) 1% loss
    (c) No profit or loss (d) 2% loss
19. A metal cube is melted and a sphere is made from it. The sphere is melted, some additional metal is added and another sphere is formed which has radius twice that of the previous sphere. This sphere is again melted and a cube is formed.
    What is the volume of this new cube as compared to the original cube?
    (b) 2 times
    (b) 4 times
    (c) 8 times
    (d) Cannot be determined
20. In the series given below what numbers would fall in the vacant spaces?
    1, 2, 6,________31, 56________
    (a) 12, 90 (b) 15, 92
    (c) 16, 84 (d) 14, 92
21. Find the missing number.

| 2 | 3 |
|---|---|
| 10 | 4 |

| 4 | 6 |
|---|---|
| 29 | 5 |

| 5 | 7 |
|---|---|
| 41 | |

    (a) 5 (b) 6
    (c) 4 (d) 3
22. A piece of square paper is folded into two equal halves as shown in Figure Y and again folded into two halves (Figure Z). If the paper in Figure Z was to be punched with three holes as shown in the Figure Z, then which pattern will emerge if the paper was to be unfolded back to its original size?

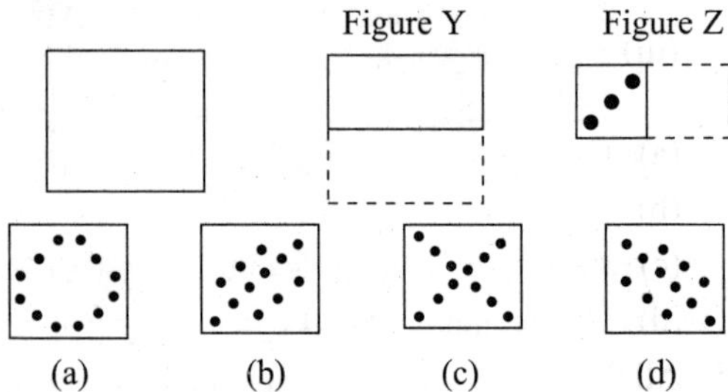


23. In the figure given below, if no two adjoining rectangles are painted with the same colour, then a minimum of how many number of colours would be required to paint the entire figure?

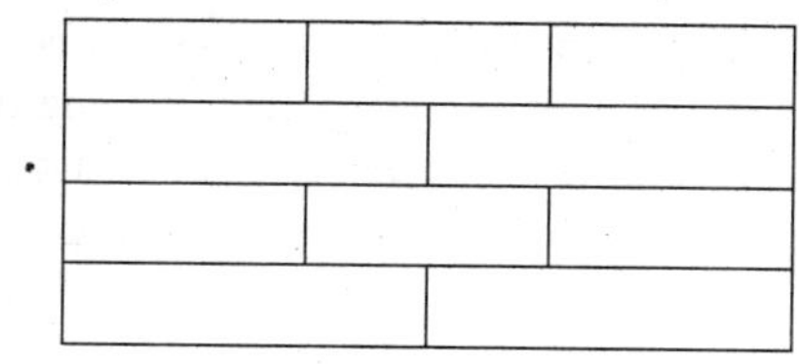

(a) 2 (b) 3
(c) 4 (d) 5

24. A

1 B C
2 3
4
5
6

D

In the figure above, rectangle A represents students of class X in a school. Circle B represents the students who have scored first division in their examination. Circle C represents students who are participating in sports competition. Triangle D represents students participating in a drama competition. Based on the information which of the conclusions mentioned below can be drawn?

(i) Some students participating in drama competition are not from class X.
(ii) All students participating in sports competition have scored 1st division in exams.
(iii) Some students participating in sports competition are from class X.

(a) Only conclusion (i) can be drawn.
(b) Both conclusions (i) and (ii) can be drawn.
(c) All the three conclusions can be drawn.
(d) Only conclusions (i) and (iii) can be drawn.

25. All the six faces of a cube are painted with green colour. The cube is then cut into 27 equal sized smaller cubes.

How many of the smaller cubes will have only one face painted green?

(a) 4 (b) 5
(c) 6 (d) 8

26. How many cubes will have no faces painted green?

(a) 0 (b) 1
(c) 6 (d) 8

27. How many cubes will have two or more faces painted green?

(a) 8 (b) 14
(c) 12 (d) 20

28. Find the figure coming next in the series?

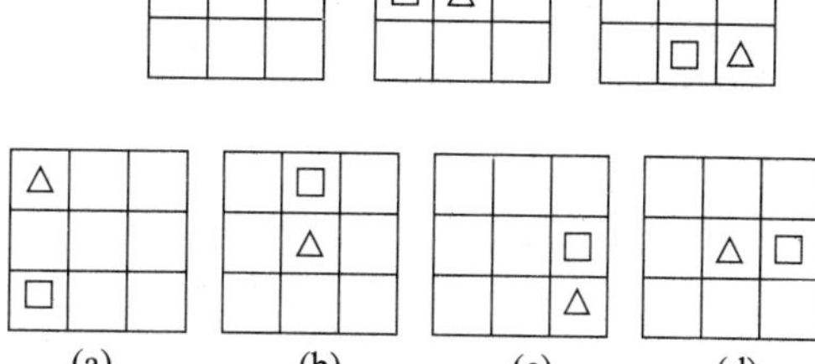

(a) (b) (c) (d)

**(D) Study the pie charts above. The contributions of the major sectors of economy to the G.D.P of country A and country B is given below. Answer the questions given as follows.**

Country A

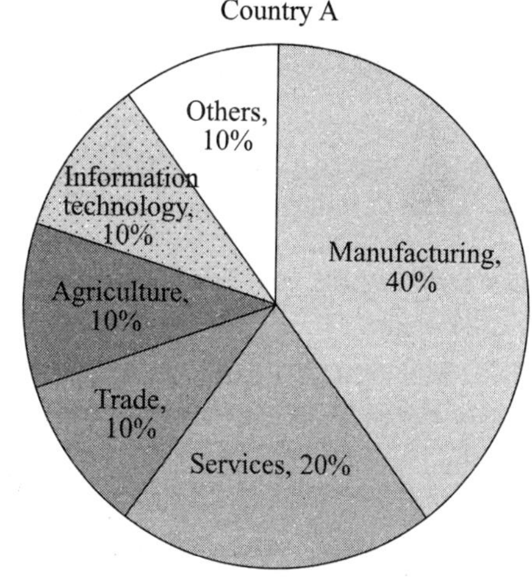

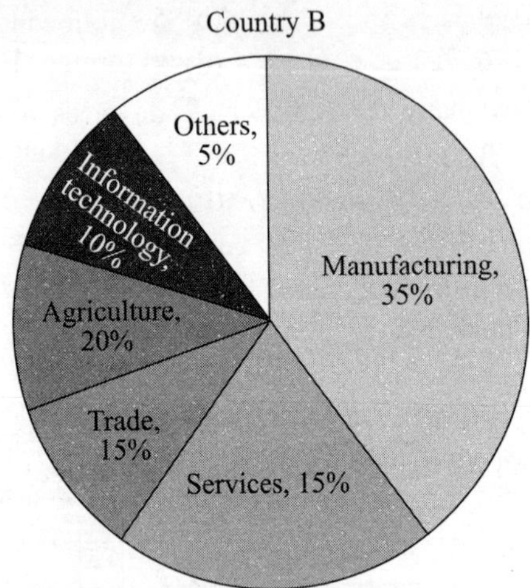


29. In absolute terms, which sector can be said to be an equal contributor to the GDP of country A as well as country B?
   (a) Information Technology
   (b) Agriculture
   (c) Others
   (d) Data insufficient

30. If the size of GDP of country B is greater than that of country A by 15%, then, in absolute terms, in which country is the manufacturing sector bigger?
   (a) Country A (b) Country B
   (c) Equal (d) Data insufficient

31. If the GDP of country A is equal to ₹100 billion and that of country B is 15% greater than that of country A, then by what amount is services sector of country A greater than that of country B?
   (a) ₹2 billion
   (b) ₹2.75 billion
   (c) Smaller by ₹2.00 billion
   (d) Equal

32. For the data given in preceding question what will be the size of agriculture sector in Country B?
   (a) ₹20 billion
   (b) ₹22 billion
   (c) ₹23 billion
   (d) Cannot be determined

33. Take the present GDP of country B to be 15% more than that of country A. If in next year the GDP of country A increases by 15% and that of country B by 10% and the contribution of services in terms of percent of GDP increases by 10% in both the countries, then the service sector of which country would be larger?
   (a) Country B (b) Country A
   (c) Equal (d) Data insufficient

34. Three statements S1, S2 and S3 are given below followed by a question.
   **S1:** The profit margin on the sale of a product is 10%.
   **S2:** A customer bargains with the shopkeeper who gives the customer a discount of 5% on the selling price of this product.
   **S3:** The shopkeeper makes a profit of ₹9.
   **Question:** What is the cost price of the product?
   Which of the following are correct in respect of the above statements and the question?
   (a) All S1, S2 and S3 together are sufficient to answer the question.
   (b) S1 and S2 together are sufficient to answer the question.
   (c) S2 and S3 together are sufficient to answer the question.
   (d) S1, S2 and S3 even together, are not sufficient to answer the question.

35. Two statements S1 and S2 are given below followed by a question.
   **S1:** A hollow cylinder has an outer radius of 10 cm with its length twice the radius.
   **S2:** The thickness of the metal sheet used in the cylinder is 2 mm.
   **Question:** What is the outer surface area of the cylinder?
   Which of the following are correct in respect of the above statements and the question?
   (a) Both S1 and S2 are sufficient to answer the question but neither S1 alone nor S2 alone is sufficient to answer the question.
   (b) S1 alone is sufficient to answer the question.
   (c) S2 alone is sufficient to answer the question.
   (d) S1 and S2 alone together are not sufficient to answer the question.

36. Two statements S1 and S2 are given below followed by a question.

**S1:** A prime number is multiplied by 4 and 1 is added to the product which gives another prime number.

**S2:** The product of the prime number and 5 is less than 40.

**Question:** What is the prime number?

Which of the following are correct in respect of the above statements and the question?

(a) Both S1 and S2 are sufficient to answer the question but neither S1 alone nor S2 alone is sufficient to answer the question.

(b) S1 alone is sufficient to answer the question.

(c) S2 alone is sufficient to answer the question.

(d) S1 and S2 together are not sufficient to answer the question.

37. Two statements S1 and S2 are given below followed by a question.

**S1:** A cricketer scored 61, 63, 17 in three innings. In the 4th innings, he scored one run more than double the average of the previous three innings.

**S2:** His score in the 5th innings reduced the average by 5.

**Question:** how much did he score in the 5th innings?

Which of the following are correct in respect of the above statements and the question?

(a) Both S1 and S2 are sufficient to answer the question but neither S1 alone nor S2 alone is sufficient to answer the question.

(b) S1 alone is sufficient to answer the question.

(c) S2 alone is sufficient to answer the question.

(d) S1 and S2 alone together are not sufficient to answer the question.

**(E) Read the conditions for the questions given below. Answer the questions correctly.**

38. A cube of cheese is of size 10 cm × 10 cm × 10 cm. It is cut vertically along the diagonal of the top face, so that it is split into two pieces of equal size. Which amongst the following is correct about the two new pieces formed? Each of the two new pieces has,

(a) Six faces: 3 square faces, two triangular faces and one rectangular face.

(b) Five faces: 2 square faces, two triangular faces and one rectangular face.

(c) Five faces: 3 square faces and two triangular faces.

(d) Four faces: two square and two triangular face.

39. In the above problem what is the total surface area of all the faces of both the pieces put together?

(a) 600 $cm^2$

(b) 741.4 $cm^2$

(c) 882.8 $cm^2$

(d) None of the above

40. In the above problem the two pieces formed on cutting the cheese are molten and then frozen in a new shape and then cut into 10 equal sized square slices of each, 1 cm thickness. Presume that there is no loss of cheese in this process, what is the size of each side of the squares?

(a) 10 cm

(b) 15 cm

(c) 20 cm

(d) None of the above

**(F) Answer the following questions correctly.**

41. How many triangles are there in the figure given below?

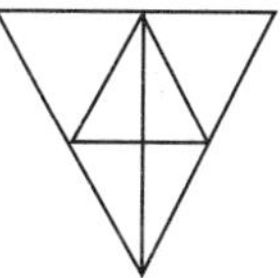

(a) 9 (b) 11

(c) 13 (d) 15

42. A person whose house is facing east, comes out of his house, takes a left turn and travels in that direction for 7 kilometres, after which he takes

another left turn and travels for 6 kilometers. He again takes a left turn and travels for 3 kilometers and again takes a left turn and travels for 3 kilometers. From this point what is the shortest distance to his house?

(a) 19 km (b) 10 km

(c) 5 km (d) $3\sqrt{2}$ km

43. A street vendor of dolls sells 2 dolls more than half the number of dolls he has. The next day he again sells 2 dolls less than half of the remaining number of dolls available with him. If he was left with 26 dolls. How many dolls did he initially have?

(a) 100 (b) 96

(c) 104 (d) 92

44. Rajat walks along a road which has lamp post at regular intervals. He took 6 minutes to walk from the first lamp post to the fourth lamp post. At which lamp post would Rajat be if he walked continuously at a constant rate for 20 minutes?

(a) $10^{th}$ (b) $11^{th}$

(c) $12^{th}$ (d) $9^{th}$

45. Ashok travels in a car from town X to town Y. Benoy travels in another car from town Y to town X starting at the same time. The ratio of their speeds was 4:3. Ashok's car reduced its speed by $1/4^{th}$ and Benoy's car increased its speed by $1/6^{th}$ after they had crossed each other. When Ashok reached town Y, then Benoy is still 20 km away from town X. The distance between town X and town Y is,

(a) 280 km (b) 210 km

(c) 200 km (d) 140 km

46. The ratio of A's age to B's age is 1:3. The ratio of their ages after 8 years will be 1:2. How many years ago was the ratio of their ages 1:5?

(a) 3 years (b) 4 years

(c) 5 years (d) 6 years

47. The selling price of a toy was 30% above the cost price. It was sold at 70% of the selling price. The loss was ₹54/. What was the cost price of the product?

(a) ₹100/- (b) ₹540/-

(c) ₹600/- (d) ₹900/-

48. Devansh travels from Delhi to Patna on a motor bike. The distances between the two cities is 1000 km after Devansh has travelled 200 kms, Madhav starts from Delhi in a car. He overtakes Devansh on way to Patna. When Madhav reaches Patna, Devansh was still 300 kms away. If the speed of both of them is constant then how far from Delhi did Madhav overtake Devansh?

(a) 200 km (b) 500 km

(c) 400 km (d) 600 km

49. In a class of 60 students, 45 play cricket, 30 play football, 5 play none. How many students play both the games?

(a) 20 (b) 15

(c) 10 (d) 5

50. In a study group consisting of 10 students, the average marks scored by them in an examination is 90%. The teacher gives the student who scored the highest marks second a target of improving his marks by 1% in the next examination. The student scoring second highest is given a target of improving his marks by 2% while the one scoring third highest has to improve by 3% and so on. Thus, the student scoring least has to improve by 10%.

If all the students were to improve their marks exactly as per the target, then a how much would be the new average?

(a) 95%

(b) 95.5%

(c) 97.5%

(d) So much increase would not be possible

51. Consider the following statements followed by two conclusions:

**Statements:** Some men are great.

Some men are wise.

**Conclusion I:** Men are either great or wise.

**Conclusion II:** Some men are neither great nor wise.

Which one of the following is correct?

(a) Only conclusion I is valid

(b) Only conclusion II is valid

(c) Both the conclusions are valid

(d) Neither of the conclusions is valid

52. Consider the following statements:

1. Some claim to have seen UFOs (Unidentified Flying Objects).
2. Life on other heavenly bodies is considered to be a possibility.
3. Voyage to space is now an established fact.

From the above statements, it may be concluded that

(a) UFOs are heavenly bodies
(b) UFOs are sent from other heavenly bodies
(c) Some living species in other heavenly bodies are more intelligent than man
(d) Nothing definite can be said about the UFOs

53. Usha runs faster than Kamala, Priti runs slower than Swati, Swati runs slower than Kamala. Who is the slowest runner?

(a) Kamala (b) Priti
(c) Swati (d) Usha

54. *Geeta:* Naresh has become a better boxer since he started meditation,

*Radha:* Impossible. A boxer's most important asset is his aggressiveness.

Radha's statement reflects her belief that

(a) meditation tends to make a person less aggressive.
(b) meditation has little or no effect on the person who practices it,
(c) Naresh was a poor boxer earlier because he was not aggressive enough.
(d) Naresh would not have taken to meditation as he was a boxer.

55. In which Indian state is the harvest festival of Pongal celebrated?

(a) Kerala (b) Odisha
(c) Tamil Nadu (d) Andhra Pradesh

56. Through which of the following states, does the river Kaveri flow?

(1) Kerala (2) Karnataka
(3) Tamil Nadu (4) Andhra Pradesh

(a) 1, 2, 3, 4 (b) 2, 3,4
(c) 2,3 (d) 1,2,3

57. Which of the following institutions are referred to as the Bretton Woods sisters?

(a) International Monetary Fund (IMF) and the World Bank
(b) International Monetary Fund (IMF), OECD and the World Bank
(c) International Monetary Fund (IMF) UNESCO and the World Bank
(d) UNESCO and the UNHRC

58. In which of the following city is the Common Wealth Games 2022 to be held?

(a) Glasgow in Scotland
(b) Birmingham in England
(c) Gold Coast in Australia
(d) None of the above

59. Which of the following places has a nuclear power plant?

(1) Rawatbhata in Rajasthan
(2) Kundakulam in Tamil Nadu
(3) Narora in Uttar Pradesh
(4) Kakrapar in Gujarat

(a) 1, 2, 3, 4 (b) 2, 3, 4
(c) 1, 3 (d) 2, 4

60. Which of the following female Indian golfer, stood 4$^{th}$ in the 2021 Olympics (Tokyo 2020), missing the bronze medal by a whisker?

(a) Aditi Ashok (b) Diksha Dagar
(c) Tvesa Malik (d) Manika Batra

## Answers of Practice Question Paper-9

| | | | | | |
|---|---|---|---|---|---|
| **1.** (b) | **11.** (c) | **21.** (b) | **31.** (b) | **41.** (c) | **51.** (d) |
| **2.** (b) | **12.** (a) | **22.** (a) | **32.** (c) | **42.** (c) | **52.** (d) |
| **3.** (d) | **13.** (d) | **23.** (b) | **33.** (b) | **43.** (a) | **53.** (b) |
| **4.** (c) | **14.** (b) | **24.** (a) | **34.** (a) | **44.** (b) | **54.** (a) |
| **5.** (a) | **15.** (d) | **25.** (c) | **35.** (b) | **45.** (a) | **55.** (c) |
| **6.** (d) | **16.** (a) | **26.** (b) | **36.** (d) | **46.** (b) | **56.** (c) |
| **7.** (c) | **17.** (b) | **27.** (d) | **37.** (a) | **47.** (c) | **57.** (a) |
| **8.** (a) | **18.** (b) | **28.** (d) | **38.** (b) | **48.** (c) | **58.** (b) |
| **9.** (d) | **19.** (c) | **29.** (d) | **39.** (c) | **49.** (a) | **59.** (a) |
| **10.** (d) | **20.** (b) | **30.** (b) | **40.** (a) | **50.** (b) | **60.** (a) |

# Practice Question Paper 10

**(A) Read the questions carefully and answer them.**

1. There were 50 questions in an objective type test. 5 marks would be awarded for every right answer. 1 mark would be deducted for every wrong answer. All questions had to be answered. If Neela scored 190 marks, how many questions did she answer right?

   (a) 40 (b) 44
   (c) 38 (d) None of these

2. A square field has a perimeter of 800 metres. Cyclist A can cycle 500 metres in one minute. Cyclist B can cycle 400 metres in one minute. If A starts to cycle one minute after B has started cycling, then how much distance has B covered when A is able to catch up with him?

   (a) 1500 m (b) 1600 m
   (c) 1800 m (d) 2000 m

3. The sum of a number and 1001 is divisible by 17 and 19. What is the smallest possible value of this number?

   (a) 201 (b) 222
   (c) 292 (d) 291

4. In 1000 ml bottle of milk, sugar content is 5.5%. How much sugar must be added so that the sugar content becomes 10%?

   (a) 45 gm (b) 50 gm
   (c) 60 gm (d) 70 gm

5. The cost of manufacturing of a television set has increased by 20% as compared to last year. The television company maintains the same selling price of the TV sets. As a result the profit for each TV set drops by 30%. The number of TV sets sold however increases by 50%. What is the percentage increase or decrease in the profit?

   (a) 5% increase (b) 5% decrease
   (c) 20% increase (d) 10% decrease

**(B) Read the information given below and answer the questions which follow:**

A family of six comprises of three males and three females. It has two fathers and two sons. Following information is known.

- Anne is John's daughter and is not married.
- John is the eldest and Jane is the youngest in the family.
- The lawyer is the father of the architect and also of the business man.
- Jack is Jane's brother. Both are students and the professor is their mother.
- The only married couple in the family are Wilson and Susan.

Answer the following questions:

6. Who is John's son?

   (a) Jack
   (b) Wilson
   (c) Both Jack and Wilson
   (d) Data insufficient.

7. Who are the only married couple of the family?

   (a) John and Susan
   (b) John and Anne
   (c) Wilson and Anne
   (d) Wilson and Susan

8. Who is the professor?

   (a) Susan (b) Wilson
   (c) John (d) Anne

9. What is the relationship between John and the architect?

   (a) John is son of the architect.
   (b) John is the father of the architect.
   (c) John is the brother of the architect.
   (d) John is the husband of the architect.

10. Anne is a
    (a) Lawyer (b) Professor
    (c) Architect (d) Data insufficient
11. Wilson is Anne's
    (a) Brother (b) father
    (c) Son (d) Husband.

**(C) Read the information and answer the questions.**

An office comprises of five divisions which are operations, management, advertisement, accounts and personnel. The offices of these divisions are placed in a sequential order with the accounts division coming first. These divisions are headed by A. Kumar, Brijesh Sharma, Damodar Das, Naresh Jain, and Ravi Singh (not in any specific order) Following information is also known.

- A. Kumar has no experience of either advertisement or operations.
- Offices of operation and managements are after that of advertisement.
- N. Jain has been handpicked for operations.
- Division headed by Ravi Singh is ahead of advertisement in order of placement.
- Damodar Das heads a division the office of which is placed last in the order.
- Accounts is not headed by Ravi Singh.

Based on the above information answer the following questions.

12. Who heads accounts department?
    (a) A. Kumar (b) Brijesh Sharma
    (c) Naresh Jain (d) Damodar Das
13. Which division comes last in the placement order?
    (a) Personnel (b) Management
    (c) Advertisement (d) Operations.
14. What is the position of advertisement division in the order in which the offices are placed?
    (a) Second (b) Third
    (c) Fourth (d) Fifth
15. Which division is headed by Ravi Singh?
    (a) Accounts (b) Management
    (c) Personnel (d) Advertisement
16. Consider the following statements.
    (i) All sports persons are hard working.
    (ii) Some sports persons take banned drugs.
    (iii) People who are indisciplined are more likely to take banned drugs.
    
    Which amongst the following conclusion can be drawn from the aforesaid three statements?
    (a) All sports persons are indisciplined.
    (b) All people who take banned drugs are indisciplined.
    (c) Some people who take banned drugs are sports persons.
    (d) Indisciplined people cannot become sports persons.
17. Laptops, though still quite expensive, are not considered to be an item of luxury nowadays, as they have become essential for studies in many schools and colleges, particularly for higher studies.
    
    Which amongst the following can be said to be a logical inference drawn from what is stated above?
    (a) All things which are essential are not to be regarded as luxury.
    (b) All things which are luxury cannot be essential.
    (c) Laptops are essential for higher studies.
    (d) Laptops are a luxury item for students.
18. Examine the following statements.
    (i) All Australian tourists visiting Taj Mahal wear an orange colour badge on their T shirts.
    (ii) Some Australian tourists also carry black umbrellas.
    (iii) Australian tourists who are above 50 years of age always carry an umbrella.
    (iv) All tourists to Taj Mahal are not Australians.
    
    Which of the following conclusion can be drawn from the statements given above?
    (a) All persons carrying black umbrellas are Australians.
    (b) All persons having orange badge on their T Shirts are Australians.

(c) All Australians carrying an umbrella are above 50 years of age.

(d) None of the above.

19. Consider the following statements.

(i) All scientists display attributes of strong logical understanding.

(ii) Home taught students, who have not undergone regular schooling, often tend to be very creative.

(iii) Only some scientists are very creative.

Based on above facts, which amongst the following conclusion can be drawn?

(a) Home taught students rarely become scientists.

(b) People with strong logical understanding are likely to become scientists.

(c) Home taught students do not display strong sense of logical understanding.

(d) None of the above.

20. Examine the following statements.

(i) Those who travel with bags with wheels do not hire porters at the railway station.

(ii) Poor cannot afford to travel in air-conditioned trains.

(iii) Some of those who travel in air-conditioned trains carry bags with wheels.

Based on the above which of the following conclusion can be drawn?

I. Poor do not hire porters at railway station.

II. Rich do not hire porters at railway station.

III. Porters do not carry bags with wheels.

(a) Conclusions I, II and III can be drawn.

(b) Only conclusion I and II can be drawn.

(c) Only conclusion II and III can be drawn.

(d) Only conclusion III can be drawn.

21. Examine the following statements and conclusions.

Television of brand X has the largest volume of sales. The company selling X had gross sales receipts of ₹ 10 crore from this brand while the gross sales receipts of next brand was only ₹ 8 crore, which is brand Y.

**Conclusion**- The maximum number of TV sets that sold were of brand X.

Which of the following if true would weaken the conclusion the most?

(a) Brand X was launched earlier than brand Y.

(b) The advertisement budget of brand X was three times that of Y.

(c) The cost of each unit of brand Y was 70% of that of each unit of brand X.

(d) 15% of customers of brand X returned the TV sets within a month as compared to 5% of brand Y.

22. A theatre has 10 row of seats. The last row has 40 seats. There are two seats less in each successive front row. How many seats are there in the theatre?

(a) 300 (b) 310

(c) 320 (d) 340

23. A square of side 12 cm is divided into two smaller squares of different sizes and two rectangles of equal size as shown below. If the area of the larger square is 9 times that of the smaller square then what is the area of each rectangle? Take the length of sides of each square to be a natural number.

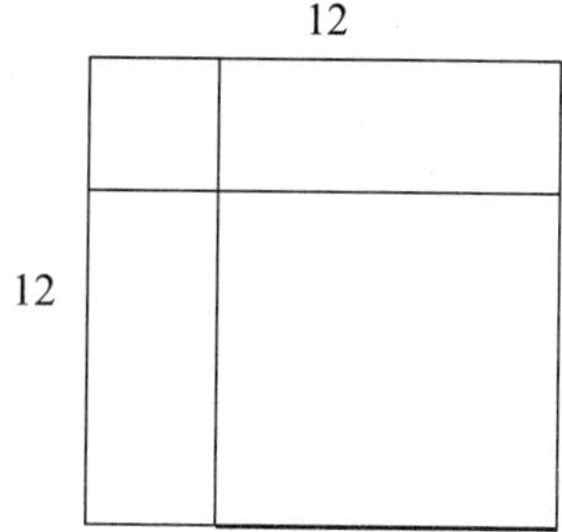


(a) 36 $cm^2$ (b) 27 $cm^2$

(c) 15 $cm^2$ (d) Data insufficient

24. Sarthak and Daksh jog around a square park which has each side of 50 m. Sarthak runs at a speed of 40 meters in a minute while Daksh at 50 meters per minute. If they start together then after how many rotations of the park by Daksh will they meet again?

(a) 5 rotation (b) 4 rotation

(c) 3 rotation (d) 10 rotation

25. Two statements S1 and S2 are given below followed by a question.

**S1:** A vehicle travels half the distance between two cities at a certain fixed speed and the remaining half at twice that speed.

**S2:** It takes 15 minutes less in the second half of the journey.

**Question:** What is the distance between the two cities?

Which of the following are correct in respect of the above statements and the question?

(a) Both S1 and S2 are sufficient to answer the question but neither S1 alone nor S2 alone is sufficient to answer the question.
(b) S1 alone is sufficient to answer the question.
(c) S2 alone is sufficient to answer the question.
(d) S1 and S2 alone together are not sufficient to answer the question.

26. Two statements S1 and S2 are given below followed by a question.

**S1:** Two boys who work at the same pace, do a job together in two hours.

**S2:** A third boy who works at half the pace joins them.

**Question:** In how much time will all three will complete the whole job together?

Which of the following are correct in respect of the above statements and the question?

(a) Both S1 and S2 are sufficient to answer the question but neither S1 alone nor S2 alone is sufficient to answer the question.
(b) S1 alone is sufficient to answer the question.
(c) S2 alone is sufficient to answer the question.
(d) S1 and S2 alone together are not sufficient to answer the question.

27. Two statements S1 and S2 are given below followed by a question.

**S1:** Kumaran scores 5% more marks than Lalitha in three subjects and 5% less than her in the remaining two subjects.

**S2:** Lalitha scored the same marks in all five subjects.

**Question:** By what percentage, marks of Kumaran were more than Lalitha?

Which of the following are correct in respect of the above statements and the question?

(a) Both S1 and S2 are sufficient to answer the question but neither S1 alone nor S2 alone is sufficient to answer the question.
(b) S1 alone is sufficient to answer the question.
(c) S2 alone is sufficient to answer the question.
(d) S1 and S2 alone together are not sufficient to answer the question.

28. Two statements S1 and S2 are given below followed by a question.

**S1:** The HCF of two numbers is 16 and their difference is also 16.

**S2:** The total of both the numbers is more than 100.

**Question:** What are the two numbers?

Which of the following are correct in respect of the above statements and the question?

(a) Both S1 and S2 are sufficient to answer the question but neither S1 alone nor S2 alone is sufficient to answer the question.
(b) S1 alone is sufficient to answer the question.
(c) S2 alone is sufficient to answer the question.
(d) S1 and S2 alone together are not sufficient to answer the question.

29. Two statements S1 and S2 are given below followed by a question.

**S1:** The interest on a certain sum of money in 5.5 years at the simple rate of interest, is 77% of the capital.

**S2:** He earns each year an interest 11% less than the rate which would have doubled the capital in four years.

**Question:** What is the rate of interest?

Which of the following are correct in respect of the above statements and the question?

(a) Both S1 and S2 are sufficient to answer the question but neither S1 alone nor S2 alone is sufficient to answer the question.
(b) S1 alone is sufficient to answer the question.
(c) S2 alone is sufficient to answer the question.
(d) Both S1 and S2 alone are sufficient to answer the question.

30. A group of 100 girls at a school are to choose from amongst the following three activities, dancing, singing or playing a musical instrument. None of the students choose to undertake all the three simultaneously, 25% of the total students choose to undertake two activities together. The number of students who undertake only dance is 50, while 15 students play only musical instruments. How many students sing but do not participate in any other activity?
    (a) 20 students (b) 15 students
    (c) 10 students (d) 5 students
31. In the above problem if there are 3 girls who do not undertake any of the activities and another (ii) who are undertaking all the three activities together, then what is the total number of students who sing but do not participate in any other activity ?
    (a) 20 students (b) 15 students
    (c) 10 students (d) 5 students

**(D) Read and answer the questions carefully.**

32. Examine the matrix of numbers and determine what are the possible values of A and B?

| 5 | 24 | 48 |
|---|---|---|
| 6 | 35 | 70 |
| 7 | A | B |

    (a) 45, 85 (b) 46, 92
    (c) 40, 80 (d) 48, 96
33. Examine the pattern in the three groups of numbers given below and identify which set of numbers would fall in the fifth group?
    ((ii), (iv), 5) ((iv), 8, 25) (6, 1(ii), 125)
    (a) 8, 16, 625 (b) 10, 20, 625
    (c) 10, 20, 3125 (d) 8, 16, 3125
34. Consider the following matrix of numbers.
    Find the value of X ?

| 3 | 7 | 208 |
|---|---|---|
| 4 | X | 309 |
| 5 | 6 | 704 |

    (a) 8 (b) 11
    (c) 13 (d) 15
35. In a machine power is transmitted through four wheels as shown in the figure below. If wheel A is the driving wheel and it is rotating in clockwise direction then in which directions wheel C and D are rotating respectively?

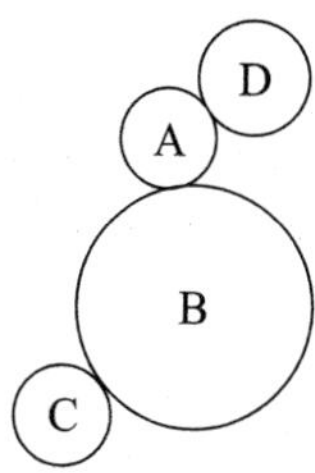


    (a) Clockwise, anticlockwise
    (b) Anticlockwise, clockwise
    (c) Clockwise, clockwise
    (d) Anticlockwise, anticlockwise
36. How many rectangles are there in the figure below?

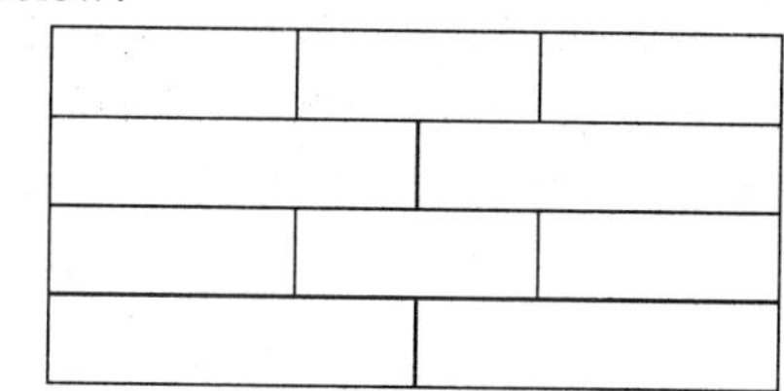

    (a) 18 (b) 24
    (c) 26 (d) 14
37.

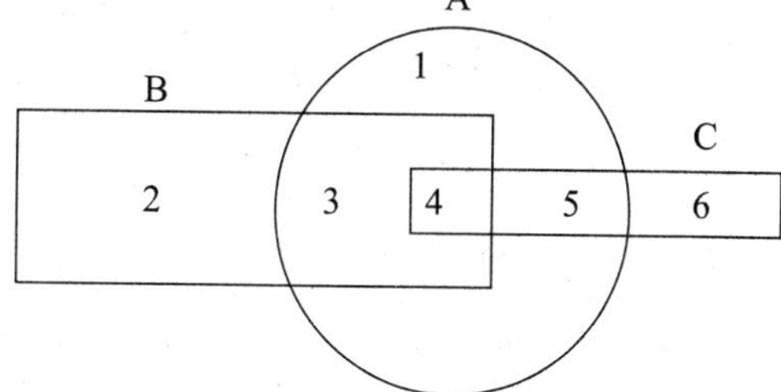


In the figure above circle A represents predators, rectangle B represents birds, while rectangle C represents nocturnal creatures. An owl will fall in which portion of the figure?
    (a) 1 (b) 5
    (c) 4 (d) 6

38. Find the missing letters in the series.
Y, T, O,_________, _________
(a) H, E (b) J, D
(c) K, F (d) J, E

39. During a period of 24 hours how many times do the minute hand and hour hand overlap?
(a) 21 times (b) 22 times
(c) 23 times (d) 24 times

40. Find the figure coming next in the series.

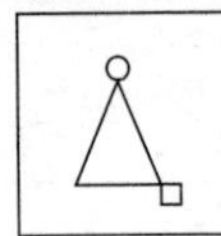 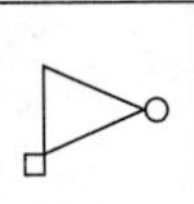 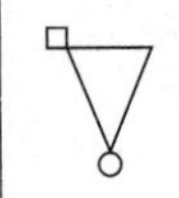

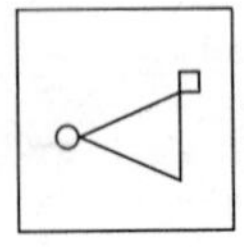 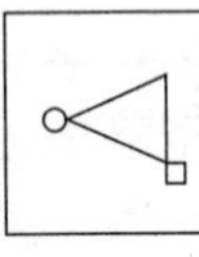 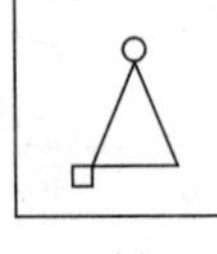 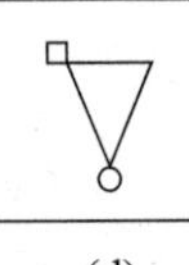

(a) (b) (c) (d)

**(E) Study the graph below and answer the questions which follow. The graph represents the velocity of a car over five equal intervals of time.**

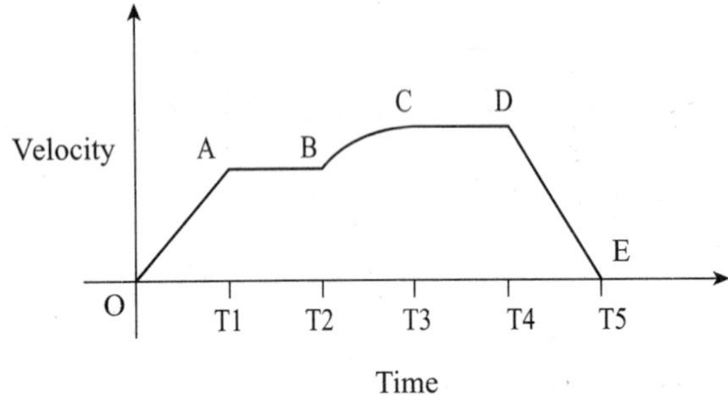


41. In which phase of car's movement is the velocity maximum?
(a) O-T1 (b) T1-T2
(c) T2-T3 (d) T3-T4

42. Which phase of the graph represents constant acceleration?
(a) O-A (b) A-B
(c) B-C (d) C-D

43. In which time interval the motorist covers the maximum distance?
(a) T1-T2 (b) T2-T3
(c) T3-T4 (d) T4-T5

44. The portion B-C on the graph represents,
(a) Constant velocity
(b) Constant acceleration
(c) Deceleration or retardation
(d) Changing acceleration

45. The motorist covers a greater distance in which of the two time intervals, O-T1 or T4-T5.
(a) O-T1
(b) T4-T5
(c) Equal distances in both
(d) Cannot be determined

**(F) Directions for the following 2 (two) items:**

The following pie charts show the break-up of disease categories recorded in the patients from two towns, Town A and Town B. Pie charts plot the disease categories as percentage of the total number of patients. Based on these, answer the two items that follow the charts.

Distribution of diseases in Town A

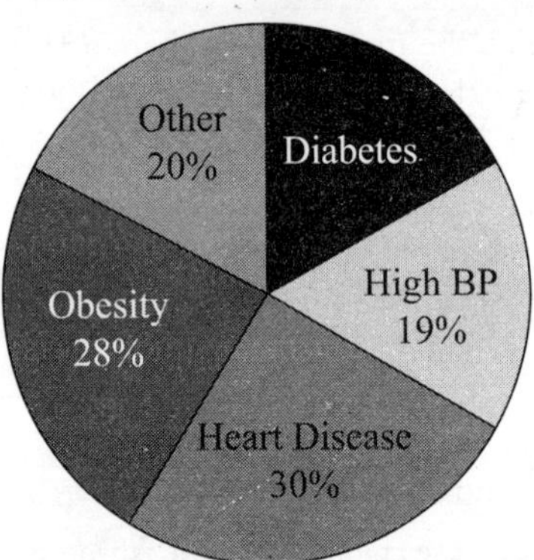


Distribution of diseases in Town B

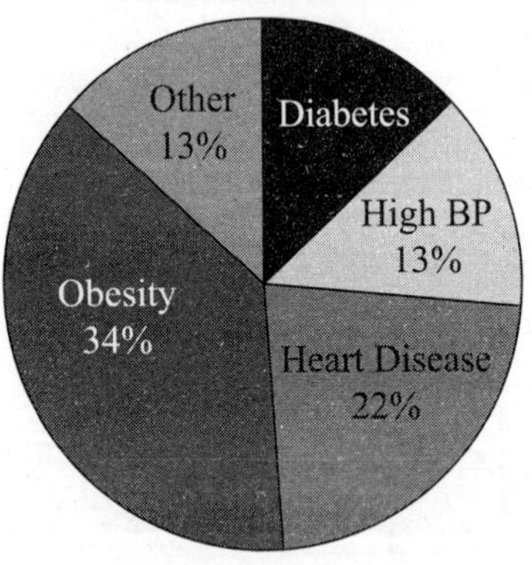